Jo van Gogh-Bonger

Jo van Gogh-Bonger
The Woman Who Made Vincent Famous

Hans Luijten

Translated by Lynne Richards

BLOOMSBURY VISUAL ARTS
LONDON • NEW YORK • OXFORD • NEW DELHI • SYDNEY

The translation of this book was made possible by the generous support of
the Vincent van Gogh Foundation and a private donor.

BLOOMSBURY VISUAL ARTS
Bloomsbury Publishing Plc
50 Bedford Square, London, WC1B 3DP, UK
1385 Broadway, New York, NY 10018, USA
29 Earlsfort Terrace, Dublin 2, Ireland

First published in Dutch, under the title *Alles voor Vincent: Het leven van Jo van Gogh-Bonger*
Author Hans Luijten

Originally published in 2019 by Uitgeverij Prometheus, Amsterdam

First published in English by Bloomsbury Visual Arts
Translation Lynne Richards

For legal purposes the Acknowledgements on p. 515 constitute an extension of this copyright page.

Cover design: Tjaša Krivec
Cover image: Jo Cohen Gosschalk-Bonger, *c.* 1904. Unknown photographer.
Van Gogh Museum, Amsterdam (Vincent van Gogh Foundation).

A catalogue record for this book is available from the British Library.

A catalog record for this book is available from the Library of Congress.

ISBN: HB: 978-1-3502-9958-0
ePDF: 978-1-3502-9960-3
eBook: 978-1-3502-9959-7

Typeset by RefineCatch Limited, Bungay, Suffolk
Printed and bound in Great Britain

Contents

Introduction

'An Amsterdam girl'

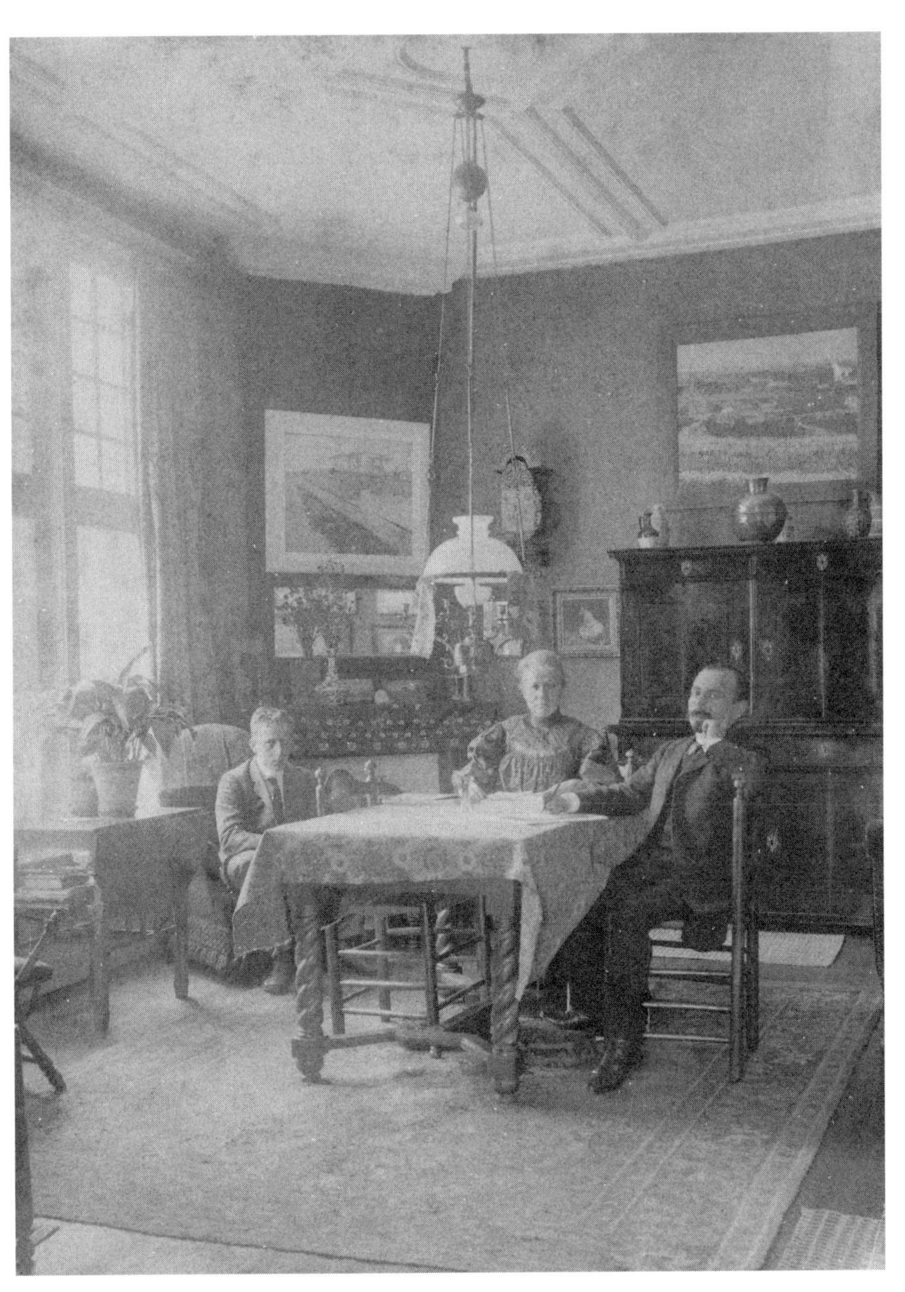

The Van Gogh Museum in Amsterdam is one of the most famous museums in the world. It attracts millions of visitors every year, and even people who have never been there know that it exists. Few people, however, know about the background to this museum—how it came into being, its foundation, its history. And even fewer know that the greater part of the collection of Van Gogh paintings in the museum today was once stored in the attic of a large detached house in Bussum, a small town some eighteen miles to the south-east of Amsterdam.

Jo van Gogh-Bonger (1862–1925) and her infant son Vincent had moved into that house, Villa Helma at number 4 Koningslaan, in April 1891. She had spent eighteen happy months in Paris with her husband Theo, the artist Vincent van Gogh's younger brother, whom she had married in 1889. But fate was cruel. Not long after Vincent's death, Theo died too, in January 1891. From that moment on—Jo was twenty-eight—she bore sole responsibility for raising their child, who was not even a year old. She was also left as a widow with an immense inheritance; Theo, who had been an art dealer, had acquired most of his brother Vincent's works in return for supporting him financially. All these paintings and drawings, along with Theo's art collection, went to Jo and Vincent, half each. Because Vincent was only a year old, Jo automatically became his guardian with control over his property until he came of age when he was twenty-one.[1]

Jo did not go back to Paris after Theo died. Acting on the advice of friends, she moved to Bussum, and a few months later opened Villa Helma as a boarding house—something single women quite often did at that time. She set to work with energy and determination. As soon as she moved in, she took out fire insurance in the amount of 12,600 guilders. The policy, dated 18 April 1891, includes the following items:

f 2,000 200 paintings by V. van Gogh
f 600 1 portfolio of drawings by V. van Gogh.[2]

An interesting source, this insurance policy, but the numbers and amounts strike us as quite odd from the perspective of our current knowledge. We know, for a start, that there were far more works of art: between April 1891 and Jo's death in September 1925, at least 247 Van Goghs were sold from the collection—192 paintings and fifty-five works on paper—according to Jo's account book, which was not even a full record.[3] The figure of two hundred must have been far too low an estimate. In 1962 Jo's son Vincent made over 209 paintings and 490 drawings to the Vincent van Gogh Foundation.[4] Taken together these works are now the nucleus of the collection in the Van Gogh Museum.

The walls of Jo's house in Bussum were covered in paintings, and all the letters and documents left by Theo and Vincent (including photographs and sketchbooks) were stored in cupboards. Even so, most of the Van Goghs were in the attic. 'Safe' and 'insured' are relative concepts. Fire insurance is a fine thing, reassuring even, but what would have happened if Villa Helma really had gone up in flames in

1891? The consequences would have been incalculable and the development of modern art in Europe would have been very different.

Understandably enough, Vincent and his brother Theo have always been the focus of attention, and Jo, Theo's widow, has been overshadowed. And yet she more than deserves to have the spotlight turned on her. The fact that Vincent van Gogh became so famous after his death is due in no small measure to her unremitting diligence and effort, and not simply and solely to the quality of his work. This biography is about Jo's tenacity, her boundless dedication and her surprisingly multilayered life.[5] For thirty-five years she single-mindedly pursued her goal of achieving recognition for Vincent van Gogh's artistic oeuvre, doing everything in her power to establish his reputation all over the world. Thanks to her great love of his art, her unshakable faith in his talent and her own energetic personality, she eventually succeeded. She was able to stand her ground in a male-dominated world and take responsibility for both the stewardship of Van Gogh's work and its dissemination. As the guardian of the legacy, she was the foundation on which the later Van Gogh cult was built. After her death, her son conscientiously took over the task, although he did remark that it was something that had been thrust upon him. In his speech at the opening of the Van Gogh Museum in 1973 he said: 'I didn't ask to be born amongst all those paintings, but like it or not, I had to deal with the collection'[6] (Plate 1).

Turning points in Jo's life

The story of someone's life is determined as much by events, successes and disasters as by birth, environment and the times. Such culmination points occur several times in this biography.[7] The break-up of Jo's relationship with the junior anatomy assistant Eduard Stumpff was one of them, as were the deaths of Mien Doorman and Cateau Stumpff. Jo struggled to come to terms with the tragically premature deaths of these dear friends. The departure of her brother Andries, who moved to Paris at an early stage, also had a profound effect on her. She had always idolized him. For years she sought someone to whom she could devote herself in the same way, and Theo van Gogh was the first person with whom this was really possible. Throwing in her lot with him was without doubt the most decisive moment in her life. Jo was twenty-six. Their marriage was happy but lasted a scant two years. And yet this step set the course for the rest of her life: Theo gave her not only a son, Vincent ('he's my solace and my treasure, my everything'[8]), but the immense legacy of his brother Vincent. Jo was to devote the rest of her life to these two Vincents—out of love for them both, but above all out of love for Theo. It was her way of bearing his premature death, which came as such a devastating blow, and to some extent rising above it. Concentrating on the two namesakes kept her closest to Theo. Later pivotal moments in her life stemmed from this: the hugely successful Van Gogh exhibition she organized in the Stedelijk Museum in Amsterdam in 1905, and her well-received publication of

Vincent's letters to Theo in 1914, which gave the public a new way of finding out about his life and work.

Another important transitional moment was Jo's second marriage in 1901, to the artist and art critic Johan Cohen Gosschalk. It was a marriage that was very difficult at times. The hesitant run-up to the wedding was a portent of trouble to come. Johan was intelligent and artistic, but at the same time fickle and neurotic; he led a retired life. He felt that Jo's drive and perseverance caused a certain hardness in her personality that should not be allowed to get the upper hand, as he wrote to her at the very outset of their relationship:

> You, my darling, alongside much persistence and toughness, have much true feminine softness, tenderness, fineness of feeling and thought. Don't think that I don't appreciate those qualities of persistence that perhaps became hardness. But all the same I might not love you if you did not also have that true femininity.[9]

Despite the difficulties and the great difference in their characters, they supported one another in the ten years they were together. These were not easy years. And Jo was unlucky in her two husbands: Theo died when he was thirty-three, Johan was thirty-eight when he died.

All this aside, there were two other interesting paths Jo trod during her life. Firstly, there was her work as a teacher and translator. After high school she took a course qualifying her to teach English and taught at various girls' schools in the Netherlands for some time. She then developed into a respected translator of novels and stories that were published in papers like *De Amsterdammer*, *De Kroniek* and *Belang en Recht*. The training, the translation work, the teaching and a permanent cultural hunger contributed to her education and development, which more or less coincided with the first wave of female emancipation in the second half of the nineteenth century.

The second path opened up within the socialist movement. Early in life Jo showed herself to be someone with a strong sense of justice, encouraged by her upbringing. She was socially aware and optimistic about the perfecting of mankind and society, and the new position of women in it. For a long time, she was active in the Social Democratic Labour Party (SDAP) and the women's movement, and wrote reviews for the moderate feminist magazine *Belang en Recht*.

In the end, her son Vincent, who took a degree in mechanical engineering, was the only person for whom she felt unconditional love—a love that he sometimes felt was stifling and from which he managed to wrest himself with considerable difficulty. In her later years he was able to tolerate it with greater equanimity.[10] Jo was very close to him and his wife Josina Wibaut and relied heavily on them. At the end of her life her grandchildren brought her great joy. 'When she got older, young people liked her very much and she was fond of them,' wrote Vincent about her role in this last period, when she took things a little more calmly: 'She enjoyed simple things and was always good company.'[11] In the family Jo was known as the 'nice aunt'.[12] Although she took things a little easier in this period, she continued to negotiate about Van Gogh's work and went on selling it. She also devoted herself wholeheartedly to translating his letters into English and trying to find a publisher for them. She had translated two-thirds of the letters when she died in 1925. She was sixty-two.

An Amsterdam girl

'Did you know that Theo is engaged and will marry an Amsterdam girl quite soon?' wrote Vincent van Gogh to his fellow artist Arnold Koning in Winschoten in January 1889, suggesting that this might have been why his younger brother was not his usual self: 'I've seen absolutely nothing of your studies sent to Theo (*I believe*), despite urging you to make an exchange. Is this to do with Theo, who possibly had other things on his mind, or with the not inconsiderable distance between us?'[13] Vincent had not yet met Jo—that would happen later—but Theo had already told him about her at length when he visited Vincent in the hospital in Arles at the end of December 1888. They lay side by side on the bed, talking, as they had often done as children in North Brabant. Theo had told his mother, who immediately responded with tenderness: 'How touching about Zundert, together on one pillow.'[14] A few days later, Theo also told Jo about Vincent's situation. It was the first letter in which he involved her in his brother's fortunes. It was not encouraging news. The brother who so fervently wanted Theo to marry Jo could not, when it came to it, be a full part of it because he had lost his mind:

> Last year he kept urging me to try to marry you, so I believe that in different circumstances, if he knew what things were like between us, he would give his wholehearted approval. You know how much he has meant to me & that it was he who fostered and nurtured whatever good there might be in me. Even when *we* are living together, I would have wanted him, whether near or far, to remain that same advisor & brother to both of us, in every sense of the word. That hope has now vanished & we are both the poorer for it.

A profoundly sad situation, and Theo's sole concern was to prevent people later on from regarding Vincent as mad or disturbed. He assumed that Jo felt the same way:

> We shall honour his memory, shan't we, dearest? For even now, I sense from the letters from home that their words of sympathy, all except Wil's, barely disguise their conviction that he was actually insane all along.[15]

It is a revealing passage, which with hindsight reads almost like a compelling summons—a summons to a shared alliance, a pact against the world, to which in this case his own family belonged. Vincent's memory had to be preserved and protected, that was what mattered. Theo felt how crucial and essential this was, but it was for Jo that it was to have the most far-reaching consequences. Her fate was sealed for ever. While her son's happiness always came before anything else with her ('I have only one goal—to make him healthy and happy—in so far as I can'[16]) Jo was immediately faced with a second goal as soon as Theo died: looking after the legacy of her brother-in-law Vincent. The title of the Dutch biography, *All for Vincent*, reflects this dual purpose in life—and always, in the background, we hear 'and all for Theo'.

The Amsterdam girl from the Weteringschans was an intelligent woman, who wrestled throughout her life to gain insight into herself. She wanted to be a noble person and was acutely aware of shortcomings she detected in herself. She had dark brown eyes, a faintly oriental cast to her round face, and dark hair. She stood barely five foot three inches tall. Both her loves, Theo and Johan, were short too.[17] She liked clothes in which 'harmony in colour' prevailed and wore long skirts that hid her feet. Jo took life very seriously and had virtually no sense of humour. According to friends she was a good chess player, seldom let things get on top of her, was sensible, sensitive and kind, and she spoilt the guests in her boarding house.[18] Her friendships were very close and she had a strong sense of responsibility. She took a great many tasks and duties upon herself, particularly when it came to bringing up Vincent. Jo's character was a complex amalgam of diffidence—more than once she described herself as quiet and inward-looking—and rebellion, with a fierce desire for independence. Before her marriage she was insecure, rather dreamy and in constant need of guidance. After 1891, when she suddenly had to face things alone, this irresolution swiftly made way for determination and drive. Although she could count on a great deal of assistance and support from family and friends, which she did not hesitate to accept (at various times in her life she was aided by some influential people), as far as etiquette permitted at that time she made her own choices and took her own decisions. In this she was tenacious and resolute.[19] The foundations for this were laid, as everyone's are, in her childhood.

Sources for the research

Writing a biography means many hours spent in the legacy of someone's life, and it is often difficult to gauge the precise circumstances. Describing a life is an attempt to bring the person in question back to life and at the same time a voyage of discovery. What someone does or omits to do, what their motives and reasons are—these are questions whose answers can be hard to find. Needless to say, a substantial number of sources provide a foothold for the reconstruction of these visible and invisible things. I had at my disposal numerous letters, Jo's diaries, extracts from her son Vincent's diaries, some household books, an account book, dozens of photographs, her own publications and translations in different daily and weekly papers, and various written accounts by eyewitnesses. But how much certainty can you derive from dry ink?[20]

It goes without saying that sources like this have to be used carefully. Jo warned herself against this when she realized, halfway through her first diary, how she had been writing about herself up to that point: 'I wager if someone ever leafed through this book, he would get the wrong impression of my character.'[21] And, even more disconcerting for a biographer: 'Of the real state of my mind and feelings I never write.'[22] This cannot, though, be a reason to abandon the quest. There is, after all, plenty left over. Jo's diaries include a great many passages written straight from the heart and, tellingly in 1881, she described their contents as 'the mirror of my inner life.'[23] She was strikingly critical of herself in her youth.

The four diaries, written between the ages of seventeen and thirty-four (from March 1880 to May 1897, sometimes with lengthy interruptions), provide a good insight into her occupations and thoughts. They have recently become fully accessible in a digital version.[24] Written in an even hand and covering hundreds of pages, serious reflections are interspersed with trivia. Jo wrote about the people she knew, about her family, friends and teachers, and about the clergymen whose churches she attended. She reflected on what she read and on the concerts and performances she went to. Writing in her diary made her more self-aware. Re-reading certain passages cheered her up from time to time. She always endeavoured to put into words as honestly as she could her motives and ambitions in life, her shame, disappointments, longings and loves. The diaries thus paint a conscientious self-portrait, albeit necessarily a fragmentary one. In February 1892 she realized only too well what its greater importance might be:

> I've brought my diary more or less up to date, and will keep it up faithfully. Later on, the child should at least be able to form an opinion about his mother's life—what she thought, felt and wanted. Her diaries and the letters from his father and his uncle—he'll be able to use them to reconstruct their lives from the past.[25]

Her notes undoubtedly fulfilled this function for Vincent; in any event he quoted several passages from them in his later edition of Van Gogh's collected letters.[26] In his turn, he too kept a diary, another important source for this biography because it reveals much about his relationship with his mother and what he thought about her.

Aside from the diaries, letters are a crucial source for the reconstruction of Jo's life. Hundreds of them have survived, received from and sent to friends, her parents, her brother Andries, Theo, her son Vincent and many others. Most of these letters are in the Van Gogh Museum. Sometimes, even now, remarkable acquisitions are added to the collection. In May 2008, for instance, Sylvia Cramer, a trustee of the Vincent van Gogh Foundation, made available a surprising addition: 102 unpublished letters from the artist Isaac Israëls to Jo, including thirteen postcards and two picture postcards. All this time the letters had been in the possession of Sylvia's mother, Mathilde Cramer-van Gogh, who was Vincent's daughter and Jo's granddaughter. They are now part of the collection of the Vincent van Gogh Foundation. Most of the letters are undated, they cover the period from February 1891 to January 1924, and reveal a short but intense relationship that until now was unknown to the public at large.[27] Isaac and Jo began as friends, became lovers for a while and later established a close friendship. As far as we know, there are no surviving letters from Jo to Isaac.

The letters her brother Andries wrote to their parents, which Jo also read, shed considerable light on Jo's early years. They tell us what issues occupied the family and which subjects were regarded as relevant: everyday subjects like food, clothes and personal hygiene, but also more elevated matters such as maintaining social contacts and furthering one's artistic and intellectual development through literature, music and visits to museums and theatres. Jo was curious and read a great deal, not solely for pleasure and diversion, but because it was an absolute necessity for her from an early age. The ideas and actions of characters in novels she found sympathetic more than once provided her with something to hold on to.

Jo's most intimate and intense correspondence was with Theo. The greater part dates from the period of their engagement and there are a few letters written while they were married. There are 101 letters altogether. Until now, of all Jo's correspondence only these letters between her and Theo have been published in book form, in part because of their fascinating and touching contents, but also because the last tragic years of Vincent's life can be largely traced through them.[28]

Although many of Jo's personal letters have survived, the majority of her correspondence relates to business. As time passed, her contacts with exhibition makers, art dealers and publishers expanded ever further and the stacks of correspondence from at home and abroad grew steadily.

A good deal has been preserved, but by no means all. In part this was Jo's own doing, if we are to believe what she wrote in 1889. It was in January, she was getting ready to leave for Paris and she wrote to Theo: 'You know I've always been fanatical about keeping letters of any interest to me, but now I must finally start disposing of them.'[29] There is a good chance that she actually did so, but even if that were not the case, her son had no qualms—at least so the sources tell us, for a passage in Vincent's diary (written several decades later) reveals an even more drastic bout of tidying mania:

> Also came across a box of letters my mother had kept, from Jos and from me, from before 1920 and some after that. It was all personal with few general things, some opened by the censor. I burnt the whole lot in the fireplace in my room—and without reading them all again.[30]

There are considerably fewer letters dating from the last period of Jo's life, because she and the members of her family were living close to one another and the telephone had been introduced.[31]

The account book mentioned previously provides crucial information about Jo's life that supplements the diaries and letters.[32] The organizations and people to whom she sold Van Gogh's work are recorded in it, and she kept a reasonably accurate record of the sums she received for paintings and drawings, so that it is possible to follow the massive rise in the price of his work during her lifetime. Nevertheless, Jo's account book cannot serve as the only source for this biography, for there were of course exhibitions at which she did not put in works for sale or sold nothing. For the purposes of this book I have therefore worked on the basis of all the Van Gogh exhibitions on which Jo collaborated, in other words not only those where she actually sold. My reconstruction of exhibitions is based on the extensive documentation and literature in the Van Gogh Museum library. This means that examples of both categories—selling exhibitions and 'ordinary' exhibitions—will crop up throughout the book. No attempt has been made to cover every exhibition. I discuss only the most salient and noteworthy of the countless exhibitions to which Jo contributed with her collection. Similarly, I have only treated the most striking of her contacts with private individuals. Exhibitions could be important to Jo for a variety of reasons: sometimes she was persuaded by the artistic views and ideals of the organizers or the international importance of a show, on other occasions she acted chiefly for social motives.

This translation follows the Dutch edition *Alles voor Vincent: Het leven van Jo van Gogh-Bonger* (2019). Corrections have been made here and there. The translations from the correspondence between Theo and Jo, *Kort geluk* (1999), were taken from the English edition, *Brief Happiness* (1999), save for a few minor changes. There are also two important revisions. Firstly, the year in which Vincent came of age. It was 1911, not 1915. The second revision relates to an important note Gustave Coquiot made (see Chapter 14 (p. 266). He wanted to find out more about Van Gogh, so in June 1922 he paid Jo a visit at 77 Koninginneweg in Amsterdam. Coquiot jotted down what he saw and heard there in a small notebook; later he typed out his observations and added them to his extensive documentation on Van Gogh, which he kept in a large exercise book. This book reveals that Anton Kröller and Helene Kröller-Müller once proposed buying the whole collection from Jo.[33] On this revelation see Zwikker 2021.

In this biography I show how Jo went to work, the paths she trod, the decisions she took, the people she met—in short, how she managed to accomplish the task she had set herself. The fact that she also had an everyday life, with boarding house guests, maids, a growing son, parents, brothers and sisters, friends, books, pets and a garden full of flowers, will play its full part in the chapters that follow, if for no other reason than that Jo particularly appreciated this intimate minutiae in a biography. Writing about the biography of George Eliot in her diary, she commented that it contained everything about the intellectual relationship between Eliot and her partner George Henry Lewes, but regrettably nothing about the details and particulars of their relationship: 'something about their daily life—those small, revealing features are missing.'[34] To her that was clearly a missed opportunity.

Jo was a passionate reader and lover of biographies throughout her life. One of her earliest portrait photographs shows her sitting with a book on her lap.

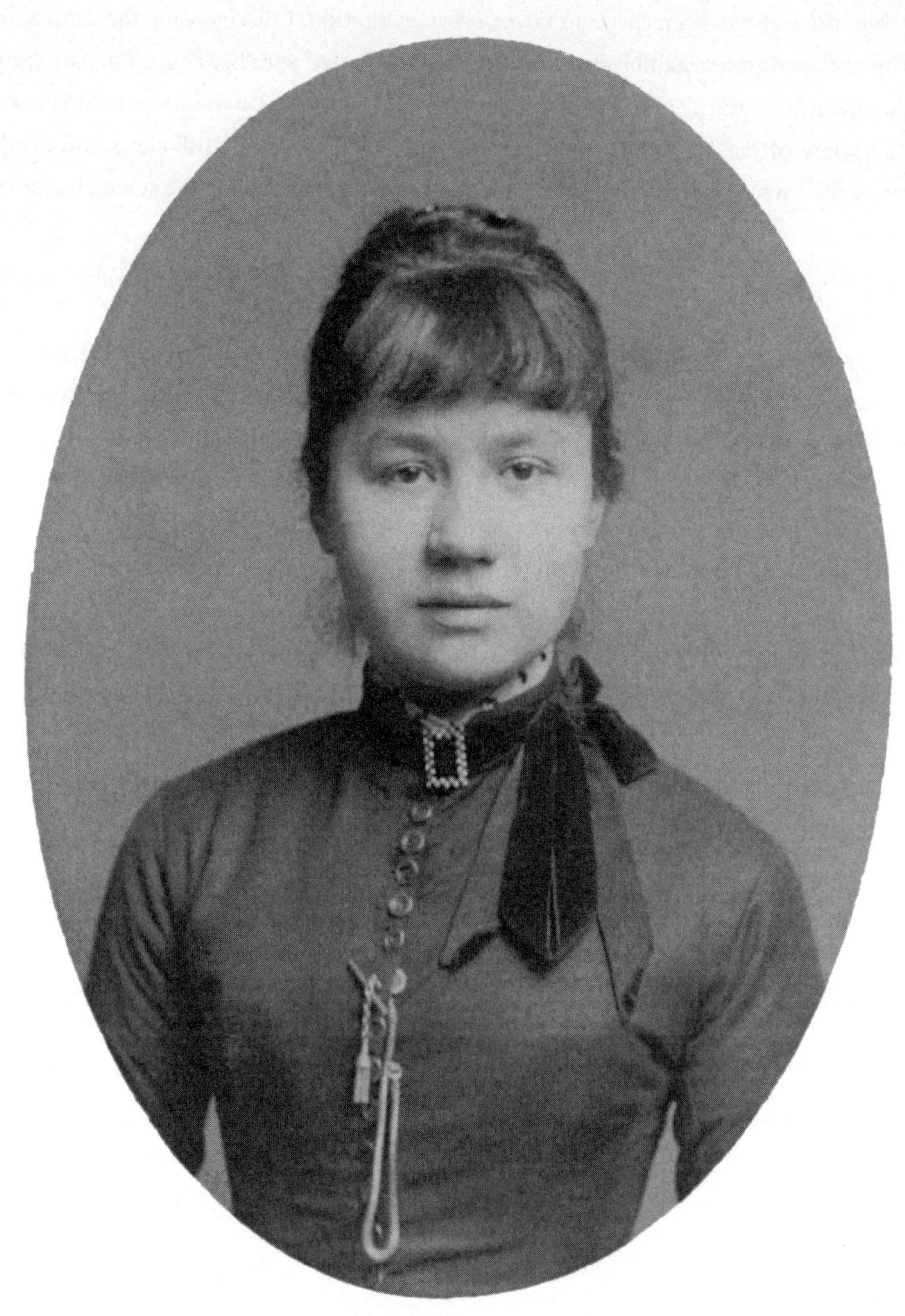

Part One

A respectable middle-class family—the Bongers

1862–88

Then how about just you, Enid Parker?
Would you like to gather up your voluminous skirts
and ride side-saddle on the crossbar
and tell me what happened between 1863 and 1931?

BILLY COLLINS[1]

1

A carefree childhood in a harmonious family

The fourth of October 1862 was a windless day; the temperature fluctuated around sixteen degrees. In the early hours of the morning, Johanna Gezina Bonger was born at number 504 Egelantiersgracht in Amsterdam. A notice in the *NRC* newspaper announced to the world that Hermina Louise Weissman and Hendrik Christiaan Bonger Jr had 'by the grace of God' had a healthy daughter. Two days later, her father (then a thirty-four-year-old insurance agent) registered the newborn. In the family, they would call her Jo and 'Net'. She was named after her spinster aunt, Johanna Gezina Weissman, her mother's sister. Jo heartily disliked her second name, Gezina, and never used it.[1] The clergyman Willem Moll, a professor of church history, baptized her in the Nieuwe Kerk on 2 November.

A notebook reveals that she caught the usual childhood illnesses at the time, including chickenpox, whooping cough and measles.[2] Nearly a year after her birth, on 24 September 1863—according to her mother Jo was 'an angelic little mite'—Hendrik and Hermine Bonger moved with their family to Zeist, where they lived in Zusterplein.[3] Hendrik was one of the three directors of the Algemeene Brandwaarborg- & Verzekeringsmaatschappij *Ultrajectum*. He was the 'liquidator', responsible for winding up companies in trouble. But *Ultrajectum* did not prosper, and in 1865 the company itself went into liquidation.[4]

The family returned to Amsterdam.[5] Hendrik was thirty-seven, Hermine thirty-four. By now they had six children and they moved into number 320 Keizersgracht[6] (Plate 2). Hendrik Bonger now became the editor and publisher of the *Zee-post*, a daily bulletin of international shipping news.[7] In 1866 they moved to 159a Weteringschans. They lived there, on the outskirts of the city, for twelve years, then moved a few doors down to number 121, opposite the Weteringplantsoen. From April 1895 they lived in a house in Weteringschans overlooking the Rijksmuseum, which had opened in 1885.[8]

For a portrait of her, the photographer sat Jo on a table with her feet on a chair and a book of prints on her lap (Plate 3). During the same session in Spiegelstraat, Hermine posed with her three daughters. Jo's head was slightly tilted (Figure 1). Not all of the family would be recorded for posterity, for Jo was confronted with death at an early age: she lost three little brothers before she was seven.

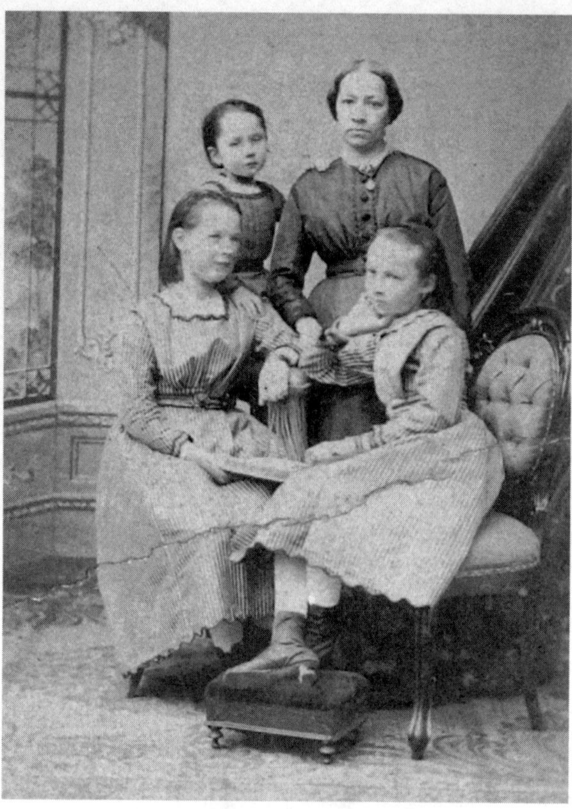

Figure 1 Hermine Bonger-Weissman and her daughters: Jo (beside her), Lien and Mien, *c.* 1869.

The only information about her primary school days that we have relates to a single year. She was at the Tesselschade School, the local primary school for pupils from the ages of six to thirteen, in Plantage Muidergracht. Christina Louisa Theunissen was the senior teacher in the second year. Jo thought this was the best period of her school years; 'never have I been as spoilt as I was there,' she recalled.[9] She was then sent to the 'French school', which provided general, non-vocational education across a wide range of subjects, including French. In a birthday diary, her oldest brother, Henri, noted the name Eugenie Petit; Jo's son later added: 'The daughters of H.C. Bonger Jr were at Miss Petit's "French school".' Eugenie Charlotte Petit wrote the poem 'Op de reize door dit leven' (On Life's Journey) in Jo's album. Jo was fourteen and about to move on to high school. These French schools for girls sought to educate their pupils for their future ideal life, as wives and mothers, but for some it was an incentive to continue their studies and become a teacher.[10] Jo, who did well at school, was one of them. There is a surviving portrait photograph of her taken at that time, showing her with a perfect centre parting (Figure 2).[11]

She had started her album at the end of 1876. Her parents were the first to write in it.[12] Her father quoted a Dutch translation of some lines by Lord Byron: ''t Geloof is veel,/ de liefde is meer:/ 't Geloof heft/ uit alle aardsche Smarte/ het Hart omhoog/ naar 's Hemels sfeer,/ Maar in de liefde/ Daalt de

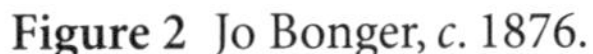
Figure 2 Jo Bonger, *c.* 1876.

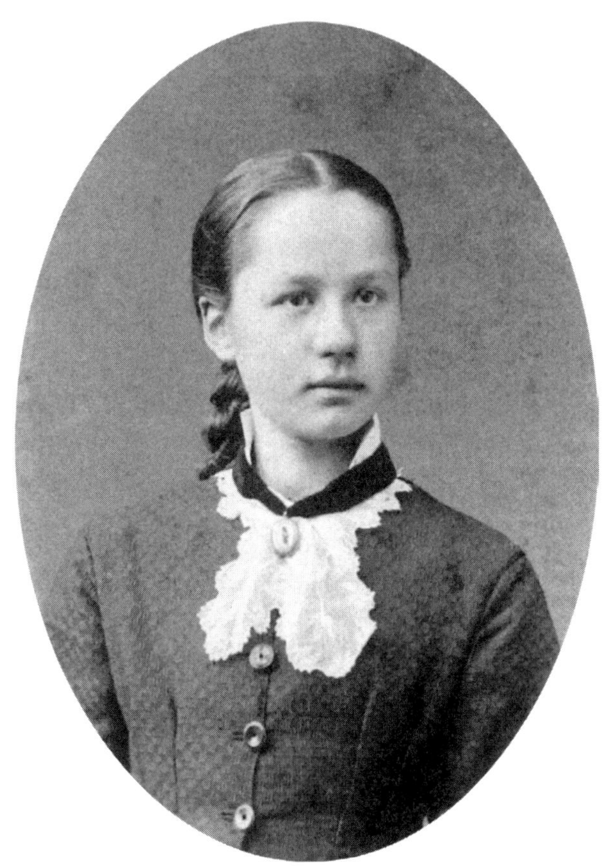

hemel neer/ in 't Harte', with the message: 'if you are profoundly aware of the truth expressed here, then you will learn to know that comforting inner peace which is of inestimable value to mankind.'[13] Her mother copied the poem 'Jonge roeping' (Youthful Vocation) by the then popular poet P.A. de Génestet. The poem is about the fresh zest for life that stems from a heart that 'rests in God'.[14] Both parents chose this means to emphasize the power of the divine support that can lead to inner peace. In this period of Jo's life, everything in the garden was seemingly lovely, but peace of mind later proved very elusive.

In 1885, Jo described her father thus: 'My dear father is what they call very liberal but a truly pious, religious man who does not pay lip service to the divine doctrine "love thy neighbour as thyself", but acts upon it.' And she spoke of her 'dear, good mother with her childlike, boundless faith'.[15] A few years later, she explained these qualities, which her parents had passed on to their children, to her future husband, Theo van Gogh:

> Father has something persistently solid in his character, which Mother lacks entirely. She relies solely on her feeling, which is exceptionally well developed so she can trust it implicitly, because her instincts are always right, but she wouldn't have been like that if she'd had to be on her own.

What she called *weakness of will* gnawed away at several members of the family; she suffered, but Andries was much worse:

> He *wants* something, but hasn't his father's strength to accomplish it, while the sensitivity he got from his mother makes him take things far too much to heart and suffer because of what he lacks—and I recognize the same in myself, which is the very reason I'm always afraid to give in to it. *This* is what has always driven me to seek my own way, to leave home, to be independent, because I know that if I didn't use the strength I have, if I didn't harden myself a bit, I wouldn't realize my potential.

Theo replied to this, expanded on it and also sensed in Jo 'something slightly more modern, something slightly more revolutionary if you will'.[16] These character traits emerged later: the hardness, when she had to stand up to all sorts of art dealers and buyers of Van Gogh's work, and the revolutionary, when Jo's convictions led her to join the socialists.

Her early years were idyllic. That, at least, is how she looked back on them as a twenty-year-old, after she had visited the Foundling Hospital in London and been touched by the orphans who did not have the blessing of a 'happy home'. She herself was particularly sensitive to affection. Until she was twenty-two, she always received her first birthday kiss from her mother, followed by hugs and kisses from her brothers and sisters—her father had already left for work at seven.[17] Jo had a carefree childhood in this harmonious family. Later she wrote that she always loved Sundays so much as a child because they were so cosy and pleasant at home.[18]

When Jo was growing up, the population of Amsterdam was about 265,000. The area around the Weteringschans still had quite a rural feel, but in 1875 a great deal began to change: Vondelstraat and P.C. Hooftstraat were built and the network of streets in the neighbourhood expanded rapidly. The city became ever more metropolitan. The industrial revolution and modern capitalism continued apace. By the middle of the century, the middle class had acquired an individual identity. Schooling, vocational education and business evolved alongside. The North Sea Canal was completed in 1876; nine years later the Rijksmuseum opened its doors on Stadhouderskade, followed in 1888 by the Concertgebouw, soon after that by the new Amsterdam Central Station and in 1895 the Stedelijk Museum. The Amsterdamsche Omnibus Maatschappij began operating a horse-drawn tram service between Leidseplein and Plantage. Around 1890, the nine thousand hand carts and countless barrel organs set the street scene. Most things were done on foot.[19]

Jo was a real city child. This came home to her most clearly in March 1892, playing in the garden of her house in Bussum with her two-year-old Vincent: 'How new this is for me—those birds, those flowers, those plants—I see for the first time now that I was brought up in an upstairs flat in the city and never, never went to the country as a child!'[20] Her 'country' was the Vondelpark, which opened when she was three. The greater part of it, designed by L.P. Zocher, was laid out between 1875 and 1877. Looking back on her carefree youth, she recalled her evening walks in the park, arm in arm with Andries. In the winter they skated.[21]

Parents and family

Jo was the fifth child of Hendrik Christiaan Bonger (5 January 1828–28 April 1904) and Hermine Louise Weissman (19 February 1831–18 June 1905). Their wedding on 5 July 1855 was quite an event, and more than a hundred people came to the reception held to congratulate them on their wedding.[22] The minister Louis Meijboom solemnized their marriage in Sloterdijk. Hendrik was the son of the bookkeeper Hendrik Christiaan Bonger and his wife Carolina Sabel. When he was eleven, his father had taken Hendrik to a church where the writer and cleric Nicolaas Beets presided, and this had made a profound impression on him. When he congratulated Beets on his fortieth anniversary in office in 1880, he wrote that he still remembered his first sermon.[23] Hermine's parents were the wine merchant Gerrit Weissman and Hermina Drinklein; Johanna Gezina was her only sister and she had two brothers, Adriaan Willem and Gerrit.

Jo's father went to a commercial college and worked in the offices of Johannes Rahder Hzn from 1843 to 1859.[24] With Charles Faber Boissevain, a member of the firm of Boissevain & Kooy, shipowners and merchants, Rahder set up the insurance company N.V. *Maatschappij van Verzekering De Phoenix*; in this period he owned several ships. His vessels imported coffee and pepper from Padang, and indigo from Batavia (present-day Jakarta).[25] Hendrik Bonger's work in this firm must have been good preparation and set him on the path for his job as editor and publisher of the *Zee-post* a few years later. In April 1885 he also became a partner in the insurance brokers Brak & Moes and from then on his financial situation was more comfortable. In 1896 he became a director of this company.[26] The family never went short of anything, but they were not especially affluent either. Bonger belonged to the middle class, he was not wealthy. He must have been a careful man. In a portrait photograph he looks thoughtfully into the lens (Figure 3).

But work was not everything. Bonger loved music and it was a part of family life. He played the viola in a string quartet, whose members varied. His nephew Willem Weissman recalled that his uncle used to play quartets with the surgeon A.A. de Lelie, the notary J.C.G. Pollones and the professional musician Henri Viotta. Willem was allowed to sit in the next room and listen, and so became familiar with Haydn, Mozart, Beethoven and Schubert. Bonger regularly attended the concerts at *Maatschappij Caecilia*; his nephew often accompanied him—as, when they were old enough, did his children.[27]

There was no scrimping on music lessons and musical instruments. The children Mien, Jo and Betsy played the piano, Henri the cello, Wim the violin and Betsy sang. Andries did not play an instrument, but he often went to concerts. Things musical could sometimes get out of hand in their home. In October 1889, Lien wrote to Theo van Gogh: 'I hope you can read this scribble, but they're so busy playing music that I can hardly write for the noise,' and the same day Wim told Jo: 'Betsy is singing scales so loud that I keep on making mistakes.'[28] Mr Bonger paid for his children's education and the members of the family bought books. They could also afford outings: they frequently went to

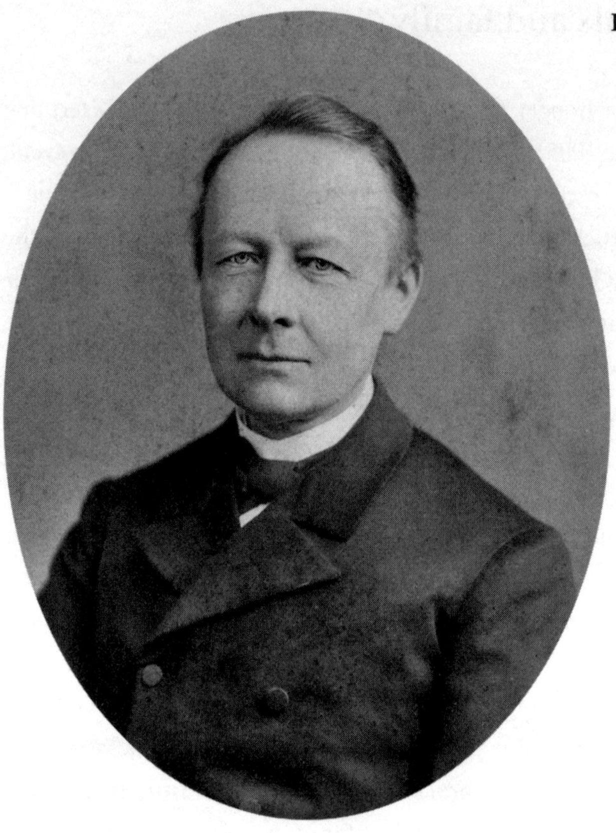

Figure 3 Hendrik Bonger, undated.

the theatre, to concerts and to Artis, where concerts were staged in the Artis Theatre (known as the Hollandsche Schouwburg after 1894). And they very much enjoyed boat trips on the Amstel. All the same, they lived frugally. Tellingly, a planned boat trip to Muiderberg was called off in 1889 when it was discovered that Jo was ten weeks pregnant. Mrs Bonger wanted to set the money aside for her trip to Paris, where she would support Jo in the days before she gave birth.[29] She was already saving up months in advance.

In everyday life, the family was unmistakably middle class, which meant that they had particular interests and a certain reserve in their conduct. When Andries visited the celebrated writer Conrad Busken Huet and his family in Paris, they gave him *Sara Burgerhart* (1782) by Betje Wolff and Aagje Deken. He told his parents: 'It surprises me, since we pride ourselves on being a real Dutch family, that we never had this novel at home.' They owed it to their class, in fact, and he regarded this neglect as a deficiency in their education, for he added pointedly that this novel, in which the heroine strives to become the perfect bourgeoise, had been read aloud in Mrs Huet's childhood home.[30] What the Bongers read were the weeklies *The Family Herald: A Domestic Magazine of Useful Information & Amusement* and *L'Illustration: Journal Universel*, which took a wide-ranging look at developments in the world; they may have been provided by a magazine subscription service.[31] And they kept pets.

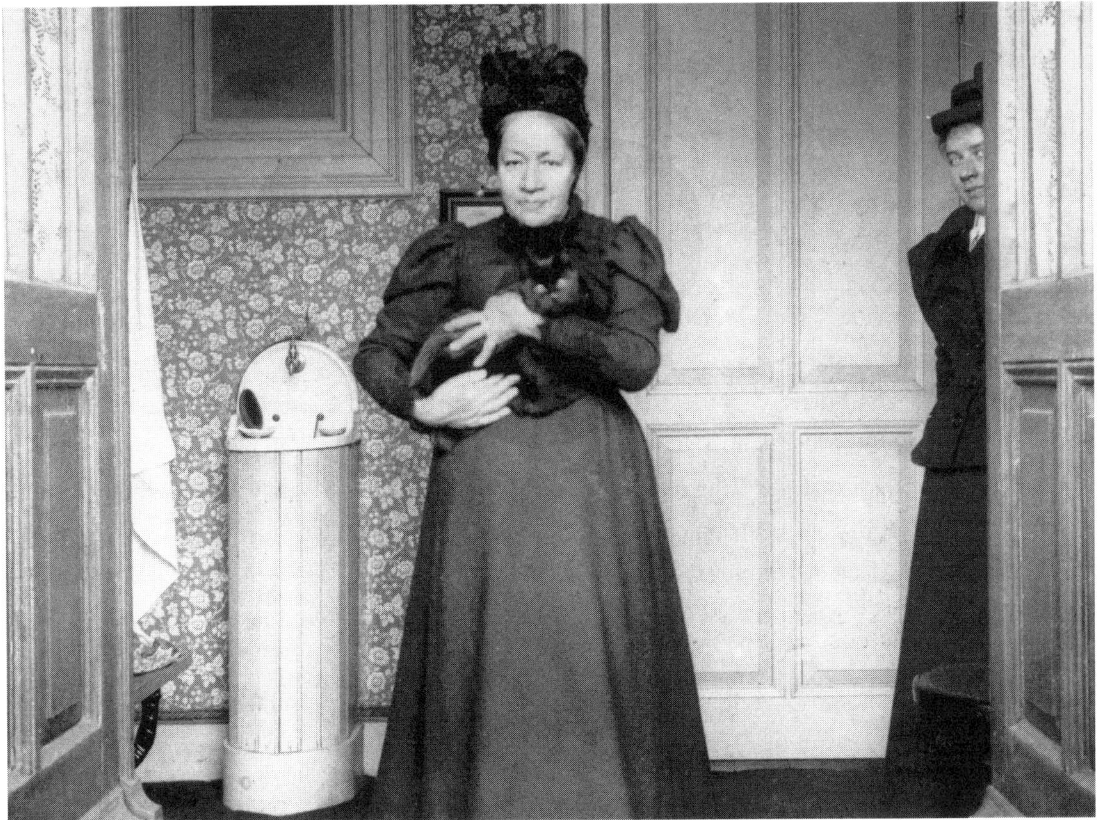

Figure 4 Hermine Bonger-Weissman with the cat in her arms; her daughter Betsy looking round the door to the right, undated.

There was always a cat, and they had a little dog called Tommie (Figure 4). Like her mother, Jo loved cats and dogs.

In all the letters and anecdotes, Mrs Bonger emerges as a simple, caring and devoted woman who found it hard to sit still. She never fretted over big things, was cheerful and enjoyed life.[32] She was very loving, but never really a confidante for Jo—that was what friends and sisters were for. Although she had been to school, she neglected her languages.[33] The maid and her two oldest daughters helped her with the housekeeping, which was impeccable. Jo was very evidently sidelined here, and consequently had considerable difficulty later, when she had to manage her own household. People in the Bonger home treated their things with great care; in 1903 Mrs Bonger was still using the dozen top sheets she had had on her wedding day in 1855.[34] Jo's son Vincent, who compiled information about the members of the Bonger and Weissman families, noted: 'The younger the children, the more they were able to get away from their controlling mother.'[35] He phrased it thus, however, after he had been in therapy.

The family saw a great deal of Adriaan Weissman's family. He was Hermine's brother and married to Wilhelmina Stoerhaan. In April 1866 they moved into an upstairs flat at 147 Weteringschans. Their son Willem was a frequent visitor at the Bongers'. He was the boy who had so enjoyed listening to Jo's father's string quartet, and he kept in touch with Jo until at least 1914. An architect, he designed, among other things, the Stedelijk Museum in Amsterdam and a number of splendid residences.[36]

Sisters and brothers

Jo's oldest sister Carolina ('Lien'; 27 October 1856–5 January 1919) was a home-loving, tidy and contented woman whose main focus was the household (Figure 5). It was a task that was made for her. In 1889 Jo wrote: 'Henri, Lien and Mien accept themselves as they are—that's fine for Lien because she *is* somebody, but not for the others.'[37] Lien comes across in her letters as a clever woman, chiefly concerned with day-to-day worries. Everyone benefitted from her skill with a needle. She went rowing with her brother Henri and loved reading. She contributed the poem 'Look Aloft' by Jonathan Lawrence to Jo's album. She was so afraid of thunder and lightning that she could not eat.[38] When Jo was living in Paris, Lien empathized with her and Theo. Jo, for her part, always thought of Lien 'in her grey cotton dress with the little hat with the daisies'.[39] We know little about the relationship between the two sisters after Jo returned to the Netherlands. We do know, though, that Lien adored her nephew, Vincent—when the telegram announcing the birth arrived, she ran full-tilt down the street to show it to her father.[40] She never married.

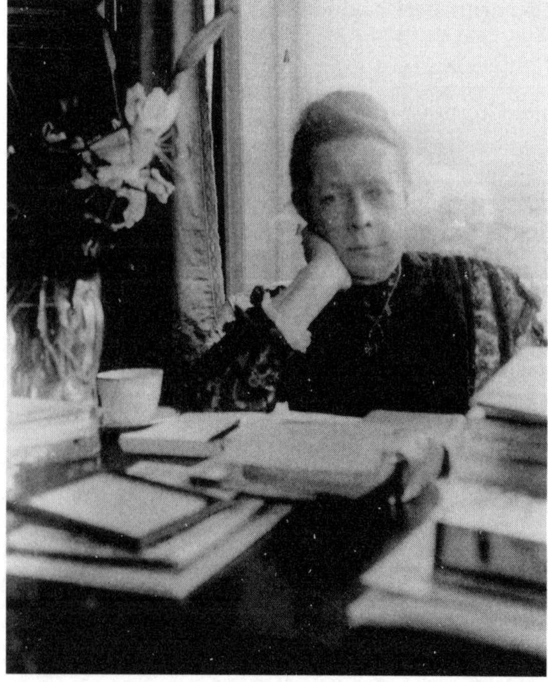

Figure 5 Lien Bonger, undated.

The second sister, Hermina Louise ('Mien'; 27 April 1858–15 July 1910) was likewise unmarried and helped with the work in the house (Plate 4). When Jo married, she turned to Mien with tricky problems relating to soapy water and carpet-beating.[41] Mien hardly ever travelled, exceptions being trips to Cleves in 1887 and Paris in 1889, where she went to help Jo when the baby was born. She liked going out and there were weeks when she attended performances of Wagner on three successive days.[42] Mien was musical, wrote lively letters, loved reading and was involved in sending books back and forth.[43] Jo and Mien were very close.[44] She lovingly called her Minnie or Minkie, embracing her time after time on paper and sending 'a thousand kisses' in the envelope. In April 1889 Jo declared: 'I've got so much to tell you that a box of paper wouldn't be enough to contain it all.'[45]

Jo's oldest brother Hendrik Christiaan ('Henri', 'Han'; 15 July 1859–19 May 1929) wore a moustache and was a passionate rower (Figure 6). He had a light rowing boat, an English wherry, in which, appropriately dressed and with Jo in the stern, he rowed on the Amstel.[46] Henri went to the commercial college, became an insurance broker and publisher of the *Zee-post*, like his father. He, too, remained unmarried. Henri was a great opera lover and enjoyed the theatre. He was extremely musical, played the cello and had a large collection of chamber music.[47] His nephew Frans Bonger inherited his instrument. In his family this cello was jokingly described as 'Uncle Han's beauty'.[48] In 1896 Henri became a partner in the insurance firm of Brak & Moes, where his father was a director and joint

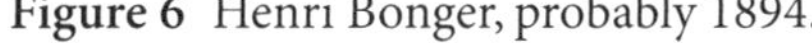
Figure 6 Henri Bonger, probably 1894.

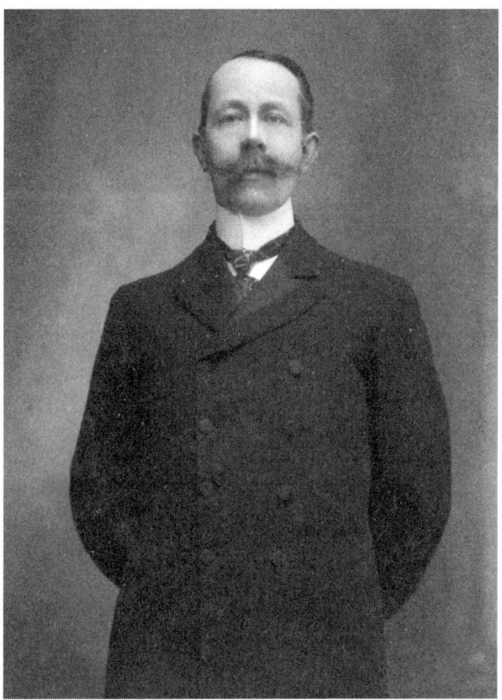

owner. He went on countless trips abroad. In his travel notes, which run from 1882 to 1912, we see him expand his horizons as he explores European cities and regions.[49] He will certainly have told Jo about his experiences, fuelling her desire to see more of the world. Henri was a rather formal, but at the same time sympathetic man, who suffered from bouts of depression.

Jo's second brother Andries ('Dries', 'André'; 20 May 1861–20 January 1936) was likewise rather formal. Like Henri, he attended the commercial college, where he was taught Dutch by Willem Doorenbos and English by Cornelis Stoffel. They awoke in him a love of literature that was to remain with him all his life. Andries read voraciously; the works of Lord Byron and Percy Bysshe Shelley were early favourites. He thought that he had had a 'hard childhood',[50] a claim later put into perspective by his nephew Henk Bonger: 'that may well have been so, but the Bongers do have a tendency to exaggerate'.[51]

For years Andries and Jo were extraordinarily close. They always went to church together on New Year's Eve, and on Good Friday they went to the old Walloon Church.[52] Their intimacy was based on their shared interests. Andries instructed, discussed and indoctrinated, while Jo faithfully followed where he pointed, took it all in and allowed herself to be lectured. Time after time, they picked up their pens and wrote to one another, because in Andries's view Jo raised subjects that required 'exhaustive discussion'.[53]

Andries worked briefly in an office in Amsterdam. In Germany he gave private lessons in English and French to the children of a well-to-do family, and at the end of 1879 he moved to Paris, where he lived for twelve years.[54] He got a job with Geo Wehry & Co, established in Amsterdam in 1867. The company dealt in tobacco, coffee, tea, rubber and artificial flowers. In 1883 Andries was yearning for a different sort of position. 'I feel I'm capable of something better than an artificial flower broker,' he lamented (Plate 5).[55]

He wrote home almost every week. Writing helped him bear his lonely existence and he recorded virtually every tiny day-to-day incident in his letters. He was a devout Christian and hated anything that tended towards the Bohemian. In 1881 he met Theo van Gogh at the Hollandsche Club in Paris. They went to museums together and became close friends. Their friendship dictated the course of Jo's life: it was through Andries that she met Theo in 1885. In 1888 Andries married Anne Marie Louise van der Linden ('Annie'; 1859–1931). His father surprised them on their wedding day with three notices in an issue of the *Zee-post*, which he had got the printer to set especially for this one copy: 'Amsterdam, departed 3 May THE WEDDING VESSEL commanded by Captain A. Bonger, to the silvery mooring.'[56] Sincere as his parents' good wishes may have been, his marriage to their former neighbour was a miserable affair. The couple remained childless and Andries and Annie were weighed down by their lack. They led a stressful and unhappy life together. Jo confessed that Annie could be 'insufferable', and Andries was sometimes not much better: 'He gave his opinion with almost theatrical, pathetic seriousness and nothing much was ever any good. These opinions were usually bristling with indignation, I never saw or heard him laugh and I actually don't think he ever did laugh.'[57] In 1934, three years after Annie died, Andries married again in Rome. His second wife was Françoise Wilhelmina Maria van der Borch van Verwolde (1887–1975), a member of a Dutch aristocratic family. He was seventy-three, she was forty-seven. Andries suffered from a 'nervous disposition heightened almost to the point of super-sensitivity', according to Françoise.[58] The marriage was short-lived; he died less than two years later.

Jo was born just over a year after Andries, and she was followed three years later by another brother, Bernard Johannes (12 September 1865–23 June 1867), who died of croup. The twins Johannes (10 December 1867–14 March 1869) and Bernard (10 December 1867–16 March 1869) died in infancy, both from a respiratory disease. In the mid-nineteenth century one in five babies died in their first year.[59]

Jo's youngest sister Elizabeth Hortense ('Beb', 'Betsy'; 16 November 1870–17 January 1944) played the piano and studied singing at the conservatory: she was a soprano (Figure 7). Until Jo moved to Paris in 1889 (she was twenty-six and Betsy was eighteen) they shared a room.[60] They both loved Beethoven and played duets. Betsy increasingly behaved like a grand lady and Wim nicknamed her 'posh Beb'. Willem Weissman reported: 'Betsy is already walking arm in arm with one of our foremost Wagner singers, proof of how popular she is at the conservatory.' Betsy was the life and soul at home; Jo often found it very dull without her. They sometimes played whist in the evenings, and their father joined in.[61]

Jo and Betsy maintained close ties for the whole of their lives. They both had an idealistic attitude to life. In September 1892, Jo went to see Betsy perform in the concert hall in the Volkshuis *Ons Huis*, an educational association in the heart of Amsterdam's Jordaan district. The Dutch *volkshuizen* (people's houses) were established in the belief that class harmony could be advanced by bringing the middle and working classes together.[62] Jo had made a point of watching the audience's response, and her observation reveals just how aware she was of class differences:

> It was quite a sight, the auditorium was not full of ladies and gentlemen in fine clothes—but of people in their shabby things with tired, weather-beaten faces, who also had an evening of enjoyment and relaxation at last. . . . the Grieg sonata left them cold—nobody understood any of it—the songs that Beb sung were enjoyed very much—and they became very sentimental during the sad endings—their eyes were full of tears.[63]

Like her two oldest sisters, Betsy never married. When she completed her training, she became a singing teacher and continued to perform regularly in the Netherlands and abroad. Her admiration for the conductor Willem Mengelberg was so great that she later presented him with Van Gogh's drawing *Two Cottages in Saintes-Maries-de-la-Mer* (F 1440 / JH 1451). She must have received it as a gift from Jo at some time.[64]

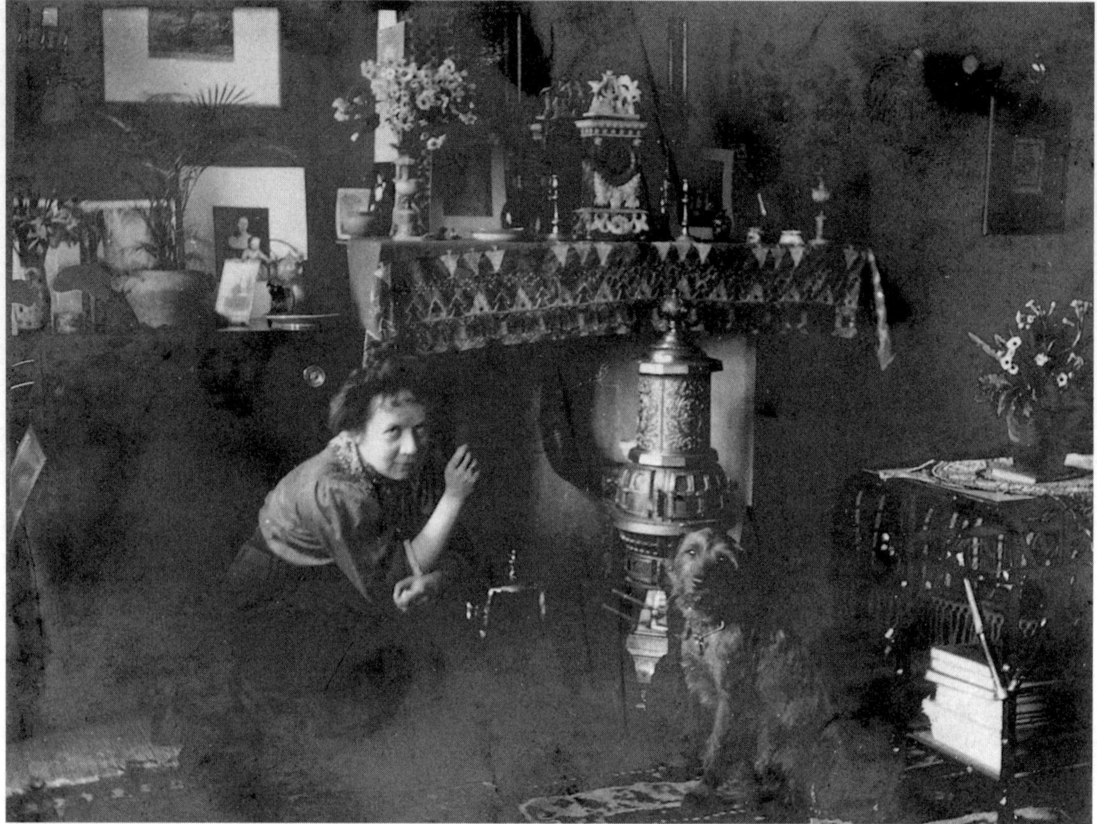

Figure 7 Betsy Bonger with her dog in the living room at 89 Weteringschans in Amsterdam, undated.

In the spring of 1904, Jo, her son Vincent and Betsy went to Switzerland. They had a wonderful holiday—it was the first time they had been away together.[65] That summer, Betsy urged her to move from Bussum to Amsterdam. Their mother had recently been widowed, and this influenced Jo's decision to make the move. They went to Switzerland again in the summer of 1906. Little is known about their relationship later on, save for birthday visits. We do know that between 1916 and 1919 (the period Jo, Vincent and his wife Josina spent in America) Betsy joined with Andries to look after their interests. She lived with her brother Henri all her life.[66]

Jo's youngest brother Willem Adriaan ('Wim'; 16 September 1876–15 May 1940) was an afterthought. Although fourteen years separated them, Wim and Jo got on very well (Figure 8). He began a letter to her: 'Dearest black gazelle!'[67] Wim attended the Amsterdam Barlaeus High School, played cricket and collected stamps. He liked to sing and until halfway through his student years took violin lessons from Christiaan Timmer, the leader of the Concertgebouw Orchestra. In 1895 he began a law degree. As a member of the Amsterdam Student Corps, and later rector, he belonged to the Clio debating society, which had many members interested in socialism and sociology. In 1898, shortly after the parliamentary

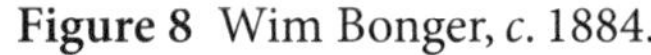

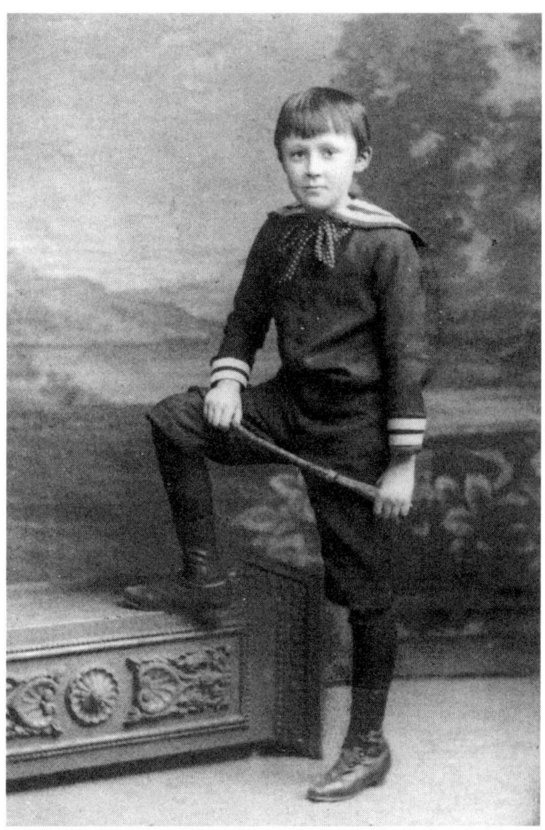

Figure 8 Wim Bonger, *c.* 1884.

elections at which the Social Democratic Labour Party (SDAP) were successful, Wim joined the party; Jo had already been a member for several years. Wim became a committed defender of socialism. He wrote lively columns in the socialist daily *Het Volk*. As chair of the Socialistisch Leesgezelschap (a socialist reading circle) he invited leading socialists for readings and he took part in political polemics in the student magazine *Propria Cures*.[68] In 1914 Wim became chair of 'Kunst aan het Volk' (art for the people) and in later years he often contributed to *De Socialistische Gids* (1916–38), the SDAP's monthly scientific journal. In the last twenty years of Jo's life, when she was living in Amsterdam, he was a regular visitor. They shared their deeply held socialist sympathies.[69]

Wim joined Brak & Moes as a deputy manager and member of the firm, like his father and his brother Henri—evidence of the close family ties and of the strength of Hendrik Bonger's position, which meant that he could secure good jobs for his sons. Wim was awarded his doctorate for his legal thesis *Criminalité et conditions économiques* on 3 March 1905. It reflected the 'scientific socialism' which gave social democrats their theoretical basis during the Second International (1889–1914) and was promulgated in the Netherlands chiefly by Frank van der Goes.[70] Six days after he received his doctorate, Wim married Maria Hendrika Adriana van Heteren ('Mies'; 1875–1961). Jo gave the newlyweds Van Gogh's drawing *Montmajour* (F 1446 / JH 1504), which Wim hung above his desk. They had two sons, Henk (1911–99) and Frans (1914–94).[71] Henk, who published his memoirs in 1986, called Jo his favourite aunt.[72] He recalled her special position in the family: 'In matters of everyday life (clothes, table manners, gestures, and in matters of taste in music, literature and painting) almost all the Bongers (with the exception of my Aunt Net) are extremely conservative.'[73]

On 12 June 1922 Wim accepted a post as professor of sociology and criminology at the University of Amsterdam; Jo would doubtless have been present at his inauguration. His life ended tragically: he and his wife decided to commit suicide when the Germans invaded the Netherlands in May 1940. Against all the odds, Mies survived because her stomach was pumped out in time.[74]

A family with a measured lifestyle

All the members of the Bonger family lived according to the rules of their class, in other words respectable, devout and with a strong sense of duty. Andries was very conscious of his father's love and felt 'a thousand times blessed' above others 'to have a father as respected and honoured as ours. God help me never to do anything to disgrace him.'[75] They were all fully aware of their filial duty. Hendrik Bonger was in a position to assist his children to study and to put them in touch with the right people, so that they could progress within their class or even move a rung higher. As a youth, Andries became increasingly convinced of the validity of their parents' lesson that mixing with the right people was a prerequisite in life.[76] One should not aim too high, but should nonetheless move up in the world. This called for a measured lifestyle.

Andries's congratulations to his brother Wim on his birthday epitomize this attitude—he expounded the family morals with his paternalistic admonitions:

> I hope that you will know that a good, honest, frank boy, always inspired by good intentions, can become a respected citizen.— If the boy has not been good, then the man will not be either.— So the best thing I can do is encourage you to be obedient and industrious so that you will be able to meet that condition.[77]

And the nine-year-old Wim had to make do with that.

The determination to regulate the passions was a constant theme in the Bongers' middle-class life. The highly-strung Andries explicitly preached self-control: 'Resisting all the passions is the prerequisite for a noble life.' The respectable position in society he wanted to occupy was part of this. He felt middle-class to his core.[78] Andries was disgusted by plays in which characters displayed 'tigerish passions' and consequently came to the unshakable conclusion: 'There can be no more beneficial influence than that of civilized company!'[79] Andries was extraordinarily class-conscious and hated bad manners, slang and smut. He was horrified by unkempt hair, he wanted a 'decently cut head'. He believed in all seriousness that 'the hairstyle of a nation generally has a deep philosophical significance'.[80] Unkempt brains were no good. Personally, he did everything he could to be a gentleman and act as an example to others. His father must have nodded in approval as he read all this.

It emerges from the letters that Andries wrote to his parents that the family had a wide-ranging interest in literature, music, art and theatre. Much of what he wrote was read by everyone at home, or read aloud to them: 'It goes without saying that my letter to Net, apart from a few personal remarks, was meant to be read by the family.'[81] It is clear from phrases like 'you remember how. . .' and 'as you know', that they knew what he was writing about. He assumed that they were familiar with classics by Molière, Racine and Shakespeare. He gave unsolicited advice about what to read and recommended plays that would be appearing on stage in Amsterdam. Books, magazines and newspapers flew back and forth, and time and time again he described with fervour a work of art he really liked, or professed his endorsement of the moral choices made by characters in novels. Andries liked character studies and frequently quoted his favourite extracts at length or even entire poems.[82] His visit to the annual Salon was a regular feature of his letters. This continuing correspondence enabled Jo to keep abreast of the latest cultural trends and doubtless stimulated her interest in art.

It was generally pleasant in the family circle, but boredom and detachment lurked. They were kept at bay by friendships outside the house. Jo's close relationship with Anna Dirks began at an early age. Justus Dirks (the chief engineer on the construction of the North Sea Canal), his wife Alida Clasina Kruijsse and their family lived nearby on Stadhouderskade.[83] Years later, in May 1892, Jo wrote in her diary: 'We walked up and down as we used to in the old days, when as young girls we accompanied each other from the Schans to the Kade and from the Kade to the Schans . . . we had an old-fashioned cosy chat about everything as we used to.'[84]

Jo's parents were members of the Dutch Reformed church and had their children baptized and confirmed. Later they joined the Remonstrants, something many free-thinkers did in the nineteenth century. The Protestant, liberal family—Jo went to a non-denominational school—was quite close.[85] In the summer of 1889, when Jo had only just settled in Paris, the tone of her letters betrayed how much she missed the day-to-day contact: she mentioned every member of the family one by one.[86]

All the children had a sheltered upbringing, but with emotional distance. When she was about twenty, Jo complained about the lack of intimacy and felt that the situation was less idyllic than it had been in her childhood. Her parents were certainly ready to help when it came to practical matters, but according to her they were lacking when it came to spiritual support. During a service taken by the minister Taco Kuiper in 1883, Jo realized what she missed in her own father. This serious and engaging clergyman appealed to her. Not that her father was unfriendly or not serious, but 'he never gives us such spiritual help', Jo wrote in her diary—she expressed herself in English in that period.[87] Well-meaning they certainly were. Anna Dirks described how sympathetic she found Mrs Bonger: 'Your dear Ma, Jo, would produce a piece of bread and butter with nothing besides at twelve o'clock with a

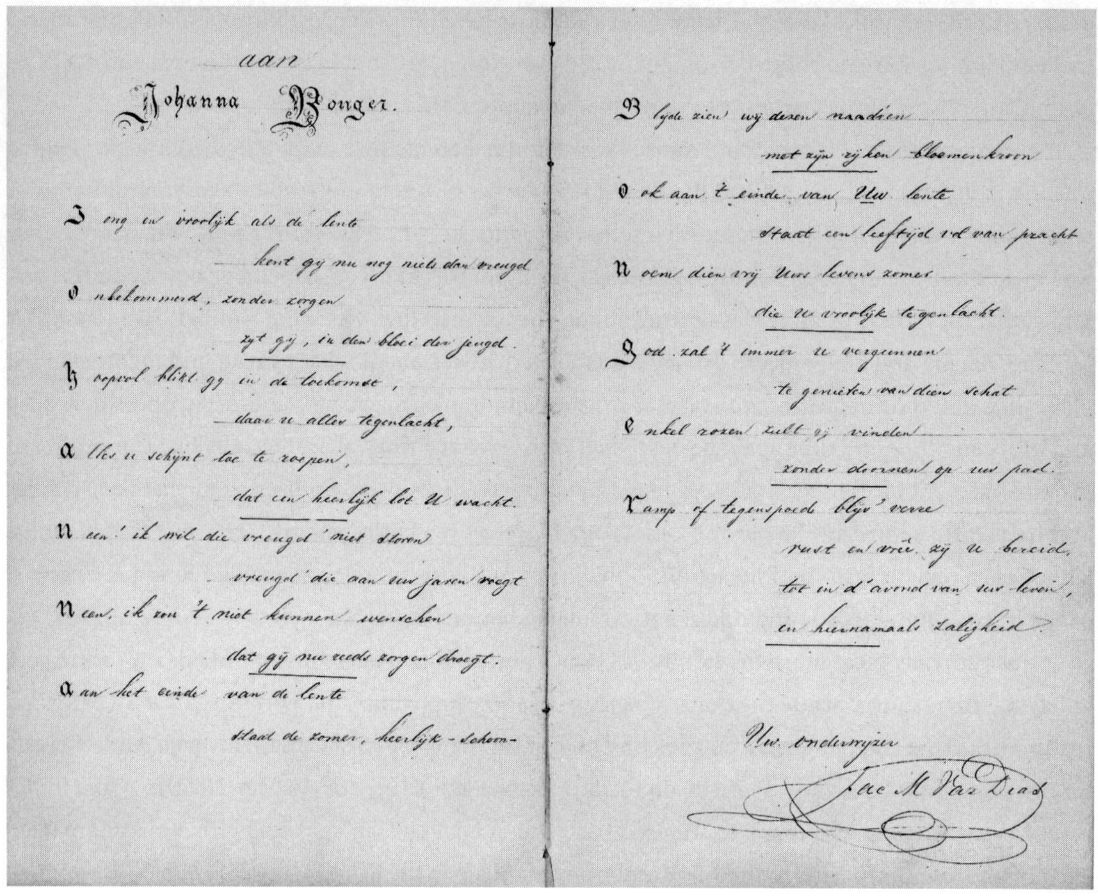

aan
Johanna Bonger.

Jong en vroolijk als de lente
kent gij nu nog niets dan vreugd
Onbekommerd, zonder zorgen
zijt gij, in den bloei der jeugd.
Hoopvol blikt gij in de toekomst,
daar u alles tegenlacht,
Alles u schijnt toe te roepen,
dat een heerlijk lot U wacht.
Neen! ik wil die vreugd niet storen
vreugd die aan uw jaren voegt
Neen, ik zou 't niet kunnen wenschen
dat gij nu reeds zorgen droegt.
Aan het einde van de lente
staat de zomer, heerlijk - schoon-
Blijde zien wij dezen naadren
met zijn rijken bloemenkroon
Ook aan 't einde van Uw lente
staat een leeftijd vol van pracht
Neem dien vrij Uws levens zomer
die u vroolijk tegenlacht.
God zal 't immer u vergunnen
te genieten van dien schat
Enkel rozen zult gij vinden
zonder doornen op uw pad.
Ramp of tegenspoed blijv' verre
rust en vreê zij u bereid,
tot in d' avond van uw leven,
en hiernamaals zaligheid

Uw onderwijzer
Jac M Vaz Dias

Figure 9 Jacob Mozes Vaz-Dias, 'Aan Johanna Bonger' ('To Johanna Bonger'), in *Poëziealbum van Jo Bonger*, between 1877 and 1880.

cheerful face and if someone was ill she would be kind and keep a cheerful atmosphere in the house.'[88] Even if the lunch might sometimes be meagre, the atmosphere was relaxed and harmonious, so that Jo came through her childhood unscathed. Her early years in the Bonger family gave her a strong basis for a well-grounded cultural life, with enough freedom for personal development. The roll-call of writers in her album proves that she did not lack for friends. As well as contributions by the immediate and extended family, there were entries by teachers and classmates from her high school days.[89] The mathematics teacher J.M. Vaz-Dias made a real effort, with a rhyming acrostic of Jo's name on rest, peace and divine bliss (Figure 9). In the years that followed, Jo expanded her view of the world and her friendships became closer. It was the perfect prelude to further study.

2

HBS and training as an English teacher

From 1877 to 1880 Jo attended the Amsterdam Hoogere Burgerschool (Higher Secondary School) for girls. This type of school was still in its infancy in the Netherlands—the progressive liberal statesman Johan Thorbecke established the HBS in 1863 and seven years later Aletta Jacobs became the first girl to attend this new type of school.[1] Jo was at the municipal HBS, housed in impressive premises at 264–6 Keizersgracht.[2]

There were eighteen pupils in the class in her first year. Her report for the autumn term (September to December 1879) reveals that she was good at French and English, and had satisfactory marks for history, geography, arithmetic and drawing. She failed physics and chemistry. Jo was apparently seldom ill at this time; she had only been absent fourteen hours that year. There were ten girls in the sixth form. Four pupils, Marie Stumpff, Helene de Ruyter, Ralphine Hooglandt and Anna Kehrer, went with her all the way through school from the first to the last year and Jo spent a lot of time with them.

The school principal was B.T. de Bouvé. She taught history, and English language and literature.[3] She must have been a compelling and inspiring teacher, conveying her enthusiasm to her pupils, for Jo continued her English studies as soon as she left school. She obtained three teaching certificates between 1880 and 1883, and in September 1884 she took up a post as a schoolmistress. She also started making translations, something she continued for many years.

Jo projected her ideals on to one of her teachers, whom she found friendly, natural and sociable. 'And should I ever see my dream realized, should I ever write a book, it will be she who will be in my mind when I describe the heroine.'[4] Her ideal woman was the twenty-one-year-old drawing mistress Adolfina Giesse, who published *Landschapteekenen met waterverf* (landscape drawing in watercolour) in 1882, and in 1883 married Pieter Jacobus Dirks, the brother of Jo's friend Anna.[5] Jo long cherished the dream of one day writing a novel with a woman as the central character. At the end of 1885 and again in 1886, looking ahead to a new year, she expressed a desire to become a writer. At the same time, she was aware that she should not set her literary ambitions too high; she felt that her own ideas were too vague and ill-defined.

There is a group photograph of fourteen girls dating from 1878–9. Young girls, all with smooth, centre-parted hair, long skirts and a completely uncertain future. Jo is at the front on the left, sitting on a low stool (Plate 6).[6] She was a 'cheerful, lively child', Vincent was to write in a brief biographical essay on his mother, but this can only have been hearsay and it may simply have been wishful thinking on his part.[7] This supposed cheerful and lively demeanour certainly does not always chime with the way Jo saw herself.

> As a child I was quiet and withdrawn and devoured every book I could, the good with the bad. It never did me any harm; on the contrary, it developed my mind, but physically I remained a child for a long time, when I was 18 I looked 14 and sadly lacked experience, I had never been out in the world and seldom among strangers, was desperately shy and awkward.[8]

Jo was constantly aware of her shyness and ineptness. She often withdrew into her own world of books, while the members of the family were playing their music.[9]

Andries as a role model

Jo did very well at school, although according to Andries she was cursed with a tendency to sluggishness and often forgot things.[10] She took her brother's departure for Paris at the end of 1879 very badly. 'I've never really known sorrow, except when Dries left,' she wrote in 1880[11] (Figure 10). When he arrived in Paris he obviously had to start at the bottom: he initially had to sleep in the shop, 'a showcase with the top on', as he told his father. This inventive bed under the counter was in the office of the firm of 'G. Wehry / H. von der Horst Successeur' in rue d'Hauteville.[12] All that was left for Jo was for them to correspond regularly, and they agreed to write once a fortnight.[13] Letters were regarded as 'conversations at a distance', which in the case of the Bongers strengthened the existing bonds between them.[14] To save on postage, the family often put several letters in one envelope; they also folded letters inside the newspapers and magazines they sent one another.[15] Sometimes Andries complained that Jo was not nearly forthcoming enough.[16]

As well as giving Jo advice on her studies and suggestions for books she should read, he also described at length life in Paris and the art that he saw. Quite early on he gave her an idea of Impressionism.[17] Although he could be a bully, he did give Jo pushes in the right direction to expand her knowledge. The Trippenhuis in Amsterdam, forerunner of the Rijksmuseum, was, he said, a must. He wrote about the Rembrandt etchings that were kept in portfolios there and could be viewed on specified days. 'If Net doesn't write and tell me that she's seen them next week, I shall have a bone to pick with her.'[18]

Jo and Andries also shared their doubts with one another—about affairs of the heart, about social issues and about religion. In these confessions they usually bypassed their parents. They were a devoted

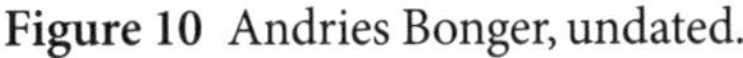
Figure 10 Andries Bonger, undated.

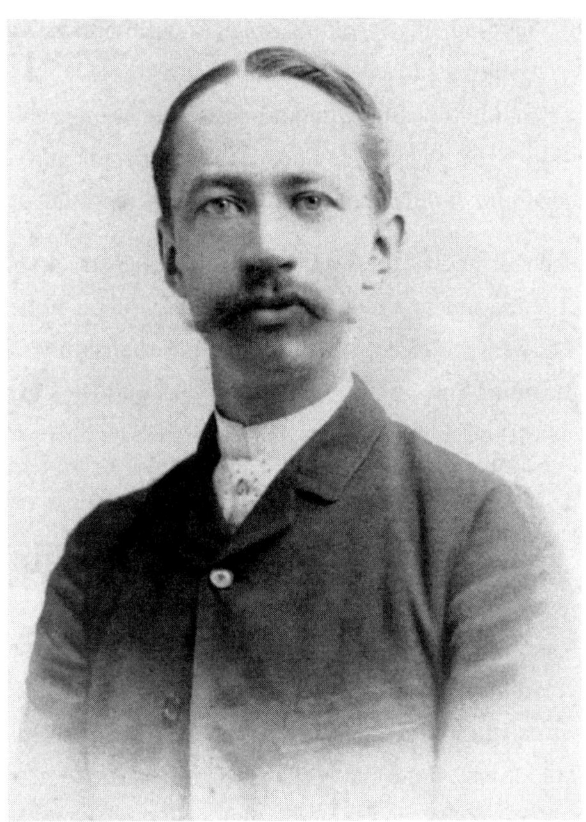

pair: he usually the wise speaker, she the eager listener. The teasing and at the same time patronizing way the eighteen-year-old Andries wrote to his sixteen-year-old sister was typical: 'Child, pay serious attention to your work and learn to look more to your brother. . . . And yet again you ignore my good advice to revise everything for your test; now I can't keep you on reins any more it will all go wrong.'[19] Although these reins were loosened slightly, Jo was happy to yield to him, impressed as she was by his self-assured attitude. A didactic young man, he advised her to be extremely active when she read English literature: 'With your pen in your hand, don't read another word until you've understood everything that went before, and write down every turn of phrase that seems strange.'[20] Andries was aware that people found him arrogant, knew that he was serious and took life seriously. Jo found a way of dealing with his condescension.

Sometimes brother and sister saw each other for several days in a row; one such occasion was their parents' twenty-fifth wedding anniversary. Jo eagerly anticipated his arrival by putting flowers on the windowsill in his room, and a posy on the table. He had scarcely left before she was already looking forward to seeing him again—she believed that together they could go into things deeply.[21] In 1880, without a shred of irony, she called him her 'pride' and 'glory':

> He's gradually becoming a man now, a man who's learned to be independent and to trust in his own strengths, and so would he confide all his ideals, his dreams, all his plans for the future to his simple, stupid little sister who knows so little of life? Oh, I'm afraid he won't, but all the same no one will love him as much as I do; he's my pride, my glory, oh may he one day become everything I expect of him. If only I could just see him there in that great bustling Paris . . . I long to see him so much.

She repeatedly expressed this yearning in a stream of engaging letters that had to compensate for his absence and prove that she was worthy of his notice.[22] Jo blamed herself for rushing her letter for Andries's nineteenth birthday. While the family were playing their instruments downstairs, she imagined him sitting alone in Paris and wallowed in remorse. In her relationship with Andries, Jo was always the submissive one. For years she saw him as her ideal mentor.

Seeking insight into herself

It may have been this constant correspondence that in the spring of 1880 prompted the seventeen-year-old Jo to start keeping a diary, as her brother did.[23] Jo's diary is an invaluable source from which we can glean a great deal about a part of her life: 'Doing it will make me learn to reflect on everything I do or have done and it will perhaps help me to become better.'[24] In her quest for self-knowledge she tried to analyze her thoughts and feelings. She felt vulnerable and often misunderstood by the rest of the family, so she could not open up to them as she would like to. 'They think I'm grumpy and bad-tempered, but it isn't that. I just feel unhappy.'[25] When she thought about her late friend Mien Doorman, who had spread happiness and love, she felt selfish. Above all, she wanted to be simple and friendly and live a useful life. This desire went very deep.[26] Mien's tragically early death led Jo to reflect on fundamental questions and she tried with all her might to organize her inner thoughts: 'No one who ever helps me, no one who does something for me, for they don't know me, they don't know what goes on inside me, oh I don't know myself: it is a "mess"' (Plate 7).[27]

Art also got her thinking. She saw Théodore de Banville's play *Gringoire* (1866) about the injustice of Louis XVI's power. She would have loved to have a husband like Gringoire: great, noble and a poet, and quoted with admiration his expressions of social compassion.[28] On the streets the difference between the classes was very evident. There Jo was confronted with poverty, poor hygiene, slums, alcoholism and begging.[29] What she saw of it, and what she heard and read fuelled her social conscience.

She enjoyed music and the theatre: she attended the oratorio *Die Schöpfung* (1796–8) by Joseph Haydn and saw Ambroise Thomas's opera *Hamlet* (1868). Prompted by these performances, which posed existential questions about God and life, she tried to penetrate deeper into the mysteries of existence, seeking more certainty about her 'inner innermost self', a phrase in her diary she borrowed from the novel *Kenelm Chillingly* (1873) by Edward Bulwer-Lytton, but she got no help in finding satisfactory answers. Sometimes she abandoned her quest for a while; she enjoyed a walk and directed her efforts towards being morally pure and charming. After going to a dance, she had an ethical insight:

> There is something impure, something shameful about it; the light, the music, the gaiety, everything serves to entangle your senses; people talk, laugh and walk to and fro, but I, at least, wasn't myself; it was as if I was doing everything in a dream; no, I shouldn't want to go often.[30]

This observation typifies the seriousness with which Jo viewed life at this time and how she wanted to be in control; here again, Andries's influence is unmistakable. This girl who always had so much difficulty feeling at ease in a group of people, believed that she had to act more freely and straightforwardly, hard though that was. She looked for support and guidance in learning how to live, but did not find it in her father: 'Pa is very good and would want to help me if I talked to him about it, but he wouldn't understand me anyway.'[31] On the eve of her last day at school in June 1880 she wanted her father and mother to have a serious talk with her and help her to decide how to spend her life, but she knew it would not happen. Now she felt a dreadful lack of real involvement. She confided her need for help and guidance to her brother, and Andries sent 'private words to Jo'.[32] Such letters were really private.

Jo concentrated on her own development and her search for something to hold on to. She longed for a more open-minded environment, a broader horizon, so that she could gain some experience of life. This she found with the Stumpff family. Her classmate Marie Stumpff had become a friend, but Mrs Bonger did not really like her going to their house. They were much more 'worldly' and 'conceited', as Jo described it.[33] This warning did not prevent her from forming strong bonds of friendship with Marie and her sisters and later with her brother.

Religious considerations also helped her: 'I wish I'd heard Hugenholtz's sermon yesterday, it might have helped. I so need a word of encouragement, of comfort.'[34] The family had joined the Vrije Gemeente—a nonconformist group founded in 1877 by the brothers Philip Reinhard and Petrus Hermannus Hugenholtz, who had left the Dutch Reformed Church and set up their own community. They preached the freedom of personal faith, an ethical faith without dogma. The Bongers had to walk only a few hundred yards to the building on Weteringschans (since 1968 the iconic music venue Paradiso); there were lectures on religious, philosophical and social subjects, accompanied by music.[35] Here, too, Jo sought support and enlightenment.

The road to greater independence—studying English

Jo had completed HBS successfully, but she was not convinced that anyone at home thought it was really important. She was strong-willed and wanted nothing more than to be independent and not cling to the parental nest like her sisters. This attitude was one of the factors underlying her decision to acquire more skills, and she immediately began preparing for the English examination that could qualify her as a teacher. She undoubtedly had help from a tutor—Andries had offered to write a recommendation to his former English teacher Cornelis Stoffel, asking him to coach her.[36] Jo worked hard and was relatively free to organize her own time at home. She revised her views about the theatre, recognizing that it could be a force for good: 'It's just for entertainment, I thought, but not for the improvement of people, foolishness; now, however, I think differently. "Liefdadige Dames" has converted me.'[37] This comedy by the German playwright Adolf L'Arronge, a parody on the charity craze among certain women, whose true goal was to attend fancy parties and find opportunities to push themselves into the limelight, had changed her mind. The play's message is that true charity is humble and expressed without outward show.

Just how someone was encouraged to be generous had always been a topic of discussion in the family. In the balance were the pulpit on the one hand and literature on the other. Andries informed his parents that clergymen did an infinite amount of good, more than reading good novels and visiting the theatre could ever do.[38] And this while Jo was so entranced by Louis Bouwmeester's superb performance in the role of Narciss Rameau, in Albert Brachvogel's tragedy *Narziß* (1857).[39] The play is based on Denis Diderot's *Le neveu de Rameau*, in which this cynical scrounger, who puts pleasure above morals, regards brilliance as greater than ethics and decency. In the tragedy, he holds a mirror up to the audience: 'I'm a sort of universal fool in which all the other fools are bound up. Who sees me, sees himself in the mirror . . . Narcissus the self-centred, the selfish, the egotist.'[40] Jo detected narcissistic tendencies in herself and immediately started to question herself; she came to the disconcerting conclusion that she suddenly did not know how to pray.[41] Her innermost thoughts were still quite confused.

On 5 September 1880 she passed her examination and was awarded her first diploma: the certificate of competence as a governess. Her passion for reading continued unabated, in part in pursuance of her studies. Again, Andries was the spur. That week he wrote about his inspiring visit to the writer Conrad Busken Huet, who had recommended him to read Sainte-Beuve, Shelley, Potgieter and Heine.[42] Jo took this advice, for the work of the last three was on her reading list. When she spent some months in London in 1883, the study of Shelley was her principal concern.

She now wrote a few pages of her diary in English. She had rested, done some household chores and visited friends, and now wanted to begin preparing for her second examination. From her reading of *My Novel: Or, Varieties in English Life* (1853) by Edward Bulwer-Lytton, in which there are numerous well-drawn characters, she concluded that most vices arose from indifference. And she asked herself doubtfully: 'Shall I always remain as I am now or will the great passion that stirs all human hearts visit me also, shall I know Love?'[43] On her eighteenth birthday she resolved to become 'kinder', 'better' and 'steadier'. This threefold resolution was a key aspect of her life for the next few years.

The witty verse attached to Jo's Sinterklaas present that year (written in a disguised hand by her father or her brother Henri) reveals that Jo received a book of poetry by the famous eighteenth-century Scottish poet Robert Burns.[44] That week she was standing at the window, knitting, and enjoying the beauty of a red and pink sunset—Burns's romantic verses may have coloured her view here. A few days later she reflected on her volatile character, which was subject to such drastic mood swings:

> They often talk about self-knowledge, but I don't believe that I will ever get to know myself, for I don't know what I'm like; sometimes I think I'm very steady and prosaic, then terribly fickle and very sentimental. I'm not the same two days in a row, sometimes my ideal is a life of calm, domestic happiness, then again I imagine all sorts of impossible things and want to be a writer, poetess or actress. I'm sometimes convinced that I have absolutely no character at all, but that is foolishness, I should rather say: I don't know what the prevailing tone of it is.[45]

Jo clearly still had to discover her 'inner innermost self' if she was to fathom her own individuality, so she joined a study club with friends of her own age, and she and Marie Stumpff took Latin lessons from the classical languages student Aegidius ('Gidius') Timmerman. One of the other members of the group was Eduard, Marie's brother.

Andries was no longer her sole mentor. Her friend Mary Westendorp and Gidius acted as confidants and sounding boards; they talked at length about the books they had read and were yet to read. In 1885, in a candid letter to Lies van Gogh, Jo looked back on this period:

> Then I got a friend who was two years older than me and had been out in the world much more; she was attracted by my knowledge of books. We started to study for our English exam together and compensated for one another's weaknesses. At her house I met a young man, a language and literature student who was a daily visitor like me; he was very handsome and bursting with enthusiasm about art and science; he noticed that I was very well-read and always turned the debate to subjects that attracted me, and you can guess what happened next! I was in love—no, not really, but I enjoyed his company, he taught me so much, I owe him an immense amount, a new life began for me, much of what had previously been unknown and vague to me now became clear—it was a time full of moonlight and roses, more beautiful than I'd ever dreamed of. He also came to our house, in the end he even gave us Latin lessons, he gave me Multatuli—then there was a time of doubt, a period of transition—how I enjoyed that time—and suffered. . . . Our platonic friendship was suddenly broken off. . . . Then I became hard and indifferent, I had to, so as not to appear too weak. . . . I shall always be grateful to him for his interest in me, stupid little teenager as I was then![46]

Her intimacy with Aegidius Timmerman was a completely new experience: an adolescent girl, she had never had a boyfriend before (Figure 11). Later she described this period as the 'blissful time of first

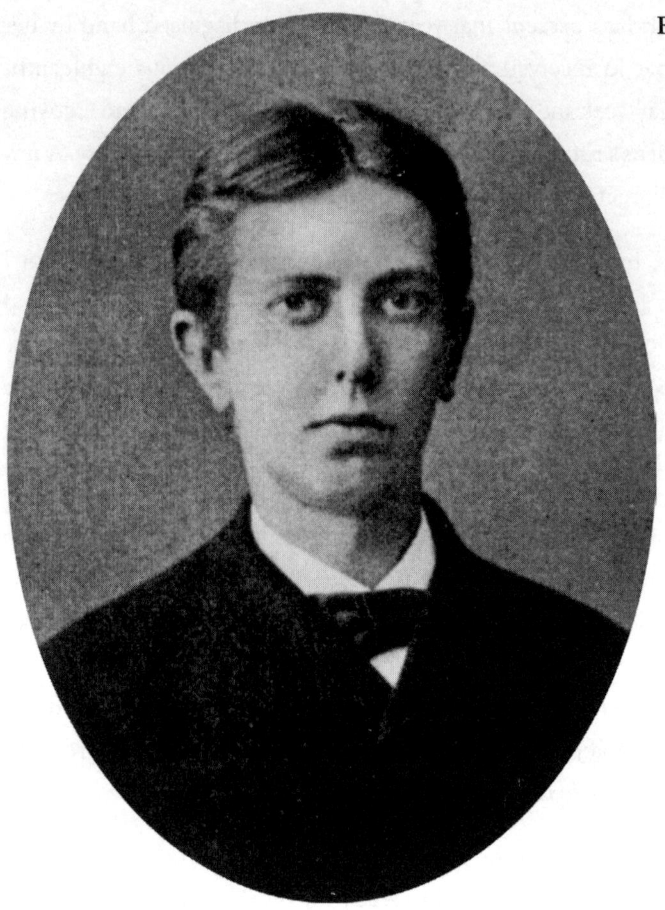

Figure 11 Aegidius Timmerman, *c.* 1876.

love!'[47] What Gidius thought about it remains unclear; in his memoirs Timmerman wrote that at that time he had the 'sweetest girls as friends', without mentioning them by name.[48]

The number of negative judgments Jo made about herself piled up frighteningly high: she thought that she was not kind and reliable enough, too withdrawn, shy and discontented, she lacked self-knowledge and felt that however much she studied she was still far too naive. She lamented: 'When shall I ever understand what life actually is?'[49] She preferred to read on her own, but the classics were often read aloud together. She had agreed to read Goethe's *Torquato Tasso* with one friend, and Multatuli's *Max Havelaar* with another. For her own amusement she translated a piece in the *Family Herald*.

At the end of 1880 she dedicated herself to a charitable cause helping young, working-class people. Andries commended her for her praiseworthy endeavours.[50] These efforts had a good deal to do with her dissatisfaction with the way she filled her life. She berated herself for her selfishness, and it was some time before she became more at home in social life and less focused on herself. Spiritual and worldly activities followed hard on one another's heels. After she had been to hear Camille de Magnin preach in the Nouvelle Église, she went skating. Her slow moral progress was in stark contrast to the speed she could achieve on her skates. Her longing to spread her wings intensified. Jo's plan was to visit Andries in Paris, but the trip never materialized. We do not know why.[51]

As we have seen, Jo often felt a need for exemplars, people who could teach her how she should live. She heard the minister François Haverschmidt preach that pain and suffering were part of human existence. In his view, there could be no victory without a battle.[52] In the preparations for her confirmation she discussed her religious convictions at length with Aegidius, and responding to what Andries had written about his visit to the Huets she remarked that 'it made me happy to hear that to some extent at least she [Mrs Huet] shares my opinion and doesn't believe in Darwinism. Gidius wouldn't think *she* was so very stupid.'[53] Her ideas about Darwinism were coloured by her personal situation at that time. On 6 April 1881 she was accepted and on 10 April confirmed by Gerrit van Gorkom, a born orator and an acquaintance of her father's who had also confirmed Henri and Andries three years earlier. Van Gorkom had broken away from the Dutch Reformed Church and in 1875 was called to be a minister in the Remonstrant Church in Amsterdam, which focused on undogmatic piety and advocated self-examination and moral idealism.[54] This position explains much of Jo's desire to be of use to other people. Van Gorkom's optimistic philosophy of life—his attention was not confined to religion and ethics, but encompassed modern literature, socialism, reprehensible antisemitism and animal protection—certainly contributed to Jo's wish to become freer and more independent in her thinking.

She found simplicity, in the sense of a modest life without any desire for wealth, to be the most attractive trait in a woman, and she continued in that view for the rest of her life. In this period, she set the bar high and forced herself to work hard; she wrote an essay on *The Lady of the Lake* by Sir Walter Scott and her appetite for reading remained immense. As soon as she and her friends finished Heine's *Harzreise* during one of their reading evenings, Jo was looking for a new 'solid' book, in other words a book from which one could learn. This need was fuelled by the fact that both Andries and Gidius had pointedly commented on her naivety. She felt that she still had so much to learn. On the very day she went to Communion, she received an 'extremely sweet, affectionate letter' from Andries. During Holy Communion the congregation remembers Christ's death on the Cross as the expiation of all our sins. The service had had a profound effect on Jo, but it was short-lived. At such a moment an affectionate letter from Andries in Paris was a true comfort.[55]

There were two sides to her constant modelling of herself on her brother: sometimes it would lift her up, then it would confront her with herself. She idolized him, of course, and her father was complicit in this. 'Pa says that Dries is so clever, so abreast of everything. I envy him, if only he were here again, what a wonderful life we could have. I always feel as if I'm only half, so empty and dissatisfied.' At such times the contrast with him reinforced her sense of failure.[56]

In May 1881 she declared that Edward Bulwer-Lytton's *Kenelm Chillingly: His Adventures and Opinions* (1873) was the best book she knew. Kenelm, the protagonist of this novel, a dreamer and idealist, tries to discover how best to approach life. He sums up his thoughts in a conversation with his father at the end of the book and this must have struck a chord with Jo: 'Perhaps we must—at whatever cost to ourselves—we must go through the romance of life before we clearly detect what is grand in its realities.'[57] And she read John Milton's poems 'L'Allegro' and 'Il Penseroso' (1631), confessing that she would rather live with the latter. She meant not with the cheerful merrymaker, but with the contemplative walker in the woods, who withdrew into study. Later that month, when she was talking with her friends about what their future husbands would be like (Marie Stumpff had meanwhile become her bosom friend), she said again that she would rather have a quieter one, 'because that's what I am myself'.[58] She endeavoured to become freer and more independent in her thinking, but continued to see herself as vain and small-minded, and reproached herself for it. All afternoon before she went to a performance of *Mignon*, the only thing she thought about was how nice she looked in her dress.[59]

Influenced by her reading and the sermons she heard, Jo wrote her confession of faith:

> There is something higher than mankind. There are higher powers, spirits or one power, one spirit, but who can say? After all, these are the mysteries of life. But still, the light, the heavenly, divine light "is it not God's breath?" and the glorious, pure feeling that can sometimes make the chest swell, that can set us aglow and flow through us, that we can as it were fathom the whole world, even eternity, in an instant, isn't that a spark of the divine in our heart? I can understand that someone sitting in his cramped room, overcome and overwhelmed by fear and doubt, confused and hard pressed by all sorts of propositions and arguments by philosophers, might say: there is no God, but go outside into the wonderful fresh air, let the mild spring coolness cool your heated forehead, enjoy the lovely scent of the flowers, the song of the birds, let the calm of the evening bring peace into your mind, is all that not just a foretaste of the divine, can a person in the world give you such pleasure, is that not holy, not divine?[60]

At the same time as her desire to be touched by the divine, her longing to fall in love grew. She thought that Gidius had pressed her hand between both of his when he took his leave, but she could have imagined it.[61] Her hormones were clearly raging.

On 12 October 1881 she passed the examination for her second teaching certificate, which qualified her to work as an English teacher in secondary schools. She contemplated her future: she wanted to earn her own money and do useful work, and she had clear motives for giving greater meaning to her as yet insignificant life:

> Oh God, if life is nothing but mending stockings and washing up cups and doing the washing, what is the point of it? I should have lived in a different age; I'm not in my place here, I think, in our

> civilized nineteenth century. Of course I know that life hangs on a thread of small things, but surely it shouldn't be *so* hollow, *so* meaningless.[62]

She went to a fancy dress ball, which she described to Andries in vivid terms, and read Willem Kloos's obituary of the poet Jacques Perk in *De Spectator*, rekindling her higher ideals.[63] She pondered on the two sides she detected in herself: 'I'm prosaic and sentimental, dreamy and practical at the same time; there is something in me that breaks down and something that builds up, and there is always conflict between these two minds!' It was with this observation that Jo ended her first diary in December 1881; she did not embark on the next one for another eighteen months.[64]

There was no lack of culture. She saw a performance of Shakespeare's *Hamlet* and in May 1882 her parents replaced their old piano, which meant that they could host 'large musical soirées'.[65] Throughout this year Jo's time was wholly occupied in looking after her aunt. Andries dwelt at length on the impending demise of their Aunt Net, who always had something to say about everything. Jo assisted her, but the task made her anything but cheerful. 'You will certainly have a difficult time looking after her and you won't be able to study as much as you would wish,' wrote Andries.[66] The situation continued until 14 August 1882, when Johanna Gezina Weissman died and Jo could heave a sigh of relief. She resumed her studies, first in Amsterdam and then in England.[67]

London

It was decided that Jo should go to England for a while to improve her knowledge of the language and concentrate on her studies. In June 1883 she set off for London, where she stayed for more than two months. On 4 July she began a new diary (which she wrote largely in English), so we can keep up with her busy life.[68] For her advanced English examination she studied the work of the romantic poet Shelley and other literary figures in the British Museum Reading Room. She loved being able to consult every book she needed, the chairs were comfortable and her desk was large; the only drawback was that visitors walked about and made too much noise.[69] In the immense library, Jo momentarily looked down at herself and saw

> a very small, shy girl who very quietly crept into this temple of erudition in the morning and looked around and above her in awe at all these scholars surrounding her. Never did I feel my own smallness more profoundly and never—did I feel happier.[70]

Jo became very fond of the Australian Elizabeth Gostwyche Gard, a forty-three-year-old spinster, from whom she rented a room at 118 Gower Street.[71] Among the other lodgers were the garrulous Miss Brandon with her fund of stories, the not unfriendly but 'thoroughly Kraut' Dr Schmaltz, her friend Mary Westendorp and Messrs Van Buren and Landsman (the latter 'odious'), Miss Salmon, Mr Landis and Mr Blanco. Blanco lent Jo works by Ernest Legouvé, who had progressive ideas about women's rights and the raising of children—subjects in which she developed a great interest.[72] Gower Street was also the site of the University of London, which had been running international programmes since 1858, and in 1878 offered women the same rights as men—the first university in the country to do so. The proximity to both the British Museum with its huge library and the university explains the large number of cosmopolitan guests.[73] Mr van Buren was Jo's guide and possibly her chaperone. As soon as she arrived, he took her to Hyde Park and Regent's Park.

She visited the most important sights of the city, walked down Oxford Street and Regent Street, and was impressed by all the carriages. But what had the greatest effect on her were the sermons of Stopford August Brooke. She often went to listen to him, sometimes with Miss Gard. She thought that he had a very melodious voice.[74] For several years Brooke preached to the Unitarian congregation in Bedford Chapel, Bloomsbury. In 1873 he was 'one of the Queen's chaplains, delivering a series of lectures on the "Theology in Poets" in St. James's Chapel, of which he is the incumbent. A recent lecture was entitled "The Theology of Robert Burns".'[75] Inevitably, a man who quoted Shelley and Burns from the pulpit had Jo's interest.

She made the best possible use of her time. In the Gaiety Theatre she saw Sarah Bernhardt perform in *Fédora* (1882), a play especially written for her by Victorien Sardou, but Andries's influence was evident in Jo's critical account of her acting: 'She is a beautiful woman, splendidly dressed; she is languissante, charmante, but not full of "high art" as I should like to call it.'[76] The next day she was overcome by the angelic singing and superb organ playing in church. Two days later she went to the Lyceum Theatre, where she saw Henry Irving's production of Shakespeare's *The Merchant of Venice*. She was proud that she had been able to understand the play and enthused to her brother about the Shakespeare performances.[77] Needless to say, she visited the National Gallery and listed her favourite works, including Edwin Landseer's portraits of dogs and Joshua Reynolds's heads of angels. She bought a reproduction of *A Child with an Apple* by Jean-Baptiste Greuze (Plate 8). Not long after this she had a very agreeable visit to the Victoria & Albert Museum, the Natural History Museum and the Science Museum in South Kensington. She had more affinity with fine art than with natural history, which she confessed she knew little about. During her months in London she reflected constantly on her own actions and ideas.

She bought *The Illustrated Birthday Motto Book and Calendar of Nature*. In this miniature book, slightly larger than a calling card, with a catchy quotation from literature for every day, Jo wrote in all the birthdays of her family, friends and loved ones; even the great Goethe was included. She also pressed flowers in it. Browsing through it, one gets a bird's-eye view of her life, for she continued to use the little book: in 1915 she noted down her son's wedding day, and later the births of her grandsons Theo, Johan and Floor. On 5 November we find the name of her daughter-in-law Josina Wibaut, and that of her first grandchild, Theo, born in 1920. Touched, she wrote: 'He will do honour to the name his grandfather made beloved by men and by artists.'[78] Notes like this make the book much more than a list of birthdays.

Again: self-knowledge and self-criticism

When Miss Gard kissed Jo goodnight twice on 28 July, it was her happiest moment in London—further evidence of her longing for affection. Her admiration for this woman led to Jo to castigate herself even more for her shortcomings and she detested her selfishness. She still thought that she was too quiet and awkward in social situations. In such a very different environment, she observed, 'you are not spoiled as at home where everything you do is applauded, but must make a way for yourself to the hearts of your companions'.[79] This sort of critical remark shows that she wanted to become a nobler person, and she used this endeavour as a mantra. Again, she noted that if Elizabeth Gard kissed her at breakfast, it made her happy for the whole day.[80] Sometimes she would kneel by her chair and they would chat. It is likely that Jo confided in her much more than she did her own parents. At the end of her stay, she wrote that experiencing Miss Gard's nobility had been one of the highlights. In Jo's album Miss Gard quoted from—who else?—Shelley: Asia's words in *Prometheus Unbound* (1820) about the inspiring power of love.[81]

Jo wanted to be as talkative and agreeable in company as possible, but found that she rarely succeeded. It is one of the constants in her life: social events and obligations were ordeals and she admitted that she preferred the company of her books to that of people.[82] She felt more at ease and cheerful when she knew she looked nice. She put on her light cream dress, enjoyed the music and danced a little in the boarding house drawing room.

She visited some of the major sights, including Hampton Court Palace, the Houses of Parliament and Westminster Abbey, where she was thrilled to see Poets' Corner, with the graves of great writers. Accompanied by her fellow-lodger Mr Landis she visited Windsor. Jo's musical and literary education advanced apace. In Covent Garden she heard work by Beethoven, Meyerbeer and Rossini. She was swept away by Byron's *Childe Harold's Pilgrimage* and had also studied Shelley's letters and biographies of him. She approved of *The Life of Percy Bysshe Shelley* by Thomas Jefferson Hogg (1858), because the biographer did not idolize the poet, instead describing him as an ordinary person and giving an account of his day-to-day life. She could read for a great many hours in one day, but she discovered that this was by no means exceptional: 'Now that I heard that Shelley read sixteen hours a day I know that my six hours can't hurt me. . . . I want to have done with always *preparing* for action only; I want to begin to set to work in earnest.'[83] Shoulder to the wheel, in other words. She would spend her evenings reading and studying.

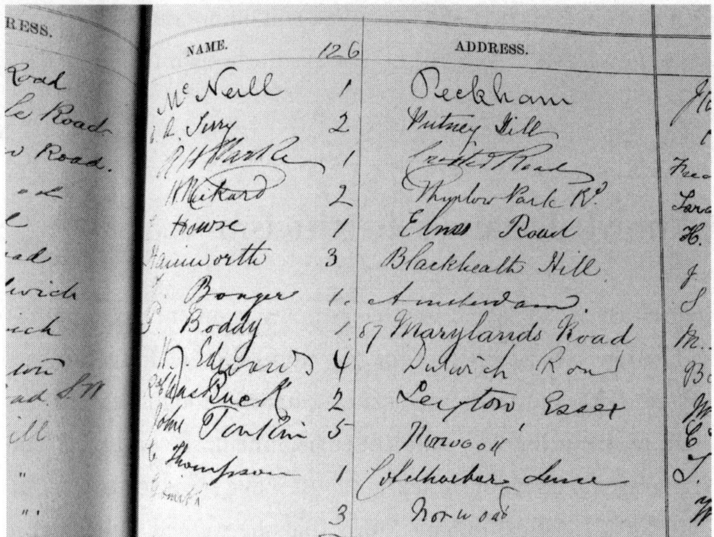

Figure 12 Jo Bonger signs the visitors' book at the Dulwich Picture Gallery in London on 24 August 1883.

Figure 13 Vincent van Gogh signs the visitors' book at the Dulwich Picture Gallery in London on 4 August 1873.

Just how much Jo wanted to be seen as engaging and how unsure she still was became apparent when there were several guests at the table. She had spoken barely a word at lunch and was gratified afterwards by the reaction of the lady of the house: 'Miss Gard saw they liked me so much! It is more than I expected.'[84] Yet more proof that as an adolescent Jo had far too negative opinion of herself. Although she believed she got on better with books than people, she spent a morning showing a party of French women around the British Museum. For the last three weeks of her stay, she was the only Dutch person left in the boarding house. She was now confident enough to set out without a chaperone and went on her own to the Dulwich Picture Gallery, where she greatly enjoyed the paintings. What she could not have known, of course, was that Vincent van Gogh had done the same thing ten years earlier: they both signed the museum's visitors' book (Figures 12, 13).

She frequently doubted her faith, her hesitancy kindled by the Multatuli reader Gidius, with whom she had often discussed religion. After attending church one day she wrote: 'I really think if I stayed long enough here I should grow quite religious again. O my love, my love, why did you take from me my heart and my faith!'[85] She had once found 'simplicity' in a woman important, now she added that she thought that 'pleasantness' was more important than 'elegance'. She longed to see more of the world and seriously considered becoming a governess in England.[86] Five years before it actually happened, she expressed a desire to go to Paris and hoped that Andries would help her find work there.[87]

Just before the end of her stay in London, Jo went to the theatre again. This time, it was a lower-class venue, and she saw how the audience reacted to the play, drank brandy they had brought with them and continually had to be called to order. It was a performance of *The Silver King* (1882) by Henry A. Jones and Henry Herman in the Princess's Theatre in Oxford Street. Wilson Barrett, English actor and author of melodramatic plays, and his company attracted huge audiences. Jo was very aware of the working class: 'You can clearly see that it is the hard working, drudging class of people who all day long busy themselves in the crowded streets, who come for relaxation there in the evening.'[88] And she realized only too well how privileged she was.

On 6 September 1883 she rode a tricycle—the fact that she managed without falling off she described as a heroic feat. She had been accompanied by her fellow lodger, Miss Salmon. Jo had never ridden any sort of bicycle before. It was a novelty to the general public; in 1881 Dunlop had invented the pneumatic tyre. Bicycles soon became safer; appropriate cycling dress for women came on to the market: decorative metal clips adorned with butterflies prevented the wind from getting under their skirts.[89] Four days after this exciting experience, Jo boarded a boat and left England.

Back in Amsterdam

London had done her good, she had been able to work on her social skills there, but within a week she was dissatisfied with herself again: she thought she had been unkind and haughty, even though everyone in the house had been kind and loving. She began taking private English lessons from Mr van Kampen and also carried on studying with Mary Westendorp, who lodged with her uncle Daniel de Clercq: 'A most comfortable, elegant, refined surrounding; how nice for Mary to live there always!' she noted with barely concealed jealousy.[90] For the first time, Jo played a piano trio with her father (viola) and Henri (cello). She also wrote an essay on *Macbeth*; Van Kampen checked it for her and told her it was good.

Beginning to study hard, she borrowed Macaulay's essays from the library to compare with Thomas Carlyle's writings for a composition.[91] Because it reminded her of London, she attended the English Church in the Begijnhof. She walked along the Amstel with a friend, they crossed the river in a little boat and laughed a lot. Her friends came to congratulate her on her twenty-first birthday; she received a 'delightful' letter from Andries, with a book by the popular French writer Ludovic Halévy, and a card from Miss Gard with forget-me-nots. One sour note was that she had quarrelled with a friend over a game of chess.[92] She read Charles Dickens's *David Copperfield* and thought that it might be one of the best books she had ever read. This *Bildungsroman* centres on the emotional, moral and intellectual development of the protagonist, who comes face to face with the appalling conditions of child labourers in the factories—he learns how important it is for a person to control his impulses. This must have touched a chord with Jo.

She wanted to use her diary to improve her style, and reading the work of good writers was a means to this end. Books by William Makepeace Thackeray were among those she read in preparing for her examination. Gazing at the blue sky and white clouds, she thought she could begin to understand the poetry of William Wordsworth. Her studies put her in touch with feelings that were essential to her: 'I always longed to learn and to penetrate a little deeper than usual into other people's thoughts and ideas and I *have* penetrated to the very sources.' She was conscious of the blessing conferred upon her in this encounter with the greatest and noblest English men and women: Shelley, Byron, Brontë and Carlyle.[93] She pondered on the latter's words: 'Doubt of any sort cannot be removed except by *Action*. . . . Do the Duty which lies nearest thee, which thou knowest to be a Duty'—and decided that her very first duty was to be kind to everyone and then take action. It was evidently in the air, for Vincent van Gogh referred to precisely these ideas of Carlyle's in his letters to Theo at this time.[94]

Jo and Mary spent days working together in the library. They most probably went to the Leesmuseum voor Vrouwen, a reading room for women in Hartenstraat. In the mornings they sat there on their own by the fire, the books within reach, testing one another. Jo really wanted to write about George Eliot or Charlotte Brontë, but she felt that 'a poor stupid thing as I am' could add little to what these superior women had achieved.[95] If she had a talent for writing, she would love to write beautiful sketches, witty anecdotes or spirited remarks about everything she had read during the day, including Elizabeth Gaskell's *Life of Charlotte Brontë* (1857). She regarded Brontë as someone who was infinitely noble.[96]

In her view, meeting new writers and their works could have a better effect on a person's character than encounters with flesh and blood people. At the same time, she learned from the melancholy four-hundred-page poem *Aurora Leigh* (1856) by Elizabeth Barrett Browning that love surpasses art, and she internalized that idea. In her diary Jo confessed from the bottom of her heart:

> I try to live only for my books and my study, make teaching my highest ideal and aim in life but that cannot take away the feeling of loneliness, the craving after love which we poor women possess. Oh

> if there were only one person in the world whom I might love passionately and fondly! A friend, a brother, a sister, it would not matter what! but people are so cool and slow in their love. What good does it do me to have one little bit of another's heart, I want to have the whole! . . . There is papa, I know he loves me, if tomorrow he could do anything for me to help me, he would, I am sure, but why does he never speak to me kindly, why does he never take me to his heart and makes me *feel* that he loves me. Am I so passionate?

As she had three years earlier, she regretted the unsatisfactory nature of her relationship with her father: he never stopped to wonder who his daughter really was and had not the slightest notion of her turbulent feelings.[97]

Despite this uncomfortable realization and the pain it caused her, on 26 November 1883 Jo passed her examination and obtained her third teaching certificate, which enabled her to teach English language and literature in secondary schools.[98] Her friend Mary Westendorp passed too. Jo had studied diligently for this national examination and her store of literary knowledge was by now extensive; it is not clear whether she was able to choose her titles for herself or they were all set texts. Aside from the works we have already seen, they included among others Dickens, *Our Mutual Friend*; Catherine Sinclair, *The Journey of Life*; Thomas Moore, *Lalla Rookh*; Nathaniel Hawthorne, *Transformation: Or, The Romance of Monte Beni*; and Bernard Mandeville, *The Fable of the Bees: Or, Private Vices, Publick Benefits*. Her marks were sent to her by post. What is striking is that she and Mary were assessed together. The explanation about Jo was brief: 'Mr Sennett writes to me as follows: "Miss B was better able to give a fair account of what she had read, she has a better grip of the scope and drift of a work than Miss W."'[99] Jo got the top mark for her knowledge of the history of literature. She passed all her oral examinations, was awarded satisfactory marks for the style and language of her essays, but failed on their content—a result she would not have been at all happy with. She urged herself on to work even harder and tried to live up to her ambitions: 'Dreams of great things, of making men happier and better!' Ambitions like these were by no means unusual for women at the end of the nineteenth century.[100] She had now achieved what she wanted, but at the same time felt confused, for after two years of study, everything was open again. It was a well-known phenomenon: like countless well-educated middle-class girls, she felt a pressing need to get out of the situation at home and do something useful for society. Many of them went abroad to work as governesses or found posts at boarding schools.[101] Jo asked Andries to look for a job in Paris for her, but to her regret his efforts were unsuccessful.[102]

In early December 1883, a man identified only as Albert, about whom we know nothing at all, asked her to marry him; he may have been a boyfriend of one of Jo's girlfriends. It was the first proposal she had received, and she turned him down because she had never felt anything for him.[103] She had to make a choice between life as a married woman or that of a lonely but free and independent governess, and for the time being at least she chose the latter. With an almost dispassionate attitude, Jo looked back on the eventful year 1883: her stay in London, the examination and the unexpected proposal: 'Three great events truly. But they have left me all the same.'[104] She realized that she would never be a pupil again, but had to begin work as a teacher. She set about applying for posts, armed with the splendid testimonials her teacher Mr van Kampen had written for her. For six months she neglected her diary—and she did not pick it up again until she started work as an English teacher in a girls' boarding school in Elburg, a job she had seized with both hands to get away from life at home that had become increasingly patronizing, as she later described it.[105] Her most important occupation in the intervening months was translating articles for *De Amsterdammer*. The money she was paid for her work and the prestige it brought her took her a step closer to greater independence.

3

Translator, teacher and love for Eduard Stumpff

The writer Justus van Maurik, editor of the daily newspaper *De Amsterdammer*, asked Jo to translate the novel *I Say No: Or, The Love-Letter Answered* by the popular author Wilkie Collins. He proposed that she deliver eight instalments within ten days, and then some eight further instalments every fortnight.[1] He was satisfied with the translations and the speed with which she delivered them. 'Well done! Keep going, this is just what I want! Now we can make progress, if you remain as diligent as this.' Jo was nothing if not diligent and the Dutch version (entitled *Ik zeg: Neen!*) appeared in sixty-eight instalments in *De Amsterdammer* between 18 June and 4 September 1884. She earned a total of a hundred and fifty guilders for her work.[2] It was published in book form under the title *'Neen'. Antwoord op eene liefdesverklaring* in two volumes with a total of 457 pages, and sold for five guilders.[3] The book's protagonist turns detective to unearth the truth about the death of her father. The plot is full of coincidences. Andries was pleasantly surprised and praised the fluent translation. This commission and all the positive responses boosted Jo's self-confidence and gave her considerable pleasure. What's more, she had proved that she could earn money for herself.[4] It is not clear how Jo first came into contact with Van Maurik or how she succeeded in establishing business relationships in the world of daily newspapers and weekly magazines, where translated literature played an important role. Her teacher Van Kampen, who had provided her with glowing testimonials, may have been instrumental in this.

Teacher at the Kinsbergen Institute in Elburg

In 1884 Jo applied for and obtained a position as an English teacher at the Admiraal Van Kinsbergen boarding school for girls in Beekstraat in Elburg, a town some fifty miles to the northeast of Amsterdam (Figure 14).[5] That summer, Aagje Visscher was appointed headmistress. She was assisted by her sister

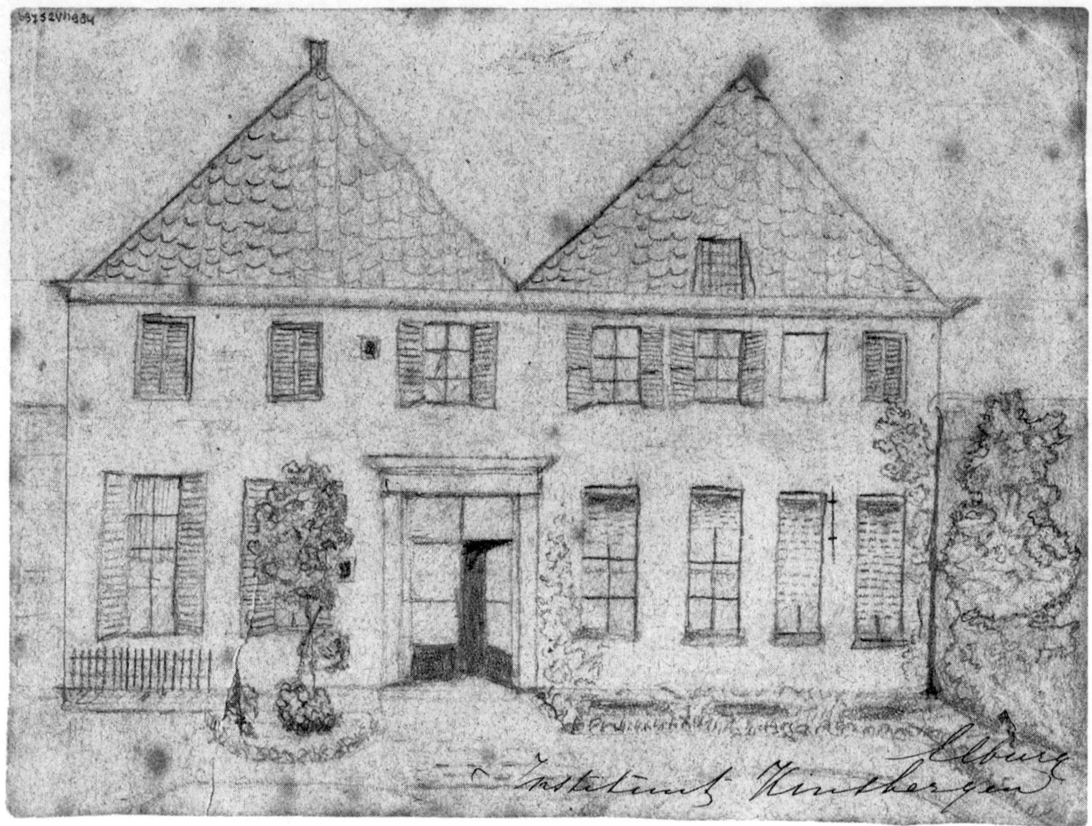

Figure 14 *Rear of the Kinsbergen Institute in Beekstraat, Elburg*, 1884–5. Jo Bonger may have made the drawing herself.

Cateau (Cato).[6] Pauline Perrin taught French and Constance (Con) Lüders gave German conversation lessons and taught piano and singing. Hermine Gericke and Allegonda (Gonne) van Holte were assistant teachers. At that time there were fifteen boarders and twenty day girls. By May 1885 those numbers had dropped to ten and eighteen respectively.[7] Music was an important part of the school day, and there was a good deal of reading aloud. Jo shared a bedroom with Gonne, which she brightened up with flowers.

She was curious to see how she would get on without any classroom experience, accustomed to a relatively undemanding life as she was. Her first lesson went better than she expected. She was in her element and within a day she was walking arm in arm with her pupil Sijtske van Mesdag, whom she took under her wing. There was also supervision outside lessons. She got on very well with this fifteen-year-old girl and they continued a confidential correspondence for a year after Jo left Elburg.

The transition was considerable and she found it difficult to adapt to her new environment. Jo loathed the extremely formal mealtimes at the Institute, and in no time at all she was longing for the

Christmas holidays. She feared the monotony of winter in the country, but compensated for this by taking extra music lessons with Constance. The most important thing was for her to get teaching experience. Every day, between three and four o'clock, she and two of her colleagues walked to the Zuiderzee, now Lake IJssel, where the fresh breeze would blow away the musty school atmosphere.[8]

Jo had only been there for ten days when she started hoping she would get a new translation job from Van Maurik because her work at the school did not really satisfy her. Within three weeks, there were also increasing tensions under the surface. Two combative clans had formed in that microcosm. 'It is here the world on a small scale—all kinds of passions, of intrigues going on; under a mask of commonplace indifference.'[9] To add to the internal troubles, there was also an outbreak of scarlet fever—an epidemic so serious that it claimed the life of little Henry Webb, the brother of Jo's pupil Mary. It was a dramatic, but not exceptional, event at that time. In the mid-nineteenth century, scarlet fever, measles and whooping cough were responsible for one death in twelve. The epidemic was still not over in January 1885.[10]

Jo celebrated her birthday away from home for the first time in her life. Now she received greetings and presents from the group in the boarding school. She concluded that she had become softer and nicer, although she was 'dreadfully jealous' of Constance, who was always in the headmistress's company. In the evenings Jo was on duty between seven and eight, and she used the time to write her diary. She went for walks with Cateau Visscher and they talked about love—books were not the only source of insights into affairs of the heart. Discussions with women in her immediate circle also contributed, which conflicted with her earlier theory about the value of book learning.

The postal service to and from the provincial town was excellent. Shortly after her birthday in 1884, she received a comforting letter full of jokes after the severe storms that had battered Elburg. Many sympathized. There were contributions from her parents, Henri, Mien and Betsy, Antoinette Stumpff and Mary Westendorp. Not everything was equally inspiring. The best Hermine could come up with, for example, was: 'As Mother of our family institution / This is my well-intended contribution.'[11] (Figure 15). That same month, Jo's cousin Willem Weissman thanked her for recommending James Anthony Froude's *Life of Carlyle* (1884) to him, and assured her that from then on she could address her requests for books to the librarian at the University of Amsterdam Library [12] She doubtless availed herself of this generous offer.

That winter she was profoundly affected by Goethe's *Faust*:

> I sat in a corner of that great cavernous dining room, by the window, and read Ach neige du Schmerzensreiche and it felt as if my heart would break, *I* who never cry over a book. But it isn't a book, it's reality![13]

This emotional response to what she read was undoubtedly strengthened by her crush on Gidius. In November 1884 she was still 'in the full ecstasy of my first love!'[14] Jo had a particular weakness for Goethe, the writer she quotes, and learned a great deal about him by reading George Henry Lewes's

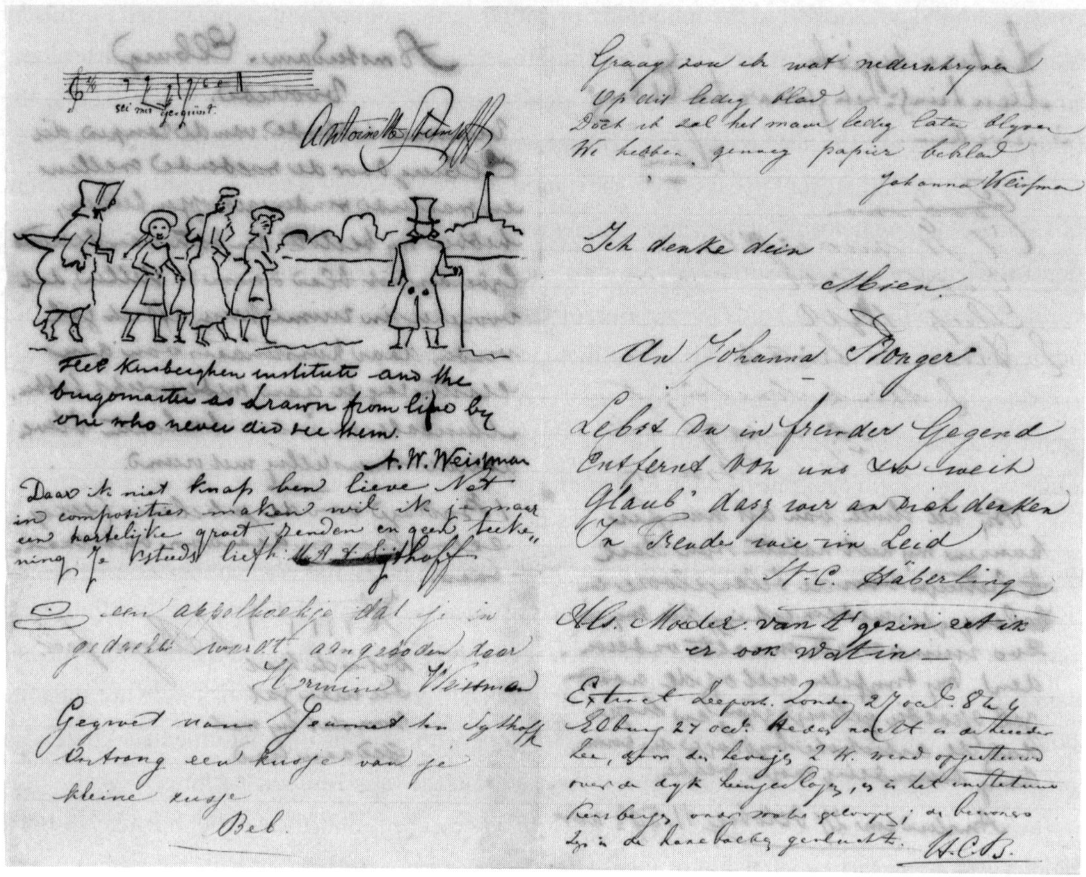

sei mir gegrüsst

Feel Kinsbergen institute and the burgomaster as drawn from life by one who never did see them.

A.W. Weissman

Daar ik niet knap ben lieve Net in compositie maken wil ik je maar een hartelijke groet zenden en geen teekening. Je steeds liefh. M.A. Sijthoff

een appelkoekje dat je in gedachte wordt aangeboden door Hermine Weissman

Gegroet van Jeannet ten Sijthoff

Ontvang een kusje van je kleine zusje

Bel.

Graag zou ik wat nederschrijven
Op dit ledig blad
Doch ik zal het maar ledig laten blijven
We hebben genoeg papier beklad

Johanna Weissman

Ich denke dein

Mien.

An Johanna Bonger

Lebst du in fremder Gegend
Entfernt von uns so weiss ich
Glaub' dass wir an dich denken
In Freude wie im Leid

H.C. Häberling

Als Moeder van 't gezin eet ik er ook wat in—

Extract Report. London 27 oct. 84.

H.C.B.

Figure 15 Letter from family members and friends to Jo Bonger in Elburg, 27 October 1884.

Life of Goethe (1855). She felt small beside such great names, who had fathomed out how to live a fruitful life. She daydreamed of having enough money to travel—to go to Weimar, or Paris, or London—and brushed aside the idea of saving this imaginary money: 'Let us be young and happy for once and enjoy our life thoroughly.'[15]

Shortly before Christmas, Jo had her portrait taken by the photographer F.W. Deutmann in Zwolle. Reflecting her new social status as a teacher and translator, she looked resolutely into the lens (Plate 9). The epidemic kept her at home for longer than planned during the Christmas holiday. Some of the pupils were confined to bed and not allowed out of the house. Jo sent letters and a parcel to the Institute, and received a very grateful reply.

The year 1885 got off to a flying start. On 4 January Van Maurik sent her a new translation job, this time the novella *Die Geschichte eines Genies. Die Galbrizzi* by Ossip Schubin. Jo must have started straight away and worked really hard, because she finished it on 11 February. She was paid fifty guilders for her translation, *De geschiedenis van een genie. Novelle*, which was a great incentive.[16] The serial ran from 22 February to 26 April in the weekly *De Amsterdammer*. Again, Andries was unstinting in his praise. 'The translation reads well; the language is natural and does not smell in any way of our neighbours.'[17] Meanwhile, Jo had been to the opera and the theatre in Amsterdam and had taken part in tea parties. The best thing that had happened to her, though, was this commission. Solitary work like this clearly suited her temperament better than the ladylike socializing and rigidly ordered life in the closed community of a boarding school. Successful translations improved her opportunities in the market should she ever want to get out of education, but for the time being she carried on teaching. Once the epidemic came to an end, all the wallpaper in the school was stripped and the whole place was disinfected, so Jo could go back.[18] The five weeks at home had done her good.

Jo settled down again by the fire with her books, Pauline sang lieder and the snow glistened outside. She went skating with Louise Gericke, the sister of the assistant teacher Hermine, something she had not done for a long time, and threw herself into it. Thinking of getting her certificate as an assistant teacher, she took lessons with Mr Alblas.[19] She cherished her peaceful evenings, but suffered from splitting headaches on several occasions.

What she heard about life in fashionable Paris fired her imagination. She wanted to know, for instance, all about Andries's soirée with the Huet family (where Theo van Gogh was also among the guests) and he was happy to oblige. At length he described the recitals, the dancing and the supper. His impressions painted an extremely attractive picture of Parisian nightlife for Jo. He was keen to hear her reaction and asked her to reply by return of post. Exceptional events like this briefly lifted his spirits above the mundane on the spot and his sister's in her imagination.[20]

They had squabbled while Andries was staying with their parents over Christmas. Jo had spoken about him disdainfully and said that he was not studying enough and becoming too frenchified. The letter he wrote to her afterwards gives us a good idea of the tension that had built up. He took a severe tone and criticized the heated way she spoke which, he said, precluded a proper view of things. She showed little evidence of empathy:

> I should like to give you a piece of my mind about your fencing with words and ideas (you really must start studying psychology) but I don't want to be too harsh.— . . . I always comfort myself with the idea that when I think about you, you're also thinking about me, and then it's as if I hear you talking, sometimes fiercely, sometimes blindly rattling on, and then I try to calm you down and forcibly argue the point.—

He ends his tirade with the nasty remark: 'just stick with the cheerful philosophy of life of your friend Goethe', because he knew she was engrossed in Goethe's *Hermann und Dorothea* (1797) at the time.[21]

Once she was back in Elburg Jo's thoughts turned to her friend Gidius. She remembered the spring when he had brought her lilac blossom and looked at her with a look that had made her tremble with bliss. Meanwhile she felt stronger and her 'thirst for happiness has been reawakened, the stupor I was in when I arrived here has gone—I'm starting to live again and what is life? To dream of love and wake to sorrow.'[22] A month later, in neighbouring Nunspeet, she was finally able to give her feelings more of a free rein. There, on a visit to the physician Johannes Schut and his family, she met a young man called Van den Bergh, who clearly impressed her. He may have been the junior notary Constantijn Leonoor van den Bergh. He seemed really manly and she thought about him for months.[23]

Mrs Bonger, Mien and Wim had descended for a while on Nunspeet, a village where tourism had really taken off in the second half of the nineteenth century since it had acquired a railway station. Jo went to see them there and Henri went too. They walked through the fields and in the park of the country house De Grote Buunte, and had tea parties together. Jo enjoyed the time spent with the family, but noticed that she drew apart mentally during the midday meals.[24] When they had gone back to Amsterdam, she sat on a hillock with Van den Bergh and there was no sense of seclusion: 'with the fantastic view over the waving wheatfields with the dark pine trees in the background. Everything slumbering in the silver moonlight—the exhilarating stillness—and (who can look at a July moon alone?) pleasant company—it was idyllic!'[25]

Andries, too, was enjoying pleasant company. He told his parents that he would like to introduce them to his sympathetic friend Van Gogh. This would prove to be crucial to the course Jo's life would take, although she was not particularly looking forward to it at first. Without Andries, though, there would have been no Theo for her. In 1881 Andries joined the Hollandsche Club, a place where Dutch people in Paris could meet. The reading room and the library were full of books, newspapers and magazines, including the *Handelsblad*, the *NRC*, *The Times*, *The New York Herald* and the *Revue des Deux Mondes*. For a while Andries was the society's librarian.[26] He thought most of the members were too narrow-minded for words, but Theo van Gogh was different: 'He is civilized and entertaining.'[27] Their friendship endured and they had a shared love of art and literature, although Andries, unlike Theo, had no time for Émile Zola's naturalistic novels.[28] They read books together, went to the Louvre on Sunday mornings and to the Théâtre français in the evening. It was not only literature, art and the theatre that bound them together, they were both concerned with the *ars amatoria*. They often discussed the pros and cons of marriage.

On 26 July 1885 the two friends went to the Netherlands.[29] Theo stayed in the parsonage in Nuenen with his mother, sisters and brothers, and with them mourned their father, who had died in March. He responded to Andries's urging to come and visit him in Amsterdam, writing:

> It will give me very great pleasure that we will have got to know one another's family, it seems to me that a visit has the same importance for us as e.g. two painters who visit one another's studios, for although the world is the greatest school, family life as we have known it from childhood was the a.b.c. for it.[30]

Andries appreciated Theo's 'gifts heart and soul' and was delighted that his parents had been so taken with him.[31] Jo saw Theo for the first time at the beginning of August, but during the visit she was much more impressed with her brother than with Theo, whom she did not even mention. She called Andries 'my boy, my pride, my darling'. As they hugged, he had whispered 'I still love you the best'. These sentimental words reflected a profound bond. The fact that he had said he loved Jo so much clearly reassured her. She was distinctly afraid of losing him now that her unique position was no more, for Andries had openly declared his love for Annie van der Linden, and Jo could not get on with Annie, who she thought was dull and distant.[32]

Jo ended her diary on 9 August 1885. Three weeks later she started a new one, which ran until 6 November 1888. We read that she often had a difficult time of it in Elburg, although she sometimes disguised it from Andries.[33] According to Cateau Stumpff, whom Jo had meanwhile got to know well, her friend had left a large hole in their Amsterdam circle of friends when she left for Elburg after the summer holiday.[34] This hole did not last long, however, for at the end of September Jo decided not to return to the boarding school after Christmas. The same Cateau recommended her to read *Zijn ideaal* by Johanna van Woude—a novel about the ministering role of a wife in marriage and the sacred ideal of motherhood, which they had talked about together. Women in the Netherlands devoured this book.[35]

On her twenty-third birthday, Jo counted herself fortunate in her independence: 'I've become a *person* now and meet at least the first requirement in that regard: I can keep myself.'[36] Cateau Stumpff, who was a teacher, also thought it was important to earn her own keep. She thanked Jo for her letter, said she was sorry to hear that she was 'not very well' and urged her to put on a bold front.[37] This encouragement hit home: the formerly so biddable Jo developed a growing need to unbend, to be freer and think more freely, away from the regimen at home in Weteringschans, because she found it suffocating there. However, she would still have to put up with it for some time to come.

Literature as a mirror

Theo and Andries encouraged their sisters Elisabeth (Lies) and Jo, who did not know one another, to correspond (Figure 16). The women obliged and their epistolary friendship soon took off. Lies was three years older than Jo and since 1879 had nursed Catharina du Quesne van Bruchem-van Willis, left bedridden by an illness. Du Quesne's house in Soesterberg had seventeen rooms, and it was from this house that Lies wrote her first letter to Jo in October 1885; it was answered at once. They confided to one another that the two young men in Paris were their favourite brothers. Lies sent Jo's letter on to her 'noble and unselfish' brother Theo, giving him a good insight into Jo's thinking. Jo confessed that she owed her taste for literature wholly to Andries.[38] Lies leapt on this remark. Her favourite poet was

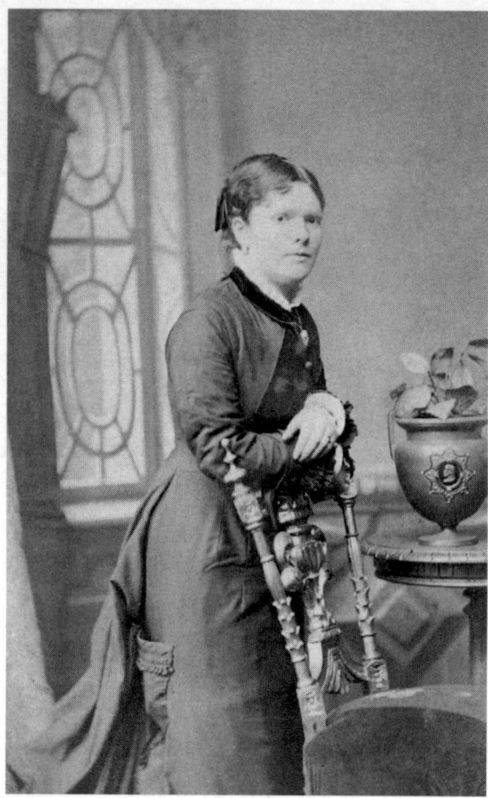

Figure 16 Elisabeth (Lies) van Gogh, undated.

Henry Wadsworth Longfellow and she also found the poetry of François Coppée extremely sympathetic. 'May poetry gain the upper hand over prose in your life,' she told Jo.[39] Jo immediately replied that George Eliot was her favourite writer and *The Mill on the Floss* (1860) her favourite book. She wrote of the protagonist Maggie Tulliver:

> Poor, dear Maggie, I love her so much, almost like one of my sisters. She has such noble aspirations . . . always tries to do the right thing, and it is sometimes so hard, so dreadfully hard!

Jo expanded further on Maggie, her brother Tom, Stephen and Lucy, and told Lies that the 'duet in paradise' appealed to her most because singing had such a compelling effect on her.[40] In the chapter of the same name, the power of music plays a very important role.[41] Lucy Deane and her fiancé Stephen Guest sing arias from *Die Schöpfung* by Joseph Haydn. Eliot writes then: 'Surely the only courtship unshaken by doubts and fears must be that in which the lovers can sing together.' The line 'Mit dir geniess ich doppelt, mit dir ist Seligkeit das Leben' is a constant refrain.[42]

There are striking parallels between the character and occupations of the protagonist Maggie and what Jo wrote about herself in her diary, about her desires and motives and her relationship with Andries. The young Maggie dislikes sewing patchwork; it is 'such foolish work', she loves boat trips, she is eager to learn, can always be found with her nose in a book (she loves Latin) and has a great love for her brother Tom, although he thinks that she is not strong-willed enough.[43] She is impulsive and has a lively imagination. Her inner struggle—she mocks cosiness and so-called bourgeois respectability, and longs for contact with the world—leads to self-denial and she often suffers from self-reproach. What repeatedly recurs in both of them is the longing for independence. They are prepared to take on an uncongenial job in a school to achieve this end (even if Jo had thrown in the towel pretty quickly). Eliot spends a lot of time on reflection and shows that the life of an adult is never without trouble: it is a 'thorny wilderness'.[44] Both Maggie and Jo strive for a clear conscience and inner perfection.

'In their death they were not divided', the book's closing sentence, also appears prominently on the title page. The quotation comes from the King James version of 2 Samuel 1:23. When Jo had her first husband, Theo van Gogh, reburied beside Vincent in Auvers-sur-Oise in 1914, she published part 1 of the *Brieven aan zijn broeder*, in which she chose precisely these words as an epitaph. There can be no doubt that she had the tragic end of *The Mill on the Floss* in mind. There, the line was engraved on the gravestone of Maggie and Tom Tulliver. Jo internalized what she read in literature into the core of her own life.

She read to get a better grasp of her own setting, identifying strongly with characters in novels and the way they handled love. She confessed to Lies:

> Perhaps I have a wholly mistaken idea of love, I really don't know anything about it, but I imagine that it can't exist without a complete understanding of each other's character and ideas, without agreement on them! . . . Do you ever have such a longing for someone much older than we are, who would teach you how you should actually live?[45]

Jo knew that Lies had literary aspirations and wanted to know more about them. Lies said Shelley was her favourite poet. She did not like French literature; it made her melancholy.[46] Lies dreamed of what it would be like to form a writing duo with Jo, like Betje Wolff and Aagje Deken or Emile Erckmann and Alexandre Chatrian. She said she had never been as frank with anyone as with Jo and told her about her earlier amorous adventures. But it was different now. For six years she had lived retired in Soesterberg, 'where I have never met a single male creature'.[47] Ironically, less than a month later, her employer Jean Philippe du Quesne van Bruchem got her pregnant in one of those seventeen rooms. He was already the father of four children.[48] Literature and real life collided. Lies quoted the character Jenny Wren's view of men in Charles Dickens's *Our Mutual Friend*: 'I know their tricks and their manners!'[49]

Jo formulated her ideal: she wanted to live in a circle of literary figures and artists, so that some of their inspiration would reflect on her: 'just admiring them would make me feel happy'.[50] Around the turn of the year 1885, the two young women met in person for the first time. They went for walks and were confirmed in their spiritual affinity.[51] Jo told Lies that she would like to read Goethe's *Faust* with her. The writer and critic Piet Boele van Hensbroek, who worshipped Goethe, had previously suggested to her that she should write an essay on *Faust*. Piet and Jo were related.[52]

A year later, when Jo read Tolstoy's *Anna Karenina* in the recently published French translation, she wrote a description of the characters in the novel in order to analyze her own feelings and give an account of her actions. Again, figures from literature acted as mirrors—something that could also apply to the authors themselves: they, too, could act as inspiring examples.[53] The man or woman behind the work was essential to her, and she shared this view with a great many contemporaries, including Vincent van Gogh. 'I make an image of the person for myself through biographies or criticism by others—when I read his works later on it is not to find his ideas in them but himself.'[54]

In Nunspeet, where she had returned, she continued to idolize Van den Bergh. They listened to 'Im wunderschönen Monat Mai' by Robert Schumann and then played billiards in the hotel.[55] And yet Jo still had a low opinion of herself. She castigated herself for being 'such a useless piece of furniture in the cosy family parlour', because she was so dreadfully bad at contributing to other people's enjoyment.[56]

Not long before she met Lies she had described her appearance: 'Figure—quite tall, taller than your brother[57]—eyes—dark brown—hair—even darker, black in fact, and I was foolish enough to have it cut very short last week.' At home they teased her because she spent so much time looking in the mirror. As she had done previously in her diary, she now candidly presented Lies with quite a sharp analysis of her half-and-half character. She very clearly did not feel she was enough of a whole person and wanted nothing more than to rise above the mediocre:

> I'm serious, to the point of melancholy, and then again crazy and high-spirited as a schoolgirl, I love a simple, quiet, industrious life, and yet I can get on really well in a large, easy setting and I love to go out; I want to raise myself above petty-minded people and yet I sometimes lack the courage to break with old habits for fear of being thought eccentric.

So at one moment she was the 'sensible, serious Miss Bonger', and then the 'silly worldly Jo'. She thought that her sister Mien and her brother Andries were among the few people who really knew her.[58]

That winter she went skating for one last euphoric time in Elburg, but in mid-December 1885 Jo left the school, where she had worked for just over fourteen months. In the end she found the place too petty and narrow-minded, although the teaching itself had gone well. She was barely back home before she plunged into 'hubbub and commotion': she saw a performance of Sophocles's *Antigone* by pupils at the Amsterdamsch Gymnasium and the following day she attended a concert in the Paleis voor Volksvlijt, where Johannes Verhulst conducted the Toonkunstkoor Amsterdam in a performance of Handel's oratorio *Samson and Delilah*. On Christmas Eve she listened to her sister singing 'Weihnachtsglocken' and enjoyed the fragrance of the violets Andries had sent.

She kept in touch by letter with friends and colleagues in Elburg. Her pupil Mary Webb thanked her for the novel *John Halifax, Gentleman* by Dinah Maria Mulock Craik she had sent her; she wrote that she looked back with great pleasure on Jo's literature lessons.[59] There are several letters from Elburg at this time expressing great affection for her. And in Amsterdam, too, there was someone who began to have increasingly warm feelings towards her. Eduard Stumpff, the brother of her friends Marie, Antoinette and Cateau, suddenly flung himself into her arms.

Love for Eduard Stumpff

In the winter of 1885–86 Jo saw operas, went to the theatre numerous times and attended a lecture on French drama. A turning-point was the waltz she danced with the medical student Johann Eduard Stumpff at the student ball in the Paleis voor Volksvlijt. She promptly fell in love with him. 'I can laugh, cry, go into raptures again; thank God I'm not yet completely and utterly frozen inside as I thought at first.'[60]

Jo had known Eduard for years. She had started going to the Stumpffs' in June 1880, when she first made friends with Marie. They lived then at number 13 Plantage Kerklaan, around the corner from Artis zoo.[61] The following year, Jo and Eduard were in a small group studying Latin. He was an assistant physician in 1885–6 and became a doctor in 1889 (Figure 17). Eduard, who inherited his musical and artistic aptitude from his father, played the violin for many years. His father, Willem, was conductor and manager of the Koninklijke Vereeniging Het Nederlandsch Tooneel and chairman of the professional orchestra Maatschappij Caecilia. He and Jo's father must have known one another.[62]

Everything points to the idea that Jo, now that Andries was slowly drifting away from her, had found the perfect replacement in Eduard. A year later it was he whom she called 'my boy', an appellation previously reserved exclusively for her brother.[63] Andries reproached her meanwhile for taking a far too sentimental attitude to life and paraded his superiority yet again as he laid down the law to her:

> I'm sure you've never wondered what art is, and . . . I was almost going to say that you don't even know what literature is.— What on earth! You gush about art and you've only been to the museum once.— It is a shame! It's because you're bored by the art you gush over, so your enthusiasm has been false, in other words . . . sentimentality. (I shall talk or write to you about art later; in the circle you move in in Amsterdam I don't believe there is anyone who understands a single painting; — music is only understood there because this manifestation of art moves people most easily.)

He thought that she ought to achieve a balance between her reason and her imagination and ended his sermon on a slightly less censorious note: 'You have such a bright mind and such a loving heart, but the mind doesn't exclude the sentimentality.'[64] He was not altogether wrong. Jo's knowledge of fine art was at a sadly low level, even though she wanted so much to live among artists. He advised her to study Dutch art for three hours every day and go to the museum regularly. She certainly had something to work on again.

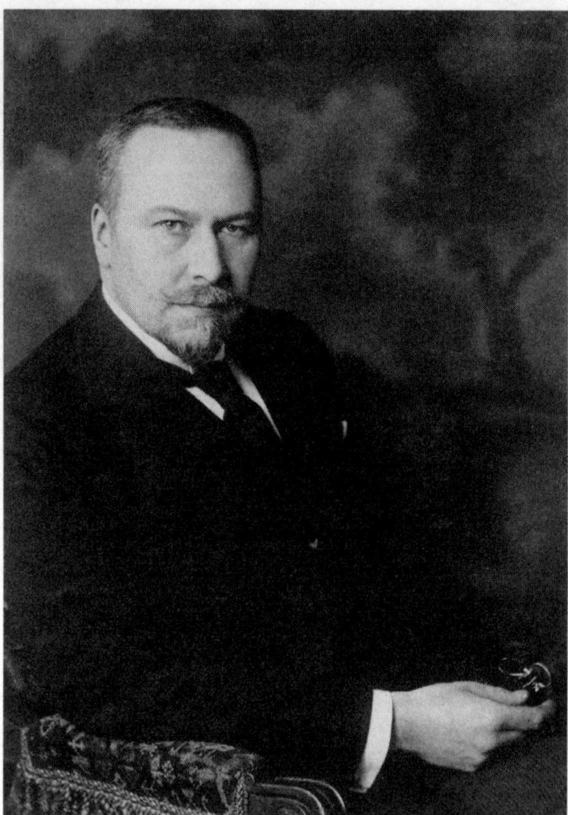

Figure 17 Eduard Stumpff, undated.

For the time being, though, Jo set aside all her brother's useful advice and achieved her goal by other means: she had danced divinely with Eduard five times at the masked ball and spent a whole day skating on the ice rink at the Amsterdamsche IJsclub in Willemspark. Dancing and skating put her in an extremely good mood—so good, in fact, that after a successful job interview she accepted a new teaching post.[65]

Teacher at the Anna Vondel Institute

Between May 1886 and July 1887, Jo taught at the Anna Vondel Institute in Nieuwer-Amstel, where J.S.L. de Holl was principal. The Institute was at number 50 Verlengde Vondelstraat, on the corner of Anna van den Vondelstraat. At this private school for girls from the upper classes, Jo helped pupils prepare for their transition to secondary education. It provided lessons in reading, writing, arithmetic, Dutch, French, German, English, history, geography, nature study, needlework, drawing and gymnastics.[66] The school organized charity events: the proceeds of a raffle and a concert were used to provide meals for a hundred needy children in Nieuwer-Amstel for three months.[67] Jo wrote virtually nothing about her teaching in her diary, except that everything was going well at school—unlike the evenings at home, which she found extremely dull without Eduard. She felt feeble. Her brother had noticed that she was going to bed far too late, and said perhaps she should be eating better. Andries thought that the gastronomic senses were not really stimulated in the Bonger household: 'At home the meat isn't cooked, it's cooked to death. There's absolutely no goodness left in it.'[68]

Although she had sailed carefree through the year, according to her friend Anna Dirks, at the end of 1886, for the umpteenth time, Jo abhorred her selfishness and reserve, and she still, as she said herself, could not manage under her own steam to get some direction in her life. It was a pattern that had been going on for years and kept recurring: 'If only I had someone who worried about me, or rather worried about *my mind*, someone who urged me to study and think, who showed me the way, who gave me books.'[69] It was against the background of this longing that her fear of losing her contact with Andries played out. He was her springboard to a life beyond Amsterdam. Andries put heart into her: 'You know how I take an interest in everything you're feeling and how much I love you.'[70]

At the beginning of 1887 she enjoyed skating again, with gusts of snow blowing into her face. Eduard was also constantly in the picture. He did not waltz with Jo, as he had a year earlier, but carried on deep conversations and lent her difficult books and articles. Thus she came to read Dostoyevsky's *Notes from Underground* in a French translation, and the article 'Balzac en Newman' by W.G.C. Byvanck in the latest issue of *De Gids*.[71] He also got her to read a contribution to the *Revue Scientifique* by Charles Richet, who was doing research into asthma, epilepsy and tuberculosis. Jo understood very little of it and hoped 'that we'll have an opportunity to discuss it at length one day'.[72] The reading matter he was giving her demanded considerable effort on her part, but she ploughed on. She also embarked on the French translation of Dostoyevsky's *Crime and Punishment*. She had once said that a lot of French literature made her depressed; this grim Russian literature must surely have had a similar effect.

This was offset, though, for amidst all the seriousness there was time for fun. On 5 February Jo went to the masked ball in the Odéon on Singel as Little Red Riding Hood.[73] Eduard must have been her escort, although it seems unlikely that this serious young man unbent enough to dress up as the Big Bad Wolf. Reading *Braves gens: roman parisien* (1886) by Jean Richepin did Jo good, for she felt desperately dull inside, a feeling made worse by the difficulties her twenty-seven-year-old brother was having: 'Henri's in a sad mood again, it creates a sense of oppression in the house that weighs on Pa in particular and that everyone feels more or less.'[74] They had had some anxious days with him in April. He suffered from bouts of deep depression. Eighteen months later, Jo lifted a corner of the veil when she put herself, Henri and Andries on the same wavelength.

> Lack of willpower, or rather weakness of will, an uneven and unself-controlled working of the will—oh yes, most people suffer from that nowadays—and alas, alas, it is our malady, too. Henri has it to a high degree, for Dries it is the bane of his life and *I*—has it not been *my* malady too, in the last two years?[75]

Jo struggled to constantly spur herself on to mean something in a demanding world.

To add to her troubles, she was dealt another heavy blow. Entirely unexpectedly, Eduard's sister Cateau died at the age of twenty. Jo was absolutely distraught. She had always felt better when she was with her, although at the same time she was ashamed of her own selfishness. When she said her last farewell, she kissed the cold forehead of her friend, laid out with flowers all round her and roses and camellias in her hair.[76] Later she made several visits to Cateau's grave at Zorgvlied, to the south of the city. She linked what Eduard had to go through and her own separation from Andries, which had caused her so much suffering: 'I've missed my boy all the time for seven years, every hour of every day, his place has never been taken by anyone.'[77] On Eduard's twenty-second birthday Jo felt powerless, unable to offer him any consolation. When they stood together in his room, looking at the photograph of Cateau, she could not suppress the thought that Eduard might also think of her now and then when he looked at it—evidence of her strong desire to be with him.

While Jo spent these months doing everything she could to develop her relationship with Eduard, spending hours with him, clearly feeling his intellectual inferior, Theo van Gogh was mulling over a plan to win Jo, who was more than five years his junior, and how he could find the appropriate words to declare his love for her. Although he hardly knew her, he regarded her as the woman of his dreams.[78] His sister Lies and Andries knew about it. In April 1887, Theo wrote candidly to Lies:

> As you know, I've only seen her a couple of times, but what I know of her really attracts me. She gave me the impression that I can place my trust in her in a completely indefinable way, as I could in no one else. I would be able to talk to her about *everything* and I believe that if she wanted to, she could be oh so much to me. Now it's just the question as to whether she thinks the same.[79]

But Jo's thoughts were wholly wrapped up in Eduard. At this time Honoré de Balzac's *La peau de chagrin* (1831) was the subject of many discussions between the two of them. She tried to fathom Eduard's nature and had her suspicions. She had trouble handling his steadiness, because she herself showed up so starkly in contrast. Sometimes she wanted to give him a good shaking, to make him 'seem more like an ordinary person.'[80]

Jo felt chastened after she had read aloud a sermon by Domela Nieuwenhuis to an old lady and her blind sister, and talked to them about it. She briefly considered becoming a nurse, probably influenced by Eduard, but she was afraid she did not have the moral strength for it, showing a degree of self-knowledge. In her diary she described how they spent Whit Monday together with their heads bent over the novel *La recherche de l'absolu* by Balzac. Eduard's sister Antoinette played a love song by Beethoven:

> E. reads aloud, a bit hastily and hurriedly and I do my best to listen properly and not think the whole time about how lovely I find it to be so close to him; now and then our fingers touch. . . . If I could express the mood in colours, I'd say gold and rose pink.

The following Sunday, the affair moved up a notch:

> He carried me in his arms more or less upstairs and larked around, if I close my eyes, I can still feel his arms around me . . . if only he knew that I'd do anything for him, how I love him.[81]

She was even more taken up with him.

After working as a teacher for more than a year, Jo gave in her notice at the Anna Vondel Institute during the summer holidays. The reason is not clear, but in any event it had nothing to do with her teaching abilities. Her testimonial states that she was a competent teacher who had been able to keep order and discipline, and could be recommended.[82] She had long talks with Eduard in Artis and on the balcony of his parents' home. The romance and intimacy gradually moved to a higher level during the summer and he gave her a bouquet of roses. They went rowing, laughed and floated in a boat: 'Yes I believe I almost lay in his arms; it was so mysterious, enchanting on the water, the lights of the city in the distance were reflected in the water'.[83] She could scarcely believe it.

Two days later, in the afternoon of 22 July 1887, Theo van Gogh caused an embarrassing scene. He had screwed up his courage and gone to visit Jo. Completely out of the blue, he proposed to her. His timing could not have been worse: the roses Eduard had given her few days earlier were still on the table. Jo was utterly overwhelmed and could only reject his proposal. She described the event in her diary and reflected on the effect it had had on her:

> It would sound improbable in a novel—yet it really happened; after being in my company for 3 days at most, he wants to spend his whole life with me, he wants to put all his happiness in my hands. How can it be? And I'm desperately sorry that I had to cause him distress. . . . But after all I couldn't say "Yes" to something like that. What he conjured up for me was the ideal that I've always dreamed of; a rich life full of variety, full of food for the mind, a circle of people around us who wish us well, who want to do something in the world, my vague searching and longing changed into an obligation that's ready and waiting for me: to make him happy! Oh, if only I could, why does my heart feel nothing for him! And when he asked me if I was free, or if I loved someone else, what could I, what should I have replied? Free, yes, that I am, completely and utterly; do I love somebody else? I'm afraid I do, but will it last? Which of them would make me happiest, which of them would *I* make happiest?[84]

A few days after this agonizing, she walked with friends from Breukelen to Loenen; they danced and messed around and rowed on the River Vecht. Jo sat shoulder to shoulder with Eduard.

Theo did not let it lie, declaring that there were many points of mutual understanding between them. It is interesting to see that in his very first letter to Jo he immediately filled her in about his brother Vincent, about Vincent's life at that moment, and about their intense relationship. Theo wanted to start up as an art dealer in his own right, with Andries as his partner. He believed that as his wife Jo would fit perfectly in this exciting new undertaking, but in the end the plan came to nothing.[85] He returned to something she had said—that there had to be 'perfect harmony of thought' in order to enter into marriage, and wrote in well-chosen words:

> I think it is far more important, knowing that we are what we are, to extend a hand to one another and, in the faith that we are stronger together than alone, to hope and strive, by living together, to reach a point where we see each other's faults and forgive them and try to nurture whatever is good and noble in one another. To seek light, not only as far as literature and art are concerned, but in the big issues in life that sooner or later confront us all.[86]

Not an hour passed without his thinking of her.

She did not read this confession and the attractive future he held out to her, which must have very much appealed to her, until later, for Jo spent the first two weeks of August in Scheveningen with Anna Dirks. They went to Anna's studio near the Kurhaus, and told each other their secrets. After a few days away, her 'foolish, wild sense of longing' for Eduard had abated a little. Together they went to see the painter Paul Gabriel, who was giving Anna lessons. When he suddenly asked Jo what she thought of his art, her heart sank; she didn't have the vocabulary for it: 'what could *I*, a poor lay person, say about all those studies and drawings, and I couldn't just stand there and say nothing.'[87] A trip to rural Voorschoten, where they picked waterlilies and ate cream, was much more to her taste.

Eduard and Jo saw each other as soon as she got back, but the meeting was a big disappointment. Their characters seemed to contrast more and more; she thought that he was too ambitious and that she herself was too lazy.

At the end of August 1887, she went with her sister Mien, her brother Henri and a friend on a three-day trip to Cleves by way of Nijmegen, the last stretch in an open landau to Hotel Robbers. They visited Moyland Castle, where Jo enjoyed the view and imagined that she was the wife of the baron. They walked in the Kermisdahl and rowed past the Schwanenthurm. The silence in the beautiful woods gave her a feeling of well-being and the trip kindled her wanderlust.

She could scarcely get down to work because she felt so unsettled. Eduard and she had to study hard for their examinations. (Which subject Jo planned to take the exam in is not clear; but she definitely failed it.) Gone were the 'gold and rose pink' of their time together in May: 'I shan't see him at all either; this horrible winter—no Artis, no rowing, no walks, nothing. Mood dull grey.'[88] For four months Jo did not write in her diary. Amidst all this greyness she did not know which way to turn. Mr Bonger had briefed Andries that Jo was rather mournful, and she found herself at an impasse. One ray of light was that she could give private lessons. Andries observed: 'It will certainly tire you a great deal less than having to drill a whole class.'[89] And yet just such a class was on the horizon.

Teacher at the Utrecht HBS for girls

On 6 December 1887, in response to her application for a vacancy that had been posted in *Het Nieuws van den Dag*, Jo received an invitation to go for an interview with Sara J.C. Buddingh, principal of the five-year HBS for girls at 4 Wittevrouwenkade in Utrecht.[90] A week later, Buddingh informed her that she had got the job as a temporary substitute teacher for English language and literature. She hoped that Jo would be able to complete the current course. Her annual salary for teaching sixteen hours a week—1,500 guilders—was extremely generous.[91] Jo found a room at 33 Tolsteegsingel, which was within an easy walk of the school. She lodged with Joanna Frederica Bruijn and George Allen Taylor, who had two daughters. There were other lodgers and sometimes they played whist together, but Jo preferred to stay in her room on her own.[92]

She started in a depressed mood and was anxious in the new city. 'I've had a desperately dismal time; a failed examination, poor health, an empty, dissatisfied feeling.' She slept at home on Saturday and Sunday nights, because she wanted to keep on seeing Eduard; he tried to cheer her up and took her to see a comedy at the theatre. She certainly needed it. She heard from Andries that after her silence, Theo van Gogh had thrown himself into the bohemian nightlife of Paris, and that gave her pause for thought. 'Do *I* have that on my conscience now, that he's ruining his health and living his life such that he's bound to regret it later? If only I knew whether I did the right thing!' she confided to her diary.[93]

Her doubts were not unconnected to the attitude of her *inamorato*, who was wholly engrossed in his studies. Although he was still good to her, she was annoyed that he did not answer her letters. He had explained why this was, but we do not get to know the reason—we do know, though, that Jo was anything but happy with his excuse. Day-to-day life was also very difficult. She suffered from toothache and stomach cramps, and often lay crying on her bed in Utrecht. When things got difficult, she inevitably drew in on herself. Eduard eventually did write, but his letter was 'as cold as a block of stone and unfriendly, oh E., you're such a wonderful mixture of tender sensitivity and harshness'.[94] She complained that he gave so little of himself, and began to doubt him to such an extent that she took steps to leave the Netherlands. She applied in vain for a job which—had she got it—would have taken her to England; it was probably a post as a governess. Soon afterwards, she again asked Andries to see if he could find something for her in Paris.

At Easter 1888 she went to stay with Anna Dirks in Scheveningen again so they could have a quiet old-fashioned conversation. The talks and the sea air were to no avail: she came back from her trip seriously ill. A final attempt to start work again in Utrecht failed, and in a panic she handed in her notice: 'I was as thin and pale as a ghost, half wasted away. I couldn't sacrifice my health utterly and completely.'[95] Within five months she had had to call it a day. On top of the exhaustion from which she was suffering, Eduard's distant attitude affected Jo's debilitated condition. She could not get over his lack of interest and felt badly hurt, which was disastrous to her already poor health.[96] As chance would have it, that same week Theo's doctor in Paris prescribed him potassium iodide. They were both ailing at the same time although they were unaware of each other's problems. Jo kept pestering Andries to look for a job for her. He wanted her to come, he told her, but it was not a convenient moment. He wrote that Annie and he were worried about trouble at the firm he worked for and they did not have a housekeeper yet.[97] All too soon, however, it became clear that the tensions in their marriage were the real reason for putting Jo off. She could forget about Paris for the time being.

In June 1888 she went to the seaside again, and in the dune landscape and the Scheveningense Bosjes, the woods between Scheveningen and The Hague, her ambitions to be a writer were rekindled:

> At the moment I have a fancy to walk in the dunes armed with my portable writing case one of these days and write calmly at my ease in the open air. First of all I want to get some practice, try to put down on paper an impression that nature makes on me, to analyze my sensation to a degree; I want—as Flaubert says—to get originality—if I don't possess it. I prefer to walk in the Bosjes because the sea breeze on the beach makes me anxious; in the woods it's warm, sunny, sheltered, a wonderful sensation of well-being settles on me and I breathe with pleasure the wonderful smell of the pines while with my eyes I enjoy the delightful shades of green, the young oak leaves, the brown beech trees whose leaves still look red, the darker pine trees, it's enchantingly beautiful.[98]

Ten days later she was still recording her impressions:

> The sea murmurs and sparkles and sings, sometimes it sounds so indignant, like a loud protest against all those unpleasant people on the beach, some of them come down the steps from the Kurhaus, walk across the beach in a dead straight line, and then stand at the edge of the water with mouths open wide with amazement—I hate bourgeois people on the beach with a passion.

She complained that the lower middle class, from whom she wanted to distance herself, had no sense of propriety, and the same applied to the fashionable clothes they wore to stroll along the promenade.[99] At the end of her stay in Scheveningen she returned home. Eduard might be cold and indifferent, but on Sunday 24 June they lay together in the dunes near Zandvoort at sunset, but it was the last time they were together. His name would not be mentioned again.

First to Seraing, later to Paris after all

On 1 August 1888 Jo and 'Mien S.' had arrived in Seraing, not far from the coal mines in the industrial district of Liège but at the same time quite rural, as she wrote in her diary. The identity of this Mien is unknown. The aim of her stay was to build up her strength, to stop agonizing over her unrequited love, escape the possibility of running into Eduard and not burden everyone at home with her moaning and brooding. They stayed for a whole month, lodging with the family of the clergyman René Peterson, who ministered to the Protestant workers in the immense industrial complex established in 1838 by the British entrepreneur John Cockerill. To her great dissatisfaction, Jo found—again—that she had no talent for conducting a general conversation in company; she was unable to 'take the lead'.[100] They visited Liège and Esneux on the River Ourthe. Jo tried to put her future into words. On the one hand she knew 'I can't be content with crocheting silly bits of lace', but at the same time she still tired easily and was moody, with the result that she worried herself sick about the cause.[101] She slept badly and often had exhausting dreams.

While they were in Seraing they visited the Cockerill blast furnaces, steel foundry, rolling mills, smithies and construction workshops. Ten thousand people worked there. In one of the huge halls she witnessed the fate of the factory worker. She was outraged at the injustice and inequality—an early sign of the social democratic beliefs that would become increasingly evident later in her life:

> In that hall there was a deafening roaring and humming, poor men who have to spend their lives in smoke, ash and carbon monoxide; why all this inequality, why do those people struggle and labour so to earn their meagre wages, while the director and the other engineers live off them so calmly?[102]

During a church service she was much impressed by a young minister and she saw him preach again at a meeting of La Société de la Tempérance, where he warned a group of craggy-faced men not to give in to their passions, particularly succumbing to drink: 'And I thought: oh, it's so much harder for the poor workman, who has so much that can excuse him if he surrenders to disastrous drinking, to cure himself of a deficiency than it is for us, who have so many resources to lead us back to the right path.'[103] This experience, too, probably sowed a seed for Jo, who in June 1901 manned a stall for teetotallers at the fair in Bussum. Drunkenness was prevalent and from the mid-1870s crusaders warned against the dangers of the demon drink in all sorts of ways.[104] When one of the delegates confessed that he had thrown away his life selfishly, it touched a nerve with Jo. That evening in her room, she wrote a shamefaced confession:

> How badly, how foolishly, how sinfully I've been living recently, sacrificing everything, everything, my own happiness and that of all those around me solely so that I can surrender to that one unhappy

> thought that has all along possessed me—I've done *nothing* for others, I've been *nothing* to others, I've put everything down to my fragile health—alas, alas, how much I myself am to blame.[105]

While she was in Belgium, Jo had felt a great 'need to write', which was expressed in a short snippet of prose that she wrote in a notebook after her stay there. It is one of the few pieces of her creative writing to have survived:

> Dusk begins to fall, the sky is grey and misty and the train carrying us from Liège to Amsterdam speeds through the landscape, where the autumn colours are already beginning to appear.— I wish I could have stayed there in that cheerful, friendly minister's family. I felt content there. A wonderful smell of new-mown grass penetrates the carriage, the mowers are working everywhere in the fields. Preparations for winter are already under way.[106]

Back in Amsterdam, it seems that she again urged Andries and Annie to let her come and visit them, but again they fobbed her off. Now he confessed to her that his marriage was sheer torture and wrote with bone-chilling candour: 'Sometimes I think that she's been lying on a marble tomb for years.— We are sadly unable to cheer one another up at all.— There is no question of an intellectual life. . . . We just have to struggle through as best we can.' After less than five months of living together, Andries was forced to admit that he and Annie were completely incompatible.[107]

Jo had duly been warned against the pernicious consequences of a relationship without harmony and decided to make a decisive change in her life after her twenty-sixth birthday on 4 October 1888.[108] In the middle of October she realized that her love for Eduard would never be returned, that she had ascribed to him feelings that he did not have. It was finally over and it had broken her spirit. Eduard had refused to commit himself and she was cast adrift. Looking back, she called him a dissembler and a coward, who had acted dishonestly. It was this injustice that most upset her. The gnawing pain dragged on until November, as she kept torturing herself with the agonizing question as to why he had done this to her; then she utterly forswore her love for him.[109] It is not clear whether thoughts of Theo van Gogh were a factor in this process of letting go. She decided that she had to make a decision, she had to act, something else had to come in its place, and this must have had a positive effect, because less than three months later she accepted Theo's proposal. Jo manifestly wanted to get away. She had to 'tear herself away from all those thousands of memories', from her shattered illusions, and she wanted nothing more than to erase them. If she went abroad, she could make a drastic change of course. As she had done before, she considered getting a job in Paris.[110]

At the end of 1888 she left Amsterdam. Jo had already expressed a desire to go to Paris in 1883. She overrode all the alarming messages from Andries and Annie and went to stay with them at 127 rue du Ranelagh. The change came about remarkably quickly and the woman who had long envisaged a bourgeois life with a humourless Amsterdam doctor became the wife of a Paris art dealer, who knew what life among artists in a busy metropolis was all about. Whether she would be equal to it, with her limited experience of life, remained to be seen.

Theo wrote to his sister Willemien at the beginning of December. He did not mention his meeting with Jo, but he may have kept quiet about it on purpose.[111] There was remarkably little time between the moment of the meeting and Jo's conviction that she could give her consent without any qualms. If she had kept the door shut against Theo until then, now she threw it wide open. Before the end of the year the matter was settled and together they made the long-awaited leap into a wholly new life.

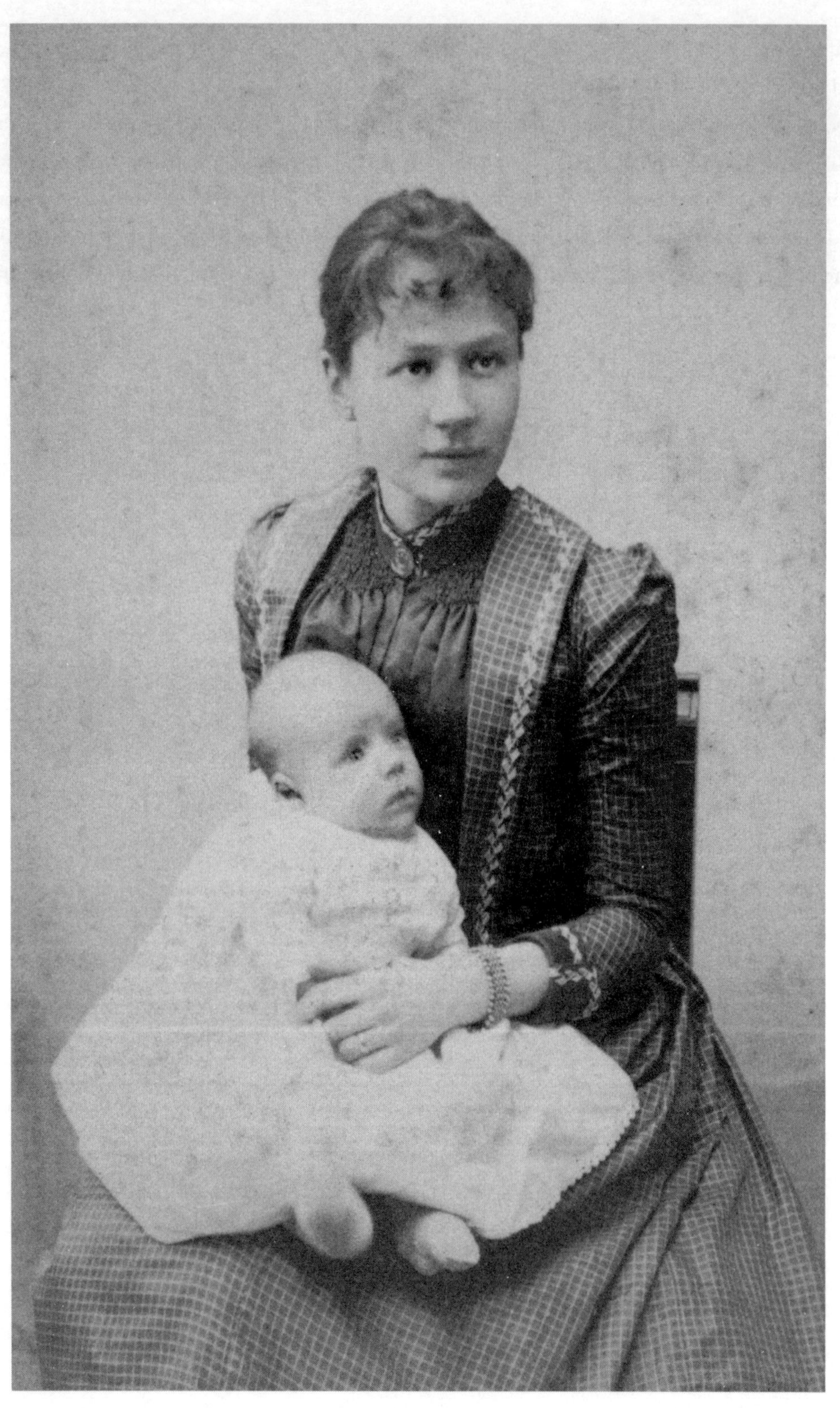

Part Two

Initiation into art—the Van Goghs

1888–91

The past is a foreign country: they do things differently there.

LESLIE POLES HARTLEY[1]

4

Prelude to her marriage to Theo van Gogh

Just before Christmas 1888, Theo told his mother the big news. He had no longer dared to count on it, but this time Jo had taken the initiative, and with considerable tact had brought about the rapprochement. 'I do believe, though, that she knew in advance I was still in love with her.'[1] He must have based this on his discussions with Andries. Jo was on the verge of exchanging her relative freedom for a role as spouse and soon as a mother too. There was no question of a relationship that gradually developed over time such as she had experienced with Eduard. Theo had a demanding job and had meanwhile become a reasonably successful art dealer. He began his career in the Goupil & Cie gallery in Brussels in 1873. At the end of 1879, having worked in their branch in The Hague for a while, he found himself in one of the firm's three establishments in Paris. From 1881 he was in charge of the branch in boulevard Montmartre and responsible for the purchase and sale of contemporary art. This continued after Goupil & Cie became Boussod, Valadon & Cie in 1884. Theo was a sensitive and conscientious dealer with good business sense. He was modern and progressive in what he dealt in, promoting the work of such artists as Paul Gauguin, Claude Monet, Camille Pissarro and Edgar Degas, which at that time were still little appreciated. He also started an art collection of his own.[2]

Theo asked his mother for her permission and hoped that she was willing to give her 'loving mother's heart' to Jo. That same day he wrote to Jo's parents and, as a result, all the members of the family heard the surprising news. Jo's brother Henri sent them a congratulatory greetings telegram on the twenty-third.[3] Theo's mother and his sisters Willemien and Anna also responded immediately. They wrote of their delight about the planned engagement and marriage. Willemien admitted she had been afraid that Theo would marry a foreigner and she was glad her future sister-in-law was not French because 'they really are a different race'.[4] From that moment Jo's life fused with the Van Gogh family.

Great joy, therefore, in the families in the Netherlands and Paris, but things were going less well in the South of France, where Vincent's problems claimed everyone's attention. Jo was still staying with Andries and Annie when Theo wrote to her on 24 December 1888 that he had to drop everything and make haste to Arles, where his brother had been taken 'gravely ill'. They were just able to say goodbye at the station.[5] In a bout of confusion Vincent had cut off virtually all of his ear and been admitted to hospital. It has been suggested that there was a direct link between Vincent's act of self-mutilation and his fear of losing Theo's support when he read about the intended marriage. This, though, is unlikely.[6] Such a conjecture is not consistent with what Theo wrote about Vincent a week later in a letter to Jo: 'Last year he kept urging me to try to marry you, so I believe that in different circumstances, if he knew what things were like between us, he would give his wholehearted approval.'[7] Soon after this, Vincent told Theo:

> Jo Bonger wrote me a line in response to the fact that I had congratulated her, that's very kind of her. It has always seemed to me that you owed it to your social position and to the one you have in the family to marry, and it has been Mother's wish for years. And by doing thus what you must do, you'll perhaps have more tranquillity than before, even amidst a thousand-and-one difficulties.[8]

Jo put her faith in the future despite the depressing events in Arles. She returned to Amsterdam on Boxing Day. Theo was still with Vincent.[9]

Before the New Year, Theo sent her an honest account of Vincent's situation in the hospital. He was worried and wondered whether his brother would remain deranged for ever. He wrote to her that he felt very attached to his brother. Jo was fully aware of their intimate bond of trust from the outset:

> The prospect of losing my brother, who has meant *so* much to me and has become so much a part of me, made me realize what a terrible emptiness I would feel if he were no longer there. And then I imagined you before me, and remembered the way you looked at me when we promised to try and build a good life together and fulfil each other's deepest needs.

Theo eagerly looked forward to Jo's father's official permission for their marriage.[10] She felt for him, wrote to him twice a day and reproached herself for not staying longer in Paris, because she wanted to support him, particularly during these wretched days. She understood that now he could not make any plans to come to the Netherlands. Jo thought back to the wonderful hours they had spent together. The best were those in Theo's apartment, where she had seen her first Van Goghs. 'I love hearing you say I can mean so much to you, it doesn't seem possible. Will you not be disappointed in me? There's so much you shall have to teach me. Does that not put you off?'[11] No one let themselves be put off—neither Theo nor Mr Bonger, who shortly afterwards consented to the marriage. Three years before, Andries had written reassuringly to his parents that Theo came from a family 'with the same standards as you'.[12] So that was not a problem in any event.

Now everyone teased Jo about how she spent the whole day writing letters—but she had to tell all her relatives, friends and acquaintances the happy news. Altogether she sent some 125 announcements.[13] In her congratulations, Mrs van Gogh wrote she had prayed for the union to receive the blessings of heaven.[14] And they certainly needed them because there was a turbulent year ahead that would draw heavily on the fortitude of them both. Theo despaired of Vincent's condition and prepared Jo for every imaginable setback. Over and above the fact that Vincent's state was poor, his own physical condition was far from good. He wrote to her that, 'Though the life I am offering you may not be carefree, together we shall try to see the sunlight as well as the storms, which I know we both consider equally sacred.'[15] He drew great strength from Jo's letters.

Theo loved 'talking to Jo on paper' about his brother—and about the wedding date. He wrote that he could barely wait to get on the train to Amsterdam. He would prefer to get married before May 1889. He realized that a great deal of time would be lost in the Netherlands on people getting acquainted with one another, but he would 'meekly submit to the role of paschal ox'—a reference to a centuries-old Eastertide custom of parading an adorned and fatted ox through the streets.[16] This is how Theo jokingly described his future role: cajoled along as a trophy, while Jo triumphantly held the rope around his neck. The comparison was very apt, for the wedding took place on 18 April—three days before Easter.

Anna Veth, who had been married to the artist Jan Veth for nearly six months, congratulated Jo with the encouraging message that 'you will have moments of happy richness and possessions, you will have a good life and feel safe, and above all independent.'[17] That independence related to her parental home. It was certainly quite a change for the two of them to be together, and for Jo not be surrounded every day by three sisters, two brothers and both parents. Meanwhile, Vincent was doing a little better, so there was no longer any reason for Theo to postpone his arrival in Amsterdam. He wrote to Jo that there was nothing he wanted more than to make her happy.[18]

The engagement

Theo took the night train on 5 January 1889. Four days later the engagement reception was held at 121 Weteringschans and shortly thereafter the young couple went to Leiden, where they visited Theo's sister Anna, her husband Joan van Houten and their two children, Sara and Anna.[19] While in The Hague, Jo and Theo bought some Rozenburg vases and visited Elbert Jan van Wisselingh's art gallery in Buitenhof.[20] They also visited Theo's former mentor Hermanus Tersteeg, who at the time was his colleague in the Boussod, Valadon & Cie branch in Plaats. They went to Bussum as well to see Jan and Anna Veth.[21]

Theo returned to Paris after a week and during the months that followed the engaged couple, wearing their engagement rings with their names engraved on them, corresponded intensively. As a result their intimacy grew. They exchanged sixty-six letters and got to know each other better and better. They formulated their ideas about marriage, art and their future home in Paris. A couple of hours after Theo's departure it was 'so empty now, so quiet' for Jo, who sat gazing at his photograph.

She expressed her joy and put her future husband very much on a pedestal, coming across as dependent—a complete reversal of her earlier ideas:

> I feel so fortunate, so happy. You have no idea what a difference you have already made to my life, how aware I have become of its pointlessness, banality, how you have inspired me to something higher and better—you did so much for me in just that one week. I'm quite sure that if I stay with you always, you might still be able to make *something* out of me.

She also asked about Vincent's letters. If Theo would rather not tell her about them, that was fine, but she hoped he wanted to give her his trust.[22]

Theo thought that all was well between them. He yearned to 'achieve one of the goals in my life, and be able to set that goal higher, since two can do more than one' and pre-empted future setbacks by assuring her that the struggle that was life was something they could cope with together.[23] Jo read the sentence 'you would make me as happy as I ever wished to be' over and over again. She wrote that all this was what she wanted. In Amsterdam she and Mrs van Gogh paid visits together. On these occasions she met family members, friends and acquaintances, and learned much more about Theo. On one visit she had a meal with Theo's cousin Kee Vos-Stricker, whom Theo had described as the most likeable member of the Stricker family. Jo was given twelve silver teaspoons and some sugar tongs that had belonged to grandmother Van Gogh. 'See how fortunate we are,' Jo wrote to Theo.[24] She reread all Theo's letters, could not understand why she had rejected his earlier proposal and asked him to forgive her. She then changed the subject to progress in society, about which she had her own ideas: 'Humanity as a whole only benefits when each of us tries to do good in our own, small circle.' The 'scatterbrain', as she called herself, had consulted Thomas Carlyle again.[25]

Theo ran himself ragged in Paris and viewed dozens of flats. Jo was regaled with possible locations, price levels and floor plans. The distance to Theo's work and the rent were both important to her. While Theo had been writing to her, the artist Meijer Isaac de Haan made a sketch of him and he enclosed it with the letter (Figure 18). De Haan lodged with him for a while starting in October 1888 and had heard that Theo was in excellent spirits: 'I am a fortunate person and sometimes catch myself whistling or humming a tune. It's your fault,' wrote Theo to her. Reflecting this mood, he sent her *L'Oiseau* by Jules Michelet, one of his favourite books with no end of songbirds.[26] He revealed even more preferences to her: Émile Zola as an author and Edgar Degas as a painter. Theo looked forward to talking to Jo about books and visiting exhibitions with her.[27] She wanted to be engaged in the discussion and wrote to him:

> At the moment we have a Nieuwe Gids—an article by Van Deyssel on *Le rêve*—and very nice book reviews by Verwey. That's all I have read so far. Were you also so impressed with Zola's latest book? To me he is still an unknown quantity.[28]

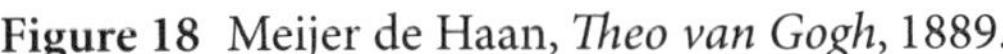

Figure 18 Meijer de Haan, *Theo van Gogh*, 1889.

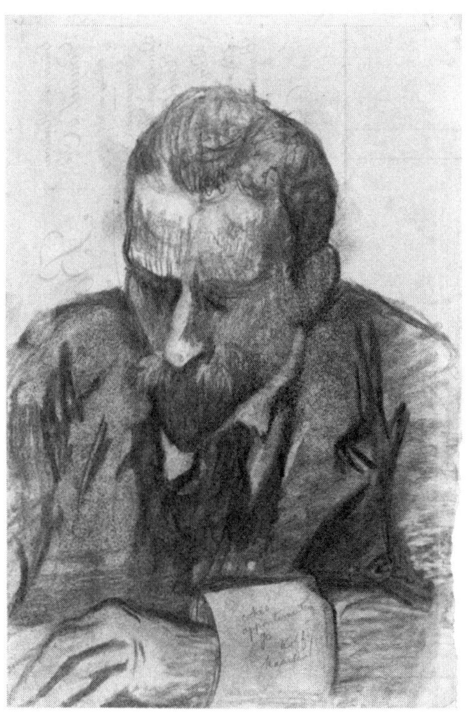

Theo forwarded to Jo the letter from Vincent in which he wrote that their parents had been exemplary in their marriage, and urged them to follow in their footsteps.[29]

Thoughts about marriage

Jo sorely needed these comforting words because, although she had her ideals, she had no illusions about wedlock. And they both understood they would have to compromise because their lives had been so very different: he had been completely free to go his own way, while she was used to a bourgeois and, in her view, narrow existence.[30] She warned him of her mood swings, which from one moment to the next could change her from being cheerful to being sad.[31] But Theo was just like that. Like her, he described himself as a dreamer and spectator who could be dissatisfied with himself. He sent her the recently published *Le livre d'or de la comtesse Diane*, a slim volume full of wisdom presented in the form of questions and answers.[32] A prepublication had aroused Jo's curiosity.

In Bussum Jo had gone walking over the heath and, on the basis of her discussions with Anna Veth, came to the conclusion that she needed to mature more. As she wrote to Theo: 'I've come to the realization that even model couples have *something* they *cannot* share, but I'd rather talk to you about it than discuss it in a letter.' She sent him a recent photograph even though she was not happy with it.[33]

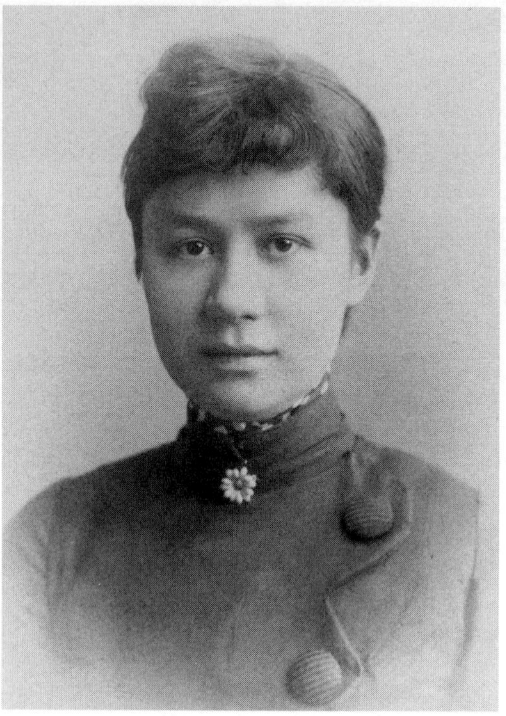
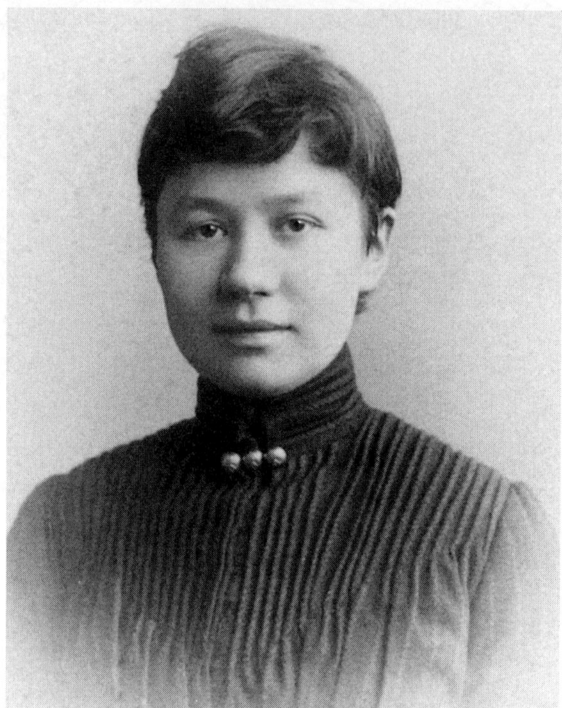

Figures 19, 20 Jo Bonger, 1889.

It must have been one of the photographs shown here (Figures 19, 20). Theo also admitted he preferred another photograph because Jo's eyes came out better on it. He was referring to the small portrait which, together with one of him, has survived in a purple velvet case (Plate 10).

Jo wrote that she and Anna's sister, Lida Dirks, had played Beethoven's Fifth Symphony on the piano, and Theo told her that he often recalled how beautifully Jo had interpreted Mendelssohn's *Songs Without Words* and a work by Rubinstein.[34] He really longed for a hot-blooded person next to him who also loved music. A concert where he heard Beethoven had refreshed him. 'It was wonderful, wonderful and as I sat there listening I wanted to hold your hand in mine.'[35] Mrs van Gogh also thought that her future daughter-in-law played the piano well. In Paris they would be clearing a space for the piano that aunt Cornélie van Gogh, uncle Vincent's widow, had given them.[36] Meanwhile Jo had started on a piano arrangement of Beethoven's Pastoral Symphony. She would like to play it in the evenings for Theo so he could relax on the couch.[37] She demonstrated her familiarity with great names of literature by quoting two lines from Goethe's *Faust*: 'Erquickung hast du nicht gewonnen,/ Wenn sie dir nicht aus eigner Seele quillt',[38] and she remarked that she was now personally experiencing how true those words were. She had ambitious ideas about marriage and assumed that the feelings of powerlessness she sometimes felt would disappear when Theo was present.[39]

A cookery book was another of the gifts she received. That was certainly necessary because Jo was only too aware of her limited housekeeping skills. She took the recipe book with her when she went to see Maria Hugo, who was married to the merchant Willem Sethe and lived in P.C. Hooftstraat. This French lady gave Jo comprehensive cookery lessons, which sometimes lasted all day. And she talked French to her. Maria gave her a silver soup ladle as a wedding present.[40] Despite all her good intentions, however, the cookbook and the cookery lessons had little effect. Nor did the soup ladle. Three weeks after she got married Jo had to confess: 'I can't do anything—I've already burnt the rice twice and the plums once.'[41]

She stayed for a few days with Anna and Jan Veth in Bussum, where they had had a little house in the style of the cottages on the island of Marken erected in their garden. 'They are absolutely delighted with it—there's even a little goat shed—goat's milk will be *the* drink at the Veth residence—they're really going to play the landed gentry!'[42] she wrote to Theo. Veth had bought this little building in 1888 and used it as a studio.[43] All Jo could say about their own future home was to advise Theo to choose soon between the flat in the cité Pigalle and the one in rue Rodier, but she would be pleased if there was also a separate guest room.

Now that they were looking for suitable accommodation themselves, they became more aware of the poor living and working conditions of workers and artists. This issue, along with women and child labour and low wages, would gradually play a major role in Jo's life. She brought up the subject of social inequality with Theo, and she now revised her earlier views about how best to resolve it. Jo was a supporter of radical social change and the abolition of capital:

> I well remember how, even as a child, I was plagued by this feeling of injustice towards the poor, and how I would keep asking Father what could be done about it. . . . Father's sermons about the small things we could do in our own lives were too narrow-minded, to my way of thinking. A major revolution, that would put everything right.

Theo, who had been in the company of avant-garde artists for years, was in complete agreement with Jo's revolutionary ideas. He found it unjust that young painters had to struggle to keep their heads above water, while they devoted their best energies to their work.[44]

He put into words why he loved Jo so much—something she had asked him to do. Each time he began 'I love you because . . .', and then he catalogued her charms one by one: the expression on her face, the sound of her voice, her helpfulness, her feel for goodness and beauty, her openness to joy and sadness, and her thoughtfulness. And, last but not least, the fact that it was him she wanted as a husband, which he could hardly imagine because at times his head felt as though it was made of cork.[45] Jo wrote to him about how important it was for her to be intimate and frank in a marriage, 'and though I know far less about things than you, silence isn't always boredom!'[46] She wanted to tell him her innermost feelings, but she was unable to.[47] He promised to tell her everything about her that bothered him, and then she would do everything she could to change. This was followed by another confession—that she considered herself 'amazingly ignorant' and that thinking logically was not her strong point.[48] Her noble thoughts about equality faltered, and once again she held Theo in higher esteem than herself.

It was a comfort for her, though, to read that he could also be 'unpleasant sometimes'—at least they had nothing to blame each other for on this head because she was far from perfect and she detected contradictions in herself, from being cautiously prosaic to extremely sentimental. Jo had been to a Catholic wedding mass and found it very hypocritical. She wanted nothing to do with church ceremonies. She was also critical about her parents' home: now she found the atmosphere increasingly petty.[49] Paris and the man who made her happy beckoned more and more.

The new home

At the beginning of 1889 Theo chose a fine flat for them. On 4 February the deal was sealed: it was on the third floor of 8 cité Pigalle (Saint-Georges), at a basic rent of 820 francs per year. The flat was not posh. According to Theo one did not need to wear 'lacquered boots' when entering.[50] Jo used a map of Paris to show everyone where they were going to live. It was a cul-de-sac, and therefore quiet, around the corner from rue Chaptal. She was in her element and signed her letters to Theo with a cheerful 'am I really the sunshine in your life?', or a roguish 'your topsy turvy Jo'.[51] Theo sent an initial floor plan of the flat (Figure 21). It was close to the neighbourhood where he worked, so he could come home for lunch. That would also be nice for her, 'because otherwise Jotje would have a really long day,' wrote Jo's father to his future son-in-law, while thanking him for all his efforts. He also assured Theo that Jo had made good culinary progress: 'Yesterday she was learning how to make custard, and from what I heard the outcome was surprising.'[52]

Theo asked Jo for some recommendations about furnishing the flat. Every morning on his way to work he inspected the progress being made by the painters and decorators and he sent a new floor plan, now with the furniture sketched in and with the dimensions of the rooms. He promised to leave some jobs for Jo.[53] She insisted on fitting out the kitchen herself, if necessary with Annie, but she definitely did not want her sister-in-law to do anything without her.[54] Jo let her imagination run riot about the flat, the furniture and the curtains and carpets, as well as whether or not to buy a tea service:

> I've been astoundingly impractical all my life, always in the clouds or in the underworld—only rarely with my feet on the ground. . . . I know you have many earnest matters on your mind at the moment, but I still want to tell you about a lovely blue morning gown I received, and other nonsense like that.[55]

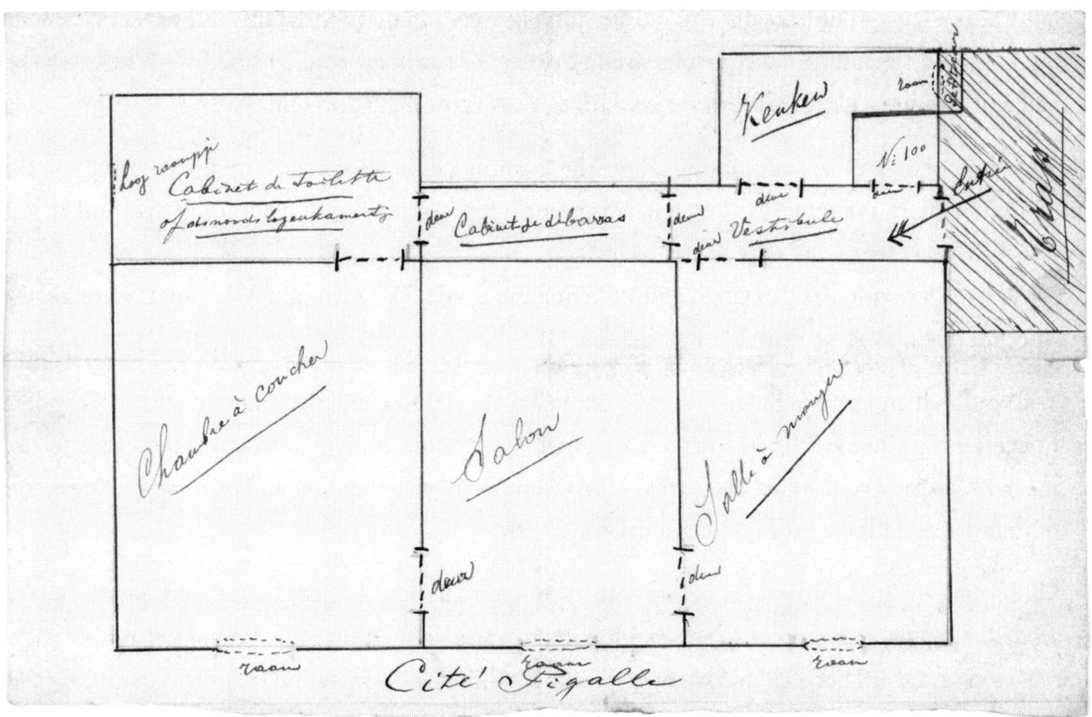

Figure 21 Theo van Gogh, *Floor Plan of the Flat at 8 cité Pigale in Paris*, 1889.

But Theo liked nothing better than to hear about such everyday matters. In fact, he wanted to know more about the dress because he was always worrying about Vincent and was sometimes so empty that he sat 'like an oyster in its shell'. He involved Jo in his plan to buy curtains made from Indonesian fabric (in yellow, with blue and green peacocks) for the dining room.[56] A month later he asked her about another dress and wrote: 'What does your wedding gown look like? I can't wait to see it, but a hundred thousand times more she who is to wear it.'[57]

Theo was extraordinarily sensitive to colour, as we also learn from a detailed description of colour schemes and the possible positioning of the furniture. He enclosed samples of the wallpaper in the envelope. Like a true aesthete, he did not take any risks, and Jo must have sat beaming as she read it all:

> The dark paper is for the dining room with dark brown boiserie. The old furniture which, as you know, is speckled mahogany, orange with dark flecks, will look well against it. Those beautiful oriental sarongs would be a comble. . . . The white and blue paper is for the corridor and the cabinet de débarras. The salon is still all right, white with grey floral decorations. The grey and pink is for the bedroom. It will go well with some curtains I saw in the Louvre. A type of cretonne, but mat and

> quite heavy. Background cream with red and pink flowers and twigs with fairly large spaces between them. A reddish-pink, not too purple, would be nice for the bedspread. The bedroom furniture i.e. bed and armoire à glace is rosewood i.e. dark red. It's varnished at present. . . .[58]

He preferred to have no curtains in the salon. The incoming light would show up the paintings on the wall to better effect. When the workmen had finished, he longed passionately for Jo's arrival and he was glad that their 'sentence' was now nearly over.[59]

Jo went to stay with Mrs van Gogh and Willemien in Breda for a fortnight. Willemien, elated at the prospect of her arrival, wrote to her beforehand:

> Yes, I can well understand that you're busy with all sorts of things and that there's a scary hotchpotch of everything all mixed up in your head, right, that's terrible. But you also know of course what I mean by 'clearing your mind', that's what I did last week in my loneliness, and now everything is sort of in order and I hope that it'll long remain so.[60]

Jo liked being in Breda very much. She heard new stories about Theo and she could devote herself without constraints to her enthusiasm about going to Paris—something she did not permit herself at home because she did not want to give her father and mother the impression that she did not care that she would be the first daughter to leave the parental home. She read letters from Theo's youngest brother Cor, who was employed in an engineering works in Lincoln, England, and she wrote inviting him to the wedding, which he attended.[61] She looked at the Japanese woodcuts that Theo had given to Willemien. As well as discussing art with Theo, Jo also talked about it at length with Willemien, who according to him had a good eye (Figure 22).[62]

Later, in an impressive letter, Willemien would refer to Jo's naive view of the world at that time:

> When I first met you in Amsterdam . . . I got to know you as you are, your individuality—strong, resilient, healthy, cheerful. When you came to Breda, I saw another side of you, something delicate and tender, something surprisingly childlike, and knowing nothing about the everyday, petty, tedious, prosaic world of worry and misery. I had had a bitter time and could barely countenance the possibility that you were heading for a bruising contact with the world—and yet an indefinable feeling made me almost certain that something or other was hanging over your head. . . .[63]

Willemien hit the nail on the head with this honest and insightful analysis because until her marriage, Jo had lived in quite a protected environment and, indeed, at that time had no inkling of the demanding tests that she might face in the real world.

But she was not completely ignorant. Theo admitted that the news from Arles about his brother saddened him. Vincent suffered a second mental crisis at the beginning of February 1889. The people around him were frightened of him. On 7 February the minister Frédéric Salles advised Theo that

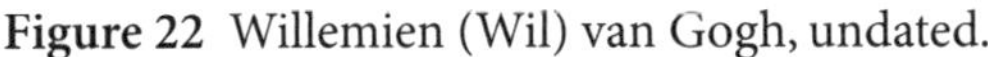

Figure 22 Willemien (Wil) van Gogh, undated.

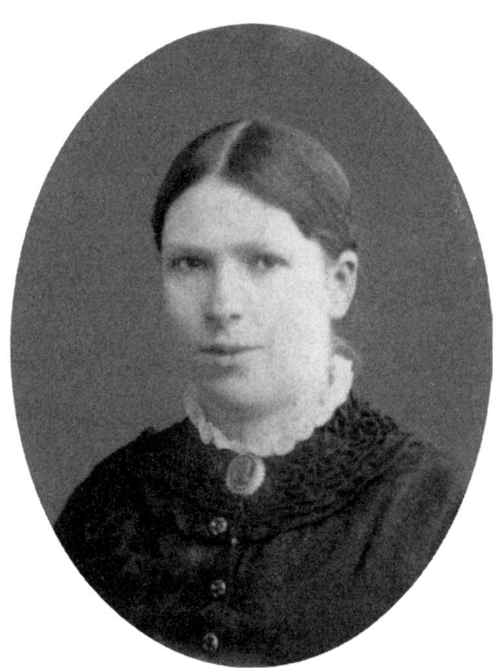

Vincent had been admitted to hospital again that same day, and that the doctors recommended having him put in a psychiatric institution. Vincent lay on his own in a room. He did not speak. He only cried and was troubled by hallucinations and nightmares. Vincent's doctor, Félix Rey, also kept Theo informed. Theo told Jo what was happening and enclosed the last letter he had received from Vincent. When Jo read it, she felt 'so terribly sorry'.[64] Theo longed to be close to Jo in trying times and looked to her for solace. At the same time, he needed practical information from her, such as her year of birth, so he could register her with the local council in advance. He had requested this information from Andries, who knew the day but was not sure about the year, just like him. Teasingly she pulled his leg by saying it was 1863 instead of 1862.[65] He dashed from haberdasher to upholsterer for his young lady, but he knew why he was doing it and felt 'as rich as a king'. He sent Jo a sample of the bedroom curtain material, which she kept (Plate 11).[66]

She was surprised that she got to know Theo so much better by reading his letters and through all the stories and anecdotes about him that family members told her. 'And I'm getting a far, far clearer picture of your relationship with Vincent.' She had profound conversations with Willemien, who not only told her in detail about the symbiosis between the two brothers, but also let Jo read letters that Vincent had written to her.[67] Those warm letters about his views on art and artistry, as well as the frank recommendations to his sister, made a deep impression on Jo.

Vincent's painful situation continued to haunt Theo, and that made him restless. He consulted doctors about where his brother could best be admitted. In his letters to Jo, his worries about Vincent led seamlessly to comments about the loving relationships in Breda, but he pointed out to her that 'there's a huge difference between them and me and don't harbour any illusions. They are so pure and have been so little exposed to the evils of the world.'[68] Theo's warning was sincere and would certainly prove relevant.

In Leiden Jo visited the home of Anna van Gogh and Joan van Houten. Willemien suspected that Jo got on best with the latter: 'You need to know Anna well before you can love her.' Shortly thereafter she urged Jo above all to remain full of high spirits, to counterbalance the Van Goghs: 'We're often so awfully serious.'[69] Jo sketched the mood in Leiden for Theo; she found it formal and forbidding to go there, and their two girls 'a bit too well brought up.'[70] According to her, Anna was burdened by an extraordinarily strong sense of duty and she was not well suited to Joan. She regretted that.[71] On the eve of her own wedding day, she had so far encountered few model marriages, and the spectacle of that flawed and cold relationship gave her further grounds for reflection. Jo admitted to Theo that she could sometimes be very unfriendly to people despite the fact that she wanted to be nice. She attributed this to her mood. When she was not feeling good, she retreated into herself and did not want anyone to notice her. Giving serious thought to preparing for her position as a married woman, she realized that she still had a lot to learn:

> My conscience has been pricked by a book I found in Father's bookcase on the subject of marriage . . . the honeymoon—the young couple's finances—good temper—(that takes up a big part), how people have to learn to get along with one another, and all manner of useful things . . . there's a lot of nonsense in it but also a lot that is good. But it made me very aware of my own imperfections.[72]

The book, with the telling title *Gelukkig—ofschoon getrouwd. Een boek voor gehuwden en ongehuwden* (1886) was by Elise van Calcar. Jo was clearly affected by it. It is not surprising that she felt inadequate. This manual contains a staggering list of recommendations, commandments and things to avoid. A model wife must not just have her heart in the right place. She also has to be prudent and healthy, and ideal matrimonial love is presented as a blend of dedication, self-sacrifice, gentleness, patience, thrift, good manners, tolerance and submission. Above all, a jovial attitude was extremely important because, according to Van Calcar, 'nothing makes a woman as pleasant to her husband as being bright and cheerful.'[73] Jo therefore sometimes brooded for hours about whether she would be able to fulfil her obligations properly. She had learned, however, that the purpose of life had to be sought close by and 'that I can and must devote myself to making both of us happy.'[74] Theo became the husband who would have to help her find her way in the overwhelming world. The transition to this new life also manifested itself in a material sense. Wedding presents trickled in as Jo studied *Gelukkig—ofschoon getrouwd*. They ranged from a tea table with cups and saucers to an embroidered footstool.

5

Married life and motherhood in Paris

After the date of the wedding had been settled, one more tricky hurdle had to be taken—whether or not to get married in church. Jo was adamant. She thought it would be a sham. She asked Theo if his mother would be very upset if they did not, because she did not want to hurt her, 'but otherwise I would a hundred thousand times prefer not to'.[1] Theo had also turned his back on the church, describing himself as unbelieving as far back as 1881.[2] Jo, who was staying with Theo's sister Anna in Leiden, did not get involved in discussing the church issue with her father, awaiting his reply to Theo's letter on the subject, and was not looking forward to the general discussions awaiting her when she got home.[3] Initially Mr Bonger pressed for a church wedding, and Theo was prepared to go along with it because he had no desire for a debate about it either.[4] In the end, the subject had to be aired because Jo's father had had second thoughts, and shortly thereafter, to their great relief, he let them decide for themselves. Theo's mother also changed her mind but, as the devout widow of a clergyman, she was obviously unhappy about it.

On 30 March 1889, Theo left for Amsterdam on the night train and notification of the marriage was given on 4 April. Two days before the wedding, Theo and Jo had dinner at 8 Keizersgracht with Mina Carbentus, widow of the clergyman Johannes Stricker and mother of Kee Vos-Stricker and Jan Stricker, who would be a witness at the wedding. Mina was Mrs van Gogh's sister. Afterwards they went to the Carré Theatre, where circus director Oscar Carré and equestrienne Mademoiselle Godlewsky put on a glittering performance. There was also a *Pas de deux comique* featuring clowns on horses. The show concluded with a pantomime with ballet—the *Schelmstreken van Reintje de Vos*.[5] They ended the evening with supper.[6]

Jo's parents and Theo's mother ordered wedding invitations printed in French. The names of the happy couple were given as Theodore and Jeanne.[7] On 18 April, the day of the wedding, it proved no easy task to get Jo into the bodice of her white wedding gown with its train. According to her sister Mien, they had to 'hoist her in'.[8] Jo was exhausted by all the fuss attendant on the wedding, and they were both dreadfully embarrassed by the surprise the family had in store for them—a glass wedding coach. There they were, on show like two goldfish in a bowl. Shortly afterwards she confided in Lies and Willemien: 'All that fuss—and then the climax of the wedding day with the veil and that glass display case of a coach. That morning I was so angry and felt so ridiculous. Really, what a farce, and Theo thought exactly the same.'[9] The witnesses—the two mothers, Jo's father, Joan van Houten (Theo's brother-in-law), Jo's brother Henri, Willem Sethe and Theo's cousin Jan Stricker, headmaster of the HBS—signed the marriage certificate. [10] Jo's sisters Lien, Mien and Betsy, brother Wim, Theo's brother Cor, his sisters Willemien, Lies and Anna, with her eight-year-old daughter Sara, and Maria Sethe were all certainly at the ceremony. The reason Andries and Annie did not attend beggars belief: he thought the whole affair was too expensive. He complained that it would cost too much money to make the trip, and on top of that Annie would have to buy a new dress. Jo's parents gave her 250 guilders and paid for her trousseau. Theo suggested that she should put some of the money towards a dining table.[11] Exactly three years later, Jo wrote in her diary that she had gone through life with her eyes half closed, but then Theo taught her to see and opened her window on the world.[12] This step was to seal her happiness and destiny.

On the way to Paris, the newly-weds spent a day in Brussels, where they visited the Cathedral of St Michael and St Gudula, before coming home to their apartment in the ninth arrondissement. Jo thought their flat upstairs was just like 'a cosy little nest' in 'that lovely, big tree that stood outside the door'. Depending on the social context, if she left the nest and wanted to introduce herself, she could choose from three different visiting cards that Theo had had printed for her: 'M^r^ & Mme Théo van Gogh / 8, cité Pigalle', 'Madame T. van Gogh' and 'Madame Théo van Gogh'.[13]

Life in Paris

Right from the outset the newly-weds felt cosy, with the teapot within easy reach. Jo felt at home in her new abode. The concierge brought them their post and posted any letters they had written. She shared her domestic bliss with her family, writing about the apartment:

> On those two Sundays in particular, when we walked around like two children playing with their dolls' house, we organized and hung everything, then reorganized everything all over again, opening and closing our 10 doors, *I repeat 10*, in turn and strolling around our palace.[14]

She remarked that with all those doors you could play hide and seek all day long. Jo had a lot to do with her feather duster and cloth, and Theo's gentle love was like a safe haven for her.

They both preferred the comfort of eating Dutch cooking. They had enjoyed their favourite, brown beans, even though the housekeeper could not believe they ate them boiled rather than sautéed in butter. Jo described the flat, the splendid colours and the art on the walls for Willemien and Lies. Vincent was everywhere: in the bedroom,

> light, cheerful—a rose pink tint in the room from the flowers on the curtain fabric—Vincent's lovely peach trees in blossom on the wall—now we've still got the Mauve to hang. The living room is more colourful: the curtains are a warm yellow, the mantelpiece covered with a red shawl—paintings (some of them with gilt frames), no mirror above the fireplace but a piece of tapestry with all sorts of lovely things on it, including a beautiful yellow rose by Vincent. The salon hasn't been finished yet so I'll say nothing about it—only that Vincent's paintings have a place of honour—and the negresses.[15]

This last reference was to *The Mango Trees, Martinique* (1887) by Paul Gauguin, which would always remain one of her favourites.

Jo missed her sister Mien and wanted to tell her everything, for example that she had been suffering from nettle rash for some time. She did not have words enough for her new husband. He was so good and loving, and there was nothing forced between them when they were together. She thought he was so straightforward and natural—exactly the same qualities she had always endeavoured to have herself. But housekeeping was still 'a farce', so it was just as well that Madame Joseph helped her to cook lunch and do all the other chores. She still had to find her feet outside the home, too. Jo was very shy when Theo introduced her to one of his superiors in the gallery in rue Chaptal. She found it hard to speak French spontaneously and breathed a sigh of relief when the ordeal of the introduction was over.[16] For the moment she was enthusiastic about Paris's bustling street life.

In the mornings Theo left at around nine. By noon he was back home again with his feet under the table and talked about the day's events during lunch:

> I didn't always understand him, but I so *wanted* to understand him—and often still managed to *feel* it by instinct—and we matched each other so well, 'you're a little woman made just for me,' he sometimes said—oh, oh, oh!![17]

She wrote this lament in June 1892, when she had been a widow for nearly eighteen months.

Theo had a basic annual salary of 4,000 francs. He was paid in more or less monthly instalments of 333 francs. On top of this he got a bonus of 7.5 per cent of the net profit of the branch he managed. This annual bonus was calculated after the inventory was drawn up in the January of the following year, and was paid out around May. It is evident from the recorded profits that Theo was entitled to a respectable sum: the average annual bonus was over 8,000 francs. When this was added to his basic salary, his substantial annual income therefore hovered around 12,000 francs (6,000 guilders at the prevailing exchange rate), of which, on average, Vincent received some 1,750 francs. In other words, for ten years Theo paid approximately 15 per cent of his income to his brother. The agreement was that, in return, the artworks Vincent sent Theo would be his property.

Shortly after the wedding, Theo started recording expenditure in an account book, which he kept up until 30 September 1890; Jo started making entries on 29 January 1891. During the seventeen months they were together, he gave her a total of 3,180 francs for housekeeping, an average of 187 francs a month, as well as forty francs to buy things for herself on ten occasions. He also gave her presents, including two hats, slippers, a dressing gown, a bodice, a corset, a muff and a ring, totalling over two hundred francs. Theo paid for the larger items himself: the rent, gas, insurance, the laundress, help in the house (initially Madame Joseph, and later Victorine—costing 12.50 francs a week), Dr Crequi, who would assist when Jo gave birth (two hundred francs), purchases relating to the birth of baby Vincent, including costly asses' milk, and doctors' appointments (to Louis Rivet and David Gruby, five francs per consultation), and the wine merchant. They must have been modest drinkers, when at home at least, although there was one exception of 180 francs for wine in December 1889. Total expenditure on beer remained steady at sixty francs. The nature of the expenses hidden behind the recurring items in the 'Miscellaneous' column remains an intriguing puzzle. Altogether Theo recorded the substantial sum of 1,005 francs, without ever specifying the purpose, whereas in the case of other sums, even very trivial ones, he did.[18]

Jo started her own housekeeping book, in which she noted all the expenses day to day between April 1889 and September 1891. As a result, she soon learned what things cost. She undertook her task diligently, scrupulously correcting 'vegetables' to 'soup vegetables', for instance.[19] She paid the baker, the milkman and the butcher, and the book also lists the ingredients for each day's meals. The housekeeper took her around the neighbourhood so that Jo knew where all the shops were. There are strikingly large numbers of lettuces and eggs, as well as countless references to meat. Chicken and veal were expensive, and she also spent a lot of money on joints of beef.[20] Turkey was served only once. With time, various French terms began to appear in the housekeeping book, such as *chair à saucisse* and *nouilles*. Potatoes were the staple, but from time to time the menu included rice, lentils or pearl barley. Asparagus was served up for the first time on 14 May 1889, and from December onwards oysters featured regularly—they were probably intended to build up Jo's strength, since she was due to give birth within a few weeks. She bought wood and charcoal for their stove, methylated spirit and cut flowers.

Jo also had a notebook cum cash book, in which she made occasional calculations, wrote down names and addresses, including those of the housekeeper, the laundress, the charwoman (*frotteur*) and the dressmaker, and recorded various expenses, such as what she spent on clothes, bus tickets, stamps and food.[21] Details reveal her habits and activities. Jo bought *eau de violette*, gave money to a beggar and in December 1889 purchased wool and knitting needles. Later in the book, she described everything in the nursery, and later still little Vincent used it to make drawings and do writing exercises (Figure 23). A hat (36.10 francs) and a dress (36.25 francs) were expensive items for herself. Such

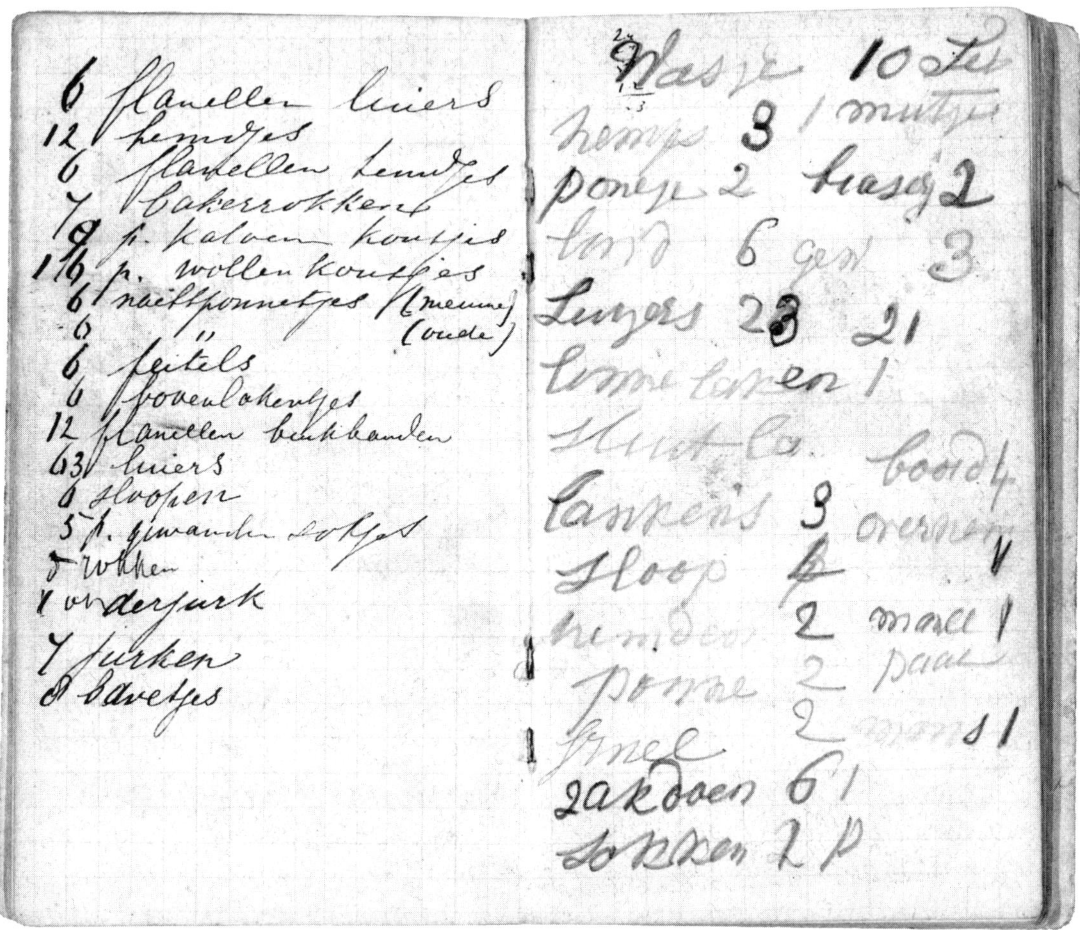

Figure 23 Jo van Gogh-Bonger's note and cash book. Jo's handwriting on the left, her son Vincent's on the right.

purchases were exceptional and she duly wrote to Mien about them: 'Yesterday afternoon I bought a hat—it's black with two black bird's wings and an old rose ribbon which I might have changed to cream—I think it suits me—I can't bear those flat hats with all those flowers that are so popular here.' For relaxation she went for walks with Theo and they visited people together.[22] Jo did not look at all like a married woman. She appeared so young that when she was out shopping, people in shops addressed her as 'Mademoiselle' rather than 'Madame'.[23]

Her new duties as wife and hostess left her with much less time to read, but initially she was very happy. She wrote as much to everyone at home in Weteringschans, telling them that the flat was like a jigsaw puzzle, where everything had yet to be given a permanent place. She did not lack diligence when it came to household tasks, but her shortcomings as a cook were really embarrassing. She had been preparing turnip tops for Theo and Andries and, to her surprise, after she had slaved over them for two and a half hours there was virtually nothing left. Her menfolk had teased her mercilessly.[24]

The flat was popular with visitors and they had little time to themselves. Cousin Vincent van Gogh (the son of uncle Cor, who like his father was also an art dealer), the artist Joseph Isaäcson and Theo's friend François Spijker dropped in from time to time. It could also be busy on the third floor of 8 cité Pigalle in the evening, with visits from the painters Camille and Lucien Pissarro, Ferdinand Hart Nibbrig and Andries.[25] Isaäcson and Hart Nibbrig did not speak French and Jo did not dare open her mouth, so unsure of herself was she among all the artists, collectors and friends. It surprised her, though, that Andries could not speak the language well either.[26] She could manage when she went shopping and when she was with the housekeeper, 'but carrying on a conversation, and particularly when Theo's there—I find that awful,' Jo confessed to Vincent in a letter.[27] She felt ashamed in front of her husband.

Jo focused completely on her role as lady of the house and now and again went to the gallery to collect Theo. In May she, Theo and Andries visited the annual Salon—Annie was in the Netherlands (just a month after the wedding, it appeared that they could afford it after all) and Andries joined them for lunch every day. She wrote in detail about her housekeeping efforts, which she took extraordinarily seriously, and about the activities of her housekeeper. Madame Joseph arrived at around half past ten, swept the passage, cleaned the shoes and the copper, and did the bedroom because Jo could not turn the heavy mattress over on her own. Sometimes Madame Joseph did the shopping for lunch, and after the meal she washed up, sharpened the knives and tidied up the kitchen. 'So I don't have her for more than 5 hours a day, and you'll understand there's enough left to do.'[28] Everything looked spick and span. Meanwhile, everyone at home was missing Jo dreadfully.[29]

Discussions about art

Shortly after their engagement had been announced, Theo wrote to Jo saying that he hoped she would come to love the artists he admired and their work.[30] He must have told her in great detail about his contacts with artists, about their work and about the art trade from the moment in January 1889 when they both visited the Van Wisselingh and Boussod, Valadon & Cie galleries and also the artists Jan Veth and Anna Veth-Dirks.[31]

He used his musical sensibility to explain to Jo what painting meant to him in a lengthy description of a Paul Gauguin painting he was trying to sell at the time. It was most probably *Autumn at Pont-Aven* (Plate 12). This work affected him in the same way as 'a beautiful symphony'. He brought the painting to life for her in a colourful evocation full of synaesthetic associations:

> A dead beech, whose leaves have prematurely turned reddish orange, stands in a hilly landscape full of trees in their resplendent foliage. That particular tree is in the centre of the picture beside a moss-covered hut, forming, as it were, a magnificent plume; the deep bluish and violet shadows of the full trees stand out against the orange, like two melodies in counterpoint. The orange harmonizes with the rich variety of browns and Havanas in the tilled fields, hard roads cutting through the woods and vanishing in the distance in the hills that rise up to the sky. The blues and violets are echoed in unusual shades of green and fade in parts into the blue of the sky above. A white cloud, a couple of peasant women in pale blue costumes, a verdant meadow in the foreground, add a few eye-catching tones which, like little melodies, relieve the counterpoint of the instruments. A musician who felt about this painting the way I do, would be able to give each colour the name of an instrument and make a musical composition of it. There is nothing material in the picture, yet it captures a moment when everything in nature is alive and burgeoning. The strange combination of colours transforms the dead tree into a sonnet of light and where life is most intense one finds the very saddest colours of mourning.[32]

This, then, this was one way to look at art. Theo enjoyed talking to Jo about what artworks did to him, and he skilfully tried to instil modern literature, art and art appreciation in her. He knew that during her visit to uncle Cor van Gogh, who had an art gallery on Keizersgracht, she had felt very unsure of herself when he talked to her about certain paintings.[33] Theo explained to her that a viewer had, as it were, to complete a work of art. He loved art that could touch people's souls. To him, even the most unappealing image could inspire poetry, and the greatest lyricism was born out of suffering. You had to be able to let go of pure aesthetics in order to understand art properly and plumb its depths. His perception of art and literature was fundamentally different from Jo's, or at least much more educated. She had barely concerned herself with modern movements in literature and art, and had certainly not yet developed a practised eye.[34] She still had a lot to learn.

Theo had also been busy with a selling exhibition of recent work by Claude Monet, some pastels by Edgar Degas and a sculpture by Auguste Rodin. He was charting a progressive course. Apparently his employer, Boussod, once said that the misshapen modern art Theo dealt in undermined the firm's dignity.[35] If this is true, it illustrates the organization's conservative stance. Artists did not just visit Theo at the gallery in boulevard Montmartre, they also came to see him at home, and so Jo got to know them.[36] During the run-up to the wedding, Jo had wanted Theo to tell her what exactly 'that new movement' in painting actually involved and she began to wonder how an artist felt and thought.[37] That was what occupied him day in and day out, and if she could talk about it, it naturally benefitted their relationship and the atmosphere at home.

As early as July 1887, Vincent thought that marriage for Theo would be more than beneficial to his health. It would also be good for his business affairs. Later he expressed himself with greater precision when he referred to 'your wife, who anyway will join with us to work with the artists'. The idea was that Theo would launch his own business, for a new generation of painters, with Jo as his right hand, so she would also have to know how the art world worked. The issue of starting his own gallery or not became a repeated subject of discussion.[38] Everything in Jo's life had changed. In Amsterdam she had been surrounded by music every day, whereas in Paris art dominated from the outset.

Theo did more than enlarge her knowledge of art, he also extended the range of her travel in the city. He took her, for example, to the viewing day of a sale of 350 artworks, where she saw *The Angelus* by Jean-François Millet. Despite the painting's great fame, however, she was unimpressed.[39] She had read about Millet's life a few months before the wedding, and afterwards urged Theo to keep writing to her about painting.[40] They went together to St Cloud, where they visited their friends Emmanuel and Clara van Praag. He had a diamond factory. When they returned, they had dinner in one of the twelve restaurants in the popular Bouillons Duval chain, where they ate from time to time.[41] Jo continued to struggle with cooking, so it was fortunate that her sister Mien was soon coming to stay. She was an excellent cook and gave Jo many practical tips.[42]

Theo had a cough and a painful leg. In response he bought a barrel of wine. They worked out that Jo could go to Amsterdam the following spring, and they would put 250 francs aside for the trip. 'So, that's arranged!' she wrote euphorically to Mien, who read how Jo had dreamed about their little brother Wim and wanted so much to go rowing on the Amstel with the family again. She also told her how she put her hair up. Jo was sorry that Theo did not like the style of her red dress because she did not have much to choose from in her wardrobe.[43]

At the beginning of June, Hermanus Tersteeg, Theo's former mentor at the Goupil gallery and now his colleague in The Hague branch, took the young couple to Le Doyen, a restaurant on the avenue des Champs-Élysées, where they ate outside. The day before, he had eaten with them in their flat using the silver cutlery that Boussod, Valadon & Cie had given them as a wedding present (Plate 13).[44] Bursting with pride, Jo told Mrs van Gogh all about it: 'We have the place settings—a beautiful case monogrammed V.G. with the letters intertwined, and inside on red cloth there are 12 pairs of heavy silver spoons and forks with lovely patterns and also a monogram.'[45] She had kept three pairs out for everyday use. Theo and Jo had been to the World's Fair several times. (It ran from 5 May to 5 November.) Soon after one of these visits, they were invited to have dinner in the restaurant high up in the Eiffel Tower by the painter Vittorio Corcos and his wife Emma Ciabatti, who moved in Italian literary circles. The Eiffel Tower, the iron wonder, had been officially opened a month before. Jo was eagerly looking forward to the ride up in the lift and the spectacular view.[46]

She was not very decisive. Jo had still not bought a light cotton frock because she was afraid she would make the wrong choice. All the while, though, the temperature rose. She did not like hot weather; it was a torment. For want of anything better, she wore her red blouse and a brown woollen floor-length winter skirt. No wonder she had problems with the heat. She also hated the crowds and the stench in the

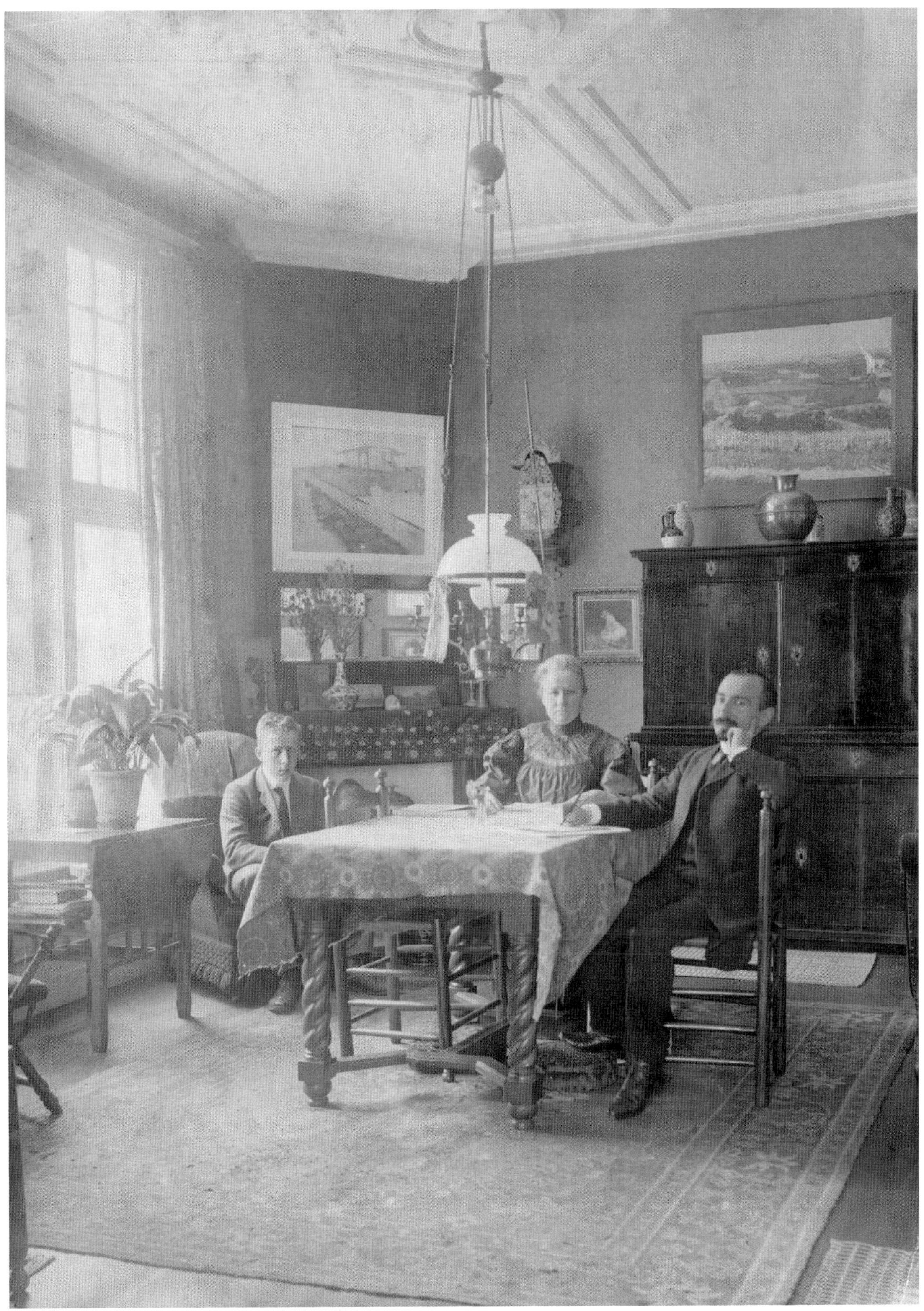

Plate 1 Vincent van Gogh, Jo Cohen Gosschalk-Bonger and Johan Cohen Gosschalk in the dining room at 77 Koninginneweg in Amsterdam, late 1910 or early 1911.

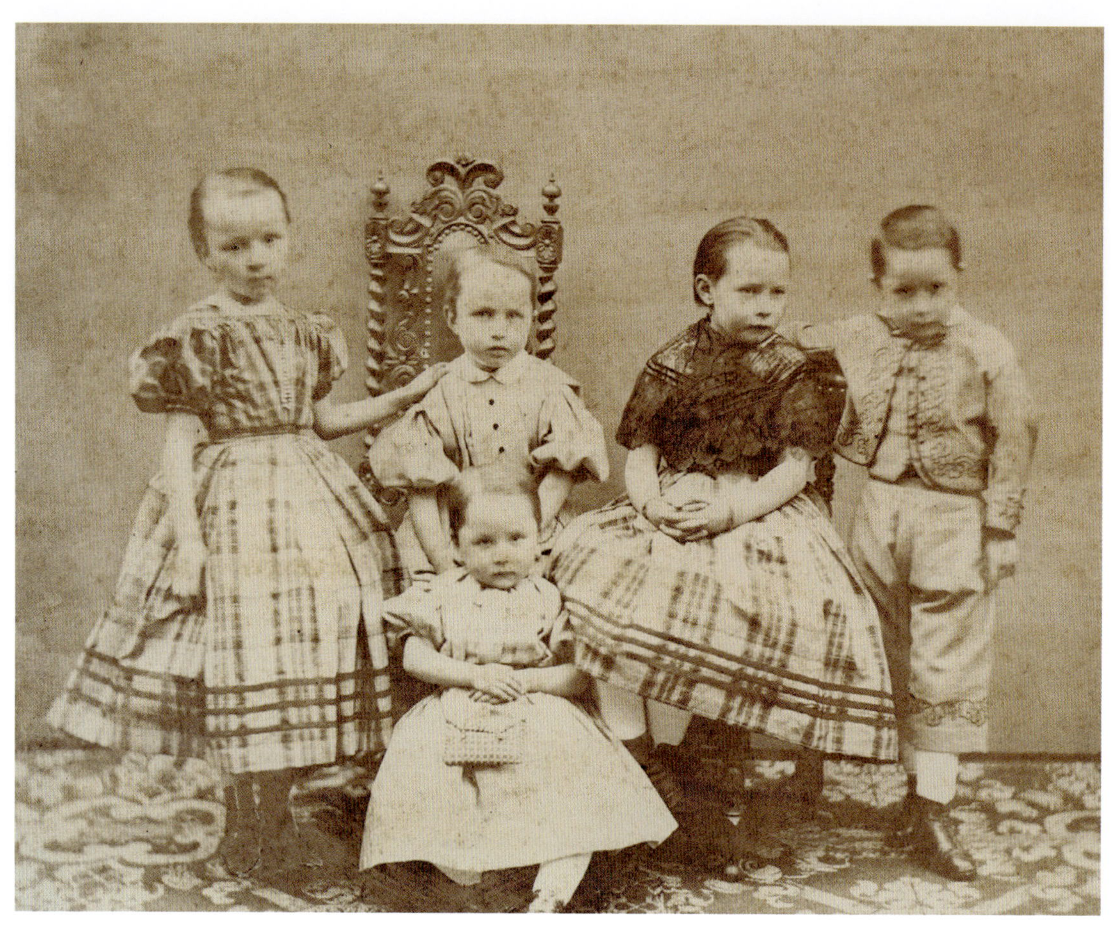

Plate 2 Five of the Bonger children: Jo at the front, and behind her Mien, Andries, Lien and Henri, *c.* 1864–5.

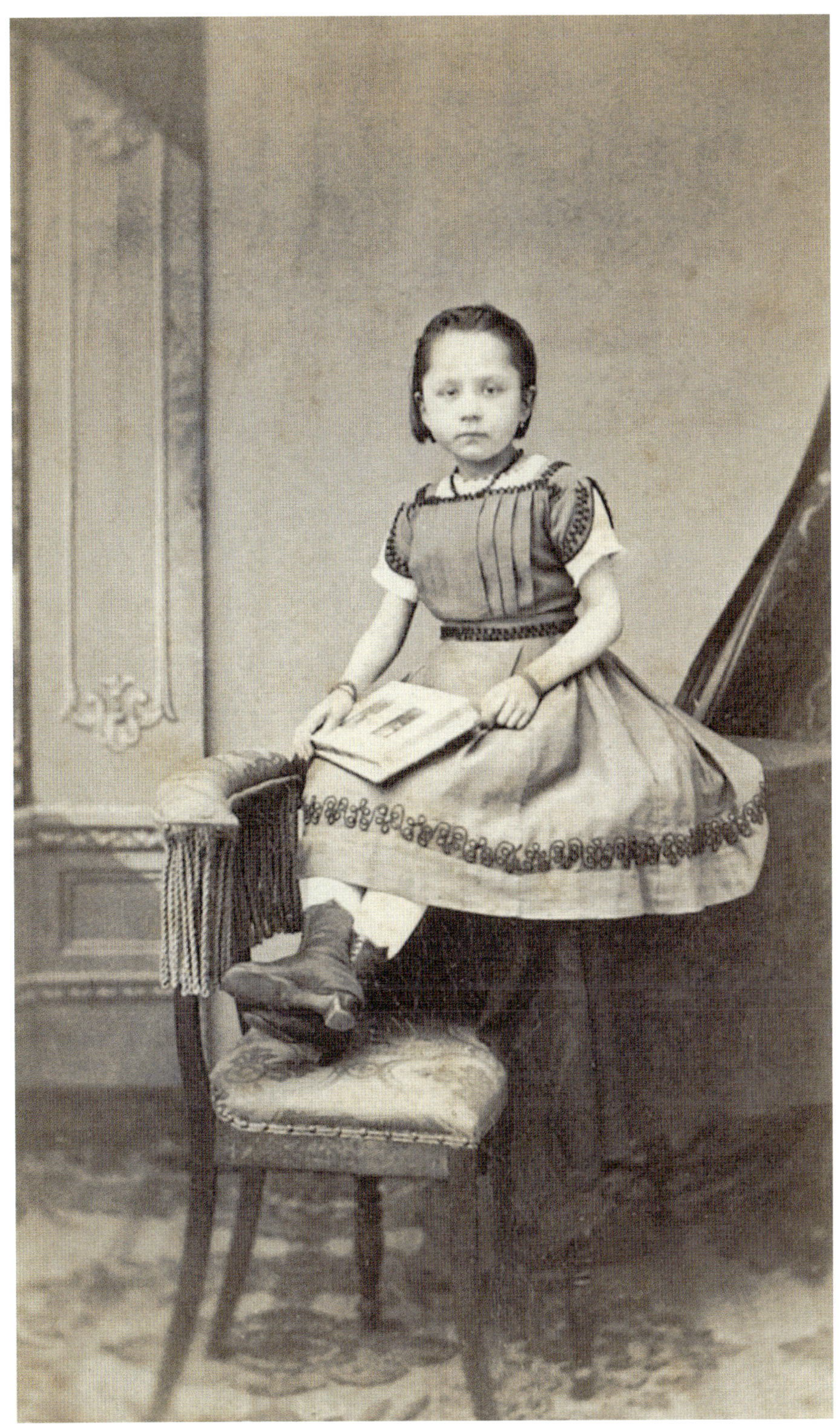

Plate 3 Jo Bonger, *c.* 1869.

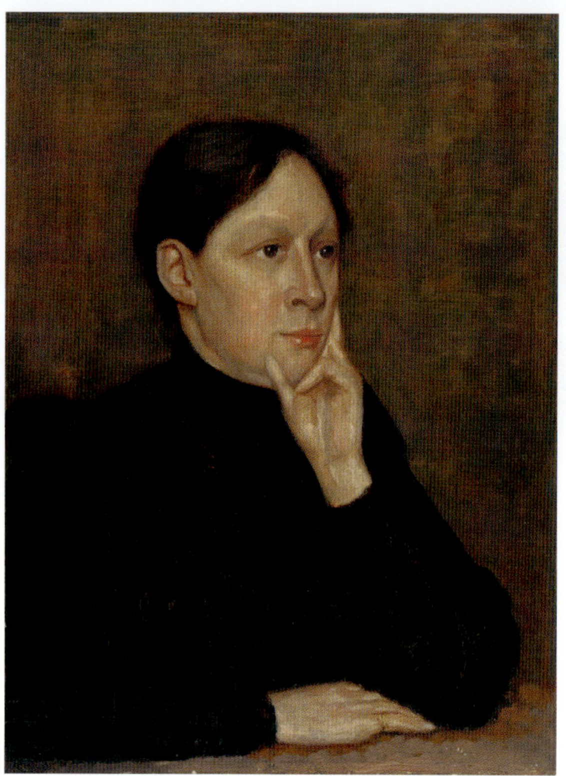

Plate 4 Johan Cohen Gosschalk, *Hermien Bonger*, 1907.

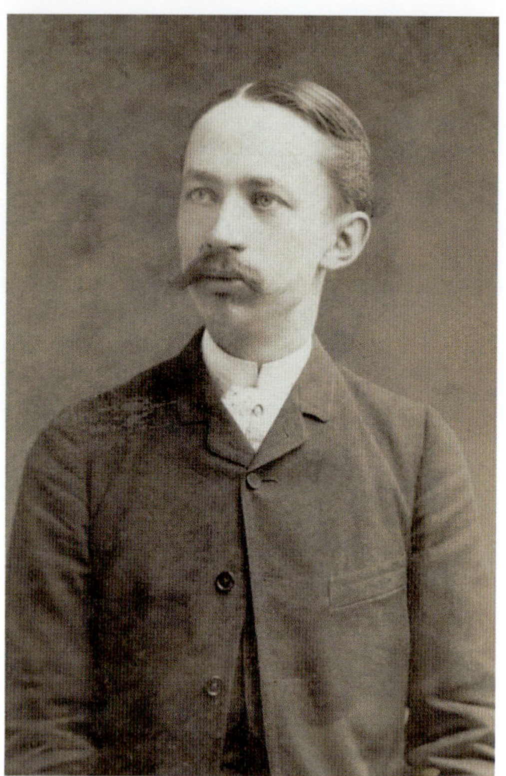

Plate 5 Andries Bonger, undated.

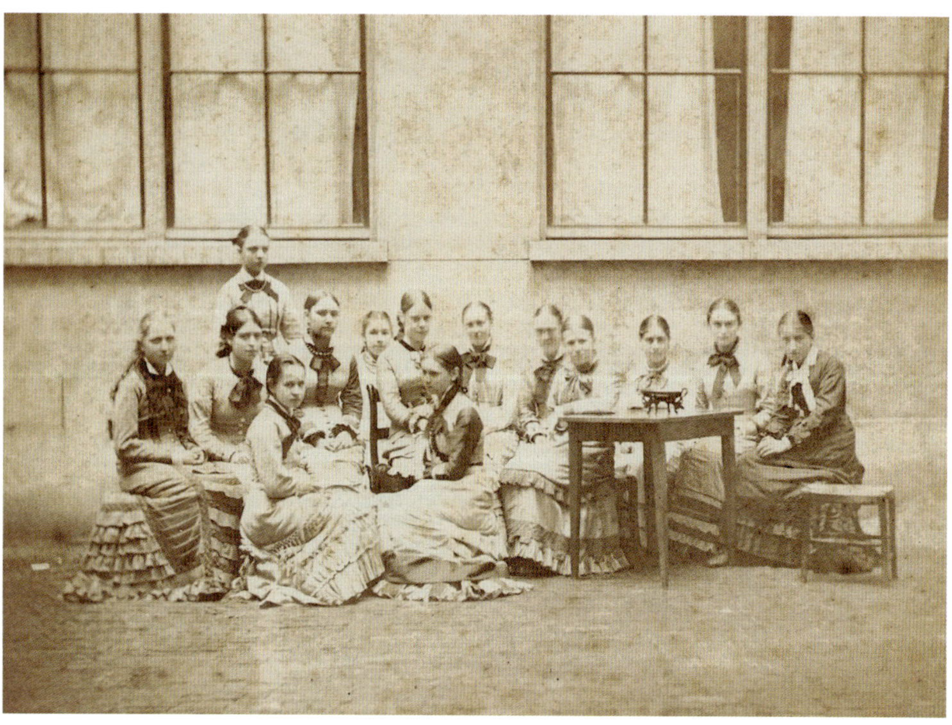

Plate 6 Second form of the high school at 264–6 Keizersgracht in Amsterdam. Jo Bonger sits at the front, third from left, 1878–9.

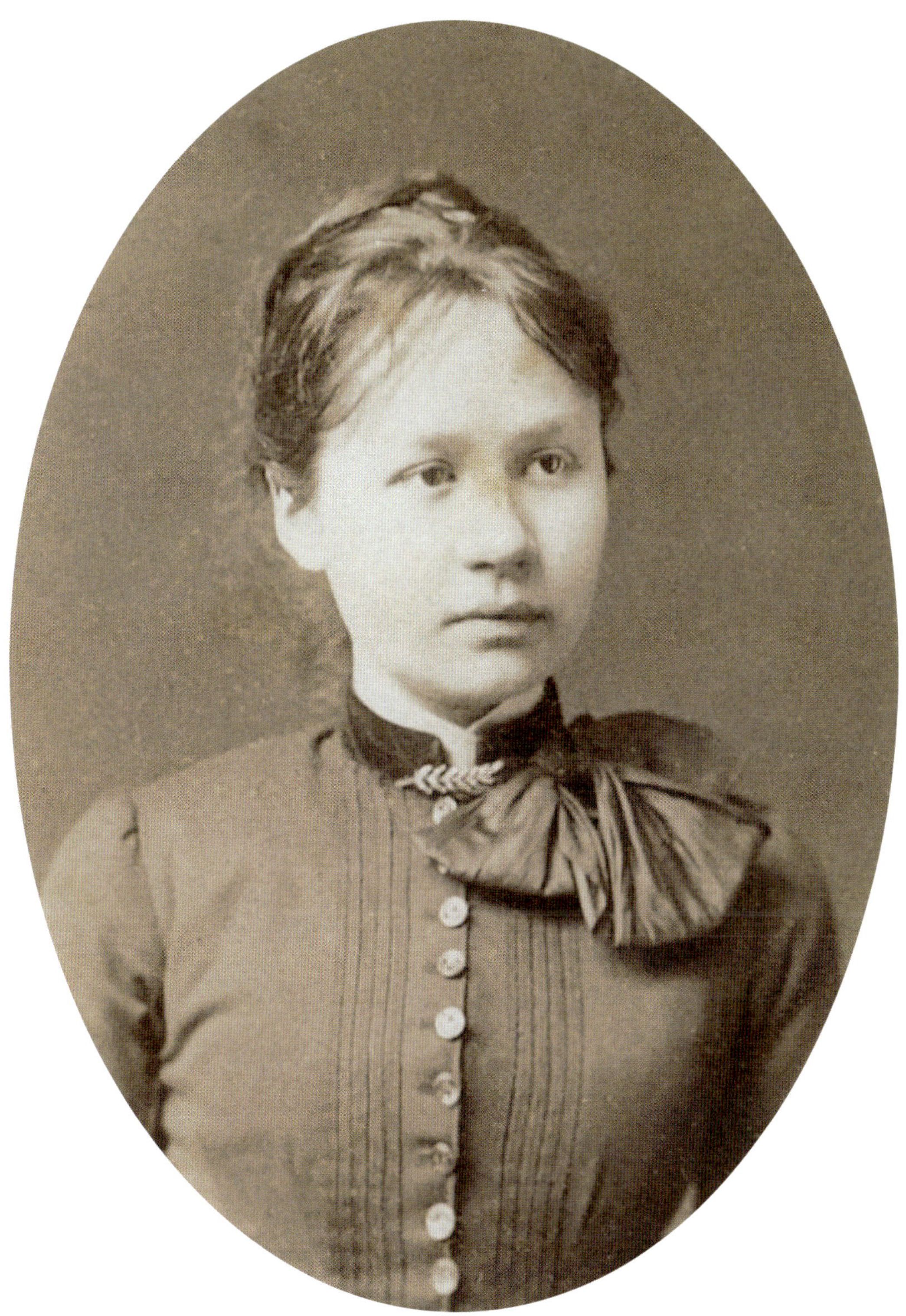

Plate 7 Jo Bonger, *c.* 1880–2.

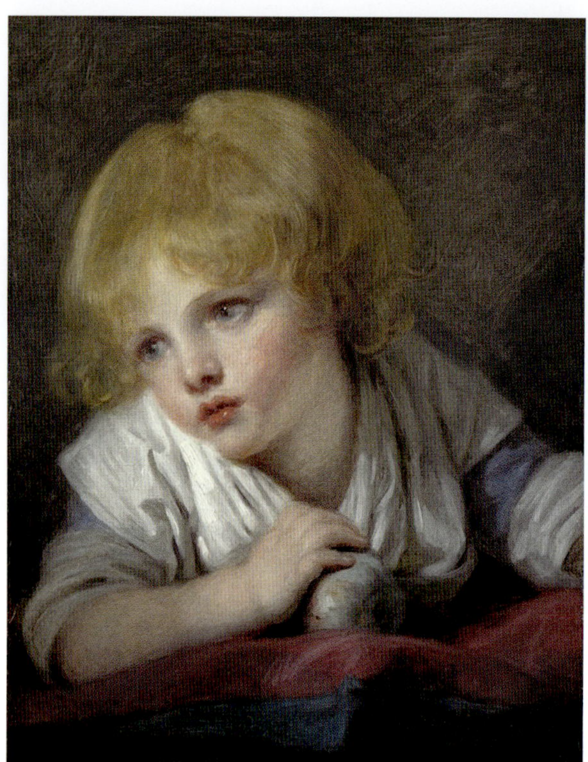

Plate 8 Jean-Baptiste Greuze, *A Child with an Apple*, late eighteenth century.

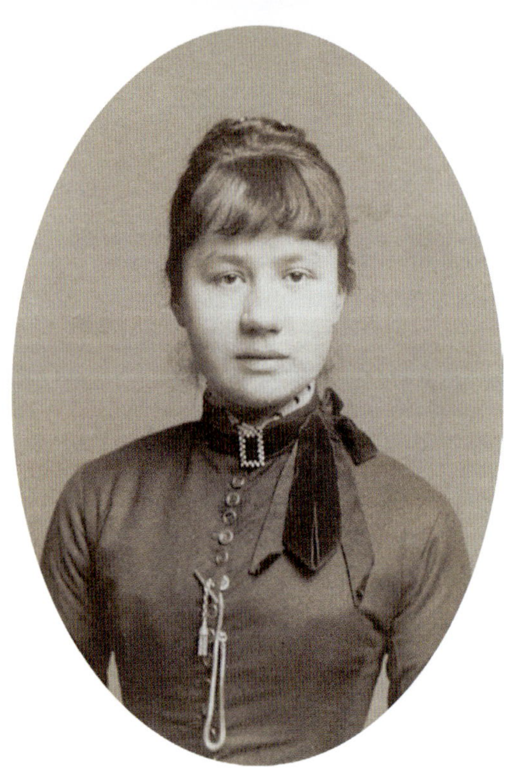

Plate 9 Jo Bonger, 1884.

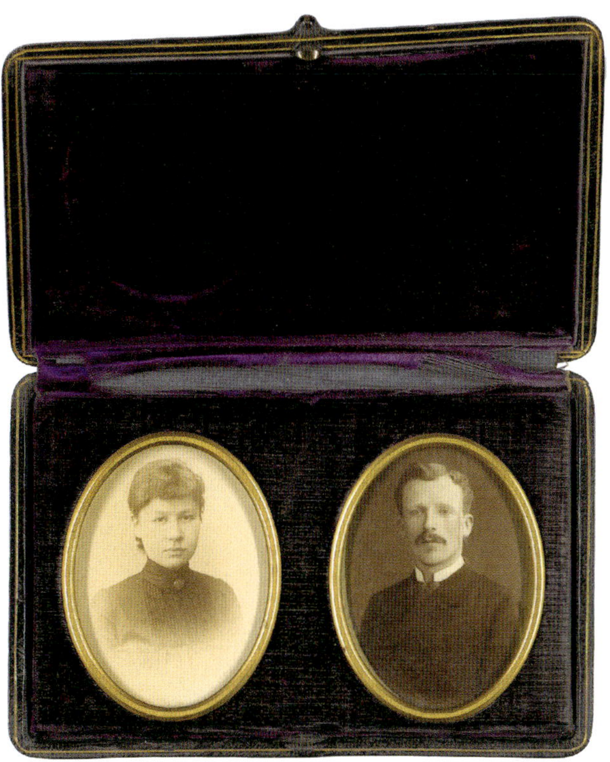

Plate 10 Case containing framed portrait photographs of Jo Bonger and Theo van Gogh, 1889.

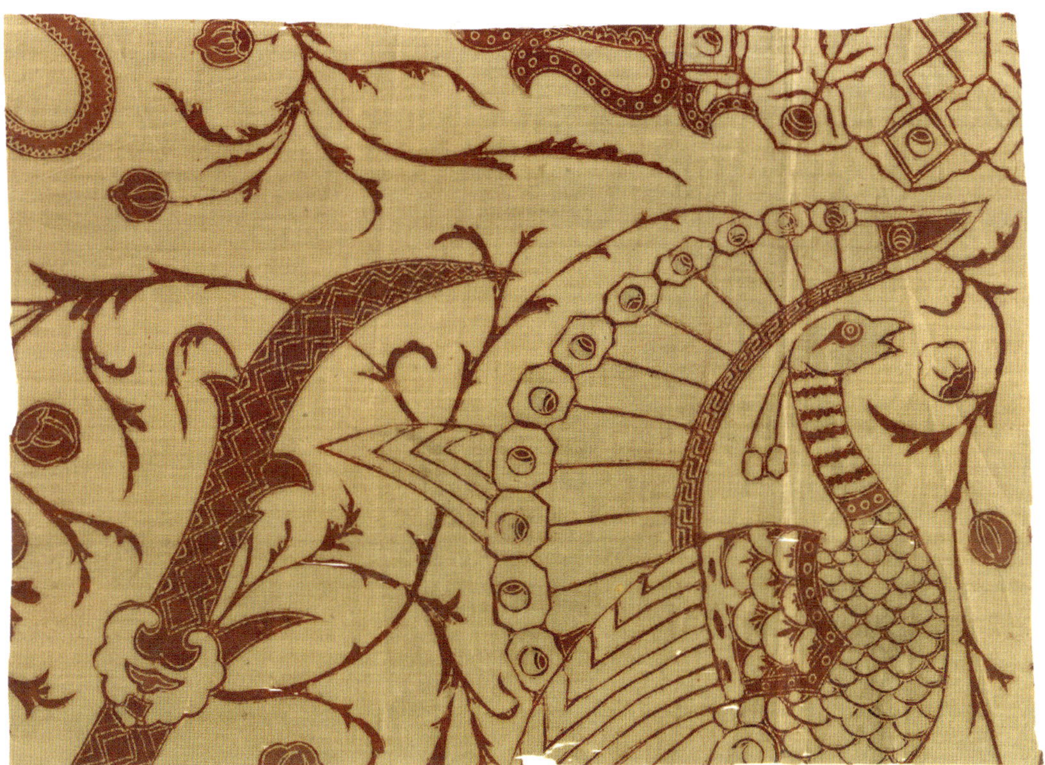

Plate 11 Sample of the Bedroom Curtain Material in the Flat at 8 Cité Pigale in Paris, 1889.

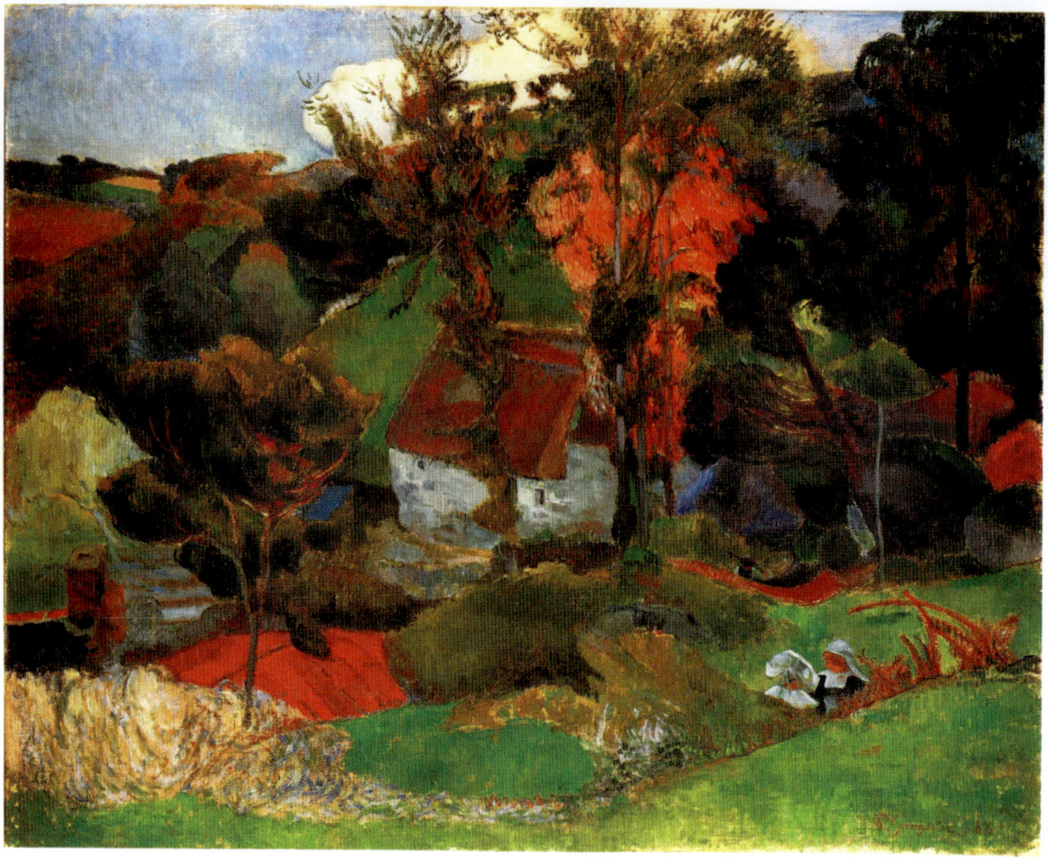

Plate 12 Paul Gauguin, *Autumn at Pont-Aven*, 1888.

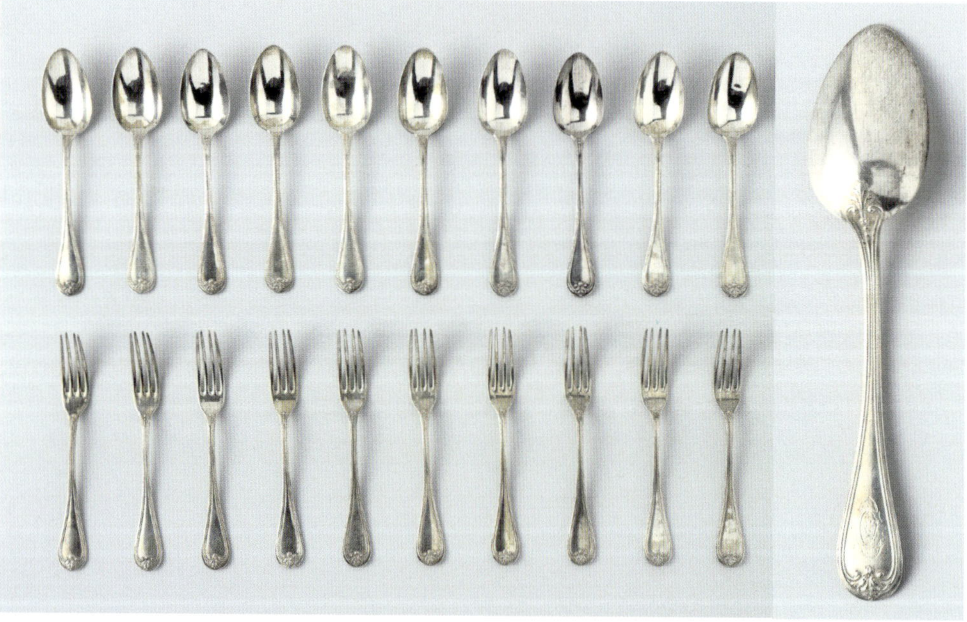

Plate 13 Cutlery with the monogram 'VG'. Wedding present from Boussod, Valadon & Cie to Theo van Gogh and Jo van Gogh-Bonger, 1889.

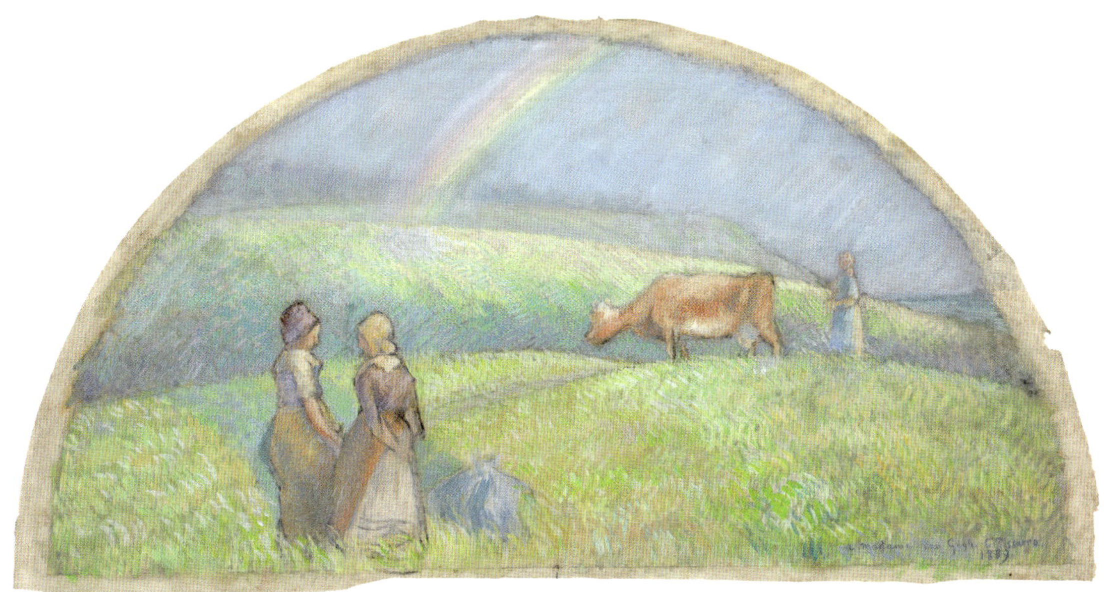

Plate 14 Camille Pissarro, *Landscape with Rainbow*, 1889.

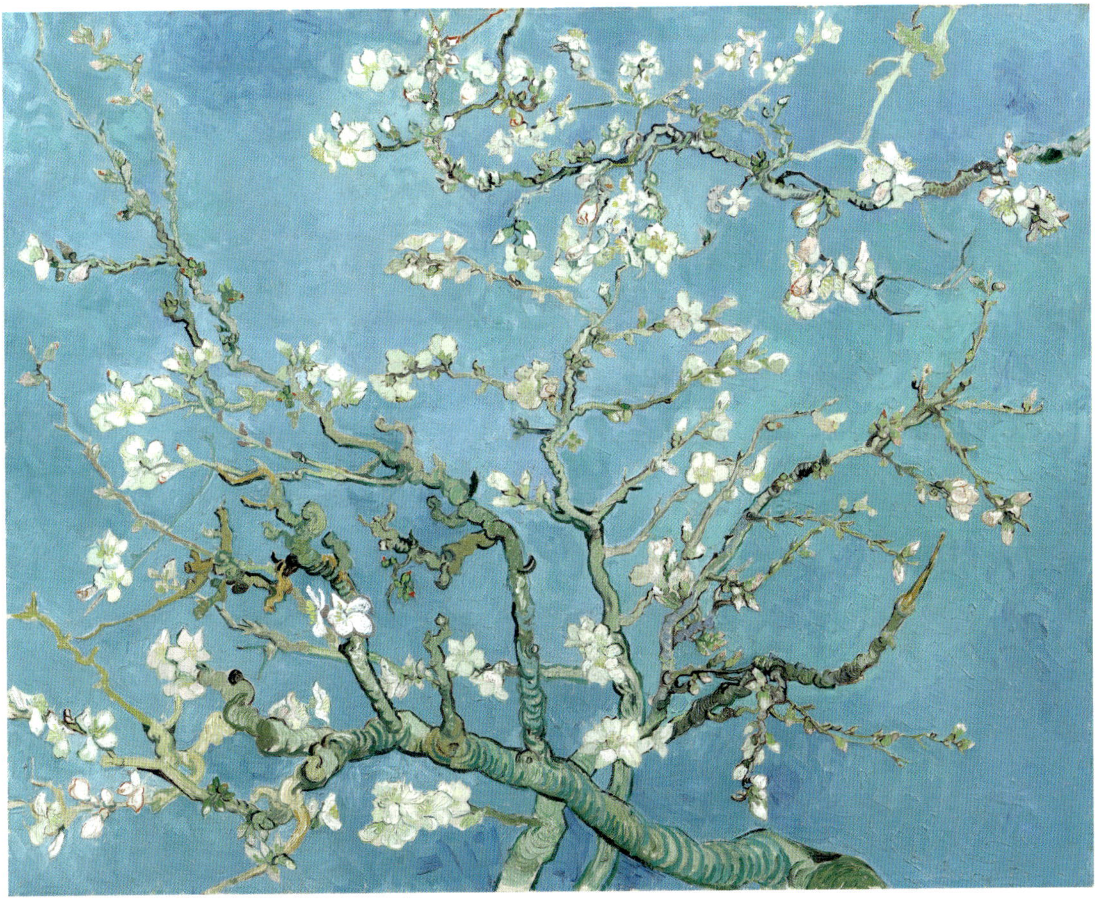

Plate 15 Vincent van Gogh, *Almond Blossom*, 1890.

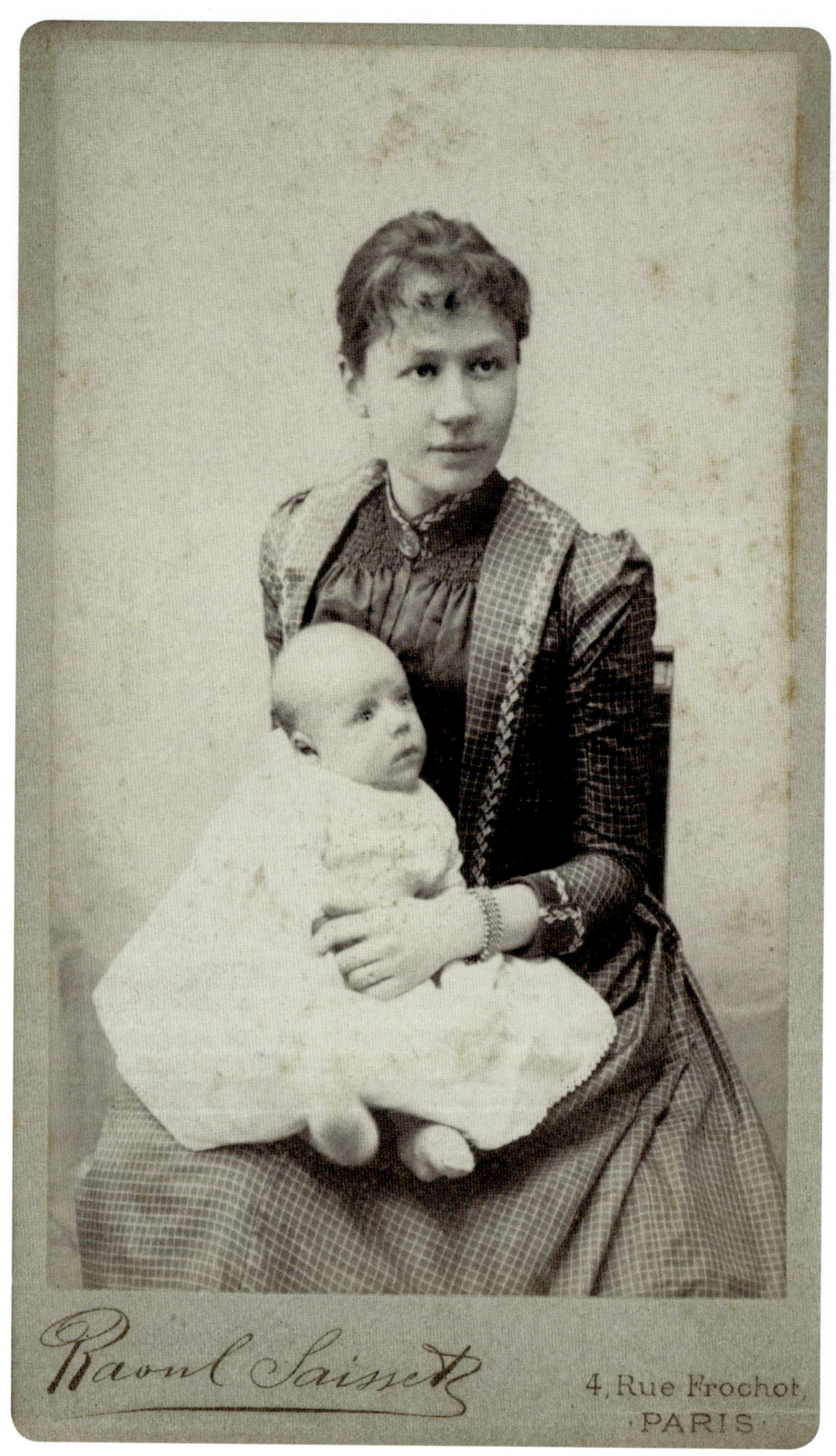

Plate 16 Jo van Gogh-Bonger and Vincent van Gogh, 1890.

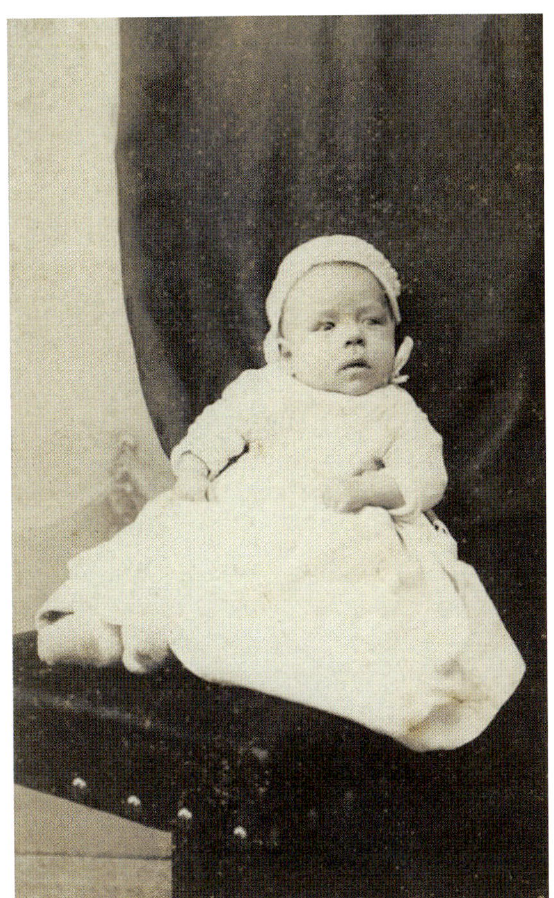
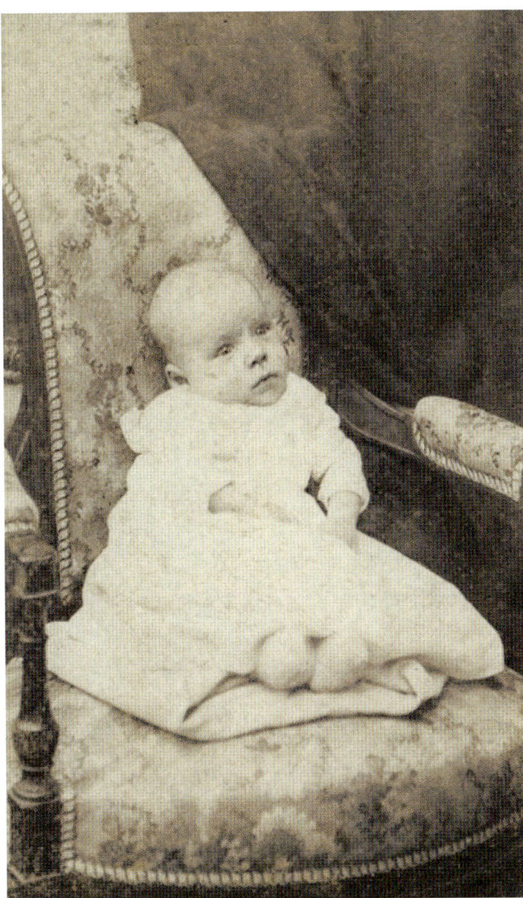

Plates 17–18 Vincent van Gogh, 1890.

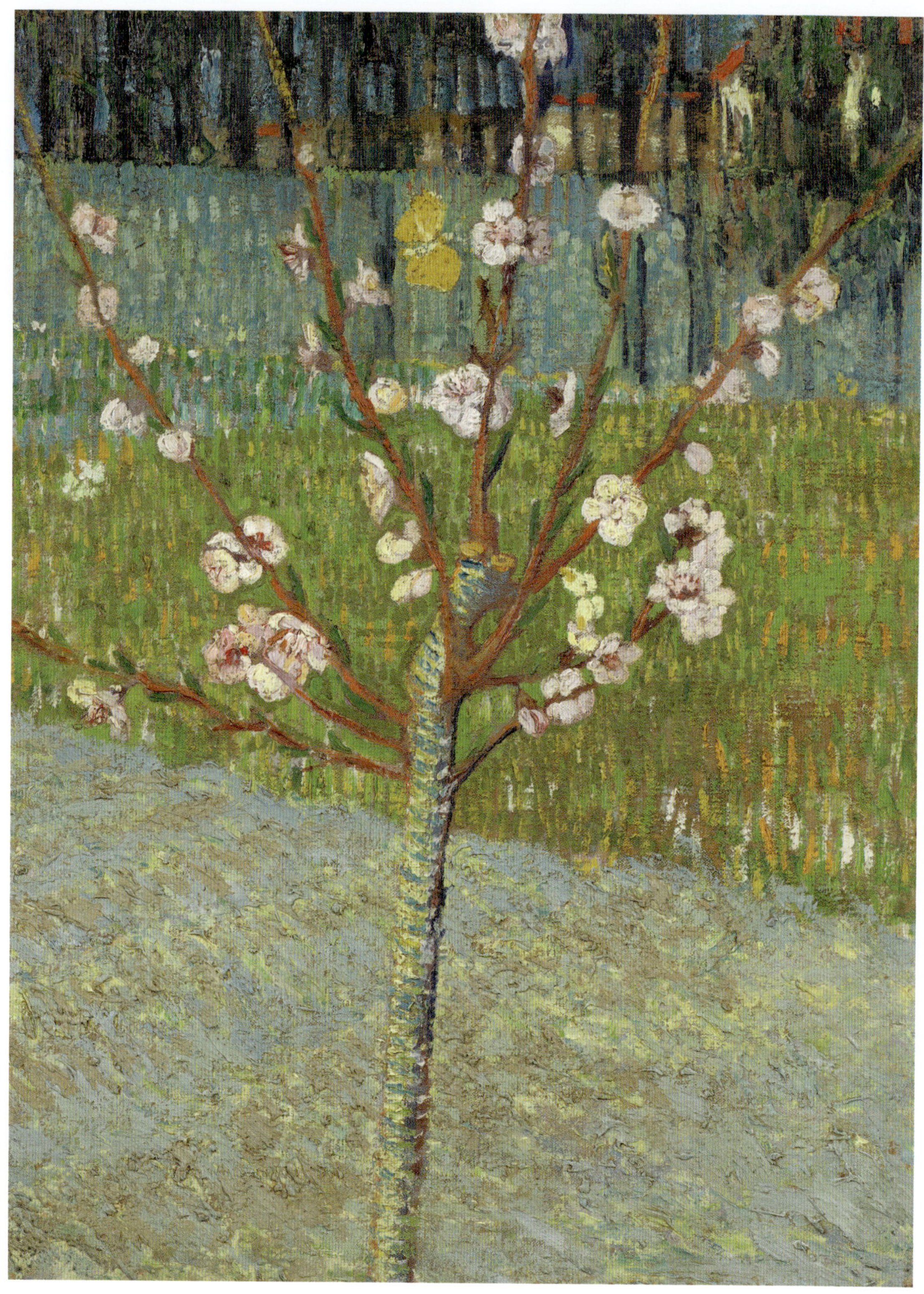

Plate 19 Vincent van Gogh, *Peach Tree in Blossom*, 1888.

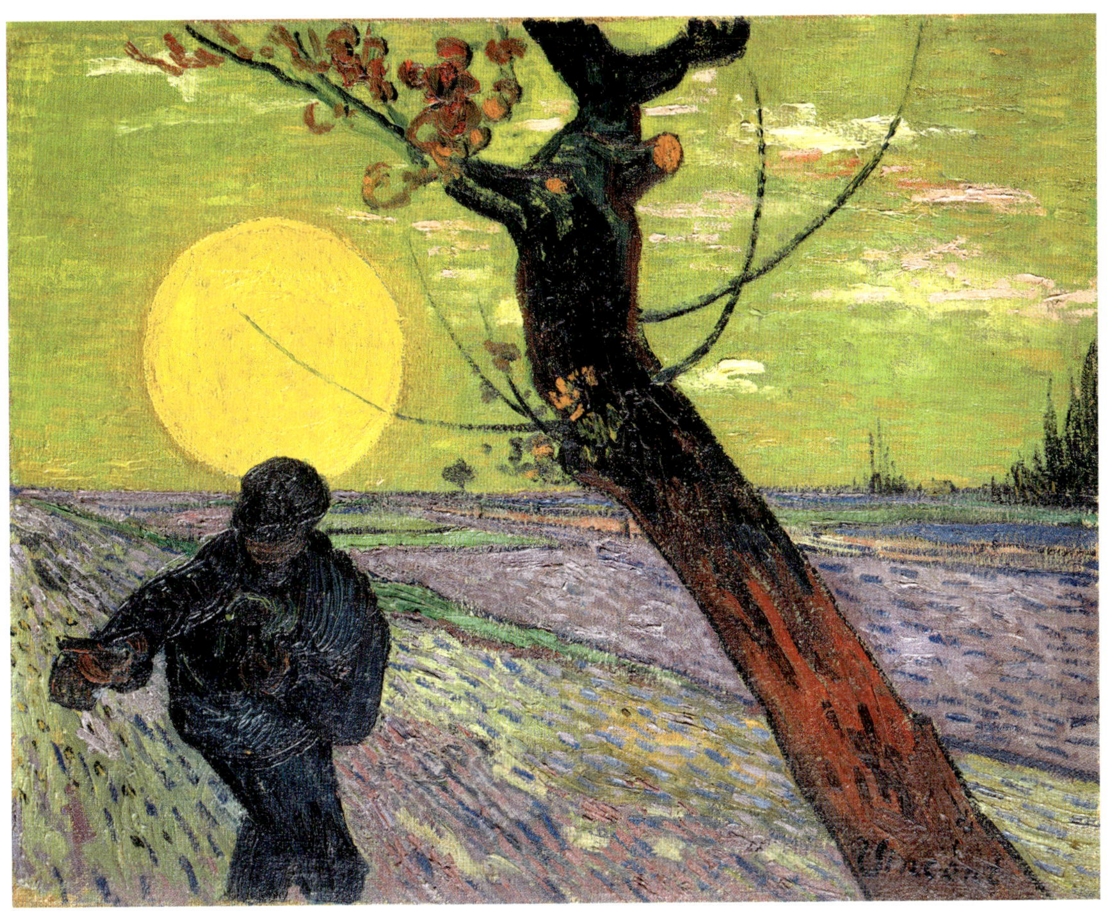

Plate 20 Vincent van Gogh, *The Sower*, 1888.

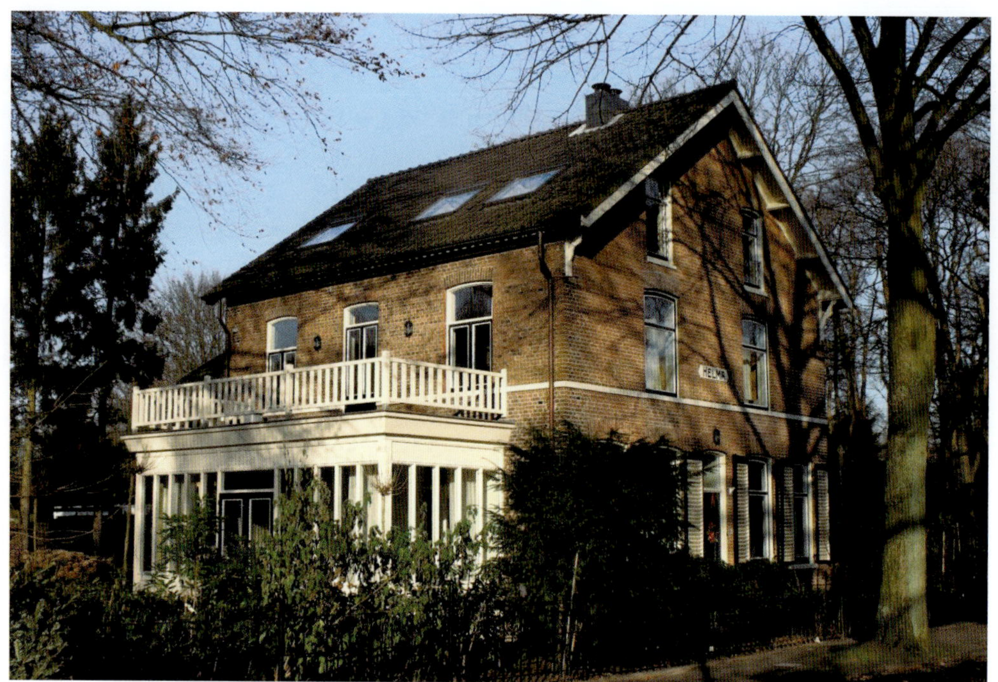

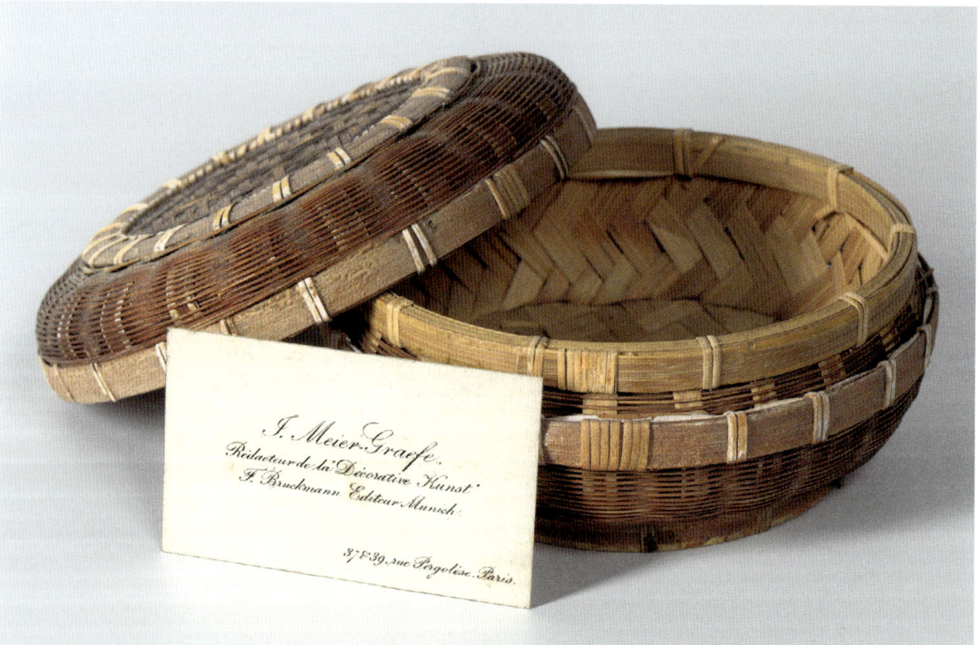

Plate 21 Villa Helma, 4 Koningslaan in Bussum, undated.
Plate 22 Jo van Gogh-Bonger's wicker basket for post and visiting cards, undated.

Plate 23 *(facing page)* Deed of gift in which all recipients officially relinquish their part of the estate of the artist Vincent van Gogh, in favour of the young Vincent van Gogh; Jo van Gogh-Bonger signed as his guardian, July 1891.

De ondergeteekenden:

1. Anna Cornelia Carbentus weduwe van den heer Theodorus van Gogh, zonder beroep wonende te Leiden, als welke zij optreedt en tevens als volgens hare verklaring gemachtigde van haren zoon den heer Cornelis Vincent van Gogh, werktuigkundige wonende te Johannesburg in de Transvaal.
2. Anna Cornelia van Gogh echtgenoote van en ten deze bijgestaan en gemachtigd door Joan Marius van Houten, kalkbrander wonende te Leiden.
3. Elisabeth Huberta van Gogh, zonder beroep wonende te Soesterberg.
4. Willemina Jacoba van Gogh, zonder beroep wonende te Leiden.
5. Johanna Gesina Bonger, zonder beroep wonende te Bussum, in wettelijke gemeenschap van goederen gehuwd geweest met den heer Theodorus van Gogh overleden te Utrecht den 25 Januari 1891, als voogdes over haar minderjarig kind ¶

Verklaren:

dat op den 29 Augustus 1890 te Auvers (Frankrijk) is overleden de heer Vincent Willem van Gogh, zonder over zijne nalatenschap te hebben beschikt en zonder achterlating van nakomelingen, zoodat zijne nalatenschap is geërfd door zijne moeder, de ondergeteekende sub 1o. genoemd, zijne zusters en broeder sub 1 en 2, 3 en 4 genoemd en zijn na overleden broeder sub 5o. genoemd.

dat zij bij deze het leven van den heer Theodorus van Gogh sub 5 genoemd, de nalatenschap van den heer Vincent Willem van Gogh met onderling goedvinden hebben ƒ gescheiden en verdeeld en [illegible] zonder eenig voorbehoud hoe ook genaamd, onder vrijwaring als volgens de wet.

Geteekend ter respectieve woonplaatsen in de maand Juli 1800 een en negentig.–

A. C. van Houten van Gogh

J. M. van Houten

Wed: Th. van Gogh

A. C. Carbentus

Wed: Th. van Gogh gem: van C. V. van Gogh

J. G. Bonger

Wed: Th. van Gogh

E. H. van Gogh

W. J. van Gogh.

Margin notes and initials:

L. Vincent Willem van Gogh. Bijvoeging goedgekeurd.
J. G. B.
Wed: Th. v. Gogh
E. H. van Gogh
A. C. v. H. v. G.
J. M. v. H.
Wd Th. v. G. C.
Wed: Th. v. G.
gem: van C. V. v. G.
W. J. v. G.

ƒ afgestaan aan den minderjarigen Vincent Willem van Gogh voornoemd zonder daarop eenige aanspraken te behouden en [illegible] de Bijvoeging goedgekeurd.
J. G. B.
Wed. Th. van Gogh
E. H. van Gogh
A. C. v. H. v. G.
J. M. v. H.
Wd Th. v. G. C.
Wed: Th. v. G.
gem: van C. V. v. G.
W. J. v. G.

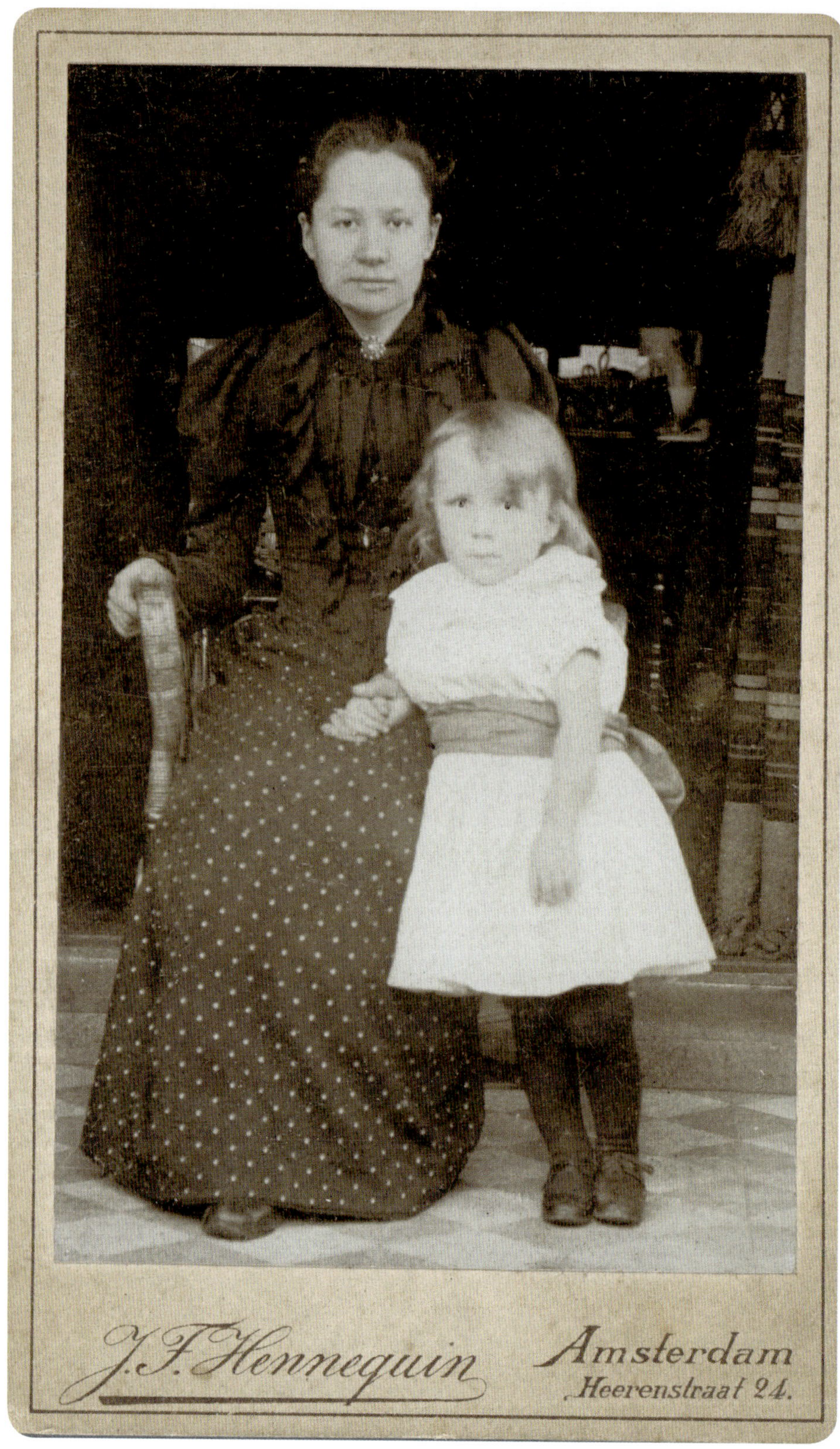

Plate 24 Jo van Gogh-Bonger and Vincent van Gogh, 1892.

sun-baked city. Jo wrote to Mien that the railway line around Paris, which she used to get to Andries and Annie, was just as filthy as the London underground.[47] Soon after this, she did buy material for a new blouse and asked her sisters to remove the train from her wedding gown so that she could still wear the dress should the occasion arise.[48] Such an opportunity came up three months later.

Pregnancy

Mrs Bonger was the first to respond to the news that ten weeks after her wedding day, Jo was pregnant. Characteristically blunt, she airily assured Jo that there was nothing special she needed to know, although it was blindingly obvious that she had no idea what was in store for her:

> What a momentous letter I received from my strong, reliable Netje. What are you afraid of? Dear heart, I'm so very glad you wrote ... there's nothing you need to know or do, just everything as you're used to, not too fussy and don't think about it all the time. It's still so early, I know it's a feeling you can't describe but you'll get used to it, and if your mother may give you some good advice, go to the market in the mornings, because that will be a distraction and you see all the activity, and be outdoors in the open air as much as you can. Don't you like milk? Water and wine, in moderation, is also very good. At the moment you don't need any bigger clothes, dearest one, you'll be in plenty of time when you're about halfway, don't leave your corset off yet. If you've been dizzy and nauseous, try to eat a little something. There aren't any rusks, are there? Make sure you go to the lav. The only snag is that we're so far away.... Now tell me, my little treasure, how are you getting on with the piano, try to play now and again, it can be such a pleasant distraction when your husband's not there. There'll be very long mornings.... If it wasn't necessary, I wouldn't want to leave Lien on her own. She'd jump through fire for you two.[49]

Sister Lien was thrilled about Jo's pregnancy and indeed wanted to do everything for them. She gave the same sort of advice as her mother. According to her, slim women usually had the sturdiest children. Above all Jo had to be cheerful, then the baby would be too.[50]

The members of the Van Gogh family were also delighted by the news. Theo and Jo were hoping that Willemien would come and stay around the turn of the year to help in the run-up to the lying in. Looking ahead, Theo thought of a decorative element to have in the flat that would instantly remind them of the familiar Dutch landscape, and asked her to look for a couple of wheat stalks: 'we have these lovely little Rozenburg vases and two others that we wanted to put stalks of wheat and peacock feathers in during the winter. The common wild oats are already over, right?'[51] There is a very good chance that they were intended for the small vases that can be seen in a later photograph of Jo's home (Figure 24).[52]

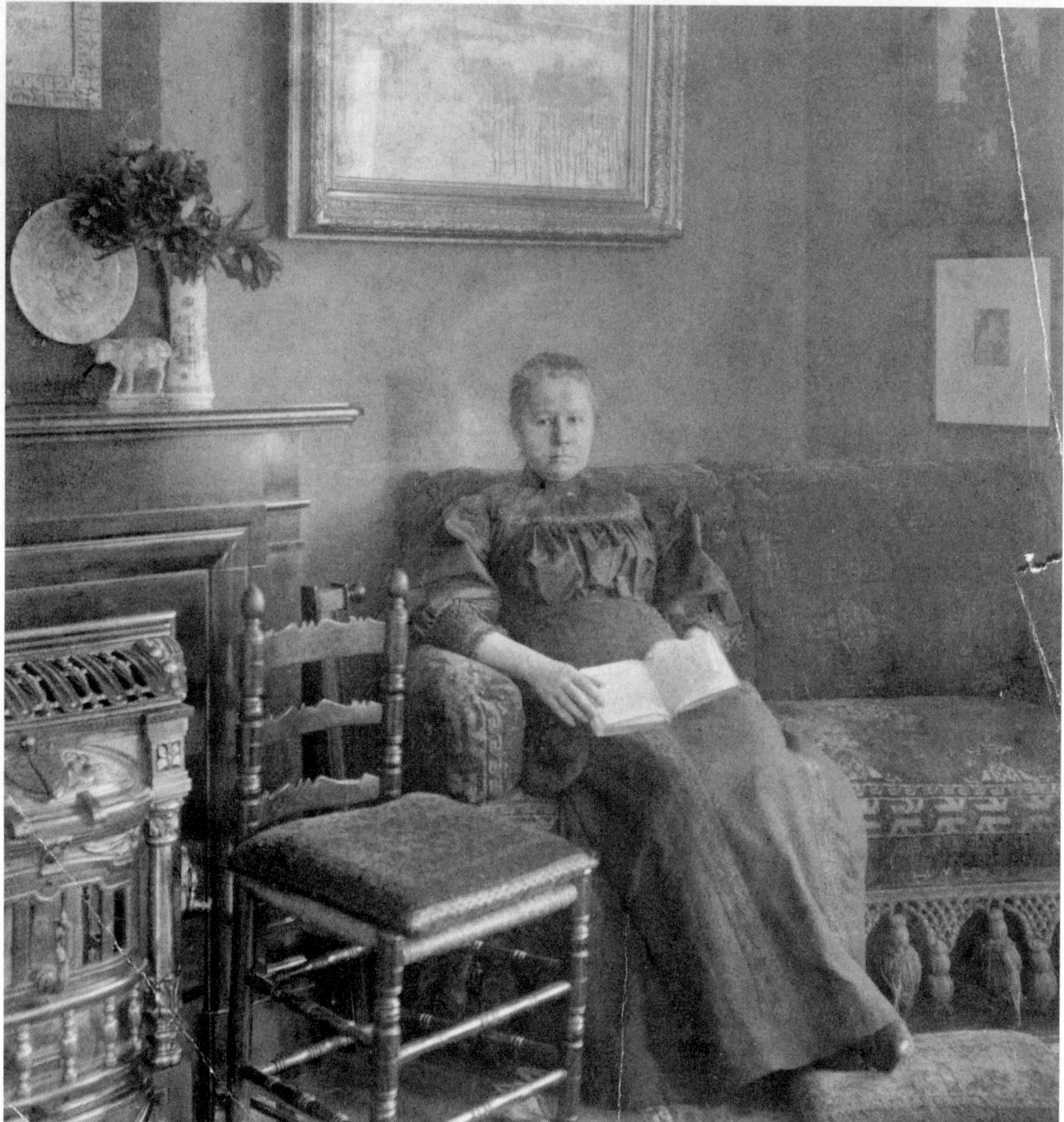

Figure 24 Jo van Gogh-Bonger in the living room in Koninginneweg in Amsterdam, with a Rozenburg vase on the mantelpiece (detail), 1910.

Despite the good news, their health and condition were far from good. Jo felt awful at the beginning of the pregnancy when she stopped menstruating, but things got better after she took the drops the doctor had given her. Drinking a lot of freshly squeezed lemon juice had made her throw up. She could not bring herself to use the word 'spugen' (vomit) in her letter and instead wrote 'sp---'. In subsequent letters she used the expression 'playing rendez-vous' as code. Like many other expectant women, she 'wanted to eat the most impossible things'. Theo had been feeling unwell for ages. At Jo's urging, he went to Dr Rivet because he was always coughing and looked dreadful.[53]

Theo's correspondence with Vincent about this issue shortly before the wedding had been rather grim. When he told his brother about his very poor health, the latter sent a coarse reply: 'Sickness or mortality, my word, that doesn't surprise me.... But how come that you're thinking about the little clauses of marriage and the possibility of dying at this moment, wouldn't you have done better quite simply to have screwed your wife in advance?'[54] With black humour he was saying, you should have done that first and seen what the result was before you married her. Sensitive it was not. This can only have made Theo's uncertainty worse. Six months later he tried to reassure himself about the condition of their unborn baby: 'If only the child is viable. I think that children generally inherit their parents' kind of constitution rather than the latter's state of health at the moment when they made it.'[55] He has to have realized only too well that with his weak constitution he took a risk by fathering a child with Jo, who was not all that strong either.

Jo and Theo talked about the baby's name. 'Theo would prefer "Vincent", oh I don't think names are that important,' wrote Jo matter-of-factly to her parents. Whether that was really the case is open to question; she thought very differently about it when her first grandson arrived. She also told her parents that she had made her own strawberry jam and gooseberry jam. She was very pleased with herself.[56]

She wrote in French to Vincent for the first time—since he started living in France he barely corresponded in Dutch any more. Jo addressed him respectfully using *vous*. Apologizing in advance for her grammatical mistakes, she got straight down to business with the news of the big event expected at the end of January. The baby would certainly be 'a pretty little boy—whom we'll call Vincent if you'll consent to be his godfather'. She had no doubt that he would be a fine little chap, but because neither Theo nor she were in good health, she was concerned that the child would be sickly. To her mind, a sound constitution was the greatest gift that parents could give their child. She wrote that she was curious about Vincent's reaction to being a future godfather. She also told him about how much she liked Shakespeare, that a performance of *The Merchant of Venice* in London once made a deep impression on her, and that she had also seen productions of *Hamlet* and *Macbeth*. Three days before, Vincent had written to Theo about Shakespeare and thanked him for sending the *Complete Works*, which he had begun to read immediately. This explains Jo's response about the Bard of Avon.[57]

A lack of artistic sensibility

Jo was lyrical in a letter to Mien about how she, Theo and Hart Nibbrig had spent hours on the Seine in a small rowing boat, three-quarters of the way out of the city, in the fresh air among willows and acacias. But nothing seemed to do Theo any good. He looked thin and pale, even though he was eating like a horse. First thing in the morning he had an egg with cognac, then breakfast with a large cup of chocolate and he took a piece of chocolate to have at four o'clock. He ate meat twice a day, but all to no avail. 'He says he'd like to take a week's holiday at some point and go to the country! If only that were true, it's too wonderful to think about—Oh Mien, I don't like Paris *at all*.' By now the city had lost all its charm for her. She thought her situation was depressing and disastrous for her constitution.[58] Jo's parents spent the last two weeks of July in Paris: her mother stayed with her and Theo, her father with Andries and Annie. It was a burden for Jo because at that time she was feeling so 'weak'.[59] Mrs Bonger had learned a few French expressions 'primarily with a view to your cook,' reported Henri.[60] Unfortunately, nothing has survived of these discussions between Hermine Bonger and Madame Joseph.

Jo now gave free rein to her thoughts about living with Theo in her letters to the unmarried Mien: 'You're infinitely less free—nothing, nothing belongs to just you any more and I can assure you that it was difficult for me to get used to it.'[61] She felt alone in the maze that was Paris, and that made her feel restless. She consequently clung even more to Theo and everything had to come from him. It is striking that a crucial part of the painful confession below from the letter to Mien was cut out (we do not know who did it—it is filled in here between square brackets):

> There's one huge stumbling block—that I have [so little?] artistic sensibility—how often have I longed to be a bit like Anna Dirks—who would certainly have appreciated him and sympathized with him—I can't. . . . I feel or think only of the most ordinary prosaic things—that bothers Theo now and again. . . . And I don't like it when I hear all those theories about art and don't understand anything, but how can I change just like that and throw everything that I used to think overboard. . . . Sometimes I think that I won't survive to see our baby—I feel so weak sometimes—but then again I don't believe that it would be so terrible because I've [received?] a great deal in my life . . . my goodness, how I've always lived in a little world of my own making without having a clue about the real world.[62]

She clearly thought she had fallen short and by choosing Theo had perhaps overreached herself; above all she lagged far behind in her knowledge of and affinity with art, and she had to acknowledge that she had little to contribute when some subjects were being discussed. And now there was more bad news from that 'real world', which was making life so difficult for her. Vincent, who had had himself admitted to the Saint-Paul-de-Mausole mental asylum in Saint-Rémy a few months before, had tried to poison himself with his own paints. Theo immediately started to look worse than he had before.

Jo also took Willemien into her confidence in the way she wrote about Vincent's art and her love for Theo. Theo had submitted *Irises* (F 608 / JH 1691) and *Starry Night Over the Rhône* (F 474 / JH 1592) for the fifth exhibition staged by the Société des Artistes Indépendants. Jo thought they were 'very, very lovely!'. Of all the paintings Theo had, she thought there was 'so much that was so very strange to me', but she understood those by Vincent best. Suddenly she confessed for the first time: 'Wil, there's something I want to tell you. We no longer love each other more every day. I'm telling you this in strictest confidence, as though I'm whispering in your ear—but it's *true*!'[63] Probably the aforementioned 'one huge stumbling block', namely Jo's barely developed feeling for matters artistic, which bothered Theo, was not the only reason for this. Jo appears to have found it difficult to get on the same intellectual, social and emotional wavelengths in that world full of obligations and stresses that was so much bigger and more hectic for her. In later reflections on her marriage, such reservations were not referred to and she idealized these years.

At the time there was also a lot going on, over and above all the concerns about Vincent. Theo's youngest brother Cor, who was then twenty-two, came to stay for a few days. They showed him all the sights of the city. Afterwards he travelled to South Africa to start working for the Cornucopia Gold Company near Johannesburg. A month later, he wrote to Theo and Jo saying how much he had enjoyed staying with them and how wretched the situation in South Africa was.[64]

Willem Weissman visited the World's Fair and dropped in, as did Jan Veth. Jan Stricker had a meal with them in the Le Petit Tourne-Bride, a restaurant in La Celle-Saint-Cloud. Fortunately, her confidante Mien would shortly be coming to stay for seven weeks, a thought that gave Jo great comfort.[65]

Theo and Jo quite often moved in exalted circles. They were invited to eat in the commune Le Vésinet by the wealthy banker and art collector Daniel Franken Dzn, the brother of uncle Cor van Gogh's second wife, Johanna Franken. And Jo could hardly believe her eyes at the soirée in the Hotel Continental, organized by Commissioner-General W. van der Vliet of the Dutch section of the World's Fair for 'the leading members of the Dutch community in Paris'. There was a Javan dance company and there were tableaux vivants of Jan Steen's *The Feast of Saint Nicholas* and Rembrandt's *Night Watch*. Jo wrote to Mrs van Gogh: 'And even though I won't be wearing powder and a low-cut dress—don't you think I'll go unnoticed among those 2,000 guests?'[66] Almost all the women at this ball wore gowns with plunging necklines and were dripping with jewellery, while the men wore decorations. Theo wore his wedding suit and Jo was in her wedding dress (without the train) and a fur coat she borrowed from Annie. There was a buffet and dancing. They met the artists Jozef Israëls and his son Isaac. They did not leave the party until half-past one in the morning.

The run-up to the birth

Both families were now hard at working knitting blankets, camisoles and caps for the new arrival, and Theo bought a large number of nappies.[67] Anna Veth-Dirks, who had become a mother herself in the meantime, told Jo all about breastfeeding, and Anna's sister Lida advised her to read a book on parenting by Dr G.A.N. Allebé. This must have been *Het kind in zijne eerste levensjaren: wenken voor ouders* (1853). Jo did not go out enough, and so Mien encouraged her to go outside for a while every day.[68]

Three years later, Jo looked back at this period and her twenty-seventh birthday on 4 October 1889:

> I can still see Theo's face so clearly when he surprised me in the morning with that lovely workbasket and then the flask—'it comes from a long way away—it comes from the little boy', oh that sweet, friendly face and that soft, fond voice. And how friendly the little drawing room was with all those lovely flowers and a comforting fire—I recall how I sat in front of the fire with a pretty dress for the child, who hadn't yet arrived, on my lap. How rich we were, how happy we were together.[69]

Yet a few weeks after that birthday Jo took Mien into her confidence about a very worrying and ominous piece of news—and asked her earnestly to keep it a secret. Theo had been refused life assurance on medical grounds: 'I keep saying I don't think it matters and I'm doing my best to put it out of his mind, but I'm so sorry for him and I'm so afraid that he'll fret about it.'[70] In her innocence, Jo apparently looked on this setback primarily as something annoying for Theo and did not realize that, if things went wrong for him, she would have no future income. And yet she could have known how important life assurance was from *Gelukkig—ofschoon getrouwd*, the book by Elise van Calcar, which she had read nine months before.[71] It was a bad sign: Theo's general physical malaise was undeniable and much more sinister than Jo was prepared to admit. It remains a question as to how much she was alarmed by the rejection and whether it made her start thinking about what exactly was wrong with Theo and what it could signify to their immediate future.

The worries under the surface did not stop them from going to a party, where Jo's stomach was severely tested because lobster with mayonnaise and pheasant were served. 'I really do prefer Dutch cooking! Lobster is enough to give you nightmares,' she wrote to her parents. She could do without experimental food.

Although she was six months pregnant, she barely showed. That same month a worried Mr Bonger earnestly urged her to organize a midwife in plenty of time, which she did indeed do.[72] As a distraction from their worries they went to see a concert by the popular Orchestre Lamoureux, which performed weekly between 1881 and 1897 under conductor Charles Lamoureux. And they polished the silver cutlery until it gleamed when Emmanuel and Clara van Praag came for dinner.[73]

Theo was feeling cold all the time so he bought a thick undershirt.[74] This was nothing new, however, as Willemien—attentive as ever—had written to Jo: 'Is Theo already enjoying the cold? He really feels the cold doesn't he, that husband of yours? When he was a little boy, he always wrapped himself around the hot stovepipe first thing in the morning.'[75] Theo's shivering, restlessness and coughing really got on Jo's nerves. They sometimes lay awake until three in the morning, so they decided they should sleep separately. Jo continued to suffer from indigestion. She looked for ways to relax: she played piano duets with Annie, bought an astrakhan muff and slowly but surely had to unpick the pleats in her coat because it really was getting too tight now. She also made enquiries about the price of cradles. Jo had less time to read and limited herself to stories by Frederik van Eeden in *De Nieuwe Gids*, and now and then a serial in the newspaper.[76] Annie tried to reassure Mrs Bonger by writing: 'Net always looks blooming,' but that was certainly not true.[77] When Mrs Bonger was getting ready for her trip to Paris, Jo asked her to bring a bottle of blackcurrant juice and a small bottle of eau de cologne, because she thought the French version smelt odd.[78]

The tension increased noticeably as the due date approached. Jo must have been horrified by the experiences that her friend Anna Veth-Dirks had told her about down to the last detail. During labour Anna had squeezed her husband's hand so hard she 'almost crushed it' and, according to her, breastfeeding could result in all kinds of complications—the pain made her ill and when the baby latched on it made her scream. On the advice of a friend she had used a mixture of coconut oil and cologne to ease the pain.[79] These discomfiting troubles would certainly not have been discussed on Christmas Day, when Jo and Theo went to Andries and Annie for lunch. They had rented a piano, which they put in the salon under one of their Van Gogh paintings.[80] Camille Pissarro was thoughtful and at New Year he sent his *Landscape with Rainbow*, 'destiné à Madame Van Gogh', asking Theo to give this design for a fan to Jo. This colourful and subtle gift—the rainbow symbolizes hope—would have delighted her (Plate 14).[81]

Willemien was there to help from the first week of 1890. In retrospect she concluded that she and Jo had not succeeded in 'deeply exploring' each other's emotions.[82] These were confusing times anyway. Theo contracted severe influenza and his illness hung 'like a threatening sword over our heads'. People were dying in Paris at that time within two or three days. This greatly increased Jo's restlessness. She asked Mien what she should use to cover the bed during the birth because rubber smelt so nasty. 'Now that I'm no longer struggling with bowel movements, my stomach is back to normal—and although I'm walking slowly, I still go out for at least an hour every day.'[83]

Mrs Bonger arrived. Jo drew comfort from the idea that while she recuperated, her 'dear little Ma' would be pottering around the room. The cradle had been decorated and she had dreamt that it was trimmed with her wedding dress. In the evenings they read George Eliot's *Middlemarch* together. Jo and Theo were both fervent admirers of Eliot. Theo's health improved slightly, and so did Vincent's. Jo thought that he had sent beautiful paintings again.[84]

Jo wrote a long letter to Vincent immediately before the birth. She had kept an unfinished letter to him in her writing case for ages and now, during the early hours of 30 January, Theo, Willemien and Mrs Bonger sat with her at the table waiting for what was going to happen. When they had gone to bed, deep emotions flowed from her pen. Jo was afraid she would not survive labour, but said she would pluck up her courage. She wrote openly about her love for Theo and about his all-encompassing allegiance to his brother:

> This evening—all these last few days in fact—I've thought about it so much, whether I really have been able to do something to make Theo happy in his marriage. He's done it for me. He's been so good to me; so good—if things don't go well—if I have to leave him—you tell him—*for there's no one in the world whom he loves as much*—that he must never regret that we were married, because he's made me so happy.[85]

Vincent replied by return, saying how much he was longing for the moment when he would hear that Jo had done well and the baby was healthy. He wrote: 'How happy Theo will be, and a new sun will rise in him when he sees you recovering,' and ended it warmly with: 'Your brother Vincent'.[86]

A bouncing baby boy

Little Vincent Willem was born on 31 January 1890. Congratulations telegrams followed and everyone was delighted.[87] People in the Netherlands were told in a birth announcement in the newspaper *Het Nieuws van den Dag* of 3 February. The paper reported that Jo had 'successfully been delivered' of a child; the Amsterdam newspaper *De Standaard* also printed the news the following day. No end of congratulatory greetings were sent. Few people knew that the birth had been very painful for Jo because her waters had broken too soon.[88] Theo was hugely relieved and joked that the baby's head looked like the head of an elderly concierge.[89]

Mrs Bonger stayed for seven weeks in all and helped, particularly at night, which Jo appreciated. Out of pure goodness she was so keen to tidy up that she once nearly knocked Theo over. Henri came for a few days and accompanied her back to Amsterdam. Jo thanked her mother at length and realized that she would now have to manage on her own. Motherhood had been transferred to the next generation, and now she took on the role traditionally assigned to women. This included dealing with the baby's green bowel movements. She gave him lime blossom tea as a remedy. Jo wondered whether it might be due to the fact she had drunk too much beer before and after the birth, which was said to be beneficial for producing milk.

Paul Gauguin dropped in, but Jo would have barely spoken to him because she had to walk around with the baby continually in order to keep him quiet, singing his favourite nursery rhyme 'Tussen Keulen en Parijs'. Once again, she did not want to call a spade a spade when she indirectly told her mother that her menstruation was still not back to normal. The doctor had prescribed an iron supplement, which she drank through a straw, 'and then powder to brush my mouth with afterwards—cinchona wine and good food and going out every day with the little boy,' she explained to her mother.[90] The other grandmother also wanted to know everything about what was happening, from nutrition to breastfeeding. Once back in the Netherlands, Willemien asked after the other Vincent even before enquiring about the baby boy. At the end of her letter to Theo and Jo, Mrs van Gogh had mentioned the 'poor chap' and Willemien picked up on this and pursued it in an addition to her mother's letter. Vincent's thirty-seventh birthday on 30 March was coming up.[91]

Jo wrote to him at length—she congratulated Vincent, adding the best wishes of his godchild, who always looked at his uncle's work with great interest, as did she:

> they're the eyes of a grown-up, and then with a great deal of expression—could he have the makings of a philosopher?
>
> He doesn't leave his mother much free time at all, but I did escape briefly for the opening of the Independents to see your paintings hanging—there was a bench just in front, and while Theo talked to all sorts of people I spent a quarter of an hour enjoying the wonderful coolness and freshness of the undergrowth—it's as if I know that little spot and have often been there—I love it so much.
>
> It's like summer here—indescribably hot and I think with dread of the hot days still to come—it sounds a bit like sacrilege—with that first delicate tender green on the trees now, but after all I like the winter much better.[92]

The sixth exhibition of the Société des Artistes Indépendants was staged from 20 March to 27 April 1890 in the Pavillon de la ville de Paris on the Champs-Élysées, where ten paintings by Van Gogh were on show. The 'undergrowth' Jo mentioned was a reference to *Trees with Ivy in the Garden of the Asylum* (F 609 / JH 1693). What she could not have known at that moment was that Vincent had made the painting *Almond Blossom* (F 671 / JH 1891). He had started it after the news of his nephew's birth and had painted it especially for him (Plate 15). It arrived in a shipment at the beginning of May and was immediately given a prominent place—not in their bedroom as Vincent had imagined, but where everyone could see it above the piano in the living room.[93] Later it hung in the bedroom Jo shared with little Vincent in Bussum.

Jo described to her parents how she had been busy in their 'hanging garden' on the balcony with its nasturtiums and convolvulus. She watched the chestnut tree in the Place de la Trinité, where she sat every afternoon, turn green, and became intrigued by the nannies and the 'ladies of the Parisian bourgeoisie ... my goodness how they cackle'. She thought the children were much too overdressed. Madame Joseph always took them to this square, wearing Jo's old coat, which long ago had been purchased at the fashion house Hirsch & Cie in Amsterdam's Leidseplein. The doctor vaccinated mother and son, who was still struggling with constipation, an ailment little Vincent shared with his mother. As well as breastmilk, he also drank mixtures of three-quarters cow's milk and one quarter water. 'Do you know that the little lad does exactly as I do? He sticks his thumb between his first two fingers—it makes me think how Beb would laugh because she always laughed at me for doing it.' The naive Jo appears to have been completely unaware of the erotic double meaning behind this gesture.[94]

The painter Victor Vignon came for lunch—Theo dealt in his art and two of his landscapes hung in the dining room. Jo enjoyed listening to Vignon because he spoke so beautifully. She arranged a surprise for Theo on their first anniversary, giving him a ring she had asked Andries to purchase for her.[95] She had made some eggnog and they drank beer. The couple received congratulations from all sides, but the fond enquiries about the infant Vincent in Paris inevitably segued into concerns about Vincent in St-Rémy.[96] During those first months, anxiety about the wellbeing of the baby's namesake was never far from people's thoughts. And after his death, many correspondents suggested that the presence of a chuckling baby would help compensate for the painful loss of the artist.

In the afternoon of 20 April, they had a lively photography session at Raoul Saisset in rue Frochot, a few streets away (Plates 16, 17, 18). Jo sent Mien an evocative description, including the farcical role of the new parents:

> At first, with him and me together, it went quite well . . . but then came the big moment—him on his own on a chair. He began to look so sleepy that we tried everything to liven him up. Imagine Theo with the rattle in one hand, waving a white handkerchief in the other. I had a guitar (which made a terrible noise) in one hand and a bunch of cherries, coloured bright red, in the other. Both of us were jumping up and down, dancing and calling out, which resulted in that silly portrait of him in a bonnet. . . . We're sending you all three. If you combine all three expressions, you'll get a good idea of what he looks like, but of course in reality he's much, much sweeter. One of the portraits is *too* smart, while the other is too sentimental.

No amount of hilarity and happiness could mask the fact that Theo continued to cough and shiver all the time, so he went to see the homeopath Alix Love. Jo was also struggling. For the second time she had a 'very heavy period' and contracted smallpox. Madame Joseph now came to her all day. She 'works like a horse—I've made a schedule for every day of the week'. Despite her ailments, Jo nevertheless had the wind in her sails.[97]

At first the news from Saint-Rémy was depressing. The doctor wrote that Vincent had been sitting with his head in his hands for weeks and did not want to talk to anyone.[98] However, the situation changed remarkably quickly, because within a month he had discharged himself from the institution and taken the train to Paris. It remained to be seen whether it had been a prudent decision, but it happened. He stayed with the family from 17 to 19 May 1890 and met Jo and little Vincent for the first time.[99] The big question was what the chemistry would be like between the tormented artist, who had been out of touch with the real world for a year, his brother, who was so seriously ill that he was unable to get life assurance, and his sister-in-law, a mother for barely three months, who wanted so much to understand her brother-in-law's art and who knew that his existence was so intimately linked to her husband's.

6

Life with the duality of Theo and Vincent

Theo's concerns about Vincent—this was the first Jo ever heard about the Van Gogh brothers. She knew Theo's life in Paris had been turned upside down in March 1886 when Vincent moved in with him. After working for years in the Netherlands and a brief period in Antwerp, the artist had decided to study at the Paris studio of Fernand Cormon. It was in this period that Andries Bonger got to know his friend's painter brother and heard his modern ideas about life and art. The three of them ate together in Theo's flat in Montmartre and had no shortage of things to talk about but, according to Andries, Vincent disagreed with everybody and Theo had his work cut out to handle him.[1] At the beginning of June 1886, the brothers moved to a different flat in Montmartre at 54 rue Lepic. Theo's health was going downhill quickly and Andries told his parents, who had met Theo the previous summer, that he was in a very bad way. 'He looks absolutely dreadful. The poor beggar has so many worries. His brother constantly makes his life a misery and blames him for things he's had absolutely nothing to do with.'[2] That summer Andries wrote to Jo, telling her the same thing, so she knew only too well how Theo was doing and that living with Vincent was a trial for him.[3]

In a letter home, Andries reported that the doctors were saying that Theo was suffering from a 'severe nervous disorder' and for some time had been barely able to move. This news appears to have been the first serious mention of Theo's illness, the symptoms of which varied but became more manifest and more grave in 1890.[4] If Jo had seen this letter it would certainly have influenced her understanding of Theo's condition at the time.[5] Even so, there were brighter moments, too, and not everything was doom and gloom. During the two years that the brothers lived together in Paris, Vincent introduced Theo to the avant-garde painters and they had heated discussions about social issues and about the direction modern art would take. Theo described Vincent in a letter to Willemien. 'He's a curious fellow, but he has such a head on him, it's enviable.'[6] On a few occasions they attended concerts of Wagner's music, which they both admired.[7] It was not until Vincent left for Arles in February 1888, however, that Theo finally had some peace and quiet, and an opportunity to get his breath back.

Everything she had heard about him had given Jo great respect for Vincent from the outset, and this inevitably played upon her insecurities at first. In December 1888, in a letter from Willemien, she read the great compliment that the painter Jozef Israëls had paid her future brother-in-law when he saw Vincent's painting *Pink Peach Trees ('Souvenir de Mauve')* (F 394 / JH 1379) at Jet Mauve-Carbentus's. 'This is a clever chap!'[8] Soon afterwards, Jo asked Theo: 'Do you think he'll ever grow to like me?'[9] It was not a foolish question. Jo had rapidly come to recognize the strong bond between the brothers and knew that by marrying Theo, she would automatically get Vincent into the bargain.

Shortly before her engagement, she wrote to Theo saying how happy and proud she would be if Vincent wanted to be a brother to her, too. 'I keep seeing the little peach tree he painted in my mind's eye!'[10] She was referring to *Peach Tree in Blossom*; Jo had seen the painting in Theo's bedroom and she continued to cherish it for the rest of her life (Plate 19).[11] After she had read a letter from Vincent that Theo had enclosed, Jo's sympathy rose to great heights and she was once again full of admiration for him:

> you had often talked about him, about how much you loved him—but now I *know* what you mean and realize what an influence he must have had on your life—it reflects such a noble, lofty spirit ... his letter has made my longing to get to know him and love him much, much stronger, and I can now wholeheartedly endorse something you once wrote to me when he was ill: 'whether near or far may he remain the same advisor and brother to both of us'. ... Shall I ever be able to do anything for him when we are married? I'm afraid he'll see me as a nuisance—even now, he thinks that when I'm there, there'll not be room in your apartment for all his paintings. Write and tell him your little wife will take up hardly any space and everything will be just the same as before, will it not?[12]

The way Jo described her position vis-à-vis Vincent was crucial. If there was one thing she absolutely did not wish for, it was for her presence to push Vincent and his art aside. More than that, she desperately wanted to mean something to him. She wrote this again two months later, when she urged Theo to go and see Vincent if he needed to, saying, 'I would be most upset if, instead of doing something to help him, I were to deprive him of something he'd like.'[13] This was without doubt the source of all the efforts she made on his behalf after his death.

When she told Theo in the middle of January 1889 that she had written a short letter to Vincent, she explained that she wished she had been more candid. The reason she had not succeeded was that she held him in too high regard, and she was well aware of it. When she thought about him, she felt 'so small—completely insignificant'.[14] The feeling was intensified by what Theo wrote about Vincent's independent personality and unconventional ideas in this telling and far-sighted sketch.

> He is one of the most progressive of the painters and even I, who am so close to him, find him difficult to understand. He holds such sweeping ideas on questions of what is humane and how we

should regard the world, that one first has to relinquish all one's conventional ideas in order to grasp what he means. But one day he will be understood.

Besides thoughts about this struggle against the accepted views about what was appropriate in society and in art, Theo also sent Jo a euphoric description of the vitality and freedom of Monet's work, full of light and sun; as far as he was concerned these paintings were rays of sunshine that gave him encouragement. Such aesthetic experiences buoyed Theo up and he conveyed to her the insight that art—in two respects—could be so enlightening.[15] The key idea was that reality can only be bearable if it is placed beside another reality.

This is how her preferences developed in the early years. Not long before their wedding, she asked Theo whether Vincent's orchard triptych could hang in their sitting room because she was so fond of these paintings.[16] She was referring to *The Pink Orchard* (F 555 / JH 1380), *Pink Peach Trees* (F 404 / JH 1391) and *The White Orchard* (F 403 / JH 1378), which were to have a prominent place on the walls during her later life, initially in her bedroom and later in the living room (Figure 25). In May 1889, when Theo and Jo had just got married, the painter Polak came to have a meal. He talked to Theo

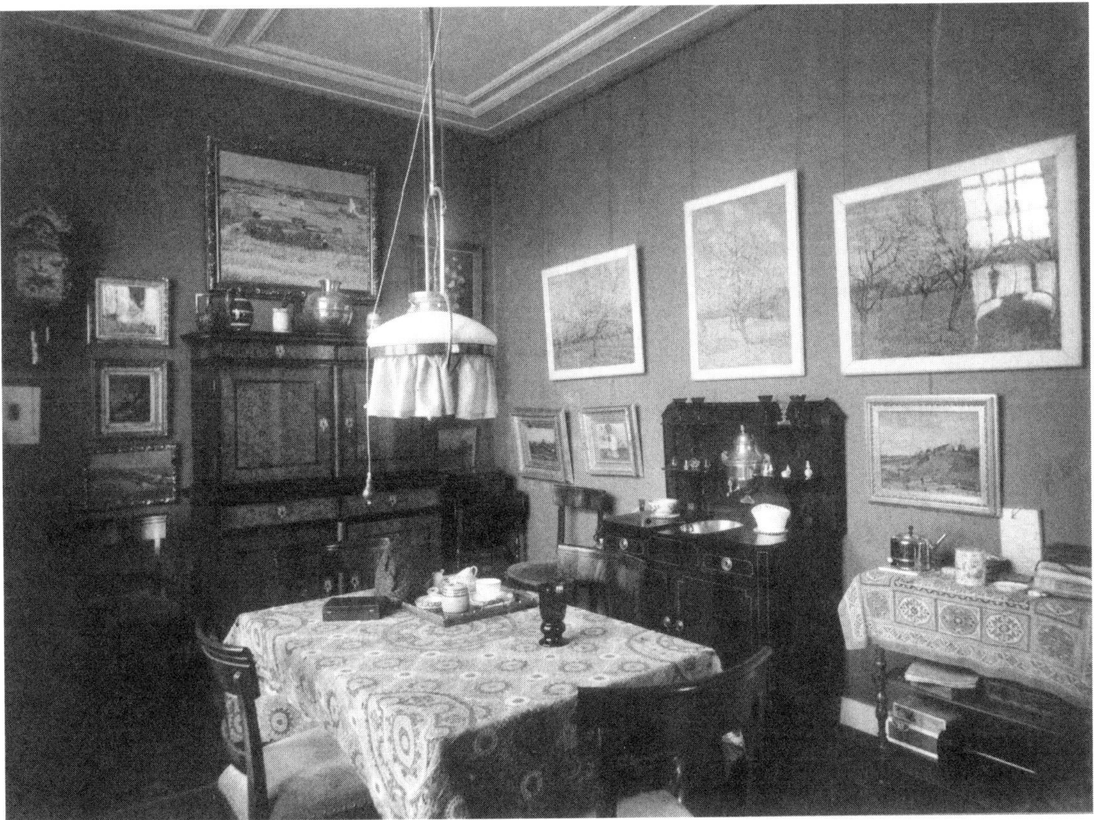

Figure 25 Dining room at 77 Koninginneweg in Amsterdam, between 1922 and 1925.

about art and artists, and they both looked through piles of drawings by Vincent, while Jo listened and watched. She wrote to Mien about it and also commented on Vincent as a letter writer: 'He always writes so cleverly—I've seldom read such letters—but that mind is rather worn out.' Vincent did indeed feel exhausted. All this was going on during the week when he had himself admitted to the institution in St-Rémy. She admitted that she had had to get used to his art in the beginning: 'What I first saw of his work were such strange things—but there are also paintings that are much easier to understand and oh so beautiful!'[17]

Her thoughts drifted from Amsterdam, via Paris, to St-Rémy. She wrote to Mien about how sad she felt inside and about the other side of the coin of brotherly love:

> I haven't played the piano much yet—I don't know why, but I still have that feeling that there's something dead inside—I can't enjoy anything any more—I'm not interested in reading, or in paintings—it's so unpleasant, but what can I do about it? Theo so wants me to read Zola, and now I've started *La faute de l'abbé Mouret*—but it leaves me cold—I think it's so unnatural, but Theo raves about it! . . . If I can just always make Theo happy, everything is good. Yet it's always Vincent, Vincent who doesn't share that happiness and satisfaction because it's better to do too much than too little—working, struggling, and that's what he's inculcated into Theo.

Vincent also, she said, demanded his attention everywhere in the apartment. Not just on the walls but under the bed and on the floor because there were unframed canvases scattered around so they could be viewed in different places.[18] It meant that she had not really been able to make their flat a real home as she so wanted to do. Jo's pregnancy may have had a negative effect on her mood and perception, but that was certainly not the only factor. Years later, in a letter to the artist Paul Gachet Jr, she expressed similar ambivalence about Vincent's all-pervasive presence in their home and lives. She could hardly be blamed for her feelings. In the intense and complicated relationship between Theo and Vincent, she was secondary, and this inevitably affected the happiness of her marriage. Looking back, it made her bitter, but she mostly kept that to herself.[19]

The first time Jo met Vincent

Vincent wrote hundreds of letters, most of them to Theo. In 1914, Jo published them under the title *Brieven aan zijn broeder* (*Letters to His Brother*). In the book's introduction she described with some panache the first time she met Vincent, who came to Paris after he had been discharged from the institution in St-Rémy:

> I had expected to see a sick man, but before me stood a sturdy, broad-shouldered fellow with a healthy complexion, a cheerful expression and something very determined in his appearance; of all

the self-portraits, the one with him in front of the easel is the best likeness of him at that time. Evidently there had again been a sudden, indescribable reversal in his condition . . .

'He's perfectly healthy, he looks much stronger than Theo,' was my first thought.

Then Theo led him into the bedroom, to the cradle of our little boy, who was named after Vincent. Silently the two brothers looked at the peacefully sleeping child—they both had tears in their eyes. Then Vincent turned to me laughing and said, pointing to the simple crocheted coverlet in the cradle, 'Don't mollycoddle him too much, little sister.'

He stayed with us for three days, and was happy and lively the whole time. St-Rémy was not discussed. He went out on his own to buy olives, which he was accustomed to eating every day, and insisted we try them. He got up really early that first morning and stood in his shirtsleeves looking at his paintings, which filled our apartment. The walls were covered with them, . . . while others were everywhere else—to the utter despair of our housekeeper—under the bed, under the sofa, under the cupboards, in the spare room, large piles of unframed canvases, which were now spread out on the floor and being studied intently. Lots of visitors came round, too, but Vincent soon realized that the hustle and bustle of Paris was not doing him any good and longed to get back to work.[20]

Vincent was now staying in Auvers-sur-Oise, a village just north of Paris. Camille Pissarro had approached Dr Paul Gachet, a physician there, who promised Theo he would keep an eye on Vincent. Vincent wrote to Theo and Jo from the Auberge Ravoux, where he was lodging, telling them that he was very pleased to have seen the young family. Not long after this, he confessed he had no disposition for social contacts, but he hoped the three of them would come and visit him one Sunday.[21] On 8 June, accordingly, they visited Vincent at Gachet's. The doctor had arranged for a substantial meal in the garden. Gachet's son Paul remembered how the two Vincents had had fun together chasing after a couple of ducks.[22] Later that month, though, there was less to laugh about. Annie told Mr and Mrs Bonger that 'Net and Theo are not looking well. Last week they barely slept.'[23] Little Vincent had a temperature and diarrhoea. According to their family doctor he was teething, but Jo was not so sure. Fortunately, little Vincent started eating a little more and he took well to the asses' milk purchased to supplement Jo's shortage of breast milk. It was the ideal solution. A donkey would visit twice a week and be milked there and then. Vincent responded to the news about the sick baby boy. He was convinced that country air would do the boy a power of good and that Jo would produce twice as much milk, so he magnanimously offered to change places with her for a fortnight.[24]

Tensions and strife

At the end of May 1890, to their great satisfaction, Theo and Jo got a new housekeeper, Victorine Izle, who was much younger than Madame Joseph.[25] Meanwhile Jo had more colour in her cheeks and had been to the dentist's.[26] Theo, who was surprisingly busy, was full of good intentions and decided to travel to the Netherlands with Jo and little Vincent. Perhaps they might even go to Auvers for a fortnight first. 'He needs it so much,' wrote Jo to her sister Mien.[27] At the beginning of July they decided to rent the first-floor apartment at 6 cité Pigalle, which was larger and two floors lower than their own at number 8. This would be less tiring with the child, and there would be more storage space for Vincent's paintings.[28] Jo was delighted, but she was never to make the move because fate struck a cruel blow.

July was the month of truth for Vincent, while for Theo it would be October. Vincent had visited the family on 6 July and had met Albert Aurier, Henri de Toulouse-Lautrec and Sara de Swart while there. The get-together was entertaining. After they had left, though, the conversation turned to Theo's thoughts about leaving Boussod and starting his own art gallery with Andries. These discussions, in which Jo also joined, were by no means straightforward. Afterwards the relationships between Theo, Vincent, Jo and Andries were strained, as emerges from the correspondence at the time.[29] Jo addressed this thorny issue in her introduction to *Brieven aan zijn broeder*. The bickering about how to proceed and what the financial implications would be was too much for Vincent, who left for Auvers, 'overtired and stressed, as emerged from his last letters and his last paintings, in which the viewer can feel the impending catastrophe approaching, like the black birds scudding above the wheatfield in stormy weather'.[30] Jo thus linked his art directly to his personal circumstances, establishing the myth that Van Gogh's destruction announced itself in the last canvases.

Andries and Annie were also very much involved in the decision on how to approach the investment, but Theo was absolutely furious about the way they kept changing their minds. He wrote to Vincent that Andries had shown himself to be a great coward when it emerged that in the end he was not prepared to join forces in a shared art gallery after all. 'It's the second time he's withdrawn at the decisive moment, and however you were there when we were talking, and he answered me squarely that I could count on him. I can't understand it except by attributing this hesitation to his wife. Much good may it do him.'[31] It goes without saying that this did no good to their relationship. It may well be that Andries and Annie were hesitant to participate in a business venture with Theo because of his poor health—so they had a good reason for their decision.

At the end of the month, a guilt-ridden Jo confessed to Theo that she could have been nicer to Vincent when they were so focused on squabbling about what to do and what the implications could be.[32] Yet what she had done had already had a positive impact because Vincent had responded with relief on 10 July to a letter from Jo (which has not survived), although he remained circumspect about all the circumstances relating to the issue:

> Jo's letter was really like a gospel for me, a deliverance from anguish which I was caused by the rather difficult and laborious hours for us all that I shared with you. It's no small thing when all

> together we feel the daily bread in danger, no small thing when for other causes than that we also feel our existence to be fragile.
>
> Once back here I too still felt very saddened, and had continued to feel the storm that threatens you also weighing upon me. What can be done—you see I usually try to be quite good-humoured, but my life, too, is attacked at the very root, my step also is faltering. I feared—not completely—but a little nonetheless—that I was a danger to you, living at your expense—but Jo's letter clearly proves to me that you really feel that for my part I am working and suffering like you.

He wrote that since then he had painted three pictures: immense stretches of wheatfields under turbulent skies, in which he had tried to express extreme loneliness.[33]

Initially Vincent had written a much more indignant letter, but he did not post it after receiving Jo's letter, which had reassured him. The letter he did not send, which was torn up and later stuck back together again, was dated 7 July 1890 and included the following: 'You surprise me a little, seeming to want to force the situation, being in disagreement.' Yet alongside this irritation about the disagreement, it emerged that there was nevertheless also scope for a more resigned tone, because seeing them all had given him a great deal of pleasure.[34]

Recuperation in the Netherlands

Shortly after Vincent had written these letters, Theo, Jo and little Vincent went to Leiden, to where Mrs van Gogh had moved in the meantime. She saw the baby boy, who was now nearly six months old, for the first time. Theo visited artists, dealers and collectors in The Hague, Antwerp and Brussels, and returned to Paris alone. On 19 July 1890 he wrote to Jo from there asking whether she had taken the opportunity to visit the exhibition of modern art in the Lakenhal's new art gallery. From Leiden, Jo went on to Amsterdam to stay with her family and, with the baby, get her strength back after her poor physical recovery following the birth. Theo regretted not being able to witness how warmly the little boy was welcomed in Amsterdam.[35] He was planning to return to the Netherlands again without delay and go on holiday with his family. Their correspondence continued until 1 August, but by no means everything was kept.[36]

Theo had been unhappy at Boussod, Valadon & Cie for some time. His bosses were only interested in increasing turnover. He had the idea that they would not put the slightest obstacle in his way if he said he wanted to leave. He told Jo that he was not counting on a pay rise. No matter how much he wanted to leave his employer, for the time being there was no alternative because of the dispute with Andries. Uncertainty about his future made Theo very gloomy. He described the disagreement with Andries as a business conflict, whereas Vincent talked about 'domestic quarrels', as can be seen in a letter from Theo to Jo: 'I understand from Vincent's letter that what he means by domestic quarrels are my attempts to achieve my own ends in the matters I discussed with Dries. That's the only explanation I can think of, it's certainly not clear.'[37]

Jo tried everything she could think of to reassure him and cheer him up. They were doing so well together and she could easily economize more. She was not worried about whether or not Theo stayed with Boussod. 'I will do my *utmost* not to be a burden but to help you. When I'm just a *tiny* bit stronger you'll see that I'm not always so hard to please.' What demands she had been making remain unclear. What is clear, however, that is Jo must have complained often about the ambiguous situation and expressed her dissatisfaction. It was only now that they were apart that she realized that their marriage was something sacrosanct and saw that she had meanwhile come to understand Theo much better than at the beginning.[38] Two letters crossed in the post. Theo had agreed with his superiors that he would stay after all. The idea of being independent appealed to him, but he was too concerned about the uncertainty it would entail.[39] The following day Jo urged him to come without delay and relax in Amsterdam, where the pace of life was so much slower than in Paris. She thought about him all the time. She once again raised what the three of them had said to one another. 'Do you still hear from Vincent? Tell him we will resolve our querelle domestique—because we still love one another, do we not?'[40]

The spotlight switched continually from one Vincent to the other. Theo very much approved of the baby eating rusk porridge so that he could benefit from Dutch cow's milk. He sighed: 'Will the little one still remember me? I do hope so.'[41] Little Vincent had just received his very first post. Anna Veth-Dirks wrote to the baby on behalf of her tiny daughter Saskia, who would like to visit him as a 'girlfriend'. She hoped that he would not cry and chuckle in French because she would not understand it.[42] Jo wrote to Theo at length about these sorts of everyday things. She had been having problems with losing blood when she was not menstruating, although that had now almost stopped so she was allowed to get out of bed. But she had not yet gone out because she was nervous about using the stairs, so her sisters took the little boy to Weteringplantsoen. Jo slept a lot—her 'usual complaint'.[43] Theo wanted nothing better than to give her a big hug, even if she was sleepy. 'I am so nervous and when I'm worried about something I'm easily thrown off balance,' he wrote. He wanted to be in Amsterdam within two weeks so he could put his arms around her and their son.[44]

Jo now went for a walk on her own for the first time and proudly pushed the pram through the Vondelpark she knew so well. She enjoyed all the compliments she received. She wrote triumphantly to Theo that an acquaintance had told Mrs Bonger that she had become such a fine, strapping woman. 'I was glad, because here they keep nagging about me being frail.' Her mother and sisters smothered her with care and Jo longed for the return of Betsy, who had been away all the while. Being close to her high-spirited youngest sister always made her feel much better.[45]

The atmosphere between the Van Gogh brothers remained uneasy. Theo had received a letter from Vincent that he once again found 'incomprehensible', but we do not know what he was referring to. He wrote to her reassuringly: 'We've not fallen out, either with him or with each other.'[46]

And yet Theo's unease conveyed itself to her. On 26 July 1890 Jo confessed to Theo 'I do apologise for yesterday's letter, what must you have thought?' That letter of the twenty-fifth has not survived, and there may well have been a reason why this particular letter disappeared. Given that Jo was to play such a decisive role in managing the brothers' estates, it is not unlikely that she came across things she found embarrassing when she was organizing all the correspondence, and deliberately suppressed a difficult side of herself. The question of exactly how far she went with her censorship can no longer be answered. The Van Gogh researcher Jan Hulsker concluded on the basis of the correspondence at the beginning of the month that Jo had tried 'as far as possible to conceal the dramatic character of the events'. He was referring to Theo's request on 8 July for a pay rise at Boussod's. Hulsker contended that Vincent had responded to what Theo had told him about his request to his employer 'with a new letter that was so desperate and perhaps even so sharply worded, that Jo probably destroyed it, and in any event never published it'.[47] This appears to be a plausible hypothesis, unless Theo took the decision to spare her its contents.

Theo hoped to be able to arrange to travel to Amsterdam somewhat earlier than planned. Meanwhile Jo brooded: 'What might be the matter with Vincent? Did we go too far the day he came? My dearest, I have firmly resolved never to squabble with you again—and always to do what you wish.' But she was rather on the late side with that firm resolve. This was followed by trivial questions, for example: 'have you got a little pot of honey for breakfast?' and 'would you take the books back to the library?'[48] But Theo had very different things on his mind. Failure by the caretaker of the flat to fulfil agreements led him to abandon the plan to move to 6 cité Pigalle. The commitment to rent for a period of three years also deterred him and he postponed his decision. He felt hounded, he did not belong anywhere and he longed to get away from it all.[49]

Jo gave him moral support and promised to be very thrifty in future. In her view, Theo should not have let himself be influenced by all those 'sombre musings' of Andries's (who has to have sketched a pessimistic future scenario) and likewise should not have been thinking about the possible closure of branches at Boussod, but about their being together in the Netherlands. She pointed out that they would be seeing each other within a week.[50] But tragedy intervened; on the day Jo wrote this, Theo received alarming news about Vincent from Auvers.

He rushed to his side. Vincent had tried to commit suicide—he had pointed a revolver at his chest and pulled the trigger. The situation was very grave and Theo wrote to Jo from Auvers, without describing the distressing event, that Vincent's life was in danger: 'He was lonely, and sometimes it was more than he could bear.' Theo was terrified of what would happen to his brother. He promised to be brave because 'after all, I have you to live for; I'll not be alone as long as I have my wife and my little boy'. He sent her 'a thousand and thousand embraces'.[51]

At that moment Jo, who was sitting in the public gardens with the baby, knew nothing about it. Friends visited her and everyone told her she was looking well. Betsy had sung and the family all had 'a mania for going for walks'. She had absolutely no idea of the gravity of the situation in Auvers and assumed that Theo would be coming as planned.[52] Untroubled and unsuspecting, she wrote that little Vincent had been feasted on by the midges, but nevertheless he was as round as a barrel. She waited to seal the envelope until the post came in case there was a letter from Theo. There was, and in a postscript she reacted to the sad news, although Theo had not described the actual circumstances in his letter. Now there was a new worry, Jo pondered the implications: 'Thank God you're no longer so far away from him—at least that's a comforting thought.' On that thirtieth of July she asked Theo to pass on her regards, but it was too late. In the meantime, with Theo at his bedside, Vincent had died at half-past one in the afternoon of 29 July 1890. They buried him on the day that Jo had written.[53]

Sorrow and guilt

There was something macabre about the confluence of circumstances. The fact that Jo was not told about the tragic news until a day after Vincent's death was entirely due to the advice Dr Gachet gave Theo—it was better not to upset his wife because it could disrupt her breastfeeding.[54] This was indeed a sensitive issue. It made Jo cross that she produced too little milk and she was fed up with the way Lien patronized her: 'they act as if the child arrived here starved and is only starting to perk up now because of them and their bottles.' She wrote that she was very sorry to have left Paris and now she hoped, 'as if clutching at a straw', that Theo would arrive that Sunday.[55]

Theo sent one letter to the Netherlands to tell the family about Vincent's death. He sent the letter with the tragic news to his brother-in-law Joan van Houten in Leiden, asking him to go and tell Mrs van Gogh and Willemien personally. Jo finally learned about it a day after that when she got a letter from them; Mrs van Gogh and Willemien were both 'heartbroken'. In her words of solace, Mrs van Gogh made the inevitable connection: 'Oh my dear Jo, what a comfort it is that your darling baby is called Vincent Willem.'[56] Although she was upset and grief-stricken, Jo wrote to Theo the following day—she sorely needed to be with him to bear the pain. Her conscience also started to nag her: 'Oh, how I should have liked to see him again and say how sorry I was for having been impatient with him the last time.' She was still haunted by guilt about her earlier tactless attitude. Although it is not clear which issue was concerned, it was probably connected to her opinion about Theo's decision about work and the associated implications for Vincent's financial support. She understood only too well how disoriented Theo was feeling: 'I would do anything, if I only could, to make up for his loss—love you far, far more even, if that were possible.'[57]

Theo, who had just had an extremely bad few days, now told Jo what had happened. This was the last letter of their correspondence. He wrote that Vincent had found the peace he had been unable to find on earth, and mentioned the friends who had been present at the funeral. He was sleeping at Andries and Annie's, despite the earlier discord, because everything at home reminded him of Vincent. He wanted Jo to go to Mrs van Gogh and Willemien in Leiden on the following Sunday and he would see her there. That same day he also wrote to Leiden, poignantly summarizing his sadness: 'Oh Mother, he was so much my own brother.'[58]

Theo went to the Netherlands and both families were grieving. After their departure, Mr Bonger wrote a heartening letter, at the same time stressing that although Jo really was better, she was by no means fully recovered. Theo and Jo received a flood of letters of condolence from family, friends and acquaintances.[59] Some time later Jo revealed to Anna Veth-Dirks:

> During the night before he died Vincent said to Theo, speaking of me, 'elle ne connaissait pas cette tristesse là'. Now I have to think about it all the time—I didn't understand then what he meant—but now I do. If only I hadn't had to learn it![60]

Powerless eyewitness to Theo's decline

Something over a month after Vincent's death, Theo told his mother that the art critic Albert Aurier was considering writing a book about Vincent and had explained how valuable he thought the correspondence with his brother was. 'I find such interesting things in Vincent's letters and it really would be a remarkable book if people could see how much he thought and remained true to himself.'[61] Theo had every confidence in Aurier and handed over the letters from the St-Rémy period. Jo knew all about it.[62] Theo had talked to her about them immediately after Vincent's death and had said 'something of those letters should be made public'.[63] He was absolutely certain that it would happen one day. Aurier died two years later at the age of twenty-seven without ever bringing his plan to fruition.

Jo wished Mrs van Gogh happy birthday and herself brought up the link between the namesakes: 'The absence of a letter from your oldest child will cast a long shadow over any joy—one thinks about it all the time, but it seems as if the grief is twice as difficult to bear on such anniversaries.' And she ended: 'Next year you'll receive a letter from little Vincent, today he is disinclined to write.'[64] She meant well, but the forced levity jars.

Theo could not shake off his melancholy. In Andries's words, the loss of his brother had 'gnawed at him dreadfully'.[65] Theo asked Émile Bernard if he could help make a selection from the overwhelming number of his brother's paintings for an exhibition. Bernard had made this suggestion himself at the funeral in Auvers and agreed the same day. At that point the venue was undecided.[66] The Durand-Ruel gallery was approached, but rejected the proposal, so Theo decided to use the empty rooms in the first-floor apartment at 6 cité Pigalle, which he had meanwhile started renting.[67] The paintings were indeed exhibited there, even though the preparations for their own move were still in full swing. Theo and Jo would never move into number 6.[68]

Theo hoped that the exhibition would get art dealers and other relevant individuals interested in Vincent's work; after years working as a dealer in modern art, he knew only too well how essential it was for an artist's work to be talked and written about. By 14 September the lion's share of Vincent's paintings—some 360 altogether—that Theo had stored with the dealer Julien Tanguy had already been relocated.[69] Although he was exhausted, with Bernard's help Theo managed to show a large number of works in the spacious flat. All the walls were fully utilized and the rooms looked like a suite of museum galleries.[70] The same impression emerges from the art critic Johan de Meester's review in the *Algemeen Handelsblad*. He referred to 'a few hundred' works.[71]

Theo sold two paintings to an artist for three hundred francs each (about a hundred and fifty guilders); there is no information about which they were or who bought them. In February he had already sold *The Red Vineyard* (F 495 / JH 1626) to Anna Boch for four hundred francs. These sales gave Jo an indication of the works' value. In a letter to Willemien, Theo talked about sales and the layout of the exhibition. He used the pronoun 'we', meaning both Bernard and Jo as well as himself: 'We thought it would be good to put a few of them up for sale in order to prompt people to start talking about him.' This was precisely the role that Jo would adopt not long afterwards for the coming decades. Theo also told his sister about his poor health. He had taken drops that the doctor had given him, but they made him hallucinate. He said that if he had continued to take them, he would have jumped out of the window or finished himself off in some other way.[72] At the beginning of October 1890 his health deteriorated shockingly fast. Nevertheless, he continued to work like a horse and all the signs were that, driven by his illness, he still had a lot he wanted to do. The presentation of Vincent's paintings made great emotional demands on him, and at the same time he was also engaged in selling works by Degas, Guillaumin, Pissarro and Constant Troyon, which earned ten thousand francs for his employer, Boussod. And all the while, in his heart of hearts, he would have preferred to leave the gallery.

Jo's birthday on 4 October started well, but this was not to last: 'everything was still good in the morning—how kindly he came to meet me with the little boy on his arm—and how generous he had been to me—but in the evening—that was the beginning of all that long misery—*that* I cannot describe!'[73] After struggling with poor health for years, Theo suffered a complete mental and physical collapse. Without any warning he could suddenly no longer urinate, and on 12 October he was admitted to Maison Dubois, a nursing home in rue Faubourg-Saint-Denis. Jo was at her wits' end and asked Paul Gachet in three sentences, scribbled in pencil, if he would visit him.[74] Two days later, Theo was moved to Maison Émile Blanche (Maison de Santé de Passy) in rue Berton, where mental patients were treated. There is nothing to suggest that he ever went home again. For the first few days after he was admitted, Jo and Vincent stayed with Andries and Annie, who had moved shortly before to 54 rue Blanche, close to cité Pigalle.[75]

Family members and friends, including Caroline van Stockum-Haanebeek, a friend of Theo's who had also known Vincent, attributed Theo's collapse to the unbearable pain and immeasurable grief arising from Vincent's death:

> Who would ever have thought that he would have to pay such a high price for his all care and dedication! How terrible that, even after his death, Vincent does not leave him in peace, and saddled him with a legacy, an unattainable task, in pursuit of which he was now sacrificing, so to speak, so much of his vitality and energy that his poor tortured head is now suffering. It's so dreadful and for you, dear Jo, distress that's almost too much to bear, poor young woman.[76]

First, the death of his brother, with whom he had become so profoundly bonded, had been a devastating blow for Theo. Now, the illness he was suffering from also began to take its toll.

Andries sent a telegram to Theo's colleague Hermanus Tersteeg in The Hague, who came to Paris immediately to talk to old Mr Léon Boussod. The upshot was that Theo would in any event remain their *gérant* until the end of the year.[77] Andries then reassured his parents about the financial position. Theo was owed just under nine thousand francs, so there was no need to worry about money. Willemien also came at once, and went with Jo to see the doctor treating Theo. Jo found it difficult to reconcile herself to the situation and, according to Andries, took him to task: 'Net is not satisfied with what is being done, and constantly wants something different because she thinks she knows Theo better and knows what he needs. I don't need to tell you how preposterous everything she wants is.' She evidently wanted to have Theo repatriated, but at that moment he was too ill to be taken to the Netherlands. Andries did not mince his words and said there was no hope whatsoever. The family doctor had explained that the case was far more serious than Vincent's. The situation was 'deeply gloomy' and Maison Blanche's medical director refused to allow visits to the patient.[78]

Theo lost control completely on 17 October 1890. There were shocking scenes. The artist Jean-François Raffaëlli told the writer Octave Mirbeau that seven male nurses could barely restrain Theo, who had been fitted with a catheter and was lashing out wildly in all directions.[79] And Camille Pissarro wrote to his son Lucien about Theo's suffering, which was so terrible that it seemed that, in his hopelessness and madness, he had wanted to kill Jo and their child.[80] There was complete panic and total despair.

Jo turned to her last resort. A few years earlier, in the Netherlands, Theo had met the physician Frederik van Eeden, and in consultation with Anna Veth-Dirks, Jo decided to get him to come to Paris in the hope that there was something he could still do for Theo. Anna thought that he could certainly have a beneficial effect: 'If he sees and recognizes Free, that face will make an impression on him and bring him peace, and Free will stop his disastrous thinking about his brother.'[81] Although he had been cautious at first and had written telling Jo that his treatment 'might not achieve what you expect of it', the thirty-year-old doctor did eventually visit the patient—on or around 23 October.[82]

Van Eeden tried to treat Theo using hypnotic suggestion.[83] He had studied the field in depth since 1886 and had written on this subject in his article 'Het hypnotisme en zijn wonderen'.[84] In 1887, with Albert van Renterghem, he opened a clinic for therapeutic hypnotism, in which there was a lot of interest. Van Eeden gave lectures about the role of the subconscious, the 'Double I', obsessional neuroses and psychotherapy, in which he stressed the power that the mind could have over the body. He wrote to Lodewijk van Deyssel that he tried to make the heads of his patients 'somewhat clearer and their mind somewhat stronger'. His progressive therapies were successful—during the first two years more than four hundred people were treated and there was improvement in approximately eighty per cent of them.[85]

After Theo had been treated it was a matter of waiting to see what the effect of the hypnosis would be. Van Eeden charged Jo 120 guilders.[86] During his stay in Paris he had also studied Van Gogh's paintings in the apartment and made glowing notes for a piece about Vincent in *De Nieuwe Gids*. In gratitude for his efforts, Jo gave him a superb version of a sower as a present (Plate 20). This extraordinarily generous gift was not entirely altruistic, because she knew Van Eeden would write positively about Van Gogh's art. Soon after this, in his article, he remarked on the unusual colours in *The Sower*: 'The evening sky is green, and the earth in the field below is purple—he paints these two things strong green and purple next to each other and it was beautiful.' For him 'this coarse, strongly accentuated, raw colour expression' had 'a very strong, direct effect of beauty'.[87] Back in Bussum, Van Eeden encouraged Jo and told her in a letter that he was coming to love the painting more every day and had meanwhile shown it to his friends—which was of course exactly what she had wanted to achieve: 'Witsen sat in front of it for a very long time and was very taken with it. I've already had many conversations with Veth about it. I also continue to enjoy the little drawings.' Jo had also given him a few drawings, including *Road with Trees* (F 1518a / JH 1495). Who knows, he thought, he could also stage another exhibition at some time.[88] Jo had successfully planted the first Van Gogh seed in the Netherlands.

At that moment Octave Maus was already engaged in organizing an exhibition in Brussels for the artists' group Les Vingt, in which he wanted to include works by Van Gogh. James Ensor and Theo van Rysselberghe were also part of that group. Maus heard from Maurice Joyant, who worked at Boussod, that Theo had had to stop working abruptly. The painter Paul Signac suggested Maus should select some of the canvases that had remained behind at Tanguy in Paris—'almost all very fine'.[89] Jo let Maus know that she was now in the Netherlands, so she was not able to carry out the honourable task of selecting the most interesting pictures, and she asked him to get in touch with Andries.[90] Andries wrote to Maus shortly before Christmas; he listed the eight works by Van Gogh he was sending in for the exhibition, with prices. It would appear that Andries had nevertheless consulted Jo about the final choice and the prices because Van Eeden's *Sower* was at the top of the list. The asking price for three paintings was five hundred francs, and the other four were eight hundred francs.[91]

The artist Charles Serret, who had visited Theo and Jo in the spring of 1890 and had been very enthusiastic about Vincent's paintings, took the opportunity in November to make two pencil drawings of Jo and little Vincent, one with the inscription: 'à Monsieur Van Gogh. Souvenir très affectueux' and one with: 'à Madame Van Gogh. Hommage affectueux' (Figure 26). These were no doubt intended to cheer Theo and Jo somewhat, although the effect will not have been significant given all the consternation about Theo's decline.

Three tense months

Anna Veth-Dirks wrote to Jo twice on the day that Van Eeden travelled to Paris. She invited her friend to stay with her in peaceful Bussum if it proved that Theo could be nursed in the Netherlands. The affectionate Anna offered to provide children's clothes, a baby bath and sterilized milk. As far as she was concerned, Jo could turn up in the middle of the night. Martha van Eeden-van Vloten, Van Eeden's wife, was also prepared to lend a hand.[92]

Van Eeden's treatment did not have the hoped-for effect. After making enquiries, he proposed that Theo should be nursed in Utrecht, where there was a skilled psychiatrist and he could easily visit Theo himself. Van Eeden advised Jo to address the application to medical director A.T. Moll, and this she did without delay.[93] After Moll had agreed to Theo's admission, he left on 17 November 1890 accompanied by two male nurses in a first-class compartment from the Gare du Nord to the Netherlands—during the journey he wore a straitjacket and could no longer understand French. Jo was kept out of everything and in the preceding days she must have been distraught. Annie asked Mr and Mrs Bonger about what was happening: 'Has Net not been allowed to see him at all, not even from a distance or through a keyhole?' Theo was taken to the Geneeskundig Gesticht voor Krankzinnigen in Utrecht, the present Willem Arntsz Huis.[94] In his referral, Dr Meuriot in Paris gave the diagnosis as 'acute maniacal excited state with delusions of grandeur and progressive generalized paralysis'. The latter part is identical to the diagnosis of dementia paralytica, which was put in the Utrecht file with the admission data, with as causes: heredity, chronic illness, excessive strain and grief.

The neurologist Piet Voskuil later carefully formulated his ideas about Theo's condition: 'The symptoms could be evidence of the diagnosed dementia paralytica or of lues cerebri.'[95] At the time it was known that dementia paralytica, also known as organic psychosyndrome, leading to severe damage to the brain, could be the result of a syphilitic infection, but it is unclear whether this specific cause was mentioned then.[96] The mercury and potassium iodide administered to Theo were in any event used to combat cerebral syphilis, but not exclusively that.[97]

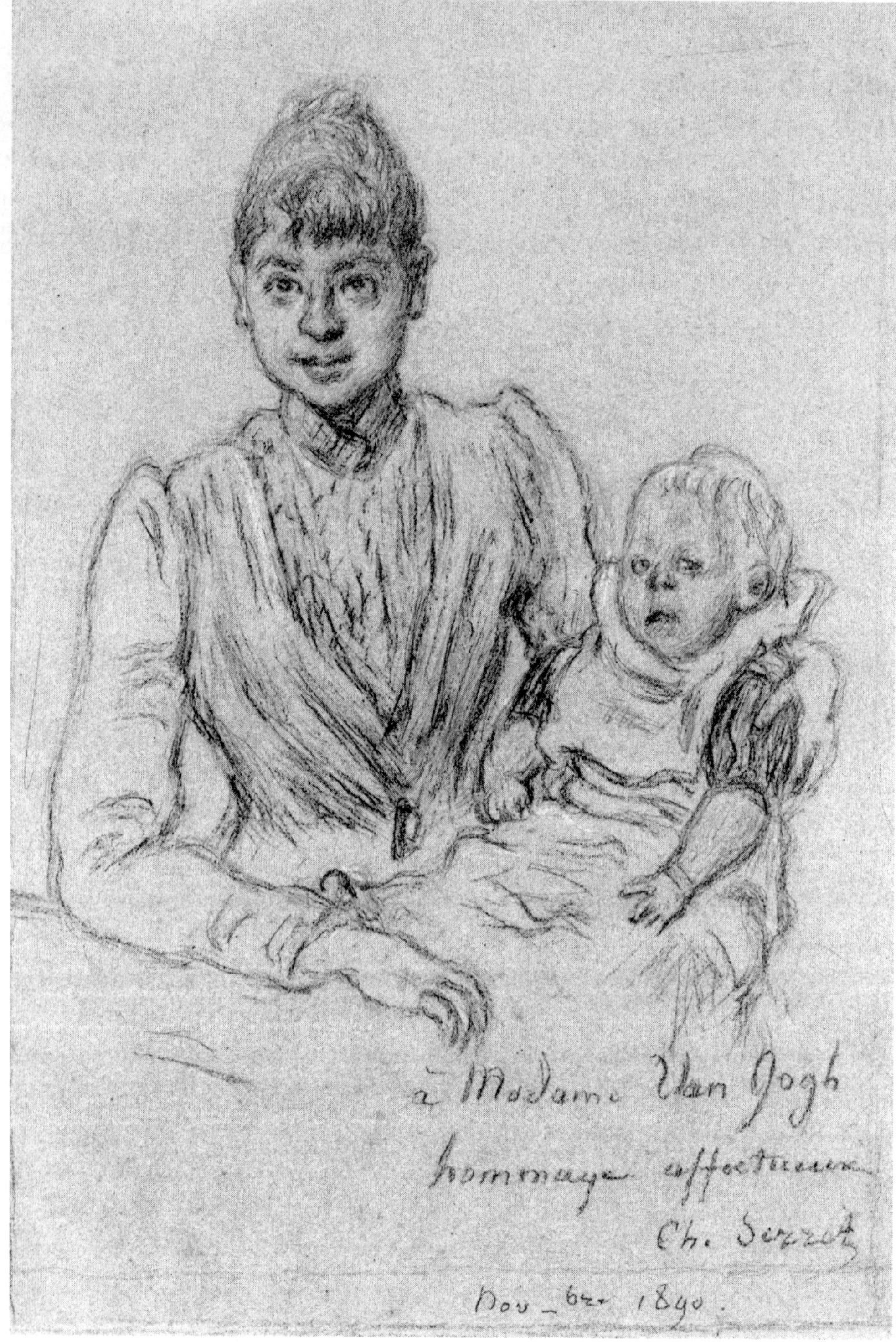

Figure 26 Charles Emmanuel Serret, *Jo van Gogh-Bonger and Vincent van Gogh*, 1890.

The question as to what Jo knew about the exact cause of Theo's decline remains unanswered. Did she take into account the possibility that their son could have hereditary symptoms or suspect that she or little Vincent might have been infected? Theo was fearful of the degeneration of future generations (Vincent had been frank about that with his brother—their physical condition was a recurring subject of discussion) and he also knew the dangers to which he had exposed himself in his many sexual contacts in the past. Theo had talked about this during appointments with his doctors, but he was probably less candid with Jo, even though she knew perfectly well about his earlier visits to brothels, to which she had resigned herself. In May 1888 Vincent had commented as follows after Theo's visit to Dr David Gruby: 'I think he'll urge you not to see women except in case of necessity, but as little as possible. . . . Have you seen Gruby's face when he pinches his lips tight and says "*No* women"?' Dr Louis Rivet, whom Theo also consulted, had prescribed potassium iodide for him. It is quite likely that Theo had started visiting brothels in 1875.[98]

Nowadays, doctors split the clinical picture of syphilis into two phases. The dividing line is the degree of communicability of the disease, which begins with a painless sore, typically on the genitals, rectum or mouth:

> Primary, secondary and the early latent stage of the disease are called early infectious syphilis. During the second stage, late syphilis, which includes the later period of latency and the tertiary symptoms, the disease can no longer be passed on.[99]

The latent period can last for years. In 1906 two previously held beliefs were overturned: the terms *syphilis ex patre*, meaning a direct infection from father to child, and *syphilis par conception*, for a healthy mother contracting the disease from her infected foetus, vanished from use.[100] If this disease was in fact the cause of all the misery, Theo did not infect either his wife or his son.

When he arrived in Utrecht, Theo was confused and disoriented. He was incoherent, speaking a jumble of languages, he gave the wrong answers to questions, had difficulty walking, coughed a lot and had a wildly erratic pulse. Now and then he was incontinent. He also kept trying to tear his clothes. The doctors gave him sedatives and sleeping pills.

On the day before Jo left for the Netherlands, she paid the doctors' hefty bills and Theo's train journey. She booked her own journey on 18 November.[101] Willemien travelled with her and little Vincent.[102] On the nineteenth, she went from her parents' house, where she was staying, to Utrecht to see how Theo was and then straight to Leiden to tell Mrs van Gogh and Willemien about the situation. That same evening, she returned to Amsterdam.

As soon as Theo, Jo and Vincent left Paris, Andries began to take action. He told his father: 'Yesterday, in my own name, acting on behalf of Theo or third parties, I insured all the paintings at Tanguy's and those in the apartment for twenty thousand francs.'[103] The relatively modest sum reflects the lowish value of Vincent's works at that moment.

Jo was facing an extremely difficult and uncertain time. On 24 November 1890, Theo was a little calmer and she went to see him, but the visit did not last long. He spoke gibberish and knocked furniture over. Soon after that he destroyed his palliasse. He was given a sleeping draught and a decoction (mercury and potassium iodide). Again, the doctors observed that his pupils were very small and unequal.[104] Mrs van Gogh and Willemien shared in the misery. Jo told them all about it and Willemien realized just how painful the visit must have been for her. 'It's a good thing Lies wasn't with you, she's so nervous and it would have done her harm.'[105] It seemed to be an inherent Van Gogh complaint: Willemien, Vincent, Theo and Lies all suffered from their nerves.

Van Eeden visited Theo, who was even more vacant than before, was eating badly and could not keep his food down. Although the doctors had previously removed Theo's catheter, they tried to insert a new one because of the pain he had in urinating, but failed. In mid-December the reviewed diagnosis was rapidly progressing dementia paralytica; the symptoms were disordered speech and walking, unequal pupils. Theo was alternately cheerful and destructive, occasionally incontinent and disoriented in place and time. Jo did not visit him because he was too distraught. She sent him a bunch of flowers, but he trampled on them as soon as they were given to him.[106]

Jo's new task

While she was staying with Mrs van Gogh and Willemien, Jo wrote to Octave Maus in Brussels again. She was pleased with the 'hommage posthume' for Vincent and wanted to send some drawings for it, 'which connoisseurs have always considered are as important as his paintings'. Theo had thought the same and Jo acted entirely in his spirit: 'It is my most earnest desire to act in all things in accordance with the wishes of my poor husband.'[107] In his reply, Maus asked her to select some drawings for the exhibition.[108]

It was a pivotal moment. Jo assumed Theo's mantle. Despite all the stress, she had made a point of packing certain of Vincent's drawings in her luggage. Amidst all the concerns about Theo's rapidly deteriorating health, she was keeping a close watch to ensure that Vincent's work would be represented as effectively as possible at the Brussels exhibition. This marked the start of the honourable task she was to undertake for the rest of her life—promoting and disseminating Van Gogh's legacy. This one-woman action brought a rebuke from Andries; two weeks later, he lectured her: 'My question was not "didn't you hesitate for a moment in selecting the drawings", what I told you was that in any event you mustn't forget to send the one with the well . . . if you didn't send that one, you'd have done better to hesitate and ask.'[109] But Jo knew Theo's favourite *Fountain in the Garden of the Asylum* (F 1531 / JH 1705), which was what Andries meant by the 'well'. She had indeed picked this pen-and-ink drawing, and it hung in the exhibition (Figure 27).[110] It was one of the fifteen drawings she chose: four were 'Brabant Types' and the rest were works from the Arles period, seven of which were included in the

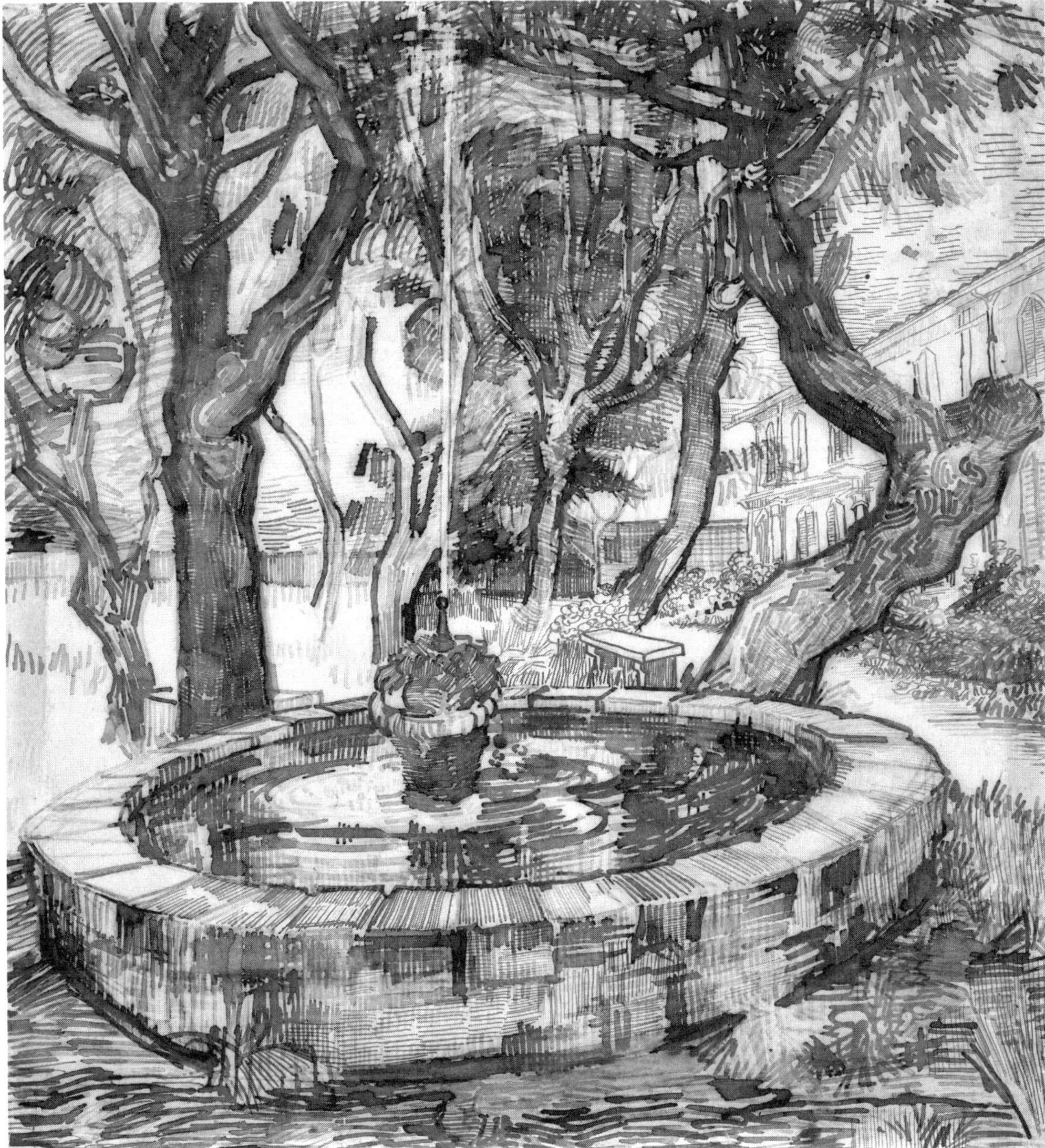

Figure 27 Vincent van Gogh, *Fountain in the Garden of the Asylum*, 1889.

show. Jo asked Maus for the address to which Van Eeden should send *The Sower*, 'one of Vincent's principal works', for she had arranged that the painting would also be exhibited. It is evident that Jo knew only too well that she had not gifted Van Eeden a lesser work, and she asked him to lend it to Les Vingt for the duration of the exhibition: a Van Gogh from a Dutch private collection—it was a shrewd tactical move.[111]

She had realized by now that there was absolutely no chance that she would ever return to Paris with Theo. Accepting this fact, she had asked Anna Veth-Dirks for advice, and yet again her friend encouraged her to move to Bussum. They thought aloud about the future and these discussions determined the course of Jo's life thereafter. Anna suggested that one solution would be for her to open a bed and breakfast or boarding house. There was one good establishment of the kind in the neighbourhood, but it was very bourgeois.[112]

Bussum was the source of a real boost for Jo in the shape of Frederik van Eeden's article 'Vincent van Gogh', which appeared in *De Nieuwe Gids*. He was enthusiastic about the work, admired the artist's tenacity in his quest for the truth in his art, and expressed himself with an abundance of exclamation marks. Van Eeden called Van Gogh a genius and even a saint.[113] Johan de Meester also wrote about Van Gogh, but he took a different tack and placed the painter in the democratic camp. In the *Algemeen Handelsblad* he described him as an out-and-out democrat, who wanted 'art to be more for the general public'.[114] Both authors made a connection between the tragedy of Van Gogh's life and his art, giving sentimentality free rein. These pieces must have made their readers curious about the work of the as yet unknown artist, which was apparently so deeply human.

Andries wrote a furious letter to Jo telling her how she should act from now on. He was vehemently opposed to her taking the reins into her own hands because he saw that she was inclined to let things drift. He also thought it ridiculous that he should have to ask her permission for the sale of two paintings for four hundred francs by Tanguy: the art dealer had not been able to believe his ears when he heard that he had had to ask for his little sister's approval first. 'Instead of answering yes or no to my telegram, you tried to be clever again.' Andries had had enough of Jo's high-handed actions and responded caustically: 'Your stupid scribbling means nothing and only serves to prove to me how extremely badly you would be able to trade, if it were to get that far.'

And there was another issue. Victorine, the maid, had lodged a complaint and the court had passed judgement. Theo should have appeared. Obviously he had not, and strictly speaking he had now been found guilty. The nature of Victorine's complaint was unknown, but it appeared to be about arrears of wages. Since the cost of compensating her would be lower than if Jo were to turn the matter over to a bailiff, Andries strongly advised her to pay the woman. But if he was to do this for her, Jo had to tell him where the 'certificate' Theo had written (by which he probably meant the employment contract), and the judgement might be. Andries would then personally ensure that the matter was settled by paying Victorine. Jo had casually mentioned the matter to her brother and had wanted to let it ride, without realizing what the legal consequences might be. Andries thought that serious measures had to be taken and he lashed out at her. 'A *conseil de famille* must be appointed (it should already have happened), without whose permission you may do *nothing*, understand me, *nothing*. . . . You know better about everything and you know nothing.'[115] Although he had put his finger on this sore spot, a demoralizing attack like this made things even harder for Jo at this already nerve-wracking time. She immediately poured her heart out to Anna Veth-Dirks.[116]

That day, Andries also roped in their father to persuade Jo to resolve all the outstanding issues as he saw fit. He made her out to be a know-it-all and told her off. In Andries's eyes, Jo's criticism of Johan de Meester's article in her letter was 'put on', for there was nothing in it that could have upset her: according to him she had 'given more proof that she had understood something of Vincent and his paintings by describing the comparison with Claude as nonsense'.[117] (De Meester compared Van Gogh with the character Claude Lantier in Émile Zola's novel *L'Œuvre* (1886). Lantier feels he has failed as a painter and hangs himself. In a letter to De Meester, Andries disputed this erroneous comparison.) More than a year later, Jan Veth and Richard Roland Holst were of the opinion that Jo had little understanding of art—which in a sense was true: the initiation into art Theo had given her came to a very abrupt end and should certainly have gone on longer.

The same letter contained yet another nasty dig at her. Andries thought that Jo's 'quasi strength' was nothing but 'a cover for boundless inexperience and frivolity'. He wrote of the choice of drawings for Maus: 'You have aplomb to spare, but substance is something else.' Arrogantly he ended: 'If you were to be honest, don't write so much, but admit that you always want to get your own way and know better about everything.'[118] These scoldings, coming as they did in the heat of the battle, did their relationship no good—their obstinacy and cocksureness drove brother and sister apart, and her former obedient attitude towards Andries was a thing of the past. Nothing ever came of the family council he had suggested, but there must have been discussions in the family about how to proceed. Jo, however, refused to be pushed around. Soon after this she made her plan.

Jo's son Vincent was not very fond of Andries, later writing in his diary that his uncle had shown little understanding of Van Gogh's art and had even once suggested simply disposing of the whole collection. This, though, is highly questionable.[119] The opposite—the conclusion that he acted as 'an important intermediary' for people who were interested in the work—is probably also too hasty. He was likewise not 'his sister's authorized agent', nor was there ever any idea that Andries 'was himself preparing to publish the letters', as was later asserted.[120] It would be more accurate to say that he acted on her behalf when necessary, representing her interests, but without any formal instructions.[121] Andries was anything but indifferent. He had a strong sense of responsibility and had conscientiously compiled a list of the Van Gogh works that were in Paris. He also took care of moving the collection to the Netherlands and dealing with the works that were still with Tanguy. In 1903 Andries himself owned seven Van Goghs.[122]

While brother and sister wrangled on paper, Theo was in a wretched state: boracic acid solution was used in an attempt to treat a 'sort of wartlike abrasion' with 'a small bleed' on his penis.[123] He became increasingly vacant, slept in a padded cot and was extremely noisy at times. He had two epileptic fits during the last couple of days of his life and then never regained consciousness, Jo visited him for the last time on 25 January 1891, and he died at half-past eleven that evening. He was thirty-three. There was no official death certificate, and the family refused a post-mortem examination. Four days later he was buried in Soestbergen cemetery in Utrecht.[124] Years afterwards, in April 1914, Jo had Theo's remains removed and reburied beside Vincent in Auvers-sur-Oise.

Condolences flooded in—from Sara de Swart, Albert Aurier, Odilon Redon, Isaac Israëls, Meijer Isaac de Haan, Émile Bernard, Octave Maus and many more. In *De Amsterdammer* Jan Veth described the death of the passionate and unforgettable art dealer as an irretrievable loss for a large group of modern artists.[125] Jo placed an acknowledgement of all the messages of condolence in *Het Nieuws van den Dag* of 10 March 1891. Within the space of six months, she had had to cope with two deaths, and her future in Paris had been shattered for all time. The visiting cards she had printed read 'Mevrouw de Wed. Th. Van Gogh-Bonger', reflecting her status as Theo's widow.

Jo's youth and illusions were gone and her life was turned upside down. Back in the Netherlands, she had to try to reconcile herself to her daunting fate and build a new life for herself as a young widow and for little Vincent. It would always be dominated by the brothers, for although life with the duality of Theo and Vincent had come to a horribly abrupt end, her care for their extensive legacy would always continue.

It was not only Theo who had persuaded her of Vincent's exceptional talent as an artist during their marriage; the artists and critics in their immediate circle, including Bernard and Aurier, did so too. In the years that followed, Jo would acquire more and more contacts in the art world in the Netherlands and beyond, with like-minded people who saw the importance of Van Gogh's art: artists, writers, dealers, exhibition makers and museum directors. They all eagerly championed their views. Their enthusiasm gave Jo an added incentive to keep promoting Vincent's work.

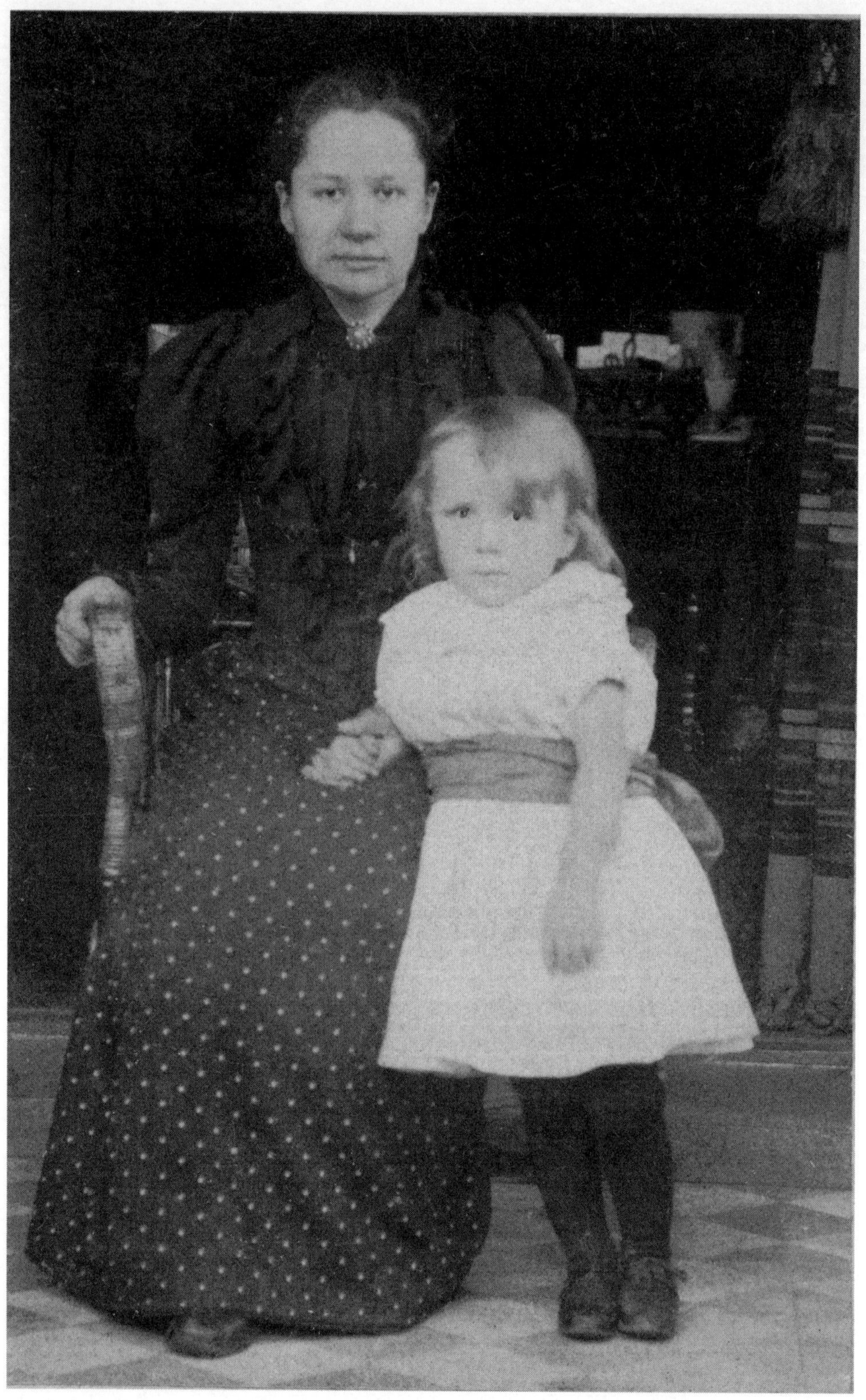

Part Three

Boarding house keeper with an attic full of art

1891–1901

There is no unmediated access to the past.
All 'pasts' are constructed in a present.

RICHARD TARUSKIN[1]

7

Back in the Netherlands—Villa Helma in Bussum

Jo knew Bussum from her visits to Anna Veth-Dirks, who had repeatedly encouraged her to move there, too, and she decided to take her advice immediately after Theo's funeral. At that time, the village had a population of about 3,500.[1] She and her son moved into Villa Helma at number 4 Koningslaan, on a site covering more than 1,300 square metres. The house was in a recently built development of large detached houses known as 'Het Spiegel' (Figure 28). Beyond the residential part of Koningslaan the street became a dirt track. The house was built in 1888 for the tobacco planter and broker Pieter

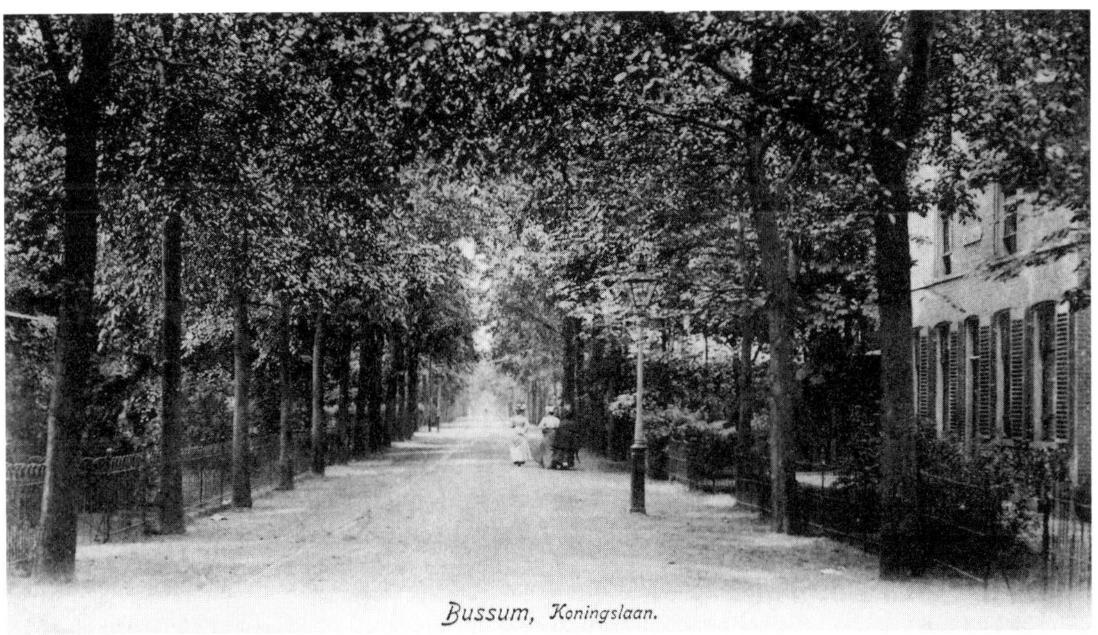

Figure 28 Koningslaan in Bussum, Villa Helma right foreground, *c.* 1900.

Wijnand. Jo paid him six hundred guilders rent a year.[2] When she arrived, she was delighted by the flowering fruit trees in her own garden.

Residents of the village welcomed Jo. Frederik van Eeden hoped that it would suit her and even Jan Veth was eventually happy that she had come to live in Bussum. She was already seriously considering the move not long before Theo died. Veth was in Berlin at the time and in a letter to his wife Anna he wrote that he suspected that Jo was afraid 'of being uncongenial', and that 'she wanted to be livened up first' when she arrived in Bussum, 'which I shall be happy to do'. Jo's initial response to his approach was restrained, but this is hardly surprising since it was all happening during the last days of Theo's life. Veth appears not to have been fully aware of this: 'I don't know why Jo B. was so cool about my letter,' he commented. 'I'm sure I wrote to her very warmly.'[3]

Jo had had made a conscious choice not to live too close to her family. Well-intentioned as its members may have been, she saw that environment as a world that threatened her personality. Her son Vincent later observed: 'My mother had an independent spirit and her ideas consequently sometimes differed from her family's.'[4] She now bore sole responsibility for her fourteen-month-old son, on whom she projected all her hopes. The people in her immediate circle also expected the child to fill the void left by Theo's death. He represented for her the comfort, the beauty and the purpose of life. Everything she did was for the welfare and advancement of her little 'golden curly-head' and her own desires came second. Mother and son became an ever-tighter unit. In the thirty-five years granted to them in which they undertook a great deal together, they developed a close bond. Vincent would never be able to wholly free himself from her, and parallel to his strong mother fixation, she had a lifelong unbreakable tie with him.

Hundreds of works from Paris

On 3 February 1891, while she was still in Amsterdam, staying at her parents' house in Weteringschans, Jo had written to Émile Bernard. She appreciated his proposal to stage an exhibition of works by Van Gogh, but regretted that she did not have the resources to cover the costs at that moment. Of course she gave him her permission to organize something were he to see an opportunity to do so, and she was grateful to him in advance for his desire to bring about 'my poor husband's plan'. The rent for number 8 cité Pigalle had been paid up to 1 July, so she suggested using their apartment for it. If they took the furniture out, they would have three rooms they could use; the bedroom in particular was spacious and the light in there was good.[5] Bernard set to work and wrote back to tell her that he would like to involve the artist Odilon Redon and the writer Joris-Karl Huysmans in the preparations.[6]

Jo soon started to receive requests for loans of artworks from all quarters—requests that sometimes came at her in waves. She also initiated many projects herself. Between 7 February and 8 March 1891, Les Vingt staged their eighth 'Exposition annuelle' at the Musée d'Art Moderne in Brussels. Like the

Parisian Société des Artistes Indépendants, Les Vingt's goal was to promote modern art; one of the ways they did this was in their annual exhibitions. They also published the magazine *L'Art Moderne. Revue Critique des Arts et de la Littérature*. Octave Maus asked Jo for the prices of the drawings she would be prepared to sell.[7] Jo sent him a list by return; they ranged from a hundred to four hundred francs. If a buyer were to take two, he would be given a discount.[8] She wrote the letter on paper with a wide black border, customary during the period of mourning at that time. Jo also continued to wear mourning for some considerable time.[9]

Jo agreed to the two hundred francs for a drawing offered at the end of the exhibition and asked Maus to use the money to have mounts made for the remaining drawings.[10] She also asked him to send her reviews of the exhibition—something she did without fail in correspondence with exhibition makers in the years that followed. She assiduously collected all the reviews, articles and catalogues to keep abreast of the reception of Van Gogh's work.[11] When the exhibition closed, she gave Maus the small drawing *Fishing Boats at Sea* (F 1430b / JH 1541) as a token of her gratitude for his efforts.[12] A few months later, when he wrote to Jo on behalf of his cousin, Eugène Boch, to find out whether Jo would part with the *Eugène Boch ('The Poet')* (F 462 / JH 1574), which was with the art dealer Tanguy, she gave Boch the painting.[13] Boch had shown sympathy to both Theo and Vincent, who he believed had done everything for the sake of pure art, and Jo had met Boch when he visited the Paris apartment exactly a year earlier.[14]

Jo was occupied with the question of how best to get the paintings to the Netherlands. The artist Sara de Swart, a friend of hers, replied to a letter from her asking for the address of the firm she wanted to approach to do the job: 'You asked for Meganck's address, Daverveldt's, it's rue Paul Lelong.'[15] In her letter, De Swart reflected that Theo had left Jo more than works of art:

> Thank God that you have your child, a legacy isn't it—something you can live for—in which you can see that his principles live on. The dear little chap will give you so much love. Particularly when he gets a little bigger. He will be a constant reminder of those inexpressibly good times; that will cause you sorrow, great sorrow—but at the same time a gentle luxury. It is so good that you want to work for him; otherwise you would be entirely without a purpose.[16]

Jo was only too aware of that purpose. Being a good mother unmistakably came first, but that other task ran parallel with it: taking countless decisions about the Van Gogh legacy. It was a constant round of lending, gifting, offering and selling works or deliberately keeping them back.

Émile Bernard advised her to leave the canvases in Paris, because the market for Van Gogh was better there than in the Netherlands: 'It's a fortune you've got there, don't spoil it—a double fortune—a fortune in glory, a fortune in money.'[17] She thought differently, however, and asked him to send the works nonetheless. He filled twenty-seven crates with a maximum of ten paintings in each and advised her to get the canvases put on stretchers, which she later did.[18] Probably around November 1890,

Andries made a list of titles; on it were 311 numbers and 361 works altogether. This overview, known as the 'Bonger list', served as a key document at the time and has since proved to be an indispensable source for research into Van Gogh. There are crosses in the margin beside 258 paintings—this is probably the number of works in the twenty-seven crates. Andries was undoubtedly present when they were packed.[19] Aside from these, there were still more than eighty works in store with Tanguy. Some of the Van Goghs that had been left in Paris may have come back when Andries and Annie moved to the Netherlands in early 1892. What Jo wrote to Willem Steenhoff shortly before her death—'In '91 I came to Holland and brought all the French paintings with me'—is therefore not true.[20] A Dutch removals firm brought the household goods, but not the works of art. There was no mention of the fate of the hundreds of drawings that likewise went to the Netherlands.

Jo thanked Bernard for his trouble and hoped that the works that had been left behind and were still in the apartment could be exhibited. She saw to it that he was given six hundred francs for the purpose.[21] Meanwhile, the Société des Artistes Indépendants had staged its annual exhibition from 20 March to 27 April 1891 in the Pavillon de la Ville de Paris. As it had the year before, it included ten works by Van Gogh. Andries had acted as the intermediary.

The fire insurance policy taken out for Villa Helma in April for a total of 12,600 guilders provides an overview of the contents and their estimated value. The works of art accounted for more than half of this sum. The list included:

f 6,000	for furniture, clothes, beds, table, linens, jewellery, gold, silver, that which further belongs to the household effects, hardly anything excepted.
f 960	for 5 paintings by Monticelli
f 40	for 1 painting by Breitner
f 150	for 2 paintings by Lautrec
f 300	for 3 paintings by Gauguin
f 160	for 4 paintings by De Bock
f 150	for 2 paintings by Renoir
f 100	for 4 paintings by Guillaumin
f 2,000	for 200 paintings by V. van Gogh
f 600	for 1 portfolio of drawings by V. van Gogh
f 60	for 1 drawing by Manet
f 1,000	for a collection of etchings by modern French artists
f 500	for a collection of prints.[22]

The estimated number of works by Van Gogh referred to here was only a proportion of his complete oeuvre. It is difficult to say just how large that proportion was since the size of the total is not certain either. For various reasons it is impossible to give an exact number, because that depends on how they are counted. There are supports that have an image on the front and back, whether all the letter sketches and all the sheets in the sketchbooks should be included is debatable, the authenticity of a great many works is questioned, and so on. To give an indication: in his first oeuvre catalogue in 1928, De la Faille arrived at a total of 863 paintings and 919 drawings, etchings and lithographs. In the ten years that Van Gogh had been an artist, he had moved several times and left behind, given away or exchanged a considerable proportion of his work. These works, scattered around Europe, gradually began to appear on the market or were donated to public collections. Jo certainly did not own everything, but all the same she had an impressive number of Van Goghs in her safekeeping in 1891.

Her son Vincent later recalled how the paintings were spread around the house:

> The Potato Eaters hung over the fireplace; opposite, above the large cupboard, the Harvest—above the door the Boulevard de Clichy.... next to the chimneybreast the vase of flowers by Vincent (the purple vase).... Vincent's drawings of the courtyard of the hospital in Arles and the fountain at St. Rémy hung in the downstairs passage; in the bedroom the three flowering orchards, the almond blossom, the Pietà after Delacroix and La Veillée.[23]

Jo and her son shared an upstairs room at the back of the house. If the downstairs was well filled with Van Goghs, the six paintings in the bedroom left virtually no space on the walls. The classicist and composer Alphons Diepenbrock wrote that when he had called, 'the whole house was full of Vincents'.[24] Van Gogh's paintings were stored in rows in the attic along with albums and portfolios of drawings, all in worrying conditions: in the winter the space was bitterly cold and damp; in the summer the temperature could soar and it must have been as dry as a bone. Countering stories that children were not allowed to play there under any circumstances are intriguing anecdotes of little boys playing hide and seek among the precious artworks and even children swinging on that art. There is no question, however, that Jo would ever have treated it so cavalierly.[25]

She arranged the paintings in her house as nearly as possible to the way they had hung in Paris. It brought Theo closer: 'It took me months—the whole of the spring—hanging the paintings—I lived with him all that time.'[26]

The young boarding house keeper

On the threshold of a new life, Jo found herself thrown back on her own devices and tried to get her life back on track by giving it structure that she determined herself. Gradually, she overcame the shortcomings she recognized in herself and succeeded in freeing herself of her negative self-image. As I have already remarked, those recurrent passages of self-loathing in her early diaries should not be taken all too seriously: as a doubting teenager and young woman she had needed them so that she could 'improve' herself, as she repeatedly described it. We know that she had also had periods of joy in her youth. She described her years with Theo as the happiest in her life. After coming through the appalling months of his illness leading up to his death, she was forced to start rebuilding her own life. It was her opportunity to show that she could cope as an independent woman—something that she had not had a chance to do during her marriage. Even so, it was a very long time before she recovered any appetite for life. Caring for her son and the pleasure she derived from him certainly helped her in this: 'I've come to live here, in Bussum, to give him healthy fresh air; I've started a boarding house to earn a living for both of us.'[27] The boarding house opened on 1 May 1891 (that was on Theo's birthday). She knew from the months she spent in London in 1883 what it was like to stay in lodgings. Many widows ran boarding houses at that time; the occupation was regarded as a respectable source of income for women.[28]

The account book Jo kept contains a wealth of clues about the day-to-day events in and around the house (Plate 21). In Bussum Jo generally looked after three guests. Three modest rooms were available for them on the first floor above the front and back rooms. A dumb waiter next to the kitchen was used to send meals up to the guests.[29] Some of them were undergoing psychiatric treatment with Van Eeden, who lived in Villa Beukenoord in Nieuwe 's-Gravelandseweg, a few streets away. The teacher Adeline Andria Muller was a guest for several years and she taught little Vincent to read. Jo also rented out an annexe on the ground floor with its own kitchen.[30]

Villa Helma, which at that stage did not have mains gas or water, certainly looked very large, but the space for Jo and Vincent was quite small: aside from the boarding house guests in the house and in the ground floor annexe—which in the summer of 1891 was occupied by a family with five children—there were also a nursery maid and a maidservant.[31] Vincent seems to have been a well-behaved toddler, but if he ever did start screaming there were plenty of people to hear him.

On 26 June 1891 Jo and her father, acting in his capacity as Vincent's legal guardian, signed a deed before the notary Harm Pieter Bok concerning 'all the property belonging to the continued community' between Jo and Theo, 'including the estate of the latter'. This Deed of Inventory, a requirement for inheritance tax and guardianship purposes, lists estimated values of the moveable property (which included part of Theo's art collection to a total of 4,871 guilders) and the household contents and effects (2,275 guilders). This inventory also allows us to reconstruct the furnishing of the house.[32] All the furniture, china, glassware, gold and silver, rugs, curtains and kitchen equipment are listed room by room. The living room was full of walnut furniture—the tall light brown linen cupboard, the well-filled bookcase, the 'art cabinet' with drawings and prints, the sideboard and the writing desk. There were rugs on the lino-covered floors. In the annexe there were small tables with cane-seated chairs and

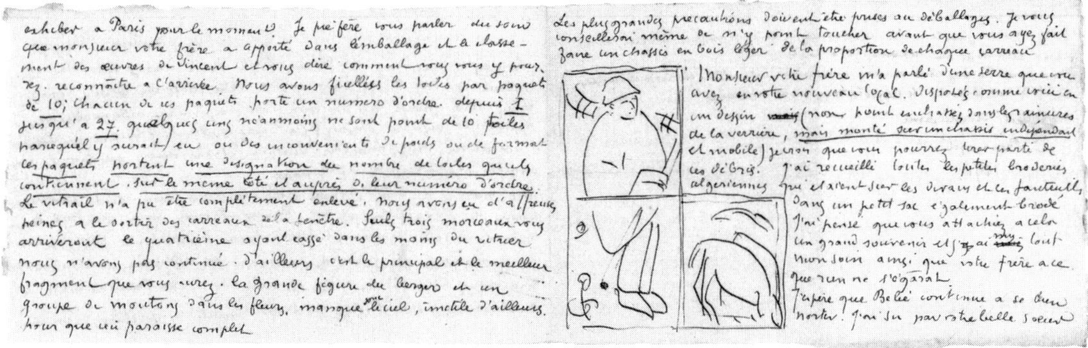

exhiber a Paris pour le moment. Je préfère vous parler du soin que monsieur votre frère a apporté dans l'emballage et le classement des œuvres de Vincent et vous dire comment vous vous y pourrez reconnaître a l'arrivée. Nous avons ficellés les toiles par paquets de 10; chacun de ces paquets porte un numero d'ordre. depuis 1 jusqu'a 27. quelques uns néanmoins ne sont point de 10 toiles parcequ'il y aurait eu ou des inconvenients de poids ou de format les paquets portent une designation du nombre de toiles qu'ils contiennent. sur le meme coté et auprés de leur numéro d'ordre. Le vitrail n'a pu être complètement enlevé. nous avons eu d'affreuses peines a le sortir des carreaux de la fenêtre. Seuls trois morceaux vous arriveront le quatrième ayant cassé dans les mains du vitrier nous n'avons pas continué. d'ailleurs c'est le principal et le meilleur fragment que vous aurez. la grande figure du berger et un groupe de moutons dans les fleurs, manque seul le ciel, inutile d'ailleurs pour que ceci paraisse complet

Les plus grandes precautions doivent être prises au déballage. Je vous conseillerai même de n'y point toucher avant que vous ayez fait faire un chassis en bois léger de la proportion de chaque carreau

Monsieur votre frère m'a parlé d'une serre que vous avez en votre nouveau local. disposez comme voici en un dessin (non point enchassez dans les rainures de la verrière, mais monté sur un chassis indépendant et mobile) je crois que vous pourrez tirer parti de ces débris. J'ai recueilli toutes les petites broderies algeriennes qui étaient sur les divans et les fauteuils dans un petit sac également brodé J'ai pensé que vous attachiez a cela un grand souvenir et j'ai mis tout mon soin ainsi que votre frère a ce que rien ne s'égarât.

J'espère que Bébé continue a se bien porter! J'ai su par votre belle soeur

Figure 29 Émile Bernard, sketch of a shepherd and sheep in (three-quarters of) a stained-glass removable inner window, in a letter to Jo van Gogh-Bonger, 7 April 1891.

the stained-glass window with a shepherd painted by Bernard had pride of place. He had painted this window panel in 1890 and shown it at the exhibition in cité Pigalle to express Van Gogh's love of the countryside. A sketch in a letter gives an impression of the design (Figure 29). There was an iron bedstead in the maids' room; the beds in the other rooms were made of wood. Jo had a washstand and a mirror-fronted wardrobe in her bedroom.

The kitchen maid did the shopping and cooked the meals in consultation with the lady of the house. When Jo was out, the housemaid received visiting cards or letters and put them aside for her in a wicker basket (Plate 22). In the ten years that Jo lived in Bussum, she employed a whole procession of maids. In the 1894 to 1901 period they earned an average of twenty-eight guilders a quarter, plus bed and board. Jo found them through advertisements like the one in the *Gooi- en Eemlander* of 19 March 1892: 'Wanted, a respectable, alert maidservant who can cook well.' Some of them received earnest money when they took up their post; a servant would have to return this—it amounted to a few guilders—if she failed to carry out her duties as agreed. An incentive like this was apparently effective. Anna Dirks had warned Jo against spoilt maids, who, she said, could lie and cheat to your face. A bluestocking, she spoke disparagingly about the 'riff-raff'.[33] With their help, though, Jo coped, and at the end of the first year in Bussum she was able to survey the situation: 'Now, at last, the household machine is pretty much in one piece and although it keeps me busy all the time during the day, it doesn't occupy my *thoughts* so much any more and I can work in the evenings again.'[34] By this she meant organizing Van Gogh's letters. It took her a while to find her feet, as she noted in her diary in March 1892: 'At first I felt as though I'd been thrown down here—there wasn't a corner anywhere that appealed to me.' Now, though, she was able to say with satisfaction: 'As time passes I'm getting fonder and fonder of Helma.'[35]

Finances

Theo and Jo had had bonds in their joint names and also invested in shares. In 1903 Jo herself bought a considerable quantity of mortgage bonds, debentures and shares for at least 12,240 guilders, probably having taken advice from her father and her brother Henri. Among other things, she owned shares in the railway companies Maatschappij tot Exploitatie van Staatsspoorwegen, the Hollandsche IJzeren Spoorweg-Maatschappij and Russisch Spoor. She declared resolutely: 'Serenity—harmony in all things—(in expenditure and income, too) that's the secret of all happiness.'[36] Harmony was certainly assured in the financial sense: between 1891 and 1919 she received 54,725 guilders in interest alone.[37] Over the years, she also benefitted to the tune of 19,049 guilders from inheritances and bequests.

Around the turn of the century, a new household of some status could get by on 2,500 guilders a year; a labourer earned about 350 guilders.[38] On average, Jo's lodgers paid between ten and twenty-five guilders a week, depending on whether they took half or full board, but the sums varied. For the first six years she more or less broke even: her income from the boarding house in this period averaged 2,000 guilders and her outgoings totalled around 2,250 guilders. After that, her earnings from her paying guests declined. Since Jo did not separate the records of her income and expenditure in her account book, it is impossible to work out exactly what her balance sheet was at any given time. As we can see from her income and capital, she had sufficient financial reserves. She never had money worries. Between 1896 and 1901 she was paid 750 guilders for her translations for *De Kroniek*. Jo gave up her translation work shortly before her second marriage in August 1901, and she continued to run the boarding house until then.

For those first ten years she was able to use some of the money she received from the sale of art for their living expenses. During that period, she made around 12,500 guilders from the sale of Van Gogh works—a very considerable sum.[39] She rapidly discovered that she had to stand her ground time after time among the mainly men who dominated the national and international art trade. Hesitant at first, she later acted with growing self-confidence—she obviously still had a great deal to learn about the value of art and about the trade. Again and again, dealers and private individuals asked Jo to drop the prices, and each time she had to decide where to draw the line. In the early stages, unaccustomed as she was, that meant agreeing to a lower return and trying to disperse the works of art through various channels as tactically as possible.

The legacy

Theo had supported his brother financially for years, so Vincent believed that he was entitled to regard the works he made and sent him as his own property. When Vincent died unmarried and childless in

July 1890, the paintings and drawings Theo had meanwhile received belonged to him and to Jo, for their marriage was based on community of property.

Theo did not leave a will when he died in January 1891. This meant that half of the Van Gogh paintings and drawings passed to Jo and the other half to their son Vincent. As the natural guardian of her underage son, Jo was responsible for and could determine what happened to his half until he came of age in 1911, although needless to say it was nowhere recorded who would get which half. The works could be left out of the estate inventory because of Theo and Jo's 'continued community'; the Deed of Inventory of 26 June 1891 did not include Vincent's works in Theo's estate for this reason. They did, though, appear on the List of Paintings, Drawings and Etchings Belonging to the Estate of Mr T. van Gogh, which Jan Veth had compiled on 23 June 1891. He had estimated the value of the two hundred Van Gogh paintings at a very modest two thousand guilders and the drawings at a thousand guilders.[40]

Soon after notary Harm Bok drew up the Deed of Inventory and in the same month that inheritance tax had to be paid, Bok confirmed a deed of gift in which Vincent's brother Cor, his sisters Anna, Lies and Willemien, and his mother Anna had already relinquished their shares in Vincent's estate in favour of the underage Vincent Willem while Theo was still alive. On balance, that was a 17/20th part (Plate 23). This estate included everything Vincent owned when he died, but not what meanwhile belonged to others; the major part of the collection was already in Theo and Jo's possession, and that did not change. The paintings Vincent had given to his mother and his sisters Willemien and Anna likewise remained theirs.[41]

According to the estate duty account relating to Theo's estate, drawn up for the purposes of inheritance tax, the total sum in moveable property, mortgage bonds and cash in the marriage of Theo and Jo was set at 9,687 guilders. Inheritance tax was due on half of this sum less the two hundred and fifty guilders funeral expenses for Theo. Jo paid the tax on 25 July; calculated down to the last half cent, it amounted to just 71.15½ guilders.[42]

Until her death in 1925, Jo continued to sell and occasionally give away paintings and drawings from the half that had passed to her. Vincent came of age in 1911 and from then on Jo consulted him on the approach to take.[43] Up to that point Jo had dealt with his part as she saw fit. She decided for herself which of his uncle's works she would and would not sell; in the end she kept more than half of the hundreds of paintings and drawings from Vincent's estate for her son. He also received a significant sum of money: Jo's spending was modest, so in due course the lion's share of the proceeds of sale went to her son. We know that Jo purposely kept a small group of works that she would not sell and the outside world had no say in the matter. It is not clear which other paintings Jo had in mind to reserve for Vincent. It is also possible that after he turned twenty-five (the age of majority), Vincent kept specific works to one side for himself, but if he did, we do not know which they were. What we do know is that from then on he and Jo often discussed decisions as to whether or not to sell something.

Little written evidence has survived, but Jo's advice to him about a possible sale to a New York museum in a letter of 1915 is doubtless typical of their relationship: 'If you can sell a drawing for the museum I would *certainly* do it, there are so many of them! But don't ask too little, I should think 1,000 dollars at the very least.'[44]

An intriguing question is where, for them, the long road to exposure of the works and by this means largely realizing the value of the works of art came to an end. In all the exhibitions (selling and otherwise) and private transactions, Jo consciously sought to have a decisive influence on Van Gogh's posthumous fame.[45] She knew Theo's views about specific works and must certainly have taken them into account in her dealings; she must also have been guided by what she read in Van Gogh's letters about the works that he regarded as successful. At the same time, the fact that she continued to sell was a sort of retrospective vindication of her husband, who had been so convinced of Vincent's qualities. Jo thus constantly honoured the importance of Theo's years of investment in his brother.

Friendships in Bussum

When she moved to Bussum, Jo looked for ways to recover her peace of mind. With hindsight, she was pleased with how she had gone about it:

> Working is the best diversion and I earned a lot of money. I sat quietly in my room in the evenings—open windows—the lamp with the pink shade—I wrote letters, always letters—I heard all the walkers passing by the house—everyone had company, talked and laughed—*I* was always alone, but not unhappy in my solitude—I had a great sense of serenity, of fulfilment—that everything was going well and my work was successful.[46]

She was fond of the people around her and fascinated by their individual quirks. Her contacts with Van Eeden and his wife Martha became more frequent and she made friends with Karel Alberdingk Thijm (the writer Lodewijk van Deyssel) and his wife Cato. Little Vincent, her 'enfant chéri', often played with Joopie Alberdingk Thijm, who was more than a year older. Their favourite game was hide and seek.[47]

In the last decade of the century, Het Gooi became a centre of writers, artists and intellectuals. Most of the men in the group known as the Tachtigers had meanwhile abandoned their Bohemian lifestyles. Jo was in touch with Willem Kloos and his fiancée Jeanne Reyneke van Stuwe, with Herman Gorter and his wife Wies (who moved into number 66 Nieuwe 's-Gravelandseweg in 1893), with Alphons Diepenbrock and his wife Elisabeth, and with Jacobus van Looy and his wife Titia. She also got to know the architect Hendrik Berlage.[48] Richard Roland Holst frequently stayed with Jan and Anna Veth. At the beginning of 1893 he had met Henriette van der Schalk, whose literary career took off soon afterwards. Through them Jo also got to know Albert and Kitty Verwey, Jan Toorop and Antoon and Johanna Derkinderen.

In the autumn of 1891, Mrs Maria Johanna Ballot-Cool from The Hague came to stay at the boarding house. Jo took to her quite quickly, describing her as 'the most delightful paying guest one could imagine'. It is a telling insight into Jo's inner self—she attributed to her the qualities she was always seeking in herself: 'the greatest modesty, a person who's completely forgotten herself—friendliness—good judgement, very well read.'[49] Marie Cremers, a student at the Rijksakademie van Beeldende Kunsten in Amsterdam, who later trained with Jan Veth, also got on very well with Jo and often went to have coffee with her. Later she wrote of her surprise on seeing particular works: 'I was allowed to browse through Vincent's works in the attic. There was one painting, nothing but a heavy shower of rain on a piece of ground; this was *the* Rain, fierce and aromatic on a dark purplish bit of land.' She was talking about Van Gogh's unconventional canvas *Rain* (F 650 / JH 1839).[50] Cremers was not the only person Jo introduced to the treasures by Van Gogh.

Getting Vincent's work as widely seen as possible

Jo had not kept a diary for three years, but on 15 November 1891 she picked it up again; she continued it—with interruptions—until 8 May 1897. She carefully formulated her beliefs:

> For a year and a half I was the happiest woman on earth; it was a long, beautiful, wonderful dream, the most beautiful one *can* dream. And following it was all that untold suffering that I cannot touch upon—I lost him, my dear, faithful husband—who made my life so rich, so full, who awakened everything that was good in me, who not only *loved* me but who understood what I was lacking and wanted to teach me. I had yearned for it all my life and in him I found it.— "I would rather be *perfectly* happy for one year than have to spread it over a whole lifetime," I used to say as a very young girl. My wish was granted—I have had my *happiness*, now *duty* remains. The duty to live and to care for my darling little boy, *our* wonderful child, our dear little Vincent. "Wouldn't you like to have a baby, my baby?" Theo whispered to me that first blissful wedding night—but I didn't know then what it meant and I was so amazed and overjoyed at the happiness of being his wife that I didn't yet count on being a *mother* at all. But he knew, and the child he gave me, his image with *his* blue eyes and his friendly features, his gentle, tender nature, *his* rich talents, his child is now my treasure, my comfort, my support, my all, to whom I cling and who gives me the courage to go on living.
>
> And so I've started writing my diary again—not for the sentimental outpourings I wrote down as a young girl—(what a lot of nonsense I often proclaimed)—but for a moment of self-analysis

> and self-examination now and then, to keep a better watch on myself and develop a little, if possible. I must use all my strength to learn again so that I may be of some use to my boy later and he will not look down on his mother with contempt—as so many boys, and rightly, have to do alas. Will I ever be able to be a support and help to him? I can do no more than my best. I've come to live here, in Bussum, to give him healthy fresh air; I've started a boarding house to earn a living for both of us—*now* I have to make sure that all the domestic worries don't reduce me to a household *machine*, but I have to keep my mind alert. That's why I want to write down here from time to time things that occur to me about what I've read or about the people I meet or receive. Living here, I'm in close contact with Anna and Jan Veth again, their house is the "centre of culture" for me; it's where many of the people connected with *De Nieuwe Gids* meet, from where the light must shine. Martha v. Eeden promised me as many books as I want—that's a great many—in the past I so often suffered from *book starvation* of the mind, just as bad as actual starvation—I don't have to fear that now.
>
> I'm reading *Utamaro* by De Goncourt, the biography of one of the greatest Japanese painters, alongside Hokusai. Theo taught me a lot about art—no, let me say rather that he taught me a lot about *life*, I learned everything through him: the greatest bliss—the greatest suffering, that teaches us to understand everything else! As well as the child, he has left me another task—*Vincent*'s work—getting it seen and appreciated as much as possible—keeping all the treasures that Theo and Vincent had collected intact for the child—that, too, is my work.
>
> I'm not without purpose—but I do feel lonely and abandoned—all the same, there are moments of great serenity—that the satisfaction of my work gives me. If I may just maintain the health to work for our child—then my life will not have been devastated by the loss of my husband—but I shall always bless him and thankfully love him for all the happiness he once gave me (Plate 24).[51]

Once Jo had restored order in her life, she had space to read and reflect again. She read George Eliot's biography and admired the courage with which the writer had lived her life. She also noted down a number of quotations about Italian painting and some extracts from books by Émile Zola about the importance of being strong and setting oneself a goal. She copied passages from *Impressions and Opinions* by George Moore on literature, theatre and art. The sentence she picked out is revealing: 'If we do not always know where we are going—we always know the fatigues of the *journey*', for making every effort, to the point of exhaustion, is what she did herself.[52] Jo bought and was given books, and joined the 'Leesgezelschap Utile Dulci', where she borrowed art books and illustrated magazines.[53] She was a member of various libraries for the rest of her life.

During her years in Bussum, she constantly thought up ways to draw attention to Vincent's art. Selling his works was an essential element of this endeavour. Vincent and Theo had had very limited success, but as time passed Jo got better and better at it. In September 1891 she sold one of Vincent's copies after Millet in Paris for four hundred francs; this may have been *Sower (after Jean-François Millet)* (F 689 / JH 1836). Then in November she sold six works that were still with Tanguy in Paris for 2,200 francs. One was Van Gogh's *The Good Samaritan (after Eugène Delacroix)* (F 633 / JH 1974).[54] On 19 December 1891, the artists' society Pulchri in The Hague held an art appreciation session for the members of the society, offering the possibility of studying a number of Van Gogh's works of art, 'made available by the Van Gogh family', according to Piet Boele van Hensbroek in *De Nederlandsche Spectator*. It is more than likely that Boele van Hensbroek had approached Jo about the event. The works were then exhibited for two weeks.[55]

Jo had instructed the painter and decorator Dirk Bouwman to make stretchers and frames. He transported the paintings on his handcart, using glass crates padded with straw. When she offered to let him choose something from Van Gogh's work for his troubles, he appears to have said that he did not need anything extra. The story that he had paintings by Van Gogh in his attic workshop in Nassaulaan for some time and that children played football around them—a tale that gained considerable currency—is highly unlikely to be true.[56] Over the years Jo also paid a good deal to the Bussum frame and crate maker Cornelis van Norren, who also transported paintings for her.[57] Transporting works for exhibitions was a recurring concern. They could be damaged if they were not properly packed, and sometimes they even got lost in the post. Over the years, Jo had to devote a good deal of thought, time and effort to compiling lists, deciding asking prices, getting the works ready to transport, unpacking them and storing them again when they came back.

Contacts and intermediaries

Jo often acted herself, but she was grateful for the help of intermediaries—her brother Andries acted for her in Paris, where she also established contact with Ambroise Vollard; later the art dealers Gaston Bernheim, Paul Cassirer and Johannes de Bois were extremely important to her. In some cases, even her paying guests acted on her behalf.[58] As time passed, Jo put countless works into circulation, but always conscious of the need to avoid flooding the market. She turned to various people for advice on her contacts with the art trade. Joseph Isaäcson visited her to discuss things and acted for her in dealings with the Oldenzeel and Buffa galleries. The firm of Oldenzeel had taken over the business of Hendrik van Gogh ('uncle Hein'). According to Jo, there was 'endless correspondence' at the time and it did not abate.[59] Isaäcson had prepared the ground well and Christiaan Oldenzeel wanted to stage a Van Gogh selling exhibition in the near future. It took some time before that exhibition came together, because many works were still without frames. Jo recommended getting simple white frames made. She suggested this solution because some of the paintings already had frames of that kind and because she knew that Vincent himself favoured them. Oldenzeel was not convinced—'white frames are not very popular here'—and he also advised her not to set 'exaggerated' prices. He charged 10 per cent commission.[60]

In February 1892 the Frans Buffa & Zonen gallery in Amsterdam's Kalverstraat showed ten paintings by Van Gogh. Jo had hoped that critics would write about them, and her hope proved well-founded. Willem Du Tour (the pseudonym of Richard Roland Holst) published a piece in the weekly *De Amsterdammer* and Leo Simons wrote a review for the *Haarlemmer Courant*. Roland Holst recommended that people should look at this uninhibited work, full of 'fierce expression, with sharp outlines', uninfluenced by Van Gogh's dramatic life. The strong colours had also affected him profoundly, as they had Van Eeden before him.[61] It was most probably Jacobus Slagmulder, a partner in Buffa's, who wrote to Jo:

> The only admirers were among some of the younger artists; the public generally responded with disbelief and distrust about the future of art. In any event, it made people think, provoked discussions, and we are very grateful to you for having given us this opportunity to provide a new sensation for ourselves and many others.[62]

Despite the excitement the exhibition stirred up, it was to be a long time before a wider public began to appreciate Van Gogh's art.

On the anniversary of Theo's death, Jo visited his grave in Utrecht. She laid upon it roses like the one he had given her on the day after their wedding. She was so overcome by her emotions that she could barely stand: 'I had wanted to stay and lie there beside him in the cold earth—I am so tired, so tired of all the worrying and thinking about everything, and the future weighs me down so!' But it was three days later, while the wind howled around the house, that despair really hit her. She was overcome by an overwhelming feeling of loss:

> I'm glad it's stormy outside, just as it is here inside—but the child lies snug and warm and safe in his cot. Theo, my darling, my own dear husband, I shall take good care of him, look after him well—with all my powers—the thought of you helps me and will help me when my powers sometimes fall short. Oh, if only I could think that your spirit is with us—close to us. My darling, my darling—why did you leave us so early? We needed you so much and I loved you so much—you were making me a better person—what will become of me now![63]

She could not allow herself to indulge such feelings for long. Her other task called. Julien Tanguy wrote to her that week to tell her that he was trying to sell the seven Van Gogh paintings he had on commission as profitably as possible. These were the very last works he had left. Most buyers thought six hundred francs was too much—the works generally sold for three or four hundred each. Tanguy asked her if she was prepared to drop the price.[64] Like Tanguy, Oldenzeel also enquired about Jo's ideas on the asking prices.[65] It must have been very complicated for Jo to keep on setting prices and then deciding whether or not to stick to her guns. She may have asked the artists she knew for advice, but there are no indications that she consulted anyone. As is the case today, it was customary to bargain, and Jo continued to feel her way in working out the prices she could ask.[66] When the works arrived in Rotterdam, Oldenzeel had discovered that some of them had small holes and three-cornered tears in them; in the years that followed she was quite often alerted to the precarious condition of some of the works. These, too, were issues on which she had to take a stand.

Organizing Vincent's letters

Making the transcripts was difficult enough, but determining the chronology was particularly complex, since Van Gogh generally failed to date his letters. Jo numbered the letters in pencil and we can see on the original manuscripts where she rubbed the numbers out and corrected them again and again. Working out which pages together constituted a letter was another tremendous puzzle. When she found a loose page she could not place anywhere, she gave it a separate number.[67] She asked her cousin Jan Stricker for a book by Jules Michelet, and he sent her *Du prêtre, de la femme, de la famille* (1845) as Van Gogh had once raved about it in his presence. What she was actually looking for, though, was *L'Amour*, because in one of his earlier letters to Theo, Vincent had written: 'That book was a revelation to me.'[68] Jo attached great value to such a book, and reading it encouraged her as she studied the letters.

Theo remained a strong presence in her life in all sorts of ways. She slept under the familiar blanket they had had in Paris—'I felt indescribable pleasure, almost as though I were with him again.'[69] And Jo received a visit from the artists Jan Verkade and Paul Sérusier, who responded enthusiastically when they saw the Van Goghs. This was exactly what she needed. Verkade had written to Jo, saying that they wanted to meet 'the wife of the man who so selflessly fought for the new art'.[70] The next day she went to the artists' society Arti et Amicitiae in Amsterdam, where they staged an art appreciation session on Van Gogh like the earlier one at Pulchri. The secretary Jan Hillebrand Wijsmuller had asked her to provide drawings for it.[71] She looked back on it in her diary:

> Everyone I wanted to see the works came—Breitner, Israëls, Witsen—Jan Veth—Jan Stricker and Kee Vos—Martha v. Eeden. It was packed, the people liked them. . . . Now I'm going to start on the letters seriously and diligently, they have to be ready before the busy summer period starts.[72]

This, written in the euphoria of the moment, proved far too optimistic, for it was to be years before things reached that point. She did, though, devote every spare hour to the letters in the first few days of March, establishing the chronology and making transcripts. As she worked, she became increasingly familiar with them and with the 'infinitely fine and tender and loving' relationship between the brothers, who understood one another so well. With every sentence she thought of Theo and often wept as she read—'may your spirit continue to inspire me—then things will go well, with our little one too. Who'll write that book about Vincent?'[73] Encouraged by Theo's inspiration as she read the letters, Jo tried to keep going: following the art appreciation session she wanted to mount a representative exhibition at Arti et Amicitiae, but was disappointed when her proposal was turned down.[74] She must have realized that she could not achieve her goals entirely on her own, so throughout her life she sought the right people to stand by her in her mission.

8

Contacts with Jan Veth, Jan Toorop and Richard Roland Holst

When she was young, Jo was treated like one of the family by Justus Dirks and Alida Kruijsse. She and their daughter, Anna, became friends when the two girls attended the HBS together. In 1883 Anna moved to the Amsterdam fine arts academy, the Rijksakademie van Beeldende Kunsten, where Jan Veth was also a student.[1] Anna and Jan were betrothed in 1884 and married in August 1888. They went to live by the harbour in Bussum (Figures 30, 31).[2]

The friendship between Jo and Anna was very close. In the summer of 1885, Jo had stayed with the Dirks family, who were then living in The Hague. She and Anna had once lain awake talking until five

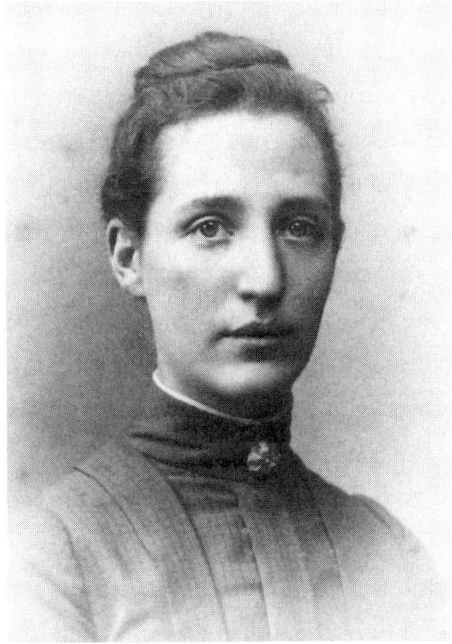

Figure 30 Anna Dirks, undated.

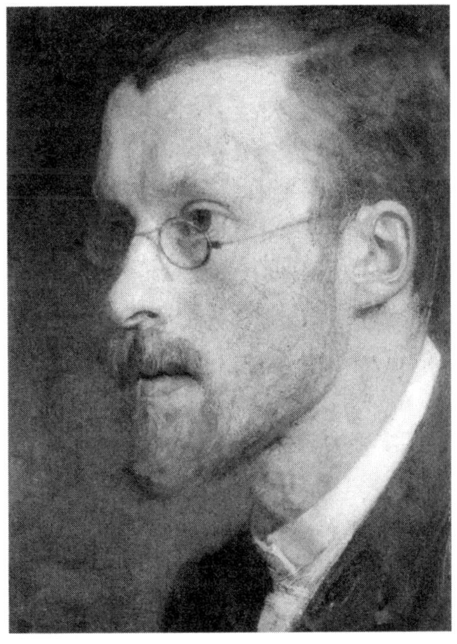

Figure 31 Jan Veth, *Self-Portrait*, 1884.

in the morning.[3] Anna became pregnant soon after her marriage and kept her friend constantly informed about her experiences of pregnancy, labour and the weeks after the birth, repeating all the details in 1889, when Jo herself was expecting. Some matters remained strictly between the women: 'Now you mustn't let your husband read this, but I'm so proud of it: I shall be able to feed it myself, because that's all in order too.'[4] Anna wrote about getting the baby to latch on, and advised Jo to place linen cloths soaked in brandy on her breasts a few times a day, and to massage them, which would make it easier for the baby to feed and would be less painful. Jo had absolutely no idea of what was in store for her and it was clearly the job of friends to give one another this sort of advice. The night she went into labour, she wrote to Vincent in Arles—and also to her dearest friend, who had empathized with her and supported her throughout. Anna had been extraordinarily frank about her own fear of the pains of childbirth.

They continued to keep in constant touch. Anna and Jan wrote words of encouragement when they heard about Theo's illness.[5] And, as we have seen, when Theo was admitted to the institution in Utrecht, Anna strongly urged Jo to come to them in Bussum: 'come here *at once. Promise me that*.'[6] A little later, as we know, Jo moved to Bussum.

Jan Veth must come round

Anna and Jo continued to share their intimate thoughts, but the relationship with the reserved Jan was more complicated. He would never really become a true friend, but Jo was determined to convince him of the value of Van Gogh's works: 'I won't rest until he likes them too,' she wrote resolutely in her diary.[7] Veth, who had seen paintings and drawings by Vincent in Theo and Jo's apartment in Paris at the end of 1889, had difficulty appreciating the radical nature of his art.[8] She had to enter into a debate with him—in public as well as in private—before she could get him to change his mind.

In the spring of 1890, the Veths moved to Villa Op den Akker in Parklaan, a few hundred yards from Villa Helma.[9] Their proximity brought Jo many new contacts, particularly from the circle around the magazine *De Nieuwe Gids*, the mouthpiece of the literary Beweging van Tachtig (Movement of Eighty). Jo regarded their house as the 'centre of culture'.[10] Veth wrote opinion pieces on art for *De Amsterdammer*, *De Nieuwe Gids* and *De Kroniek*, covering a wide field and fervently defending the new art. Among the contributors to *De Nieuwe Gids* and the Tachtigers, he honed his view of the world and developed his artistic, literary and critical faculties. In his letters to Anna he wrote at length about his aesthetic views and ambitions.[11] Veth had a lyrical, evocative style and his writings often focused on feeling, emotion and mood. He took a conscientious approach to his art, working almost like a artisan.[12] Jo observed him at a party for his twenty-eighth birthday: 'Jan was stiff—talked a lot but not jovial, not open, not simple, sometimes there's something very artificial in the way he speaks.'[13] She herself was quiet and rather shy and her thoughts often wandered. Although she had always longed to be part of such gatherings, she never really felt at ease among all these intellectuals.

At first, Veth did not know what to make of Van Gogh's art, and in this respect he believed he had found an ally in Émile Bernard. In an article in *De Amsterdammer* of 26 July 1891, Veth wrote that Bernard had not regarded Van Gogh as a 'unique painter' and thought that many of his paintings were unfinished. They were not, and Jo denied it forcefully. In a letter to the editors published in *De Amsterdammer* of 9 August 1891, she quoted Bernard's remarks about Van Gogh to demonstrate just how much he appreciated his work. A month later, a resentful Veth wrote his riposte in a letter: he thought that she had little understanding of art criticism and was prejudiced. He declared that an artist's intentions should not be confused with what he had achieved, and he derided Jo's 'ridiculous triumphant concluding sentence', which read: 'It was unfortunate that in seeking someone who shared his opinion of Vincent, Mr V. should have lighted upon one of Vincent's greatest admirers.'[14] The controversy put pressure on their relationship. Veth thought that Jo had tried to force admiration on him. He wrote that her 'feeble prodding' was frightening, because it 'drove him round the bend'.[15]

This tension persisted, at a time when Jo desperately needed friendship. In April 1892, she wrote in her diary that Veth had made a new painting 'with strong colours, a complete departure from the dull matt colours he used before—*he has Vincent to thank for that*—he won't want to admit it, that's why he's avoiding me', continuing: 'I wish he was my friend and that I dared to trust him completely!'[16] For the moment, however, that was out of the question. When she refused to drop the price of the painting of *Cypresses*, he asked her—supposedly on behalf of an enthusiast—whether she wouldn't like to sell 'that little seascape that hangs above the door'.[17] He offered 125 guilders (in the first instance incognito), but Jo thought the bid was too low. This anonymous person, however, proved to be none other than Veth himself. Soon after this, he came clean: 'I don't blame you for valuing it properly, but you will understand that I couldn't give any more. . . . You can see from this development that my delight in what I call the fine Vincents was not wholly platonic.'[18]

For weeks Jo debated with him about the quality of Van Gogh's oeuvre. And for the whole of this time Jo found their relationship 'most disagreeable' and thought that he saw her as negligible. She noted resignedly, all too aware of her position in the nineteenth-century man's world: 'we women are largely what our husbands make us!'[19] But gradually something seemed to change. Veth had found out that Van Eeden wanted to help in editing the letters, and offered his services too.[20] He was soon completely converted and, with his art critic's hat on, became an important champion of Van Gogh as a writer and painter (albeit that Huizinga's contention that Veth initiated the Netherlands into admiration of Van Gogh gave him far too much credit).[21]

The following, extraordinarily frank letter to Jan Veth sheds considerable light on their relationship and on Jo's interaction with Van Gogh's letters, which had such a profound influence on her. From her opening sentence ('another little epistle') we can deduce that the Bussum housemaids were kept busy delivering mail between the two houses.

> I just have to write you another little epistle—if I have something to say—I can write it more easily than say it. I am so glad that you think the letters are so good, too—I knew you would! But now I ask you if—you—who say now that you've read only the smallest and least important part 'I dream of them'—would just put yourself in my place as far as you can! I have lived with them from the moment Theo fell ill—the first lonely evening I spent in our home . . . I picked up the bundle of letters—for I knew that I would find him in *them*—and evening after evening *that* was my solace in all the great misery.
>
> I was not looking for Vincent *then*, only for Theo—every word, every detail that concerned him—I hankered after them—I read those letters—not just with my head—I was absorbed in them with the whole of my soul . . . .
>
> I read them and reread them until I had the whole figure of *V.* clearly before me. And now think about when I came to Holland—completely sure in myself about the great—the indescribable height of that solitary artist's life—what I felt then, faced with the indifference that met me on all sides where Vincent and his work were concerned. Do you still blame me so much for being so sensitive on that point—that so denounced little article in the *A.*[22] Do you understand now that it was not the desire to see myself in print that you accused me of—but only the burning sense of injustice, of the whole world against him—and that I now had a chance to speak out on one single point. It sometimes got so bad—I remember how on the anniversary of Vincent's death last year—I went outside late at night—I couldn't stand it in the house—it was blowing and raining and it was pitch black—and everywhere in the houses—I saw lights and people sitting companionably together—and I felt so abandoned—that I understood for the first time what he must have felt—at those times when everyone turned away from him and it was as if 'there was no place for him on earth'. And when you reproached me that evening, saying that I had damaged his reputation and that I couldn't *mean* that I loved his work—and all those other things—you hurt me so much it made me ill. I'm not saying this to blame you—but I wish I could make you feel what Vincent's influence on my life has been. He helped me to order my life such that I can find peace in myself—serenity—that was their favourite word, the two of them, and something that they regarded as the ultimate.[23] I have found serenity—I haven't been unhappy this long, lonely winter—'sorrowful, yet always rejoicing'; that is also one of his sayings that I have only now learned to understand.[24] And although it's true that I did many things clumsily and wrong—I really didn't deserve for you to judge me *on that*—when I was so alone and yet acted as best I could! I just had to get all this off my chest![25]

Jo was someone who could not disguise her feelings, and her assertion that Van Gogh had a huge significance for her was obviously sincere. She was determined to establish his name as an artist and tell the world about the battle he had fought in his life. Once Veth had spent time looking in depth at Van Gogh's self-portraits, he began to appreciate them more. In *De Amsterdammer* of 27 March 1892 it became clear that he wholeheartedly accepted him as a painter. Jo was delighted by this public recognition. Her giving him Vincent's letters to read—she described this as 'the most sacred thing that exists for me, which no one has known anything about before you'—was the greatest proof of her trust she could have given him.[26] She had wanted to say that when she handed over the bundle, but it had been too difficult for her (just how many letters were in the bundle is not clear). She was often able to express herself on paper better than she could when she was face to face with someone.

The bickering over the value of Van Gogh's art may have ceased, but that was not the end of it. Their continued clashes were not just about their views of Van Gogh. Their personalities were very different. Veth admitted that he had a high opinion of himself and that he was 'intellectually proud'.[27] Although their paths crossed on various occasions, the relationship between the rather arrogant Veth and the retiring Jo was never close—a far cry from her intimacy with Anna.

Vincent's work gains recognition

Piet Boele van Hensbroek had suggested to Jo that they should put together an exhibition for the newly founded artists' society the Haagsche Kunstkring in 1891. He asked if she would lend him a portfolio of drawings, so that he could persuade his fellow members Théophile de Bock and Pieter de Josselin de Jong that it was a worthwhile idea. Boele van Hensbroek, who had been a friend of Theo's, had good contacts with Jo.[28] The Haagsche Kunstkring's liberal approach offered a chance to present progressive art and it embraced this attitude towards modern art: it was a perfect opportunity to show the work to artists and art lovers. The exhibition was eventually staged in May and June 1892.[29]

Jo took the initiative and wrote to De Bock through the intermediary of Marius Bauer.[30] Jan Toorop, like De Bock one of the founders of the Kunstkring, then asked if he could come and make a selection.[31] He was also a member of Les Vingt, was familiar with European avant-garde painting and played a crucial role in the introduction of Neo-Impressionism in the Netherlands. Like Isaäcson, he probably put Jo in touch with art dealers. Toorop had asked Van Eeden to produce a modest publication about Van Gogh's life and work, with excerpts from the letters to Theo, possibly in combination with his earlier article in *De Nieuwe Gids*.[32]

Veth and Toorop were not the only players in this run-up phase to proclaiming Van Gogh's importance. Richard Roland Holst was also of great significance to Jo at this time; he was touched by the art—to him it was the essence of colour and expression—and he loathed people who regarded the works as an illustration of the drama of Van Gogh's life or a symptom of his mental illness. He had expressed this view in *De Amsterdammer*. Jo then wrote to him, saying that she thought it a shame that he had not dared to admit his admiration generously and openly. Roland Holst told Toorop that he had not responded to this and remarked condescendingly:

> Mrs van Gogh is a charming little woman, but it irritates me when someone goes into raptures about something they do not understand at all, and blinded by sentimentality are still supposed to be able to be purely critical. It's schoolgirlish drivel, that's all. . . . Mrs van Gogh would think that the best work was the one that was most overblown and sentimental—that made her cry the most; she forgets that her grief turns Vincent into a God.[33]

And so Jo was scornfully dismissed as a novice—an attitude doubtless informed by the fact that these men were not accustomed to such an independent woman with an opinion. Despite his vexation, Roland Holst promised Jo he would write an article about the Hague exhibition in which he would show her that he was by no means afraid of proclaiming his admiration for Van Gogh 'very openly and very loudly', as he wrote to her.[34] Nothing ever came of the article, but in the autumn Roland Holst made considerable efforts to help Jo in organizing an important exhibition.

Encouraged by the positive reactions to Van Gogh's work she had received, Jo began knocking on doors like a travelling salesman. She called at Elbert Jan van Wisselingh's gallery in Amsterdam's Kalverstraat. 'I had a small thing by Vincent with me—but a very, very fine one—which I showed and now they want a couple of his works on commission. What a triumph!'[35] Six days later she received a bid of 125 guilders for the painting 'poplars with two small pink figures, which you brought to us in person'.[36] Jo must have decided that the offer was too low, for the little painting in question, *Cypresses and Two Women* (F 621 / JH 1888), has never left the collection.

In the same month, the Oldenzeel gallery in Rotterdam showed twenty paintings and drawings by Van Gogh. Jo was extremely pleased, particularly because it was widely covered in the press. Oldenzeel did, though, tell Jo that four or five hundred guilders each was 'MUCH TOO HIGH'. Jo went to Rotterdam to discuss prices with him and look at the exhibition. The drawings showed to advantage, but she thought the paintings did not look good, chiefly because of the ugly frames.[37] Oldenzeel sold the drawing *A Corner of the Asylum Garden* (F 1505 / JH 1697) for a hundred guilders.[38]

The winter of 1891–92 had taken a lot out of Jo. At the end of March, she sat quietly in the garden with her little son for the first time that year, enjoying the flowering bird cherry, the berberis twigs and the song of the blackbirds. When Mrs van Gogh came to stay for a few weeks, Jo saw her as 'a piece of Theo' and reflected on how difficult it would be ever to live with someone else again.[39] She found running her boarding house a more onerous task than it had been in the first year, and she had to put aside her work on the transcriptions and on abridging the letters for the time being because she felt 'too overstrained'.[40] In the meantime she had managed to put the huge piles of correspondence in order and had realized that the St Rémy letters were missing. Albert Aurier had borrowed this set from Theo so that he could write his biographical sketch, and Jo asked him to send them back: 'It was such an important period, and save for those there is nothing missing from the correspondence, which I am currently preparing for the press.' It is evident that she already knew for certain that she wanted to publish the letters, although it was to be another twenty-two years before the edition appeared. She said that she was happy with the attention Van Gogh's work was getting and was only too aware of her own share in it: 'It is the only thing I can do in memory of my husband and for Vincent.'[41]

Meanwhile, she was fully engaged in promoting Van Gogh in her immediate circle. She had let Jan Veth read a great many of the letters, and she and Toorop were making the arrangements for the planned exhibition in The Hague. He wrote: 'I'm pleased you've had all the paintings mounted; I shall see to wooden frames.'[42] An exhibition of sixteen Van Gogh paintings organized by Émile Bernard at the Le Barc de Boutteville gallery opened in April. Jo actually went to Paris to see it.[43] Bernard had commissioned photographs of twelve works, which he offered for sale in order to cover the cost of the exhibition.[44] This was at the same time a deliberate move to bring the work to a wider audience. Her conversations with Bernard in Paris would have encouraged Jo to continue on the same path.

Amidst all the exertions, she paused on her wedding anniversary, profoundly aware of what she was missing:

> There's something of the infinite in my love for my boy—but it's not enough for me—every day he takes a step further away from me, becomes more independent—he needs me less. That's good—that's what must happen—but I—I remain with my poor, discontented heart, that still wants so much, desires so much. . . . Is everything over for me now?

It happened less often than before, but there were still 'days of dullness and grimness—of nothing'.[45]

And yet, it was in this period that she felt the urge to start writing again. She often looked at situations from a literary point of view. After a concert given by her sister, the soprano Betsy, and the violinist Aafje de Lange, she tried to capture something of the atmosphere in words, describing De Lange as 'indescribably energetic—powerful—nervous with only that slightly Chinese curved line in her eyes—something languorous—something of an odalisque or a sphynx'. Not long before this she had wondered: 'Shall I ever learn to use my pen to write something original? . . . it always stirs and swirls within me.'[46] She turned again to the life and letters of George Eliot, in which she found much that resonated with her, 'including the urge to create—but the creation itself, alas—will probably never come to me'.[47] It rekindled Jo's love of reading and she devoured, among other things, a biography of Alfred de Musset and Huysmans' novel *En ménage*.

Van Gogh in The Hague and Antwerp

The selling exhibition of forty-five paintings, forty-four drawings and one lithograph by Van Gogh ran from 16 May to 6 June 1892 at the Haagsche Kunstkring. The society had taken three rooms on the top floor of Café Riche in the Passage. This extensive overview fulfilled one of Jo's long-held wishes, although she was not entirely happy with Toorop's layout: 'It was not *splendid*—not enough trouble had been taken for that—but there was space and light for viewing the paintings—that was all.'[48] She went to the opening with Willemien van Gogh and had a pleasant conversation with Jozef Israëls. He compared Van Gogh's efforts to paint the impossible, such as the sun, with the bold, trail-blazing artistic endeavours of Richard Wagner. Afterwards Jo went back to Leiden with Willemien, and stayed the night there.

It emerges from the exhibition catalogue that a number of works were not for sale. This was a clever tactic that Jo used throughout her life. By interspersing works that were for sale with star pieces that she wanted to keep in the collection, she did justice to Van Gogh's oeuvre and sparked visitors' interest in buying. She was quite clear from the outset about which paintings and drawings she wanted to keep herself. They included *Self-Portrait as a Painter* (F 522 / JH 1356), *Peach Tree in Blossom* (F 557 / JH 1397), *Almond Blossom* (F 671 / JH 1891) and *Orchards in Blossom* (several versions of this). Jo was keen to know the name of the buyer of *Wheatfield after a Storm* (F 611 / JH 1723), which had sold for two hundred and seventy guilders in The Hague, and learned that it was the Danish artist Johan Rohde.[49] According to Théophile de Bock, the exhibition provoked considerable debate, and at the last moment Jan Veth, writing in *De Amsterdammer*, encouraged art lovers not to miss it.[50]

While everyone in her circle was involved in their own affairs, Jo often felt alone. Her work in the boarding house did nothing to improve her mood: 'I have to keep devising meals the whole time—and get cross with the maids—those are my two main occupations.'[51] She frequently thought about her little Vincent's future. She had heard that Lies van Gogh, who had married Jean Philippe du Quesne van Bruchem in December 1891, was pregnant and secretly hoped that the baby would be a girl. 'If it's a boy, it will be called Theo—oh—I wouldn't like that—little Vincent's oldest son—he must be a little Theo.'[52] But Lies gave birth to a son on 20 November 1892—and he was called Theodore.

Meanwhile, Van Gogh's art had become more widely known and the hoped-for snowball effect took hold. In April, the Belgian artist Henry van de Velde, through the intermediary of Jan Toorop, had asked Jo if he could borrow some works by Van Gogh for the first exhibition of L'Association pour l'Art, the Antwerp counterpart of Les Vingt in Brussels. The young artists wanted to conscript Van Gogh into their generation, a notion that pleased Jo.[53] She consequently seized the opportunity and had seven works sent from The Hague to Antwerp, which meant that she had to provide alternatives for the Kunstkring. De Bock wrote to her, saying that their arrangement had been broken, but he was nevertheless happy that she could fill in the gaps.[54] And so the Antwerp Ancien Musée de Peinture showed nine paintings and three drawings in May and June 1892. As they had at the time of Les Vingt, the public, with the exception of a few enlightened souls, were indignant and sometimes downright scandalized by Van Gogh's art.[55]

In June Jo went to the opening of the 'Keuze-tentoonstelling van hedendaagsche Nederlandsche schilderkunst' (Exhibition of Selected Contemporary Dutch Painting) in Arti et Amicitiae, held on the occasion of Amsterdam University's anniversary celebrations. Jan Veth and Johan Ankersmit, who later became a journalist, had selected Van Gogh's paintings *Pink Peach Trees* (F 404 / JH 1391) and *Rain* (F 650 / JH 1839), but she did not think it had been a good choice. Clearly, she had had no say in the matter. She would much rather have staged a one-man show in Arti.[56] It was a success, though: in the end 3,993 paying visitors came in the space of five and a half weeks.[57]

Jo felt harried and tried to combat this nervous agitation. Although she would have far rather played happily with little Vincent, she often had to draw back—sorrowful and lonely—in her grief at Theo's death. One of the ways she kept herself in hand was to try to be more objective and describe her surroundings.[58] Meanwhile she and Anna Veth-Dirks devoted themselves to studying the art of the Renaissance. They read the biography *Michel Ange* by Émile Ollivier, and their studious evenings together did her good. Again, she expressed her wish: 'The desire in me to write is becoming stronger than ever, I see and feel much more clearly ... I have to wait until the urge to create becomes so strong—that I can't ignore it.' As an exercise she wrote a description of one of her boarding house guests in her diary.[59]

Willemien van Gogh came to call and enjoyed her visit at Villa Helma, where she met the ladies Mensing and Liernur. Miss Liernur rented a room in the boarding house that summer.[60] After they left, Marie Mensing and her niece Line Liernur, headmistress of a girls' school, wrote that they had enjoyed playing with the 'little sweetie' and had felt 'comradeship.'[61] In 1897 the militant Mensing co-founded a female suffrage movement, the Vereeniging voor Vrouwenkiesrecht (VVVK), in Kampen. She wrote about cooperative household management, sexual liberation and marriage in social democratic and feminist papers.[62] Jo kept in close touch with her until at least 1915—in the discussions with Mensing she heard about the ideals of the socialists Pieter Troelstra, Floor Wibaut, Herman Gorter and Henriette Roland Holst, which struck a chord in her.

Throughout the summer of 1892, Jo's melancholy was compounded by earache and deafness. At the end of August, she actually had a minor operation for the problem. She found it very difficult on her own. She had, though, been wholly absorbed in Louis Couperus's recently published novel *Extaze. Een boek van geluk*. 'It gripped me—as no other book has done in ages—it's as though it was written from my soul—I think it's so good that I'd like to thank him for having written it.'[63] Unsurprisingly, Jo identified strongly with the protagonist: Cecile van Even was also thirty years old and had been a widow for eighteen months. Sensitive and melancholic, Cecile has been left with two young boys and has quite emancipated ideas. She fears continuing loneliness and the emptiness in herself. In the novel,

Cecile is attracted to Taco Quaerts. She speaks of a kind of magnetism and their love develops as emotional mysticism. She experiences a moment of divine empathy and their being together is ecstatic. When Taco leaves her at the end of the book, despite her despair and bitterness she is grateful for the happiness she has experienced.[64]

The parallels between Jo and the character in this novel are remarkable. Jo, too, experienced every impression intensely and yearned for someone to love. Thoughts of what had been and the loss of what might have been played constantly in her mind. A large part of her ability to love was stifled. She found most affection and love in little Vincent, in the books she read and in her cat. 'My abundance of tenderness or love, whatever it is—I now devote solely to the child—who can never have too much of it—and the cat. My sweet little black puss, I never thought that I'd become so attached to you.'[65] This remark is an interesting contribution to the history of domestic pets in the Netherlands, for it was in precisely this period that the cat was embraced as a pet by the middle class and emotional attachment to companion animals grew.[66]

Jo looked back on her two birthdays with Theo, and the last two without him. She addressed him directly in her diary:

> Theo, darling, I shall look after our little boy well and do my best to be a good example for him—I promise you that, my own, dear husband, whom I love so much, oh so much. Stay around us with your spirit—your spirit of love, of humility and simplicity—I need it so badly.[67]

When she lapsed again into such a melancholy mood, she stayed up late into the night re-reading her correspondence with Theo. Jo so longed for comforting warmth that she could understand that a man in such circumstances would visit a prostitute:

> Oh, how I understand Theo's life in Paris—poor darling, how often he felt unhappy and then sought—sought solace—which only resulted in remorse. We women bear it, but—it makes us ill and miserable, and what's the good of that!![68]

She tried with all in her power to change her mood by reading. She read *Serres chaudes* (1889) by Maurice Maeterlinck, *La maison d'un artiste* (1881) by Edmond de Goncourt and *Bonheur* (1891) by Paul Verlaine—this last probably in preparation for Verlaine's appearance in Amsterdam. On 8 and 9 November he read aloud from his work at Maison Couturier on Keizersgracht. Jo wrote wryly in her diary that she could barely hear what he was saying—'my observations about him in public were all I got out of that evening (which cost me two and a half guilders)'.[69] This disappointing outing did not really encourage her to go to such events more often; she preferred to spend time talking with her emancipated friends or settle down under her trusty reading lamp. She read Frederik van Eeden's *Johannes Viator—het boek van de liefde* (1892), in which the protagonist concludes that physical love is only acceptable when it has its roots in spiritual love. After she had read it, Jo turned to her diary and wrote: 'Anyone who's truly experienced love . . . will already know that it's the highest, the only, the great, absolute happiness—creation, with all the urges there are in us for something good, something great.' Approvingly, she quotes Jules Michelet, who wrote of a loved child 'the mother conceived it in heaven'.[70] Jo believed that women understood love better than men like Van Eeden. She saw it in herself and in Martha van Eeden, and in the character Cecile van Even in Couperus's *Extaze*. In her view, Van Eeden himself lacked depth in life. At the same time, she had to admit that his search for different forms of love in *Johannes Viator* had resulted in a good book.

Success in Amsterdam

After Rotterdam, Paris, The Hague and Antwerp, at the end of 1892 it was Amsterdam's turn. The Van Gogh exhibition in the grand Panorama building on Plantage Middenlaan demanded Jo's full attention. Roland Holst had agreed to help back in September and felt honoured that in this pleasant task he could 'openly prove my admiration for Vincent's talent'.[71] He kept Jo informed about progress, and about his contact with Henry van de Velde, who was going to supply extra fabric for the wall covering—it was turquoise and gave the space a fresh feel. Jo started preparations for transporting the works.[72]

Letters flew back and forth discussing how everything should be hung and what sort of invitations should be sent out. For Roland Holst, one thing was non-negotiable: 'The opening *must* be lavish and solemn, and having paying public at the opening would spoil that.' He also expected Jo to keep the vernissage exclusive. Roland Holst proposed hanging 'orchards in blossom in the middle, to the left of them the olives and the blue-toned paintings, and St Rémy mountains and the yellow-toned paintings on the right', and asked Jo what she thought.[73]

The exhibition opened in Panorama's gallery on 17 December 1892. It was scheduled to run until 5 February 1893, but was so successful it was extended for a week. Jo had established the chronology of the eighty-seven paintings and twenty drawings. *The Potato Eaters* (F 82 / JH 764) was the only work made in the Netherlands in the show. Magazines carrying favourable articles by Octave Mirbeau, Albert Aurier and others lay open on tables. Roland Holst had been the driving force behind this. In consultation with Jo, he had written a short introduction to the catalogue, which included quotations from the letters, and he had designed a lithograph for the cover—a withered sunflower with dry leaves and a halo encircling the stem above the drooping flower, against a dark background with a setting sun. Below was the name 'Vincent' (Figure 32). The halo was traditionally reserved for Christ or saints. Although Roland Holst had said not long before that he was against seeing Van Gogh's work purely as an illustration of the drama of his life, his lithograph was in fact the earliest known image of Van Gogh as a martyr to art.[74] Four years later, this romantic picture of the suffering artist was magnified still further when the makers of an exhibition in Groningen saw fit to hang a crown of thorns above a portrait of Van Gogh that Jo had provided.

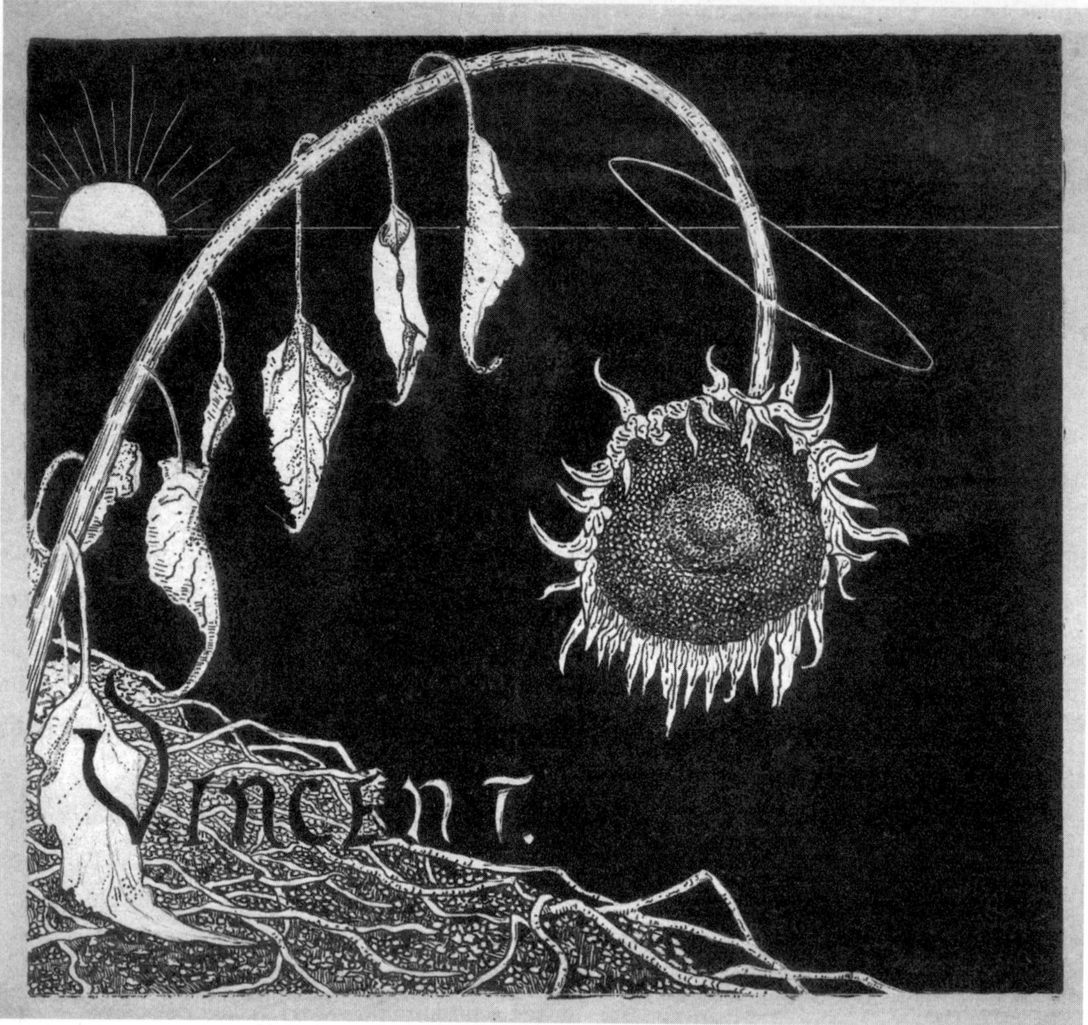

Figure 32 Richard Roland Holst, cover illustration for the catalogue of the exhibition *Tentoonstelling der nagelaten werken van Vincent van Gogh in kunstzaal Panorama in Amsterdam*, December 1892.

As thanks for all his efforts, Jo gave Roland Holst the drawing *Landscape with Arles in the Background* (F 1475 / JH 1435) and told him he could also choose a painting. He picked *The Alyscamps ('Leaf-Fall')* (F 487 / JH 1621). This large canvas hung above the fireplace in his house at 25 Noordermarkt in Amsterdam, where it was a conversation piece for visitors—as *The Sower* had proved to be at Van Eeden's. Again, Jo was very well aware of what the beneficial effect of such a gift could be.[75] During the exhibition, two paintings, a drawing and a lithograph were sold for a total of six hundred and thirty guilders—the annual rent for Villa Helma.[76]

Jan Veth wrote a blazing review in *De Nieuwe Gids*, which pleased Roland Holst no end, and Jo doubtless as much. In the article, Veth placed Van Gogh's oeuvre in what was called Synthetism, a style of art in which the form is synthesized with the major idea or feeling of the subject, as Aurier had formulated it; Veth argued that Van Gogh 'synthetized the impressions of reality as revelations of a life of fierce pathos'.[77] Roland Holst informed Jo about several newspaper articles and responded in similar terms:

> All we who see the work distinct from the person admire above all the powerful rigour, the Old Testament in him, his dramatic force, which was so strong that even his most delicate subjects, 'the orchards in blossom', were works of great intensity.[78]

When the exhibition ended, he asked Jo to come to Amsterdam so that she could decide how the works were to be packed and where they were all to be sent.[79]

Although there was no question of general appreciation—some reactions were downright hostile and it would be years before the general public would really accept and understand Van Gogh's art—interest had been kindled.[80] Van Gogh was no longer an unknown in the Netherlands and all the attention in the press provided a sound foundation on which to increase familiarity with his oeuvre in future shows, selling exhibitions, presentations and art appreciation sessions. Publications by Joseph Isaäcson, Adrien Obreen, Richard Roland Holst, Ida Heijermans, Jan Veth, Leo Simons, Etha Fles and others had prepared the way for more publicity. Jo saw the importance of this from the outset and kept a close eye on the process.

Despite the successes of 1892, Jo remained profoundly unhappy. If we are to believe her diary, aside from Van Gogh's work there were only two real factors in her life: emptiness and her son. On New Year's Eve she wrote: 'Everything's empty, everything around me has gone—except the child, the child.'[81] A day later, she wrote that she could accept anything as long as little Vincent could remain a source of eternal joy for her. This bond between mother and son became increasingly intense as time passed. To her, he was the most important thing she had and for years they were inseparable.

Jo began 1893 seriously depressed. She had long felt tired and weak, and she only wrote in her diary a few times that year because the struggle to exist and constant sorrow took such a toll on her. Theo was in her thoughts every day and she lived part of the time in a parallel universe: she often dwelt on the past and tried to endure Theo's absence in the present.[82]

Van Gogh's letters in the *Mercure de France*

The editor Alfred Vallette and Émile Bernard set about publishing Van Gogh's letters to Bernard in the art journal *Mercure de France*. Vallette asked Andries Bonger if he could supply translations of letters to Theo written in Dutch and Bernard asked Jo for additions.[83] She was instantly on board. As she was organizing the letters Van Gogh had written in Arles, a period that included the events involving Paul Gauguin, she had seen how 'very remarkable' these letters were. And she knew that she had a strong supporter in Bernard: 'You know better than I that they must be published.'[84] By return he asked if she would send all the letters in French, not just those from Arles. He wanted to print extracts from them: 'those that may be interesting about Vincent's oeuvre and through which I can show his temperament.'[85] Jo's faith in the postal service is remarkable: she sent Van Gogh's original letters to Bernard, who was in Pont-Aven in Brittany at the time. He promised to send them back quickly, but that did not happen.[86] He hung on to the originals for a very long time, even while he was touring around Italy and then staying in Constantinople (now Istanbul). Jo was naturally concerned about the fate of the vulnerable manuscripts, but Vallette reassured her, writing that Bernard kept sending him transcripts and was keeping the originals carefully. By the end of August, Bernard had finished the transcriptions in a monastery on the Greek island of Samos, where he had ensconced himself as a monk.[87]

Jo was prudent enough to help illustrate the important publication in the *Mercure*. Vallette asked her to send drawings packed between two pieces of strong cardboard. She sent ten. With two attractive illustrations per issue they had enough for five instalments.[88] A month later she received three copies of the *Mercure* and immediately ordered some more.[89] Bernard had cut repetitions, trivial facts and family matters out of the letters because, in his view, they said nothing about Van Gogh's ideas on art.[90] Vallette kept the drawings so that he could put them on sale and suggested that Jo should note down the prices on the proofs he had sent earlier. If she liked, he could also take the drawings to Tanguy, who still had a few Van Goghs in stock.[91]

In *De Amsterdammer* of 4 February 1893, Jan Veth informed the Dutch public about the noteworthy foreign publication. He wrote about Vincent's self-portrait in the *Mercure*: 'The expression on the face of this fearful, resolute man, who could paint and write, so strong and also as robust as if he was wielding a sledge hammer.'[92] Veth meanwhile had come to understand precisely what sort of telling blows Van Gogh could deliver—not just as a painter, but as a writer, too. His words prove that Jo's efforts to get him on her side had had the desired effect. *De Telegraaf* also featured the French publication.[93] Responding to all the attention, Piet Boele van Hensbroek, writing in *De Nederlandsche Spectator*, expressed the wish and expectation that Vincent's letters to Theo would one day be published in their entirety and in a respectful manner.[94]

It was 1896 before Jo got back the letters she had lent to Bernard. It must have been a huge relief when she finally got her hands on the package, which had been sent from Egypt. Bernard hoped that Van Gogh's complete correspondence would one day be published and in a dignified manner. If there was anything he could help Jo with, she should not hesitate to let him know.[95]

Van Gogh in Denmark

Johan Rohde followed up his purchase of Van Gogh's *Mountain Landscape* in the spring of 1892 a year later, when he asked Jo if she would let him have paintings for an exhibition in Denmark. Jo sent him twenty paintings and some drawings, acting as Theo would have done:

> I perfectly recall that my husband often talked to me about Mr Mourier Petersen and the free exhibition—and said that in Denmark they are more advanced in painting than Holland because they like modern painting more. I am convinced that he would also have sent you his brother's pictures. It's because of this that I immediately accept your invitation to exhibit them in Copenhagen.[96]

Again, Richard Roland Holst offered his services and helped her to make the selection.[97]

Rohde asked Jo to finalize the arrangements with the Danish artist Georg Seligmann, who was in Haarlem at the time. Seligmann wrote to Jo in his capacity as ambassador of the artists' society 'Den Frie Udstilling' Rohde had founded, which staged annual exhibitions.[98] He visited the 'quite young, extremely friendly widow' and also met Van Gogh's mother on this occasion, as he told Rohde. He also reported on the odd way the prices were arrived at: 'There are several paintings whose prices and titles I don't know, but you will have them as soon as I get them in. By the way, I helped set the prices for other things that had not yet been valued. But anyway, the lady is also prepared to receive an offer if need be.'[99] It is clear that Jo needed to toughen up her act as a businesswoman.

Things moved fast: the exhibition ran in Copenhagen from 26 March to the end of May. Some of the works were damaged in transport because of the poor condition of the crates—they contained twenty-nine Van Goghs from his last couple of years. The prices were low and three works were not for sale; those three did not include the *Sunflowers*, of which Jo still had different versions. Although the exhibition was due to end within a month, Seligmann visited her again in April and chose some more works. Evidently there was room to extend the exhibition.[100]

Rohde reported that the works had been well received by the critics and the public. He sent Jo the catalogue and a newspaper cutting with a favourable review, and wrote that he was sure that Van Gogh's work would now become better known in Denmark.[101] She got one of her friends to translate the article.[102] At the end of May he let Jo know that if she was willing to reduce the prices there might still be buyers, and sent her two more pieces from the newspapers. In her surprised response, 'Mon Dieu', she hoped that work would be sold in Copenhagen and said she would be prepared to drop the prices slightly for a combination purchase (a painting with a drawing) or two drawings together.[103] Three weeks later, Rohde made a counter-offer. The tug-of-war put a considerable strain on her resolve, but she stuck to her guns and did not yield. In the end, all this toing and froing came to naught and the correspondence between the two petered out.[104]

Van Nu en Straks and Henry van de Velde

At the beginning of 1893, the magazine *Van Nu en Straks* asked Jo if it could print some of the Van Gogh letters. The editor, Henry van de Velde, humbly requested her assistance; it was the first of thirteen letters he wrote to Jo.[105] Before contacting her, Van de Velde had sought Roland Holst's advice and asked him if he would send a recommendation. An amused Roland Holst wrote to Jo: 'It's funny that they think you're unapproachable—you, of all people, for whom nothing is too much trouble where Vincent is concerned.'[106]

The socially engaged Van de Velde supported the consolidation of artists and workers in a hoped-for glorious future—he credited the working class with purity of heart and simplicity of mind, and was convinced that art which expressed social involvement was capable of bringing about people's moral improvement. He believed that it was only when the working class could engage with high culture to some extent that class distinctions could be reduced, and proclaimed this ideal in articles and lectures.[107]

Jo did not hesitate for a moment in agreeing to publication in the magazine. Van de Velde expressed his admiration for the way she devoted herself to promoting this 'great deceased painter'.[108] He sent Jo proofs to correct and asked if she was happy with the way the letters had been shortened.[109] This was her initiation into editing and it helped her build up experience that would be very useful in later years.

The August issue of *Van Nu en Straks* was devoted in its entirety to Van Gogh. Its thirty-seven pages included three reproductions of drawings and an illustration of the *Portrait of Van Gogh* that the Englishman Horace Mann Livens had made when he and Van Gogh were students together at the art academy in Antwerp in the winter of 1885–6. There were also illustrations by Johan Thorn Prikker, Richard Roland Holst and Jan Toorop, and an introduction by Henry van de Velde. There was a generous selection of extracts from thirteen letters; in August, a satisfied Jo placed it on her desk beside the copies of the *Mercure de France*.[110]

Karel Alberdingk Thijm

In the same month, Jo got in touch with an important Dutch author who could well be of importance in widening knowledge of Van Gogh's letters. Jo had met Karel Alberdingk Thijm, who wrote as Lodewijk van Deyssel, through Van Eeden. He and his wife Cato had moved into Villa Villetta in Dillenburglaan in Baarn, where they lived until 1901.[111] Back in January 1889, Jo had read Van Deyssel's enthusiastic review of Émile Zola's *Le rêve* in *De Nieuwe Gids* and soon afterwards extracts from his own controversial novel *Een liefde* (1887), in which the sensual life of his character Mathilde was evoked in considerable detail, including a notorious scene in which she pleasures herself.[112]

Meeting Alberdingk Thijm was a bright spot in her life. He came to her house to look at Van Gogh's paintings and thought they were wonderful.[113] She was invited for a return visit, and the host and his little son Joopie met Jo and Vincent at the station. They had a splendid time in the idyllic house in the woods, although Jo was surprised to see how shabby his study was.[114] Soon afterwards, she sent him some of Van Gogh's letters. In her lengthy accompanying letter she addressed him with considerable respect:

> It is not much—for I was afraid to tire you with too large a batch—and if you finish them and would like to read what follows—I can send them to you at once. If I have made a mistake in giving you the *first* letters to read—and you would rather have something from a later period—the error is easily rectified.[115]

She was eager to hear his opinion. Alberdingk Thijm assured her: 'I hope to speak or write to you in more detail about the letters.'[116] It apparently went no further than conversations, since no letter about what he thought has survived. Thereafter, too, there is no trace; his reading of Van Gogh's letters, surprisingly, did not lead him to make an effort to bring them to the public's notice, an omission that Jo regretted. The recommendation of an author of his stature could have been an important stimulus in getting the letters published. With hindsight, it would have been better if she had let him read part of the later correspondence, for instance the letter in which Van Gogh declares his enthusiasm for the character Angélique—'very very beautiful'—in Zola's *Le rêve*, the book that had cast Alberdingk Thijm into raptures.[117]

In May 1895 she asked him to approach his old friend Jack Thomas Grein, founder of the Independent Theatre in London that had been established in 1891. She had come up with the idea of staging an exhibition of a few works by Van Gogh in the foyer of one of the theatres. Soon afterwards Alberdingk Thijm let her know that the location was unsuitable and that Grein had referred him to the Brook Street branch of Van Wisselingh's gallery. However, Jo knew that this was a dead end because she had already approached Van Wisselingh and had been turned down.[118]

Over the next few years Jo continued to visit Alberdingk Thijm and his family.[119] They had a great deal to talk about, particularly literature. Karel discussed books with her endlessly and lent her many, for instance, the recently published *En route* (1895) by Joris-Karl Huysmans. In 1899 Herman Gorter and his wife Wies Cnoop Koopmans, together with their friends Albert Verwey and Jacobus van Looy and their wives, invited Jo to join them for a meal at Hotel Groeneveld in Baarn to celebrate Karel and Cato's copper wedding anniversary—proof that she had been accepted into their circle.[120] Their friendship endured at least until 1914.

Domestic life between art movements

From October 1893 to February 1896, Jo kept a second cashbook for household expenditure. She used the standard *Huishoudboek voor Nederlandsche vrouwen* (Household Book for Dutch Women), in

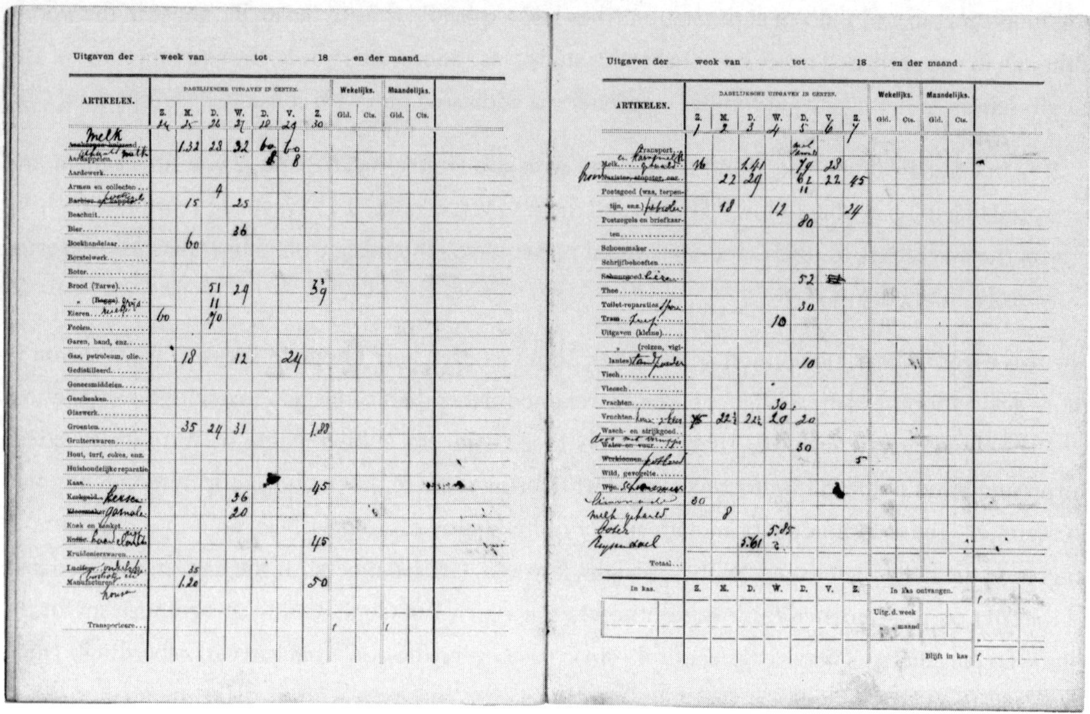

Uitgaven der week van tot 18 en der maand

ARTIKELEN.	Z. 24	M. 25	D. 26	W. 27	D. 28	V. 29	Z. 30	Wekelijks. Gld.	Cts.	Maandelijks. Gld.	Cts.
Melk		1.32	28	32	60	60					
Aardappelen					8	8					
Aardewerk											
Armen en collecten			4								
Barbier of kapper		15		25							
Beschuit											
Bier				36							
Boekhandelaar		60									
Borstelwerk											
Boter											
Brood (Tarwe)			51	29			39				
" (Rogge)			11								
Eieren	60		70								
Fooien											
Garen, band, enz.											
Gas, petroleum, olie		18		12		24					
Gedistilleerd											
Geneesmiddelen											
Geschenken											
Glaswerk											
Groenten		35	24	31			1.88				
Grutterswaren											
Hout, turf, cokes, enz.											
Huishoudelijke reparatie											
Kaas							45				
Kersen				36							
Garnalen				20							
Koek en banket											
Koffie							45				
Kruidenierswaren											
Lucifers		35									
Manufacturen		1.20					50				
Transporteere								f		f	

Uitgaven der week van tot 18 en der maand

ARTIKELEN.	Z. 1	M. 2	D. 3	W. 4	D. 5	V. 6	Z. 7	Wekelijks. Gld.	Cts.	Maandelijks. Gld.	Cts.
Transport											
Melk	16		1.41		79	28					
Naaister, stopster, enz.		22	29		61	22	45				
Poetsgoed (was, terpentijn, enz.)		18		12			24				
Postzegels en briefkaarten					80						
Schoenmaker											
Schrijfbehoeften											
Schuurgoed					52						
Thee											
Toilet-reparaties					30						
Tram				10							
Uitgaven (kleine)											
" (reizen, vigilantes)					10						
Visch											
Vleesch											
Vrachten				30							
Vruchten	[illegible]	22½	22½	20	20						
Wasch- en strijkgoed											
Water en vuur					30						
Werkloonen							5				
Wild, gevogelte											
Wijn											
	80										
		8									
			5.61	5.85							
Totaal											

In kas.	Z.	M.	D.	W.	D.	V.	Z.	In kas ontvangen.	f
								Uitg. d. week	
								" " maand	"
								Blijft in kas	f

Figure 33 Jo van Gogh-Bonger's everyday expenses between 1893 and 1896.

which daily outgoings could be neatly organized in columns.[121] All the important items, including 'matches' and 'the poor and collections', were pre-printed across two pages for a week. Jo entered everything in such tiny writing that she only used one double page in two weeks. This meant that she made the book last two years instead of one (Figure 33).

On her thirty-first birthday, she looked back in her diary at a year full of worry, struggle and sorrow. Every day she was filled with melancholy thoughts of Theo, and this was fuelled by the many contacts in the family and beyond. Meijer de Haan, for instance, wrote that he would really like to talk about Theo, 'this irreplaceable artist friend'. Jo replied immediately. De Haan thanked her and told her that, like her, he so longed to share their thoughts.[122] Jo spent Christmas in Amsterdam, over the new year she stayed in Leiden, and in between she had been to see Line Liernur and Marie Mensing in Haarlem.[123] She wrote sadly about her visit to Willemien, Mrs van Gogh and Anna in Leiden: 'It does so much good to feel that there are still people who are fond of you.'[124] This strong bond with the Van Goghs would continue to help motivate her.

Vincent's fourth birthday was celebrated on 31 January. A little flag fluttered outside; indoors Hans and Paultje van Eeden, Saskia and Lidaatje Veth and Joopie Alberdingk Thijm played with the birthday boy. At the end of the day, Jo mused:

> I'm sitting alone in the small drawing room—it's pleasant in the lamplight—I can *feel* the fine, special—tenderness of the atmosphere in this little room—there are flowers on the table beside me—a delicate, pinkish tulip, slender on its pale green stem . . . books on the table—the fairy tale of the ugly duckling—a book by Tolstoy that I once discussed with Theo.[125]

There were always children's books all over the house. When the grown-up Vincent read Randolph Caldecott's *The Farmer's Boy* with his own children, he recalled, 'it is one of my oldest books; I can still see myself sitting beside my mother, who always did so much with me.'[126]

Julien Tanguy died in Paris on 6 February 1894. The next day, his widow wrote to Andries about the last batch of Van Gogh paintings they still had in their storeroom. She had contacted him because she did not have Jo's address.[127] In the months that followed, Jo received several requests from French Van Gogh admirers who were interested in the works at Tanguy's. She answered a letter from the artist Émile Schuffenecker, whom she had never met. Because he said he had profound respect for Van Gogh's work, she agreed to the sale.[128] He offered three hundred francs for a painting of flowers and two hundred for a landscape. Jo agreed rather precipitately. We do not know which landscape she sold to Schuffenecker, but the other painting was the now iconic *Sunflowers in a Vase* (F 457 / JH 1666). Tanguy's widow asked for seventy-five francs commission.[129]

The remaining works she had went to the Durand-Ruel gallery, which kept them on consignment for a while. Charles Destrée, a partner of Durand-Ruel, asked Jo to send him the prices but she proposed that he could suggest prices himself—Destrée was more au fait with the market value of art in Paris.[130] She did, though, tell him boastfully that she had sold several works for eight hundred and a thousand francs in the Netherlands. As was to be expected, he set the prices extremely low. One collector offered five hundred and fifty francs for three works. Jo wrote that she would agree to two for that sum, but even that asking price was not accepted.[131]

In this same period, Paul Gauguin let Jo know that she probably had three Van Goghs that belonged to him: a *Augustine Roulin ('La berceuse')* (F 506 / JH 1670), an *Arlésienne* (possibly *Marie Ginoux ('The Arlésienne')* (F 542 / JH 1894) and a *Sunset in Arles*, which he had left with Theo when he set off on his travels. He was prepared to be flexible: he would be happy with equivalent works if she no longer had them.[132] When Jo replied that she did not know which sunset it was, Gauguin sent a sketch in a letter, from which it was clear that the painting he meant was *Reaper* (F 617 / JH 1753). She sent him the three works. In exchange, she received his painting *Women on the Banks of the River* (Plate 25).[133]

Meanwhile domestic life in Bussum continued, with difficult days, but plenty of high points, too, like the performance of 'Snow White, a fairy tale with music in five scenes', in which Saskia Veth, Paul and Hans van Eeden and Vincent van Gogh played dwarfs. And Jo was indulgent enough to treat herself with shrimps and with cherries in the summer.[134] She had to do something, for the older she got the more difficult she found this time of the year: 'Oh these dusty sunny summer days, I hate them.'[135] This was the only sentence she wrote in her diary in nine months. When she was seventeen, she had thought very differently about it. Then she knew: 'Yes, when summer comes I shall be perfectly happy again.'[136]

On the few occasions she went out, she did not enjoy herself at all. Over two evenings in mid-November, Frederik van Eeden read *De Broeders, tragedie van het recht* in the Gebouw der Maatschappij van den Werkenden Stand on Kloveniersburgwal in Amsterdam. A ninety-strong audience listened for two hours to the author's droning delivery, while the temperature in the room soared to an alarming height.[137] Jo was there and found it 'impossibly boring'. She was not alone in her opinion: the reviewer for *De Telegraaf* had been bored to death during the torture in the stifling room. The writer Herman Gorter had enough and left early.[138]

On New Year's Eve, Theo was, as always, close by. She addressed him as if in a prayer:

> I look back with yearning at those long, quiet evenings last year—alone with my books, with my memories! The child is delightful—he's sleeping peacefully in his little bed. Theo, darling, be with us again this year—your love, your gentleness, your goodness, let them come over us.[139]

An influential contact: Ambroise Vollard

The ambitious Ambroise Vollard, who was to become one of the most important dealers in contemporary art, recognized the value of Van Gogh's works at an early stage (Plate 26). He bought them in quantity and sold them at a handsome profit. In May 1895, he asked Jo if she would send him some works for the upcoming show in his gallery at 39 rue Laffitte. Émile Schuffenecker, Paul Gauguin and Madame Gramaire-Aurier had already agreed to make their Van Goghs available. The exhibition ran from 4 to 30 June and included some twenty paintings by Van Gogh. On 7 June, Vollard reported that the show was a great success, and again asked Jo whether she would like to send something. She certainly wanted to, but she responded so slowly that by the time she finally sent them it was too late.[140] She sent him a list of the titles of the paintings and drawings, and concluded: 'I hope you will do good business with what I have sent you. It would have been too late to send you others, and in any case you will write to me before selling, won't you?'[141] In December she told him that the Dutch in Paris and the French art lovers who had been to see her regretted that there had been so little by Van Gogh in Paris. It must have been this that prompted her to make good this lack and at the same time extend the scope of her activities. Gradually the situation began to change: instead of Jo having to take the initiative herself, curiosity increasingly brought interested individuals, dealers and artists to her.

Vollard had acquired a taste for this and looked for other ways of getting hold of the artist's work. Shrewdly, he approached Joseph Ginoux, patron of the Café de la Gare in Arles. Ginoux had been Van Gogh's friend and owned a number of his paintings. Vollard pounced, and managed to extract works from Ginoux's collection for a pittance: three canvases for a hundred francs.[142] He also sold for Jo. In March 1896 he let her know that he had sold *Interior of a Restaurant* (F 549 / JH 1572) for a hundred and eighty francs.[143] Several artists had told him about Jo's extensive collection and he wanted to know which other paintings she would be willing to sell. He went to see her in the autumn and they came to an agreement.[144] The list of titles and prices she drew up reveals that a great many superb works went to Paris (Plate 27).[145]

Vollard confirmed receipt of fifty-six paintings, fifty-four drawings and a lithograph by Van Gogh. He had discussed the prices with her, but saw to his surprise that she had put down higher sums. He cunningly made her a counter-offer, putting the ball back in her court.[146] Jo refused to give ground and now the dealer in Vollard came to the fore. He talked about a collector who wanted to buy a specific group of paintings on certain conditions, and made a new proposal. He also wanted to buy the Renoir and the Guillaumin in Jo's collection.[147] The selling exhibition eventually went ahead from December 1896 to February 1897. The works on offer were impressive and there was great interest in them, but Vollard was disappointed that sales did not really take off. Again, he raised the issue of changing the deal that had previously been proposed and haggled with her.[148] Jo was continually forced to recalculate and must have had difficulty fathoming Vollard's marketing strategy. In the end they reached an agreement and the sale went ahead.[149]

A few months before, Vollard had taken over from Alfred Vallette the drawings that were still with the *Mercure de France*, and at the end of March Jo called on him to return them 'with GREAT speed'—for she had to send them off that week for an upcoming exhibition in Groningen.[150] He sent back a crate of works and presented payment for a total of 2,340 francs for the works he had sold. The entry in her cashbook was not very specific: she put down 1,120 guilders for '3 triptychs, 1 portrait, Dr Gachet and 1 pair of drawings'.[151] The business of getting the money dragged on and on because Vollard had sent a cheque that could only be cashed in Paris. Jo was livid and looked for somebody to act for her. The relationship deteriorated after these experiences. Vollard turned his back on Jo and set his sights on the Van Goghs owned by Joseph Roulin and Émile Bernard.[152]

Vollard remained the most important dealer in Van Goghs in Paris until the turn of the century, contributing to the painter's early reputation in France. Between 1896 and 1899, he sold some twenty-five works from Jo's collection. He later acknowledged that it had been a great mistake to stop dealing in Van Gogh's work.[153]

At the same time as Jo was first in touch with Vollard in Paris, in May 1895 Lucien Moline of Galerie Laffitte wrote that he had a customer who was interested in buying a Van Gogh. He asked if Jo was prepared to sell and, if so, whether she could send three or four works to choose from with a list of prices.[154] Jo sent him seven works instead of three. Moline tried to persuade her with arguments—Pissarro had not been ashamed to sell a work for sixty francs so Jo could certainly make concessions; after all, she had enough works in stock. He wrote that he knew someone who would pay eight hundred francs for six of the seven canvases.[155] Shortly afterwards the offer was dropped even lower: eight hundred francs (less than four hundred guilders) for all seven works. Astonishingly, Jo agreed. She may have felt intimidated or that she had no choice.[156] Given that *Cypresses* (F 613 / JH 1746) was one of the works sold, it proved to be a very poor bargain for her. By way of comparison: in January 1896 Arti et Amicitiae in Amsterdam exhibited two paintings by Van Gogh that the C.M. van Gogh gallery was offering for four hundred and fifty and four hundred guilders, according to the *Algemeen Handelsblad*.[157] Had Jo been following the market for Van Gogh at the time—which one would be entitled to expect—such huge discrepancies in asking prices must have given her food for thought. She yielded far too easily in transactions like these—a clear sign of her uncertainty as a novice among seasoned art dealers. It took some time before she became more cautious about what she offered and gradually raised her asking prices. Her desire to see the paintings gain international recognition more than once won out over her satisfaction with what she earned. Or perhaps her mind was not wholly on the matter, for although life seemingly jogged along quietly in Koningslaan in Bussum, under that calm surface there was turmoil. This became more intense in the latter months of 1895: 'Oh, that longing for some fullness, richness of love in my life!'[158] It was not long before that wish was fulfilled. Over the next two years she had an affair with the painter Isaac Israëls—a relationship that was kept secret for a long time.

9

Playing with fire—Isaac Israëls

In September 1889, the twenty-seven-year-old Jo van Gogh-Bonger met the artist Isaac Israëls, three years her junior, at a soirée at the Hotel Continental in Paris. She thought he was 'very pleasant'.[1] After that Israëls visited Theo's gallery in boulevard Montmartre and viewed works by Van Gogh in the young couple's home.[2] In 1891, looking back on that visit, he wrote to Jo saying that he had delightful memories of it and that he had always found Theo to be such a likeable friend. He sounded her out: 'I wonder perchance if I could come and visit you, or perhaps one of these days you might visit me, which I would very much enjoy.'[3]

Israëls came from a prosperous Jewish family. He was not a practising Jew and his work shows barely any traces of Judaism. His father was the successful Hague School painter Jozef Israëls, and his mother was Aleida Schaap, who was apparently rather overbearing.[4] Isaac Israëls and George Breitner had studied at the Amsterdam Academy at the same time and they both captured street scenes populated by working class figures. In the 1890s the Amsterdam authorities gave Israëls permission to paint townscapes at his easel in the street. In these works, he tried to depict the fleeting hustle and bustle with swift line drawings and dynamic brushstrokes. He developed into a versatile painter. He lived in Paris for a while. In his own words, he had to be there so he could 'live like a vagabond'.[5] Israëls made several trips; in 1894, for example, he went to Spain and Morocco with his father and the writer Frans Erens, one of his best friends.

Erens described Israëls as restless, astute and well read. In Erens's eyes he was a virtuous, gentle man with a sense of humour, not afraid to make fun of himself. There is no end of anecdotes about their experiences. Israëls read the books of Giacomo Leopardi in Italian and knew passages from Cervantes's *Don Quixote* by heart. He loved writers like Verlaine, Zola and Huysmans. His friend wrote of his lifestyle without ties: 'He wanted to be independent and not be constrained by the possessions that life piles on us.'[6] Israëls had contacts with many Tachtigers and *Nieuwe Gids* contributors, including Van Eeden, Van Looy, Van der Goes, Van Deyssel, Veth and Kloos—precisely the circles in which Jo had found herself since she moved into Villa Helma.[7]

Erens and Israëls went on evening walks together through Amsterdam, hunting for street prostitutes. They strolled along Zeedijk, Warmoesstraat and Nes, visiting dance halls, variety theatres and cabarets.

A photograph taken at that time shows Israëls in the pose of a freethinking person who was full of himself (Plate 28). He sympathized with Domela Nieuwenhuis's Social Democratic League and jokingly described himself as 'a simple worker in search of a fortune'.[8] Israëls was of modest stature and had piercing dark eyes. This highly volatile, sandy-haired charmer went through life as a libertine, and Jo was not impervious to his charms.[9]

Renewed acquaintance

In 1891 and 1892 they came across one another now and then. Israëls had visited her once and they both attended an art appreciation event about Van Gogh at Arti et Amicitiae.[10] Starting in 1894, however, they had more frequent contact. Jo visited his studio on a number of occasions and sent him flowers more than once.[11] Although she missed Theo and still felt an emptiness inside, on the day before her thirty-second birthday she sensed that something was changing: 'It is as if something more powerful is growing up inside me—but sometimes so weak—oh so weak!'[12] She was someone who found it difficult to admit to her feelings, and a conversation with a young widow reminded her of this: 'But she's a pretty, worldly woman—she'll find solace sooner than I,' she reflected.[13] Jo withdrew into herself all too easily.

In their correspondence (Jo's letters to him have not survived), Isaac commented on how different their lives were: Jo in her home full of warmth, where she was seldom if ever alone; he an unmarried man, who always had to eat in cafés.[14] In November 1894, he arrived at Villa Helma with a portrait of little Vincent in a red shirt that he had painted at her request.[15] They looked at the art in Jo's home and walked to Van Eeden's together. Afterwards Isaac stayed for a meal with her. She analyzed her feelings and doubted whether he would want to visit her again: 'I'd like to know what he thought—oh, it's always the same—they come once and then I never see them again.'[16] It would seem that she had already had disappointments with other men in similar circumstances. In fact, they saw each other again the following day at a lecture given by Van Eeden. She had thought to speak to him there, but there was no more than a handshake. She was content when she was home again safe and sound. Less than two months later, she felt a sense of security when she was with him in his home, although she had a guilty conscience about enjoying an extramarital relationship so much.[17]

Israëls lived at 82 Oosterpark in Amsterdam, in what is now known as the Witsenhuis (Witsen House).[18] He had a studio on the ground floor, where he also slept. Over time, the studio above was occupied by, among others, George Breitner, Willem Witsen, Willem Kloos and Sara de Swart, who lived there with Anna Vis. Later Israëls had both storeys to himself. The location was agreeable, but it was rather noisy (Figure 34).

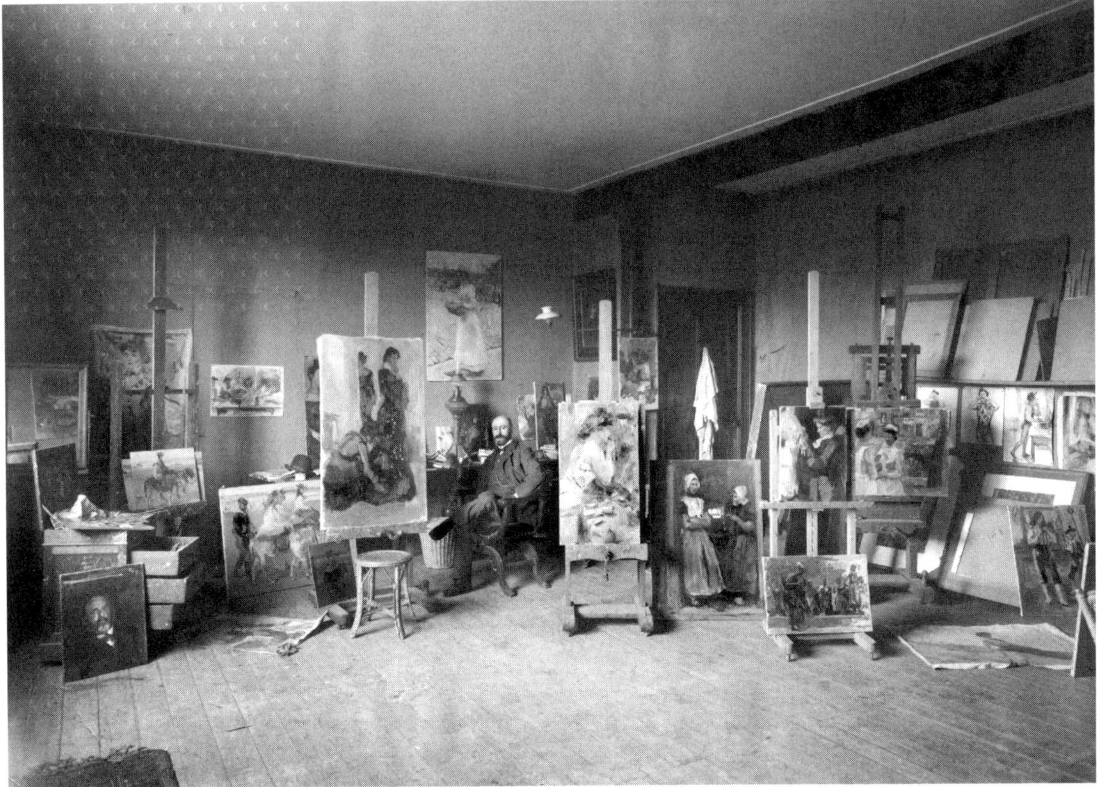

Figure 34 Isaac Israëls in his studio on the first floor of 82 Oosterpark in Amsterdam, 1903.

Jo found it pleasant there, as she wrote in her diary in January 1895:

> I only felt safe and comfortable in the studio with Israëls—they were wonderful afternoons, lazy I believe—he drew a little portrait of me—crayon—I just sat very still—resting easily and he talked—talked—brought back to me all sorts of thing from the past. It was very pleasant—very good—our feelings—then.[19]

The portrait she referred to must have been the sketch of her in black chalk (Figure 35).

They had a shared interest in art, literature and the theatre. Isaac had seen Victorien Sardou's *Gismonda* and told her all about it in a letter. He also advised Jo to read *Rêves étoilés* (1888) by Camille Flammarion. And he hoped she would visit him again: 'Do come and see me one afternoon some time. But drop me a line beforehand. It's much better than me coming to you.'[20] It goes without saying that they had greater freedom and latitude in Oosterpark than in Koningslaan in Bussum.

Their relationship became more intimate during the summer of 1895. Jo realized that 'he shook me awake out of my sad dreaming—my indifference—I want to dress a little better—still very, very

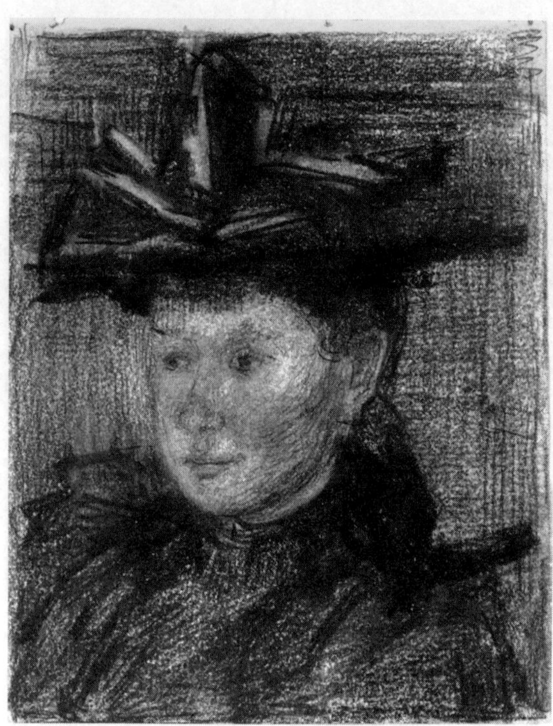

Figure 35 Isaac Israëls, *Jo van Gogh-Bonger*, 1895.

simply—but there must be something of myself in it.'[21] They had a surprise evening out together, which he had organized. It emerges from casual remarks that he was getting to know her better and better. When he wanted to arrange to see her he had meanwhile switched from the formal version of 'you' ('u') to the familiar ('je'): 'Let me know if you'll come,' and he continued as though they had known each other for years, 'but then don't change your mind (I can never be sure about you). And if you perhaps would rather not go, I will *absolutely* not be *cross* about it.'[22] But Jo very much wanted to go, and that week they saw a show with poets, comedians and cabaret artistes staged by the Chat Noir company in the Grand Théâtre in Amstelstraat. One of the numbers was a musical setting of the poem 'Berceuse bleue' by Gabriel Montoya, and she recorded the romantic opening lines in her diary: 'They were two lovers,/ who dreamt of distant love.'[23]

'My lovely young body'

After such preliminaries, a physical relationship was inevitable. 'I wrote nothing about that afternoon with Isaac Israëls—it was just an impulse, we played with fire—but there's no trifling with love . . . he pretended he loved me—it was *still* wonderful,' she confided in her diary.[24] So although she was not convinced of Isaac's love for her, she really enjoyed their shared intimacy. (The ellipsis . . . represents where three lines were cut out of the diary. What she had written there was clearly not intended for posterity. These words were permanently removed either by Jo herself or by her son, Vincent.)[25] Jo and Isaac found out a lot about one another while he was drawing her portrait. In December he wrote that he was not happy with the likeness he had made of her.[26] He then drew a portrait in red chalk from a photograph (Plate 29). Jo realized that the ties they had would never develop into marriage, but things might have turned out differently had she not had a child:

> oh, that wonderful, friendly—actually bare and empty studio with its memories! He gave me that fine calendar by Nieuwenhuis—we sat together in the chair and played—yes, what we do is really playing together. Then he brought me home—through the silent grey park, with the lights of the city in the distance. I've now put an end to the ambiguous nature of our relationship—I don't want to play with fire any longer. He is not a man for marriage—oh, if I was free and independent—how I would give myself to him—how he would enjoy my beautiful young body—how I would stand free and pure before him—no egoism—no tiresome aftermath of everything—I would want to give him nothing but pleasure—how happy we could be—pleasure is happiness. But I may not, if I did—I would make it impossible to earn for the child—so it's better that we don't see each other for the time being.[27]

After an inner struggle she decided to end the relationship. She was rather hurt when Isaac agreed immediately that it would indeed be better not to see one another for the time being.[28] Now she felt as though 'everything that was good in my life had been taken away'. Sobbing, she threw herself on her bed. After they exchanged a few letters their relationship had become 'an armed peace'.[29] The fact that, despite her closeness to others, Theo was still very much in her thoughts did not make life any easier for Jo.[30]

Sometimes she dropped in to see Isaac after she had visited her family: 'he was glad that I went—it was wonderful—just half an hour perhaps.'[31] In the summer he wanted to paint another portrait of her and urged her to make some time free to sit for him.[32] And in the autumn he looked forward to seeing her again.[33] Like Jo, Isaac had a cat, which he was very fond of. He drew some sketches of it for her and enclosed them in a letter (Plate 30). The cat used to curl up in the lining of his jacket when he was reading the paper in the evening.[34]

This picture was typical of their relationship for they were equally unable to let each other go, and their more or less platonic affair continued to be very fluid. Isaac was frank and tried to change Jo's expectations—unlike him, she sometimes still seemed to be seeking a more enduring union. He thought that she mistakenly saw him as a someone who had 'arrived', and wrote with a degree of irritation: 'you have no concept of the reality and the trouble one has to achieve anything, or nothing.' He clarified the situation with a metaphor:

> While you think I'm in a safe little cabin with my work and need nothing more than a sweet little woman, in fact I'm adrift at sea buffeted by several hurricanes. It's my duty to reject a passenger, even though that person still really wants to come with me. As I've told you many times before, I can't even *think*, about something more permanent I mean, in the way that you mean it.... If I thought or felt that we must and we *shall belong* together, I would say so. But let me be completely honest, that's not how I feel. I've always considered it as a magnificent mistake of yours, undeserved and unique *bonne fortune* [an incomparable success in love] and it was actually not kind of me to want to profit from it, but it was too enjoyable for me—and I'll never meet another person like you.... But I do think that it's the best thing for you if we don't see each other again.[35]

Despite these unambiguous words, they nevertheless went on seeing each other and Jo continued to take the train back and forth between Bussum and Amsterdam. From 1896 she no longer left the train at the Central Station but at the new Muiderpoort stop. Isaac assured her that he would collect her 'at the normal time, around half past seven.'[36]

They met regularly: 'Another delightful afternoon in the studio, oh, so delightful—at every meeting "we get closer together"—he was so sweet to me yesterday—so friendly,' she wrote in her diary in February 1896, but when she looked back on their relationship on New Year's Eve that same year—it had occupied Jo for much of her time—and they continued to meet frequently—she was not sure: 'it causes doubt and anxiety and trouble in my soul, and my peace and contentment are gone.'[37] This was as true, if no more so, of Isaac, as emerges from a 'key letter' in which he expressed his own restlessness in no uncertain terms: 'I think you were well on your way to forgetting me. Weren't you?' And he set out his ultimatum:

> I would much prefer it if we could agree on a set day, once a week for instance, during the day or in the evening.
>
> But it's true that you now have a seriously guilty conscience and that you've always been in such a dilemma.
>
> My dear, let me say once again honestly what the situation is.
>
> I really love you *very* much (there, are you happy now?) and I'm very happy with your friendship. Please don't doubt that I hate the fact that you are so often sad and fearful.
>
> I sometimes get upset about it, and then I feel guilty myself because inwardly I have guilt, too. Please don't say no.
>
> I shouldn't enjoy keeping you as my friend whilst knowing that I can't do what you would prefer.
>
> Perhaps this is the right moment for you to think hard about what's really best for you. Think about it very carefully, then take a bold decision and keep to it.
>
> Either comply with the voice of your conscience, family and tradition. Always tell them everything that's on your mind (what a spoilt child to find that so comforting).

Or—you know very well. Do it now because now is the moment that the family will engulf you again. Or—I'll never have no feelings about it. I can sense that's coming.

I'm taking this seriously, Jo, think carefully, ponder profoundly.

I shall abide by what you think is best, but you must also abide by it, if possible. (I shouldn't have written that last phrase). It's too much à la you to say 'if possible'. So let us, or rather you, decide now whether it's over, or it should be continued on a wider and more comprehensive scale. (Please excuse this poor metaphor).

Farewell or see you soon.[38]

The language could not have been clearer. The ball was now in Jo's court, but she continued to put off the decision. In the months that followed, Isaac visited Bussum a number of times, as he did on the evening of 1 April 1897. After that visit, Jo wondered whether it would be his last, but a month later she visited him—and what she wrote about it was the very last sentence in the fourth and final volume of her diaries: 'another afternoon at the studio brought us closer together again—and now another period of truce?'[39] Israëls's magnetic studio created a comforting atmosphere. Although the diary says nothing more about their on-again off-again affair, Isaac's letters provide a clear picture of their continuing relational struggles.

The fault lines became more evident. 'You're absolutely right to think that it's not worth the trouble. Only a moment or two in six months! You're much too good for that,' he wrote to her. He wondered whether he was actually capable of loving someone and concluded: 'So the best advice I can give you is to ditch me.'[40] Isaac felt that she should preserve her honour. Yet despite these blunt words, two weeks later he invited her to come to Scheveningen, Katwijk or Egmond aan Zee for a couple of days so they could spend some time wandering around together.[41] The plan did not go ahead, however, because Jo was struggling with her health, which made Isaac think that he should collect the 'poor little wretch' for a change.[42]

Sense of duty to the family and her little son

Isaac very much disliked the way that Jo interacted with her own family. This emerges from a letter, probably written in August 1897, containing a sketch of a girl on the beach—he was working in Scheveningen at the time (Figure 36).

Jo and her family had returned from their summer holiday at the seaside. Her independence, which she had always argued for so passionately, proved extremely relative. She could clearly not arrange a day with Isaac without having to account for herself to her family. He compared their influence to a malignant spider: 'I might still be here in September and of course I hope to see you then. I'd watch

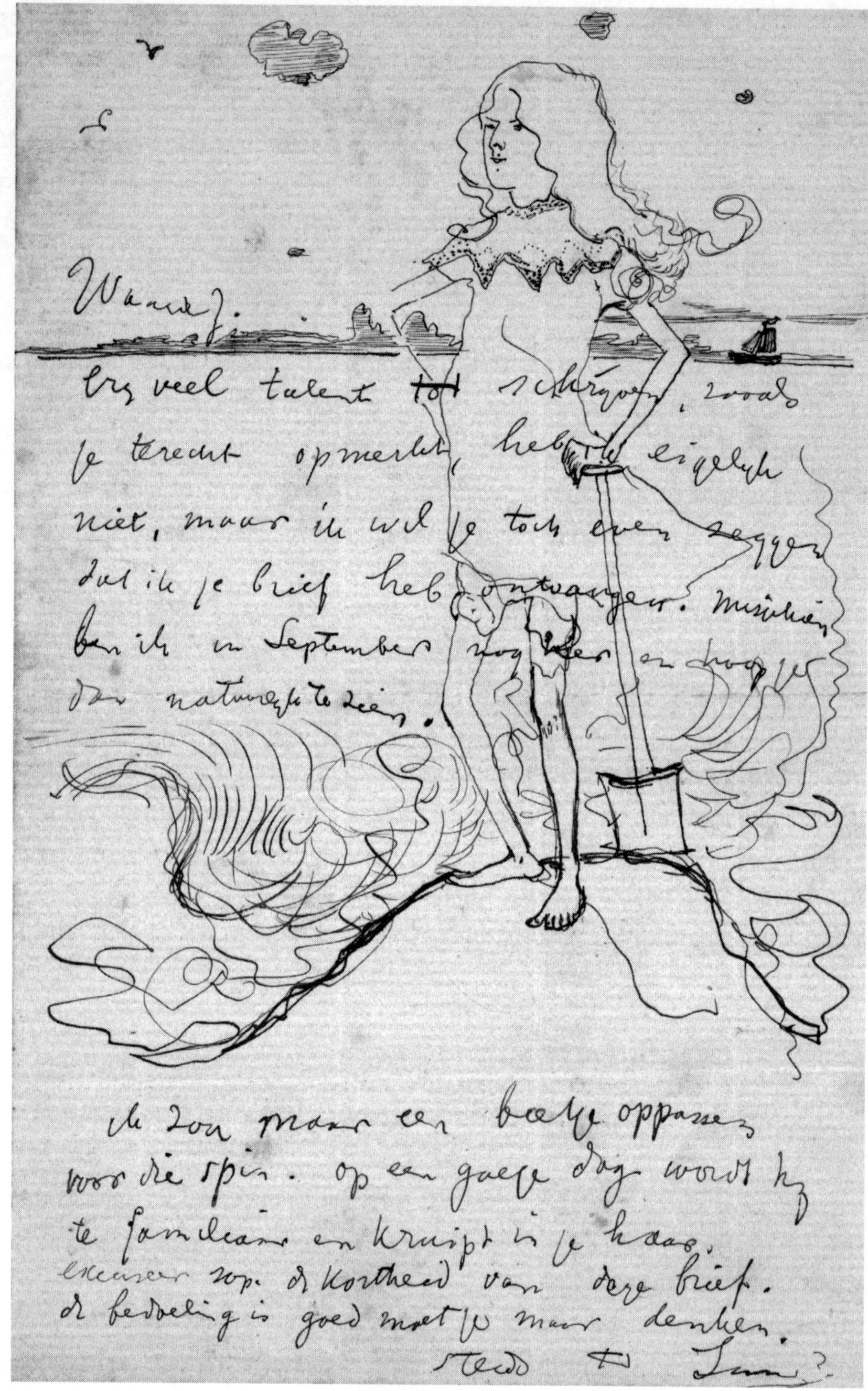

[illegible]

veel talent tot schrijven, zooals je terecht opmerkt, heb ik eigenlijk niet, maar ik wil je toch even zeggen dat ik je brief heb ontvangen. Misschien ben ik in September nog hier en hoop je dan natuurlijk te zien.

Ik zou maar een beetje oppassen voor die spin. Op een goeie dag wordt hij te familiaar en kruipt in je haar.
Excuseer svp. de kortheid van deze brief.
[illegible] is goed met je maar denken.
Steeds t. t. [illegible]

Figure 36 Isaac Israëls, Sketch of a girl on the beach, in a letter to Jo van Gogh-Bonger, probably August 1897.

out a bit for that spider if I were you. One of these days it will get too familiar and crawl into your hair.'[43] He remarked in another letter from Scheveningen during this period: 'the best thing would be if you could come for a late afternoon and evening—the families needn't be involved.'[44] He sensed exactly how difficult it was for Jo to free herself from her familial straitjacket and go her own way.

Reflecting on their stalemate, he looked back at their summer, when his hopes of a meeting had been dashed. Now they had finally planned to see each other north of Purmerend, but that, too, came to naught. He and Jo had gone by different routes. They missed one another and Jo was left waiting in vain.

> My dear,
>
> I'm sorry you waited there so long—but how could I have known—I went back a completely different way, through Kwadijk—Hoorn.
>
> Oh, what good would it have done us anyway, you would have had to dash away immediately as the eternal slave to your duty or your sense of duty—still it's going too far when your family has you so firmly under its thumb that you don't dare to go out with me even for a day for the whole of the summer—and then I'm supposed to say that I'm sorry I'm not more intimate with you! . . . That quiet corner of yours, what continent do you think it's on? Jopie, I hope that you feel a bit content.[45]

Inevitably the relationship foundered and in the late summer of 1897 the decision was final. Although Isaac, who was much more realistic, still had to impress this on Jo:

> It's all very well and good, but just for one minute don't let yourself be swept along by emotion and admit to yourself—
>
> Nothing will ever come of marriage *anyway*. You know it and more: never, ever would I want to persuade someone to do something that they would later regret or be nagged about. You are *completely* and absolutely right that you don't want that. I don't want it either. . . . I'm sorry that it's so, but that's the way it is.
>
> We'll meet again one day.[46]

Although he did not regret his harsh words, he was nevertheless concerned when he had still not heard from her after four days.[47] Evidently they found a way of keeping in touch after that: in September and October 1897 Isaac was working in Zeeuws-Vlaanderen and on Zuid-Beveland; he wrote from Goes that he would like it if she would come and see him one evening when he got back. Jokingly, he wrote: 'You could say that Zuid Beveland is the Andalusia of Zeeland and Goes the Seville,' but there was not much more to laugh at and their earlier intimacy had vanished altogether.[48] Against their better judgement, they had managed to keep each other dangling for a distressingly long time.

Throughout his life, Israëls was terrified of tying himself to one woman and losing his freedom—more than once he was infatuated with models and embroiled in complicated relationships. Full of bravado, Israëls boasted to Frans Erens of a successful conquest—in two respects. 'That's perhaps the ideal thing about being a painter: selling paintings to a woman and making love to her afterwards.'[49] Later he confessed to Erens that the perfect situation for him would be to have a woman he could see now and then.[50] He expressed his opinion in a pithy note to Willem Witsen and his wife Augusta Schorr: 'People are just like cakes, if they're stuck together for too long, they go stale.'[51] He had no desire to start a family, and Jo in her turn was wary of surrendering to such an unconventional artist. It is possible that she came to regret it later. A few years after this, she did remarry. Her second husband was the timid, bourgeois artist Johan Cohen and her sedate relationship with him could not have been more unlike her passionate affair with Israëls. When their engagement was announced in January 1901, Israëls wrote to Erens, with his typical arrogance: 'I ran into Mrs v. G. in the street the other day, now betrothed as you know. We stood stock still for some time without saying a word to each other. They were a few lovely seconds (particularly for her).'[52]

Aside from an occasional note in the years that followed, there seems to have been virtually no contact between them. Around 1914 their friendship was resumed; Jo lent him some Van Gogh paintings and later he made several sensitive portraits of her.

Van Gogh in Groningen, Rotterdam and Haarlem

Despite all the romantic goings-on, Jo had continued to contribute to a number of exhibitions, which involved her in a good deal of work. One such was staged in the Groningen Museum of Antiquities in 1896. Jakob Huizinga, the brother of Johan Huizinga (later a distinguished historian), approached her and she acceded to his request for works.[53] His fellow organizer Willem Leuring asked her if she would like to make a selection and put forward a very particular proposal of his own: 'Do you still happen to have a portrait of Vincent? If so, we would like to hang a wreath around it, consisting chiefly of thorns, with a few laurel leaves here and there.'[54] He also asked if she still had copies of the catalogue with the Roland Holst cover illustration of the withered sunflower and the halo. As in 1892, they wanted to present Van Gogh as a martyr—by adorning his portrait with a crown of thorns and laurels, they were unmistakably associating him with the suffering and triumphant Christ—and Jo let it happen. She apparently had no objection to their representing Van Gogh in this way and sent them a portrait drawn by Henri de Toulouse-Lautrec. Leuring asked if Johan Thorn Prikker might come to Bussum and make a selection with her assistance. He duly appeared, and within a few hours they picked out a hundred and two paintings and one lithograph.[55]

The articles on Van Gogh in *Les Hommes d'Aujourd'hui*, *Mercure de France* and *Van Nu en Straks* were also put on display.[56] Albert Aurier's piece in the first of these magazines was regarded as the international confirmation of Van Gogh's greatness, but only a small group were aware of it. In

Groningen, August Vermeylen, the young Belgian founder of *Van Nu en Straks*, gave a lecture on Van Gogh attended by two hundred people. Jo kept the reports on the event in *De Telegraaf* and the *NRC*, which contained lengthy summaries of Vermeylen's discourse. Leuring thanked her for all her support and noted with satisfaction: 'People are now recognizing that there really is something to the so-called "modern" and being not yet able to wholly sympathize with it, the public wants to see more and better. In short, without exaggeration, we have a huge success.'[57]

Around 1,600 paying visitors went to see the exhibition, which ran from 21 to 26 February 1896. Boys from the technical school and workmen could go in free—a concession that must have pleased Jo.[58] They had 'let the residents of the cold north get warm for once and given them a firm shove,' Vermeylen told Leuring.[59] The artist Albert Hahn later recalled how when he was a student at the Academie Minerva in Groningen he had stood eye to eye with the 'pure madnesses' of Van Gogh. He was constantly drawn to the *Wheatfield with Crows* (F 779 / JH 2117), which had had an oppressive effect on him and made him look at art differently.[60] The student Reintjo Rijkens was also very engaged by the show and told Jo about the reactions in the gallery:

> Among the crowds, a good fifth were highly appreciative and of those there were several who were decidedly enthusiastic. People pushed and shoved one another to the best positions from which to see a picture. People gesticulated. It was amusing. Obviously there were those who laughed—but not that many.[61]

When the exhibition closed, some of the works were put on display at the Oldenzeel gallery in Rotterdam. Later that year, Pieter Haverkorn van Rijsewijk, in his capacity as chairman of the 'First Selected Exhibition of Dutch Watercolours', approached Jo and asked her if she would be prepared to lend some works.[62] At the last moment, she sent him two watercolours and hoped that she was in time: 'The opportunity to show something of Vincent's work—is so rare, alas, that I would be very sorry—if it was too late,' she wrote.[63] The exhibition opened on 5 September 1896 at the Rotterdamsche Kunstkring with two Van Goghs on display—a landscape and a garden, each for sale at a hundred and fifty guilders.

Jo used a variety of sales channels in her task as the promotor of Van Gogh's work. Among the outlets she chose was the gallery known as 'Maison Hals, Salon d'exposition des tableaux anciens et modernes' at 45 Kruisweg in Haarlem.[64] Jacqueline Royaards-Sandberg wrote about it to Lodewijk van Deyssel (Karel Alberdingk Thijm) on 7 February 1896: 'She seems to be selling them, I would never do that. I shall go again soon; they're getting new ones all the time.'[65] The paintings Royaards-Sandberg saw there made a great impression on her. Earlier, in May 1895, there had been a little show of Van Goghs at Maison Hals, on which Jo had evidently cooperated. The admission fees went to 'Weldadigheid naar Vermogen', a poor relief charity.[66]

In March 1896, as part of her endeavours to gain more attention for Van Gogh, she had asked the Museum Committee at the Stedelijk Museum in Amsterdam if they would submit a request to the city authorities for permission to show drawings by Van Gogh in some of the museum's smaller galleries. She would have to pay one and a half guilders per room per day to rent the space.[67] For reasons that remain obscure, this plan failed despite her efforts. It was to be another nine years before she succeeded in staging an exhibition in the Stedelijk Museum.

Sometime later, a new Van Gogh admirer appeared on the scene in the shape of the art critic and novelist Julius Meier-Graefe, who had acquired Van Gogh's *Row of Cypresses with a Couple Strolling ('The Poets Garden')* (F 485 / JH 1615) in 1893. He had visited Jo and reminded her of their conversation. He was working on a book and wanted to include images he had seen in her house, so he asked her whether she knew someone who could come and take photographs of the paintings. He believed that these illustrations would be a perfect fit for his publication and could also encourage sales of the paintings.[68] Jo could not have agreed more and seized the opportunity with both hands. Meier-Graefe's book *Die Entwicklungsgeschichte der modernen Kunst* appeared in 1904 and proved extremely influential. Jo and Meier-Graefe were to cross paths more than once after this.

At the beginning of 1898 a good chance presented itself abroad, which Jo took full advantage of. She had sent a card to the French poet, critic and exhibition organizer Julien Leclercq by way of Emile Schuffenecker.[69] Jo was familiar with the obituary of Vincent that Leclercq had published in the *Mercure de France* of September 1890. He was a friend of Albert Aurier's and had met Van Gogh at that time. Now he was putting together an exhibition and wanted to include some of Van Gogh's works.[70] He would take responsibility for these paintings with the Maison Blomqvist gallery.[71] Jo lost no time in sending three star works—Leclercq listed the titles and prices: *Bd St Remy* at five hundred, *Parc à Arles* at eight hundred and *Jardin* at twelve hundred francs. These three, together with two Van Goghs that may have come from Vollard, were exhibited in Stockholm, Gothenburg and Berlin. There were no sales, but people in Scandinavia and Berlin did at least have a chance to see some of Van Gogh's better works.[72]

Translator for *De Kroniek*

In the spring of 1896, Jo had also started translating serials from French, German and English for *De Kroniek*. This socially committed magazine started by the socialist Pieter Lodewijk Tak was effectively the successor to *De Nieuwe Gids*, of which he had been the editor (Figure 37).

The weekly was established at the end of 1894. It kept abreast of cultural developments, and also covered social, political and economic affairs and the art and literature of the new generation. The impressive group of contributors included, alongside Tak as editor-in-chief, J.F. Ankersmit, Marius Bauer, Frans Coenen Jr, Alphons Diepenbrock, Frank van der Goes, Johan de Meester, Aegidius Timmerman, Jan Veth and Floor Wibaut.[73] The debate about the emergence of socialism was carried

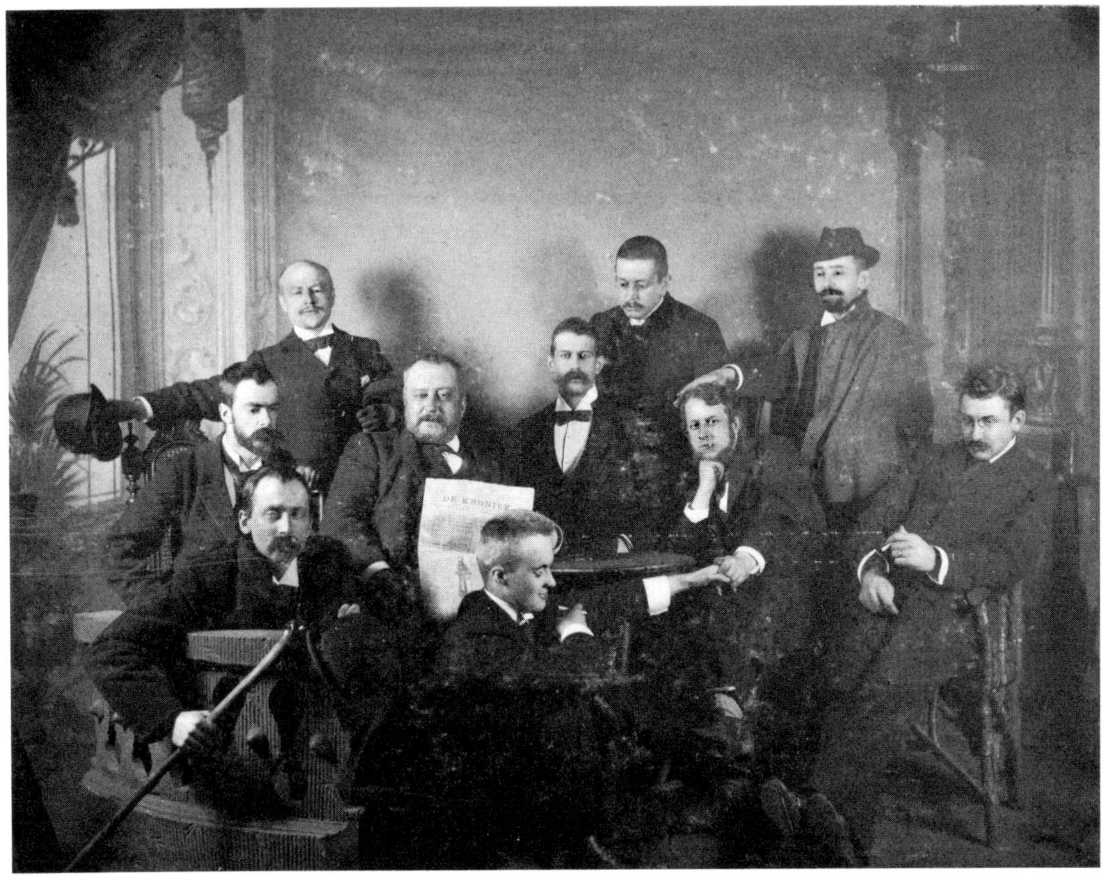

Figure 37 Founding meeting of *De Kroniek* in the Amsterdam Doelen, 30 December 1894. H.J. Haverman, A. Timmerman, J.F. Ankersmit, F. Coenen Jr, P.L. Tak, V. van Gogh, J. Kalff, A. Molkenboer, C.G. 't Hooft and A. Jolles.

on enthusiastically in *De Kroniek*. The discussions tended to focus on the one hand on the relationship between the individual and the ideal society, and on the other that between the intellectual and the working man. Art, according to the supporters of socialism, was an essential part of this ideal society, in which beauty and intellectual development had to be open to all.[74]

Tak lived in Bussum from 1890 to 1893 and was friendly with Van Eeden and Veth, so Jo might have met him through them. Since both Tak and Jo were members of the SDAP (see Chapter 15), however, they could have encountered each other at a party meeting. Tak was an advocate of legal workers' protection for women.[75] Women's wages at that time were much lower than men's. In 1898, girls working at Ruttenberg & Van Zanten, a metalware factory in Dordrecht, earned only around four guilders for a nine-hour working day, whereas the average wage for a man at the Zaalberg textile factory was about nine guilders.[76] Jo translated serials for *De Kroniek* for years, but it is impossible to tell which were her work. Countless serials by various named authors appeared in the magazine, but the translators were never credited.[77] Between March 1896 and April 1901 she received a total of seven hundred and fifty guilders for her translation work.

In May 1896, Cor van Gogh, Vincent and Theo's younger brother, arrived back in the Netherlands on leave from South Africa. He was in the country for four months and Jo must have met him during that period.[78] At the same time, Maude Stephenson Hoch, a woman from Chicago of Icelandic origins, took a room in Villa Helma because she was being treated by Van Eeden. She gave Jo all sorts of advice about her health, recommending hydrotherapy and a natural diet according to the precepts of the German naturopath Sebastian Kneipp. Jo may have developed an interest in such alternatives, for she made a note of the address of the Pomona, a vegetarian restaurant in The Hague.[79]

As she did every year, Jo spent the turn of the year 1897–98 at her parents' house.[80] She also always took Vincent to visit her parents and Mrs van Gogh on their birthdays. In early 1898, Jo's brother Wim and Carel Steven Adama van Scheltema, who was a member of the same debating society, stayed with her in Bussum.[81] Adama van Scheltema and Jo got on very well and liked to philosophize about life—later, in 1907, she recalled that time with affection when she wished him happiness on his engagement. She was sorry that they saw one another so infrequently: 'Couldn't something be done about that?'[82] Adama van Scheltema wrote socialist poetry and, like Jo, had joined the SDAP. In 1900 he published his first volume of poetry *Een weg van verzen*. Jo wrote a critical review of it in the magazine *Belang en Recht*, as we shall see in Chapter 11.

The women's movement and feminism

Jo's life now was a busy one. She was a mother, boarding house owner, translator and art promotor, and at the end of the 1890s she also started to work for women's emancipation. On 22 May 1897, the regional newspaper *De Gooi- en Eemlander* reported that Jo and Martha van Eeden were the local committee of the Vereeniging Nationale Tentoonstelling van Vrouwenarbeid (Society for the National Exhibition of Women's Work). 'We urgently invite everyone who wishes to support this Society in a financial or moral respect to apply to these ladies.'[83] Anyone who wanted a copy of the brochure written by Marie Jungius, a member of the board of the Society, could obtain one from Jo. A day later, Cécile Goekoop-de Jong van Beek en Donk wrote to Jo from The Hague. She was president of the exhibition and had written to check that Jo had a sufficient stock of brochures. She was warm in her thanks for everything Jo had done for 'our fine cause'.[84]

In 1898 the Vereeniging Nationale Tentoonstelling van Vrouwenarbeid organized an exhibition exposing the conditions in which women had to work and highlighting their achievements. Its aim, supported by lectures, conferences and musical performances, was to promote employment opportunities for women and improve their wages and working conditions. The event, staged to coincide with the inauguration of Queen Wilhelmina, ran from 9 July to 21 September at Scheveningseweg in The Hague, in a building constructed especially for it, and attracted 90,000 visitors. The profit of 20,000 guilders was used to establish the Nationaal Bureau voor Vrouwenarbeid in 1901 with the aim of exploring, enlarging and improving Dutch women's occupational fields.[85]

Like Jo, Willemien van Gogh, who worked as a teacher of religion in The Hague, was a loyal adherent of the women's movement. She was a member of the committee in charge of the preparations for the women's work exhibition, involved in the organization by her housemate Margaretha Gallé and her friends Emilie Knappert, Margaretha Meijboom and Marie Jungius (Figure 38).

Knappert gave catechism lessons to youngsters from a liberal Protestant background and Willemien had trained with her from 1890 onwards. Knappert encouraged women in all sorts of ways to make the best possible use of their opportunities, for the benefit of the general good. The work gave Willemien satisfaction, at the same time offering her the structure in her life she so desperately needed.[86] Jo and Willemien must have discussed the exhibition at length, because both stood firmly behind the objectives. The event had a huge effect, both on the women's movement and on the thinking about the position of women, and inspired the establishment of countless organizations concerned with education, child-rearing, working conditions and housekeeping.

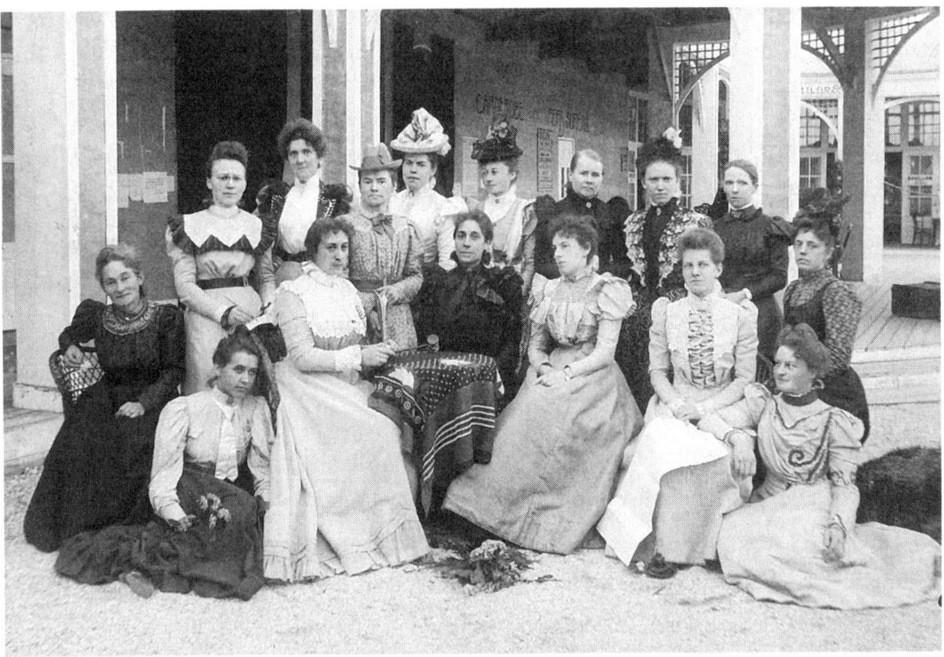

Figure 38 Organizing committee of the Nationale Tentoonstelling van Vrouwenarbeid (National Exhibition of Women's Work) in The Hague, 1898. Willemien van Gogh is on the far right with her hand on the back of the chair Marie Jungius sits on.

By the end of 1897, *De Kroniek* was running more and more articles about socialism, and directly coupling them with pieces on feminism. P.L. Tak's contribution on women's work, 'Vrouwenarbeid', focused on the rise of the feminist movement.[87] From June 1898, debates raged. Jo ('J.v.G.') also felt obliged to dive into in this melee of arguments, responding to the article 'Over het feminisme' ('On Feminism') by 'M.E.P.' This was the author Maria Barbera Boissevain-Pijnappel, who described the women's movement as 'an ugly, unnatural growth of our fin-de-siècle civilization and development' and wanted to silence the troublesome feminists.[88] In her response, Jo wrote that 'M.E.P.' had not treated the subject with sufficient dignity and seriousness. Worse, in fact—she had brought it into discredit. In Jo's view, the principal thesis, 'that there is no intellectual difference between men and women', was inadequately underpinned. She reproached the writer for a piece that was 'inconsequential' and 'illogical'. She did not consider herself a feminist, 'nor any other *ist*' and wondered whether Boissevain-Pijnappel's criticism had been fanned by reading the emancipation novel *Hilda van Suylenburg* by Cécile Goekoop-de Jong van Beek en Donk.[89] Jo believed that if women wanted to earn their own living, they had to try to do what men did. The question of women was not one to be trifled with. Her own experience is evident in the following paragraph:

> I am utterly unable to find the case of the woman who needs a housekeeper as foolish as you make it appear. I think, on the contrary, that it is a very wise, sensible woman who would prefer to spend her time with her children, rather than always washing up the cups, mending and doing the laundry. A person can only do one thing at a time and sadly I know a lot of women who put their *house* before their *children*.[90]

From the 'extreme left', the champion of women's emancipation Cornélie Huygens had already responded to Boissevain-Pijnappel's article, which in her view came from the 'extreme right'.[91] Arguing calmly, Huygens showed that the subordinate place of women in society had to and would change. In her view, this was an economic necessity. In the same issue that contained Jo's contribution, the feminist Annette Versluys-Poelman had stumbled over the quoted definition of feminism—it was not about *equality*, but *equivalence* of men and women, about the right to choose education and an occupation if one wanted to and had an aptitude for it. Jo would have nodded in approval when she read this: 'They want the woman to stand beside the man and with him not only bring up her own children but also take responsibility for the care of Society as a whole.'[92] On 26 June, Boissevain-Pijnappel acerbically defended herself against all the criticism: she felt that her piece had not been properly judged 'for what it *is*: an emotional protest'.[93] And this, for the time being, was the end of the matter. In taking the position she had, Jo had become caught up in a heated discussion about women's freedom to develop and about social inequality—issues that were very dear to her heart.[94]

After the exhibition of women's work in The Hague, the subject remained topical for some time: that same year Cornélie Huygens published the brochure *Socialisme en 'Feminisme'* and Pieter

Troelstra's collection *Woorden van vrouwen. Bijdragen tot den strijd over Feminisme en Socialisme* appeared. Huygens argued that women had to battle side by side with men and be prepared to recognize their own 'mental flabbiness' and 'hothouse existence'.[95] It was both a gender war and a class war. Troelstra referred to the discussion that had arisen out of Huygens's position and 'the difference between the bourgeois (ideological) ideology of feminism and the proletarian (historical materialistic) ideology of social democracy'.[96] This was debated at one of the conferences during the exhibition. Tak, editor of *De Kroniek*, also linked socialism and feminism more than once because both sought greater justice in society.[97]

Tak was very pleased with Jo's translations and she received payments for her work every month. Shortly after the polemic exchange he asked Jo: 'I hope I'm not too late but would you translate Le Chômage from the enclosed little book (p. 58) this week? To conclude the debate in which you took part, I hope before long to write an article designed to bring some clarity to the position of the women's movement vis-à-vis socialism.'[98] Tak had followed the discussion closely and obviously knew that Jo had written one of the letters to the editor.

Exactly a week after the request, Jo's fluent translation 'Werkeloozen' (Unemployed) of Émile Zola's 'Le chômage' appeared in the magazine. In this sad tale, Zola perfectly captured the misery of the working class: it describes the distressing situation of a young family where the breadwinner cannot find work. In the closing sentence, the little daughter asks her mother 'with a burning pain in her chest and huge eyes' *why* they are so hungry.[99] Tak complimented Jo on her translation and encouraged her to suggest texts herself: 'I so much prefer to get things from you, both because of the long-standing relationship and because you translate so much better than those other ladies. In any event I shall try to send you something else this week, but if you find something yourself I would very much welcome it.'[100]

In the summer Jo usually went on holiday with Vincent and her family; this time they stayed in Noordwijk aan Zee. During one of these breaks, Jakob Braakman took their photograph (Plate 31). In the middle of August 1898, she invited Cato Alberdingk Thijm to come and visit them in Villa Jacoba, right on the beach:

> Be my guest in the afternoon and evening (if you would like to). The guest bedroom is small, but there's a spare bed for Jopie—and Vincent would love it if he came too. So bring him with you if you can—and add on an extra night.[101]

They accepted the invitation and thoroughly enjoyed themselves. Cato's husband Karel, who had come to collect them, wrote in a thank you note to Jo: 'It was a real pleasure to meet your parents, and your sister and brother, and to see Vincent playing by the sea like a little brown sailor.'[102]

Mother and son were always active. The marriage manual Jo had read in March 1889 told its readers that a sluggish mother raised sluggish children, so she made every effort to give Vincent, now eight, a broad education over and above his formal schooling. At the beginning of autumn 1898, she bought a handicraft course based on the *slöjd* principle, a Swedish teaching method aimed at promoting a child's development through play with cards, clay and wood.[103] And in February 1899 he started drawing lessons. Vincent himself looked back on these with mixed feelings—not just the drawing lessons but the piano lessons that followed—because they were always taught by old spinsters. From 1900 onwards he also did gymnastics.[104] Vincent began to collect stamps and learned various board games, including draughts and Halma. The poet Willem Kloos usually brought stamps for Vincent on his visits to Villa Helma—while the boy arranged them, Kloos and Jo played chess.[105]

Jo had always been very interested in ideas about child-raising and had progressive views. She responded to the article 'Ooievaarspraatjes in de kinderkamer' ('Stork tales in the nursery') in *De Kroniek* with a contribution entitled 'Moeder en kind' ('Mother and Child'). It was a passionate plea to talk to children openly and honestly about reproduction and not surround the subject with fairy tales. Then, there is 'more chance that the sex life will develop in a healthy body with a healthy mind'.[106] The anthroposophist Jo Hart Nibbrig-Moltzer, who had been married to the painter Ferdinand Hart Nibbrig for four years, wrote to Jo congratulating her on her piece.[107] Others noticed her article, too. Two years later, Jo's argument in favour of honesty towards children, the closing words of her contribution, appeared as an aphorism on a page in a block calendar (Plate 32).[108]

The end of the first decade in Bussum

Between October and December 1898, forty-four paintings and drawings by Van Gogh were on display in the newly opened Arts and Crafts Art Gallery on Kneuterdijk in The Hague.[109] Johan Uiterwijk, its manager, had contacted Jo on the eighth of October and the opening took place just nine days later.[110] The Dutch artist Albert August Plasschaert wrote a two-page, lyrical introduction to the illustrated catalogue, which he inscribed to Jo: 'To Mrs van Gogh, for her beautiful love for the beautiful work of Vincent the man.' Plasschaert's bombastic and overblown prose pushed Van Gogh even more firmly into martyrdom: 'The poor, great man Vincent. He was crucified, this man. The light erected a burning cross for him, where, scorching, his body hung writhing; from his beautiful lips most beautiful words ran into the purple-red day.'[111]

The painting *Field with Poppies* (F 636 / JH 2027) was sold for four hundred guilders, to everyone's great satisfaction, and this enabled Jo to arrange for fifteen works to remain on consignment with the Hague gallery.[112] Within a month another three sold, two for five hundred and forty guilders each, and one even for nine hundred guilders: they were *The Garden of the Asylum with Dandelions and Tree-Trunks* (F 676 / JH 1970), *Starry Night over the Rhône* (F 474 / JH 1592) and *Avenue of Chestnut Trees in Blossom* (F 517 / JH 1689). The commission was highly lucrative at 27 per cent, and Uiterwijk made a handsome five hundred and thirty guilders on the sale—Jo noted a total of 1,450 guilders in her account book.[113] This price rise reflected the gradually growing appreciation of Van Gogh.

At the request of Pieter Haverkorn van Rijsewijk, director of Museum Boymans from 1883 to 1908, Jo wrote an overview of Vincent's life, intended for the museum's catalogue; they had apparently asked for this biographical information for their records.[114] It is possible that the museum was already toying with the idea of buying a Van Gogh. In any event, Jo issued an invitation: 'If you would like to come and see the collection here—I shall be happy to receive you.'[115] It would seem that the approach was successful, for in 1903 Museum Boymans acquired *Poplars near Nuenen* (F 45 / JH 959) (Figure 39; see also p. 210). This was the very first Van Gogh painting to enter a Dutch public collection.

Jo had done well in her first ten years in Bussum, even though her love life had not been what she hoped. Although she was financially secure, her sense of duty towards others and her desire to conform

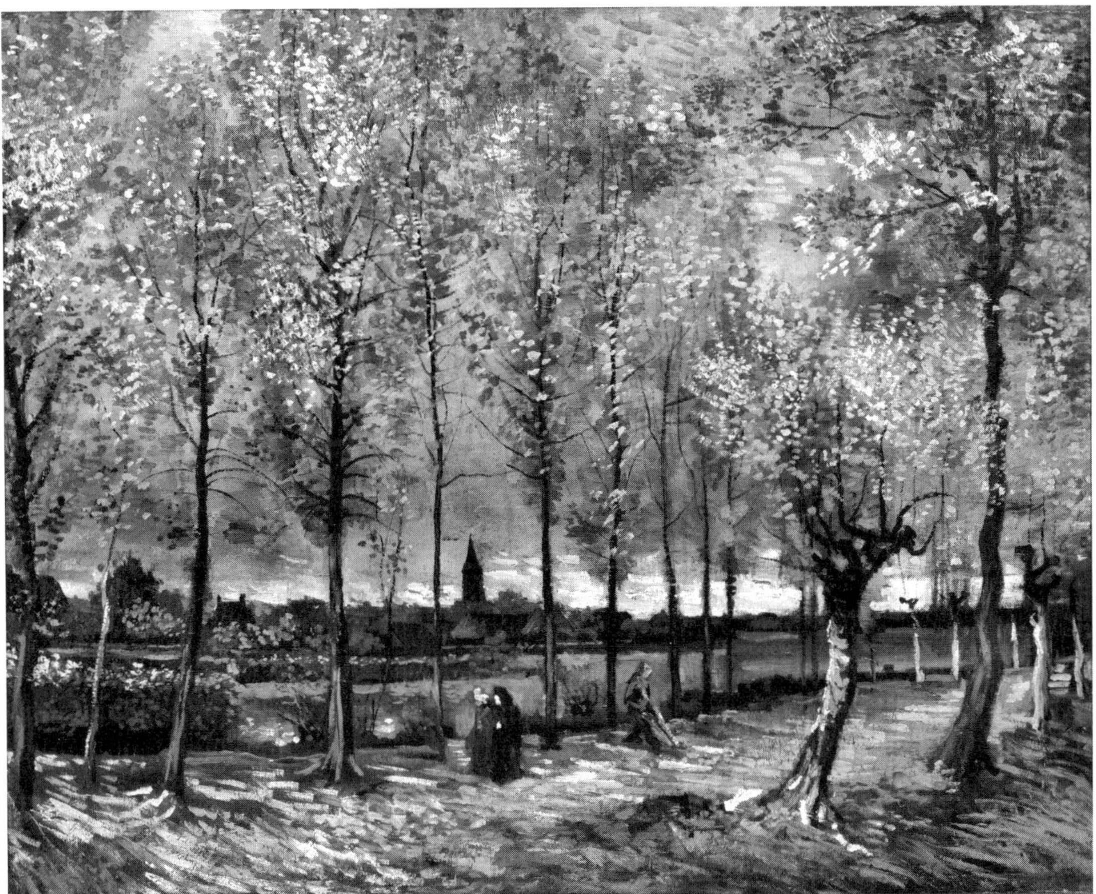

Figure 39 Vincent van Gogh, *Poplars near Nuenen*, 1885.

to social conventions left her less independent than she had probably wished to be. Israëls had recognized that Jo's family and the standards that prevailed there had an inhibiting effect on her freedom to run her own life. But young Vincent was glowing with health and doing well at school, and that was certainly worth a very great deal to her.

She had undeniably been successful in raising Van Gogh's profile and spreading awareness of his work, and the upward trend continued after 1900. A combination of factors had helped to bring this about. The first was the recognition by artists in Van Gogh's own circle, among them Bernard, who himself acted as a champion of the work. The growing number of publications (starting with Albert Aurier's favourable article in the *Mercure de France*) and the various exhibition reviews contributed to this. In the second place, a new generation of collectors who were receptive to modern art emerged around the turn of the century. As time passed, more and more dealers, collectors and museums bought works by Van Gogh, in the Netherlands and abroad. And lastly, after a rather hesitant start, Vincent's work began to impinge on the consciousness of a wider public. Jo's tireless efforts: establishing and maintaining contacts, lending and selling paintings and drawings, and her work on the publication of Vincent's letters in the years that followed had a strong influence on this process. Large shows at Bernheim-Jeune in Paris in 1901, in the Amsterdam Stedelijk Museum in 1905 and in the Städtische Ausstellungshalle in Cologne in 1912 created momentum.[116] Jo's support in all this came from the young artist Johan Cohen Gosschalk. He was to become her second husband and would encourage her in the crucial task she had so selflessly taken on. But there were many ups and downs before the marriage actually took place.

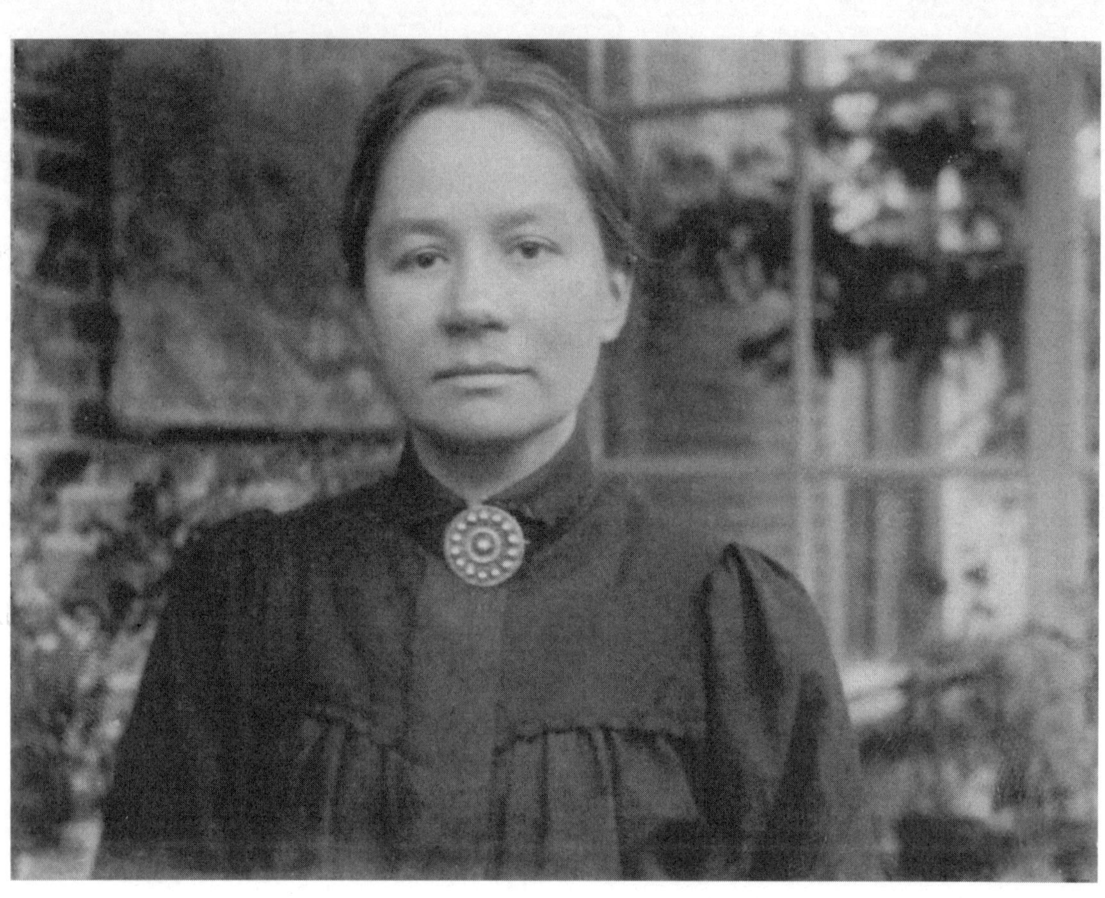

Part Four

Second marriage and concentrated promotion of Van Gogh's work

1901–5

'I was thinking that a life is just the history of what we give our attention to,' said Patrick. 'The rest is packaging.'

EDWARD ST AUBYN[1]

10

Johan Cohen Gosschalk—Villa Eikenhof in Bussum

Johan Henri Gustave Cohen was the new man in Jo's life. He was the son of Christina Gosschalk and the insurer Salomon Levi Cohen, who had died in 1893. There are no indications that Johan was a practising Jew. He had his mother to thank for his double-barrelled surname. A Royal Decree granted the Cohen children the right to add their mother's surname to their own from November 1902. For years Johan took lessons in drawing and graphic techniques from Jan Veth in Bussum, and Jo must have met him at Jan and Anna's in the second half of the 1890s.[1] He was a guest at Jo's boarding house during the summer of 1900, and they got to know each other better.

When he was at Veth's, Johan worked in a summerhouse that served as a studio, preferring to be alone. As one of Johan's models, a rather bewildered fisherman from Huizen, wondered: 'What does this broody hen do in there?'[2] A member of the Amsterdam artists' societies Arti et Amicitiae and the Guild of St Luke, Johan Cohen became a painter, draughtsman, etcher and lithographer. He also wrote popular art reviews for magazines, including *De Kroniek*, *Elsevier's Geïllustreerd Maandschrift*, *Onze Kunst* and *The Burlington Magazine*.[3] On 16 December 1896 he was awarded a doctorate by the law faculty of the University of Amsterdam for his thesis *Beleediging door caricaturen* (Insult by caricature).

Jo and Johan got engaged just before Jo's thirty-eighth birthday on 4 October 1900—Johan was twenty-seven—and they married in August 1901.[4] Her sister Lien and Vincent had put their heads together for that birthday, and she had persuaded him to suggest some special treats for his mother. The list he came up with included 'gloves, nice stockings, paper, a brooch, a new flower basket or an umbrella'.[5] Marie Mensing sent Jo a letter asking her friend certain questions about general suffrage for women and the Sociaal-Democratische Arbeiderspartij (SDAP—Social Democratic Labour Party). She also remarked that Jo had spent her birthday 'in the old way for the last time'. She was referring to the new phase in Jo's life.[6]

The laborious run-up to marriage

It was some considerable time before Jo and Johan finally tied the knot. Doubts set in as soon as the engagement was announced, and they decided to keep their distance for the time being. There were concerns about Johan's financial position, which was by no means rosy, and his poor health—and neither of them was sure about how compatible their characters were.[7] They constantly questioned one another's moods, and their confidence in the success of their relationship fluctuated. Meanwhile Johan was staying in a room in Laren and wrote to her:

> In such a serious matter, after all the experiences we have had together, we shall have to feel *very much* responsible to one another. But it *is* wonderful that we can both have such complete and profound trust in each other (because I have that in you, as, I may say, you also have in me, and I shall try to be worthy of it) and—no matter how everything turns out—we shall certainly know that we mean well towards each other & each other's vital interests. . . . Now, my love, I shall no longer be so serious.[8]

They met a few times while he was in Laren, and they corresponded. Nine letters from him to her from this period, mostly undated, have survived. They contain all sorts of revelations, analyses of their personalities and disclosures about daily trials and tribulations, such as the problems associated with purchasing the 3,700 square metres of land on which Villa Eikenhof, their future home at 39 Regentesselaan, would be built. The land was bought from Constant Wattez, who had a tree nursery close to Regentesselaan, and Johan advised Jo to have the purchase put in her name. They had a rather uncomfortable exchange about it:

> I know perfectly well that you may have been touchy and I'd like to forget what you said, but it bothers me all the same. Foolish of me, perhaps, because *I know* that in your heart you don't think badly of me, but I don't hear you say so! Darling, please don't think that I'm cross with you, but I don't want to give even the impression of not being good in all respects . . . and *fair* to you.[9]

On more than one occasion Johan expressed his love for her, and in his imagination he gave her the most passionate kisses while looking into her eyes in her portrait. He thought her letters were severe, melancholy and suspicious, but he forgave her for it:

> You may perhaps have something hard in your nature, but you're too *honest* to want to be *unfair*. I know a different you, and I've grown to love her, and I have nothing to forgive that other you, but a *lot* to thank her for because she was good and gentle. She could think so generously and purely about everything and she is the thing that I miss very much indeed in my life, and I feel that almost every instant. . . . I've never thought anything bad about you. I always trusted you, even though I've sometimes seen you make mistakes.[10]

Johan's approach to life was far from cheerful. And although he was full of good intentions, that pessimistic attitude would never change. They had not even seen one another very often. In the same letter he wrote that he thought it was annoying that he actually knew so little about her. And that when people were together—no matter how painful it was—they could become estranged. He was enthusiastic about what he'd been reading: Cornélie Huygens's *Barthold Meryan* (1897), a key novel about the fledgling SDAP, and *Kamertjeszonde* (1898) by Herman Heijermans, a novel set in artistic circles where traditional marriage was denounced. That latter book obviously focused his thinking about his own situation. He also said that he had come to love young Vincent very much.[11] Not long before his eleventh birthday Vincent wrote to his Bonger grandparents from Leiden, where he was staying with Anna van Gogh, and told them he had been to Katwijk, where he had enjoyed playing football. He wrote the same to Jo and in that letter, the first one he is known to have written to his mother, he also sent greetings to his future stepfather.[12]

The engagement was not a joyful time. Johan expected that if Jo and he went for a walk in the woods at Crailo, they would rediscover their 'healthy real human feelings' and would be able to enjoy life again instead of 'brooding morosely'. He recognized that it was important for Jo to have something to do and he admired her determination and perseverance, provided it did not descend into doggedness. At the same time, he acknowledged something feminine in him, which Jo by now knew about:

> Theosophy would suggest that a female soul has been reincarnated in me! I sometimes feel that my thinking is particularly feminine. You already know that because you know me well. I hope you don't think it's sickly. I shall certainly also have masculine factors in my soul—assuming I possess one! And you, my darling, as well as so much tenacity and toughness, also have a lot of real feminine softness, tenderness, delicacy of feelings and thoughts. Please don't think that I don't appreciate those qualities of persistence, which perhaps became a hardness. But I might nevertheless not love you if you didn't have that real femininity. I'm too masculine not to love that most of all.[13]

At Jo's urging, he promised to read the article 'Socialisme en feminisme' by Frank van der Goes, which had been published in the *Tweemaandelijksch Tijdschrift*.[14]

While they were trying to get to grips with their relationship, Jo received a frank letter from Theo's aunt Cornélie van Gogh-Carbentus, uncle Vincent's widow. She must have been able to overcome her embarrassment and put her cards on the table for Cornélie, who felt that Jo should not get involved with a neurotic personality like Johan. She did not mince her words:

> If it would make him calmer to know that he would not face you with the possibility of having a mental patient for a husband again, then he would act nobly, but who can say *what* would be best. In any event, dear Jo, I really feel for you because you have a difficult struggle and no easy life. . . . If

> it's truly better to *be done with* it, I think it would be torture for you two to continue seeing and writing to each other or working together. Or do you still have hope? Can't doctors or professors shed some light on it![15]

Yet despite all these problems, in the end Jo did not shy away from the potential risks. Johan also remained optimistic, kept his courage up and wrote that it did not appear impossible that everything would still turn out well: '*We can in any event hope*; because we still love one another after all.' He suggested meeting at an inn, De Gooische Boer, to talk about the problems. He pointed out in passing that sometimes Jo was not resilient enough: 'I'm not laughing at you because you think you might be getting ill. . . . I already told you, I think Vincent's letters are unsuitable work for you *now*. I know how memories can make someone weak and in your circumstances this would be undesirable now.'[16] He contrasted her present toughness with her sentimentality about the past.

Johan's moods fluctuated. Now he was working again cheerfully; he had written a piece about Théophile Steinlen and purchased a new bicycle. He hoped Jo would soon also learn to ride a bicycle so they could go cycling to places together.[17] She did, and quickly developed into an accomplished cyclist. It did Johan good to see that she was beginning to be her old self again after all their squabbling.[18] Jo wanted to see something of the world and wrote to him about 'the need to keep constantly in touch with life'.[19] The exact opposite applied to him. He experienced his best times 'in contemplation, quietly immersing myself in everything around me and *in* me'. He asked her exactly what she meant by 'in touch with':

> I do not suspect you, dear, of 'wanting to go out' for the sake of it. You want to see and hear good things, and you're right. I also really love good music and the theatre too, as you know, but sitting there like a tailor's dummy for an entire evening at concerts and comedies. . . . I don't always enjoy it . . . now I'd prefer to listen to music in a tranquil room in the evening in the twilight and quietly enjoy it . . . that's being really uplifted by music.[20]

Nevertheless, he went along with her wishes and proposed they should go together to Richard Wagner's *Lohengrin*, which was to be conducted by Henri Viotta in the Amsterdam Stadsschouwburg in May 1901.[21] Jo knew Viotta because he had played in the same string quartet as her father.

Johan called Jo a 'dear angel', but also a 'naughty woman', because despite their agreement to leave one another alone a few weeks later, ink continued to flow from her pen and consequently from his, too. But needless to say, it came to nothing. 'You *really* wanted to write to me again, didn't you?' he observed, and he continued, searching for the right tone:

> Sometimes I still love you such a very, very little bit. And sometimes I still think of you *just for a moment* and I long—a very, very little longing, of course—to have you with me, to see you, to be able to love you. . . . If we were just to speak to each other again, perhaps we would know more clearly again *what we see in one another. Because it's essential* we know that.

Again he proposed meeting at De Gooische Boer to consider their situation; 'a sort of peace conference about our feelings'. If Jo would nevertheless prefer to meet in Koningslaan, she would have to ask whether Mrs Cramer could be in the villa to prevent someone finding the two of them there together. This comment reveals how strictly he complied with social etiquette. He ended playfully, with pursed lips: 'Dearest, I long to see you and to kiss your dear mouth, and not only in my thoughts, as I do now.'[22]

Second marriage

The marriage between Jo and Johan went ahead despite the difference in their characters and ongoing uncertainty about whether they were suited to one another. Apparently, the expected protection and closeness, and the fact that Johan loved young Vincent very much, finally persuaded Jo to join him in jumping in the deep end. Johan's hoped-for support for all the plans she had to promote Van Gogh's work and publish his letters must also have been an important factor in her decision. She discussed a lot of things with Johan, as she had with Theo, and he backed her up in art-related matters. 'Looking at paintings with him was always wonderful, exactly as it had been with your dear father,' she wrote to Vincent later.[23] There would in any event be no shortage of discussion and he was certainly also fascinated with Jo's sweet lips (Plate 33).

As Vincent's supervisory guardian, Jo's father signed a statement that, prior to Jo's marriage to Johan Cohen, he 'had received a detailed schedule of the aforementioned minor child's property'.[24] Official notice of an intended marriage was given two days later on 9 August, and Jo and Johan married in Bussum on 21 August 1901. The witnesses were Jacob Hartog Hamburger, Wim Bonger, Frans Jas and Albert Boks. The names of the bride and groom were published in the *Algemeen Handelsblad* of 22 August.

Two days before their wedding, Jo and Johan made a prenuptial agreement before a notary in which general community of property was excluded. They married in community of 'gain and loss' (*Dutch Civil Code* book 1, article 210), which meant that all gains and losses from the day of the marriage would be added up and divided in two periodically. Gains comprised, for example, Jo's income from dividends and interest, and Johan's income from selling his paintings. Premarital debts and possessions remained outside the community. The notarial deed of prenuptial agreement lists the property brought into the marriage, including bonds, lottery tickets, an antique oak cupboard, a piano and an American harmonium worth 260 guilders, and an undivided share in his parents' estate from Johan, and immovable property and furniture worth 1,331 guilders from Jo. The property brought into the marriage by each of them therefore remained their individual property and was not part of any community. On that same day, 19 August, they also made their wills, in which they bequeathed all tangible movable and immovable goods to each other.[25] Jo's portion of the collection of Van Goghs was not included. Upon her death that would go to Vincent.

The members of the Bonger family and Johan's sisters must have been present on the day of the wedding: Fréderique, who married Jacob Hartog Hamburger in 1891, and Meta, who like her brother was also an artist. She married the architect Salomon Franco in 1906. Jo saw them often. The relationship between Jo and Mrs Cohen-Gosschalk, Johan's mother, remains obscure. The only surviving document is an inconsequential postcard from her to Johan and Jo. There is a single indication that she visited Jo and Johan in 1904; she was with her daughter, Meta.[26]

Now she was married, Jo stopped running her boarding house and was able to divest herself of all sorts of domestic duties. She, Vincent and Johan moved into Villa Eikenhof at 39 Regentesselaan, a large house surrounded by oak trees, only a couple of streets away from her former address in Koningslaan. A few months before, the three of them had placed the first stone by the front door. It bore the inscription VINCENT VAN GOGH / 9 APRIL 1901. Their new home was designed by the architect Willem Bauer (Figure 40). We do not know how Jo and Johan arranged between themselves to pay for the villa. The total building costs were 6,430 guilders, half of which was paid to the contractor Bernard Jurriëns in May. There is no record of what Bauer received.[27] He also designed De Lelie, a house for Frederik van Eeden and his family built at 86 Nieuwe 's-Gravelandseweg in 1899. Bauer was being treated by Van Eeden for depression and also worked with him in the Walden cooperative Van Eeden had established. Bauer had been a guest at Jo's boarding house between December 1897 and June 1898.[28] Most of the furnishings in Villa Eikenhof must have been Jo's. Together they bought some new things, including a lamp designed by Jan W. Eisenloeffel.[29] Jo's wardrobe was sober, and included

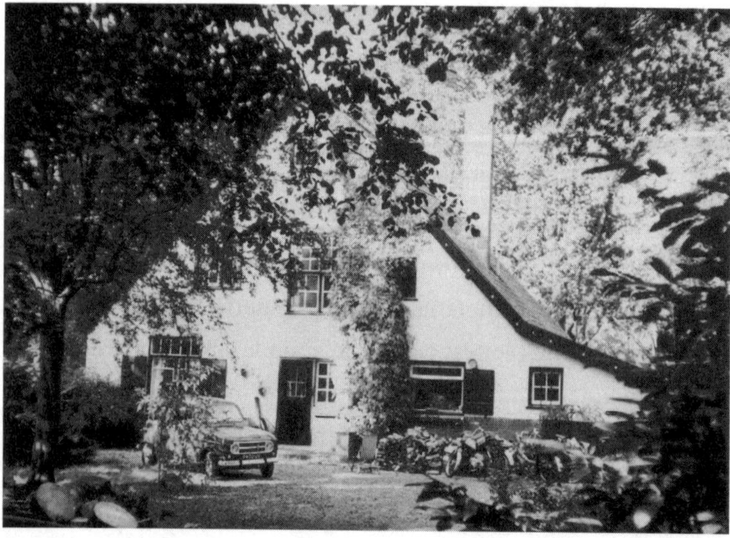

Figure 40 Front of Villa Eikenhof, 39 Regentesselaan in Bussum, between 1968 and 1973.

'*two* blouses, what luxury; you look so nice in the red one, you should wear it all the time, it suits you so well', Johan had assured her.[30]

The feast of St Nicholas was celebrated in high style right from the start. A few poems in Johan's handwriting have survived. They are witty and also give an insight into their day-to-day lives. One of them, which accompanied a bicycle basket, refers to how Jo always cycled down the road 'like lightning'. And that, in addition to money and keys, as 'interior decoration', her purse contained 'cooperative coupons'. In other words, they did their shopping at Van Eeden's Walden cooperative. Later, in Amsterdam, Jo joined the Algemeene Arbeiders Coöperatie De Dageraad cooperative and, like Johan, the civil servants' cooperative Eigen Hulp.[31]

Aunt Mietje van Gogh thanked Jo for the letter on her birthday and the plant she sent. Jo had told her that in Bussum they were primarily engaged in painting and writing.[32] The writing referred to her translation work and reviews for the feminist magazine *Belang en Recht*.[33] Her son Vincent, who retained an interest in plants and flowers throughout his life, had his own little patch in the garden, but that year he was unlucky; the spring plants did not want to grow.[34] So instead he passed the time playing card games. When he played bezique with his own children in the 1930s, he recalled 'the old game my mother played as a child', which he had played with her.[35] Meanwhile the young Vincent was excelling at school and was top of the class, and had great fun with Bobbie, 'a real free country dog'.[36] Mrs van Gogh wrote that the yearly spring cleaning in The Hague was over and done with, and shared their pleasure in the delights of Bussum: 'It's lovely weather for the studio and Cohen will no doubt enjoy it and you have no cleaning to do, how nice. Have you got a good servant?' They had a housekeeper in the new house too.[37] During the summer of 1902 Vincent went on a steam train and told grandmother Van Gogh about it. The three of them had stayed with Johan's sister in Zwolle, and during the summer holidays they also went to Kampen. When they arrived home in Bussum they were very relieved to find that their missing cat had returned.[38]

Mrs van Gogh was pleased with the long letter she received from Jo in the autumn. She was delighted to hear that everything was going so well and that Cohen (she never used his first name) had his own space: 'How lovely that the studio has already been completed. It can surely be made nice and warm. . . . Bauer also worked there during the winter, and the books were there too, so was everything together in his own little world.'[39] So, it was Bauer's work space that was constructed again in the garden of Villa Eikenhof, albeit in a different form, as Vincent was to remark later. This timber studio was on their own land and was now Johan's property. Mrs van Gogh understood completely: Johan worked there in his own manageable world. He needed seclusion and could stay there in peace and quiet, even though, or precisely because, he was married. The epithet 'broody chicken' continued to apply to the introverted artist throughout his life. And that was by no means always positive. Johan's mental and physical absence was one of the reasons why his relationship with Jo was anything but smooth.

The dubious portents turned out to be true and a symbiosis between the married couple did not develop. Not long after the wedding, Jo told her good friend Bertha Jas about her disappointment. Bertha responded sympathetically: 'I so much wanted you to have happiness again, but now I find myself worrying about you. . . . I had such a wonderful impression of you, the three of you together, so it was all the more painful to find you in such a state yesterday.'[40] Johan's nervous tension and depression was causing him to act unpredictably—he was someone who could wander off; he would disappear suddenly for days on end, which left Jo unsettled and disheartened. In 1914 she wrote candidly about this to Vincent, following a visit to the Alberdingk Thijm family, when Karel was more anxious than ever because of financial problems. On the day of his son Joop's official engagement, he had sneaked off and stayed away for ten days without anyone knowing where he was. Jo reflected on the state of affairs: 'How will this situation end? I really feel for them because I've been through the same thing with Johan—but not to such an extent thank God!'[41] She must have had a very difficult time with him. Depression and agitation in one person in a relationship can have a devastating effect on the other person's nerves. At times his anxiety made him unpredictable. In a later letter to Vincent, for example, Jo told him how she had once been in Antwerp with Johan 'and these are not all happy memories because even then he had that problem of not being able to go where he wanted to; he didn't want to go to the Plantijn Museum then—and I thought all along how much he would have enjoyed it if he'd seen it.'[42] It is clear that in certain situations he felt completely locked, he shut down or he simply walked out. There was clearly no prospect of Jo living a straightforward life with Johan, let alone of his ever playing football in the garden with Vincent.

Van Gogh exhibitions until the summer of 1905

Selling exhibitions continued in the Netherlands and beyond, and Jo was involved in them. There were some fifteen between her engagement and the major exhibition in Amsterdam's Stedelijk Museum in the summer of 1905; that one she managed herself and it heralded a turning point in the public appreciation of Van Gogh. In order to keep her records straight she always made lists of titles and prices for herself.

Among these exhibitions were the sixty-six drawings from Jo's collection shown by the Rotterdamsche Kunstkring from 23 December 1900 to 10 February 1901. Prices ranged from forty to two hundred and fifty guilders.[43] Three were sold, fetching five hundred and forty guilders.[44] From Rotterdam, the exhibition travelled to Zwolle, where the general public was given much less time to see them—from 10 to 15 March in the upper gallery of the Sociëteit de Harmonie in Grote Markt. The Rembrandt Society and the Vereeniging tot bevordering van Vreemdelingenverkeer organized it. Members could go free of charge while other visitors had to pay twenty-five cents. (By way of comparison, at that time Jo paid eleven cents for a loaf of bread.) Extracts from glowing essays about Van Gogh by Jan Veth and Frederik van Eeden were quoted in the *Provinciale Overijsselsche en Zwolsche Courant* of 9 March in order to encourage members of the public. Nicolaas Beversen, dean of the grammar school, wrote to Jo: 'It went as could have been expected—much exasperation and surprise, but also a lot of admiration, profound admiration and delight that these drawings had come here.' Someone wanted to buy two for two hundred guilders, whereas they were priced at a hundred and twenty-five each. 'Now, I consulted with my fellow organizers: if we waived our ten per cent and you dropped the price by twelve and a half guilders, the deal could go ahead. We would like it if something was sold.'[45] Jo thought so too, and agreed. She realized that this sale would generate publicity, which it did.

In March 1901, in the middle of all the emotional entanglements between Jo and Johan in the run-up to their wedding, there was also an exhibition at the Utrecht society 'Voor de Kunst', to which Jo loaned sixteen paintings.[46] It prompted Willem Steenhoff to make a striking appeal on 24 March in *De Amsterdammer*—striking in that it was the first time in history that someone put forward the idea of a museum devoted specifically to Van Gogh:

> It was clear to me at that exhibition in Utrecht how the prices of Vincent's works have risen considerably. And there's already greater demand for them! And so it may be that ultimately his works will be scattered far and wide. A large part of Vincent's legacy is still under one roof, however, so further fragmentation can still be avoided. The government will do nothing to that end, though, either now or in the foreseeable future, so there is an opportunity here for a patron to do something really laudable at a cost that will not be that huge. A collection of works by Vincent van Gogh, brought together either in a separate building or as a separate department in an existing museum, and therefore always easy to access, would be of very great benefit to artists and art lovers. I hope that I will not be alone in thinking like this or expressing such a desire.[47]

Seven years later it emerged he was not alone, when someone wrote something comparable in the *NRC* of 9 November 1908. It is not known whether Jo ever took this provocative suggestion seriously. We do know, however, that she was familiar with Steenhoff's article because it had been specifically pointed out to her.[48] It goes without saying that at the time, with all the uncertainties about her relationship with Johan and her impending move to Villa Eikenhof, Jo could not even begin to think about such an ambitious undertaking. Besides, she would first have to discuss the matter with her son, who was entitled to half of the works. It is possible that when he made his appeal for a benefactor in the Netherlands, Steenhoff had in mind someone like Karl Osthaus, who had been involved in founding the Museum Folkwang in Hagen. Be that as it may, this was the first time the idea of a Van Gogh Museum was suggested. Steenhoff also foresaw that prices in the national and international art trade would rise steeply during the first twenty years of the twentieth century.

The physician Willem Leuring wrote to Jo at the end of March 1901, saying that he wanted to buy the painting *Field of Flowers Under a Stormy Sky* (F 575 / JH 1422). The work had been on his mind since he had visited Jo, but he had not yet been able to come up with the asking price of a thousand guilders. He asked if he could reserve the painting and pay her later. Jo took an accommodating view and agreed. Later Leuring also went on to acquire Van Gogh's *Landscape with Snow* (F 391 / JH 1358). At Jo's request, he loaned both works for the exhibition in the Stedelijk Museum in 1905.[49]

The critic Julien Leclercq contacted her from Paris again. To his regret he had been unable to sell any works on his trip through Germany, Sweden and Norway. Now he asked Jo whether she could let him have other paintings. The timing was favourable because the World's Fair was running from 15 April to 12 November 1900. He wanted some half dozen works on commission for six months. Presumably in the hope of putting Jo in a good mood, he disclosed his plan to write a biography of Van Gogh. Leclercq was living in Paul Gauguin's former flat and studio and realized that it would be an excellent setting for presenting Van Gogh's works. He was primarily interested in landscapes and parks, and he told Jo at the outset that she had to write his address (6 rue Vercingétorix) on the crate in large letters.[50] She agreed to his proposal and sent eight paintings and three drawings.[51]

Leclercq was also pleased that Jo wanted to help him obtain information for a planned article on Van Gogh that they had corresponded about earlier.[52] They discussed what the best month would be for an exhibition in Paris. He told her about the growing interest in the Impressionists, including from such important dealers as Durand-Ruel and Bernheim-Jeune. Jo kept abreast of developments in the art world and the more commercial aspects through contacts like Leclercq and by reading *La Gazette des Beaux-Arts*. Leclercq and Jo talked about market forces. 'What you say is very true,' he wrote. 'It will be difficult to raise the prices while the exhibition is running, should it be a success.' He was convinced that in due course it had to be possible to establish a 'permanent reputation' for Vincent's oeuvre. Leclercq placated her by saying how much he would like to acquire a painting by Van Gogh for himself.[53] He also wrote that Émile Schuffenecker had shown an interest in eight works. For Jo's benefit he calculated that if Schuffenecker were to buy them, only six would be left to sell during the exhibition. So perhaps she could send a further ten or so, but preferably no dark, early paintings. In his mind's eye he walked through Villa Helma, probably on the basis of his notebook, and identified the works that he had seen hanging in the veranda, on the staircase and in the vestibule. He also wrote: 'At the beginning of the catalogue, I shall print an article running to ten pages or so, covering Vincent's origins, his life and the place he occupies in the Impressionist School.' He asked her what she thought about all this.[54] That put Jo on the spot, but at the same time it must have been good for her to know that another attempt was being made to stimulate interest in Van Gogh's work in Paris.

Jo sent a further ten paintings for the exhibition in Leclercq's Paris home in rue Vercingétorix in addition to the eleven works he had already received. They were reasonably priced at between a thousand and sixteen hundred francs.[55] At the end of December, eight went to Émile Schuffenecker, as agreed, for a total of nine thousand four hundred francs, Leclercq bought four for himself for three thousand eight hundred francs and he returned five to Jo.[56] He had asked her a few questions, about the dating of the paintings, among other things, and she also became involved in an interesting appraisal case. Bernheim-Jeune had purchased a painting as a Van Gogh, but doubted its authenticity and was curious to know her opinion. Over the years she received several such requests.[57]

Leclercq made efforts to have an ambitious exhibition staged at Galerie Bernheim-Jeune. They already had fifty-nine canvases and five drawings, but they wanted Jo to help out so that there would be more saleable works by Van Gogh than the seven or eight that Bernheim had. Leclercq consequently asked for paintings that could provide a more complete picture and listed some he had noted during his first visit to Jo. As was so often the case, it had suddenly become urgent: 'I need these canvases *right away* to get the frames made, and the drawings as well.' With regards to the catalogue, he asked Jo a series of difficult questions about Van Gogh's work.[58] She would normally have answered immediately, but now, suddenly, it all became too much for her. The complications with Johan (at that time they were still in the middle of their mutual wavering about their decision to get married) were occupying her too much, and overnight she withdrew from further cooperation. Leclercq was surprised and disappointed. This was followed by a plea to at least send *The Zouave* (F 423 / JH 1486) and the one of the *Arlésiennes Walking*, as he called it.[59] But Jo pulled out, and in so doing missed an excellent opportunity; as a result her name did not appear in the catalogue.

Leclercq sent her a copy of the catalogue of the *Exposition d'œuvres de Vincent van Gogh*, Galerie Bernheim-Jeune, Paris, 8 rue Laffitte, with the dedication 'To the widow of Theo van Gogh-Bonger, in memory of Vincent.'[60] Thanks to all his contacts—most works came from collectors, the majority being artists, art dealers and art critics—Leclercq succeeded, without Jo's input, in staging an impressive Van Gogh exhibition of seventy-one works, which ran from 15 to 31 March. He went on to send Jo photographs of the paintings about which visitors had asked questions. One was *Portrait of Théodore van Gogh*. In his opinion, this actually had to be a self-portrait, something that Jo must have agreed with wholeheartedly because she was later to assert emphatically that Vincent had never painted a portrait of his brother.[61] According to the correspondent from the *NRC* the exhibition was 'poorly laid out' and badly lit. Nevertheless, it aroused the interest of the German art dealer Paul Cassirer. This proved to be a significant step in the development of Van Gogh's reputation, for Cassirer, as emerged some time later, had a huge influence on the distribution and reception of Van Gogh's work.[62]

Leclercq acquired a taste for exhibitions and launched the most ambitious plans. He asked Jo to lend him at least a hundred drawings for an exhibition and for another fifty or sixty paintings. He also proposed writing an introduction to a publication of letters, but he did not explain precisely what was involved. He had already referred to the importance of the letters in his foreword to the catalogue (he knew the letters that had been published in the magazines referred to above): 'Eye to eye with his work and with his correspondence within reach, it is possible to make a complete and significant study.' His request was precipitate: he asked whether Jo could arrange for all letters in Dutch to be translated into French.[63] It must have surprised her that Leclercq suggested this so enthusiastically, not just as the seller of the work but as a passionate advocate of the letters too.

Nonetheless, she did not enter into any of these enthusiastic proposals. The only thing she did through him was to try to persuade the owner of the *Portrait of the Artist's Mother* to exchange it, but without success. Leclercq's letter reveals how shrewd he was. He had purchased Van Gogh's *Daubigny's Garden* (F 776 / JH 2104) and he tried to coax Jo into exchanging *Sunflowers*, which she had sent him earlier, for that painting plus three hundred francs.[64] She did not fall for it though. Leclercq sent *Daubigny's Garden* together with *Starry Night Over the Rhône* (F 474 / JH 1592): 'It will give you pleasure to see a Vincent you don't know.' He hoped that she would send a work of comparable quality and summarized his wish list.[65] He was to become an important intermediary for her again on one further occasion. Three months later he asked her if she wanted to release works for an exhibition at Cassirer's in Berlin.[66] By then, things had calmed down a little for Jo and she sent him fifteen paintings (all from the French period), with modest prices ranging from four hundred and fifty to twelve hundred francs.[67]

Leclercq, who was thirty-six, died unexpectedly at the end of October 1901. News of his death came as a shock to Jo and she wrote a letter of condolence to his wife, the pianist Fanny Flodin. She sympathized with her in her grief, which she could well imagine, and told her what had happened to her ten years before with Theo; that pain was still very real. She asked Flodin to send the Van Gogh works on to Berlin.[68]

The exhibition there, at Paul Cassirer's, which ran from 28 December 1901 to 12 January 1902, included nineteen paintings from Jo's collection. It was the first solo Van Gogh exhibition in Germany. In the years that followed, Jo made substantial progress thanks to Cassirer. He traded in works by Impressionists and Post-Impressionists, and through him many Van Goghs were to end up in public and private collections. A few months before, five paintings by Van Gogh had hung at the 'Dritten Kunstausstellung der Berliner Secession' in Charlottenburg. The exhibition included works from the collections of Graf Kessler, Leclercq and Amédée Schuffenecker. Julius Meier-Graefe, who had written about Van Gogh in May 1900 in the magazine *Die Insel*, had probably been hard at work behind the scenes.[69]

Cassirer was able to interest the collector Karl Ernst Osthaus of Museum Folkwang in Hagen, referred to earlier, in Van Gogh. Osthaus was one of the first collectors in Germany to buy a Van Gogh. He hung the painting *Reaper* (F 619 / JH 1792) in his newly established museum in 1902. He developed a good relationship with Jo. Osthaus wanted to elevate the ordinary people through art and he regarded his collection as a social prestige project.[70] That certainly appealed to Jo, even though throughout her own life she actually endeavoured to distribute Van Gogh's work among people all over the world rather than gather them in one location. She apparently felt that the former had to take place before the latter. It was not until after her death that her son Vincent took the decisive step to house the work in a museum.

11

Reviewing books and promoting Van Gogh—back in Amsterdam

Around 1900, Jo had a little more time, and as well as running the boarding house and promoting Van Gogh, she ventured into other fields. She began to work with a number of feminist women, becoming a member of the first generation of champions of women's rights. Her interest in the issue became public when between October 1900 and May 1905 she contributed twelve reviews to the moderate feminist magazine *Belang en Recht: Orgaan van de Vereeniging tot Verbetering van den Maatschappelijken en den Rechtstoestand der Vrouw in Nederland, van 'De Vrouwenbond' te Groningen en 'Thugatêr' te Amsterdam*, which appeared fortnightly.[1] Marie Mensing, who was in the editorial team of the feminist paper *Evolutie*, had asked Jo as far back as 1893:

> Do you support the movement? In that regard, I can only imagine, if you agree with us, that a woman, contrary to the attitude of the law, most men and even the majority of her own gender, does well to defend herself, or better yet to see that this attitude makes way for a more just and fairer one through her robust and skilful actions.[2]

Jo's first review in *Belang en Recht* was about *Van het viooltje, dat weten wilde*, a book of fairy tales by Marie Marx-Koning. She thought it was affectedly naive and mawkish. If someone wanted to raise serious existential questions, they should treat them seriously. In her view, the book was 'childish in form and yet not suitable for children'. Its style and composition were clumsy, and where the book talked about stinging nettles that know they will be picked by God, Jo commented scornfully: 'This has to be one of the weirdest occupations that has ever been ascribed to God.'[3]

Immediately after that first review, the editor, Henriette van der Meij, sent her the collection of poems *Een weg van verzen*, Carel Steven Adama van Scheltema's debut: 'I suspect that you and he are members of the same party.'[4] This assumption was correct. In her review, which was published on 15 December 1900, Jo again did not spare her criticism. She displayed her literary knowledge by writing that she heard echoes of Willem Kloos and Herman Gorter in the sonnets of the talented young man. Jo saw promising elements in his poetry, but she thought the format was pretentious. She felt that the reader did not enter an imposing edifice of socialist rapture, as the solemn preface to the collection suggested, but only the author's own humble 'flower garden'. Jo felt there was a lot of noise, but little substance.

The third book she was asked to review, Baromètre's *Beau temps—Mauvais temps*, did not appeal to her either. As the heading of her review Jo quoted a sentence, quite deadly in this case, from Elizabeth Barrett Browning's *Aurora Leigh*: 'Of writing many books there is no end.'[5] In her opinion *Beau temps—Mauvais temps* was an unnecessary little book, full of clichés. If only the author had looked at *Le livre d'or* by the Comtesse Diane, she critically remarked, which at least contained some pithy thoughts.[6] Mr Baromètre, whom she suspected was Dutch, presented only triteness, kicked in open doors and had not a shred of literary talent. She felt that he could have expressed himself better 'in his mother tongue' than in French—referring to the winged words in the popular novel *Camera Obscura* by Hildebrand.

In the summer of 1901 Jo reviewed the substantial novel *Halfmaagden* (*Les demi-vierges*) by Marcel Prévost, translated into Dutch by E. van der Ven. She criticized not just the abominable translation, full of Gallicisms and solemn dialogues (which were 'so fluent and witty' in French), but also let fly at the abject content. The flippant book was cleverly written, but with its disgusting scenes and upsetting passions it should be kept out of the hands of young girls. It was of little interest to mothers, either. Instead of the perverse *semi-virgin*, Jo preferred the *new woman*: 'the young girl of this new era, who chooses a purpose in life and works and seeks, alongside men, to prepare a better future for society'.[7] This ideal of freedom and service is what Jo and the readers of *Belang en Recht* had in their sights. Two months before, she had heard a great deal about it at the seventh SDAP conference on 7 and 8 April 1901 in Utrecht, during which the SDAP's youth organization 'De Zaaier' was established. This organization arose out of Rosa Luxemburg's call to set up national movements for young socialists, made the year before during the Second International in Paris. Henriette Roland Holst took up the challenge in the Netherlands. A committee formulated the objectives: bring about improvement in the material, spiritual and moral position of youth, provide insight into the essence of anti-militarism and raise class-conscious workers.[8]

Elisabeth Dauthendey's *Over de nieuwe vrouw en hare liefde*, translated from the German, was another study about the role of the individual—and women in particular—in society that Jo reviewed. She was enthusiastic about this book. She believed that it could be a good support and stimulus in the search for new missions in life.[9]

Van der Meij was pleased with Jo's book reviews: 'I want to send you a new supply as soon as something of more interest than the usual rubbish turns up. And are you thinking about the translations for the serial?'[10] Apparently Jo also did translations for the magazine at this time but, as we saw earlier with *De Kroniek*, the translators were never credited, so it is impossible to identify her contributions.

Henriette van der Meij became a good friend of Jo's. She lived with Ant de Witt Hamer, at first in Zeeland, later in Amsterdam and finally in Laren, in D'Ackerwoning at 10 Rozenlaantje. In 1910, when Jo and Johan had moved to Amsterdam, they had a summerhouse built on the adjoining plot. Van der Meij worked as a journalist for various periodicals. She got to know the progressive couple, Floor Wibaut and Mathilde Wibaut-Berdenis van Berlekom, which led in 1895 to Van der Meij and Mathilde founding the Middelburgse Vereniging voor Vrouwenkiesrecht. In Amsterdam, Pieter Tak and Henri Polak put her in touch with workers, and for years Van der Meij endeavoured to improve the position of working women.

Jo wrote nothing for *Belang en Recht* between July 1901 and April 1902.[11] Apparently the first eight months of marriage had been uninspiring, but after this she started publishing reviews again. Her first was of C.S. Adama van Scheltema's *Uit den dool*. She advised everyone to buy this collection of poems because the verses were 'so fresh, so young, so real'[12] and because a lovely, wistful autumn breeze blew through them. The next review was of *Vrije liefde* by Charles Albert, translated from the French by P.M. Wink. She could certainly recommend this book about the history of love and prostitution (the 'slaves of capital')—particularly to 'ignorant, indifferent, unaware women who are impossible to mobilize', quoting Van der Meij in this piece approvingly.[13]

Jo had nothing but praise for *Van zon en zomer* by the prolific Adama van Scheltema. She thought that the musical 'mood poems' in this third collection were 'enchanting'. In her opinion, however, the poetry deserved a more colourful jacket (which it was indeed given in later editions).[14] After that she tackled a collection of novellas, *Liefde*, written by M.E. delle Grazie and translated from the German by B. de Graaff van Capelle. After quoting the persuasive blurb, Jo commented: 'But it soon disappoints.' As far as style was concerned, she concluded that the collection was full of clichés, although that might have been the fault of the poor translation. It was inferior reading, no more than that: 'full of sentimentality, false sensibility, superficiality, sometimes morbid exaggeration!'[15]

Jo was much more positive about *Das Jahrhundert des Kindes* by the Swedish writer Ellen Key. This book was written by someone 'who loves and understands children', not just neglected children but also those 'who have been educated *too much*'. Educators and parents should be able to leave children alone and let them be free to do what they want because they will have to shape the 'society of the future'. Hitting children is altogether wrong and forcing them to ask for forgiveness is undesirable—it can lead them to lie for fear of being punished. Jo wanted the book to be translated into Dutch (it was later that year) 'and made available for the lowest possible price so that someone parenting or teaching children could learn from it!'[16] Key attributed more influence to life at home than going to school. In the school system children were completely overloaded and a child's individuality was underappreciated. Jo agreed. It was perfectly clear to her. The government would do better to invest in improving education rather than in defence. She would get confirmation of this again fifteen years later when, in

New York, she met a fervent supporter in Carl Zigrosser, who was expressing similar ideas about education in his *Modern School*.

After two further reviews, Jo's brief and modest career as a reviewer came to an end. The first dealt with Johan de Meester's *Over het leed van den hartstocht*, a series of stories describing the misery someone without lust for life and the will to live brings upon themself. Jo praised the sharp observations and penetrating analyses (egoism and weakness made relationships disastrous), and she linked the way the author mercilessly dissected feelings with Marcellus Emants's descriptions of ennui and emptiness. She also suggested that in his sketches De Meester had learned the art from Guy de Maupassant and Alphonse Daudet. She spoke with unmistakable authority.[17]

The subject of her last review for *Belang en Recht* (we do not know why she stopped reviewing) was not a book, but a talk—also about child-rearing, the subject that was so close to her heart. She had listened to Ellen Key's speech 'Die Individualität des Kindes' in the Concertgebouw in Amsterdam. She enthusiastically reported on the presentation of this 'simple, witty and engaging woman'. Jo described her as a strong personality who subtly and humorously addressed the reproach directed at her by some parents, who complained that their children were uncontrollable and difficult, even though they had been raised on the basis of the proposals in Key's book *De eeuw van het kind* (1903). With a chuckle, the author responded by saying that the error was not in her principles, but in the way they were applied. Parents should not automatically give in to a child's moods and tricks. Jo summarized: 'Child-rearing must not be based on *suppressing* faults through fear of punishment but on guiding children so that they learn to realize and understand that those faults are wrong.' This pathway to developing a character is lengthy and demands dedication from the parents. What is considered a shortcoming in children is in many cases a negative characteristic of what is in fact a positive disposition. If you guide obstinacy prudently, a child's willpower can be developed and strengthened. This means that attention must be devoted to 'the hygiene of the soul', not just knowledge of the body. Peace of mind and satisfaction make children harmonious beings, and from there they must be able to develop freely.[18] Jo agreed wholeheartedly with these views and tried to put them into practice in her own life. Later, her son sometimes ventured to doubt that she always succeeded.

Starting in 1903, the magazine *Belang en Recht* also made space available for the Nederlandsche Vrouwenbond voor Geheelonthouding, a women's teetotal organization that had been active since 1897. Jo supported this mission too. In June 1901 she manned a tent at the Bussum Fair where teetotalism was advocated. We know this because the writer Tine Cool wrote to her sister Dien: 'It's a wonderfully big fair this year. Ma and Gerrit are also going from time to time because Mrs v. Gogh is also there in a teetotalism tent. She's selling all sorts of things, including strawberries, which I feasted on!'[19] Their young brother Gerrit was at school with Vincent. The labour movement and the churches were trying to combat the harm caused by alcohol consumption. Jenever (Dutch gin), beer and wine were looked upon as absolute enemies of the people. In August 1888, at a meeting about alcoholism, the accounts of its disastrous effects had made a lasting impression on Jo and now she was happy to make a contribution to the campaign in the teetotalism tent. Shortly before, brochures and books warning of the problem had appeared, among them the *Verslag van het Eerste Nationaal Congres voor Geheel-onthouding van Alcoholhoudende Dranken, gehouden te Utrecht, 6 en 7 November 1896*, which launched an offensive against what it termed this 'terrible monster'. The report contained the presentations by Nellie van Kol about 'Sociaal-democratie en onthouding' (Social democracy and abstinence) and Titia van der Tuuk on 'De rol der vrouw in den drankstrijd' (Women's role in the fight against drink). Jo would certainly have discussed the subject with her brother Wim, because in the spring of 1901 he had become embroiled in a controversy with the law student Leo Polak about the influence of social conditions on alcoholism. He concerned himself with the issue for a long time.[20] The fact that Jo did not particularly like alcohol and that she turned against it publicly did not, though, mean that her guests were never offered any to drink. In June 1891 her cellar in Bussum contained a selection of wines worth thirty-five guilders.[21]

Paintings sold for Willemien van Gogh

With the deaths of Vincent, Theo and meanwhile also Cor van Gogh—he committed suicide in Brandfort (South Africa) on 24 April 1900—there was still no end to the psychological afflictions of the Van Gogh family. Now it was Willemien who fell prey to a mental disorder, which Jo found very distressing. Willemien had had a breakdown years before, after Theo's disastrous last months. At the time, out of self-protection, she had had to leave Jo alone in the institution where Theo was being cared for:

> That Sunday evening in Utrecht I broke down and I didn't have the strength to stay with you. Later I felt such remorse, bitter remorse about it—but the feeling, 'I can't do Theo or you any good', and the great harm it was doing me by staying, drove me to leave. . . . I lost all self-respect and self-confidence. . . . Slowly but surely, I've begun to see things more clearly, I've muddled through on my own—I'm used to that; in difficult times I need to be alone.[22]

Willemien's condition began to give cause for concern in August 1902. She became more depressed and was receiving treatment.[23] She had been able to suppress the chaos in herself for a while by focusing on her studies. She wrote to Jo about the importance of child-rearing: on the one hand it required a light touch, while on the other it had to ensure that a child could cope with the world—both of which, in her opinion, had been lacking in the Van Gogh family. 'Perhaps nobody can know that better than I do and I'm equally convinced that the suffering that was too much for Vincent and Theo could to some extent have been prevented.'[24] That last comment was as revealing as it was sweeping.

In her view, the sternness of their upbringing and the lack of trust contributed to the brothers' inability to cope with life. And that applied equally to herself.

Willemien had lived with her mother for years and had never really succeeded in creating a life of her own. After her nervous breakdown in late 1890 and early 1891, when Theo was being treated in the Netherlands, things appeared to have gone well for a long time. And Mrs van Gogh reminded Jo of that. 'You'll recall how she was completely overcome by the breakdown that night, but it didn't last.'[25] Nevertheless, things went wrong again later on. In October 1902 Willemien was admitted to the 'Rusthuis voor zenuwzieken' mental nursing home in Prinsevinkenpark in The Hague and seven weeks later she was transferred to the Veldwijk psychiatric hospital in Ermelo. When she was admitted her doctor noted: 'Repeatedly angry and wild, screaming, biting, scratching and hitting. At other moments she is still and silent and is almost completely remote from her environment. Refuses to eat. Suffering from hallucinations.'[26] The situation never improved. For the rest of her stay—until her death in 1941 at the age of 79—Willemien stared blankly ahead of her and spoke rarely, if at all. She was fed artificially and made several attempts to commit suicide.[27] Jo visited her a few times, even though it was a very daunting task. It was terrible for her to see one of her closest friendships deteriorate in such a way.[28]

Now it looked as though Willemien would never be coming home again, Jo took custody of a few Van Goghs from Willemien's collection and arranged for them to be sold. The proceeds were used to pay for her care. One of those paintings was *The Bedroom* (F 484 / JH 1771). The art teacher H.P. Bremmer, who at that time occasionally acted for Jo as an intermediary, wrote that he knew a buyer for this work. Five hundred guilders had been offered. In May 1904 he asked her what she thought and involved her in his considerations: 'Bearing in mind that prices are rising, you might object to this, so please let me know what you want me to do.'[29] And indeed, Jo elected to wait. Five years later another interested party materialized: 'Do you want to write to him yourself, or would you prefer to tell me the price and let me handle it?' asked Bremmer in a letter to her. 'Please do what you think is appropriate.'[30] She did, and soon afterwards Galerie Bernheim-Jeune purchased *Bedroom* for three thousand guilders—in just a few years the price had increased sixfold.[31] Anna van Gogh's husband Joan van Houten was delighted and complimented Jo: 'It's such a reassuring feeling to know there's enough money for Wil's care for several years. We entirely agree with you that we can afford to arrange something different for her now, and perhaps there can be some diversion in her sad existence.'[32] Joan and Anna managed the money for Willemien, and a surprised Anna concluded: 'Who would have thought that Vincent would ever contribute to Wil's care?'[33] Years later Jo arranged the sale of two more works from Willemien's collection, a wheatfield and a landscape, for a combined price of two thousand guilders. Again, Joan was grateful, as he had been in 1920, when he wrote to Jo's son Vincent to thank him for depositing three thousand guilders for *The Blute-Fin Windmill* (F 348 / JH 1182) from Willemien's collection, even though the painting had not actually been sold at that moment: 'In the meantime thank you once again for the way you and your Mother have been willing to take action in this matter in W's interests.'[34] Acting on Jo's instructions, J.H. de Bois from the Artz & De Bois gallery also succeeded in selling Van Goghs that Willemien owned, among them *Field with a Ploughman* (F 625 / JH 1768) in 1908 in Zurich.[35] Although it was of little comfort, Jo was able to mean at least something to Willemien for years.

Friendships

In the end, the friendship with Karel Alberdingk Thijm did not achieve the result Jo had hoped for. They kept in touch, they ate at each other's homes and birthday cards were sent, but at the end of 1902 he fended off Jo's proposal to give a lecture about Van Gogh.[36] Their friendship was not profound, although a 1905 letter from Alberdingk Thijm to Jo—headed Confidential—might suggest otherwise. As editor of the magazine *De XXe Eeuw* he had received a contribution and had grave doubts about its originality. Since Jo was well informed about the offer of translations from the French in *De Kroniek*, he wondered if she might know its source. He asked her not to talk to anyone about it were she indeed to unmask it as plagiarism. We do not know what Jo replied.[37]

Her relationship with Willem Steenhoff had a much greater influence on Jo's life (Plate 34). He had been an assistant in the Rijksmuseum since 1899, and would go on to serve as deputy director from 1905 to 1924. Jo got to know him better after 1903 and they became firm friends. He was married to Cornelia van der Kellen and had three daughters, when he fell in love with the young Coba Snethlage. Jo knew about the affair because she arranged for a nurse to care for Coba when she was ill in 1909. Steenhoff had an extramarital relationship with Coba for years, but it was not until 1922 that they married.[38] It must have come as a relief to Jo that her friend was unconcerned by Johan's aloof manner: 'Steenhoff was perhaps the only person, or at least one of the very few, who was undeterred by my step-father's weakness and came to visit us from time to time,' wrote Vincent in his diary years later.[39] Johan's problems were clearly not conducive to sociability in the home. His inhibited behaviour created a stifling atmosphere.

Over the years, Steenhoff emerged as an enthusiastic advocate of modern art, and Van Gogh's in particular. He recalled this in a letter to Vincent in 1928: 'How times change—twenty-five years ago I found Six very disinclined to show a small collection on loan in the Stedelijk in Amsterdam when your mother was prepared to do so!'[40] Jan Six was on the committee of the Vereniging tot het Vormen van eene Openbare Verzameling van Hedendaagsche Kunst te Amsterdam (VvHK) and this initiative to show work by Van Gogh in the Stedelijk on a permanent basis should have played a role in the run-up to the major exhibition of 1905, in which Steenhoff played an important role. In 1931 Vincent loaned a large part of his collection to the Stedelijk.

Works by Van Gogh in Breda

Van Gogh worked as an artist for two years in Nuenen, in the Province of North Brabant. When he went to Antwerp at the end of 1885, he left a large part of his work behind. At the time, Theo had already acquired a considerable number of the early paintings and drawings. After Mrs van Gogh and Willemien moved away from Nuenen at the beginning of 1886, the remainder of the household effects were put into storage with Janus Schrauwen in Breda and left there. For years nobody did anything, and after that, at the beginning of the twentieth century, objects began to be distributed without anyone knowing in what circumstances or where they were. In 1903 Jo tried to find out what had happened to the 'Breda crates': 'Since I managed the estate for Vincent's then minor heir, in the interests of the beneficiary I had to launch an investigation into the fate of the paintings.'[41] Jo instructed the lawyer Johan Jolles to investigate the matter on her behalf.

Rumour had it that the dozens of works from Van Gogh's Dutch period that had been stored in the crates ended up with the second-hand dealer Jan Couvreur for a symbolic sum of one guilder, after Schrauwen had already given away a few canvases. Couvreur treated them with the same sort of indifference and sold works to, among others, the Breda art collector Kees Mouwen, who, together with his nephew Lieutenant Willem van Bakel, went in search of the works that had already been sold. They were apparently afraid that the Van Gogh family would demand the paintings and drawings, so they sold them on. They got in touch with H.P. Bremmer, who in turn referred them to the Oldenzeel gallery in Rotterdam. All this was going on behind Jo's back. Starting in the autumn of 1902, Margareta Oldenzeel-Schot (whose husband had died in 1896) staged three selling exhibitions. Encouraged by Bremmer, several of his students purchased Van Goghs.[42]

Bremmer played an important part in publicizing Van Gogh, to whom he devoted a great deal of attention in his courses and publications. In the years before the First World War he became the leading Van Gogh specialist in the Netherlands. He saw the work as the result of a heroic life that eventually, after sacrifice and extreme struggle, achieved profound spirituality. In his eyes that made Van Gogh a true artist. This enthusiasm meant that over the years more and more of his students, or 'Bremmerians', bought works by Van Gogh.[43]

Jo may have travelled to Rotterdam between 4 January and 5 February 1903 to see the unknown Van Goghs. Newspaper reports about the exhibitions in May and in November-December (around a hundred works) must surely have aroused Jo's curiosity and sent her to Oldenzeel. She certainly visited the autumn exhibition.[44] She enquired about the provenance of the art exhibited at the Hague branch of Boussod, Valadon & Cie, where Hermanus Tersteeg still worked. The people there assumed that it belonged to Van Bakel.[45] Tersteeg had had a few drawings framed for Van Bakel and recognized the Van Goghs. And he told Jo about 'an exhibition about Vincent here, which included seven paintings from the later period that belonged to Mr L.C. Enthoven of Voorburg'. He gave her the name of the location: Binnenhuis 'Die Haghe' in Scheveningsche Veer.[46] Mrs van Gogh had also told Jo that same month that a man had called to ask about those paintings. She thought it was someone from Die Haghe. Works from the Mouwen-Van Bakel collection were also exhibited here.[47]

Jo also asked Bremmer what he knew about it. He referred to 'an officer' and maintained he had not seen the works prior to the exhibition. Seventeen had been sold 'for very good prices, but to my mind they still don't mean much compared with what the future holds in store'. He protected the owners and, against his better judgement, held back information—and went even further by suggesting that the officer had to be 'a relative of Vincent's'. He went on to say that in April he would be publishing a Van Gogh issue in the series *Moderne Kunstwerken*, which he had just started.[48]

A sale at Frederik Muller & Cie in Amsterdam on 3 May 1904 included forty-one paintings, watercolours and drawings by Van Gogh from the Mouwen collection. Only eleven of the works were sold for a total of four hundred and fifty guilders, which was a pittance.[49] A month later five unknown Van Goghs from the Mouwen-Van Bakel collection were exhibited at Oldenzeel, and in November so too were the unsold items from the sale at Muller. Only a few were sold.[50] During his investigation into the 'Breda crates', the lawyer Johan Jolles had received assistance from Frans Pels Rijcken in Breda and they produced, as best they could, an analysis and overview of the situation. Jo had to pay Jolles a hundred and twenty guilders for his services, and that was the end of the matter as far as she was concerned.[51] So all in all it was a great deal of trouble for nothing, although now she knew better than before what was what. We do not know whether she ever considered taking legal action.

During the same period, Jo succeeded in bringing Van Gogh's work to the attention of art lovers over a larger geographical area. Between 17 January and 1 February 1903 there was an exhibition in Vienna entitled 'Entwicklung des Impressionismus in Malerei u. Plastik', with five paintings by Van Gogh. Jo agreed with one of the organizers, the painter Wilhelm Bernatzik, that she would lend *Sunflowers*, *Fruit Tree in Blossom* and *Portrait of Van Gogh* by Toulouse-Lautrec.[52] And Jan Toorop wrote to her saying he was pleased she was prepared to lend Van Goghs for the 'Frühjahr-Ausstellung des Vereins Bildender Künstler Münchens Secession'. He asked her if she would select seven herself and tell him what she chose. She had to send the works within a week 'express' by the carrier Van Gend & Loos.[53] All seven were for sale, and Jo sold two paintings privately to Hugo von Tschudi, director of the Nationalgalerie in Berlin. They were *Orchard in Blossom with a View of Arles* (F 516 / JH 1685) and *Rain* (F 650 / JH 1839). She received two thousand guilders after paying commission.[54]

The first Van Gogh in a Dutch museum

As early as 1888, in a letter to Theo, Vincent had opportunistically suggested donating paintings not just to influential people in the art world, but to the modern museum in The Hague too.[55] In the end—

but not until 1903—it was not the Hague museum, but Rotterdam's Museum Boymans that acquired the very first work by Van Gogh to go into a Dutch public collection. Twenty-six art lovers put up the money, in what was an early form of crowdfunding, to buy the 1885 painting *Poplars near Nuenen* (F 45 / JH 959) (see Figure 39). Jo and Johan supported the purchase and even contributed fifty guilders themselves. Director Pieter Haverkorn van Rijsewijk expressed his thanks for their generous cooperation: 'Truly, a work by Vincent is needed, sorely needed, to raise people out of their parsimony,' he wrote pugnaciously. 'Today I'm beginning to collect the contributions. The official price remains 800 guilders as you asked.'[56] The painting went first to the restorer and a splendid frame was ordered. The *NRC* wrote a piece about it and also reported the sale of *Wheatfields* (F 775 / JH 2038) to the Moderne Galerie in Vienna, which paid a comparable price for it—816 guilders. Jo sent this press cutting to Mrs van Gogh, who answered 'What a movement in the Art World' and thought it a 'wonderful Crown' on all the work. Theo was mentioned in the article, and she wrote her letter on his birthday, remembering her beloved son.[57] Haverkorn van Rijsewijk was content and dreamed of being able to add *Orchard in Blossom* to the collection as well. It was priced at twelve hundred guilders. He implored Jo not to sell this work without giving him first refusal.[58]

That year there were even more movements in the art world associated with Van Gogh. In the spring, the 'Niederländische Kunstausstellung' in het Kaiser-Wilhelm-Museum in Krefeld included three paintings from Jo's collection. That autumn she sent fifteen works, eleven of them for sale, for the 'Ausstellung der Holländische Secession', which was staged in the function room of Wiesbaden Town Hall by the Wiesbadener Gesellschaft für Bildende Kunst.[59] Increasingly, appreciative voices were beginning to make themselves heard, and in *De Gids* G.H. Marius openly described Van Gogh as the last great sensation of the preceding century who had struck like a meteor.[60]

Briefly but effectively, the artists' society Kunstlievend Genootschap Pictura exhibited a series of drawings and watercolours by Van Gogh in the upper gallery of De Harmonie in Groningen, on 13, 14 and 15 February 1904. The newspapers reported that they came 'from the portfolio of Mrs Cohen Gosschalk-Bonger'.[61] Following on immediately, and running until 20 February, there was an exhibition in the Leidsche Volkshuis featuring seven paintings from Van Gogh's French period and twenty drawings and prints from the collection of Hidde Nijland. The director, Emilie Knappert, had asked Jo at the last minute whether she would be prepared to loan a few works 'because it's so seldom that we can show people paintings'.[62] She had seen landscapes hanging in Jo's living room that would fit in perfectly. Knappert made great efforts to reconcile class-related conflicts and elevate the morals of the proletariat. She focused attention on the objective of Dutch community centres and advocated democratization of cultural heritage as a social obligation of the citizenry. Her views were informed by the ideas of Arnold Toynbee, who strove to improve the living standards of workers. What she wrote to Jo about an early lithograph by Van Gogh is telling in this context. It was the one 'of the old man with his hands in front of his face, on which V. wrote: "il faut que ces feuilles se vendent à

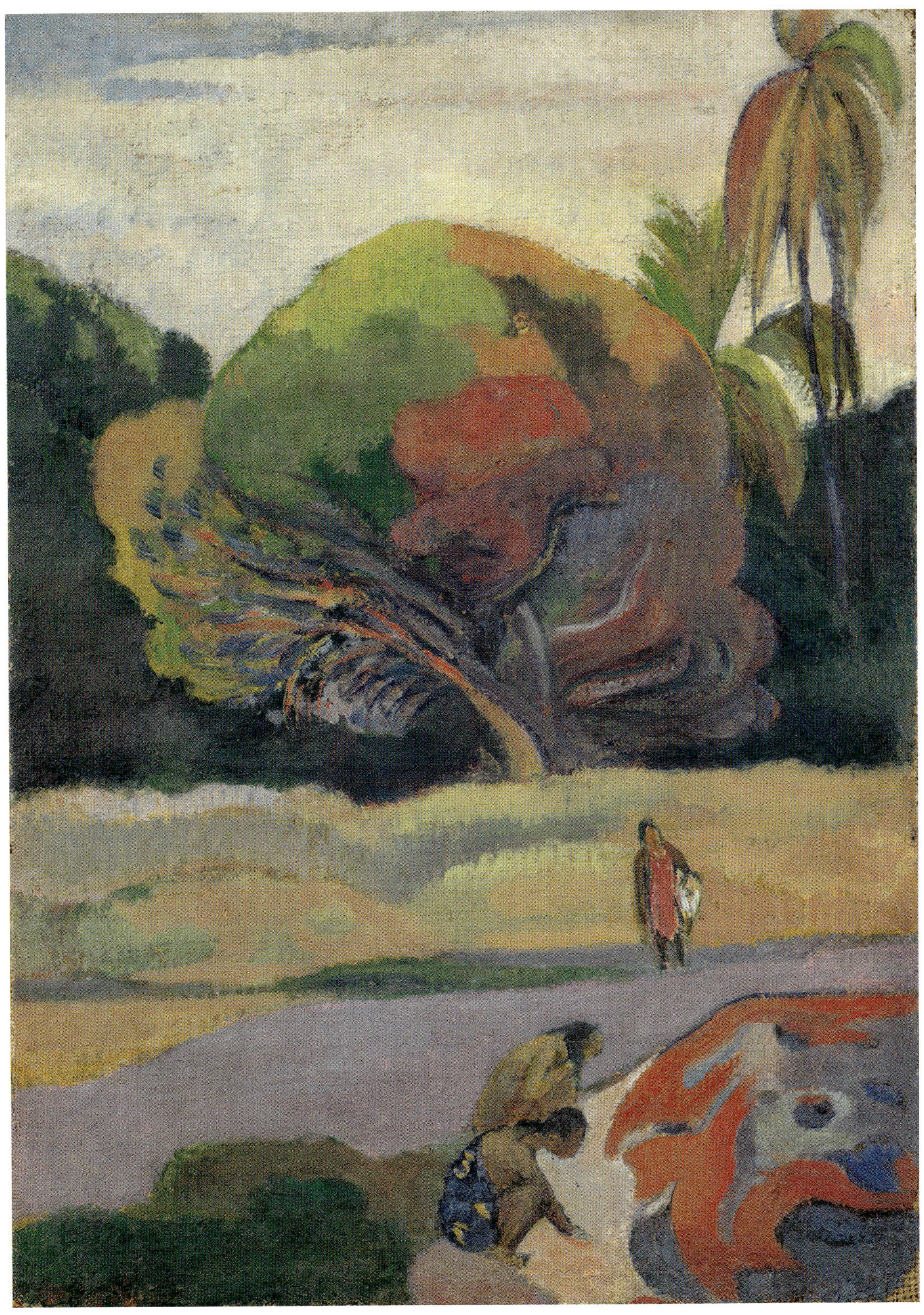

Plate 25 Paul Gauguin, *Women on the Banks of the River*, 1892.

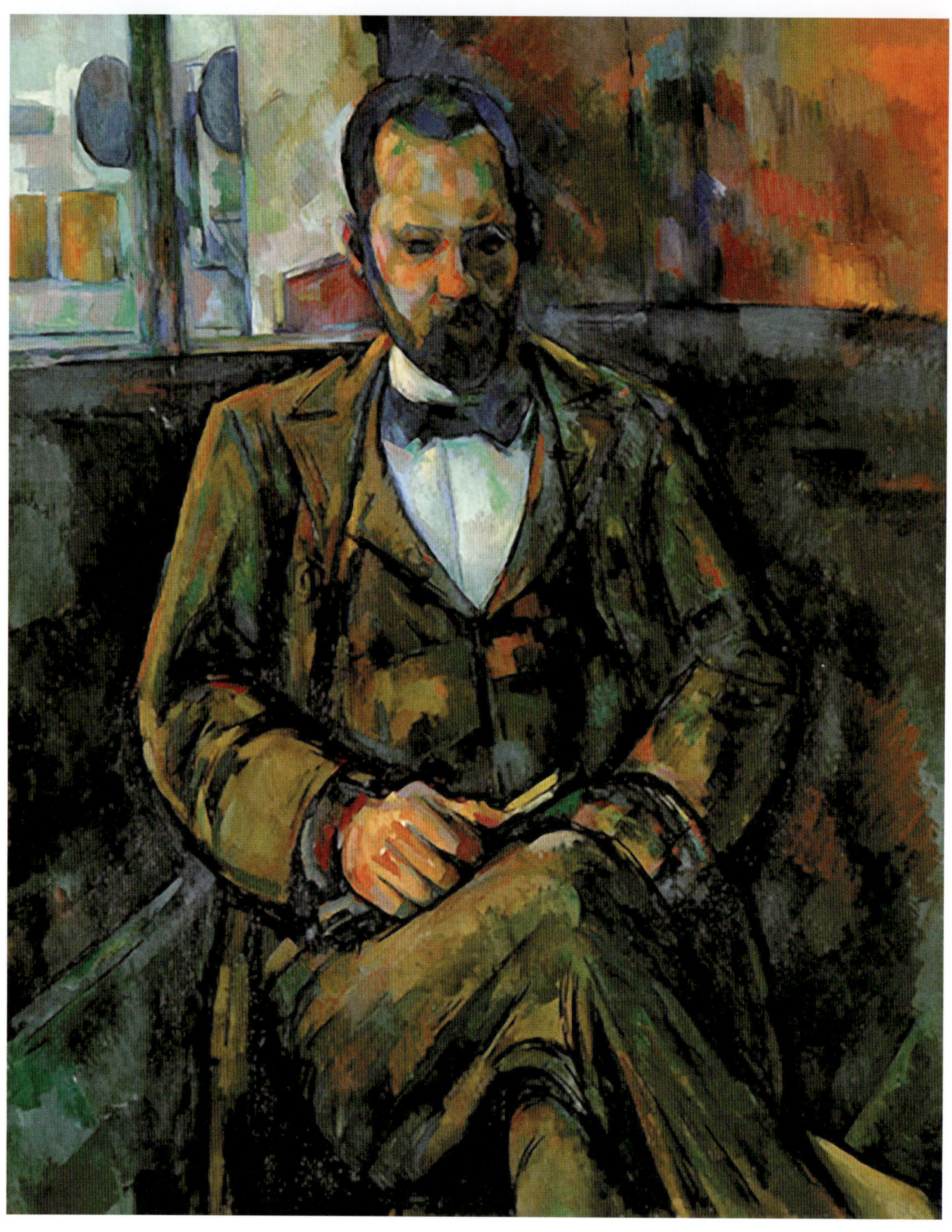

Plate 26 Paul Cézanne, *Portrait of Ambroise Vollard*, 1899.

b 1437 V/1962

Lijst van de schilderijen bij Vollard 6 Rue Laffitte Parijs

November 1896.

1	- 121	Rhône le soir	1000
2	- 1	mangeurs de pommes de terre	
3	- 95	soleils (fond bleu)	800
4	235	champs de blé (moissonneur) mauve	600
5	328	les pêchers arbres en fleurs	500
6	118	parc à Arles	500
7	181	étoiles tournantes (astres)	500
8	297	champs de coquelicots	500
9	94	soleils (fond vert	800
10	236	maison à Arles	400
11	47	moulin de la galette	250
12	76	moulin de la galette	250
13	87	bord de Seine à Asnières	400
14	128	effet de neige	300
15	261	effet d'orage (oiseaux)	600
16	260	gerbes de blé	400
17	70	la grande jatte tryptique	600
18	81	bords de Seine à Asnières	600
19	82	bords de Seine à Clichy	600
20	237	portrait de Vincent malade.	
21	147	oliviers (niet opgezet	400?
22	201	village	500
23	84	tournesols fanés	500
24	317 -	marronnier en fleurs	200
25	168	arlesienne	400
26	251	Dr Gachet verpocht	300
27	101	laveuses sur les bords du Rhone	300
28	215	oleandres (lauriers roses)	400
29	312	paysage Auvers	300
30	51 -	livres jaunes	300
31	11 -	paysanne coiff rouge	200
32	12 -	" " blanch	200
33	16 -	nid d'hirondelles	150
34	24 -	chaussures	150
~~35~~			

Plate 27 Jo van Gogh-Bonger, list of the Van Gogh paintings and the asking prices for Ambroise Vollard in Paris, November 1896.

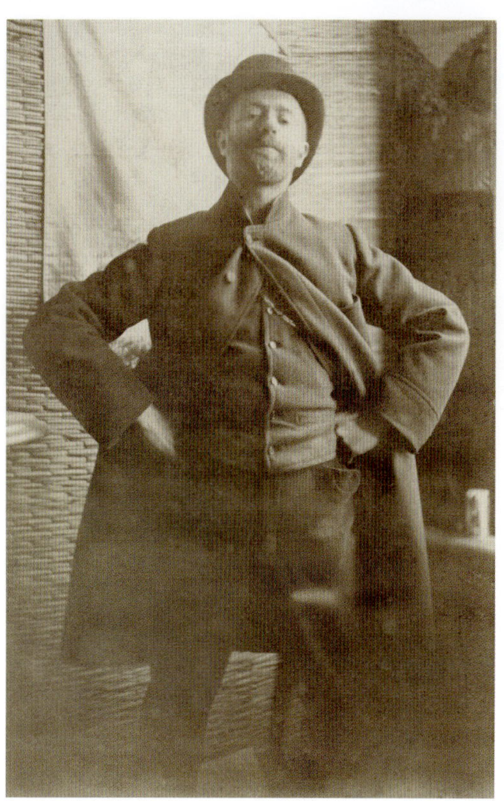

Plate 28 Joseph Jessurun de Mesquita (attributed to), *Isaac Israëls*, *c*. 1888.

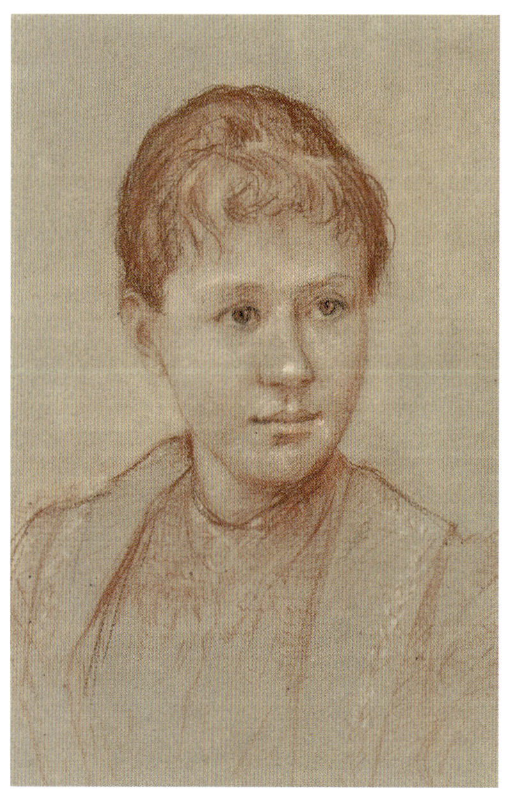

Plate 29 Isaac Israëls, *Jo van Gogh-Bonger*, 1895–6. Drawing from an 1890 photograph (see Plate 16).

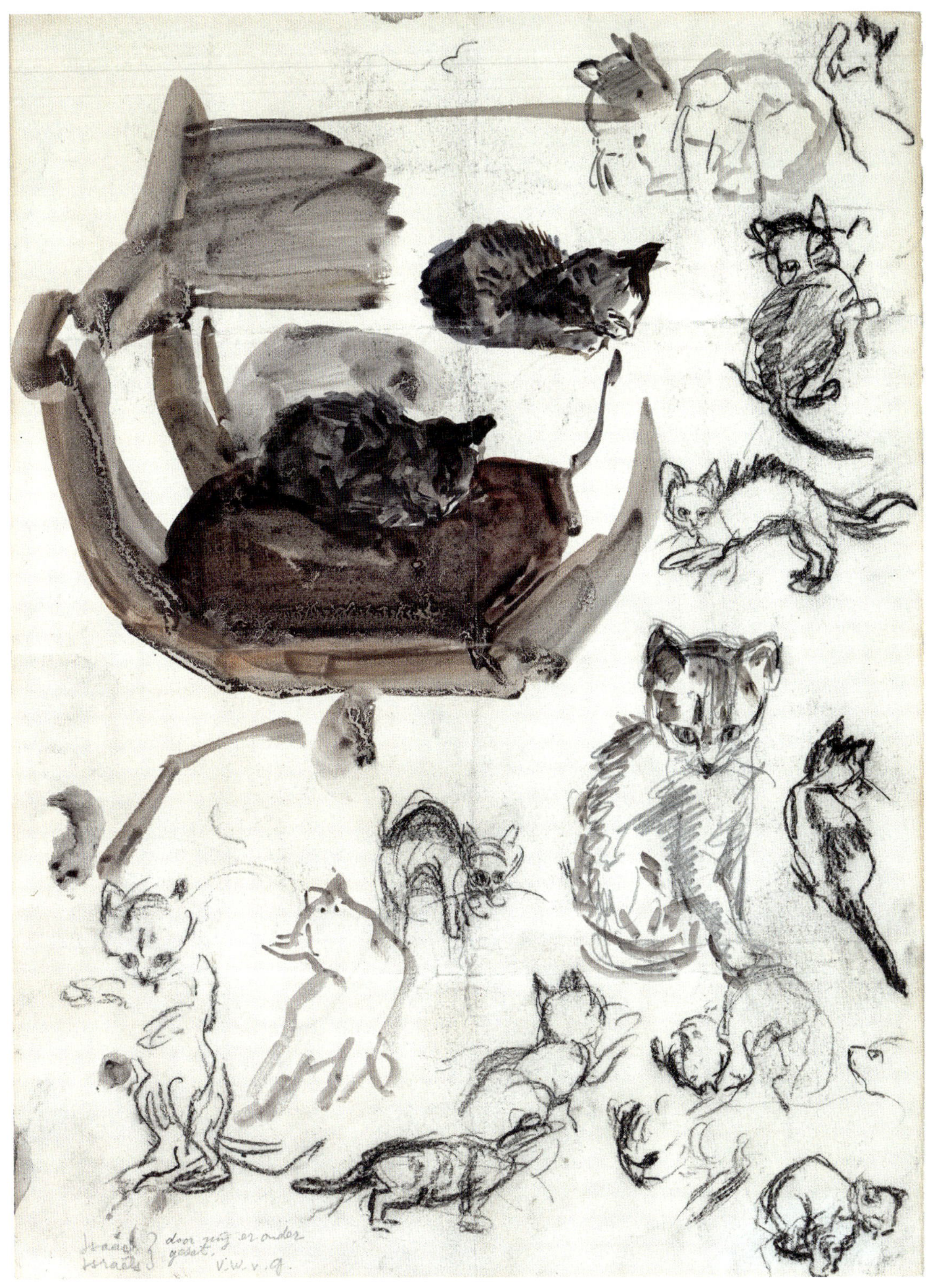

Plate 30 Isaac Israëls, *Kitten in Different Positions*, 1896. Enclosure with a letter to Jo van Gogh-Bonger.

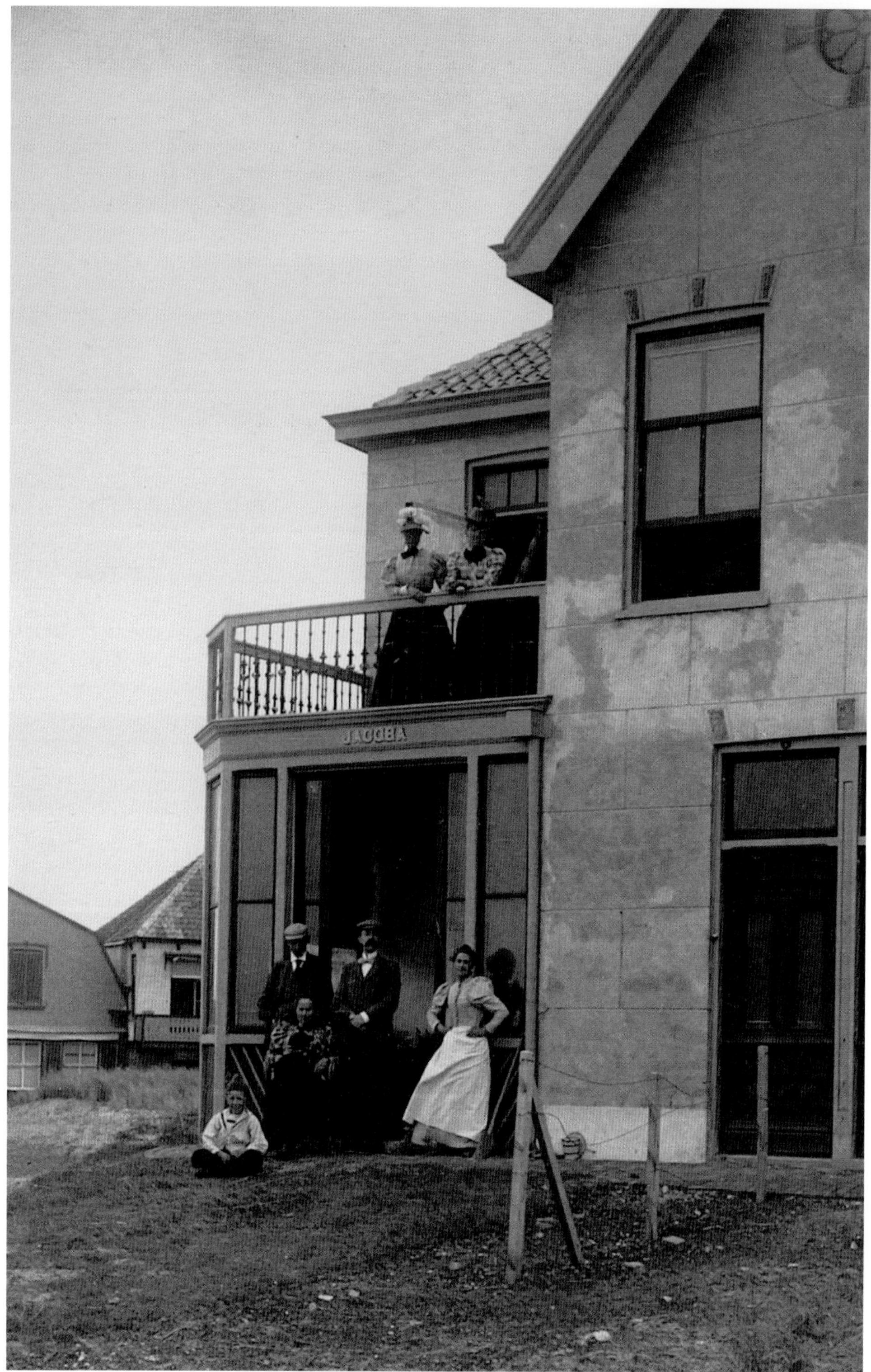

Plate 31 Villa Jacoba, Noordwijk aan Zee, summer 1898. Jo van Gogh-Bonger sits on the chair on the left, Vincent van Gogh sits cross-legged on the ground in front of her. The man with a moustache behind her in the centre may be her brother Henri. On the right, wearing a white apron, is the maid Gerritje.

Plate 32 Calendar page for Wednesday 22 May 1901 with a quotation by Jo van Gogh-Bonger. 'Preserving our children from prejudice and misconceptions is one of the few things we can do to make their life's struggle easier. They are entitled to that.'

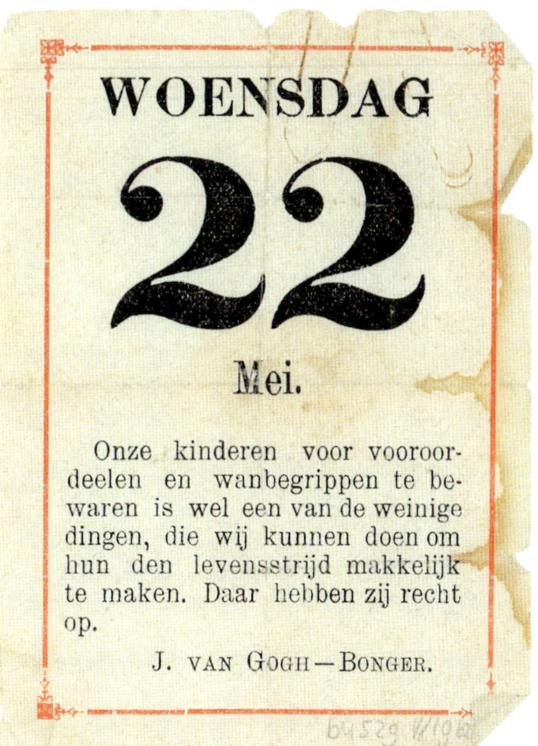

WOENSDAG

22

Mei.

Onze kinderen voor vooroordeelen en wanbegrippen te bewaren is wel een van de weinige dingen, die wij kunnen doen om hun den levensstrijd makkelijk te maken. Daar hebben zij recht op.

J. VAN GOGH—BONGER.

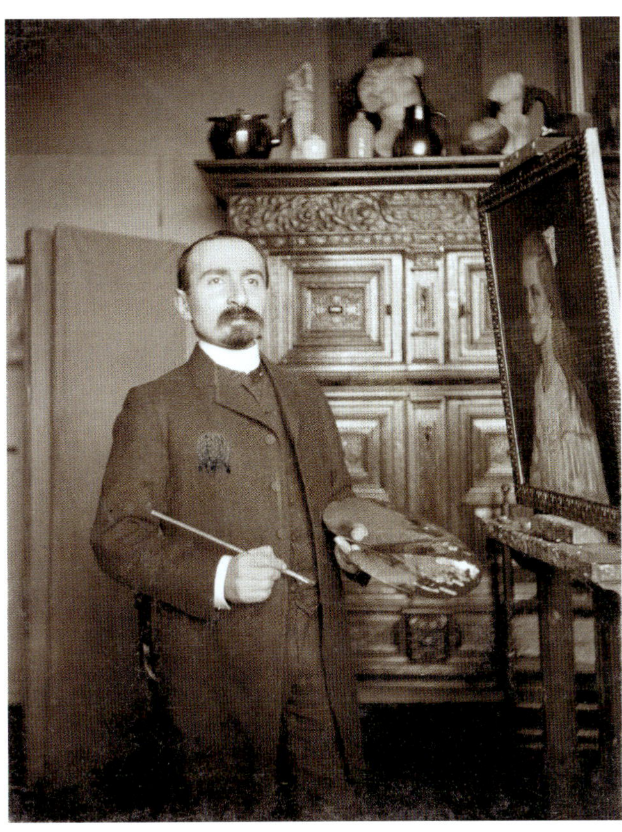

Plate 33 Johan Cohen Gosschalk at his easel on which there is a portrait of a girl, undated.

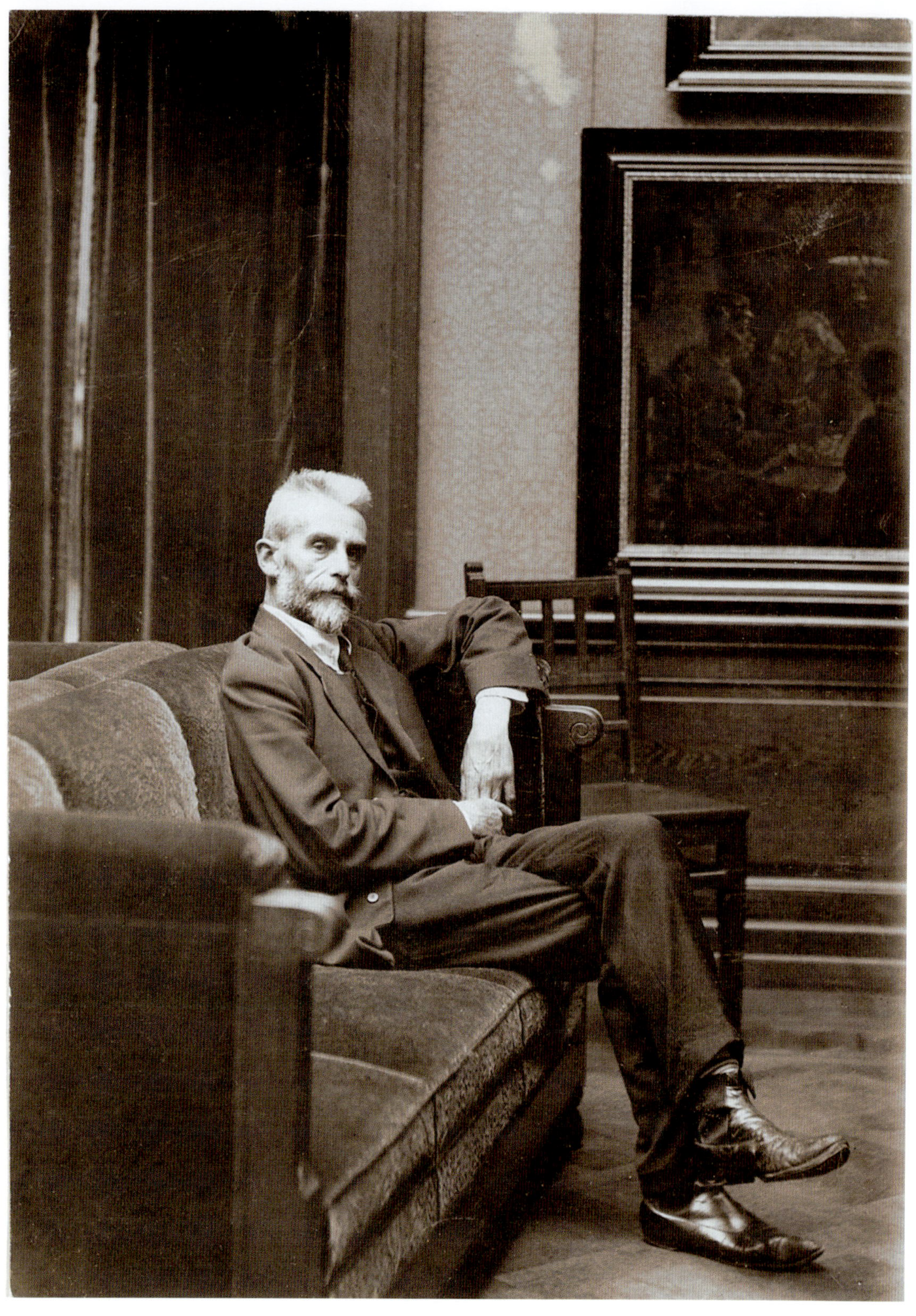

Plate 34 Willem Steenhoff in the Rijksmuseum, with Van Gogh's *The Potato Eaters* behind him, *c.* 1918.

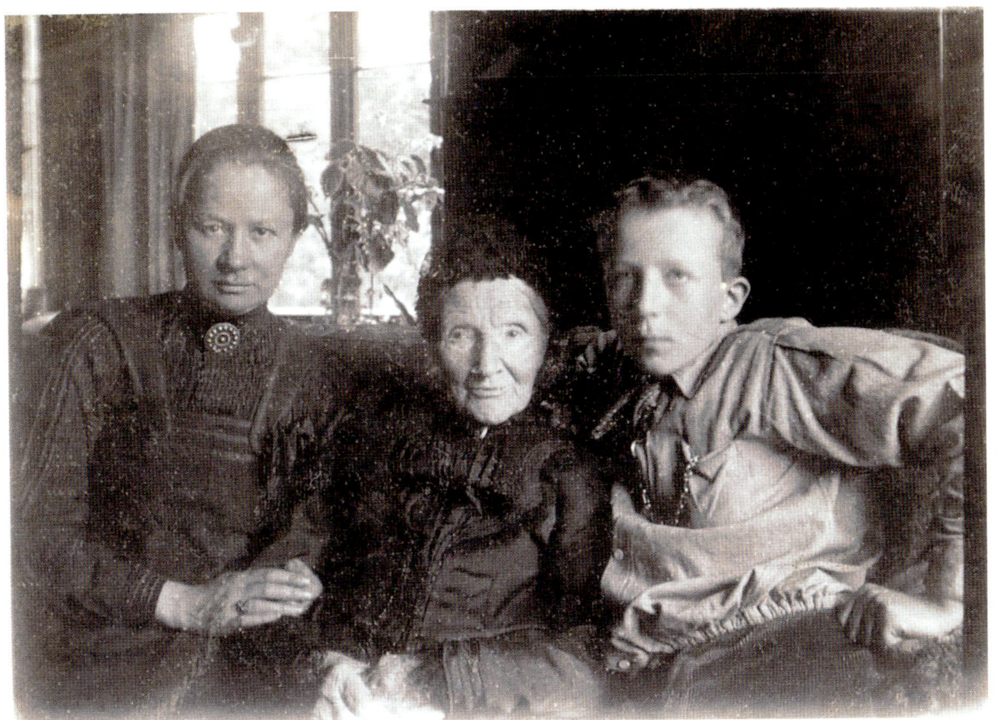

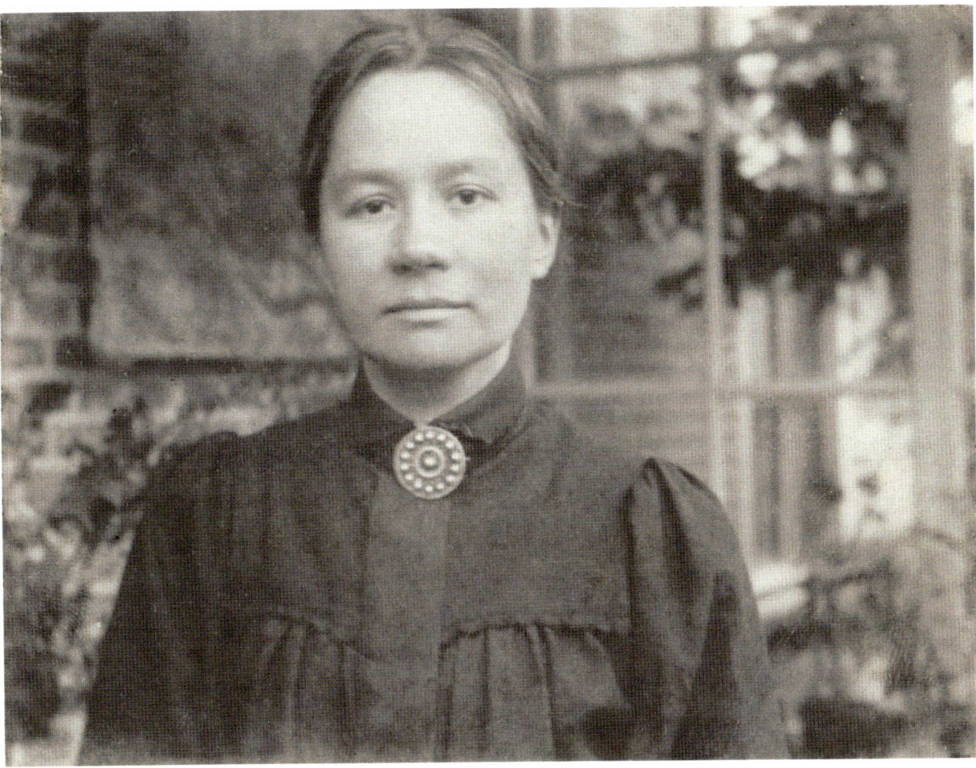

Plate 35 Jo Cohen Gosschalk-Bonger, Anna van Gogh-Carbentus and Vincent van Gogh in Bussum, 1903.
Plate 36 Jo Cohen Gosschalk-Bonger, *c.* 1904.

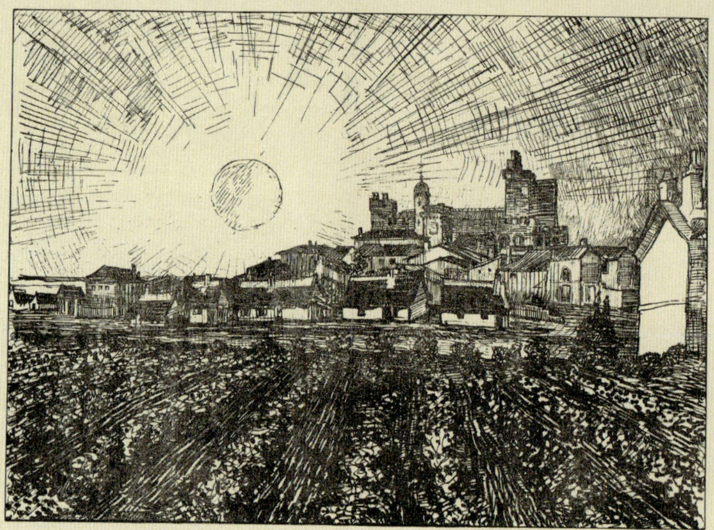

Plate 37 Poster 'Tentoonstelling Vincent van Gogh, Stedelijk Museum Amsterdam, juli-augustus 1905'.

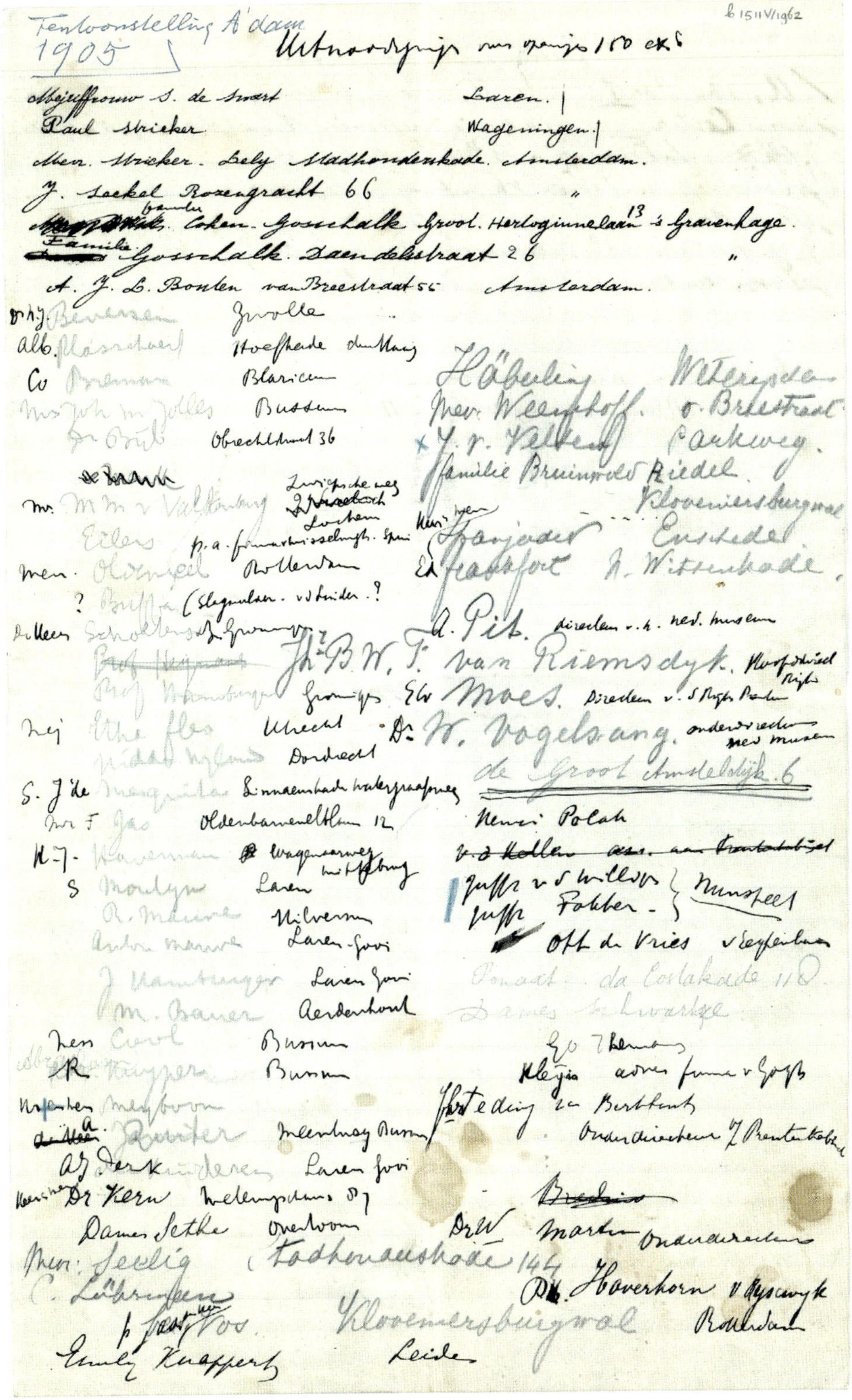

Plate 38 List of invitees to the opening of the exhibition in the Stedelijk Museum, 1905. Handwriting of Jo Cohen Gosschalk-Bonger and her son Vincent.

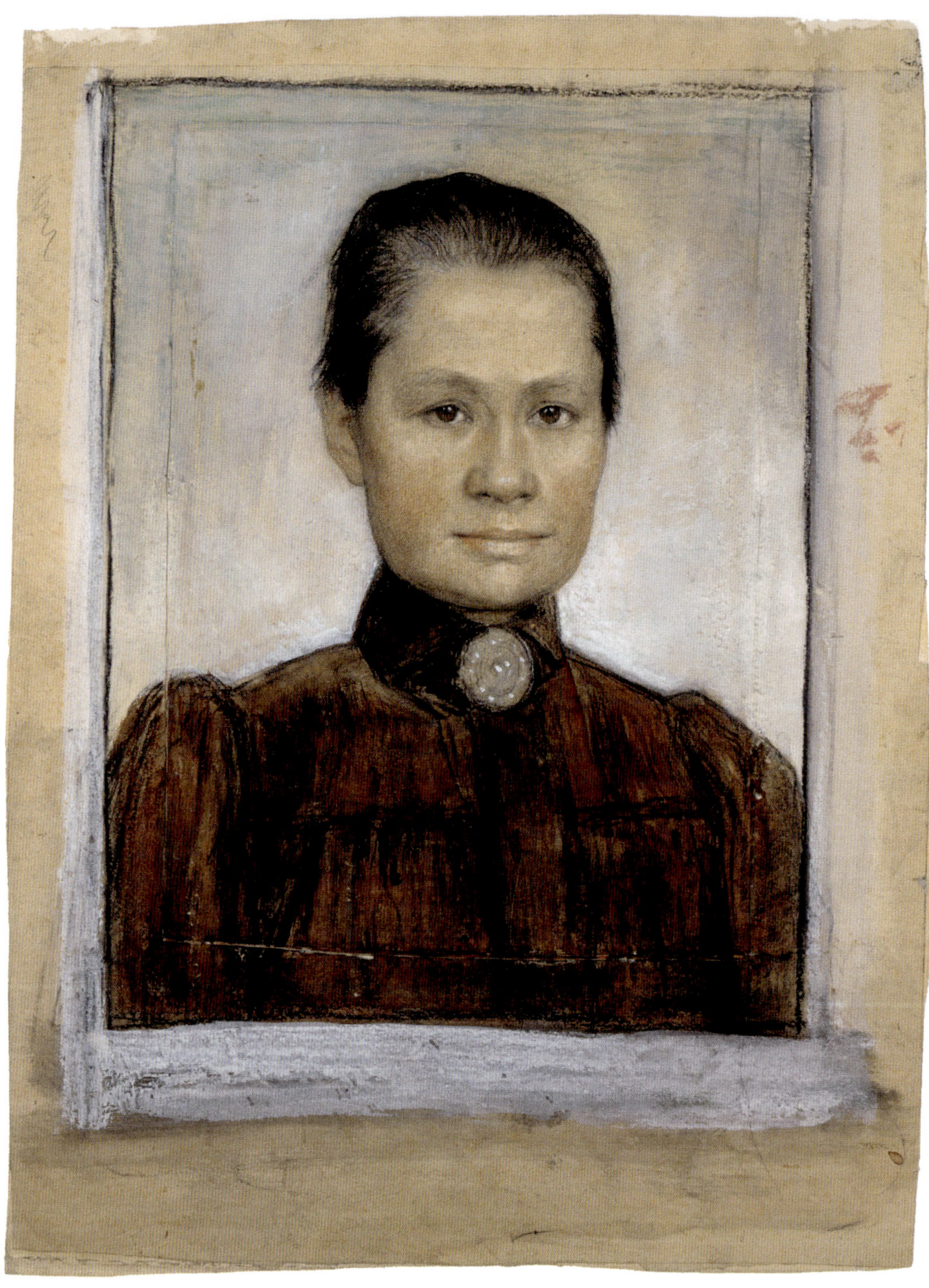

Plate 39 Johan Cohen Gosschalk, *Jo Cohen Gosschalk-Bonger*, *c*. 1905.

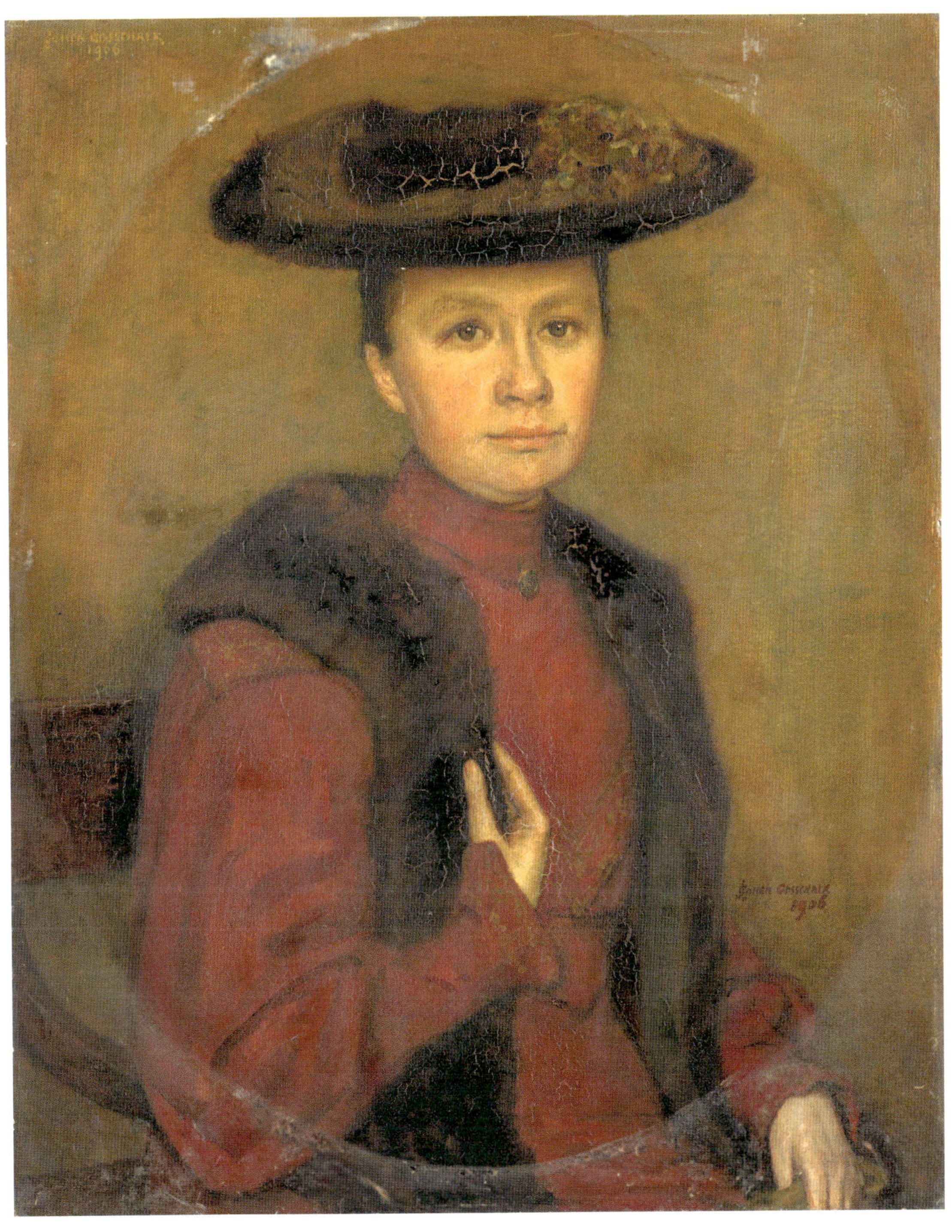

Plate 40 Johan Cohen Gosschalk, *Jo Cohen Gosschalk-Bonger in a Red Dress, Fur Hat and Fur Stole*, 1906.

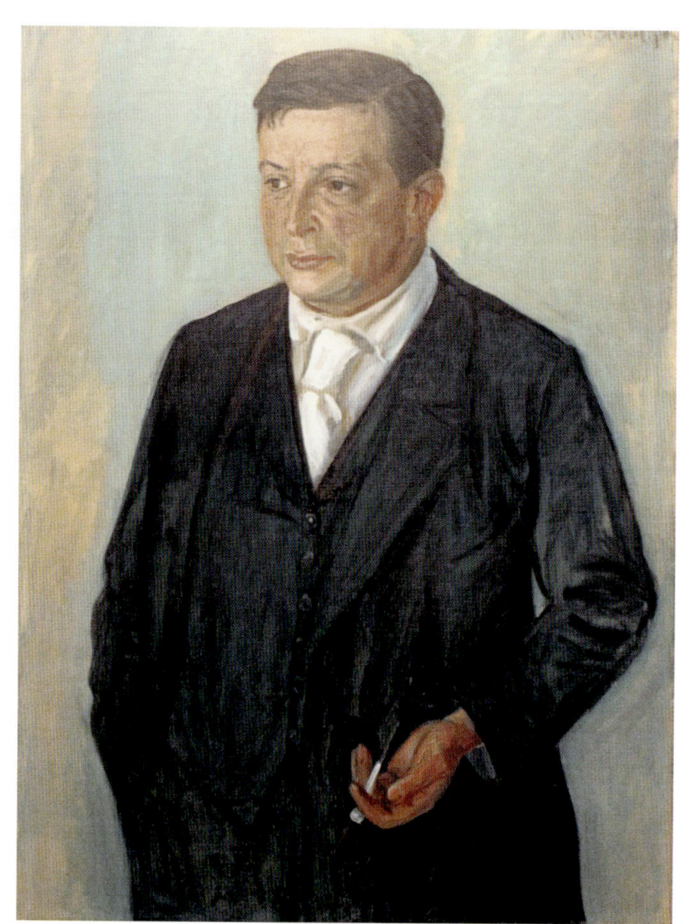

Plate 41 Leopold Graf von Kalckreuth, *Portrait of Paul Cassirer*, 1912.

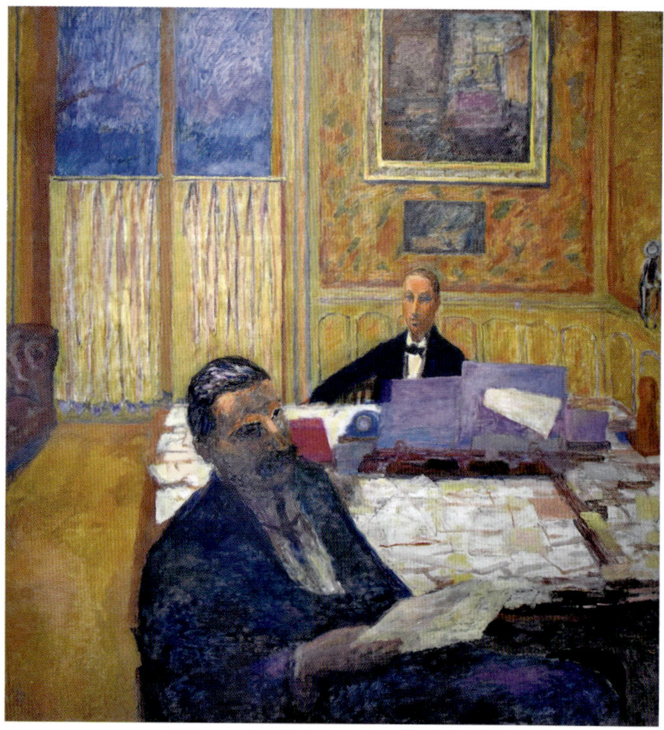

Plate 42 Pierre Bonnard, *The Bernheim-Jeune Brothers*, 1920. Josse in the foreground and Gaston behind him.

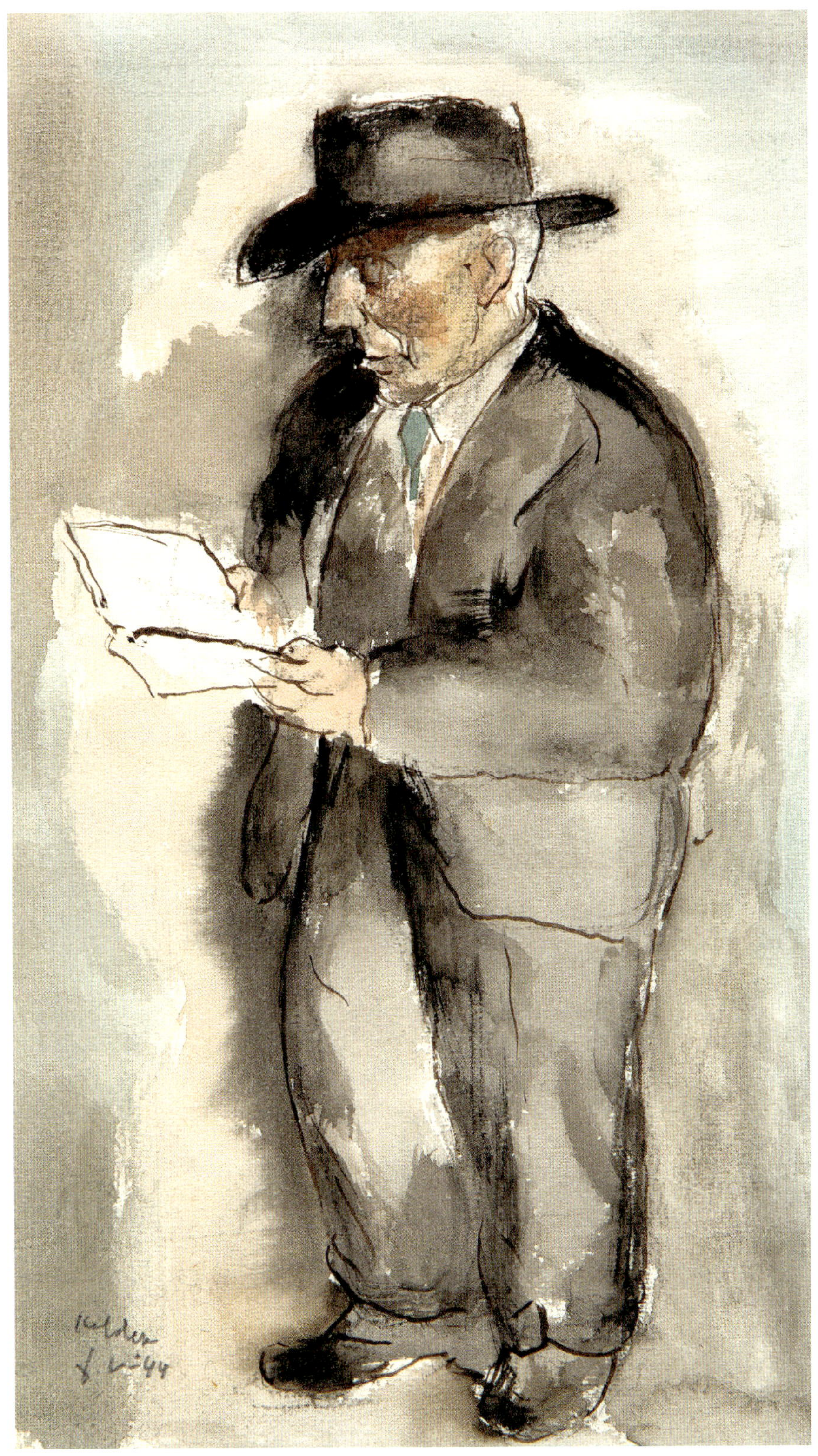

Plate 43 Anthonius (Toon) Bernardus Kelder, *Portrait of J.H. de Bois, Art Dealer, Haarlem*, 1944.

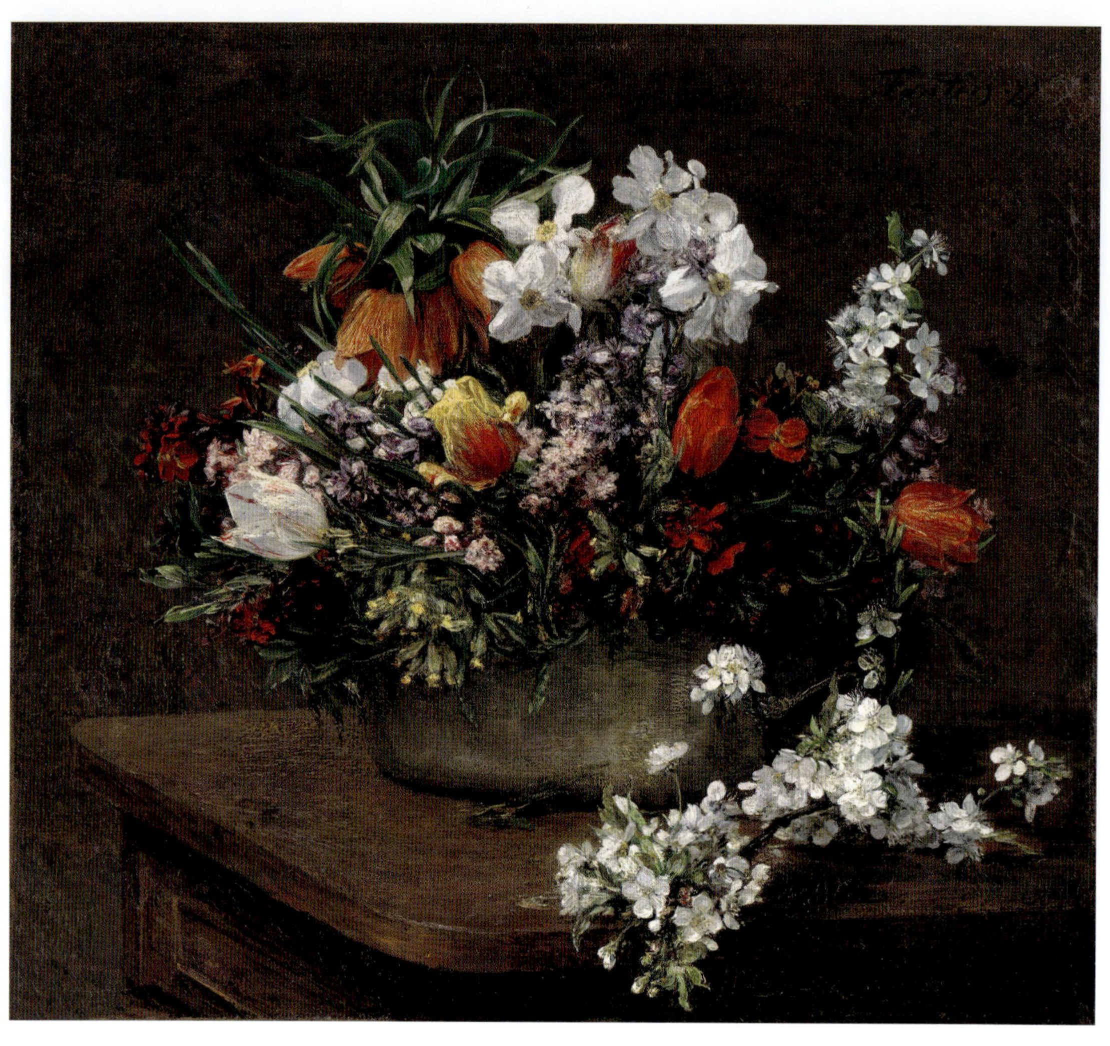

Plate 44 Henri Fantin-Latour, *Flowers*, 1877.

15 centimes!", which is very appropriate here, isn't it?' Vincent's insistence that the sheets were to be sold for just fifteen centimes chimed with the principles of the Volkshuis, which lent out art reproductions.[63]

Physical discomfort

At home things were going relatively well under the circumstances. Mrs van Gogh had come to stay shortly after Whitsun in 1903 and been delighted at what she found there. 'I keep seeing your beautiful home with everything and everybody who moves and lives and works there, and the impressions of your Great love in my mind's eye, for which I once again give profound, heartfelt thanks.'[64] Photographs were taken during that visit—'everyone thinks the one on the couch is the best' (Plate 35).[65] It must have been around this time that Johan made the portrait drawing of her that was included in the introduction to *Brieven aan zijn broeder* (1914). He also drew Jo and Vincent, who progressed to the third form of the HBS (Higher Secondary School) in Amersfoort.[66]

Things started to go wrong in September, when Johan contracted pleurisy. It was the start of a chronic complaint that repeatedly recurred with severe attacks. Johan's bed was brought downstairs and Jo had a nurse to assist her at night. Vincent stayed elsewhere for two months. Things did not look good. Jan Veth was in Berlin and was kept up to date about Johan's condition by his wife, Anna. He wrote: 'I can only hope that he'll come through it. It would be terribly tragic.'[67] Anna did what she could to provide support during that period. 'Please do everything you can think of to help Cohen and Jo in particular.'[68] Henriette van der Meij also understood the gravity of the situation and sent her best wishes: 'What a stressful time, you'll be exhausted in body and soul and now there's that awful weakness. And you're no giant yourself.'[69]

The following month Johan's situation improved slightly and the nurse left. Jo's parents were opposed to her taking all his care on her own shoulders, knowing as they did that their daughter's constitution was far from robust. On top of the pleurisy, Johan developed mysophobia—a pathological fear of germs—which did not make her life any easier.[70] Jo felt powerless. She even had to undergo an operation at the beginning of 1904. It involved her being admitted for two days, but the reason was not disclosed, which suggests it was a delicate matter. When her father suffered from kidney stones during these months, for example, the problem was discussed openly. We know, for instance, that he drank plenty of Java tea to get relief from the complaint.[71] Jo had not told her mother about the mysterious operation beforehand. Clearly concerned, Mrs Bonger wrote: 'I'm so worried. How do you get it? Could that have been the reason you suffered? Heaven help you to recover soon. Still, you'll really need to need to build up your strength, and take things easy at the moment, and don't cycle anywhere.'[72] Mrs van Gogh also urged Jo to be careful: 'such an experience is a clear message.'[73]

Nevertheless, all the stops were pulled out to celebrate Vincent's birthday. Jo gave him red tulips as usual and wrote to Mrs van Gogh about the festivities. She answered immediately, writing she was a 'wonderful, loving, mother'. She also took advantage of the opportunity to give Jo some advice and the names of clergymen in Amersfoort to whom Vincent could go at lunchtime for confirmation classes—something she felt his education was still lacking. Well intentioned as this was, Jo was completely opposed to the idea, and so was Vincent.[74]

Like Johan, Jo's nerves were fragile. At the beginning of 1904 all the worries and stress became too much for her. She had a relapse and was admitted to the Lutherse Diaconessenhuis, on the corner of Van Eeghenstraat and Koninginneweg in Amsterdam.[75] Vincent was once again sent elsewhere temporarily.[76] Her friend J. Mante-Aalders empathized and hoped that Jo was not suffering too much from all the nervous exhaustion: 'I was so sorry to learn that you and your husband were in such a bad way. Mrs [Bertha] Jas wrote and told me that you were very overwrought because of the stress you've been under and that you spent some time in the Diaconessenhuis, which didn't surprise me. You certainly have a lot to cope with in your married life.'[77]

After she was discharged from hospital, Jo went to Switzerland to convalesce. To begin with, she travelled with her sister Betsy and Vincent, and later with another Betsy, apparently a paid companion who happened to have the same name. While in Lucerne, Jo wrote a few undated letters to Johan and one dated 15 April 1904—by then they had already been to Wiesbaden, Locarno and Basel. She sent them from Pension Kaufmann, where she and her sister shared a room with a view of Mount Pilatus. Vincent's room had a view over Mount Rigi. Jo saw mountains for the first time in her life, and she thought they were 'much more beautiful than I thought, so solemn and serious, so immune to the actions of human hand', she wrote to Johan.[78] They projected something comforting and brought the beginning of Psalm 121 to mind: 'I will lift up mine eyes unto the hills'. Reclining in her easy chair in front of the open window looking out over Lake Lucerne, she contemplated how 'decrepit' she was and how much good the pure air was doing her. She regretted she had not brought *Tartarin sur les Alpes* by Alphonse Daudet with her because it was so well suited to this environment. Jo ate a lot. She was always hungry when she travelled.

She visited the museum in Basel, where she bought Holbein reproductions for Johan and his sister Meta. 'I miss you, I wish that you were with me, then it would be perfect here—how beautiful and big the world is,' she wrote to him affectionately.[79] She described their boat trip to Brunnen, through the mist and the rain, as unforgettable. While they were on board Betsy had softly sung 'Es schrie ein Vogel' by Christian Sinding, and Vincent, who was wearing his cape, walked around the boat. 'He glistened in the rain and radiated enjoyment.'[80]

Jo also told Johan that she got on well with a few British, American and Canadian boarding house guests. At the same time, she often thought about the Netherlands. She knew there had been an exhibition of Jan Toorop's work at Frans Buffa & Zonen in Amsterdam and her thoughts turned to the tenth SDAP conference, which was held between 3 and 5 April 1904 in Dordrecht. She was worried about Johan's inability to handle money and wondered whether their housekeeper Rika was thrifty enough. When Jo was at home she kept a tight rein on things, but now she had no control. 'But I'll get things back on track once I'm home!'[81] In the boarding house she found the complete works of Goethe and decided to read his *Briefe aus der Schweiz*. She still felt utterly wretched, though.

In bed she listened to the rhythmic lapping of the lake, but to her it sounded like the sea. Meanwhile she had taken leave of her sister and son, and continued on her travels with the second Betsy. She was not comfortable with strangers, so Jo was with her a lot of the time. They both bought large summer hats and went for regular walks. Jo loved the cool air—she hated hot weather. In one of her letters to Johan, she asked whether Dr Beyerman was still examining him weekly and wanted to know what he had said about the state of Johan's lungs. She also wrote that Vincent had been a competent traveller and knew all about trains and boats. He had sent her a postcard from the Netherlands—'he'll never be a writer,' she concluded resignedly.[82] 'I would like to put Siegmund's 'Siehe der Lenz lacht in den Saal' as a motto at the top of my letter—I keep hearing it in my head,' she admitted in her last letter home, in which she described a trip to Küssnacht.[83] The line she quoted comes from Wagner's opera *The Valkyries* and it refers to the moment at which Siegmund senses that the month of May is approaching. As far as Jo was concerned Switzerland was 'utterly and completely the country of Wagner . . . a land for giants and gods.'[84] While travelling she saw unbelievably beautiful colours that kept on making her think about all sorts of paintings. The landscape 'was just like a Segantini—how annoying, all those comparisons that always go round in someone's mind.'[85] Betsy and she philosophized together a lot:

> about how people spoil so much—and yet a small human heart can take in the greatness of everything and enjoy it—but in the end what can that person do with it? Then you come back down to earth and listen to the people at the dining table all saying the same old things every day—it's as if they aren't aware of all the beauty around them.[86]

She read on the façade of an inn in Küssnacht that Goethe had stayed there, and in the village she found various references to Friedrich Schiller's *William Tell*. 'They certainly honour their great men,' she commented tellingly. It will certainly have stimulated her. By then she had been striving for nearly fifteen years for such a 'great man' and she would continue to do so for at least another twenty years.[87]

She had only just returned to the Netherlands safe and sound when her father died on 28 April 1904. All the brothers and sisters were there at home when he passed away. Shortly before his death Jo sent news about her father's ordeal to Mrs van Gogh, who replied to Jo and wrote about the comfort that the members of this 'exemplary family' would offer one another in these difficult times.[88] Johan made a portrait of Jo's father as a tribute, and Jo's mother was very pleased with it. She praised her husband: 'How hard Pa worked throughout his life and kept everything in good order.'[89] It took some time before Jo's grief at this loss lessened a little. Their relationship had not been intimate, but she had always been able to call on her kind father. Her great love of music also came from him.

A pioneering study on modern art

The art critic Julius Meier-Graefe, who had been immersing himself in Van Gogh's work for a considerable period, told Jo that he had found a publisher for his 'very profound study', devoted to the development of modern art. He sent her a long list of requests and fired no end of questions at her. He needed an overview of the principal Van Gogh works that she possessed or had possessed, preferably including dates, and he sent a list of owners' names and asked Jo whether she knew any others. He also wanted to know which six works she thought were the most important and her views on the short biography of Van Gogh that Bernard had written for the *Mercure de France* in 1893. And he was eager to hear what she felt about Gauguin's pronouncements concerning his determining influence on Van Gogh.[90]

Jo foresaw how important this publication would be and answered his questions. However, when she read what Meier-Graefe eventually asserted in his book about Gauguin's influence on Van Gogh, she was very far from pleased. When she wrote to him later, she told him in no uncertain terms that Vincent had never addressed his friend Gauguin as 'maître', and asked him to stop publishing such inaccurate accounts of what happened, which she rightly described as nonsense. Vincent had praised Gauguin to Theo as 'un bien grand maître', but this had been a strategic move aimed at convincing his brother to do everything in his power to bring about a hoped-for cooperation with Gauguin, and never went much further than that. She felt that the assertion of Vincent's esteem for Gauguin was too suggestive.[91]

Meier-Graefe also asked Jo about the collection of Van Gogh letters. Like Leclercq two years before, he put himself forward as editor of the correspondence and enthusiastically explained his plans. He suggested that Jo could perhaps translate the letters written in Dutch into French or German in the evenings. It was clear that he had absolutely no idea of what that would involve for her.[92] He had a very clear vision of a publication of the letters: 'Here it is, winter—prepare a little of the correspondence. I'm dying to deliver it to the public.'[93] Before this, however, his study *Die Entwicklungsgeschichte der modernen Kunst. Vergleichende Betrachtung der Bildenden Künste, als Beitrag zu einer neuen Aesthetik* was published at the end of May 1904 in three bulky volumes. She told Gachet in 1907 that, a couple of misgivings aside, she thought the section about Van Gogh was very good.[94] Meier-Graefe saw Van Gogh as an example for painters, but assumed that the public at large would never learn to appreciate him. Jo's opinion was without doubt favourably influenced by the way he stressed Van Gogh's socialist motives and focused on humanist values in his work. He wrote that he hoped one day to publish Van Gogh's collected letters and included a list of Van Gogh collectors. Jo had the most, followed by the

Schuffenecker brothers with around thirty paintings, then Paul Gachet Jr with twenty-six and Bernheim-Jeune with fifteen. The list ended with some others with eight or fewer.[95] Meier-Graefe's essay about Van Gogh had a significant influence on interest in his work in Germany. As a dealer, Paul Cassirer for example, profited from the publication, in which Van Gogh, Gauguin and Cézanne were identified as the founders of modern art.[96] Later, Meier-Graefe expanded the piece about Van Gogh and published it separately in 1910. By that time, a third edition of *Die Entwicklungsgeschichte* was being prepared.

Another individual interested in Van Gogh's letters appeared on the scene. On the advice of Jan Veth, who emerged once again as advocate, Paul Cassirer's nephew Bruno had read the letters in *Mercure de France* and *Van Nu en Straks*. He was profoundly impressed and surprised at the extent of the correspondence, and told Jo that he would like to publish the letters.[97] Bruno Cassirer published the magazine *Kunst und Künstler* from 1902.[98] Cassirer and Jo came to an arrangement, and fifteen instalments of 'Aus der Korrespondenz Vincent van Goghs', illustrated with letter sketches, drawings and paintings, were published in the course of 1904 and 1905.[99] Immediately afterwards, Cassirer published Vincent van Gogh, *Briefe* in book form. The title page of the anthology credits Margarete Mauthner with editing the passages from the letters. The inexpensive and successful 1906 edition was reprinted frequently and reached a wide audience. The fourth, expanded edition (1911) was the basis for the first English translation: *The Letters of a Post-Impressionist, Being the Familiar Correspondence of Vincent van Gogh* (1912) by Anthony M. Ludovici.[100] Jo was not involved in any way with this rather sloppily compiled publication. Meanwhile she was thinking about putting out a better English language version herself.[101]

Back in Amsterdam

Staying in Hotel Beau Site in the North Sea resort of Zandvoort during the hot summer of 1904, Jo had tried to restore her equilibrium, but it was very difficult. 'Yes, the sea can affect people's nerves in different ways. And then there's that heat!' confirmed an unknown correspondent on a postcard. Johan avoided the seaside and had wisely withdrawn to Nunspeet to paint.[102] While in her holiday accommodation, Jo thought a lot about the future. Life in Bussum might well have seemed idyllic, but old familiar Amsterdam began to draw her more and more. Her sister Betsy had clearly exerted pressure on her to move house: 'If you were to move to Amsterdam, you'd see what a lovely time we'd have. . . . We could easily find a cheap place to rent. Then you could have a nice maid and you could also come here for the day.'[103]

The decision was made at the end of August. Both Jo and Johan let themselves be persuaded to return to the city where she was born. They found a tenant for Villa Eikenhof, their home in Bussum that would remain in Jo's possession for many years. This house was to generate significant rental income, initially for her and later for her son.[104] A few improvements were made during the 1930s and the property was not sold until 1978.[105]

The three of them moved to Amsterdam and from September 1904 they lived on the corner of Brachthuijzerstraat and Koninginneweg. They rented a new modern two-storey apartment in the building that H.H. Baanders had designed the year before.[106] Jo continued to live there until her death in 1925. The entrance was at 2 Brachthuijzerstraat, but on her notepaper Jo used the more chic-sounding 77 KONINGINNEWEG. Beneath their flat there was a grocer, who also rented the cellar.[107] Johan rented a room elsewhere that he used as a studio, but exactly where it was is unclear.[108]

The surviving construction drawing shows the floorplan of their apartment: they had a large sitting room, with a bay window, and a dining room that led off it. The kitchen was at the back. Upstairs there were two bedrooms and a maid's room. Given the size of the art collection, Jo probably stored part of it, perhaps at her haulier's premises. There was not enough space in the small room adjoining the kitchen and the attic to store all the artworks, even though the majority were unframed. (It is possible that Jo also used part of Vincent's bedroom.) In his memoires, the socialist Henri Wiessing wrote about a visit he and Willem Steenhoff paid her in 1908: 'With Steenhoff's help, that Mrs Bonger, shall I say, brought a number of canvases from a small room in the attic and took some drawings out of a cupboard.'[109] They were already well settled in on her forty-second birthday, 4 October 1904. The interior was pretty much full of furniture and knickknacks, while the walls were covered in paintings, as had been the case in Bussum (Figure 41).[110]

Vincent attended the HBS in Roelof Hartplein. Jo wrote to Jan and Anna Veth saying that the proximity of Vincent's school was one of the reasons why they moved. When he read that letter many years later, a disgruntled Vincent noted the following in his diary:

> It says, among other things, that it was good for me because it was less tiring since there was no travelling (to Amersfoort, 2nd class HBS). And also that she liked living closer to her mother again. Both are fallacies and incorrect. Her marriage was a disappointment, and she then fell back, not on her independent lifestyle in Bussum, but on her family. And her domineering mother actually hindered the development of her children. She also repeated a number of those inaccuracies in conversations with others: that the flat was so much better and so on. She did me a lot of harm through that move—and by getting married to that neurotic. She could have found a better husband. I've already written previously that I benefitted from his fine mind, but he didn't help me develop.[111]

Nowhere else in his diary or correspondence did Vincent express himself in such a frankly negative way about his past home situation. In their household at that time there was a depressing, almost deathly atmosphere, which Johan obviously did not create deliberately, but was oppressive for Vincent and sometimes rendered Jo powerless. Starting in 1939 and continuing for some time, Vincent received

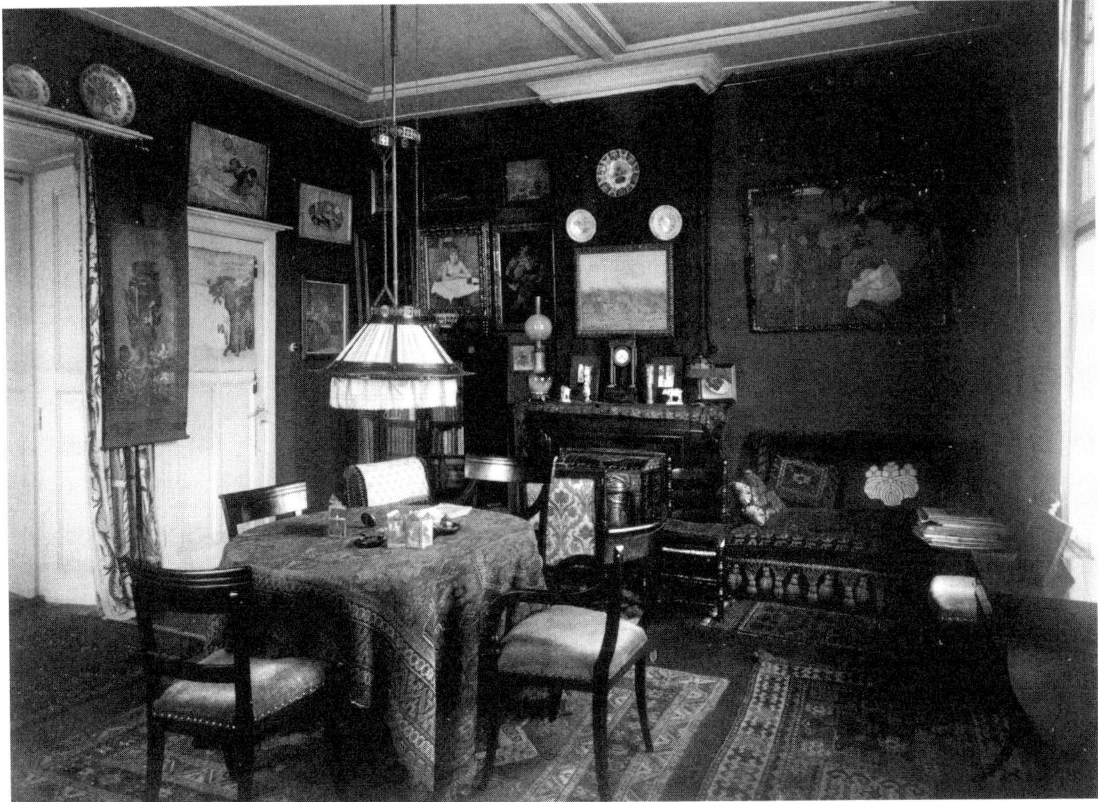

Figure 41 The sitting room at 77 Koninginneweg in Amsterdam, between 1922 and 1925.

treatment from a psychiatrist—this difficult period in his family life must have been discussed at length during consultations.

Not everything was doom and gloom. He could get on well with his mother and what he wrote about her was therefore predominantly positive. Jo talked to him about the art of Pieter Breugel the Elder, for instance, and she taught him that this painter was the first 'who depicted ordinary things. I so clearly recall my mother telling me that.' And prompted by a visit to Museum Boymans in 1935 with his own son Theo: 'I'd already been there with Theo in the holidays to see the Vermeer exhibition, which had many Pieter de Hooch's. My mother always told me that my father loved them so much, which I can well imagine.'[112] Over the years mother and son learned a lot about Dutch Renaissance art and together they also studied the huge number of engravings that Van Gogh had collected. In 1904 it must have done Jo good to read that Aunt Mietje was moved when she saw the young Vincent. She was surprised by how much he looked like his father at that age: 'the same head of curly hair and the friendly face.'[113] It goes without saying that such observations did nothing to bring Johan any closer as a husband and stepfather.

Grave rights in Auvers-sur-Oise

In September 1904 Paul Gachet Jr wrote to Jo about extending the grave rights in Auvers-sur-Oise (Figure 42). He contacted her because she had told him that Mrs van Gogh had granted her power of attorney with regard to the estate of her oldest son, Vincent. Gachet suggested placing a simple statue on Vincent's grave.[114] A modest monument certainly met with Jo's approval, although nothing ever came of it. She had planned to go to Auvers in August, but the trip did not go ahead because of the move and her exhaustion. In the autumn of 1890, Jo and Theo had stood at Vincent's grave and now she asked Gachet if it was possible to buy a second grave and at the same time to buy the grave rights for both graves in perpetuity. This is an interesting detail in her correspondence with Gachet. It shows that as early as 1904 Jo was toying with the idea of a reburial for Theo.[115] He replied that even if they were to buy the grave rights in perpetuity, Vincent's mortal remains would still have to be moved because of a change in the layout of the cemetery. If she did nothing now, the grave would be cleared. Gachet offered to act on her behalf, but she would have to agree in writing. Shortly afterwards he told Jo about the options and the prices.[116] She discussed this with Mrs van Gogh and in June 1905 Vincent was reburied in the same cemetery. Jo attended.

Meanwhile the developments associated with Van Gogh's work continued. The collector Gustav Schiefler of Hamburg wrote to Jo to say how much he had enjoyed visiting her and that he very much wanted to organize an exhibition in his city.[117] His plan came to nothing, however; he could not drum up enough support and Jo left him in limbo in favour of Paul Cassirer.[118] In September 1905 Schiefler

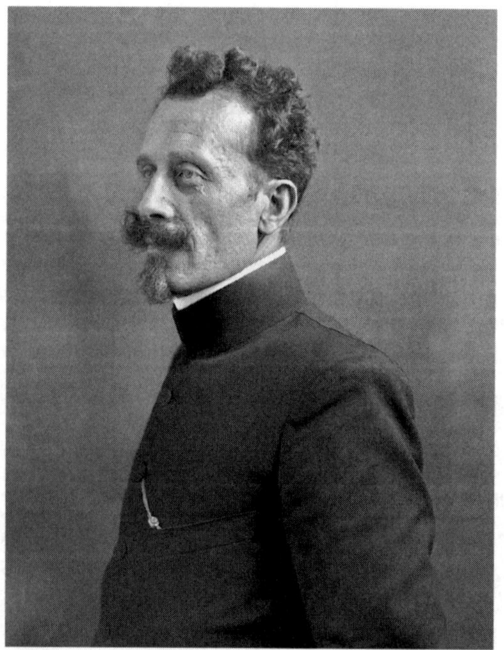

Figure 42 Paul Gachet Jr, 1909.

thanked her at length for two works that he had purchased directly from her. He told Jo they had made his heart race with joy and his wife was elated too. He paid two and a half thousand guilders for the paintings, which were *Canal with Bridge and Washerwomen* (F 427 / JH 1490) and *Garden with Flowers* (F 430 / JH 1510).[119] Six years later, Schiefler contacted her with another request. The works were unsigned and so he asked Jo if she would confirm on the backs of the photographs he had had made that she had sold him the paintings, as evidence for posterity.[120] Jo wondered whether it might not be better to do that on the backs of the canvases themselves, but she did not follow this up and wrote on the photographs concerned, returning them with a declaration drawn up by a notary.[121] It was a good thing she did, because Schiefler had to sell *Garden with Flowers* in the economic depression after the First World War. This was followed in 1924 by *Canal with Bridge*, which was bought by Cassirer—of all people—for his wife. It is striking how polite, pleasant and accommodating Jo had been in her letters to Schiefler.[122]

Paul Cassirer set to work enthusiastically and within six months sold fourteen works by Van Gogh at five exhibitions.[123] Jo received a letter from H.L. Klein, who ran the C.M. van Gogh gallery in Amsterdam. In it he asked for confirmation of the net prices of seven paintings by Van Gogh that she had placed with him on commission. The prices she set were high and ranged between six hundred and a thousand guilders. He asked whether she was prepared to drop the highest category to eight hundred and fifty guilders, arguing that the asking prices were really too high compared with those in Paris.[124] It was through such contacts as this that Jo increased her knowledge of the current art market.

1905: a year of contrasts

As we have seen, Jo did not confine her sales to private collectors. She also placed works with a number of galleries, which helped her to meet her goal of spreading Van Gogh's work like a fan all over Western Europe. By now, she had no need to offer art herself because interested parties approached her.[125] Over the years, more and more artists were exposed to works by Van Gogh, and this increased his influence on modern art. Van Gogh's opinions about art during his early period also became known through other channels. In 1905 the art critic Albert Plasschaert published excerpts from letters from Van Gogh to his artist friend Anthon van Rappard in *Kritiek van Beeldende Kunsten en Kunstnijverheid*. The letters to Van Rappard were not published in book form until 1936 (in English) and 1937 (in Dutch and German).[126]

Van Gogh's commercial breakthrough came in 1905, culminating in the major Van Gogh exhibition in the Stedelijk Museum in Amsterdam. Before that, though, the correspondence between Paul Cassirer and Jo intensified. He wanted to stage an exhibition again and asked for her help. After his recent experience in Germany he could envision successful future collaboration. Being a businessman, he spoke eagerly of 'pecuniary success'. On 14 April he confirmed receipt of thirty works, and the exhibition opened two weeks later in Berlin. He suggested to Jo that nine of them be offered for sale (at a higher commission). Cassirer told her regularly about offers and asked for her response. Suggested prices moved up and down; the final result was a cheque for 14,000 marks. Jo noted 8,259 guilders for the nine works in the cash book. This was followed on 30 April by the sale of a further work for 1,059 guilders. When the exhibition closed, the remaining artworks were shipped back in five crates.[127] This was indeed a favourable transaction for Jo, both in terms of getting Vincent's work seen and financially. But it did not end there. Cassirer turned out to be the right man in the right place for her.

Van Gogh's triumphal march in Germany was an extraordinary contrast to the impending emotional event in Auvers-sur-Oise. Jo received an agreement from the local mayor for a double cemetery plot of four square metres, which was now assigned in perpetuity. It cost her over four hundred francs. The carpenter sent a bill for a hundred and thirty francs for a new lead-lined oak coffin.[128] Jo travelled to Paris with her sister Betsy. They went by train from the Gare du Nord to Chaponval, and on Friday 9 June 1905 they arrived in Auvers. Paul Gachet Sr and his son Paul were present at the official reburial.[129] Jo saw how Vincent's mortal remains were exhumed from the grave and transferred to the coffin. For a moment she stood face to face with his skull, as she later recounted to Gustave Coquiot: 'I assisted at Vincent's exhumation. I clearly recognized the shape of his head.'[130] The sight of his skull made a profound impression on her. The emotions engendered by the reburial—she had not been present at the funeral in 1890—and her stay in Auvers took Jo back fifteen years. She wrote to Gachet when she arrived home, telling him that it reminded her of the happiest time of her life. Those years were engraved indelibly on her memory.[131] To express her gratitude for all their help and hospitality, she sent the Gachets an original letter from Vincent; it was the letter he wrote to Theo on 28 June 1890, with a letter sketch of Marguerite Gachet at the piano. She kept a transcript for herself.[132]

Jo's decision to have Theo reburied too dated from the moment that the grave rights issue arose. To that end she had not only bought a double burial plot in Auvers, she had also asked about the costs of having Theo's mortal remains taken from Utrecht to France and ascertained what authorizations were required. Gachet complimented her on her determined attitude in this matter by describing her as 'a stoical woman'[133] (Plate 36). Nevertheless, the plan was not actually put into effect until years later. Theo's reburial finally took place in April 1914, when Jo's publication of the letters was about to be released.

Jo and Betsy had barely returned from this memorial trip to Auvers when their mother died on 18 June 1905, aged seventy-four. Jo was with her in her last hours and present as her mother gently slipped away, surrounded by her four daughters. Her three sons were not able to be there. Johan and Vincent arrived shortly before she died, although Jo's mother no longer recognized them. Jo had lost both her parents within a year. Now she was aware of a huge void.[134] In her message of condolence, Johan's sister Meta expressed the hope that Jo's nervous system would not 'be overset again' by the shock.[135] That remained to be seen.

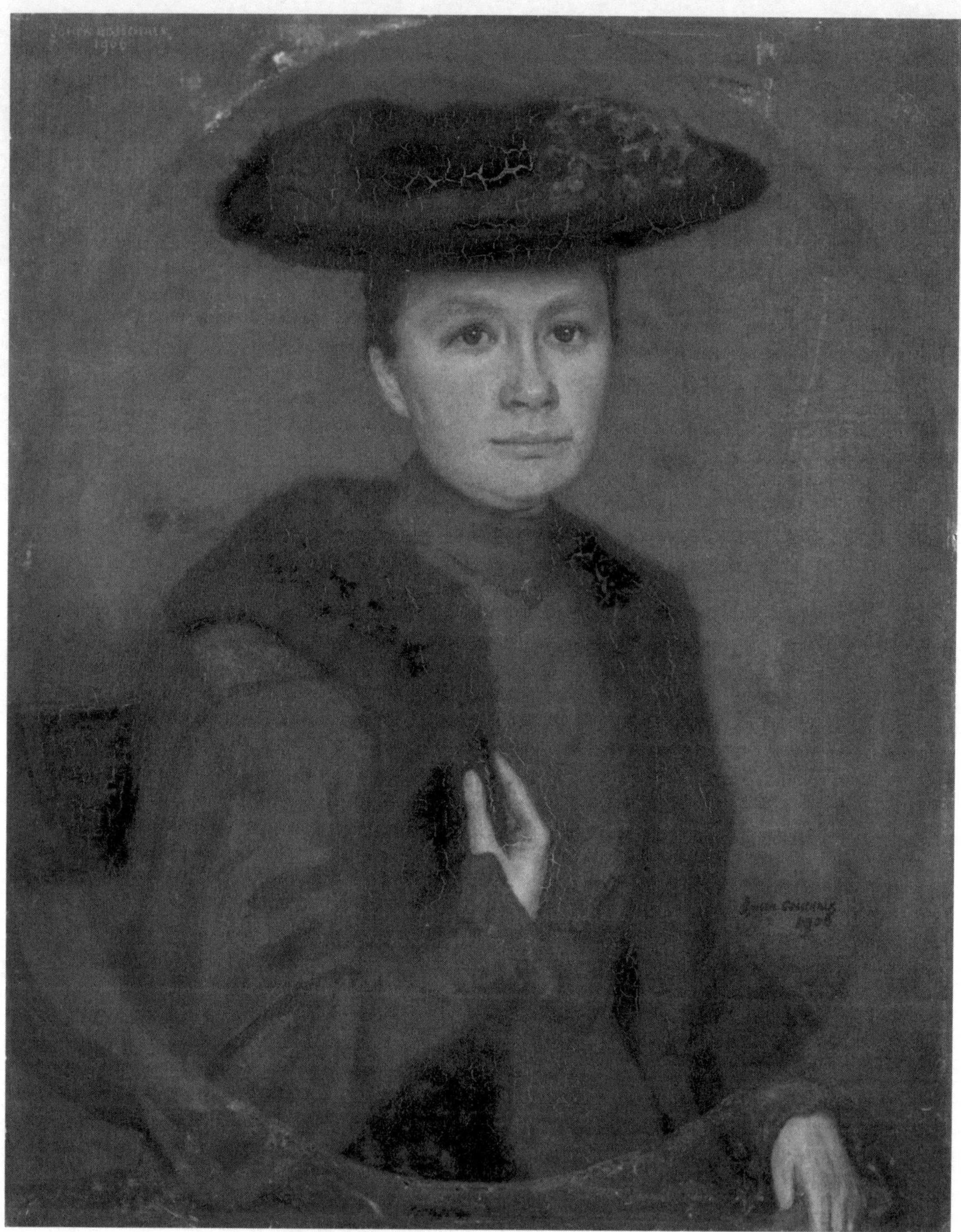

Part Five

Van Gogh goes from strength to strength

1905–12

It is quite true what philosophy says: that Life must be understood backwards. But that makes one forget the other saying: that it must be lived—forwards.

SØREN KIERKEGAARD[1]

12

A magnificent exhibition in the summer of 1905

Despite her grief following the death of her mother, Jo kept a cool head and continued steadily with her activities. For the rest of the year she actually outdid herself, and was more visible than ever. She decided that the time was ripe for her to organize a major exhibition in Amsterdam's Stedelijk Museum, and asked a number of owners to lend their Van Goghs. Such loans were important and the names of the owners looked impressive in the catalogue as evidence of Van Gogh's popularity among collectors in the Netherlands and abroad. The first loans arrived in the same week as the messages of condolence. Jo received a total of twenty-nine, including those from family members.[1]

She started making preparations as early as March, tackling the enormous task efficiently and calling on her experience with previous exhibitions.[2] With Johan's assistance, she made lists of the selected works, searching assiduously for suitable titles, as the many corrections and additions show.[3] Five days before the opening, Hugo von Tschudi, director of Berlin's modern art museum, sent a further two paintings by express.[4] Jo's ability to maintain an overview of all the shipments and the piles of correspondence confirmed her organizational talent. She had 'season tickets' and a striking poster printed (Plate 37).[5] Jo selected eighteen passages from Van Gogh's letters to Theo for the exhibition catalogue, most of them relating to paintings and drawings dating from the period when Vincent was working in France. Johan wrote the introduction with input from her. In it, he underlined the generous support Theo had always given Vincent and referred to Theo's 'rare brotherly love and self-denial'. Of Vincent's period in Arles (1888–9) he wrote vividly: 'The sun, the bright, happy colours, the cascading light—they affected him like sparkling wine.' Given the biographical particulars he described, at that time Jo was clearly already well on the way organizing and transcribing the stacks of letters written by Vincent and Theo.[6] Towards the end of the exhibition, they had a second, revised edition of the catalogue printed.

Applying for permission from the Amsterdam city authorities to rent out galleries in the Stedelijk Museum to a private individual, the supervisory committee asked curator Cornelis Baard whether

Jo was organizing the exhibition for 'sales or advertising, or purely in the interests of art'. Baard put everyone's mind at ease and assured them that the interests of art were at the forefront. No sales would be made during the exhibition and, on specific days, admission would be free for students taking drawing courses.[7] The contract with the city stipulated that Jo would be responsible with Baard for day-to-day management.[8]

The exhibition, simply called 'Vincent van Gogh', opened at two in the afternoon of Saturday, 15 July 1905. It ran for seven weeks and was open every day until 30 August between 10 a.m. and 5 p.m., except on Tuesdays, when the museum was closed. Admission was twenty-five cents, but on Thursdays it was fifty cents—that day was apparently reserved for a more exclusive type of visitor.[9] The invitation list for the opening reflects the extensive network Jo had meanwhile built up. Altogether, a hundred and fifty invitations were sent to family members, lenders, art dealers, museum directors, collectors, art critics, editors of daily newspapers and weeklies, artist friends, writers and architects, and to her contacts in the Amsterdam Sociaal-Democratische Vrouwenpropagandaclub (SDVC), which she had helped to found shortly before (see Chapter 15). The fifteen-year-old Vincent contributed to the preparations by keeping a neatly written list of invitees and helping to arrange and hang the works (Plate 38). It was Jo's way of involving him in this major event.[10] In the meantime, Johan helped her in all sorts of ways with both moral and practical support.[11] He took care of some of the correspondence, for instance, as can be seen from a letter addressed to him by a potential buyer who wanted a discount on a painting because there was no artist's signature on it and the composition had been painted on 'common strawboard'.[12] Many interested buyers wrote to Jo directly, while others talked to her or contacted her through third parties. The catalogue encouraged readers to ask the attendant or enquire at the desk for information.

Jo was able to stage her impressive exhibition in the summer of 1905 with Johan's help and the assistance of Willem Steenhoff, who had just been appointed deputy director of the Rijksmuseum's paintings department. She was given nine days to arrange and hang the works. There were 443 of them, divided between five large galleries in chronological order. Jo added another forty-one works soon after the opening, which most probably meant that she needed to rent two more galleries.[13] There are no known photographs showing how everything was displayed, but the art historian Willem Vogelsang, who had just joined the Rijksmuseum, thought the exhibition was 'superbly organized'—although he was less impressed by the 'bathroom shades' of the walls and the 'funereal black' of the panelling.[14] In terms of sheer size, this Van Gogh exhibition has not been equalled and never will be.

Jo succeeded in attracting large numbers of visitors and encouraging people to talk about what they saw, in both positive and negative terms. Although the Stedelijk Museum concentrated on contemporary art—it had accommodated the City of Amsterdam's modern art collection since 1895—the modernity of Van Gogh's work was too extreme for many, including some professional art critics. There were journalists who described the exhibition as a madhouse, and of course that did the museum's reputation no good. The art reporter A.C. Loffelt wrote mercilessly in *Het Nieuws van den Dag*, 'daring to exhibit such shoddy work is scandalous,' and sneered that the stars in Van Gogh's *Starry Night* (F 612 / JH 1731) looked like doughnuts.[15] Fifteen years after his death, Van Gogh's work was still controversial. There were enthusiasts, for example the art editor Jan Kalff Jr, writing under the pseudonym 'Giovanni' in the *Algemeen Handelsblad* of 24 and 25 July, was quick to shower praise in his two articles. Opposing them there were those with reservations and even aggressive attitudes, bristling with open enmity.[16] This generated heated discussions during and after the exhibition, with the beneficial and very welcome side effect of focusing attention on Van Gogh. Willem Steenhoff also joined in the debate with four articles in *De Groene Amsterdammer*, in which he contended that this retrospective of Van Gogh's oeuvre would make it necessary for very many opinions about the paintings and drawings to undergo a 'serious review'. He praised the artist's originality and individuality and urged the general public most earnestly to go and look: 'The work will grip you and never let you go.'[17]

Jo set a special price of admission of ten cents for members of the association 'Kunst aan het Volk' because she sympathized with its goals. It had been founded in 1903 by artists who were members of the SDAP, or were kindred spirits, in order to foster understanding and enjoyment of art among workers. The first chair was Pieter Lodewijk Tak. The working members (a few dozen) organized theatre performances, concerts, talks and exhibitions for the two thousand or so art loving members. Amsterdam City Council supported the association with an annual grant between 1910 and 1924.[18] Vice-chair and artist Marie de Roode-Heijermans thanked Jo for the discount on the price of admission and wrote a glowing article about the exhibition that was published in *Het Volk* on 12 August.[19] She was convinced that workers could love this art—a view that Van Gogh would have enthusiastically endorsed, which also coincided with that of the French art critic Albert Aurier. He had asserted as early as 1890 that simple folk and illiterates would be able to understand Van Gogh's work.[20]

Jo received a letter from Julius Meier-Graefe enclosing a list of people whom he believed she should not fail to tell about her exhibition. It included Julius Stern (Potsdam), Harry Graf Kessler (Weimar), Karl Osthaus (Hagen) and Curt Herrmann (Berliner Secession). He also wrote that the exhibition at Cassirer's in Berlin had been a success—*Sunflowers in a Vase* (F 456 / JH 1561), which Jo had sold to him, had been on show there (currently in Munich, Bayerische Staatsgemäldesammlungen, Neue Pinakothek): 'Vincent will have a true homeland for his glory here. We talk about him all the time and he wins admirers every day.'[21] He finally came to Amsterdam himself in mid-August and walked through the galleries after hours with Jo. He was completely overwhelmed by the sheer volume of artworks, and above all by their beauty.

A group of French people actually came by car from Paris—a highly unusual undertaking because at that time cars were still very few and far between. In 1908, for example, only twelve cars a day used the road between Amsterdam and Haarlem. 'They already knew Uncle Vincent's work from before—I had a nice chat with them,' wrote Jo in a letter to Vincent on 20 July.[22] Other foreign visitors included Paul Cassirer, Hugo von Tschudi and Max Liebermann from Berlin. Mrs van Gogh was moved and commented admiringly about her two sons: 'How hard Vincent worked and how much Theo saw the value in everything. That's a bond between all of us and you and your dear child, which I hope and trust all our family will keep up.'[23] Jo was only too well aware of that bond, and if there was anyone who made efforts during her lifetime to maintain it, it was her.

The state of affairs before and during the exhibition

Jo recorded all expenses and income associated with the exhibition in a separate notebook.[24] It gives a surprising insight into the practical ups and downs of her adventure in the Stedelijk Museum. She was incredibly busy and tackled things very professionally. Nothing escaped her notice. The gallery rental (fifty guilders), the salary and black bow tie for the attendant (she had hired just one), the appointment of a cashier, ensuring there was enough change in the cash register, paying the cleaners and handymen, payments to the florist and the carpenter, tips, coffee and transport: she arranged all these things herself and she paid for everything (Figure 43).

On 28 April Jo had sold five hundred guilders' worth of shares to get some start-up capital. It soon emerged that she needed much more, however, because during the following weeks she spent hundreds of guilders on publicity, among other things. She acted shrewdly, and had a keen feel for marketing. She did business with the printers P.C.J. Faddegon & Co, which specialized in advertisements, the Nederlandsche Kiosken Maatschappij and the Scheltema & Holkema bookshop. Posters appeared on billboards and kiosks all over the city, and striking typographical advertisements were published in national newspapers. Jo paid the frame maker J.H. Leuning six hundred guilders and 644 guilders to the firm of M. van Menk, which made frames as well as providing transport services. The hauliers and frame makers J.S. Fetter & Co received 363 guilders. She had asked Paul Gachet Jr what types of frames art lovers in Paris favoured at that moment; she certainly did not want sumptuously gilded ones.[25]

The overall cost of the exhibition amounted to 4,130 guilders and admission tickets generated around 1,200 guilders, plus a further 273 guilders from paying visitors on the last day, which Jo forgot to note during all the upheaval.[26] It is no longer possible to determine the ratio between visitors who paid fifty cents (on Thursday), those who paid twenty-five cents and the 'Kunst aan het Volk' members, who paid ten. Nor do we know how many 'season tickets' Jo had distributed, but the total number of visitors is more likely to have been around four and a half thousand than the two thousand that was once estimated. By way of comparison, the exhibition in Groningen in 1896, which only lasted six days, drew some sixteen hundred visitors.[27] Jo had invested a great deal of her own money in the overall organization, but this was more than offset by the numerous works she sold between August 1905 and October 1906 in the wake of the exhibition, bringing in the substantial sum of more than thirty-four thousand guilders.

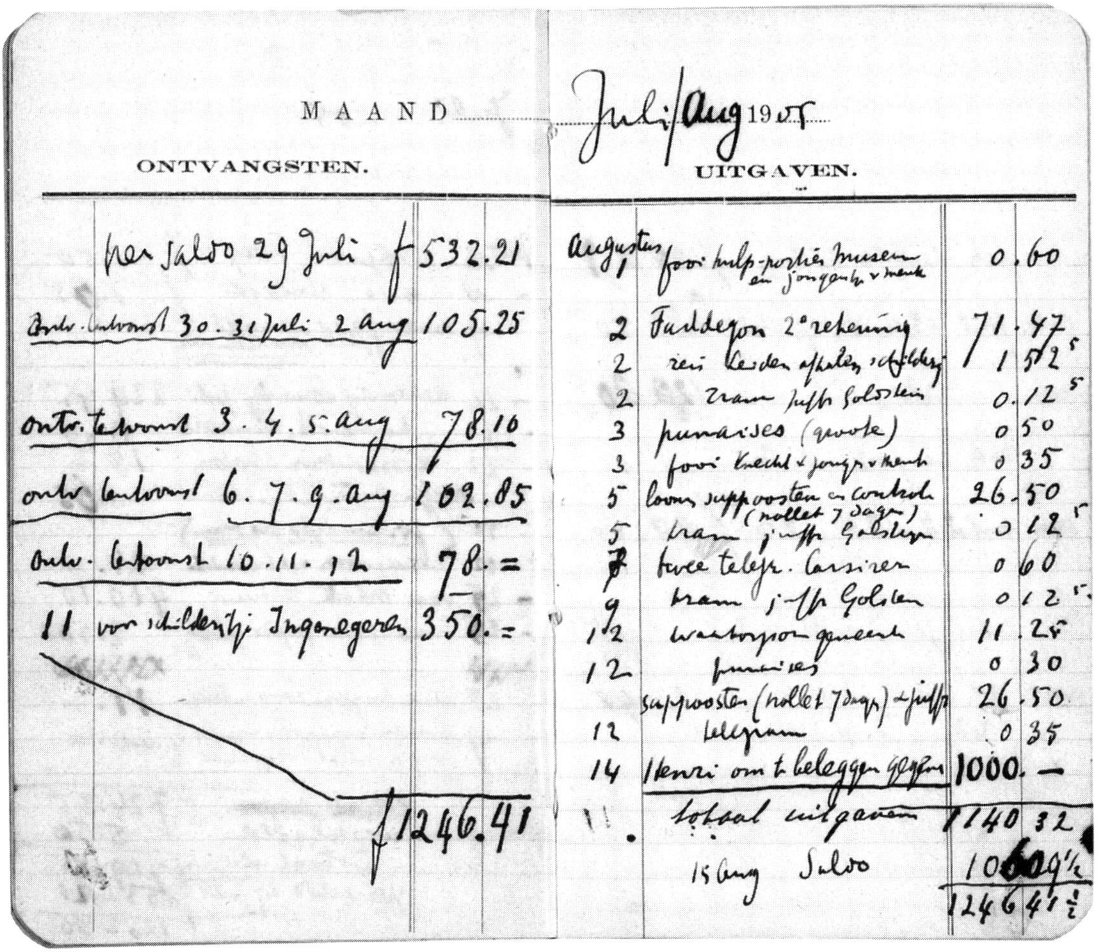

MAAND Juli/Aug 1905

ONTVANGSTEN. UITGAVEN.

Figure 43 Jo Cohen Gosschalk-Bonger, Notebook containing receipts and expenses associated with the exhibition in the Stedelijk Museum, 1905.

She noted all the asking and selling prices in her own proofs of the catalogue. Insurance was something else she had had to take care of, and she used another copy of the exhibition catalogue to record all the amounts for which the works were insured. The total insured value was 102,505 guilders. Jo made a fair copy of all the selling prices in a third.[28]

Once the exhibition was under way, Johan decided he had had enough of Amsterdam and in August he retreated to the De Valk boarding house in Nunspeet in order to paint. He had been in the same accommodation, which was very popular with artists, the year before. He was able to use a studio in the garden. Jo had sent Vincent to spend his holidays elsewhere, and in mid-August she relaxed for a few days in Anna's Oord, a boarding house in peaceful Groesbeek to get her breath back. All the same, her workload did not diminish in the slightest.

She was bombarded with letters from Paul Cassirer, who, after seeing so many Van Goghs in the flesh at the exhibition, saw endless possibilities for his gallery. Cassirer wanted Jo to make an exception for the museum in Berlin by selling Von Tschudi a number of drawings at half price. She needed to understand that the 'moral success' could be significant when it became known that the prestigious Nationalgalerie had purchased work by Van Gogh. Jo would certainly not have been immune to his reasoning, but she found this proposal too much to swallow and rejected it. Cassirer wrote back, emphasizing that he would earn nothing at all from this specific transaction and giving the impression that he wanted to do it purely and simply for the good of the cause; what he failed to mention, however, was that a purchase like this would inevitably strengthen his position as a dealer.[29] Cassirer was only too keen to sell Van Goghs himself and suggested to Jo that he should stage an exhibition in his Hamburg gallery, sending her a contract straight away. It stipulated that she would place the artworks with him on commission until 1 April 1906, after which they would be exhibited in Austria. In this case she did agree to his proposal. She selected thirty-five works and, as she invariably did, kept a list of them with prices. As always, some of the works were not for sale.[30] While in Groesbeek, Jo also answered all sorts of biographical questions she had received from Paul Gachet Jr. She apologized for the bad writing, but the pen and ink, which she had apparently borrowed from the boarding house, were dreadful.[31]

She was back in Amsterdam on 17 August. The following day she gave the monthly *Elsevier's Geïllustreerd Maandschrift* permission to photograph three paintings. They were intended for the article about Van Gogh that Johan had written for *Elsevier's*. It was lengthy, and in it he portrayed the artist as someone who had sacrificed his life for his art, again comparing him directly to the suffering and triumphant Christ: 'Fate did not give Van Gogh's life a peaceful course. He was nailed to his art as though to a cross. He bore it in ecstatic resignation until the end.'[32] There were sixteen illustrations in the article. The publication was further evidence of Johan's important role in the entire undertaking of publicizing Van Gogh.

After Jo had left Groesbeek and before she returned to her own home, she stayed for a few days with her sisters and brother in Weteringschans. They were all still living at home. Although she had been feeling unwell for a week, she did manage to walk through the galleries in the museum every day and kept Johan in Nunspeet fully informed, writing to him with the bouquet of flowers he had sent beside her on the table: 'I enclose the reply from Architectura—we surely can't ask them *again* can we?' (This concerned the Amsterdam society 'Architectura et Amicitia', which would be taking over the galleries on 1 September.) She told him she felt that the article by Querido in the magazine *Op de Hoogte* was 'bombastic' and that she was preparing for an SDAP meeting that evening at Carry Pothuis-Smit's.[33] Jo and Johan wrote to each other every day. In answer to a question from him she wrote: 'you bad man, how can I say *when* I'll come to Nunspeet when I haven't the faintest idea how long it'll take to tie things up—it's no small matter and then everything for Cassirer has to be packed up and sent off immediately!' She also told him L.C. Enthoven had bought *Sower* (F 494 / JH 1617) that morning for fourteen hundred guilders and that she had had an unpleasant encounter with Jan Veth in front of the paintings: 'He's so insufferably caustic! . . . He's too much!!' After all those years, the relationship with Veth had clearly not improved.[34]

Jo was not prepared to take the cash and cheques received during the exhibition to the bank on foot, so for safety's sake she took a taxi to her brother Henri, who looked after her banking. So business was certainly done outside the museum and the purview of the city authorities. She also told Johan that the 'maid crisis' was finally over because she had taken on a new housekeeper, who was also a good cook. Jo was desperate without a maid, particularly now she realized how exhausted she was. Andries and Annie, who were staying in Bordeaux, had sent some French grapes, and she sent them on to Johan.[35] At that time the postal service still operated like greased lightning.

Final chord in the Stedelijk museum

The exhibition was coming to an end. There were days with as many as a hundred and seventy to two hundred visitors. During this period Jo continually updated Johan on everything that happened. She wrote happily 'very good, don't you think?' about the sale to the collector Gustav Schiefler referred to in Chapter 11. And she asked him: 'How much extra shall we give the attendant?'[36] She was clearly up to her ears in work, and she had discussions with one person after another: Steenhoff, the haulier Van Menk and the photographer who came to take photographs of some of the works. In this euphoric mood, Jo presented Van Gogh's etching *Doctor Gachet with a Pipe* (F 1664 / JH 2028) to Ernst Moes, Director of the Rijksmuseum Print Room—a formal event that was reported in the *Netherlands Government Gazette*.[37] Steenhoff again demonstrated his influential role by accompanying Jo to see Barthold van Riemsdijk, General Director of the Rijksmuseum, to discuss loans. He brightened up considerably when Jo said she wanted to donate two works to the nation's treasure trove. Van Riemsdijk could make a selection from a number of works. The decision was made in March 1906. The works were the drawings *Road behind the Parsonage Garden in Nuenen* (F 1129 / JH 461) and *Farm in Provence* (F 1478 / JH 1444). Jo received thanks for her exceptional gesture not just from the Rijksmuseum. Pieter Rink, Minister of the Interior, wrote to her saying: 'I have the honour to thank you on behalf of the Government for this proof of your interest in the Rijksmuseum's collections.'[38] The *Algemeen Handelsblad* reported that the drawings were hanging in the Rijksmuseum's Waterloo gallery two days after the donation. This acknowledgement in a newspaper drew the donation to the public's attention, which was without doubt Jo's intention.[39]

She had a bad cold and there were workmen in the flat, but she remained stoic: 'Today they finally found the leak in the gas pipe. Yesterday they took the front room floor up, and today the living room floor. I hardly need tell you how delightful it was!'[40] Marie Mensing was staying with Jo temporarily—she was considerate and did not interfere or get in the way. Mensing had set her sights on a job at the Sociaal-Democratische Vrouwenpropagandaclub and had applied to Mathilde Wibaut.[41] Jo would certainly have put in a good word for her. (In 1906 Mensing became the secretary and organized the publicity for *De Proletarische Vrouw. Blad voor Arbeidsters en Arbeidersvrouwen.*)

On 30 August 1905, Jo was overwrought and wrote to Johan no fewer than three times. It was the last day of the exhibition. By eleven o'clock there were already sixty people in the galleries, and by the end of the day there had been 273 paying visitors. At closing time, the attendant had had to tell members of the public twice to leave. The painter George Breitner, who had initially viewed the art with indifference but later gave it his full attention, remained until the very last moment. After that the handymen emptied the entire Gallery of Honour at lightning speed. Jo expressed her gratitude to Steenhoff by giving him the painting *Poplars in the Mountains* (F 638 / JH 1797). He took it home under his arm.

'It's such a pity that it couldn't have stayed open for another couple of weeks,' she wrote to Johan, 'but I still don't have any regrets about doing it in the summer—because oh what a difference—with sunlight, or like the day before yesterday—a grey day! I would've liked to walk around the exhibition with you one more time this afternoon—we did very well, didn't we? "even though I say it myself".' It is not difficult to sense her deep satisfaction now that everything had turned out so admirably. And although she had not been completely out of touch with events around the world, such as developments in the Russo-Japanese War, for the whole of that period she was focused primarily on her task in Amsterdam.

Her mind was full of all sorts of impressions. In her third letter on that Wednesday she reviewed what she still had to do:

> It all went off very well; the shipment to Utrecht has gone—and is ready for Hagen—fortunately. Now I'll be with you on *Saturday*, at a quarter to one. Tomorrow I'll pay tax and go to the town hall for the admission books and settle up with Baard. On Friday I'll reorganize my wardrobe somewhat and tidy up my desk, which is covered in paper again, and on Saturday I'll drop everything and fly to you. Don't doubt that I'm also longing to be in the lovely countryside in that pure exhilarating air. Really, I've been nothing but a mechanical automaton for the last week.... Because three or four letters are needed for every unresolved issue.... It's lovely for me that Marie Mensing is staying in the flat—with Vincent—because at the moment all sorts of things are still happening!

She had been looking forward to having more time for other things—for Johan's work, but also for music and literature. Her sister Betsy had sung a love song by Robert Schumann and recalling it had stimulated her longing:

> Flutenreicher Ebro, it's in my head as I write. I longed for the piano to be open for a change—if only I'd had the time, I'd have played myself. . . . I wish I had some pleasant reading material here to bring with me—it'll have to be Heine again I think—because I won't have time now to go out and borrow anything. I'd like to have Flaubert's letters or something similar because I won't keep you from your work—you know that.

She sent Johan 'heaps of kisses' for the night.[42]

But for the time being she still had her hands full. She had meanwhile started to send back all the loans, each of which demanded great attention. Gachet Jr, for example, was very particular and gave specific instructions—so the crates were packed with the greatest care before they were returned to him. He assumed, not without reason, that the exhibition had made his Van Goghs even more valuable and he complimented Jo on her achievements.[43] It was a while before she replied because she was, as she wrote, 'really overwhelmed with work'.[44] The growing volume of correspondence had swamped her, and it was only now that she realized how tired she actually was. So she went to Nunspeet to recover.[45] It was around then that Johan made her portrait in chalk (Plate 39).

The family was finally reunited in Amsterdam at the end of September 1905, but sadly the peace and quiet was short-lived; Johan contracted pleurisy again and had to stay in bed for two months. She begged Gachet not to write anything about Johan's illness: 'He doesn't like people to know.'[46] Writing or talking about it in public was a very sensitive issue for him.

The merry-go-round keeps turning

In the meantime, Jo had started to correspond with the collector Karl Osthaus. He had previously introduced the German public to Van Gogh's early work, which he had on loan from the Rotterdam art dealer Margareta Oldenzeel-Schot. Now he wanted to organize an exhibition in Museum Folkwang in Hagen and listed some works that he felt were indispensable.[47] He had gone to the Stedelijk Museum twice to make the best conceivable selection. A month later Jo sent him eleven paintings and three drawings.[48] Osthaus went on to include them in his exhibition. He also set his sights on some works that he wanted to add to his own collection. Initially Jo offered to sell *Sunflowers in a Vase* (F 454 / JH 1562) for the astonishingly high sum of eleven thousand guilders, but she changed her mind about selling it, to Osthaus's great disappointment. He wanted to pay seven and a half thousand marks for four paintings and three drawings, and he promised he would give them a prominent place in the museum afterwards. It was typical of Jo that she did not give in immediately, even though her asking price in this case remained very reasonable: eight thousand marks, to which he naturally agreed. The money was transferred on 6 February 1906; when converted it was 4,732 guilders. Among the works he bought was the sublime *Olive Trees with the Alpilles in the Background* (F 712 / JH 1740).[49]

In Utrecht the society 'Voor de Kunst' staged an exhibition in Nobelstraat from 9 September to 2 October 1905. Jo lent fifty-nine works for it, a third of which were not for sale. The *Algemeen Handelsblad* of 13 September described the carefully selected works as very representative of Van Gogh's oeuvre. The catalogue contained Johan's introduction as well as the passages from Vincent's letters that had also been in the Stedelijk exhibition catalogue. Eleven hundred and fifty visitors came.[50] *Garden with Flowers* (F 429 / JH 1513) was sold for a thousand guilders to the botany professor Jan Willem Moll on behalf of his wife Anna Cornelia Moll-Fruin, who was elated and wrote to Jo: 'We are utterly enchanted by our purchase, which we shall honour in our home.'[51] Some of the works in the Utrecht exhibition then went on to the 'Leidsche Kunstvereeniging', where they were shown between 7 and 16 October. There were more than forty artworks spread over two galleries. Here, too, there was a great deal of interest.[52]

Jo wanted to continue the success of Amsterdam, Utrecht and Leiden in Rotterdam and Middelburg. A geographical spread like that had to be lucrative, so she asked Margareta Oldenzeel-Schot if she would like to take over the exhibition. Oldenzeel-Schot agreed and included in her own catalogue the front and back matter from the catalogues prepared for Amsterdam and Utrecht, thus giving the texts concerned national distribution (the only thing that differed on each occasion was the list of exhibited works). Between 26 January and 28 February 1906, there were fifty-seven paintings and eight drawings on display in Rotterdam, which means that Jo had supplemented the shipment from Leiden again.[53] According to the *Rotterdamsch Nieuwsblad* of 29 January, this extremely important exhibition made a lasting impression, and the *Algemeen Handelsblad* of 8 February published a glowing article about 'unprecedented things'. Jo had forgotten to send *Irises*, but she rectified this later.[54] A number of offers were made, and time after time she had to decide whether or not she wanted to haggle. Brief notes flew back and forth between the Oldenzeel gallery in Rotterdam and Jo in Amsterdam. *The Starry Night* (F 612 / JH 1731) was eventually sold to Georgette Petronelle van Stolk for a thousand guilders, on which Oldenzeel received fifteen per cent commission.[55]

The crates were to be taken by water from Rotterdam to Middelburg on 13 March, provided that the stormy spring weather had improved.[56] Oldenzeel-Schot warned Jo that a number of works

> are very sorely in need of restoration or varnish, otherwise they will be completely lost before long. There are some that are cracked, for example the apples, the brass cauldron (the background), the pansies, in which somebody was interested but was afraid that the cracks would grow, the sky over the fields etc. Since most of the canvases weren't prepared, sooner or later you're going to have to face the fact that some of the paint will flake off.

She hoped that Jo would not take this meddling amiss. All she wanted was 'to achieve the enduring good condition of the works'.[57] It is no longer possible to establish whether or not it was wise, but Jo did nothing, and for the rest of her life remained extraordinarily reluctant to have works restored, and categorically prohibited the use of varnish.

The correspondence with Middelburg was conducted through Mies van Benthem Jutting, secretary of the society 'Voor de Kunst' in Zeeland.[58] The exhibition was short and sweet—sixty-four paintings and drawings were on show at Sociëteit Sint-Joris between 25 March and 1 April.[59] The works had 'the same effect on some visitors as a red rag to a bull, while others, with great respect and admiration, praised the work to the skies', wrote the *Middelburgsche Courant* of 27 March, and this was a particularly neat summary of the reception of Van Gogh at that moment. Jo's eyebrows shot up, however, when the newspaper went on to comment that so much of the heritage had meanwhile been sold 'that what remains now is not the best'.[60] She reached for her pen and sent an immediate rectification, which the *Middelburgsche Courant* quoted on 29 March. She wrote incisively that it was not an 'inferior remainder, but a selection of the best Van Goghs that are currently being exhibited in your city, including a few of the *very best*, which have not been for sale and never will be.'[61] People must not think that she sold her soul to commerce and had held a clearance sale.

Jo sent presents for the feast of St Nicholas and New Year to Mrs van Gogh, who wrote back saying that she was thinking all the time about her 'dear Willetje', who lived 'in darkness'. The people in her immediate circle were struck by how Mrs van Gogh, who missed Willemien terribly, repeated herself continually and was sometimes very forgetful.[62] She told Jo pathetically: 'It's just as if I really long to receive a note from you?' and her daughter-in-law therefore continued to write to her, sometimes including comforting press cuttings of exhibition reviews. Mrs van Gogh responded to the passages from the *Middelburgsche Courant* saying: 'Thanks for letting me read this. How much everything is being seen and discussed.' Jo went to lengths like this to maintain close family ties. Aunt Mietje van Gogh also very much enjoyed her letters: 'you write and tell things so comfortably.'[63]

Jo also continued to work energetically on her ideals and philanthropic activities. After the brutal suppression of the Russian Revolution, a committee ('Comité tot het houden van een Bazar tot ondersteuning der Slachtoffers in Rusland') was set up to organize a sale to support the victims in Russia. The Federatie SDAP Amsterdam organizing committee, of which Jo was a member, called on people to give as much as possible to the support campaign: 'Our embattled comrades in Russia are sacrificing everything, and the little we can do must be done well.'[64] Four rooms in Bellevue were set up for the charity bazaar. Visitors were made to feel welcome: a barrel organ played, and the attractions included a shooting gallery and a test your strength machine. Jo was on the art stall, where the works for sale included something by Van Gogh, which she must have donated herself. More than three thousand guilders were raised for the victims.

Jo looked back with satisfaction at all her efforts during this busy year. It had demanded a great deal of her, but at the same time had brought her to new heights—and right in the middle of the summer, when the Tour de France reached the first mountain stages. The Van Gogh exhibition in the Stedelijk Museum had been like cycling up a mountain for her, and it was without doubt one of the pinnacles of her life. Soon afterwards, Johan painted a delicate portrait of her in a red dress. Unlike earlier modest portraits, this time she looked more prosperous and did not shrink from wearing fur (Plate 40).

Paul Cassirer

In the meantime, Paul Cassirer and Jo had intensified their collaboration (Plate 41). In consultation with Johan, she had amended a few things in his contract. He sent her confirmation from Berlin that an art shipment had arrived and he told her that a cheque for five thousand guilders was on its way. The paintings were hung in three successive galleries: in Hamburg (September-October), Dresden (October-November) and Berlin (December) 1905. The catalogue listed fifty-four works and they were by no means the worst. Nevertheless, sales were disappointing. By 4 December only one painting had been sold.[65] The reason Cassirer gave was that a circular had been distributed among dealers and collectors (he had not been able to get hold of a copy) asserting that the prices he was asking were incorrect and had to be halved and that this had been confirmed personally by Jo. He could not believe it and asked for her response. Jo replied immediately that this was, of course, complete and utter nonsense.[66] That clarified the matter and things got back to normal, although not all negotiations were equally smooth.

Cassirer complained, for example, that he had to pay the same prices as an ordinary private individual. In future he wanted a substantial 30 per cent of the asking price as commission instead of 15 per cent, because he put in so much effort: 'I think you can see that it is no bad thing for you if I represent you here in Germany.'[67] He was undeniably entitled to express his views, but it is doubtful that Jo ever agreed to such a high percentage. Whatever the outcome may have been, he continued to do his best. That autumn an excited Cassirer informed Jo that he had succeeded in getting the twenty-two-year-old millionaire Alexandre Louis Philippe Marie Berthier, the fourth Prince of Wagram, interested in Van Gogh. He told her this in confidence and he assumed that Jo would not approach Berthier personally. Cassirer expected a great deal to come of it and believed that Van Goghs would soon match the prices that were meanwhile being paid for Monets. The prince had made offers for three paintings and it looked as though this collector, who already owned fifty Cézannes, wanted to have a respectable number of Van Goghs in his collection as well. 'I definitely hope that you have enough of a head for business not to let this opportunity pass you by and that you immediately telegraph your approval,' wrote a jubilant Cassirer.[68] He asked her to send ten works or so by express and not to keep him waiting a minute longer. In the end, however, it was all for nothing. The urgency with which Jo had been admonished to act contrasted sharply with the snail's pace of the potential buyer. At the beginning of 1907 Berthier had still not bought anything.[69]

Requests for loans for exhibitions continued to arrive. In January 1906 essentially the same paintings that had been on show in Berlin were exhibited in Galerie Miethke in Vienna. Five of them from Jo's collection (all of which were for sale) then went to the Internationale Kunstausstellung in Bremen, which ran from mid-February to mid-March.[70] Van Gogh was now becoming better and better known in Germany and increasingly sought after, with the result that Jo, who by now was a skilled negotiator, received 3,853 guilders.[71] At the end of the year, Cassirer asked her to supply drawings for an exhibition of the Berliner Secession in the Nationalgalerie, where Max Liebermann was president. She sent thirty sheets, of which seven were not for sale.[72] An offer was received a week after the opening. Jo had to decide once again. The upshot was the sale of seven sheets for 1,857 guilders. Five of them ended up in Hugo von Tschudi's hands.[73]

Cassirer sent her 'some volumes of the great German national poet' as a gift to mark the feast of St Nicholas.[74] He remained enthusiastic and had now set his sights on staging a major Van Gogh exhibition. He was prepared to pay seven and a half thousand guilders for nine of the best works, whereas Jo had asked for ten thousand net. Cassirer put forward the following ingenious argument: he acknowledged that prices had risen, but felt that it was nevertheless not fair 'that you should also pass the increase on to me, since I am in no small measure the cause of this rise, which mainly benefits you.' In the end they softened their positions and compromised at nine thousand guilders.[75] Jo was very attached to Van Gogh's *Armand Roulin* (F 493 / JH 1643), but she nonetheless sold it. Afterwards Cassirer played on her conscience: 'I hope, though, that you recognize that it is right to treat me with some kindness. After all, I have really provided great benefits.'[76] The cat-and-mouse game did no damage at all to their collaboration. He was already looking forward to visiting Jo again in April.'

More and more potential buyers came to see her, including the brothers Émile and Amédée Schuffenecker, two visitors who, to Jo's delight, had known Theo. She sold Van Gogh's *Olive Grove* (F 585 / JH 1758) and five other works to Amédée for a total of five thousand eight hundred guilders.[77] She wrote to Gachet that she was very disappointed, though, because they had come solely to do business.[78] She would have liked to talk to them about the art itself, and without doubt would also have wanted to hear more recollections of Theo. She always wanted more than to just do business, especially when it came to contacts with artists.

An overwhelming proposal and influential reproductions

In the spring of 1906, the forceful art dealer Gaston Bernheim made Jo an unheard-of proposal (Plate 42). He wanted to do one huge all-encompassing deal:

> I find that you are asking me for very high prices, but what I want to know is if you would be willing to sell everything that was at the Exhibition last year and especially the ones you have reserved for yourself. If I bought everything for a large sum, I would like to have the good ones and not so much

those that were for sale. Please drop me a line and tell me whether you would agree to sell all your 'Van Goghs' on those conditions.[79]

Effrontery on this scale must have taken Jo's breath away. There was, of course, no question of her entertaining the proposal. Such a bloodletting would mean that little or nothing of her own collection would remain. It did, though, put some new ideas into her head and prompted her to go systematically through all the works again and consider which could be sold in due course and, if so, at what prices, which she would have to reassess. The increase in value was obvious, and she made a radical change of course. In consultation with Johan, she put up the prices of some Van Goghs by thousands of guilders overnight. He wrote '*May 1906*' on the cover of the 1905 catalogue, and all the higher prices were meticulously recorded in it. The prices of some paintings were increased fourfold.[80] The selection of works that Jo thought should stay in the family became more structured, although outsiders would repeatedly try to get their hands on them. She wrote to Gachet Jr, saying she had rejected Bernheim's impertinent proposal in no uncertain terms. 'I enjoined him *not* to come, because I had absolutely no desire to get rid of the paintings at a stroke.'[81]

Besides informing him about Bernheim's brazen move, Jo told Gachet about the high quality of the isographic reproductions made for her by Willem van Meurs in Haarlem.[82] She explained she was in favour of reproductions because they were so useful for publicity or record-keeping and because they would enable more people to surround themselves with Van Goghs. She commented enthusiastically: 'if only his business of these photographs succeeds!'[83] And it did. G.H. Marius praised this photographic reproduction method in a newspaper article, writing that many people were already familiar with the reproductions by 1907.[84] Twenty-four Van Gogh drawings, which had been isographically reproduced and then mounted on cardboard, were offered for sale in an undated brochure issued by the 'Maatschappij Voor Goede en Goedkoope Kunstreproducties', affiliated to the 'Maatschappij Voor Goede en Goedkoope Lectuur'. The prices ranged from five and a half to ten guilders, which was not cheap. An illustrated prospectus with eleven small reproductions cost twenty-five cents. The same works were the first to be mentioned in the catalogue *Isographieën. Systeem W. van Meurs*, which listed 166 art reproductions for sale, but that was not until years later.[85] It was a successful undertaking, but there is no evidence as to whether Jo benefitted from it financially. While Vincent, who had meanwhile married Josina Wibaut, was in America in 1916, Jo wrote: 'I hope the Washington Square Gallery orders a large number (*of the photographs*) one of these days.'[86] These reproductions introduced Van Gogh to countless thousands of people all over the world, and played an increasingly important role as time passed—a process that has never stopped. Sometimes Jo accepted payment. For example, she gave the editor of Velhagen & Klasings Monatshefte in Berlin permission to reproduce four works for two hundred marks (118 guilders). She came up with sums like these herself so that she could have some sort of control over the market, because at that time there were no legal provisions on which she could base them. The Dutch Copyright Act, which protects artists and their legal successors, did not come into force until 1912.[87]

Switzerland revisited

Jo had a relapse in the spring of 1906. She felt wretched and for some time stayed in bed when dealing with her correspondence. When Émile Bernard met her in Amsterdam that summer—they had not seen each other for sixteen years—he wrote how 'utterly white and sad' Jo looked.[88] Johan was also struggling. He had ventured outside for the first time since the winter and contracted pleurisy again. In consequence, he sometimes spent long, uninterrupted periods indoors, which did nothing to improve the atmosphere between the two of them. Jo was advised by her doctor to recuperate somewhere else.[89]

As she had done two years before, she chose to go to Switzerland. Jo went there, again accompanied by her sister Betsy, in August 1906. This time they stayed in the Hotel des Alpes, Engelberg, near Lucerne. Johan addressed her as his 'gnädige Frau (because you speak such excellent German!)' and she wrote to him about their exploits. While she was away, he spent the time reading Gustave Flaubert's letters and travel journals. He ended on a cheerful note: 'make sure you really benefit from the wonderful air without tiring yourself out with trips. Is there a wood where you can lie down?'[90] It is certain that the Swiss air did her good; what we do not know is exactly what she did during those weeks because her letters have not survived.

Once Jo had returned home, she told Paul Gachet Sr about her health and described the satisfaction that Vincent's involvement gave her: 'You can have no idea how much my son, young as he is, shares my feelings, particularly those that touch on the story of his dear father and revered uncle.' She had put the publication about the letters on the back burner and hoped she would make progress with it in due course: 'if only we didn't have any invalids!'[91] By the end of December, Jo had recovered sufficiently to travel to Berlin with Betsy. She enjoyed their stay in this *Großstadt*, where she undoubtedly visited Paul Cassirer.[92] Upon her return, she received the French artist and collector Gustave Fayet. Afterwards he wrote to Jo from the Hôtel de l'Europe in Amsterdam to thank her for her hospitality and for showing him Van Gogh's work. He purchased two watercolours for 912 guilders.[93] Jan Veth had also come calling and expressed his pleasure at seeing Johan and Jo again. But Veth would not have been Veth unless he had something to complain about. He thought it took far too long to get from the Central Station to Koninginneweg and commented coldly: 'All I can say is that when I come to Amsterdam, regrettably I won't always come to see you!'[94] His words must have provoked a wry shrug from Jo. At that time, she was more concerned with a major sale that was impending.

Giving in to Bernheim and Cassirer

At the beginning of 1907, the young French millionaire suddenly appeared on the scene again. This time, though, it was not Cassirer but the art dealer Bernheim who had contact with this Alexandre Berthier, Prince of Wagram. He wrote to Jo explaining that the prince had expressed interest in four works, which he might eventually bequeath to the Louvre. In Bernheim's view this was positive, because the more of Van Gogh's work there was in major collections the better. He was just as devious as Cassirer and thought that, in return for all his great efforts, Jo could now let him have works she had classified as 'not for sale' (which he had referred to a year earlier as 'the ones you have reserved for yourself'). She made all kinds of calculations at the bottom of his letter. She had previously offered him fifteen works for forty thousand francs. His counteroffer was now twenty-five thousand.[95] She quite understandably rejected it, but Bernheim thought that she really could not turn down such a first for France. Once again, she did sums for herself on his letter.[96] The upshot was that she agreed to an exhibition. In response he asked Jo to send only saleable works in addition to the fifteen in question.[97] After an interim bid of thirty-two and a half thousand francs on 1 March, and thirty-three and a half five days later, the deal was done on the eleventh for thirty-four thousand francs (16,200 guilders). Among the fifteen there were such masterpieces as *Olive Pickers* (F 587 / JH 1853), *Augustine Roulin ('La berceuse')* (F 504 / JH 1655), *Entrance to the Public Garden* (F 566 / JH 1585) and *Wheatfield with Sheaves and Rising Moon* (F 735 / JH 1761).[98] After her refusal a year before to sell all the exhibited works in one go, Jo now agreed to a substantial transaction.

She wrestled continually with the question of whether to sell to private admirers or to influential art dealers, who were cleverer at negotiating lower prices and also asked for commission. Dealers usually bought several works at once, so they appeared to be running a degree of risk. On the other hand, past masters of dealing in art like Bernheim and Cassirer knew exactly which works could earn them greater profits. It was not for nothing that Cassirer wrote: 'I ask you to send only saleable drawings from the later period.'[99] Most negotiations involved incessant shifts in prices and terms and conditions. Sometimes additional cash was paid, but only if that extra drawing was thrown in. Jo was often unable to keep on top of all the numbers. She gave in to Cassirer, too, and sold him nine drawings for 2,600 guilders, whereas she had initially asked 2,760 guilders for eight. She was momentarily confused and forgot to note the amount in the cash book.[100]

Mrs van Gogh dies—Vincent starts at university

Mrs van Gogh died on 29 April 1907. Jo's brother-in-law Joan van Houten told Jo in a letter that she had passed away in her sleep and commented warmly: 'We know we're in your thoughts. You were always so good to Mother.' Van Houten acted as executor and drew up a list of things for Jo, including teaspoons, a butter warmer, a sideboard and six dining chairs, and Van Gogh's painting *Seascape*.[101] She admitted to Paul Gachet Sr: 'The death of my dear mother-in-law has distressed me very much and it is always quite difficult for me to write in times of great emotion.'[102] With Mrs van Gogh's death, possibly the most important reservation about publishing Vincent's outspoken letters had been removed. After Willemien had read the letters to Bernard in 1893, she wrote to Jo saying: 'I sometimes think it'd be better to postpone publishing all the letters for as long as Ma's alive, and then afterwards everything, holding nothing back.'[103] It is highly probable that Jo respected Willemien's opinion. She did not sign the contract for the publication until three years after Mrs van Gogh's death.

A second major milestone that year was Vincent's success in passing his final HBS exam, which meant that he could start studying at Delft University of Technology in September 1907. Jo told Carel Adama van Scheltema of her fear of the empty nest syndrome: 'I don't have to tell you that I'll miss him dreadfully.'[104] She could hardly bear to let him go. Mother and son had shared an intense mutual dependence, and it took a while before he had—and took—the opportunity to spread his wings as he saw fit. Jo had been extraordinarily protective while bringing him up. When he looked back at his childhood, he realized that this had been the main cause of his uncertainty and lack of boldness. He had great difficulty breaking the ties, some of them restrictive, and freeing himself from the grip of motherly love.[105] Reminiscing, Vincent considered himself as having been far too timid in his new life as a student. He thought that he had received too little support, and with 'somewhat different guidance at home' could have completed his studies better and faster (it was to take him six years before he graduated, which was not exceptionally long).[106] When he was a young student he would have liked more encouragement than his mother and stepfather had been able to give him.

Nevertheless, he settled down well in Delft. Van Gogh's *Fishing Boats at Sea* (F 415 / JH 1452) hung in his room there. He had a subscription to publications by the publishers Wereldbibliotheek, and this enabled him to add to his library Dutch literary works and translations, including Marx's *Das Kapital* translated by Frank van der Goes.[107] He became a member of the 'Sociaal-Democratische Studenten-Vereeniging'.[108]

At the end of August 1907, before the start of the academic year, he went to Zandvoort for a few days with his mother and his aunt. It was not the first time they had done something of the kind: during the summer they also occasionally stayed at other seaside resorts—Katwijk aan Zee or Noordwijk aan Zee.[109] Not for the first time, Jo felt unwell for weeks on end during the summer, so she abandoned the plan to go to Auvers-sur-Oise. Johan informed Paul Gachet Jr by telegram.[110]

She regretted that. It was very important for her to maintain all the Van Gogh contacts. Jo remained in touch with the daughters of Joan van Houten and Anna van Gogh (Theo and Vincent's eldest sister) for years. Sara de Jong-van Houten married the clergyman Broer de Jong, and Anna Scholte-van Houten wed Johan Scholte, who was also a churchman. When Jo wrote to Sara in 1908 to congratulate her on her pregnancy, she also talked about her love of cats ('you know what a cat-lover I am—the mother gave birth to her five kittens on my lovely new summer hat!') and declared herself an enthusiastic supporter of a liberal upbringing:

> believe me Saar, the happiest children are the ones who are free to move and let off steam—they don't *have* to act like other children—let them be *themselves*. You'll say to yourself, what a tirade—but just a few days ago I stayed with two married girlfriends, each with four children. One foursome has been 'trained' or educated, while the other has grown up freely—the latter are infinitely more original, fresh, cheerful and therefore happier![111]

Six years later Jo wrote to her once again about this educational issue:

> Children are such a treasure, particularly if they can thrive and grow up in the countryside. That gives them a lifelong foundation of freshness, poetry and health, which is absolutely priceless! Later, though, the move from country living to urban life, which must inevitably come, may be difficult. But prudent parents who understand their children can be very accommodating and help in this.

That last, according to Vincent, she had done far too little, in any event when he was a university student.

At the time Jo had sent Sara a copy of Van Gogh's letters and was pleased with her response:

> I like what you wrote about the book, Saar, that you think the past is important, because then you understand yourself better. Yes, that's right and I'm sure that it'll help in bringing up your children, as it helped me to always understand my Vincent. You're a Van Gogh too, Saar![112]

The tone of their letters reflects just how close the women were.

Jo left Sara and her sister Anna ten thousand guilders each in her will. In their letter of thanks to Vincent, they praised her sympathy, friendliness and kindness.[113] Since her marriage to Theo, Jo always felt 'a Van Gogh' in her heart. At the beginning of 1889, she had jumped on to the moving Van Gogh train, which would never come to rest again.

13

The art dealers Gaston Bernheim, Paul Cassirer and Johannes de Bois

Jo was still spending a great deal of time corresponding with art dealers. The most important players in her business dealings remained Bernheim in Paris and Cassirer in Berlin. A newcomer for her, who appeared on the scene in 1908, was the Dutch art dealer Johannes de Bois.[1] He started by trading paintings in Switzerland and arranged for an exhibition to be staged in Zurich in the summer. From time to time these dealers bought large numbers of works because they were speculating or because they had buyers lined up.

Before that, though, there were other major exhibitions that year. At the beginning of 1908 the Galerie M.M. Bernheim-Jeune & Cie in Paris opened a large exhibition of Van Goghs. Jo had received requests regarding it months before from Félix Fénéon, the 'directeur Expositions'. The art critic Octave Mirbeau had agreed to write the introduction to the catalogue and needed information from her.[2] Jo became so absorbed in this that she lost count—she was worried she had sent a hundred and one works instead of a hundred, but Fénéon assured her, after a recount, that the latter number was correct. He deeply regretted that a quarter of the works were not for sale, and asked her to think seriously about changing her mind. Obviously the prices should not be so high that potential buyers were discouraged. There was also some financial squabbling before the exhibition opened. Jo had priced the works in guilders and felt that they should be multiplied by 2.1 to convert them into francs. But Fénéon decided without consultation to make the conversion factor 2 because otherwise there would be some odd prices. Jo was prepared to agree to 15 per cent commission, whereas Fénéon insisted on 25 per cent. In her letter of 27 December 1907, she stood firm, refusing to go higher than 15 per cent, and Fénéon grudgingly consented.[3] She was not easily swayed. The exhibition was going ahead come what may.

And indeed, the exhibition 'Cent tableaux de Vincent van Gogh' ran at Bernheim-Jeune at 15 rue Richepanse from 6 January to 1 February 1908.[4] Jo went to Paris, most probably with her son Vincent, to see it with her own eyes and touch base with her contacts. She will without doubt also have visited Galerie Druet, where a further thirty-five Van Goghs were on show at the same time. She stayed in the Grand Hôtel at 29 boulevard des Capucines and on 9 January met Dr Paul Gachet Sr, who had meant so much to Vincent and Theo in 1890.[5] Jo became so ill during her visit that months later Lies du Quesne-van Gogh was still asking her about her health and commented: 'That came as a shock to me too. The operation and all the unpleasantness of being ill while you're abroad! I felt so sorry for you and I hope from the bottom of my heart that all traces of the condition have disappeared.'[6] What ailed Jo is unknown, but it was clearly something serious. When Fénéon sent a message to the hotel on 18 January asking her to respond to an offer before five o'clock that day, she did not have the strength to write a reply.[7] Ten days later, she was still not well enough to correspond; her recovery was so slow that Fénéon dealt with Johan, arranging with him to send ninety-four works on to Cassirer in Berlin and four back to Amsterdam after the exhibition. Only two paintings were sold: *Wheatfield and Cypresses* (F 743 / JH 1790) and *Pièta (after Eugène Delacroix)* (F 757 / JH 1776). They went for 4,020 francs to Gustave Fayet, who had purchased two watercolours from Jo when he visited her at home the year before.[8]

Although the sales results were disappointing, the exhibition's organization and the cooperation went well. Soon, however, there was disturbing news. After the crates of paintings had been opened in Germany, Wiedmann, a Cassirer employee, wrote: 'several pictures have holes, however these seem to be of an older date.' According to him the damage was not done during transport, but that did not make the problem any less embarrassing.[9] Paul Cassirer exhibited twenty-three works from the shipment, supplemented by four from his own stock, between 5 and 22 March 1908. At Jo's request he sent the remaining works on to Munich.

She made that request at the end of February, when she was well enough to write again. *Irises* and *Roses* were among the works sent to Munich. Ten drawings went to the Ausstellungshaus am Kurfürstendamm in Berlin. Cassirer sent her a list of titles.[10] He also told her he had kept back three paintings. These were *Irises in a Vase* (F 680 / JH 1978), *Roses in a Vase* (F 682 / JH 1979) and *Daubigny's Garden* (F 814 / JH 2107). He offered 8,000 guilders. Jo agreed in principle, but insisted on 8,150 guilders. Her cash book records only 1,650 guilders for *Garden in Auvers* because the other two paintings came from Mrs van Gogh's estate. The remainder of the money would therefore have been divided between the three daughters, Willemien, Lies and Anna. At the end of April, Cassirer, the spider in the middle of the web, sent works to Dresden and asked Jo whether he could have them on consignment if they still did not sell.[11]

It is clear that Cassirer was also in direct contact with Munich. It was from there that in November 1907 Franz Brakl and Heinrich Thannhauser of Moderne Galerie had expressed their appreciation for Jo's willingness to provide works for their exhibition. She told these newcomers they could charge 10 per cent commission. They then tried to persuade Jo to agree to their request to release some works that were specifically not for sale (as always, they wrote, 'forbidden fruit tastes the sweetest'), but their request fell on deaf ears.[12] Van Gogh's *The House of Père Pilon* (F 791 / JH 1995) was for sale and was bought by the Russian artist Alexej von Jawlensky. He financed his purchase from Brakl & Thannhauser by selling some of his own work first. Jo agreed to his paying in four instalments. The painting remained her property until he had paid in full. An elated Jawlensky thanked Jo, whose 'gracious accommodation' had enabled him to acquire this painting.[13]

With Jo's permission, Thannhauser shipped the works to the Emil Richter gallery in Dresden when the exhibition in Munich closed. This gallery was owned by Herrmann Holst, who wrote to tell her he had received seventy-five paintings and twenty drawings from Munich and seventeen paintings from Berlin. The exhibition caused a 'sensation', so Holst asked Jo if he could extend it. Like the organizers in Berlin and Munich, he reported that damage had been observed. He also asked her if she would agree to 20 per cent commission for one work.[14] She agreed and sold *Thatched Cottages and Houses* (F 805 / JH 1989) for 1,200 guilders.[15] Again there was a frequent exchange of letters, and it was all Jo could do to maintain an overview.

Johannes de Bois appeared on the scene in the summer of 1908 (Plate 43). The contact was established through the C.M. van Gogh gallery, where De Bois had been manager of the Hague branch since 1906. He and Jo hit it off immediately and they worked together closely. He confirmed receipt of a list of works that Jo had placed with him on commission until 15 September 1908, with their prices, and advised her to ask reasonable prices, except of course for the best works. He offered 6,500 guilders for five paintings he had specified. He expected to find interested parties for them in Switzerland. At that moment he was in Zurich and he asked Jo to send him a telegram. As was the case everywhere, people had the greatest interest in the works that were not for sale and he tried to get her to change her mind: 'Are you adamant?' De Bois did not mince his words, asking what she thought about having works restored, because some of them looked 'as though they've just been fished out of the gutter'.[16] In his opinion, investing in restoration would most certainly be worthwhile. Worrying observations about the condition of Van Gogh's paintings came thick and fast, and descriptions like this spoke for themselves. On every occasion Jo continued to respond warily, or did not respond at all, to suggestions about restoration. She must have thought that it was better to do nothing than to harm the works unintentionally.

In July 1908, with De Bois's help, Elmar Kunsch, director of the Züricher Kunstverein, organized a successful exhibition. Seven of the forty-one paintings were sold during the exhibition, even though Kunsch looked on them as second-rate at best. During this period De Bois regularly travelled through Europe promoting Van Gogh works that he had in stock to private collectors and museums.[17]

Jo's personal correspondence continued as normal despite all these commercial goings on. Letters often concerned the other Vincent, in whom Jo had an emotional interest. Aunt Cornélie told her he had delighted her by dropping in to see her: 'How lovely to have such a child . . . nothing but praise for the mother who was able to develop that gift and give him such a wonderful childhood by bringing him up so soundly.'[18] Such a huge compliment pleased Jo no end, of course, and she left no stone unturned in her efforts to spoil her son. She stayed with Vincent in Delft that summer. It is not clear how large an allowance he received as a student, but he will have not have wanted for anything. There is only one reference to its being 150 guilders.[19]

Helene Kröller-Müller

In the first two decades of the twentieth century there was one other woman, apart from Jo, who contributed significantly to the rise in interest in Van Gogh's work. Helene Kröller-Müller lived in The Hague and was married to the fabulously wealthy businessman Anton Kröller. Supported by her closest advisor, H.P. Bremmer, she rapidly built up an impressive collection of Van Goghs. Bremmer had been a part-time employee of hers (for one to one-and-a-half days a week) since 1907 and was also her private art history teacher. She had read his book *Vincent van Gogh. Inleidende beschouwingen* and was impressed by Van Gogh's 'spiritual elevation' and the way he 'transcended hardship', as Bremmer had described it. Helene spent more than 1.2 million guilders on art between 1907 and 1919. At the end of 1919, her husband Anton's personal fortune was estimated at twenty million.[20] Her purchases attracted the art trade's attention to Van Gogh. She made her collection available to the general public at an early stage, and in so doing gave the introduction and acceptance of modern art in the Netherlands a strong shot in the arm.[21] The Kröller-Müllers' appreciation of Van Gogh's work must have delighted Jo.

It is remarkable that while Helene was amassing a collection in The Hague that starred Van Gogh, there was someone living in Amsterdam who owned just such a collection. It is even more remarkable that the two women never met. As far as we know, the paths of Jo and Helene, who was seven years her junior, never crossed. It is possible that they deliberately kept out of each other's way. For one thing, they held very different views and Jo, with her social democratic ideas, probably felt little need to seek out the immensely rich couple who could buy whatever they wanted. In her view they were out-and-out capitalists. As far as Helene was concerned, she probably thought that a visit to Jo was beneath her dignity. Evert van Straaten, who later became director of the Kröller-Müller Museum, wrote that he could well imagine 'that the class-conscious Mrs Kröller would prefer not to climb the stairs to a first-floor flat in Amsterdam'.[22] In any case, Helene was not someone who found it easy to meet new people or develop new friendships. She was obstinate, proud and a loner. In her dealings with people her usual attitude was that 'he who pays the piper calls the tune'.[23] There was a telling example of her behaviour at the beginning of the 1930s, five years after Jo's death. She did not want Van Goghs from her collection to be hung in among those from Vincent's in the Stedelijk Museum.[24] This was despite the fact that in the end more than thirty Van Goghs that had originally been in Jo's and Vincent's collection had ended up with the Kröller-Müllers through dealers and intermediaries.[25]

In 1913 Helene Kröller-Müller told her husband she wanted to stop buying Van Gogh's art:

> Recently I've thought a great deal about my collection, and I've come to the conclusion that we shouldn't buy any more Van Goghs now, unless something really special turns up. . . . In general, though, I feel that we have a real wealth of Van Gogh's work, the largest in the world along with Mrs Cohen. That sounds proud, doesn't it? We have Van Goghs from all his periods . . . and it's easy to trace developments in his ability and as a painter.[26]

She had started collecting Van Goghs seriously in the summer of 1908, when she paid 4,800 guilders for *Four Sunflowers Gone to Seed* (F 452 / JH 1330). This still life was sold to her by Jo's closest advisor De Bois, with Bremmer as intermediary.[27] What Helene wrote to her confidant Sam van Deventer on 23 November 1913 is revealing: 'I believe in a greater continued existence for myself in my intellectual life than in what I leave behind, I believe that the intellectual edifice I leave will bear more certain fruits than the corporality I could give through the children.' She looked on the art she had accumulated as the fulfilment of her life. On another occasion, she wrote: 'At the end of the day, a person is defined by what they leave behind.'[28] Once again Helene was not referring to her children, with whom she had a troubled relationship. In that regard, the two women could not have been more different. Jo's priorities in life were her child and art in equal measure.

It was usually Helene who bought art, but on occasion Anton made impulse purchases. In 1928, for example, he was the one to effectively negotiate the acquisition of over a hundred drawings from the Dutch collector Hidde Nijland. And he encouraged Bremmer to 'track down all the best Van Goghs'.[29] It is difficult to overestimate the significance of Bremmer's appreciation of and admiration for Van Gogh. He showed how crucial 'aesthetic emotion' was when contemplating a work of art. As a rule, Helene blindly accepted her adviser's opinion. While she made the choices, it was he who proposed purchases, and her selection was in turn based on the artistic taste he had instilled in her. The only time that man and wife departed from this pattern, things immediately went very wrong. In November 1910, when Helene and Anton bought Van Gogh's *Reaper with a Scythe (after Jean-François Millet)* (F 688 / JH 1783) from Paul Cassirer in Berlin without involving Bremmer, the latter said as soon as he saw the painting—undoubtedly prompted by his pique about being left out of the deal—that it was a fake. He was the expert and he brushed aside the argument that the work had come directly from the Van Gogh estate. The sale was promptly cancelled and the painting went back to Berlin. Cassirer told Jo about it and asked her for a certificate of authenticity. As for Bremmer's opinion, he wrote: 'Has the man gone mad?'[30] This was one of the few times that the name Kröller appeared in a letter to Jo. Helene even felt it necessary to take the matter to court, and her suspicious attitude must have been all the more reason for Jo, to whom it came as a most unpleasant surprise, to have nothing to do with her.

Bremmer's biographer Hildelies Balk wrote that a degree of rivalry swiftly developed in relations between Bremmer and Jo because they shared the objective of distributing Van Gogh's work far and wide.[31] The Van Gogh researcher Stefan Koldehoff makes a similar comment about the relationship between Helene Kröller-Müller and Jo: 'The two women ... saw themselves as rivals—although they both contributed significantly to his fame. ... The rivalry between the two was so great that they barely spoke to one another.'[32] It is actually doubtful that Jo saw any rivalry at all. Both acted effectively, each in their own way, and the fact that Bremmer was able to interest more and more buyers can only have been good for Jo. It did no harm to her endeavours whatsoever.

She was certainly aware of some purchases. In April 1912, for instance, the Kröller-Müllers hit the headlines when they spent 115,000 guilders on fifteen paintings and two drawings by Van Gogh in Paris. Such an exorbitant purchase attracted the attention of international collectors and dealers, as did the sale of Cornelis Hoogendijk's collection a month later. On the latter occasion the couple acquired four more Van Goghs, paying 16,000 guilders for *The Langlois Bridge with Washerwomen* (F 397 / JH 1368) alone. That was more than five times the guide price. Such astronomical sums caused a sensation and pushed up prices. Jo knew there had been fiercely competitive bidding at the auction and that in the end the painting was knocked down to a Dutch art lover, according to the *NRC* of 12 May 1912.[33] The huge numbers were indeed impressive. In that one year the couple bought nearly a hundred works and paid a total of over 280,000 guilders for them. By way of comparison, at that time a university professor's annual salary was around four thousand guilders.[34] Needless to say, Jo went along with this price war. Her cash book reveals that she put fewer paintings on the market than before. The prices of Van Gogh's works, which she had increased in 1905, were boosted again after 1912.[35]

Outside the Netherlands, most of the buyers were Germans, who purchased more and more Van Goghs with increasing frequency. The profit Cassirer made on the fifty-five works he bought from Jo between 1902 and 1911 at a cost of some 50,000 guilders was substantial. Thanks in part to Cassirer, by 1914 there were 210 Van Goghs in Germany in sixty-four collections. Josse and Gaston Bernheim of Galerie Bernheim-Jeune were active in France, as were Émile and Amédée Schuffenecker. The fabulously wealthy Prince Alexandre Berthier also played a major role. He bought and sold some twenty-seven paintings by Van Gogh between 1905 and 1912.[36] There was interest in Russia too, where there were ten Van Goghs at the beginning of the century. They had ended up there in various ways.

Jo buys a Fantin-Latour

In August 1908 Jo stayed in central Germany, close to the Thuringian Forest. Letters from the Netherlands were addressed to 'Poste Restante Oberhof Thüringen'. At that time it was a popular holiday area. It would appear that Jo liked it too because she went back a year later, again without Johan.[37]

With help from Jo, the C.M. van Gogh gallery exhibited eighty-four paintings and forty-one drawings by Van Gogh, first at 16 Kneuterdijk in The Hague and then at 453 Keizersgracht in Amsterdam. During that exhibition in the summer of 1908, Van Gogh's *Mousmé* (F 431 / JH 1519) was sold for 3,400 guilders, and Jo used the money to buy a still life, *Flowers* by Henri Fantin-Latour, from the gallery (Plate 44).[38] It was the only painting she ever bought for herself. It was given a place of honour above her desk, where she so often sat and worked (Plate 45).

In the *NRC* of 9 November an anonymous reviewer made a rousing appeal, not unlike the one made by Willem Steenhoff seven years before:

> Is this not the time, now, while important work by Van Gogh can still be obtained, for our museum boards to get involved? To begin with, for instance, that very poignant 1889/90 self-portrait, which because of its completeness is so particularly appropriate for retention in this artist's homeland.[39]

But the time was still not ripe and the appeal had no effect. The idea drew no attention, and all the key players continued to follow their chosen course.

Jo received a summary from H.L. Klein of the C.M. van Gogh gallery. Without any warning she had increased the prices of eighteen works by over five hundred guilders on average. He asked her to reconsider the prices of one particular work—Van Gogh's *Restaurant*—because an offer exactly five hundred guilders below the asking price had been received. That same day Klein also dispatched six crates, containing ninety-five paintings and a few drawings, to Cassirer by train.[40] On her own list Jo indicated which of those works came from the collections of Willemien and Mrs van Gogh, which titles were not for sale, and the prices of the remaining works.[41] Six months later, Cassirer asked whether he could keep the shipment for a while longer. Jo noted on his letter: 'Answered 18 February—50 paintings returning—the other 50 until 1 May.'[42] She wrote down exactly which works stayed behind on the list of the objects in the return shipment, and worked constantly at her desk to maintain an overview.

The previous generation continued to be overtaken by the inevitable. After Jo's parents and Mrs van Gogh, the next to die was Paul Gachet Sr, on 9 January 1909. Jo wrote an obituary for the *NRC* of 14 January about this loyal friend and admirer of Vincent van Gogh and sent a letter of condolence to his next of kin in which she lamented: 'Oh what a good friend to the Van Gogh family he always showed himself to be' and paid Paul and Marguerite a lovely compliment: 'You have done *everything* for him—there are few children who have the satisfaction of having done their duty to their parents so well!'[43] Devotion to duty was taken very seriously and the satisfaction it gave rise to was substantial. Paul Gachet Jr was profoundly touched by Jo's letter and told her he would look after it with care.[44] He kept his word and, nearly half a century later, even had it printed in his book *Deux amis des impressionnistes: le docteur Gachet et Murer* (1956).[45]

Fearful of new crises

Johan wrote to Jo from Laren three days after she had completed the brief Gachet obituary for the newspaper. Their relationship was far from easy and again they had to talk seriously about their marriage. They loved one another of course, but clearly that was not enough:

> I've already admitted that we are not happy because I fall short in many ways, for example because of my health and peculiarities. It is not the case that I don't realize this and that I'd be ashamed to admit it wholeheartedly. But—I don't believe I'm *guilty* in the sense that I can be accused of something serious I can be *blamed* for.... I always live in hope of improvement, but I should not continue living in fear of new crises for that reason. I say this candidly because I feel, as do you, that we should not have to go through the same thing again.

He promised not to get so stressed about little things that irritated him. The absence of a feeling of togetherness was evident. Johan was also worried because he had sold little work and he complained about the level of council taxes.[46]

Jo responded immediately, as he did too. They were good at writing letters, but relations between them were difficult and their finances remained an issue. 'You are, of course, right when you say that we're far from being able to live on my income the way we *do now*,' he wrote to her.[47] He would have liked to earn more. In 1908 his income was significantly less than in the preceding years, when he had almost always earned about 3,500 guilders, a reasonable income at the time. He did not profit from the proceeds of the sales, which had resulted in a substantial increase in Jo's bank balance. Vincent benefitted from that money at a later stage. Jo also always bore in mind the share of the Van Gogh works that would become Vincent's when he reached the age of majority in 1911. That share was half of the total. Johan tried to approach the situation positively and afterwards changed the subject: 'We must stop all this contemplation. We should take our courage in both hands and begin again and try to make it work between us.'[48] He then moved on to Jo's successful visit to the Rijksmuseum in January 1909—a preliminary discussion about lending Van Goghs for the opening of the gallery featuring Impressionists scheduled for later that year: 'That Jonkheer is a fool—(and an arrogant one) never to have heard of Sisley.'[49] This was a dig at the art historical baggage of Hendrik Teding van Berkhout, deputy director of the Rijksmuseum Print Room. Jo had clearly put him in his place with her knowledge of modern French art.

A few days later, Johan tried to insist that Jo should come to Laren, but she dreaded the idea and put it off. In reply he asked her to give the carrier the hot water foot warmer: 'Do you recall that we always said the first step in acquiring a car was to get a carriage warmer?'[50] They certainly had a foot warmer but they never bought their own car. When he was back home again a month later, Jo told Gachet Jr that Johan rarely went out, and so she had little news. In that same letter she corrected an inaccuracy.

She was annoyed that Bernard, unhindered by any knowledge of the matter, had announced that Tanguy had *given* Vincent canvas and paints. That was not true because she knew that Theo had paid for them. 'This is how history is written!' she wrote indignantly.[51] Sometimes Jo could be brusque and peremptory, but in her view the facts had to be correct and, in this case, her pent-up anger served a purpose. When Johan wrote to her again from Laren that summer, he called her a 'naughty little woman' because she had been offended that on the day they had talked in Amsterdam he had not written to her as well. He had, in fact, dutifully written to her the following morning, but the letter was delayed. 'This time why don't we just kiss and make up again?' he wrote, trying to placate her. 'And let's not have any resentment about such villainy.'[52] So they continued to have things to blame one another about.

Meanwhile, Jo received another request for a certificate of authenticity, this time through Johannes de Bois, who asked on behalf of a client. She sent a certificate written in German to Fritz Meyer-Fierz for the painting concerned, *House under a Night Sky* (F 766 / JH 2031). A reproduction was attached on which she added her name followed by: 'Widow of Th. van Gogh.'[53] De Bois, too, discovered that Jo was sometimes overenthusiastic when it came to setting her asking prices and wondered whether she thought increasing the asking price for *Interior of a Restaurant* (F 342 / JH 1256) from 1,300 guilders to 3,000 guilders within a year was not rather quick and excessive. Her pricing policy was usually to stick to her asking prices or simply increase them. De Bois showed this canvas in the 1909 summer exhibition at the gallery's branch in The Hague. Three years later, when he was working for Artz and De Bois, he went on to sell it to the Kröller-Müllers, and Jo received 5,000 guilders for it.[54]

Publication of Van Gogh's letters in Germany

The 1906 German selection of Van Gogh's letters, which had been published in magazines, had been fairly successful, so Paul Cassirer and his nephew Bruno began to shape their ideas about a more comprehensive publication of the letters to Theo. Bruno believed that publishing all of Vincent's letters to his brother would have a beneficial impact: 'As you know, the publication of the letters in Germany contributed a great deal to Van Gogh's art catching on here, and it is safe to assume that the publication of further letters will have the same effect.'[55] No matter how sound his reasoning about the snowball effect of a publication undoubtedly was, Jo initially rejected the proposal because, apparently, Bruno had not properly honoured agreements made with regard to the production of his anthology. She also invoked her ownership rights and demanded a reasonable fee. She stuck to her guns in such cases. Bruno humbly apologized for his previous behaviour. He discussed the issue with Paul, who then developed a detailed proposal. Jo could supply the letters from Vincent to Theo in French (approximately a third of the total) as they were, but that was not the case for the ones in Dutch: 'However, we must have the ones in Dutch translated into German.'[56] As the publisher, Paul Cassirer promised to pay for the translation, and asked her to give him a preliminary estimate of the magnitude of the manuscript. Jo replied, but in his opinion her response was far too cursory, and consequently it was impossible for him to calculate the expenses, selling price and Jo's royalty per copy sold. He wrote back somewhat irritably:

> I don't know why you keep coming back with this strange distrust. Have you done bad business with me? Or do you think that the exhibition at my gallery and everything I've done for Van Gogh's reputation have been unfavourable? You told me at the time that the money aspect would not weigh heavily with you when it came to the publication.[57]

Jo objected to the tone of the letter, particularly to the reproach of 'distrust'. But that dissatisfaction soon disappeared because in a third letter Paul said he had no objections to a somewhat more expensive edition, even though he personally believed a popular edition would do better. He asked her once again to spell out exactly what her ideas were.[58]

Jo and Johan discussed the proposal at considerable length and sent their answer. On 8 July 1910 a long letter from Bruno arrived. Among other things, he promised royalties of 20 per cent of the selling price, which meant that an edition of a thousand copies and a price of eight marks would generate a total of 1,600 marks for Jo. He hoped that this would make up for his earlier mistake. The deal was finally sealed at the end of that month with a contract for the German publication of the letters.[59] The exclusive two-volume edition *Briefe an seinen Bruder* eventually appeared in mid-1914. Bruno asked Jo if he could include a selection in an anthology of artists' letters. This substantial book, *Künstlerbriefe aus dem 19. Jahrhundert*, in which Van Gogh featured at the end in the form of a few letters and extracts, also appeared in 1914.[60]

In the summer of 1909, Jo combined business and pleasure while on the way to her German holiday address in the Thuringian Forest. She went to Museum Folkwang in Hagen to see again the paintings she had sold to Karl Osthaus a few years before. While there, she discovered a Van Gogh she had never seen before, *Armand Roulin* (F 492 / JH 1642), which Osthaus had bought from Ambroise Vollard in Paris in 1903. It is highly likely that she also talked to Osthaus while in Hagen.[61]

Gachet, who kept her abreast of developments in sales of Van Gogh's paintings in France, reported that he had heard that *The Red Vineyard* (F 495 / JH 1626) had been sold for 30,000 francs to the Russian collector Ivan Morozov (the actual price was 33,000 gold roubles). He did not have a good word to say about such dealers. They were only interested in the money, and Jo also thought the reported price was ridiculous.[62] She asked whether Gachet could find out what the Druet gallery had actually asked for the painting. 'If it was possible, I would like to buy it back—I loved this painting so much!'[63] This was the second time she considered buying a Van Gogh for herself. Her first attempt, in

April 1901, had been to get hold of the *Van Gogh's Mother (after a Photograph)* (F 477 / JH 1600). Jo knew how enthusiastic Vincent had been about *The Red Vineyard* and recalled that shortly after she married Theo it had hung in their flat. Anna Boch bought the canvas in February 1890, when it was part of the Les Vingt exhibition in Brussels. But Jo was never to acquire the painting. It remained in Moscow with Morozov, who took the opportunity to buy more Van Goghs from Druet.

Jo thanked Gachet for the Druet catalogue he had sent. She was surprised by the number of portraits she did not know:

> too many perhaps, because I have never sold any of the portraits in *our* collection—where do they come from? But it's true that Vincent was very generous, to Bernard, to Gauguin—and many other painters got portraits from him. After all, one never knows![64]

Again she praised the reproductions, because they at least gave an impression to people who did not have the means to buy art. She was convinced that without reproductions, Van Gogh's work would never have become so well known.

The official opening of a gallery in the Rijksmuseum containing only Impressionists on 2 December 1909 was a major step in publicizing and gaining recognition for Van Gogh in the Netherlands. They were works by Paul Cézanne, Alfred Sisley, Gustave Caillebotte and Édouard Vuillard. Jo loaned Van Gogh's *Self-Portrait as a Painter* (F 522 / JH 1356), *Wheatfield* (F 411 / JH 1476) and *Reaper* (F 618 / JH 1773) for an indefinite period. 'This is the first time we will see them in our museum!' she wrote to Gachet with a delighted exclamation mark.[65] The availability of a new wing meant that the paintings could be hung in a small gallery on the ground floor, together with works from the Hoogendijk Collection. Not everyone was impressed by the space. An anonymous chronicler in the *Algemeen Handelsblad* of 12 December wrote: 'In these sober surroundings, with good light, hang works by forceful artists like Sisley, Cézanne and Vincent van Gogh, as though in sombre cells.'[66] In his opinion, the way the works were arranged could also have been more refined. Willem Steenhoff wrote a number of articles about these 'odd men out' in the world of paintings. Among the works there were seven paintings and three drawings by Van Gogh and eleven paintings by Cézanne.

As this successful museum breakthrough was generating welcome publicity, Jo also made a financial killing. On behalf of the Bernheim-Jeune gallery, Félix Fénéon confirmed the purchase of six Van Gogh paintings for 42,000 francs. In reply to her question about whom to approach about a French publication of the letters, he wrote: 'The Bernheim-Jeune house would be happy to publish it, just as it has already published an important work on Eugène Carrière.'[67] Jo thought about his proposal, but remarkably she did not follow it up. It is not clear why she let this opportunity slip through her fingers. Other factors must have played a role such that she decided to keep her cards close to her chest. Her attitude was very different later on when it came to an English edition. It was more than a year before there was further contact between Jo and Fénéon.

Van Goghs on tour through Germany

An exhibition of forty-nine paintings and six drawings toured Germany between October 1909 and April 1910. It opened in Munich (until December 1909 with Franz Brakl, who had meanwhile left Thannhauser and opened his own gallery), before going to Frankfurt (in January 1910 in the home of Carl Marcus, director of the Frankfurter Kunstverein) and in Cologne (also in January at the Kunstverein Köln). It then went to Frankfurt (in February at Moderne Kunsthandlung Marie Held), Dresden (in February and March at Galerie Ernst Arnold) and finally Chemnitz (in April at Kunstsalon Gustav Gerstenberger). All the parties involved kept up an exhaustive correspondence with Jo. The general thrust was that there would be little chance of success if she continued to ask such high prices.[68] There was also a great deal of consultation about transport because it was inevitable that during this long series of relocations by train, the art would suffer; needless to say, there was no climate control or ways to absorb vibration. Repeated packing and unpacking and being exhibited for months at different locations were likewise not conducive to maintaining the condition of the paintings.

The way the works were packed in the crates was downright scandalous. Ernst Arnold told Jo that he had never come across anything so bad. The only damage to some works was to the frame, but he also listed several works that were more seriously damaged. Jo was shocked and tried to do something about it from a distance. She sent an uncompromising telegram to Arnold: 'Forbid any restoration of the pictures and ask for the costs of damage to the frames first.'[69] She wrote to the Frankfurter Verein saying: 'I need not tell you how disappointed I am. I thought that the valuable pictures I entrusted to you would be handled with care. I will have the damage assessed in Dresden and hold you responsible for it.'[70] Franz Brakl also became involved in the debate, writing to Marcus about how he shook his head when he saw how some crates had anything from six up to as many as twelve works crammed into them. He believed that an end should be put to such scandalous practices. According to him things could start going wrong when the works were packed because they were 'placed more or less directly on top of each other'. By referring to a furious Jo in his letter as 'a very distinguished lady', Brakl hoped that he could calm her down somewhat. She received a carbon copy of this letter via Marcus.[71]

In the end Marcus came to the conclusion that the damage had to have been done previously. Various letters were exchanged, and on 10 March he sent three damaged works back to Amsterdam.[72] Arnold asked whether the exhibition could be extended by a month. Jo noted her answer, which was 'impossible'. Arnold had a new crate and new frames made at a cost of twenty-five marks before the works went on to Chemnitz. The amount of money involved was not that much after all, and it was Jo's fault that the crates had not been replaced earlier.[73] Gerstenberger also observed when the shipment of works arrived in Chemnitz that there was previous flaking of the paint.[74]

Johannes de Bois was fully involved in the organization. He saw to it that the works were transported from Cologne to the correct address in Frankfurt. He had a problem with an angry client who had expressed interest in *Stone Bench in the Garden of Saint-Paul Hospital* when the asking price was 1,200 guilders, but now he saw that the price had gone up within a year to 2,000. De Bois was concerned about it because he was being accused of deliberately driving up the price. He therefore asked Jo if she could agree to 1,800 guilders, 'in which case we would like to reach agreement and reduce our own profit'. And that was how the game was played in some cases. It then emerged for the first time in black and white that Jo had meanwhile consulted Vincent about the sales: 'I would also like to know from you whether the big "Montmartre" can be sold and for what price. During my last visit you promised you would speak to your son about it.' On 23 January Jo scribbled the prices at the bottom of the letter: 1,900 guilders for *Stone Bench in the Garden of the Asylum* (F 732 / JH 1842) and 16,000 guilders for *Vegetable Gardens in Montmartre* (F 350 / JH 1245), which was extremely high. Jo's discussion with the twenty-year-old Vincent might have had an effect on this.[75] On 31 January 1911 Vincent celebrated his twenty-first birthday and reached his majority, and his mother's guardianship ended. From that moment he formally had control over his half of the Van Gogh Collection; Jo retained the other half of Theo's estate.[76] De Bois was in contact with the secretary of the Rotterdamsche Kunstkring and asked Jo: 'You probably have no objections to helping us, even though your latest intention was to stop shipping works hither and thither.'[77] She had indeed stopped temporarily, but she nevertheless complied with this request from Rotterdam. De Bois was in good form and shortly afterwards succeeded in selling *Girl against a Background of Wheat* (F 774 / JH 2053) for 4,000 guilders to Gustav Henry Müller (Helene Kröller-Müller's brother) and his wife Wilhelmina Maria Anne Müller-Abeken, who lived in The Hague.[78]

At the end of the year, a fine batch of drawings was shipped to the Berliner Secession, but that was before the disturbing news about the damage to works. Jo sent a crate containing thirty sheets, which was exactly the number that Max Liebermann had requested.[79]

As the years passed Jo came increasingly to understand that the modernity of Van Gogh's art was unequalled. She learned a great deal from her countless discussions and extensive correspondence with artists and people in the art trade, and from the responses she received at exhibitions and the ever-growing number of publications about Van Gogh.

It had all begun with her conversations with Theo. As a result, she knew Vincent's own opinions about some of his works. She subsequently absorbed Bernard's views about Van Gogh's art as well as those of a number of other artists in her circles, initially in Paris and later in the Netherlands. Among them were Richard Roland Holst, Jan Toorop and Jan Veth. The opinions of the art dealers Gaston Bernheim, Paul Cassirer and Johannes de Bois, and of museum directors, curators and leading collectors also affected the way she viewed Vincent's oeuvre. There was a great deal of discussion about the quality of Van Gogh's art, and from that Jo was able to deduce which types of paintings and drawings attracted special interest. Through comments from exhibition visitors and buyers, she increasingly understood how Van Gogh's oeuvre was appraised. In common with the art experts Willem Steenhoff, Grada Marius, Johan Rohde, Henk Bremmer, Julius Meier-Graefe and her husband Johan, she looked on Van Gogh as a trailblazer of modern art. Jo was convinced that he had reached very great heights, particularly in his last two years.

She had her own decided favourites, particularly his landscapes and works with themes that drew much from Van Gogh's own life, such as *The Harvest* (F 412 / JH 1440), the triptych of orchards in blossom, *The Pink Orchard* (F 555 / JH 1380), *Pink Peach Trees* (F 404 / JH 1391) and *The White Orchard* (F 403 / JH 1378), the drawing *La Crau seen from Montmajour* (F 1420 / JH 1501) and *The Bedroom* (F 482 / JH 1608).

't Lanthuys, Laren

During the summer months the peace and coolness of the countryside formed a pleasant contrast to life in the busy and muggy city. In 1910 Jo and Johan, who knew from experience the blessings of living in the country, decided to have a summer home built in rural village of Laren. They named it 't Lanthuys (Figure 44). The architect was Herman Ambrosius Jan Baanders, the son of the architect who had designed the building in Koninginneweg. Later Baanders extended 't Lanthuys to create a large villa on the instructions of Vincent, who decided in 1926–27 to live there with his family. It was not until then that gas pipes and mains water were installed. Before that they used oil lamps for lighting and the gardener always had to pump water by hand (three hundred strokes) from the water reservoir up to a tank on the first floor so that water could be drawn off on the ground floor. Vincent lived in this house until the end of his life in 1978 (Figure 45).[80]

Jo's friends Ant de Witt Hamer and Henriëtte van der Meij kept her updated about progress with the construction at 12 Rozenlaantje (now number 20). They lived at number 10 and were looking forward to becoming neighbours. De Witt Hamer wrote with a generous offer: 'If you come to live here, please feel free to ask us for help, at any hour of the day or night. If unexpected visitors arrive, for instance, our larder door is open.'[81] In March, Van der Meij updated Jo about the good progress with the building: 'The walls of your house are going up quickly. The studio window and the others have already been fitted.'[82] She had written to Jo in 1906, four years previously, saying that the village of Laren had a soothing effect on 'nervous types'.[83] There is no doubt she wrote this because she knew about the mental state of the newcomers. Johan found it necessary to be alone and this house met his needs with a studio and a separate bedroom for him downstairs. This meant that from the summer of 1910 onwards he had two studios to choose from: one in Laren and one in Amsterdam. He had probably meanwhile rented out the one in Bussum in the garden of Villa Eikenhof.

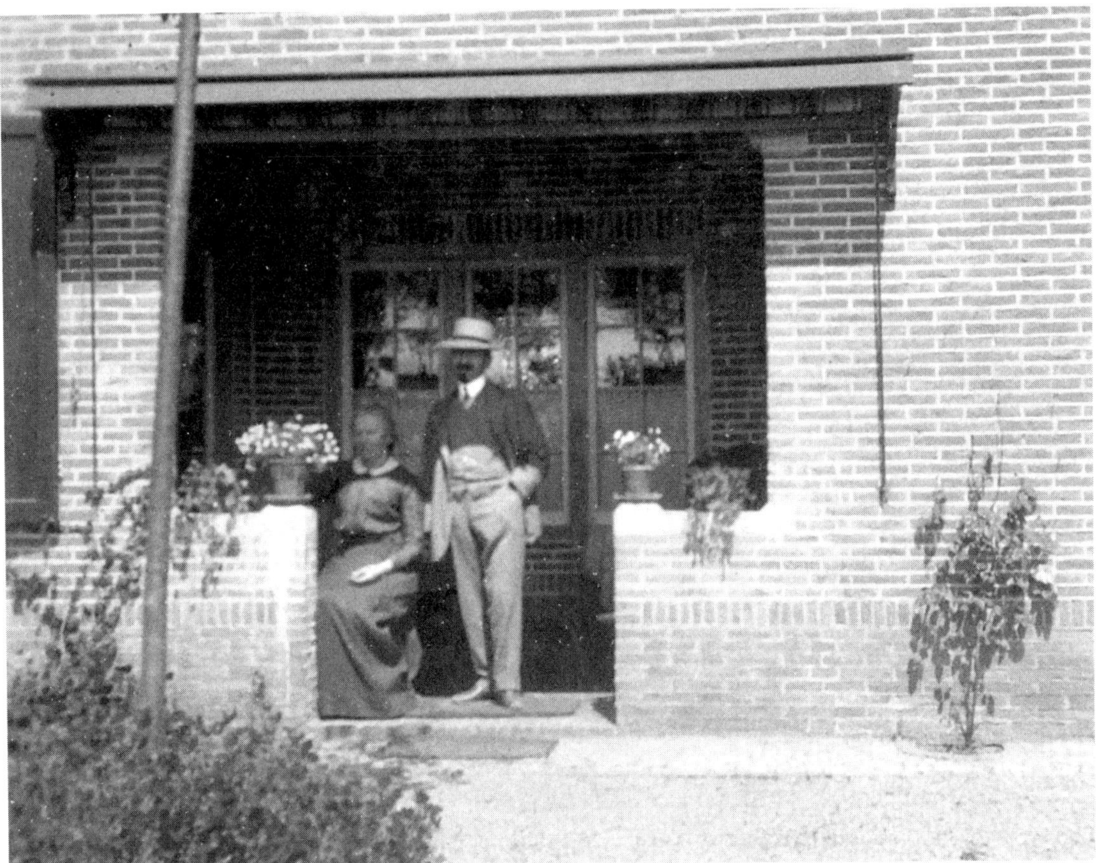

Figure 44 Jo Cohen Gosschalk-Bonger and Johan Cohen Gosschalk at the back of their summer home 't Lanthuys in Rozenlaantje in Laren, in or around June 1910.

Laren was easy to reach from Amsterdam. A train went from Muiderpoort Station to Hilversum, from where a steam tram went to Laren. There was also a direct connection using the Gooische steam tram from Weesperspoor station. The journey time varied depending on the time of day and the number of stops, but it was never more than an hour. It is not clear when Jo started to use the services of the car hire firm of Crayé or how often she called on them—the foot warmer mentioned earlier is in any event a clear indication that she certainly did not always travel by public transport.[84]

Five men were working on building the house. They started work at 6 a.m. every day. The roof went on very quickly, and there was not a drop of rain during that period.[85] The house was reaching completion as early as 10 May 1910. A sundial was cemented into the back wall. The plot measured 1,450 square metres and had unobstructed views over fields. Vincent recalled there was beautiful weather during Jo's first birthday in Laren. 'At that time the garden, except for behind the house, was full of lupins. It was always a real celebration,' he wrote in his diary.[86] Jo invariably had flowers on the

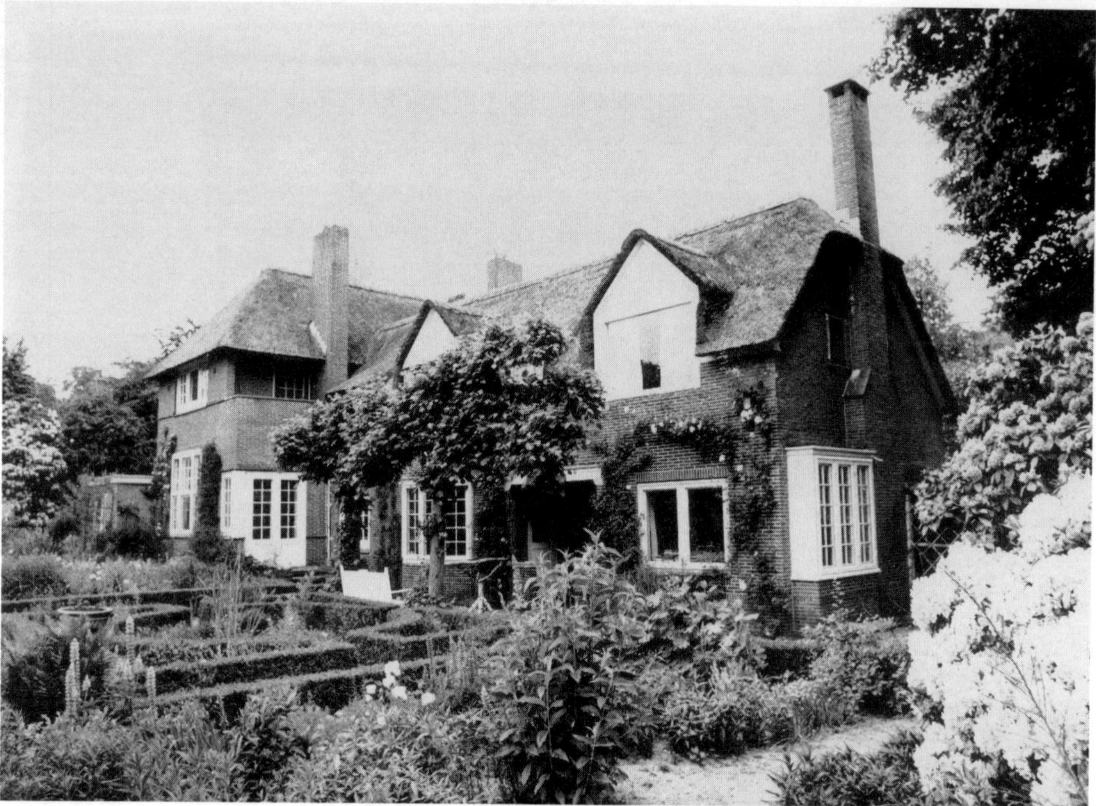

Figure 45 't Lanthuys in Rozenlaantje in Laren after the later enlargement (see the extension on the left), after 1927.

dining table on birthdays. She was not minded to do the housekeeping on her own and advertised in the *De Gooi- en Eemlander* for a suitable maid.[87]

Many like-minded people lived in Laren. The painter Wally Moes welcomed them as new friends. Johan should feel free to come and play her organ, and the three of them could discuss the news of the day. During the first summer they were there Moes 'rolled up' several times in her wheelchair and entered through their 'hospitable gate'.[88] Wally's next-door neighbour was the painter Marie van Regteren Altena; she knew the artists Lizzy Ansingh and Nelly Bodenheim, both of whom became good friends of Jo's. Vincent later judged Bodenheim as being the most unassuming and socially perceptive. 'The others (including Lizzy Ansingh, whom my mother was also really fond of) are too precious, and have a conservative bourgeois mentality that's unbearable.'[89]

Catharine van Tussenbroek was Jo's doctor. Jo had deliberately chosen her. Van Tussenbroek was a family doctor who specialized in treating women and girls and, like Jo, was a contributor to *Belang en Recht*. Between 1910 and 1916 she was vice-president and president of the women's workers association Nationale Vereeniging voor Vrouwenarbeid. When Jo had severe pain in her ears in the spring of 1910,

Van Tussenbroek advised her to go to bed early and drink lots of yoghurt. Jo wrote about it to Henriëtte van der Meij, who responded to this doctor's recommendations with interest.[90]

Jo provided sixteen paintings from Van Gogh's French period for an exhibition at the Rotterdamsche Kunstkring, which ran from 11 June to 10 July 1910. They were not intended for sale. Jo was aware of some imperfections: 'If the white picture frames get dirty during transport, could you arrange to have them cleaned up for me?' she asked the secretary.[91] But it was an unpleasant surprise for her to learn that yet again damage had been found. The telegram that confirmed the arrival of the works asked 'did you know that the branch in blossom has a hole in the canvas?'[92] Jo continued to loan magnanimously, and as a result Van Gogh's art became even better known—but at the expense of the works, more and more of which sustained damage.

This was a huge problem, but she spent little or no time on it. Her thoughts were wholly occupied by her sister Mien, who had been seriously ill for some time and finally died on 15 July 1910, while she was on holiday in Zandvoort. She had had repeated 'attacks' a few months before and had suffered frequently for long periods. Jo was extraordinarily sad—while they might no longer have had such intensive contact, the two sisters had always been very attached to one another. It was a severe blow but, as she wrote to Kee Vos-Stricker, Vincent had comforted her at this sorrowful time. In her letter of condolence Kee answered: 'He's such a dear part of the whole family. It's lovely that he's already such a mature person and really feels for you.'[93]

Quarrel with Lies du Quesne-van Gogh

While Jo was grieving the loss of her sister Mien, she was infuriated by her sister-in-law, Lies. Previously they had got on so well together, but that was now over for ever. In 1910 Lies du Quesne-van Gogh published *Vincent van Gogh. Persoonlijke herinneringen aangaande een kunstenaar,* a book in which she wholeheartedly praised Jo's efforts:

> Using her knowledge of art and her commercial acumen, and more importantly being driven by a sense of inner piety, one woman's tactful handling achieved the well-nigh impossible for this art, and broke through the brick wall of convention that this art had initially been rejected as 'not being art'.

But as Jo read it, she became more and more vexed. She underlined all the factual errors in her copy and in the margin made feisty comments such as 'completely fabricated', 'ridiculously exaggerated', 'utterly untrue assumption' and 'nonsense'. One of Lies's footnotes about the alleged descent of the family was also targeted by Jo: 'hypocrisy', she commented.[94] Spiteful or not, she pointed out to several reviewers that *Persoonlijke herinneringen* was full of errors. Willem Steenhoff responded in *De*

Amsterdammer,[95] Jan Greshoff in *Onze Kunst*[96] and Johan de Meester in *De Gids*. Greshoff condemned the book, which was steeped in 'offensive vanity', as 'one of the most annoying and trivial publications of recent years', and De Meester published a 'list of rectifications' that went on for pages.[97] Albeit indirectly, this was how Jo got even.

It goes without saying that this was not lost on Lies. Vindictively, she cut out her previous praise of Jo in the subsequent publication *Vincent van Gogh. Herinneringen aan haar broeder* (1923). She also made all sorts of corrections. Jan Hulsker described the tension that had arisen between the two women, each of whom was convinced she knew what the relationship between Vincent and Theo had been like, as a feud. Jo again explicitly challenged her sister-in-law in her own introduction to *Brieven aan zijn broeder* (*Letters to His Brother)* (1914), which was itself not completely free of errors. Lies, for instance, described Vincent's love of teasing when he was a child, while Jo stated, based on information from Theo, that in fact he 'could make up such wonderful games'.[98] Incidentally it is not true that Jo deliberately erased references to Lies in her letters edition, as Hulsker later alleged in *Vincent and Theo van Gogh: A Dual Biography*. She certainly did mention her.[99] The fact that Jo referred to living people using an initial was not meant unkindly. She did the same for people other than Lies. It was consistent with her approach of maintaining people's privacy and not disclosing intimate sensitivities. In any event, after Jo had publicly denounced Lies, their friendship was at an end. Meanwhile the planned edition of the letters was becoming ever more imminent.

14

Contracts for publication of Van Gogh's letters

From mid-1910 onwards, Jo worked very hard on preparing for the publication of Vincent's letters to Theo in both a German edition and a Dutch one. Jo and Paul Cassirer set aside their previous difference of opinion about the German edition and he now presented her with an accurate calculation, noting that he could not produce it for less than twenty-five marks a copy. After Jo agreed, Cassirer sent her a new contract, with her changes incorporated in it. This last contract was the definitive one and included Jo's deadline for completing all her texts. Jo's goal was to have her three-volume edition *Brieven aan zijn broeder (Letters to His Brother)* published shortly after the two-volume *Briefe an seinen Bruder* in 1914. Both works duly appeared. They included reproductions of all the sketches Vincent had made in his letters or enclosed with them.[1]

On 25 July 1910, Jo signed the contract with Verlag Paul Cassirer in her own capacity and as the legal representative of her minor son, who needless to say knew all about it. She undertook to deliver a clearly legible transcript of the letters, guaranteed absolute accuracy and agreed that the translator of the Dutch letters, the painter Leo Klein-Diepold, would be given access to the original manuscripts if he needed it. The art historian and art critic Carl Einstein translated the letters that had been written in French. Jo had to produce a biographical introduction. It was agreed that she would not publish the letters in any other language before the German publication was ready. Cassirer wanted to beat everyone else to the market. The first edition ran to 2,080 copies, eighty of which were a luxury version. A further 215 copies were produced; not for sale, these were intended as complimentary copies for gifts. Jo received six luxury copies and thirty-two standard ones. Under the contract she would be sent sales figures and receive 20 per cent of the selling price. In the event of a reprint, that would be 25 per cent.[2]

The Wereldbibliotheek (WB)

Between February and July 1910 Jo also conducted negotiations with the publishers Elsevier. She was toying with the idea of putting Dutch, German and French editions on the market. The potential publishers would have to pay the translation costs. She calculated the numbers of letters, pages, lines and even characters that would be involved for the managing director Jacobus George Robbers. He expressed surprise in his response of 12 May: '3,619,200 characters is not nothing!' Jo would transfer all publication rights and would have to work out what that would cost. Robbers took a lengthy vacation and consequently the final decision was delayed. Jo wrote to him at the beginning of July saying that in the meantime there was a publisher in Germany and asked him if Elsevier wanted to publish only the Dutch edition. Robbers replied that the cost of paper and printing meant that it would only have been worthwhile to put both editions on the market, and the negotiations ceased. Soon afterwards Jo started a dialogue with publishers the Wereldbibliotheek (WB) in Amsterdam, who *were* interested in working with her.[3]

In view of Jo's socially driven attitude to life, the WB or 'De Wereldbibliotheek (Maatschappij voor Goede en Goedkoope lectuur)' to give it its full title, was in fact a more logical choice for her than Elsevier. Literature and art were crucial in the social advancement of ordinary people, and the WB endeavoured to distribute books to new groups of readers. Associations promoting art for the working class such as 'Kunst aan het Volk' and 'Kunst voor Allen' had similar objectives. Reducing the length of the working day, raising workers' standard of living, and improving housing and education should go hand in hand with more broadly based development. Needless to say, encouraging literary and cultural knowledge and awareness among an untapped group should be beneficial in promoting the sale of books. The businessman and SDAP politician Floor Wibaut was one of the shareholders in the Amsterdam publishing house. Nevertheless, managing director Leo Simons, who established the WB in 1905, observed years later that despite all the good intentions, 'ordinary people' remained almost completely out of reach as buyers. The books were purchased primarily in the circle of 'more educated folk with modest incomes'.[4] This must have disappointed Jo, who wanted to keep the selling price as low as possible.

Letters flew frequently between her and the Wereldbibliotheek, dealing with the detailed cost calculation, including the size of the edition, the font, the font size, the paper, the electrotype plates, typesetting, printing, proofreading, binding, advertising, stock figures, statements and commissions. Payments would be made through an accountant and through Jo's brother Henri, who always took care of her banking.[5] She signed the contract for the publication of *Brieven aan zijn broeder* on 18 January 1911. The selling price for the three volumes was set at 7.50 guilders stitched and 10 guilders for the bound edition. The edition ran to 2,100 copies, which was more or less the same as the German one. Jo would receive information about sales annually. The contract reveals that she paid for the printing, which cost forty-three guilders per sheet (a sheet was folded to produce a quire of sixteen pages), and that she would pay for additional correction costs.[6] She arranged for the set type for the first edition to be retained should there be a reprint. It is remarkable that Jo was also responsible for all the advertising. As the editor, she would only receive six stitched and six bound complimentary copies, which was not overly generous. Now that she was bound by contract again, she really had to get cracking—and she did, but it was a struggle. She had badly misjudged the enormous amount of work involved in transcribing the letters, and as a result more than three years passed before both editions were in the bookshops. In other words, not until the summer of 1914.

Van Gogh's art in the United Kingdom

In October 1910, Félix Fénéon of the Bernheim-Jeune gallery told Jo about an exhibition featuring Post-Impressionists that was being organized in London by the painter and art historian Roger Fry. A substantial event, it was to include a hundred and twenty works by Manet, Van Gogh, Cézanne, Seurat, Gauguin and others. Fénéon asked Jo on Fry's behalf whether she could provide ten or so works by Van Gogh, but two weeks later the secretary, Desmond MacCarthy of the Grafton Galleries, had still not heard anything even though it was a matter of urgency.[7] He asked which works she was intending to send. Jo jotted down twelve works on the back of his note. She did the same with the asking prices; they are on the back of a later letter from MacCarthy. Johannes de Bois, who was still working for the C.M. van Gogh gallery, acted as intermediary and sent her confirmation in October that the works, packed in three crates, had been shipped from Vlissingen. His colleague H.L. Klein told Jo about the design of the exhibition and the way the works were arranged on the walls. Meanwhile Jo had had second thoughts and also sent *Self-Portrait as a Painter* (F 522 / JH 1356) and four drawings for the exhibition.[8] She realized that a self-portrait always appealed to the public's imagination, particularly this one in which Van Gogh stands with his palette in his hand.

Only one letter from Jo to MacCarthy, dated 7 December 1910, has survived. In it she asks what he wrote in his letter to *The Spectator* and she talks about Van Gogh's illness.[9] MacCarthy was planning to give a lecture on Van Gogh and Gauguin, and he accepted Jo's invitation to visit her in Amsterdam. Sitting in front of Gauguin's *The Mango Trees, Martinique*, they talked about the two artists (Plates 46, 47).[10] It was a memorable visit, which he recalled years later with awe. They discussed the prices of the paintings: 'They were still admirably cheap. When we came to price them, she was asking a hundred and twenty pounds or less for some admirable examples of his art.'[11]

Everything was ready by the beginning of November. The exhibition *Manet and the Post-Impressionists* ran from 8 November 1910 to 15 January 1911 in the Grafton Galleries. Jo's name was mentioned in the catalogue as a member of the 'Honorary Committee'. She was more difficult to trace for readers of the book *The Post-Impressionists* by Charles Lewis Hind, which was published in 1911.

The name of the owner in the caption to the *Self-Portrait* appeared as 'Madame Gossehalk Berger'. Either Hind had mangled it or the typesetter did his best to read bad handwriting.[12] It was the first time that so many Van Goghs—nearly thirty—had been exhibited in England and it attracted a great deal of attention from the press. There were 25,000 visitors.[13] Jo wanted to buy a work by Odilon Redon, but it had already been sold. She shared her interest in Redon with her brother Andries, and at the time Johan was also very keen on Redon's art; he had published an article about him shortly before.[14]

On 9 December Jo received a copy of Roger Fry's article in *The Nation* that MacCarthy sent her. Fry tried in his publications to dispel the stubborn image of Van Gogh as a 'disturbed artist'. His efforts were certainly desirable, for alongside many enthusiastic responses there had also been disappointingly negative reactions to the exhibition. The *Bystander* of 23 November 1910 published a cartoon showing people roaring with laughter as they stood face to face with Van Gogh's art. 'I trust you are not wounded by the silly criticisms,' MacCarthy wrote to Jo.[15]

After the exhibition closed, two paintings went on to an exhibition at the United Arts Club of Dublin. They had been requested by the co-founder of this cultural society, Ellen Duncan, and Jo agreed immediately. Between 25 January and 14 February, eight works by Van Gogh hung in the Modern Gallery among paintings by Camille Corot, Gustave Courbet, James McNeill Whistler and Claude Monet. After Dublin they could also be seen in March at the Sandon Studios Society in the Liberty Buildings in Liverpool.[16] Sales in the United Kingdom were not very brisk, however. By 1896 some eight collectors had a Van Gogh, and during the period prior to the First World War only a few new buyers appeared.[17] One of them was Cornelis Frank Stoop of London, who had previously purchased a Van Gogh from Cassirer. At the beginning of 1911, Johannes de Bois announced that this collector wanted to visit Jo. In March, De Bois gave him nine drawings on approval. Stoop bought three and Jo received 2,700 guilders for them. The C.M. van Gogh gallery retained the works he had not selected 'in order to be able to show foreigners something in that area too'.[18]

Meanwhile De Bois had succeeded in selling *Head of a Girl* (F 518 / JH 2056) and *Chestnut Tree in Blossom* (F 752 / JH 1991). He worked on a 'tit for tat' principle and wrote to Jo, saying: 'Presumably you are satisfied with what we have achieved, so we should like to count on your continuing cooperation if we ask.' Wasting no time, he immediately proposed that certain works he still had on consignment should be replaced.[19] This initiative had particularly beneficial consequences for the C.M. van Gogh gallery. Before the end of the year they bought *Shoes* (F 461 / JH 1569) and *The Painter on the Road to Tarascon* (F 448 / JH 1491) at 4,800 guilders for both. *Shoes* was subsequently sold on for a lucrative 3,600 guilders.[20]

Jo's agreement boosted the momentum of the Van Gogh machine. By June 1910, Paul Cassirer had sold ten of the works she held for 14,000 guilders, and in October and November he staged an exhibition of seventy-four works in Berlin that later travelled to Hamburg and Frankfurt.[21] Jo had sent twenty-three paintings and twenty-one drawings. She received numerous offers, all demanding that she respond 'immediately, please'. Only two drawings were sold because people continued to complain that prices were too high.[22] Bruno Cassirer asked Jo if he could take photographs of some of the works she had provided—they would always come in handy—and she agreed. He sent her eleven prints three weeks later.[23] That autumn Emilie Knappert came to discuss an exhibition in the Leidsche Volkshuis, agreeing to something Jo must have written to her about the gap between rich and poor in society, and what art could mean in mitigating the need: 'Yes, there's much sorrow and much sadness, but there is also a great deal of joy.'[24] Members of the public did indeed derive considerable enjoyment from the cross-section of Van Gogh's oeuvre on show at that modest exhibition in Leiden.

Vincent came home for two weeks during the Christmas holidays. Jo brought him up to date with recent events, including the exhibitions in the United Kingdom, De Bois's sales and the seven outstanding works from Cassirer's stock which the Kunsthalle in Bremen exhibited that month.[25] The painting *Fields with Poppies* (F 581 / JH 1751), which Jo had sold to Julien Leclercq in 1900 along with three other paintings for only 3,800 francs, was purchased in 1911 by the museum in Bremen with help from the Galerieverein, for 30,000 marks. This spectacularly expensive purchase—of a work by a foreign painter to make matters worse—caused ructions in the German art world, incensing dealers and artists alike.[26]

Van Gogh's reputation was given further shots in the arm in 1911 by some important publications, particularly H.P. Bremmer's study *Vincent van Gogh. Inleidende beschouwingen*, Johan de Meester's article 'Over kunstenaar-zijn en Vincent van Gogh', which was published in *De Gids*,[27] and *Lettres de Vincent van Gogh à Émile Bernard*, published by Ambroise Vollard. Vollard sent Jo a copy with a personal dedication.[28] Later, in the foreword to her own letters publication, Jo complimented Bernard, describing his introduction as being 'without doubt the most beautiful pages ever written about Vincent'.[29]

Jo had also been working on a rectification for *The Burlington Magazine for Connoisseurs* and her contribution appeared in the January 1911 issue. Rudolf Meyer-Riefstahl had commented in a previous issue that the letters from Van Gogh's early years 'are lost beyond all possibility of discovery', and that was something Jo had to emphatically dispute. She strategically referred to her impending edition, to the letters that had already been published in *Mercure de France* and to Vollard's attractive Bernard edition. A comment she made about the *Mercure* publication is telling: 'It was impossible then to publish the whole. The reasons that prevented this no longer exist twenty years after his death.'[30] She deemed that the time was now ripe because there was sufficient historical distance. The *Algemeen Handelsblad* of 5 January 1911 reported on Jo's letter, so people in the Netherlands knew about it at the same time.

Jo knew better than anyone that the letters to Theo held a key position in the totality of correspondence, if only because of the 820 letters that Vincent wrote, 651 were to his brother and seven to Theo and Jo. Those 658 letters covered a period of eighteen years and give a penetrating insight into Van Gogh's life and what drove him: how, after twelve occupations and thirteen disasters, he eventually decided to become an artist when Theo had suggested it to him. The fact that it was Theo who persuaded his brother to do it had a significant influence on their relationship in later years. He clearly considered it his duty to support Vincent, particularly in a financial sense, after he made his choice. Theo proved to be an accommodating patron. His support, which never wavered, was a driving force behind the progress of Van Gogh's artistic career and its importance cannot be overestimated.

Vincent was able to devote himself completely to art from the age of twenty-seven. The hundreds of letters to his brother spell out the breathtaking development he underwent, as a person and as a self-taught artist, during the ten years that followed. That extraordinary process can be followed step by step in the letters.

They bear witness to his views on art, to the eagerness with which he threw himself into drawing and painting, and to his growing conviction that colour was crucial in his quest for truth. His goal was to intensify and sublimate experience of life in a work of art. Much, if not everything, was permitted in order to achieve that ideal. That emerges, for instance, from a letter to Theo in 1885 in which he formulated his great desire to 'learn to make such inaccuracies, such variations, reworkings, alterations of the reality, that it might become, very well—lies if you will— but—truer than the literal truth'.[31] Many of his letters contain lively sketches, which he included to keep Theo abreast of his progress and show him the compositions he was working on. Jo realized from the outset how unique the letters from this passionate artist to his brother were. And history has proved her right.

No lack of interest

In the summer of 1911 Jo encountered another grasping Van Gogh devotee, who wanted to buy her collection in one fell swoop. She wrote nothing about it herself, but Johannes de Bois revealed it later in the *Haarlemsche Courant*:

> Now, perhaps, it is time to publish a curious incident; in the summer of 1911 this author approached Mrs Cohen Gosschalk (as she then was) with a virtually unlimited authorization from a principal, who wanted to acquire this particular collection in its entirety for his museum. But he was refused and, despite the indeed extraordinarily high offer he made, he was firmly sent packing with a calm smile. If you want, you can call this a commercial defeat, but it increased my respect even more for her, as she declined my offer.[32]

Evidently Jo dealt with the issue in person, smiling affably the while.

It is highly probable that the principal was H.P. Bremmer, acting on the instructions of Anton and Helene Kröller-Müller, because after a visit to Jo in 1922, Gustave Coquiot noted something that she must have told him: 'She refused to sell all her works by Vincent to Mrs Kröller, even though Mrs Kröller had offered her an unlimited sum!'[33] Jo had no interest whatsoever in

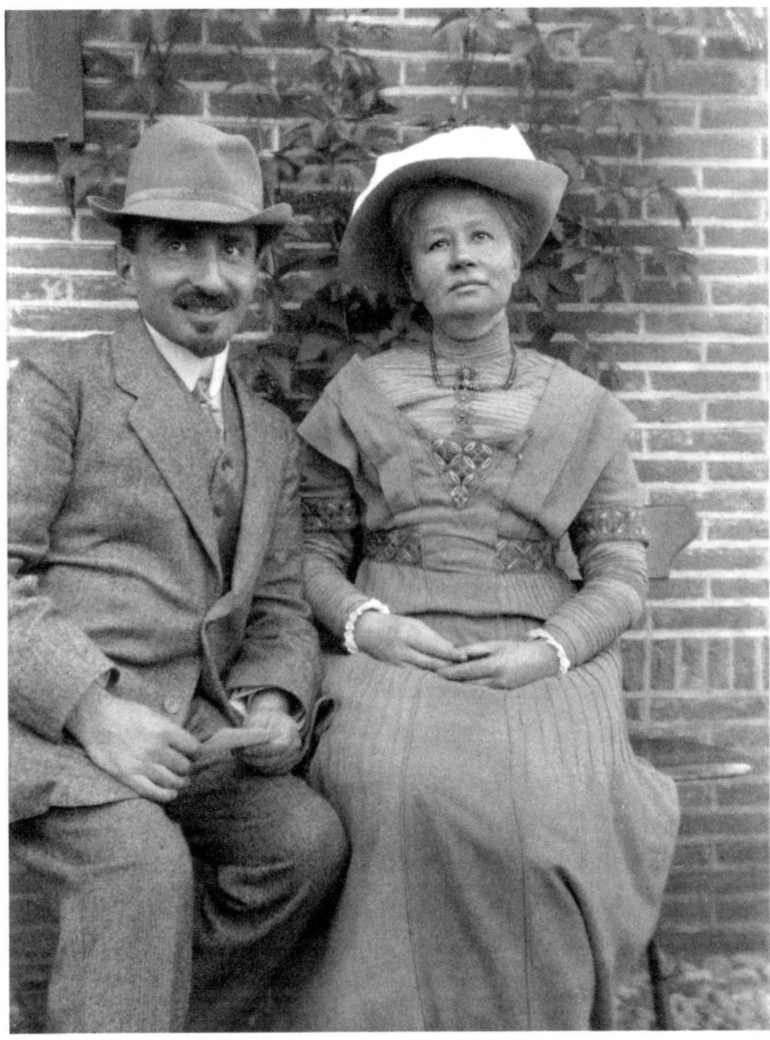

Figure 46 Johan Cohen Gosschalk and Jo Cohen Gosschalk-Bonger, *c.* 1911.

disposing of the collection and the twenty-one-year-old Vincent would have wholeheartedly agreed. She was satisfied with how things were going and wanted to continue along the route she had chosen.

Jo also wrote to her son in Delft about everyday events. She told him she had enjoyed a beautiful summer's evening. She had sat under a lamp in her garden with a lovely book by William Makepeace Thackeray she had borrowed from Hilversum library on her lap. Johan was much less comfortable in high summer because 'the heat really does affect him', she added (Figure 46). The flowers wilted in the heat, but the pumpkins grew like weeds. She wrote that her brother Henri and sister Lien would be visiting and gently reminded her son to send a card to Aunt Annie (his Uncle Andries's wife), whose birthday was coming up. Something like that was easy to forget![34]

Johannes de Bois left the C.M. van Gogh gallery and became a partner at the Artz gallery in Lange Vijverberg in The Hague. Tactfully, he had put himself forward as a dealer in modern art. He told Jo that he had found that when it came down to it, he had received little support for this segment of the market from his former employer. De Bois hoped he could continue to count on Jo's support and played on her emotions: he was sure she would sympathize with this new business, where such enthusiastic young people were working.[35] And that indeed proved to be the case; when he wanted to exchange works by Van Gogh again, Jo sent him eight paintings and six drawings straight away. He also discussed with her his plans to exhibit works in the United States. He had previously proposed getting the Durand-Ruel gallery interested because they had contacts in New York.[36] He proudly announced on 1 March 1912 that he had made his first sales in his new position: two Parisian landscapes by Van Gogh for a total of 5,000 guilders. *Bank of the Seine with the Clichy Bridge* (F 302 / JH 1322) went to the Unger & Van Mens gallery in Rotterdam, and *Labourer on a Country Road* (F 361 / JH 1260) went to Thannhauser's Moderne Galerie in Munich.[37] Between 1908 and 1913, as an extremely dedicated intermediary, De Bois succeeded in selling thirty-three Van Goghs for a total of some 80,000 guilders on Jo's behalf.[38]

But Jo also continued to sell directly, for example to the collector and art critic Klas Walter Fåhraeus of Stockholm, who at the end of 1911 recalled his visit to her with such pleasure. He was delighted with the purchase of the drawings *Quay with Sand Barges* (F 1462 / JH 1556) and *Cypresses* (F 1524 / JH 1749). 'The cypresses act like a fanfare—wonderful!' he wrote triumphantly, and he enclosed for Jo a biography of the artist Ernst Josephson, undoubtedly because he had seen a preliminary study of Josephson's painting *The Waternix* in her home.[39]

She was still frequently asked for advice. This time it was about the estate of Vincent van Gogh, Uncle Cor's son, who had owned a large art collection. Anton G.C. de Vries acted on behalf of his aged father R.W.P. de Vries, who had an auction house at 146 Singel in Amsterdam and was the deceased's executor. Among the prints were some by Van Gogh, impressions of which were also in Jo's collection. She was asked what should be done with them. At the bottom of the letter from the auction house she noted: 'Reply 27 Febr. include in the sale', which they duly did.[40]

Although she had stated previously that she wanted to hold on to portraits of Van Gogh, at the beginning of 1912 Jo nevertheless sold the Frankfurter Kunstverein his *Self-Portrait* (F 345 / JH 1249) for 5,000 marks. She enclosed a certificate of authenticity because the new owner doubted whether the cardboard on which it was painted dated from Van Gogh's time.[41]

Alongside all these activities, her work on the letters was going well. She made transcripts of Van Gogh's last letters from Auvers-sur-Oise and tried to put them in sequence. She asked Paul Gachet if she could borrow the letter she had given him in 1905 because she wanted to include all the letter sketches, and this letter contained a particularly fine example. She ensured consistency in the quality of the reproductions by having this letter sketch, as well as all the others, photographed at Maison Van

Leer. As she read the letters from Auvers, she recalled her visit to the Gachet family with Theo and their baby. She asked what Gachet knew about Van Gogh's last days because she had been in the Netherlands during that dramatic period. She wanted to find out—probably just for her own peace of mind, because during those last months there had been a great deal of tension between those involved—whether Van Gogh's suicide was connected to his illness ('une crise de sa maladie'). She was still wrestling with the question of whether he had really felt so wretched: 'it remains a mystery'.[42] In her introduction Jo did not after all use the information that Gachet sent her later, including what he said about the motives that he believed had led to the suicide. She commented as follows about her letters edition:

> I assure you that it gives me a great deal of work and there is a lot more to do—because although the manuscript is ready now (there were 638 letters and most of them are not dated) I still have to add the notes and correct all the proofs.

She showed him the letter in which Vincent wrote about Paul Gachet Sr's illness. In her opinion it was not necessary to delete that passage because who, after all, never had a nervous disorder? As far as she was concerned, this was a rhetorical question. The aside that she made afterwards speaks volumes in this context. Things were alas still not going well with her husband, and Gachet was not to write anything about it because she did not want Johan to see it. Jo kept her anxiety about his health largely to herself. Yet what is crucial about her letter, in particular, is her comment that she would do anything to arrange for Theo's mortal remains to be buried next to Vincent's for ever.[43] And so her thoughts jumped from her current husband, who was so very poorly and with whom she had an unsatisfactory marriage, to her previous love, with whom she had briefly been so blissfully happy. Both were ill and weak, and it was a morbid coincidence that, in the end, the dates of Theo's reburial and Johan's funeral, which was now on the horizon, were not to be that far apart.

Johan's death

Johan's pleurisy was fatal. After suffering for months, he died on 18 May 1912 in Amsterdam. He was only thirty-eight. Three days later he was buried at 12.15 p.m. in Zorgvlied cemetery in the simplest of ceremonies without any speeches at the graveside. The death announcement was also sober. Those present included Jan Veth and Willem Steenhoff. The newspapers mentioned Johan's fragile constitution and 'a lingering illness', but did not give details. Johan's contributions to the *NRC* were praised for their soundness, keen analysis and polished style, which was sometimes 'gently ironic'.[44] Jo placed announcements of his death in *Het Volk*, the *Algemeen Handelsblad* and the *NRC*.[45]

At the end of that year, there was the 'Exhibition of works left by Johan Cohen Gosschalk' at the C.M. van Gogh gallery at 115 Rokin. The exhibition was advertised on a grand scale in *De Amsterdammer* of

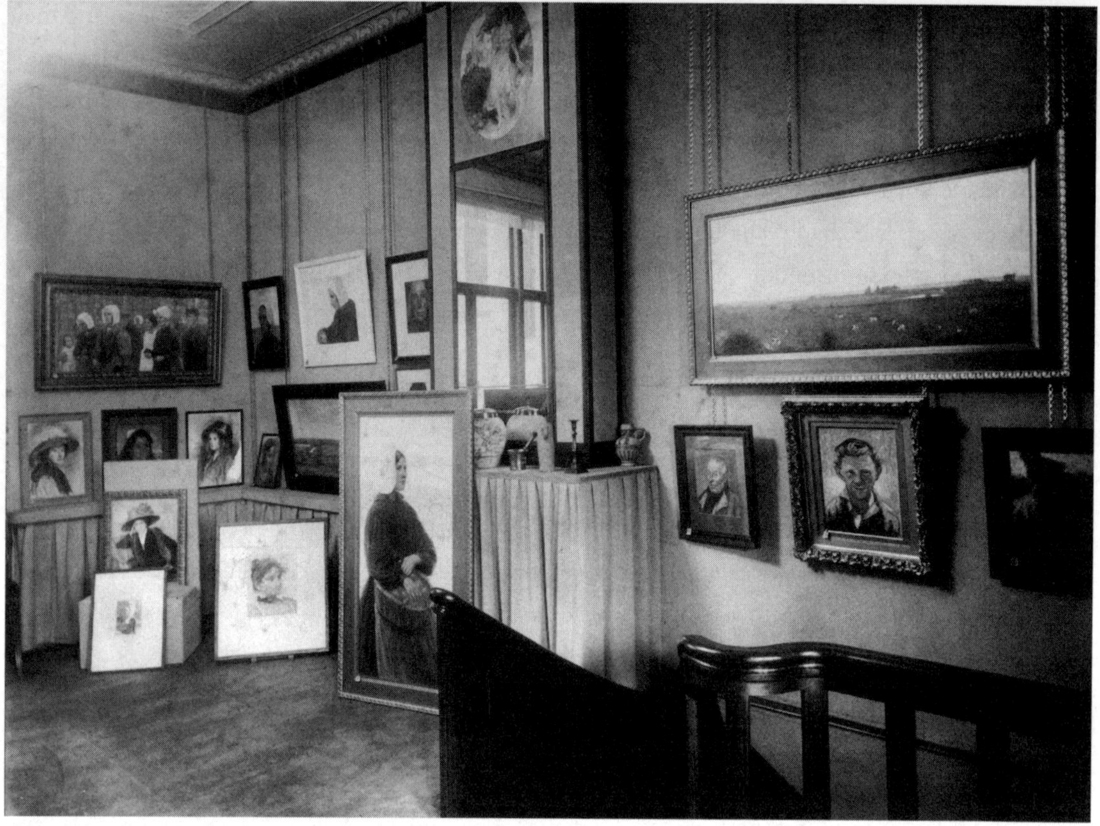

Figure 47 Exhibition of works by Johan Cohen Gosschalk at the C.M. van Gogh gallery. Amsterdam, 1912.

15 December. There was a catalogue with an introduction written by Steenhoff. He did this with input from Jo, who drew up a preliminary list of seventy-one works (the final number was eighty). The portraits that Johan had made of Jo and Vincent were also in the exhibition. Steenhoff described his work as restrained and he detected in it traces of 'serious effort' by a principled artist. 'And so, working against a backdrop of steady self-criticism, he was very hard on himself.'[46] In a previous contribution in *De Amsterdammer* he had emphasized Johan's modesty and remarked that he could be gloomy in his work, while in conversation, on the other hand, he was often witty (Plate 48).[47] Kee Vos-Stricker was struck by the colourful paintings, as she wrote to Jo: 'How clever he was. He was the same in his work as he was in person, so precise and yet powerful at the right time. . . . You did important and good work by enabling a wider circle to make the acquaintance of all those treasures and to value him.'[48] De Bois was also enthusiastic: 'The work looks very good in those intimate spaces, don't you think?' but he also made a cautious comment: 'In fact there might have been slightly too many works, I thought' (Figure 47).[49]

In *Elsevier's Geïllustreerd Maandschrift* Cornelis Veth wrote about Cohen Gosschalk's 'utterly unobtrusive life' and appreciated the purity and sincerity of his work. He used such words as 'spare' and 'laborious' in referring to the execution. Johan's former teacher Jan Veth detected such nervous traits or traces of timidity, particularly in the artist's later work, but thought they had been made on the basis of an 'aristocracy of mind and spirit'.[50] Jo asked Veth what he would think if a small anthology containing a selection of Johan's writings were to be published. He supported the idea and even wanted to write an introduction for it.[51] It is not clear why this plan did not go ahead in the end, but it does show that Jo, despite all the problems she had had with him, did respect her second husband and wanted to utilize the expertise and perseverance she had meanwhile acquired on behalf of Johan's reputation and the work he left behind. She donated his pastel drawing *Girl from Laren* (c. 1910) to the Rijksmuseum.[52]

A memorandum Vincent wrote in 1977 sheds additional light on their relationship and also how the estate was settled. This memorandum was prompted by a letter sent by Elisabeth du Quesne-van Gogh on 15 February 1923 to Benno J. Stokvis about her visit to a Van Gogh exhibition in Utrecht. Jo and Vincent had also seen that letter at the time. Now Vincent wanted to clarify matters for himself and apparently also for posterity. He started by quoting the following from Lies's letter:

> It was Mrs Cohen Gosschalk who exhibited, calling herself, *pour la raison de la cause*, Van Gogh-Bonger again, thus ignoring her second marriage to the honourable Jewish worker Cohen Gosschalk, whose principal heir she was.[53]

Vincent commented as follows:

> My mother's second marriage did not bring her what she expected. Her husband was very neurotic. . . . After his illness started, Cohen Gosschalk constantly struggled with his health. Because he was so sombre, he gradually lost touch with his friends and acquaintances, who no longer wanted to visit him. . . .
>
> She gave her husband the greatest possible care and dedication. Each of them had a modest income. His only contacts with his family were with his younger sister Meta, Johan Franco's mother, who was also a painter, and with his brother-in-law Professor Hamburger. He had no dealings with his mother and older brother. After their deaths, my mother did not want, on emotional grounds, to accept the part of the estate she was entitled to. After I reached the age of majority, she and I made an arrangement concerning our joint property. She was able to continue her modest lifestyle after my education was completed. . . . In retrospect she could certainly have used her bequests from the family of her second husband in order to make her life somewhat more comfortable. She had had enough unpleasantness from that side. She did, however, have the satisfaction of independence. The reference in Mrs du Quesne-van Gogh's letter to a legacy, which she lived on, does not hold water.

Vincent's son Johan noted later on this document that Jo and Vincent were extremely upset about Lies's letter.[54]

The notarial deed for the execution of Johan's last will and testament, drawn up by the Bussum notary Sytse Scheffelaar Klots on 13 December 1912, states that Jo was the heir to seven-eighths and his mother Christina Gosschalk to one-eighth of his estate. The instrument contained a detailed report on what he left in the way of shares and bonds, and the estimated value of his possessions, for example 'Two Delft Cows' (fifteen guilders), a few books (five guilders) and his easel (six guilders). The value of the forty-nine paintings by him was estimated at only six hundred guilders. There is also a list of unpaid accounts—funeral expenses, of course, but also strikingly large bills from the tailor and the dentist, plus the rent of an upstairs flat in Amsterdam where Johan had a studio. Mrs Gosschalk was not at the meeting; she had authorized a representative to sign the document on her behalf.[55] The paintings and drawings that Johan left—in so far as Vincent's heirs did not want them—were transferred to the 'Stichting Schone Kunsten rond 1900', a foundation established in 1964, and accommodated in the Drents Museum in Assen.

HERE LIES MY DEAR HUSBAND. This was the text Jo chose for the gravestone. A weeping rose, dwarf periwinkle and ivy were planted on the grave, and a box hedge was added a year later. At the end of June, Jo sent cards to thank everyone for their condolences. She also expressed her gratitude in an announcement in the *Algemeen Handelsblad* and the *NRC* of 1 July. Jo wrote to Paul Gachet that Johan's death had dealt her a 'cruel blow'.[56] She was strong, though, as ever in such difficult circumstances. Jo was a widow for the second time. She had to carry on her way of life, which Vincent described as 'modest', without all the worries about Johan but at the same time without his support.

A new stimulus in Cologne

Immediately after Johan's death, Jo had no time to grieve, and not just because of everything she had to arrange and organize for his funeral. Again, Van Gogh forced himself into the foreground because, as one of the guests of honour, Jo was invited to the opening of the major exhibition 'Internationale Kunstausstellung des Sonderbundes westdeutscher Kunstfreunde und Künstler zu Cöln', which ran from 25 May to 30 September 1912 in the Städtische Ausstellungshalle am Aachener Tor. Jo clearly considered the invitation to be important for on 21 May, when Johan had only just been buried, she went to Cologne and put in an appearance. The exhibition attracted a great deal of attention, and with good reason. There were some 130 works by Van Gogh, who was being put forward as the progenitor of modern art. Jo and the Kröller-Müllers provided works (there were more works from their collections than those listed in the catalogue). Some forty-six Van Goghs came from the Kröller-Müllers' collection, and Jo lent at least twenty-two, a few of which were for sale.[57] It is a matter of conjecture whether she knew at the time that Helene and Anton were the buyers who paid 9,000 marks for *Paul Eugène Milliet ('The Lover')* (F 473 / JH 1588), a painting that came from her collection—something the catalogue did not mention.[58]

The organizers had only approached Jo for loans a month before the opening. The letter explained that several private Van Gogh owners, including 'Herr Kröller, Scheveningen', would be providing works. She agreed at once, and a few days later Alfred Hagelstange, director of the Wallraf-Richartz-Museum, visited her.[59] Between them they made the selection for this important exhibition—Johan had no say because he was already ill and had distanced himself from such matters.

The work of promoting Van Gogh's oeuvre continued in the months after Johan's death and the requests kept on coming. Jo also took action for Berlin. Cassirer, who had had a particular work on commission in 1910, now asked if she still owned it and what its price was. It can be deduced from her note on his letter that Jo increased the asking price from 1,500 guilders to 4,000 guilders. A few days later he asked her to send him five drawings because he had a potential buyer. If she no longer had one of the specified works, could she please send an alternative. Jo had meanwhile developed such an efficient record-keeping system that she could retrieve the drawings on demand, and then pack them up and ship them.[60]

During the summer months there was an exhibition of forty drawings at the Artz & De Bois gallery in The Hague. In consultation with De Bois, Jo compiled an 'ensemble' of thirty-one works from her collection. A watercolour, *Outskirts of Paris, View from Montmartre* (F 1410 / JH 1286), was sold for 2,000 guilders to the foundation 'Vereeniging tot het vormen van eene openbare verzameling van hedendaagsche kunst', which loaned it to the Stedelijk Museum in Amsterdam.[61] De Bois also sold two painted copies by Van Gogh after works by Jean-François Millet, which he had exhibited in Cologne, as well as a few Van Gogh drawings.[62] Shortly afterwards he told her about a disagreement with Fénéon of Galerie Bernheim-Jeune, who had asserted that a watercolour by Van Gogh was a forgery, even though it had come from Jo's collection. 'You know so much about the art trade, Madam, that you will understand I *cannot sit idly by* when such an assertion is made.' De Bois, who had meanwhile formed a united front with Jo, considered Fénéon's comment to be 'offensive' and was furious about it: 'These are the *un*pleasant aspects of our profession.'[63] The watercolour concerned was *Fishing Boats on the Beach at Saintes-Maries* (F 1429 / JH 1459), which he was to sell in 1913. Jo received 2,000 guilders for this drawing too. Jealousy could have been a reason for the dispute; De Bois found clients outside the Netherlands so Bernheim-Jeune sold less. He provided Jo with an overview of the works he had received from her on consignment and noted which of them he had sold (Plate 49).[64]

In the summer of 1912, Jo found herself alone in 't Lanthuys in Rozenlaantje for the first time. She tried to get over her grief following Johan's death by concentrating on Van Gogh's letters. During this period Willem Steenhoff consulted her on several matters. In one case, for instance, the Oldenzeel gallery had asked him about the authenticity of a work. He also studied Bremmer's book *Vincent van Gogh. Inleidende beschouwingen* (1911) in depth and in connection with this raised the subject of

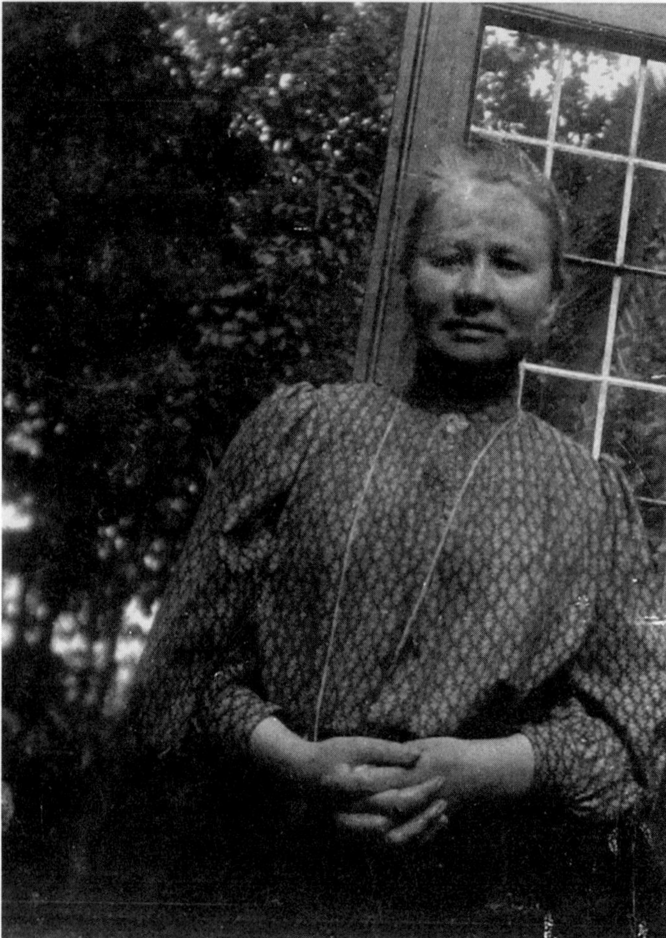

Figure 48 Jo Cohen Gosschalk-Bonger, undated.

Johan: 'Behind [Bremmer's] schoolmasterish façade there is so much seriousness and warmth. I recall how pleasant it was to discuss such subjects with Cohen.'[65] That must also have applied to Jo. Much of her understanding of art had certainly come from her discussions with Johan.

That summer she was also in contact with Gachet. This time he asked her about Van Gogh's etchings and she answered on the back of a picture postcard of *The Bedroom*. It was one of the Van Gogh reproductions sent to her from Cologne and she thought it looked very good.[66] She told her friend about the two cornerstones of her existence: 'Here I am, alone again, and the only thing that sustains me and gives me the courage to continue is the love for my dear son and the duty to look after the interests of Vincent's work'[67] (Figure 48).

By way of relaxation, Jo visited her 'dear son' in Sheffield in late August, early September. Vincent worked there for a few months in the drawing office of Hadfields Limited, a British steel manufacturer, which received many orders from railway companies. Together they went to Scotland, where they visited Glasgow and its environs. Vincent's landlady, E. Harrison of Beighton near Sheffield, wrote later that she had received postcards from Jo in 'Lake-Land' (the Lake District); she was pleased to read she had had a lovely holiday in the midst of 'some of Scotland's grand scenery down the Kyles of Bute'. She and her husband missed Vincent at breakfast, and in particular the passionate conversations the three of them had had about flowers. Jo met the Harrisons and probably also stayed with them, or somewhere near them, for a brief period.[68]

When Jo got back, Cassirer began to exert ever greater pressure on her. He was left completely high and dry in the absence of the promised biographical introduction for his edition of Van Gogh's letters. She had still not delivered it, and meanwhile the typesetters had completed everything else. He urged her to take immediate action and also asked her whether, upon reflection, a fee of 15 per cent of the actual retail price would be acceptable, so that he could at least make the exercise profitable. If not, he might have to drop everything, citing the delay that had built up as one of the reasons. This last point struck a chord with Jo. She had just turned fifty and she understood that she now had to really put her shoulder to the wheel. Nonetheless, her reply did not reveal a trace of anxiety; she remained matter-of-fact and businesslike, and was adamant about the previously agreed 20 per cent of each copy sold, to be settled at the end of every calendar year.[69]

She must have discussed these developments and her plans with Vincent, who gave her a great deal of support at that time. Shortly thereafter Josina Wibaut, who was engaged to Vincent and was to marry him in 1915, added more colour to Jo's existence. Their future life was to take Jo far beyond the Netherlands, to the south of France, New York and elsewhere, with Van Gogh's letters permanently under her wing and within easy reach. First as proofs, later on in three linen-bound volumes and finally her own English translation, which she was to work on for years. The letters formed the core of her existence in the last phase of her life. At the same time, she began to devote more time and effort to the Sociaal-Democratische Arbeiderspartij (SDAP) and the peace movement. Jo had completely overcome the dislike of appearing in public that she had had experienced now and again in the past, and she looked forward to enjoying the benefits of all her efforts and hard work.

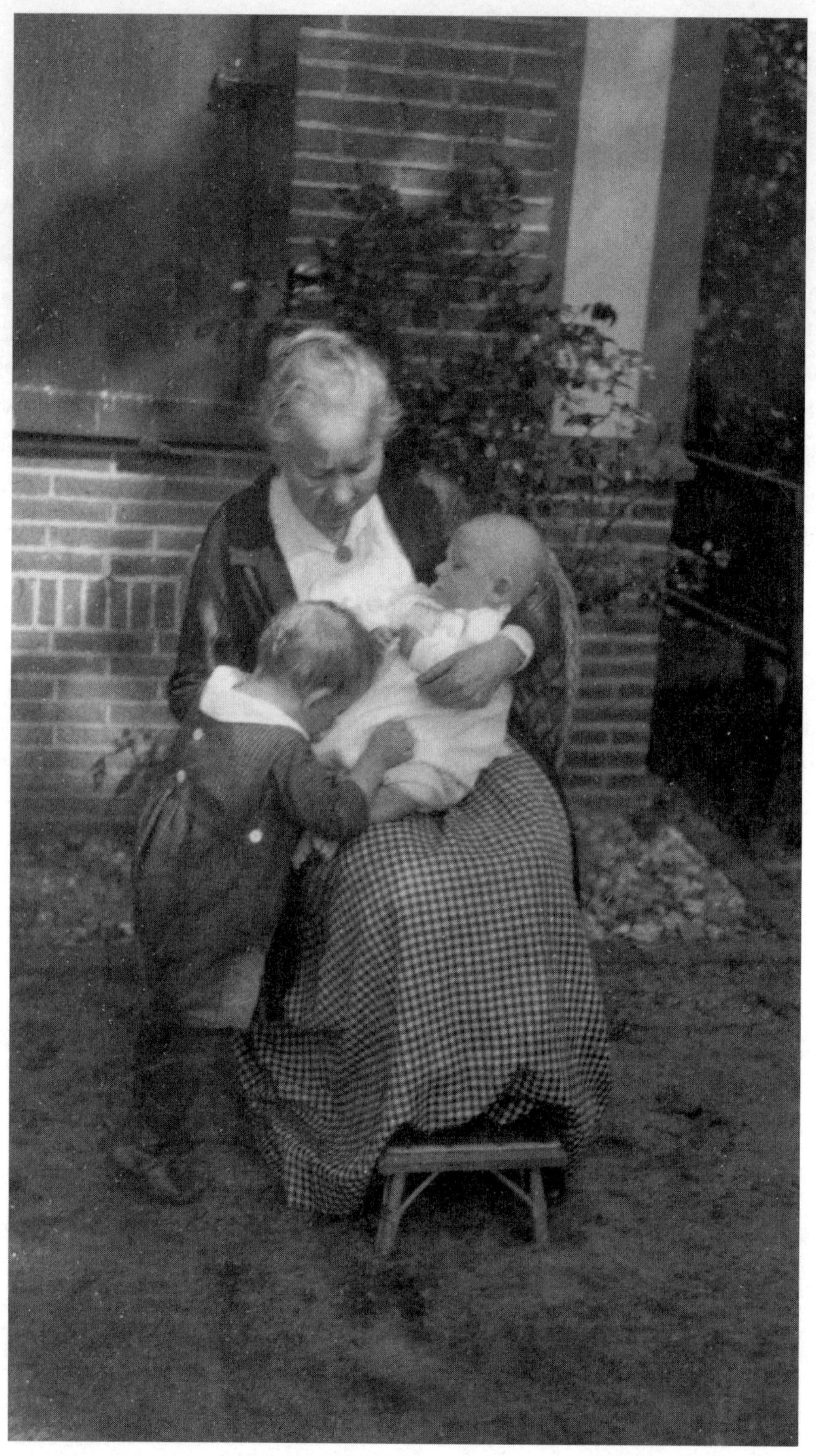

Part Six

Efforts for social democracy and publication of Van Gogh's letters

1912–25

I like biography far better than fiction myself; fiction is too free. In biography you have your little handful of facts, little bits of a puzzle, and you sit and think, and fit 'em together this way and that, and get up and throw 'em down, and say damn, and go out for a walk. And it's real soothing; and when done, gives an idea of finish to the writer that is very peaceful. Of course it's not really so finished as a rotten novel; it always has and always must have the incurable illogicalities of life about it. . . .
Still that's where the fun comes in.

ROBERT LOUIS STEVENSON[1]

15

The Sociaal-Democratische Arbeiderspartij (SDAP)

References were made now and again in previous chapters to Jo's highly developed sense of justice, her contacts with various members of the Sociaal-Democratische Arbeiderspartij (SDAP), visits to party conferences and reviews of socialist poetry in *Belang en Recht*. Her social democratic activities continued after 1912 too, and because they played such a large part in her life, they deserve more detailed analysis in context.

Jo was concerned with the lot of the oppressed in society. She became a member of the SDAP shortly after it was founded in 1894 because she had complete confidence that a better future was in store for them.[1] Many intellectuals and respected members of the bourgeoisie joined the party and gave it additional dimensions. Among them were Frank van der Goes, Henriette Roland Holst, Floor Wibaut and Herman Gorter. Jo's brother Wim and the influential Pieter Tak followed.[2] The party fought its first elections in 1897. Two years later, when Gorter took the initiative of establishing a separate SDAP branch in Bussum, Jo applied to join immediately.

The party attracted few supporters during the early years.[3] It was a socialist movement that had evolved from the revolutionary activities of Domela Nieuwenhuis in the 1880s. The upshot was that a part of the proletariat began to champion their own cause. This first workers' movement, the Sociaal-Democratische Bond (SDB), was primarily anarchic; people made little if any effort to acquire parliamentary influence. When a few social democrats grew tired of the SDB's revolutionary antics, they left the movement. They were dissatisfied and founded their own party, the SDAP, with the primary goal of engaging in a class struggle via parliamentary power. Social democratic members of parliament and the work of active propagandists resulted in growing party membership. The political spearheads were general suffrage, a state old age pension and an eight-hour working day. Socialism's three greatest enemies were considered to be capitalism, church and taverns.

Considerable energy was devoted to fostering the suffrage movement. From 1900 the party had its own daily newspaper, *Het Volk*, with Pieter Jelles Troelstra and Pieter Tak as authoritative editors. Within ten years the paper had some 40,000 subscribers. Orthodox Marxists soon split from the Revisionists: the former wanted a proletarian revolution, while the later preferred a civil parliamentary path. The SDAP membership grew by leaps and bounds, cooperation with the trade unions' association Nederlands Verbond voor Vakverenigingen became more intensive, and mass protests by tens of thousands demonstrated the workers' combativeness. During this period Jo's financial contribution to the party was limited. The party's 1905–15 'support lists' show that with effect from 1 May 1906 she paid five guilders a year to the SDAP. This was a modest sum, but was typical of what most people gave. On the other hand, her brother Wim gave twenty-five guilders annually and someone like Tak was much more generous with an annual 250 guilders.[4]

The SDAP had a victory at the ballot box during the 1913 local authority elections. The number of members of parliament rose from seven to fifteen. The party refused ministerial responsibility, however, because wartime budgets were submitted. This first opportunity to form a progressive coalition government in the Netherlands was therefore not seized. When Wibaut became Amsterdam's first socialist alderman in March 1914, the city had fifteen representatives. The party won twenty-two seats in the lower house in 1918. Employment grew and wages rose, but this changed when it emerged that the purchasing power of neighbouring countries was zero. Germany had a major economic crisis as a result of the immense reparation payments imposed on it by the Treaty of Versailles. The value of the mark collapsed and Germany defaulted on repayments of its massive war debt. After the war, the reforms that the socialists advocated only stood a chance of being implemented if the progressive wings of the centre-ground parties endorsed them. When Jo returned from the United States in May 1919, the party had close to 50,000 members. By then the revolutionary character of the SDAP was already waning. Wim Bonger saw little point in the ideology of revolution and remarked at the time: 'Oh, that sudden about-turn is a wonderful concept, but it's not possible.' According to friends, Wim was driven by outrage about injustice.[5]

It proved difficult to generate enthusiasm for goals that went beyond universal suffrage and an eight-hour working day—even though they were both achieved in the end—and it took a long time before Dutch politics was able to overcome post-war pessimism. Unemployment doubled between 1920 and 1923 and there were many strikes. At Christmas in 1921 the SDAP committed itself to helping the needy in Drenthe and alleviating the famine in the Volga region, in which Jo actively participated.[6] The economy did not begin to recover until 1925, the year of Jo's death, and the SDAP received 23 per cent of the votes in Amsterdam and 37 per cent in Rotterdam. Yet despite having twenty-four seats in parliament, the party's role in government policy remained small.

The Sociaal-Democratische Vrouwenpropagandaclub (SDVC)

Jo's friend Marie Mensing was very enthusiastic about it in March 1901. According to her, now that Jo no longer had the boarding house, she was at a stage where she could devote more time to the party.[7] She was right: Jo was indeed more interested now in worthy causes, and she became the secretary of the Bussum branch of the 'Nederlands Comité voor Algemeen Kiesrecht' ('Dutch Committee for General Suffrage'). Her name is mentioned in the invitation to participate in a national general suffrage demonstration 'Groote Nationale Betooging ten gunste van Grondwetsherziening, om te komen tot Algemeen Kiesrecht voor Mannen en Vrouwen', printed in the *Bussumsche Courant* of 10 and 13 September 1902. This demonstration took place in Utrecht on 14 September. 'Bussum demonstrators' could buy tickets for the boat from Weesp to Utrecht from Jo, from the Bussum branch of the Sociaal-Democratische Arbeiderspartij, which was chaired by Herman Gorter, from the carpenters' association 'Door Eendracht Sterk' and the Gooi branch of the temperance society 'De Nederlandsche Vereeniging tot Afschaffing van Alcoholhoudende Dranken'. The newspaper's designer cheekily inserted an advertisement for Haantje's beers underneath (Plate 50). It was a long struggle. Universal suffrage for men did not arrive until 1917, and women had to wait even longer. They were given the right to vote in 1919 but they could not use it until the 1922 general election.

In 1905 Jo co-founded the party's Amsterdam propaganda organization, the Amsterdamse Sociaal-Democratische Vrouwenpropagandaclub (SDVC—also abbreviated as SDVPC). During the first year she, together with Carry Pothuis-Smit, was superintendent and she was on the board until November 1906.[8] Prior to the inaugural meeting Jo had consulted the chair, Mathilde Wibaut-Berdenis van Berlekom, for several hours. They had ambitious plans. Their ideal was to encourage adult learning among the working class and improve women's working conditions. They fought for independence, maternity care and better child rearing. Mathilde and Jo soon became close (they were the same age) and they discussed current topics during walks together. They appeared together and spoke in turn at meetings for workers' wives. Jo did, though, find it troublesome to find the right tone and wording when explaining issues. Mathilde thought that Jo was making things too difficult for herself: 'I don't have that problem as much as you do. You have to remember that it's a popular movement.'[9] The two women were very friendly and they get to know one another even better when Vincent and Mathilde's daughter Josina fell in love and got married in 1915.

The members of the speakers group had a debating evening once a fortnight. They met in Jo's flat at 77 Koninginneweg and her address was also used for the SDVC's correspondence. On 5 May 1905, for example, they debated 'How taxation burdens women' and 'The interests of children'. Jo organized exchange programmes for children to and from the countryside and collected books for a children's library.[10]

The SDVC extended the range of its activities. The women's section in *Het Volk* was scrapped in 1902 to save money, so Carry Pothuis-Smit proposed to the leadership of the SDAP that it should publish a women's magazine. It took a while before the conference adopted the idea. The first issue of *De Proletarische Vrouw. Blad voor Arbeidsters en Arbeidersvrouwen*, edited by Pothuis-Smit, was published on 1 November 1905. Initially the magazine had seven hundred subscribers, and it developed into the periodical of the national federation of social democratic women's clubs, the Bond van Sociaal-Democratische Vrouwenclubs (BSDVC), which was founded in April 1908. In 1919, *De Proletarische Vrouw* had nearly 11,000 subscribers, and this number grew hand over fist to 63,000 in 1933. Starting in December 1909, *De Proletarische Vrouw* was accompanied by a children's magazine, *Ons Kinderblaadje*, which promoted itself as an 'ongoing source of delight for children'. This is how the women's work developed a stronger educational slant.

Wibaut-Berdenis van Berlekom, Pothuis-Smit and Marie Mensing knew how and through which subjects they could reach out to workers' wives. The annual reports show how the various women's clubs teamed up to advocate such advances as female suffrage and insurance to cover the costs associated with motherhood. They also distributed information about child rearing and sexuality. Above all, the federation was not permitted to become elitist. It was there for all groups: from factory workers and seamstresses, to office staff and shop assistants. While women were striving in the first instance to improve their own position, their ultimate goal was to create a more just society. If women were to 'awaken', men and women could achieve this goal together. Their struggle was not easy. The women's organization in the SDAP did not get broader recognition until 1914, and it took even longer before they could exert real influence. The federation had little leeway and there was barely any financial elbowroom.[11] But that did not stop the women from collectively fighting for their ideals. Mensing and Wibaut-Berdenis van Berlekom had an international outlook and in 1906 they attended the German social democratic women's conference in Mannheim. During it the feminist Clara Zetkin-Eissner made an impassioned plea for female suffrage.

As a social democrat, Jo also devoted herself fully to achieving equal rights. As far back as 1888, when she was twenty-five and staying in Seraing, amidst the coal mines in the industrial area of Liège, she had written in her diary about the social inequality there, which she found so unjust:

> Went to Cockerill today. The factory covers 37 hectares and there are 10,000 workers . . . The steam hammers exert a force of 5 to 10,000 kg. In that hall there was a deafening roaring and humming, poor men who have to spend their lives in smoke, ash and carbon monoxide; why all this inequality, why do those people struggle and labour so to earn their meagre wages, while the director and the other engineers live off them so calmly? It's the privilege of intellectual development over manual labour, but still it seems unjust. My head still throbs when I think about it—what a contrast with our lovely peaceful rowing boat trip on the Meuse yesterday evening.[12]

This must have been a memorable day for Jo. The ideal of social equality remained rooted in her ever after.

The tidal wave of social idealism that spread over Europe during the first decade of the twentieth century affected both her and her son Vincent. He recorded he had taken courses on Saturday evenings given by the well-read speaker Rudolf Kuyper—their former neighbour in Regentesselaan in Bussum—in Marxist sociology, axiology and historic materialism. That was in around 1908 on Kloveniersburgwal in Amsterdam. 'My mother came with me,' he wrote later in his diary.[13] Kuyper, as head of the Kuyper Institute, ran a school for the staff of the labour movement, with correspondence and classroom courses in business studies and social sciences. He was friends with Wim Bonger.[14]

In addition to Rudolf Kuyper, Jo also knew Wabien Andreae, who played a pioneering role for the SDAP in Groningen. Andreae had been a boarding house guest in Bussum in 1900 and Jo visited her later on in Groningen.[15] She furthermore got to know the author and literary critic Frans Coenen Jr well. He was likewise a member of the SDAP and gave active support to 'Kunst aan het Volk', of which Jo and Vincent were both members. In 1914 they jointly provided over two hundred Van Gogh drawings for an exhibition that 'Kunst aan het Volk' organized in Amsterdam's Stedelijk Museum.[16]

Van Gogh in America

Alongside all the social compassion in those years, Jo's efforts for Van Gogh continued as usual. In keeping with Roland Holst's cover design for the 1892 catalogue, in April 1913 Jo boosted Van Gogh's image as the 'sunflowers man' by lending the canvas *Vincent van Gogh Painting Sunflowers* by Paul Gauguin to the Rijksmuseum (an agreement that would be renewed by Vincent in 1926) and announcing it publicly.[17]

Jo now increasingly shifted her focus to the United States. Although there was not to be a real breakthrough during her lifetime, Van Gogh's introduction to America was in any event imminent at the beginning of 1913. The painter Walt Kuhn made a selection of ten paintings from Van Gogh's oeuvre at the Artz and De Bois gallery in The Hague for the International Exhibition of Modern Art, also called the Armory Show, which was staged at the 69th Regiment Armory in New York from 18 February to 15 March. The exhibition was more or less modelled on the earlier Sonderbund exhibition, but Van Gogh was much less prominent. The American artist and art critic Walter Pach, an admirer of Van Gogh since 1906, took care of the shipping from Paris. He played a key role in the composition of the European section and found various owners who were prepared to part with their Van Goghs. Altogether eighteen Van Gogh works were exhibited. After New York, the exhibition travelled to The Art Institute of Chicago, where it was staged from 24 March to 16 April, and then it was in the Copley Hall in Boston from 28 April to 19 May.[18]

At the beginning of the second decade of the twentieth century, readers in the United States, the United Kingdom and Japan could also make the acquaintance of some of Vincent's letters to Theo and

Bernard thanks to the publication *The Letters of a Post-Impressionist, Being the Familiar Correspondence of Vincent van Gogh* (1912–13), a translation of the German anthology that Margarete Mauthner had compiled in 1906 for Bruno Cassirer. Jo played no part in it. The British philosopher and polyglot Anthony Mario Ludovici made a very free English translation from the German, which in turn was the basis for the first translation in book form in Japanese.[19] It was translated by the artist Shōhachi Kimura and published in Tokyo in 1915.[20] There had been a few earlier translations into Japanese by Kikuo Kojima based on the German translation. They were published from February 1911 onwards in the magazine *Shirakaba*.[21]

H.P. Bremmer asked Jo's permission to make reproductions of Van Gogh's work.[22] Jo agreed: she granted him the right to include facsimiles in his art magazines 'without him paying any fee', and she also gave him permission 'to have colour reproductions made of the works of Vincent van Gogh and to have these reproductions published on the condition that Mrs J. Cohen Gosschalk-Bonger or her successors in title receive a lump sum of 100 guilders for every colour reproduction published.' In the contract it was also stipulated that she retained the right to grant the right to others to make reproductions 'of works reproduced by or for H.P. Bremmer'.[23] Later he asked Jo whether she would give him approval to publish an edition of two hundred colour reproductions: 'In return I could send you ten copies of each print or I could pay you a fee of 100 guilders.'[24] A number of the colour reproductions were offered for sale at the back of the catalogue *Tableaux et dessins. Prentkunst. Farbenlichtdrucke,* J.H. de Bois, Haarlem (1913). They were not cheap and ranged in price from fifteen to forty guilders. Bremmer called the technique for making these three-colour prints the 'Scherjon process', because Willem Scherjon had developed his own collotype process. Scherjon and Adriaan Versluys had been running the firm of Versluys & Scherjon since 1903. He later declared that Jo generously gave young painters the opportunity to come to her home to view Van Goghs—he had spent days in her flat in order to take photographs in peace and quiet.[25] Jo always tried to keep a close eye on such initiatives. As she had done previously, she gave approval based on strategic considerations (reproductions were, after all, an important vehicle for spreading Van Gogh's name far and wide, as she herself said more than once), but she was invariably annoyed at the poor quality of the colour reproductions. She was still furious about it ten years later in a letter to Julius Meier-Graefe.[26]

In the spring of 1913, Jo was on the verge of completing the proofreading of the first volume of the letters. After that she had to do the revision and write the introduction, with which progress was still not being made. In mid-June, with help from Vincent, she moved to her summer home in Laren. Jo wrote proudly to Paul Gachet that her son only had one more exam to pass before getting work experience in the electromechanical plant ACEC ('Ateliers de Constructions Électriques de Charleroi'), and then would get his engineering degree that winter. She also wrote with equal satisfaction that Vincent had got engaged to the twenty-two-year-old Josina Wibaut, a 'law student, from a very good family, with whom I've been linked for a long time' (Figure 49). Vincent and Josina met around 1910

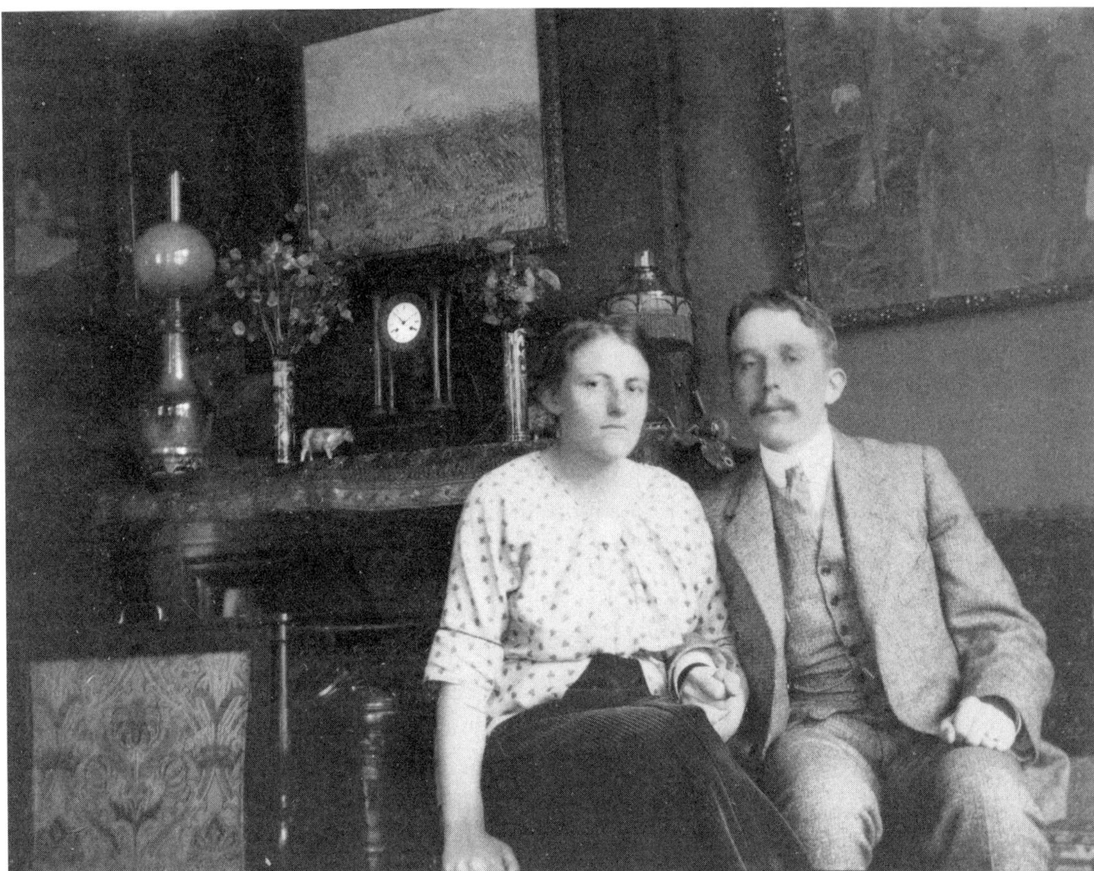

Figure 49 Josina van Gogh-Wibaut and Vincent van Gogh on the sofa in the living room at 77 Koninginneweg in Amsterdam, 1915.

at a meeting of the Delft and Amsterdam social democratic student club 'Sociaal-Democratische Studenten-Vereeniging'. Jo confided to Gachet that it had been an emotional time for her because of all these developments. Nevertheless, she had succeeded, at his request, in inventorying Van Gogh's graphic oeuvre.[27]

'The best quality'—Van Gogh in Lange Voorhout

The Kröller-Müllers, like Jo, continued to loan works by Van Gogh for exhibitions after the 1912 Sonderbund show. One of these was very special. The Van Gogh retrospective on the occasion of the centenary of the Kingdom of the Netherlands ran from 4 July to 1 September 1913 in the ground floor rooms of the head office of Müller & Co in Lange Voorhout in The Hague. It was the first large-scale permanent and private exhibition facility for modern art in the Netherlands. With over a hundred and fifty paintings and drawings, it was a large exhibition and the newspapers were enthusiastic about it. Not surprisingly the Kröller-Müllers, who owned the location and had H.P. Bremmer organize the event, topped the list of owners with fifty-seven works.

In the run-up to the imminent publication of the letters, this exhibition was a particularly good moment for Jo, though she was offended by the way everything was handled. In the first instance Bremmer had not asked her to contribute, so Jo felt bypassed. He pulled out all the stops in order to clear the air:

> In response to your letter, I have to tell you that nothing could have been further from my thoughts than the vanity that you are suggesting with regard to showing my Vincent collection, either on my part or on Mrs Kröller's. It pained me to read something like that in your letter because I believe that people could have assumed noble intentions in everything I've always done for Vincent.

Bremmer humbly apologized:

> I would be delighted if you would be kind enough to send a selection of the finest things by Vincent. If, for instance, you were to send the sixteen works that were in Rotterdam three years ago, it would make me very happy and I would be most grateful to you. Please let me know if you would like me to make any arrangements, such as insurance, shipment etc. I can visit you next Friday to discuss everything. This would be the easiest way to put you to the least trouble.[28]

In the end they reached agreement, but Jo clearly thought that sixteen was not enough. According to Bremmer in the catalogue's introduction, it became 'more than thirty of the best quality'. Jo's name was stated as the lender next to each work and information about possible purchase could be obtained from Johannes de Bois. Bremmer also lent a large number of works, but this was not explicitly stated. His works were described as being from a 'Private Collection, The Hague'. We do not know whether Jo was at the opening, but if she had been, she need not have been concerned about a confrontation with Helene Kröller-Müller, who was conspicuous by her absence.[29]

Meanwhile De Bois, who had been running his own gallery at 68 Kruisweg in Haarlem since the summer, saw to it at Jo's request that a few Van Goghs were returned from Bromberg (Bydgoszcz, now in Poland) and Essen. He talked to her about better crates for the paintings.[30] She was furthermore without doubt aware that Frederik Muller & Cie had put up Van Gogh's painting *On the Outskirts of Paris* (F 351 / JH 1255) from the estate of aunt Cornélie van Gogh-Carbentus for auction, as well as twenty drawings originating from Michiel Antonie de Zwart, Van Gogh's former landlord in The Hague.[31] Just before the end of the year she came up with a surprising sale herself. The secretary of the public contemporary art collection foundation 'Vereeniging tot het vormen van eene openbare verzameling van hedendaagsche kunst' agreed to the purchase of the painting *Vegetable Gardens in*

Montmartre (F 350 / JH 1245) for the substantial sum of 12,000 guilders. This large canvas was incorporated in the collection of the Stedelijk Museum in Amsterdam.[32] Shortly before, Jo had made a pleasing purchase herself—the complete graphic oeuvre of Odilon Redon: two portfolios bound in linen with a total of 192 reproductions for fifty guilders.[33] During this period she was certainly not short of money, because at the end of 1913 she received part of the estate of Uncle Vincent and Aunt Cornélie, who were childless. He had died in 1888, and she in May 1913. Jo invested the 8,000 guilders allocated to her.[34]

That summer 't Lanthuys in Laren was redecorated throughout.[35] Jo was not there all the time because she joined Vincent and Josina during their holiday for a tour of the Loire castles. They met up in the city of Charleroi and the three of them then enjoyed a delightful trip. Vincent recorded their journey in his diary:

> Blois (Cheverney, Chambord) and Tours (Azay-le-Rideau, Chinon, Luynes, Ussé), with Amboise in between, and separately in Loches. It was our first visit to the French province. Finally, Chartres and Versailles.[36]

When she got back, Jo again looked urgently for a maid, and to that end placed advertisements in daily newspapers.[37] She hoped that by having help with the housekeeping, she could concentrate better on completing her edition of Van Gogh's letters.

16

The publication of Brieven aan zijn broeder *(*Letters to his Brother*) (1914)*

As far back as 1892, Jo had made an optimistic start on organizing Van Gogh's letters. Not long after Theo's death, she wrote overconfidently in her diary that she wanted to immerse herself in the correspondence, using every free moment, but realized all too soon that she could not keep up the pace: 'I used to work into the night and *I* can't permit myself such excesses—my *first* duty is to remain alert and healthy in order to look after the child.'[1] And so it remained for many years thereafter. She devoted herself completely to little Vincent and did not go back to her other commitment, completing the letters edition, until 1913.

She really got down to work when the very first proofs arrived. To help her in writing the introduction, she used a notebook in which she jotted down questions for herself and copied out passages about Van Gogh's character or his working practices. At the beginning of the notebook she wrote lines from the final verse of the poem 'Mijn liefste', from the *Immortellen* (1912) by Salomon Bonn, published in *De Gids*: 'Oh, a dream of being with you one more time . . ./ And then to know nothing more/ And to die, gently.'[2] These lines could have been about the love between the two brothers, but equally about her own, still profound, feelings for Theo, which were reignited as she read through the letters.[3]

It was during this period that she took a decision that had major implications for the way she was henceforth to appear in public. At the end of December 1913, she told Paul Gachet that with immediate effect she would use the surname Van Gogh-Bonger again, and that her son was the most important reason for doing so: 'It will not surprise you that I'm reassuming my previous name in order to have the same name as my son.'[4] His happiness was her solace—mother and son had to be as one as much as possible. But that was not the only reason: obviously an editor with the Van Gogh name would look much better on the title page of *Brieven aan zijn broeder* (*Letters to his Brother*) and it would certainly serve her well in the future. Furthermore—and that was perhaps the weightiest argument for her—when it came down to it, her two years with Theo were many times more precious than the ten with Johan. As far as she was concerned, two years after Johan's death the name Cohen Gosschalk belonged to the past.[5]

The printer and publisher were hard at work on volume one of the letters. However, Jo still had to check the proofs of the introduction, which was deliberately paginated differently using Roman numerals so that it could be the very last part to be printed. She wrote to Gachet: 'I can't tell you what it cost me to bring all that past back to life.' Now that she was completely absorbed in the past and again presented herself as a Van Gogh, she finally decided to have Theo's remains taken to Auvers-sur-Oise, where Vincent was buried. She asked Gachet if he could find out what formal arrangements still had to be made for this reburial, and he did so shortly thereafter.[6]

Jo had just had a few enjoyable weeks. Immediately after he had been awarded his mechanical engineering degree on 15 January 1914, after six years of study, Vincent received an offer to supervise construction works in the Pyrenees for six months. His principal was the Hague-based 'Algemeene Bank voor Zakelijk Onderpand', known as the 'Bank van Treub', which provided loans to the Entreprise Varnoux.[7] Brimming with maternal pride, Jo asked Gachet if he thought her son was not brave, taking on such a responsible task before he had even turned twenty-four. His base would be in the mountain village of Fabian, not far from Arreau, close to the Spanish border. The only real snag was that he would be separated from his mother and fiancée (mentioned by Jo in that order). She told Gachet she felt lonely and tired, and so a trip to Auvers was out of the question for the time being.[8] Yet less than three months later she was suddenly able to come, while on the way to … of course, Fabian. She wanted to see her son, and if the mountain did not come to Jo, Jo would go to the mountain.

The visit was preceded by a blizzard of mail—postcards and letters from and to the brand-new graduate engineer were delivered with great efficiency, within two days from door to door. Jo sent postcards to Vincent on 22, 24 and 28 January 1914. She wrote to him saying he was often in her thoughts and she could imagine him sitting in the sleigh wearing a fur coat. If her 'darling' needed woollen underwear, he just had to tell her. She shared her business and social expertise with her son: 'I hope you're getting on well with the contractor. Be as friendly and accommodating as possible. You can check and conduct inspections meticulously and still be cordial to him, can't you?'[9] Josina, who lived in Amsterdam, had very frequent dealings with Jo: they discussed a whole range of things, she sometimes spent the night in her flat, and together they played Mozart sonatas for piano and violin. They also visited the Van Wisselingh gallery.[10] All the indications are that over time their relationship become more and more intimate.

Jo was hard at work revising the introduction, and for relaxation in the evening she occasionally went to the Stadsschouwburg city theatre, where she saw performances like the comedy *Lentewolken* and Richard Strauss's opera *Salome*. According to the *Algemeen Handelsblad*, it was a passionate, intoxicating performance, and Jo found all the sensuality 'beautiful and frightening at the same time'.[11] For a change she occasionally had a meal at her brother and sisters' home in Weteringschans, where they played Beethoven trios in the evenings.[12] Meanwhile, she continued to mollycoddle her son: she advised him to eat fruit every day and sent him flowers. Jo understood that her 'darling boy' would be kept very busy by his work and have little need to read. 'Life itself is much more interesting,' she told him.[13] Later, though, she sent him an essay by Oscar Wilde she had obtained from the Wereldbibliotheek. This must have been *The Soul of Man Under Socialism* (1891), translated by P.C. Boutens as *Individualisme en socialisme*. It enjoyed unrivalled popularity in Europe for a while.[14]

Jo's work on the Dutch edition and the German publication *Briefe an seinen Bruder* continued more or less in parallel and she had to work flat out. She received a request from Germany, asking her to look at the proofs of the letters from the French period and indicate exactly where the illustrations had to be inserted. Apparently, things were not going as fast as they wanted, for within two weeks she was gently reminded to get a move on. She got cracking, and for good measure added comments about errors in the translations, which prompted the editor-in-chief to compliment her on her good command of German. There is no way of knowing how thoroughly she checked the translation, but there is no doubt that she really took trouble over it.[15]

In her never-ending stream of letters to the South of France, Jo unwittingly sought reassurance all the time, as when she asked, for instance, 'Do you think I'm writing enough?' We do not know how Vincent responded, but it is clear that he has to have been more than happy with this letter because she also wrote: 'Yesterday I received more documents relating to the estate. It's now definite: you receive just over four thousand'—which was a tremendous windfall for him from the estate of Uncle Vincent and Aunt Cornélie.[16] Jo kept him abreast in detail about other matters too. She thought that Josina, who was studying full time and also having lessons at a cookery school, was starting to show much greater vitality. Jo spent a 'pleasant evening' with her brother Henri at a performance by the Polish dancer Angèle Sydow (of the Jacques Dalcroze Anstalt from Hellerau) in the Stadsschouwburg.[17] She also visited the Paleis voor Volksvlijt with Josina on Women's Day (Figure 50). The speakers included Heleen Ankersmit, who was secretary of the BSDVC between 1909 and 1914, Johan Willem Albarda (member of parliament and leader of the SDAP) and Josina's mother, Mathilde. They talked about the role of women in the workplace and advocated separate medical insurance for women. Meanwhile the number of female party members had grown to some four thousand.[18]

Antwerp—contemporary art

The Flemish writer and art historian Ary Delen learned from the art dealer Theo Neuhuys that Jo was prepared to receive a delegation to select works for the Antwerp exhibition 'L'art contemporain. Salon

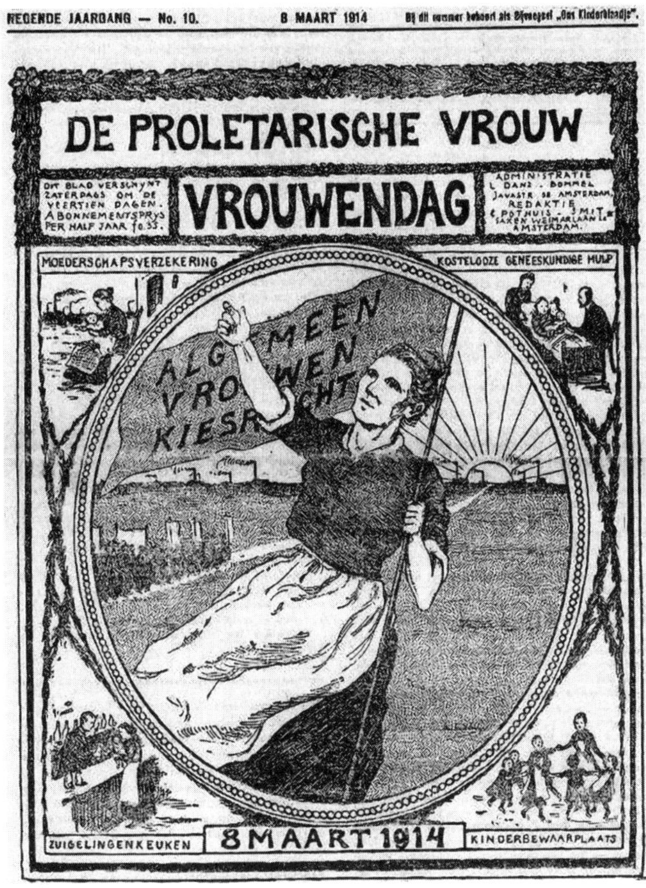

Figure 50 Adri Ladenius, *De Proletarische Vrouw. Vrouwendag*, 8 March 1914.

1914 / Kunst van Heden. Tentoonstelling 1914', which would run from 7 March to 5 April in the 'Zaal Comité voor Artistieke Werking'.[19] As had been the case at the Sonderbund exhibition in 1912 and the show in The Hague in 1913, works from the collections of the Kröller-Müllers and Jo were cheek by jowl, except that in this case the number of loans from Jo exceeded those from the Kröller-Müllers—fifty-nine (some of which were for sale) as against thirty-four. Delen thanked her for her hospitality and her permission to use the plate of Van Gogh's painting *Self-Portrait as a Painter* (F 522 / JH 1356), which was normally on loan to the Rijksmuseum, but now went to the exhibition in Antwerp. 'We have a beautifully lit gallery with fifty-nine metres of picture rail,' he wrote to Jo. 'We've reserved about half for paintings that you'll be prepared to lend us.'[20] He had asked her to date all the works, including those from other lenders. She must have known the dates of most of them; for a few of them, however, she left the date open or gave a tentative one.[21]

This exhibition gave the Belgians a good idea of Van Gogh's oeuvre. But there were still some who ridiculed his work and others who pilloried it. Jo and Josina went to see it, and also artworks by Rik Wouters and James Ensor (Figure 51). They talked to the painter Richard Baseleer, co-founder of

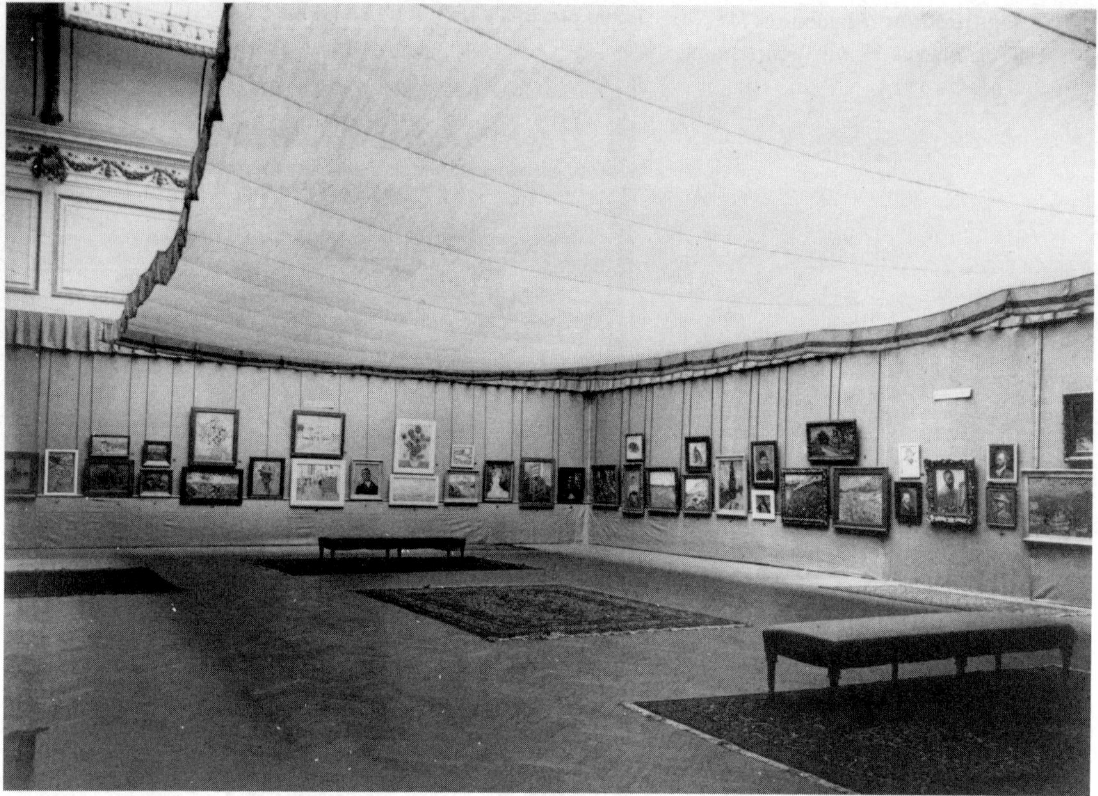

Figure 51 Works by Vincent van Gogh at the exhibition 'Kunst van heden' in Antwerp, 1914.

'Kunst van Heden', who could still remember Van Gogh from the time they had both been at the Royal Academy of Fine Arts Antwerp in 1886. Jo wrote to her son:

> We had a wonderful time together. We thoroughly explored and admired the Plantijn Museum and the cathedral, which I think is so beautiful! We stood in the little square in front of it just as dusk fell and, looking down a narrow street, we also saw the old façades of the Grande Place. There was a sense of history everywhere—an atmosphere of long ago![22]

She had little to say about the exhibition, at least nothing about the how the pictures had been hung or about the reactions of the visitors: 'I'm sure Jos told you about the exhibition. It was much better than the one in The Hague (this time I had your name put in the catalogue too).'[23] This enabled people to get used to her former surname and to that of her son, who in the meantime had obtained control over his part of the Van Gogh Collection.

Afterwards some of the works were shipped to Paul Cassirer in Berlin; Delen sent the others back to Amsterdam in crates. To be on the safe side, Jo told Vincent about it: 'the exhibition in Antwerp is going on to Berlin—I hope you agree.'[24] He was thus aware of such decisions, even though in this case it was after the fact. Delen asked her for fifty prospectuses of the impending letters edition so that potential purchasers could pre-order copies. He was eagerly looking forward to the publication.[25]

Josina often ate with Jo and together they celebrated her father's appointment as Amsterdam's public housing alderman.[26] Meanwhile, Vincent was eagerly looking forward to seeing the two women. They were to meet up in Paris first and then the three of them would travel on to Fabian after the reburial in Auvers. Jo became nervous as the departure date approached and suddenly wanted to know all sorts of things: should she take two pairs of stockings, should they be thick or thin, and how much money should she take with her. 'Should I also have some of those waterproof shoes, or galoshes, or snow shoes?' She seemed calmer as she ended the letter: 'The early blossom trees are already out, by the way, as though they're apricot trees, and in the meadows there are yellow kingcups.'[27]

Theo's reburial in Auvers-sur-Oise

Jo spent almost two months making preparations for the reburial. After she had finally received permission from the consulate, she arranged for the exhumation in Utrecht, where she had to be present in person. That was on 8 April 1914, and the same day the coffin with Theo's mortal remains went in a sealed railway wagon to Auvers.[28] She sent Gachet the documentation and the legal instruments, and authorized him to represent her in local matters. Jo asked him to reserve three rooms for one night, 'in a hotel or boarding house in Auvers (very simple) because Vincent's fiancée is accompanying me too.'[29]

They arrived in Auvers on 13 April and on the fourteenth Theo's mortal remains were reburied in their presence. It was an emotional occasion for everyone there, particularly for Vincent, who had lost his father shortly before his first birthday. The grave was still open as they left the cemetery—a sight that kept haunting Jo for days. Unnecessarily, she asked Gachet whether it had indeed been filled in. She thanked the Gachet family for all their support and hospitality around the solemn event and said that it had also benefitted Vincent: 'He is so attached to family traditions and he can never hear too much about them.' It was a comfort to her that the torch could be handed down from generation to generation. Jo asked Gachet if he would plant ivy at the foot of the two vertical gravestones.[30] Now Vincent and Theo would lie side by side always, and in no time the spot became a place of pilgrimage. Jo found it 'touching' when some young Japanese people put a plant on Vincent's grave in 1921.[31]

They caught the night train to the Pyrenees via Toulouse. The journey from Paris to Arreau took thirteen hours.[32] She wrote to Gachet that the last leg to Fabian was by horse and cart and took three hours 'by a wonderfully beautiful road in the Aure valley'. She had never seen such an overwhelming landscape, not even in Switzerland.[33] They took rooms in the little Hotel Fouga in the mountains,

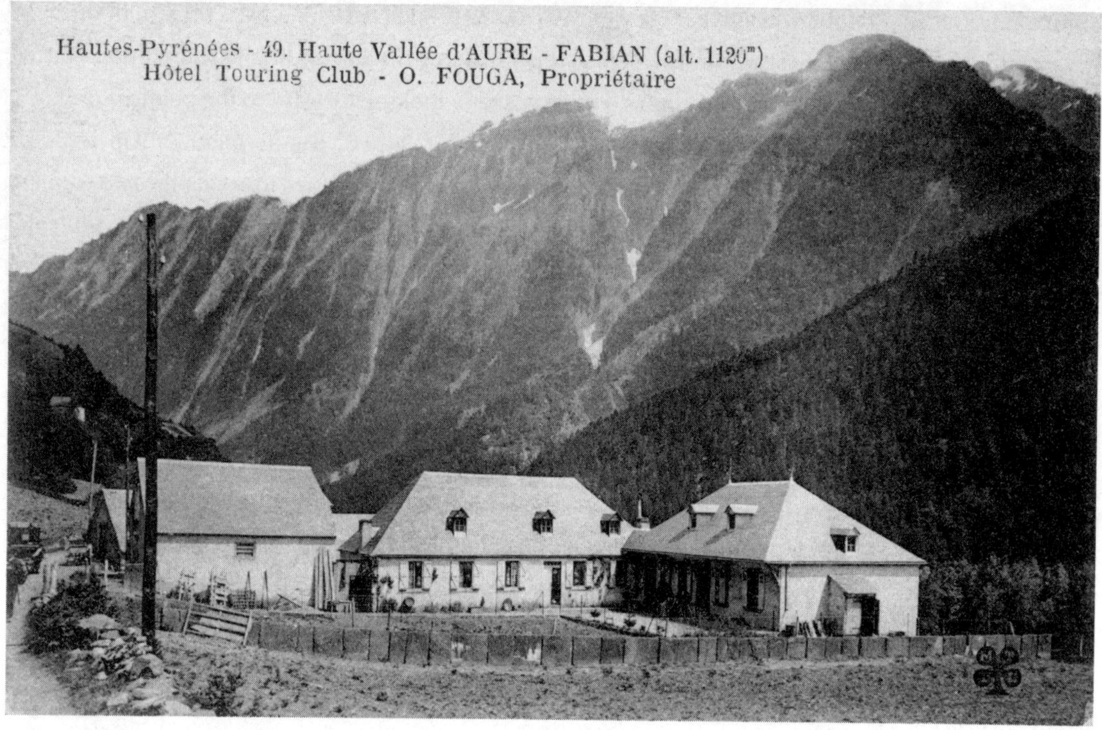

Figure 52 Hautes-Pyrénées, Fabian, Hotel Fouga, undated.

where they stayed for a few weeks (Figure 52). While they were there, Jo buckled down to correcting the second volume of the letters. It was not comfortable and miles from anywhere, but she did not mind. She felt at ease with simplicity, and the presence of Vincent and Josina more than made up for the lack of comfort. She found peace and quiet, went for regular walks and saw the most beautiful wild plants (Figure 53, Plate 51). During their rambles through the mountains they took Charles Flahault's *Nouvelle flore coloriée de poche des Alpes et des Pyrénées* with them. Jo loved the way the clear green water of the mountains cascaded onto the rocks below with the spray flying.[34]

At the beginning of May, Jo sent her neighbours in Laren a panoramic picture postcard showing the hotel. Jo invited them to eat everything in the kitchen garden behind 't Lanthuys because she was not there herself. She wrote enthusiastically about her stay:

> My favourite walks here are along the water or through the woods slightly higher up. Last week we went on a six-day trip because Vincent had to be in Périgeux—and we went to Pau and Bordeaux on the way there and came back via Tarbes. The first part of the journey was by car—it's wonderful that Vincent has a car available if he has to go on a business trip. In Périgeux we met Treub, who was most charming. Jos is back at home, but I'm staying here for the time being. I brought work with me![35]

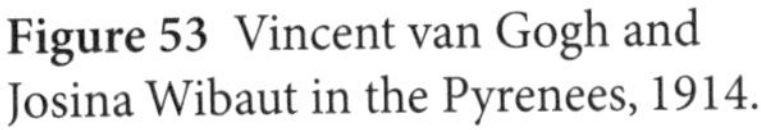

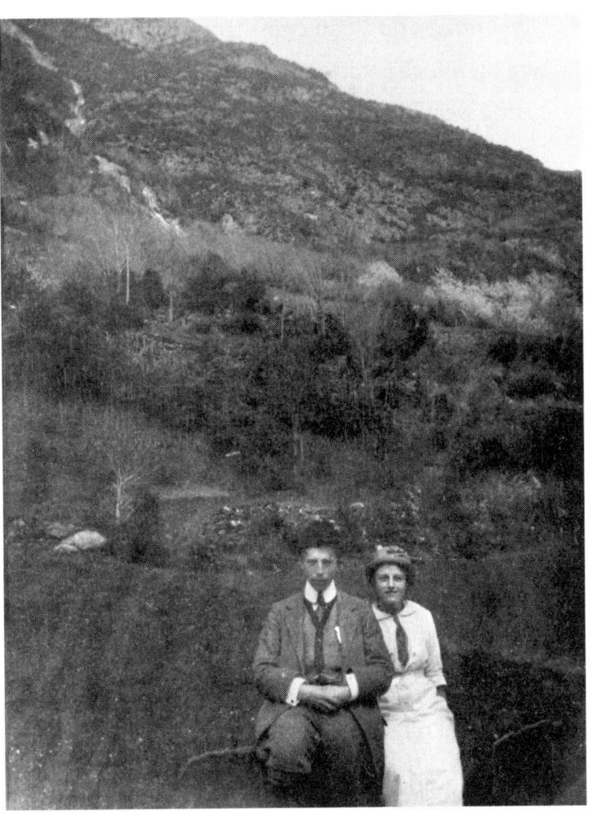

Figure 53 Vincent van Gogh and Josina Wibaut in the Pyrenees, 1914.

The hotel might have been devoid of luxury, but on the other hand Vincent apparently had the use of a chauffeur-driven car. Two weeks later, the two of them were off on their travels again. An elated Jo told her friends that they had been to Biarritz and even briefly in Spain—crossing the River Bidassoa to Fontarrabie in Hondarribia. 'The weather was wonderful—the air was balmy—quite a contrast to the snowstorm we had here last week! When we got back here, I was struck again by the fact that this landscape really is the most beautiful of all.'[36] Jo enjoyed Vincent's company and the panoramic views. She took deep breaths of the mountain air.

Brieven aan zijn broeder: 'a sensation'

As he had been at his father's reburial in April 1914, Vincent must have been moved when he opened the parcel that the publisher in Amsterdam sent to Arreau. It included the first volume of *Brieven aan zijn broeder*, containing the letters that his Uncle Vincent had sent his father, Theo, between 1872 and 1883 (the second and third volumes did not appear until later in the year). He recalled that moment very clearly many years later:

> My mother and I had come from Fabian (1,200 m) to Arreau (probably because the company car was there). The station was closed till around 4.30 p.m.—and there it was—a sensation. It was fine spring weather.

In the first copy Jo wrote a dedication in it there and then: 'To Vincent and Jos. Arreau 1 June 1914.'[37]

An extraordinary amount of work had been done to prepare for this historic event. She had added a brief introduction for each period, but at a certain point she stopped, apparently because she ran out of time. Her preferences are evident from the passages that were included. She referred, for example, to two 'touchingly beautiful letters' from the Borinage. She made concise, usually biographical, notes on the letters. Where Van Gogh called the painter Wilhelm Leibl a Swede, for instance, Jo pointed out that he was German. She noted that the physician David Gruby had also treated Heinrich Heine. And for some questions she sought information elsewhere. In the case of the painter Adriaan Madiol, whom Van Gogh mentioned, she contacted the librarian of the Rijksmuseum in Amsterdam.[38] Jo could have added much of a personal nature, but did so only very sparingly. She did, though, add a note mentioning her engagement to Theo when commenting on an 1888 letter. She drew on the messages that Dr Théophile Peyron had sent at the time about Vincent's situation in the institution in Saint-Rémy and remarked that she had thought it ridiculous that she, Theo and Vincent, 'three Dutch people, spoke French together'.[39] She only once referred to a reply from Theo to Vincent (of which just thirty-nine have survived):

> In it he talked about a plan to resign from his position and finance going into business for himself. That would take a great deal of doing, and the way things stood then, both Vincent and we ourselves would have had to tighten our belts. In this letter, Theo also expressed the hope that one of these days Vincent would find a woman who wanted to share his life.[40]

And yet, anyone who thought in 1914 that they would be reading the complete letters from Vincent to Theo was going to be disappointed. Using square brackets in pencil, Jo had indicated on the originals which passages had to be left out. In her view these were uninteresting, superfluous or embarrassing—and there were very many of them. She cut out numerous passages from the Bible and Christian texts, and in their place simply noted: 'A few psalms and religious verses'.[41] Parts that mentioned illnesses, sex, arguments or awkward family-related matters were also removed. So too were trivialities, such as sending a pair of duffel trousers. In many but not all cases, she inserted a row of dots to indicate where something had been cut. She also replaced the names of people who were still alive with initials. Jo was not entirely to blame for treating Van Gogh's writing so drastically. It was also a sign of the times. People were prudish and took offence at earthy or coarse remarks. In 1911 Bernard had also significantly bowdlerized Van Gogh's letters, possibly at the instigation of the publisher Vollard. In those days, far less stringent standards were applied to the publication of letters and personal documents than the ones used now.[42]

Jo spent years working her way through Vincent's letters. She transcribed some by hand and had some typed out. For the latter she requested the return of her Remington typewriter, which she had lent.[43] She edited the transcriptions by hand and inserted the annotations later.[44] No matter how flawed her publication is compared to contemporary editing yardsticks, Jo's edition proved very useful for the 2009 scholarly edition of Van Gogh's correspondence. There were, for instance, places that had become illegible in the intervening years, because words had suffered from ink corrosion. Her edition was also helpful in dating certain sheets, because it appeared in some cases that Jo may still have had envelopes with postmarks.[45]

In order to introduce some variety into the story of Van Gogh's life, she also used the substantial Van Gogh family correspondence—a goldmine that survived thanks to Theo. She made extracts and used them for her carefully constructed and smoothly formulated introduction. She continued to polish her text up to the last moment: she changed letters 'full of cheerfulness' to 'radiating cheerfulness', and 'with all his strength' to 'with almost desperate strength'. She stuck pieces and strips of paper with changed wording over earlier texts. She did not add more general observations until the end; for instance 'In his letters from this period there is an almost morbid oversensitivity.' Jo did not just describe Van Gogh the person—his self-sacrifice: 'he never did anything by halves!' She also stressed his environment and his social conscience as well as his qualities as a letter writer. Sometimes she was rather controlling and not free from sentiment, but on the other hand, who was more entitled than she, who through Theo had ultimately got to know Vincent at such close quarters: 'he still had to get through the bitter winter of 1879–80—the saddest, most hopeless period in his truly joyless life', and she referred to him as 'infinitely lonely'.[46] She selected only one aspect of Van Gogh's views of art, which was his comment: 'In a painting I'd like to say something consoling, like a piece of music.'[47] She refrained from art criticism, leaving that to the experts. Now and then she quoted from letters and recollections by Anthon van Rappard, Paul Gauguin, Frédéric Salles, Paul Gachet and Theo. She particularly emphasized Theo's decisive role: 'as always, it was only Theo who understood him and continued to support him'.[48]

Jo zoomed in on a few particulars. She talked, for instance, about 'the famous self-portrait at his easel', which she could do because in the meantime she had provided it for exhibitions and lent it to the Rijksmuseum. She described one of the still lifes as 'radiating and sparkling from some kind of inner glow'.[49] It was *Quinces, Lemons, Pears and Grapes* (F 383 / JH 1339), the frame of which Van Gogh also painted; in red paint he added the dedication 'À mon frère Theo'.

Jo felt that Vincent had reached the peak of his capabilities in Arles and described *The Bedroom* as one of his most famous works. Jo rightly criticized Gauguin's assertion that Vincent had just been muddling through before his arrival in Arles in 1888, and only made progress after he gave him his advice.[50] She also commented that depression dominated Vincent's life, but pointed out that he produced some of his finest works during the year he was receiving treatment. Jo ended her introduction by recounting the end of Vincent's and Theo's lives, and underlined their intimate brotherly love. In the closing sentence, which was followed by the date December 1913, she described how the brothers lay buried together in Auvers Cemetery surrounded by wheatfields. She anticipated the facts because at that moment the reburial had not happened and it did not take place until just before the book was published, but as far as she was concerned this was, rhetorically speaking, the most dramatic way to end.

She formulated a simple dedication for her introduction: 'This book is dedicated to the memory of Vincent and Theo. "And in their death they were not divided." 2 Samuel 1:23.' Jo knew this quotation from Samuel from the Bible and also from the novel she described in 1885 as her favourite book, George Eliot's *The Mill on the Floss*. 'In their death they were not divided' appears on the title page of this novel and is its closing sentence. In the story the words are chiselled into the gravestone of brother and sister Tom and Maggie Tulliver, who die tragically.[51] Jo recognized the striking similarity and reflected it in two ways: Theo's reburial and the publication of the letters. The sender and the recipient were inseparably united for ever.

In the end, the production costs of the three volumes amounted to 6,680 guilders. One reason why the costs were so high was the inclusion of illustrations of all the letter sketches and enclosed sketches. In accordance with the stipulations in the contract, the selling price for the three volumes was 7.50 guilders stitched and 10 guilders for the edition bound in pale yellow linen. Jo had deliberately wanted to keep the prices low. She marketed the books using her commercial acumen and placed advertisements in the *Algemeen Handelsblad*, *Het Nieuws van den Dag*, the *NRC*, *De Telegraaf*, *Het Volk* and *Het Vaderland*. The publishers held on to part of the edition as broadsheets, so they could stitch or bind volumes depending on demand. Jo paid all the expenses, including 140 guilders for advertising. After deducting the proceeds from the copies sold in 1914, she made a loss that year of more than 4,332 guilders.[52]

There were a number of reasons why publication was so seriously delayed. Jo gave the most important one in her introduction: 'It would have been grossly unfair to the dead artist to stimulate interest in him as a person before the work to which he devoted his life was recognized and appreciated as it deserved.'[53] She had meanwhile spent half her life on the last of these. As she said herself, she also spent a lot of time raising her son, and had gone through various difficult periods in her own life. It is also perfectly possible that she delayed publication of this frank 'memorial to the sons' until after the death of their mother, which was something that Willemien had touched on in an earlier letter.[54] As a tribute to Mrs van Gogh, Jo had included Johan's portrait of her and also the four surviving letters from Vincent to his parents, the eight to his mother and the letter to his mother and Willemien, all written in Saint-Rémy and Auvers.[55] In the end, the book was more than just a remembrance of the sons. Gachet described Jo's diligent efforts as a 'sacred duty'.[56] Her edition of the letters and the biographical introduction set the template for knowledge about Van Gogh for a long time.

Responses to the letters and exhibitions

Yet not everyone was so enthusiastic. Jo's son Vincent recalled: 'When Vincent's Letters (*Brieven*) were first published, we got quite a lot of comments from family members who were shocked that all sorts of personal things were made public.'[57] Once again, and not surprisingly, it was Van Gogh's middle sister Lies du Quesne-van Gogh who was particularly critical. Years later she openly criticized the publication in an interview in the *Algemeen Handelsblad*: 'We deeply regretted the publication of all those letters to Theo, full of intimacies. Vincent and Theo would have resented it; an anthology of the letters would have been so much better!'[58] But what was done was done, and there was no going back.

The first of June 1914 was a memorable day for Jo in several respects. She wrote a dedication to her son and soon-to-be daughter-in-law in volume one of the publication, and that same day the biggest Van Gogh solo exhibition ever outside the Netherlands opened when Paul Cassirer exhibited 151 works in Berlin. Jo and Vincent generously provided sixty-six of them (of which only seven were for sale)—the others came primarily from private collectors. In the catalogue Cassirer thanked Jo for her kindness and of course referred to the just-published *Briefe an seinen Bruder*, and, just as Jo had done in the 1905 catalogue, he included a few striking quotations from the letters as tasters.[59] The catalogue contained a list of all the owners, and this gave her an insight into Cassirer's impressive network. Meanwhile, Cassirer's employee Theodor Stoperan tried, hoping against hope, to get his hands on *Irises* (F 608 / JH 1691), a *Landscape near Arles* and the drawing *Fountain in the Garden of the Asylum* (F 1531 / JH 1705): 'During my visit to Amsterdam, you told me, of course, that there was no point asking you whether certain works were for sale.'[60] Jo had meanwhile become much more difficult to soften up; she became increasingly skilled at monitoring which paintings and drawings were popular with enthusiasts. After Berlin the works went to Galerie Commeter in Hamburg via the Kölner Kunstverein.

Jo's extraordinary book immediately attracted great interest in the Netherlands. On 2 June 1914, in the column 'Onder de Menschen' in the *NRC*, M.J. Brusse even quoted openly from a letter Jo had written to him from the Pyrenees. The public thus learned more about her personal situation and experiences, and readers could see that the whole project had been almost more than she could cope with:

> I've done nothing else for the last two years, and I've often continued working until late at night . . . it was sometimes utterly exhausting. And all the family letters I've read through in order to find a date here and there that could clarify something. . . . And all Theo's letters to me stirred up all the old grief in me and I relived everything. . . . That's why, when I'd finally finished the introduction to the first volume, I decided to escape here to be with my son and find some peace and quiet in beautiful natural surroundings.[61]

There is no way of knowing whether Jo was aware that her letter would be quoted publicly and, if so, whether she deliberately let it happen in the interests of marketing. Brusse's article was in three parts: in the first, which appeared on 31 May, he described Theo as 'truly heroic in his self-sacrifice'.[62] The quotations from Jo's letter were in the second part, published on 2 June, and the final section of the fascinating three-parter on 4 June contained passages from a few of Van Gogh's letters. Jo could not have wished for better publicity.

That same month, H.P. Bremmer gave a lecture on the occasion of Anton Müller's twenty-five years as head of the trading and shipping company Müller & Co, during which he quoted extensively from the letters. As we have seen, Bremmer had a substantial number of followers, and many of them bought Jo's edition of the letters. Among them was Helene Kröller-Müller, who in a letter of 28 June 1914 wrote to her confidant Sam van Deventer that people who were impervious to Van Gogh's work would now be converted thanks to his letters.[63] This demonstrates yet again how closely the two women mirrored one another's views about Van Gogh. And indeed, many people became familiar with the painter's life and work through this publication. The letters made it possible to follow each step of the way as Van Gogh had tried, through reasoning, courage and boundless perseverance, to shape his life as a true craftsman and to give his all for art. This gained the respect of a great many people.

After a six-week stay in the South of France, in June 1914 Jo and her son Vincent made a flying visit to the Netherlands. A week later they set out again for Fabian, stopping over in Paris on the way. While they were there, the author and publisher Ambroise Vollard presented Jo with a copy of *Cézanne*, a very expensive book.[64] In the Louvre she also saw *Fritillaries in a Vase* (F 213 / JH 1247), which had come from Isaac de Camondo's collection; Jo was delighted to see another Van Gogh she had been unaware of.[65]

Jo and Vincent missed the exhibition in Le Salon du Bon Vouloir in Mons (Bergen), for which they had loaned six paintings. Clément Benoît, secretary of the art circle concerned, was the driving force behind the organization of this exhibition. He had arranged, among other things, for the socialist Louis Piérard to give a lecture. Alongside works by Van Gogh, there were also paintings and sculptures by Rik Wouters. After the exhibition, Benoît sent the paintings back to the framers Van Menk in Kalverstraat. They arrived in Amsterdam on 28 July, just before the First World War broke out, and Benoît gave a sigh of relief when he read the telegram confirming their safe arrival.[66]

Het Volk reviewed the letters publication, unequivocally placing Van Gogh in the socialist camp: 'a worker who had to take endless trouble to learn his difficult trade, who realized that as an artist driven by primordial force he would come to grief if he stayed in the wealthy lustre of society's comfortable upper crust, a worker who felt his art root itself in the unspoilt strength of the proletariat who had to toil as he did.'[67] A response like that must have pleased Jo. The following day she wrote a letter to her niece, Sara de Jong-van Houten. It gives such a good insight into Jo's generous attitude to Vincent, and how she experienced all the events at the time, that it is quoted at length.

I get so many letters from people who enjoy the book. They say: we're so grateful for it! The German edition has just appeared and someone sent me a newspaper, *Der Tag*, which says: 'The work is done and Van Gogh enters history; the artist has become a kind of classic.'[68]

Your mother[69] wrote that all those memories of the past were painful for her—but I can't understand that—in a way it was a thousand times more painful for me—all that rummaging about in the past and reliving grief that had lessened with the years—but that wasn't what I was thinking about—my mind was on how wonderful a picture emerged of Uncle Theo alongside his brilliant brother and how loving and warm their parents—your grandparents—were! Of course, people should be broad-minded when reading the letters. We can't approve of everything Uncle Vincent did. But we can understand it all and how it stemmed from generous, heartfelt feelings! We can talk about this later, after you've read it too! I've just completed the second volume and now I'm starting to proofread the third. The German printer is ahead of us; they've already finished everything! You see I'm not just here for pleasure—sometimes I work all day long. But those excursions now and again are delightful—and so too are the lovely walks around here. Now they're bringing in the harvest, as I'm sure they are in Holland, and Vincent and I spent 14 July, Bastille Day, in the hayfield behind the hotel—a blissfully quiet day.

Last week we spent three days travelling to Gavarnie. The Cirque de Gavarnie is one of the most famous sights of the Pyrenees—the road to it is really beautiful—in an open motor coach we could see everything so clearly. When we arrived it was still snowy, not just on the tops of the mountains but on the ground too.

The flowers here are not as lovely as in the spring—I've been here now for exactly three months. So, I've experienced the seasons! The hotel is certainly too primitive; they don't lift a finger for the guests. People always have to end up here because there's nowhere else, and they take advantage of that! But you can get used to all these things, and the food, and the poor care for the rooms etc.—and if we go on a trip, we get double the enjoyment from good hotels and so on. Then we're in seventh heaven!

Being here has been beneficial for my health. The last two years were too bitter and lonely—and returning to an empty house will bring back all the sadness—but the diversion here has certainly done me good![70]

At the end of June Jo thanked her friend Paul Gachet for the photographs of the two gravestones in Auvers that he had sent her. When she looked at them, she realized the sacrifices she had made. But she was certainly happy with her decisions. 'I carry my memories in my heart; there are some among them that I am proud of, with a pride that no woman could be ashamed of.' She wrote that she recalled how Theo, after the first month of their marriage, had said he was perfectly happy with her. But then, completely unexpectedly and suddenly vexed, she accused Vincent openly for the first time—in her opinion it was Vincent's fault that Theo came to grief at the time, and she believed he was responsible for the loss of her happiness: 'Ah when I think about all these things I feel a grudge against Vincent, because he is the one who took my happiness. But I must not indulge these memories, you are the only one who really understands these things so I can express myself this way.'[71] Despite her grudge against her brother-in-law, which she confided to Gachet alone because he understood what she meant, she nevertheless worked steadily on the final stage of the publication. She was able to keep such things separate. Jo ended her letter with apologies for the marks on the paper: the hotel's dog had jumped on it. The fact that she did not rewrite the grubby letter, which she should have done, of course, is additional evidence of the bond of friendship between her and Gachet. Now she got down to work in the simple mountain hotel on the proofs of the last volume, knowing that at the end of their stay they would travel to the north, spending the night at the more luxurious Hôtel d'Angleterre in Arreau on the way.[72]

Willem Steenhoff obviously joined in. In *De Amsterdammer* of 19 July 1914 he published the first of three glowing reviews of the publication, calling it 'an exceptionally poignant book'.[73] The two other reviews appeared on 26 July and 22 November. Without doubt this passionate endorsement by an expert boosted sales. Jo contributed to the marketing when she got back to Amsterdam. She placed advertisements in the *NRC* and the *Algemeen Handelsblad* of 18 September. A week later she sent a copy of the second volume to France, where her son had gone back to work, with the dedication: 'To Vincent from Mama, Amsterdam 24 September 1914.'[74]

The publication of the letters also saw Isaac Israëls and Jo getting in touch again. He had received a copy of the first volume while he was staying in Morley's Hotel, Trafalgar Square, London, and in his response he called Vincent a 'lucky man' to have had such an understanding brother as Theo.[75] Israëls rented a studio in London, and soon afterwards received the second volume there. In his letter of thanks—which bore a stamp showing that it had been opened by the English censor under wartime regulations—he said he regretted not getting to know Van Gogh better: 'It was certainly not his fault however and I should probably not have understood him then. When you grow wise it is generally too late.'[76] He was back in the Netherlands a month later and had a meal in Jo's flat. On that occasion he praised her collection as being the finest in Amsterdam. He loved Van Gogh's work and came to own, among others, *Wheatfields with Auvers in the Background* (F 801 / JH 2123), which he must have acquired through Jo.[77] Israëls made a portrait of her in February 1915.[78] This may have been the painting of her seated in a chair with a high back (Plate 52).

Josina Wibaut

As we saw earlier, Jo's relationship with her future daughter-in-law Josina was very good right from the start. They had similar interests in culture, art, music, and certainly in politics too. Both were intelligent. As could be expected, Josina passed her final exams at the University of Amsterdam and was awarded a degree in economics, which in those days was taught in the law faculty. Jo sent her a bouquet of red roses on Vincent's behalf. Jo felt at ease during a meal with the Wibaut family in their home to celebrate. She went for walks with Josina in Amsterdam's Vondelpark and they arranged to go on all sorts of excursions together to pass the time until they saw Vincent again. Jo longed desperately for a letter from him.[79] Two women, one yearning for her son, the other for her future husband, which was now a settled thing: Floor and Mathilde Wibaut had officially consented to the marriage.

Josina came from an intellectual socialist family. In 1912 her brother Johan was awarded a doctorate in chemistry, and her brother Floor became an ophthalmologist and politician. Her parents loved their children. Josina was the apple of her father's eye and she, in turn, felt closely involved with her parents' political work.[80] At the time Mr Wibaut was making plans to replace slums and basement dwellings in Amsterdam with better housing for workers, which would have to be made affordable by subsidizing rents. It was a huge undertaking. Over 2,900 homes were built between 1914 and 1918. It was a revelation for Vincent to be part of the ebullient Wibaut family because the atmosphere was so completely different from his home life.[81]

Jo wrote proudly to Vincent about how she was refining Josina's cultural knowledge: 'Quatre-vingt-treize [a novel by Victor Hugo] is certainly stimulating; I'm so glad that you write such good French, my darling—I'll read a little French with Jos, as practice. Flaubert's letters or Uncle Vincent's letters in French!'[82] It is not clear how successful Jo was in introducing her daughter-in-law to the Van Gogh legacy through literature: in any event volume 3 of the letters edition, containing letters that Vincent wrote to Theo in French, was on the brink of being published.

The two women went to see Georges Bizet's *Carmen* in the Paleis voor Volksvlijt. It is typical of Jo that the only detail she mentioned to Vincent was a song by the mother of the soldier José: 'she thinks of the absent one night and day—I do that too.'[83] Did Josina write something similar to her beloved at the same time? Just as Jo realized in 1889 that marrying Theo would not separate him from Vincent, Josina has to have understood that her empathetic, but possessive mother-in-law was an inseparable part of her husband's baggage and would always be around. Mrs Wibaut recalled later that Jo adored her son and had remarked on the evening before the wedding: 'My Vincent has no faults whatsoever,' whereupon she had said: 'I can't say the same thing about my Jos!'[84] To Jo, however, this went without saying; she was living the words of Jules Michelet that she had quoted in her diary in 1892: 'Any mother of any worth has an unshakable conviction; it is that her child wants to become a hero: as a man of action or of science, no matter which.'[85] It was a perfectly respectable wish for a mother to be convinced her son is a hero, but it was, of course, one with an unmistakable undertone of compulsion.

At the Wereldbibliotheek, where Jo had been given a tour of the publisher's premises, she stood and looked at the stacks of copies of her publication, including volume 3, which was ready for distribution.[86] It had taken years to reach the point where the 1,678 pages were in print and, at last, on 3 November large advertisements for the complete set of letters appeared in *Het Nieuws van den Dag*, the *NRC* and

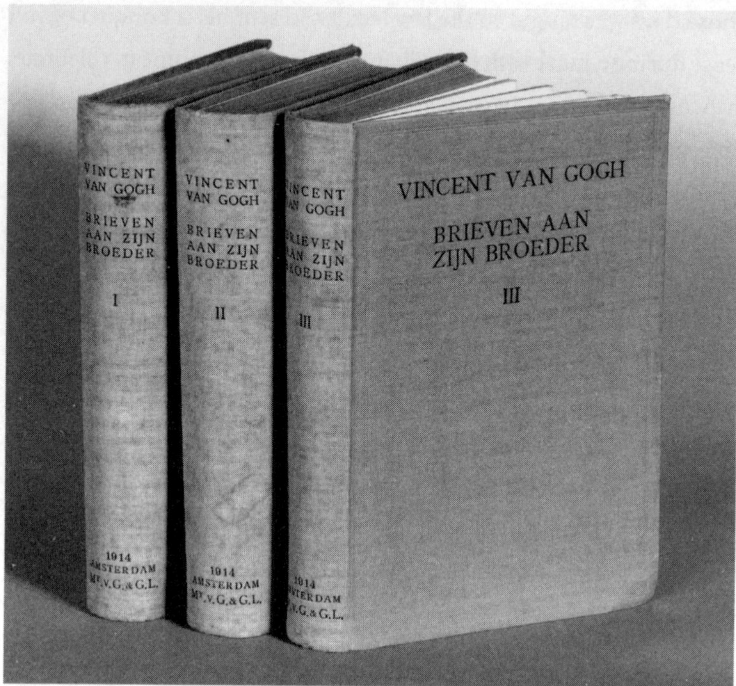

Figure 54 Vincent van Gogh, *Brieven aan zijn broeder*. Uitgeverij de Wereldbibliotheek, Amsterdam, 1914.

Het Volk. The three volumes were produced with great care (Figure 54). Two days later, on Josina's twenty-fourth birthday, Jo wrote a dedication in the third volume: 'To Vincent and Jos, Amsterdam 5 November 1914'.[87] She gave Josina a travelling case for her birthday and arranged for cyclamens to be sent on Vincent's behalf. Jo also congratulated Vincent, who at that moment was on a business trip to Champigny-sur-Marne, just outside Paris. Her letter included a pointed comment in brackets:

> What a relief it'll be when you're together—not always having to write letters (except to your poor old mother of course), togetherness and warmth and love all around—your own home—oh my dear boy, I don't have the words to express how much these thoughts please me! It will only be then that Jos's real life begins.[88]

That last sentence was, of course, based on her own experience.

During the last weeks of the year Jo kept Vincent informed in detail about her activities. She had already made enquiries on his behalf about how he could return, since travel by road or rail was no longer possible because of the war. He could cross the Channel by boat from Dieppe to the English seaside town of Folkestone, from where there were sailings to Vlissingen.[89] Jo was happy to do something for Belgians who had fled their country and offered her house in Laren to the family of the Antwerp writer and publisher Lodewijk Opdebeek. It is highly probable that she got in touch with this family through Ary Delen, most likely during her visit to Antwerp in March. She welcomed the war refugees in Rozenlaantje in person.[90] Years later Gabriël Opdebeek, Lodewijk's son, published the story 'De gouden regen' ('The Golden Rain') and dedicated it to Jo by way of thanks for her generous help. That help was certainly enduring, for they were still living in 't Lanthuys in June 1916.[91]

Jo sent a copy of *Brieven aan zijn broeder* to the artist Rik Wouters, who was among the ten thousand Belgian soldiers interned in a camp in Zeist. She had learned from the writer Jan Greshoff that Wouters was interested in the letters. 'The book will certainly be a source of comfort to you during your period of enforced idleness,' she wrote to him.[92] Wouters was grateful that she had encouraged him in this way and showed himself to be an ideal reader. He thought the letters were impressive, 'like his paintings. Your Hon. will understand with what force his words have awakened me from the sad emptiness, and how they emerge as something holy in the midst of such depressing surroundings.'[93]

Mother and son lend works to the 'Kunst aan het Volk' association

On 16 and 17 December 1914 Jo once again placed advertisements for the letters edition in the *NRC* and the *Algemeen Handelsblad*. It was a tactical move on the eve of the opening of an exhibition of more than two hundred drawings by Van Gogh, initiated by the 'Kunst aan het Volk' association in Amsterdam's Stedelijk Museum. It ran from 22 December 1914 to 19 January 1915. When she asked Vincent if he approved of lending these works, she wrote tellingly: 'That's nice and straight away I've got more work.'[94] Mother and son lent the drawings out of idealistic conviction and contributed to the catalogue, which included Johan Cohen Gosschalk's 1905 introduction.[95] Willem Steenhoff helped design the exhibition's layout. According to the *Algemeen Handelsblad* of 23 December 1914, 'many well-known figures from the art world and some painters' attended the opening, which was presided over by Floor Wibaut, one of the organizers and chair of Kunst aan het Volk.[96] Keeping it in the family, the annual general meeting was held that same evening, and Wibaut was succeeded by Jo's youngest brother Wim, who was a member of no end of associations and clubs and had developed into a true workaholic. On a surviving poster for the exhibition, a strip of paper with the number 19 had been pasted over the closing date of 12 January; the show had evidently attracted enough interest to extend it.[97]

The exhibition sparked a controversy. In his review of 29 December 1914 in *Het Volk*, Johan Ankersmit focused particularly on the drawings that Van Gogh made of the working class, which he thought conveyed so much 'urge to work'. Richard Roland Holst had a critical comment—he felt that the selection of works for the exhibition was based too much on 'sentimental beliefs', which he abhorred. Marie de Roode-Heijermans joined the fray with a counter-argument, to which Roland Holst responded immediately by reiterating his repugnance to 'a *glorification of poor Vincent* full of impure tendencies, fanatical exaggeration and a lack of proportion'. (As we saw in Chapter 8, he had expressed similar criticism in March 1892.) Steenhoff got involved in the debate, which was summarized and reviewed shortly afterwards by Cornelis Veth.[98] The divergent views about Van Gogh were thus given a thorough airing. Quite apart from this controversy, Johan de Meester wrote three pieces for the *NRC*. The first of these, dated 31 December 1914, praised the tireless efforts put in by Jo, this 'energetic woman for whom the stewardship, rescue and conservation of Vincent's entire legacy became such a magnificent vocation, which has now been crowned by publication of the Letters'.[99]

Vincent and Josina got married in Amsterdam on 14 January 1915, during the last week of the exhibition.[100] They left on their honeymoon, travelling via London to Paris, with goodbyes and a farewell serenade.[101] Vincent accepted a job there as a replacement for an engineer who had been mobilized. On 12 February they went to live in La Varenne-St Hilaire (Chennevières), Val de Marne (Saint-Maur-des-Fossés), in south-eastern Paris.[102] They rented a furnished house at 12 rue Hoche. There were three bedrooms on the first floor. It was telling that Josina, who like Vincent was a keen visitor to libraries, acquired a library card for the Bibliothèque Nationale as soon as she arrived.[103]

Into the breach for peace

In March 1915, the fifty-two-year-old Jo travelled to the International Socialist Women's Conference for peace in Berne together with Heleen Ankersmit and Carry Pothuis-Smit, whom she knew from the social democratic propaganda organization Sociaal-Democratische Vrouwenpropagandaclub (SDVC), the association of social democratic women's clubs Bond van Sociaal-Democratische Vrouwenclubs (BSDVC) and *De Proletarische Vrouw*. The journey was no easy matter in wartime conditions. Jo had a great deal of trouble obtaining a travel document so that she could go to Switzerland via Germany. It reveals that her hair had meanwhile gone grey and that her height was 155 centimetres (5 feet 1 inch). The document was issued on 22 March and before she left on the twenty-fourth it had already been stamped six times, including by the consulates of the two countries. More stamps were added as she crossed borders on 25 and 29 March, and by the German and Dutch consulates in Berne to confirm her return trip (Plate 53).

Things went wrong as soon as they reached the Dutch–German border. The German border guards decided Pothuis-Smit was a spy and arrested her. Later, looking back at Jo's life, *De Proletarische Vrouw* wrote: 'Together with her two travelling companions, she suffered at the hands of the German border guards, who deprived us of our liberty. She was a lively participant in that secret anti-war conference.'[104] The meeting was chaired by the German feminist Marxist Clara Zetkin-Eissner and took place between 26 and 28 March 1915. There were delegates from Germany, the United Kingdom, Russia, the Netherlands, Poland, Italy, France and Switzerland.

Ankersmit and Pothuis-Smit had got to know Zetkin-Eissner in 1910 at the second International Socialist Women's Conference in Copenhagen. The Berne conference ended with a resolution drafted

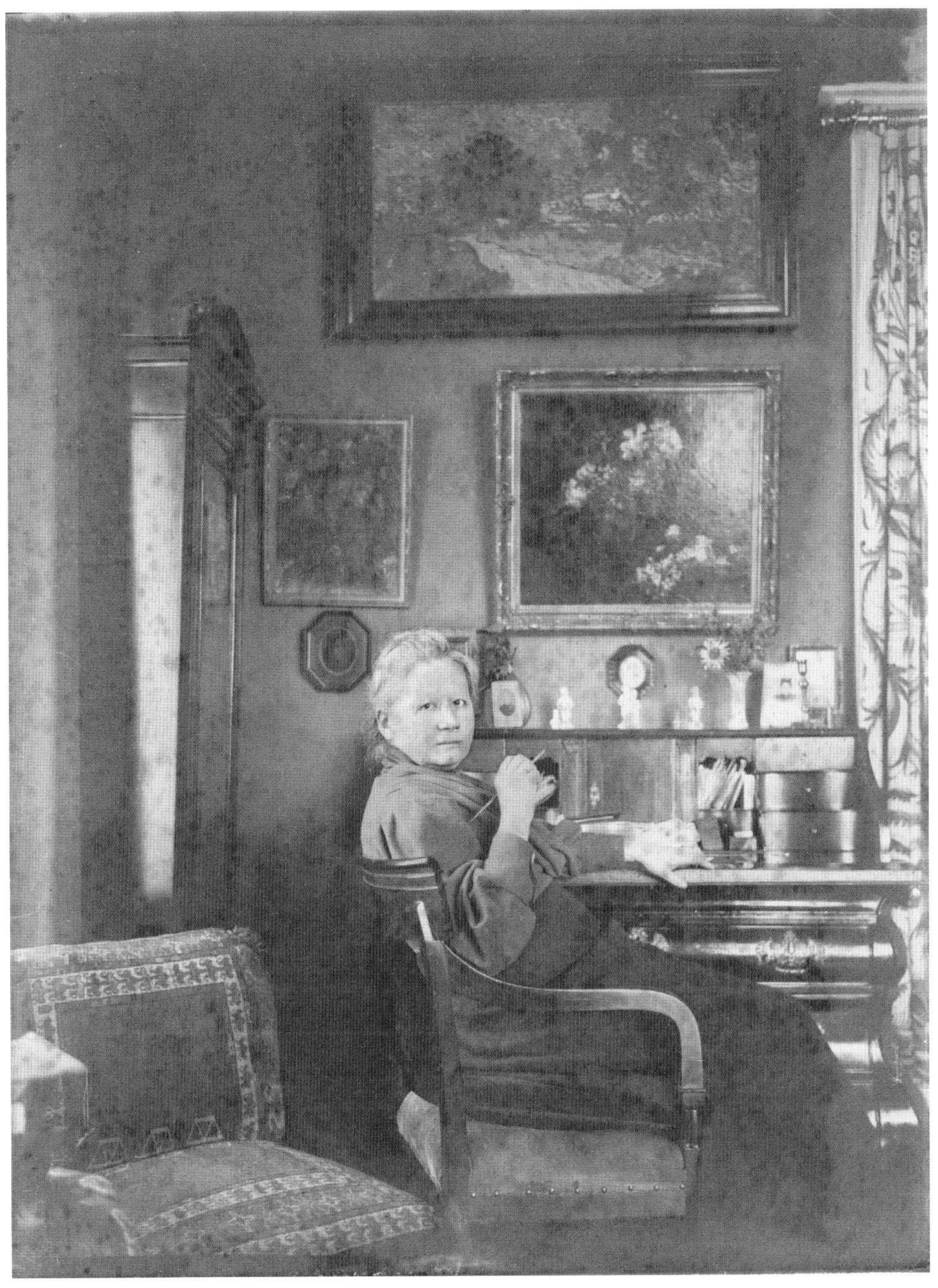

Plate 45 Jo van Gogh-Bonger at her desk in the living room at 77 Koninginneweg in Amsterdam, 1909 or later. On the wall behind the desk are Fantin-Latour's *Flowers* and Vincent van Gogh's *Vase of Honesty* (1884), with *Landscape at Twilight* (1890) at the top.

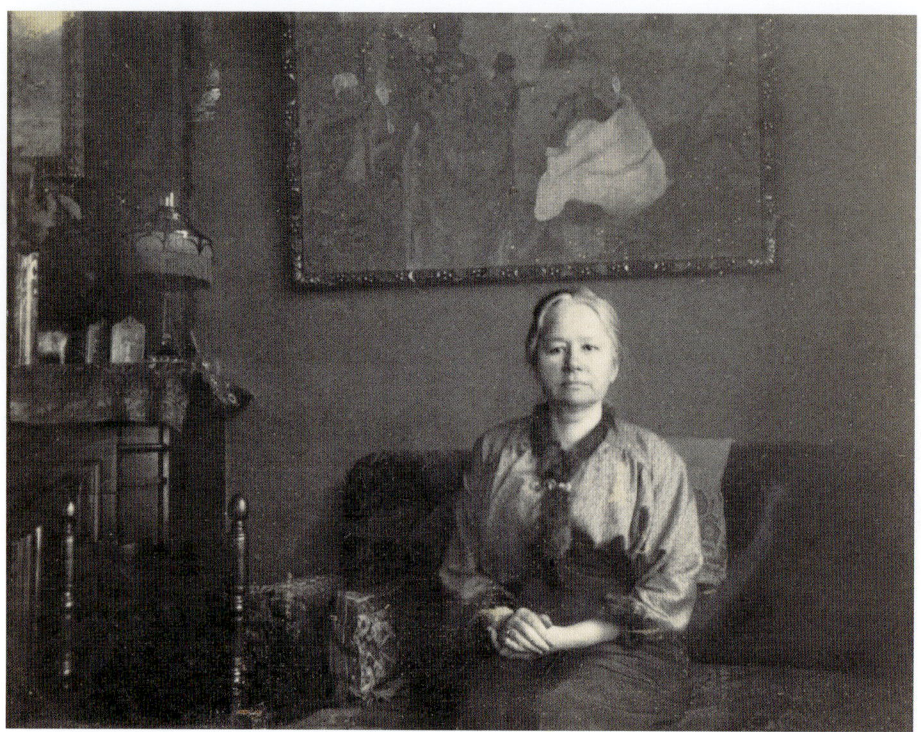

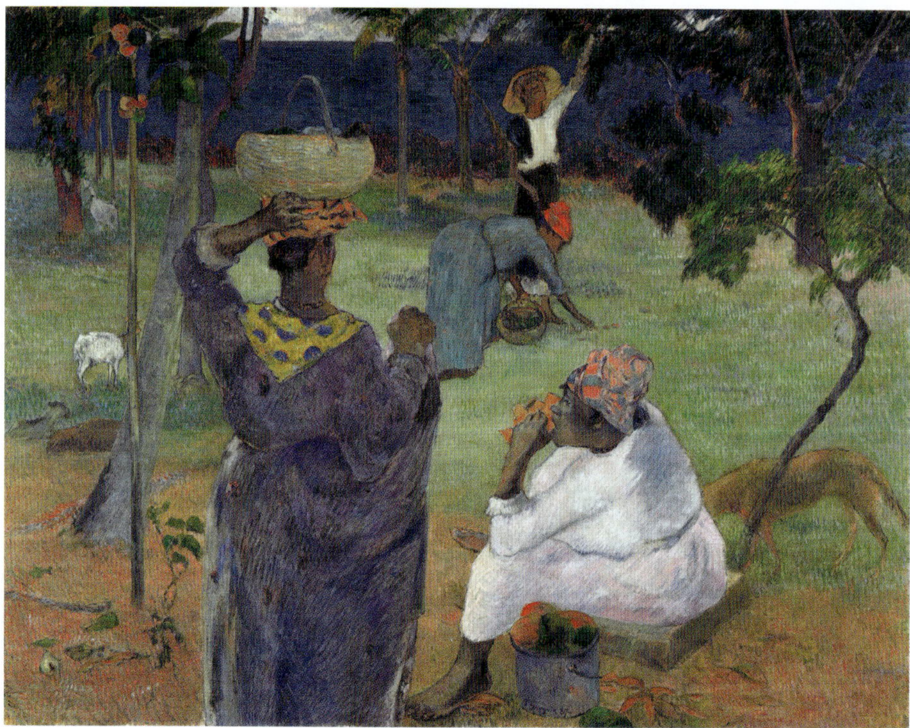

Plate 46 Jo van Gogh-Bonger on the sofa in the living room at 77 Koninginneweg in Amsterdam, 1915. On the wall behind her is Gauguin's *The Mango Trees, Martinique*.
Plate 47 Paul Gauguin, *The Mango Trees, Martinique*, 1887.

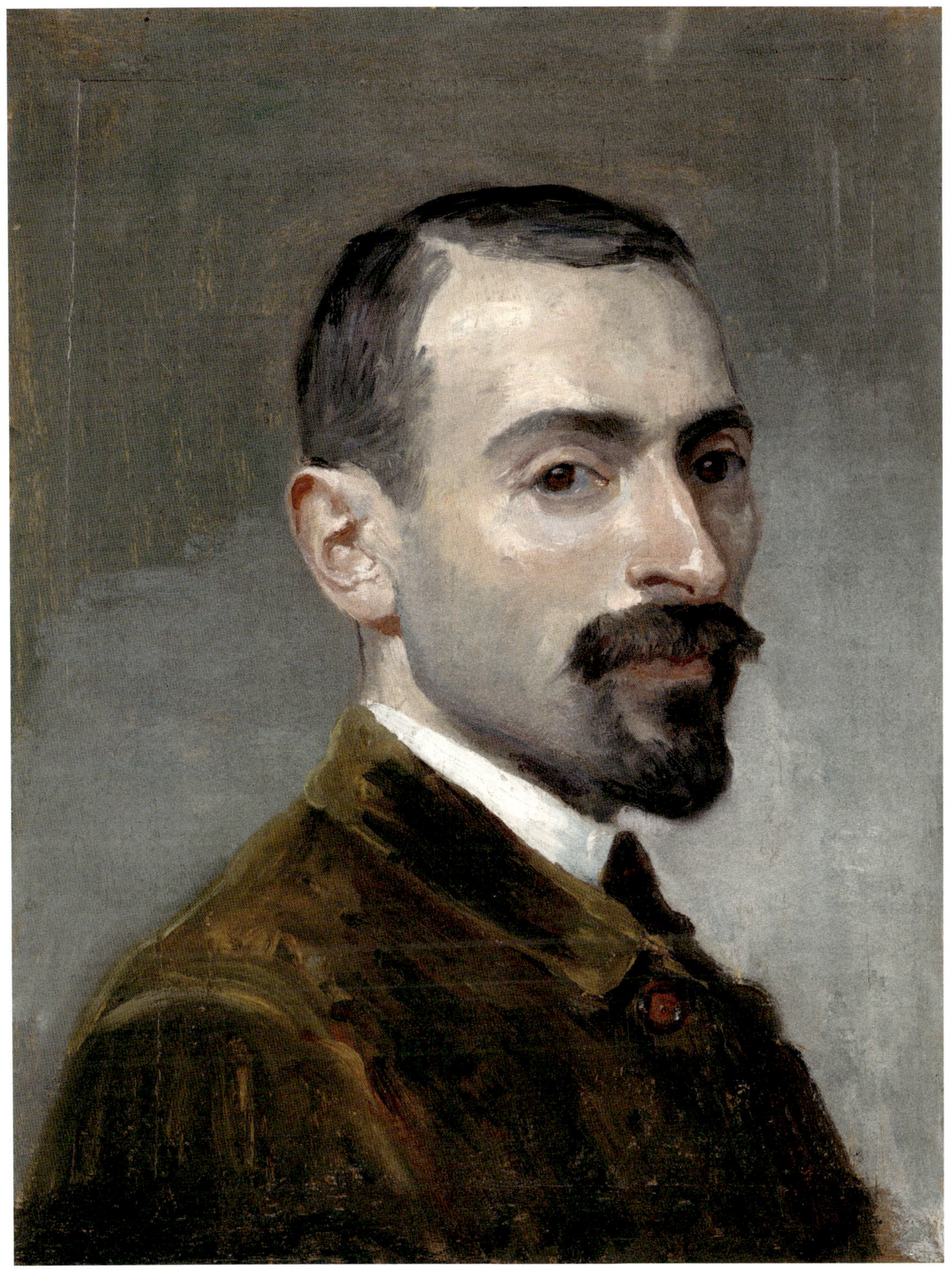

Plate 48 Johan Cohen Gosschalk, *Self-Portrait*, 1905–10.

654964/1996

SCHILDERIJEN EN TEEKENINGEN door Vincent van Gogh.
Eigendom van Mevr. J.Cohen Gosschalk-Bonger
aanwezig bij en verkocht door
ARTZ & DE BOIS.

S.A.of T.		Titel	Ovangen		Prijs.	Aanteekenig
s.		Landschap blauw figuur,	1911		3000.	
t.		Landschap Arles 2 fig.	1911		1400.	teekening
t.		Wever.	1911		600.	
s.		Appelen Brab. tijd	1911		3000.	
s.		Kreeftjes	1911		2000.	— 3000
s.		Molen Montmartre	1911		2000/	3000
s.		Meisje.blauw fond	1911	X	3500.	do heden betaald
t.		Kerkhof bij regen	1911		~~750~~ 9000	
t.		Paris-Montmartre	1911		550.	
s.		Monet? Pisarro?	1911		----	
a.		Fortifications X	1911		1800.	13 Sept 12.bet.
t.		Moestuin.	1911		1250.	
s.		Brabantsche kannen	1911		2500.	
s.	1	Groote Montmartre	19/4 12		20000.	— 30000
s		Zonnebloemen.	id.		------	wordt geretourneerd
s.		Herderinnetje	id.	X	4000.	do heden betaald
s.	2	Olijvenboomgaard klein	id.		5000	
s.	3	~~Jong opgaand hout~~	id.		~~6000.~~	terug 15000
s.		Einde van den dag	id.	X	6000.	do heden betaald
s.		Restaurant	id.		5000.	19 Juni 12.bet.
s.	4	~~Groote olijvenboomg.~~	id.		~~6800.~~	terug 10000
s.		Grasveldje.	id.		3800.	— 5500
s.		Stilleven,klompen.	id.		2000.	— 3000

Teekeningen-expositie Juni1912 — na 15 December

De nummers 2, 4, 6, 9,11, 12,17, 19,20, 23, 25, 26,29, en 31
welke alle niet te koop waren, gaan dezer dagen naar A.terug.

Nr	Titel		Prijs	Aanteekenig
1.	Zouaaf X		1000.	13 Sept 12.bet.
3.	Grasveld met struik		800.	
5.	Landschap m.2 boomen		800.	~~verkocht.bet.Jan13~~
7.	a.Gezicht MontMajor		2000.	verkocht – betaald eind Dec
8.	Molen op Montmartre		1000.	
10.	Landschap.weg m.figuur		900.	~~verkocht.bet.Jan13~~
13.	a.Gezicht op de stad museum	X	2000.	do heden betaald
14.	a.Schepen.		2000.	
15.	a.Vrouw met kruiwagen.		1400.	
16.	Soepuitdeeling.		1200.	
18.	Kerkhof.		2000.	
21.	a. Charette bleue X		1800.	12 Sept. 12 bet.
22.	Vrouwenkop.		600.	
24.	Oude man.		1000.	
27.	Garenwindster.		900.	
28.	Boom.		900.	
30.	Tuin met bank.		1000.	

3500
4000
6000
2000
15500

S.E.O.
12 Nov: 1912
Artz & De Bois

Plate 49 Schedule of works by Van Gogh on commission with the Artz & De Bois gallery in The Hague, 12 November 1912.

Plate 50 Announcement of the 'Nationale Betooging' (national demonstration) in Utrecht—*Bussumsche Courant*, 10 September 1902.

Nederlandsch Comité voor Algemeen Kiesrecht.

Groote Nationale Betooging

ten gunste van Grondwetsherziening, om te komen tot Algemeen Kiesrecht voor Mannen en Vrouwen,

op Zondag 14 September a.s. des namiddags ten één uur, te Utrecht.

Sprekers: **F. MOL, B. H. HELDT, Mr. P. J. TROELSTRA, K. TER LAAN, Mevr. VERSLUIJS—POELMAN en Mevr. TH. HAVER.**

Na afloop **OPTOCHT** door de stad, met ontplooide Banieren en begeleiding van drie Muziekkorpsen.

DE BUSSUMSCHE MEETINGGANGERS vertrekken 's ochtends met trein 7.39 (Spoortijd) naar Weesp en vandaar per stoomboot langs de Vecht naar Utrecht. Terugkomst te Bussum 's avonds 8.58 (Spoortijd). Kosten Retour Weesp **25** cents, boottocht Weesp—Utrecht en terug **40** cents. Kaarten voor de boot zijn verkrijgbaar aan een der onderstaande adressen:

Afd. »Bussum" Nederl. Comité voor Algemeen Kiesrecht:
E. WEITINGA, *Voorzitter.*
Mevr. J. COHEN—BONGER, *Secretaresse.*

Afd. »Bussum" der Sociaal-Democratische Arbeiderspartij:
Dr. H. GORTER, *Voorzitter.*
H. KEETELAAR, *Secretaris.*

De Timmerlieden-Vereeniging »Door Eendracht Sterk":
J. JANSEN, *Voorzitter.*
H. KEETELAAR, *Secretaris.*

De Afd. »Gooi" der Nederl. Vereen. tot Afschaffing van Alcoholhoudende Dranken:
Mevr. STIBBE, *Secretaresse.*

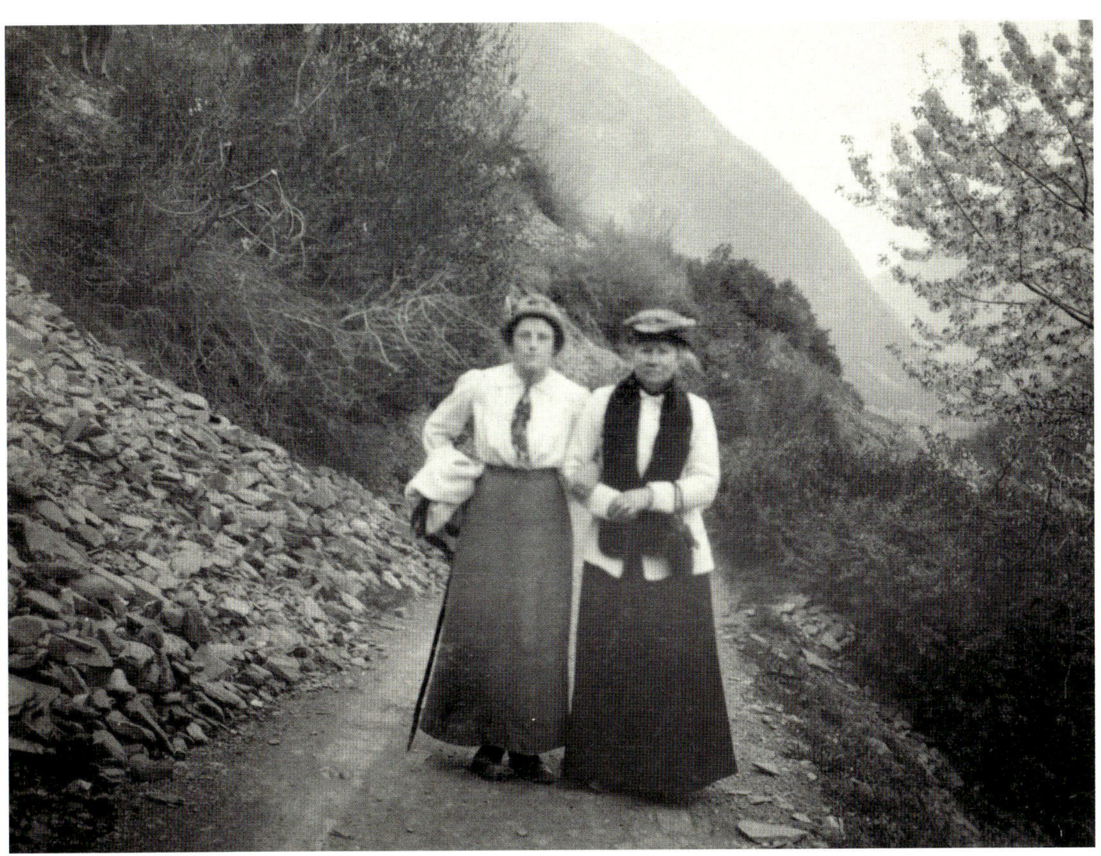

Plate 51 Josina Wibaut and Jo van Gogh-Bonger on the road to Aragnouet in the Pyrenees, 1914.

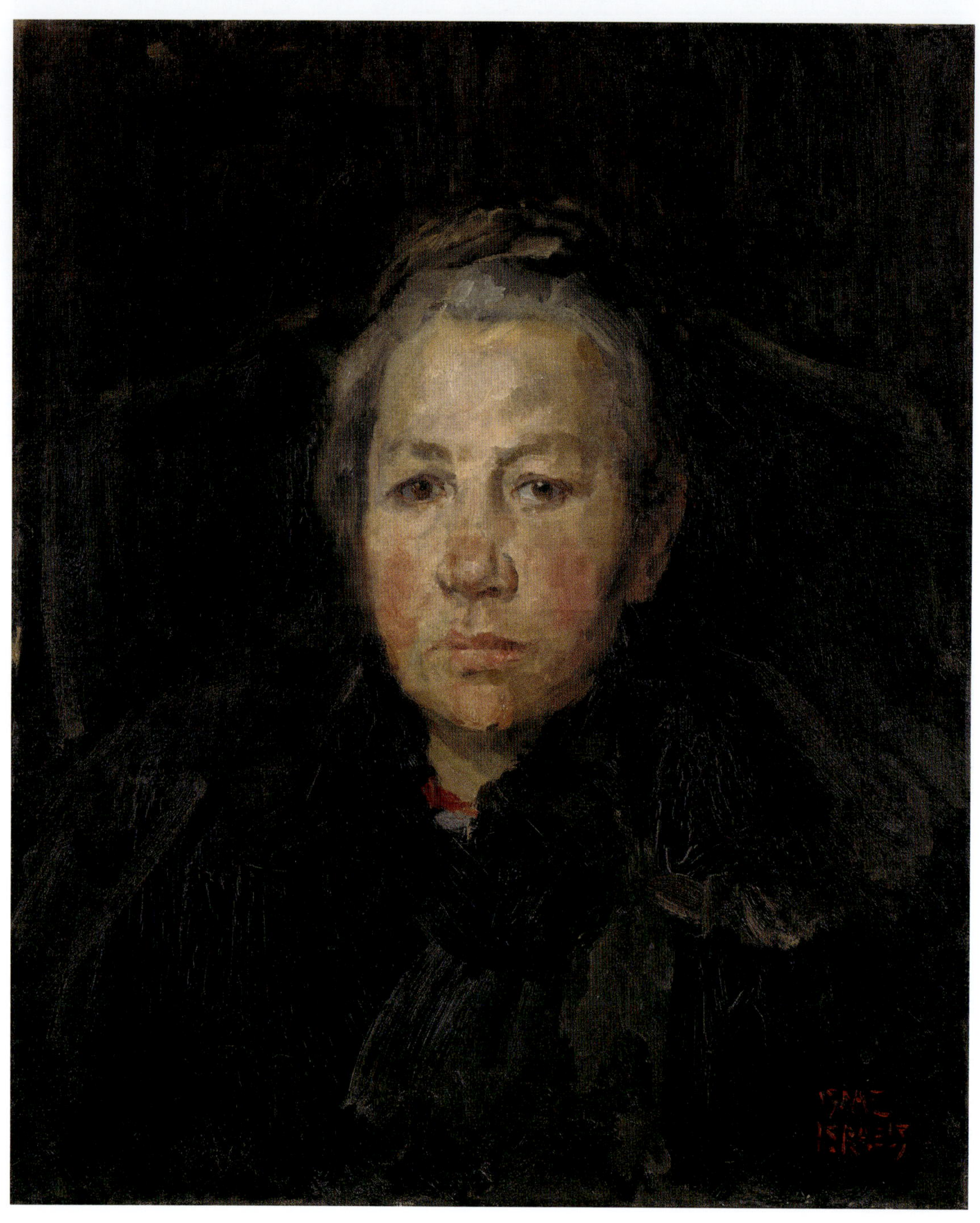

Plate 52 Isaac Israëls, *Jo van Gogh-Bonger*, undated.

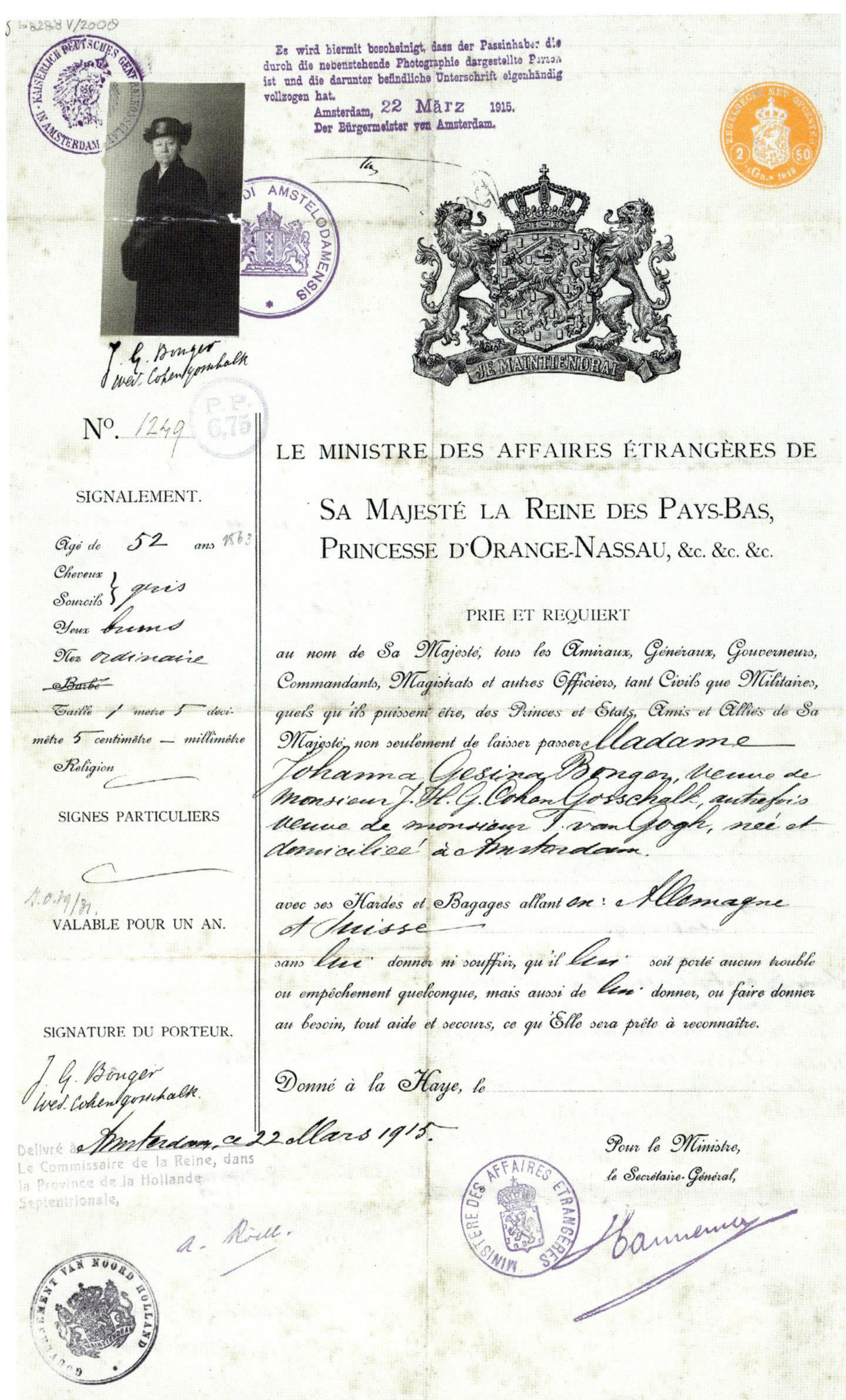
Es wird hiermit bescheinigt, dass der Passinhaber die durch die nebenstehende Photographie dargestellte Person ist und die darunter befindliche Unterschrift eigenhändig vollzogen hat.
Amsterdam, 22 März 1915.
Der Bürgermeister von Amsterdam.

No. 1249

LE MINISTRE DES AFFAIRES ÉTRANGÈRES DE

SA MAJESTÉ LA REINE DES PAYS-BAS,
PRINCESSE D'ORANGE-NASSAU, &c. &c. &c.

SIGNALEMENT.

Agé de 52 ans
Cheveux / Sourcils gris
Yeux bruns
Nez ordinaire
Barbe
Taille 1 mètre 5 décimètre 5 centimètre — millimètre
Religion

SIGNES PARTICULIERS

VALABLE POUR UN AN.

SIGNATURE DU PORTEUR.

J.G. Bonger
wed. Cohen Gosschalk

PRIE ET REQUIERT

au nom de Sa Majesté, tous les Amiraux, Généraux, Gouverneurs, Commandants, Magistrats et autres Officiers, tant Civils que Militaires, quels qu'ils puissent être, des Princes et Etats, Amis et Alliés de Sa Majesté, non seulement de laisser passer Madame Johanna Gesina Bonger, veuve de monsieur J.H.G. Cohen Gosschalk, autrefois veuve de monsieur T. van Gogh, née et domiciliée à Amsterdam

avec ses Hardes et Bagages allant en: Allemagne et Suisse

sans lui donner ni souffrir, qu'il lui soit porté aucun trouble ou empêchement quelconque, mais aussi de lui donner, ou faire donner au besoin, tout aide et secours, ce qu'Elle sera prête à reconnaître.

Donné à la Haye, le

Delivré à Amsterdam, ce 22 Mars 1915.
Le Commissaire de la Reine, dans la Province de la Hollande Septentrionale,

Pour le Ministre,
le Secrétaire-Général,

Plate 53 Permit for 'J.G. Bonger, widow of Cohen Gosschalk' to travel through Germany and Switzerland, 22 March 1915.

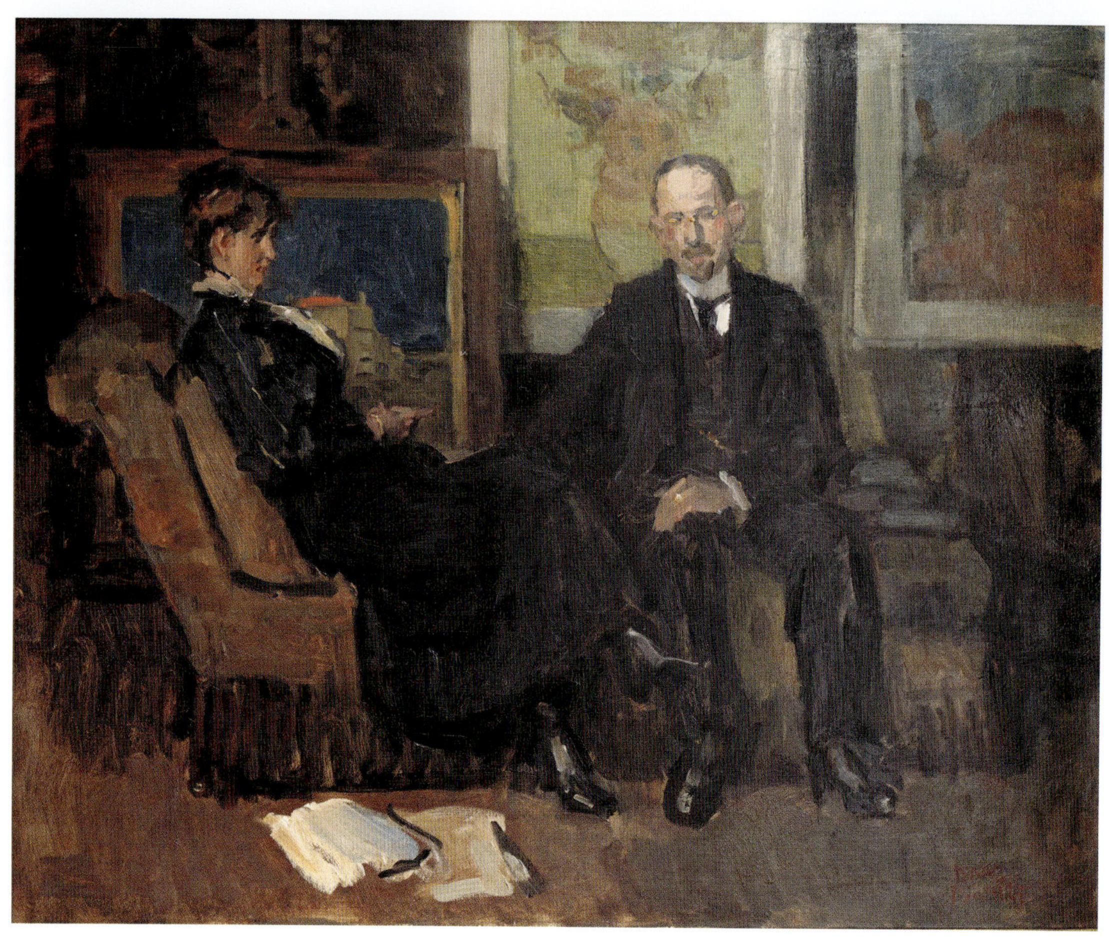

Plate 54 Isaac Israëls, *Isaac Bennie Cohen and His Wife Jacqueline Wilhelmine Longépée*, 1915–20. Parts of three Van Gogh's are depicted in the background: *The Yellow House ('The Street')*, *Sunflowers* and *The Bedroom*.

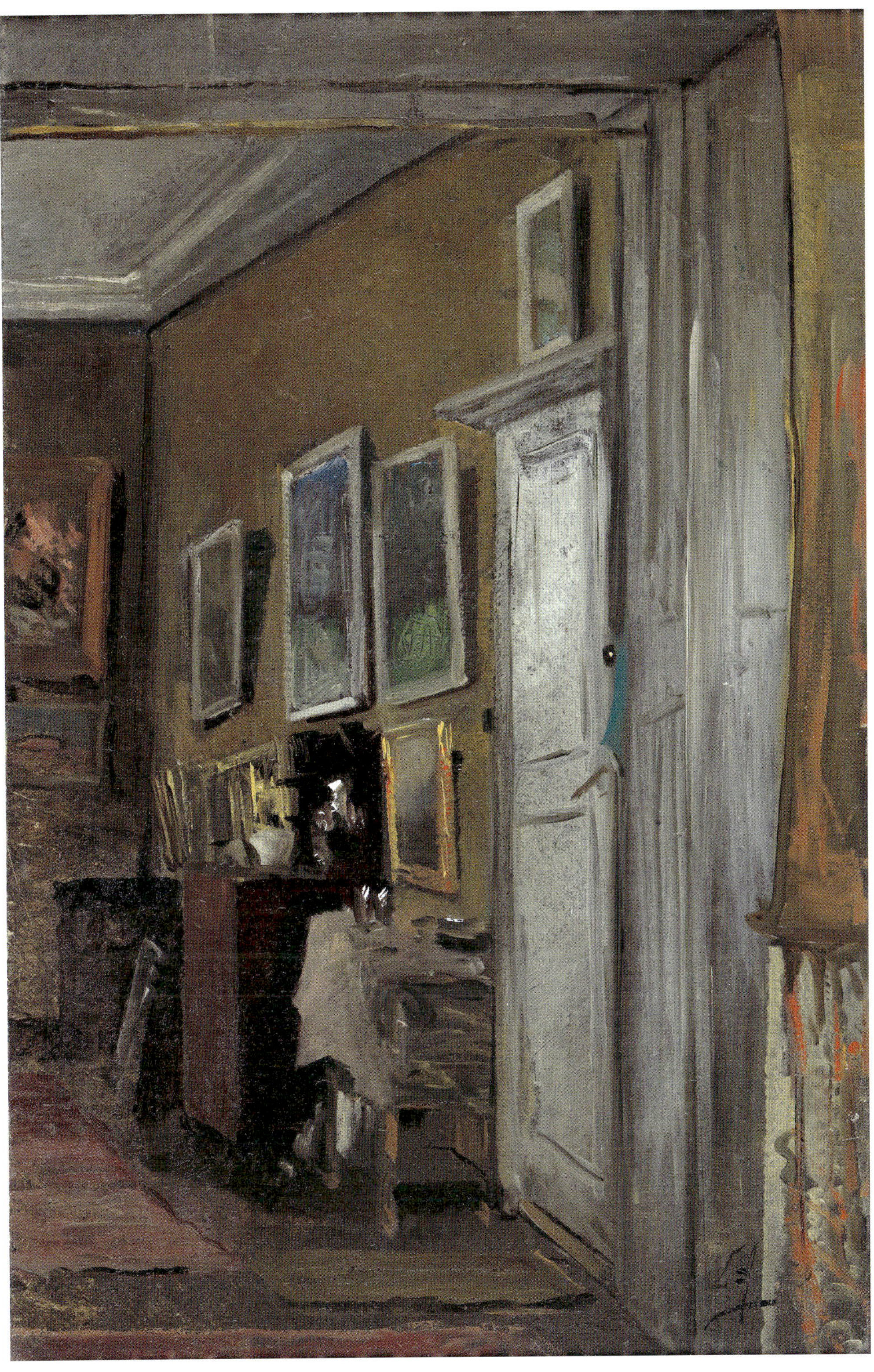

Plate 55 Lizzy Ansingh, *Interior of 77 Koninginneweg in Amsterdam*, undated.

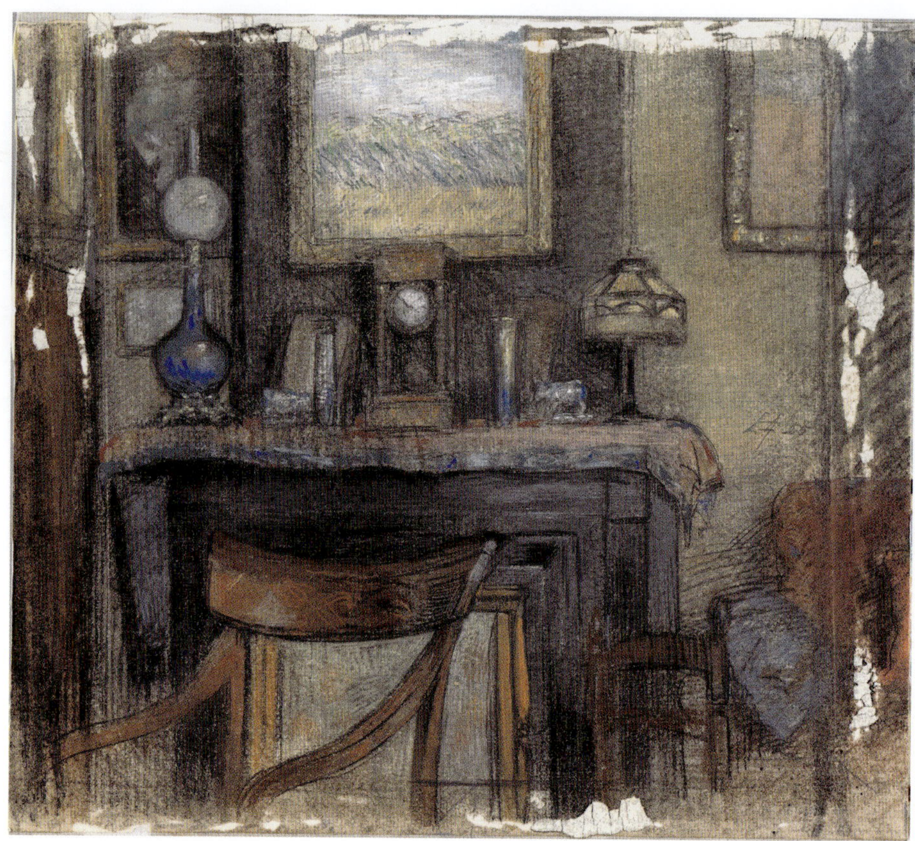

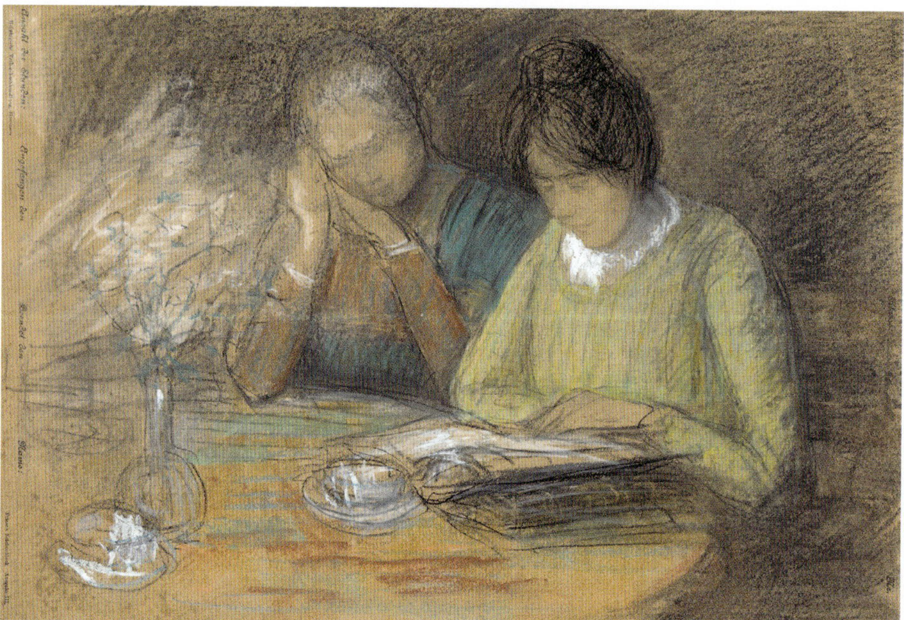

Plate 56 Lizzy Ansingh, *The Mantelpiece at 77 Koninginneweg*, undated.
Plate 57 Lizzy Ansingh, *Two Women Reading*, undated (the figure on the left is Jo van Gogh-Bonger).

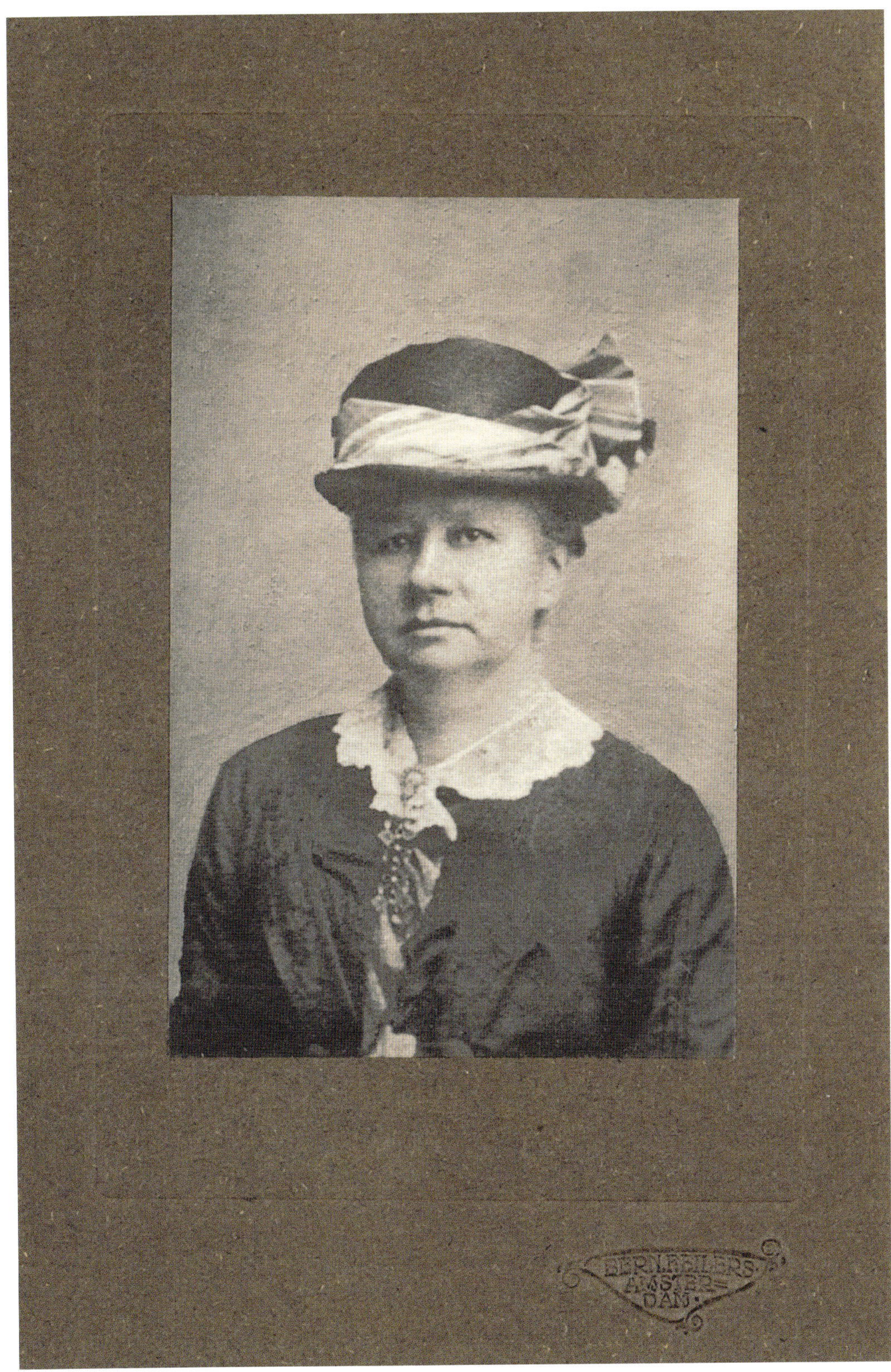

Plate 58 Jo van Gogh-Bonger, 1915–16.

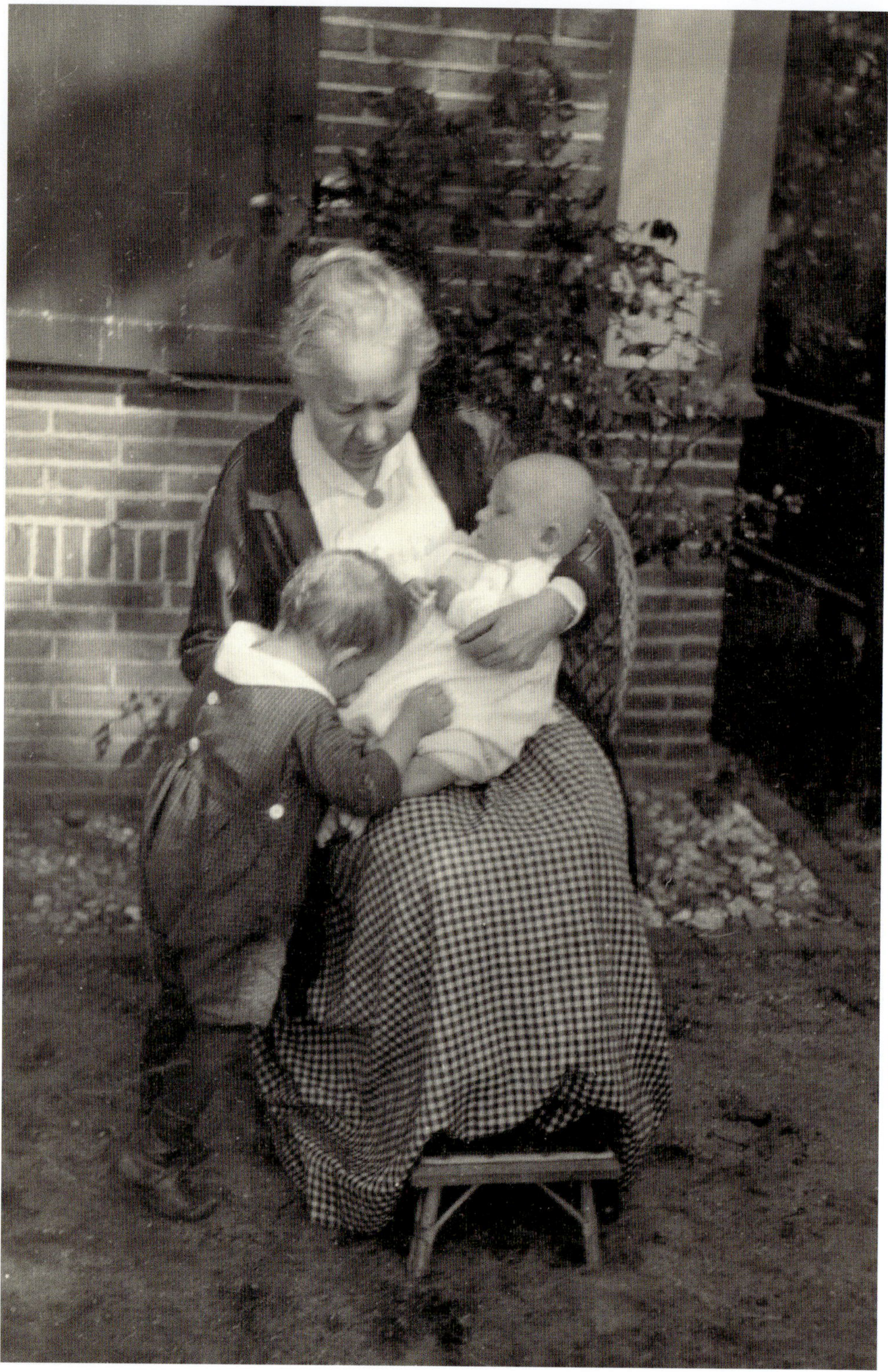

Plate 59 Jo van Gogh-Bonger with her grandsons Theo and Johan van Gogh in Laren, 1922. This small framed portrait photograph stands on the table in the living room at 77 Koninginneweg in Amsterdam, see Figure 41.

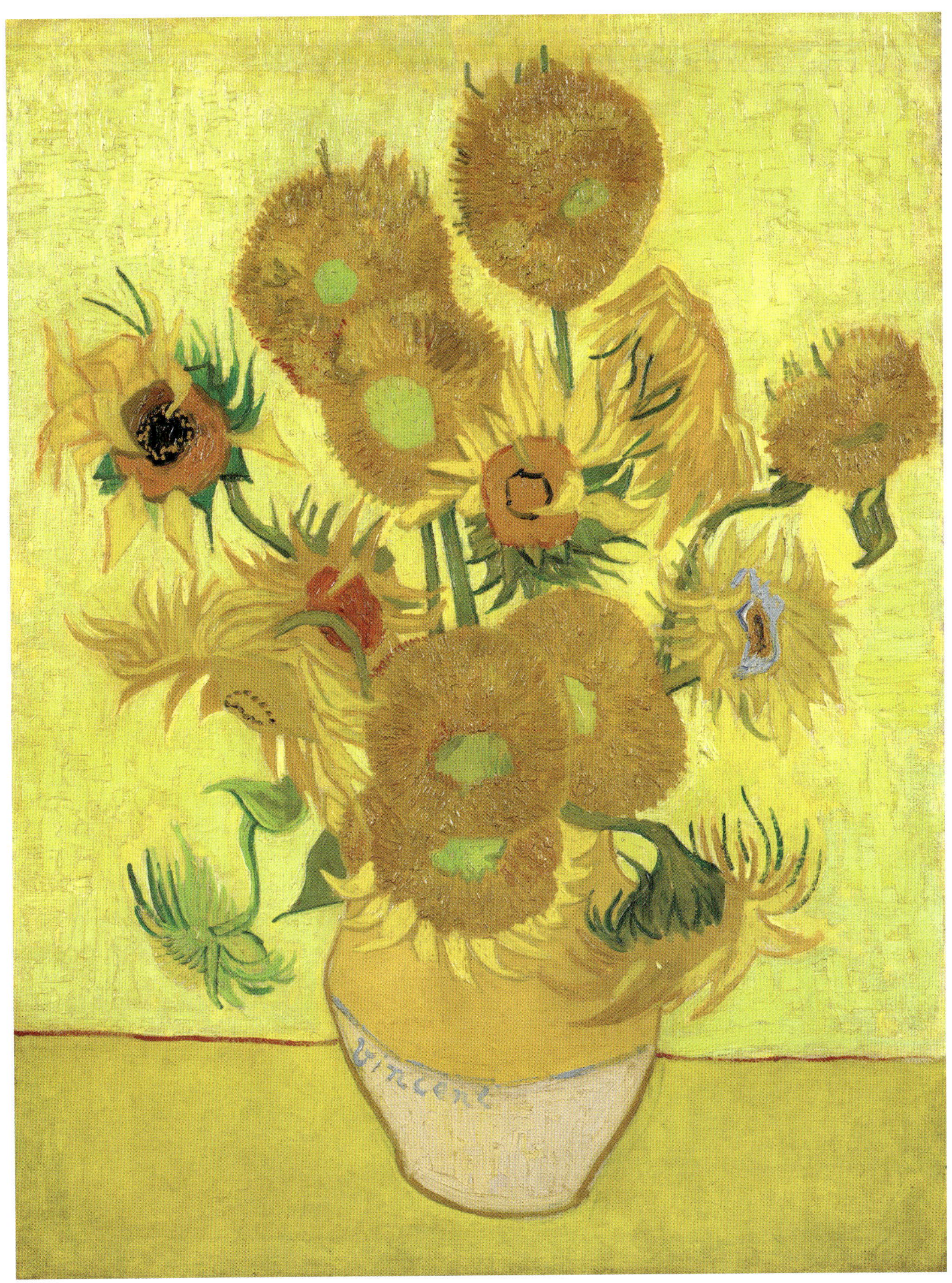

Plate 60 Vincent van Gogh, *Sunflowers*, 1889.

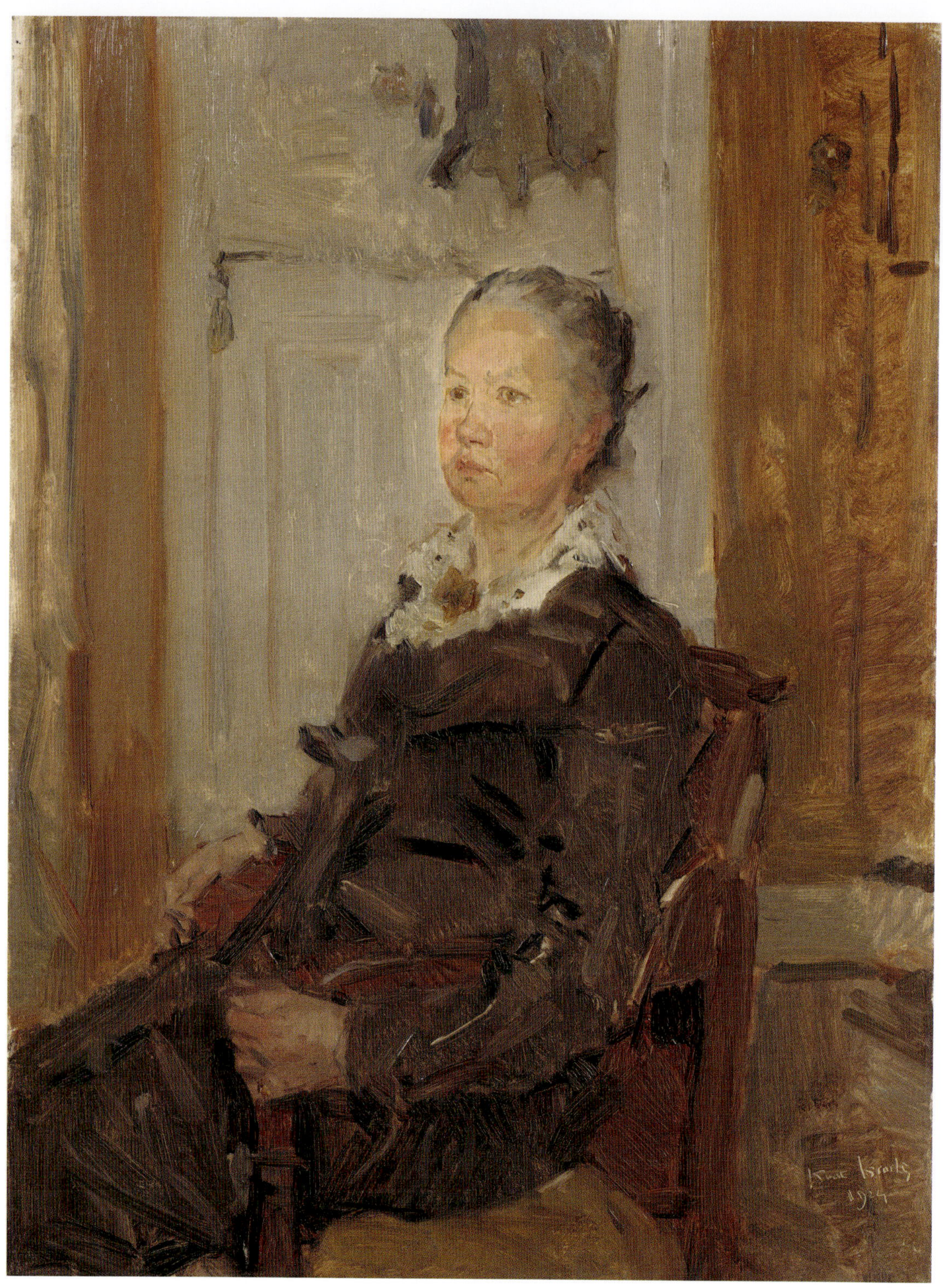

Plate 61 Isaac Israëls, *Jo van Gogh-Bonger*, 1924.

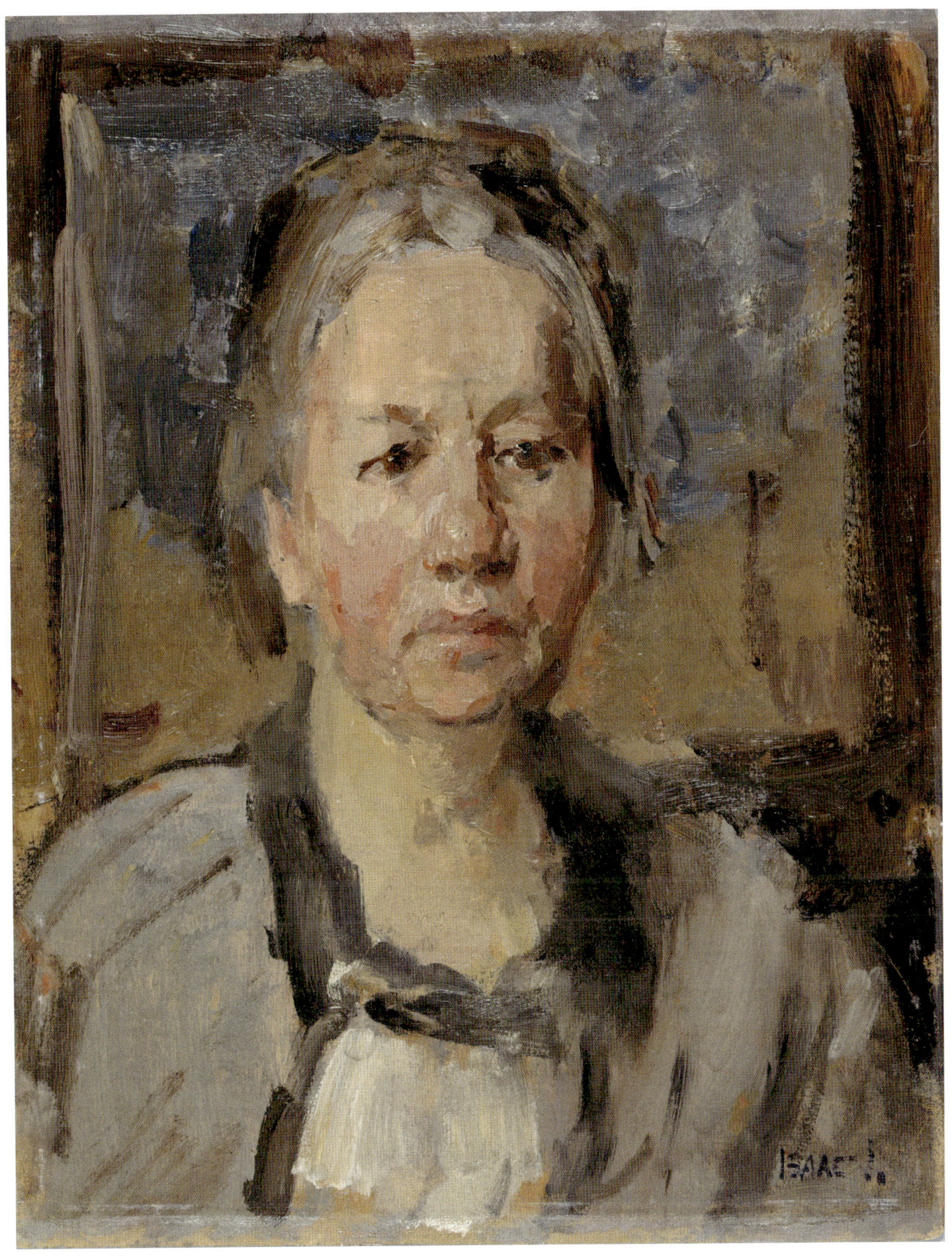

Plate 62 Isaac Israëls, *Jo van Gogh-Bonger*, 1926.

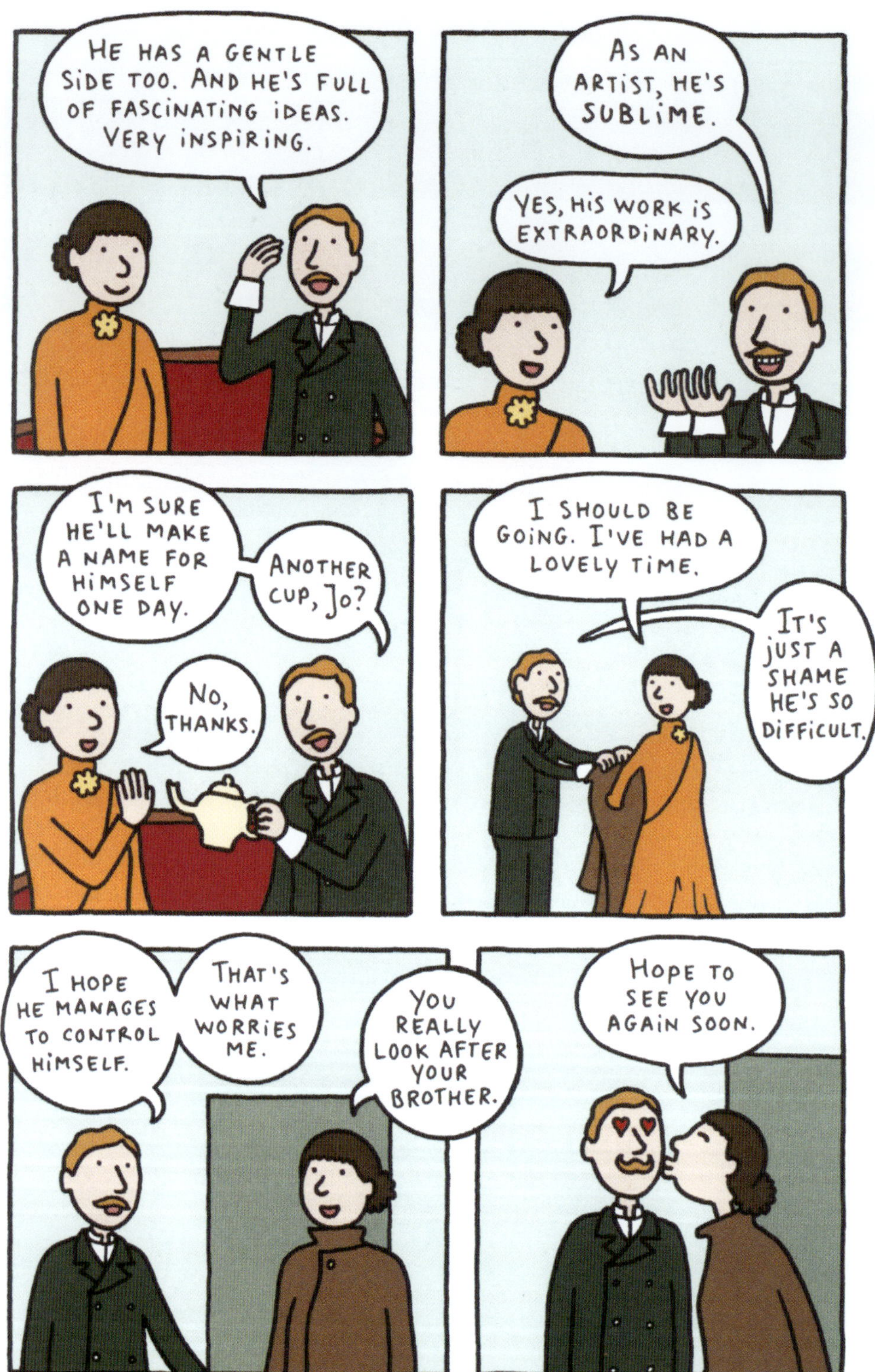

Plate 63 Barbara Stok, *Vincent*. Self Made Hero, London 2012 (p. 21).

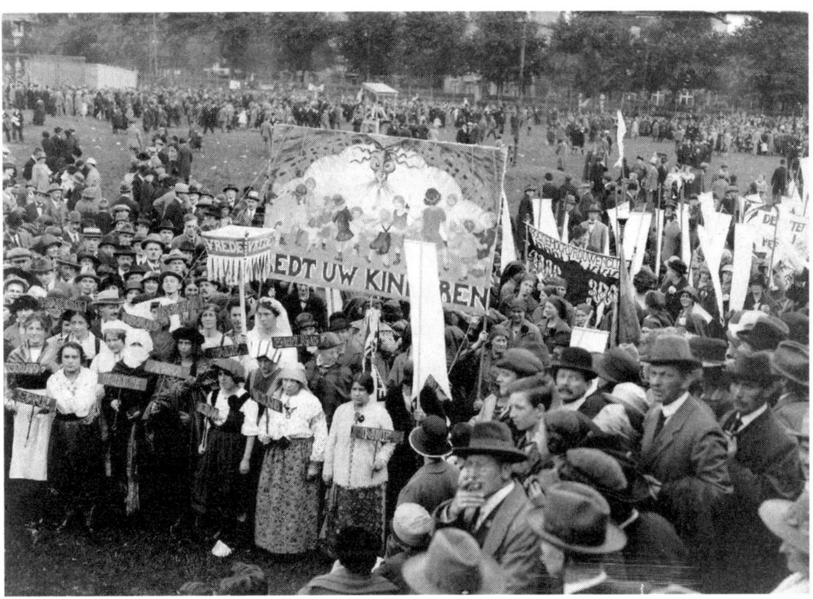

Figure 55 Internationale Vrouwendag voor de Vrede (International Women's Day for Peace). Demonstration in Museumplein in Amsterdam, 1 April 1915.

by Zetkin-Eissner together with the Dutch and British delegations, where Jo's linguistic talents came in very handy. This resolution declared war on the war. The women demanded peace without annexations, recognition of the right of peoples to self-determination, and called upon one another to use all possible means in their struggle.[105] Necessity knows no law. Together with her fellow party members, who hoped passionately for a new dawn, Jo worked hard for the good cause.

Immediately after this conference, on 1 April in Amsterdam's Concertgebouw there was the protest meeting 'Voor de Vrede' ('For Peace'), organized by the SDAP and the BSDVC. Women from all over the country came to this fourth Women's Day wearing red ribbons and holding red tulips. The BSDVC was more than an association that supported the interests of workers' wives. A substantial proportion of the members were women with a working-class background. They sang protest songs and Mathilde Wibaut-Berdenis van Berlekom spoke about the women whose husbands had been killed at the front. In so doing she followed up on the issues discussed in Berne. The war forced workers in the countries fighting the war to fight each other and consequently nothing came of the international movement. Heleen Ankersmit contended that peace and socialism went hand in hand and showed how capitalism provoked war. Jo, who had demonstrated such commitment at the Berne conference, was without doubt involved. During the demonstration 130,000 copies of a manifesto were distributed. It contained slogans such as: 'That same courage that fires up men to destroy can inspire women in the struggle to preserve life', and 'Mothers, stand up for your children'. Afterwards thousands of workers' wives took part in a march to the Oosterpark. At the front there were girls sounding gongs and marchers carrying banners and flags proclaiming such messages as CAPITALISM MEANS DEATH and SAVE YOUR CHILDREN (Figure 55).[106]

Temporary departure of Vincent and Josina

A passport issued by the French vice-consulate at the end of May gave Jo permission to travel to Paris. She went to stay in La Varenne-St Hilaire with the young couple, who had only just returned from their honeymoon. Jo followed the same route as she had mapped out for Vincent six months before: first she went by boat to England, and then crossed the Channel in the other direction and arrived in Dieppe on 1 June. Three days later she registered her presence in Paris.

She enjoyed their company, the shady garden and the rural surroundings.[107] Two weeks later, the three of them went by rail to Tarbes and then to Aragnouet, near Fabian.[108] This time they only stayed in the South of France for a fortnight. While in that Francophone environment, Jo toyed with the idea of translating her introduction to the letters into French, but she never put pen to paper. Back in Paris, they visited Émile Bernard at 10 Île Saint-Louis, 'a lovely old house where he had his studio'.[109] They returned home via England in mid-August.[110] The two months abroad heartened Jo, which was just as well because from then on she would be separated from the couple for a long time.

On 5 October 1915 Vincent and Josina, who according to the passenger list were both twenty-five years old and '5 foot 8 inches tall', left Rotterdam on the steamship *Rijndam* for New York, where they arrived on the seventeenth. Things went very wrong as soon as they arrived because Josina was diagnosed with cancer. Shortly afterwards she had to have one breast surgically removed. Jo was terribly worried and followed every step of Josina's recovery after the operation. She also had frequent contact with Josina's mother.[111] Writing later about that period, Vincent noted that his mother tried to help calm the Wibauts. 'She sent us a telegram saying "be calm and hopeful", and we were visited by someone she had met in Europe, to whom she had sent a telegram asking "kindly visit young Mrs. van Gogh who is lying ill" and giving our address. That helped us more.'[112] Thus Jo was able to support them even though she was far away.

Meanwhile, Vincent was working as a junior draughtsman in the drawing office of the Public Service Electric Company in Newark. His office was on the eighth floor of the New Prudential Building, where the Prudential Assurance Company, to which his company was affiliated, was located. He sent Jo a picture postcard of the building and drew an arrow on it indicating where he worked.[113] He left that job to join a purchasing agency of the Dutch consulting engineer Rudolf Klein. After that Vincent went to work for the Chas. T. Stork Company, where he was responsible for purchasing machinery and metals, formulating specifications and supervising. While with them he made two business trips to the West Coast.[114]

In Amsterdam Jo indulged her literary interests. She went to a lecture on Dutch literature given by Dirk Coster, author of the book *Werk en wezen der kritiek* (1912), in the Larensche Kunsthandel on Herengracht: 'he praised Mrs [Henriette Roland] Holst as a poetess to the skies. I couldn't agree more,' she wrote afterwards to Vincent and Josina.[115] During this period she received a 'fee' of 31.30 guilders from the *NRC*. It is not clear why, but it was probably for doing a small translation.[116] The art historian G.H. Marius praised Jo's conscientious approach to the letters edition and Henriëtte van der Meij also thought she had done a 'wonderful work of piety', doing justice to both brothers.[117] Jo provided two works for an exhibition of modern art organized for the benefit of the Russian Red Cross in 't Binnenhuis in Amsterdam's Raadhuisstraat. She was very unhappy about the rooms that were used, which she felt were much too dark. The proceeds from ticket sales were intended for the good cause.[118]

During this period Jo and Isaac Israëls were getting on so well again that she lent him some Van Goghs for him to study at his leisure. He wrote that he had a weakness for the painting of the green olive trees and followed up on his letter with an ingenious plan: 'I would love to paint another portrait of you, against the background of a Vincent. . . . I promise you'll get everything back safely.'[119] When it came to the point, however, Israëls had great difficulty parting with the loans, particularly the *Sunflowers*, which he believed was 'one of the most important things' that Jo possessed. He borrowed this work at least three times and it served as a background in several of his portraits (Plate 54). He challenged her: 'It's taking credit for what someone else has done. Don't you want to swap anything else??????' She accepted that challenge, and it is possible that this was how Israëls got the *Olive Grove* (F 711 / JH 1791).[120] A year later he was still lamenting that he no longer had the *Sunflowers*.[121] In 1916 Jo and Israëls tried sporadically to see one another again, although his plan to paint a version of a portrait of Jo in the foreground came to nothing.[122] He lent her the book *With Poor Immigrants to America* (1914) by Stephen Graham, and she sent it on to Vincent and Josina, together with the optimistic comment: 'A wonderful new people must surely emerge from the cross-breeding of all those different races.'[123]

Jo told Vincent and Josina in detail about the French socialist Louise Saumoneau, who was arrested on 2 October for distributing anti-war literature. She also wrote: '*Don't worry about money*, that's the only thing I'm concerned about, dear hearts.' She furthermore advised them to wear wool next the skin and expressed her views on all kinds of other matters: 'Didn't I tell you that they eat strange things in America? Bacon, chocolate—ice cream—it makes me shudder. Take care of your stomachs—avoid that ice cream because it's dreadful stuff.'[124]

Vincent and Josina took a few works by Van Gogh with them in their luggage. They lent a couple of drawings and a painting to a New York gallery, which pleased Jo greatly: 'What an incredible coincidence that the exhibition happens to be about Uncle Vincent—it's good that you added that little one to it.' This exhibition was staged at the end of 1915 in Marius de Zayas's Modern Gallery, which had opened in October of that year on the corner of Fifth Avenue and 42nd Street.[125] The painting concerned was Van Gogh's *Butterflies and Poppies* (F 748 / JH 2013), a small work that was indeed no larger than a long-playing record, and Jo wrote to them about it:

> Josje, have you already enjoyed the poppies? Once it's back you must hang it so you can see it when you're in bed—then you'll always have something of a lovely summer morning in your head and in

> your heart. My darling child, if you find yourself brooding about what's happened, always remember Goethe—'bear the inevitable with dignity'—and if you carry the burden together, it makes everything lighter. The words of the English marriage vows are so beautiful: to have and to hold, for better, for worse, for richer, for poorer, in sickness and in health, to love and to cherish, till death us do part—I plight thee my troth. That says it *all*.[126]

The letters Jo sent to America show she was leading an active and busy life. She went to see Kee Vos-Stricker, who was ill. Accompanied by Frans Coenen, she visited Jan and Anna Veth in Bussum, and she went to Lizzy Ansingh's studio. The two women were friends and Ansingh regularly painted and drew in Jo's home (Plates 55, 56 and 57).[127] She went to a party to celebrate the tenth anniversary of the Wereldbibliotheek and planned to attend the extraordinary SDAP conference scheduled for 8 and 9 January 1916 in Arnhem, where Mrs Wibaut was due to speak. At Christmas, Jo's home was full of purple lilac and yellow jasmine. She transferred money to Vincent and Josina at the beginning of 1916. Although they were far apart, mother and son continued to work together closely on their strategic and carefully considered promotion of Van Gogh's art. Jo wrote to him: 'If you can sell a drawing to the museum, I would *certainly* do it, there are *so* many of them! But don't ask too little, I would say a thousand dollars at the very least.'[128] So Vincent had deliberately taken those drawings to the United States to sell.

Jo's tough words

Jo had to conduct a lot of negotiations during her life and sometimes she could play hardball. That proved to be necessary again. She relentlessly chased Paul Cassirer to pay her the royalties for the copies of the letters that had been sold. It was almost March 1916, and she had still not received a cent despite her reminders. She threatened to hand the matter over to her lawyer if he did not respond within fourteen days.[129] Cassirer thought this threat was outrageous. He did not understand why she used such blunt language and he wondered whether she was fully aware that Germany was fighting a major war. Sales in 1915 were so bad that barely any payment could be made. He felt that her intention to instigate legal proceedings demonstrated little tact and he cynically fobbed her off: 'Under German law, it is not possible to bring a suit against a soldier during the campaign.'[130] She nevertheless received her share three months later. Cassirer did write, however, that Mauthner's anthology—the ninth edition of which appeared in 1912—had sold significantly better than their more expensive publication in two large volumes.[131]

There is no evidence to suggest that Jo was embarrassed by Cassirer's reproach. The statement she was sent in June 1916 refers to a sum of 1,904 marks. She wrote a draft of her reply on that letter, querying the number of copies sold (159 in 1914 and 65 in 1915). Was it correct? She would have thought that sales in the second year would actually have been higher. The subsequent 1916 statement gives a figure of 720 marks; so the combined figure for the whole of 1917, and 1918 up to 1 September, worked out at 1,972 marks.[132] Jo was not interested in any departures from the contract and held Cassirer to it. It is likely that her aversion to the war also played a part.

Slowly but surely, more and more contacts were established in America. The French art dealer Stephen Bourgeois and the American art critic Walter Pach visited Vincent and Josina to select drawings for an exhibition. Bourgeois, who owned Van Gogh's painting *Woman Reading a Novel* (F 497 / JH 1632), which had been in the 1913 Armory Show, wanted to see more paintings as well as the drawings, but Vincent and Josina believed that shipping works from the Netherlands would be too risky in wartime. They were right. German U-boats were operating in the Atlantic and the relationship between the United States and Germany was deteriorating. On 7 May 1915, a U-boat sank the ocean liner RMS *Lusitania*, which had 114 American passengers on board. In the end, five drawings and the paintings *Irises* and *Still Life* were exhibited in April 1916 in the Bourgeois Galleries, 668 Fifth Avenue.[133]

Vincent and Josina presented Pach with the three volumes of the letters—which they had also brought with them from the Netherlands for the purpose—and Josina asked Jo whether she was still planning to have it translated into English because Pach had offered to do so himself, although his command of Dutch was far from perfect. 'Once you're here, you would be able to help him, if you wanted to. But if you would prefer to do it yourself, that would be even better of course.'[134] They were obviously expecting Jo to come over. Jo's reply was decisive:

> I'm quite happy for Pach to do it, if he can. *I* won't do it myself. It's too much for me. I'd do the Introduction, but that's all. He would need to find a publisher, which could submit a proposal to us. That's how the German edition was organized—the publisher then pays the translator. I want to help, of course, for example I could do the editing and proofreading or something like that.[135]

Her categorical attitude was short-lived. Before long, she was thinking very differently. She suddenly realized there were opportunities for a new project over which she could keep much better control herself, and she got down to work.

When Vincent was offered a new job in the spring of 1916, an elated Jo took the letter with his good news to Vincent's parents-in-law. They too were delighted. Mr Wibaut wrote very sympathetic letters to America, in which he repeatedly addressed his daughter affectionately as 'poeseken' 'my little kitten'.[136] In her letters, Jo sometimes referred to world news, for example the failed attempt in Berlin to assassinate the social democrat Karl Liebknecht: 'Don't you think that attempt to kill Liebk. was terrible? And by a woman at that. What sort of delusions does someone have to be suffering from to do something like that?'[137] On Women's Day on 16 April she heard Floor Wibaut and Carry Pothuis-Smit speak about female suffrage. On that day Jo went to other socialist meetings in Amsterdam too,

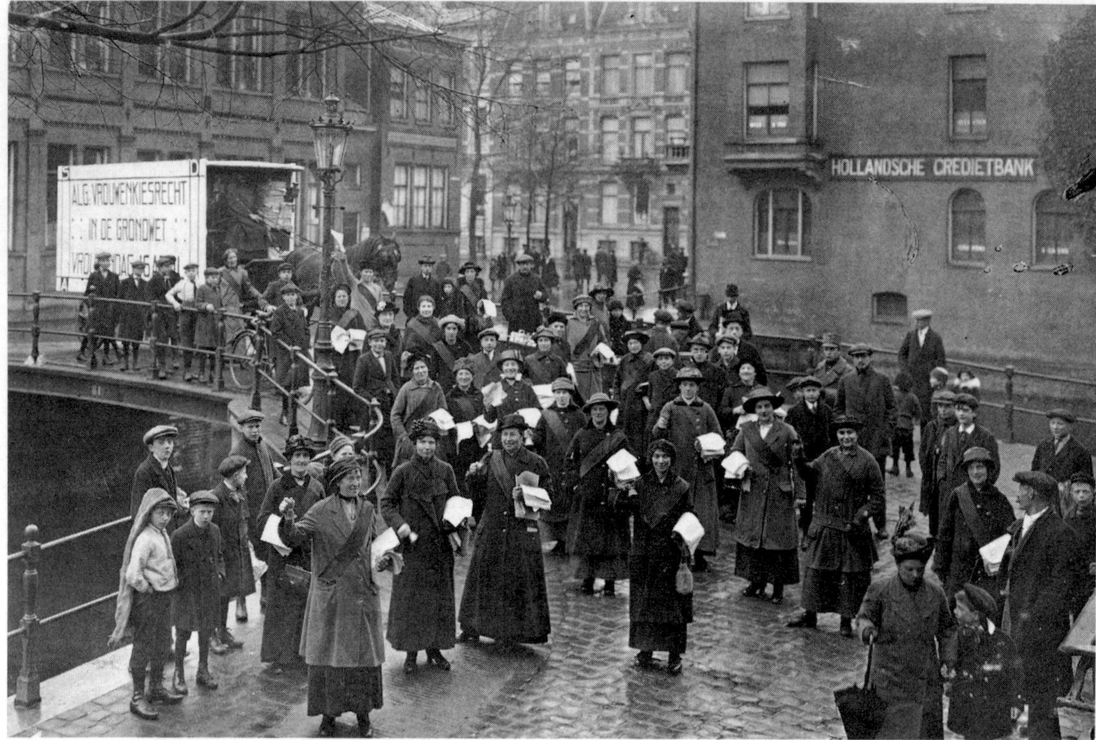

Figure 56 Street propaganda by the women's suffrage society Vereeniging voor Vrouwenkiesrecht in Reguliersgracht in Amsterdam. Vrouwendag (Women's Day) SDAP, 16 April 1916.

at the craftsmen's support group Handwerkers Vriendenkring and in Bellevue, where there were red banners with slogans, for example MOTHERS IN ALL COUNTRIES PROTEST. Wearing a red sash over her coat, she joined the march. The demonstration ended in Thorbeckeplein (Figure 56).[138]

Alongside comments about social upheavals, Jo also always wrote about everyday things. She told Sara de Jong-van Houten that she had had the interior of her home redecorated, and in her letters to Vincent she talked remarkably frequently about flowers and plants: 'In front of me are grape hyacinths in a small glass basket and a few *tiny* red tulips, just like anemones, in a little vase. . . . At the moment I eat American apples now and again. They have a *wonderful* colour and they're really fragrant.' She also told them about a lovely afternoon she spent playing chess with Willem Steenhoff, with whom she discussed recent political developments.[139]

Jo commented thoughtfully that social democracy was a wonderful thing, 'but social democrats often say and write strange things'.[140] She reported the interim results of the elections, which she had discussed in detail with her brother Wim, and she confessed she had given a substantial financial contribution to the SDAP. It is no longer possible to establish exactly how much money Jo gave or whether she did so more than once. It is possible, however, to unearth what the party received in April,

May and June 1916 in the form of payments, contributions, voluntary donations and deposits in the election fund. The total was over 10,000 guilders.[141] In the spring the SDAP advocated lower food prices and in June there was another demonstration in Amsterdam supporting universal suffrage. Jo continued to believe faithfully in a classless utopia, where everyone could live in a dignified way.

At the end of June 1916, she wrote to tell the couple in America that she was having a purple linen dress with a separate shoulder cape made for her, ready for the very hot weather. 'I have your little portraits by my bed. The last things I see when I blow out the candle at night are your sweet faces, and they're the first things I see when I wake up in the morning!' She hoped that something of her inner life was reflected in everything she had written in her long letter that she wrote over four days at the end of June.[142] Soon she would no longer need to communicate by post because they would be sitting face to face again, with fragrant American apples within easy reach.

17

New York-translations of the letters into English

In May 1916 Vincent and Josina moved to Westfield, New Jersey, to the south-west of New York. Mrs Wibaut could see their new domestic situation clearly in her mind's eye, as she wrote in a letter to her daughter: 'I was just thinking how you'll walk around that huge garden in Westfield and think about your work. . . . How lovely it will be to get away from that dreadful hustle and bustle in N.Y., and that you will find all the furnishings there and don't have to drag anything around with you.'[1]

Jo's bed was made up and ready in this spacious house, and she joined her children at the end of the summer. Shortly before that, the photographer Bernard F. Eilers took a portrait of her dressed in her Sunday best (Plate 58). On 12 August she left Rotterdam on the steamship *Rijndam* and arrived on Ellis Island on 27 August. According to the passenger list, she was '5 foot, 3 inches' tall and had brown eyes.[2] The name of the 'servant girl' Marie Eek, twenty-five years old, is immediately below Jo's name on that list. By then she had been working for Jo for five years. They must have got on well together because she remained with Jo for about a year after they returned to Amsterdam in 1919, and they continued to correspond after that.[3] While Jo was in America, Marie looked after the house and cooked the meals.

A major advantage of Westfield was that Annie van Gelder-Pigeaud lived close by. She had studied architecture at Delft University and later became an artist. Jo liked to visit her and her husband Henk. Jo did not meet Annie until she went to America, but she knew about her from all the photographs Josina had sent. She responded to them enthusiastically: 'In one of them she's holding a violin—Jos, that means the two of you can play duets.'[4] As with Jo, reading, social engagement, making music and going to the theatre were part and parcel of life for her children. They went together to a recital by the singer Yvette Guilbert and to a performance of Mussorgsky's *Boris Godunov* in the Metropolitan Opera House.[5] She could borrow books and sheet music from the library free of charge.

Jo was to spend two years and eight months in the United States. She was close to her son and daughter-in-law, and she was in an English-speaking environment, which had a beneficial influence on her as she worked on the translations of Van Gogh's letters into English. In the end she translated the introduction and two-thirds of the letters herself.[6] After her death, Cornelis de Dood translated what remained. In his opinion Jo had been a 'painstaking and honest' translator.[7]

The international art trade was essentially at a standstill during the war, so Jo was able to set aside her normal business activities for a while.[8] Before she left, however, she did agree to lend the Rijksmuseum fifty-six Van Goghs. Alongside works by a few other 'ultra-modern' artists, they were exhibited for an extended period, and this significantly enhanced Van Gogh's fame and the recognition of his work. The museum's deputy director Willem Steenhoff made a considered selection and Jo's brother Andries, who had been living in Amsterdam since 1901, supervised the way all the works were packed for shipment. There were many positive reactions, especially after the paintings were moved to an area with better lighting in November 1917.[9]

Trotsky speaks

In October 1916, two months after her arrival, they moved to 1815 7th Avenue, 111th Street, virtually bordering on Central Park.[10] They lived there for over a year. During that period Jo corresponded again with Israëls, whom she kept informed about how things were going overseas. He wrote excitedly back, encouraging her to do something else for a change: 'Go to a *good* cinema in New York from time to time and tell me if you ever see anything *there* other than my old enemy *Bunny*, and if those real American films are just as stupid as the ones that you always see here.'[11] We do not know whether Jo was a cinemagoer or was aware of John Bunny, who starred in early silent films. The visible traces she left behind in the city relate, as ever, to Van Gogh. In the spring of 1917, after careful consideration, she donated the three volumes of the letters to the New York Public Library, for which the director thanked her. The library reported her gift in its *Bulletin*.[12]

She told Steenhoff that living in a small flat on the sixth floor had become too inconvenient and claustrophobic, and in 1917 they all moved to a house with a small garden surrounded by trees at 49 Park Avenue, (Long Island) Jamaica, just outside Manhattan. Vincent commuted to work.[13] Meanwhile, one visit a week to the bustling city was more than enough for Jo (Figure 57).[14]

Vincent and Josina had various friends whom Jo also got to know: the Van Gelders, of course, and also the Rutgers and Baarslag families, Walter and Magdalene (Magda) Pach and their small son Raymond, and Algernon Lee. Lee was one of the founders of the Socialist Party of America (SPA) and educational director of the Rand School of Social Science, an educational institute and research organization closely linked to the SPA. Josina probably worked in the school's library, which she and Vincent visited frequently.[15] The school also provided education for workers, endeavoured to increase class consciousness and organized summer camps for socialists and people actively involved in the

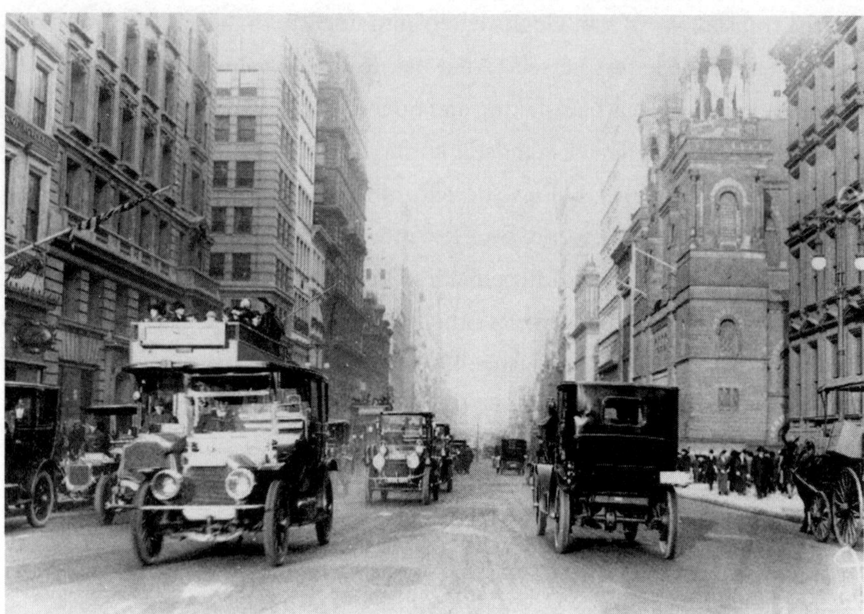

Figure 57 New York, Fifth Avenue, 1918.

unions. Lee co-authored the controversial anti-war resolution during the SPA's St Louis Emergency Convention in 1917.

Jo indulged her political interests in various ways. On several occasions between 14 January and 27 March 1917, for example, she went with Vincent and Josina to hear Russian revolutionary activist Leon Trotsky speak in public.[16] Trotsky had lived as an exile in Europe for a few years, but he was expelled when he set up a Communist organization in Paris, and moved to the United States. In New York he was welcomed as a hero by Russian emigrants with Socialist sympathies. Interviews with him and articles written by him appeared in their newspaper *Novy Mir* as well as in the Jewish newspaper *Forverts*. He made speeches at the Cooper Union, the Harlem River Park Casino and elsewhere, in Russian to begin with and later in German. A visitor described his addresses as 'powerful and electrifying'. Trotsky preached hellfire and damnation for the allies and declared that the social revolution could wait no longer. The horrors of capitalism had to be eradicated and revolution had to bring about an end to war. He observed with disappointment that on 6 April 1917 America had declared war on Germany and joined the allies. A revolt had broken out in Moscow and Petrograd (now St Petersburg) the month before, and in May Trotsky returned to Russia and became chair of the local council (soviet). Four months later, power was seized by the Marxist Bolsheviks led by Vladimir Ilyich Ulyanov, better known as Lenin. The proletariat had temporarily defeated the bourgeoisie.[17]

It is not surprising that while she was in New York, Jo did not want to miss this greatly admired speaker, who later played such a crucial role in the Russian Revolution. Her contemporary Henriette Roland Holst met Trotsky and other major players, including Lenin, Liebknecht and Rosa Luxemburg, at the International Socialist Congress in Stuttgart in the summer of 1907, and in 1915 she had extensive discussions with him at a meeting in the Zimmerwald in Switzerland, where a motion condemning the war was passed. She felt irresistibly drawn to him and wrote that revolution-leaning Western socialists glorified the young Trotsky. He was a saint with a halo, shrouded in a romantic haze.[18] Jo, too, was not immune to his charisma. Later she wrote to Steenhoff about the few times she had listened to him perform: 'he has a persuasive, powerful way of expressing himself; uncompromising—I remember thinking at the time that this man could do anything!'[19]

A letter from Willem Steenhoff brought Jo's attention once more to the name of Kröller. Steenhoff was short of money and wrote that with a very heavy heart he had been obliged to part company with Van Gogh's *Path in the Garden of the Asylum* (F 733 / JH 1845), which he had obtained from her.[20] He confessed to her it had been sold to Anton Kröller for ten thousand guilders; but tried to make the best of the situation by consoling her that it would at least stay in the country. After he had paid off his debts, he deposited what was left in an account in the name of his mistress Coba Snethlage. He wrote to Jo: 'I believe it would be even safer if, in the event of my death, you could provide some sort of proof that you had given it to her.... You see this is an emotionally painful matter for me. I would have preferred to tell you in person, but perhaps it's better to do it in writing.'[21] He was much relieved by Jo's understanding response to his confession.[22]

It was nevertheless distressing, all the more so because Jo gave Steenhoff *Path in the Garden of the Asylum* in December 1910 after he had been forced to sell *Poplars in the Mountains* (F 638 / JH 1797), again because he was in urgent need of money. Steenhoff and Coba had been so very happy with *Path in the Garden*, as he wrote to Jo: 'Its appearance changes incessantly, *as though it's alive*'. As far as they were concerned, this gesture was evidence of Jo's unconditional friendship. At the time they had given the living room a makeover so that the canvas, 'with its rich *bronze* colouring', would look at its best. 'But rest assured, it will always be at your disposal,' he promised.[23] The fact that Steenhoff risked the friendship by selling the painting after all reveals the magnitude of his financial problems. One thing was clear: come what may, the two paintings were forever beyond Jo and Vincent's reach.

1917 saw the publication of the *Catalogus van de schilderijenverzameling van Mevrouw H. Kröller-Müller. 's-Gravenhage, Lange Voorhout*, compiled by H.P. Bremmer, cataloguing Mrs Kröller-Müller's collection. It is not clear whether Jo acquired a copy, and as far as we know she never visited the collection either before or after the catalogue appeared. This might have been because it was necessary to request permission beforehand in writing from Helene Kröller-Müller. At the time the couple owned 408 works, of which seventy-three were by Van Gogh.[24] And the end of Helene's buying spree was not yet on the horizon. In December 1918 she bought Van Gogh's *Pink Peach Trees ('Souvenir de Mauve')* for twenty-five thousand guilders from Elisabeth van den Broek-Mauve, Anton Mauve's daughter. This really astronomical price was the highest that she, or anyone else, had ever paid for a Van Gogh. A month later she acquired *Sower with Setting Sun* (F 422 / JH 1470), also for a hefty sum. As time passed, her Van Gogh collection cemented its ever more impressive second place, behind that of Jo and Vincent.[25] It was extended once again on 18 May 1920, when Bremmer, acting on Helene's instructions, purchased twenty-six paintings and six drawings by Van Gogh for over 110,000 guilders at the sale of items from the estate of Lodewijk Cornelis Enthoven; three works from his period in the South of France accounted for 48,000 guilders.[26] These transactions demonstrated that the prices of Van Gogh's better paintings were increasing at an unprecedented rate, and that trend also benefitted Jo and Vincent.

Carl Zigrosser

At the end of 1917, Jo, Vincent and Josina became friends with Carl Zigrosser, a devoted art lover and conscientious objector, who had taken part in various anti-war demonstrations (Figure 58). Walter Pach, who had been Zigrosser's mentor and guide at the 1913 Armory Show, was instrumental in adding Van Gogh, Cézanne and Munch to his absolute favourites.[27] At the time, Zigrosser was working for the print dealership Frederick Keppel & Company and as editor of *The Modern School: A Monthly Magazine Devoted to Libertarian Ideas in Education.* At first the magazine, a jewel of typography and printing, was purely educational, but under Zigrosser's influence it featured poetry and art as well as liberal child rearing ideas. In his autobiographical manuscripts published after his death in *My Own Shall Come To Me*, Zigrosser describes how his friendship with Jo resulted in the inclusion of some extracts from Van Gogh's letters in *The Modern School*, together with reproductions of his drawings. Referring to seventeenth-century Dutch art, Zigrosser described Jo's vitality and youthful spirit: 'With her sparkling eyes and ruddy complexion, she looked like a Frans Hals portrait come to life. Her spirit was so youthful and her response to world events, art, drama, and education was so alert that she made us youngsters feel like greybeards.'[28]

His estate contains a few letters from Jo.[29] She wrote the earliest known one on 24 January 1918 from 49 Park Avenue, (Long Island) Jamaica, despite her doctor's advice not to write it herself because she was suffering so badly from cramps in her hands. They were the first indications of Parkinson's disease.[30] The letter is a response to Zigrosser's proposal to include passages from Van Gogh's letters. She was very much in favour of the idea. According to her, the challenge would be 'to find something in connection with art education!'—and with that goal in mind she tried to make a selection. An announcement in the June issue awakened readers of *The Modern School*'s interest in letters penned by Vincent, this 'eminent Dutch artist', who had received so much support from his brother, Theo. Jo selected eight extracts, which were published in the July 1918 issue, with the note: 'Authorized translation by J. van Gogh-Bonger'.

Zigrosser's accompanying introduction to the letters, which he could not have written without information from Jo, is interesting. In it he praised all aspects of her work, personality and modern views about raising children:

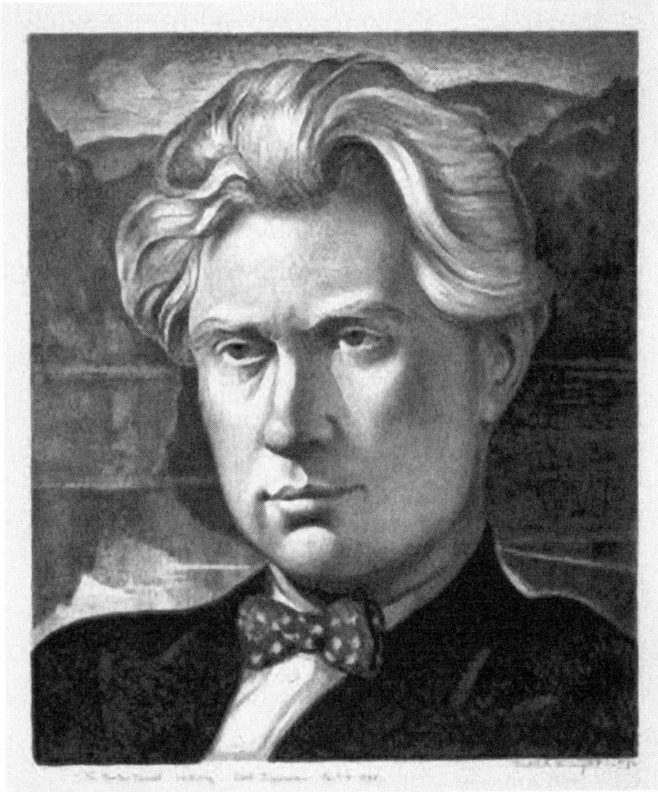

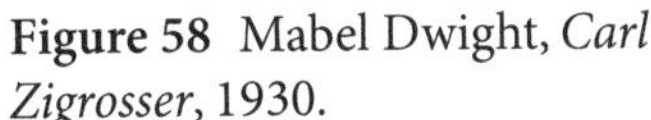

Figure 58 Mabel Dwight, *Carl Zigrosser*, 1930.

> This number contains a very important and original contribution to art and letters in the shape of extracts from letters of the great Post-Impressionist painter, Vincent van Gogh. They are written to his brother Theo and have never before been published in English. They appear here by the courtesy of Mrs. J. van Gogh-Bonger, who is translating the entire correspondence. She is the widow of Theodore van Gogh, and is herself a splendidly vigorous and alert personality. She has such a cultured, finely-balanced nature that increasing years will constantly bring her a finer and profounder insight, more serenity and an even more beautiful sense of values. She loves children and has rational ideas about education. She believes especially in the cultivation of a child's individuality without the arbitrary hindrance of parental authority.

He described Van Gogh as being 'modern in his humanitarianism and freedom from prejudice; he is, he writes, of the new generation, he must be true to it and oppose the old'. In conclusion, Zigrosser allowed himself to make an intriguing observation about Van Gogh's literary preferences: 'He loved Dickens, Harriet Beecher Stowe, Hugo, and Michelet. It is strange he never mentions Dostojevsky. He would have loved his stories had he known of them. Indeed, what is Vincent's whole life and character but an episode from a Dostojevsky novel.'[31]

The August 1919 issue of the magazine contained a further series of extracts from letters written by Van Gogh, this time while he was in The Hague. Reference was again made to this first publication in English, and it was expressly stated that Jo had authorized the translation.[32]

The Modern School was not just the magazine's title. It was also used as the collective name for the educational bastions established by the same anarchist movement. These schools were intended for workers' children and managed by workers themselves. The underlying aim was to abolish all forms of authority, and in so doing to herald a new society based on voluntary cooperation between individuals. The first school opened its doors in New York in 1911. Later on, another community was established around the Ferrer Colony and Modern School, named after the Spanish freethinker and anarchist Francisco Ferrer, who had set up a similar type of school ten years before. At this time, educational innovations based on a range of approaches emerged at several locations. Maria Montessori's method was one of them. Jo looked on the Modern School as more than just a channel to enhance awareness of Van Gogh's letters. It was also a circle of like-minded people who confirmed her ideas about progressive child rearing.[33]

At the beginning of 1918, she asked Steenhoff to lend the paintings *Sunflowers* (F 458 / JH 1667 or F 454 / JH 1562) and *The Yellow House ('The Street')* (F 464 / JH 1589) to Isaac Israëls so that they could serve as a source of inspiration and as repoussoirs.[34] She complained again about painful cramps that made it difficult for her to write. A few months after this, she was forced to start dictating her letters and took on the twenty-three-year-old Helen Opel, who would also help her translate the Van Gogh letters. She deliberately chose someone who was young. Years later, Johnson-Opel recalled that Jo loved having 'young folks around her'.[35] Jo told Steenhoff she discovered new things in the letters every day, despite having read them so often. She also wrote that she had heard that Van Gogh's works were hung very well in the Rijksmuseum, and that she was suddenly overcome by a great sense of loss: 'all of a sudden I had a terribly strong desire to have all the things I've had around me throughout my life, the trees in blossom, the Arles landscape—everything, everything.' Yet she was also very appreciative of New York. In her opinion the city was an incredible melting pot of nationalities; she furthermore detected all kinds of traces of Dutch settlers. Jo and Steenhoff were members of the same political party, and so she gave him her views about recent political developments: 'Isn't what's happening in Russia wonderful? You've always predicted it would happen in Russia! I'm following events with passionate interest; this is what we've been waiting for all this anxious time.' She also told him there were a few artists in their circle of acquaintances, including the English painter and art historian Stephen Haweis.[36] Haweis had asked Jo about the relationship between Van Gogh and Gauguin, and she had let him read her translation of the introduction to the letters, which tells us that she had completed it in the meantime.[37] It was an important trump card that could enable her to effectively expand her circle of influential people interested in Van Gogh.

Meanwhile, there was increasingly overt recognition in the Netherlands of Jo and her dedication to Van Gogh's work. In an article in the *Haarlemsche Courant* of 7 March 1918, Johannes de Bois outlined the history, starting with the 'storage shed in Bussum', and described Jo as an 'astute woman'; it was primarily thanks to her—even though there had been 'many helpful factors'—that Van Gogh's work had become so widely appreciated.[38] She heard from Willem Steenhoff that there had been a very widespread response to the Dutch edition of the letters, and he urged her to continue with the English translation. He updated Jo in detail about the latest developments in the Rijksmuseum. He had moved the loans, including Jo's, to galleries in the new wing (the current Philips Wing), part of which was intended for the Drucker-Fraser Collection of nineteenth-century paintings. Now, though, it also housed Van Gogh's paintings. 'I think I already told you that I had the collection moved to one of the Drucker galleries upstairs because of the better light.' All that remained now was to clear up the confusion among the visitors: 'The attendant downstairs told me that visitors were often disappointed because they thought the paintings had gone again'[39] (Figure 59). The way Steenhoff described the placement of the works on the walls indicates the care he took as deputy director:

> The view of Arles is in the middle, flanked by the canvas of the blue irises on one side and the Japanese interpretation on the other. This automatically brings out the view of Arles and amplifies the sunlight. Above them, as a crowning glory, are the sunflowers. I'll get the arrangement photographed one of these days. A few of the last works are on a short wall: the bedroom in the middle and the wheatfield beneath thunderclouds above it; their proximity has a very powerful effect. The interpretation of Delacroix is close by. Naturally this exhibition is a really special event for very many people. But I sense and I'm also becoming aware that it's giving rise to irritation in a certain clique here in our contrary Holland.

The precarious condition of the paintings came up once again and Steenhoff gave her the following prudent advice to consider:

> It would be highly desirable to have some paintings cleaned under professional supervision, for example the bedroom, where over time rather a lot of dirt has accumulated on the light colours. I'm convinced the work would benefit. Think about it. We have a very suitable and trusted man in the museum. This is separate from the varnish issue (a very thin layer). I know that you're completely opposed to it.[40]

From a contemporary viewpoint it remains hard to estimate whether Jo should have acted before, when De Bois and Oldenzeel-Schot made recommendations about restoring the paintings, or now when Steenhoff urged the same. Be that as it may, she was not convinced and remained extremely cautious about it throughout her life.[41] In November 1923, when Ernest Brown & Phillips proposed varnishing a few works, her response was still as implacable:

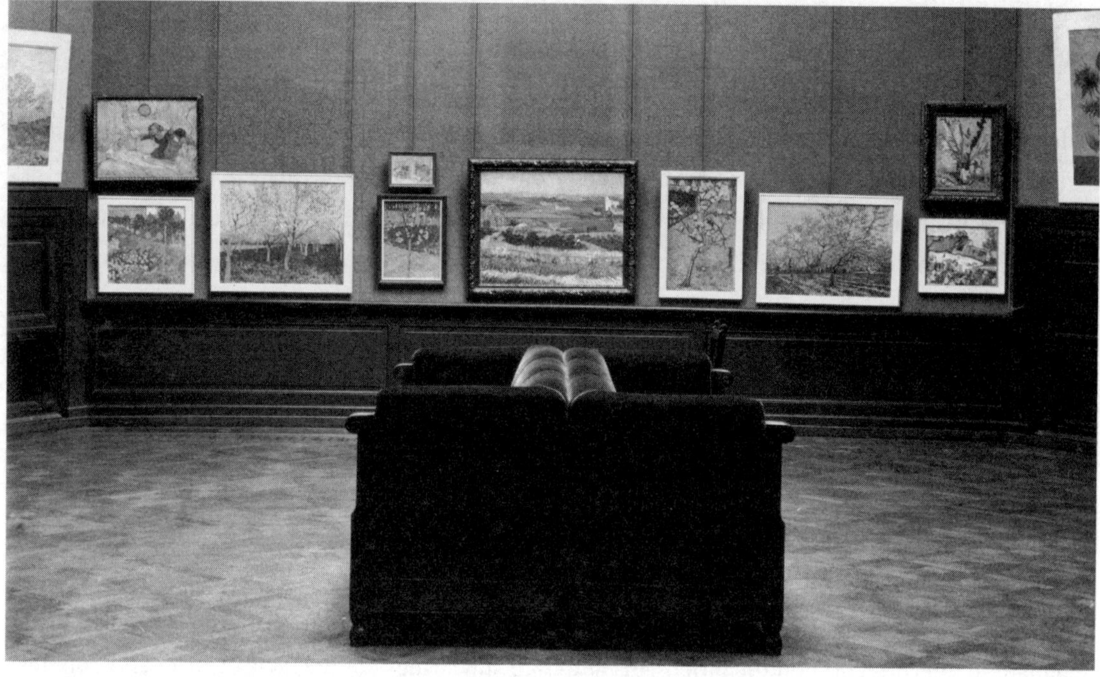

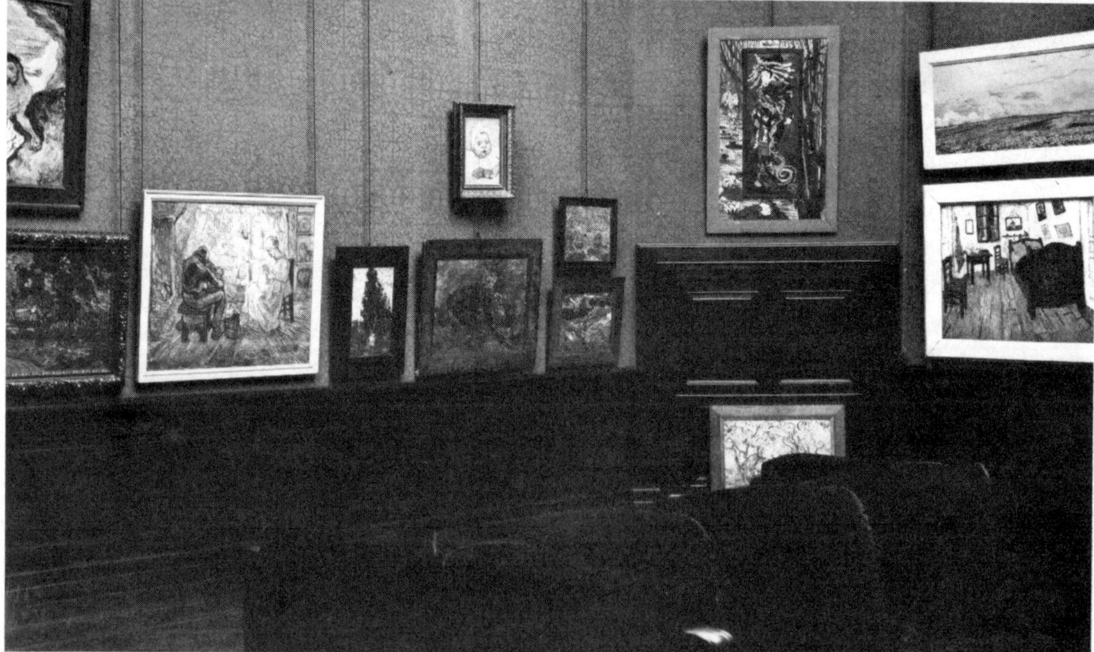

Figure 59 Works by Van Gogh exhibited in the Rijksmuseum's Drucker galleries, 1918.

> On no account do I want the paintings to be varnished; I am strongly opposed to it, and forbid it for any picture of our collection. I express myself rather strongly on this subject, because I know it spoils the beautiful aspect. I have seen some pictures, which German collectionneurs had varnished, and I found the effect horrible, Van Gogh's technique does not agree with varnish.[42]

Initially, during his Dutch period, Vincent had used varnish himself and had even suggested to Theo that varnish should be applied to enliven darker colours or prevent the paintings from 'sinking in', in other words becoming dull as oil migrates out of the paint. Later, though, in part due to the influence of the Post-Impressionists, he changed his mind and elected not to varnish the paint surface. Jo adopted a position in line with this later, revised view. The fact that in retrospect this was a fortunate decision is confirmed by the conservator Ella Hendriks, who commented as follows: 'Given current opinion in conservation and restoration circles, Jo's reservations with regard to treatment was preferable to the campaign of universal wax/resin relining followed by varnishing.'[43] Yet that dubious 'campaign' was unavoidable. It was initiated in March 1926, a good six months after Jo's death, by Steenhoff, the restorer J.C. Traas and Vincent because it was really vital to do something. Paint had begun to detach, Steenhoff had found residues of fly droppings and the relining and cleaning of the paintings simply could not be put off any longer. Van Gogh had sent many of his studies to Theo without a stretcher or strainer and, as time passed, they had been given protection in the form of a lining (some were mounted on cardboard, others on panel) but these had to be replaced. Traas set to work. Between 1926 and 1933 he replaced supports, lined the works and mounted them on stretchers. In very many cases, Traas varnished the paintings.[44]

Rockaway Park, Long Island

In July 1918, from her new address at 348 119th Beach, Rockaway Park, Long Island (on the Rockaway Peninsula, between Jamaica Bay and the Atlantic Ocean), Jo wrote to Carl Zigrosser, thanking him for sending the copies of the July edition of *The Modern School*. She and her friends found the magazine '*very* interesting'. In her letter she also told him that she had meanwhile completed the English translation of volume 1 of the letters.[45]

At that moment Vincent and Josina were staying briefly in Berkeley, California, and before long they moved to Kobe in Japan for a year, where Vincent went to work for the firm of Chas T. Stork. Josina gave Jo permission to open her mail before she forwarded it so she would immediately know the latest news, so it is clear that they kept no secrets from one another in their correspondence.[46] Just before they left Berkeley, Vincent and Josina were welcomed by Walter and Magda Pach. They wrote to Jo about it during their stopover in Honolulu. A year later, on 30 August 1919, they returned from

Yokohama on the steamship *Empress of Japan*, arriving in Vancouver on 19 September.[47] After that Vincent worked briefly for a foundry in Newark, where Rudolf Klein, whom we encountered earlier, was managing director.

While Vincent and Josina were in Japan, Pach invited Jo to come to California, but she did not take him up on the offer because she was wary of such a long journey. She looked forward to the arrival of Travis Lindquist, who was a friend of Magda Pach's, and wanted to come and help Jo to check her translations. Despite missing the children, she was very happy in her new home and this time she enjoyed the summer weather. She continued to correspond with Pach, although it was less easy for her than before: 'I dictated this letter to give my arm a rest.' Only the postscript and the signature were in her own handwriting.[48] During this period she also received support from the Baarslag family, who lived nearby.[49] Jo wrote to the Gachet family expressing her relief and delight at the ending of the First World War.[50]

At the very end of her stay, she did a translation into English for *The Modern School*. Written by the poet Maurits Wagenvoort, who had also translated poems from the famous poetry collection, it was part of the introduction to the Dutch translation of Walt Whitman's *Leaves of Grass*. Wagenvoort met Whitman in 1892 and was immediately gripped by the American's poetry. He published the first translations in 1898 under the title *Natuurleven*. The extended collection, *Grashalmen*, appeared in 1917. Jo knew that Van Gogh had been enthusiastic about Whitman's lyrical and earthy verse, which made this translation assignment particularly interesting.[51] She asked Zigrosser to review her translation critically, and then sent him a follow-up postcard because she was still in two minds about one word—evidence of her dedication and precision. Jo's translation of Wagenvoort's contribution, 'Walt Whitman: A Dutch View', ran in the April-May edition of *The Modern School*, which devoted sixty pages exclusively to the poet and his output.[52] She asked Zigrosser to send a copy of the issue to her friend Annie van Gelder-Pigeaud at Manetto Hill Farm, Hicksville, Long Island. Some time later, she told him that the Whitman special had generated a great deal of interest in Amsterdam, and then took out a subscription to the magazine on behalf of herself and Mathilde Wibaut-Berdenis van Berlekom.

Towards the end of her time in America, Jo stayed with various friends, finally spending a few days in New York, where she visited Zigrosser in his gallery. While in the city she saw 'the most modern French pictures', but it is not clear whether that was at his premises.[53] They remained in touch and sent one another New Year greetings during the years that followed. Zigrosser wrote that he had seen a few beautiful Van Goghs, whereupon Jo responded enthusiastically: 'Some day you must come over and see those in our house! They are the best of all!'[54] During the summer of 1922, Zigrosser did indeed visit her. In his memoirs he wrote about the deep impression the art collection made on him; he was almost as impressed by Jo's Persian carpet table cover, a Dutch custom completely alien to foreigners. He clearly recalled that it was removed before the table was laid. He also thought that the ritual of having coffee or tea together was very special. Many years later, in 1954, he and his wife Laura visited Vincent.[55]

Loving tyranny

Jo's years in New York had been an extraordinary experience and she looked back on them with satisfaction. Her stay had broadened her horizons, she had met many new and inspiring friends and made good progress with her translations, which were also published in *The Modern School*.[56] But she had imposed herself on her children rather too often and was very demanding, at least in the perception of her son, who confided in his diary half a century later that her inescapable presence had also had a downside: 'in some respects she made things difficult for us; she could have tried to fit in with us a bit more.'[57] When, in the 1960s, Vincent thanked J.H. Reisel for sending him the published version of the latter's thesis on Isaac Israëls, he made a remarkable comment: 'When searching for the origin of all creative work, outside the art field, too, one can always look back to a mother figure; at least that's my own experience when I look around me.' He must have recognized something about his relationship with his mother in the picture that Reisel had sketched of the influence of Israëls's mother, who was the type of dominant woman

> who wants to continue to protect her son under her wing, even though he believes he doesn't need this protection.... Loving tyranny and protective bossiness appear to be her strongest characteristics.... She is the classic overprotective mother type.[58]

It is fair to ask to what extent Vincent felt that Jo's influence on his life was coercive and oppressive. Presumably she needed a great deal of attention and there were more demanding, unspoken expectations than the sources reveal. Jo liked to retain control over things because she was afraid of losing her grip, and her Vincent, whom she always wanted nearby, must have realized that. He knew his role was crucial. He had to alleviate her feelings of loneliness and must not disappoint her in any way whatsoever. Throughout his life he must have sensed and known that she wanted to make a hero of him, as she had once written in her diary.

On 23 April 1919, Jo left New York on the steamship *Rotterdam* and arrived in the Netherlands on 4 May. The liner could carry 3,500 passengers, but there were only 827 on board. The passenger list reveals she travelled first class. Her first name was Americanized to Jeane.[59] 'Aunt Jeane' took Indian outfits, including feather headdresses, for her young nephews Henk and Frans, her brother Wim's sons (Figure 60). She had bought them in a 'real Indian village'. She also brought them the children's book *Oh Skin-nay! The Days of Real Sport* (1913) written by Wilbur D. Nesbit and illustrated by Clare Briggs.[60]

In September 1919, Floor Wibaut, accompanied by his wife Mathilde and their daughter Annemarie, went to America, where they visited Josina and Vincent. At that time things were not going well with Josina. Four years after her breast had been removed, she was treated again and had to undergo radiotherapy. The wound healed slowly, but she persevered and was discharged from the hospital on

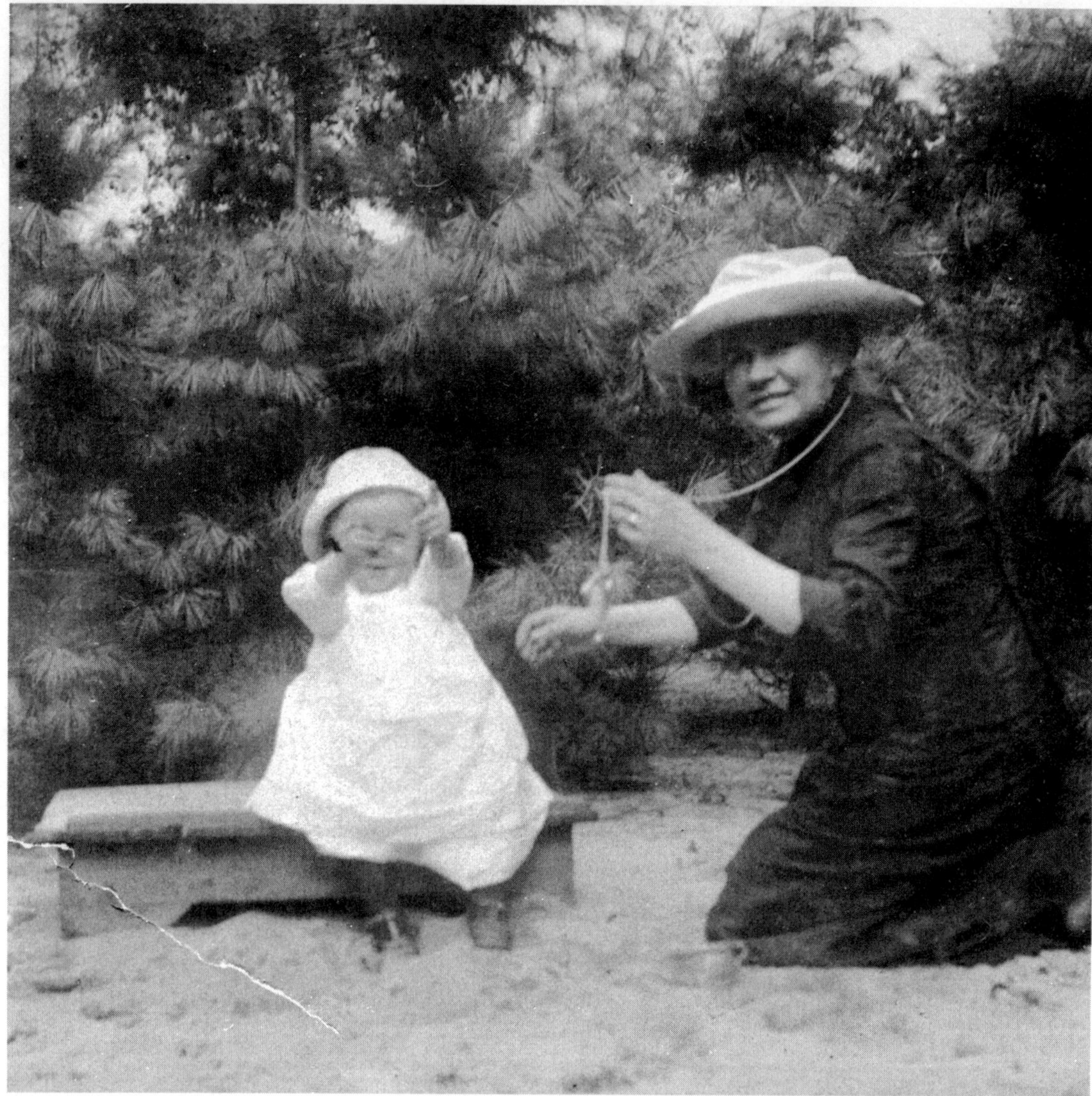

Figure 60 Henk Bonger with his aunt Jo Cohen Gosschalk-Bonger, 1912.

9 January 1920. The idea was that they would repatriate within the foreseeable future. Mathilde hoped that Vincent would be able to find work in the Netherlands and she told Floor, who had only been able to stay for a few weeks and was back in Amsterdam: 'He is so very taken with America and doesn't have a good word to say about Holland. That often makes me very anxious. But if something, or a prospect of something, comes up for him soon, he'll become more reconciled to the idea.'[61] With her two daughters and her son-in-law, she visited Morris Hillquit, one of the leaders of the Socialist Party of America.

They returned to Amsterdam on 31 January 1920. Initially Vincent and Josina were registered as living at Jo's address. A few months later, they moved into a home of their own, a kilometre away at 13 Alexander Boersstraat.[62] At the time Jo was not uncritical about them because she apparently thought they were very formal. As Vincent wrote later in his diary: 'My mother often said we were so stiff.'[63] Gustave Coquiot's opinion of the Van Goghs' attitude after a visit he made in 1922 was very clear. He thought that all three were nice enough but rather eccentric, and Vincent and Josina were extraordinarily reserved and remote:

> This whole family makes a curious impression: she, the mother, he, the son, the daughter-in-law, sickly, strange, strange. Him, looking so stupid! A wound-up automaton, guarded. The mother, ill, nervous, trembling with age (and she's not even 60); the daughter-in-law, cold, unpleasant—withdrawn! . . . Little encouragement to return—but how Mrs van Gogh-Bonger reveres Vincent![64]

Yet that supposed rigidity was not an obstacle to Vincent as far as society was concerned. He became a consulting engineer with the firm 'Organisatie Advies Bureau', which he founded with his university friend Ernst Hijmans. Initially the consultancy advised primarily in the fields of scheduling, stock management and job analysis. At a later stage the focus shifted more towards recommendations about staffing plans, building services and management audits. They received numerous commissions from the Dutch government and from domestic and foreign enterprises. Their collaboration ended in 1934, after which Vincent ran the business alone from his business address 209 Herengracht until 1965.[65]

Once Jo had become acclimatized again to her familiar surroundings at 77 Koninginneweg / 2 Brachthuijzerstraat, she continued with her translations in so far as her insidious illness permitted, and resumed her involvement with exhibitions, often in close consultation with Vincent. As a result, she was faced with some difficult decisions during the last six years of her life. Jo had a lot to do and it was always work that caused her a good deal of worry, although that was evidently not apparent to others. In 1972, in the *NRC Handelsblad*, H.A.E. Vogler-Korthals Altes, who had lived at 1 Brachthuijzerstraat, described her quiet neighbour in terms that did not wholly reflect reality: 'She lived a very retiring life. Sometimes she stood in her bay window, always soberly dressed, looking out at the traffic, which was light in those days, in Koninginneweg. . . . A quiet and consequently easily forgotten figure.'[66]

18

A sacrifice for Vincent's glory

Alongside her work translating the letters, the ostensibly 'quiet' Jo continued to conduct business correspondence relating to publications, exhibitions, searching for an overseas publisher for the letters and whether or not to donate works to reputable institutions. At the end of 1919, the art dealer Gaston Bernheim asked for her authorization to publish a book about Van Gogh's work; Octave Mirbeau was to write the introduction and the art critic Théodore Duret the remainder. He asked Jo for an overview of the most important publications about the painter all over the world and then made a bold proposal—that she should donate a painting to the Museé du Luxembourg. 'They would prefer flowers,' he added. His strongest argument for making such a gift was the fact that previously a Van Gogh from the Camondo Collection had ended up in the Louvre. Jo and Vincent knew that flower still life well. They had stood in front of it five years before. Bernheim believed that the inclusion of Van Gogh's work in such landmark collections was an ideal way to underline the artist's glory.[1] It was a nice idea and it could certainly have strengthened his trading position, but there are no indications that Jo and Vincent ever seriously considered this proposal. They probably wanted to avoid creating a precedent.

Jo did ensure, however, that her activities became known to a wider circle: 'Mrs van Gogh-Bonger is working on an English edition of Vincent van Gogh's "Letters" for publication in New York and London,' reported the *Algemeen Handelsblad* and *Het Vaderland* on 17 January 1920.[2] And she told the publisher and art collector Willem Scherjon, board member of the Utrecht art lovers' association 'Voor de Kunst', that he could borrow the *Sunflowers* and the *Irises* for 'Flower Still Lifes by Dutch Masters from the Beginning of the Seventeenth Century to the Present Day', an exhibition which was to run from mid-February to mid-March 1920. She had to retract her offer, however, because she had also received a request from abroad, and she preferred to send the painting of sunflowers there: 'So you'll be getting the *Irises*—plus a smaller one: *Gladioli*, also a first-rate Van Gogh,' she reassured Scherjon politely but firmly.[3] No one needed to tell her about the hierarchy of the works in the collection.

Attempted launches in New York

At the beginning of 1920, Jo received a telegram from the art dealer Newman Emerson Montross, whom she had met in New York. He had a gallery at 550 Fifth Avenue and wanted to organize an exhibition, and Walter Pach would be assisting him.[4] She and Vincent generously agreed to participate and entrusted the shipping of sixty-three works to the reliable firm of J.S. Fetter & Co, which restored the frames first and made five new crates for a sum of over a thousand guilders.[5] The shipment arrived in New York at the beginning of August—in plenty of time since the exhibition ran from 23 October to 31 December.[6] Mother and son hoped this wide-ranging selection would provide a comprehensive introduction to Van Gogh's work in America, and also assist Montross in finding an American publisher for the letters. Jo therefore also sent him a copy of the Dutch edition as well as her English translation of the introduction.[7]

By the end of the exhibition's first week there was an offer of 8,000 dollars for Van Gogh's *Joseph Roulin* (F 436 / JH 1675). Vincent accepted it, but for some unknown reason the transaction did not take place. As ever, people found the prices excessive. Both parties would have been very disappointed if nothing were sold, so they tried to devise a solution.[8] Jo received letters from friends saying that Montross's exhibition of the paintings was excellent, so she consented to leave the works with him until May 1922. She furthermore cut asking prices by a substantial 20 per cent, except for *Snow-Covered Field with a Plough and Harrow (after Jean-François Millet)* (F 632 / JH 1882) and a *Landscape in Arles*, whose prices were reduced by 10 per cent. Jo concluded from press cuttings she had received that only Pach really understood Van Gogh's art. During her stay in New York, she told Montross, 'I saw there the most modern French pictures and I supposed the American taste in art was advanced enough, fully to appreciate Van Gogh in which I have been rather mistaken.'[9] Cutting prices did the trick. Three works were sold to the art collector and theologian Theodore Pitcairn from Pennsylvania for 14,800 dollars (equivalent to some 35,000 guilders). They were *Adeline Ravoux* (F 769 / JH 2037), *Sower* (F 575a / JH 1596) and the drawing *Sorrow* (F 929a / JH 130). So despite the discount, the proceeds were still substantial.[10]

Within six months of the exhibition in Montross's gallery, paintings by Van Gogh were hanging in the Metropolitan Museum of Art in New York. The exhibition 'Impressionist and Post-Impressionist Paintings' was staged there from 3 May to 15 September 1921. Jo and Vincent provided four works for it, with Montross acting as intermediary.[11] They were *Joseph Roulin* (F 436 / JH 1675), *Snow-Covered Field with a Plough and Harrow (after Jean-François Millet)* (F 632 / JH 1882), *Van Gogh's Chair* (F 498 / JH 1635) and *Carafe and Dish with Citrus Fruit* (F 340 / JH 1239).[12] Van Gogh's name would become better known thanks to leading exhibitions like these in prestigious museums such as the Metropolitan, and as a result prices might start to climb again. But again, Jo was disappointed by the reviews that Montross had sent her because the reviewers had not understood Van Gogh's modernity. Vexed, she replied to him: 'It is the fate of critics to be remembered by what they failed to understand.'[13]

Montross also arranged for the Anderson Galleries, at Park Avenue and 59th Street in New York, to exhibit three drawings and six paintings by Van Gogh, including the *Pietà (after Delacroix)* and the *Irises*, under the auspices of the Holland-America Society.[14] And he wrote to Jo that five Van Goghs had been exhibited in Chicago among other Impressionist works, but there, too, they remained unsold. 'We are following the art movements in America with the greatest interest; the modern painters have to make their way still,' she observed resignedly.[15] She consented to the works staying for a further year, until May 1923. When the deadline arrived, Montross was given permission to retain a few works that he thought still stood at least a chance of being sold. The rest were shipped shortly afterwards. Only *Mill on Montmartre* remained, but the following year that painting was returned too.[16] In the end the result was evidently a disappointment for Jo despite all the efforts and good intentions.

Fact and fiction

At the end of 1920, Julius Meier-Graefe told Jo that his novel, with the working title *Vincent et Theo*, was almost ready. He sent her two chapters, which had meanwhile been published in *Der Neue Merkur*.[17] She gave a very guarded response, as do many people who suddenly see their own lives played out in fiction. She parried Meier-Graefe's idea that Mrs van Gogh was a peasant woman, asserting that she actually came from a 'very intellectual milieu in The Hague', and she was furious about the fictitious dialogues, but only intimates would notice:

> For me, who experienced their lives, who hear their voices over the space of thirty years, there is sometimes a wrong note, artificial, in the conversations you attribute to them, but it will only be so for me and the few people still alive who knew Vincent and Theo personally.

Jo found it frustrating that Meier-Graefe repeatedly gave her the impression that he wanted his story to stick strictly to the facts. Because he also wanted to focus on Theo's role, he asked her to send him transcripts of one or two notable letters. She had two typed out, both dating from October 1888, and in the accompanying letter she wrote unnecessarily that, after years of burying herself in their legacies, she was utterly convinced of the passion and enthusiasm with which the brothers had worked to create the substantial oeuvre: 'I, who have devoted my entire life to this immense work of Vincent and Theo, I know these joys.'[18] Six months later she returned to the so-called conversations that she was so bothered about.[19] In the end Theo's name was removed from the book's title in 1921, and it was just called *Vincent* (later on with the subtitle *Der Roman eines Gottsuchers*). It was reprinted several times. As late as 1923 Jo wrote to Walter Pach that she would never forgive Meier-Graefe for suggesting that after their marriage Theo was no longer able to support Vincent. Such blatant errors irritated her beyond measure.[20] Three years after Jo's death, the painter Eduard Gerdes revealed in *De*

Telegraaf another similar comment that Jo made to him about Meier-Graefe's novel: 'Oh, it's all so wrong! . . . It was all so *very* different.'[21] She was critical about several points, including the poor quality of the colour reproductions. She did not give Meier-Graefe permission to include colour reproductions in the revised version of his book: 'They are always wrong, no matter how carefully they are made.'[22]

The highly dramatized and romanticized book remained successful. An English translation appeared in 1933, spreading the distorted picture of Van Gogh's life story and character worldwide. This whole mystification was given further momentum by the American novel *Lust for life* (1934) by Irving Stone and the 1956 film based on it. As a result, ineradicable legends about Van Gogh spread far and wide, and went on to be confirmed time and again in subsequent books, films and documentaries. So, ironically enough, the art world itself is responsible for the fact that to this day the general public sees Van Gogh as a mad, passionate genius, a martyr to his art or, at the very least, a socially awkward, completely misunderstood and poverty-stricken painter. His letters reveal that he had a much more nuanced personality, which some of his fellow artists certainly understood, and that he had a reasonable income thanks to Theo's financial support.[23]

At the beginning of the 1920s, Jo also corresponded frequently with Paul Gachet. Among other things, he asked her whether she wanted the documents concerning Theo's reburial. She replied that she would certainly like to have them.[24] Shortly thereafter she asked him for the umpteenth time to send her the bill for the gravestones; it is understandable that she wanted to pay for them herself and it irritated her that he simply did not understand this. She wrote proudly how she and her son kept the past alive—there was one uninterrupted family tradition that she saw was continuing with her newborn first grandson Theo, who had come into the world ten weeks before: 'Rest assured, dear friend, that just as I initiated him into the cult of remembering his father and his uncle, my son will follow the same tradition for little Theodore as soon as he is old enough' (Figure 61).[25]

Requests for loans continued to arrive, some of them very substantial. This time Vincent was invited by the Ministry of Education, Arts and Sciences to cooperate in preparations for an exhibition of old and new Dutch art in the Galerie nationale du Jeu de Paume in Paris in April and May. This 'Exposition hollandaise' was intended to enhance the country's prestige, and the Lower House of the Dutch Parliament had allocated generous funding to the tune of 60,000 guilders. The Ministry requested only one work, *Fishing Boats at Sea* (F 415 / JH 1452), but mother and son felt that was nowhere near enough, so Vincent offered a further four masterpieces, including *Self-Portrait as a Painter* (F 522 / JH 1356) and *The Langlois Bridge* (F 400 / JH 1371). All five hung in the exhibition.[26] Jo also gave permission for the paintings to be photographed so that black-and-white reproductions could be sold, this time solely for the benefit of a good cause. She knew beforehand that the proceeds would go to supporting areas devastated during the war.[27] Jo wrote to Gachet, who had been to see this exhibition, to tell him that they had lent a few of their favourites, but that the orchard (which she had loaned as a

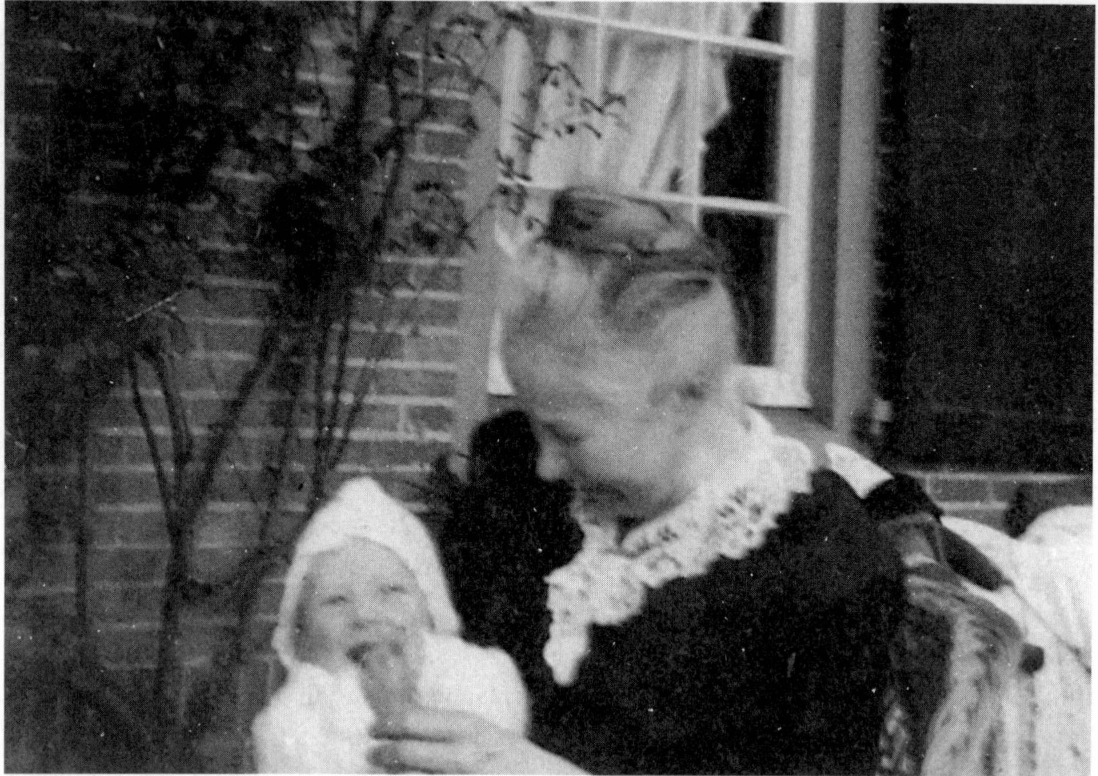

Figure 61 First grandson Theo van Gogh with Jo van Gogh-Bonger in Laren, 1921.

favour to one of the organizers) was, needless to say, not for sale. In her view, Van Gogh's exalted position in Dutch art was beyond question:

> We keep the series of orchards intact at home and it was only to please a friend of mine, a member of the exhibition committee, that I agreed to send one of these canvases to Paris. Since we even sent our Rembrandts!!

As was often the case during her last few years, the letter was typed for her rather than handwritten by her because of her ongoing writer's cramp, but tellingly she had used a pen to add the two exclamation marks herself now that Van Gogh, alongside the giant Rembrandt, was represented so prominently.[28]

Isaac Israëls also lent two Van Goghs for this exhibition: *Le Moulin de la Galette* (F 349 / JH 1184) and *Olive Grove* (F 711 / JH 1791).[29] He and Jo got in touch again during this period, and when Israëls went to the Dutch East Indies six months later, he wrote her a lovely letter from the steamship he was on in the Indian Ocean.[30] Together with Jan Veth and Anna Veth-Dirks, he visited the cities of Batavia (present-day Jakarta), Solo and Yogyakarta on Java. They then sailed to Bali. Writing from Solo, he thanked Jo for her letter and noted: 'In what you call this monkey country, I have yet to meet a single monkey. . . .' In his mind's eye he saw Jo as being very much a grandmother: 'And you, you're just like a Javanese with your grandchildren.' He went on to say: 'It's remarkable how kind they are to small children and how cruel they are to animals; which is preferable? With us it's often the other way round.'[31] Jo, however, adored both. She loved animals and doted on her grandchildren—the first was Theo, followed by Johan, who was born on 26 March 1922. She told Israëls the news. In letters she told Gachet that little Theo was 'a true Van Gogh' and Zigrosser that he was 'a perfect Van Gogh'.[32] And she waxed lyrical to Annie van Gelder-Pigeaud about him: 'he's an indescribable angel with the loveliest nature in the world, really sweet tempered.'[33]

Meanwhile she had been corresponding with Van Gelder-Pigeaud about progress with her English manuscript of the Van Gogh letters. Annie received Jo's translation of the introduction from Montross and then approached three New York publishers. She also tried to find a magazine to publish the introduction.[34] Jo wrote to her saying: 'it seems to me that it can't do any harm and it'll help generate more publicity. Everyone's saying that now's the right time for a Dutch book to appear in America.' She was still brimming over with plans. During a visit from Walter and Magda Pach she gave them transcripts of a few of the letters from Paul Gauguin in her collection. Full of determination, she told Van Gelder-Pigeaud, 'I want to publish these too'.[35]

Jo also told her she had contacted Adriaan Jacob Barnouw, a lecturer in the Germanic languages department at New York's Columbia University, who lectured on Van Gogh. She sent him a copy of the Dutch edition of the letters. He promised to do his best to bring Van Gogh's letters to the attention of American publishers and told Jo he would also approach the young publisher Alfred A. Knopf, although he warned her that she needed to be patient.[36] She was, but in the end Barnouw's efforts as a cultural ambassador did not have the hoped-for effect. It took months before a publisher responded, but they only wanted to publish the letters if they were drastically abridged. 'Obviously I wouldn't dream of it,' she wrote uncompromisingly to Van Gelder-Pigeaud.[37]

Jo's philanthropic leanings came to the fore during this period, when she donated Van Gogh's drawing *Peasant Woman, Head* (F 1181 / JH 679) for a prize draw art exhibition in Amsterdam's Stedelijk Museum. It was organized by the SDAP for the benefit of victims in the Volga region. Famine among the population threatened on a huge scale as a result of earlier confiscations of grain and failed harvests caused by a long drought. Posters and newspapers, among them the Communist *De Tribune. Orgaan van de Communistische Partij in Nederland*, called upon the generosity of artists and collectors. The response was overwhelming and over three hundred prizes were available.[38] Van Gogh's drawing was hailed as the cream of the crop and it encouraged many people to buy a ticket (for fifty cents each).[39] The draw took place on 1 April 1922 and the total proceeds amounted to approximately 14,000 guilders.[40]

Failing health

Jo was still able to do her work, but at times her physical condition let her down. She had to rest for nearly two months in the spring of 1922. She told Annie van Gelder-Pigeaud about it: 'It was a bladder infection, but all I had to do was follow a strict diet and stay in bed.' This gave her the opportunity to read the books Annie had sent. Jo liked *Main Street* (1920) by Sinclair Lewis the best. She wrote she had had a 'charming little English secretary' that winter. She still had to dictate everything, which was inconvenient because she had many translations ahead of her. The lawyer Jacob-Baart de la Faille had furthermore started preparations for the first Van Gogh catalogue raisonné, about which Jo wrote complacently 'of course I'll have to play a big part in it'.[41]

Remarkably there is a letter of thanks in her private correspondence that Jo sent to the Swiss-born clergyman Ernst Pfeiffer at the end of 1921. In 1923 Pfeiffer was appointed to a living in The Hague, and he contributed to publications of the Haagse Swedenborg Genootschap, which was founded in 1909. After meeting Jo on a previous occasion, he sent her Emanuel Swedenborg's *Conjugial Love and Its Chaste Delights*, an English translation of *Delitiae sapientiae de Amore conjugiali* (1768). There were several editions in circulation. He sent the book for a reason. The most important issue in it is whether marriage stops with death, or whether it continues after death. Jo wrote to Pfeiffer:

> I read it and reread it—oh if I could have believed—you would have done me the greatest service a man can do to a fellow creature. But I cannot—I think continually: 'what happiness it must be to believe this', but then comes the doubt and disturbs it all.[42]

Now that Jo sensed that the last phase of her life had started, she developed greater interest in spiritual issues, but to her regret she could not sign up to this theory. It remains unclear how and where she met Pfeiffer—it may have happened as a result of the Van Gogh purchases made in May of that year by Theodore Pitcairn, whom Pfeiffer knew.

Around that time, the French writer and art critic Gustave Coquiot approached Jo because he wanted to write a book about Van Gogh. She recommended what he should read, stressed the importance of the third volume of the letters and advised him to seek out Paul Gachet. Coquiot sent her three books he had written, whereupon she invited him to visit her, which he did in June 1922.[43] After Coquiot had written to Gachet, in his reply the latter expressed his respect for Jo's efforts and those of her son: 'I greatly admire her fine character and constant self-sacrifice.'[44]

Coquiot kept a notebook during his trip to the Netherlands. Apparently Jo had not been able to conceal her fatigue and poor health because he sketched her as a 'woman of 55 to 60 years old, average build, very nervous, suffering greatly, expressive eyes, but both hands tremble constantly, particularly the right hand.' He described the works of art in her home and was in awe of her dedication: 'Mrs v. G.-Bonger has been criticized for publishing certain painful letters from Vincent. And yet *she kept the most painful ones secret!* . . . what letters can these letters be!' She had evidently told him about the cuts she had deliberately made in the letters.[45]

After the birth of Johan, their second son, Vincent and Josina moved from Alexander Boersstraat to 10 Waldeck Pyrmontlaan, also close to Jo, but this time in a spacious home with front and back gardens. Her grandchildren were Jo's greatest solace during the last phase of her life.[46] They stayed with her in Laren for a lengthy period during the summer: 'I so enjoyed it,' she wrote to Annie van Gelder-Pigeaud, 'because here in the city I see them every day but never for longer than an hour or so.'[47] Who knows whether Josina and Vincent always enjoyed the obligation (because it certainly sounds like one) of that daily visit, but it was very important to Jo. At the end of 1922, she sent Gachet a photograph of herself with her grandchildren (Plate 59). Again she subtly connected the generations:

> Enclosed you will find Grandma with little Theo, who is kissing his little brother's feet; it was taken last summer. The babies have grown since then; Theo is already nearly two and is extremely intelligent and has superb vitality. Little Johan (he's my godson) is a chubby, beautiful eight-month-old baby. Looking at his beautiful clear eyes I always think of what Vincent said, that a baby has the infinite in its eyes.[48]

She thanked him for sending six yellow petals from the sunflowers on the graves in Auvers—she was profoundly moved.

Meanwhile Jo was becoming progressively affected by Parkinson's disease and was being treated for it. She took Coquiot into her confidence: 'I had an electric treatment and was absolutely forbidden to write, and having neither typewriter nor secretary here in the country, I couldn't be more disabled.'[49] It is not clear what sort of electrotherapy she received. There were several alternatives available at the time, for example galvanic or faradic therapy, with a relatively new type of high frequency or diathermic technique.[50] A patient received stimuli by holding an instrument in their hand or by having it placed on a part of their body. The treatment was local, with electrodes on the locations where the Parkinson's symptoms were most manifest.[51] Jo sensed she did not have much longer to live. She wrote to Coquiot: 'It is so good, after so many years of public indifference, even hostility towards Vincent and his work, to feel towards the end of my life that the battle is won.'[52] She had undeniably won her battle to get recognition for Van Gogh, but her struggle against her disease was to drag on for another three years. There is no mention of whether the electrotherapy gave her any relief. In any event she considered herself to be severely handicapped.

She will without doubt have been cheered by the printed dedication 'À Madame J. van Gogh-Bonger' with which Coquiot prefaced his substantial study *Vincent van Gogh*.[53] In this dedication he spoke openly of his appreciation of the diligent work Jo had done. He recalled her fiery sparkling eyes during their conversations about the two brothers and thanked her for everything she had so generously confided to him. He honoured her by giving her a copy, adorned with the number 1, specially printed on luxury Dutch paper and uncut. Jo also returned the favour. When Coquiot told her that he wanted to dedicate the book to her, it was her turn to give praise. She called him 'a true magician', a description reserved in Van Gogh's letters for the masters Rembrandt and Delacroix.[54] She wrote to him saying that if he were ever to come to the Netherlands, he should visit her—then he would be able to buy a Van Gogh drawing for a knockdown price. In other words not as a present, as she had done now and again in the past.[55] But nothing ever came of it.

'Modern Dutch art cannot be represented without Van Gogh'

On 13 January 1923 Jo was invited to a ceremony in the Rijksmuseum honouring Willem Steenhoff on the occasion of his sixtieth birthday. Jan Veth gave the speech.[56] During the proceedings she must have been profoundly aware of the crucial role Steenhoff had played in her life—his tireless efforts to establish the importance of Van Gogh's work and his unceasing support for her in fulfilling her mission. The following year he and his wife Coba—they had married shortly before—moved to The Hague, where he became director of the Rijksmuseum H.W. Mesdag.[57]

Jo continued to work, although she had been compelled to slow down. Meanwhile things were stirring in America again. She told Newman Montross about the Jacques Goudstikker gallery, which staged exhibitions of Dutch art in Saint Louis, Cleveland and Detroit, and asked him to lend the works Goudstikker wanted, ending her letter: 'Modern Dutch art cannot be represented without Van Gogh.'[58] The 'Exhibition of Dutch and Flemish Pictures XV to XX Century from the Goudstikker Collection of Amsterdam' ran from 10 March to 7 April 1923 in the Anderson Galleries in New York. Although it had been heavy going in America initially, this approach at least was successful.[59]

Ernest Brown & Phillips in London

Sights were set on the west. No work by Van Gogh had been exhibited in London since 1910, but now this was to change. In May 1923, Jo responded to a request from Ernest Brown & Phillips, a firm that organized exhibitions at the Leicester Galleries in Leicester Square, and informed them she would like to provide works for a show. The brothers Cecil and Wilfred Phillips founded the business in 1902; Ernest and Oliver Brown joined as partners shortly afterwards. From then on, they traded as Ernest Brown & Phillips. They were delighted to be able to stage this 'first "one-man" show', but on condition that the selection of works was representative and did not contain any inferior pieces. Jo replied firmly that they could trust her: 'I have arranged more than a hundred exhibitions already,' she wrote with authority and not without pride.[60]

It was impressed upon her that British collectors tended not to engage if the asking prices were extreme.[61] She countered that in the thirty years she had been managing the collection, the selling prices had done nothing but go up. She believed it was better to sell a few works for good prices than more works for prices that were too low. But in any event, she wrote, they need not worry she would ask exceptional prices in a country where the artist was less well known. It would be harmful to her interests if she threw away the chance of success by doing so. She proposed having a face-to-face discussion about the matter in Amsterdam, preferably in the short term, because she spent the summer in the country—although in that case they could also arrange to meet with her son.[62] That year, she went on several excursions while she was in Laren, including a pleasant tour with Vincent through Belgium and Northern France, visiting Ghent, Bruges, Ostend, Rouen, Amiens and Brussels.[63]

The British organizers did indeed send someone across the North Sea to discuss the arrangements. Oliver Brown made a selection with the willing assistance of Vincent because at the time Jo was 'seriously ill'.[64] The list was put before her for final approval, however, and she was pleased with the flattering statement that Jo had 'such great experience of Van Gogh Exhibitions' (paraphrasing her own words).[65] Later Brown recalled how she had haughtily answered the question about why the full scope of Van Gogh had never been seen before in the United Kingdom: 'Nobody has ever asked me.'[66]

Contrary to Jo's expectations, the preparations for the London exhibition ran into some difficulties. The first was that Brown asked if the works were glazed—because if they were not, the insurance would be significantly less expensive.[67] After that Jo received the telegram 'Kindly substitute Berceuse for Lazarus,' followed by a letter with apologies for all the trouble this put her to.[68] In the end twenty-seven paintings (unglazed) and twelve drawings made the crossing to England on the steamship *Maasstroom*. 'In case the National Gallery wants to acquire something for the museum, you know it's customary to lower the price,' pointed out Jo shrewdly to be on the safe side.[69]

Brown noted on the confirmation of receipt of the works that holes had been found in some paintings, including *Wheatfield with Crows*. There was also a tear in the *Olive Trees*. He asked whether Jo knew about this and advised her to have the painting lined without delay.[70] She acknowledged that the works needed to be restored, but she went no further than that. At that moment her focus was elsewhere: she took the opportunity to say that she would very much appreciate it if Brown could find a British publisher for Van Gogh's letters.[71] It emerges from two surviving draft notes that she had rather demanding conditions as far as that publication was concerned: she wanted 20 per cent royalties for the edition of the letters and 5 per cent for the translations, and not just any prospective publisher would do: 'it must be a big firm'. Brown asked whether the percentage she quoted referred to the trade price or the retail price. If it was the latter, 20 per cent would be extremely high. But Jo stuck to her guns about this high percentage and received the predictable response that it would never be paid—Brown was adamant that even the most successful authors could not command that sort of percentage.[72] This forced her to adopt a less high-handed approach after all.

Meanwhile, she had contacted a few publishers herself, including Harcourt, Brace and Company. They were interested, but proposed compiling an anthology. She turned the idea down; her most compelling reason was that 'these letters form the most perfect autobiography existing, and not a single letter could be left out without disturbing the perfect unity of the whole.' She then discussed proposals from Ernest Benn Limited Publishers in London with Leo Simons of the Wereldbibliotheek.[73] Further letters to the publishing house of Selwyn & Blount in London followed between January and April 1924. After they sent her a rejection, Jo felt the need to let them know her opinion: 'I cannot help feeling that you are mistaken.' She steadfastly pursued her ultimate goal and was not prepared to make concessions.[74] Her argument that many readers looked on Van Gogh's letters as their bible (Jo wrote this to several publishers) was not enough to convince them. No one wanted to take the financial risk. As regards her translation, she told the publishers Albert and Charles Boni in New York, who were the last she approached: 'it was made with the utmost care to keep the flavour of the quaint rather old-fashioned style of the original letters and I think I succeeded in this'. It is possible that those negotiations failed because of the low proposed royalty, which was only 10 per cent of the selling price. In the margin Jo had noted in pencil: 'Cassirer 20%'.[75]

Ernest Brown & Phillips's exhibition in the Leicester Galleries opened on 1 December 1923 and ran until 15 January 1924. Michael Ernest Sadler of University College, Oxford, wrote the introduction to the accompanying catalogue. 'He has to be reckoned with,' Sadler stated categorically.[76] But it was not a good time—the elections in the United Kingdom soaked up a great deal of attention and it was a turbulent period for the private sector, so many buyers kept their purse strings tight.[77] Only a few works were sold: the paintings *Olive Grove* (F 714 / JH 1858), *View of the Terrace near the Moulin de Blute-fin* (F 272 / JH 1183) and *Head of a Woman (Gordina de Groot)* (F 140 / JH 745), and the drawing *Cypresses* (F 1525 / JH 1747), for which Jo received a total of 14,540 guilders.[78] They were bought by Michael Sadler, who exhibited them at the Oxford Arts Club a few months later.[79]

The artist Frances Hodgkins, who had spoken to Johannes de Bois, wrote cattily about Jo's lucrative earnings in a letter to her friend Hannah Ritchie, who was also an artist: 'The widow sister-in-law owns most of the [Van] Gogh's & is rolling rich & fat on the sales.' That was grossly exaggerated, particularly with regard to the British situation. But even though little was sold, the exhibition had certainly made its mark and established Van Gogh's name and reputation in the United Kingdom. 'He [De Bois] says London has now seen the best—not *all* by any means,' wrote Hodgkins.[80]

Jo corresponded with Paul Gachet and Walter Pach during the summer of 1923. She sent the former a small collection of picture postcards of Van Gogh drawings. They were made for sale and the proceeds were earmarked to support needy artists.[81] She told Pach how pleased she was that thanks in part to his efforts Van Gogh's paintings had been shown in the United States, and she sang the praises of her two grandchildren. She wrote that Isaac Israëls had painted a charming portrait of little Theo.[82] What primarily concerned her, and what annoyed her, however, was the publication of Van Gogh's letters:

> I long *so very much* to see them published in English. I do hope I shall live to see it. My Dutch publisher now tries it in London, but it is always the same: 'very interesting but too long.' And every word, every line of them is so precious.

To express her gratitude to Walter and Magda Pach, Jo gave them the drawing *Landscape with Trees* (F 1518 / JH 1493).[83] This generous gesture could have been partially rooted in self-interest: Pach might perhaps still have had influence when it came to finding a publisher.

Evidence of Jo's Parkinson's disease was now becoming more and more apparent. 'She could no longer conceal her condition,' recalled her nephew Henk Bonger later,[84] and the Japanese art historian Tei Nishimura was also struck by her symptoms: 'She appeared to be suffering from rheumatism and to have difficulty walking. Her hands twitched continually.' He knew Vincent and Josina from the period in 1918–19 when they lived in Kobe. Nishimura described his impression of Jo after a visit in the autumn of 1923. He recalled a hospitable woman dressed in black with a piercing gaze who spoke fluent English. She offered him hot chocolate while he sat eye to eye with paintings crowded on the walls. He dined that evening at home with Vincent and Josina. There too he was again completely surrounded by Van Gogh's art.[85]

In the grip of the *Sunflowers*

At the end of September 1923, while he was on a boat to England, Harold Stanley Ede, also known as Jim Ede, wrote a lyrical letter to Jo, whom he had visited just a few hours before. Ede was an assistant curator at the National Gallery of British Art, on Millbank in London.[86] This museum for British art, just over a mile and a half from the National Gallery in Trafalgar Square, was opened in 1897 after the wealthy industrialist Henry Tate had donated his art collection to the nation in 1889. It was managed by the National Gallery for years. In 1917 the name was shortened to National Gallery, Millbank and in 1932 it was changed to include the name of its benefactor: the Tate Gallery. It is now Tate Britain. Tate Modern is some two and a half miles away on Bankside.

Ede's letter was prompted by his desire for her to reconsider selling one of the two versions of the *Sunflowers* that she still owned (they had discussed the matter earlier that day). He argued that it would be a great pity if Van Gogh were not to be represented in the United Kingdom by one of his very best paintings. She has to have referred again to an English edition of the letters in her reply, because Ede promised to do his best to find a suitable publisher. Jo was pleased she had met such an enthusiastic Van Gogh admirer and she expected Ede would become even more eager after reading the letters. As for the *Sunflowers*, however, she had to disappoint him: 'The sunflowers are not for sale, never; they belong in our family, just like Vincent's bedroom and his house at Arles.'[87]

Ede offered to read her translations critically if Jo thought it would be useful, although he doubted whether that was really necessary: 'I hardly think that with your wonderful knowledge of the English language there will be any need for that'—a compliment that undoubtedly pleased Jo. It was Ede who put her in touch with the publishers Selwyn & Blount, but they thought the royalty percentage Jo was asking for was much too high. Ede then suggested she should invest in the publication herself, but she did not entertain the idea.[88] She had done it ten years before for the Dutch edition published by the Wereldbibliotheek, but she appears never to have considered it seriously for the English one. She never had any doubts that the letters would retain their value.

Meanwhile, the director of the National Gallery of British Art, Charles Aitken, had also become involved in the negotiations about purchasing a painting. He followed up on what Ede had discussed with Jo and asked if she was willing to accept 9,000 guilders for Van Gogh's *Joseph Roulin* (F 436 / JH 1675) instead of 10,000 guilders. He also asked her if, after the end of the exhibition at the Leicester Galleries, she would lend three works to the National Gallery for a while. Her draft response, which she noted on Aitken's letter, shows how difficult it was for her to write, but also how unbroken her spirit was. She clearly did not want to cut the price any further. She was, however, prepared to lend the three paintings for a couple of months, 'or even a little longer if you wish'.[89]

Now Charles John Holmes, director of the National Gallery in Trafalgar Square, also became involved. He told Aitken that in his opinion the works on offer were not masterpieces. He even disparagingly referred to '"remnants", left after the better things had been picked up by more daring buyers.'[90] He did, though, very much want to borrow the *Sunflowers*, *The Bedroom* and *The Yellow House* after the exhibition was over, and he was prepared to offer 9,000 guilders for *Joseph Roulin* and 8,000 guilders for *Vincent's Chair*.

The three-part loan and the double purchase both went ahead. Jo stood firm and in the end received 10,000 guilders for Roulin's portrait. She wrote that the cheque could be made out to Vincent.[91] Ernest Brown & Phillips derived no benefit whatsoever from this transaction so Jo generously transferred 760 guilders to them for their mediation.[92] Even then the agreement was not yet entirely settled because the National Gallery sent *Joseph Roulin* back to Ernest Brown & Phillips. That was ludicrous, as Ede wrote to Jo: the trustees of the Courtauld Fund—they were ultimately the people who financed the purchase—felt that the luxuriant beard was 'too funny'. A ridiculous argument that was certainly not supported by everyone because a month later the painting was sold to Galerie Thannhauser for 10,000 guilders.[93] So the British still did not have a Van Gogh masterpiece, but they hatched a plan to get their hands on an even more significant work. Once again, their prey was the *Sunflowers* and, after seemingly endless doubts and discussions, Jo and Vincent decided to part company with one of their two versions, the painting they had cherished for over thirty years. 'It is a sacrifice for the sake of Vincent's glory,' wrote Jo to Charles Aitken on 24 January 1924, and with these solemn words she captured in a nutshell their ultimate duty (Figure 62).[94]

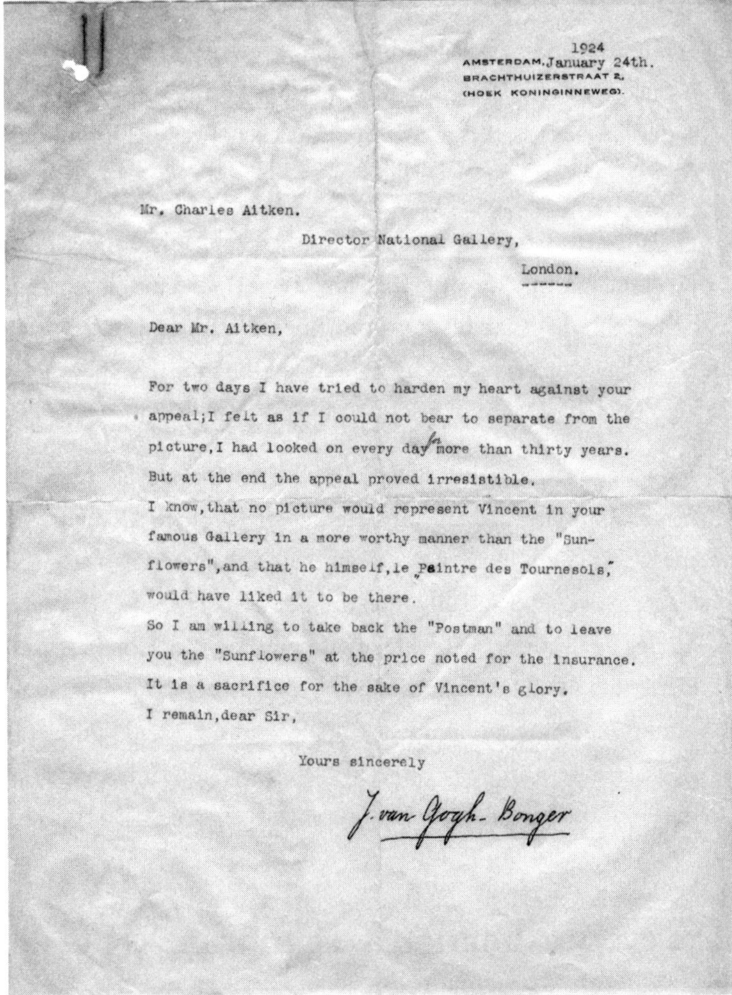
1924
AMSTERDAM, January 24th.
BRACHTHUIZERSTRAAT 2.
(HOEK KONINGINNEWEG).

Mr. Charles Aitken.
Director National Gallery,
London.

Dear Mr. Aitken,

For two days I have tried to harden my heart against your appeal; I felt as if I could not bear to separate from the picture, I had looked on every day for more than thirty years.
But at the end the appeal proved irresistible.
I know, that no picture would represent Vincent in your famous Gallery in a more worthy manner than the "Sunflowers", and that he himself, le Paintre des Tournesols, would have liked it to be there.
So I am willing to take back the "Postman" and to leave you the "Sunflowers" at the price noted for the insurance.
It is a sacrifice for the sake of Vincent's glory.
I remain, dear Sir,

Yours sincerely

J. van Gogh-Bonger

Figure 62 Letter from Jo van Gogh-Bonger to Charles Aitken, 24 January 1924.

A satisfied Aitken replied: 'Van Gogh is at last adequately represented in England.' That same day he officially confirmed that they paid 15,000 guilders for the *Sunflowers* (F 454 / JH 1562) and 8,000 guilders for *Van Gogh's Chair* (F 498 / JH 1635).[95] The votes of Samuel Courtauld and the Trustees of his Trust were decisive—Courtauld himself played a crucial role in the purchases because of the £50,000 he had paid into his fund in 1923. It was thanks in part to him that modern foreign art slowly gained a foothold in the United Kingdom. Prior to 1917 he had maintained a completely different position regarding the national collections because the National Gallery, Millbank, was only permitted to hold works by British artists.[96]

In a letter to Aitken, Vincent confirmed once again that a lot of water had flowed under the bridges across the Thames before they were able to make a decision. He also underlined his mother's wish, now Van Gogh's work had won recognition in the United Kingdom, that the letters should also be published in English. Interest in the artist was bound to grow, now that the two works were in the National Gallery. On that same day Vincent wrote the same thing to Samuel Courtauld, although interestingly in his letter he discussed the correspondence between the brothers and so not just Vincent's letters to Theo:

> It took indeed quite some deliberation before we let the beautiful Sunflowers go, but my mother yielded for the sake of having Vincent van Gogh well represented in the most important museum of England. For the same motive, of having Vincent appreciated to his full worth, she has now one more desire, namely to have the correspondence between the brothers Theo and Vincent appear in English, because it gives such a beautiful insight in his personality and work.

The desire to have Van Gogh's letters published in English clearly played a significant role in their decision to part with the *Sunflowers*.[97] Jo was convinced, as she wrote to Aitken herself, that the British public could get to know Van Gogh in great depth through his letters. She believed that they gave a much more accurate picture of his personality than did books like the ones by Meier-Graefe.[98]

Ernest Brown & Phillips finally informed Jo that they could sell Van Gogh's *Self-Portrait* (F 320 / JH 1334) for 11,400 guilders, but initially the sale did not go ahead: '14 May replied in the negative,' noted Jo on their letter. A month later the painting was finally sold for 12,000 guilders.[99] Shortly before, Samuel Courtauld and his wife Elizabeth Courtauld-Kelsey had paid a 'delightful visit' to Jo in Amsterdam, and so the emotional London adventure came to an end.[100]

'Make every exhibition as significant as possible'

After the United Kingdom, it was Switzerland's turn. In May 1923, the German art critic Friedrich Markus Hübner learned that Jo and Vincent looked favourably on the idea of an exhibition of some fifty works in Basel.[101] It was staged within a year. The painter Wilhelm Barth, curator at the Kunsthalle in Basel since 1909, told Jo he wanted to organize a really good exhibition, to which many Swiss art lovers were sure to come. Barth had an impressive track record, including exhibitions featuring works by Die Brücke, Pablo Picasso and Edvard Munch, so Jo was very willing to provide twenty-five paintings and twenty-five drawings, which would be shipped from London. She could send an additional ten paintings and ten drawings, but only if the Kunsthalle paid the transport and insurance costs.[102]

Hübner asked the art historian Hans Schneider, who worked at the Mauritshuis in The Hague and lectured at Leiden University, to act as intermediary. Schneider wrote to Barth saying he would visit 'Frau van Gogh' in person in order to try 'to find out more details from the very self-willed old lady. I

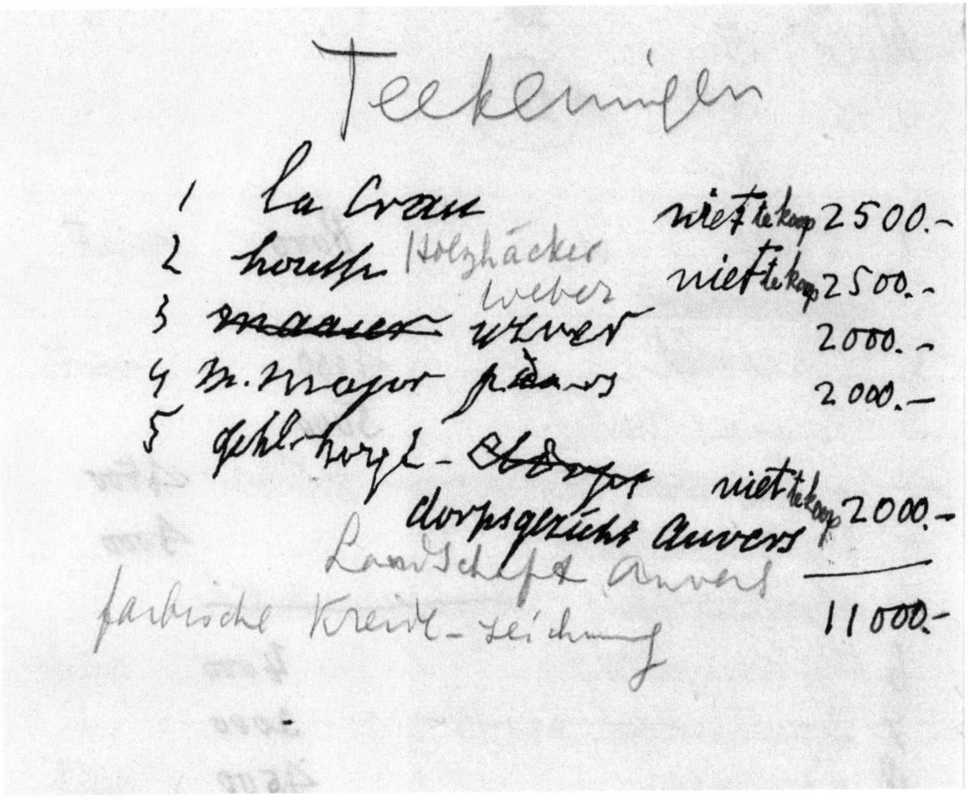

Figure 63 Jo van Gogh-Bonger, list of the titles and prices of the drawings loaned to the Kunsthalle in Basel, 1924.

will also try to make it clear to her in moving words how important it would be for Switzerland to get more than just twenty-five pictures from her.'[103] But Jo, who was indeed a very self-willed woman, preferred to discuss everything directly with Barth. She considered that 'easier and more correct', so Schneider's role was soon played out.[104] She made her intentions regarding loans crystal clear: 'It has always been my business to make every exhibition as significant as possible.'[105] She could hardly have expressed her conviction that her way was the right way more clearly.

Contrary to what she had written to Barth, Jo was actually planning to send an extra thirty-eight paintings and nineteen drawings from Amsterdam to Basel rather than ten of each. In the end she sent twenty paintings and five drawings.[106] A list of titles in her handwriting betrays once more how excruciatingly difficult it was for her to write (Figure 63).

The unflattering photograph portrait of Jo with a stoop must also date from this period. She did keep the photograph but was very dissatisfied with it. On the back she wrote, 'very ugly' (Figure 64). Despite her limitations, she was still able to climb stairs reasonably easily to the living room of her flat

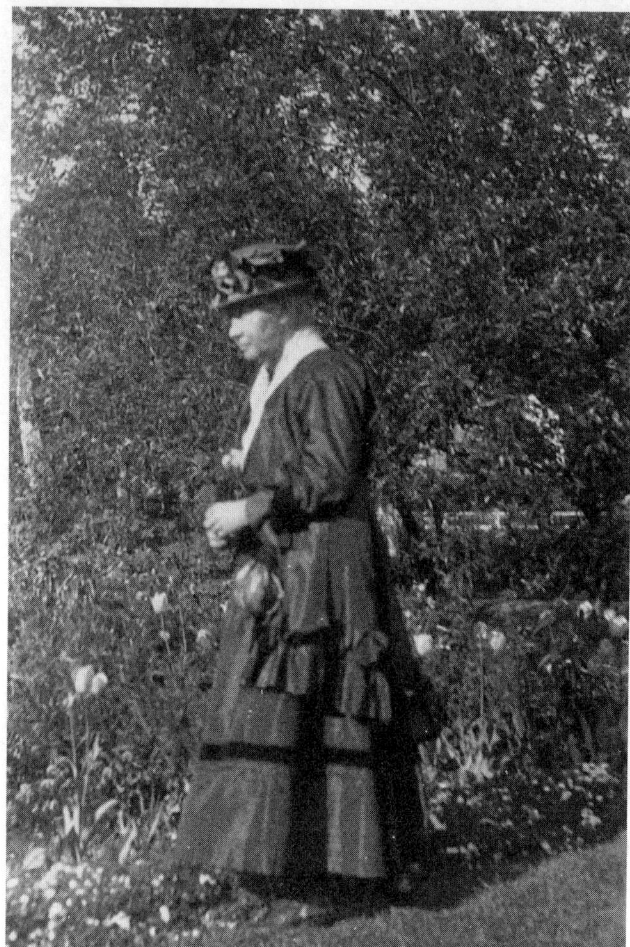

Figure 64 Jo van Gogh-Bonger, *c.* 1924.

in Koninginneweg, which was on the first floor, and her bedroom, which was on the second floor. She stayed put and apparently felt no need to move to a more convenient ground-floor flat.

The exhibition in the Kunsthalle in Basel ran from 26 March to 4 May 1924. As usual Jo made her own notes about the prices of the works she wanted to sell and sent Barth a list of works and their selling prices that her secretary had typed out. She left no room for confusion about some works: 'The drawing of "La Crau" is definitely not for sale.' An offer at a lower price was made for the *Olive Grove*, which she rejected in a terse note: 'The prices are fixed and will not change.'[107] There was no scope for haggling whatsoever.

Meanwhile Jo had found a new secretary, young like the previous one, who also helped with the English translations.[108] She was the twenty-two-year-old Willemina Sax, daughter of the funeral director Nicolaas Sax, who lived with his family in Larense Drift, near Rozenlaantje. In the summer of 1923 Willemina was awarded her diploma to teach English and put advertisements in the newspapers advertising her services as a teacher.[109] Her father was extremely interested in nineteenth-century French prints. He owned a fine collection and published articles about it, which would have appealed to Jo.

At the beginning of 1924, Jo's health was very poor and she wrote about it to Paul Gachet. He sent her a few publications about Van Gogh (we do not know which ones), about which she was extremely vexed because of all the errors they contained—'What nonsense they wrote about Vincent!!'—and she was also furious that none of the documents mentioned that all the biographical information had been taken from her introduction to the letters.[110] Jo told him of her hope that the two works purchased by the National Gallery would have a positive impact on finding a British publisher for the letters. The subject preyed on her mind constantly. With satisfaction she confirmed that they still cherished their beautiful version of the *Sunflowers*: 'My son still owns another picture of sunflowers, which will always remain in the family.'[111] That second painting, *Sunflowers* (F 458 / JH 1667), did indeed stay in the family and to this day it is one of the top attractions in the Van Gogh Museum in Museumplein in Amsterdam (Plate 60).

There was good news. The first edition of the letters had meanwhile almost sold out, so the editor at the Wereldbibliotheek, Nico van Suchtelen, proposed a second edition. Jo received the contract on 24 February 1924 and agreed to pay 5,124 guilders, half of the cost. After Jo's death, Vincent continued to work with the Wereldbibliotheek and their collaboration lasted a further five decades. The edition ran to two thousand copies. Vincent had decided that in consultation with Van Suchtelen, who in the meantime had become the publisher's managing director.[112] Jo noted with satisfaction in her brief foreword:

> What I hoped for so earnestly for the first edition turned out to be the case: they found their way into people's hearts. Comments reach me from all four corners of the globe, telling me how the sheer humanity of the great artist touches, captivates and moves the readers. This second edition—which does not differ from the first in any way—will therefore also make new friends.[113]

These proved to be prophetic words: since then Van Gogh's letters have attracted a never-ending stream of admirers and friends.

A shrewd businesswoman

Jo's friendship with Paul Cassirer came to an end in 1924. She had asked him whether he could send her the statement of sales of the German edition of the letters during the preceding years. She explained she had not wanted to approach him earlier because of the tragic situation after the war. Cassirer replied that the mark had devalued to such an extent that only a ridiculously low amount remained:

less than three hundred guilders. He proposed a new print run, and suggested paying her 6 per cent for each copy sold.[114] In her response Jo showed once again that she was not to be trifled with: 'I should like to receive your settlement for the Van Gogh letters. I received the following specification of the sales from you on 23 September 1918, but because I was in America then, we didn't settle it.'[115] She made no reference to devaluation, although she did remark that she had arrived at a sum of 2,692 marks for the January 1916 to September 1918 period. That prompted Cassirer to calculate again, but he continued to tell her the amount outstanding really was minimal; a mere hundred and twenty marks.[116] It is no longer possible to establish how exactly this financial tug of war ended and whether Jo gave up. Cassirer's letter is the last surviving communication in their correspondence. Their collaboration, once so glorious and inspired, was snuffed out like a candle by this sad financial bickering.

That year Jo also had a quarrel with Jacobus Exter, director of the Amsterdamse Gebouw voor Beeldende Kunst at 80 Vondelstraat. A number of Van Gogh's works from his Dutch period were exhibited at the institution in March and April 1924. They came from the collections of Hidde Nijland and Jo. According to *De Tijd*, the paintings were hung in this mansion's attic.[117] Exter had corresponded with Jo about her contribution for this and for a second exhibition, likewise initiated by him.[118] This was to take place in September, but at the last moment the intended exhibition space was withdrawn. This was despite the fact that at the end of August Jo had notified him that a shipment of nearly sixty works from Switzerland was on its way.[119] Upset about what was going on, she wrote to Exter: 'I fail to understand how you dared to wait until the last minute to tell me that the exhibition isn't going ahead.' Now, at the drop of a hat, she had to think of what to do with the returning shipment. 'I urgently request you to notify me when they've arrived and to send back the lists.'[120] The end of the exercise was marked by a humble letter of apology, although Exter did feel the need to say he thought it was unforgivable that she had rebuked him 'like a schoolboy'. He had after all done everything possible to let the exhibition take place.[121] It is doubtful whether she wrote to the indignant thirty-two-year-old Exter after that.

That summer she made a new inventory of all the drawings she had in her home at 77 Koninginneweg and took out insurance for them from a number of insurers for a total insured sum of 56,850 guilders.[122] That was a very different outcome compared with thirty years before, when she had just returned to the Netherlands from Paris, and insured all the drawings for six hundred guilders. That same summer Jo also corresponded with Otto Fischer, director of the Staatliche Landeskunstsammlungen in Stuttgart, who had asked her whether he could exhibit works from her collection in his museum. He considered the Van Goghs he had viewed in Switzerland to be among the best he had seen during the last fifteen years. Jo told him that the works first of all needed to come to Amsterdam (this explains her great irritation at Exter), but after that they could go to Stuttgart.[123] In response to Fischer's question about transport and customs charges, she replied that they were always paid by the organizers. She assumed he would answer by return—now she knew the Amsterdam exhibition was not going ahead, she would not have the crates unpacked, which would save her a great deal of trouble.[124] The agreement was signed and in the end there were thirty-four paintings and nineteen drawings on view in the exhibition, which took place in October and November at the Württembergischer Kunstverein in Stuttgart.[125] Jo emphasized that the works designated as being 'not for sale' were not, in any circumstances (underlined), for sale. A request that was nevertheless made after this was curtly dismissed: '*unverkäuflich*'.[126] Fischer reported there were nine institutions in Germany that had stated their willingness to take over the exhibition,[127] but Jo was decisive about that too: '*No* more exhibitions will be held in Germany.'[128] It was clear that things were beginning to get too much for her. After that, the works were to go on to Galerie Bernheim in Paris, so Fischer and Bernheim had to arrange for payment of the transport and insurance costs between them. She subtly reminded Fischer that she had yet to receive a catalogue.

Jo was in discussion with De la Faille, compiler of the catalogue raisonné, about the authenticity of a still life. She wrote that the work in question might date from Van Gogh's time in Paris or Arles, but concluded wisely: 'Assessing the authenticity of a painting is always a difficult business and it is never possible to make a proper evaluation without having seen the painting. . . . We could only be completely certain if we saw the painting for ourselves.'[129] De la Faille did not take Jo's authority all that seriously: four years later he went so far as to assert—in a crass comment that was reported in the *NRC* and *Het Vaderland*—that even if Jo had signed a declaration that a painting was from her collection, that was not 'the overwhelmingly decisive factor' for determining a painting's authenticity.[130]

That same week Jo wrote a letter to the editor of the *Times* entitled 'Once more Van Gogh and Doré'. The paper published it on 1 September 1924 headed 'Van Gogh and Doré'.[131] The background was a comment by Pelham H. Box in that newspaper about Van Gogh's painting *Penitentiary (after Gustave Doré)* (F 669 / JH 1885). He had called this work a 'copy' of Gustave Doré's print *Newgate: Exercise Yard*, but according to Jo it would be better—and she was right—to talk about an 'interpretation' rather than a 'copy'. She based her contention on Van Gogh's own words: 'That's my own interpretation.'[132] It was important to her to set the public record straight about such details, and the benefit in this case was that she could at the same time bring people's attention to the value of the letters when evaluating Van Gogh's art. The *Algemeen Handelsblad* of 3 September 1924 printed a paraphrased version of Jo's letter to the *Times*. This exchange confirmed her status as an authority on Van Gogh for the public at large.

A letter from Paul Gachet took her thoughts back to bygone times. Something he wrote made her recall the lovely catalpa, the tree with beautiful bell-shaped flowers that grew outside her and Theo's flat in the cul-de-sac cité Pigalle. She found it both pleasant and confrontational:

> Reading your letter, I relived the best memories of my life. The dear Catalpa, I see it in front of me, I was so proud of it. 'You are in the middle of the countryside,' he told me. How happy I was in that obscure little corner of Paris and . . . what I suffered there. How tragic my life was and how it took me by force! Alas, I don't have much left.[133]

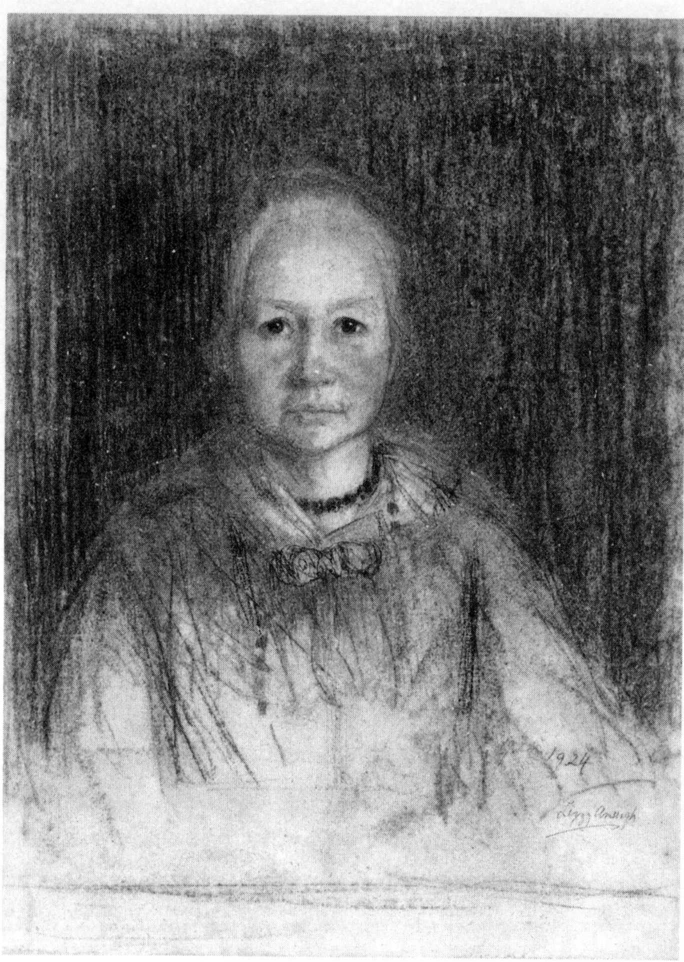

Figure 65 Lizzy Ansingh, *Jo van Gogh-Bonger*, 1924.

She dictated the letter to her secretary Willemina Sax, only writing her name at the bottom herself, but this did not make it any less personal.

Shortly afterwards Jo was quite literally suddenly in the public eye. The artists' society Arti et Amicitiae exhibited the portrait of her recently drawn by Lizzy Ansingh (Figure 65). Maria de Klerk-Viola praised both the portraitist and the by now famous subject of the portrait in the *NRC* of 24 October 1924: 'Everyone in Amsterdam knows the talented woman with a wide-ranging interest in art, whose admirable hard work we have to thank for the books of letters by her brother-in-law Vincent van Gogh—and so can form an opinion about the striking likeness.'[134] She also pointed out that Jo's dark eyes sparkled so brightly—a comment that was followed up in *De Tijd* of 29 October, in which the reviewer referred to a face 'in which the warm, intelligent eyes quiver with inner life.'[135] Her physical condition deteriorated shockingly fast, but apparently the same could not be said of her charisma.

Galerie Marcel Bernheim & Cie

There was one more Van Gogh exhibition in Paris during Jo's lifetime. It opened at the beginning of 1925, but Jo had to refuse many other requests before that. Carl Marcus of the Frankfurter Kunstverein tried, for instance, followed by Emil Richter from Dresden, the Nassauischer Kunstverein in Wiesbaden, the Münchener Neue-Secession and the Kunstverein in Hamburg.[136] There was clearly no lack of interest, but Jo barely responded any more.

Galerie Marcel Bernheim & Cie in rue de Caumartin, on the other hand, had indicated as early as April 1924 that they wanted to take over the Basel exhibition. Jo looked favourably on the idea, although she took care to tell them straight away that most of the paintings were not for sale.[137] This was followed by an exchange of letters in order to agree suitable dates, and in October she sent Bernheim a list of the titles of the works.[138] In response he sent her a form and asked her to fill it in immediately and have it countersigned by the consulate. French customs, pursuant to the French War Damage Compensation Act, levied 26 per cent tax, which was extremely high, and Jo had to confirm that German merchandise was not involved.[139] She did so, and to avoid confusion put all the works in Vincent's name.[140]

Bernheim told Jo that the opening of the exhibition on 5 January 1925 was a success, and someone wanted to pay 10,000 guilders for the *Irises*. It was a splendid sum, to be sure, but she telegraphed uncompromisingly: 'not for sale'.[141] He replied that the buyer wanted to give the work to the Louvre and hoped she would reconsider her position in light of that, but she did not. A year before, after lengthy hesitation, she had consented to sell one of her favourites to the National Gallery in London, but now she refused point blank.[142] Jo asked for press cuttings and a copy of the catalogue, which she received by return, but she had an unpleasant surprise when she read it: Vincent's name was not referred to anywhere, yet all the other owners were mentioned.[143]

She remained critical, resilient and active, but in the last year of her life she realized that all her work organizing and making arrangements was coming to an end. As she confessed to her loyal friend Paul Gachet: 'It is not for my pleasure but for the sake of Vincent's work that I arrange all these exhibitions. Once I'm gone, there will be an end to it.'[144] It was clear that her powers were gradually deteriorating, but as far as the outside world was concerned, she remained the same combative woman. That was crystal clear from her portrait with sparkling eyes by Lizzy Ansingh and the lively portrait of her that Isaac Israëls painted that same year (Plate 61). Jo's nephew Henk Bonger wrote later that during this period she had a 'slightly raspy, deep voice' when she talked about her life. He described her as a woman 'who controlled her emotions, had her own opinions, a wry sense of humour and a clear sense of values'. He said her thinking was open and progressive.[145]

Pulchri

During the rest of her life Jo only lent Van Gogh works for exhibitions three times—in The Hague, then Potsdam and finally Utrecht. In November 1924 the board of the Pulchri Studio society in The Hague requested permission to stage an exhibition of works from her and her son's collection. She consented for herself and on behalf of Vincent, but first the shipment had to return from Paris.[146] The society's secretary corresponded with her about the practical arrangements. This time she was the one to say that something had to be done to maintain the condition of the works: 'An artist friend in Paris,' this may have been Émile Bernard, 'pointed out to me that a few paintings need to be given new stretchers, which can perhaps be done immediately—at my expense of course.'[147] Six days later, the director, Johan Hendrik Christoffel Vermeer, confirmed that everything had arrived from Paris and responded to her request to have some paintings re-stretched. Shortly afterwards Jo had a few more works transported for the exhibition, which was scheduled for March and April.[148] She specified, without doubt in consultation with Vincent, the minimum prices for three paintings and even offered a bulk discount: '*Ears of Wheat*, 3,000 guilders, *L'Allée in Arles*, 9,000 guilders, *Books*, 9,500 guilders; for all three 20,000 guilders. The others are not for sale.' The attractive offer she made concerned *Ears of Wheat* (F 767 / JH 2034), *Piles of French Novels* (F 358 / JH 1612) and *The Garden of Saint Paul's Hospital ('Leaf-Fall')* (F 651 / JH 1844).[149]

Yet again, all sorts of misunderstandings about Van Gogh had to be corrected, she wrote to Steenhoff with a degree of irritation. For example, the image of him as a possessed and coarse figure, a sort of wild man 'who does everything in a daze of agitation. He was nothing like that. He possessed infinite amounts of tenderness and delicacy of feelings.' And she sighed: 'I often think: "How difficult it is to establish the pure truth about something."'[150] She wrote she was busy working on the English translation of the letters written in French (she was still hoping for an English publication) and had also parted company with a few of her 'very finest paintings', and so the walls of her rooms were bare, but she was used to that and she had always been prepared to do something for the good cause. Elated, she told him Vincent and Josina were expecting their third child around Easter. That was her grandson Floor. He was to be followed by a fourth grandchild, Mathilde ('Til'), but she was not born until 1929, four years after Jo's death.

Floor's birth coincided more or less with an equally happy event for Jo, which was the publication of the third volume of the new edition of *Brieven aan zijn broeder*. 'Interest in Van Gogh's work and in him as a person continues to grow,' observed a journalist from *Het Vaderland* on 25 April 1925, and he continued: 'The second edition of these interesting letters is proof of this, as are the exhibitions of his work in Paris and here in Pulchri.'[151] When the exhibition was over and all but three of the works had returned, they were divided between two homes—Jo's and Vincent and Josina's. The list, which has survived, shows which works Jo considered to be her 'very finest':

> Paintings in Koninginneweg: 1 Arles landscape—2 Auvers sunset—3 Cypresses with two figures—4 St. Rémy winter landscape—5 Tower in Nuenen—6 La Veillée (after Millet)—7 Woman at the cradle (Paris). To Berlin—8 Orchard in Blossom (white)—9 Orchard in Blossom (pink)—10 Fruit still life (yellow)
>
> Paintings in Waldeck Pyrmontlaan: 1 Bedroom. To Berlin—2 Painter's house in Arles. To Berlin—3 Self-portrait—4 Sea—5 Sower—6 Thresher, after Millet—7 Sheep shearer, after Millet—8 Seine at Asnières.[152]

'To Berlin': these were the paintings Jo had meanwhile committed to lend for the exhibition '50 Jahre Holländische Malerei 1875–1925' in Potsdam. Hendrik Enno van Gelder, director of the Haagse Gemeentemuseum, had acted as intermediary and managed to persuade her to part with seven works on loan.[153] Three of them usually hung on the walls of Jo's and Vincent's homes—they were *Woman at the Cradle*, *Bedroom* and *The Yellow House*—but she had asked Pulchri to send them directly to the Gemeentemuseum so they would be part of a combined shipment to Potsdam.[154]

The last loan she made during her lifetime, her *Irises* (F 678 / JH 1977), was for the 'Tentoonstelling van bloemstillevens van Hollandsche kunstenaars', a show in Utrecht's Centraal Museum, which ran in August and September. Vincent lent his *Sunflowers*. These two key paintings by Van Gogh, which were always among Jo and Vincent's favourites, symbolically marked an end, as fitting as it was powerful, to the impressive series of loans that were made over a period of more than three decades.[155]

'An uncommonly strong woman'

Wednesday 2 September 1925 was reasonably mild, with a maximum temperature of around eighteen degrees Celsius. in other words, it was not too warm and muggy for someone like Jo, who suffered in hot weather throughout her life. She had been desperately ill during the preceding days and finally, on that Wednesday in her summer home in Laren, she died peacefully in her sleep at half past six in the evening.[156] The cause of death is not known, but Parkinson's sufferers usually die from a lung infection or heart failure.

Jo was buried during a heavy rain shower at 12.30 p.m. on 5 September in Zorgvlied Cemetery in Amsterdam, beside her second husband Johan Cohen Gosschalk.[157] The *Algemeen Handelsblad* reported on it and listed among the mourners family members, friends and acquaintances, including Nelly Bodenheim, Lizzy Ansingh, Jacob-Baart de la Faille, H.L. Klein, Johannes de Bois, Frank van der Goes and his wife Marie Koens, Cornelis Baard, the writer Anna van Gogh-Kaulbach, Mrs C. Kok, treasurer of the BSDVC, and board members of that association. There were also some employees of the publishers Wereldbibliotheek. The bier was covered with wreaths of white asters and *Hesperis tristis*, alongside colourful bouquets of wild flowers; the Wereldbibliotheek's wreath had a ribbon bearing the words LOYALTY, DEDICATION, LOVE. There were no speeches at the graveside. Afterwards Vincent thanked everyone for coming. According to the newspapers he was deeply moved by all the interest that had been shown.[158]

These days, a visitor to Jo's grave will notice that her middle name, Gezina, is wrongly spelled on the gravestone as Gesina. Ironically, she always hated that name. The gravestone also has the year of her birth wrong. It should be 1862, not 1863. Apparently, Vincent based his information on a letter from Jo to Theo during their engagement in which she jokingly pretended to be a year younger than she actually was.[159] It is not known whether she ever considered being buried in Auvers-sur-Oise.

Many obituaries were published shortly after Jo's death. They praise her efforts to make Van Gogh world famous as an artist and letter writer. And her work for the 'Kunst aan het Volk' circle was also acclaimed. They are elegies to a well-spent life, during which Jo succeeded in inspiring the general public as well as herself. In the *NRC* of 4 September, Willem Steenhoff talked about the 'unquenchable enthusiasm in her dark eyes'. Admiringly, he wrote: 'She heroically completed her mission, and in so doing intellectually enriched her own life.' According to him, she had contributed 'to helping people understand the value of Vincent van Gogh as a person and an artist'.[160] That same day, Liede Tilanus commemorated her fellow party member in *Het Volk*, and a standard announcement about Jo's death was printed in other newspapers, including the *NRC*, *De Telegraaf*, *Het Vaderland*, the *Nieuwe Arnhemsche Courant*, the *Provinciale Drentsche en Asser Courant* and the *Utrechtsch Provinciaal en Stedelijk Dagblad*. *De Gooi- en Eemlander* followed a day later, praising her active mind, her talent as an organizer and her generous willingness to share her rich art collection. J.H. de Bois wrote an obituary in the *Haarlems Dagblad* lauding Jo's immense dedication and perseverance. He also observed tellingly: 'We must never forget that this was always a woman who took on the burden of all the worries, requests etc. etc.'[161] A woman who had been able to hold her own in a world completely dominated by men—at the end of the nineteenth century and beginning of the twentieth that was anything but self-evident.

Jo's influential role was acknowledged in various ways in the years that followed. In a letter of 5 May 1926 to Andries Bonger, for example, Émile Bernard talked about her death. He recalled that during her eventful life she was twice widowed and referred to her 'noble dedication' to the cause of establishing Van Gogh's fame.[162] Many years later, at the opening of the exhibition in the Stedelijk Museum in 1953 to celebrate the centenary Van Gogh's birth, it was clear that she had not been forgotten: Mark Edo Tralbaut's speech praised Jo, who 'illuminated Vincent's palette, which had blossomed in the glow of Theo's heart, and preserved it for future generations'. He tellingly called her 'an uncommonly strong woman'.[163]

According to *De Proletarische Vrouw*, Jo was always apologizing for the fact she had not done more for the socialist movement. But she had her reasons. 'She would say that raising her son and guiding him in the right direction was also a contribution to society. "That was therefore my primary task". Those were her exact words.'[164] They perfectly reflected what she had written to Vincent on the eve of his wedding: 'I know of nothing more sublime than seeing you happy. Know that it is the crowning glory of my life!'[165] And he summarized it pithily himself when writing to Gachet: 'You know well what she's been doing for the last thirty-five years; at the same time for me it was as if she only lived for me.'[166] There was no question that her son had always been her support and anchor since 1891: 'my treasure, my comfort, my support, my all, to whom I cling and who gives me the courage to go on living.'[167]

Her son and her brother-in-law—both controlled her life, and the thought of committing herself to them and using all her efforts for them became entrenched in her soul from the very beginning. For over thirty-five years Jo gave both Vincents all she had.

Epilogue

'An exceptional example for women'

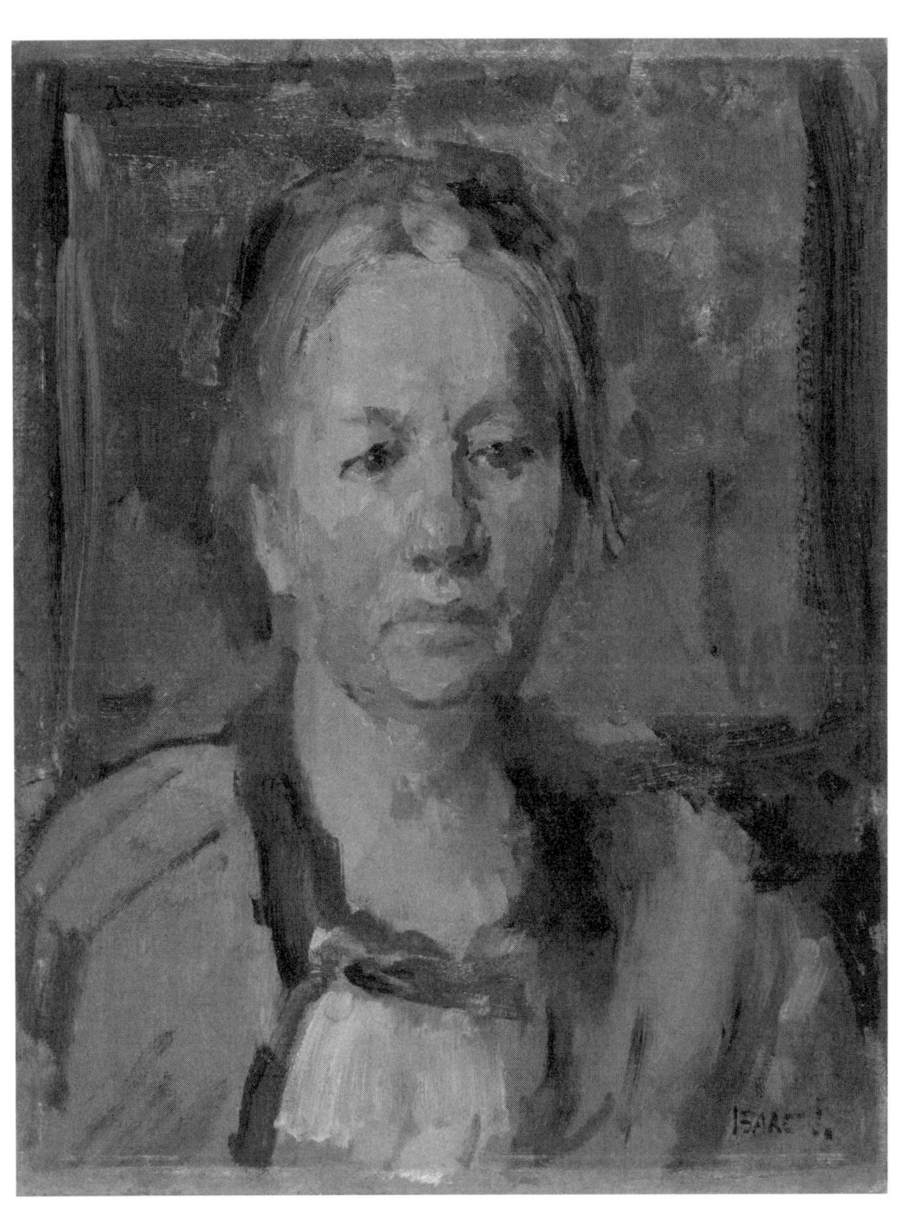

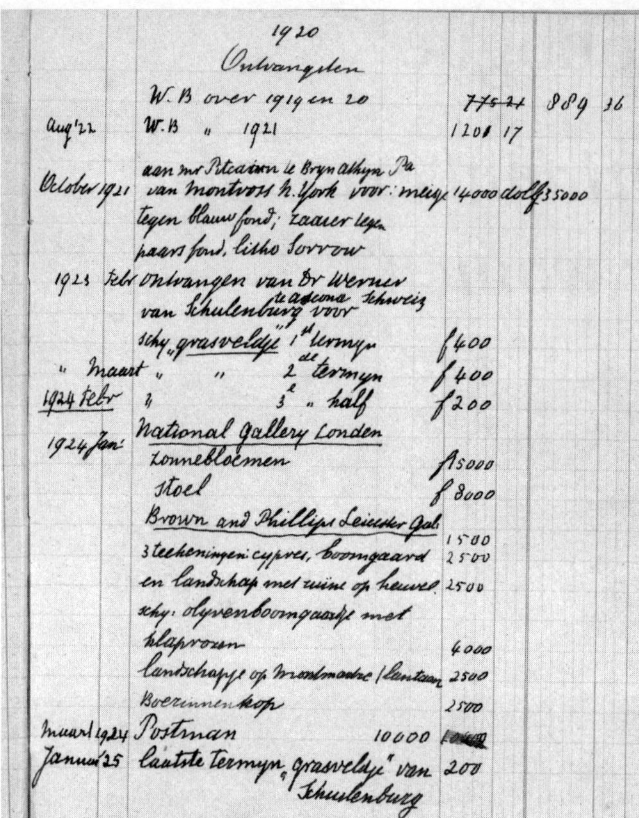

1920
Ontvangsten
W.B over 1919 en 20 ~~775.21~~ 889 36
Aug '22 W.B " 1921 1201 17
aan mr Pitcairn te Bryn athyn Pa
October 1921 van Montross N. York voor: meisje 14000 dolls 35000
tegen blauwe fond; zaaier tegen
paars fond. litho Sorrow
1923 Febr Ontvangen van Dr Werner
van Schulenburg te Ascona Schweiz voor
schy. "grasveldje" 1st termyn f400
" Maart " " 2de termyn f400
1924 Febr " 3e " half f200
1924 Jan: National Gallery Londen
Zonnebloemen f15000
Stoel f8000
Brown and Phillips Leicester Gal.
3 teekeningen: cypres, boomgaard 1500 2500
en landschap met ruine op heuvel 2500
schy: olyvenboomgaardje met
klaprozen 4000
landschapje op Montmartre (Lentetuin) 2500
Boerinnenkop 2500
Maart 1924 Postman 10000
Januari 25 laatste termyn "grasveldje" van Schulenburg 200

Figure 66 Vincent van Gogh, receipts of sales in the Account Book, between 1920 and January 1925.

Until shortly before her death, Jo was still actively negotiating and selling a final few of Van Gogh's works. During the last years of her life, Vincent noted down the transactions in the same cash book his parents had used since their wedding in 1889 (Figure 66).[1] After Jo's death the entire collection passed to him. He was also responsible for settling her estate. The first item on the inheritance tax return was the 'household contents', valued at only 3,178 guilders. The 'undivided half' of the works of art, including those by Johan Cohen Gosschalk, added up to 9,075 guilders. Among other things, Jo left debentures and mortgage bonds, as well as Villa Eikenhof in Bussum (18,000 guilders). The proceeds from selling works by Van Gogh over the years are not recorded in this document. Vincent had to pay inheritance tax on 71,069 guilders. The page listing 'liabilities' reveals that Jo had outstanding commitments when she died: current subscriptions to *De Socialistische Gids. Maandschrift der Sociaal-Democratische Arbeiderspartij*, *Het Volk* and the *NRC*, and unpaid bills from the car rental firm Crayé, her doctor W. Feltkamp, nurse Bongers (who nursed her during her last months), and a private night security service. There were also memberships of the Protestantsche Ziekenzorg medical care organization and the Leesinrichting Lectura reading material service.[2]

This last membership had been very important to Jo. She read a lot throughout her life. She bought books and was given them as presents, and she and Vincent were always devoted library users, both recognizing the great social importance of libraries. Part of Jo's substantial collection of books was given a public purpose after her death: doubtless at her request, Vincent donated more than three hundred books to the Laren-Blaricum public reading room and library. According to the *Laarder Courant De Bel* of 17 November 1925, they 'included very many important works in all manner of fields, and particularly about art and art history in many European countries'.[3]

With heavy hearts Vincent and Josina emptied Jo's flat in Amsterdam. The letters, diaries and photographs they found evoked such strong emotions that they prompted Vincent to commission Isaac Israëls to paint another portrait of his mother, with a background probably alluding to the colours of *The Yellow House ('The Street')* (Plate 62).[4] Suddenly their home was overflowing with furniture and other things. Now all the Van Gogh paintings and drawings that had hung or were stored at 77 Koninginneweg also passed to Vincent.

In 1925, he was in fact, faced with the same predicament as his mother had been in 1891: like it or not he was saddled with the collection and now he had to decide what should happen to it. Initially he declared that art did little for him and that he had a greater affinity for technology and how to organize companies. He had to prove to himself that he could earn his own living, and he did not want to go through life simply benefitting from the capital that had been acquired and his uncle's ever-growing fame. Vincent's son Johan later wrote: 'At that time my father definitely wanted to keep his Van Gogh collection intact, but not to devote any further effort to it. He was concentrating on his engineering career and did not want to be regarded as the nephew of the famous painter. . . . It was not until after the war that he took an active interest in the collection.'[5] As time passed it proved to be difficult, if not impossible, for Vincent to emerge from the shadow of his world-famous uncle, to whom he was linked throughout his life if only because of his name. Gradually he began to take on the role that Theo and Jo had previously fulfilled. After 1945 he gave no end of lectures about Van Gogh in the Netherlands and other countries, usually in connection with exhibitions. He was always very modest about his own role. In the speech he gave during celebrations of his eighty-fifth birthday in 1975, he described it as a 'derived function' and referred to Vincent and Theo as the 'key players'.[6]

In the summer of 1926, ten months after Jo's death, the art dealer Johannes de Bois contacted Vincent. He wrote that he had visited Jo now and again at the end of her life, but no longer discussed business with her, one reason being that 'a number of years ago, the decision appears to have been taken not to sell anything more from the stock of works by Vincent still in your possession. Unfortunately for me. . .' Now, however, he had seen a 'fairly large number' at Pulchri that were for sale and he therefore cautiously offered his services again.[7] He was not mistaken. Vincent remained prepared to make loans for exhibitions, and the sale of works also went on for a while, with De Bois continuing to assist.[8] Vincent sold a few further works.[9] At the end of 1926 he offered to sell two paintings to Ernest Brown & Phillips for 6,000 guilders each.[10] Sales peaked in 1927, when he sold eleven works for a total of 44,500 guilders to the Leicester Galleries in London, including *Couple Walking between Rows of Poplars* (F 773 / JH 2041) and *Portrait of Madame Trabuc* (F 631 / JH 1777).[11] This was at the same time a tactical move because publication of the letters in English was imminent. He did not decide to stop selling for good until a couple of years later. 'He explained to me that he had now enough money to educate his children and that he would not contemplate selling any more, but that I could have as many as I liked for an exhibition,' wrote the art dealer Oliver Brown, recalling a visit to Vincent in 1930.[12]

J.-B. de la Faille published the first Van Gogh catalogue raisonné in 1928. It is interesting to see how Van Gogh's art was spread over the Netherlands and the rest of the world at that time. Vincent then owned 595 works; H.P. Bremmer and his circle—including the Kröller-Müllers and other Bremmerians—had 486, and a further seventy-seven were owned by Dutch private individuals and museums. Meanwhile 513 Van Goghs had found their way abroad. The total number of located works, 1,671, was more or less equally divided between paintings and drawings.[13] Jo had noted down the sale of 192 paintings and fifty-five works on paper in the cash book, but it does not contain all sales. We know for certain that her total sales amounted to over 325,000 guilders, and this success must have given her personal satisfaction. A substantial proportion of this sum must at some point have ended up in the hands of her son Vincent. It is difficult to reconcile this with what he wrote later about the fact that Jo refused to accept her part of Johan Cohen Gosschalk's estate, remarking that she could certainly have used the money, since she obviously cannot have been hard up during all those years.[14]

Set against all the sales, in later years there were also acquisitions, some of them due to Vincent's efforts, of paintings, drawings, letters and documents as a result of donation, inheritance or purchase. These included *Woman Binding Sheaves (after Jean-François Millet)* (F 700 / JH 1781), from the estate of Jo's sister Betsy, who died in 1944, *The Garden of the Asylum* (F 659 / JH 1850), donated by Paul Gachet in 1954, and the four letters from Van Gogh to Anton Kerssemakers, which Vincent bought in London in 1964.[15] Jo's letters to Paul Gachet Sr and Jr also ultimately found their way into the growing collection. For decades she and Gachet Jr had a relatively frank relationship and Vincent also had friendly contacts with him. At the end of the 1930s, Gachet wrote how vividly he could still recall Jo.[16] He saved the correspondence because he recognized its value—'there are often very interesting passages'—but later he gave all the letters to Vincent; eventually they entered the Van Gogh Museum's collection by way of the Vincent van Gogh Foundation.[17]

After Jo died, Vincent did everything within his power to fulfil her last wish. Only a month after her death, the London publisher Constable—through the mediation of the Wereldbibliotheek—made him an attractive proposal for an edition of the letters translated into English, after which the negotiations made rapid progress.[18] Vincent stipulated that his mother's translation, in which the character of the original was respected with such emphasis, must remain intact. It was permissible to correct Americanisms, but not until they had been submitted to him. It is no longer possible to find out exactly which changes the publisher proposed because the copy of Jo's translations has not survived. Vincent also asked that his tribute to his mother should be titled 'Loyalty, Devotion, Love'. He checked all the proofs and made meticulous comments.[19]

So finally, in 1927, the first two volumes of Jo's English translation, on which she had worked for years so diligently and almost doggedly, appeared: *The Letters of Vincent van Gogh to his Brother, 1872–1886*, published by Constable & Co and Houghton Mifflin Co in London, Boston and New York, the same publishers who put the anthology *The Letters of a Post-Impressionist, Being the Familiar Correspondence of Vincent van Gogh* on the market in 1912–13. Vincent asked for complimentary copies to be sent to Jo's brothers Henri, Andries and Wim, to Walter Pach in America, to Mrs Harrison (his English landlady in 1912), and to his business partner Ernst Hijmans.[20] *The Burlington Magazine for Connoisseurs* praised Jo's 'rare devotion to the task of assuring the fame of her husband's brother Vincent' and the reviewer was also very impressed by her translation: 'Apart from an occasional slip, the translation is extremely well done.' He described the publication as a whole as 'a worthy monument to one of the most remarkable and heroic figures in the whole history of art'.[21] These were very grand words that would have given Jo great satisfaction. The third volume, *Further Letters of Vincent van Gogh to his Brother, 1886–1889*, with, again, a foreword by Vincent, followed in 1929. Jo had barely made a start on translating the letters in French it contained. Cornelis de Dood translated them.[22]

Jo conceived *Brieven aan zijn broeder* as a monument to Vincent and Theo, and her son Vincent continued down that path with the three-volume edition in English, followed by *Lettres à son frère Vincent* with letters from Theo (1932), which also contained the five letters from Jo to Vincent, and finally the impressive four-volume *Verzamelde brieven van Vincent van Gogh* (1952–54), which was *Brieven aan zijn broeder* and *Lettres à son frère Vincent* supplemented with all of Van Gogh's other correspondence and further relevant documents.[23] He included the tribute to his mother in each of these publications.[24]

Vincent did not speak much about Jo to his children: 'My father was not communicative about his mother; he told us a lot about art, but he was tight-lipped when it came to her,' said his son Johan.[25] When talking to others, however, he sometimes made telling comments about her. For instance, he told an acquaintance, William J. Gravesmill, that Jo was 'the perfect pack rat', someone who carefully hoarded everything, as a result of which there remains a unique collection of letters and documents at our disposal.[26] If *Brieven aan zijn broeder* had formed the basis for a series of new letter editions, which appeared in a range of languages, Vincent's *Verzamelde brieven* was the icing on the cake. It too was published in various languages, with the result that Van Gogh's letters are currently known all over the world, and this has obviously had a significant impact on the appreciation of his art. The most recent, digital edition of the letters: Vincent van Gogh, *The Letters: The Complete Illustrated and Annotated Edition* (2009), was a continuation of these earlier editions.[27]

Looking back at what Jo accomplished over the years as an exhibition organizer and a seller of Van Gogh's art, one is struck by the fact that in the first instance her own initiatives were limited. Right from the start, and thereafter progressively more often, she contributed to exhibitions. Her own personal successes were the shows in the Panoramazaal in 1892-1893, and above all the one in the Stedelijk Museum thirteen years later. In the course of selling Van Gogh's art she learned how to play the market shrewdly. On occasion she marketed a substantial number of works at once, and then refrained for a considerable period in order to see what effect her actions were having. This was one of the factors that created an increasingly fertile environment for Van Gogh's art. She saw for herself how the Van Gogh machine went on running ever faster. During her lifetime exhibitions of all types and sizes were organized everywhere.

Jo's perseverance was founded on idealistic motives. First and foremost, she wanted, come what may, to complete the task that Theo had set himself in 1890—publicizing Vincent's art. Secondly, and no less importantly to her, she supported the socialist view that looking at art could elevate people, and this meant that the paintings and drawings had to be displayed far and wide so people could see them. To begin with, she sold most works from her own home. Later on, she worked more and more through the mediation of successful art dealers. She was prudent enough not to give anyone the sole selling rights. Most transactions were conducted via Bernheim-Jeune (Paris), Cassirer (Berlin) and De Bois (Amsterdam, The Hague, Haarlem)—the last two of whom each sold more than fifty works by Van Gogh. According to Jo, purchases by museums were the best recognition of Van Gogh's art, so she gave a number of museums a discount. Donations and loans, including long-term ones, as in 1916 to the Rijksmuseum, also had a favourable effect. For a long time, sales in the United Kingdom and the United States lagged behind significantly. Jo was so keen on publishing the letters in English—she knew it could represent a substantial shot in the arm for his fame all over the world—that during the last decade of her life she offered some works exclusively on the British and American markets in the hope that the presence of Van Gogh's art in Anglo-Saxon collections would also stimulate curiosity about his letters.

Some of the works were always for sale in virtually every exhibition. Jo combined masterpieces that were not for sale with drawings and other paintings that could be sold. She tried to do justice to Van Gogh's oeuvre while at the same time igniting visitors' interest in buying.[28] It became ever more beneficial for her not to agree to excessively low bids or to respond to requests to drop asking prices, although she continued to have moments of weakness. Jo was aware that appreciation for a work of art was also reflected in the pricing. After 1914, by which time she had sold more than two hundred works, she throttled back significantly on selling. She categorically refused to part with a huge core of paintings, which she wanted to retain for the family. She knew from Vincent's letters, and those from Theo himself, which their favourites were, and as far as Jo's own preference for certain paintings and drawings was concerned, both aesthetic and emotional considerations would have played a role. The same will doubtless also have applied to her son. Jo did not need the proceeds of the sales for her own daily living expenses. Ultimately, they secured Vincent's financial future.

After the Second World War, Van Gogh's work acquired progressively greater fame, which spread far beyond the borders of Europe. Jo's reputation was also enhanced in its wake. In 1962 the Japanese magazine *Art Garden* published an article about Van Gogh. It included a portrait photograph of Jo between photographs of the two brothers. She was portrayed in glowing terms as an 'exceptional example' for women whose horizon extends beyond motherhood: 'The wise Madame Bonger, Johanna, is a miraculous paragon among women. One hopes that the women of the world will follow Madame Bonger's example and, not merely content to be mothers, will bear the desire to discover and cultivate genius.'[29] During that same year a small monument to Jo, Theo and Vincent was unveiled in Sanda (Hyogo), just to the north of Kobe.

There is nothing to suggest that Jo and her son ever discussed the possibility of founding a museum. Jo's reason for hanging on to certain works was more likely to have been bound up with her family's collection, rather than ideas for a possible future museum. While Helene Kröller-Müller was collecting her art primarily to show it to the general public, Jo's efforts were always aimed at both showing Van Gogh's work and selling it, which she did by deliberately not saturating the market and always ensuring that the art went to owners spread far and wide. It was not until April 1931, some years after her death, that this approach changed, when Vincent lent 239 works by Van Gogh and twenty-eight by contemporary artists to Amsterdam City Council for an indefinite period so they could be exhibited in the Stedelijk Museum.[30]

'You must come with me to Amsterdam,' said Vincent to his wife Josina shortly beforehand, after which they went to the Amsterdam alderman concerned and jointly signed a covenant. This was the first step towards making the family collection permanently accessible to the public in a museum context. Josina had a great deal of influence on this decision—she felt it was important to enable more people to enjoy the paintings, which is something Jo would certainly have agreed with. Jo never went to such lengths herself—on the one hand because only part of the collection was her property, and on the other because she always saw the purpose of her task in different terms. The decision also suited Vincent better. He no longer wanted to have too much practical involvement. By then he was comfortably off and he decided not to sell anything else. He also supported Josina's position that as many people as possible should be able to become acquainted with Van Gogh's work.[31]

The spectacular show in the Stedelijk Museum was a great success and confirmed Van Gogh's fame. In 1935 Vincent received the City of Amsterdam's Silver Medal of Honour for his services and in 1955 the Prins Bernhard Fonds granted him the Silver Carnation Award for his special significance to Dutch culture. Jo was emphatically honoured on that occasion too. According to the report, she kept the lion's share of the collection together and, with her son, introduced 'millions' of people to Van Gogh's paintings, drawings and letters thanks to their generous approach to loans and publications: 'It was her belief in the value of the work and her love of the task that Vincent had set himself in his work that in fact resulted in this decoration.'[32]

For years a substantial part of the collection was in Vincent's house in Laren, where he went to live after Jo's death, but as time passed he became aware that it would be better to look for a permanent home for it, so the first Vincent van Gogh Foundation was established in 1949. On 28 December 1960, it became part of the Theo van Gogh Foundation, which had been set up in the meantime. On the same day a new Vincent van Gogh Foundation was established. Its regulations were laid down in a deed of 10 July 1962. This second foundation still exists. Vincent sold his Van Gogh collection to this foundation in that same month, including the part which had been on loan to the Stedelijk Museum for all that time. He discussed the matter at length with A.M. Hammacher (director of the Kröller-Müller Museum) and H.J. Reinink (Director-General of Fine Arts at the Ministry of Education, Arts and Sciences). According to his son, Johan, the initiative for the foundation was taken not by his father but by the Dutch government, which also undertook to build a museum in which the newly acquired collection could be exhibited. The Dutch State paid over 18.4 million guilders for the entire collection, thus ensuring it would stay in the Netherlands. 'The Dutch State commits to pay the interest and repayments of a loan to be taken out by the foundation, which loan amounts to 18,470,000 guilders, to pay the purchase price the foundation is willing to accept.' The Vincent van Gogh Foundation was the owner. If it failed to meet its obligations, the collection would revert to the Dutch State.[33]

It was more than ten years later, on 2 June 1973, that the 'Rijksmuseum Vincent van Gogh' opened in Paulus Potterstraat in Amsterdam. It stands next door to the Stedelijk Museum and a stone's throw from the Rijksmuseum, where in 1885 the passionate painter from Nuenen was so deeply impressed by the paintings of seventeenth-century Dutch masters.[34] That painter now had his own museum, and from that moment on he and his art would fulfil a comparable role for young artists and visitors from all over the world, who as the years have passed have streamed to Museumplein in ever growing numbers.

At the outset of Vincent's engineering career it did not look as though he would devote himself to Van Gogh's art, but in the end he, like his mother, worked hard for decades to promote attention to his uncle's work and life. It remains puzzling and inexplicable, however, why he made absolutely no mention of his mother's name in his speech at the museum's opening in 1973. He died in 1978, after which his children, grandchildren and great-grandchildren took over this task. These days the family continues the work conscientiously and with tremendous involvement through the Vincent van Gogh Foundation and in other ways.[35]

Since then, there has been no lack of attention to Jo. Since 2012 a separate wall in the Van Gogh Museum has been devoted to the role Jo and her son played in looking after the collection. An entry about Jo was included in the *Digitaal Lexicon voor Vrouwen in Nederland* in 2014, and in 2019 her biography *Alles voor Vincent* was published in Dutch. Her achievements will be described in the *Art*

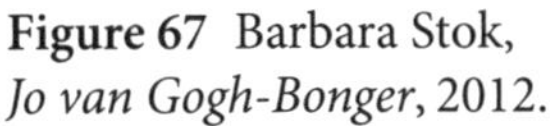

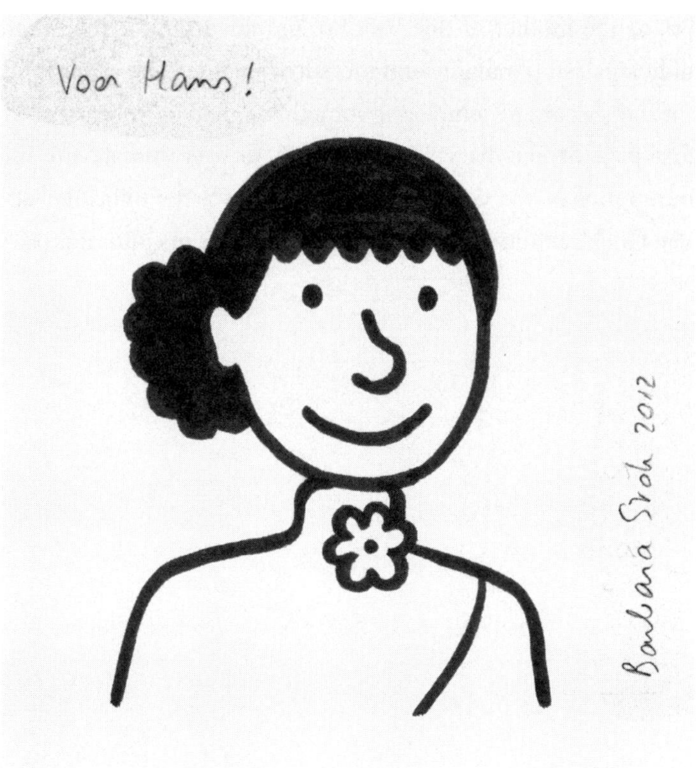

Figure 67 Barbara Stok, *Jo van Gogh-Bonger*, 2012.

Market Dictionary, launched in 2022.[36] She has also appealed more than once to the imagination of writers, who have featured her in novellas, novels, plays, screenplays and comics (Plate 63, Figure 67).[37]

Little is known about Jo's inner life during her last few years because there are no written sources. She had stopped keeping a diary long before, and she spoke to her friends more often than she wrote to them. Her medical condition was also a very serious obstacle when it came to writing. Her earlier diaries and correspondence, in particular with members of her family, and of course with Theo, Vincent, Johan, Steenhoff and Gachet Jr, remain the best sources on this point. They paint the frankest picture of her thoughts and opinions. The diaries of her son Vincent also reveal glimpses now and then. She herself was only too well aware of the unknowable nature of someone's deepest being, which is doomed to remain hidden in the hustle and bustle of everyday life. The fact that she had many unspoken longings and ideas is revealed by a passage from the novel *Kenelm Chillingly* by Edward Bulwer-Lytton that she copied into her diary on 4 April 1880: 'Where is that innermost self, so deep down, so deep, yet when it does come forth, so much higher, higher, immeasurably higher than one's every day self? It longs to get to the stars and then, ah how soon it fades back again!'[38]

Jo really wanted to know who she was, but in the end she did not permit herself time and scope to do so. From this perspective you could say that to an extent she discounted and sacrificed herself. And yet, as the mother of one Vincent and advocate for the other, she was able to lead her life in an individual, wide-ranging and measured manner. She never fulfilled her dream of writing a book, but she did succeed in completing something 'great or noble', as she had intended and written on the very first page of her diary.[39] It is difficult to overestimate the importance of Jo's work in the global recognition of Van Gogh's greatness. Thanks to her unbridled efforts, she unmistakably contributed to Van Gogh's attaining a lasting place of honour in cultural history.

Notes

Introduction: 'An Amsterdam girl'

1 By law, the guardian had to get a court-appointed joint guardian without delay. Jo's father was appointed. It was his duty to supervise Jo as guardian with regard to Vincent's property. After Mr Bonger's death in 1904, Jo's oldest brother Henri, who also managed her banking for her at the time, was probably appointed as joint guardian. Cf. the bill from the notary Ten Sijthoff that Jo settled at the beginning of 1905. *Account Book* 2002, pp. 124 and 162. Seventeen-twentieths of Vincent's estate (the part that was in Auvers-sur-Oise when he died) went to his little nephew Vincent under the terms of a deed of gift drawn up in July 1891. This deed is VGM, b2216. See also Chapter 7. On the life of Jo's son and the artist's nephew, Vincent van Gogh, see Van Crimpen 2002 and the biography of him being prepared by Roelie Zwikker.

2 VGM, b4553.

3 *Account Book* 2002, pp. 9, 20.

4 VGMD. If there are images on both the recto and verso of a canvas, panel or sheet, they are counted separately in these totals. Jo numbered a great many of the drawings herself; the highest number was 271. The watercolours and gouaches had their own numbering. *Account Book* 2002, p. 26.

5 The type of biography I have aimed for in this book is what Hans Renders would call an 'interpretive biography'. 'Its author works rather as an historian than a literary author.' Renders 2008, pp. 6–7. Previous publications with biographical information about Jo are Van Crimpen 1993 (an article about Jo's first years in Bussum and the earliest exhibitions); Meyjes 2007 (a book about Jo's great importance as a promotor of Van Gogh and the professional way she strategically disseminated his works over the years); Modderkolk 2014 (an entry with a thumbnail sketch of Jo's life and work).

6 VGM, b6621; 2 June 1973.

7 As Jan Fontijn, the biographer of Jo's contemporary Frederik van Eeden, described it: 'Such a turning point or moment of conversion can be compared with the literary phenomenon of the epiphany, the moment when the ignorance or innocence of a character in a drama or story becomes knowledge and experience.' Fontijn 2007, p. 79.

8 *Diary* 4, p. 15; 24 February 1892.

9 VGM, b7279; undated (spring 1901).

10 Cf. Chapter 12 for Vincent's difficult disentanglement from his mother.

11 Van Gogh 1952–54, p. 249.

12 Conversation with Els Bonger. Amsterdam, 9 February 2011. She died on 31 March 2014. Els was the daughter of Frans Bonger, who was the son of Wim Bonger, Jo's youngest brother.

13 Van Gogh, *Letters* 2009, letter 740.

14 Anna van Gogh-Carbentus to Theo van Gogh. VGM, b2425; 28 December 1888.

15 VGM, b2022. *Brief Happiness* 1999, p. 77. This letter dates from 1 January 1889.

16 *Diary* 4, p. 13; 24 February 1892.

17 Details taken from a letter from Jo to Elisabeth van Gogh. VGM, b3544; 15 November 1885, from a travel document dated March 1915 in which her height was given as 1.55 metres (five foot one inch) (VGM, b8288) and from the list of passengers sailing from Rotterdam to New York on 12 August 1916 where it is given as 1.60 metres (five foot three inches) (NAW). Her friend Emilie Knappert thought that a portrait of Jo looked 'Japanese'. VGM, b2882; 4 October 1892.

18 Reyneke van Stuwe 1932, pp. 354–6.

19 Heijne 2003, p. 33.

20 Free after Detlev van Heest, *Pleun*. Amsterdam 2010, p. 430.

21 *Diary* 1, p. 69; 20 December 1880.

22 *Diary* 2, p. 60; 4 September 1883.

23 *Diary* 1, p. 97. For the historical reliability and unreliability of autobiographical writings: Van Uildriks, *Dagboek* 2010, p. 10 (n. 4) and 40–2. Cf. also www.egodocument.net.

24 Bonger, *Dagboeken—Diaries* 2019: www.bongerdiaries.org.

25 *Diary* 4, p. 13; 24 February 1892.

26 Van Gogh 1952–54, pp. 244–7.

27 A digital edition of the text of these letters is currently in preparation.

28 *Brief Happiness* 1999. Introduction and commentary Han van Crimpen. Eds. Leo Jansen and Jan Robert.

29 Jo to Theo. VGM, b4254; 19 January 1889. *Brief Happiness* 1999, p. 94.

30 *Vincent's Diary*, 2 September 1973. During the First World War the censor read letters sent from the United States and London; the recipient could tell from a stamp on the item that it had been opened. VGM, Bd78.

31 Jo had a telephone from around 1907. *Vincent's Diary*, 13 September 1933.

32 *Account Book* 2002, published by Chris Stolwijk and Han Veenenbos. The account book contains an overview of all Jo's daily income and expenditure.

33 In *Alles voor Vincent* I wrote that the identity of the person who made the suggestion was unknown. Luijten 2019, pp. 359–60. Coquiot pasted new notes between numbered pages in the exercise book; those pages are not numbered separately. VGM, b7150 (notebook; unpaged) and b3348 (exercise book).

34 *Diary* 4, pp. 53–55; 9 June 1892. Cf. also Nelleke Noordervliet, 'God met een kruimel in zijn baard. Het veelzeggende detail', *Biografie Bulletin* 6, no. 1 (1996), pp. 11–20.

Part One

1 Billy Collins, 'Cemetery ride'. *Aimless Love: New and Selected Poems*. New York 2013, p. 163.

1 A carefree childhood in a harmonious family

1 Jo to Theo van Gogh. VGM, b4251; 2 January 1889. The other witnesses to the registration were the forty-two-year-old underwriter Johan Brak and the twenty-four-year-old insurance agent Christiaan Schone. ACA.

2 VGM, Bd74.

3 VGM, b3611. The address was B45k Zusterplein, probably the building that is now number 4.

4 L. Visser, *Zeist in oude ansichten*. Vol. 2. Zaltbommel 2000, no. 15. K.W. Galis, 'Ultrajectum', *Seijst* 1 (1973), pp. 14–16.

5 *GAZ*, 16 October 1865.

6 ACA, *Population Register*, KK 320, fol. 770, 6 November 1865. The house was renumbered 289 in 1875.

7 Subscribers to the *Zee-post* included the boards of shipping companies, shipowners, port authorities and the families of seafarers. The editorial offices were at number 3 Rokin, near Vijgendam, (in August 1883). VGM, b1785 and b1875.

8 ACA, *Population Register*, vol. 565, fol. 79, 133. 159a Weteringschans was later renumbered: first 33 and then 145. From 1878 the family lived at number 121. ACA, *Address Book 1887–1888*; *Address Book 1898–1899*. A servant of theirs lodged at 89 Weteringschans.

9 Jo to Theo van Gogh. VGM, b4260; 2 February 1889. *Brief Happiness* 1999, p. 134.

10 VGM, Bd75; 30 November. P.T.F.M. Boekholt and E.P. de Booy, *Geschiedenis van de school in Nederland vanaf de middeleeuwen tot to de huidige tijd*. Assen and Maastricht 1987, p. 129.

11 VGM, b4170; March 1877.

12 The contributions continue until April 1886.

13 Cf. 'The Giaour. A Fragment of a Turkish Tale': 'Yes, love indeed is light from heaven/ A spark of that immortal fire . . ./ To lift from earth our low desire./ Devotion wafts the mind above,/ But Heaven itself descends in love.' *The Poetical Works of Lord Byron*. London and Leipzig 1860, p. 74. 'Zijt gij van de daarin uitgesproken waarheid diep doordrongen, dan zult ge die behagelijke inwendige vrede leeren kennen die voor den mensch een niet hoog genoeg te waardeeren schat is.'

14 *De dichtwerken van P.A. de Génestet*. Ed. C.P. Tiele. 2 vols. Amsterdam 1869, vol. 2, pp. 18–19.

15 'Mijn lieve vader is wat men noemt zeer liberaal maar een echt vroom, godsdienstig man die de goddelijke leer: "heb uw naasten lief als U zelven" niet alleen met de lippen maar met daden belijdt.' 'lieve, goede moeder met haar kinderlijk, onbeperkt vertrouwen.' Jo to Lies van Gogh. VGM, b3546; 13 December 1885.

16 Theo to Jo. VGM, b2051; 18 March 1889. *Brief Happiness* 1999, pp. 220, 226.

17 *Diary* 2, p. 66; 9 September 1883 (quotation) and *Diary* 2, p. 129; 4 October 1884.

18 Jo to Vincent van Gogh. Van Gogh, *Letters* 2009, letter 771; 8 May 1889.

19 Brugmans 1976; *Geschiedenis* 2006, *passim* and pp. 242–4 (population growth); Van der Woud 2010, p. 44.

20 *Diary* 4, p. 35; 29 March 1892.

21 *Diary* 1, pp. 12 and 27; 1 and 18 April 1880. *Geschiedenis* 2006, pp. 348–51.

22 VGM, b8708. The reception was held at the mother of the bride's house on Looiersgracht.

23 Hendrik Bonger to Nicolaas Beets. UBL, LTK Beets 8:1; 5 October 1880.

24 VGM, b8710. Hendrik Bonger noted down information about the family; his daughter Lien supplemented it. VGM, Bd74.

25 *Nederlandsche Staats-Courant*, 13 December 1845, no. 295; *Piet's scheepsindex*. www.scheepsindex.nl. *NRC*, 28 December 1855 and *Nieuwe Amsterdamsche Courant. Algemeen Handelsblad*, 5 January 1856.

26 The other partner was the insurance broker J.S. Brak. Bonger and he had been friends since October 1862. Brak & Moes later merged with the Muntendam insurance company.

27 Weissman 1948, pp. 103–4. In 1988, Frans Bonger, the son of Jo's brother Wim, wrote a brief memoir titled 'De muzikaliteit van de familie Bonger'. Typescript. VGMD.

28 'Ik hoop dat je het gekrabbel kunt lezen maar ze zijn zoo druk aan het muziek maken dat ik er haast niet door heen kan schrijven.' Lien Bonger to Theo van Gogh. VGM, b2846; 2 October 1889. 'Betsij zit zoo van do re mi te zingen dat ik me aldoor vergis.' Wim Bonger to Jo. VGM, b2872; 2 October 1889.

29 Mrs Bonger to Jo. VGM, b2877; 24 June 1889.

30 'Het verwondert me dat wij, die er ons toch op laten voorstaan een echt Hollandsche familie te zijn, dien roman nooit in huis gehad hebben.' Andries to his parents. VGM, b1804; 25 December 1884. Andries had obtained an introduction to Huet through Gerrit van Gorkom and got to know him, his wife and their son Gideon. They often talked about literature and culture in the broadest sense. See also Praamstra 2007, chapters 14–16. Cf. for the elasticity of the concept of 'burgerij' and 'burgerlijkheid': *Bürgerkultur im 19. Jahrhundert. Bildung, Kunst und Lebenswelt.* Ed. Dieter Hein and Andreas Schulz. Munich 1996.

31 In March 1883 Andries asked whether they had read *Die Gartenlaube. Illustrirtes Familienblatt* at home. VGM, b1754. That periodical was probably provided by such a service. The Van Goghs had a subscription to one of these services at this time. VGM, b2268. Cf. also De Vries 2001, pp. 276 and 343.

32 VGM, b4257.

33 Jo's mother later regretted that she had not kept up her languages. VGM, b2877. In her letters she rambles and goes off at a tangent.

34 VGM, b3617 and b3611.

35 'Hoe jonger de kinderen, hoe meer ze zich aan de dominerende moeder hebben kunnen onttrekken. Undated carbon copy of a typescript. VGMD.

36 In March 1891 Willem moved into 46 Weesperzijde, with his sister Jeannette Adelaïde Weissman. On the family: Weissman 1948.

37 Jo to Theo van Gogh. VGM, b4278; 16 March 1889. *Brief Happiness* 1999, p. 220.

38 Jo to Mrs Bonger. VGM, b4300; 14 January 1890. VGM, b4170 (album) and VGM, b1862.

39 'aldoor in haar grijze katoenen japon met 't hoedje met de madelieven.' VGM, b2905, b4291, b2877 and b3242. Jo to Mien Bonger. VGM, b4289; 16 June 1889 (quotation).

40 VGM, b3227 and b3210. 'Van alle kanten hoor ik wonderen van Vincentje. Lien praat nooit over wat anders geloof ik. Hij is ook al weer een heel genot en een groote vergoeding in haar leven.' ('I hear wonders about little Vincent on all sides. I don't think Lien ever talks about anything else. He is a great joy and enormous consolation in her life.') Annie Bonger-van der Linden to Jo. VGM, b2866; 2 February 1892.

41 VGM, b2847. 'De deuren moeten die met warm zeepsop afgeveegd om de vingers er af te krijgen? hindert dat niet voor de verf—och hemel ik weet van al die dingen niets af.' ('Should the doors be wiped with hot soapy water to get the finger-marks off? Won't that hurt the paint—oh heavens, I know absolutely nothing about all these things.') Jo to Mien. VGM, b4291; 11 July 1889.

42 VGM b2864.

43 VGM, b2899, b1026 and b2404. In 1889 Mien read *De Nieuwe Gids*.

44 Kee Vos-Stricker to Jo. VGM, b2806; 20 July 1910. Lies du Quesne-van Gogh to Jo. VGM, b2308; 18 July 1910. Both letters date from shortly after Mien's death.

45 'Ik zou je zooveel willen vertellen dat een doos papier niet voldoende zou zijn om 't te bevatten.' Jo to Mien. VGM, b4285; 26 April 1889. Jo knew about the unrequited love that almost finished Mien. *Diary* 3, p. 126; 11 October 1888.

46 VGM, b4291.

47 VGM, b2890. *Algemeen Handelsblad*, 1 January 1896.

48 'oom Han z'n mooie'. Information from Frans's daughter Els Bonger, 9 February 2011 and son Thijs Bonger, 23 July 2015. Frans was the son of Jo's youngest brother, Wim.

49 With thanks to Els Bonger, who made Henri's travel journals available. VGM, Bd96.

50 This was something he told his second wife. See Van der Borch van Verwolde 1937, p. 112.

51 'dat zal ook wel zo zijn geweest, maar de Bongers overdrijven wel eens'. Bonger 1997, p. 3. Henk Bonger wrote his 'Herinneringen aan mijn oom Dries Bonger', in which he recorded a great many details about the family.

52 Andries to his parents. VGM, b1599; 22 March 1880. *Diary* 1, pp. 70–1; 24 December 1880.

53 'breedvoerige behandeling'; Andries to his parents. VGM, b1618; 8 October 1880.

54 ACA, *Population Register*, vol. 565, fol. 79; 28 November 1879.

55 'Ik voel me tot iets beters in staat dan Commissionnair in kunstbloemen.' VGM, b1576. Andries to his parents. VGM, b1763; 27 May 1883 (quotation).

56 'Amsterdam, vertrokken 3 Mei. DE HUWELIJKSHULK gevoerd door Schipper A. Bonger, naar de Zilver-Ree.' VGM, b8703; no. 15.613, p. 3, columns 1–2; p. 4, column 1.

57 Jo to Mien Bonger, VGM b4285; 26 April 1889. 'Met bijna theatrale, pathetische ernst gaf hij zijn oordelen en er deugde niet veel. De oordelen werden meestal verpakt in verontwaardiging. Ik heb hem nooit zien of horen lachen en ik denk dat hij überhaupt niet lachte.' According to Andries's nephew Henk Bonger, in Bonger 1997, p. 8.

58 'haast tot overgevoeligheid verhoogd zenuwleven'; Van der Borch van Verwolde 1937, p. 116 (quotation), Tralbaut 1963, Locher 1973, Hulsker 1996a, Bonger 1997, *Redon and Bernard* 2009.

59 See also Leonieke Vermeer, '"Ik heb daar zóó zijne oogjes toegedrukt, hij is gestorven." Emoties van ouders over ziekte en sterven van jonge kinderen, 1780–1880', *Tijdschrift voor Biografie* 5-1 (2016), pp. 24–34.

60 'Het vreemdste is het me nog als je 's avonds niet meer naast me ligt.' ('I still find it so strange when you're not lying beside me in the evenings any more.') Betsy Bonger to Jo. VGM, b2896; 26 April 1889.

61 Mien to Jo and Theo. VGM, b2895; 6 and 7 December 1889. Jo to Theo, VGM, b4244; 30 July 1890. 'Betsy loopt al arm in arm met een onzer eerste Wagner zangeressen, wel een bewijs hoe populair zij op het conservatoire is.' Willem Weissman to Jo. VGM, b2890; 2 October 1889.

62 Adang 2008, p. 56. Leo Simons, whom Jo met in 1911, was involved in this movement: De Glas 1989, pp. 66–7. See also Bosch 2005, p. 247. Betsy was also a 'working member' of the society 'Kunst aan het Volk'.

63 *Diary* 4, p. 70; 26 September 1892.

64 For years Betsy placed advertisements in *Het Nieuws van den Dag* to attract pupils for her singing lessons. Reviews of her performances in *The Daily Telegraph* of 10 July 1903. The drawing is now in New York, Pierpont Morgan Library.

65 VGM, b7302, b7303 and b7304.

66 After her death in 1944, Vincent's oldest son, Theo van Gogh, moved into this house at 137 Weteringschans; he and some friends were arrested there by the Germans on 8 March 1945 and shot.

67 'Lieve zwarte gazelle!' Wim Bonger to Jo. VGM, b2896; 26 April 1889.

68 Van Heerikhuizen 1987, quotation p. 169; Ger Harmsen, *Biografisch Woordenboek van het Socialisme en de Arbeidersbeweging in Nederland* 8 (2001), pp. 1–7.

69 'Wim kwam in Amsterdam geregeld bij mijn moeder, zeker iedere Zondagochtend.' ('Wim often went to see my mother in Amsterdam, at least every Sunday morning.') *Vincent's Diary*, 5 January 1934.

70 Van Heerikhuizen 1987, p. 5; Blom 2012.

71 They each had four children. One of Frans's children was Els, who was kind enough to make various documents and family photographs available. The drawing is now in Amsterdam, Rijksmuseum Print Room.

72 Bonger 1986.

73 'In zaken van het dagelijks leven (kleding, tafelmanieren, gebaren en ook in zaken van smaak in muziek, literatuur en schilderkunst) zijn bijna alle Bongers (met uitzondering van mijn tante Net) uiterst conservatief.' Bonger 1997, pp. 10–11.

74 Lucas Ligtenberg, *Mij krijgen ze niet levend. De zelfmoorden van mei 1940*. Amsterdam 2017, pp. 106–17. The Jewish writer Etty Hillesum had seen him the evening before. She, like him, was desperately worried about the future after the German invasion and the capitulation of the Netherlands. She talked to him and remarked: 'de felle Bonger was zo weerloos als een kind. . . . Alle hartstocht en felheid waren uitgeblust.' ('the fierce Bonger was as defenceless as a child. . . . All the passion and fervour had been extinguished.') *Het verstoorde leven. Dagboek van Etty Hillesum*. Eighth impression. Haarlem 1981, p. 28.

75 'duizendmaal gezegend . . . een vader te hebben zoo geacht en geëerd als de onze. God helpe me, dat ik hem nooit tot schande zal maken.' Andries to his parents. VGM, b1591; 14 February 1880.

76 Andries to his parents. VGM, b1698; 18 January 1882.

77 'Ik hoop toch dat je wel zult weten wat het is een brave, eerlijke, rondborstige jongen, steeds bezield met goede voornemens, een geacht staatsburger kan worden.— Is de jongen niet braaf geweest, dan wordt de man 't ook niet.—'t Beste wat ik dus doen kan, is je aan te sporen tot gehoorzaamheid en ijver opdat je die voorwaarde zult kunnen vervullen.' Andries Bonger to Wim Bonger. VGM, b1822; 15 September 1885.

78 'Weêrstand bieden aan alle hartstochten is de eerste voorwaarde van een edel leven.' Andries to his parents. VGM, b1718; 17 June 1882 and b1732; 15 October 1882.

79 'Geen heilzamer invloed dan die van een beschaafd gezelschap!' Andries to his parents. VGM, b1749; 6 February and b1752; 26 February 1883.

80 Andries to his parents. VGM, b1839; 5 April 1886.

81 'Il va sans dire dat mijn brief aan Net, met enkele persooneele bemerkingen uitgezonderd, ook voor de familie leesbaar was.' Andries to his parents. VGM, b1601; 6 April 1880. The letters he wrote to his father at the office were not read at home. They were either to do with business or accounts of how he struggled with his health.

82 In 1880 he copied out for them all 114 lines of the poem 'Vivere Momento' by Louise Siefert. Andries to his parents. VGM, b1623; 3 December 1880.

83 VGM, b1542.

84 *Diary* 4, p. 47; 4 May 1892.

85 Bonger 1997.

86 Jo to Mien Bonger. VGM, b4289; 16 June 1889.

87 *Diary* 2, p. 96; 28 October 1883. Jo was studying English at that time.

88 'Je lieve moe, Jo, zou met een vroolijk gezicht om twaalf uur een boterham opzetten waar niets bij was en was iemand ziek, ze zou goed doen en de vroolijkheid in huis houden.' Anna Dirks to Jo. VGM, b3769; 25 May 1886.

89 Andries copied out Thomas Moore's poem 'Heaven', and other contributions include one by the teacher M.L.J.T. Rühl, who became headmistress at the Openbare Burgerschool first class for girls.

2 HBS and training as an English teacher

1 Aletta Jacobs was the first woman to gain a university degree in the Netherlands. She became a physician and obtained her doctorate. For a quarter of a century she headed the Vereniging voor Vrouwenkiesrecht (Society for Women's Suffrage).

2 'Archief van de Gemeentelijke HBS voor meisjes', ACA, 708, inv. nos. 1–15. VGM, b3550. Brugmans 1976, p. 287. On the education they provided: Mineke van Essen, *Opvoeding met een dubbel doel. Twee eeuwen meisjesonderwijs in Nederland*. Amsterdam 1990.

3 *NNBW*.

4 *Diary* 1, pp. 10–11; 29 March 1880.

5 ACA, 708, inv. no. 10; and ACA, 15030, inv. no. 117500. A copy of Giesse's book in VGMB, Dep 674.

6 VGM, b4808; ACA, 708, inv. no. 13.

7 Van Gogh 1952–4, pp. 242–9, quotation on p. 243.

8 Als kind was ik stil en ingetrokken en verslond alle mogelijke boeken, rijp en groen. Kwaad heeft het me niet gedaan, nooit; in tegendeel, het ontwikkelde mijn geest, maar naar lichaam bleef ik lang een kind, toen ik 18 was zag ik er uit als 14 en had ook bitter weinig ondervinding, ik was nooit in de wereld geweest en weinig onder

vreemden, was wanhopend verlegen en onbeholpen.' Jo to Lies van Gogh. VGM, b3544; 15 November 1885. A year later she still felt that she lacked natural ease. *Diary* 3, p. 29.

9 *Diary* 3, p. 6; 25 October 1885.

10 Andries to Henri Bonger: 'Zeg aan Netje dat ze een vergeetal is, waarom schrijft ze niet. Als het ach. . .e niet vast zat dan vergat ze dat ook nog.' ('Tell Netje that she's got a memory like a sieve, why doesn't she write? If her back. . .e wasn't attached she'd forget that too.') Prudishness prevented him from writing the word 'achterste' (backside) in full. VGM, b1874; 22 July 1879.

11 *Diary* 1, p. 34; 20 May 1880; *Diary* 1, p. 47; 21 July 1880 (quotation).

12 Andries to Mr Bonger. VGM, b1575; 2 December 1879. For the name of the firm see VGM, b1583.

13 VGM, b1673 and b1704. 'Ik heb Jo in een dag of tien niet geschreven, maar zal het zeker vandaag of morgen nog doen.' ('I haven't written to Jo for about ten days, but I'll definitely do it today or tomorrow.') Andries to his parents. VGM, b1800; 1 November 1884.

14 Ruberg 2005.

15 Andries to his parents. VGM, b1591; 14 February 1880.

16 'Net houdt me altijd een Tantalus beker aan de lippen en vertelt me één woord.' ('Net always holds a Tantalus cup to my lips and tells me a single word.') Andries to his parents. VGM, b1623; 3 December 1880.

17 Andries to Jo. VGM, b1604; 23 April 1880—Andries to his parents. VGM, b1600; 27 March 1880. In his view, when painters exaggerated the 'indefinable', they descended into the absurd: 'Er komen dan onbeschrijflijke groene en blauwe tinten tevoorschijn, waaraan men geen mouw passen kan.' ('Then indescribable blue and green hues appear, which one can't make anything of.') Andries to Mien Bonger. VGM, b1647; 25 April 1881.

18 'Als Net me niet schrijft dat ze ze de volgende week gezien heeft dan zal ik een appeltje met haar te schillen hebben.' Andries to his parents. VGM, b1648; 29 April 1881.

19 'Kind, paar toch aandacht bij 't werk aan ernst en leêr wat meer naar je broer kijken. . . . En toch weêr mijn goede raad in den wind geslagen alles voor 't proefwerk te repeteeren; nu ik je niet meer aan de leiband kan houden zal 't wel heelemaal mis gaan.' Andries to Jo. VGM, b1566; 23 June 1879. He often made sly digs at her.

20 'met de pen in de hand en geen woord verder gaan zonder de voorgaande alle begrepen te hebben, alle zinswendingen die je vreemd voorkomen opschrijven'. Andries to Jo. VGM, b1598; 17 March 1880.

21 This was in the first week of July 1880. VGM, b1610, b1611 and b1661. *Diary* 1, p. 45.

22 *Diary* 1, pp. 12–13; 1 April 1880 (quotation) and *Diary* 1, pp. 15, 53, 59–61 and 84.

23 *Diary* 1, p. 6; 26 March 1880: 'Dries schrijft ook een dagboek, maar ik heb er nooit iets uit gelezen, dat is goed ook want onwillekeurig zou men dan anders gaan schrijven en de dingen beter en mooier voorstellen dan ze zijn en dat moet niet.' ('Dries is writing a diary, too, but I've never read anything from it; that's a good thing too for one would unconsciously start writing differently and make things seem better and nicer than they are and that mustn't happen.') Andries stipulated in his will that his correspondence should be destroyed; it is highly likely that the same thing happened to his diary. RPK, André Bonger archive, folder E 1 (20 March 1934); point 50.

24 *Diary* 1, p. 1; 26 March 1880.

25 *Diary* 1, p. 14; 3 April 1880.

26 *Diary* 1, p. 29; 2 May 1880 and p. 37; 6 June 1880.

27 *Diary* 1, p. 25; 17 April 1880.

28 *Diary* 1, p. 24; 14 April 1880.

29 Timmerman 1983, pp. 207–10. Van Heerikhuizen 1987, p. 22. The working class was concentrated in three city districts, with the Jordaan as the largest 'enclave of the poor'. Van der Woud 2010, p. 107.

30 *Diary* 1, pp. 28–9; 27 April and 2 May 1880.

31 *Diary* 1, p. 37; 13 June 1880.

32 Andries to his parents. VGM, b1609; 22 June 1880.

33 *Diary* 1, pp. 38–9; 13 and 22 June 1880.

34 *Diary* 1, pp. 40–1; 28 June 1880.

35 D. Jansen, 'Petrus Hermannus Hugenholtz jr.', in *Biografisch lexicon voor het Nederlandse protestantisme*. Vol. 5. Kampen 2001, pp. 267–9. E.H. Cossee, 'De stichting van de Vrije Gemeente, haar voorgeschiedenis en uitwerking', in J.D. Snel (ed.), *En God bleef toch in Mokum. Amsterdamse kerkgeschiedenis in de negentiende en twintigste eeuw*. Delft 2000. Raymond van den Boogaard, *De religieuze rebellen van de Vrije Gemeente. De vergeten oorsprong van Paradiso*. Amsterdam 2018.

36 VGM, b1598. Andries occasionally asked Stoffel questions about English literature. VGM, b1624 and b1622. Stoffel gathered a following with his textbook *Handleiding bij het onderwijs in het Engelsch*. Vol. I: *Uitspraak; lees- en vertaalboek*. Vol. II: *De voornaamste eigenaardigheden der Engelsche taal* (1881), which Jo may have used.

37 *Diary* 1, p. 50; 3 August 1880. *Liefdadige dames* had been performed a day earlier in the Amsterdam Stadsschouwburg.

38 Andries to his parents. VGM, b1612; 8 August 1880.

39 Albertine de Haas later wrote: 'die wonderlijke figuur "Narcis" van Bouwmeester bleef in de herinnering van een mensch!' ('Bouwmeester's wonderful character "Narcis" remained in a person's memory!') *Elsevier's Maandschrift*, 1 January 1909.

40 'Ich bin so eine Art Universalnarr, in dem alle übrigen aufgehen. Wer mich sieht, sieht sich im Spiegel . . ., Narziß der Selbstliebhaber, der Eigensüchtige, der Ichmensch.' *Narziß*. Ed. Leipzig 1909, pp. 27 and 33.

41 *Diary* 1, pp. 52–3; 28 August 1880.

42 Andries to his parents. VGM, b1615; 10 September 1880. He also recommended Mien and Jo to go to the reading of Heine's *Harzreise*.

43 *Diary* 1, pp. 56–7; 19 September 1880.

44 On the Feast of St Nicholas on 5 December, Dutch people give one another presents, accompanied by amusing verses personal to the recipient. VGM, b4445.

45 *Diary* 1, pp. 66–7; 16 December 1880.

46 'Toen kreeg ik een vriendin, die 2 jaar ouder was en veel meer in de wereld was geweest dan ik; mijn boekenkennis trok haar aan, we gingen zamen studeeren voor Engelsch examen en vulden bij elkaar 't ontbrekende aan. Bij haar aan huis maakte ik kennis met een jongmensch, student in de letteren die er even als ik een dagelijksch bezoeker was; hij was heel knap en vol enthusiasme voor kunst en wetenschap; hij merkte dat ik veel gelezen had, bracht altijd het discours op onderwerpen die mij aantrokken, het gevolg kun je wel raden! Ik was verliefd—neen toch eigenlijk niet, maar ik genoot van zijn omgang, hij leerde me o zoo veel, ik heb oneindig

veel aan hem te danken, er begon een nieuw leven voor mij, veel van wat vroeger onbekend en vaag voor mij was geweest kwam nu tot klaarheid—het was een tijd vol rozengeur en maneschijn, schooner dan ik 't ooit had gedroomd. Hij kwam ook bij ons aan huis, eindelijk gaf hij ons Latijnsche les zelfs, hij gaf me Multatuli in handen,—er kwam een tijd van twijfel, een periode van overgang—wat heb ik in dien tijd genoten—en geleden. . . . Plotseling werd onze Platonische vriendschap afgebroken. . . . Toen werd ik hard en onverschillig, dat moest ik wel om niet te week te schijnen . . . ik zal hem altijd dankbaar blijven voor zijne belangstelling in mij, dom bakvischje als ik toen was.' Jo to Lies van Gogh. VGM, b3544; 15 November 1885. Timmerman loved Shelley and Multatuli, 'die in den vermolmden stam onzer geestelijk-literaire samenleving bleef hameren, dat de stukken er afvlogen' ('who kept hammering away at the decaying trunk of our intellectual and literary society until the splinters flew'). Timmerman 1983, pp. 148 and 150 (quotation).

47 *Diary* 2, p. 147.

48 'allerliefste meisjes-vriendinnen'; Timmerman 1983, p. 42.

49 *Diary* 1, pp. 118–19; 4 July 1881.

50 Andries to Jo. VGM, b1627; 31 December 1880.

51 'Laat Net maar vast eens trachten te weten te komen of ze ook voor het komende Salon hier zal zijn.' ('Get Net to try to decide whether she will also be here for the coming Salon.') Andries to his parents. VGM, b1632; 21 January 1881.

52 *Diary* 1, p. 91; 13 March 1881.

53 *Diary* 1, pp. 94–5; 27 March 1881. Andries had quoted Huet's wife Anna Dorothée van der Tholl: 'Zoolang ik de lente zie komen ieder jaar, den zon zoo vriendelijk schijnt, geloof ik niets van hun naturalisme en Darwinisme.' ('As long as I see spring arriving every year, and the friendly sun shining, I don't believe a word of their naturalism and Darwinism.') Andries to his parents. VGM, b1643; 25 March 1881. Jo's reaction is evidence that letters to the parents were shared with the other members of the family.

54 L.H. Slotemaker, 'Levensbericht van Dr. Gerrit van Gorkom', *Jaarboek van de Maatschappij der Nederlandsche Letterkunde te Leiden*. Leiden 1905, pp. 195–224, esp. 205; L.H. Slotemaker, 'Aan de nagedachtenis van Dr. G. van Gorkom', *Opstellen van Dr. G. van Gorkom*. Leiden 1905.

55 *Diary* 1, pp. 99–101; 21 April 1881.

56 *Diary* 1, p. 107; 17 May 1881. She reformulated the same feeling in *Diary* 1, p. 116; 28 June 1881.

57 Ed. Edinburgh and London 1873, vol. 2, p. 435.

58 *Diary* 1, p. 111; 17 May 1881.

59 VGM, b1644 and b1645.

60 *Diary* 1, pp. 109–10; 21 May 1881. The quotation about God's breath comes from the poem 'Licht (bij het genezen mijner blindheid)' ('Light (on the curing of my blindness)') by Jan van Beers. *Jan van Beers' gedichten*. Amsterdam *s.a.*, pp. 2–3.

61 *Diary* 1, p. 112; 31 May 1881. Soon after this he lent her *The French Revolution* (1837) by Thomas Carlyle. She hoped that reading it would lead to more self-cultivation and self-improvement. *Diary* 1, p. 114; 24 June 1881.

62 VGM, b3730. *Diary* 1, pp. 126–7; 23 November 1881.

63 Andries to his parents. VGM, b1689; 26 November 1881.

64 *Diary* 1, pp. 127–9; 10 December 1881.

65 This was most probably the performance of *Hamlet* in January 1882 by the Koninklijke Vereeniging het Nederlandsch Toneel in Amsterdam's Grand Théâtre. See Jo to Vincent van Gogh. Van Gogh, *Letters* 2009, letter 786; 5 July 1889. Andries to his parents. VGM, b1713; 10 May 1882.

66 'Met haar te verzorgen zal je ook zeker een moeitevollen tijd hebben en zal er van studie niet zóó veel komen als je wel zoudt wenschen,' Andries to Jo. VGM, b1716; 31 May 1882. Aunt Net, who was often cantankerous and quarrelsome, features in the first diary. VGM, b7177 and *Diary* 1, pp. 47, 79, 83, 86 and 102.

67 VGM, b1725 and Bd74.

68 On 22 June 1883, Mary Westendorp wrote a contribution in Jo's album, signed with the address of the lodgings where they were both staying. VGM, b4170. Andries wrote that he was looking forward to getting Jo's address: 'We zullen een belangrijke correspondentie kunnen voeren, in zeden en gewoonten vergelijken, en elkaârs levensdingen weergeven.' ('We shall be able to conduct an important correspondence, compare morals and customs, tell one another about the things in our lives.') VGM, b1766; 1 July 1883.

69 Jo kept the house rules. VGM, b4542. Later, she showed her son this Reading Room as a memory of her time there. *Vincent's Diary*, 26 January 1936.

70 Jo to Lies van Gogh. VGM, b3548; 27 December 1885.

71 London, British Census, 'Australia Births & Baptisms, 1792–1981'. Three domestic servants worked in the boarding house.

72 His *La femme en France au XIX*^e^ *siècle* (1864, 1878²), *Enfance et adolescence* (1867) and *La jeunesse* (1869) were popular.

73 In the 1881 census, nine lodgers were recorded at Miss Gard's address; in the 1891 census there were fourteen, ranging in age from twenty-one to fifty-eight.

74 *Diary* 2, p. 73; 24 September 1883.

75 *Bruce Herald*, 12 September 1873. Among other things, Brooke published *Theology in the English Poets: Cowper, Coleridge, Wordsworth, and Burns* (1874) and *English Literature* (1876).

76 *Diary* 2, p. 9; 14 July 1883.

77 Jo to Andries. VGM, b1769; 23 July 1883. She kept the cast list of the Vaudeville Theatre in the Strand. VGM, b3683. The two corresponded frequently while she was in London. VGM, b1770.

78 VGMB, BVG 3292.

79 *Diary* 2, p. 14; 25 July 1883. She repeated exactly the same thing shortly afterwards. *Diary* 2, p. 34; 6 August 1883.

80 *Diary* 2, pp. 61–2; 6 September 1883 and pp. 70–1; 18 September 1883.

81 Signed '*E.G.G.* 118, Gower Street'. VGM, b4170.

82 *Diary* 2, p. 54; 31 August 1883.

83 *Diary* 2, p. 46; 23 August 1883.

84 *Diary* 2, p. 48; 23 August 1883.

85 *Diary* 2, p. 51; 26 August 1883 and 72; 24 September 1883. When Gidius was given the choice he rapidly turned his back on the church and religion. See Timmerman 1983, p. 36. Multatuli's influence was not restricted to Jo. Her son Vincent later wrote in his diary that Jo's brothers and sisters also admired Multatuli's *Ideeën*. He himself grew up with *Woutertje Pieterse*. *Vincent's Diary*, 17 January 1977.

86 She revealed this two years later in a letter to Lies van Gogh. VGM, b3548; 27 December 1885.

87 *Diary* 2, p. 58; 31 August 1883.

88 *Diary* 2, pp. 61–2; 6 September 1883. The play was preceded by the farce *Aunt Charlotte's Maid.* VGM, b3681.

89 It is clear from the diary of Frederike van Uildriks that cycling was not immediately acceptable for women. For a long time she rode a three-wheeler and only switched to a regular bike after she had taken lessons. See Van Uildriks, *Dagboek* 2010.

90 VGM, b3739; *Diary* 2, p. 100; 3 November 1883 and pp. 117–18 (quotation); 22 January 1884.

91 *Diary* 2, pp. 77–8. Thomas Babington Macaulay, *Critical and Historical Essays* (1843). The question for this essay, by no means easy, has survived; Jo chose option 'd': 'a. Give some account of the following prose fictions, and the special ends which their writers had in view. 1 Utopia. 2. The Pilgrim's Progress. 3. A Tale of a Tub. 4. Gulliver's Travels / b. Shakespeare's Female Characters / c. Chaucer's Influence on English Poetry / d. Macaulay's Essays.' VGM, b3763.

92 *Diary* 2, pp. 80–2; 5 October 1883.

93 In 1884, someone like Helene Kröller-Müller, Jo's contemporary and later a renowned collector of modern art in the Netherlands, regarded reading the work of 'Great Men' and finding out about their lives as the highest there was. Rovers 2010, p. 34.

94 *Diary* 2, pp. 93–5; 26 October 1883. The quotation comes from Thomas Carlyle, *Sartor Resartus* (1833–34), chapter 9: 'The everlasting Yea.' Van Gogh, *Letters* 2009, letter 274, letter 312, letter 398 and letter 400.

95 *Diary* 2, p. 99; 1 November 1883: 'reading and writing either at the museum or at home.'

96 Jo signed her own edition of 1859: VGMB, BVG 1445a–b.

97 *Diary* 2, pp. 101–3; 9 November 1883. Three years earlier she had written that her father would not understand her anyway (*Diary* 1, p. 37).

98 VGM, b3736.

99 VGM, b3742; 4 December 1883. The examiner was most probably the Irishman Joseph Graham Sennett, who taught at the Rijks Hoogere Burgerschool in Alkmaar and in 1885 was on the examining boards for the state examinations taken in North Holland. See Noord-Hollands Archief, *Population Register*, 14 March 1892 and *Verslagen eindexamens Staten Generaal* for 1885.

100 *Diary* 2, pp. 113–14; 13–14 December 1883. See for example the collection in Atria: https://atria.nl/; the *Digitaal Vrouwenlexicon van Nederland*: http://resources.huygens.knaw.nl/vrouwenlexicon and the Biografisch portaal van Nederland: http://www.biografischportaal.nl/, and cf. *1001 vrouwen uit de Nederlandse geschiedenis*. Ed. Els Kloek. Nijmegen 2013, and *1001 vrouwen in de 20ste eeuw*. Ed. Els Kloek. Nijmegen 2018.

101 England was the mecca for governesses. Greddy Huisman, *Tussen salon en souterrain. Gouvernantes in Nederland, 1800–1940*. Amsterdam 2000, p. 200.

102 VGM, b1776, b1872 and b1779.

103 She wrote of her friend Helena Coomans de Ruiter: 'Will she ever forgive me for purloining her Albert's heart, even though it was absolutely not my fault?' *Diary* 3, p. 11; 9 November 1885.

104 *Diary* 2, pp. 114–15; 31 December 1883.

105 Jo to Lies van Gogh. VGM, b3540; 13 October 1885.

3 Translator, teacher and love for Eduard Stumpff

1 Justus van Maurik to Jo. VGM, b3653; 7 June 1884. The book was published in New York in 1884. On the popularity of Wilkie Collins's book in the Netherlands, see De Vries 2001, pp. 181–2.

2 Justus van Maurik to Jo. VGM, b3654; 13 June—b3655; 14 June 1884 (quotation)—and b3656; 5 August 1884. On the payments: VGM, b3542.

3 Published in The Hague by the Gebroeders Belinfante. Brinkman 1884. The novel could also be purchased in instalments. *De Amsterdammer* of 8 August 1884 listed the '1st instalment for 60 cents' under 'New Publications in the Netherlands' (p. 7).

4 Andries to his parents. VGM, b1789; 23 June—b1790; 4 July 1884.

5 Westerink 1976. Lindenburg 1989, pp. 90–1, 277, with a photograph of the front of the premises around 1900. The Institute was founded in 1808 and named after the Dutch naval officer Jan Hendrik van Kinsbergen. See Ronald Stenvert et al., *Monumenten in Nederland. Gelderland*. Zwolle 2000, p. 164.

6 VGM, b3745, b3130 and b3766; and Lindenburg 1989, p. 265.

7 SNVN, 'Lijst archivalia Instituut van Kinsbergen, 1796–1960', Lindenburg, file 16. See also Lindenburg 1989, pp. 90–1, 262, 265.

8 *Diary* 2, p. 124; 10 September 1884.

9 *Diary* 2, p. 128; 18 September 1884.

10 *Diary* 2, p. 132; 20 October 1884. See Lindenburg 1989, p. 264.

11 'Als Moeder van 't gezin, zet ik er ook wat in.' VGM, b3472; 27 October 1884.

12 Willem Weissman to Jo. VGM, b3620; 24 October 1884: she had only to drop Hendrik Cornelius Rogge a postcard and she would get what she wanted.

13 'Ik zat in een hoekje van de groote holle eetzaal aan 't raam en las het Ach neige du Schmerzensreiche en het was mij daarbij of mijn hart zou breken, *ik* die anders nooit schrei bij een boek. Maar 't is ook geen boek, 't is werkelijkheid!' Jo to Lies van Gogh. VGM, b3542; 1 November 1885. The line she quotes comes from Gretchen's prayer as she kneels before a statue of the Mater Dolorosa: 'Ach neige,/ Du Schmerzensreiche,/ Dein Antlitz gnädig meiner Not!' Goethe 1999, vol. 1, pp. 156–7, ll. 3587–8 and ll. 3617–19. 'O Virgin Mother, thou/ Who art full of sorrows, bow/ Thy face in mercy to my anguish now!' Translation David Luke. Goethe 2008, vol. 1, p. 114.

14 She looked back on this a year later: *Diary* 3, p. 13; 24 November 1885.

15 *Diary* 2, pp. 137–8; 20 November 1884.

16 *Diary* 2, p. 142; 11 February 1885. VGM, b3657 and b3542. Ossip Schubin was the pseudonym of Lola Kirschner. Without a commission, Jo translated a short novel by Paul Lindau in the hope that *De Amsterdammer* would pick it up, but this did not happen. *Diary* 2, p. 145; 5 March 1885.

17 'De vertaling leest vloeiend; de taal is natuurlijk en riekt hoegenaamd niet naar onze buren.' Andries to his parents. VGM, b1813; 16 May 1885. Andries may have been referring to another translation in July, when he wrote: 'Ik heb met heel veel plezier een gedeelte van de novelle gelezen die je onlangs vertaald hebt.—Ik vond dat je met reuzenschreden vooruitgegaan bent.—Je zegt me dat je hoe langer hoe dommer wordt. Je slaat mij wat.' ('I read with great pleasure part of the novella you translated recently.—I thought you'd progressed in leaps and

bounds.—You say the older you get, the more stupid you become. I'm deeply moved.') She had certainly caught him on the hop. Andries to Jo. VGM, b3767; 7 July 1885.

18 VGM, b3135.

19 Jo wrote to Lies van Gogh: '[Ik heb] geen acte als hulponderwijzeres. Daarmee kun je overal terecht.' (I do not have an assistant teacher's certificate. You can go anywhere with one of those.'). VGM, b3548; 27 December 1885. Assistant teacher was the level below headmistress. See Jan Geluk, *Woordenboek voor opvoeding en onderwijs*. Groningen 1882.

20 VGM, b2266, b1804 and b1025; Praamstra 2007, pp. 775–80.

21 'Ik zou je nog wel eens een hartig woordje willen zeggen over je gescherm met gedachten en denkbeelden (je moest noodig psychologie gaan bestudeeren) maar ik wil het niet te erg maken.—. . . waarmee ik me altijd troost, is de gedachte dat als ik aan je denk, je ook met mij bezig bent, en dan is het me alsof ik je hoor praten, soms heftig, soms wat blinde-vinken doordravend, en dan tracht ik je tot bedaren te brengen en je tot klem van redenen te bewegen.'; 'blijf maar bij de vroolijke levensopvatting van je vriend.' Andries to Jo. VGM, b1026; 26 February 1885.

22 *Diary* 2, pp. 147–9; 18 April 1885. The last remark is a variation on a line in the poem 'Thou art not false, but thou art fickle' by Lord Byron.

23 *Diary* 3, p. 8; 24 and 25 May 1885.

24 To the middle class, eating a hot meal at midday with the family was a sacred occasion. Jobse-Van Putten 1995, p. 230.

25 *Diary* 2, pp. 153–4; 24 June 1885. The quotation comes from the novel *Red as a Rose Is She* (1870) by Rhoda Broughton.

26 Andries to his parents. VGM, b1679; 14 October 1881. See also VGM, b1583 and b1585.

27 'Die is beschaafd en onderhoudend.' Andries to his parents. VGM, b1673; 27 August 1881. Four years later he remarked: 'Onderhoudender gezelschap dan het zijne, kan men zich niet denken.' ('One cannot conceive of more entertaining company than his.') Andries to his parents. VGM, b1812; 4 April 1885.

28 VGM, b1754.

29 VGM, b1817 and b1818.

30 'Het zal mij vooreerst zeer veel genoegen doen dat wij onze wederzijdsche familie zullen hebben leeren kennen, mij dunkt zulk een bezoek heeft voor ons het zelfde belang als b.v. twee schilders die elkaars atelier komen bezoeken, want al is de wereld de grootste leerschool, het familie leven zooals wij het van kind af gekend hebben, was het a.b.c. ervoor.' Theo van Gogh to Andries. VGM, b889; 6 August 1885.

31 'gaven naar hart en geest'. Andries to his parents. VGM, b1820; 25 August 1885—b1821; 7 September 1885 (quotation)—and b1824; 1 October 1885.

32 *Diary* 3, p. 21; 17 February 1886. Cateau Stumpff was aware of this. Cateau Stumpff to Jo. VGM, b3768; 30 October 1885. On the very day Jo turned twenty-three, Andries asked his parents for their permission to marry Annie; they agreed immediately.

33 Andries to his parents. VGM, b1810; 21 March 1885—and b1819; 12 August 1885.

34 Andries to Jo. VGM, b1028; 3 September 1885.

35 VGM, b4448. Dianne Hamer, 'Een leven "met de pen in de éene, den stofdoek in de andere hand. . ." Sophie van Wermeskerken-Junius', *Literatuur* 9 (1992), pp. 151–6.

36 *Diary* 3, p. 3; 4 October 1885.

37 Cateau Stumpff to Jo. VGM, b3768; 30 October 1885.

38 'edele en onbaatzuchtige'. Lies van Gogh to Jo. VGM, b3539; 11 October 1885. Jo to Lies van Gogh. VGM, b3540; 13 October 1885. Lies to Jo. VGM, b3541; 21 October 1885 (quotation).

39 'Moge in je leven de poesie de overhand hebben boven het proza.' Lies to Jo. VGM, b3541; 21 October 1885.

40 'Arme lieve Maggie, ik houd zooveel van haar, bijna als van een mijner zusters. Zij heeft zulke edele aspirations (ik weet er geen goed hollandsch woord voor), tracht steeds het goede te doen, en het valt soms zoo zwaar, zoo bitter zwaar!' Jo to Lies van Gogh. VGM, b3542; 1 November 1885.

41 Eliot 2004, book VI, chapter 1.

42 Eliot 2004, book VI, chapter 1. 'With thee delight is ever new,/ With thee is life incessant bliss'. On 17 April 1880 Jo wrote: 'How I enjoyed yesterday evening. The *Schöpfung* was superb, divinely beautiful; oh, to be able to sing *like that,* life must be wonderful it seems to me.' *Diary* 1, p. 24.

43 Eliot 2004, book I, chapter 2 (quotation).

44 Eliot 2004, book II, chapter 7.

45 'Ik heb misschien van liefde een geheel verkeerd denkbeeld, ik weet er ook eigenlijk niets van, maar ik verbeeld me het kan niet bestaan, zonder volkomen kennis van elkaars karakter en denkbeelden, zonder overeenstemming daarmede! . . . Heb jij ook soms zulk een verlangen naar iemand veel ouder dan wij zelven, die je zou leeren hoe eigenlijk te leven.' Jo to Lies van Gogh. VGM, b3542; 1 November 1885.

46 Lies to Jo. VGM, b3539; 11 October 1885.

47 'waar ik nooit meer één mannelijk wezen ontmoet heb'. Lies to Jo. VGM, b3545; 17 November 1885.

48 Six years later the thirty-two-year-old Lies stayed with Jo and they discussed the ups and downs of her impending marriage to Du Quesne van Bruchem. The fifty-one-year-old was an acting cantonal judge in Amersfoort and had been a widower since May 1889. They married on 17 December 1891 and had four more children, as well as their illegitimate daughter.

49 Lies to Jo. VGM, b3551; 21 January 1886.

50 'Alleen in het bewonderen zou ik me gelukkig voelen.' Jo to Lies. VGM, b3548; 27 December 1885.

51 Lies triumphantly reported: 'Bij mijn thuiskomst vond ik een langen brief van Theo, waarin hij mij aanraadde eens naar Amsterdam te gaan, en nu kon ik hem dadelijk schrijven, dat ik er geweest was.' ('When I got home I found a long letter from Theo, in which he advised me to go to Amsterdam, and now I could actually write to him and tell him that I had been there.') Lies to Jo. VGM, b3549; 10 January 1886.

52 Jo to Lies. VGM, b3550; 19 January 1886. Piet's father, Andreas Willem Gerrit, was the son of Adriaan Willem Boele van Hensbroek and Johanna Margaretha ('Martine') Weissman. Martine was the sister of Gerrit Weissman, who was married to Hermina Drinklein. Gerrit and Hermina were the parents of Jo's mother, Hermine Weissman. This means that Piet's grandmother and Jo's grandfather were brother and sister. Piet Boele van Hensbroek had published in *De Gids* and *De Nederlandsche Spectator*. Jo apparently enjoyed his confidence.

53 *Diary* 3, pp. 35–6; 21 December 1886.

54 *Diary* 3, pp. 48–9; 23 March 1887.

55 From the cycle *Dichterliebe*, to poems by Heinrich Heine. *Buch der Lieder*: 'Im wunderschönen Monat Mai,/ Als alle Knospen sprangen,/ Da ist in meinem Herzen/ Die Liebe aufgegangen.' *Diary* 2, p. 155; 29 June 1885.

56 VGM, b3543 and *Diary* 3, p. 8; 9 November 1885.

57 'gestalte—tamelijk groot, grooter dan je broer—oogen—donker bruin—haar—nog donkerder, eigenlijk zwart, en ik heb de domheid gehad het verleden week heel kort te laten afknippen.' Theo van Gogh was clearly a short man, because Jo was barely five foot three.

58 'Ik ben ernstig, tot melancolie toe, en dan weer dol en uitgelaten als een schoolkind, ik houd van een eenvoudig, rustig, werkzaam leven, en toch kan ik me zoo heerlijk schikken in een ruime, gemakkelijke omgeving en ga dolgraag uit; ik wil mezelf verheffen boven kleingeestigheden en toch ontbreekt mij soms de moed om te breken met oude gewoonten om niet voor eccentriek te worden gehouden.' 'verstandige, ernstige Miss Bonger'; 'dwaze wereldsche Jo'. Jo to Lies. VGM, b3544; 15 November 1885.

59 VGM, b3141, b3139 and b3142. A later pupil in Utrecht returned a volume of Wordsworth's poetry Jo had lent her. VGM, b1543; 5 June 1888.

60 *Diary* 3, p. 20; 17 February 1886. Jo to Lies van Gogh. VGM, b3552; 21 February 1886.

61 The family moved to 103 Leidsestraat in May 1887.

62 J.E. Stumpff had founded the Parkorkest in 1849 and his nephew, the conductor Willem Stumpff, took over the running of it in 1871. The Parkzaal in the Plantage was owned by J.E. Stumpff. *Geschiedenis* 2006, p. 172; Timmerman 1983, p. 24.

63 *Diary* 3, p. 89; 23 February 1888.

64 'Ik ben zeker dat je je nooit heb afgevraagd wat kunst is, en… ik ging haast zeggen dat je ook niet weet wat letterkunde is.—Comment, je dweept met de kunst en je bent nog maar één maal in 't museum geweest.— it is a shame! Het is omdat je je verveelt bij die kunst waarmeê je dweept, dus is je enthousiasme valsch geweest, dus … sentimentaliteit. (Ik zal je later nog wel eens spreken of schrijven over de kunst; in den kring waarin je te Amsterdam verkeert geloof ik dat er niemand is die eene schilderij begrijpt;—muziek wordt eigenlijk alleen daar begrepen omdat die openbaring der kunst het gemakkelijkst ontroert).' 'Je hebt zoo'n helder verstand en zoo'n liefdevol hart, maar het verstand sluit de sentimentaliteit niet uit.' Andries to Jo. VGM, b1024; 24 February 1886.

65 Andries to his parents. VGM, b1840; 15 April 1886: 'Ik sta er van te kijken dat Net vandaag al onder het mes is. Ik twijfel niet of ze gedraagt zich onverschrokken tegenover die schoolvossen.' ('Well I'm astonished Net has gone back into the lion's den today. I don't doubt she'll face those pedants unflinchingly.')

66 *Algemeen Handelsblad*, 12 December 1882 and 2 February 1883. Jo's friend Cateau Stumpff had taught there in 1885. See VGM, b4448. Anna van den Vondel was the daughter of Joost van den Vondel, one of the most famous writers of the Dutch Golden Age.

67 *Diary* 3, p. 61; 17 July 1887. *Het Nieuws van den Dag*, 2 May 1887 and 24 November 1887.

68 'Het vleesch wordt te huis niet gekookt maar uitgekookt. Er is hoegenaamd geen kracht meer in.' Andries to Jo. VGM, b1029; 6 July 1886. Foreigners were often struck by the fact that more attention was given to the quantity, rather than the food itself: 'The average middle-class family wolfs down the midday meal, to the point of choking,' according to J. van Leyden, *Eten en drinken in Amsterdam*. Amsterdam 1897, p. 82; quoted in Jobse-Van Putten 1995, p. 251.

69 Anna Dirks to Jo. VGM, b1542; 3 October 1886. 'Had ik toch maar iemand, die zich om mij bekommerde, om *mijn geest* liever gezegd, iemand die mij opwekte tot studie en nadenken, die mij den weg wees, die mij boeken gaf.' *Diary* 3, p. 31; 9 December 1886 (quotation).

70 *Diary* 3, p. 62; 17 July 1887. 'Je weet wel hoe ik belang stel in alles wat er in je omgaat en hoe veel ik van je houd.' Andries to Jo. VGM, b1031; 10 December 1886.

71 *De Gids* 51 (1887), pp. 75–114, continued on pp. 298–335. The article was about the author Honoré de Balzac and Cardinal John Henry Newman.

72 *Diary* 3, p. 39; 18 January 1887.

73 *Het Nieuws van den Dag*, 1 February 1887. *Diary* 3, p. 39; 14 February 1887.

74 *Diary* 3, p. 40; 14 February 1887.

75 *Diary* 3, pp. 122–3; 19 September 1888.

76 *Diary* 3, p. 42; 6 March 1887.

77 *Diary* 3, pp. 43–6; 6 March 1887.

78 Theo van Gogh to Willemien van Gogh. VGM, b911; 25 April 1887.

79 'Zooals je weet zag ik haar maar een paar keer, maar wat ik van haar weet staat mij veel aan. Zij gaf mij een impressie als of ik vertrouwen in haar kan stellen op een geheel onbepaalde manier, zooals ik het in niemand zou doen. Ik zou met haar over *alles* kunnen spreken & ik geloof, dat als zij wilde zij o zoo veel voor mij zou kunnen zijn. Nu is maar de questie of van haar kant de zelfde gedachte bestaat.' Theo van Gogh to Lies. VGM, b910; 19 April 1887. He had visited the Bongers again in the summer of 1886. Andries had been delighted that they liked Theo: 'Hoe langer men hem leert kennen, hoe meer men zijn fijnen geest leert apprecieeren—Zijn gezelschap is altijd onderhoudend.' ('The longer one gets to know him, the more one learns to appreciate his fine mind—he is always entertaining company.') Andries to his parents. VGM, b1844; 27 August 1886.

The correspondence between Jo and Lies stopped abruptly after 7 March 1886. It was broken off because of Lies's pregnancy, but very few people knew of it. The families did everything possible to prevent a scandal, because a young woman getting pregnant out of wedlock brought disgrace, so it was put about that the reason was the ending of a fictitious engagement. Lies left the country for some time. Her daughter Hubertina Normance was born out of sight on 3 August 1886 in Saint-Sauveur-le-Vicomte (Manche). The family hushed up this shameful situation. Lies returned to the Netherlands after the birth, leaving her baby behind with a twenty-two-year-old widow, Mrs Balley. Hubertina died in 1969. See Benno Stokvis, *Lijden zonder klagen: het tragische levenslot van Hubertina van Gogh*. Baarn 1969.

80 *Diary* 3, pp. 55–6; 24 May 1887.

81 *Diary* 3, pp. 59–61; 30 May 1887.

82 VGM, b3747; 13 December 1887.

83 *Diary* 3, pp. 62–3; 20 July 1887.

84 *Diary* 3, pp. 64–5; 25 July 1887.

85 Theo to Jo. VGM, b4284; 26 July 1887. *Brief Happiness* 1999, pp. 63–5.

86 Theo to Jo. VGM, b4283; 1 August 1887. *Brief Happiness* 1999, p. 66.

87 *Diary* 3, p. 69; 8 August 1887.

88 *Diary* 3, p. 78; 5 September 1887.

89 'Het zal je zeker heel wat minder vermoeien dan een heele klasse te moeten drillen.' Andries to Jo. VGM, b1032; 3 October 1887.

90 VGM, b1280.

91 Sara Buddingh to Jo. VGM, b1281; 14 December 1887. VGM, b3748. The salary was advertised in the *Nieuwe Amsterdamsche Courant. Algemeen Handelsblad* of 14 January 1888.

92 HUA, accession number 481, inv. no. 312.

93 *Diary* 3, p. 88; 20 February 1888.

94 *Diary* 3, p. 87; 20 February 1888. None of their correspondence has survived.

95 *Diary* 3, p. 94; 10 May 1888.

96 On 14 May 1888 she was honourably discharged by the local authority 'on health grounds.' VGM, b3750.

97 Andries to his parents. VGM, b1848; 31 May 1888.

98 *Diary* 3, pp. 97–8; 1 June 1888.

99 *Diary* 3, pp. 102–3; 11 June 1888. In the nineteenth century it was regarded as objectionable if people presumed to dress above their class. Clothes that were too fashionable could be condemned as vulgar. See Ileen Montijn, *Tot op de draad. De vele levens van oude kleren*. Amsterdam 2017, pp. 101–2.

100 *Diary* 3, p. 107; 9 August 1888.

101 *Diary* 3, p. 113; 20 August 1888.

102 *Diary* 3, p. 116; 25 August 1888. In 1883 Jo had become aware in a London theatre of the fate of the labouring class. *Diary* 2, pp. 61–2; 6 September 1883.

103 *Diary* 3, p. 119; 27 August 1888.

104 J.C. van der Stel, *Drinken, drank en dronkenschap. Vijf eeuwen drankbestrijding en alcoholhulpverlening in Nederland*. Hilversum 1995. Cf. also Jobse-Van Putten 1995, pp. 228–9.

105 *Diary* 3, pp. 119–20; 27 August 1888.

106 'De avond begint reeds te vallen, de lucht is grijs en beneveld en door het landschap dat reeds de herfst tinten begint te vertoonen, snelt de trein die ons van Luik terug naar Amsterdam voert.—Ik had er willen blijven in de vrolijke, gezellige dominé's familie. Ik voelde me daar tevreden. Een heerlijke geur van versch gemaaid gras dringt naar binnen, overal op de velden zijn de maaiers bezig. Voorbereidselen voor den winter worden reeds gemaakt.' VGM, b3570.

107 'Soms denk ik dat ze jaren op een marmeren graftombe gelegen heeft.—We slagen er helaas niet in elkaâr wat op te vroolijken.—Van geestelijk leven is geen kwestie.... we moeten maar zoo goed mogelijk opsukkelen.' Andries to Jo. VGM, b1033; 12 September 1888. He was having a very difficult time and felt weak in body and mind. It would be better if Jo did not come to Paris. Andries to Jo. VGM, b1034; 3 October 1888.

108 *Diary* 3, p. 124; 29 September 1888.

109 Eduard Stumpff married Helena Wilhelmina Becht at the end of 1892. He championed the appointment of lay nurses and wrote one of the first Dutch nursing textbooks: *Voorlezingen over ziekenverpleging*. Haarlem 1906. Stumpff became a general practitioner and medical director of the Binnengasthuis in Amsterdam.

110 *Diary* 3, p. 126; 11 October 1888 and p. 134; 6 November 1888. Jo would not write her diary again for three years. She picked it up once more on 15 November 1891, when she had suffered a tragedy and her life had taken a totally different direction.

111 Theo van Gogh to Willemien van Gogh. VGM, b916; 6 December 1888.

Part Two

1 L.P. Hartley, *The Go-Between*. Ed. New York 2002, p. 15.

4 Prelude to her marriage to Theo van Gogh

1 'Wel geloof ik, dat zij vooruit wist dat ik nog van haar hield.' Theo to his mother. VGM, b917; 21 December 1888.

2 Rewald 1986a; Rewald 1986b; exh. cat. Amsterdam 1999. This catalogue contains an overview of the works Theo bought and sold.

3 Theo to his mother. VGM, b917; 21 December 1888. On this telegram: Theo to Lies. VGM, b918; 24 December 1888. Jo's letter to her parents has not survived.

4 Mother to Theo. VGM, b2389; 22 December 1888. Willemien to Theo and Jo. VGM, b2387; 23 December 1888.

5 Theo to Jo. VGM, b2019; 24 December 1888. *Brief Happiness* 1999, p. 67.

6 On the basis of the painted envelope in *Still Life with Onions* (F 604 / JH 1656), Bailey assumed that the letter in it had arrived on the twenty-third: 'It almost certainly contained news that Theo had fallen in love with Johanna (Jo) Bonger, and Vincent was fearful that he might lose his brother's emotional and financial support.' At the same time Bailey backpedalled: 'News of the love affair could well have been a trigger for the self-mutilation, although there was probably no one simple explanation for the incident.' See Martin Bailey, 'Why Van Gogh Cut his Ear: New Clue', *The Art Newspaper*, December 2009. The designation F stands for 'Faille': the numbers of the Van Gogh works in De la Faille 1970; JH stands for 'Jan Hulsker': the numbers of the Van Gogh works in Hulsker 1996b.

7 Theo to Jo. VGM, b2022; 1 January 1889. *Brief Happiness* 1999, p. 76. It was wishful thinking on Theo's part that Vincent had 'kept' urging Theo in 1888 to choose Jo as his wife (unless this was in letters that have not survived). What Vincent did write in the summer of 1887 was: 'It would please our mother greatly if your marriage came off, and for your health and business affairs you shouldn't remain single anyway.' Van Gogh, *Letters* 2009, letter 572. Theo had probably talked to Vincent about it before the latter's departure for Arles in February 1888. In fact, Vincent did not consider marriage as the principal thing in life.

8 Vincent to Theo. Van Gogh, *Letters* 2009, letter 738; 19 January 1889.

9 Jo to Theo. VGM, b4246; 28 December 1888. *Brief Happiness* 1999, p. 69.

10 Theo wrote to Jo about the self-mutilation, inflicted in a bout of lunacy and high fever. VGM, b2020; 28 December 1888. *Brief Happiness* 1999, pp. 70–1. See also Bernadette Murphy, *Van Gogh's Ear: The True Story*. Amsterdam 2016, and *De waanzin nabij: Van Gogh en zijn ziekte*. Nienke Bakker et al. Amsterdam 2016.

11 Jo to Theo. VGM, b4247 and b4249; 29 December 1888. *Brief Happiness* 1999, pp. 72–3.

12 Andries to his parents. VGM, b1832; 24 December 1885.

13 Jo to Theo. VGM, b4248; 31 December 1888. *Brief Happiness* 1999, p. 75.

14 Mrs van Gogh to Jo. VGM, b2391; 31 December 1888. Seeing Theo married was 'one of her most heartfelt wishes'. Lies to Jo. VGM, b2278; 2 January 1889. Lies's congratulations marked the resumption of the abandoned correspondence.

15 Theo to Jo. VGM, b2021; 30 December 1888. *Brief Happiness* 1999, p. 74.

16 Theo to Jo. VGM, b2022; 1 January 1889. *Brief Happiness* 1999, pp. 76–8.

17 Anna Veth-Dirks to Jo. VGM, b2075; 1 January 1889. In Atria there are eight letters from Anna Veth-Dirks to Jo during the 1889–90 period.

18 Theo to Jo. VGM, b2023; 3 and 4 January 1889. *Brief Happiness* 1999, pp. 81–3; Van Gogh, *Letters* 2009, letter 728; 2 January 1889.

19 VGM, b4250 and b4272.

20 The longer she looked at the vases, the more beautiful she found them. Jo to Theo. VGM, b4252; 16 January 1889. *Brief Happiness* 1999, pp. 90–1. See also Theo and Jo to Willemien. VGM, b946; 26–7 June 1889.

21 Jo to Theo. VGM, b4260; 2 February 1889. *Brief Happiness* 1999, pp. 134–6.

22 Jo to Theo. VGM, b4250; 13 January 1889. *Brief Happiness* 1999, pp. 84–5.

23 Theo to Jo. VGM, b2024–5; 14 and 16 January 1889. *Brief Happiness* 1999, pp. 86–9.

24 Jo to Theo. VGM, b4252; 16 January 1889. Theo to Jo. VGM, b2026; 19 January 1889. *Brief Happiness* 1999, pp. 90–91 and 92–93. Kee was the daughter of J.P. Stricker, who was married to Mrs van Gogh's sister W.C.G. Stricker-Carbentus. She was widowed in 1878.

25 Jo to Theo. VGM, b4254; 19 January 1889. *Brief Happiness* 1999, pp. 94–6.

26 Theo to Jo. VGM, b2027; 20 January 1889. *Brief Happiness* 1999, pp. 98–100.

27 Theo to Jo. VGM, b2029; 24 January 1889. *Brief Happiness* 1999, pp. 107–9.

28 Jo to Theo. VGM, b4255; 22 January 1889. *Brief Happiness* 1999, pp. 102–4. Lodewijk van Deyssel wrote enthusiastically about Zola's novel, which had moved and enraptured him: 'I read it from cover to cover sweating, gasping and weeping.' He described *Le rêve* as 'the book of Virginity and Desire'. *De Nieuwe Gids* 4, no. 1 (1889), pp. 149, 153. Albert Verwey discussed 'An ugly duckling, Jan ten Brink, Brederoo, Heine and Hélène Swarth', pp. 211–42.

29 Theo to Jo. VGM, b2049; 23 January 1889. *Brief Happiness* 1999, pp. 105–6. Van Gogh, *Letters* 2009, letter 741; 22 January 1889.

30 Jo to Theo. VGM, b4251; 2 January 1889. *Brief Happiness* 1999, pp. 79–80.

31 Theo to Jo. VGM, b2031; 27 January 1889. Jo to Theo. VGM, b4257; 27 January 1889. *Brief Happiness* 1999, pp. 116–18 and 119–20.

32 Theo to Jo. VGM, b2007; 4 February 1889. *Brief Happiness* 1999, pp. 137–8. On the flyleaf he wrote 'J. Bonger. Febr. '89' (VGMB, BVG 1446). Later Jo referred to this publication in one of her reviews published in *Belang en Recht*, 1 January 1901.

33 Jo to Theo. VGM, b4261; 5 February 1889. *Brief Happiness* 1999, pp. 139–40.

34 Theo to Jo. VGM, b2032; 28 January 1889. *Brief Happiness* 1999, pp. 121–3. Theo did not play a musical instrument.

35 Theo to Jo. VGM, b2009; 9 and 10 February 1889. *Brief Happiness* 1999, pp. 145–9.

36 Theo hoped that it was not 'ramshackle'. Theo to Jo. VGM, b2030; 26 January 1889—b2044; 7 March 1889 (quotation). *Brief Happiness* 1999, pp. 115 and 200. Mrs van Gogh on Jo's playing: VGM, b2426; 1 February 1889—and b2913; 29 April 1889.

37 Jo to Theo. VGM, b4264; 12 February 1889. *Brief Happiness* 1999, pp. 156–7.

38 Goethe 1999, vol. 1, p. 40, ll. 568–9. 'Refreshment! it's your own soul that must pour/ It through you, if it's to be anything.' Translation David Luke. Goethe 2008, vol. 1, p. 21.

39 Jo to Theo. VGM, b4256; 25 January 1889. *Brief Happiness* 1999, pp. 112–14.

40 Jo to Theo. VGM, b4259; 31 January 1889. *Brief Happiness* 1999, pp. 126–7. Jo kept in touch with Maria Sethe until at least 1916. VGM, b8293.

41 Van Gogh, *Letters* 2009, letter 771; 8 May 1889.

42 Jo to Theo. VGM, b4260; 2 February 1889. *Brief Happiness*, p. 134.

43 Pictured in Bijl de Vroe 1987, p. 35.

44 Jo to Theo. VGM, b4260; 2 February 1889. Theo to Jo. VGM, b2007; 4 February 1889. *Brief Happiness* 1999, pp. 134–6 and 137–8. Social inequality was discussed at length in articles in *De Nieuwe Gids*. See Blom 2012, p. 79.

45 Theo to Jo. VGM, b2039; 25 February 1889. *Brief Happiness* 1999, pp. 179–81.

46 Jo to Theo. VGM, b4269; 25 February 1889. *Brief Happiness* 1999, pp. 182–3.

47 Jo to Theo. VGM, b4275; 10 March 1889. *Brief Happiness* 1999, pp. 208–9. Years before she had also been unable to reach her 'inner innermost self'. *Diary* 1, p. 28; 21 April 1880.

48 Jo to Theo. VGM, b4278; 16 March 1889. *Brief Happiness* 1999, pp. 219–21.

49 Theo to Jo. VGM, b2037; 20 February 1889. *Brief Happiness* 1999, pp. 172–3—and VGM, b4269.

50 Theo to Jo. VGM, b2007; 4 February 1889. *Brief Happiness* 1999, pp. 137–38.

51 Jo to Theo. VGM, b4260; 2 February—b4262; 8 February 1889. *Brief Happiness* 1999, pp. 234–6, 143–4.

52 'want anders zou Jotje werkelijk een lange dag hebben', 'Gisteren was ze aan het artikel vla; en naar het geen ik er van hoorde waren de uitkomsten verrassend.' He evidently did not try it himself. Jo's father to Theo. VGM, b2892; 9 February 1889.

53 Theo to Jo. VGM, b2011; 13 and 14 February 1889. *Brief Happiness* 1999, pp. 158–9. Theo outlined Vincent's character and his sensitive temperament: his brother spared no one and was difficult to deal with. Theo found it painful that he could do so little for him. Theo to Jo. VGM, b2035; 14 February 1889. *Brief Happiness* 1999, pp. 160–2.

54 Jo to Theo. VGM, b4269; 25 February 1889. *Brief Happiness* 1999, pp. 182–3.

55 Jo to Theo. VGM, b4265; 15 February 1889. *Brief Happiness* 1999, pp. 163–4.

56 Theo to Jo. VGM, b2036; 16 and 17 February 1889. *Brief Happiness* 1999, pp. 165–7.

57 Theo to Jo. VGM, b2053; 25 March 1889. *Brief Happiness* 1999, pp. 236–7.

58 Theo to Jo. VGM, b2037; 20 February 1889. *Brief Happiness* 1999, pp. 172–3. A 'comble' is a high point, the 'cabinet de débarras' is the box room and the 'armoire à glace' is the mirror cupboard. By 'de Louvre' he meant 'Les Grands Magasins du Louvre'.

59 Theo to Jo. VGM, b2039; 25 February 1889. *Brief Happiness* 1999, pp. 179–81.

60 'Ja, 'k kan me begrijpen dat je 't druk hebt met allerlei en dan dat akelige gekrioel van alles door elkaar in je hoofd, hè, dat is ijselijk. Dan weet je ook wel wat 'k meen met 'je hoofd opruimen', dat heb 'k verl. week in mijn eenzaamheid gedaan, 't is nu weer wat in orde en 'k hoop dat 't lang zoo blijven zal.' Willemien to Jo. VGM, b2396; 10 February 1889. She returned to the need to sort out her confused head later that year: Willemien to Theo and Jo. VGM, b2931; 13 September 1889.

61 Cor van Gogh to Willemien and Jo. VGM, b835; 6 March 1889.

62 Van Gogh, *Letters* 2009, letter 669 and letter 670.

63 'Toen 'k je voor 't eerst in Amsterdam zag . . . heb 'k je leeren kennen zooals je zelf bent, jou ikheid—stevig, veerkrachtig, gezond, vrolijk. Toen je in Breda kwaamt zag 'k een anderen kant, iets fijns en teers, iets verbazends kinderlijks, en niets afweten van de alledaagse, kleingeestige, vervelende, prosaïsche wereld van zorg en misere. 'k had een barren tijd gehad en kon haast niet denken aan de mogelijkheid dat jou een onzachte aanraking met die wereld te wachten kon staan—en toch deed een onbestemd voorgevoel me bijna zeker weten dat 't een of ander je boven 't hoofd hing. . .' Willemien to Jo. VGM, b2920; undated.

64 Theo to Jo. VGM, b2037; 20 February 1889. Jo to Theo. VGM, b4268; 22 February 1889. *Brief Happiness* 1999, pp. 172–3 and 174–6. The letter from Vincent that Jo saw was dated 18 February, see Van Gogh, *Letters* 2009, letter 747. In it he wrote: 'The only desire I might have is to be able to continue to earn with my own hands what I spend.'

65 Theo to Jo. VGM, b2040; 27 February 1889. Jo to Theo. VGM, b4272; 2 March 1889. *Brief Happiness* 1999, pp. 184–6 and 193–5.

66 Theo to Jo. VGM, b2041; 28 February 1889. *Brief Happiness* 1999, pp. 188–90.

67 Jo to Theo. VGM, b4270; 28 February 1889. *Brief Happiness* 1999, p. 187. Willemien wrote to Theo: ''k Heb Jo zijn brieven laten lezen, die brieven waren zoo heerlijk. Ze denkt zoo lief over hem, 't is een nobele natuur, Jo.' ('I let Jo read his letters, those letters were so lovely. She's so fond of him, Jo has a noble nature.') And also: 'Jo is niet sterk en 't huishouden niet gewoon, maar ze zal 't ongetwijfeld snel aanleeren.' ('Jo's not strong and isn't used to housework, but without doubt she'll soon learn.') VGM, b2392; 16 March 1889.

68 Theo to Jo. VGM, b2042; 1 March 1889. *Brief Happiness* 1999, pp. 191–2.

69 'Anna moet je goed kennen om van haar te houden.' 'Wij zijn dikwijls zoo akelig ernstig.' Willemien to Jo. VGM, b2397; 8 March 1889.

70 Jo to Theo. VGM, b4274; 9 March 1889. Theo also thought that the situation in Leiden was 'a bit like the North Pole'. Theo to Jo. VGM, b2046; 11 March 1889. *Brief Happiness* 1999, pp. 203–4, 212.

71 Jo to Theo. VGM, b4275; 10 March 1889. *Brief Happiness* 1999, pp. 208–9.

72 Jo to Theo. VGM, b4279; 18 and 19 March 1889. *Brief Happiness* 1999, pp. 228–30.

73 Van Calcar 1886, p. 203. An adaptation of Edward John Hardy, *How to be Happy though Married: Being a Handbook to Marriage. By a Graduate in the University of Matrimony*. Chillworth and London (1885). Another aphorism was: 'Getting married means being loyal and trusting.' Van Calcar 1886, p. 62.

74 Jo to Theo. VGM, b4280; 22 March 1889. *Brief Happiness* 1999, pp. 233–5.

5 Married life and motherhood in Paris

1 Jo to Theo. VGM, b4272; 2 March 1889. *Brief Happiness* 1999, pp. 193–5.

2 Vincent to Theo. Van Gogh, *Letters* 2009, letter 187; 19 November 1881.

3 Theo to Jo. VGM, b2043; 5 March 1889. Jo to Theo. VGM, b4274; 9 March 1889. *Brief Happiness* 1999, pp. 196–7 and 203–4.

4 Theo to Jo. VGM, b2050; 16 March 1889. *Brief Happiness* 1999, pp. 222–4.

5 *Het Nieuws van den Dag*, 16 April 1889. The pantomime was about the roguish tricks of Reynard the Fox, a mid-thirteenth-century Dutch fable.

6 Jo's father looked back exactly one year later. Jo's parents to Jo and Theo. VGM, b2880; 16 April 1890.

7 VGM, b1492. An announcement appeared in the newspaper *Het Nieuws van den Dag* on 19 April 1889.

8 Mien Bonger to Jo. VGM, b2907; undated.

9 'Die omhaal—en dan tot toppunt die trouwdag met de sluier en 't glazen kastje van een koets.—Die morgen was ik zóó kwaad en vond mezelf zóó belachelijk, bah wat een comedie en Theo vond 't precies zoo.' Jo and Theo to Lies and Willemien van Gogh. VGM, b923; 26 April 1889.

10 ACA, marriage certificate, no. 692; VGM, Bd93.

11 VGM, b925, b2913, b3583; *Brief Happiness* 1999, pp. 175, 196; VGM, b2429 and b2042.

12 *Diary* 4, p. 41; 18 April 1892 and p. 75; 3 November 1892 (quotation).

13 *Diary* 4, p. 36; 31 March 1892. On Brussels: VGM b923. Visiting cards: VGM, b3709 and b1489.

14 'Vooral die twee Zondagen, toen hebben we rondgeloopen als twee kinderen—die spelen met hun poppenkamer, alles neergezet, opgehangen, dan weer eens verschikt, beurt om beurt onze 10 deuren, *zegge 10*, open en dichtgedaan en ons paleis rondgewandeld.' Jo to Lies and Willemien van Gogh. VGM, b923; 26 April 1889.

15 'licht, vroolijk—een roseachtig tintje in de kamer door de bloemen van de gordijnen—de mooie bloeiende persik boomen van Vincent aan de muur—nu komt er nog de Mauve te hangen. De huiskamer is kleuriger: de gordijnen warm geel, de schoorsteenmantel bekleed met een roode shawl—schilderijen met vergulde lijsten (sommige), boven de schoorsteen geen spiegel maar een stuk tapijt met allerlei mooie dingen er op o.a. een prachtige gele roos van Vincent.—De salon is nog niet klaar dus daarvan zeg ik niets—alleen dat Vincent's schilderijen er een eereplaats hebben—en de negerinnen.' Jo to Lies and Willemien van Gogh. VGM, b923; 26 April 1889.

16 Jo to Mien. VGM, b4285; 26 April 1889.

17 *Diary* 4, p. 61; 29 June 1892.

18 VGM, b2205; abbreviated as *Account Book* 2002. Theo put the overall expenditure figures for 1889 on a separate sheet: VGM, b2206. This shows that he also gave money to his mother and his sisters Lies and Willemien. Cf. also Van Gogh, *Letters* 2009, letter 394, http://vangoghletters.org/vg/context_3.html#intro.III.3.2.

19 VGM, b2211; abbreviated as *Huishoudboek* 1889–91.

20 The biggest pan could hold a 'small joint of beef no bigger than two and a half pounds.' Jo to Mien Bonger. VGM, b4289; 16 June 1889.

21 VGM, b3570.

22 'Gisterenmiddag heb ik een hoed gekocht—een zwarte met twee zwarte vlerkjes en een strik van vieux roze die ik misschien nog laat veranderen in mousse—hij staat goed vind ik—die platte hoeden met al die bloemen die ze hier zooveel dragen kan ik niet op hebben.' Jo to Mien Bonger. VGM, b4287; 11 May 1889.

23 'it's really too bad!' she wrote to Vincent, describing her reaction to it. Van Gogh, *Letters* 2009, letter 771; 8 May 1889.

24 Mien had to explain to Jo how to cook a head of lettuce. VGM, b2909; 12 July 1889.

25 Jo to Vincent. Van Gogh, *Letters* 2009, letter 771; 8 May 1889.

26 Jo to Mien Bonger. VGM, b4287; 11 May 1889. Andries's written French was reasonably good. Joosten 1969a, p. 156. A few months later, in August-September 1889, Isaäcson wrote a series of articles in a sensitivist, impressionist style, entitled 'Parijsche brieven' ('Parisian letters'), for *De Portefeuille. Kunst- en Letterbode*. He was the first Dutch critic to comment on Van Gogh. 'Vincent is voor het nageslacht' ('Vincent is for posterity') he asserted on 17 August 1889. Later Isaäcson discussed the analytical methods and colour laws that the neo-impressionists used in 'De revolutionaire schildersgroep in Frankrijk' ('The revolutionary group of painters in France'), *De Portefeuille. Kunst- en Letterbode* of 10 May 1890, pp. 75–6 and of 17 May 1890, pp. 88–9. He mentioned Van Gogh twice in a list of 'emotioneel-impressionnistische artiesten' ('emotional-impressionist artists').

27 Jo to Vincent. Van Gogh, *Letters* 2009, letter 771; 8 May 1889. She also wrote to him: 'But now we really have become brother and sister, and I would so much like you to know me a little and, if possible, love me a little.'

28 'Ik heb haar dus niet meer dan 5 uur per dag maar U begrijpt dat er genoeg te doen overblijft.' Jo to the Bonger family. VGM, b4286; 2 May 1889.

29 VGM, b2900 and b3613. Mien Bonger to Jo. VGM, b2900; 6 May 1889, and Mrs Bonger to Jo. VGM, b2903; 18 May 1889.

30 Theo to Jo. VGM, b2023; 3 and 4 January 1889. *Brief Happiness* 1999, pp. 81–3.

31 Jo to Theo. VGM, b4260; 2 February 1889. *Brief Happiness* 1999, p. 134.

32 Theo to Jo. VGM, b2032; 28 January 1889. *Brief Happiness* 1999, p. 121–3.

33 Jo to Theo. VGM, b4258; 29 January 1889. *Brief Happiness* 1999, p. 124–5.

34 Theo to Jo. VGM, b2034; 1 February 1889. *Brief Happiness* 1999, p. 130–3.

35 Quoted in Maurice Joyant, *Henri de Toulouse-Lautrec 1864–1901—peintre*. Paris 1926, p. 118.

36 Theo to Jo. VGM, b2008; 6 February 1889. *Brief Happiness* 1999, pp. 141–2.

37 Jo to Theo. VGM, b4277; 14 March 1889. *Brief Happiness* 1999, pp. 214–16.

38 Van Gogh, *Letters* 2009, letter 572 and letter 741; 22 January 1889 (quotation), letter 743 and letter 784. On this also see Chapter 6.

39 Jo to the Bonger family. VGM, b4290; 27 and 29 June 1889. On this sale: Van Gogh, *Letters* 2009, letter 785.

40 Jo to Theo. VGM, b4261; 5 February 1889. *Brief Happiness* 1999, pp. 139–40.

41 VGM, b4295; 9 November 1889.

42 Jo to Mien. VGM, b4287; 6 May 1889. She presented Mien with several prizes for it. VGM, b4287; 11 May 1889. Her sister wondered whether Jo could already really cook on her own. Mien to Jo. VGM, b2847; 23 May 1889.

43 Jo to Mien. VGM, b4288; 25 May 1889.

44 This cutlery was valued in June 1891 at 72 guilders. SSAN, NNAB, Archive of the notary H.P. Bok 1883–91, Deed 1891/54.

45 'De couverts zijn in ons bezit—een prachtig etui met een monogram V.G. door elkaar en daarin rusten op rood laken 12 paar zware zilveren lepels en vorken met fraaie versieringen en ook een monogram.' Jo to Mrs van Gogh. VGM, b943; 7 June 1889.

46 Jo to Mrs van Gogh. VGM, b943; 7 June 1889. In 1880 the successful society painter Corcos had signed a fifteen-year contract with Goupil & Cie.

47 Jo to Mien. VGM, b4289; 16 June 1889—b4291; 5 and 11 July 1889.

48 Jo to the Bonger family. VGM, b4290; 27 and 29 June 1889. Mien wrote to Jo: 'Mother will bring the white dress, and Jeannette will of course take off the train, but what shall we do with the bodice, which will be too suffocating in this hot weather.' VGM, b2907; undated.

49 'Wat kreeg ik nu een gewichtigen brief, mijn flinke, degelijke Netje, bang waarvoor? lief hart, ik ben zoo dol blijde je het maar geschreven . . . je hoeft niets te weten of te doen, gewoon alles zoo als je gewent bent, niet te maltentig en er niet zoo plein aan denken. 't is nog zoo kort, ik weet wel 't is een gevoel dat je niet kunt beschrijven maar 't went wel, en als Moe je een goeden raad ken geven, ga s'morgens maar na de markt, dan heb je afleiding en je ziet al de bedrijvigheid, en ga maar zoo veel als je ken in de lucht. smaakt melk je niet? water en wijn, niet veel, is ook heel goed, je hoeft nu nog geen wijt goed te hebben, mijn hart, als 't zoo tegen de helft komt, laat niet je corset uit nog hoor . . . als je draaijerig en misselijk bent geweest prebeer dan maar een stukje te eten, beschuit is er niet, wel? ga je wel na de plee, 't eenige onvolkoomene zal 't zijn we zoo ver weg zijn.—. . . Nu lieve hartebok . . . hoe gaat 't met spelen, prebeer je 't nu wel eens, 't zou je ook zoo'n afleiding geven als de man weg is, 't zullen heele ochgende zijn.–. . . als 't niet hoefde zou ik Lien niet gaarne alleen laten, die zou wel voor jelui door een vuur willen springen.' Mrs Bonger to Jo. VGM, b2877; 24 June 1889.

50 Lien Bonger to Jo. VGM, b4566; 25 June 1889.

51 'we hebben die mooie Rozenburgvaasjes & nog twee anderen waar we van de winter graag halmen & pauweveeren in wilden zetten. Het belletjesgras is al weg, niet?' Theo to Willemien; Jo continued the letter. VGM, b946; 26–7 June 1889. For a time Willemien played with the idea of becoming a florist. The Van Gogh family loved stalks of wheat. When Mr van Gogh sent a parcel with a relative who was going to see Vincent in London in 1873, he included a bouquet of stalks of wheat for his oldest son. Theodorus van Gogh to Theo van Gogh. VGM, b2664; 1 October 1873.

52 These little vases, bought when they were engaged, have not survived. Verbal communication from Johan van Gogh, October 2011.

53 Jo to the Bonger family. VGM, b4290; 27 and 29 June 1889. Jo's contemporary Frederike van Uildriks also used the expression 'rendez-vous spelen' ('playing rendez-vous') for vomiting, see Van Uildriks, *Dagboek* 2010, pp. 94 and 354.

54 Vincent to Theo. Van Gogh, *Letters* 2009, letter 745; 3 February 1889.

55 Theo to Vincent. Van Gogh, *Letters* 2009, letter 792; 16 July 1889.

56 Jo to the Bonger family. VGM, b4290; 27 June 1889.

57 Jo to Vincent. Van Gogh, *Letters* 2009, letter 786; 5 July 1889.

58 'Hij zegt hij wou nog wel eens een 8 dagen vacantie nemen en naar buiten gaan! als dat eens waar was, ik vind 't te heerlijk om aan te denken—O Mien ik hou *niets* van Parijs.' Jo to Mien. VGM, b4291; 5 and 11 July 1889.

59 Jo to Mien. VGM, b4293; 23 August 1889. Theo was extremely affectionate to his mother-in-law: 'Moe schreef maar Theo voor en Theo na.' ('All Ma could talk about was Theo this and Theo that.') Lien to Theo and Jo. VGM, b2898; 30 July 1889.

60 Henri Bonger to Jo. VGM, b2855; 17 July 1889.

61 'Vrij ben je oneindig minder—niets, niets behoort meer aan je zelf en ik verzeker je dat het me moeite heeft gekost daaraan te wennen.' Jo to Mien. VGM, b4292; 9 August 1889.

62 'Er is één groot struikelblok—dat ik [zo weinig[?] artistiek gevoel heb—wat heb ik dikwijls verlangd om iets van Anna Dirks te hebben—die eerst zou hem geapprecieerd hebben en met hem mee geleefd—ik kan 't niet. . . . Ik voel of denk niet meer dan de meest gewone prozaïsche dingen—dat hindert Theo wel eens. . . . En als ik dan al die theoriën over kunst hoor en er niets van begrijp dan vind ik 't wel naar, maar hoe kan ik op eens veranderen en alles wat ik vroeger vond over boord gooien. . . . Soms denk ik wel eens dat ik 't niet zal beleven ons kindje te zien—ik voel me soms zoo zwak—maar dan vind ik 't nog niet erg want ik heb heel veel [gekregen[?] in mijn leven . . . mijn hemel wat heb ik altijd in een wereldje van mijn eigen makelij geleefd zonder een ahnung te hebben van den eigenlijken wereld.' Jo to Mien. VGM, b4292; 9 August 1889.

63 'Wil, zal ik je wat vertellen—dat we niet iederen dag meer van elkaar houden. Zie zoo dat zet ik maar in een heel klein hoekje alsof ik 't je even influister—maar *waar* is het!' Jo to Willemien. VGM, b944; 23 August 1889. Cf. also this response from her brother Henri a month before, which was prompted by a remark of Jo's that she found being a married woman very difficult: 'Tot mijn spijt lees ik in je brief dat je in je trouwen inplaats van vooruit, achter uitgaat: "Geen slag meer kunnen roeien," jij die het zoo flink kon. Dat gaat zoo niet, ik hoop dat het spoedig een anderen wending mag nemen.' ('I was sorry to read in your letter that getting married was a step backwards rather than forwards for you. "I can't do a thing." You, who used to be so spirited. That's no good, and I hope things change soon.') Henri Bonger to Jo. VGM b2855; 17 July 1889. Theo and Jo visited the exhibition at the Société des Artistes Indépendants, which ran from 3 September to 4 October 1889. VGM, b2129. See also Van Gogh, *Letters* 2009, letter 732.

64 *Account Book* 2002, pp. 60, 153. M.H. van Meurs, 'Cor van Gogh en de Boerenoorlog', *Journal for Contemporary History. Joernaal vir Eietydse Geskiedenis* 25, no. 2 (December 2000), pp. 177–96. Cor to Theo and Jo. VGM, b838; 20 October 1889. Cf. Chris Schoeman, *The Unknown Van Gogh: The Life of Cor van Gogh from the Netherlands to South Africa*. Cape Town 2015.

65 VGM, b4293, b2861 and b2931. Atria; VGM, Bd86. Weissman 1948, pp. 122–3.

66 'En al ben ik niet gepoederd en gedecolleteerd—denkt U niet dat ik onder die 2000 gasten wel onopgemerkt zal doorslippen? Jo to Mrs van Gogh. VGM, b945. The newspaper *Het Nieuws van den Dag* of 1 October 1889 carried a report of the event.

67 Lien was curious to know what Theo thought of his son's 'wardrobe'. Lien to Theo. VGM, b2846; 2 October 1889. For nappies see *Account Book* 2002, p. 63.

68 Lida Janse-Dirks to Jo. VGM, b1429; 3 October 1889. Allebé also wrote *De ontwikkeling van het kind naar ligchaam en geest: een handleiding* (1848).

69 *Diary* 4, p. 71; 3 October 1892.

70 'Ik zeg aldoor dat ik er niets aan hecht en doe mijn best het hem uit 't hoofd te praten maar het spijt me zoo voor hem en ik ben zoo bang, dat hij er over tobt.' Jo to Mien. VGM, b4294; 28 October 1889. They had had 'een naren dag met die ellendige levensverzekering, daar moest hij onderzocht en ik hield al mijn hart vast want die docters zijn soms zoo ruw en hij *is* immers op 't oogenblik niet goed. Ik durfde niet naar hem kijken toen hij t'huis kwam maar jawel hij was heel opgeruimd—neen ze hadden niets gezegd—ik was al zoo blij—maar 's avonds kwam er een brief dat ze hem niet wilden aannemen.' ('an awful day with that dreadful life assurance. He had to be examined and I was very concerned that the doctors would be too rough with him because, after all, he really *isn't* well at the moment. I didn't dare look at him when he came home, but he was very much relieved—no, they hadn't said anything—I was so pleased—but that evening a letter arrived saying that they would not accept his application.') That letter has not survived. Specific medical issues, such as tuberculosis, heart abnormalities and chronic intestinal diseases, were normal reasons for refusing life cover; occasionally alcoholism, gonorrhoea and syphilis were listed. With thanks to Karel-Peter Companje (Kenniscentrum Historie Zorgverzekeraars, Houten).

71 Van Calcar 1886, p. 109.

72 'Ik houd toch meer van de hollandsche keuken hoor! kreeft is zoo iets om de nachtmerrie van te krijgen,' Jo to her parents. VGM, b4295; 9 November 1889. Mr Bonger to Theo and Jo. VGM, b2893; 25 November 1889.

73 VGM, b2893; 10 November 1889. The Van Praags were friends about whom Mien had written to Jo. VGM, b2899; 19 November 1889.

74 Jo to her parents. VGM, b4297; undated.

75 'Geniet Theo al van de kou, 't is een koukleum hè, die man van jou. Als kleine jongen omarmde hij 's morgens vroeg altijd de warme kachelpijp.' Willemien to Jo. VGM, b2404; 19 October 1889.

76 Jo to Mien. VGM, b4298; 25 November 1889. They also had a subscription to the weekly magazine *De Portefeuille. Kunst- en Letterbode*. See *Account Book* 2002, p. 76.

77 'Net ziet er altijd blozend uit.' Annie Bonger-van der Linden to Mrs Bonger. VGM, b1849; 28 November 1889.

78 Mien to Jo and Theo. VGM, b2895; 6 and 7 December 1889. Mandarins and marrons glacés went from Paris to the Netherlands to mark the feast of St Nicholas on 5 December. Mrs van Gogh sent traditional fondants for Theo's cough, fingerless gloves for Jo and a pastry letter filled with almond paste. VGM, b2860; 2 December 1889. The request: Jo to her mother. VGM, b4300; 14 January 1890.

79 'Het kindje zoog bij mij de tepels heelemaal kapot: de vellen hingen erbij, zoodat ze soms bloed zoog, dat het er langs liep. . . . Ik brandde met Lapis Infernalis dat ze zwart werden, en de bovenste huid er afviel.' ('The baby sucked on my nipples until they hung in tatters. The skin was broken so that sometimes she sucked blood too because it came out with the milk. . . . Silver nitrate burned and made them go black, and the top layer of skin fell off.') Anna Veth-Dirks to Jo. Atria; 19 December 1889 and 17 January 1890; VGM, Bd88 and Bd89.

80 VGM, b1850.

81 Camille Pissarro to Theo. VGM, b821; 12 December 1889. Pissarro, *Correspondance* 1980–91, vol. 2, pp. 312–13.

82 'diep in elkaar te komen'; Willemien to Jo. VGM, b2920; undated. She hoped that Jo would give her finger exercises to do on the piano. Willemien to Theo and Jo. VGM, b2859; 13 December 1889.

83 'als een dreigend zwaard boven 't hoofd'. 'Nu ik niet meer sukkel met de ontlasting is mijn maag weer in orde—en 't loopen gaat wel langzaam maar toch altijd minstens een uur per dag.' Jo to Mien. VGM, b4299; 9 January 1890.

84 VGM, b4300. In March she gave this book to Willemien as a present. *Account Book* 2002, p. 71. They also read it in the Bonger household, in English and in the Dutch translation. Mrs Bonger was reading the last volume in December 1889. VGM b2895. Jo had lent Andries her copy of *Middlemarch* years before. According to him, Eliot's novels put everything else in the shade. Andries Bonger to Jo. VGM b1029; 6 July—b1031; 10 December 1886.

85 Jo to Vincent. Van Gogh, *Letters* 2009, letter 845; 29–30 January 1890 (my italics).

86 Vincent to Jo. Van Gogh, *Letters* 2009, letter 846; 31 January 1890.

87 See VGM, b3209, b3227 and b3324.

88 Theo to Vincent. Van Gogh, *Letters* 2009, letter 847; 31 January 1890. Mien and Lien to Jo. VGM, b3246; undated. On the difficult birth see also Anna Veth-Dirks to Jo. VGM, b1433; 11 November 1890.

89 Annie Bonger-van der Linden to Jo. VGM, b2866; 2 February 1892. Andries said that the child took after Mr Bonger, 'een hoog voorhoofd, dat is veel verstand' ('a high forehead, which means high intelligence'). Lien reported this to Jo in a letter. VGM, b3246; undated.

90 'en dan een poeder om daarna mijn mond te borstelen—kina wijn en goed eten en iederen dag op straat, 't jongentje ook.' Jo to her mother. VGM, b4301; 14 March 1890. And, of course, her mother had advice for her: 'Neem als je het nodig hebt, bast of lijnzaad of wonderolie.' ('If you need to, take bark or linseed or castor oil.') VGM, b2885; 23 March 1890.

91 Mrs van Gogh and Willemien to Theo and Jo. VGM, b2924; 23 March 1890.

92 Jo to Vincent. Van Gogh, *Letters* 2009, letter 861; 29 March 1890. A.L.H. Obreen gave an insightful description in the *NRC* newspaper of 4 April 1890—Theo and Jo would have been delighted with it: 'Een van de inzenders is de heer Vincent van Gogh, die door de ware aanbidders van het nieuwe licht wordt gehuldigd als de beste hunner adepten, en die zulks ook in menig opzicht verdient. Deze stippelt zijn landschap niet, maar hij schildert met facetten zoo groot ongeveer als een lid van een vinger. . . . Deze schildertrant is inderdaad het laatste woord van bizarrerie.' ('One of the entrants is Mr Vincent van Gogh, who true believers of the new light revere as the best of their adepts, and who also deserves to be in many respects. He does not use dots in his landscape. He paints using areas about the size of a knuckle. . . . This painting style is indeed the last word in bizarreness.')

93 Van Gogh, *Letters* 2009, letters 855–7, letter 867 and letter 879.

94 'Weet U wat 't jongentje precies doet als ik? Zijn duim tusschen zijn twee voorste vingers steken—ik denk aldoor wat zou Beb daarom lachen want die lachte mij er altijd om uit.' Jo to her parents. VGM, b4302; 5 April 1890.

95 Victor Vignon, *Woman in a Vineyard* and *Winter Landscape*. VGM, s277 and s276. The ring cost 16 francs. Jo to Mien. VGM, b4303. 'Bij jellui is het maar een leventje, dat geeft mekaar maar gouden ringen cadeau of het maar niets is.' ('You live in great style, which makes giving each other gold rings seem like nothing.') So wrote Lien to Theo and Jo. VGM, b2854; 16 April 1890.

96 Willemien to Theo and Jo. VGM, b2925; 17 April 1890.

97 'Eerst met mij samen ging tamelijk gemakkelijk . . . maar toen kwam 't heldenfeit—hij alleen op een stoel. Hij begon zoo slaperig te kijken dat we alles probeerden om er wat leven in te krijgen, stel je voor Theo met de rammelaar in de eene hand een witte zakdoek wuivende in de andere—ik een guitaar (die een afschuwelijk geluid maakte) in de eene, en een tros vuurrood gemaakte kersen in de andere en alle twee springende en dansende en roepende, dat gaf dat oolijke portretje met de muts. . . . We sturen ze alle drie, omdat als je al de drie expressies combineert je een idee krijgt hoe hij er uitziet maar natuurlijk is hij in werkelijkheid veel, veel liever, 't eene portretje is *te* bij de hand, 't andere te sentimenteel.' Jo to Mien. VGM, b4303; 21 April 1890. 'werkt als een paard—ik heb een programma voor iedere dag van de week.' Jo to Mien. VGM, b4304; 26 April 1890. Theo to Mien. VGM, b4305; 25 April 1890. Theo paid the photographer 24 francs. *Account Book* 2002, p. 73.

98 Theo to Mien. VGM, b4305; 25 April 1890.

99 Theo to Paul Gachet Sr. VGM, b2012; 19 May 1890.

6 Life with the duality of Theo and Vincent

1 Andries to his parents. VGM, b1839; on or about 8 April 1886.

2 'hij heeft letterlijk geen gezicht meer. De arme stakkerd heeft veel zorg. Zijn broer maakt het leven hem buitendien altijd nog lastig en verwijt hem alles waaraan hij part noch deel heeft.' Andries to his parents. VGM, b1843; 23 June 1886.

3 Andries to Jo. VGM, b1029; 6 July 1886.

4 Voskuil 1992. Andries to his parents. VGM, b1867; 31 December 1886.

5 Andries to his mother. VGM, b1846; 18 February 1887. 'Wanneer hij niet zoo'n aards stijfhoofd was, zou hij al lang naar Gruby gegaan zijn.' ('If he weren't so cursed stubborn, he'd have been to see Gruby long ago.') Andries had already been seeing this doctor for five years.

6 'Het is een curieuse kerel, maar wat een hoofd zit er op, het is benijdenswaard.' VGM, b912; 15 May 1887. On the discussions see Johan de Meester to Albert Plasschaert. VGM, b3043; 16 January 1912, and VGM, b3044; undated, also Andries Bonger in 'Vincent', *NRC*, 5 September 1893.

7 Theo to Willemien. VGM, b915; 14 March 1888.

8 'Het is een knappe vent!' Willemien to Theo and Jo. VGM, b2387; 23 December 1888. Van Gogh painted *Pink Peach Trees* after Anton Mauve's death for Mauve's widow Jet Carbentus.

9 Jo to Theo. VGM, b4250; 13 January 1889. *Brief Happiness* 1999, pp. 84–5. Shortly before, Theo had written to her, 'You know how much he has meant to me and that it was he who fostered and nurtured whatever good there might be in me.' Theo to Jo. VGM, b2022; 1 January 1889. *Brief Happiness* 1999, pp. 76–8.

10 Jo to Theo. VGM, b4251; 2 January 1889. *Brief Happiness* 1999, pp. 79–80.

11 Van Gogh, *Letters* 2009, letters 721, 771 and 861. Formerly identified as *Small Pear Tree in Blossom* (F 405 / JH 1394). See *Vincent van Gogh Paintings, Volume 3. Arles, Saint-Rémy and Auvers-sur-Oise 1888–1890, Van Gogh Museum*. Louis van Tilborgh, Teio Meedendorp and Nienke Bakker. Amsterdam 2023.

12 Jo to Theo. VGM, b4256; 25 January 1889. *Brief Happiness* 1999, pp. 112–14.

13 Jo to Theo. VGM, b4279; 18 and 19 March 1889. *Brief Happiness* 1999, pp. 228–30.

14 Jo to Theo. VGM, b4252; 16 January 1889. *Brief Happiness* 1999, pp. 90–1.

15 Theo to Jo. VGM, b2009; 9 and 10 February 1889. *Brief Happiness* 1999, pp. 145–9.

16 Jo to Theo. VGM, b4278; 16 March 1889. *Brief Happiness* 1999, pp. 219–21.

17 '[Hij] schrijft altijd zoo knap—ik heb zelden zulke brieven gelezen—maar dat hoofd is wat afgetobd.' 'Wat ik 't aller eerst van hem zag waren meest zulke vreemde dingen—maar er zijn ook zoo veel meer begrijpelijken en o zoo prachtig!' Jo to Mien. VGM, b4287; 6 May 1889. It is not known who this Polak was.

18 'Veel piano gespeeld heb ik nog niet—ik weet niet hoe 't komt maar ik heb nog altijd dat gevoel of er iets dood is van binnen—ik vind 't zoo naar maar wat kan ik er aan doen. Theo wou zoo graag dat ik Zola las en nu ben ik aan la faute de l'abbé Mouret—maar 't kan me niets schelen—ik vind 't zoo onnatuurlijk en Theo dweept er mee! . . . Als ik Theo maar altijd gelukkig kon maken dan is alles goed. Maar altijd weer komt Vincent, Vincent die geluk en tevredenheid niet deelt omdat rust roest—werken, strijden, en dat heeft hij bij Theo zoo er in gebracht.' Jo to Mien. VGM, b4288; 25 May 1889. The painting *Augustine Roulin ('La berceuse')* hung in the spare room. VGM, b2848.

19 Jo to Paul Gachet Jr. VGM, b2166; 25 June 1914. See also Chapter 16, p. 302.

20 'Ik had verwacht een zieke te zien, en voor mij stond een stevige breedgeschouderde man met een gezonde kleur, een vroolijke uitdrukking en iets zeer vastberadens in zijn voorkomen; van al de zelfportretten geeft dat voor den schildersezel hem in dien tijd 't beste weer. Blijkbaar had er weder zulk een plotselinge, onbeschrijfelijke omkeer in zijn toestand plaats gehad . . . . "Hij is volkomen gezond, hij ziet er veel sterker uit dan Theo," was mijn eerste gedachte. Dan troonde Theo hem mee naar de slaapkamer, waar het wiegje stond van onzen kleinen jongen, die naar Vincent genoemd was; zwijgend keken de twee broers naar het rustig slapend kindje—zij hadden beiden tranen in de oogen. Toen keerde Vincent zich lachend tot mij en zei, wijzend naar het eenvoudige gehaakte spreitje op de wieg: "Je moet hem maar niet te veel in de kanten leggen, zusje." Drie dagen bleef hij bij ons en was al dien tijd vroolijk en opgewekt. Over St. Remy werd niet gesproken. Hij ging zelf uit om olijven te koopen, die hij gewend was iederen dag te eten, en die wij absoluut ook moesten proeven; den eersten morgen stond hij al heel vroeg in hemdsmouwen zijn schilderijen te bekijken waarvan ons appartement vol was; de muren waren er mee behangen; . . . verder lagen overal—tot groote wanhoop onzer femme de ménage—onder het bed, onder de sofa, onder de kasten, in het logeerkamertje, groote stapels onopgezette doeken, die nu op den grond uitgespreid en aandachtig bekeken werden. Er kwam ook veel bezoek, maar Vincent merkte al spoedig dat de drukte van Parijs hem toch niet dienstig was, en verlangde om weer aan 't werk te gaan.' *Van Gogh* 1914, vol. 1, pp. lx–lxi. Andries also noticed that Vincent was looking very well and cheerful. Andries to his parents. VGM, b1852; 21 May 1890.

21 Vincent to Theo and Jo. Van Gogh, *Letters* 2009, letter 873; 20 May 1890 and letter 874; 21 May 1890.

22 Paul Gachet Jr to Vincent van Gogh. VGM, b3409; 5 December 1927.

23 Annie Bonger-van der Linden to Mr and Mrs Bonger. VGM, b1855; 30 June 1890.

24 Vincent to Theo and Jo. Van Gogh, *Letters* 2009, letter 896; 2 July 1890.

25 VGM, b3570, b1854 and b2929. See also *Brief Happiness* 1999, p. 247 and *Account Book* 2002, p. 156.

26 VGM, b2863 and b2869. The dentist's bill was 40 francs. *Account Book* 2002, p. 75.

27 Jo to Mien. VGM, b4306; 7 June 1890.

28 VGM, b1856.

29 This tension manifested itself in two letters from Vincent, written on 7 July (not sent) and around 10 July, and in two letters from Jo of 31 July and 1 August.

30 'oververmoeid en overspannen, zoals blijkt uit zijn laatste brieven en uit zijn laatste schilderijen, waarin men het dreigend onheil voelt naderen als de zwarte vogels, die in den storm over het korenveld jagen.' Van Gogh 1914, vol. 1, pp. lxii–lxiii.

31 Theo to Vincent. Van Gogh, *Letters* 2009, letter 900; 14 July 1890. Andries's role in this was not known for many years because Jo only published letters *to* Theo and when the letter was published in the *Verzamelde brieven* 1952–4 this passage was left out.

32 Jo to Theo. VGM, b4245; 31 July—and b2060; 1 August 1890. *Brief Happiness* 1999, pp. 277–8.

33 Vincent to Theo and Jo. Van Gogh, *Letters* 2009, letter 898; on or about 10 July 1890.

34 Vincent to Theo and Jo. Van Gogh, *Letters* 2009, letter RM24; 7 July 1890.

35 Theo to Jo. VGM, b2056; 18 July—and b2057; 19 July 1890. *Brief Happiness* 1999, pp. 245–8. *Het Nieuws van den Dag*, 19 June 1890.

36 *Brief Happiness* 1999, pp. 245–8, 255.

37 It is striking that neither Vincent's letter nor one from Jo to Theo have survived. Theo to Jo. VGM, b2058; 20 July 1890. *Brief Happiness* 1999, pp. 249–50. See also Theo to Vincent: Van Gogh, *Letters* 2009, letter 900; 14 July 1890.

38 Jo to Theo. VGM, b4237; 21 July 1890. *Brief Happiness* 1999, pp. 251–2.

39 Theo to Jo. VGM, b2061; 21 July 1890. *Brief Happiness* 1999, pp. 253–4.

40 Jo to Theo. VGM, b4238; 22 July 1890. *Brief Happiness* 1999, pp. 254–5.

41 Theo to Jo. VGM, b2059; 22 July 1890. *Brief Happiness* 1999, p. 256.

42 Anna Veth-Dirks (on behalf of Saskia) to Vincent and to Jo. Atria; 19–20 July 1890; VGM, Bd90.

43 Jo to Theo. VGM, b4239; 23 July 1890. *Brief Happiness* 1999, p. 257.

44 Theo to Jo. VGM, b2062; 24 July 1890. *Brief Happiness* 1999, p. 258–9.

45 Jo to Theo. VGM, b4240; 24 July 1890. *Brief Happiness* 1999, p. 260.

46 Theo to Jo. VGM, b2063; 25 July 1890. *Brief Happiness* 1999, p. 261–2. That letter from Vincent to Theo was his last, and was dated 23 July. He wrote another one earlier that same day, but it remained incomplete and was never sent. Van Gogh, *Letters* 2009, letters 902 and RM25.

47 Hulsker 1996a, pp. 49–52. Vincent did, however, support Theo's ambitions—at least that is stated in a letter from Theo to Albert Aurier (sold at the Cornette de Saint-Cyr auction house in Paris, 14 December 2016, lot 130).

48 Jo to Theo. VGM, b4241; 26 July 1890. *Brief Happiness* 1999, pp. 263–4.

49 Theo to Jo. VGM, b2065; 26 July 1890. *Brief Happiness* 1999, pp. 265–6.

50 Jo to Theo. VGM, b4242; 27 July 1890. *Brief Happiness* 1999, pp. 267–8.

51 Theo to Jo. VGM, b2066; 28 July 1890. *Brief Happiness* 1999, pp. 269–70. He wrote: 'I shan't go into detail, it's all too distressing.'

52 Jo to Theo. VGM, b4243; 28 July 1890. *Brief Happiness* 1999, pp. 271–2.

53 Jo to Theo. VGM, b4244; 30 July 1890. *Brief Happiness* 1999, pp. 273–4. VGM, b1993. Permission for the burial: VGM, b2113; 29 July 1890.

54 Paul Gachet to Theo. VGM, b3265; 27 July 1890.

55 Jo to Theo. VGM, b4245; 31 July 1890. *Brief Happiness* 1999, pp. 275–76.

56 Mrs van Gogh and Willemien to Jo. VGM, b1003; 31 July 1890 (quotation)—and Mrs van Gogh and Willemien to Theo. VGM, b1009; 31 July 1890. Pickvance 1992, pp. 45–53.

57 Jo to Theo. VGM, b2060; 1 August 1890. *Brief Happiness* 1999, pp. 277–8.

58 Theo to Jo. VGM, b2067; 1 August 1890. *Brief Happiness* 1999, pp. 279–80. VGM, b934 (quotation).

59 Mr Bonger to Theo. VGM, b1002; 4 August 1890: 'Peace and quiet are also medicine for her.' The letters of condolence were published in Pickvance 1992.

60 'In den nacht voor zijn sterven had Vincent tegen Theo gezegd, over mij sprekende, 'elle ne connaissait pas cette tristesse là' ('she does not know such sorrow'). Daar moet ik nu aldoor aan denken—ik begreep toen niet waar 't goed voor was—maar nu wel. had ik 't maar niet hoeven leeren!' Jo to Anna Veth-Dirks. VGM, b2080; 10 November 1890. Jo's son Vincent spotted this intriguing text on the back of a telegram, which was dated 9 June

1926. It is not clear how it came into his possession. Sorrow was always an important theme for Van Gogh. Cf. Vincent's words to Theo on his deathbed: 'La tristesse durera toujours' ('Sorrow endures for ever'), and what Andries quoted in a letter to Gustave Coquiot: 'Il n'y a pas eu de cause déterminante du suicide de Vincent. Sa force était brisée il ne pouvait plus reprendre la lutte, Théo lui ayant demandé s'il voulait vivre encore, il a répondu: "Non, la tristesse demeure."' ('There was no determining cause for Vincent's suicide. His spirit was broken and he could no longer continue the fight, Theo asked him if he still wanted to live; he replied: "No, sorrow remains."') Respectively Du Quesne-Van Gogh 1910, p. 96 and VGM, b899; 23 July 1922.

61 'In Vincent's brieven vind ik nog zulke interessante dingen en het zou werkelijk een merkwaardig boek zijn als men zien kon hoeveel hij gedacht heeft en zichzelf gelijk is gebleven.' Theo to his mother. VGM, b937; 8 September 1890.

62 On 3 November 1890 Piet Boele van Hensbroek, a partner in the publishers Martinus Nijhoff, wrote to Aurier about that intention to write a biography. See A.M. Hammacher, *Les amis de Van Gogh*. Exh. cat. Paris, Institut néerlandais. Paris 1960, pp. 56–7. Theo had informed Aurier that he could provide letters and documents, to which the latter replied: 'Il laisse une œuvre qui est une partie de lui-même et qui, un jour, nous en sommes surs, vous et moi, fera revivre son nom et pour éternellement.' ('He leaves an oeuvre which is a part of him and which, one day, we are sure, you and I, will make his name live for eternity.') Respectively an undated letter, sold at the Cornette de Saint-Cyr auction house in Paris, 14 December 2016, lot 131, and Albert Aurier to Theo. VGM, b1277; 1 August 1890.

63 'iets van die brieven bekend moest worden gemaakt.' Van Gogh 1914, vol. 1, p. vii.

64 'Dat er een brief van uw oudste kind zal ontbreken zal een groote schaduw werpen op aller vreugd—men denkt er altijd om, maar 't schijnt of op zulke dagen van herinnering het verdriet dubbel zwaar weegt.... Het volgend jaar krijgt U een brief van Vincentje, hij is van daag niet gedisponeerd tot schrijven.' Jo to Mrs van Gogh. VGM, b4308; 9 September 1890. After Vincent's death Elisabeth van Gogh wrote to Theo and Jo that little Vincent 'nu nog meer een soort nalatenschap van Hem aan ons allen is geworden' ('has now become even more a sort of legacy from Him to us all'). VGM, b2002; 2 August 1890.

65 'verschrikkelijk geknauwd.' Andries to his parents. VGM, b1858; 22 September 1890.

66 Émile Bernard to Theo. VGM, b1154; 18 September 1890. And Bernard 2012, p. 122. Theo's letter was published in *Art-documents* 1952.

67 The rental agreement, which had been signed on 2 August 1890, officially came into effect on 1 October. In the event of Theo's or Jo's death, it would be dissolved. The rent was 1,070 francs a year. VGM, b2017. Cf. exh. cat. London 2015, p. 205.

68 On 11 March 1891 Jo asked Octave Maus whether he would return Vincent's exhibited works to 8 cité Pigalle. AHKB; VGM, Bd12. Later she wrote to Gustave Coquiot: 'Nous avons seulement habités 8 cité Pigalle.' ('We only ever lived at 8 cité Pigalle.') VGM, b3269.

69 Theo wrote to his mother about the preparations: 'Verbeeld U Moe, wij zitten al in het nieuwe huis' ('Just imagine, Ma, we're already in the new apartment,') and he told Willemien that things were beginning to be organized around the flat; they had already had the curtains altered. VGM, b938; 16 September (quotation)—b947; 27 September 1890. In October there were still some hundred works with Tanguy. Paul Signac to Octave Maus. AHKB; 23 October 1890; VGM, Bd67.

70 Theo announced this exhibition in the newspaper *La Bataille* of 26 August 1890. He told Aurier on August 27 he wanted to include a few letters in the accompanying catalogue in addition to a brief biography. Stein 1986, pp. 234–5. *Lettres à Bernard* 1911, pp. 3–4.

71 *Algemeen Handelsblad*, 31 December 1890. By then Theo had already been admitted to a hospital in Utrecht and Jo remained in Leiden. Andries had shown De Meester around.

72 'Wij hebben gedacht dat het goed was er nog eenigen in den handel te brengen, om daardoor te maken dat er over hem gesproken wordt.' Theo to Willemien. VGM, b947, the follow-up to letter b2055; 27 September 1890 (quotation and reference to the sales). *Account Book* 2002, pp. 23–4, 156. For *The Red Vineyard* see Van Gogh, *Letters* 2009, letter 855.

73 *Diary* 4, p. 73; 3 October 1892.

74 Jo to Paul Gachet. VGM, b2013. Two days before, Andries had also asked if there was anything he could do: 'Ma soeur est à bout de force et ne sait quoi faire.' ('My sister is at the end of her tether and doesn't know what to do.') Gachet 1956, pp. 125–6; Gachet 1994, p. 291.

75 VGM, b2079. Jo's housekeeping book shows they were at home on the 15th. *Huishoudboek* 1889–91.

76 'Wie had ooit gedacht dat hij al zijne zorgen en toewijding zóó duur zou moeten betalen!— Hoe vreesselijk dat Vincent hem nu nog na zijn dood niet met rust laat en hem als legaat, een onuitvoerbaar werk opdroeg, waaraan hij nu als het ware zóó al zijn levenskracht en energie ten offer brengt, dat zijn arm gemarteld hoofd er onder gaat lijden. 't is ontzettend en voor U, Lieve Jo, een leed dat bijna te groot is om te kunnen dragen, arm jong vrouwtje.' Caroline van Stockum-Haanebeek to Jo. VGM, b1140; 23 October 1890.

77 Hermanus Tersteeg to Jo. VGM, b1074; 24 October 1890. On 29 November 1890 Tersteeg again offered to consult Léon Boussod. VGM, b1075. Jo had kept him fully informed in the interim. In response Tersteeg wrote: 'De behandeling, die ge van de Heeren Joyant en consorten hebt moeten verduren, vind ik allertreurigst, maar komt me, helaas! niet vreemd voor.' ('I think the treatment by Joyant and colleagues you've had to put up with is so very sad, but I have to say that I'm afraid it doesn't surprise me.') It emerges from his remarks about 'die gerechtelijke omslachtigheid' ('that legal long-windedness'), which had been 'bitter onaangenaam' ('bitterly unpleasant)' for Jo, that settlement of the finances (Theo's salary and the outstanding profit sharing) still had to be dealt with through official channels. VGM, b1076; 2 December 1890. Maurice Joyant left the firm in September 1893. VGM, b779 and Bd68.

78 'Net heeft geen vrede met wat gedaan wordt, en wil aldoor wat anders, omdat ze denkt Theo beter te kennen en te weten wat hij noodig heeft.— ik behoef U niet te zeggen hoe ongerijmd alles is wat ze wil.' Andries to his parents. VGM, b1860; 16 October 1890. Boussod's statement of account of 27 April 1891 lists a sum owing of 8,280.60 francs. Prior to that, Jo had already received 2,000 francs on 3 November and, via Tersteeg, a further 798 francs from Boussod at the end of January. VGM, b4602. The medical director was André Meuriot. Andries to Paul Gachet. VGM, b887; 16 October 1890.

79 Jean-François Raffaëlli to Octave Mirbeau. Paris, Musée du Louvre. Cote BC.b7.L23; 27 October 1890: 'Il a fallu sept hommes pour l'y conduire.—Détail abominable: il avait une autre horrible maladie,—qu'il soignait sans doute lui-même (!): lorsqu'on l'a déshabillé à l'hospice, on lui a trouvé une sonde *enfoncée dans le canal!*' ('It took seven men to accompany him. Abominable detail: he has another horrible condition—which he undoubtedly treated himself (!): when they undressed him in the hospital, they found a *catheter inserted into the urethra!*')

80 Camille Pissarro to Lucien Pissarro: 'Théo van Gogh était, paraît-il, malade avant sa folie; il avait une rétention d'urine. Il y avait une huitaine qu'il n'urinait pas; joint à cela les tracas, les chagrins et une violente discussion avec ses patrons à propos d'un tableau de Decamps. Par suite de ces faits il a, dans un moment d'exaspération, remercié les Boussod, et tout d'un coup il est devenu fou. Il voulait louer le Tambourin pour faire une association de peintres. Il est ensuite devenu violent. Lui qui aimait tant sa femme et son enfant, il a voulu les tuer.' ('It seems Theo van Gogh was ill before his madness; he was retaining urine. There was a week when he did not urinate; related to this, the worries, the distress and a violent discussion with his bosses about a painting by Decamps. After this, in a moment of exasperation, he dismissed the Boussods, and all of a sudden, he went mad. He wanted

to hire the Tambourin to establish an association of painters. He subsequently turned violent. He who loved his wife and his child so much wanted to kill them.') Published for the first time in Doiteau 1940, pp. 83–4. This image of a murderous Theo came up again and again because the passage was included in, among others, Camille Pissarro, *Lettres à son fils Lucien*. Présentées, avec l'assistance de Lucien Pissarro, par John Rewald. Paris 1950, pp. 188–9; in John Rewald, 'Theo van Gogh, Goupil and the Impressionists', *Gazette des Beaux-Arts* 81 (1973), pp. 1–108 (quotation on p. 67); and in Pissarro, *Correspondance* 1980–1991, vol. 2, p. 363.

81 'Als hij dan Free ziet en herkent, zal dat gezicht indruk op hem maken en hem rust geven en Free zal dat noodlottige denken aan zijn broer eruit krijgen.' Anna Veth-Dirks to Jo. VGM, b1431; 20 October (quotation)—and b1432; 21 October 1890.

82 'niet zoude uitwerken wat gij er van verwacht'. Frederik van Eeden to Jo. VGM, b4569; 17 October 1890.

83 'Misschien hebt ge nu eenig bemoedigend antwoord van D[r] van Eeden; ik hoop het van harte; maar naar wat ik over hypnose gelezen heb, durf ik mij niet voorstellen, dat die behandeling nu reeds eenigen invloed ten goede kan hebben, later misschien, als de toestand der hersenen meer normaal geworden en de congestie geweken zal zijn.' ('You may by now have received an encouraging answer from Dr van Eeden. I hope so from the bottom of my heart, but from what I've read about hypnosis, I don't dare to imagine that such treatment can do any good at this stage, later perhaps, if the condition of the brain has become more normal and the congestion has receded.') Hermanus Tersteeg to Jo. VGM, b1074; 24 October 1890.

84 *De Nieuwe Gids* 2, no. 2 (1886), pp. 246–69.

85 Van Eeden wound up his practice in 1893. 'wat helderder en hun geest wat sterker te maken'. Fontijn 1999, pp. 230–43 (quotation on p. 238).

86 Jo paid Van Eeden 251 francs. This will have included travelling and accommodation expenses. *Huishoudboek* 1889–91; 27 October 1890.

87 'In een avondlucht is het groene, in een aard-akker daaronder het paarsche,—hij schildert die twee dingen sterk groen en paarsch tegen elkaar en het was mooi . . . deze grove, sterk geaccentueerde, rauwe kleur-expressie . . . een zeer sterk, direct effect van mooiheid.' *De Nieuwe Gids* 6, no. 1 (1891), pp. 263–70, quotations on pp. 266–7.

88 'Witsen heeft er zeer lang voor zitten kijken en was er zeer door getroffen. Met Veth heb ik er reeds veel gesprekken over gehad. Ook de teekeningetjes blijf ik mooi vinden.' Frederik van Eeden to Jo. VGM, b4570; 29 October 1890. In his biography of Van Eeden, Fontijn merely mentioned that in Paris he had 'assisted' Theo, who was critically ill. Fontijn 1999, p. 357.

89 'presque toutes fort belles'. AHKB 5752 and 5753; 23 October 1890 and 24 October 1890; VGM, Bd67 and Bd68.

90 Jo to Octave Maus. AHKB 5754; 7 November 1890; VGM, Bd10.

91 Andries to Octave Maus. AHKB 5755; 22 December 1890; VGM, Bd17. Octave Maus had previously written to Andries. VGM, b1347; 5 December 1890.

92 Anna Veth-Dirks to Jo. VGM, b1432; 20 October 1890: 'Ik kan huilen als ik denk wat je moet hebben uitgestaan.' ('I could cry when I think about what you've had to bear.') VGM, b1431; 20 October 1890.

93 Frederik van Eeden to Jo. VGM, b4571; 13 November 1890.

94 'Heeft Net hem in 't geheel nog niet weer mogen zien, ook niet in de verte of door een sleutelgat?' 'U weet niet hoe zielsbedroefd 't ons gemaakt heeft hem Maandag avond aan de gare du Nord te zien.' ('You have no idea how desperately sad it made us to see him on Monday evening at the gare du Nord.') Annie to Mr and Mrs Bonger. VGM, b1863; 16 November 1890. The information about Theo was taken from his medical records, published in Voskuil 1992.

95 'De ziekteverschijnselen zouden kunnen passen bij de gediagnosticeerde dementia paralytica of bij lues cerebri.' Voskuil 2009, p. 1 (quotation).

96 Mooij 1993, pp. 40, 57; Vijselaar 1982, pp. 64–5; Voskuil 2009.

97 Voskuil 1992; Tuong-Vi Nguyen, Erwin J.O. Kompanje and Marinus C.G. van Praag, 'Enkele mijlpalen uit de geschiedenis van syfilis', *Nederlands Tijdschrift voor Geneeskunde* 157 (2013), pp. 1–5, esp. p. 4.

98 See Van Gogh, *Letters* 2009, letter 42. When Theo was transferred to Paris, his father warned him of the dangers of seeing prostitutes. VGM, b2481; 30 May 1879. For ideas about sexuality and visiting brothels see Nop Maas, *Seks! . . . in de negentiende eeuw*. Nijmegen 2006. On Gruby and Rivet: Van Gogh, *Letters* 2009, letter 611; 20 May 1888. On degeneration: ibid. letter 603. Jo's knowledge of Theo's brothel visits: *Diary* 4, p. 77; 3 November 1892.

99 Mooij 1993, pp. 36–40; the quotation on p. 36.

100 Mooij 1993, pp. 57–60. People often had medical check-ups before marriage to rule out marital venereal diseases and reduce the risk of hereditary problems. Mooij 1993, pp. 99–101.

101 *Huishoudboek* 1889–91; 17–19 November 1890: 'Dr Rivet: 30,00; Dr Blanche: 661,25; 1e [klas]reis: 271,30; reis van mij: 22,50; bagage: 28,00'. ('Dr Rivet: 30.00; Dr Blanche: 661.25; 1st class train tickets: 271.30; my ticket: 22.50; luggage: 28.00'.)

102 Andries to Mr Bonger. VGM, b1861; 20 November 1890.

103 'Gisteren heb ik, op mijn naam, handelend voor Theo of derden de gezamentlijke schilderijen liggend bij Tanguy en die van het appartement voor fr. 20.000.- verzekerd.' Andries to Mr Bonger. VGM, b1861; 20 November 1890. It is possible that it was for this purpose that he compiled the list of titles of Van Gogh's works—the 'Bonger List'. VGM, b3055.

104 Taken from Theo's medical records. See also Mooij 1993, p. 39.

105 'Goed [dat] Lies niet bij je was, ze is zoo zenuwachtig en 't zou haar kwaad gedaan hebben.' Willemien to Jo. VGM, b2403; 25 November 1890 (quotation). She urged her: 'Blijf maar moedig & dapper & vertrouwend, zooals je 't altijd zijt geweest.' ('Stay courageous and brave and trusting, as you've always been.') Willemien to Jo. VGM, b3597; undated.

106 Taken from Theo's medical records; 23 December 1890.

107 'qui par les connaisseurs ont toujours été considérés aussi importants que ses tableaux'; 'Mon plus vif désir étant d'agir en toute chose d'après les voeux de mon pauvre mari.' Jo to Octave Maus. AHKB 5756; 26 December 1890; VGM, Bd60: 'J'ai emporté les dessins avec moi en Hollande.' ('I brought the drawings back to Holland with me.')

108 Octave Maus to Jo. VGM, b1348; 29 December 1890.

109 'Ik heb je niet gevraagd of je "geen oogenblik geaarzeld hebt in de keus van de teekeningen" maar heb je gezegd dat je vooral niet vergeten moest die te sturen met den put. . . . Als je die niet gestuurd hebt, hadt je beter gedaan te aarzelen en te vragen.' Andries to Jo. VGM, b1868; 8 January 1891.

110 Theo thought the drawing was 'superb'. Theo to Vincent. Van Gogh, *Letters* 2009, letter 838. See also Sanchez 2012, p. 385.

111 'une des principales des œuvres de Vincent'. Jo to Octave Maus. AHKB 5757; 31 December 1890; VGM, Bd61. Jo thanked Maus for framing the drawings: AHKB 5758; 10 January 1891; VGM, Bd63.

112 Anna Veth-Dirks to Jo. VGM, b1434; 28 December 1890.

113 *De Nieuwe Gids* 6, no. 1 (1891), pp. 263–70; dated 25 November 1890. Also published in Tibbe 2014, pp. 123–9. In a letter to Jan Veth of 17 December 1890, Roland Holst described it as a 'pathetic article', because to his mind Van Eeden placed too much emphasis on Van Gogh's struggles and suffering, and expressed his opinion of the art poorly. Tibbe 2014, pp. 21 and 128. Veth had been against running the article.

114 'dat de kunst méér voor het groote publiek zou zijn'. *Algemeen Handelsblad*, 31 December 1890. See also Leeman 1990, p. 208.

115 'In plaats van op mijn telegram ja of neen te antwoorden, heb je wêer slim willen zijn.' 'Je domme geschrijf beteekent niets en bewijst me alleen maar hoe bitter slecht je zoudt kunnen handelen, als 't zoo ver komen moet.' 'Er moet ('t had al gebeurd moeten zijn) een conseil de famille benoemd worden, zonder wiens toestemming je *niets*, versta je me, *niets* doen mag. . . . Je weet alles beter, en je weet niets.' Andries to Jo. VGM, b1868; 8 January 1891. In terms of Andries's assistance, the idea that he had done everything he could to help Jo in October 1890 needs to be put into perspective. See Hulsker 1996a, p. 53. Cf. in this context what Jo's son Vincent wrote about his uncle's interference: 'Hij heeft het mijn moeder lastig gemaakt toen zij in Holland kwam.' ('He made things difficult for my mother when she came to Holland.') *Vincent's Diary*, 6 November 1933.

116 Jo to Anna Veth-Dirks. VGM, b1436; between 10 and 12 January 1891.

117 'meer bewijs gegeven iets van Vincent en zijne schilderijen te begrijpen, met de vergelijking met Claude nonsens te vinden'. See Stein 1986, pp. 257–8. Theo had previously expressed this view in a letter to Willemien. VGM, b911; 25 April 1887.

118 'kwasi flink zijn'; 'dan een dekmantel voor grenzelozen onervarenheid en lichtzinnigheid'. 'Je hebt aplomb te over, maar degelijkheid is iets anders.' 'Wanneer je nu eerlijk bent, schrijf dan niet zooveel, maar zeg dat je een kop toont en alles beter wil weten.' Andries to Jo. VGM, b1868; 8 January 1891.

119 *Vincent's Diary*, 27 September 1973: 'Volgens hem had ze alles weg moeten doen, maar zij verzette zich.' ('He said that she should have disposed of the lot, but she resisted.') He wrote the same in his diary on 26 January 1936 and noted it again on 1 January 1963 and on 29 October 1974. His son Johan was alluding to these notes when he commented: 'Fortunately she did not listen to her brother Andries (Dries) when he advised her to throw out the entire Van Gogh collection.' Van Gogh 1987, p. 3. Disposing of something is very different from throwing it out, however. The exact circumstances and context can no longer be discovered, but there can be no doubt that Andries was well aware that Jo and Vincent were each entitled to half of the estate, which makes the suggestion even more unlikely.

120 Locher 1973, pp. 113–14. Equally inaccurate is the comment 'Na de dood van Vincent en Theo bleef hij zich op allerlei niveaus inspannen voor de bekendwording van Van Gogh.' ('After the deaths of Vincent and Theo, he continued to work on all sorts of levels to promote Van Gogh's work.') Locher 1973, p. 123.

121 Fred Leeman in *Redon and Bernard* 2009, p. 25.

122 Locher 1973, pp. 106–7 and *Redon and Bernard* 2009, p. 120. Six of them were *Sunset in Montmartre* (F 266a / JH 1223); *Self-Portrait* (F 295 / JH 1211); *Le Moulin de la Galette* (F 348a / JH 1221); *Orchard with Peach Trees in Blossom* (F 551 / JH 1396); *Wheatfield* (F 564 / JH 1475); *Houses* (F 759 / JH 1988).

123 Taken from Theo's medical records; 30 December 1890.

124 The refusal of an autopsy is noted in Theo's medical records. The grave rights were purchased for an indefinite period. VGM, b3065; 28 January 1891.

125 *De Amsterdammer*, 29 January 1891.

Part Three

1 Richard Taruskin, *Text and Act: Essays on Music and Performance*. Oxford 1995, p. 218.

7 Back in the Netherlands—Villa Helma in Bussum

1 Paul Schneiders, *Het Spiegel. Geschiedenis van een villawijk van 1874 tot heden*. Laren 2010, pp. 56–8. Fontijn 1999, p. 208. Jo had already notified the authorities in Amsterdam and Bussum of her move with Vincent on 19 March 1891. ACA, *Population Register*, vol. 565, fol. 79.

2 ANG, Bussum Land Register, no. 871, p. 1780 and no. 3041. *Account Book* 2002, p. 160.

3 Frederik van Eeden to Jo. VGM, b4572; 31 January 1891. Jan Veth to Anna Veth-Dirks; 10 and 19 January 1891 respectively. Private collection.

4 Van Gogh 1952–4, p. 248 (quotation). Vincent later told his son Johan that it had been Jo's conscious decision to live at some distance from her family. Information provided by Johan van Gogh, 18 July 2011.

5 'projet de mon pauvre mari'. Jo to Émile Bernard; 3 February 1891. Published in *Art-documents* 1952. Also in Bernard 2012, p. 141, n. 1.

6 Émile Bernard to Jo. VGM, b1089; 8 March 1891. The aim of this exhibition was to ensure 'that we know in France what a remarkable and extraordinary artist my very dear friend Vincent was' ('que nous sachions en France quel artiste curieux et extraordinaire est mon ami très aimé Vincent'). See also Bernard 2012, pp. 137–8.

7 Octave Maus to Jo. VGM, b1349; 5 February 1891.

8 Jo to Octave Maus. AHKB 5759; 7 February 1891; VGM, Bd62. She thanked him for his letter of condolence.

9 Bill for 'mourning wear' in *Account Book* 2002, pp. 80, 158. The duration of the mourning period and the type of garments varied. Willemijn Ruberg, 'Rouwbrieven en rouwkleding als communicatiemiddelen in de negentiende eeuw'. *De Negentiende Eeuw* 31, no. 1 (2007), pp. 22–37, esp. 26–9.

10 Jo to Octave Maus. AHKB; 7 March 1891; VGM, Bd11.

11 She and Andries compiled impressive collections of newspaper cuttings with reactions, in VGMB, BVG 3116 and BVG 3117 respectively.

12 Jo to Octave Maus. AHKB; 11 March 1891; VGM, Bd12. *Account Book* 2002, p. 26, n. 38. She asked him for the third time to send accounts in the newspapers; this time he complied. Jo to Octave Maus. AHKB; 24 March 1891; VGM, Bd64 and Octave Maus to Jo. VGM, b1352; 6 April 1891.

13 Octave Maus to Jo. VGM, b1353; 21 June, and b1354; 29 June 1891 Maus also reported that Bernard had written about Van Gogh. He was referring to a piece in *La Plume*. See Bernard 1994, vol. 1, pp. 26–7.

14 Eugène Boch to Jo. VGM, b1184; 22 July 1891. The painting hung in Boch's parents' house. Boch to Jo. VGM, b1186; 30 November 1891. Later he gifted it to the Louvre; it is now in the Musée d'Orsay. For the visit: Van Gogh, *Letters* 2009, letter 890.

15 Transport company Charles J. Daverveldt & Co., with branches in Paris, Brussels, Rozendaal, Rotterdam and Amsterdam, which worked with Danger & Méganck (Sutton & Co.).

16 'God dank, dat gij Uw kind hebt, een erfenis nietwaar—iets waar ge voor leven kunt—waar ge zijn principes in kunt doen voortleven. Het lieve ventje zal U zoo veel liefde geven. Vooral als hij wat grooter wordt. Hij zal U steeds herinneren aan dien onuitsprekelijk goede tijden, dat zal U droefheid geven, groote droefheid—maar te gelijk een zachte weelde.—Het is zoo goed dat gij voor hem werken wilt, gij zoudt anders zoo geheel zonder doel zijn.' Sara de Swart to Jo. VGM, b1336; March 1891.

17 'C'est une fortune que vous avez là, ne la gâtez pas—double fortune—fortune de gloire, fortune d'argent.' Émile Bernard to Jo. VGM, b833; undated.

18 Émile Bernard to Jo. VGM, b1090; 7 April 1891. Bernard also sent her all the 'little Algerian embroideries that were on the divans and the armchairs' ('petites broderies algériennes qui étaient sur les divans et les fauteuils'). Cf. also Bernard 2012, pp. 141–2.

19 'Bonger list'. VGM, b3055. See also *Account Book* 2002, pp. 23–6.

20 Jo to Willem Steenhoff. VGM, b7426; 1 April 1925.

21 Jo to Émile Bernard; 9 April 1891. Published in *Art-documents* 1952.

22 VGM, b4553; 18 April 1891. The risk was shared between the 'Nederlandsche Assurantie Compagnie te Amsterdam van 1776' and the 'Brand Verzekering Maatschappij Holland' in Dordrecht. This latter policy was brokered by Brak & Moes, where Jo's father worked.

23 Van Gogh 1952–4, p. 248.

24 Alphons Diepenbrock to Andrew de Graaf, 10 August 1892. Alphons Diepenbrock, *Brieven en documenten*. Ed. Eduard Reeser. The Hague 1962, vol. 1, p. 366.

25 Story told by the son of A.G. Dake, who was also called A.G. Dake. His father was on holiday there in the summer of 1896 and clearly remembered this prohibition. Conversation with Johan van Gogh, September 2011. Cf. in contrast the account of one of the little friends, later told to Frédéric Bastet: 'They played hide and seek among all those paintings, the products of some loony uncle or other. Sometimes they kicked them, but never went right through them, because they were nice little boys at heart.' ('Tussen al die schilderijen, de producten van de een of andere verknipte oom, speelden ze verstoppertje. Soms schopten ze ertegen, maar gingen er nooit doorheen, want het bleven nette jongetjes.') See Prick 2003, p. 363. There is also the suggestive report of how Jan Toorop 'got together the paintings that the Widow Van Gogh's children used to swing on in the attic' ('de doeken bijeenzocht, die de kinderen van de Wed. Van Gogh op zolder gebruikten om op te schommelen') for the Haagsche Kunstkring in 1892. *Algemeen Handelsblad,* 8 February 1917, anonymous. After Jo's death some of the works were in the unheated attic of her house in Laren, where her son and his family went to live. Tromp 2006, p. 165.

26 *Diary* 4, p. 5; 24 February 1892.

27 *Diary* 3, pp. 138–9; 15 November 1891.

28 Shortly before this, in 1889, Wilhelmina Drucker had set up the Vrije Vrouwenvereeniging (Free Women's Association, VVV). They championed women's right to better education and to practise a profession. See Braun 1992, p. 92.

29 The three boarding rooms were later converted into one large room—the positions of the partition walls can still be seen on the wooden floors.

30 *Account Book* 2002, p. 158. RHCM. *Diary* 4, p. 32. *Vincent's Diary*, 3 October 1973.

31 In 1904 Villa Helma had been connected to the gas and water mains. *De Gooi- en Eemlander*, 17 September and 1 October 1904.

32 SSAN, NNAB. Archive of the notary Harm Pieter Bok 1883–91, inv. no. 12, deed no. 54. The abridged deed (without the list of furniture etc.) is VGM, b2214. 'Continued community' meant that the surviving spouse in a marriage could continue to enjoy the deceased's goods; this continued community was dissolved when Jo remarried in 1901.

33 Anna Dirks to Jo. VGM, b1436; January 1891. Cf. Elise van Calcar, who wrote: 'A good housewife trains good servants.' Van Calcar 1886, p. 121. Without a servant, a bourgeois or middle-class family was not only 'inconvenienced', but also 'socially déclassé', according to Stokvis 2005, p. 140.

34 *Diary* 3, p. 141; 18 November 1891.

35 *Diary* 4, p. 25; 21 March 1892.

36 At the beginning of 1892, Jo sold French stocks in the amount of 1,568 francs. *Account Book* 2002, pp. 15, 39–42. The maxim quoted: *Diary* 4, p. 34; 27 March 1892.

37 In 1919 her stocks stood at 40,789 guilders, on which she received 2,050 guilders in interest. *Account Book* 2002, p. 134.

38 Menno Tamminga, 'D.G. van Beuningen (1877–1955) heerste over stad en arbeiders', *NRC Handelsblad*, 1 October 2004, p. 31. Van der Woud 2010, pp. 63–80.

39 Vincent tried to play this down: 'My mother also sold paintings but she had secured her living by hard work. Those first prices were very low, as well.' *Vincent's Diary*, 11 March 1976.

40 Lijst van Schilderijen, Teekeningen en Etsen behoorende tot de nalatenschap van den Heer Th. van Gogh. This list had been drawn up two months earlier for the purposes of the fire insurance policy. VGM, b2215 (list signed by Veth; 23 June 1891) and b4553 (policy; 18 April 1891); in this policy the drawings are listed with an approximate value of 600 guilders. *Dutch Civil Code* 1, art. 444 obliges the guardian to make a list of the minor's assets.

41 This deed of gift is VGM, b2216. Jo co-signed as Vincent's guardian. On Theo's death, Jo was entitled to half of 3/20ths of Vincent's estate, because when Vincent died on 29 July 1890, his heirs inherited as follows (*Dutch Civil Code* 1, art. 902): his mother Anna 5/20ths; Theo, Anna, Lies, Willemien and Cor 3/20ths each—Theo's share in this estate was included in the community of property between him and Jo.

As early as August 1890, Joan and Anna van Houten, Lies and Willemien had let it be known that they would like Theo to inherit Vincent's estate, but this declaration had no legal grounds because the names of Mrs van Gogh and Cor were missing. All the persons mentioned to Theo van Gogh. VGM, b2217; August 1890. See also Van Gogh 1987, p. 3.

42 'Memorie van aangifte der nalatenschap van den heer Theodorus van Gogh', 6 August 1891. HUA, 137–7, inv. no. 463.

43 'After I attained my majority, she and I came to an agreement concerning our joint property,' by which he meant their two halves. VGMD, memorandum by Vincent; 27 May 1977.

44 'Als je een teekening kunt verkoopen voor 't museum zou ik 't *zeker* doen, er zijn er zóó veel! Maar niet te weinig vragen, ik zou denken 1000 Dollar op zijn allerminst.' Jo to Vincent and Josina. VGM, b8294; 29 December 1915.

45 It has been suggested that Vincent was always averse to the sales, but no source has been found for this. Cf. Van Crimpen 2002, p. 256.

46 *Diary* 4, p. 6; 24 February 1892.

47 Prick 2003, p. 361, 363. Alberdingk Thijm talked about Jo's 'always busy management'.

48 According to Vincent, Jo always reproached Berlage because he 'did not join the workers' movement (the SDAP), despite his social conscience'. *Vincent's Diary*, 13 August 1934.

49 *Diary* 4, p. 7; 24 February 1892.

50 Marie Cremers, *Jeugdherinneringen*. Amsterdam 1948, p. 36; later reprinted as *Lichtend verleden*. Amsterdam 1954, p. 32. In 1892, this painting appeared at the exhibition of contemporary Dutch painting, 'Keuze-tentoonstelling van hedendaagsche Nederlandsche schilderkunst', in Arti et Amicitiae.

51 *Diary* 3, pp. 136–42; 15 November 1891.

52 *Diary* 3, p. 145. Jan Veth gave her this book as a thirtieth birthday present. VGMB, BVG 1462.

53 This reading circle was associated with Boekhandel R. Los, the bookshop at number 23 Nassaulaan in Bussum; Jo paid subscriptions in the 1894 to 1900 period. VGM, b3524 and b3525.

54 This information comes from a list of calculations Andries drew up for Jo in Paris. VGM, b2209. The buyers of these works are unknown. *Account Book* 2002, pp. 140–41; Cat. Otterlo 2003, pp. 347–50.

55 We do not know how many works there were. Flanor (Boele van Hensbroek's pseudonym), *De Nederlandsche Spectator*, 9 January 1892. Willemien van Gogh to Jo, VGM, b2914; 7 December 1891. See also Joosten 1969b.

56 Bouwman 1992; *Account Book* 2002, 20 October 1891; Geel 2011; Van der Heide 2015a, 2015b and 2015c.

57 *Account Book* 2002, pp. 49, 141, 163. Klaas Oosterom, 'Cornelis van Norren, een ware bouwer. Een "kleine luyde" met betekenis voor Bussum', *Bussums Historisch Tijdschrift* 29, no. 1 (2013), p. 10.

58 In May 1893, for example, Miss Schleier received 10 per cent commission for negotiating the sale of the painting *Two Crabs* (F 606 / JH 1662) to William Cherry Robinson, the British consul in Amsterdam. She was paid twenty guilders. *Account Book* 2002, pp. 141, 180.

59 Joseph Isaäcson to Jo. VGM, b1902; 7–8 January 1892; *Diary* 4, p. 12 (quote).

60 Christiaan Oldenzeel to Jo. VGM, b1283; 25 January—and b1284; 31 January 1892. For the white frames see Van Gogh, *Letters* 2009, letters 615, 707, 718, 812, 825, 834 and 837.

61 Joosten 1969b. *De Amsterdammer*, 21 February 1892. On 16 February and on 6 March 1892 articles appeared in the *NRC*; Leo Simons, in the *Haarlemmer Courant*, 25 February 1892. See also Tibbe 2014, pp. 159–61 (including the article by Roland Holst).

62 F. Buffa & Zonen (Jacobus Slagmulder) to Jo. VGM, b1928; 10 March 1892. Slagmulder had been a partner since 1891. See *Kunsthandel Frans Buffa & Zonen (1790/1951). Schoonheid te koop*. Eds. Sylvia Alting van Geusau, Mayken Jonkman and Aukje Vergeest. Exh. cat. Laren, Singer Museum, 2016–17. Zwolle 2016.

63 *Diary* 3, p. 146; 28 January 1892.

64 Julien Tanguy to Jo. VGM, b1426; 31 January 1892. Andries and Annie moved from Paris to Hilversum in January. VGM, b2866; 2 February 1892.

65 Christiaan Oldenzeel to Jo. VGM, b1285; 12 February 1892.

66 Richard Bionda in exh. cat. Amsterdam 1991, p. 53.

67 Van Gogh 1914, vol. 2, p. 72.

68 Jan Stricker to Jo. VGM, b2917; 17 February 1892. Van Gogh, *Letters* 2009, letter 26.

69 *Diary* 4, p. 4; 24 February 1892.

70 Jan Verkade to Jo. VGM, b1278; shortly before 24 February 1892.

71 Jan Hillebrand Wijsmuller to Jo. VGM, b1906, b1907 and b1908; 14, 20 and 26 February 1892. On the admission ticket it says that Jo was giving the session: VGM, b1500. It is unlikely that she actually spoke on that occasion. Had she spoken herself she would surely have made some comment about it, and giving an art appreciation session could also mean providing the opportunity to look at and appreciate works of art. Jo left the works (including some watercolours) at Arti for some time and they were displayed there. VGM, b1286.

72 *Diary* 4, pp. 12–13; 25 February 1892.

73 *Diary* 4, pp. 18–19; 6 March 1892.

74 Jan Hillebrand Wijsmuller to Jo. VGM, b1501; 14 March 1892.

8 Contacts with Jan Veth, Jan Toorop and Richard Roland Holst

1 On Veth: Huizinga 1927; Bijl de Vroe 1987; Blotkamp in exh. cat. Amsterdam 1991, pp. 75–8; *Kunstschrift* 49, no. 1 (2005).

2 Anna Dirks to Jo. VGM, b3559; 21 September 1884. Bijl de Vroe 1987, pp. 45–6. Jo had been afraid that Jan Veth would think her 'impossibly boring'. *Diary* 3, p. 97; 1 June 1888.

3 Anna Dirks to Jo. VGM, b4532; 10 May 1886.

4 'Je moet dit nu niet aan je man laten lezen, maar ik ben er zoo trotsch op: ik zal het zelf kunnen voeden, want ook dat is in orde.' Anna Veth-Dirks to Jo. VGM, b3230; 3 February 1890.

5 Anna Veth-Dirks and Jan Veth to Jo. VGM, b2076; 18 October 1890.

6 'kom dan *dadelijk hier. Beloof me dat*.' Anna Veth-Dirks to Jo. VGM, b1433; 11 November 1890.

7 *Diary* 4, p. 3; 24 February 1892.

8 Theo to Vincent. Van Gogh, *Letters* 2009, letter 813; 22 October 1889.

9 Anna Veth-Dirks to Jo. Atria; 29 May 1890; VGM, Bd92.

10 *Diary* 3, p. 139; 15 November 1891. Van Eeden got on well with Veth and with Isaac Israëls. Fontijn 1999, pp. 168, 182, 208, 217.

11 Bijl de Vroe 1987, pp. 192–3.

12 Bijl de Vroe 1987, pp. 89–92.

13 *Diary* 4, p. 51; 18 May 1892.

14 'Het was ongelukkig dat de heer V. in zijn zoeken naar iemand die zijn opinie omtrent Vincent deelde, juist terecht moest komen bij een van Vincent's grootste bewonderaars.' Jan Veth in *De Amsterdammer*, 9 September 1891. Cf. also Joosten 1970c, pp. 155–6.

15 'zachte drijverij'; 'tureluurs'. Jan Veth to Jo. VGM, b2077; undated.

16 *Diary* 4, pp. 39–40; 15 April 1892.

17 'dat zeetje dat boven de deur hangt'. Jan Veth to Jo. VGM, b2083; undated (in 1892).

18 'Ik geef je geen ongelijk dat je ze op waarde houdt, maar je begrijpt dat ik niet meer kon geven. . . . Je kunt uit dit verloop zien, dat mijn ingenomenheid met wat ik de mooie Vincenten noem niet heelemaal platonisch was.' Jan Veth to Jo. VGM, b2078; undated.

19 *Diary* 4, p. 21 (first quotation), pp. 23, 27 (second quotation); 20 and 21 March 1892.

20 Jan Veth to Jo. VGM, b2084; undated.

21 Huizinga 1927, pp. 31, 47. On Veth's revision of his opinion of Van Gogh see also exh. cat. Amsterdam 1991, p. 82.

22 Jo's letter to the editor appeared in *De Amsterdammer* on 9 August 1891.

23 Van Gogh used the word 'serenity' dozens of times in his letters.

24 2 Corinthians 6:10; Van Gogh quoted this more than twenty times.

25 'Ik moet je weer even een episteltje schrijven—als ik iets te zeggen heb—kan ik 't eerder schrijven dan zeggen. Ik ben zoo blij dat je de brieven ook zoo mooi vind—ik wist 't wel! Maar nu vraag ik je of—jij—die nu je nog maar 't kleinste en minst belangrijke deel gelezen hebt, zegt: 'ik droom er van'—stel je nu eens even in mijn plaats voor zoover je het kunt! ik heb van 't oogenblik dat Theo ziek werd daarmee geleefd—den eersten eenzamen avond dien ik in ons huis weer doorbracht . . . nam ik 't pak brieven op—want ik wist dat ik hem *daarin* terug zou vinden—en avond aan avond was *dat* mijn troost in al de groote ellende.

Ik zocht er *toen* niet Vincent maar enkel Theo in—ieder woord, iedere bizonderheid die hem betrof—ik hunkerde er naar—ik las die brieven—niet met mijn hoofd alleen—ik was er in verdiept met heel mijn ziel . . . .

Ik heb ze gelezen en herlezen tot ik de heele figuur van *V.* duidelijk voor mij had. En denk nu eens toen ik in Holland kwam—voor me zelf zoo volkomen bewust van het groote—het onbeschrijfelijk hooge van dat eenzame kunstenaarsleven—wat ik toen gevoeld heb bij de onverschilligheid die me van alle kanten werd betoond waar het Vincent en zijn werk betrof. Neem je het me nu nog zoo kwalijk dat ik zoo gevoelig was op dat punt—dat zoo gewraakte artikeltje in de *A.*[25]—begrijp je nu dat 't niet was le désir de se voir imprimer zooals je me verweet—maar alleen 't brandende gevoel van onrechtvaardigheid van de heele wereld tegen hem—en dat ik nu eens op één enkel punt kon uiten. Het is me soms zoo bar geworden—ik herinner me hoe verleden jaar op Vincent's sterfdag—ik s'avonds laat nog uit liep—ik kon 't in huis niet uithouden—'t woei en regende en 't was stikdonker—en overal in de huizen—zag ik licht en zaten de menschen gezellig bij elkaar—en ik voelde me zóó verlaten—dat ik voor 't eerst begreep wat hij moet gevoeld hebben—in die tijden toen iedereen zich van hem afkeerde en 't hem was 'of er voor hem geen plaats was op de aarde'. En toen je me verleden op dien avond verweten hebt, dat ik kwaad had gedaan aan zijn reputatie en dat ik 't niet kon *meenen* dat ik van zijn werk hield—en al die dingen meer—toen heb je me zoo gegriefd—dat ik er ziek van ben geweest. Ik zeg dit niet om je iets te verwijten—maar ik wou dat ik je kon doen voelen wat de invloed is geweest van Vincent op mijn leven. Hij heeft me geholpen om mijn leven zoo in te richten dat ik vrede kan hebben in me zelf—sereniteit—dat was van hun beiden 't geliefkoosde woord en iets dat zij beschouwden als 't hoogste. Sereniteit heb ik gevonden—ik ben dezen langen, eenzamen winter niet ongelukkig geweest—'bedroefd—maar nogthans blijde' dat is ook een van zijn spreuken die ik nu eerst heb leeren begrijpen. En nietwaar al heb ik nu veel dingen onhandig en verkeerd gedaan—'t was immers niet verdiend dat je me *daarna*[*ar*] beoordeelde—waar ik zoo alleen stond en toch volgens mijn beste weten handelde! Dit alles moest er eens even uit!' Jo to Jan Veth. VGM, b2079; undated. Jo's son Vincent published part of this letter later, saying that his mother had written it 'to a girlfriend', but this is impossible because she had never engaged in such a quarrel with any of her women friends. See Van Gogh, *Lettres à son frère Vincent* 1932, p. 12; Van Gogh 1952–4, p. 247.

26 'het heiligste dat voor me bestaat, waarvan niemand vóór jou iets geweten heeft'. Jo to Jan Veth. VGM, b2081; 3 April 1892. *Diary* 4, pp. 31–2; 27 March 1892.

27 'geestelijk trotsch'. Veth's biographer Huizinga noted that others found his pernicketiness unpleasant and that his 'irritating vehemence' could lead to needless disputes. Huizinga 1927, pp. 17, 162–3.

28 Piet Boele van Hensbroek to Jo. VGM, b1182; 11 August 1891. He had met Vincent in the early 1870s. See Van Stipriaan 2011, p. 22.

29 Ton van Kalmthout, 'Een gezellige en nuttige vereniging', in *De Haagse Bohème op zoek naar Europa. Honderd jaar Haagsche Kunstkring*. Eds. Ellen Fernhout et al. Zutphen 1992, pp. 21–39.

30 Marius Bauer to Jo. VGM, b1910; 30 January 1892.

31 Jan Toorop to Jo. VGM, b1911; 4 February 1892. The paintings were sent on 25 March; Veth had helped in making the choice. *Diary* 4, p. 30; 25 March 1892. His assistance had not been entirely wholehearted—there was still tension between him and Jo: 'Maandagavond reisde ik n.b. met Toorop. Ik had, meegetroond door Holst, bij de familie gegeten. 't Was goed dat ik niet in Bussum was want anders was ik tot ergernis van Jo vanzelf weer in het Vincent-kijken van Toorop gemoeid geworden.' ('I travelled with Toorop on Monday evening; cajoled into going by Holst, I had eaten with the family. It was a good thing I wasn't in Bussum, because if I had been I would inevitably have got involved in Toorop's Vincent-viewing, to Jo's annoyance.') Jan Veth to Anna Veth-Dirks; undated (early February 1892). Private collection.

32 Jo knew about this. Jan Toorop to Jo. VGM, b1912; 3 March 1892. De Bock and Van Gogh had gone around together in the 1880–3 period. Van Eeden 1937, p. 56; 1 March 1892.

33 'Mevr. van Gogh is een charmant vrouwtje, maar het irriteert mij wanneer iemand fanatiek dweept met iets waar zij toch niets van begrijpt, en door sentimentaliteit verblind toch vermeend zuiver kritiesch te kunnen zijn. Het is bakvischjes gekwezel voilà tout . . . mevr. van Gogh zou dát stuk best vinden dat het opgeschroefst en sentimenteelst was—dat haar het meest deed huilen, zij vergeet dat haar verdriet Vincent maakt tot een God.' KBH, Toorop Archive, T.C. C 142; 3 March 1892. Quoted in Joosten 1970c, pp. 157–8, n. 61. Leeman 1990, p. 211: 'Certainly Johanna's reaction does not seem to have done justice to the self-searching way in which Roland Holst formulates his critical stance. He was in fact the first who seemed to realise that to judge Van Gogh's work, new artistic values might be required.' On Roland Holst's contribution to *De Amsterdammer* of 21 February 1892: exh. cat. Amsterdam 1991, p. 83.

34 'heel openlijk en heel luid'. Richard Roland Holst to Jo. VGM, b1220; 30 March 1892.

35 *Diary* 4, pp. 16–17; 3 March 1892.

36 'populieren met 2 rose figuurtjes, die U ons persoonlijk gebracht hebt'. P.C. Eilers Jr (working at Van Wisselingh's) to Jo. VGM, b2939; 9 March 1892. See also Heijbroek and Wouthuysen 1999, p. 42.

37 Christiaan Oldenzeel to Jo. VGM, b1287; 3 March 1892. *Diary* 4, pp. 19–20; 20 March 1892.

38 Christiaan Oldenzeel to Jo. VGM, b1288; 23 March—b1289; 27 March—and b1290; 19 April 1892. See also Joosten 1969b.

39 *Diary* 4, p. 37.

40 *Diary* 4, pp. 25–7; 21 March 1892.

41 'C'était une période si importante et sauf celles-là il n'y a rien qui manque à la correspondance, que je suis en train de préparer pour la presse.' 'c'est là la seule chose que je peux faire en souvenir de mon mari et pour Vincent.' Jo to Albert Aurier. VGM, b1510; 27 March 1892. When Alfred Vallette, editor of *Mercure de France*, informed Jo that Aurier had died on 5 October 1892, just twenty-seven years old, Jo was shocked at his untimely death. She was relieved, though, when Aurier's brother-in-law reassured her that Vincent's letters had been found. Alfred Vallette to Jo. VGM, b1291; 19 October 1892. T. Gramaire to Jo. VGM, b1541; 23 November 1892.

42 'Het doet mij genoegen dat U al de schilderijen hebt laten opzetten, dan zal ik wel voor houten lijsten zorgen.' Jan Toorop to Jo. VGM, b1913; on or about 23 March 1892.

43 Jo's visit to Paris is referred to in a letter from Sara de Swart to her. VGM, b2857; undated (between April and October 1892).

44 See Larsson 1993, pp. 127–8; Van Gogh, *Letters to Bernard* 2007, p. 19. On the photographs: VGM, b4759.

45 *Diary* 4, pp. 41–3; 25 April 1892.

46 *Diary* 4, pp. 46–7; 1 May 1892. *Diary* 4, pp. 23–4; 20 March 1892.

47 *Diary* 4, p. 53; 9 June 1892. Jo previously read Oscar Browning, *The Life of George Eliot* (1890). She would have been familiar with the letters and diaries through *George Eliot's Life, as Related in her Letters and Journals*. Ed. John Walter Cross. 3 vols. New York 1885.

48 *Diary* 4, p. 50. In this period Toorop wrote several letters to Jo. VGM, b1911–16. See also Tibbe 2014, pp. 162–5, including on pp. 170–2 the article 'Vincent van Gogh' by Ferdinand Keizer (pseudonym of Ida Heijermans) in *De Nederlandsche Spectator*. Cf. Van Kalmthout 1998, p. 32.

49 Jo to W.C. Tengeler (Kunstkring administrator), 20 June 1892. VGM; Bd82 (copy). His reply is VGM, b1304; 22 June 1892. See also Joosten 1969c, pp. 269–73; Joosten 1970a, pp. 47–9; Op de Coul 1990; *Account Book* 2002, pp. 46, 141. On Rohde's enthusiasm for Van Gogh see Stein 1986, pp. 290–2 and Larsson 1996, pp. 26–7.

50 Théophile de Bock to Jo. VGM, b1915; 28 April 1892. *De Amsterdammer*, 5 June 1892.

51 *Diary* 4, p. 55; 9 June 1892.

52 *Diary* 4, p. 57; 23 June 1892. Vincent acceded to Jo's wishes; she adored her first grandchild, Theo, and described him as a prince who radiated light.

53 Jan Toorop to Jo. VGM, b1914; 16 April 1892. 'Er exposeeren niets dan nieuwe en jonge kunstenaars. Daarom hadden wij volgaarne het werk van Vincent daar ook gehad. Hij hoort daar t'huis.' ('Only new and young artists are exhibiting. That's why we would have gladly had Vincent's work there too. He belongs there.')

54 Théophile de Bock to Jo. VGM, b2072; 21 May 1892.

55 For the poster and a photograph of the extremely crowded hang see Daloze 2015, pp. 190–2.

56 The two Van Goghs were among 'the least unusual' and this cautious choice was intended not to scare off the public at large, who were not yet familiar with his work, J.F. Ankersmit later declared in 'De keuze-tentoonstelling van 1892', *Propria Cures* 48, no. 32 (12 June 1937), pp. 305–7. See also J.F. Ankersmit, *Een halve eeuw journalistiek*. Amsterdam 1937, pp. 20–1 and Tibbe 2014, pp. 154–8.

57 *Diary* 4, pp. 58–9. VGM, b1502 and b1505. See also Joosten 1970a, p. 49; Joosten 1970b, p. 100, and Joosten 1970c, p. 155. When someone later suggested including a few works in an exhibition at the Lakenhal, Jo reiterated her wish and turned the request down. She would rather have 'een heele expositie van Vincent, want zoo'n paar schilderijen tusschen Israëls, Maris en al die donkeren in voldoet absoluut niets.' ('a whole exhibition devoted to Vincent, because a few paintings between Israëls, Maris and all those dark ones is no use at all.') Jo to Anna van Gogh. VGM, b2972; 6 October 1893.

58 *Diary* 4, pp. 61–3; 4 July 1892.

59 *Diary* 4, p. 65–6; 8 July 1892. 'She's seventy-four, small and a bit lopsided—a pleasant, impressive face—I'd say a French type from the days of the Revolution—fine straight nose, proud blue eyes and silver white hair that she wears combed up high in front and then covered with a small black lace scarf, so that the forehead remains

completely exposed. If she's tired or a bit listless she's an ordinary old woman—almost a witch in a simple brown dress, stumbling along on her stick—but when she ignites during a conversation—then everything changes and she becomes the proud noble lady that she in fact is—she bridles—her eyes sparkle—and all her features relax or rather become a noble, fine whole.'

60 Willemien van Gogh to Jo. VGM, b1038; 15 August 1892. *Account Book* 2002, pp. 87–8.

61 Marie Mensing and Line Liernur to Jo. IISG; 28 August 1892.

62 Marie Mensing, 'Eisch eener vrouw van 't heden, ten opzichte van 't sexueele leven'. *De Dageraad* 1897–98, pp. 473–82, 627. On her: IISG; Atria; *BWSA* 2 (1987), pp. 89–91; Fia Dieteren, 'Men is niet ongestraft feminist', *Rooie Vrouw. Landelijk Blad van Rooie Vrouwen in de Partij van de Arbeid* (September 1988), pp. 12–15; Hofsink and Overkamp 2011, pp. 58–69.

63 *Diary* 4, p. 68; 3 September 1892.

64 *Extaze*. Eds. H.T.M. van Vliet, Oege Dijkstra and Marijke Stapert-Eggen. Utrecht and Antwerp 1990, pp. 70 and 51.

65 *Diary* 4, p. 71; 26 September 1892.

66 The increase in pet lovers was part of a wider middle-class civilizing offensive. See Hanneke Ronnes and Victor van de Ven, 'Van dakhaas tot schootpoes. De opkomst van de kat als huisdier in Nederland in de negentiende eeuw', *De Negentiende Eeuw* 37, no. 2 (2013), pp. 116–36.

67 *Diary* 4, pp. 73–4; 3 October 1892. Willemien congratulated Jo on her birthday. She empathized strongly with her friend and paid her a consoling compliment: 'Ik dacht zoo dikwijls van den zomer, als Theo 't zag wat zou hij veel goed vinden.' ('I thought so often in the summer, if Theo saw it, how much he would approve.') Willemien van Gogh to Jo. VGM, b2915; 3 October 1892.

68 *Diary* 4, p. 77; 3 November 1892. Jo must have meant that women's misery serves some purpose after all—in any event they do not take their problems to whores.

69 *Diary* 4, p. 78; 7 November 1892. Verlaine had mumbled poems from the collection *Romances sans paroles* so indistinctly and inaudibly that the *Algemeen Handelsblad* of 10 November 1892 described the evening as 'drearier than dreariness itself'. Verlaine had stayed with Willem Witsen and Isaac Israëls for five days. Exh. cat. Amsterdam 2012, pp. 78–80; J.F. Heijbroek and A.A.M. Vis, *Verlaine in Nederland. Het bezoek van 1892 in woord en beeld.* Amsterdam 1985.

70 *Diary* 4, p. 81; 17 November 1892. 'La mère l'a conçu dans le ciel.' Jo had evidently managed to get hold of Michelet's *L'Amour*, which she had been trying to find in February. The quotation in the ed. Paris 1858, p. 158.

71 *Diary* 4, p. 70; 26 September 1892. 'door dat plezierig werk, openlijk mijn bewondering voor Vincents talent te kunnen bewijzen'. Richard Roland Holst to Jo. VGM, b1221; 24 September 1892. She was sent a floor plan so that she could decide on the layout. Christiaan Lodewijk van Kesteren to Jo. VGM, b1421; 11 October 1892.

72 Richard Roland Holst to Jo. VGM, b1230; 20 November 1892.

73 'de opening *moet* royaal en plechtig zijn, en betalend publiek op de opening zou daarom kwaad doen', Richard Roland Holst to Jo. VGM, b1231; 10 December 1892. The Haagsche Kunstkring sent thirty-two frames for the works. Richard Roland Holst to Jo. VGM, b1232; 11 December—b1233; 'bloeiende boomgaarden in 't midden' 'links daarvan de olijven en de blauwe-toon schilderijen, rechts bergen van St Remi en de geele-toon schilderijen'; 13 December, b1234 and b1236; both 14 December—and b1235; 15 December 1892 (about the catalogue).

74 Exh. cat. Amsterdam 1892. Van Gogh called the halo the symbol of the '*je ne sais quoi* of the eternal'. Van Gogh, *Letters* 2009, letter 673. Cf. also Evert van Uitert, 'De legendevorming te bevorderen: notities over de Vincent van

Goghmythe', in exh. cat. Amsterdam 1977, pp. 15–27. *De Amsterdammer*, 5 February 1893. For the extension see *Algemeen Handelsblad*, 9 February 1893.

75 The drawing was offered for sale by J.H. de Bois in October 1919 and shown at an exhibition staged at Pictura in The Hague. Despite its provenance, H.P. Bremmer questioned its authenticity at the time. Balk 2006, p. 408. Richard Roland Holst to Jo. VGM, b1242; 15 February, b1244; 27 February—and b1245; 8 March 1893. Etty 2000, p. 57 (the hang).

76 Joosten 1970b, pp. 101–2. *Account Book* 2002, pp. 46, 141. VGM, b1422; 23 February 1893.

77 'de indrukken der werkelijkheid synthethizeerde als levensopenbaringen van fellen pathos.' Jan Veth to Jo. VGM, b2085; undated. *De Nieuwe Gids* 8 (1893), pp. 427–31; reprinted in *Hollandse teekenaars van dezen tijd.* Amsterdam 1905, pp. 49–53. Also included in the DBNL and in Tibbe 2014, pp. 177–80. Huizinga 1927, p. 49, reports that Roland Holst was moved by the article.

78 'Wij allen die het werk zien buiten den persoon om, bewonderen vooral de machtige rigoureusheid, het oud-testamentische in hem, zijn dramatische kracht, die zoo sterk was dat zelfs zijn teerste sujetten, "de bloeiende boomgaarden", werken worden van groote felheid.' Richard Roland Holst to Jo. VGM, b1249; undated.

79 Richard Roland Holst to Jo. VGM, b1240; 30 January 1893.

80 By no means everyone was persuaded. The art dealer Van Wisselingh wrote that he did not think much of what he saw at the exhibition in the Panorama. E.J. van Wisselingh to Jo. VGM, b2938; 2 December 1893.

81 *Diary* 4, p. 83; 31 December 1892.

82 *Diary* 4, pp. 86–7; 3 October 1893.

83 Alfred Vallette to Andries Bonger. VGM, b893; 19 January 1893. Émile Bernard to Jo. VGM, b828; 1 February 1893. For the articles in *Mercure de France* between 1893 and 1897 see http://vangoghletters.org/vg/publications_2.html#intro.IV.2.3.

84 'Vous saurez mieux que moi ce qu'il faudra publier de cela.' Jo to Émile Bernard; 26 January 1893. Published in *Art-documents* 1952. Cf. also Leeman 2013, pp. 224–5, 253. Jo also let Roland Holst know how pleased she was: Richard Roland Holst to Jo. VGM, b1240; 30 January 1893.

85 'ce qui peut être intéressant sur l'œuvre de Vincent et sur ce que j'ai à prouver de son tempérament'. Émile Bernard to Jo. VGM, b830; February 1893.

86 Émile Bernard to Jo. VGM, b832; March 1893.

87 Émile Bernard to Jo. VGM, b829; undated. Alfred Vallette to Jo, VGM, b1293; 28 May 1893—b1294; 7 June 1893. See also Bernard 2012, p. 221.

88 Jo thanked him for sending her the article 'Eugène Delacroix' by Théodore de Wyzewa in *Le Figaro*, 12 June 1893, in which the author made a connection between Van Gogh and Delacroix, although she thought it was a shame that he had focused on the maniacal aspects of their personalities. 'Mais cela m'a beaucoup touché de les voir nommé ensemble—Delacroix et Vincent—il doit y avoir quelque chose de commun entre ces deux. Vincent parlait toujours de Delacroix avec une belle admiration!' ('But it touched me greatly to see them mentioned together—Delacroix and Vincent—they must have had something in common, those two. Vincent always talked about Delacroix with great admiration!') Jo to Alfred Vallette, 16 June 1893. Pedro Corrêa Do Lago Collection, Brazil. Alfred Vallette to Jo. VGM, b1295; 23 June 1893.

89 Alfred Vallette to Jo. VGM, b1296; 25 July 1893.

90 Émile Bernard to Andries Bonger. RPK, André Bonger Archive; 25 December 1894. Bernard 2012, pp. 350–3. See also *Lettres à Bernard* 1911, p. 41.

91 Alfred Vallette to Jo. VGM, b1297; 27 July 1893. Vallette hung on to the drawings for a year, then at Jo's request he took them to Ambroise Vollard to sell in his gallery. AVP (2,2); 7 November 1896.

92 'Treffend is de uitdrukking in den kop van dezen angstig vastbeslotene, die schilderen kon en schrijven, zoo sterk en ook zoo zwaar alsof hij een moker hanteerde.' Veth had seen to it that they used his reproduction of the portrait of Van Gogh (from Andries Bonger's collection), which had appeared in the *Gedenkboek keuze-tentoonstelling van Hollandsche schilderkunst uit de jaren 1860 tot 1892.*

93 *De Telegraaf*, 8, 11 and 21 May 1893.

94 *Mercure de France* 3, no. 40 (April 1893), pp. 324–39. Boele van Hensbroek: 'Hij, die de hand slaat aan het werk, om die brieven uit te geven, moet niet slechts kunstenaar zijn, maar hij moet hen gekend hebben, hen, beide de Van Goghs. En hij volvoere het werk met piëteit.' ('Whoever takes on the task of publishing these letters must not only be an artist, he must have known them, them, both the Van Goghs. And may he carry out the work with piety.') *De Nederlandsche Spectator,* 6 May 1893. Veth supported him in *De Amsterdammer* of 21 May.

95 'Dieu permette qu'elles soient editées un jour dignement et en leur entier.' Émile Bernard to Jo. VGM, b831; 28 June 1896.

96 'Je me rappelle parfaitement que mon mari m'a souvent parlé et de Mr Mourier Petersen et de l'exposition libre—et que en Danemarc on était plus avancé en peinture qu'en Hollande qu'on y aime plus la peinture moderne, je suis convaincue que lui aussi vous aurait envoyé les tableaux de son frère. C'est pour cela que j'accepte tout de suite votre invitation pour les exposer à Copenhague.' Jo to Johan Rohde. KBK; 8 February 1893; VGM, Bd59. In the Royal Library in Copenhagen there are six letters from Jo dated between February and August 1893. Jo was referring to the Danish artist Christian Vilhelm Mourier-Petersen (1858–1945). He had met Vincent in Arles in the spring of 1888 and had stayed with Theo in Paris in the summer of that year.

97 Richard Roland Holst to Jo. VGM, b1241; 10 February 1893.

98 Johan Rohde to Jo. VGM, b1988; 20 February 1893. Georg Seligmann to Jo. VGM, b1984; 22 February 1893.

99 Georg Seligmann to Johan Rohde. KBK. On Jo: 'En ganske ung, meget elskverdig enke'; on the prices: 'Til et par av Billederne (Annas) mangler jeg endnu Priser og Titler, men du skal faa dem saa snart jeg faar dem. Jeg var forresten med til at sætte Priser på Flere Ting, da de ikke alle var taxerede. Men forresten modtager Fruen ogsaa Bud, hvis det skal være.' With thanks to Eve-Marie Lund for her translation from Danish into Dutch, on which the English is based. See also Kirsten Olesen, 'From Amsterdam to Copenhagen', in *Gauguin and Van Gogh in Copenhagen in 1893.* Ed. Merete Bodelsen. Copenhagen 1984, pp. 29–30.

100 Georg Seligmann to Jo. VGM, b2175; 1 May 1893. For the versions of the *Sunflowers* Jo owned at that time see Martin Bailey, *The Sunflowers are Mine: The Story of Van Gogh's Masterpiece.* London 2013, pp. 202–5.

101 Johan Rohde to Jo. VGM, b1986; 9 April 1893.

102 Jo to Johan Rohde. KBK; 12 April 1893; VGM, Bd119.

103 Johan Rohde to Jo. VGM, b1987; 30 May 1893; Jo to Johan Rohde. KBK; 26 May—3 June 1893 (quote); VGM, Bd120 and Bd121.

104 Johan Rohde to Jo. VGM, b1989; 24 June—and b1990; end of June 1893. Jo to Johan Rohde. KBK; 14 July 1893; VGM, Bd122. Rohde wrote that he was planning to write a piece about Van Gogh and Jo sent him information, but nothing was done with it. Johan Rohde to Jo. VGM, b1991; 20 August 1893—and b1992; 2 October 1893. Jo to Johan Rohde. KBK; 24 August 1893; VGM, Bd123.

105 Henry van de Velde to Jo. VGM, b1356; undated.

106 'Grappig dat zij u zoo voor ongenaakbaar houden, u, die juist als het Vincent geldt geen moeite te veel is.' Richard Roland Holst to Jo. VGM, b1241; 10 February 1893—and b1247; 13 April 1893.

107 Lieske Tibbe, *Art Nouveau en Socialisme. Henry van de Velde en de Parti Ouvrier Belge*. Amsterdam 1981.

108 'grand Peintre mort'. Henry van de Velde to Jo. VGM, b1357, b1358 and b1361; all 30 April 1893.

109 Henry van de Velde to Jo. VGM, b1364; July 1893.

110 It probably appeared on 12 August 1893. A detailed view of this issue: Van Kerckhoven 1980 and Greer 2007.

111 Prick 1986, p. 19; Prick 2003, pp. 355–6.

112 *Brief Happiness* 1999, pp. 103, 140.

113 *Diary* 4, p. 85; 17 September 1893.

114 *Diary* 4, p. 87; 15 October 1893 Karel Alberdingk Thijm to Jo. LMDH, LM A 245 B 1; 13 October 1893. Prick 1986, p. 20.

115 'Het is maar weinig—doch ik vreesde u te vermoeien door een te groote bezendingen—en indien u ze uit hebt en er het vervolg van wilt lezen—kan ik ze u onmiddellijk zenden. Indien ik verkeerd gedaan heb door u juist de *eerste* brieven te laten lezen—en u liever iets uit lateren tijd had—dan is ook die fout gemakkelijk goed te maken.' Jo to Karel Alberdingk Thijm; 22 October 1893. Prick 1981–6, vol. 2, p. 121; also quoted in Prick 1986, p. 20 and Prick 2003, p. 359. The confirmation of receipt: LMDH, LM A 245 B 1; 26 October 1893; VGM, Bd100. Prick called the fact that Van Deyssel did not seize the chance to promote the letters in 1893 with both hands as an 'insoluble mystery'. Prick 2003, p. 358. That they had discussed it: *Diary* 4, p. 87.

116 'Over de brieven hoop ik U nader te spreken of te schrijven.' Karel Alberdingk Thijm to Jo. LMDH, LM A 245 B 1; 8 June 1895. Her letter of thanks is VGM, b2940; 9 June 1895. See also Prick 1986, p. 21 and Prick 2003, p. 360.

117 Van Gogh on Zola: Van Gogh, *Letters* 2009, letter 777.

118 E.J. van Wisselingh to Jo. VGM, b2938; 2 December 1893.

119 She was invited on a number of occasions between 1895 and 1898. Karel Alberdingk Thijm to Jo. LMDH, LM A 245 B 1; 20 December 1895; VGM, Bd103—LM A 245 B 1; 27 November 1896; VGM, Bd102—and VGM, b5344; 18 April 1897. She visited on 18 May 1898: Lodewijk van Deyssel, *Het leven van Frank Rozelaar*. Ed. Harry G.M. Prick. The Hague 1982, p. 315.

120 The copper wedding anniversary is celebrated in the Netherlands after twelve and a half years of marriage. VGM, b1251; 15 November 1899.

121 Second edition. Leiden. VGM, b2213; abbreviated as *Huishoudboek* 1893–6.

122 'deze onvervangbaaren artistenvriend'. Meijer Isaac de Haan to Jo. VGM, b1321; 12 October—and b1044; 16 October 1893.

123 Line Liernur and Marie Mensing to Jo. VGM, b2876; 1 January 1894.

124 *Diary* 4, p. 88. Mrs van Gogh had meanwhile moved to 25 Prins Hendrikstraat in The Hague, where Willemien lived.

125 In 1889 Theo had written to her about the character Lewin in *Anna Karenina* (1877). See *Brief Happiness* 1999, p. 231. The other one was probably Hans Christian Andersen's tale *The Ugly Duckling*.

126 ''t is één van mijn oudste boeken; ik zie telkens mezelf weer bij mijn moeder zitten, die zooveel altijd met mij heeft gedaan.' *Vincent's Diary*, 5 September 1933. In Samuel Foote, *The Great Panjandrum Himself* (London 1885), illustrated by Randolph Caldecott, Jo wrote on the flyleaf: 'Vincent v. Gogh'. VGMB, BC0001.

127 Renée Julienne Tanguy-Briend to Andries Bonger. VGM, b1447 and b1448; 7 and 15 February 1894. See also Pissarro, *Correspondance* 1980–91, vol. 3, pp. 437–8.

128 Jo to Emile Schuffenecker. UBA, Special Collections. Gd65a; 3 March 1894; VGM, Bd113. Schuffenecker had made the request on 27 February. Tanguy's widow let Andries know that he had shown an interest. VGM, b1446; undated.

129 Émile Schuffenecker to Jo. VGM, b1427—and b1428; 7 and 15 March 1894. *Account Book* 2002, pp. 96, 141, 159.

130 Charles Destrée (of the Durand-Ruel gallery) to Jo. VGM, b1207; 19 April 1894. He sent a list of eight titles; they charged ten per cent commission: VGM, b1449; 12 April 1894—this list was a copy of VGM, b1450; April 1894. Both were written on Tanguy's letterhead.

131 Charles Destrée to Jo. VGM, b1208; 2 May 1894. References to Jo's letters in Rewald 1986b, pp. 245–6. Rewald refers to Charles Durand-Ruel's archive. Cf. exh. cat. London 2015, p. 205. The unsold works were sent to Bussum on 7 February 1895. See Georges Durand-Ruel to Jo. VGMD; 29 November and 27 December 1894.

132 Paul Gauguin to Jo. VGM, b1482; 29 March 1894. *Gauguin lettres* 1983, pp. 330–3. There are only three letters from Gauguin to Jo—the two she wrote to him are unknown.

133 Paul Gauguin to Jo. VGM, b1483 (sketch)—and b1484; 14 April and 4 May 1894. *Gauguin lettres* 1983, pp. 334–41. According to Feilchenfeldt, Gauguin had forgotten that *Reaper* (F 617 / JH 1753) and *Madame Ginoux ('The Arlésienne')* (F 542 / JH 1894) were with Georges Chaudet in Pont-Aven, but it is not clear if that actually was the case. Feilchenfeldt 2013, pp. 117, 201, 214. Rewald conjectured that Gauguin also sent Jo his painting of *Paris in the Snow* (VGM, s223) at the same time as *Women on the Banks of the River*; Rewald 1986a, pp. 85–6.

134 Jo made a note of the cast: VGM, b5088; 14 May 1894. She bought the shrimps and cherries on 27 June 1894. *Huishoudboek* 1893–6.

135 *Diary* 4, p. 90; July 1894.

136 *Diary* 1, p. 14; 2 April 1880.

137 *Algemeen Handelsblad*, 16 November 1894.

138 *Diary* 4, pp. 91–2. *De Telegraaf*, 14 and 15 November 1894. Fontijn 1999, pp. 366–7.

139 *Diary* 4, p. 92; 31 December 1894.

140 Ambroise Vollard to Jo. VGM, b1306; 9 May—and b1369; 7 June 1895. See also Feilchenfeldt 2005, pp. 110–11; exh. cat. New York 2006, p. 276. Vollard had already sold some works by Van Gogh in 1894. On Vollard and Van Gogh: Pratt 2006, pp. 48–60.

141 'J'espère que vous ferez de bonnes affaires avec ce que je vous envoie alors je pourrai plus tard vous enverrez d'autres, en tous les cas vous m'écrirez avant de vendre n'est-ce pas?' Jo to Ambroise Vollard; 3 July 1895. AVP (2,2)—the second part of the letter, known in a transcript, is VGM, b4559; 3 July 1895. On her letter of 14 December 1895 see also Pratt 2006, p. 58, n. 5.

142 Exh. cat. New York 2006, pp. 249, 276–7; Pratt 2006, pp. 51–3; Feilchenfeldt 2005.

143 Ambroise Vollard to Jo. VGM, b1307; 25 March 1896. She noted 85 guilders in her cashbook. *Account Book* 2002, pp. 47, 142, 178. AVP (4,3) and (2,2).

144 Jo to Ambroise Vollard; 27 March 1896. AVP (2,2). Ambroise Vollard to Jo. VGM, b1308; 8 July 1896—b1370; 2 November 1896.

145 VGM, b1437; November 1896. See also 'Liste des tableaux chez M. A. Vollard'. AVP (4,4). Feilchenfeldt 2005, pp. 110–12; exh. cat. Amsterdam 2005, pp. 30, 38–9; Pratt 2006, pp. 54–7.

146 Ambroise Vollard to Jo. VGM, b1372; 23 November 1896.

147 Ambroise Vollard to Jo, VGM, b1309; 30 November 1896.

148 Ambroise Vollard to Jo. VGM, b1373; 3 February 1897. On the exhibition: Pratt 2006, pp. 54–5.

149 Ambroise Vollard to Jo. VGM, b1374; 16 February 1897.

150 'par GRANDE vitesse'. Jo to Ambroise Vollard; 27 March 1897. AVP (2,2).

151 '3 triptieken, 1 portret, Dr Gachet en 1 paar teekeningen'. *Account Book* 2002, p. 47, 142–3.

152 Ambroise Vollard to Jo. VGM, b1376; 29 March 1897. For the reconstruction of the works: *Account Book* 2002, pp. 47, 142–3. Jo to Ambroise Vollard; 15 May 1897. AVP (2,2). In August 1897 she sold *The Langlois Bridge with Washerwomen* (F 397 / JH 1368) to Vollard after all. (Not recorded in the account book.) *Account Book* 2002, p. 142. See also exh. cat. New York 2006, p. 277. AVP (4,3) and (4,4). Pratt 2006, pp. 53–8. Jo sought help at the time for a matter of business in Paris, as emerges from several letters from Isaac Israëls to her. This probably related to Vollard, with whom she was embroiled in negotiations. Israëls suggested three intermediaries—his cousin Herman Louis Israëls, who was a lawyer who concerned himself specifically with dealings between Dutch and French people, Charles Destrée, commercial manager at the Durand-Ruel gallery, and Petrus Christiaan Eilers, who worked for the art dealers E.J. van Wisselingh & Co in Amsterdam. Isaac Israëls to Jo. VGM, b8661; 9 March and b8623; 23 July 1897.

153 'I was totally wrong about Van Gogh! I thought he had no future at all,' he told Raymond Escholier. Quoted in Brassaï, *The Artists of My Life*. Translated from the French by Richard Miller. London 1982, p. 212.

154 Lucien Moline to Jo. VGM, b1311; undated (around May 1895).

155 Lucien Moline to Jo. VGM, b1312; 14 June 1895.

156 Lucien Moline to Jo. VGM, b1313; 17 December 1895.

157 Lucien Moline to Jo. VGM, b1314; 20 December 1895 (enclosing the cheque). *Account Book* 2002, pp. 29, 47, 105, 142, 167. On the prices at Arti: *Algemeen Handelsblad*, 9 January 1896.

158 *Diary* 4, p. 96; 31 December 1895.

9 Playing with fire—Isaac Israëls

1 'heel aardig'. Jo to her parents. VGM, b4297; undated.

2 Theo wrote to Vincent, telling him that Isaac Israëls had come to his flat to look at paintings. Van Gogh, *Letters* 2009, letter 813; 22 October 1889.

3 'Mag ik U bijgeval eens komen opzoeken of heeft U soms eens lust aan te komen dan zal mij dit zeer aangenaam zijn.' Isaac Israëls to Jo. VGM, b8564; 2 February 1891.

4 Moes 1961, pp. 151–2, 156. Exh. cat. Amsterdam 2012, p. 12. She died in January 1894.

5 'vagebonderen'. He told Erens this in May 1897. Exh. cat. Amsterdam 2012, p. 46. The letters quoted from here are in the Erens Archive in Nijmegen.

6 'Los wilde hij zijn en niet vastgehouden door de dingen, die het leven op ons stapelt.' Frans Erens, *Vervlogen jaren*. Amsterdam 1989, pp. 316–41, quotes on pp. 316, 322–3.

7 's-Gravesande 1956; G. Stuiveling, *De Nieuwe Gids als geestelijk brandpunt*. Amsterdam 1935; Enno Endt, *Het festijn van Tachtig. De vervulling van heel grote dingen scheen nabij*. Amsterdam 1990; Vergeer 1990, esp. pp. 112–19; exh. cat. Amsterdam 1991, esp. p. 75.

8 Exh. cat. Amsterdam 2012. The quote 'een eenvoudige arbeider, op zoek naar fortuin' is from a letter to Erens of 21 May 1897. See exh. cat. Amsterdam 2012, p. 51.

9 Exh. cat. Amsterdam 2012, pp. 14–15. There was gossip about him 'chasing skirts'. Vergeer 1990, p. 55. Willem Kloos, who created a sensation with his debut poem collection *Verzen* in 1894, sketched Israëls as a philanderer in some unpublished insulting sonnets. See 's-Gravesande 1956, pp. 410–11, 444; Stokvis 2005, p. 99.

10 Sara de Swart wrote to Jo: 'Aardig dat Israëls U opzocht.' ('It was nice of Israëls to call on you.') VGM, b1336; March 1891. For the art appreciation event see *Diary* 4, p. 12; 25 February 1892.

11 Isaac Israëls to Jo. VGM, b8570; undated (about flowers that were sent)—b8571; 13 March 1894 and b8580; 25 September 1894. He lent her books by Edgar Allen Poe (13 March 1894). Isaac Israëls to Jo. VGM, b8595; 5 December 1896—and b8576; undated (also about flowers that were sent).

12 *Diary* 4, p. 90; 3 October 1894.

13 *Diary* 4, p. 74; 20 October 1892.

14 Isaac Israëls to Jo. VGM, b8576; undated. He ended: 'amuseer je maar goed. Je vriendje' ('enjoy yourself. Your boyfriend.')

15 Isaac Israëls to Jo. VGM, b8575; undated. The portrait is Isaac Israëls, *Portrait of Vincent Willem van Gogh*, 1894. Oil on panel, 15.7 x 13 cm. VGM, s516. He also drew a portrait in chalk and pastel, 14.2 x 10.3 cm. VGM, d1145.

16 *Diary* 4, p. 91; 13 November 1894. Six days later he wrote: 'Ik kom u toch als u 't goedvindt nog eens opzoeken.' ('If it's all right with you, I'll come and visit you again some time.') He had given her the portrait. Isaac Israëls to Jo. VGM, b8574; 19 November 1894.

17 Isaac Israëls to Jo. VGM, b8565; 16 December 1894. Je moet altijd maar doen wat je denkt dat 't beste is, dat doe ik ook, maar die scrupules van je begrijp ik wel.' ('You must always do what you think best, that's what I do, too, but I understand those scruples of yours.')

18 Until February 1895 this was 438 Eerste Parkstraat. Israëls continued to live there until the autumn of 1905.

19 *Diary* 4, p. 94. He also challenged her, as he did in a letter that he must have written around that time: 'laat je eens spoedig aanschouwen' ('do come and see me soon'); Isaac Israëls to Jo. VGM, b8568; undated. Jo did not reminisce about those lovely afternoons until August 1895.

20 'Komt u zoo maar eens een middagje of zoo. Maar schrijf het dan even vooruit. Het is veel aardiger dan dat ik bij u kom.' Isaac Israëls to Jo. VGM, b8572; 7 February 1895.

21 *Diary* 4, pp. 94–5.

22 'Meld mij even of je 't doet . . . maar blijf er dan ook bij ('t is met jou altijd onsekuur). Als je misschien liever niet gaat ben ik *volstrekt* niet *boos* erom.' Isaac Israëls to Jo. VGM, b8666; 6 August 1895.

23 'C'étaient deux amoureux/ Qui rêvaient d'amours lointaines.' *Diary* 4, p. 95. The song had an unhappy ending for the lovers: they drown.

24 *Diary* 4, p. 96; 3 November 1895.

25 Later, possibly at the beginning of the 1920s, Jo certainly filled in the names of two people in the first diary and rewrote the final paragraph. Shreds of paper in the spine of the diary indicate that the last page was torn out.

26 Isaac Israëls to Jo. VGM, b8662; 4 December 1895. The portrait he was dissatisfied with might have been the small panel *Portrait of Jo van Gogh-Bonger*. VGM, s284.

27 *Diary* 4, pp. 97–8; 2 January 1896. When Jo wrote 'home' she meant 'to the station'.

28 Isaac Israëls to Jo. VGM, b8567; 5 January 1896. He told her he wanted to concentrate solely on his work.

29 *Diary* 4, pp. 98–9; 24 January 1896.

30 'Darling, darling, don't think that I shall ever forget you—even though there are sometimes moments when I think I might have new happiness and a new life—you will always live in the depths of my soul.' *Diary* 4, p. 101; 25 January 1896. Five years had passed since Theo's death.

31 *Diary* 4, p. 102; 13 April 1896.

32 Isaac Israëls to Jo. VGM, b8587; 16 August 1896.

33 Isaac Israëls to Jo. VGM, b8594; 11 October 1896.

34 Isaac Israëls to Jo. VGM, b8585; undated.

35 'je hebt geen begrip van de realiteit en van 't gedonder dat iemand heeft om iets te bereiken, of niets.' 'Terwijl jij denkt dat ik in een veilig hutje zit met mijn werkje en niets meer behoef dan een lief vrouwtje zwalk ik intusschen op zee te midden van verschillende orkanen. Is 't niet mijn plicht om een passagier af te wijzen al wil die nog zoo graag mee. Ik heb 't je al dikwijls gezegd: ik kan er niet eens over *denken*, over iets duurzaams bedoel ik, in den zin waarin jij 't bedoelt. . . . Als ik nu dacht of voelde: wij moeten en we *zullen* bij elkaar *hooren* dan zou ik 't zeggen. maar laat ik volkomen eerlijk zijn: zo voel ik 't niet. ik heb 't altijd beschouwd als een magnifieke vergissing van je, een onverdiende en unieke bonne fortune [een onvergelijkelijk succes in de liefde] waar 't toch eigenlijk niet mooi van was dat ik wilde profiteren, maar 't was te prettig voor me—en iemand als jij zal ik wel niet meer ontmoeten. . . . Maar wel geloof ik dat 't voor jou het beste is om elkaar niet meer te zien.' Isaac Israëls to Jo. VGM, b8566; undated.

36 'om de gewone tijd, tegen ½ 8.' Isaac Israëls to Jo. VGM, b8664; undated.

37 *Diary* 4, pp. 101–2; 25 February 1896 and 31 December 1896 (this single page in the diary covers an entire year).

38 'Je was net al goed op streek om me te vergeten geloof ik? Is 't niet?' 'Veel liever zou ik willen dat we een vaste dag afspraken, eens in de week bijvoorbeeld, overdag of s'avonds?—maar 't is waar, je hebt nu ernstige gemoedsbezwaren en je hebt altijd zoo'n tweestrijd. My dear laat ik je nu nog eens eerlijk zeggen waar 't op staat. Ik hou heusch *heel* veel van je (daar, ben je nu tevreden) en ik ben heel blij met je vriendschap. denk je nu niet dat ik 't ook naar vind dat je daar zoo dikwijls verdriet en angst mee hebt. Ik vind het heusch soms beroerd, dan voel ik mijzelf schuldig want ik heb innerlijk ook schuld, zeg maar niet van nee. Ik moest 't niet prettig vinden om je als vriendin te willen houden terwijl ik weet dat ik niet doen kan wat jij 't liefst zou willen. Het is misschien een goed moment voor je om er nogeens goed over te denken wat nu heusch voor jou 't beste is. denk er eens driedubbel en dwars over na, neem dan een kloek besluit en hou je er bij. òf schik je naar de stem van 't geweten, familie en traditie. vertel hun altijd alles wat je op je hartje hebt (wat een bedorven kindje om dat nu zoo heerlijk te vinden). òf—je weet wel. heusch doe het nù want nu is het oogenblik daar dat de familiegolf je weer moet verzwelgen—òf ik heb er nooit geen gevoel meer voor, dat voel ik aankomen. Ik neem het ernstig, Jo, denk na, overweeg rijpelijk. Ik zal mij houden aan wat jij 't beste vindt, maar hou jij je der dan ook aan, als 't kan. (dat laatste zinnetje had ik niet moeten zeggen). dat is te veel à la jou 'als 't kan'. laten we nu of liever jij nu decideren, of 't is er geweest, of 't moet op ruimer en uitgebreider schaal worden voortgezet. (excuseer deze slechte beeldspraak). Vaarwel of tot ziens.' Isaac Israëls to Jo. VGM, b8583; undated. Doubts arose from time to time about whether it was good for them to continue seeing each other: VGM, b8589; probably 10 February 1897—and b8590; probably 29 April 1897.

39 *Diary* 4, p. 103; 1 April and 8 May 1897. On the same page there is an ode to little Vincent, in between two laments of love for Isaac. On 17 May 1897 Isaac wrote to her from London. VGM, b8596.

40 'Je hebt volkomen gelijk dat je dat niet de moeite waard vindt, zoo'n oogenblikje eens in de zes maanden! daar ben je toch veel te goed voor'; 'Het beste wat ik je dus kan aanraden is dit: laat mij stikken.' Isaac Israëls to Jo. VGM, b8591; probably 2 July 1897.

41 Isaac Israëls to Jo. VGM, b8622; 18 July 1897.

42 'arme stakkertje.' Isaac Israëls to Jo. VGM, b8623; 23 July 1897. There was little to do in the boarding house because there was only one guest at the time.

43 'Misschien ben ik in September nog hier en hoop je dan natuurlijk te zien. ik zou maar een beetje oppassen voor die spin. op een goeje dag wordt hij te familiair en kruipt in je haar.' Isaac Israëls to Jo. VGM, b8624; probably August 1897.

44 Isaac Israëls to Jo. VGM, b8620 and b8621; both probably August-September 1897.

45 'My dear, 't Spijt me dat je daar zoolang gewacht hebt—maar hoe kon ik dat weten—ik ben een heel andere weg terug gegaan, over Kwadijk—Hoorn. och wat hadden we er ook aan gehad, je had toch direkt weer weggemoeten als eeuwige slavin van je plicht of je plichtsgevoel—enfin het is toch bar dat die familie je zoo onder de plak heeft dat je zoo'n heele zomer niet eens een dag met mij uit durft gaan—en dan zou ik nog zeggen dat 't me spijt dat ik er niet meer intiem mee ben! . . . dat rustige hoekkie van je, in welk werelddeel denk je is dat? Jopie ik hoop dat je je een beetje prettig voelt.' Isaac Israëls to Jo. VGM, b8655; probably September 1897. For the sake of discretion, she had entered Israëls in her birthday calendar by his initials only. VGMB, BVG 3292; 3 February.

46 'Het is allemaal heel lief en goed maar laat je nu toch eens een oogenblik niet alleen door 't gevoel meeslepen en erken nu eens zelf. Van trouwen komt *toch* nooit iets. Je weet het, en verder, Nooit en nimmer zou ik iemand willen brengen tot iets waar hij naderhand spijt of gezanik om zou krijgen. Je hebt *volkomen* en absoluut gelijk dat je 't niet wil. Ik wil 't evenmin. . . . Het spijt me dat 't zoo is maar 't is niet anders. We zien mekaar nog weleens terug.' Isaac Israëls to Jo. VGM, b8592; probably 17 September 1897.

47 Isaac Israëls to Jo. VGM, b8593; probably 21 September 1897.

48 'Zuid beveland is het andalusie van Zeeland en Goes het Sevilla zou je kenne zegge.' Isaac Israëls to Jo. VGM, b8618; 2 October 1897. Isaac Israëls to Jo. VGM, b8619; undated.

49 'Dat is wellicht het ideaal van een schilder: schilderijen verkopen aan een vrouw met wie je daarna de liefde bedrijft.' Letter dated 2 October 1898. Exh. cat. Amsterdam 2012, p. 48. At that time the twenty-two-year-old actress Jacqueline Sandberg was one of his sitters. For Israëls's letters to her see Royaards-Sandberg 1981, pp. 470–82. He had written to her in March 1898: 'Ik ben je slaaf, je hoeft maar een wenk te geven en ik rol in 't stof' ('I am your slave, you have only to give me a hint and I will grovel at your feet' (p. 471)). There are no such declarations of subjection in his letters to Jo.

50 Isaac Israëls to Frans Erens; 3 September 1913. In 1888 he was bewitched by 'onbetrouwbare vrouwen' ('untrustworthy women'), later by the married Sophie de Vries-Dalberg. See exh. cat. Amsterdam 2012, pp. 26–7, 54.

51 'De menschen zijn net als koekjes, als zij lang op elkaar geklit zijn bederven zij.' Isaac Israëls to Augusta Maria Witsen-Schorr and Willem Witsen. KBH, 75 C 51; 11 November 1921.

52 'Ik ben onlangs op straat Mme v. G. tegengekomen, nu verloofd zoals je weet. We bleven stokstijf staan gedurende enige tijd zonder iets tegen elkaar te zeggen. Het waren enkele mooie seconden (vooral voor haar).' Isaac Israëls to Frans Erens; 26 January 1901. See exh. cat. Amsterdam 2012, p. 50. It is clear from the wording that Erens knew about their former liaison.

53 Jakob Huizinga to Jo. VGM, b1252; 28 January 1896.

54 'Heeft U ook soms nog een portret van Vincent, dan zouden we daarom gaarne een krans willen hangen, voornamelijk uit doornen bestaande, met hier en daar wat lauwerbladen.' Willem Leuring to Jo. VGM, b1253; 4 February 1896.

55 Willem Leuring to Jo. VGM, b1905; 8 February 1896. Thorn Prikker had seen 'sublieme dingen' ('sublime things') there, he wrote in a letter to Henri Borel on 12 February 1895. *De brieven van Johan Thorn Prikker aan Henri Borel en anderen, 1892–1904*. Ed. Joop M. Joosten. Nieuwkoop 1980, p. 243. On Toulouse-Lautrec's portrait drawing: VGM, b1259; it is in the Van Gogh Museum (VGM, d639).

56 Willem Leuring to Jo. VGM, b1254, b1255 and b1256; 8, 12 and 15 February 1896.

57 'Men ziet nu in, dat er in 't z.g. "moderne" toch iets zit en nog niet geheel mee kunnende voelen, wil 't publiek toch meer en beter zien. Enfin, zonder overdrijving, we hebben een succès fou.' Willem Leuring to Jo. VGM, b1257; 25 February 1896.

58 Cf. Lieske Tibbe, 'Verheffing, nut, of pret maken? Georganiseerde bezoeken van werklieden aan nijverheidstentoonstellingen in de negentiende eeuw', *De Negentiende Eeuw* 34, no. 3 (2010), pp. 249–68. In 1860, some 54 per cent of the Dutch visitors to the Rijksmuseum in Amsterdam were skilled workmen and 9 per cent were unskilled labourers. See Ellinoor Bergvelt and Claudia Hörster, 'Kunst en publiek in de Nederlandse rijksmusea voor oude kunst (1800–1896). Een vergelijking met Bennetts *Birth of the Museum*', *De Negentiende Eeuw* 34, no. 3 (2010), pp. 232–48.

59 'de bewoners van 't koude Noorden, eens warm laten worden en een fermen stoot gegeven'. Willem Leuring to Jo. VGM, b1259; 5 March 1896.

60 'pure krankzinnigheden'. Albert Hahn, 'De brieven van Vincent van Gogh (fragment)', in *Schoonheid en samenleving. Opstellen over beeldende kunst*. Amsterdam 1929, pp. 133–44 (quote on p. 133). Previously published in *De Socialistische Gids* 1919.

61 'Onder die massa was wel een vijfde, dat zeer apprecieerde en onder dat gedeelte weer enkelen, die bepaald enthousiast waren. Men haalde elkaar naar plaatsen, van waaruit een schilderij het best te zien was. Men gesticuleerde. 't was grappig. Natuurlijk ook lachers—maar ook dat viel mee.' Reintjo Rijkens to Jo. VGM, b1260; 25 February 1896.

62 Pieter Haverkorn van Rijsewijk to Jo. VGM, b5384; 9 June 1896.

63 'De gelegenheid om iets van het werk van Vincent te laten zien—is helaas zoo zelden, dat het mij zeer zou spijten—indien het niet meer kon.' Jo to Pieter Haverkorn van Rijsewijk. RPK; 28 August 1896; VGM, Bd110. The catalogue with prices in RKD, D4.4 e 14.

64 At the home of Frans Vos, who lived there between 1894 and 1897. Haarlem, *Population Register* 1860–1900, V 886d.

65 'Zij schijnt ze te verkoopen, dat zou ik nu nooit doen. Ik ga er gauw weer heen krijgen telkens nieuwen.' Royaards-Sandberg 1981, pp. 14–17. The name 'Maison Hals' is mentioned in a letter of 3 March 1896.

66 *De Tijd*, 10 May 1895.

67 Curator J.E. van Someren-Brand to Jo. VGM, b5382; 12 March 1896.

68 Julius Meier-Graefe to Jo. VGM, b7585; 19 October 1897. He asked for photographs of some small pictures in the drawing room and left it to Jo to choose the rest. Julius Meier-Graefe to Jo. VGM, b7586; 12 December 1897.

69 Emile Schuffenecker to Jo. VGM, b1894; 17 January 1898.

70 Julien Leclercq to Emile Schuffenecker. VGM, b1535; 1 January 1898. See also Supinen 1990, p. 7.

71 Julien Leclercq to Jo. VGM, b4127; 22 January 1898. On Leclercq and Van Gogh: Supinen 1990.

72 *Road Menders ('The Tall Plane Trees')* (F 657 / JH 1860 or F 658 / JH 1861); *Avenue of Chestnut Trees in Blossom* (F 517 / JH 1689) and *The Public Garden ('The Poet's Garden')* (F 468 / JH 1578) respectively. Julien Leclercq to Jo. VGM, b4126; 28 January 1898. The prices were high and so, too, was the commission at 25 per cent. Leclercq had asked that the paintings should be sent rolled and *Avenue of Chestnut Trees in Blossom* was damaged in the process. VGM, b3468. The works may also have been shown in Helsinki and Copenhagen; they were sent on to Berlin in mid-June. VGM, b3469. See Supinen 1990, pp. 7–8; Larsson 1996, pp. 99–128.

73 Thys 1956; Borrie 1973; Blom 2012, pp. 142–9.

74 The magazine had a limited number of subscribers—around eight hundred. See Bijl de Vroe 1987, p. 166.

75 Tak was secretary of the Comité Honger en Schrik, which was founded in 1893 on the initiative of Floor Wibaut to support the needy families of workers who had been arrested because of their political activities. See Van Uildriks, *Dagboek* 2010, pp. 262–3.

76 See Grever and Waaldijk 1998, pp. 250–8, and Sjaak van der Velden, 'Lonen bij de dekenfabriek van Zaalberg te Leiden, 1896–1902', *Jaarboek der sociale en economische geschiedenis van Leiden en omstreken*. Leiden 2012, pp. 49–72.

77 Reyneke van Stuwe 1932, p. 355. Thys 1956.

78 Van Beek 2010, pp. 99–100. Jo never saw Theo's brother again after that.

79 Maude Stephenson Hoch to Jo. VGM, b7182; incomplete and undated (soon after October-November 1896, when she was staying in Villa Helma). See *Account Book* 2002, p. 108. For Pomona: VGM b8598.

80 IJsbrandina (Dien) Reinhold-Brandligt to Jo. VGM, b3675; 5 January 1904: 'Ik weet nog hoe jij en Vincent dan altijd naar A. gingt, en allen thuis vereenigd waren.' ('I remember how you and Vincent always went to A. then, and everyone was reunited at home.') Dien and her husband, the engineer Huibert Reinhold, moved to Bussum around 1896 and Vincent played with their son Tom.

81 Carel Adama van Scheltema to Jo, VGM, b1415 and b1416; 10 January and 29 January 1898 (quote). Jo to Carel Adama van Scheltema. LMDH, LM A 192 B2; 7 July 1898; VGM, Bd98.

82 'Zou daar niets aan te doen zijn?' Jo to Carel Adama van Scheltema. LMDH, LM A 192 B2; 24 August 1907; VGM, Bd97. On 24 October 1907 Adama van Scheltema married fellow party member Annie Kleefstra.

83 'Wij noodigen ieder, die deze Vereeniging op financieele of moreele wijze wil steunen, dringend uit, zich tot deze dames te wenden.' *De Gooi- en Eemlander*, 22 May 1897.

84 'onzen mooien zaak.' Cécile Goekoop-de Jong van Beek en Donk to Jo. VGM, b3775; 23 May 1897. Cf. Elisabeth Leijnse, *Cécile en Elsa, strijdbare freules. Een biografie*. Amsterdam 2015. Jungius's brochure is in the Atria in Amsterdam.

85 On the position of women in the latter years of the nineteenth century and female suffrage: Grever and Waaldijk 1998.

86 Willemien van Gogh to Jo. VGM, b2919; 17 January 1892—and b2920; undated. See also Kramers et al. 1982, pp. 101–2.

87 *De Kroniek*, 20 February 1898.

88 'een leelijk, onnatuurlijk groeisel van onze fin-de-siècle beschaving en ontwikkeling.' M.E.P., 'Over het feminisme', *De Kroniek*, 5 June 1898. Boissevain-Pijnappel was chair of the Nederlandsche Bond voor Vrouwenkiesrecht (Dutch Union for Female Suffrage).

89 On the best seller *Hilda van Suylenburg*, which unleashed a controversy: the introduction by Tessel Pollmann in the Amsterdam 1984 edition, and 'The Life of Women' in Bank and Van Buuren 2004, pp. 451–68.

90 'dat er geen geestelijk geslachtsverschil tusschen man en vrouw bestaat'; 'noch tot eenige andere *isten*'; 'Het geval van die mevrouw die een huishoudster noodig heeft, kan ik volstrekt maar niet zoo dwaas vinden als u 't doet voorkomen. Ik denk integendeel dat het een zeer wijze, verstandige vrouw is, die zich liever met haar kinderen veel bezig houdt, dan altijd kopjes wasschen, verstellen en de wasch doen. Een mensch kan maar één ding tegelijk doen en ik ken helaas veel vrouwen die hun *huis* stellen boven hun kinderen.' J.v.G., 'Nog eens feminisme', *De Kroniek*, 19 June 1898.

91 'Eenige beschouwingen over het artikel van M.E.P.', *De Kroniek*, 12 June 1898.

92 'Zij willen, dat den vrouw staat naast den man en met hem niet alleen haar eigen kinderen opvoedt, maar ook de zorg op zich neemt voor de geheele Maatschappij.' *De Kroniek*, 19 June 1898.

93 'naar wat het *is*: een gevoelsprotest.' *De Kroniek*, 26 June 1898.

94 According to Van Boven, there was no one who brought Boissevain's concept of 'feminism' into the debate—but Jo and Versluys-Poelman did precisely that. Van Boven 1992, p. 164. On 17 July, *De Kroniek* also published the response 'To M.E.P.' by Aga S. (Agatha Snellen?), which proclaimed in italics: '*Gezegend de vrouwenbeweging en het recht voor de vrouw, haar gaven te ontwikkelen en haar krachten te gebruiken in de richting, waarin haar persoonlijke aanleg gelegen is!*' ('*Blessed be the women's movement and a woman's right to develop her gifts and use her strengths in the direction in which her personal aptitude lies!*') In the early years of the century, this abstract feminism with its ideal of equality gave way to a focus on the female that acquired its own mental content and was an enrichment of social good, according to Van Boven 1992, pp. 164–6.

95 'geestelijke vadsigheid'; 'broeikassen bestaan.' Cornélie Huygens, *Socialisme en 'Feminisme'*. Amsterdam 1898, p. 4.

96 'het verschil tusschen de burgerlijke (ideologische) levensbeschouwing van het feminisme en de proletarische (historisch materialistische) levensbeschouwing der sociaal-demokratie.' Pieter Troelstra, *Woorden van vrouwen. Bijdragen tot den strijd over Feminisme en Socialisme*. Amsterdam 1898.

97 In *De Kroniek* of 1897. See also Grever and Waaldijk 198, p. 245. In 1898 Frank van der Goes and Frans Coenen Jr engaged in a polemic exchange in *De Kroniek* about how socialism should be deployed to combat social abuses.

98 'Ik hoop niet dat ik erg laat kom, maar wilt u voor deze week uit bijgaand boekje Le Chômage (p. 58) vertalen? Tot slot van het debat waaraan U hebt deelgenomen, hoop ik eerdaags een artikel te schrijven met de bedoeling wat klaarheid te brengen in de verhouding van de vrouwenbeweging tot het socialisme.' Pieter Tak to Jo. VGM, b1419; 10 July 1898.

99 'brandende pijn in haar borstje en grote ogen'. *De Kroniek*, 17 July 1898 (appendix). The story appeared in Émile Zola, *Nouveaux contes à Ninon*. Paris 1896, pp. 110–19 (first edition 1874). Jo also knew the story 'Le forgeron' in the same collection; see *Diary* 3, p. 104.

100 'ik heb zooveel liever van u, én om de oude relatie én omdat u ze zooveel beter vertaalt dan die andere dames. Ik zal in elk geval trachten u deze week nog wat te zenden, maar als u zelf eens wat vindt, houd ik mij toch zeer aanbevolen.' Pieter Tak to Jo. VGM, b1420; 15 August 1898.

101 ''s middags en 's avonds ben je mijn gast (als je 't goed vindt). We hebben wel een klein logeerkamertje maar er is een bed over voor Jopie—en Vincentje zou 't heerlijk vinden als hij meekwam. Als het kan breng hem dan mee—en knoop er nog een nachtje aan.' See Prick 1986 and Prick 2003, p. 563; 14 August 1898.

102 'Het heeft ons veel genoegen gedaan je ouders te leeren kennen, en je zuster en broer, en Vincent als een gebruind matroosje aan de zee te zien spelen.' Karel Alberdingk Thijm to Jo. LMDH, LM A 245 B 1; 20 August 1898; VGM, Bd104. See also Prick 1986, p. 20, and Prick 2003, pp. 362, 563.

103 Van Calcar 1886, p. 48. *Account Book* 2002, pp. 113, 161.

104 *Account Book* 2002, pp. 112, 117, 161. In December 1901 Mrs van Gogh asked Jo: 'Nam Vincent nog steeds les. 't Zou heerlijk zijn als muziek ook genot voor hem werd.' ('Is Vincent still taking lessons. It would be wonderful if music became a pleasure for him too.') VGM, b3631. Jo had modern views on gymnastics: ''t moest veel meer gedaan worden door meisjes—onze opvoeding is zoo verschrikkelijk eenzijdig.' ('Girls should be doing a lot more—our education is so terribly one-sided.') When she was twenty-seven, Jo had an hour's gymnastics lesson every day. Jo to Theo. VGM, b4260; 2 February 1889. *Brief Happiness* 1999, pp. 134–6.

105 See Prick 2003, p. 1275. *Vincent's Diary*, 4 December 1933. The draughtboard was a present from his grandfather: VGM, b5092; 12 March 1900. When he grew up, Vincent still used the board that had been Jo's when he played Halma with his children. *Vincent's Diary*, 3 January 1934.

106 'meer kans dat het sexueele leven zich ontwikkelen zal in een gezond lichaam met een gezond verstand'. *De Kroniek*, 15 October 1899; 'Ooievaarspraatjes' in *De Kroniek*, 8 October 1899 was signed 'H.G.S. Ez.' For the prevailing views on sex education for children see Bakker 1995.

107 Jo Hart Nibbrig-Moltzer to Jo. VGM, b3121; 17 October 1899.

108 'Onze kinderen voor vooroordelen en wanbegrippen te bewaren is wel een van de weinige dingen, die wij kunnen doen om hun den levensstrijd makkelijk te maken. Daar hebben zij recht op.' ('Preserving our children from prejudice and misconceptions is one of the few things we can do to make their life's struggle easier. They are entitled to that.') VGM, b4529.

109 VGMB, BVG 5345 and VGM, b3046. The drawings were not in the catalogue.

110 Johan Theodoor Uiterwijk to Jo. VGM, b1264; 8 October—and b1265; 10 October 1898.

111 'Aan Mevrouw van Gogh, om haar schoone liefde om 't schoon werk van 't mensch Vincent'. ''t arm groot mensch Vincent. Die is gekruist, dit mensch. Hem heeft het licht een zengend kruis gericht, waar, schroeiend, zijn lijf, wringend hing; waar-van zijn schoone lippen schoonste woorden stieten tot den paars-rooden dag.' VGMB, BVG 1123a. In 1910 Plasschaert became manager of the Oldenzeel gallery. See Geurt Imanse, *Albert August Plasschaert (1866–1941)*. The Hague 1988, p. 35.

112 *Account Book* 2002, pp. 47, 143, 182. Balk 2006, pp. 238–9. Johan Uiterwijk to Jo. VGM, b1267; 9 December—and b1269; 31 December 1898.

113 *Account Book* 2002, April 1899, pp. 47, 143, 175, 176, 184.

114 Museum Boymans changed its name to Museum Boymans-Van Beuningen in 1958 and to Museum Boijmans van Beuningen in 1996.

115 'voor de catalogus van het Museum'; 'Indien U de collectie hier eens wilt komen zien—zal ik U gaarne ontvangen.' Jo to Pieter Haverkorn van Rijsewijk. RPK; 3 February 1900; VGM, Bd106.

116 See Rovers 2009b, and Alan Bowness, *The Conditions of Success: How Modern Art Rises to Fame*. London 1989. According to Bowness it usually takes twenty-five years before a great artist gains public recognition (pp. 47–9).

Part Four

1 Edward St Aubyn, *At Last*. London 2011, p. 9.

10 Johan Cohen Gosschalk—Villa Eikenhof in Bussum

1 Cohen began studying with Veth in 1894. VGM, b1377–80, b1385 and b1389. Exh. cat. Assen 1991, pp. 8–9. He lived at various addresses in Amsterdam between 1891 and 1897. ACA, *Population Register*, vol. 33, fol. 49.

2 Marie Cremers, *Jeugdherinneringen*. Amsterdam 1948, p. 36; later reprinted as *Lichtend verleden*. Amsterdam 1954, p. 32.

3 Between 1900 and 1910 Johan recorded all his income from articles and reviews in a notebook. VGM, b7362.

4 *Account Book* 2002, pp. 121, 161. Mrs Cohen to Johan: 'Het nieuws vond men zeer heureux pour toi. . . . Groet Jo voor mij.' ('Everyone was very happy for you when they heard the news. . . . Give Jo my best wishes.') VGM, b7309; 15 September 1900. There are two series of letters from Johan to Jo and two from her to him—a modest crop because in the twelve years they were together, there must have been many more letters and documents.

5 'handschoenen, mooie kousen, papier, een broche, een nieuwe bloemenmand, of een paraplu'. Vincent to Lien Bonger. VGM, b5093; 25 September 1900.

6 'voor het laatst onder den ouden vorm'. Marie Mensing to Jo. IISG, 4 October 1900. Mensing had been in Jo's boarding house that summer. *Account Book* 2002, p. 122.

7 Mrs van Gogh to Jo. VGM, b3595; undated (shortly after 19 February 1901). She wanted to know whether, if people asked her why Jo had not got married yet, it would be all right for her to say 'for health reasons'.

8 'In zulk een gewichtige zaak zullen we na al de ervaringen, die we opdeden, ons wel *heel goed* tegenover elkaar verantwoord moeten voelen. Maar het *is* heerlijk, dat we allebei zo'n vol en groot vertrouwen in elkaar kunnen hebben (want dat heb ik in jou en ik mag wel zeggen, dat heb je ook wel in mij en ik zal probeeren het waard te zijn) en—hoe dan ook alles gaat—zeker zullen we weten dat we het goed meenen met elkaar & met elkaars hoogste belangen). Nu, mijn lief, ik zal niet langer zwaar op de hand zijn.' Johan to Jo. VGM, b7279; undated.

9 'Nu weet ik wel dat je misschien prikkelbaar was en vergeet ik gaarne wat je zeide, maar toch hindert het me. Dwaas misschien van me, want *ik weet wel* dat je in je hart niets slechts van me denkt, maar ik kan het ook niet van je hooren! Lieveling, denk nu niet dat ik boos op je ben; maar ik wil zelfs niet den schijn hebben van niet in alles goed . . . en *fair* tegenover je te zijn.' Johan to Jo. VGM, b7276; undated. If Johan gave the postman a letter at half past eight in the evening, Jo would be able to read it at breakfast next morning.

10 'Je mag misschien iets hards in je natuur hebben, maar je bent toch te *eerlijk* om *onbillijk* te willen zijn. Ik ken een andere jij en daar ben ik van gaan houden en die andere, die heb ik niets te vergeven, maar wel *veel* te danken, want die was goed en mild, die kon zoo ruim en zuiver over alles denken en die is het, die ik wel héél érg mis in mijn leven, dat voel ik haast elk oogenblik. . . . Van jou heb ik nog nooit wat slechts gedacht; ik had altijd vertrouwen in je, al heb ik je wel eens vergissingen zien doen.' Johan to Jo. VGM, b7277; undated. *Vincent's Diary*, 27 December 1935.

11 Johan to Jo. VGM, b7278; 11 March 1901. Both these books were popular at the time, particularly in socialist libraries. See De Vries 2001, p. 320.

12 Vincent to Jo's parents. VGM, b5090; 31 December 1900. Vincent to Jo. VGM, b8287; 31 December 1900.

13 'De theosofie zou zeggen dat een vrouwenziel in mij is gereïncarneerd! Ik voel soms het bepaald vrouwelijke in mijn denken. Je weet dat ook wel, want je kent me goed. Ik hoop dat je het niet naar vindt; ik zal ook nog wel mannelijke factoren in mijn ziel—als ik die heb!—bezitten. En jij, mijn schat, jij hebt naast veel doorzettends en taais, ook veel echt vrouwelijke zachtheid, teerheid, fijnheid van voelen en denken. Denk niet dat ik die eigenschappen van doorzetten, dat misschien wel een hardheid werd, niet apprecieer. Maar ik zou toch misschien niet van je houden, als je niet ook dat echt vrouwelijke had. Ik ben toch te veel man, om daar niet vooral van te houden.' Johan to Jo. VGM, b7279; undated.

14 Johan to Jo. VGM, b7283; undated (April 1901). Van der Goes's article is on pp. 113–54.

15 'Zou het hem kalmer maken te weten hij u niet weer voor een feit zou stellen van misschien weer een zenuw patient tot man te krijgen, dan handelt hij edel maar wie zal nu hierin kunnen zeggen *wat* het best zou zijn. In elk geval, beste Jo, heb ik bitter met je te doen want ge hebt een moeijelijke strijd en geen gemakkelijk leven . . . als het waarachtig beter *af* is, vind ik het eene marteling elkander te blijven zien en schrijven of zamen te blijven werken. Of hoopt gij nog? Kunnen doctoren of professoren geen licht geven!' Cornélie van Gogh-Carbentus to Jo. VGM, b3599; 24 March 1901.

16 '*Zeker mogen we hopen*; want we houden immers nog van elkaar . . . Ik zei je toen al, dat ik de brieven van Vincent *nu* ongeschikt werk voor je vond. Ik weet hoe herinneringen iemand week kunnen maken en in jou omstandigheden was dit nu ongewenscht.' Johan to Jo. VGM, b7280; undated (30 March 1901).

17 Johan to Jo. VGM, b7282; undated.

18 Johan to Jo. VGM, b7284; 1 April 1901.

19 'de noodzakelijkheid om met het leven voortdurend in aanraking te komen'. Johan to Jo. VGM, b7283; undated (April 1901).

20 'in contemplatie, stil verdiepen in alles om me en *ín* me'. 'Ik verdenk jou niet, lief, van per se "lust tot uitgaan"; je wilt graag mooie dingen zien en hooren en daar heb je gelijk aan. Ik houd ook zooveel van mooie muziek en van toneel ook, dat weet je wel, maar van concerten en comedies, een heele avond opgeprikt zitten . . . dat is niet altijd een genot voor mij; . . . nu zou ik liefst muziek willen hooren, in een rustige kamer, 's avonds bij schemering en dan stil genieten . . . dát is werkelijk stijgen door muziek.' Johan to Jo. VGM, b7283; undated (April 1901).

21 'Soms houd ik nog wel eens zoo'n heel, heel klein beetje van je. En soms denk ik nog wel eens *eventjes* aan je en verlang ik—een heel klein verlangentje natuurlijk—om je bij me te hebben, om je te zien, om van je te mogen houden. . . . Als we elkaar dan nog maar eens spraken, misschien zouden we dan weer eens zuiverder weten, *wat we aan elkaar hebben. Want het is noodig* dat we dat weten . . . een soort vredes-conferentie voor onze gevoelens'. Johan to Jo. VGM, b7283; undated (April 1901).

22 'Lief, ik verlang je te zien en je lieve mond te zoenen, niet enkel in gedachten, zooals ik nu doe.' Johan to Jo. VGM, b7281; 11 or 25 April 1901.

23 'Het schilderijen zien met hem was altijd heerlijk, precies zoo als met je lieven vader'. Jo to Vincent. VGM, b2105; 31 March 1914.

24 'een behoorlijken staat van de bezittingen van genoemden minderjarige'. This was done to comply with the *Dutch Civil Code* book 1, article 407; currently article 355. The statement was registered in Hilversum on 14 August (vol. 50, folio 26 recto box 3). It states that the subdistrict court can demand the preparation within a specified period of a description of the assets of the children and its submission to the clerk of the court. VGM, b4558; 7 August 1901.

25 SSAN (Regional Archives), Bussum Registry of Births, Deaths and Marriages, Marriage Certificate 1901, no. 37. VGM, b3635. SSAN, NNAB. Repertory of notary Sytse Scheffelaar Klots in Bussum, nos. 2615–2617. Perhaps unnecessarily, the deed stated that 'terwijl zij onder zich heeft en mitsdien moet uitkeeren het aan haar zoon Vincent Willem van Gogh toekomend erfdeel uit de nalatenschap van diens vader den heer Theodorus van Gogh voornoemd, ten opzichte waarvan door haar wordt verwezen naar een acte van boedelbeschrijving' ('whereas she [Jo] possesses and therefore has to pay to her son Vincent Willem van Gogh the part of the estate of his father, the aforementioned Theodorus van Gogh, he is entitled to, in regard to which she refers to a deed of estate inventory'). It was executed by a notary on 26 June 1891: SSAN, NNAB. Archive of the notary Harm Pieter Bok 1883–91, inv. no. 12, deed no. 54. Vincent obtained the estate of his father Theo (*Dutch Civil Code* book 1, article 182).

26 VGM, b1104; 3 February 1904.

27 *Account Book* 2002, pp. 124, 162.

28 *Account Book* 2002, p. 161. Bauer, who had contracted syphilis, committed suicide in 1904.

29 *Vincent's Diary*, 3 August 1936.

30 '*Twee* blouses, wat een luxe; je bent zoo aardig in die roode, die moet je maar altijd dragen, hij staat je zoo goed.' Johan to Jo. VGM, b7282; undated.

31 VGM, b7326–8. The cooperative society was granted legal status in 1876. All sorts of forms of collaboration developed in the agricultural industry. Van Eeden ran into financial difficulties with his Amsterdam cooperative, De Eendracht, and as a result Walden became insolvent in 1907. The number of consumer cooperatives rose from seventeen in 1907 to fifty-one in 1920. Brugmans 1976, pp. 284–5, 377–8. National Cooperative Museum, Schiedam. On Jo's membership of De Dageraad and Eigen Hulp see *Vincent's Diary*, 21 November 1968.

32 Maria van Gogh to Jo. VGM, b2578; 4 April 1902.

33 See Chapter 11.

34 In April 1892 Jo wrote in her diary: 'if my boy doesn't develop into an artist, I'd like to make a tree nurseryman out of him—what a wonderful, healthy life.' *Diary* 4, p. 38.

35 'het oude spel uit de jeugd van mijn moeder'. *Vincent's Diary*, 18 February 1934. Frederike van Uildriks also played bezique often. See Van Uildriks, *Dagboek* 2010, pp. 172, 177, 181 and 140.

36 On Bobbie see Bertha Cramer to Jo. VGM, b3779; 3 October 1904. Johan made two drawings of this dog. Assen, Drents Museum, inv.nos. E1983–1441 recto and verso. The family in Weteringschans had a dog called Tommie. VGM, b3517; 15 April 1901. VGM, b3609 and b3614.

37 ''t Is heerlijk weer voor 't atelier en Cohen zal daar wel van genieten, en gij geen schoonmaak, heerlijk. Hebt ge een goede gedienstige?' Mrs van Gogh to Jo. VGM, b3632; 9 May 1902 (quotation)—b1131; undated.

38 VGM, b1091, b1131 and b1108.

39 'Heerlijk het Atelier nu ook klaar zal zijn. Zeker kan 't lekkertjes verwarmd worden. . . . Bauer werkte er toch ook 's winters in, heerlijk ook de boeken daar, zoo alles bij elkaar een eigen kleine wereld.' Mrs van Gogh to Jo. VGM, b3630; 16 November 1901. *Vincent's Diary*, 4 December 1933. Johan left this timber studio in his will. SSAN, NNAB. Archive of the notary Sytse Scheffelaar Klots 1892–1925, inv. no. 53, deed no. 7523.

40 'Ik had je dat nieuwe geluk zoo zielsgraag gegund en toch moet ik voor je vreezen. . . . Ik had zoo'n mooien indruk van jullie zijn, dáár verleden met zijn drieën, des te pijnlijker was het mij gisteren je zóó te treffen.' Bertha Jas-Bosscha to Jo. VGM, b3529; undated. In 1888 she married Frans Jas, who was a witness at Jo's second wedding, and lived close by in Villa De Noord in Beerensteinerlaan (GAGMN). Vincent wrote: 'Mijn moeder zei altijd van mevrouw Jas, dat zij een van de weinige menschen was geweest, die haar met vriendschap tegemoet gekomen was zonder eenige terughouding. Het zijn intellectueel fijne menschen.' ('My mother always said that Mrs Jas was one of the few people who had reciprocated her friendship without any reservation. These were fine intellectual people.') *Vincent's Diary*, 6 November 1933.

41 'Hoe zal die toestand eindigen? Ik voel er zoo mee omdat ik 't zelf met Jo [Johan] zoo heb meegemaakt—maar niet zoo erg goddank.' Jo to Vincent. VGM, b2109; 26 October 1914. For this episode in Alberdingk Thijm's life see Prick 2003, pp. 827–30.

42 'en dat waren niet alle goede herinneringen, want hij had toen ook al dat niet kunnen gaan waar hij wou, het museum Plantijn wilde hij toen niet—en ik dacht nu aldoor hoe aardig hij het zou hebben gevonden als hij het had gezien.' Jo to Vincent. VGM, b2105; 31 March 1914.

43 VGMB, BVG 3462 (the catalogue).

44 Secretary B.P. van IJsselstein to Jo. VGM, b4155; 9 February 1901. He also told her the names of the buyers. VGM, b4156; undated. *Account Book* 2002, pp. 48, 144, 198. SAR, Rotterdamsche Kunstkring Archives, 76, inv. nos. 6 and 169.

45 'Het is gegaan zooals men kon verwachten—veel ergernis en verbazing, maar toch ook veel bewondering, groote bewondering en blijdschap dat deze teekeningen hier geweest zijn.' 'Nu overlegde ik met mijn medebestuurders: als wij onze 10% lieten vallen en U *f* 12,50, dan zou de zaak in orde kunnen komen. Wij zouden het prettig vinden als er iets verkocht werd.' Nicolaas Beversen to Jo. VGM, b4158; on or around 16 March (quotation)—b1459; 25 March 1901. Frits Schoemaker Lzn reported it in *Het Centrum*, 24 March 1901. The price of bread: VGM, b3519.

46 This list is in HUA (The Utrecht Archives), 'Archief Vereeniging "Voor de Kunst"', inv. no. 777–2: 7. VGM, Bd66.

47 *De Amsterdammer*, 24 March 1901.

48 Nicolaas Beversen to Jo. VGM, b4159; 25 March 1901. 'U hebt natuurlijk het stukje van Steenhoff in de Amsterdammer gelezen.' ('Of course, you've seen Steenhoff's piece in the Amsterdammer.')

49 Willem Leuring to Jo. VGM, b4160; 31 March 1901. VGM, b1925 and b3696. These sales are not mentioned in the cash book.

50 'Et comme, dans un livre de critique que je publierai après l'exposition, je veux écrire une longue biographie de Vincent.' ('And so, in an art review I shall publish after the exhibition, I want to write a long biography of Vincent.') Julien Leclercq to Jo. VGM, b1895; 14 March (quotation)—and b5739; 8 April 1900.

51 Julien Leclercq to Jo. VGM, b5740; 15 June 1900. Jo made a list for her own records: VGM, b5738.

52 Julien Leclercq to Jo. VGM, b4128; 23 September 1900.

53 'Vous disiez une chose très juste, Il sera difficile pendant la durée de l'Exposition d'augmenter les prix en cas de succès.' 'réputation définitive'. Julien Leclercq to Jo. VGM, b4129; 12 October 1900. He was referring to the *Exposition Universelle*. On *La Gazette des Beaux-Arts* see VGM, b2137.

54 'Je ferais en tête du catalogue un article d'une dizaine de petites pages pour indiquer les origines de Vincent, sa vie et la place qu'il tient dans l'école impressionniste.' Julien Leclercq to Jo. VGM, b4130; 25 November 1900. By 'veranda' he was referring to the extension to the living room.

55 The second list of works that Jo sent is VGM, b1533.

56 He calculated four hundred francs commission. He held on to the *Sunflowers* (priced at fourteen hundred francs) for a while so that it could be lined by a restorer. Julien Leclercq to Jo. VGM, b4131; 28 December 1900. *Pine Trees with Setting Sun* (F 652 / JH 1843) was sold to Amédée Schuffenecker. Not recorded in the cash book. Cat. Otterlo 2003, pp. 323–27. *Wheatfields with a Tree and Mountains* (F 721 / JH 1864) and *Ravine* (F 661 / JH 1871) went to Émile Schuffenecker, together with a few other works. *Account Book* 2002, pp. 29, 48, 144.

57 'J'ai conseillé à Bernheim de vous envoyer cette toile que vous connaissez peut-être si elle est de Vincent.' ('I advised Bernheim to send you this canvas to see if you might know whether it's by Vincent.') Julien Leclercq to Jo. VGM, b4133; 25 January 1901. Cf. Julius Meier-Graefe, who doubted the authenticity of a work that Osthaus had and wanted to know Jo's opinion. He made a sketch of the work, including descriptions of the colours. VGM, b7590; 2 August 1903.

58 'J'ai besoin *tout de suite* de ces toiles pour faire faire les cadres, et aussi les dessins.' Julien Leclercq to Jo. VGM, b4134; 6 February 1901. She must have answered quickly because he reverted to the matter within a fortnight. VGM, b4136; 20 February 1901.

59 Julien Leclercq to Jo. VGM, b4135; 13 February 1901. It is not clear which works by Van Gogh he meant here, possibly *The Zouave* (F 423 / JH 1486) and *The Green Vineyard* (F 475 / JH 1595).

60 'A Madame Vve Th. Van Gogh Bonger en souvenir de Vincent.' Julien Leclercq to Jo. VGM, b4138; 15 March 1901—the catalogue with dedication is VGM, b5737.

61 Julien Leclercq to Jo. VGM, b4139; 20 March 1901. On 3 November 1922 she wrote the following to Gustave Coquiot, underlined and with two exclamation marks: 'Il n'existe pas de portrait peint de lui.' ('No painted portrait of him exists.') VGM, b3274.

62 'slordig ingericht': *NRC*, 26 March 1901. Feilchenfeldt 1988, pp. 12–14; Feilchenfeldt 1990, p. 19; Grodzinski 2009.

63 'On pourrait devant son œuvre et sa correspondance en main, fournir une étude complète et significative.' Julien Leclercq to Jo. VGM, b4139; 20 March 1901. Quotation: catalogue, pp. 5–6.

64 Julien Leclercq to Jo. VGM, b4141; 5 April 1901.

65 'Cela vous fera plaisir de voir un Vincent que vous ne connaissiez pas.' Julien Leclercq to Jo. VGM, b4142; 15 April 1901.

66 Julien Leclercq to Jo. VGM, b3470; 18 July 1901.

67 This list is VGM, b2186; 8 October 1901. He confirmed receipt a week later. Julien Leclercq to Jo. VGM, Bd112; 15 October 1901 (postcard; in the possession of Johan van Gogh in 2015).

68 The two letters, which are in a private collection in Helsinki, were published in Supinen 1988, pp. 106–7 and Supinen 1990, p. 14. VGM, Bd7; 9 November—Bd8; 21 November 1901.

69 The exhibition opened on 8 May 1901. See Feilchenfeldt 1988, pp. 14, 144; Feilchenfeldt 1990, p. 20; Lenz 1990, p. 25.

70 Jo added five hundred guilders in her cash book in April. *Account Book* 2002, pp. 48, 144; *Kunstsalon Cassirer* 2011, vol. 2, pp. 71–88; Feilchenfeldt 1988, pp. 14–15. Exh. cat. Essen 2010.

11 Reviewing books and promoting Van Gogh—back in Amsterdam

1 IISG, microfilms 2944–7.

2 'Heeft de onderneming je sympathie? Op dat punt kan ik je niet anders voorstellen, of je bent 't met ons eens, dat de vrouw tegen de opvatting, die de wet en die het gros der mannen en zelfs het gros van haar eigen sexe van haar heeft, goed doet zich te verdedigen, of beter die opvatting door haar flink en kundig optreden, voor een juistere en meer billijke te doen plaats maken.' Marie Mensing to Jo. VGM, b2883; 16 March 1893.

3 'kinderachtig van vorm en toch niet geschikt voor kinderen'; 'Dit is wel een van de zonderlingste occupaties die men God ooit heeft toegedicht.' *Belang en Recht*, 15 October 1900.

4 'Ik vermoed een partijgenoot van U.' Henriette van der Meij to Jo. VGM, b3536; 19 October 1900.

5 *Belang en Recht*, 1 January 1901; *Diary* 2, p. 100. It is a quotation from Ecclesiastes 12:12.

6 Theo had given Jo this book as a present in February 1889.

7 'het jonge meisje van den nieuwen tijd, dat zich een levenstaak kiest en werkt en zoekt, om met en naast den man een betere toekomst te bereiden aan de maatschappij'. *Belang en Recht*, 15 July 1901.

8 Ger Harmsen, *Blauwe en Rode Jeugd. Ontstaan, ontwikkeling en teruggang van de Nederlandse jeugdbeweging tussen 1853 en 1940.* Assen 1961 (reprint Nijmegen 1973).

9 *Belang en Recht*, 1 April 1903.

10 'Graag zend ik U nieuwe voorraad, zoodra er iets van meer belang dan de gewone rommel komt. En U denkt immers aan de vertalingen voor [het] feuilleton?' Henriette van der Meij to Jo. VGM, b3535; 29 November 1900.

11 Henriette van der Meij to Jo. IISG, 28 March 1902.

12 *Belang en Recht*, 15 April 1902.

13 'slaven en slavinnen van het kapitaal'; 'onwetende, onverschillige, onbewuste vrouwen, die niet mobiel zijn te maken'. *Belang en Recht*, 15 April 1902.

14 'stemmingsverzen'; 'bekoorlijk'. *Belang en Recht*, 15 June 1902.

15 'Maar het valt al dadelijk niet mee.' 'vol sentimentaliteit, valsch gevoel, oppervlakkigheid, soms ziekelijke overspanning!' *Belang en Recht*, 1 November 1902.

16 'die kinderen liefheeft en begrijpt'; 'die *te veel* opgevoed worden'; 'toekomstmaatschappij'; 'en zoo goedkoop mogelijk verkrijgbaar gesteld; welk een opvoedende kracht zou daarvan uitgaan!' *Belang en Recht*, 13 January 1903. Bakker 1995 discusses the place of Key in thinking about child-rearing in the Netherlands.

17 *Belang en Recht*, 1 February 1904.

18 'eenvoudige, geestige en beminnelijke vrouw'. 'Opvoeden moet zijn: de gebreken niet *onderdrukken* door vrees voor straf, maar het kind zóó leiden, dat het leert inzien en begrijpen dat die gebreken verkeerd zijn.' 'de hygiëne van de ziel'. *Belang en Recht*, 1 May 1905. See also Bakker 1995, esp. pp. 86–7.

19 ''t Is van 't jaar een prachtige groote kermis. Moe en Gerrit gaan er ook al eens heen, want Mevrouw v. Gogh staat er ook met een onthoudingstent. Zij verkoopt van alles, ook aarbeien, waar ik al wat van gesmuld heb!' Tine Cool to Dien Cool; 19 June 1901. Johan Cohen drew a portrait of their father, the artist Thomas Cool. See also, for the quotation, http://www.thomascool.eu/Painting/TC1851-VanGogh.html.

20 *Diary* 1, p. 111; Van Kol was adamant: 'Waar het socialisme verschijnt, daar verdwijnt, althans voor een groot deel, de dronkenschap' ('Where socialism appears, drunkenness disappears, or at least for the greater part' (p. 181). For Wim Bonger see Van Heerikhuizen 1987, pp. 56–60, 203; *NRC*, 23 June 1923.

21 SSAN, NNAB. Noted in the archive of the notary Harm Pieter Bok 1883–91, inv. no. 12, deed no. 54.

22 'Die zond. avond in Utrecht zakte 'k in elkaar en 'k had niet de kracht met je te blijven. Later heb 'k er berouw, bitter berouw over gehad—maar 't gevoel, "ik kan noch Theo noch jou goed doen" en 't groote kwaad dat 'k me zelf deed door te blijven, deed me heengaan . . . 'k verloor alle zelfrespect en zelfvertrouwen. . . . Langsamerhand ben 'k de dingen weer uit elkaar gaan zien, 'k ben er alleen doorgescharreld—dat ben ik gewend, 'k moet in moeilijke tijden alleen zijn.' Willemien to Jo. VGM, b2920; undated. She had talked about it to the psychologist Professor Oost.

23 VGM, b3578 and b3565. Van Dalen, the doctor treating Willemien, continued to ask after her condition until into 1905.

24 'Misschien kan niemand dat zoo goed weten als ik en even stellig ben 'k ervan overtuigd dat voor een deel 't leed dat Vincent en Theo te zwaar is geworden had kunnen worden voorkomen.' Willemien to Jo. VGM, b2936; undated and incomplete.

25 'Ge weet nog wel die blokkering vroeger van die nacht maar die werd niet bestendigt.' Mrs van Gogh to Jo. VGM, b3647; 16 August (quotation)—b3644; 14 October 1902.

26 'Treedt telkens nog woest en wild op, schreeuwen, bijten, krabben, slaan. Andere momenten is zij stil en zwijgend en neemt nauwelijks deel aan de omgeving. Voedselweigering. Onder den invloed van hallucinaties.' Willemien was admitted on 4 December. See Vijselaar 1982, p. 31; Erik van Faassen, 'Willemina van Gogh. Zundert 1862—Veldwijk 1941', *De Combinatie* 5, no. 6 (1986), pp. 6–12 (quotation); Hofsink and Overkamp 2011, p. 140.

27 Cf. Mrs van Gogh to Jo. VGM, b1094; December 1902—b1102; 22 January 1904.

28 VGM, b1132; undated (before 3 April 1903)—b3565; 25 April 1904—and b3641; undated (shortly before 25 June 1904). They kept each other informed about Willemien's condition. VGM, b3634. According to Cornélie van Gogh-Carbentus in a letter to Jo, Mrs van Gogh 'snapped' as a result of all the bad news. VGM, b3584; 25 June 1904. On one occasion there was a brief remission, when Jo was able to talk to Willemien. VGM, b3713; 21 September 1905.

29 'Daar de prijzen stijgende zijn zoudt U er bezwaar tegen kunnen hebben en zoo zou ik gaarne eenig bericht van U ontvangen hoe te handelen.' Henk Bremmer to Jo. VGM, b4162. 2 May 1904.

30 'Wilt U hem daarover nu zelf schrijven of wilt u mij den prijs opgeven dat ik hem verder bericht? Doe zooals U dat goed lijkt.' Henk Bremmer to Jo. VGM, b6922; 6 September 1909.

31 Johannes de Bois to Jo. VGM, b5410; 12 November 1909. Although Bremmer said that he acted altruistically now and again, he also profited from certain transactions. In this case he received ten per cent commission as an intermediary. The art dealer Douwe Komter gave him a Van Gogh watercolour as a fiftieth birthday present. See Balk 2006, pp. 361, 391.

32 ''t is zoo'n rustig gevoel, dat er nu voor verscheiden jaren geld genoeg is voor Wil's onderhoud. We zijn 't geheel met je eens, dat het nu best lijden kan om haar voor een keer eens wat anders, en kon 't zijn wat afleiding, in haar droef bestaan te verschaffen.' Joan van Houten to Jo. VGM, b4143; 22 November 1909.

33 'Wie had gedacht dat Vincent nog eens zou voorzien in het onderhoud van Wil?' Anna van Houten-van Gogh to Jo. VGM, b4144; 22 November 1909.

34 'Dank intusschen nogmaals voor de wijze waarop gij en je Moeder deze zaak in het belang van W. hebt willen behandelen.' Joan van Houten to Vincent. VGM, b4147; 28 November 1920.

35 Two thousand guilders were set aside for Willemien's nursing. *Account Book* 2002, pp. 52, 148–9. (In 2017 the painting was sold at Christie's in New York for over eighty-seven million dollars.) In September 1912 De Bois asked her whether she would drop the two-thousand-guilder asking price for *The Harvest* (F 1484 / JH 1438) by four or five hundred guilders. Johannes de Bois to Jo. VGM, b5485; 7 November 1912. For an overview see Heijbroek and Wouthuysen 1993, pp. 196–8, 205 and exh. cat. Haarlem 2017.

36 Karel Alberdingk Thijm to Jo. LMDH, LM A 245 B 1; 11 December 1902 (the lecture)—9 June 1903 (invitation to come for a meal)—17 November 1903 (interest in Johan's health)—and 28 July 1908 (a thank you for Cato's birthday card). On 22 September 1924 Jo congratulated him on his sixtieth birthday. Prick 2003, p. 914.

37 Karel Alberdingk Thijm to Jo. LMDH, LM A 245 B 1; VGM, Bd105; 6 February 1905.

38 Willem Steenhoff to Jo. VGM, b1940; 7 February 1909. They had a son.

39 'Steenhoff was misschien de eenige of althans een van de heel weinige die zich niet door de slapte van mijn stiefvaader liet afschrikken om van tijd tot tijd bij ons te koomen.' *Vincent's Diary*, 13 May 1975. The difficult relations between the men were confirmed by P.J.H. Steenhoff on 21 October 2013. Sometimes the criticism of Johan was evident, such as in Steenhoff's opinion of this 'possibly too scrupulously zealous painter.' *De Amsterdammer* of 7 June 1908. The frank letter that Maria Steenhoff-Bogaert wrote in confidence to Vincent contained some details about her father's personal life and the impact it had on her as a young girl. VGM, b7428; 1 May 1975.

40 'Wat brengt de tijd toch 'n verandering—een 25 jaar terug vond ik bij Six voor 't stedel. te Amsterdam een afwerende houding om een kleine collectie daar in bruikleen op te nemen toen ik je moeder daartoe bereidwillig had gevonden!' Willem Steenhoff to Vincent. VGM, b5636; 10 May 1928. See also Heijbroek 1991, pp. 180–5.

41 'Daar ik voor den toen nog minderjarigen erfgenaam van Vincent diens nalatenschap beheerde, moest ik in het belang van den rechthebbende een onderzoek instellen naar den herkomst dier schilderijen.' *Algemeen Handelsblad*, 13 May 1911. Jo wrote this in response to incorrect assertions by Elisabeth du Quesne-van Gogh in the same newspaper on 11 May. See also exh. cat. Breda 2003, pp. 41, 47.

42 Van Tilborgh and Vellekoop 1998, p. 31; Op de Coul 2002, pp. 104–19; Balk 2006, pp. 240, 359.

43 Balk 2006 and Rovers 2010, p. 103.

44 VGM, b1557 and b3035. Jo visited Mrs van Gogh in The Hague shortly before 23 January 1903. See VGM b1111; 23 January 1903.

45 Teunis van Iterson to Jo. VGM, b1556; 13 February 1903.

46 'een tentoonstelling hier van Vincent, waarop een zevental schilderijen uit de latere periode het eigendom zijn van den Heer L.C. Enthoven te Voorburg.' Hermanus Tersteeg to Jo. VGM, b4148; 28 February 1903. Jo also wrote about it to Meier-Graefe, who told her in the winter of 1903–4: 'Je suis tout à fait étonné de ce que vous écrivez de cette exposition à Rotterdam et envieux d'apprendre à qui appartiennent ces tableaux. Binnenhuis m'en a envoyé un tas de dessins de Vincent de son tout premier temps, peu intéressant.' ('I'm absolutely astonished by what you write about this exhibition in Rotterdam and would dearly like to know who these pictures belong to. Binnenhuis sent me a bunch of drawings from Vincent's very earliest days, of little interest.') Julius Meier-Graefe to Jo. VGM, b7592; undated. Between 1899 and 1904 Meier-Graefe, together with Henry van de Velde, ran the Berlin gallery 'La Maison Moderne.'

47 Mrs van Gogh wrote about what her son had thought at the time: 'ge weet hij stelde wel belang in 't werk als studie maar kende geen waarde. Zeker zijn de schatten in 't bezit van wie dan ook aanmerkelijk gerezen.' ('you know he thought the work was important as a way to study but gave it no value. To be sure, the treasures in the possession of whoever have also increased substantially.') Mrs van Gogh to Jo. VGM, b1113; undated (probably February 1903)—b1096; 20 February 1903 (quotation). Exh. cat. Breda 2003, p. 36.

48 'tegen flinke prijzen maar die m.i. nog niet veel betekenen bij wat de toekomst hierin brengen zal'; 'familie van Vincent'. Henk Bremmer to Jo. VGM, b1557; undated (January-February 1903).

49 VGM, b1559; 6 June 1905; exh. cat. Breda 2003, pp. 28, 36, 43; Balk 2006, p. 239; Heijbroek 2012, pp. 42, 46.

50 At the beginning of 1906 the value of what was left in The Hague and Rotterdam was estimated at 6,500 guilders and in Amsterdam, at Van Bakel, at 4,000 guilders. Exh. cat. Breda 2003, p. 37.

51 VGM, b1560 and b4169; 28 October 1905 (invoice).

52 Bernatzik organized this exhibition together with Meier-Graefe for the Vereinigung Bildender Künstler Österreichs Secession Wien. VGM, b3939; 27 November 1902—b3940; 5 March 1903.

53 Jan Toorop to Jo. VGM, b1272; 8 February 1903.

54 VGM, b3938; *Account Book* 2002, pp. 49, 144–45, 176, 183. For the role played by Von Tschudi in the recognition of modern art see Johann Georg Prinz von Hohenzollern and Peter-Klaus Schuster, *Manet bis Van Gogh: Hugo von Tschudi und der Kampf um die Moderne*. Exh. cat. Berlin, Nationalgalerie and Munich, Neue Pinakothek, 1996–7. Munich etc. 1996.

55 Van Gogh, *Letters* 2009, letter 592; 3 April 1888.

56 'Waarlijk, een werk van Vincent is noodig, broodnoodig om de lui wat te verheffen uit hun krenterigheid.' 'Vandaag begin ik ook te incasseeren de bijdragen; volgens uw verzoek, blijft de prijs officieel *f* 800,-.' Pieter Haverkorn van Rijsewijk to Jo and Johan. VGM, b5387; 3 April 1903.

57 *Account Book* 2002, pp. 48, 144, 168. Mrs van Gogh to Jo. VGM, b3633; 1 May 1903. The undated press cutting in VGMB, BVG 3116. Jo decided it would be a good thing to reduce the price: 'Ik heb er natuurlijk ook gaarne iets voor over om Vincent's werk in Uw museum te zien.' ('Of course, I would like to help make it possible to see Vincent's work in your museum.') Jo to Pieter Haverkorn van Rijsewijk. VGM, Bd109; 1 April 1903 (original in the Rijksmuseum Print Room, Amsterdam). The purchase was made by 'eenige vermogende Rotterdammers' ('a few prosperous residents of Rotterdam'), wrote the *Haagsche Courant* on 30 April 1903. According to Balk, they were inspired by H.P. Bremmer, see Balk 2006, p. 202. On average each of the donors contributed thirty guilders. The museum's annual report stated that the acquisition became part of the collection on 23 April 1903 (p. 4).

58 Pieter Haverkorn van Rijsewijk to Jo and Johan. VGM, b5387; 3 April 1903.

59 VGM, b3937 (Krefeld) and b3257 (Wiesbaden).

60 G.H. Marius, 'De Idealisten III. Vincent van Gogh', *De Gids* 67 (1903), pp. 311–22; also included in her *Geschiedenis der Hollandsche schilderkunst in de negentiende eeuw* (1903).

61 'uit de portefeuille van Mevrouw Cohen Gosschalk-Bonger'. *Het Nieuws van den Dag* and *Het Nieuwsblad van het Noorden*, both 13 February 1904.

62 'omdat wij zoo zelden het volk schilderijen kunnen laten zien'. Emilie Knappert to Jo. VGM, b1273; 9 February 1904. Kramers et al. 1982, pp. 97–108; Bosch 2005, p. 65. Jo had known Knappert since 1892. VGM, b2882.

63 'van den oude man met de handen voor het gezicht, waar V. op schreef: "il faut que ces feuilles se vendent à 15 centimes!", aardig hè, juist voor hier.' Emilie Knappert to Jo. VGM, b1273; 9 February 1904. For this lithograph see

Van Heugten and Pabst 1995, p. 93 (no. 5.6). The painter Paul Signac spoke to Van Gogh in March 1889 in Arles. According to him he had talked continuously about 'peinture, littérature, socialisme' ('painting, literature, socialism'). Referred to in Gustave Coquiot, *Vincent van Gogh*. Paris 1923, p. 194.

64 'Steeds staat me U.L. liefelijke woning met al wat en wie zich daar beweegt en leeft en werkt voor oogen en binnen in mij de indrukken van UL. Groote liefde waar ik nog eens innig hartelijk voor dank.' Mrs van Gogh to Jo, and to Jo and Johan. VGM, b1112; 22 May—b1097; 8 June—and b1098; 13 June 1903 (quotation).

65 'dat op de canapé vindt ieder zoo best'. Mrs van Gogh to Jo. VGM, b1125; 15 June 1903.

66 Johan Cohen Gosschalk, *Portrait of Vincent van Gogh*, 1905 (private collection). Some of these drawings of Jo and Vincent are held in the Drents Museum in Assen.

67 'ik hoop maar dat hij er door komt. Het zou wel vreeselijk tragisch wezen.' Jan Veth to Anna Veth-Dirks; 6 September 1903. Private collection.

68 'Doe voor Cohen en Jo vooral maar wat je voor hen doen en bedenken kunt.' Jan Veth to Anna Veth-Dirks; 13 September 1903. Private collection.

69 'Wat een tijd van spanning, van afmatting van ziel en lichaam zal je gehad hebben en nu nog die ellendige zwakte. En jij zelf die ook al geen reus bent.' Henriette van der Meij to Jo. VGM, b3114; 21 September 1903.

70 Bonger 1986, p. 484.

71 Mrs van Gogh advised Jo: 'Verzuim U niet genoeg, vertrouw de raad, beste Jo, maar blijf liggen' ('Don't neglect yourself, trust the advice, dear Jo, and don't get up.'). Mrs van Gogh to Jo and Johan. VGM, b4567; 23 January 1904. On the kidney stone: Jo's father to Jo and Johan. VGM, b3616; 20 January 1904.

72 'ik ben er zoo bang voor, hoe komt een mensch er aan? zou je daar het erg van hebben gehad? de hemel geeft het nu beter word, toch zal je erg je moeten versterken, en die dagen rust houden, niet rijden.' Jo's mother to Jo. VGM, b2867; undated.

73 ''t is toch een wenk zoo eene ondervinding.' Mrs van Gogh to Jo. VGM, b3648; undated.

74 *Vincent's Diary*, 30 January or 2 February 1934. Mrs van Gogh to Jo. VGM, b1104; 3 February 1904. Six months before she had already mentioned that the minister Van Loenen Martinet 'toch zoo aangenaam catechisatie les geeft, nu dat kan ik denken dat zou ook heerlijk voor 't jongetje zijn.' ('gives such nice confirmation lessons, and I can imagine that they would also be delightful for the lad.') Later on, she made another attempt in a similar vein. VGM, b1119; 10 October 1903 (quotation)—b3568; 31 December 1904.

75 Antonie Johannes, *Luthers Diakonessenwerk. Geschiedenis van 100 jaar Lutherse Diakonessen Inrichting te Amsterdam*. Zutphen 1986.

76 Yda, the daughter of Jo's friend Dien Reinhold, wrote to Vincent: ''k Hoop, dat je nu weer thuis zijt en Mama weer terug is, hersteld en uitgerust. Hoe gaat het met de heer Cohen, wat een guur weer voor een halve zieke!—Kunt ge met Paschen bij ons komen, dan vinden wij dat allen recht prettig.' ('I hope that you're home again and that Mama is back again, recovered and rested. How is Mr Cohen, what awful weather for someone who's recuperating! If you could come to us at Easter, we would all really like it.') VGM, b3674; 24 March 1904.

77 'Wat speet het mij erg dat U en Uw man zoo lijdende was. Mevrouw [Bertha] Jas had mij wel geschreven dat U door groote overspanning zeer zenuwachtig was en eenige tijd in het Diaconessehuis doorbracht en dat verwonderde mij niet. U maakt toch waarlijk ook veel mee in U huwelijksleven.' J. Mante-Aalders to Jo. VGM, b3778; 22 July 1904. She was the mother of Jan Mante, one of Vincent's school chums. *Vincent's Diary*, 21 July 1972; *Account Book* 2002, p. 161. VGM, b6921.

78 'veel mooier dan ik gedacht, zoo plechtig en ernstig, zoo waar menschenhanden niets aan af kunnen doen'. Jo to Johan. VGM, b7302; undated.

79 'Ik verlang naar je, ik wou dat je bij me was, dan was 't volmaakt hier—wat is de wereld toch mooi en groot'. Jo to Johan. VGM, b7302; undated.

80 'glom van de regen en straalde van genot'. Jo to Johan. VGM, b7303; undated. Johan's letters to Lucerne are missing from the estate. Betsy had also sung during a performance at the beginning of the year in Berlin: *Berliner Tageblatt*, 10 January 1904.

81 'Enfin dat komt allemaal weer terecht als ik terug ben!' Jo to Johan. VGM, b7304; undated.

82 Jo to Johan. VGM, b7305; 15 April 1904. This postcard has not been found. Beyerman was the Bussum-based doctor Diederik Hendrik Beyerman, who was awarded a doctorate for his work on the influence of the nervous system on respiration. *Nederlands Tijdschrift voor Geneeskunde* 83, no. 47 (25 November 1939), p. 5595.

83 'Ik zou als motto boven mijn brief willen zetten Siegmund's Siehe der Lenz lacht in den Saal—dat klinkt me aldoor in mijn hoofd'. Jo to Johan. VGM, b7306; undated.

84 'op en top het land van Wagner . . . een land voor reuzen en goden'. Jo to Johan. VGM, b7306; undated.

85 'precies een Segantini—eigenlijk naar al die vergelijkingen die een mensch altijd door 't hoofd spoken'. Jo to Johan. VGM, b7306; undated.

86 'dat de menschen zooveel bederven—en toch dat een klein menschenhart het groote van alles in zich kan opnemen en er van genieten—maar ten slotte wat kan hij er mee doen? Dan kom je weer beneden op de aarde en hoort de menschen aan tafel allemaal dezelfde praatjes houden iederen dag—'t is of zij niets zien van al dat mooie om hen heen.' Jo to Johan. VGM, b7306; undated.

87 'Ze eeren hun groote mannen wel.' Jo to Johan. VGM, b7306; undated.

88 'voorbeeldige gezin'. Mrs van Gogh to Jo. VGM, b3637; 28 April 1904. She offered her condolences to the family on 30 April. VGM, b3640.

89 'Wat heeft Pa zijn heele leven gewerkt en alles in orde gehouden.' Jo's mother to Jo. VGM, b3606; 7 May 1904. In 1905 Jo received 3,550 guilders from her father's estate and 4,671 guilders from her mother's. Three years later she received 2,011 guilders from Mrs van Gogh's estate. *Account Book* 2002, pp. 124–6, 149. For the portrait drawing see exh. cat. Assen 1991, p. 29.

90 Julius Meier-Graefe to Jo. VGM, b7588 ('étude très approfondie'); 5 July—b7589; 20 July and b7587; 15 October 1903.

91 Jo to Julius Meier-Graefe. VGM, b7606; 25 February 1921. Van Gogh, *Letters* 2009, letter 694.

92 Julius Meier-Graefe to Jo. VGM, b7590; 2 August—b7591; 12 August 1903.

93 'Voilà l'hiver—préparez un peu la correspondance. Je brûle de la livrer au public.' Julius Meier-Graefe to Jo. VGM, b7592; undated (winter 1903).

94 Jo to Paul Gachet. VGM, b2143; 12 June 1907. She sent Meier-Graefe reproductions: Julius Meier-Graefe to Jo. VGM, b7600; 22 February 1907.

95 Jo tried to maintain an overview of which collections included Van Goghs. VGM, b5388. Julius Meier-Graefe to Jo. VGM, b7593; 17 May—b7595; 6 June 1904. The quotation in vol. 1, p. 117.

96 For Meier-Graefe and his writings about Van Gogh see Lenz 1990. See also Feilchenfeldt 1990, p. 20.

97 Bruno Cassirer to Jo. VGM, b3941; 25 June 1904. 'Es tut mir sehr leid, dass unsere Korrespondenz nicht zu dem erwünschten Resultat geführt hat!' ('I deeply regret that our correspondence has not led to the desired result.')

98 Brühl 1991, pp. 246–86.

99 She gave permission to have works reproduced. He immediately asked her if she would agree to someone coming to make transcripts of the letters. She prudently refused the request. Bruno Cassirer to Jo. VGM, b3942; 15 September 1904. Ten years later Paul Cassirer published *Briefe an seinen Bruder*. See Chapter 16.

100 F. Melian Stawell praised the German edition in 'The Letters of Vincent van Gogh', *The Burlington Magazine* 19 (1911), pp. 152–4.

101 Jo to Annie van Gelder-Pigeaud. VGM, b3719; 6 October 1921: ''t werd zonder mijn toestemming uitgegeven onder de misleidende titel: familiar correspondence. 't zijn citaten zonder eenig verband.' ('it was published without my permission under the misleading title: familiar correspondence. They are quotations without any context.')

102 'Ja, de zee heeft zo'n verschillende uitwerking op zenuwmenschen. En dan die hitte!' This hotel's address is on this postcard. VGM, b7316; 24 July 1904. In Nunspeet Johan stayed in a boarding house, De Valk, where there was also a studio. While there he could also use his sister Meta's studio. SNVN, land registry ledger, sheet II–III; Roodenburg 1992, pp. 75–9, 193.

103 'Komen jelui toch maar naar Amsterdam, je zou zien hoe gezellig we 't zouden hebben . . . We kunnen best een goedkoop huis vinden, dan nemen jelui een aardig meisje in huis maar dan kun je ook een dag hier komen.' Betsy Bonger to Jo. VGM, b3609; summer 1904. The decision had still not been taken by mid-August. Cf. Elise Josephine Gosschalk to Jo. VGM, b3554; 19 August 1904.

104 VGM, b3585. There is only one reference to rental income in the cash book. It was in 1919 and the annual rent was 700 guilders. *Account Book* 2002, p. 164. In April 1926 the house was valued at 18,000 guilders, with a rent of 1,200 guilders a year. VGM, b2219.

105 Verbal communication from Johan van Gogh, 18 July 2011.

106 SSAN, Bussum Land Registry, no. 2018. Construction drawings of 69, 77 Koninginneweg / 1, 2 Brachthuijzerstraat. ACA, 5221.BT. In November 1915 the bathroom was redecorated and tiled. VGM, b3717. After H.H. Baanders died in 1905 his heirs became the building's owners. His son, H.A.J. Baanders, lived at 955 Prinsengracht. The cash book has an entry for rent in 1919: 850 guilders. *Account Book* 2002, pp. 134, 164.

107 In the population register records, the address is given as 2 Brachthuijzerstraat, and all three of them are listed on the family registration cards as living at this address. So too were the maids Johanna Wagenmaker (1883–?) and Catharina Noor (1877–?) for a while in 1905–06. ACA, 5417 K 77, and *Population Register*, neighbourhood AL, vol. B 67, fol. 237. The layout of the residences has been changed since then.

108 It is stated in the notarial deed of Johan's last will and testament that, after his death, Jo would have to pay Baanders a further 182.50 guilders for the year 1912 for rent arrears of an 'upstairs flat'. SSAN, NNAB. Archive of the notary Sytse Scheffelaar Klots 1892–1925, inv. no. 53, deed no. 7523.

109 'Die mevrouw Bonger, zal ik maar zeggen, haalde met de hulp van Steenhoff een aantal doeken tevoorschijn uit een zolderkamertje en tekeningen uit een kast.' H.P.L. Wiessing, *Bewegend portret. Levensherinneringen*. Amsterdam 1960, pp. 249–50. From 1907 Wiessing was editor of the *De Amsterdammer*, for which Steenhoff wrote as an art critic. Jo kept Van Gogh's drawings unframed and probably some of them also without mounts. Jo to Montross. VGM, b6275; 30 August 1923.

110 Sara van Houten to Jo. VGM, b3582; 4 October 1904. Meta Cohen Gosschalk gave Jo a blue and white umbrella stand. VGM, b3473.

111 'Daarin staat o.a. dat het voor mij zo goed was, wegens mindere vermoeidheid door vervallen van het reizen (naar Amersfoort, 2e klas hbs). En ook dat ze het prettig vond weer dichter bij haar moeder te wonen. Beide drogredenen en onjuist. Haar huwelijk viel haar tegen, en toen viel ze terug, niet op haar onafhankelijk bestaan in Bussum maar op haar familie. En haar dominerende moeder belette juist de ontplooiing van haar kinderen. Ze heeft ook mondeling een aantal van die onjuistheden verkondigd tegenover anderen: dat het huis zoveel beter was e.d. Wat heeft ze mij met die verhuizing een kwaad gedaan—ook met haar huwelijk met zo'n neuroticus. Ze had wel een betere man kunnen krijgen. Ik heb wel eens eerder geschreven dat ik aan zijn fijne geest wel wat had, maar me helpen ontplooien niets.' *Vincent's Diary*, 15 August 1971.

112 'die de gewone dingen weergaf. Ik herinner me zoo goed dat mijn moeder me dat vertelde.' 'Met Theo was ik er al geweest in de vacantie, om de Vermeertentoonstelling te zien, met de vele Pieter de Hooghen. Mijn moeder heeft me altijd verteld dat mijn vader daar zoo veel van hield, wat ik me best begrijpen kan.' *Vincent's Diary*, 25 September 1934, 22 September 1935 and 29 March 1936 respectively. Cf. Hans Luijten, 'Rummaging Among My Woodcuts': Van Gogh and the Graphic Arts', in *Vincent's Choice: the Musée imaginaire of Van Gogh*. Eds. Chris Stolwijk et al. exh. cat. Amsterdam (Van Gogh Museum), 2003. Amsterdam and Antwerp 2003, pp. 99–112.

113 'dezelfde krullenbol en 't vriendelijke gezicht'. Maria van Gogh to Jo. VGM, b3589; 2 October 1904. As Mrs van Gogh had done, she raised the subject of confirmation.

114 Paul Gachet to Jo. VGM, b3411; 25 September 1904.

115 Jo to Paul Gachet. VGM, b2127; 5 October 1904. Later Paul and his sister Marguerite gave back Jo's letters and those of Johan and Vincent. VGM, b2126–71. Marguerite died in 1949, Paul in 1962. Jo and Theo's visit to Vincent's grave took place between 12 September and 4 October 1890. It was a poignant occasion for both of them.

116 Paul Gachet to Jo. VGM, b4574; 13 October 1904.

117 On this visit see Schiefler 1974, pp. 24–6; Indina Woesthoff, *'Der glückliche Mensch'. Gustav Schiefler (1857–1935). Sammler, Dilettant und Kunstfreund*. Hamburg 1996, pp. 222–33, esp. 226–9.

118 Gustav Schiefler to Jo. VGM, b3689; 6 November 1904. There were subsequent letters: VGM, b3690; 27 April—b3924; 14 June—b6927; 21 August 1905. Cassirer complained to Schiefler that Jo did not want to sell many works for speculative reasons and asked for prices that were too high. He asked Jo not to get involved with Schiefler, advice that she followed.

119 Gustav Schiefler to Jo. VGM, b3926; 10 September 1905. *Account Book* 2002, pp. 50, 145, 172.

120 Gustav Schiefler to Jo. VGM, b3928; 30 July 1911.

121 Jo to Gustav Schiefler. SUBH, Carl von Ossietzky, Nachlass Gustav Schiefler, B:23:1911,1:126; 7 August 1911.

122 Jo to Gustav Schiefler. SUBH, Carl von Ossietzky, Nachlass Gustav Schiefler, B:7:1904:84; 10 August 1904; B:7:1904:85; 12 November 1904; B:8:1905,1:112; 17 June 1905; B:8:1905,1:113; 23 August 1905; B:8:1905,1:114; undated (August 1905); B:8:1905,1:115; 4 September 1905; B:8:1905,1:119; 13 September 1905 respectively.

123 See *Kunstsalon Cassirer* 2011, vol. 2, pp. 571–98; Feilchenfeldt 1988, p. 16; Feilchenfeldt 1990, pp. 21, 145.

124 H.L. Klein to Jo. VGM, b5419; 23 November—b4163; 28 December 1904.

125 Various examples in exh. cat. Essen 1990.

126 VGMB, TS 3564. The Van Rappard letters were owned by Johan de Meester. In 2006 the Van Gogh Museum was able to add essentially all of them to its collection.

127 VGM, b4005 ('pecuniären Erfolg')—b4006–12. *Account Book* 2002, pp. 49 and 145. He exhibited a total of twenty-three works. VGM, b2185. Cf. Feilchenfeldt 1988, p. 18 (with an image from the purchases book 'Mai 1905'); Feilchenfeldt 1990, p. 20 and *Kunstsalon Cassirer* 2011, vol. 2, pp. 685–708.

128 Albert Vavasseur to Jo. VGM, b3063–b3064; 24 and 26 May—b3061; 13 June 1905. The receipt is VGM, b3062. The bill for the coffin: VGM, b2115. On this reburial see Gachet 1994, p. 258; exh. cat. Paris 1999, p. 284 and Andreas Obst, *Records and Deliberations about Vincent van Gogh's First Grave in Auvers-sur-Oise*. Lauenau 2010. Published privately. VGMB, BVG 21462.

129 VGM, b2130, b1973 and b3368. On the attendees: Gachet 1994, p. 257–8—VGM, b3364 and b2131. Vincent did not accompany her. He was to meet Gachet Sr (who died on 9 January 1909) on a later occasion. Vincent to Paul Gachet Jr. VGM, b2808; 4 September 1925.

130 'J'assistais à l'exhumation de Vincent. Je le reconnus nettement à la structure de sa tête.' Gustave Coquiot notes. VGM, b3348, p. 19—and VGM b7150 (unpaged; June 1922). See also Gachet 1994, p. 258.

131 Jo to Paul Gachet. VGM, b2131; 14 June 1905. She repeated this to him a year later. VGM, b2138; 20 May 1906: 'Je n'oublie rien—ni personne de ce temps à Paris.' ('I've forgotten nothing and no one from that time in Paris').

132 Van Gogh, *Letters* 2009, letter 893. Jo to Paul Gachet. VGM, b2131; 14 June 1905. She borrowed the manuscript when she wanted to make an image of the letter sketch for her publication of the letters. Three letters to Paul Gachet. VGM, b2151–3; 15, 21 and 27 February 1912.

133 VGM, b3062; 9 June 1905 (the agreement regarding 'une concession double'). Paul Gachet to Jo. VGM, b3413; 20 June (including the costs of transporting the mortal remains by rail, as well as the morbid addition: 'Conditions—Bière chêne, enfermée dans une caisse de Zinc soudée pour ne laisser passer ni odeur ni liquide' ('Conditions—oak casket enclosed in a zinc box, soldered to prevent the passage of odours and liquids'))—b3368; 4 July 1905 ('une femme stoïque'). A reburial was not exceptional in Europe at the time. With thanks to W.G.H.M. van der Putten, legal advisor of Velp, specialist in funeral services law; email of 7 June 2015.

134 Jo to Paul Gachet. VGM, b2171; 1 July 1905: 'Il y a un grand vide autour de nous que rien ne peut combler.' ('There is a great void around us that nothing can fill.') See also Anna van Houten-van Gogh to Jo. VGM, b3562; 19 June 1905 and Cornelia van Gogh-Carbentus to Jo. VGM, b3587; 20 June 1905.

135 'weer in de war'. Meta Cohen Gosschalk to Jo. VGM, b3503; 19 June 1905. Henriette van der Meij to Jo. VGM, b3115; 30 June 1905: 'Het is zoo, of nu voor goed alles wat nog met je jeugd verbandt houdt, weg is.' ('It is as if everything that was still associated with your childhood has gone for good.') Mathilde Wibaut-Berdenis van Berlekom also sent Jo a fond letter of condolence. IISG, 20 June 1905.

Part Five

1 *The Diary of Søren Kierkegaard*. Ed. Peter Rohde. New York 1988, vol. 5, part. 4, no. 136; Diary 1843.

12 A magnificent exhibition in the summer of 1905

1 Among those who sent messages were Bas Veth, Richard Roland Holst, Paul Gachet Sr (who proposed that Vincent's self-portraits should be draped in mourning veils on the anniversary of his death. VGM, b1974) and Henk Bremmer, who provided Jo with some names and addresses at her request. VGM, b1969 and b1970; both 10 July 1905.

2 Jo to Paul Gachet Jr. VGM, b2129; 12 March 1905.

3 VGM, b5422–4.

4 Hugo von Tschudi to Jo. VGM, b3807; 10 July 1905. In May 1905, when Paul Cassirer returned crates of paintings from Berlin that he had received on commission from Jo, he was able to send them directly to the Stedelijk Museum. VGM, b4012.

5 VGM, b2177.

6 'zeldzame broederliefde en zelfverloochening'; 'De zon, de helle, blije kleuren, het klaterende licht, zij werken op hem als schuimende wijn.' Quotations on pp. 10–11. At the end of the introduction Vincent is referred to as the (underage) heir to the collection (p. 14). Johan's handwritten outline of the biography has survived. VGM, b3710. He consulted with Jo, who selected the letters herself, as she wrote to Gachet Jr. VGM, b2134. Gachet replied: 'Quant à la *préface* je pensais bien que vous et votre mari seriez tous deux auteurs.' ('As to the *Preface*, I was thinking that both you and your husband would be the authors.') VGM, b3400; 23 August 1905. (Johan's introduction was used again, for the exhibitions in the Larensche Kunsthandel gallery (June-August 1911), in the Stedelijk Museum (December 1914 –January 1915) and others.)

7 'verkoop, of reclame, of zuiver uit het belang der kunst'. The process of approval for this exhibition can be traced in detail in various documents in the Amsterdam City Archives (ACA)—Algemene Zaken, Brievenboeken and the 'Deliberatieboek'. With thanks to Eveline Lambrechtsen.

[1] Algemene Zaken. Archive 5181, inv. no. 3471, no. 1620. Jo had submitted a request in person on 18 March, and on 27 March Cornelis Baard advised the city authorities to approve this proposal. Members of the supervisory committee asked for additional information on the 30th. Baard's reassurance followed on 7 April. Subsequently the committee consented (10 April) and Jo received a green light (3 May).

[2] Brievenboeken, containing letters from Baard to the city authorities. Accession number 30041, inv. no. 5. Permission was granted on 20 April (pp. 26–7) and from 19 July admission would be free for students at Amsterdam art academies and drawing schools, except on Tuesdays and Thursdays (p. 41). On 11 August permission was given to extend the exhibition until 1 September, although Jo would have to take into account that 'Architectura et Amicitia' would have the galleries at its disposal from that day on (p. 44).

[3] Algemene Zaken. Archive 5181, inv. no. 3479, no. 4736. On 9 August Johan submitted a request in writing for permission to extend the exhibition, which Baard laid before the city authorities 'without objection' on the 11th. On 12 August Jo received confirmation of permission by letter for an extension until 30 August. The Museum was closed on the 31st for Queen Wilhelmina's birthday.

[4] 'Deliberatieboek'. Archive B&W, accession number 5166, inv. no. 189, pp. 567–8.

[5] Algemene Zaken. Archive 5181, inv. no. 5979, no. 17215. On 25 September Jo submitted a request to the city authorities concerning 'restitution of tax paid on Public Entertainments', which is how she referred to the exhibition, but her request was rejected on 24 November.

8 VGM, b1921.

9 Announcements in *Het Nieuws van den Dag*, between 19 July and 30 August 1905.

10 VGM, b1511.

11 This emerges from a letter from Kee Vos-Stricker to Jo. VGM, b3016; 12 July 1905.

12 'ordinair stroo karton'. Willem Pieter Ingenegeren to Johan. VGM, b1964; 7 August 1905. He paid 350 guilders for *Landscape with Sunset* (F 191 / JH 762), which is painted on cardboard. *Account Book* 2002, p. 50.

13 Jo to Paul Gachet Jr. VGM, b2171; 1 July 1905. See also Schiefler 1974, p. 26. Gustave Coquiot noted '7 Salles' ('7 Galleries') in his catalogue: VGM, b7197. Most of the works were numbered sequentially, with eleven that had a- and b-numbers. The forty-one additions were [1] the inserted numbers 156a and 432, and [2] the 'Supplement', at the back of the catalogue on pp. 43–45. The extra works were also reported in *Het Volk* of 21 August 1905.

14 'badkamerachtige tint'; 'doodkisten-zwart'. *Onze Kunst* 4 (1905), pp. 59–68; quotations: pp. 61–2.

15 ''t is een schandaal om zulk prulwerk te durven exposeeren'. *Het Nieuws van den Dag*, 26 July 1905. Johan responded in the edition of 7 August 1905, which was followed by a rejoinder from Loffelt. Three days later Loffelt poured more scorn on top when he wrote that, 'in despair and torment', he fled the building to escape from the 'hell of immature clumsy colouring' ('wanhopig en gepijnigd'; 'hel van onrijp kleurengeschetter'). Loffelt's own catalogue has survived—he scribbled his indignant remarks alongside various works (RKD).

16 See Joosten 1970c, pp. 157–8; and Heijbroek 1991, p. 180.

17 'ernstige revisie'; 'Het werk zal u grijpen en u niet meer loslaten.' *De Groene Amsterdammer*, 23 July, 6 and 13 August (quotation) and 3 September 1905.

18 For detailed information about this association see Adang 2008; on this exhibition: pp. 492–8 and 506. Jo's son Vincent became the treasurer in 1924 (p. 628).

19 *Het Volk*, 21 August 1905. Marie de Roode-Heijermans to Jo. VGM, b3110; 1 August 1905. They discussed publicity and logistics. VGM, b3111.

20 This contribution, 'Nog iets over Vincent van Gogh', is included in Tibbe 2014, pp. 264–8. For Albert Aurier's text see Aurier 1890. On this view see *Primitivism in 20th Century Art: Affinity of the Tribal and the Modern*. Ed. William S. Rubin. Exh. cat. New York (The Museum of Modern Art), 1984–5. Fifth edition. New York 1994.

21 'Vincent aura ici une vraie patrie pour sa gloire. Nous parlons beaucoup de lui et il gagne tous les jours des admirateurs.' Julius Meier-Graefe to Jo. VGM, b7597; 3 July (quotation)—b3464; 5 July—b7598; 11 August—b7599; 25 August 1905.

22 'Zij kenden het werk van Oom Vincent al van vroeger—ik heb prettig met hen gepraat.' Jo to Vincent. VGM, b3712; 20 July 1905. Vincent was staying in Haarlem with the Reinhold family. On low numbers of road users: Brugmans 1976, p. 372.

23 'wat heeft Vincent toch gewerkt en wat heeft Theo alles gewaardeert. Dat is voor ons allen een band aan U en Uw lieve kind, die ik hoop en vertrouw al de onzen onderhouden.' Mrs van Gogh to Jo. VGM, b3004; 5 July 1905. In the meantime she had moved to 46b Zoeterwoudsesingel in Leiden, where she lived until her death in 1907. The story goes that Mrs van Gogh, who could no longer cope with stairs, wanted to visit the exhibition but there was only a goods lift, which she refused to use. 'Een fatsoenlijk mens doet dat niet' ('A respectable person does not do that.') she is supposed to have said. Communication from Johan van Gogh (17 March 2016), who heard the anecdote from his father.

24 VGM, b4169.

25 See also *Account Book* 2002, p. 163. Jo to Paul Gachet Jr. VGM, b2126; 29 March 1905. In response to her question, he sent a detailed description of the frames that would be most suitable. Paul Gachet Jr to Jo. VGM, b3417; undated (early April 1905)—b3364; 29 June 1905.

26 On 14 August she gave her brother Henri a thousand of those guilders to invest.

27 No sources were found for that low estimate or the fact that Cornelis Baard was held to account by Amsterdam's city authorities for the negative comments made by some visitors. This comes from John Jansen van Galen and Huib Schreurs, *Het huis van nu, waar de toekomst is. Een kleine historie van het Stedelijk Museum, 1895–1995*. Naarden 1995, pp. 36–8. For the number of visitors in Groningen see VGM, b1259.

28 VGM, b2192 (proofs), b5353 (insurance) and b7196 (insurance after the exhibitions in 1905–6). VGMB, BVG 3465a (handwritten prices). A further copy of the 1905 catalogue contains the 'Specification and Valuation of the works at 77 Koninginneweg': VGM, b5421. The dating has to be 1906–7 because the works sold in the meantime were no longer noted and all the individual amounts were increased.

29 'moralischer Erfolg'. Paul Cassirer to Jo. VGM, b4013 (quotation), b4014 and b4016; 12 and 21 August 1905, and undated (the same month) respectively.

30 Paul Cassirer to Jo. VGM, b4015; 24 August—b4017; 31 August 1905 (contract). VGM, b2183; September 1905 (list).

31 Jo to Paul Gachet Jr. VGM, b2134; 15 August 1905. She told him that she had wanted to respond to an article in *La Plume*, but Johan had advised her most earnestly not to do so. She had written to him previously about Adolphe van Bever, 'Les ainés—un peintre maudit: Vincent van Gogh (1853–1890)', *La Plume* 17, no. 373, 1 June 1905, pp. 532–45 and no. 374, 15 June 1905, pp. 596–609. Jo thought that the malicious comments about Gachet (on p. 605) and about Gauguin's scornful and intimate vision of Van Gogh's personality were 'horrible'. Jo to Paul Gachet Sr. VGM, b2133; 23 July 1905. She wrote 'fout' ('wrong') next to assertion in her copy of the magazine. VGMB, BVG 821a-b. Van Bever viewed Van Gogh as a deranged but at the same time brilliant artist searching for extremes. See also Zemel 1980, pp. 88–91.

32 'Het noodlot had geen vredigen loop beschikt voor Van Gogh's leven. Hij was genageld op zijn kunst als op een kruis, hij droeg het in extatische gelatenheid tot het einde toe.' *Elsevier's Geïllustreerd Maandschrift* 15, no. 10 (1905), pp. 218–34. A translation of the article appeared in *Zeitschrift für Bildende Kunst* 43, no. 9 (1908), pp. 225–35. Cf. editor Herman Robbers to Jo. VGM, b1515; 18 August 1905.

33 Jo to Johan. VGM, b7294; 24 August 1905. I. Querido wrote 'Vincent van Gogh', *Op de Hoogte. Maandschrift voor de Huiskamer* 2, no. 8 (August 1905), pp. 478–82.

34 'stoutert, hoe kan ik nu zeggen *wanneer* ik in Nunspeet zal komen, als ik geen flauw besef heb hoe lang dat opruimen zal duren—'t is geen kleinigheid, alles voor Cassirer moet dan immers meteen gepakt en weggestuurd!' 'Wat is hij toch onuitstaanbaar vinnig! . . . 't Is er toch een!!' Jo to Johan. VGM, b7295; 25 August 1905. Enthoven bought a further two works for a total of 3,600 guilders. *Account Book* 2002, pp. 50, 145–6.

35 Jo to Johan, VGM, b7296; 26 August—b7298; 29 August 1905. She put an advertisement in the newspaper *Het Nieuws van den Dag* of 3 August 1905 for a 'skilled maid'. The salary was 120 guilders.

36 Jo to Johan. VGM, b7297; 28 August 1905.

37 Paul Gachet Jr to Jo. VGM, 3374; 5 July 1905. Gachet Sr had wanted to donate it to the Stedelijk Museum, but there must have been a reason why Jo nevertheless took it to the Rijksmuseum. See also Van Heugten and Pabst 1995, pp. 101–2.

38 'Voor dit bewijs van belangstelling in 's Rijks verzamelingen heb ik de eer U den dank der Regeering te betuigen.' Barthold van Riemsdijk to Jo. VGM, b5447; 27 March 1906. Pieter Rink to Jo. VGM, b5448; 12 April 1906.

39 *Algemeen Handelsblad,* 13 April (donation) and 15 April 1906 (presentation).

40 'Eindelijk is vandaag het defect in de gasleiding gevonden. Gisteren was de voorkamer opgebroken, vandaag de huiskamer. Ik hoef je niet te zeggen, hoe prettig!' Jo to Johan. VGM, b7298; 29 August 1905.

41 Jo to Johan. VGM, b7297; 28 August 1905. Marie Mensing to Jo. IISG, 29 March, 11 May, 4 June and 18 June 1905.

42 ''t Is ook ontzettend jammer dat 't niet nog een paar weken kon duren maar toch heb ik geen spijt, dat we 't in den zomer hebben gedaan—want o dat verschil—met zonlicht of zooals eergisteren—een grauwe dag!—Ik had graag van middag er nog eens met jou rondgewandeld—we hebben 't toch maar knap gedaan "al zeg ik 't zelf", hè.' 'Tout cela s'est bien passé; de zending naar Utrecht is weg—en voor Hagen staat klaar—gelukkig. Ik kom nu *Zaterdag* bij je, kwart voor één. Morgen zal ik de belasting betalen, naar het stadhuis gaan voor de entreeboeken en met Baard afrekenen—vrijdag mijn garderobe wat in orde maken en het permanente bureau—dat weer in volle gang is—opruimen en Zaterdag schud ik alles van me af en vlieg naar je toe. Geloof je niet dat ik er ook naar verlang om heerlijk buiten te zijn in die zuivere opwekkende lucht. Heusch, ik ben de laatste week niet anders geweest dan een werkmachine. . . . Want voor iedere zaak die hangende is moeten 3, 4 brieven eer 't in orde is. . . . 'k vind 't heerlijk dat Marie Mensing in 't huis blijft—met Vincent—want op 't oogenblik zou je het huis niet kunnen sluiten, er komt zoo van alles!' 'Flutenreicher Ebro, dat heb ik aldoor in mijn hoofd onder 't schrijven. ik verlangde er naar dat de piano eens openging—ik zou er toe gekomen zijn om zelf eens te spelen, als ik maar tijd had gehad. . . . Ik wou dat ik wat prettige lectuur had om mee te nemen—'t zal weer Heine worden denk ik—want tijd om iets te gaan leenen heb ik niet meer. 'k Zou graag brieven hebben van Flaubert of zoo iets want ik zal je niet van je werk houden hoor—dat weet je wel.' 'een boel zoenen'. Jo to Johan. VGM, b7299–7301; all three 30 August 1905. The admissions books she referred to have not been found.

43 Paul Gachet Jr to Jo. VGM, b3372; 26 September 1905. Paul Gachet Jr to Jo. VGM, b3369; 29 August (packing)—b3371; 16 September 1905 (increased value).

44 'vraiment accablée d'ouvrage'. Jo to Paul Gachet Jr. VGM, b2135; 4 September 1905.

45 She sent Vincent a telegram and a postcard: 'Ik voel 't beter is een dag uit te rusten vóór ik naar A. kom. Anders zou ik half ziek aankomen en dat wil ik niet!' ('I think it'd be better if I rest for a day before I come to Amsterdam. Otherwise I'd arrive still half ill, and I don't want that!'). VGM, b3713; 21 September 1905.

46 'il n'aime pas qu'on le sache'. Jo to Paul Gachet Sr. VGM, b2136; 18 October 1905. Johan was better again two months later, as Jo wrote to Lies du Quesne-van Gogh. VGM, b2299; 21 November 1905.

47 Karl Osthaus to Jo. VGM, b3936; undated. Jo kept a copy of the 1905 catalogue with private notes, which she wrote during and after the exhibition, including about the works that went to Hagen. VGM, b7195.

48 He asked whether she would agree to a ten per cent commission if he sold something. Karl Osthaus to Jo. VGM, b3930; 27 August—b3478; 28 September 1905.

49 VGM, b2103 (list). Karl Osthaus to Jo. VGM, b3931; 10 October—b3932; 31 October 1905. VGM, b3933 (money transfer). See also *Account Book* 2002, pp. 50, 146.

50 VGM, b5424 (list); b7192 and b7202 (catalogues); b5602 and VGMB, BVG 3465a (catalogues with prices). *Tiende Jaarverslag der Vereeniging 'Voor de Kunst' te Utrecht, 1904–1905*. Utrecht 1905, p. 4.

51 'Wij zijn ontzaggelijk bekoord door onzen aankoop, die in ons huis in hooge eere zal worden gehouden.' A.C. Moll-Fruin to Jo. VGM, b3005; undated (probably October 1905). She continued: 'De verpakking liet wel wat te wenschen over, de twee dunne planken waren met kartonnetjes aan elkaar bevestigd. De lijst der schilderij heeft dan ook nog al geleden.' ('The packaging left much to be desired. The two thin boards were held together with pieces of cardboard so the frame of the painting suffered quite a bit.') Moll-Fruin was a student in Groningen with Johan's sister Fréderique Hamburger-Cohen Gosschalk. See Dorien Daling, *De krans. Hoogleraarsvrouwen in de Groningse academische gemeenschap, 1914–2014*. Hilversum 2014, p. 28. For *Flower Garden* see VGM, b5420 and *Account Book* 2002, pp. 146, 172.

52 A. van der Elst to Jo. VGM, b1952; 11 October 1905. In a copy of the Utrecht catalogue there are sixteen crosses and one crossing out indicating the works that did not continue to Leiden. See VGM, b7202 and the catalogue of the Rotterdam exhibition at Oldenzeel, which followed the one in Leiden.

53 The catalogue is in the RKD.

54 Margareta Oldenzeel-Schot to Jo. VGM, b5426; 11 October—b5427; 19 December 1905—b5428; 8 January—b5430; 17 January—b5432; 26 January 1906.

55 Oldenzeel-Schot sold a further two works. VGM, b5438. *Account Book* 2002, pp. 51, 146, 193. Van Stolk was a board member of the Rotterdamsche Kunstkring from 1903 to 1911.

56 Margareta Oldenzeel-Schot to Jo. VGM, b5540; 13 March 1906.

57 'zeer noodige restauratie of vernis noodig hebben, om ze niet over eenige tijd geheel verloren te laten gaan. Er zijn er die gebarsten zijn zooals de appelen, de koperen ketel (de achtergrond), de violen, waarvoor hier een liefhebber was, maar die bevreesd was het verder zou springen, de lucht van de akkers, e.a. Daar de meeste doeken niet geprepareerd zijn, staat u een of anderen dag voor het feit er een gedeelte verf uitvalt.' 'de blijvende, goede staat der werken op het oog'. Margareta Oldenzeel-Schot to Jo. VGM, b5439; 7 March 1906. In 1901 Mrs van Gogh told Jo that they were in the throes of their annual spring clean. Contemporary restorers will be horrified by their merciless cleaning methods: 'O Jo, de schilderijen van Vincent hangen toch zoo mooi bij ons, Wil heeft die grooten afgesponst en tegen de schoone muren voldoen ze zoo en hangen ze zoo mooi in 't licht.' ('Oh Jo, Vincent's paintings hang so well here. Wil sponged off the large ones and against the clean walls they look so good in the light.') It does not appear that Jo, in so far as she knew better, ever discussed with them the best way to treat the works or told them that too much light was disastrous for the paint. Mrs van Gogh and Willemien to Jo. VGM, b3594 (quotation); 20 April—b3596; 22 April 1901.

58 Mies van Benthem Jutting to Jo. VGM, b1949–51 and b5444–6, between 13 October 1905 and 23 March 1906. Jo had made the proposal for Middelburg before 13 October. In 1905 the society had 162 members. See Ada van Benthem Jutting, *Mies. Een uit de hand gelopen reportage. Over het (on)gewone leven van een Middelburgse boekverkoopster (1876–1928), een vrouw die klaarstond voor de vluchtelingen in de Eerste Wereldoorlog*. Amsterdam 2015, p. 30.

59 VGM, b5443.

60 'hadden op sommige toeschouwers de uitwerking van een rooden lap op een stier, terwijl anderen in diepen eerbied en vol aanbidding het werk tot in de wolken prijzen'; 'dat niet het beste is wat nu is overgebleven'. *Middelburgsche Courant*, 27 March 1906.

61 'inferieur overschot, maar een keus van de beste Van Goghs die thans bij u geëxposeerd zijn en waaronder enige van de *allerbeste* die niet te koop zijn geweest of zullen zijn'. *Middelburgsche Courant*, 29 March 1906.

62 'lief Willetje'; 'in duisternis'. VGM, b1117, b3003 (quotation), b3020 and b2996 respectively.

63 ''t Is me net of ik erg naar een briefke van je verlang?' 'Bedankt voor 't lezen, wat wordt alles gezien en besproken'. Mrs van Gogh to Jo. VGM, b1106; 15 April 1906—b3592; 3 April 1906 respectively. 'gij weet zoo gezellig te schrijven en te vertellen.' Maria van Gogh to Jo. VGM, b2297; 8 February 1906. Her last surviving communication was when Aunt Mietje thanked Jo for the spirea. VGM, b2298; 23 July 1909. She died on 10 April 1911; Jo and Vincent attended her funeral in Leiden.

64 Archive of the SDAP, Federatie Amsterdam 1894–1946, Steunakties, 551. Jo noted the following: 'Ontvangen op de bazaar *f* 438,50 / Afgedragen *f* 270,–'. ('Received at the bazaar 438.50 guilders / Handed over 270.–'.) Theo van Hoytema sent her three of his lithographs—Albert Neuhuys donated a drawing. IISG, 21 and 23 December 1905; 15 May 1906. *Algemeen Handelsblad*, 6, 30 and 31 December 1905; 13 January 1906.

65 Paul Cassirer to Jo. VGM, b4019; 13 September 1905. *Account Book* 2002, pp. 50, 145. VGM, b4020 (catalogue). Her personal list of titles and prices: VGM, b2183. There were forty-seven works from her collection on show in Hamburg. Feilchenfeldt 1988, pp. 20–3. See also Walter Stephan Laux, 'Die Van Gogh-Ausstellung der Galerie Arnold, Dresden 1905', *Oud Holland* 106 (1992), pp. 33–4.

66 VGM, b4021–2.

67 'Ich glaube, Sie sehen, dass es nicht für Sie zum Schade ist, wenn ich Sie hier in Deutschland vertrete.' Paul Cassirer to Jo. VGM, b4026; 23 January 1906.

68 'Ich hoffe ganz bestimmt, dass Sie geschäftskundig genug sind, um diese Gelegenheit nicht vorübergehen zu lassen, und dass Sie mir telegraphisch sofort Ihre Zustimmung melden.' Paul Cassirer to Jo. VGM, b4029; 20 March 1906.

69 Paul Cassirer to Jo. VGM, b4031; 25 September 1906. Theodor Stoperan, a Cassirer authorized signatory, to Jo. VGM, b4035; 5 February 1907. (On the works acquired from Jo that Cassirer sold to Wagram see Cat. Otterlo 2003, pp. 414–18.) In March 1906 Cassirer sent Jo a cheque for 1,190 guilders for the sale of the painting *Field with Green Wheat* (F 807 / JH 1980). (Not recorded in Jo's cash book.) See Feilchenfeldt 2013, p. 264. Cassirer exhibited three works in Posen in Prussia (now Poznań in Poland). VGM, b4030; 11 May 1906. In October Jo received 2,295 guilders for the sale of three paintings. *Account Book* 2002, pp. 51, 147.

70 *Account Book* 2002, pp. 50–1, 146–7. Feilchenfeldt 1988, pp. 22, 145.

71 Paul Cassirer to Jo. VGM, b4026; 23 January 1906. *Account Book* 2002, pp. 51, 146–7.

72 VGM, b4033; 20 November 1906—b3923 (list of prices).

73 VGM, b2202; 7 December 1906. VGM, b4035–6. Cf. Feilchenfeldt 1988, p. 145. *Account Book* 2002, pp. 51, 147–8.

74 'einige Bändchen des grossen Deutschen Nationaldichters'. Paul Cassirer to Jo. VGM, b2960; 4 December 1906.

75 'dass Sie diese Steigerung auch mir gegenüber zum Ausdruck bringen, da ich doch zum nicht geringsten Teil der Veranlasser dieser Steigerung, die hauptsächlich Ihnen zum Vorteil gereicht, bin.' Theodor Stoperan to Jo. VGM, b4035; 7 February—b4036; 13 February 1907 (quotation). *Account Book* 2002, p. 51, 148; VGM, b4038 and b2202.

76 'Ich hoffe aber, dass Sie einsehen dass es richtig ist, mich mit einiger Freundlichkeit zu behandeln. Ich habe doch wahrhaftig grossen Nutzen verschafft.' Paul Cassirer to Jo. VGM, b4037; 16 February (quotation)—b4038; 20 February 1906 (visit).

77 Emile Schuffenecker to Jo. VGM, b1889; 5 April—b1890; 11 April 1906. *Account Book* 2002, pp. 51, 147; VGM, b2179 (titles).

78 Jo to Paul Gachet Jr. VGM, b2138; 20 May 1906.

79 'Je trouve que vous me demandez des prix très forts, mais ce que je tiens à savoir, c'est si vous voulez vendre tout ce qui était à l'Exposition l'année dernière et surtout ceux que vous réserviez pour vous. Si j'achetais en tout pour une grosse somme je désirerai avoir les beaux et moins ceux qui étaient à vendre. Voulez-vous m'écrire un mot pour me dire si dans ces conditions vous consentiriez à vendre tous vos "Van Goghs".' Gaston Bernheim to Jo. VGM, b1959; 9 May 1906. She received a telegram about it on the ninth and the letter on the tenth: VGM, b5744.

80 VGM, b2178. The prices and the names of the buyers during and in the wake of the exhibition, including Cassirer, Bernheim, De Bois, Sternheim, Fayet and the Prince of Wagram. Higher prices were noted in black ink and even higher ones in red ink (this latter category might have been added later). Jo noted alongside twenty-five works that they were no longer for sale. She added the same annotation on the 'Bilder aus Berlin' list for the Emile Richter gallery in Dresden with regard to *Sunflowers* (F 454 / JH 1562), *The Bedroom* (F 482 / JH 1608), *Van Gogh's Chair* (F 498 / JH 1635) and *Self-Portrait as a Painter* (F 522 / JH 1356). VGM, b2191; 24 April 1908.

81 'Je lui ai engagé de ne *pas* venir, parce que je ne désirais nullement me défaire tout d'un coup des tableaux.' Jo to Paul Gachet Jr. VGM, b2138; 20 May 1906.

82 Paul Gachet Jr to Jo. VGM, b3379; 9 May 1906. In 1904 Henk Bremmer instructed the publisher Willem Versluys to issue a portfolio of forty Van Gogh reproductions. It included works from Jo's collection.

83 'mais si son affaire de ces photographies réussira!' Jo to Paul Gachet Jr. VGM, b2138; 20 May 1906.

84 *Het Nieuws van den Dag*, 28 October 1907.

85 VGMB, TS 593 and TS 736. There were notes to eight illustrations stating they were in Jo's collection and referring to her three-volume 1914 edition of the letters.

86 'Ik hoop maar dat die kunsthandel Washington square Gallery eens een flinke bestelling er van doet (*van de foto's*).' Jo to Vincent and Josina. VGM, b3715; 17 April 1916.

87 VGM, b3919–20 (April 1908). *Account Book* 2002, p. 149. On reproduction law: Robert Verhoogt, *Art in Reproduction: Nineteenth-Century Prints After Lawrence Alma-Tadema, Jozef Israëls and Ary Scheffer*. Amsterdam 2007. Cf. also Balk 2006, p. 393.

88 'toute blanche, comme triste'. Émile Bernard to Jo. VGM, b1977; undated (shortly before 22 May)—b1978; 22 May 1906. Bernard 2012, pp. 715–16, 722 (quotation from a letter to Juliette Andrée Fort).

89 Jo to Paul Gachet Sr. VGM, b2139; 22 June 1906: 'C'est toujours chez nous des maladies—vraiment ce n'est pas gai!' ('It's always illnesses in this house—it's really not cheerful!')

90 'gnädige Frau (dit ter eere van je schitterend Duitsch-spreken!)'; 'doe je nu eens echt te goed aan de lekkere lucht zonder je moe te maken met tochten. Is er een bosch om in te liggen?' Johan to Jo. VGM, b7288; 15 August 1906.

91 'Vous ne savez pas combien mon fils, si jeune qu'il soit, partage mes sentiments surtout ce qui touche à l'histoire de son cher père et son oncle vénéré.' 'si seulement nous n'avions pas de malades!' Jo to Paul Gachet Sr. VGM, b2142; 14 November 1906. It was not possible for a meeting of the Sociaal-Democratische Vrouwenpropagandaclub in Jo's flat to go ahead because she was struggling with her health. *Het Volk*, 10 November 1906.

92 Kee Vos-Stricker told aunt Cornélie about Jo's trip. Cornélie van Gogh-Carbentus to Jo. VGM, b3015; 22 January 1907.

93 Gustave Fayet to Jo. VGM, b1961; 20 January—b1962; 23 January—b1963; 27 January 1907. *Account Book* 2002, pp. 51, 147. Fayet's wife and Maurice Fabre travelled with him. See Magali Rougeot, *Gustave Fayet (1865–1925). Itinéraire d'un artist collectionneur*. Paris 2013, pp. 79, 206.

94 'Ik wil maar zeggen, dat als ik in Amsterdam kom, ik helaas nog niet altoos bij U langs de deur ga!' Jan Veth to Johan. VGM, b1403; 15 March 1907.

95 Gaston Bernheim to Jo. VGM, b5746; 4 February 1907.

96 Gaston Bernheim to Jo. VGM, b5747; 9 February 1907. Jo kept a copy of the 1905 catalogue with the name 'Bernheim' written next to the works concerned. VGM, b7194.

97 Gaston Bernheim to Jo. VGM, b5748; 14 February 1907.

98 VGM, b5749–51. The works were in Paris on 19 March 1907 and Jo received a cheque. VGM, b5752. *Account Book* 2002, pp. 52, 148. VGM, b2195 (Jo's list of the works sold to Bernheim).

99 'Ich bitte Sie möglich nur verkäufliche Zeichnungen aus der späteren Zeit zu senden.' Paul Cassirer to Jo. VGM, b4042; 19 November 1907.

100 Paul Cassirer to Jo. VGM, b4044; 30 November 1907. Theodor Stoperan to Jo. VGM, b4043; 22 November 1907—b4045; 8 December 1907.

101 'We weten wel, dat je met je gedachten bij ons zijt; je bent ook altijd voor Moeder zoo lief geweest.' Joan van Houten to Jo. VGM, b3002; 29 April 1907 (quotation)—b2973 (the list).

102 'La mort de ma chère belle mère m'a causé beaucoup de peine et dans les temps de grande émotion il m'est toujours assez difficile d'écrire.' Jo to Paul Gachet Sr. VGM, b2143; 12 June 1907.

103 'Ik denk soms: zou 't niet beter zijn te wachten met 't uitgeven van al de brieven zoolang Moe leeft en dan ook zonder achterhouding, alles.' Willemien van Gogh to Jo. VGM, b2921; 22 May 1893.

104 'Ik hoef je niet te zeggen dat ik hem onuitsprekelijk missen zal.' Jo to Carel Adama van Scheltema. LMDH, LM A 192 B2; 24 August 1907; VGM, Bd97.

105 He wrote the following in his diary on 5 October 1971: 'Gisteren was ook de verjaardag van mijn moeder waaraan ik telkens dacht—veel goeds, maar ook heeft ze het me met de beste bedoelingen wel lastig gemaakt.' ('Yesterday was also my mother's birthday, which I thought about every year—much that was good, but with the best of intentions she certainly made my life difficult.')

106 'een wat andere leiding thuis'. *Vincent's Diary*, 14 October 1967.

107 Vincent Memorandum, 28 August 1965. VGM, b7435: speech given by Vincent at the annual meeting of the Wereldbibliotheek on 25 May 1974.

108 On that organization: *Vincent's Diary*, 3 January 1970.

109 Two postcards from the Gachet family were forwarded to the 'Bonger family' and the 'Bonger ladies' at 6 Poststraat in Zandvoort. VGM, b3354–5. Vincent recalled: 'Mevrouw Jas kwam iedere zomer in Katwijk een keer bij ons.' ('Mrs Jas came to visit us in Katwijk once every summer.') *Vincent's Diary*, 6 November 1933.

110 VGM, b3387; 26 August 1907.

111 'je weet hoe 'n poesenhart ik heb—moederpoes bracht haar 5 jongen ter wereld op mijn mooie nieuwe zomerhoed!!', 'Geloof me Saar, 't zijn de gelukkigste kinderen die zich vrij uit mogen bewegen en uitleven—ze *hoeven* niet te doen als andere kinderen—laten zij zich *zelve* zijn. Je zult zeggen wat een tirade—maar ik logeerde juist eenige dagen bij twee getrouwde vriendinnen van me, die ieder vier kinderen hebben. 't Eene viertal is 'gedresseerd' of opgevoed, 't andere groeide vrij op—de laatste zijn zoo oneindig oorspronkelijker, frisscher, vrolijker en daardoor gelukkiger!' Jo to Sara de Jong-van Houten. VGM, b2281; 17 September 1908. It has not been possible to unearth which friends these were. Seventeen years before Jo had indeed commented that the young Saar had been 'a bit *too well* brought up' ('een beetje *te veel* opgevoed'). Jo to Theo. VGM, b4274; 9 March 1889. *Brief Happiness* 1999, p. 203.

112 'Kinderen is een groote schat en vooral als zij buiten kunnen tieren en opgroeien—dat geeft hun in 't heele leven een ondergrond van frischheid, poëzie en gezondheid, die met geen schatten te betalen is! Alleen is later de overgang van buitenleven naar stadsleven die onvermijdelijk komen moet, wel eens moeilijk—maar verstandige ouders die hun kinderen begrijpen, kunnen daar erg in tegemoet komen en helpen.' 'Ik vind aardig Saar wat je schreef van het boek, dat je belang stelt in het verledene, omdat je dan jezelf beter begrijpt, ja dat is het juist en ik weet zeker dat het je helpen zal in de opvoeding van je kinderen, zoals het mij geholpen heeft mijn Vincent altijd te begrijpen. Jij bent ook een Van Gogh Saar!' Jo to Sara de Jong-van Houten. VGM, b3107; 17 July 1914.

113 Vincent to Sara de Jong-van Houten and to Anna Scholte-van Houten. And their replies. VGM, b4563 and b4564 (both 22 March 1926); b6933 and b8276 (both 24 March 1926).

13 The art dealers Gaston Bernheim, Paul Cassirer and Johannes de Bois

1 Heijbroek and Wouthuysen 1993. Exh. cat. Haarlem 2017.

2 Félix Fénéon to Jo. VGM, b5756; 30 October—b5757; 6 November—b5758; 5 December 1907.

3 VGM, b5755 and b5759 respectively; 2 January 1908. The estate contains a catalogue with prices. VGMB, BVW 362.

4 VGMB, BVG 3444. The catalogue contains passages from letters that were published in *Mercure de France* in 1893. VGM, b7218 (Jo's invitation). Jo also loaned twelve drawings for the '14. Ausstellung der Berliner Secession', which opened in December. See Feilchenfeldt 1988, p. 146.

5 Paul Gachet Jr wrote the following to Jo on a calling card: 'Je viens de voir l'Exposition de Vincent chez Bernheim—il y en a une chez Druet 114 fg. St Honoré—mon père sera à Paris Mercredi 9 Janvier, respectueuses amitiés pour Vous et votre fils. P. Gachet. (Ne parlez pas de moi si vous allez chez Druet).' ('I just saw Vincent's exhibition at Bernheim's—there's one at Druet's, 114 fg. St Honoré—my father will be in Paris on Wednesday, 9 January, with very best wishes to you and your son. P. Gachet. (Don't mention me if you go to Druet's).') VGM, b3425. Jo would have received this communication in Paris, and given that he asked her to give his best wishes to Vincent, we know that her son had accompanied her. Later on, Vincent wrote to Paul Jr: 'J'ai bien songé à la fois que j'ai visité Monsieur votre père (à Paris il y a déjà bien des années).' ('I thought about the time I visited your esteemed father (in Paris many years ago).') VGM, b2808; 4 September 1925. Jo recalled her meeting with Dr Gachet in a letter to his children Paul and Marguerite. VGM, b2146; 13 January 1909.

6 Lies du Quesne-van Gogh to Jo. VGM, b2300; 19 May 1908. The following question, which Gachet Jr asked her shortly afterwards, is an indication of Jo's visit to Druet: 'Ce Portrait est-il le même qu'un intitulé "Gardien de Fous"? (exposé en Janvier dernier chez Druet à Paris).' ('Is this portrait the same as the one titled "Asylum Superintendent" (exhibited last January at Druet's in Paris)?') Paul Gachet Jr to Jo. VGM b3390; undated (shortly after 20 May 1908). Jo knew the names of the exhibited works' owners from the catalogue *Quelques œuvres de Vincent van Gogh* at Galerie Druet (6–18 January 1908): Aubry, Boch, Druet, Fabre, Fayet, De Heymel, Keller, Kessler, Michelot and Schuffenecker.

7 Félix Fénéon to Jo. VGM, b5761; 18 January 1908.

8 Félix Fénéon to Johan. VGM, b5762; 28 January 1908. VGM, b5743 and 5763; the sales were not recorded in the cash book.

9 'Verschiedene Bilder haben Löcher, diese scheinen jedoch älteren Datums zu sein.' Wiedmann to Jo. VGM, b4048; 20 February 1908. See Feilchenfeldt 1988, pp. 66–7.

10 VGM, b4049; 24 February 1908—b4051–b4052 (lists).

11 Paul Cassirer to Jo. VGM, b4053; 10 March 1908—b4054 (the offer)—b4055; 14 April 1908 (the cheque). *Account Book* 2002, pp. 52, 148, 184. Paul Cassirer to Jo. VGM, b4056; 28 April 1908 (the request).

12 'smaken de verboden vruchten het best.' VGM, b3906; 25 November 1907—b3907 and b3909–b3911; 21 March 1908 (forbidden fruit). On Thannhauser's significance in promoting Van Gogh see *Thannhauser Gallery* 2017.

13 'Liebenswürdiges Zuforkommen.' Alexej von Jawlensky to Jo. VGM, b3915; 28 March 1908. VGM, b3914 (payment in instalments). The work cost 1,100 marks, equivalent to 591 guilders. *Account Book* 2002, pp. 52, 127, 148. *Thannhauser Gallery* 2017, pp. 104–5.

14 'grosse Sensation.' Herrmann Holst to Jo. VGM, b3905; 9 May 1908. VGM, b3916 (the request).

15 The cheque was enclosed in the envelope. VGM, b3917; 17 April 1908 and *Account Book* 2002, pp. 52, 148.

16 'Is dat onwrikbaar?' 'of ze zóó uit den goot zijn opgevischt.' Johannes de Bois to Jo. VGM, b5416; 23 July 1908. In September De Bois paid Jo 8,000 guilders for four paintings. Three came from her collection and one from Willemien van Gogh's. *Account Book* 2002, pp. 126, 148–9.

17 Feilchenfeldt 1990, pp. 21–2; Heijbroek and Wouthuysen 1993, pp. 31, 33, 197.

18 Cornélie van Gogh-Carbentus to Jo. VGM, b3019; 3 July 1908. *Account Book* 2002, 1 December 1908.

19 *Account Book* 2002, 1 December 1908. The cash book does not note any other payments to Vincent.

20 There is an overview of the purchases in Cat. Otterlo 2003, pp. 443–6. Rovers 2010, p. 323.

21 Rovers 2010. Ariëtte Dekker, *Leven op krediet: Anton Kröller (1862–1941)*. Amsterdam 2015.

22 'dat de standsbewuste mevrouw Kröller liever niet de trap opklom van een Amsterdams bovenhuis.' Van Straaten in Cat. Otterlo 2003, p. 11.

23 'Wie betaalt, bepaalt.' Rovers 2010, pp. 242–3, 319. Richard Roland Holst was likewise far from enamoured of moneyed art-loving women like Mrs Kröller-Müller. Rovers 2010, pp. 224–5.

24 Van Gogh 1987, p. 5.

25 VGMD; *Account Book* 2002; Cat. Otterlo 2003 and Cat. Otterlo 2007.

26 'Over mijn verzameling heb ik de laatste tijd nog allerlei gedacht & ik ben tot den overtuiging gekomen dat wij nu geen van Goghs meer moeten kopen, of er moet zich dan iets heel bijzonders voordoen.... Maar over 't algemeen denk ik zoo: Wij hebben een heele van Gogh rijkdom, met Mevrouw Cohen den grootsten der wereld. Klinkt dat niet trotsch? Wij hebben van Goghen uit alle tijden ... & men kan zijn ontwikkeling zoowel in zijn capaciteit als schilder goed volgen.' Helene Kröller-Müller to Anton Kröller. Kröller-Müller Museum Archive, inv. no. HA502195; 11 January 1913. With thanks to Eva Rovers.

27 *Account Book* 2002, pp. 52, 149; Cat. Otterlo 2003, pp. 181–4.

28 'Ik geloof aan een groter voortbestaan van mijzelf in mijn geestelijk leven, dan in de materie die ik achterliet, ik geloof dat de geestelijke bouw, dien ik achterliet zekerder vruchten zal brengen, dan de stoffelijkheid die ik kon geven door de kinderen.' 'de mensch is toch per slot wat hij achterlaat.' Helene Kröller-Müller to Sam van Deventer. Kröller-Müller Museum Archive, 23 November 1913 and 27 February 1913 respectively. See Rovers 2010, pp. 189, 217.

29 'alle beste Van Goghs op te sporen'. Between 1892 and 1904 Nijland acquired 122 drawings and watercolours, two lithographs and two paintings by Van Gogh. See Rovers 2010, pp. 189–91, 241.

30 'Ist der Herr verrückt geworden?' Paul Cassirer to Jo. VGM, b4075; 18 December 1910. See also Balk 2006, p. 408; Rovers 2010, esp. pp. 96–106 (quotations on 98–9), 194–5. The court found in Cassirer's favour, without doubt on the grounds of Jo's declaration: 'In dem Prozess Kröller-Bremmer hat das Gericht zu meinem Gunsten entschieden. Die Klage der Frau Kröller ist auf Grund Ihrer Aussage glatt abgewiesen worden.' ('In the Kröller-Bremmer trial, the court ruled in my favour. The action brought by Mrs Kröller has been rejected outright on the basis of your testimony.') Theodor Stoperan (Cassirer's employee) to Jo. VGM, b3986; 2 March 1912.

31 Balk 2006, p. 241.

32 'Die beiden Frauen ... sahen sich als Konkurrentinnen—obwohl sie beide maßgeblich zu seinem Nachruhm beitrugen.... Die Konkurrenz zwischen beiden war so groß, dass sie kaum miteinander sprachen.' Stefan Koldehoff, *Ich und Van Gogh. Bilder, Sammler und ihre abenteuerlichen Geschichten*. Berlin 2015, p. 79.

33 Rovers 2010, pp. 184–5, 189, 192–5; Heijbroek 2012, p. 369.

34 Rovers 2010, pp. 208, 295.

35 *Account Book* 2002, pp. 124–31; Rovers 2010, pp. 195–6.

36 *Account Book* 2002, p. 28; Cat. Otterlo 2003, p. 414; Rovers 2010, pp. 194–5. Berthier's sister, Elisabeth de Gramont, reported that in 1908 he owned forty-seven Van Gogh paintings, but only twenty-two of them could be identified.

See Elisabeth de Gramont, *Souvenirs du monde de 1890 à 1940*. Paris 1966, p. 219; M.G. de la Coste Messelière, 'Un jeune prince amateur d'impressionnistes et chauffeur', *L'Œil*, no. 179 (November 1969), p. 24.

37 Mien Bonger to Jo. VGM, b3622; 11 August 1908.

38 VGM, b5415, b5403 and b2068. Heijbroek and Wouthuysen 1993, p. 29. *Account Book* 2002, pp. 52–3, 149.

39 'Zou het geen tijd worden, nu er nog belangrijk werk van Van Gogh te krijgen is, dat onze museumbesturen er de hand op legden? Te beginnen bijv. met dat sterk aangrijpende zelfportret uit 1889/90, hetwelk ook om zijn kompleetheid zich voor een behoud in het geboorteland des kunstenaars zoo bijzonder leent.' See also Heijbroek and Wouthuysen 1993, p. 29.

40 H.L. Klein to Jo. VGM, b5417; 15 September 1908—b5418 (the final price).

41 VGM, b4058; October 1908 (list); Feilchenfeldt 1988, p. 147.

42 '18 Februari beantwoord—50 sch. terug—de andere 50 tot 1 mei.' VGM, b4059; 13 February 1909—b4061; 17 March 1909.

43 'Oh quel bon ami il s'est toujours montré pour la famille van Gogh.' 'Vous avez fait *tout* pour lui—Il y a peu d'enfants qui ont cette satisfaction d'avoir si bien fait leur devoir envers leur parents!' Jo to Marguerite and Paul Gachet. VGM, b2146; 13 January 1909.

44 Paul Gachet to Jo. VGM, b3392; 21 January 1909.

45 Gachet 1956, pp. 12, 140–1.

46 'Dat er aan ons geluk ontbrak, omdat ik, ook—o.a. door mijn gezondheid en eigenaardigheden, in veel te kort moest schieten, dat erkende ik reeds.—Er is geen sprake van, dat ik dit niet inzie en dat ik mij zou schamen dit volmondig toe te geven. Maar—dat ik *schuld* zou hebben, in den zin, dat mij hierin iets als ernstig *verwijt* mag worden toegerekend, dat geloof ik niet. . . . Ik leef altijd in hoop op verbetering, maar ik zou in het vervolg niet in angst voor nieuwe krisissen om die reden moeten leven. Ik zeg dit openhartig, want ook ik voel, zooals jij, dat wij niet nóg eens hetzelfde moeten doormaken.' Johan to Jo. VGM, b7289; 17 January 1909. The sum concerned was 220 guilders.

47 'Natuurlijk zeg je terecht dat we van mijn inkomsten op geen stukken na konden leven *als nu*.' Johan to Jo. VGM, b7290; 19 January 1909. Johan noted down all the income from his articles and reviews. VGM, b7362.

48 'We moeten dan maar niet meer bespiegelen—en met nieuwe moed beginnen en trachten het samen goed te hebben.' Ibid.

49 'Die Jonkheer is toch een uil—(en een aanmatigende) om nooit van Sisley gehoord te hebben.' Ibid.

50 'Weet je niet dat we altijd zeiden, dat het de eerste stap tot een auto was, om alvast een rijtuig-stoof te hebben?' Johan to Jo. VGM, b7291; 23 January 1909. He was fascinated by cars and hoped a 'car shop' would open in Laren. VGM, b7292; 26 January 1909; b7293; 17 September 1909 ('auto-winkel').

51 'C'est bien ainsi qu'on écrit l'histoire!' Jo to Paul Gachet. VGM, b2147; 1 March 1909.

52 'Voor ditmaal zullen we het dus maar weer afzoenen nie-waar?' 'En geen rancune om zooveel snoodheid.' Johan to Jo. VGM, b7293; 17 September 1909.

53 Jo to Fritz Meyer-Fierz. VGMD (copy). Meyer-Fierz purchased the painting from C.M. van Gogh. *Thannhauser Gallery* 2017, p. 162.

54 Johannes de Bois to Jo. VGM, b5405; 15 March 1909. *Account Book* 2002, pp. 148–9.

55 'Wie Sie wissen, hat die Veröffentlichung der Briefe in Deutschland sehr viel dazu beigetragen, dass die Kunst van Goghs bei uns Boden fasste, und es ist anzunehmen, dass die Veröffentlichung weiterer Briefe in demselben Sinne wirken wird.' Bruno Cassirer to Jo. VGM, b3946. 4 May 1909.

56 'Die holländisch geschriebenen mussten wir allerdings in deutscher Übersetzung haben.' Bruno Cassirer to Jo. VGM, b3948; 7 June 1909.

57 'Ich weiss nicht, weshalb Sie immer wieder mit diesem seltsamen Misstrauen kommen. Haben Sie schlechte Geschäfte mit mir gemacht? Oder finden Sie, dass die Ausstellung bei mir und mein ganzes Verhalten für den Ruf von van Gogh ungünstig gewesen sind? Sie sagten mir damals, dass der Geldpunkt für Sie keine grosse Wichtigkeit bei der Veröffentlichung haben könnte.' Paul Cassirer to Jo. VGM, b4063; 13 May—b3979; 22 May 1909 (quotation).

58 Paul Cassirer to Jo. VGM, b3982; 14 June 1909.

59 Bruno Cassirer to Johan. VGM, b3956; 8 July—b3957; undated (shortly after 8 July 1910).

60 Bruno Cassirer to Jo. VGM, b3950; 28 September 1909. The letters are in the 1914 first edition of *Künstlerbriefe* on pp. 678–91; in the 1919 second edition on pp. 638–51.

61 Jo to Paul Gachet. VGM, b2148; 22 November 1909. She thought the portrait was 'bien beau' ('very good'). Julius Meier-Graefe had written to Jo about it in 1903 and had made a sketch of it. VGM, b7590; 2 August 1903.

62 Paul Gachet to Jo. VGM, b3393; 29 November 1909.

63 'Si c'était possible je voudrais le racheter—je l'aimais tant ce tableau!' Jo to Paul Gachet. VGM, b2150; 1 December 1909.

64 'trop peut-être, car de tous les portraits de *notre* collection, je n'en ai jamais vendu un—d'où proviennent ils donc? Mais c'est vrai que Vincent était très généreux, que Bernard, que Gauguin—et beaucoup d'autres peintres ont eu des portraits de lui. Enfin on ne sait jamais!' Jo to Paul Gachet. VGM, b2148; 22 November 1909. Van Gogh, *Letters* 2009, letters 781 and 855 respectively. The catalogue is *Cinquante tableaux de Vincent van Gogh*: VGMB, BVG 3446 (the exhibition took place in November 1909). In the end Jo sold at least twenty portraits and heads, as well as four self-portraits, by Van Gogh. *Account Book* 2002.

65 'C'est le premier fois qu'on le verra dans notre musée!' Jo to Paul Gachet. VGM, b2150; 1 December 1909. See Heijbroek 1991, pp. 163–6–4; E.P. Engel, 'Het ontstaan van de verzameling Drucker-Fraser in het Rijksmuseum', *Bulletin van het Rijksmuseum* 13 (1965), pp. 45–66. Jo requested the temporary return of the self-portrait on 3 March 1914. Vincent renewed the loan agreement for the three works in January 1926 and November 1927: VGM, b5450 and b5459.

66 'In deze nuchtere omgeving, met goed staand licht, hangen de hevigen, als Sisley, Cezanne, Vincent van Gogh, als in nuchtere cellen.' *Algemeen Handelsblad* , 12 December 1909.

67 'La maison Bernheim-Jeune l'éditerait volontiers de même qu'elle a déjà édité un ouvrage important sur Eugène Carrière.' Félix Fénéon to Jo. VGM, b2180; 31 October 1909. On 12 November Jo recorded 10,092 guilders and on 8 February a further 10,105 guilders. *Account Book* 2002, pp. 52–3, 149–50. VGM, b5768; 4 February 1910. On the French edition of the letters: VGM, b5766; 20 November 1909. Fénéon got back to her three years later to ask her to send a copy of her publication as soon as it appeared: VGM, b5773; 5 June 1912.

68 Jo adjusted a few prices upwards when the works were shipped to Brakl. VGM, b2201 and b2182 (the return list). Johan also noted everything down. The lower prices on his list show that it was made first. VGM, b2204. They tried to sort the prices out together, as can be seen from an overview, which is a complete hotchpotch in pencil. VGM, b4058 *verso*.

69 'Verbiete jede Restauration der Bilder und verlange erst Aufgabe der Kosten von Rahmenbeschädigung.' VGM, b3845, b3846 and b3848 (telegram).

70 'Ich brauche nicht zu sagen wie sehr Ich enttäuscht bin. Ich meinte man würde die kostbaren Bilder, die Ich Ihnen anvertraute, mit Sorgfalt behandeln. Ich werde in Dresden die Schade taxieren lassen und stelle Ihnen verantwortlich dafür.' VGM, b3875; 12 February 1910 (carbon copy).

71 'ziemlich direkt aufeinander gelegt'; 'eine sehr vornehme Dame'. Franz Brakl to Frankfurter Kunstverein. VGM, b3876; 17 February 1910. Carl Marcus to Jo. VGM, b3878; 18 February 1910.

72 Marcus sold *Portrait of a Woman* (F 357 / JH 1216) for 1,800 guilders. VGM, b3877–82. Marie Held stated that the mats of the drawings needed replacing and she tried to get a discount. On the letter Jo noted 'Antwort: Kleine Reduction bei Gesamtpreis' ('Answer: small reduction in total price'). Marie Held to Jo. VGM, b3860; 1 February—b3861; 15 February 1910 (including Jo's answer). Held sold two drawings for 949 guilders. One of them was Gauguin's *L'Arlésienne, Madame Ginoux*, which was thought to be by Van Gogh. VGM, b3862-b3863. *Account Book* 2002, pp. 53, 150, 200.

73 Ernst Arnold to Jo. VGM, b3850; 14 March 1910—b3851 (new crate).

74 Gustav Gerstenberger to Jo. VGM, b3836; 6 April 1910.

75 'in welk geval wij gaarne met onze winst het op een accoordje brengen'. 'Ook zou ik nog gaarne van U vernemen of het groote "Montmartre" verkocht mag worden en tegen welken prijs. Bij mijn laatste bezoek beloofdet U mij daarover met uwen zoon te spreken.' Johannes de Bois to Jo. VGM, b5396; 21 January 1910, giving the prices (*Vegetable Gardens in Montmartre* was sold in 1913; see also Chapter 15, p. 286–7.). Cf. *Account Book* 2002, pp. 53, 150. He went on a selling trip and wanted to make agreements beforehand. Johannes de Bois to Jo. VGM, b5398; 14 February 1910.

76 'Zij en ik hebben na mijn meerderjarigheid een regeling getroffen over ons gezamenlijk bezit.' ('After I attained my majority, she and I came to an arrangement concerning our joint property.') VGMD, memorandum by Vincent; 27 May 1977.

77 'Vermoedelijk hebt U geen bezwaar ons te helpen, al was Uw laatste voornemen voorloopig het rondzenden te staken.' Johannes de Bois to Jo. VGM, b5399; 31 March 1910. Albert Reballio to Jo. VGM, b5466; 29 March 1910.

78 *Account Book* 2002, pp. 53, 150.

79 VGM, b3894; 22 November 1909. Max Liebermann to Jo. VGM, b3895; 19 November 1909. The works were not for sale. VGM, b2203. See also Feilchenfeldt 1988, p. 147.

80 Jo paid 2,000 guilders for the plot in February and a further 2,000 guilders in April. *Account Book* 2002, p. 128. Van Gogh 1987. On the water reservoir: Bonger 1986, p. 489 and verbal communication from Johan van Gogh, 9 September 2007.

81 'Beschik over ons als je hier mocht komen wonen, op elk uur van den dag; kunnen wij ooit met iets helpen b.v. bij onverwachte bezoeken met onze provisiekast: hij staat voor je open.' Ant de Witt Hamer to Jo. VGM, b9053; 16 November 1909.

82 'Jelui huis vliegt de lucht in, het atelierraam en de andere staan er al in.' Henriëtte van der Meij to Jo. VGM, b9056; 29 March 1910.

83 'zenuwmenschen'. Henriëtte van der Meij to Jo. IISG, 30 April 1906.

84 VGM, b2219.

85 Ant de Witt Hamer to Jo. VGM, b9057; 8 April 1910.

86 'De tuin was toen, behalve achter het huis, één groot lupine-veld. 't Was altijd een heele feestdag.' *Vincent's Diary*, 4 October 1933. A few years after that he reminisced: 'Vandaag was de verjaardag van mijn moeder—dat geeft de herinnering aan iets feestelijks. . . . Hoe gezellig was zo'n feestdag. Met liefde denk ik aan haar.' ('Today was my mother's birthday--that makes me recall something festive. . . . Such a celebration was such fun. I think of her with love.') *Vincent's Diary*, 4 October 1939.

87 *Vincent's Diary*, 13 September 1933. *De Gooi- en Eemlander*, 24 September 1910 and 18 March 1911. The maid was paid 130 guilders a year.

88 Wally Moes to Johan. VGM, b1411; 16 November 1909. 'binnenrollen' through their 'gastvrij hekje'. Wally Moes to Jo and Johan. VGM, b1412; 18 November 1910.

89 'De andere (Lizzy Ansingh o.a., waar mijn moeder ook zo op gesteld was) zijn te precieus, van een conservatief burgerlijke mentaliteit die niet te harden is.' *Vincent's Diary*, 27 December 1935. In the summer of 1910, the composer Alphons Diepenbrock and his wife Elisabeth de Jong van Beek en Donk moved into their house in De Drift in Laren. It is not known whether Jo met them at the time. The same applies to the American art collector William Singer, who in 1911 moved into Villa De Wilde Zwanen, part of the current Singer Museum, with his wife Anna Spencer Brugh. The artist couple Sara de Swart and Emilie van Kerckhoff also lived in the village. De Swart and Jo knew each other. Cf. Lien Heyting, *De wereld in een dorp. Schilders, schrijvers en wereldverbeteraars in Laren en Blaricum, 1880–1920*. Amsterdam 1994.

90 Henriëtte van der Meij to Jo. VGM, b9056; 29 March 1910. For Tussenbroek see *BWN* and Bosch 2005, pp. 296–301.

91 'Mochten de witte lijsten door het vervoer vuil zijn geworden, wilt U ze dan wat laten opknappen van mij?' Jo to Albert Reballio. SAR, Rotterdamsche Kunstkring Archive, 76, no. 303c; 5 June 1910. Jo's list is VGM, b2200.

92 'in het doek van bloeiende tak zit een gaatje, dit is U bekend?' VGM, b5467; 9 June 1910. The work in question was *Almond Blossom* (F 671 / JH 1891).

93 'Hij hoort zoo innig bij de geheele familie. Heerlijk hij al een mensch is en geheel met je mee voelt.' Kee Vos-Stricker to Jo. VGM, b2806; 20 July 1910. Cf. VGM, b2985 ('aanvallen'), b2986 and b2991. On 29 November 1911 Jo had new planting put on the family grave in Zorgvlied cemetery, where Mien was buried alongside her parents. VGM, b7341.

94 'Door kunstzin en door handelsgeest geleid, meer nog gedreven door een gevoel van innige piëteit, heeft de tactvolle hand eener vrouw het schier onmogelijke gedaan voor deze kunst, er voor baan gebroken dwars door een muurharde conventie heen, die deze kunst aanvankelijk had uitgeworpen als 'geene kunst' zijnde.' Du Quesne-Van Gogh 1910, pp. 97–8. Jo's comments ('geheel verzonnen', 'bespottelijk overdreven', 'volkomen onware veronderstelling', 'onzin', 'huichelarij') on pp. 25, 28, 30, 35, 38 and 54 in the copy VGMB, BVW 178. As he grew older Vincent likewise could not refrain from writing these types of critical comments in the margins of his books.

95 Willem Steenhoff, *De Amsterdammer*, 18 December 1910.

96 'grove ijdelheid'; 'een van de ergerlijkste en onbeduidendste'. J. Greshoff, 'Rond Vincent', *Onze Kunst* 10, no. 2 (1911), pp. 73–6.

97 'reeks van corrigenda'. Johan de Meester was the only one to reveal Jo's name as the source in 'Over kunstenaar-zijn en Vincent van Gogh', *De Gids* 75 (May 1911), pp. 274–92, esp. pp. 289–92.

98 Van Gogh 1914, p. xx [= 20].

99 Hulsker 1990, p. 5, n. 4. See also Molegraaf 2012, pp. 31–3. Lies clearly based the title of her new edition in 1923 (*haar broeder [Her Brother]*) on that of Jo's letters edition (*zijn broeder [His Brother]*).

14 Contracts for publication of Van Gogh's letters

1 Paul Cassirer to Jo. VGM, b3983; 27 June—b3984; 25 July 1910.

2 VGMD, 25 July 1910 (copy). Cassirer had recommended Klein-Diepold as a translator to Jo years before. VGM, b4039; 19 March 1907. Klein-Diepold, whose wife Hermina Tappenbeck was Dutch, lived in Noordwijk aan Zee. He had been hoping to work from a typed version of the transcripts, but that was not yet available. He visited Jo because he was not always able to decipher her writing. Leo Klein-Diepold to Jo. VGM, b6870; 15 September—b2953; 30 November 1910.

3 The documents are in VGM, b6870. Jo to J.G. Robbers. VGM b6870; 6 May (draft)—25 June (draft)—5 July 1910. J.G. Robbers to Jo. VGM, b6870; 12 May (quotation)—27 April—25 June (Robbers's secretary)—8 July 1910. Jo to the editors of WB. VGM, b6849; 17 August 1910 (draft).

4 'meer ontwikkelden met beperkte inkomens'. See De Glas 1989, pp. 65–92; quotation on p. 92.

5 These documents, from the 1910–1925 period, are all filed under VGM, b6849–6850. According to Vincent in his presentation at the annual general meeting of the WB on 25 May 1974, Jo had involved her son in the discussions with Simons (VGM, b7435).

6 The amounts are rounded. Cf. also *Account Book* 2002, p. 20.

7 Félix Fénéon to Jo. VGM, b5771; 8 October—b5772; 20 October 1910. Anna Gruetzner Robins, 'Marketing Post-Impressionism: Roger Fry's Commercial Exhibitions', in *The Rise of the Modern Market in London, 1850–1939*. Eds. Pamela Fletcher and Anne Helmreich. Manchester and New York 2013, pp. 85–97.

8 Desmond MacCarthy to Jo. VGM, b5863; 19 October 1910 (titles)—b5865; 1 November 1910 (prices). Johannes de Bois to Jo. VGM, b5400; 21 October 1910. On the later shipment: VGM, b5868. See also Heijbroek and Wouthuysen 1993, p. 193.

9 University of Indiana. Lilly Library, MacCarthy MS. Also included in Bailey 2010, p. 798.

10 VGM, b5866.

11 Desmond MacCarthy, 'The Art-Quake of 1910', *The Listener*, 1 February 1945, pp. 123–9; quotation on p. 124. See also Bailey 2010, p. 795.

12 VGM, b5859 and VGMB, BVG 5070 (catalogue). This garbled version is in the 1911 London edition, p. vii. Jo received an enquiry about whether they could make colour reproductions of the *Self-Portrait* and the *Irises*. VGM, b5871.

13 Anna Gruetzner Robins, *Modern Art in Britain, 1910–1914*. London 1996, pp. 35–40, 187–8; exh. cat. Compton Verney 2006, p. 22; Bailey 2010.

14 Desmond MacCarthy to Jo. VGM, b5870; 9 January 1911. Redon felt honoured by the article that Johan had written about his work in *Elsevier's Geïllustreerd Maandschrift* 19, no. 8 (1909), pp. 72–6. Odilon Redon to Johan. VGM, b1333; 13 August 1909. The artist was also taken with Johan's article 'Odilon Redon' in *Zeitschrift für Bildende Kunst* 46, no. 3 (1910), pp. 61–70: VGM, b1279. For Andries see *Redon and Bernard* 2009.

15 Desmond MacCarthy to Jo. VGM, b5867; 9 December 1910. Cat. Amsterdam 1987, p. 27.

16 Ellen Duncan to Jo. VGM, b6026; 10 January—b6027; 13 January—b6028; 27 January 1911. Fanny Dove Hamel Calder to Jo. VGM, b1958; undated (about Liverpool).

17 On these collectors: exh. cat. Compton Verney 2006.

18 'vreemdelingen ook op dat gebied iets te kunnen toonen'. VGM, b5391, b5393, b5394 (quotation) and b5395. *Account Book* 2002, pp. 53, 151.

19 'Vermoedelijk zult U over onze werkzaamheid voldaan zijn, en mogen wij dus uwerzijds weer op mede werking rekenen als wij U verzoeken.' Johannes de Bois to Jo. VGM, b5401; 1 November 1910. He paid her 4,652 guilders. He also reported that he had sold a further two paintings for 6,000 guilders. All four went to the Kröller-Müllers. *Account Book* 2002, pp. 53, 150. See also Heijbroek and Wouthuysen 1993, pp. 31–2.

20 The purchase took place on 29 December 1910. *Account Book* 2002, pp. 53, 151.

21 *Account Book* 2002, pp. 53, 150.

22 The list of what she held back is VGM, b4064. Theodor Stoperan to Jo. VGM, b4074; 8 November 1910 ('gefälligst umgehend'). She received a copy of the catalogue: VGM, b4073.

23 Bruno Cassirer to Jo. VGM, b3960; 21 November—b3961; 10 December 1910 (the prints).

24 'Ja er is veel droefheid en veel ellende maar ook heel veel vreugde.' Emilie Knappert to Jo. VGM, b5472. There were twenty paintings and twelve drawings on display: VGM, b1953 and b2198. Cf. Kramers et al. 1982, pp. 102–5.

25 VGM, b4076; 24 December 1910. VGM, b3018 (Vincent in Amsterdam).

26 Exh. cat. Bremen 2002. *Account Book* 2002, p. 144.

27 *De Gids* 75 (1911), pp. 274–85.

28 'À Madame Van Gogh, Hommage de l'éditeur Vollard.' VGMB, BVG 1241a.

29 'wel de schoonste bladzijden gegeven die over Vincent geschreven zijn', *Brieven* 1914, vol. 1, p. l [= 50] in the foreword). Earlier Bernard had approached her with the idea of publishing a complete letters edition in the *Mercure*. His plan was to publish everything that he had written about Van Gogh. Émile Bernard to Jo. VGM, b834; 4 January 1910.

30 J. Cohen Gosschalk-Bonger, 'The Letters of Vincent van Gogh', *The Burlington Magazine for Connoisseurs* 18, no. 94 (January 1911), p. 236.

31 Van Gogh 1914, letter 418. Van Gogh, *Letters* 2009, letter 515.

32 'Nu mag wel eens als curiositeit gepubliceerd worden, hoe in den zomer van 1911 schrijver dezer zich tot (toen nog) mevrouw Cohen Gosschalk wendde met een nagenoeg onbeperkte volmacht van een lastgever, die juist deze collectie in haar geheel voor zijn museum wilde bezitten. Maar bot ving en ondanks de inderdaad bijster hooge offerte die hij maken mocht, met een kalmen glimlach, vastberaden naar huis werd gestuurd. Een zo ge wilt commerciële nederlaag, die echter mijn respect voor haar, die mijn aanbod afsloeg, nog vermeerderde.' *Haarlemsche Courant*, 23 March 1918.

33 'Elle a refusé de vendre à Mme Kröller toute l'œuvre de Vincent, bien que Mme Kröller fit l'offre d'une somme illimitée!' VGM, b3348, p. 20. See Zwikker 2021. Cf. the comment, referred to above, that Helene made to her husband Anton in 1913: 'I've come to the conclusion that we shouldn't buy any more Van Goghs now, unless something really special turns up. . . . We have a real wealth of Van Gogh's work, the largest in the world along with Mrs Cohen.' Helene Kröller-Müller to Anton Kröller. Kröller-Müller Museum Archives, inv. no. HA502195; 11 January 1913. Coquiot loathed the Köllers' overwhelming wealth. He had been to The Hague, where he had stood outside their mansion in Lange Voorhout, but found it closed. He was not sorry: 'Ces collections à coups de millions me dégoûtent.' ('I detest such collections, created by spending millions.'). VGM b3348, on a separate sheet, in front of p. 20. At that time the Kröller-Müllers had twelve Van Goghs. Rovers 2010, p. 155.

34 'doet de warmte nog al aan.' Jo to Vincent. VGM, b2088; undated (before 20 August)—b2087; 20 August 1911.

35 Johannes de Bois to Jo. VGM, b5480; 15 October 1911.

36 Johannes de Bois to Jo. VGM, b5482; 8 February 1912—b5494 (list of works). On New York: VGM, b5481; 22 December 1911.

37 Johannes de Bois to Jo. VGM, b5483; 1 March 1912. *Account Book* 2002, pp. 54, 151. *Thannhauser Gallery* 2017, p. 112.

38 Heijbroek and Wouthuysen 1993, pp. 191–207. *Account Book* 2002, p. 28.

39 'Die Cypressen wirken wie eine Fanfare—herrlich!' He sent a bill of exchange for 2,400 guilders. Klas Walter Fåhraeus to Jo. VGM, b6031; 12 December—b6032; 29 December 1911. The book was probably the first volume of Karl Wåhlin, *Ernst Josephson, 1851–1906: en minnesteckning*. 2 vols. Stockholm 1911–12. In 1946 Vincent donated Josephson's sketch to the Nationalmuseum in Stockholm.

40 'Antw. 27 Febr. in de veiling opnemen.' Firma R.W.P. de Vries to Jo. VGM, b8543; 29 December 1911. Two Van Gogh prints went under the hammer in November 1912. See Van Heugten and Pabst 1995, pp. 89 and 93.

41 Carl Marcus to Jo. VGM, b3889; 23 January 1912. Jo noted 2,943 guilders in her cash book in February. *Account Book* 2002, pp. 130, 151.

42 'Cela restera toujours un mystère.' Jo to Paul Gachet. VGM, b2151; 15 February 1912.

43 'Je vous assure que cela me donne énormément d'ouvrage et j'en aurai encore pour bien longtemps—car quoique le manuscript est prêt maintenant (il y avait 638 lettres et la plupart pas datées) je dois encore ajouter des notes et puis corriger toutes les épreuves.' Jo to Paul Gachet. VGM, b2153; 27 February 1912 (the number of 638 she mentioned should have been 658). See Chapter 6 for the tension between those involved. According to Gachet, Van Gogh had been perfectly calm when he decided to kill himself. He insisted that Jo leave the passage about his father (the current letter 877) intact. At that time Gachet also owned Vincent's letter to Aurier, which Theo had given Gachet Sr (the current letter 853; in the collection of the Van Gogh Museum since April 2019). Paul Gachet to Jo. VGM, b3397; 4 March 1912.

44 *Algemeen Handelsblad*, 18 and 20 May 1912.

45 *NRC*, 19 May 1912; *Algemeen Handelsblad*, 20 May 1912; *De Tijd*, 21 May 1912. VGM, b2154 (the card).

46 'zwaarwichtige inspanning'; 'En zoo, in gestadige zelfkritiek arbeidende, was hij zeer ongemakkelijk jegens zichzelf.' *Tentoonstelling der nagelaten werken van Johan Cohen Gosschalk*. Inleiding Willem Steenhoff. Amsterdam 1912, p. 5–6. VGMB, BVG 8182.

47 *De Amsterdammer*, 26 May 1912; later he wrote for *Onze Kunst* 11, second half of the year (1912), pp. 31–2.

48 'Wat was hij knap, wat was hij de zelfde in zijn werk als in persoon, zoo in fijn en toch op tijd krachtig. . . . Ge deedt er een groot en goed werk aan al die schatten in wijder kring te leeren kennen, ook ter zijner waardeering.' Kee Vos-Stricker to Jo. VGM, b3598; 30 November 1912.

49 'Het werk doet in die intieme zaaltjes wel fijn, vindt U niet?' 'Misschien hing er zelfs iets te veel, dacht ik.' Johannes de Bois to Jo. VGM, b5488; 11 December 1912. VGMB, BVG 8182 (the catalogue) and VGM, b7367 (the handwritten list of seventy-one works).

50 'ganschelijk onopzichtig leven.' *Elsevier's Geïllustreerd Maandschrift* 23 (1913), pp. 194–5.

51 'aristocratie van geest en gemoed.' Jan Veth to Jo. VGM, b1406; 23 February 1913.

52 *Algemeen Handelsblad* and *NRC*, both 12 April 1913. An illustration in exh. cat. Assen 1991, p. 20. Mrs Cohen Gosschalk, Johan's mother, contributed by establishing a fund—she donated 3,000 guilders and the interest was to be used to award the annual Johan Henri Gustave Cohen Gosschalk Prize to a student at the National Academy of Visual Arts in Amsterdam. *Het Nieuws van den Dag* and the *Algemeen Handelsblad*, both 15 July 1913, and *De Tijd*, 9 July 1914 (the amount).

53 'Het was Mevr. Cohen Gosschalk die exposeerde, zich pour la raison de la cause nog eens noemende van Gogh-Bonger en daarmede negerende haar 2[e] huwelijk met den achtbaren Israëlitischen werker Cohen Gosschalk, van wie zij in hoofdzaak erfgename was.' Elisabeth du Quesne-van Gogh to Benno J. Stokvis; 15 February 1923.

54 'Het tweede huwelijk van mijn moeder bracht haar niet wat zij ervan verwachtte. Haar man was een sterk neuroticus. . . . Sinds zijn ziekte is Cohen Gosschalk altijd blijven sukkelen met zijn gezondheid. Hij raakte door zijn zwaar op de hand zijn langzamerhand al zijn bekenden kwijt, die hem niet meer wilden opzoeken. . . .

Zij heeft haar echtgenoot de grootste zorg en toewijding gegeven. Zij en hij hadden ieder een bescheiden inkomen. In zijn familie had hij alleen kontakt met zijn jongere zuster Meta, de moeder van Johan Franco, die ook schilderes was, en met zijn zwager Prof. Hamburger. Met zijn moeder en oudere broer onderhield hij geen kontakt. Na hun overlijden heeft mijn moeder uit gevoelsargumenten het haar toekomende deel van de nalatenschap niet willen aanvaarden. Zij en ik hebben na mijn meerderjarigheid een regeling getroffen over ons gezamenlijk bezit; zij heeft haar bescheiden leven kunnen voortzetten, toen mijn opvoeding achter de rug was. . . . Achteraf bezien had zij de nalatenschappen van de familie van haar tweede echtgenoot best kunnen gebruiken om haar leven wat makkelijker te maken; zij had van die kant ook genoeg narigheid meegemaakt. Zij heeft echter de voldoening van onafhankelijkheid beleefd. De verwijzing in de brief van mevr. Du Quesne-van Gogh naar een erfenis, waarvan zij leefde, houdt geen steek.' VGMD, memorandum 27 May 1977. Cf. *Vincent's Diary*, 22 April 1975: 'Mijn moeder beging vroeger de fout niets te willen ontvangen van de naalaatingschap van de moeder van mijn stiefvaader. Ze had er volkoomen recht op want ze verzorgde hem tot en met zonder enig genot terug behalve de huiselijke, ten deele onmoogelijke sfeer (hij ging heele winters de deur niet uit e.d.). Van mijn moeder's kant was dat een misplaatste trots—het zou haar het leeven iets vergemakkelijkt hebben.' ('My mother previously made the mistake of not wanting to receive the estate of my step-father's mother. She was perfectly entitled to it because she had cared for him until the end without getting any pleasure in return except the domestic, sometimes impossible atmosphere (he stayed indoors all winter etc.). That was misplaced pride on my mother's part—it would have made her life a bit easier.')

55 SSAN, NNAB. Archive of the notary Sytse Scheffelaar Klots 1892–1925, inv. no. 53, deed no. 7523. The blue Delft cows graced the mantelpiece in the living room. VGM, b7339–42. The inheritance tax Jo had to pay was calculated a year later; it worked out at 1,514 guilders. VGM, b7343; 12 April 1913.

56 'cruellement frappé.' Jo to Paul Gachet. VGM, b2160; 16 June 1913.

57 VGM, b3815, b3812 and b3816. Feilchenfeldt 1988, p. 149. A reconstruction in exh. cat. Cologne 2012, pp. 542–3. J.H. de Bois also sent in paintings that he had received from Jo on commission.

58 On 28 June, Jo received a telegram from Cologne reporting that *Young Man with a Cap* (F 536 / JH 1648) had been sold for 7,200 marks (it had already been shown at more than fifteen exhibitions), and the following month she received a message about *The Lover*. VGM, b3813 (anonymous) and W. Klug to Jo. VGM, b3814; 22 July 1912. The asking prices had been 4,000 and 5,000 guilders respectively. Fifteen per cent commission was deducted from the selling prices. *Account Book* 2002, pp. 54, 152. Exh. cat. Cologne 2012, pp. 82, 541–42.

59 Curator Richart Reiche to Jo. VGM, b3810; 23 April—b3811; 29 April 1912. Hagelstange had delivered the lecture 'Von Manet bis Van Gogh' at Galerie Thannhauser in Munich (*Berliner Tageblatt*, 17 October 1911).

60 Paul Cassirer to Jo. VGM, b4079; 8 June—b4078; 12 June 1912.

61 VGM, b5494–5 (price lists drawn up by Jo). Johannes de Bois to Jo. VGM, b5484; 24 July 1912. For the transactions in this section see *Account Book* 2002, pp. 54, 151–2.

62 Johannes de Bois to Jo. VGM, b5485; 7 September 1912.

63 'U weet zooveel van den kunsthandel af, mevrouw, dat U wel begrijpen zult dat ik dat niet zoo kalm *laat* beweren'; 'onbeschoft'; 'Dat zijn de *on*aangenaamheden van ons vak.' Johannes de Bois to Jo. VGM, b5486; 30 September 1912. De Bois also passed on to Jo and Vincent greetings from the family of the artist Odilon Redon.

64 Johannes de Bois to Jo. VGM, b5492; 18 November—b5488; 11 December—b5489; 20 December 1912.

65 Willem Steenhoff to Jo. VGM, b2073; 18 July 1912.

66 Jo to Paul Gachet. VGM, b2157; 22 July 1912, with the reproduction of *The Bedroom*.

67 'Me voilà de nouveau seule et la seule chose qui me soutient et me donne le courage de continuer c'est l'amour de mon cher fils et le devoir de veiller sur les intérêts de l'œuvre de Vincent.' Jo to Paul Gachet. VGM, b2156; 15 July 1912. In the same letter she wrote: 'Je suis seule dans notre petite maison de campagne—où je tâche de soulager mon profond chagrin en travaillant à mon livre—les lettres de Vincent.' ('I'm alone in our little country house—where I try to relieve my profound sorrow by working on my book—Vincent's letters.')

68 *Vincent's Diary*, 12 July 1934. VGM, b2095. E. Harrison to Jo. VGM, b3785; 6 September 1912. Jo sent Vincent a card addressed to 206 Abbeyfield Road, Pitsmoor; it was slightly to the north of Sheffield, where the steel plants were. VGM, b3711; 22 July 1912.

69 Paul Cassirer to Jo. VGM, b3987; 28 December 1912. Jo to Paul Cassirer. VGM, b3988; 19 January 1913.

Part Six

1 R.L. Stevenson to Edmund Gosse, 18 June 1893. *The Letters of Robert Louis Stevenson to His Family and Friends*. London 1899, p. 294.

15 The Sociaal-Democratische Arbeiderspartij (SDAP)

1 Van Gogh 1952–4, p. 248. Vincent reported elsewhere that Jo had been a member for thirty years (*Het Volk*, 15 September 1925). Surviving membership records only start in 1909.

2 Van Hulst et al. 1969, esp. pp. 3–83; Blom 2012, pp. 141–256. Tak and Wibaut developed the principles underlying socialist local politics. Borrie 1973, pp. 89–183. As early as 1885 Jo's brother Andries had called himself 'an arch-enemy of all socialism'. VGM, b1826.

3 The following historical overview of the SDAP is based on Van Hulst et al. 1969; Ger Harmsen, *Historisch overzicht van Socialisme en Arbeidersbeweging in Nederland*. Vol. 1: *Van de begintijd tot het uitbreken van de Eerste Wereldoorlog*. Nijmegen 1971; and J. Outshoorn, *Vrouwenemancipatie en socialisme. Een onderzoek naar de houding van de SDAP ten opzichte van het vrouwenvraagstuk tussen 1894 en 1919*. Nijmegen 1973.

4 These lists are in the International Institute of Social History (IISG) in Amsterdam. This institute holds several letters sent to Jo during the 1892–1910 period. They were donated by the Vincent van Gogh Foundation in 1984–5 because of their social democratic content. The Van Gogh Museum holds copies of them. The letters were

from Frederik van Eeden (1), Theo van Hoytema (1), Marie Mensing (11), Henriëtte van der Meij and Ant de Witt Hamer (6), Albert Neuhuys (1), Henriette Roland Holst (1), Pieter Tak (1), Theo van der Waerden (4) and Mathilde Wibaut-Berdenis van Berlekom (8). Some have the salutation 'W.P.', for 'Waarde Partijgenoot' ('Valued Fellow Party Member').

5 Van Hulst et al. 1969, pp. 97–8.

6 See Chapter 18.

7 Marie Mensing to Jo. IISG, 5 March 1901. After Jo had moved to Amsterdam, she asked once again whether she could be more active in the party's affairs. IISG, 21 November 1904.

8 *Het Volk*, 11 March 1905. The regulations were adopted and the board members were chosen by fifty-six members of the federation. Henriëtte van der Meij was also involved in setting the movement up.

9 *De Proletarische Vrouw*, 10 September 1925; Henriëtte van der Meij to Jo, 14 November 1906 (IISG); 'Ik heb dat niet zoo sterk als jij. 't Is een volksbeweging moet je rekenen.' Mathilde Wibaut-Berdenis van Berlekom to Jo, 11 March and 30 March 1905, and two undated letters (IISG). On Mathilde see De Liagre Böhl 2013, pp. 194–209.

10 'Hoe de belastingen de vrouw drukken'; 'Het belang der kinderen.' Announcement of the debating evening in *Het Volk*, 5 May 1905; on the exchange programmes: *Het Volk*, 6 June 1906; on the children's books: *Het Volk*, 30 September 1905.

11 Ulla Jansz, *Vrouwen ontwaakt. Driekwart eeuw sociaal-democratische vrouwenorganisatie tussen solidariteit en verzet*. Amsterdam 1983 and *Vrouwenstemmen. 100 jaar vrouwenbelangen, 75 jaar vrouwenkiesrecht*. Eds. M. Borkus et al. Zutphen 1994. For all the preparatory work done by the women's associations in the SDB see Fia Dieteren and Ingrid Peeterman, *Vrije vrouwen of werkmansvrouwen? Vrouwen in de Sociaal-Democratische Bond (1879–1894)*. Amsterdam 1984. On the political struggle for more just social relationships and the significance of the feminist movement see Marianne Braun, *De prijs van de liefde. De eerste feministische golf, het huwelijksrecht en de vaderlandse geschiedenis*. Amsterdam 1992.

12 *Diary* 3, pp. 115–16; 25 August 1888. In 1838 John Cockerill established the integrated industrial complex with blast furnaces, a steel foundry, rolling mills, forges and construction workshops. These installations played a key role in the economy around Liège for more than a century.

13 'Mijn moeder ging ook mee daar heen.' *Vincent's Diary*, 14 January 1934.

14 *BWSA*. In 1907 Kuyper was a member of the committee that revised the party's manifesto. At the end of Jo's life many members of the SDAP were studying socialization and democracy in businesses. Wim Bonger, Floor Wibaut and Rudolf Kuyper were on the socialization committee. It is therefore not surprising that later on Jo's son Vincent became knowledgeable in the field of business organization and employee participation. Van Hulst et al. 1969, pp. 36, 96–107 and 143–4 (in 1969 Frans Bonger, Wim's son, alerted Vincent to this recently published study by Van Hulst et al.). Van Gogh 1995, p. 3.

15 Cf. *Account Book* 2002, p. 122. *Vincent's Diary*, 29 October 1971 and 2 March 1975.

16 *Vincent's Diary*, 22 April 1936. Jo's friend Bertha Jas-Bosscha recommended that they become members. VGM, b3671; 7 October 1904. For this association, which was chaired by Pieter Tak, see Kalmthout 1998, p. 255.

17 VGM, b5450; 1 April 1913.

18 Milton W. Brown, *The Story of the Armory Show*. New York 1988, pp. 271–2; Heijbroek and Wouthuysen 1993, pp. 43–5; McCarthy 2011, esp. pp. 76–7; *The Armory Show at 100: Modernism and Revolution*. Eds. Marilyn Satin Kushner and Kimberly Orcutt. Exh. cat. The New York Historical Society. New York and London 2013, pp. 443–4.

19 It was published in London in 1912 by Constable & Co, and in Boston and New York in 1913 by Houghton Mifflin Co. The set type is the same—only the title page is different. Ludovici also wrote the introduction. Jo commented on the 1912 edition to Annie van Gelder-Pigeaud: 'de vertaling van een duitsch boekje, vertaald uit 't fransch—korte citaten niet eens chronologisch uit brieven, alleen uit de laatste periode, die ik na Vincent's dood aan de Mercure de france afstond. . . . 't werd zonder mijn toestemming uitgegeven onder de misleidende titel: familiar correspondence. 't zijn citaten zonder eenig verband' ('the translation from a German book, translated from the French—short quotations, not even in the chronological order of the letters, only from the last period, which I let the Mercure de France use after Vincent's death. . . . Published without my permission under the misleading title: familiar correspondence. There are quotations without any context.') VGM, b3719; 6 October 1921. In 1927 the same publishers, Constable & Co and Houghton Mifflin Co, published *The Letters of Vincent van Gogh to His Brother, 1872–1886* and in 1929 *Further Letters of Vincent van Gogh to His Brother, 1886–1889*. See 'Epilogue'.

20 A few of these letters had been published in the magazine *Seikatsu* from September 1913 onwards. See Nakatani Nobuo, 'Van Gogh's Influence on Modern Japanese Painting', and Kinoshita Nagahiro, 'Van Gogh in Modern Japanese Literature', in Kōdera and Rosenberg 1993, pp. 88 and 185 respectively.

21 See Takashina Shui, 'The Formation of the "Van Gogh Mythology" in Japan', in Kōdera and Rosenberg 1993, pp. 151–3.

22 H.P. Bremmer to Jo. VGM, b8530; 21 April 1913.

23 'zonder eenige vergoeding zijnerzijds'; 'tot het laten maken van kleurenreproducties van het werk van Vincent van Gogh en deze reproducties te doen uitgeven op voorwaarde, dat Mevrouw J. Cohen Gosschalk-Bonger of hare rechtverkrijgenden bij verschijnen van elke kleurenreproductie 100 gulden inééns zullen ontvangen'; 'of works reproduced by or for H.P. Bremmer'. VGM, b2941; 15 May 1913. Hildelies Balk was not aware of this letter and concluded incorrectly that Jo had not entertained Bremmer's proposal. Balk 2006, p. 394. The letter to which Jo responded was VGM, b2943; 12 May 1913. To say that Bremmer and Jo 'crossed swords' from 1904 about the reproduction rights is putting it too strongly: Balk 2006, p. 242.

24 'Als tegemoetkoming zou ik U van elken druk 10 exemplaren of een bedrag van f 100,- kunnen doen toekomen.' H.P. Bremmer to Jo. VGM, b2942; 6 November 1913.

25 See Balk 2006, p. 88 and Ebbink 2006, p. 14. For Jo see Willem Scherjon, 'De vermeende Van Gogh-vervalschingen', *NRC*, 31 January 1929.

26 H.P. Bremmer to Jo. VGM, b2942; 6 November 1913. RKD catalogue. For this see Ebbink 2006, p. 46. Jo to Julius Meier-Graefe. VGM, b7609; 27 April 1923.

27 'étudiante en droits, de très bonne famille, avec laquelle j'étais liée depuis longtemps'. Jo to Paul Gachet. VGM, b2160; 18 July 1913.

28 'In antwoord op Uw brief moet ik U melden dat bij mij niets heeft voorgezeten van wat U meent dat ijdelheid zou zijn om mijn Vincent collectie te vertoonen, noch bij mij noch bij Mevrouw Kröller. Het heeft mij leed gedaan zooiets uit Uw brief te lezen, daar ik meen dat men, naar wat ik steeds voor Vincent gedaan heb, zuivere bedoelingen had kunnen veronderstellen.' 'Ik vind het heerlijk als U een collectie van de mooiste dingen van Vincent wilt zenden, indien U er b.v. de zestien heen wilde sturen die 3 jaar geleden in Rotterdam waren dan zou mij dat een groote vreugde en zou ik U daarvoor dankbaar zijn. Indien U mij nu even wilt berichten of ik tot regeling van een en ander, assurantie, verzending enz. Vrijdag a.s. bij U aan kan komen om alles te bespreken, dan zou dit de eenvoudigste weg zijn die U het minst moeite bezorgde.' H.P. Bremmer to Jo. VGM, b8531; 16 June 1913.

29 'een ruim dertigtal van de beste kwaliteit'. VGMB, BVG 5346 and Balk 2006, p. 242.

30 Johannes de Bois to Jo. VGM, b5491; 15 November 1913. See also Heijbroek and Wouthuysen 1993, pp. 192, 195, 197 and 207.

31 The sale was on 25 and 26 November 1913. The figure '3,300.–' is written in the margin of an annotated catalogue (RKD). That same year the painting went to a collector in Hamburg. See Meike Egge, 'Van Gogh in Hamburg', in Ulrich Luckhardt and Uwe M. Scheede, *Private Schätze. Über das Sammeln von Kunst in Hamburg bis 1933.* Hamburg 2001, pp. 74–5. The drawings went under the hammer for amounts ranging from two hundred to 1,100 guilders.

32 J.H. Mentendorp to Jo. VGM, b1947; 18 December 1913. *Account Book* 2002, pp. 132, 163. This was a case where she dropped the price; cf. Chapter 13, p. 255.

33 *Odilon Redon, Œuvre graphique complet.* Collotype: Willem Scherjon, Utrecht. Ed. Artz & De Bois. The Hague 1912. VGMB, BVG 526–7. Heijbroek and Wouthuysen 1993, pp. 36–7; *Account Book* 2002, p. 131.

34 *Account Book* 2002, p. 131.

35 The contractor L. Klerkx from Bussum did the work. VGM, b3660; 14 May 1913. In 1912–13 he had done plastering and painting in Laren (after electric lighting had been installed) and he also did work on Villa Eikenhof in Bussum. VGM, b3659; 14 February 1913.

36 'Blois (Cheverney, Chambord) en Tours (Azay-le-Rideau, Chinon, Luynes, Ussé) en tusschen die twee in Amboise, en afzonderlijk Loches. 't Was onze eerste kennismaking met de Fransche provincie. Tot slot Chartres en Versailles.' *Vincent's Diary*, 15 October 1933.

37 *Het Nieuws van den Dag*, 5 July 1913; *De Gooi- en Eemlander*, 4 October 1913 and *Het Nieuws van den Dag*, 9 October 1913. The annual salary was 140 guilders.

16 The publication of *Brieven aan zijn broeder*

1 'Zulke buitensporigheden mag *ik* mij niet veroorloven—mijn *eerste* plicht is wakker en gezond te blijven om voor het kind te zorgen.' *Diary* 4, p. 18; 6 March 1892.

2 'O een droom van nog eenmaal met U te zijn . . ./ En dan niets meer te weten/ En te sterven, zacht.' *De Gids* 76 (1912), p. 377.

3 VGM, b2954. In her introduction she used facts about the Van Gogh family drawn from notes made by Uncle Jan and Aunt Mietje van Gogh. VGM, b4530. For the proofs see Jo to Paul Gachet. VGM, b2149; 13 September 1911.

4 'Il ne vous étonnera pas que je reprends mon nom d'autrefois pour porter le même nom de mon fils.' Jo to Paul Gachet. VGM, b2161; 1 January 1914.

5 Jo gave Hartog Hamburger and Fréderique Hamburg-Cohen Gosschalk a copy of *Brieven aan zijn broeder* because, according to their granddaughter A.H.C. Kliphuis-Leopold in a letter to Aly Noordermeer (employed at that time in the Van Gogh Museum), 'zij de enigen in de familie waren, die geen bezwaar maakten, toen Mw. Cohen Gosschalk de naam van haar eerste echtgenoot weer wilde voeren' ('they were the only ones in the family who did not object when Mrs Cohen Gosschalk wanted to return to her first husband's name'). VGMD; 1 September 1991.

6 'Je ne peux vous dire ce que cela m'a couté de faire revivre tout ce passé.' Jo to Paul Gachet. VGM, b2161; 1 January 1914.

7 VGM, b5108; 15 January 1914 (degree). Jo and Josina attended the graduation ceremony. Van Gogh 1995, p. 3. The member of parliament M.W.F. Treub was director of the 'Bank van Treub'. See Diederick Slijkerman, *Enfant terrible. Wim Treub (1858–1931).* Amsterdam 2016. Vincent sent his mother a postcard with a photo of the 'Electrification des Lignes de Pyrénées - Tunnel d'Eget - Entreprise Varnoux', no. 6. VGM, b9123; 18 February 1914.

8 Jo to Paul Gachet. VGM, b2162; 20 January 1914.

9 'Ik hoop dat je goed op schiet met den aannemer, wees maar zoo vriendelijk en toeschietelijk als 't mogelijk isje kunt best scherp controleeren en toch vriendelijk tegen hem zijn nietwaar?' Jo to Vincent. VGM, b2093; 24 January 1914.

10 Jo to Vincent. VGM, b2099; 8 March 1914 (Mozart). Jo to Vincent. VGM, b2091; 22 January 1914 (Wisselingh).

11 'prachtig en griezelig tegelijk'. Jo to Vincent. VGM, b2098; 23 February 1914. For the comedy see *Het Nieuws van den Dag*, 22 January 1914. The Wagner-Vereeniging performed the opera, with Edyth Walker in the title role. *Algemeen Handelsblad*, 21 February 1914.

12 Jo to Vincent. VGM, b2101; 9 February 1914.

13 ''t Leven zelf is veel interessanter'. Jo to Vincent. VGM, b2090; 6 February—b2101; 9 February 1914 (quotation).

14 Jo to Vincent. VGM, b2099; 8 March 1914.

15 Theodor Stoperan (Cassirer employee) to Jo. VGM, b3989; 20 February 1914. A. Gold to Jo. VGM, b3990; 9 March—b3991; 25 March 1914. Cf. Van Gogh 1952–4, p. 249.

16 'Vind je dat ik genoeg schrijf?' 'Gisteren weer papieren van de erfenis, 't is nu definitief: jij krijgt vier mille en nog iets.' Jo to Vincent. VGM, b2096; 26 February 1914.

17 Jo to Vincent. VGM, b2104; 1 March 1914. That evening was 27 February 1914 (*Algemeen Handelsblad*, 21 February 1914).

18 Jo to Vincent. VGM, b2099; 9 March 1914. Ankersmit had spoken at the first International Women's Day in the Netherlands in May 1912. This meeting of women's clubs was given over to emancipation of women and female suffrage. *De rode canon. Een geschiedenis van de Nederlandse sociaal-democratie in 32 verhalen*. Eds. Karin van Leeuwen et al. The Hague 2010, pp. 22–3.

19 Ary Delen to Jo. VGM, b3699; 20 January 1914.

20 'Wij beschikken over eene prachtig verlichte zaal van 59 m. cimaise. Daarvan hebben wij ongeveer de helft voorbehouden voor het plaatsen der schilderijen die U ons zult willen leenen.' Ary Delen to Jo. VGM, b3700; 30 January—b3701; 6 February 1914 (quotation).

21 VGM, b3698; b5703–4. For the exhibition see Daloze 2015, p. 197.

22 'We hebben 't erg best samen gehad: het Museum Plantijn hebben we grondig bekeken en bewonderd en de cathedraal vind ik zoo prachtig! We stonden op het pleintje er voor juist toen de schemering viel en door een nauw straatje zagen we ook die oude gevels op de Grande Place—en er hing zoo iets van die oude tijden over alles—een geur van vroeger!' Jo to Vincent. VGM, b2105; 31 March 1914.

23 'Jos[ina] vertelde je zeker van de tentoonstelling, 't was veel mooier dan in den Haag (ik had nu ook jouw naam in de catalogus laten zetten).' Jo to Vincent. VGM, b2105; 31 March 1914.

24 'de tentoonstelling in Antwerpen gaat naar Berlijn—ik hoop dat je 't ook goed vindt'. Jo to Vincent. VGM, b2100; 9 April 1914.

25 Ary Delen to Jo. VGM, b3702; 8 April 1914.

26 Jo to Vincent. VGM, b2105; 31 March 1914.

27 'Zou ik ook van die waterdichte schoenen moeten hebben, of overschoenen, of sneeuwschoenen?' 'Hier bloeien ook al die vroege bloesemboompjes, je weet wel, net of 't abrikozen boompjes zijn, en in de weilanden de gele

dotters.' Jo to Vincent. VGM, b2095; 2 April 1914. She hoped that Vincent wanted to wait for them in Paris, 'want als ik aan die Quai D'Orsay denk—denk ik zooiets van een chaos waar ik niet wijs uit zou worden!' ('because when I think of the Quai D'Orsay—I think of all sorts of chaos where I can't made head or tail of it!'). Jo to Vincent. VGM, b2105; 31 March 1914.

28 The burial register of Soestbergen Cemetery records the exhumation: VGM, Bd124.

29 'dans un hôtel ou pension à Auvers—bien simple—car la fiancée de Vincent m'accompagnera aussi'. Jo to Paul Gachet. VGM, b2158; 4 April 1914. In the end only one room was booked; Jo and Josina stayed at Gachet's home. VGM, b2100.

30 'Il tient tellement aux traditions de famille et jamais il peut en entendre parler trop assez.' Jo to Paul Gachet. VGM, b2163; 21 April 1914. It was Jo's favourite plant for these circumstances. Vincent to Paul Gachet. VGM, b2815; 18 August—b2816; 22 August 1927.

31 Jo to Annie van Gelder-Pigeaud. VGM, b3718; 21 December 1921.

32 VGM, b2159 and b2167. *Vincent's Diary*, 15 May 1975 (onward travel). VGM, b2165 (arrival in Fabian: 16 April).

33 'par une route merveilleusement belle dans la vallée d'Aure'. Jo to Paul Gachet. VGM, b2163; 21 April 1914.

34 The guide was the 1906 Paris edition, with 298 illustrations (private collection). Jo to Paul Gachet. VGM, b2163; 21 April 1914.

35 'Hier wandel ik 't liefst, langs dat water of door 't bos iets hooger op. We maakten vorige week een reisje van 6 dagen want Vincent moest in Périgeux zijn—en we gingen naar Pau en Bordeaux er heen en over Tarbes terug. 't Eerste gedeelte per auto—dat is zoo heerlijk dat Vincent daar beschikking over heeft als hij voor zaken op reis moet. In Périgeux ontmoetten wij Treub; hij was erg aardig. Jos is weer naar huis, ik blijf voorlopig maar hier, ik heb werk bij me!' Jo to Henriëtte van der Meij and Ant de Witt Hamer. VGM, b3117; 3 May 1914. Vincent's son Johan recalled that his father never had a driving licence (interview on 6 May 2013). It was quite a distance to travel: Périgueux is some hundred kilometres northeast of Bordeaux. M.W.F. Treub was director of the 'Bank van Treub'.

36 ''t Weer was prachtig—de lucht als balsem—een groot contrast met de sneeuwstorm die we vorige week hier hadden! Bij 't terugkomen hier trof 't me weer dat dit landschap toch het allermooiste is.' Jo to Henriëtte van der Meij and Ant de Witt Hamer. VGM, b3116; 17 May 1914. A day later she also wrote to Paul Gachet, on the back of a picture postcard of the new power station where Vincent was working. VGM, b2164; 18 May 1914.

37 'Mijn moeder en ik waaren van Fabian (1200 m) naar Arreau gekoomen (waarschijnlijk was de auto van de entreprise er). Het station zat dicht tot 16.30 of zo—en daar was het—een sensatie. 't Was mooi lenteweer.' *Vincent's Diary*, 17 December 1977. The dedication in copy VGMB, BVG 17195 I. She gave him volume 2 on 24 September and volume 3 on 5 November 1914. The production of the German edition by Paul Cassirer was somewhat earlier and was completely ready on 1 July: VGM, b3992.

38 'ontroerend schoone brieven'. *Brieven* 1914, vol. 1, p. 179 (quotation); vol. 2, p. 142 (Leibl); vol. 3, p. 45 (Heine). Max Ditmar Henkel to Jo. VGM, b1942; 5 March 1911 (Madiol).

39 'drie Hollanders, Fransch samen spraken'. *Brieven* 1914, vol. 3, pp. 421 and 435.

40 'Daarin sprak hij ook over een plan om zijn betrekking op te geven en zich voor eigen rekening te vestigen; er was zóóveel noodig en zooals 't nu was moesten én Vincent en wij zelven ons toch altijd bekrimpen; ook wenschte Theo in dien brief Vincent toe dat hij ook eenmaal een vrouw mocht vinden die zijn leven wilde deelen.' *Brieven* 1914, vol. 3, p. 456. Theo's letter was dated 30 June 1890. Van Gogh, *Letters* 2009, letter 894.

41 'Eenige psalmen en godsdienstige versjes'. *Brieven* 1914, vol. 1, p. 105.

42 Pieces of text were still missing and passages had been mangled in Van Gogh, *Verzamelde brieven* 1952–4 and the reprint in 1973. For Bernard see Van Gogh, *Letters to Bernard* 2007, p. 22. For developments in editing practice see Marita Mathijsen, *Naar de letter. Handboek editiewetenschap*. Assen 1995; and http://vangoghletters.org/vg/about_1.html.

43 Theo van der Waerden to Jo. IISG, 21 November 1910, thanking her for the generous loan. The typewriter was one of the Standard Models (No. 5–10) or a Noiseless Standard No. 2, see http://Typewriterdatabase.com. Jo's handwritten copy has also survived: initially written extremely neatly, but later gradually covered with additions and corrections. It became neater again from the French period—possibly because she had rewritten that part previously. VGM, b3262.

44 VGM, b4523 and b4535. She compiled data, for example about Paul Gauguin: VGM, b2971.

45 Van Gogh, *Letters* 2009, letter 485 (ink corrosion). http://vangoghletters.org/vg/about_5.html#intro.VI.5.2.1.

46 'vol van opgewektheid'; 'stralend van opgewektheid'; 'met alle kracht'; 'met bijna wanhopige kracht'; 'Er is in zijn brieven uit dien tijd een haast ziekelijke overgevoeligheid.' 'nooit deed hij iets ten halve!'; 'den barren winter van 1879–'80 moet hij nog doorworstelen—dien droevigsten, meest hopeloozen tijd uit zijn waarlijk niet vreugderijk leven'; 'grenzenloos eenzaam'. *Brieven* 1914, vol. 1, pp. xxiii, xxvi–xxvii, xxxi and xxxv respectively.

47 'dans un tableau je voudrais dire quelque chose de consolant comme une musique.' *Brieven* 1914, vol. 1, p. xxxii. Cf. Van Gogh, *Letters* 2009, letter 673.

48 'als altijd is het Theo alleen die hem begrijpt en hem blijft steunen'. *Brieven* 1914, vol. 1, p. xxxvi.

49 'het beroemde zelfportret voor den schildersezel'; 'stralend en fonkelend als van een innerlijke gloed'. *Brieven* 1914, vol. 1, p. l (= 50).

50 *Brieven* 1914, vol. 1, pp. lii–liii.

51 For *The Mill on the Floss* see also Chapter 3, p. 55. Maggie and Tom drown in each other's arms during a flood.

52 Cf. for this, and the accounts for the 1914–21 period (in total 7,813 guilders): *Account Book* 2002, pp. 132–6. The correspondence with the Wereldbibliotheek has been combined under VGM, b6849–50. On the selling price: 'Vincent van Gogh als boekverkoopersbediende, 2', *NRC*, 2 June 1914.

53 'Het zou een onbillikheid geweest zijn jegens den doode belangstelling te wekken voor zijn persoon eer het werk waaraan hij zijn leven gaf, erkend werd, en gewaardeerd werd zooals het verdiende'; 'gedenkteeken voor de zoons' *Brieven* 1914, vol. 1, pp. vii and xvi respectively.

54 Willemien van Gogh to Jo. VGM, b2921; 22 May 1893.

55 VGM, b3056 and b3057 (annotations). The 1903 portrait drawing is also in exh. cat. Assen 1991, p. 29.

56 'devoir sacré'. Paul Gachet to Jo. VGM, b3414; 17 July 1912.

57 'Toen Vincents Brieven voor het eerst gepubliceerd waren, kregen we nog al eens aanmerkingen van familieleden die zich gechoqueerd voelden dat allerlei persoonlijke dingen gepubliceerd werden.' Speech given by Vincent at the annual meeting of the publishers Wereldbibliotheek on 25 May 1974. VGM, b7435.

58 'Dat al die brieven aan Theo, vol intimiteiten, zijn uitgegeven, hebben wij heel diep betreurd. Vincent en Theo zouden het verfoeid hebben; wat zou een bloemlezing daaruit niet veel beter geweest zijn!' *Algemeen Handelsblad*, 5 May 1934. Lies had previously launched a lie about the publication into the world when writing to Jos Verwiel, co-initiator of the Hildo Krop Monument in Nuenen: 'Dit is een geldquestie geweest, daar ze aan den meest biedenden zijn verhandeld. Ik heb er mijn sanctie aan ontzegd, daar geen mijner beide broeders, bescheiden en in zich zelf gekeerd naar hun kunstenaarsnatuur, toestemming bij leven zouden hebben gegeven tot het openbaar maken dezer uitingen van hart tot hart.' ('This was a matter of money, because she did business with the highest bidder. I refused to give my blessing because neither of my brothers, who were modest and introspective by virtue of their artistic nature, would have ever given permission to publish their innermost heartfelt thoughts.') Baarn, 26 October 1927. Las Vegas, Nevada, Gallery of History. Copy in VGMD. Jo financed the publication in full from her own resources.

59 *Vincent van Gogh: 30. März 1853–29. Juli 1890. Zehnte Ausstellung*. Berlin 1914. VGMB, BVG 3414. See also Feilchenfeldt 1988, pp. 40 and 150. Paul Fechter described Van Gogh as a trailblazer of modern art: 'Van Gogh ist die höchste Steigerung, die der Naturrausch des Impressionismus erreicht hat.' ('Van Gogh is the highest improvement that Impressionism's ecstasy of nature has achieved.') *Der Expressionismus*. Munich 1914, p. 9.

60 'Bei meinem Besuch in Amsterdam sagten Sie mir freilich, dass es keinen Zweck habe, bei Ihnen nach der Verkäuflichkeit des einen oder anderen Stückes zu fragen.' Theodor Stoperan to Jo. VGM, b4080; 14 June 1914.

61 'De laatste twee jaar heb ik niets anders gedaan, en dikwijls tot laat in den nacht zitten werken . . . het was soms om overspannen van te worden. En wat al familiebrieven heb ik doorgezocht om hier en daar een datum te vinden, die iets kon ophelderen. . . . En al Theo's brieven aan mij, al het oude leed weer opgerakeld en opnieuw doorleefd. . . . Daarom ben ik, toen eindelijk de Inleiding bij het eerste deel klaar was, hierheen gevlucht om bij mijn zoon wat rust te zoeken, hier in de heerlijke natuur.' 'Vincent van Gogh als boekverkoopersbediende, 2', *NRC*, 2 June 1914.

62 'waarlijk heldhaftig van opofferingsgezindheid', *NRC*, 31 May 1914.

63 Rovers 2010, pp. 248–51 and 256 (quotation); Balk 2006, p. 305.

64 VGMB, BVG 525. Vincent wrote on the title page: 'Persoonlijk door haar gekregen van Vollard. Parijs 1914.' ('Given to her personally by Vollard. Paris 1914.')

65 Jo to Henriëtte van der Meij and Ant de Witt Hamer. VGM, b3118; 17 June 1914. The still life is presently in the Musée d'Orsay.

66 They included *The Old Church Tower at Nuenen ('The Peasants' Churchyard')* (F 84 / JH 772), *View of Arles with Irises in the Foreground* (F 409 / JH 1416) and *Sunflowers* (F 454 / JH 1562 or F 458 / JH 1667). Jo to Clément Benoît, 14 June 1914. Bibliothèque Centrale Université de Mons. Inv. no. Ms Pt. 1724, B.U.E. Mons; *Catalogue du XIXe Salon, Le Bon Vouloir*, 1914, p. 18. B.U.E. Mons 1987/1046. See also Daloze 2015, pp. 197–9.

67 'een arbeider die met eindeloos sloven zijn moeilijke werk moet leeren, die beseft dat hij als oerkrachtig kunstenaar ten onder zou gaan, als hij in den verfijnden weelde-glans der behagelijke bovenste lagen der maatschappij vertoefde, een arbeider die zijn kunst voelde wortelen in de onbedorven kracht van het volk dat zwoegen moest als hij zelf.' *Het Volk*, 16 July 1914.

68 Probably *Der Tag, Populärste Illustrierte Zeitschrift der Welt*. In the *Berliner Tageblatt* of 29 July 1914. Adolf Bene praised the publication, which 'gehört zu den wertvollsten und kostbarsten Veröffentlichungen der letzten Zeit' ('is one of the most valuable and precious publications of recent times.')

69 This is Anna, Theo and Vincent's eldest sister.

70 'Ik krijg zóóveel brieven van menschen die genieten van het boek, die zeggen: wij zijn er zoo dankbaar voor! De Duitsche uitgave is net al verschenen en iemand stuurde me een courant, 'Der Tag', waarin staat: 'Das Werk ist vollendet und Van Gogh tritt in die Geschichte ein, der Künstler ist ein Art Klassiker geworden'.

Moeder schreef me dat het haar pijnlijk was al die herinneringen aan vroeger—maar dat kan ik niet goed begrijpen—voor mij was het in zeker opzicht duizendmaal pijnlijker—al dat vroeten in het verleden en leed dat de jaren had verzacht weer opnieuw te moeten doorleven—maar 't was niet dááraan dat ik dacht—wel hoe prachtig Oom Theo's figuur uitkomt naast zijn geniale broer en hoe liefderijk en hartelijk de ouders—jou grootouders—waren! Natuurlijk moet men de brieven lezen met een ruimen blik—niet alles kunnen wij goedvinden wat oom

Vincent deed.—Maar wel alles begrijpen, hoe 't toch voort kwam uit een rijk, warm gemoed! We zullen 't er later nog wel eens over hebben als jelui 't ook gelezen hebt! Ik ben nu juist klaar met 't tweede deel en begin aan de proeven van 't derde. De Duitsche drukker is ons nog vóór geweest, die zijn helemaal klaar! Je ziet, ik ben niet enkel voor plezier hier—soms werk ik den heelen dag. Maar die reisjes er tusschen door zijn verrukkelijk—en de mooie wandelingen hier niet minder. Ze zijn nu, net als in Holland zeker, aan het maaien, en 14 Juli, de nationale feestdag in Frankrijk, brachten Vincent en ik door op het hooiveld achter het huis, een zalig rustige dag.

Vorige week waren we drie dagen op reis naar Gavarnie. Het Cirque de Gavarnie is een der beroemdheden van de Pyrenëen—de weg daarheen zéér prachtig—in een open auto-car zagen we alles heerlijk—toen we daar kwamen lag er nog sneeuw, niet alleen op de toppen der bergen maar ook op den grond.

De bloemen hier zijn niet meer zóó mooi als in de lente—ik ben hier nu juist drie maanden. Dus heb zoo de seizoenen mee gemaakt! Het hotel is wel wat al te primitief, ze doen niets geen moeite voor de gasten—men moet altijd hier terecht komen, er is niets anders en daar profiteeren ze van! Maar och men went aan al die dingen, en eten, en weinig verzorgdheid der kamers enz.—en als we dan op reis zijn genieten we dubbel van goede hôtels enz., dan zijn we in de rijke dagen! . . .

Mijn gezondheid is er hier op vooruit gegaan, de laatste twee jaar waren ook al te bitter en eenzaam geweest—en 't terugkomen in 't leege huis zal weer alle droefheid oprakelen—maar de afleiding hier heeft me toch goed gedaan!' Jo to Sara de Jong-van Houten. VGM, b3107; 17 July 1914.

71 'Mes souvenirs à moi, je les porte dans mon coeur; il y en a parmi eux dont je suis fière, d'une fierté dont aucune femme n'aurait à rougir.'; 'ah quand je pense à toutes ces choses il me vient comme une rancune contre Vincent, car c'est lui qui m'a pris mon bonheur. Mais je ne dois pas me laisser aller à ces souvenirs, c'est à vous seul qui comprenez bien ces choses que je peux m'exprimer ainsi.' Jo to Paul Gachet. VGM, b2166; 25 June 1914. She had hinted at such rancour a month after her wedding in a letter to her sister Mien. VGM, b4288; 25 May 1889. See Chapter 6, p. 104.

72 Jo to Floor Wibaut on this hotel's stationery. IISG; 22 July 1914.

73 'een zeldzaam aangrijpend boek'. *De Amsterdammer*, 19 July 1914.

74 'Voor Vincent van mama, Amsterdam 24 September 1914.' VGMB, BVG 17195 II.

75 'geluksvogel'. Isaac Israëls to Jo. VGM, b8602; 20 July 1914.

76 Isaac Israëls to Jo. VGM, b8603; 21 September 1914.

77 Jo to Vincent. VGM, b2106; 29 October 1914. Cf. for *Wheatfields with Auvers in the Background*: Isaac Israëls to Jo. VGM, b8650; 23 June 1923. He sold the painting on 26 June 1934, shortly before his death.

78 Isaac Israëls to Jo. VGM, b8610; 5 February—b8611; 9 February 1915.

79 Jo to Vincent. VGM, b2110; 28 October 1914.

80 Oscar Wibaut Sr, *Floor en Mijntje en hun nazaten*. Eindhoven 2002; Eric Slot and Hans Moor, *Wibaut: onderkoning van Amsterdam*. Amsterdam 2009, and De Liagre Böhl 2013, pp. 276–80.

81 *Vincent's Diary*, 28 February 1976.

82 'Quatre vingt treize is zeker wel boeiend; ik ben toch zoo blij dat je zoo goed Fransch schrijft, lieve schat—ik zal met Jos een beetje Fransch gaan lezen, dat oefent nog, de brieven van Flaubert—of de Fransche brieven van Oom Vincent!' Jo to Vincent. VGM, b2106; 31 October 1914.

83 'elle pense à l'absent nuit et jour—dat doe ik ook.' Jo to Vincent. VGM, b2102; 2 November—b2107; 5 November 1914). The aria contained the word 'songe' not 'pense' (*Carmen*, first act). That morning Jo had put flowers on Johan's grave because it was his birthday.

84 'Mijn Vincent heeft geen enkel gebrek.' 'Dat kan ik van mijn Jos niet zeggen!' Johan van Gogh told me the anecdote about Mathilde Wibaut in a conversation on 9 September 2007. Cf. Jo to Vincent. VGM, b2106; 31 October 1914.

85 'Toute mère de quelque valeur a une ferme foi, c'est que son fils doit être un héros, dans l'action ou dans la science, il n'importe.' *Diary* 4, p. 15. On the first page of this diary she wrote: 'J'ai donné un homme au monde.' ('I gave the world a man.') Both quotations come from Michelet's *Du prêtre, de la femme, de la famille*.

86 Jo to Vincent. VGM, b2102; 2 November 1914.

87 VGMB, BVG 17195 III. Israëls also received a copy. He invited Jo out for a simple meal: 'if you don't mind something in Pyrenean style!' Isaac Israëls to Jo. VGM, b8606; 10 November 1914.

88 'Wat zal het toch een rust zijn als je bij elkaar zult zijn—niet altijd meer die brieven te schrijven (alleen nog maar aan de oude moeder!), gezelligheid en warmte en liefde om je heen—een eigen thuis—o mijn jongen, ik kan je niet zeggen hoe ik me verheug in die gedachte! Jos haar eigenlijke leven zal dan ook pas beginnen.' Jo to Vincent. VGM, b2107; 5 November 1914.

89 Jo to Vincent. VGM, b2108; 9 November 1914.

90 In 1922 Lodewijk Opdebeek published the monograph *Rik Wouters, zijn leven, zijn werk, zijn einde* by Ary Delen. Jo carefully calligraphed her name in her copy, one of the twenty-five printed on 'Imperial Japanese paper'. VGMB, BVG 1032.

91 Published under the pseudonym Gabriele Violanti in *Nederland. Verzameling van oorspronkelijke bijdragen door Nederlandsche letterkundigen*. Ed. M.G.L. van Loghem. Amsterdam 1917, pp. 49–63. On the refugees in Laren in 1916: VGM, b2168.

92 'Het boek zal u zeker tot troost worden in uwe gedwongen werkeloosheid.' Olivier Bertrand, *Rik Wouters, visies op een levensloop. Nel Wouters, Onuitgegeven herinneringen*. Brussels 2000, p. 384.

93 'net als zijn schilderen. Ue[dele] zal best begrijpen met welke macht die lectuur me uit het droevige niets doen wekt, en als iets heiligs voorkomt te midden dit zoo lastige milieu.' Rik Wouters to Jo. VGM, b3704; 4 December 1914.

94 'Dat is wel aardig en dan heb ik meteen weer werk.' Jo to Vincent. VGM, b2110; 28 October 1914.

95 It is telling that one of the surviving copies has corrections and additions in the handwriting of both Jo and Vincent. They are evidence of his growing active involvement. VGMD, 'Amsterdam 1914–1915'; VGMB, BVG 5307b. Needless to say there is an advertisement for the letters edition on the back flap.

96 'vele bekende persoonlijkheden op kunstgebied en enkele schilders'. *Algemeen Handelsblad*. 23 December 1914.

97 VGM, b7372.

98 'sentimenteele overtuigingen'; 'een *zielige Vincent verheerlijking* vol onzuivere tendenzen, dweepzieke overdrevenheid, en gemis aan proportie'. *De Nieuwe Tijd* 1915, pp. 60–61 and 199–200; Veth in *De Nieuwe Gids* 30 (March 1915), pp. 437–9.

99 'energieke vrouw voor wie het beheeren, het redden, het handhaven van heel Vincent's nalatenschap zoo schoon een levensroeping werd, welke nu is bekroond door de uitgaaf der Brieven'. *NRC*, 31 December 1914.

100 VGM, b5118.

101 This was the song 'Sint-Jans gheleide', which was traditionally sung for those about to leave. The lyrics and musical notation have survived on a page from *De Nieuwe Amsterdammer* of 19 December 1914. There is a handwritten note: 'Vincent: wedding day'. VGM, b5117.

102 They stayed in the Arundel Hotel and visited Oxford. IISG. When first in Paris they were in the Grand Hôtel Terminus, rue St Lazare. The sent a telegram to Jo on 5 February. IISG.

103 VGM, b5128 (library card)—b5114, b5120 and b5121.

104 'Ze heeft met die twee moeten lijden door het optreden der Duitsche grensofficieren, die ons de vrijheid ontnamen. Aan die geheime anti-oorlogsconferentie heeft zij levendig deelgenomen.' *De Proletarische Vrouw*, 10 September 1925.

105 *BWSA*. This German 'Manifest', a powerful call for peace, is in the IISG.

106 'Dat eenzelfde moed, die de mannen aanvuurt in de daad der vernieling, de vrouwen zou kunnen bezielen in den strijd voor behoud van het leven', and 'Moeder ga voor je kindje staan'. 1916 Annual Report about 1915 (IISG, BSDVC); *De Telegraaf*, 2 April 1915; *De Tribune*, 7 April 1915; *De Lokomotief*, undated (press cutting IISG, BSDVC); *De Vrouw in Indië*, 15 May 1915.

107 Jo to Henriëtte van der Meij and Ant De Witt Hamer. VGM, Bd114; 11 June 1915.

108 They were in Tarbes on the seventeenth and in Aragnouet on the twenty-second. VGM, b7221 and b8289, with the note in her visa: 'But: accompagner son fils'. VGM, b8290. Vincent made further business trips on 9 July and 9 August 1915. VGM, b5127, b5129 and b5132.

109 Jo to Paul Gachet. VGM, b3453; 29 June 1915. 'een mooi oud huis waar hij zijn atelier had'. Vincent to Johan van Gogh. VGM, b4429; 3 July 1951 (visit to Bernard). There is a French translation of Jo's introduction to the letters, with annotations and improvements by Gustave Coquiot, which he used in his 1922 book about Van Gogh. Coquiot will have had this translation done. VGM, b3344.

110 VGM, b5130; 20 August—b5131; 27 August 1915.

111 Jo to the Gachet family. VGM, b3454; 1 January 1916.

112 'Zij telegrafeerde ons toen het "be calm en hopeful", en er kwam iemand bij ons die zij ontmoet had in Europa, aan wie zij had getelegrafeerd: "kindly visit young Mrs. van Gogh who is lying ill" en ons adres. Dat hielp ons meer.' *Vincent's Diary*, 28 August 1933.

113 VGM, b5133; 13 December 1915.

114 Van Gogh 1995, p. 3.

115 'hij roemde mevr. Holst als dichteres zoo. Dat ben ik zoo eens'. Jo to Vincent and Josina. VGM, b8293; 28 October 1915. Announcement in the *NRC* of 8 October 1915.

116 *Account Book* 2002, p. 133.

117 'mooie daad van piëteit'. G.H. Marius, 'De brieven van Vincent van Gogh', *Onze Kunst* 14, no. 2 (1915), pp. 51–65 (quotation on p. 52), and Henriëtte van der Meij in *Soerabaja. Bijblad van het Weekblad voor Indië voor Dames*, 28 February 1915.

118 VGMB, BVG 3123 and Dep 38. Jo to Vincent and Josina. VGM, b3717; 14 to 18 November 1915.

119 'Ik wil met plezier nog eens een portret van je maken en zal je dan tegen de achtergrond van een Vincent maken. . . . Je krijgt alles eerlijk terug.' Isaac Israëls to Jo. VGM, b8614; 25 November 1915.

120 'een van de belangrijkste dingen'; 'Het is pronken met een andermans veeren. heb je niet lust om nog wat te ruilen??????' Isaac Israëls to Jo. VGM, b8617; 20 December 1915. She exchanged the portrait Israëls had made of her son 'tegen een studie van Oom Vincent' ('for a study by Uncle Vincent'): Jo to Vincent and Josina. VGM, b8294; 29 December 1915. Shortly thereafter Israëls invited her to come and see a couple of paintings he had made with a Van Gogh in the background. He found them of immense use ('enorm nut'). On 20 February he was 'nog steeds erg aan 't Vincenten' ('still very engaged with the Vincents'). Isaac Israëls to Jo. VGM, b8627; 6 January—b8630; 10 February—b8631; 20 February 1916. He returned three paintings at the end of April. They were 'het interieur, de zonnige heuvel en het laantje' ('the interior, the sunny hill and the avenue'). The first was *The Bedroom* (F 482 / JH 1608), the second might have been *Montmartre: Behind the Moulin de la Galette* (F 316 / JH 1246) and the third was *The Yellow House ('The Street')* (F 464 / JH 1589). Two further works followed on 15 May. Isaac Israëls to Jo. VGM, b8632; 26 April—b8635; 14 May—b8636; 15 May 1916. It is not clear which version of *Sunflowers* Jo lent him at the end of 1915 and in 1918. It was either *Sunflowers* (F 458 / JH 1667 or F 454 / JH 1562). In any event the latter was returned to her in 1920 (b8645).

121 Isaac Israëls to Jo. VGM, b8640; 15 October 1916.

122 'Ik verneem dat je naar Amerika gaat. Indien je nog hier komt voor die tijd hoop ik je te zien!' ('I understand that you're going to America. If you have a chance to come here before you leave, I hope to see you!') He invited her to come for a meal. Isaac Israëls to Jo. VGM, b8638; 23 July—b8639; 1 August 1916 (quotation).

123 'Uit de kruising van al die verschillende rassen moet wel een nieuw prachtig volk ontstaan.' Jo to Vincent and Josina. VGM, b3716; 26–29 June 1916. Graham argued: 'In the New World the peoples are joined in co-operation and friendship, working out in peace and trade the synthesis of a new race.... None can tell what the new American nation will be. We can only watch the wonderful patterns and colours that form in the great ballet and choir dance, the mingling in the labyrinths of destiny, the disappearances and the emergences, the involution and the evolution. It is something enacted within the mystery of the human race itself.' Stephen Graham, *With Poor Immigrants to America*. New York 1914, pp. 287 and 293.

124 'Zei ik 't niet dat ze rare dingen eten in Amerika? spek, chocola—ice cream—'t is om van te rillen. Spaar je magen voor dat ice cream—dat is uit den boze. Hoe vreeselijk toevallig dat juist die tentoonstelling van Oom Vincent is—goed dat je die kleine erbij gedaan hebt.' Jo to Vincent and Josina. VGM, b3717; 14 to 18 November 1915.

125 Marius De Zayas, *How, When, and Why Modern Art Came to New York*. Ed. Francis M. Naumann. Cambridge, Massachusetts 1996. Cf. John Rewald, *Cézanne and America. Dealers, Collectors, Artists and Critics, 1891–1921*. London 1989, p. 287 with a reference to an announcement in *The New York Evening Post* of 20 November 1915. Vincent to Mark Tralbaut. VGM, b7787; 1 November 1955. According to Vincent, there was barely any interest in it at the time.

126 'Josje, heb je wel plezier gehad van de klaprozen al? Je moet als het terug is, het zóó hangen dat je uit bed er op kijkt—dan heb je ineens iets van een mooie zomermorgen in je hoofd, in je hart. Kindje, denk maar altijd—als je eens tobt over wat gebeurd is—aan Goethe—'das unvermeidliche mit Würde tragen'—en jelui draagt het samen, dat maakt alles lichter—het Engelsche huwelijksformulier is zoo mooi: to have and to hold, for better, for worse, for richer, for poorer, in sickness and in health, to love and to cherish, till death us do part—I plight thee my troth. Daarin ligt *alles*.' Jo to Vincent and Josina. VGM, b8294; 29 December 1915.

127 Jo to Vincent and Josina. VGM, b8697; 10, 12 and 13 February 1916. The lines of poetry come from 'Denkspruch' by Karl Streckfuß.

128 'Als je een teekening kunt verkoopen voor 't museum zou ik 't *zeker* doen, er zijn er zóó veel! Maar niet te weinig vragen, ik zou denken 1000 Dollar op zijn allerminst.' Jo to Vincent and Josina. VGM, b8294; 29 December 1915. *Account Book* 2002, p. 133.

129 Jo to Paul Cassirer. VGM, b4561; 22 February 1916.

130 'Durch deutsches Gesetz ist eine Klage gegen einen Soldaten während des Feldzuges nicht möglich.' Paul Cassirer to Jo. VGM, b3992; 1 March 1916.

131 Paul Cassirer to Jo. VGM, b3994; 4 July 1916. She received six deluxe copies. Cassirer lamented: 'Leider wird unser Buch nicht so viel gelesen, wie die gekürzte Ausgabe.' ('Unfortunately, our book is not read as much as the abridged edition.')

132 VGM, b3993, b3995 and b3996 respectively.

133 Catalogue *Exhibition of Modern Art: Arranged by a Group of European and American Artists in New York.* New York 1916, pp. 11 and 13. VGMB, TS 4911.

134 'Vooral als U hier bent, zou U hem er goed aan kunnen helpen, als U wou. Maar als U 't liever zelf doet is dat natuurlijk nog beter.' Josina to Jo. IISG, 20 March 1916.

135 'Ik zou 't best vinden als Pach 't deed, als hij 't kan—*ik* doe het niet zelf, 't is me te veel, de Inleiding doe ik wel—dat is alles. Hij moet dan maar een uitgever uit zoeken en die ons een voorstel doen. Zoo is 't met de Duitsche ook gegaan—de uitgever betaalt de vertaler dan. Ik wil natuurlijk wel helpen, b.v. één correctie op me te nemen, of zoo.'' Jo to Vincent and Josina. VGM, b3715; 17 April 1916.

136 These letters from Wibaut are in the IISG.

137 'Vindt jullie niet gruwelijk die aanslag op Liebk. en dat heeft nog wel een vrouw gedaan, wat moeten een wanbegrippen in zoo iemand's hoofd zitten die dát doen kan!' Jo to Vincent and Josina. VGM, b3715; 17 April 1916.

138 *Het Volk* and *De Tribune*, both 17 April 1916.

139 'Ik heb voor me een klein glazen mandje met druifhyacinthjes—en een vaasje met een paar *kleine* rode tulpjes, net anemoontjes. . . . Ik eet wel eens Amerikaanse appelen tegenwoordig—die zijn *prachtig* van kleur en heel geurig.' Jo to Vincent and Josina. VGM, b3715; 17 April 1916.

140 'maar sociaal democraten zeggen en schrijven dikwijls rare dingen'. Jo to Vincent and Josina. VGM, b8697; 10, 12 and 13 February 1916.

141 IISG, SDAP Archives.

142 'Ik heb jelui portretjes bij mijn bed staan, als ik 's avonds de kaars uit blaas is mijn laatste blik op je lieve hoofden en 's morgens de eerste ook weer!' Jo to Vincent and Josina. VGM, b3716; 26–9 June 1916.

17 New York-translation of the letters into English

1 'Nu dacht ik hoe je in die groote tuin in Westfield zult lopen en denken over je werk. . . . Wat zal het heerlijk zijn uit die vreeselijke drukte van N.Y. daar buiten te komen, en dat je 't huishouden daar vindt en niets hoeft mee te sjouwen.' Mathilde Wibaut-Berdenis van Berlekom to Josina. IISG, June 1916.

2 'List or manifest of alien passengers for the United States immigration officer at port of arrival'. NAW.

3 On 26 October 1911 Marie notified the population register that she was living at 2 Brachthuijzerstraat. SGVH, *Dienstboderegister*; ACA; Annie van Gelder-Pigeaud to Jo. VGM, b3720; 17 March 1922.

4 'Op één staat zij met de viool—Jos, jelui kunt dus duo's spelen.' Jo to Vincent and Josina. VGM, b3716; 26, 28 and 29 June 1916.

5 *Vincent's Diary*, 19 February 1940. They went to the opera in mid-November 1917: Frank Cullan, Florence Hackman and Donald McNeilly, *Vaudeville Old & New: An Encyclopedia of Variety Performances in America.* 2 vols. New York and London 2007, vol. 1, p. 464.

6 Jo got as far as letter 526 before she died in 1925. That marked the end of volume 2 of *Brieven aan zijn broeder*. The three-volume publication contained a total of 652 letters. Number 526 is in Van Gogh, *Letters* 2009, letter 666. Van Gogh 1952–4, p. 249 and Van Gogh 1927, p. LXXII.

7 Cornelis de Dood to Vincent. LMDH, D 652 B 1, 15 November 1954. Cf. Van Gogh, *Complete Letters* 1958, pp. XI–XII.

8 Kenneth E. Silver, *Esprit de Corps: The Art of the Parisian Avant-Garde and the First World War, 1914–1925*. London 1989. The severity of the economic downturn was unprecedented: there was a great deal of profiteering, and in September 1918 the prices of everyday articles shot up, some of them by a factor of fourteen.

9 Willem Steenhoff to Jo. VGM, b5611; undated. Willem Steenhoff, 'Een tentoonstelling Vincent van Gogh', *De Kroniek*, August 1917. *Algemeen Handelsblad*, 17 November 1917.

10 Jo to Marguerite Gachet. VGM, b3456; 26 October 1916.

11 'Gaan jelui eens naar een *goeje* bioskoop in New York en vertel mij eens of je *daar* eindelijk eens wat anders ziet, als mijn oude vijand *Bunny*, en of die echte Amerik. films zoo idioot flauw zijn als die je hier altijd ziet.' Isaac Israëls to Jo. VGM, b8640; 15 October 1916.

12 Edwin Hatfield Anderson to Jo. VGM, b6849; 18 May 1917. The set's shelfmark is 3-MCH G61.A1b.

13 Jo to Willem Steenhoff. VGM, b7427; 20 January 1918 (photocopy (VGMD) from the documents left by Steenhoff. Private collection). *Vincent's Diary*, 27 December 1935.

14 IISG, 10 October 1917. Jo to Willem Steenhoff. VGM, b7427; 20 January 1918. Jo described Jamaica as a place 'zoover als Bussum van Amsterdam is' ('as far as Bussum is from Amsterdam'). Prior to that—in any event in May and June 1917—Vincent and Josina had lived at 90 Beach, 45th Street, Edgemere (Queens, Long Island), near Jamaica Bay.

15 She received an envelope addressed to the Rand School Library, 7 E. 15th St NYC. IISG, March 1918. Sebald Rutgers and his wife Bartha left for Moscow in 1918.

16 *Vincent's Diary*, 14 October 1967.

17 Ian D. Thatcher, 'Leon Trotsky in New York City', *Historical Research: The Bulletin of the Institute of Historical Research* 69 (1996), pp. 166–80; R.B. Spence, 'Hidden agendas: Spies, Lies and Intrigue Surrounding Trotsky's American Visit of January-April 1917', *Revolutionary Russia* 21 (2008), pp. 33–35; Robert Service, *Trotsky: A Biography*. London 2009, pp. 154–60, quotation on p. 156. Most of his speeches have remained unpublished.

18 Etty 2000, pp. 221–4 and 313–20.

19 'hij heeft een overtuigend krachtige expressie, onverzettelijk—ik dacht toen al, wat zal die man kunnen doen!' Jo to Willem Steenhoff. VGM, b7427; 20 January 1918 (photocopy (VGMD) from the documents left by Steenhoff. Private collection).

20 Cat. Otterlo 2003, pp. 314–16 and 444.

21 'ik verneem dat het nog veiliger zou zijn bij eventueele dood (van mij) als U een soort bewijs wildet geven dat U het aan haar gegeven hebt. . . . Ziezoo, deze pijnlijke geschiedenis is me van 't hart; ik had het u zelf willen vertellen, maar 't lijkt me toch beter schriftelijk.' Willem Steenhoff to Jo. VGM, b5610; 17 April 1917.

22 Willem Steenhoff to Jo. VGM, b5607; 25 September 1918.

23 'dat het onophoudelijk, *als iets dat leeft*, van aanschijn wisselt'; 'met z'n rijken *bronzen* kleuraard'; 'Maar U weet, U kunt er steeds over beschikken.' Willem Steenhoff to Jo. VGM, b1941; 5 December 1910.

24 VGMB, BVG 14998. Works acquired after 1 April were not in the catalogue. This is why *Path in the Garden of the Asylum* is not in it.

25 Rovers 2010, pp. 318 and 333.

26 Cat. Otterlo 2003, pp. 424–7. Rovers 2010, pp. 189 and 334–5.

27 McCarthy 2011, pp. 46–7 and 76–7; Allan Antliff, 'Carl Zigrosser and the Modern School: Nietzsche, Art, and Anarchism', *Archives of American Art Journal* 34, no. 4 (1994), pp. 16–23, esp. p. 19; Allan Antliff, *Anarchist Modernism: Art, Politics, and the First American Avant-Garde*. Chicago 2001, esp. pp. 167–75.

28 Zigrosser 1971, p. 85.

29 Zigrosser 1971, p. 85. See also CZPP.

30 Henk Bonger wrote that it was clear to see that Jo was suffering from Parkinson's, but she was always cheerful and chatty despite this. Bonger 1986, p. 488.

31 The letters are on pp. 194–203; the comments on pp. 221–2. Van Gogh only referred to Dostoyevsky after reading an article about the writer. See Van Gogh, *Letters* 2009, letters 680 and 812.

32 *The Modern School*, August 1919, pp. 215–23, and 'Editorial Note', p. 240. This issue was Zigrosser's swansong as editor. Zigrosser 1971, p. 82.

33 http://friendsofthemodernschool.org/. Their idealistic principles are summarized in Carl Zigrosser's manifesto *The Modern School: Ferrer Colony, Stelton N.J.* New Jersey 1917 (IISG). It stresses the free development of the personality of each pupil, who learns how to cope with society and help it to progress with an 'open mind and concentrated powers' (p. 5). Concepts such as will and free spirit occur frequently, and courage, independence, sincerity, sensitivity and esteem for ideals are considered to be cardinal virtues (p. 17). See also Paul Avrich, *The Modern School Movement: Anarchism and Education in the United States*. Princeton 1980. For Zigrosser and the magazine see pp. 79, 115–17, 161–3; on the idea that avant-garde art and radical politics were part of a comparable revolutionary process: pp. 136–41.

34 Israëls received *Sunflowers* on 3 March 1918. Willem Steenhoff wrote to Jo that he had signed a receipt for it. VGM, b5611; undated. Later, when Israëls had to part company with this painting, he wrote that it would leave behind 'een ontzettende leegte op de muur' ('an incredible void on the wall'). Isaac Israëls to Jo. VGM, b8625; undated (end of 1919). Jo got the canvas back in February 1920. Isaac Israëls to Jo. VGM, b8645; 20 February 1920.

35 This secretary had a French father and a Norwegian mother. Helen married Augustus Johnson, and lived in Trenton, New Jersey at least between 1927 and 1936. Helen Johnson-Opel to Vincent. VGMD; 18 February 1936. At the end of 1927, Vincent got the publishers, Constable, to send her the translation of the letters: Vincent to Constable and Company. VGM, b6857; 18 December 1927.

36 'ik verlangde op eens vreselijk naar al de dingen die ik mijn leven lang om mij heb gehad, de bloeiende bomen, het landschap van Arles—alles, alles.'; 'Is 't niet heerlijk wat er in Rusland gebeurt? U hebt altijd wel voorspeld dat het uit Rusland komen zou! Ik volg het met hartstochtelijke belangstelling, dat is waar we op gewacht hebben heel deze bange tijd.' Jo to Willem Steenhoff. VGM, b7427; 20 January 1918 (photocopy (VGMD) from the documents left by Steenhoff. Private collection). Haweis studied in Paris with Alphonse Mucha and Eugène Carrière. He married the poetess Mina Loy in 1903. They divorced in 1917.

37 Jo to Stephan Haweis, 12 February 1918. Columbia University in the City of New York, Stephen Haweis Papers, 1860–1969.

38 'Bussumsche voorraadschuur'; 'schrandere vrouw'; 'veel factoren meegewerkt'. Johannes de Bois, *Haarlemsche Courant*, 7 March 1918.

39 'Ik zei u reeds, meen ik, dat om beter licht ik de collectie liet verhuizen naar een der Druckerzalen boven.' 'De suppoost beneden vertelde me dat telkens bezoekers teleurgesteld waren meenende dat de schilderijen weer weg waren.' Willem Steenhoff to Jo. VGM, b5606; 10 April 1918.

40 'Het gezicht op Arles in het midden geflankeerd door het stuk met de blauwe irissen en aan den anderen kant die japansche interpretatie. Zoodoende komt het gez. op Arles zelfstandig en zonne-lichtend uit. Hier boven als kopstuk de zonnebloemen. ik zal toch eens zien de schikking te laten fotografeeren. Op een korten wand eenige der laatste werken: de slaapkamer in 't midden en daarboven het korenveld met onweerslucht, die zeer krachtig tegen elkaar werken ook de interpr. van Delacroix hangt daarbij. Natuurlijk is die tent. voor zeer velen een evenement. Maar ik voel en word ook al gewaar dat het bij een zekeren kliek nog hier in ons chineesche Holland ergernis wekt.' 'dat het voor sommige schilderijen toch wel zeer wenselijk zou zijn ze met beleid te laten schoonmaken. bijv de slaapkamer, waar de lichte kleuren door den tijd nog al vuil op aangeplakt stof hebben aangenomen. ik geloof zeker dat het werk er mee winnen zou. Denkt u er eens over. We hebben ervoor een zeer geschikt en vertrouwd man aan het museum. De verniskwestie (een zeer dun laagje) staat hier buiten. Ik weet, dat u daar volstrekt op tegen is.' Willem Steenhoff to Jo. VGM, b5605; undated (shortly before 25 September 1918)—b5607; 25 September 1918. See also Heijbroek 1991, pp. 206–9.

41 There is a reference to having two works restored by the Amsterdam restorer Hesterman. That was in February 1903. It is not known which two works these were. *Account Book* 2002, pp. 48, 144.

42 Jo to Ernest Brown & Phillips. VGM, b5896; 17 November 1923.

43 'Vanuit de huidige opvatting van conservering en restauratie gezien, is Jo's terughoudendheid ten aanzien van behandeling te prefereren boven de campagne van universele was-harsbedoeking en vernissen die daarop volgde.' Ella Hendriks in an e-mail to me dated 16 February 2013.

44 VGM, b5618 and b5627. For this episode see Heijbroek 1991, pp. 212–18. For the restorations see Cat. Amsterdam 1999, pp. 25–6, and Ella Hendriks, 'Treatment History of the Collection', in *Vincent van Gogh Paintings: Volume 2. Antwerp and Paris 1885–1888, Van Gogh Museum.* Louis van Tilborgh and Ella Hendriks. Amsterdam 2011, pp. 28–36. Ella Hendriks, 'Jan Cornelis Traas, Paintings restorer of the Van Gogh Family Collection. The Art of Conservation: XVII', *The Burlington Magazine* 164, February 2022, pp. 164–77.

45 CZPP; 20 July 1918.

46 On 18 July 1918 Vincent noted 'Dana Street' on the back of a photograph of their house. VGM, b5135. Josina to Jo. VGM, b8698; 27 September 1918. According to the Japanese researcher and translator Ryusaburo Shikiba, they took some works by Van Gogh with them at that time, but no evidence of this has been found. Cf. Kōdera 2002.

47 'List or manifest of alien passengers for the United States immigration officer at port of arrival'. NAW.

48 WPPW; 20 August 1918.

49 '[Zij] zorgden voor mijn moeder toen wij in Japan waren.' ('They looked after my mother while we were in Japan.') *Vincent's Diary*, 6 January 1934.

50 Jo to the Gachet family. VGM, b3457; 15 November 1918. Gachet had been stationed as a soldier and as a militiaman: VGM, b8533; 16 January 1915—b2168; 2 June 1916.

51 Vincent had written to his sister Willemien about Whitman. Van Gogh, *Letters* 2009, letter 670. Jo read his letters to Willemien in 1889. See Willemien van Gogh to Theo van Gogh. VGM, b2392; 16 March 1889.

52 *The Modern School*, April-May 1919, pp. 155–6; Zigrosser 1971, p. 82.

53 Jo to N.E. Montross. VGM, b6262; 17 February 1921.

54 28 March; 14 April (request to send magazine to Van Gelder-Pigeaud); 29 July 1919 (subscription and quotation); 15 January 1921 and 12 January 1922 (New Year greetings) respectively. See CZPP. The copies from the Wibaut Library are in the IISG. Vincent and Josina had taken out a subscription to *The Modern School* earlier.

55 Zigrosser 1971, p. 85; with a photograph of them in the garden in Laren.

56 Jo to Annie van Gelder-Pigeaud. VGM, b3721; 3 October 1922: 'Je leert zooveel dingen zooveel beter begrijpen.' ('You learn to understand so many things so much better.')

57 'zij maakte het ons in sommige opzichten wel lastig; ze had zich wel íéts meer kunnen voegen.' *Vincent's Diary*, 13 May 1975.

58 'Voor de oorsprong van alle creatief werk, ook buiten de kunst, kan men altijd terug kijken naar een moederfiguur; dat is ten minste mijn eigen ervaring als ik om me heen kijk.' 'die haar zoon onder haar vleugels wil blijven beschermen, ook als hij meent deze bescherming niet van node te hebben. . . . Vooral liefdevolle tyrannie en beschermende bazigheid blijken eigenschappen te zijn die haar kenmerken. . . . Zij is het klassiek "overprotective mother-type".' Carbon copy of letter, 24 October 1966 (VGMD); Reisel 1967, pp. 104–8, quotation on p. 108.

59 SAR.

60 Years later Henk wrote: 'Als ik, een enkele keer, bij tante logeerde hingen de *Aardappeleters* boven mijn bed in de kleine logeerkamer. Ik was bang van die smoelen.' ('If I stayed with Auntie, as I did on occasion, *The Potato Eaters* hung above my bed in the small guest room. I was scared of those ugly mugs.') Bonger 1986, pp. 484 (the presents) and 486 (ugly mugs).

61 'Hij is zoo enorm ingenomen met Amerika en niets in Holland is goed, dat maakt mij zoo ongerust dikwijls. Maar als hij nu maar gauw iets heeft of een uitzicht, dan zal hij er meer mee verzoend raken.' Mathilde Wibaut-Berdenis van Berlekom to Floor Wibaut. IISG, several letters dated between November 1919 and January 1920.

62 *Vincent's Diary*, 26 October 1969. On 9 August 1920 their particulars were transferred to their own family registration card (ACA).

63 'Mijn moeder zei dikwijls dat we zoo stijf waren.' *Vincent's Diary*, 28 August 1933.

64 'Impression bizarre, de toute cette famille Van Gogh, Elle, la mère; lui, le fils, la bru, malades, bizarres, bizarres. Lui, l'air si bébête! Un automate remonté, doucement. La mère, malade, nerveuse, tremblement sénile (et elle n'a pas 60 ans), la bru, froide, pas agréable—renfermée! . . . Ce n'est pas encourageant à revoir—et cependant quel culte Mme V. G.-Bonger garde à Vincent.' VGM b3348, p. 21; Coquiot wrote the following in his notebook: 'En somme, famille Van Gogh-Bonger, hospitalité mesurée—aimable, mais rien au-delà.' ('In short, the Van Gogh-Bonger family: measured hospitality—cordial, but nothing more.') VGM, b7150.

65 VGM, b5339. Van Gogh 1995, p. 3. Vincent wrote the book *Bedrijfsorganisatie*. Leiden 1935; second, revised edition: Leiden 1949.

66 'Ze leefde er zeer teruggetrokken. Soms stond zij in haar erker, altijd stemmig gekleed, wat uit te kijken naar het destijds rustige verkeer van de Koninginneweg. . . . Een stille en daardoor spoedig vergeten figuur.' *NRC Handelsblad*, 15 December 1972.

18 A sacrifice for Vincent's glory

1 'On aimerait de préférence des fleurs.' Gaston Bernheim to Jo. VGM, b3703; 4 December 1919.

2 'Mevrouw Van Gogh-Bonger bereidt eene Engelsche editie der "Brieven" van Vincent van Gogh voor ter uitgave in New-York en Londen.' Both in the *Algemeen Handelsblad* and *Het Vaderland*, 17 January 1920.

3 'U krijgt dus de *Irissen*—en een kleiner: *Gladiolen*, ook een eersterangs Van Gogh'. Jo to Willem Scherjon. VGM, b3152; 20 January—b3148; 3 February 1920 (quotation). *Vase with Gladioli and Chinese Asters* (F 248a / JH 1148), measuring 46.5 cm x 38.4 cm, or *Vase with Chinese Asters and Gladioli* (F 234 / JH 1168) measuring 61.1 cm x 46.1 cm. The catalogue is in HUA.

4 N.E. Montross to Jo. VGM, b3150; 22 January 1920. He wrote later to Vincent: 'Am glad that I had the pleasure of meeting her and shall cherish the memory of that visit.' N.E. Montross to Vincent. VGM, b6279; 5 July 1927.

5 N.E. Montross to Vincent. VGM, b6248; 21 May 1920. Vincent to N.E. Montross. VGM, b6249; 29 May 1920.

6 Draft and final lists of works with prices. VGM, b6250–6.

7 VGM, b6240–2, b6245, b6246, b6259. In the end there were sixty-seven numbers in the catalogue, in other words four more than on the shipping manifest. VGMB, BVG 3489. Vincent reused the frames for the exhibition in London in August 1923.

8 N.E. Montross to Vincent. VGM, b6257; 2 November 1920. Vincent to N.E. Montross. VGM, b6258; 2 November 1920. N.E. Montross to Jo. VGM, b6259; 7 December 1920—b6260; 6 January—b6261; 25 January 1921.

9 Jo to N.E. Montross. VGM, b6262; 17 February (quotation)—b6263; 23 March 1921. Pach had visited Jo, as recorded in N.E. Montross to Jo. VGM, b4087; 7 October 1921. She must have been familiar with Pach's contribution 'Vincent van Gogh', *International Studio* 74 (November 1920), pp. 72–3. Later Pach published the slim volume *Vincent van Gogh, 1853–1890: A Study of the Artist and His Work in Relation to His Times*. New York 1936.

10 N.E. Montross to Jo. VGM, b4085; 27 May 1921. *Account Book* 2002, pp. 54, 136 and 152. Jo and Vincent must have agreed that they would retain the payments for the time being.

11 N.E. Montross to Jo. VGM, b4085; 27 May 1921. See also the *Algemeen Handelsblad*, 19 April 1921 and Rebecca A. Rabinow, 'Modern Art Comes to the Metropolitan: The 1921 Exhibition "Impressionist and Post-Impressionist Paintings"', *Apollo* 152, no. 464 (2000), pp. 3–12.

12 Edward Robinson (The Metropolitan) to Jo. VGM, b6264; 23 September 1921.

13 Jo to N.E. Montross. VGM, b4084; 20 June 1921—b4088; 25 October 1921 (quotation). Jo wrote in her diary: 'The lot of critics is to be remembered by what they failed to understand.' It was taken from *Impressions and Opinions* (1891) by George Moore. Jan Veth gave Jo this book as a thirtieth birthday present (VGMB, BVG 1462). If she took the quotation from this copy, as would seem obvious, she did not copy it into her diary until after 4 October 1892. *Diary* 4, p. 144.

14 According to the catalogue *Modern Art of Holland: An Exhibition* and a report in the *NRC* of 10 June 1921.

15 N.E. Montross to Jo. VGM, b6266; 28 January 1922. Jo to N.E. Montross. VGM, b6267; 23 February 1922 (quotation).

16 Jo to N.E. Montross. VGM, b6270; 11 May—b6272; 9 June 1923—b6276; 27 February 1924 (Montmartre).

17 Julius Meier-Graefe to Jo. VGM, b7602; 2 August 1920.

18 'milieu très intellectuel de la Haye'; 'Pour moi qui ai vécu de leur vie, qui entend leurs voix à travers l'espace de trente ans, il y a quelquefois une note fausse, artificielle, dans les dialogues que vous leur attribuez, mais ce sera ainsi seulement pour moi et les rares personnes encore en vie qui ont connu Vincent et Théo personnellement.' 'Moi, qui ai consacré ma vie entière à cet œuvre immense de Vincent et de Théo, je connais ces joies.' Jo to Julius Meier-Graefe. VGM, b7604; 23 October 1920.

19 Jo to Julius Meier-Graefe. VGM, b7606; 15 February 1921.

20 Jo to Walter Pach. WPPW; 27 June 1923.

21 'Ach, het is er allemaal zoo naast! ... Het was allemaal zoo héél anders.' *De Telegraaf*, 4 December 1928. Jo expressed no opinion concerning Meier-Graefe's views about Van Gogh's art.

22 'Sie sind immer falsch, wie sorgfältig sie auch gemacht sind.' Jo to Julius Meier-Graefe. VGM, b7609; 27 April 1923.

23 Cf. Lenz 1990, Kōdera and Rosenberg 1993, Stefan Koldehoff, *Meier-Graefes Van Gogh: wie Fiktionen zu Fakten werden*. Nördlingen 2002, and Stefan Koldehoff, *Van Gogh: Mythos und Wirklichkeit*. Cologne 2003. For the letters see Van Gogh, *Letters* 2009.

24 Paul Gachet to Jo. VGM, b3401; 22 December 1920. Jo to Paul Gachet. VGM, b1518; 31 December 1920.

25 'Soyez persuadé, cher ami, que mon fils comme moi, a le culte du souvenir de son père et de son oncle et dès qu'il en aura l'âge, le petit Théodore sera initié dans la même tradition.' Jo to Paul Gachet. VGM, b1516; 19 January 1921. Years later he had still not sent the bill for the gravestones. Jo found it insufferable to think she would die without having settled it. Jo to Paul Gachet. VGM, b1526; 12 March 1924. Jo emphasized to Coquiot that everyone had to leave the graves of Theo and Vincent alone: 'Mme V. G-Bonger me l'a nettement exprimé: elle ne veut pas que l'on touche, en quoi que ce soit, aux tombes des deux frères Van Gogh! Tant pis pour les mangeurs de cadavres!' ('Mrs van Gogh-Bonger has made her views very clear. She does not want anyone whatsoever to touch the graves of the two brothers! So that's too bad for the vultures!') VGM, b3348, p. 21.

26 VGM, b5778–84. VGMB, BVG 2937.

27 Jo to an unknown addressee: VGM, b5784; May 1921 (carbon copy of letter).

28 'Nous gardons chez nous intacte la série des vergers et c'était seulement pour faire plaisir à un de mes amis, membre du comité de l'Exposition que j'ai consenti à envoyer une de ces toiles à Paris. Puisqu'on en envoyait même nos Rembrandts!!' Jo to Paul Gachet. VGM, b1517; 2 May 1921. Her 'ami' Jan Veth was in the organizing committee.

29 Both works were once more on show at the E.J. van Wisselingh gallery in Amsterdam from 27 April to 18 May 1932: 'Hollandsche en Fransche schilderkunst der 19^e^ en 20^e^ eeuw', nos. 19–20. Vincent to Anna Wagner. VGMD, 2 March 1961.

30 Isaac Israëls to Jo. VGM, b8646; 22 November 1921.

31 'In dit apenland zooals jij het noemt, heb ik tot dusver geen enkele aap ontmoet. ...' 'Ja jij, je bent heusch een echt Javaantje met je kleinkinderen.' ''t is merkwaardig hoe aardig of ze hier met kleine kinderen zijn en hoe hardvochtig met dieren. wat is preferabel? Bij ons is 't dikwijls andersom.' Isaac Israëls to Jo. VGM, b8647; 28 February 1922. Isaac Israëls to Jo. VGM, b8648; 6 July 1922: 'Jij sprak van oerwouden, maar mijn lieve menschje, die *zijn* er op Java niet!' ('You talked about jungles but, my dear little woman, there *aren't* any on Java!') He asked her to do him a favour as a friend—at least if she got the chance: 'do your darling grandchildren give you any time for yourself??????' ('laten je kleinkindertjes je tijd??????')

32 'un vrai Van Gogh'. Jo to Paul Gachet. VGM, b1518; 31 December 1920. Jo to Carl Zigrosser; 15 January 1921. See CZPP.

33 ''t is een onbeschrijfelijke engel met het liefste humeur van de wereld, echt sweet tempered.' Jo to Annie van Gelder-Pigeaud. VGM, b3719; 6 October 1921.

34 This was in February 1921 and the publishers were Dodd, Mead and Company, The Macmillan Company and Boni & Liveright. VGM, b6857.

35 'Me dunkt, dat kan nooit kwaad en zal er meer bekendheid aan geven. Iedereen zegt, dat het nu wel het moment is voor een Hollandsch boek om in Amerika te verschijnen.' 'die ik ook wil uitgeven'. Jo to Annie van Gelder-Pigeaud. VGM, b3719; 6 October 1921. During that visit Jo also gave them a copy of the luxury edition of *Briefe an seinen Bruder*, with inside the dedication: 'In Freundschaft gewidmet'. Sale San Francisco, PBA Galleries, *Fine Literature & Fine Books*, 18 May 2017, lot 178. The publication of Gauguin's letters to Vincent, Theo and Jo did not appear for another sixty years, see Gauguin, *Lettres* 1983.

36 Adriaan Jacob Barnouw to Jo. VGM, b6265; 12 January 1922.

37 'waar ik natuurlijk niet aan denk'. Jo to Annie van Gelder-Pigeaud. VGM, b3721; 3 October 1922.

38 The prize draw art exhibition ran from 10 to 31 December 1921. *Algemeen Handelsblad*, 12 December 1921.

39 *De Tribune*, 9 and 22 December 1921–8 March and 5 April 1922. De la Faille 1928, p. 80 lists the owner of the drawing after Jo's as the Amsterdam gallery 'Caramelli & Tessaro'. Alberto and Jan Caramelli and Philippe Tessaro had been employed by Frans Buffa & Zonen.

40 *Catalogus der prijzen voor de Kunstverloting. De opbrengst is ten behoeve van den hongersnood in Rusland.* Centraal Lotenbureau Algemeen Comité tot Steun aan de Hongerenden in Sowjet-Rusland. Schoolstraat 26 Utrecht (RKD copy).

41 'Het was een blaas-catahrr, waarbij ik echter nergens last van had dan een streng dieët en blijven liggen.' 'charmant Engelsch secretaresje'; 'waar ik natuurlijk veel bij te pas moet komen'. Jo to Annie van Gelder-Pigeaud. VGM, b3720; 17 March 1922. Later she asked Gachet to show De la Faille his Van Goghs. Jo to Paul Gachet. VGM, b1521; 17 February 1923.

42 Jo to Ernst Pfeiffer. VGM, Bd95; 20 December 1921 (photocopy). Accompanying this letter was a bookmark with a small drawing after Van Gogh's *Sorrow*, which Theodore Pitcairn bought in May 1921. Cf. www.philippesmit.com/biographies/ernst-pfeiffer/ and Guus Janssens, 'Swedenborg en Nederland, 1712–2010', *Swedenborgiana. Tijdschrift voor Swedenborg Publikaties* 71 (2010). www.swedenborg.nl.

43 Jo to Gustave Coquiot. VGM, b3270; 27 December 1921—b3271; 2 May 1922—b3268; 11 June 1922.

44 'J'ai une grande vénération pour son beau caractère et sa constante abnégation.' Paul Gachet to Gustave Coquiot. VGM, b3313; undated.

45 'femme de 55 à 60 ans, moyenne, très nerveuse, fort souffrante, des yeux expressifs, mais elle a un tremblement perpétuel des deux mains, surtout de la main droite'. VGM, b3348, before p. 20; Coquiot amended his text on the basis of his notes in VGM, b7150. 'C 'est une quinquagénaire, taille moyenne, très rouge de figure surtout par moments, tremblement perpétuel des deux mains, surtout de la droite, l'air froid, puis souriant tout d'un coup avec chaleur. Les yeux sont vifs et agréables.' ('She is in her fifties, average height, now and then very flushed, continuous trembling of both hands, particularly the right, cold, and the next moment friendly and smiling. Her eyes are lively and engaging.') He made a few further remarkable notes about Jo, including her veneration for everything in the estate: 'Elle a le culte des souvenirs, même jusqu'au fétichisme, c'est ainsi qu'elle conserve des petits calepins ayant appartenu à Vincent, choses sans intérêt absolument.' ('She wallows in everything that holds memories; in fact it borders on fetishism. For instance, she carefully keeps Vincent's notebooks, things of absolutely no importance.') 'On a reproché à Mme v. G.-Bonger d'avoir publié certaines lettres douloureuses de Vincent.— Et, cependant, *elle a gardé secrètes les plus douloureuses!* . . . quelles lettres peuvent être ces lettres-là!' VGM, b3348, p. 20.

46 Jo to Paul Gachet. VGM, b1519; 24 April 1922.

47 'Ik heb er zoo van genoten, want hier in de stad is het toch altijd maar een uurtje dat ik ze zie, elken dag.' Jo to Annie van Gelder-Pigeaud. VGM, b3721; 3 October 1922.

48 'Ci-inclus vous trouverez Bonne-Maman avec le petit Theo, qui embrasse les pieds de son petit frère; ça date de l'été dernier. Les bébés ont grandi depuis; Theo a deux ans déjà et est extrêmement intelligent et d'une vitalité superbe. Le petit Johan (c'est mon filleul) est un gros, beau bébé de 8 mois. En regardant ses beaux yeux limpides je pense toujours à ce que Vincent dit, qu'on voit l'infini dans les yeux d'un enfant.' Jo to Paul Gachet. VGM, b1520; 26 November 1922. For the quotation see Van Gogh, *Letters* 2009, letter 656.

49 'J'ai eu un traitement électrique avec défense absolu d'écrire et n'ayant ici à la campagne ni machine à écrire, ni secrétaire j'étais on ne peut plus handicapé.' Jo to Gustave Coquiot. VGM, b3272; 2 September 1922. Draft letter written by her secretary, containing a few spelling mistakes.

50 Images in Étienne Piot, *Indications cliniques de l'électroradiothérapie*. Paris 1927, pp. 25–35. A Dutch manual about high-frequency current published in the 1930s describes its application to patients with rheumatic, muscular or nervous pain as positive.

51 H.P. Baudet, 'Indicaties voor electrotherapie', *Nederlandsch Tijdschrift voor Geneeskunde* 49 (1905), pp. 1478–90; Hazel Muir, 'The Ultimate Recharge', *New Scientist*, 16 February 2013, pp. 41–3. With thanks to Mieneke te Hennepe, curator of medicine at the Rijksmuseum Boerhaave in Leiden.

52 'C'est si bon, après tant d'années d'indifférence, de hostilité même du public envers Vincent et son œuvre, de sentir vers la fin de ma vie que la bataille est gagnée.' Jo to Gustave Coquiot. VGM, b3275; 10 November 1922.

53 On pp. 7–9. This dedication was mentioned in the *Algemeen Handelsblad*, 22 March 1923 and 14 April 1923.

54 VGMB, BVG 869a; Coquiot also produced a special dedication for the fourth edition of his book *Les Indépendants, 1884–1920*. VGMB, BVG 372. 'un vrai magicien'. Jo to Gustave Coquiot. VGM, b3273; 17 October 1922.

55 Jo to Gustave Coquiot. VGM, b3276; 19 January 1923—b3277; 5 March 1923. The book was reprinted three times in 1923.

56 *Het Vaderland*, 15 January 1923.

57 Heijbroek 1991.

58 Jo to N.E. Montross. VGM, b6268; 25 October 1922. Jo had told Goudstikker which paintings Montross was holding, but Goudstikker probably did not pursue the matter.

59 Jo and Vincent lent Goudstikker four paintings and a watercolour. VGM, b5500–b5503. The loans came about through the mediation of Cornelis Baard. The *NRC* of 28 March 1923 reported on the exhibition.

60 Ernest Brown & Phillips to Jo. VGM, b5873; 2 May—Jo's reply: b5874; 9 May—their response: b5875; 14 May—her reply: b5876; 29 May 1923.

61 Ernest Brown & Phillips to Jo. VGM, b5877; 7 June 1923.

62 Jo to Ernest Brown & Phillips. VGM, b5878; 18 June 1923.

63 *Vincent's Diary*, 15 October 1933.

64 Brown 1968, pp. 83–4. Vincent used the lists compiled for the 1920 exhibition in New York as preparation for the show in London. VGM, b6243, b6244 and b6247.

65 Ernest Brown & Phillips to Jo. VGM, b5880; 24 September 1923.

66 Brown 1968, pp. 83–4.

67 Oliver Brown to Jo. VGM, b5884; 11 October 1923.

68 Ernest Brown & Phillips to Jo. VGM, b5887; 17 October—b5888; 19 October 1923. Jo to Ernest Brown & Phillips. VGM, b5885; 18 October 1923.

69 Jo to Ernest Brown & Phillips. VGM, b5889; 24 October 1923. Nine works were not for sale. VGM, b5935.

70 Jo to Ernest Brown & Phillips. VGM, b5891; 7 November 1923. Ernest Brown & Phillips to Jo. VGM, b5892; 7 November 1923.

71 Jo to Ernest Brown & Phillips. VGM, b5894; 12 November—b5896; 17 November 1923.

72 Jo to Ernest Brown & Phillips. VGM, b5901; 15 December (quotation)—b5902; 17 December 1923. Ernest Brown & Phillips to Jo. VGM, b5904 19 December 1923—b5906; 2 January 1924.

73 Jo to Joel Elias Spingarn (Harcourt, Brace and Company). VGM, b6857; 22 November 1922 (quotation). Leo Simons to Jo. VGM, b6857; 19 May 1923.

74 VGM, b6857; 11 January—6 April 1924 (quotation).

75 Jo to Albert Boni. VGM, b6857; 14 January 1925 (draft letter). Boni, who married Cornelia van Leeuwen in 1917, was a correspondent for the *NRC* in the 1920s and 30s. He knew Jo, Vincent and Josina from their time in New York. Albert Boni to Jo. VGM, b6857; 3 April 1925.

76 VGMB, BVG 3427.

77 Ernest Brown & Phillips to Jo. VGM, b5900; 13 December 1923—b4090; 18 January 1924.

78 VGM, b4092–3. *Account Book* 2002, pp. 164–5.

79 Exh. cat. Compton Verney 2006, pp. 24–5.

80 Letter of 29 December 1923, see *Letters of Frances Hodgkins*. Ed. Linda Gill. Auckland 1993, p. 374.

81 Jo to Paul Gachet. VGM, b1522; 25 June 1923.

82 Israëls made the portrait in June 1923 (private collection).

83 Jo to Walter Pach. WPPW; 27 June 1923 and 18 October 1923.

84 'Haar kwaal kon zij niet meer verbergen.' Bonger 1986, p. 488.

85 *Chuo Bijutsu*, July 1924. Reprinted as 'A Visit to Van Gogh's Sister-in-Law', in exh. cat. Sapporo 2002, pp. 266–9.

86 H.S. Ede to Jo. VGM, b5883; undated (end of September 1923). Cf. for the negotiations also exh. cat. Compton Verney 2006, pp. 25–7.

87 H.S. Ede to Jo. VGM, b5940; 1 October 1923. Jo to H.S. Ede. VGM, b5886; 18 October 1923.

88 H.S. Ede to Jo. VGM, b5942; 26 November—b5943; 27 November—b5945; 19 December 1923—b5946; 3 January—b5953; 1 April 1924. On the manuscript of the English translations see Ernest Brown & Phillips to Jo. VGM, b5930; 1 July 1924—b5933; 4 November 1924. Jo to H.S. Ede. VGM, b5954; 9 April 1924.

89 Charles Aitken to Jo. VGM, b5958; 30 November 1923. Jo to Charles Aitken. VGM, b5957; undated.

90 C.J. Holmes to Charles Aitken. TGAL. VGM, Bd23; 29 November 1923.

91 C.J. Holmes to Jo. TGAL. VGM, Bd24; 30 November 1923. Jo to Charles Aitken. TGAL. VGM, Bd25; 3 December 1923. Oliver Brown to Charles Aitken. TGAL. VGM, Bd26; 7 December 1923. Charles Aitken to Jo. VGM, b4106; 9 January—b5947; 15 January 1924. Jo to Charles Aitken. VGM, b5948; 16 January 1924.

92 Jo to Ernest Brown & Phillips. VGM, b4089; 15 January 1924.

93 VGM, b4115, b4094 and b4095. This gallery in Lucerne opened in 1919. This work is currently in the Museum of Modern Art in New York. *Account Book* 2002, pp. 136, 164–5. Exh. cat. Compton Verney 2006, p. 25 (Ede quotation) and *Thannhauser Gallery* 2017, pp. 48–9 and 156–7.

94 The original, signed by Jo, is in the TGAL. VGM, b5951 (carbon copy). Martin Bailey described Jo's English in this letter as being 'slightly stilted'. That may well have been the case, but she meant what she said. See exh. cat. Compton Verney 2006, p. 27 and Martin Bailey, *The Sunflowers Are Mine: The Story of Van Gogh's Masterpiece*. London 2013, p. 160.

95 Charles Aitken to Jo. VGM, b4108; 6 February 1924.

96 VGM, b5950. *Account Book* 2002, pp. 136, 164. On the exclusion of non-British purchases before 1917: John House, *Impressionism for England: Samuel Courtauld as Patron and Collector*. London 1994, p. 9.

97 Vincent to Charles Aitken. TGAL and carbon copy: VGM, b4106; 9 February 1924. Vincent to Samuel Courtauld. VGM, b4112; 9 February 1924. TGAL. VGM, b4113; 14 March 1924. VGM, Bd34–Bd35. Cf. also Ernest Brown & Phillips to Jo. VGM, b5912; 6 June 1924.

98 Jo to Charles Aitken. VGM, b5952; 27 February 1924.

99 Ernest Brown & Phillips to Jo. VGM, b5919; 12 May 1924. '14 mei afwijzend geantwoord.' Ernest Brown & Phillips to Vincent. VGM, b5926; 12 June 1924. Not recorded in the cash book. The portrait is currently in Musée d'Orsay, Paris.

100 Jo to Charles Aitken. VGM, b4110; 13 May 1924.

101 Vincent to F.M. Hübner. VGM, b6042; 3 May 1923. F.M. Hübner to Jo. VGM, b6044; 10 July 1923. Jo to F.M. Hübner. VGM, b6046; 25 September 1923.

102 Wilhelm Barth to Jo. VGM, b6048; 8 October 1923. Jo to Wilhelm Barth. VGM, b6049; 25 October 1923 (carbon copy). Jo's original letters are in the Staatsarchiv des Kantons Basel-Stadt (SAKB).

103 'von der sehr eigenwilligen alten Dame mehr Details in Erfahrung zu bringen. Ich will auch versuchen, ihr in bewegten Worten klar zu machen, wie wichtig es für die Schweiz wäre, mehr wie nur 25 Bilder von ihr zu erhalten.' Hans Schneider to Wilhelm Barth, 13 November 1923. SAKB.

104 'einfacher und korrekter'. Jo to Wilhelm Barth. VGM, b6051. Wilhelm Barth to Jo. VGM, b6052; 14 November 1923.

105 'Es ist mir immer gelegen, jede Ausstellung so bedeutend wie möglich zu machen.' Jo to Wilhelm Barth. VGM, b6053; 17 November 1923.

106 VGM, b6059; 5 February—b6060; 16 February 1924.

107 Wilhelm Barth to Jo. VGM, b6064; 28 March—b6067; 19 April—b6068; 23 April 1924 (offer). SAKB. 'Die Zeichnung "La Crau" ist definitiv unverkäuflich.' 'Die Preise sind festgestellt und es ist nicht davon zu ändern.' Jo to Wilhelm Barth, 2, 15 and 26 April 1924 respectively. The drawings were *La Crau seen from Montmajour* (F 1420 / JH 1501) and *Olive Grove* (F 1555 / JH 1859).

108 Cf. Vincent in a letter to Paul Gachet. VGM, b2813; 22 August 1926: 'Sa fille a aidé ma mère la dernière année avec la traduction anglaise des lettres.' ('His daughter helped my mother with the English translation of the letters last year.')

109 *Algemeen Handelsblad*, 31 July 1923; *De Gooi- en Eemlander*, 1 December 1923.

110 'Ce qu'on a écrit des bêtises sur Vincent!!' Jo to Paul Gachet. VGM, b1524; 12 January 1924.

111 'Mon fils possède maintenant encore un tableau de tournesols, qui restera toujours dans la famille.' Jo to Paul Gachet. VGM, b1526; 12 March 1924.

112 *Brieven* 1923–24. (The dating of 1923 was incorrect; it should have been 1924.) Speech given by Vincent at the annual meeting of the publishers Wereldbibliotheek on 25 May 1974. VGM, b7435. The shared investment is described in a document dated 15 June 1925. VGM, b6850.

113 'Wat ik bij de eerste uitgave zoo vurig hoopte, is waarheid gebleken: zij hebben hun weg gevonden tot de harten der menschen. Uit alle oorden der wereld komen de getuigenissen tot mij, hoe de zuivere menschelijkheid van den grooten kunstenaar, de lezers van zijn brieven treft, boeit en ontroert. Zoo zal zich ook deze tweede uitgave—die in geen enkel opzicht van de eerste verschilt—nieuwe vrienden maken.'

114 Jo to Paul Cassirer. VGM, b3998; 9 March—b4003; 29 March 1924. Paul Cassirer to Jo. VGM, b4002; 28 March 1924.

115 'Ich möchte gerne Ihre Abrechnung der Briefe von van Gogh empfangen. Die folgende Angabe des Absatzes habe ich am 23sten September 1918 von Ihnen empfangen, aber weil ich damals in Amerika war, haben wir es nicht verrechnet.' Jo to Paul Cassirer. VGM, b4004; 5 April 1924.

116 Paul Cassirer to Jo. VGM, b4568; 29 April 1924.

117 *De Tijd*, 31 March and 16 April 1924.

118 J.J.N. Exter to Jo. VGM, b5504–b5509; these six letters were written between 12 February and 8 May 1924.

119 Jo to J.J.N. Exter. VGM, b5510; 25 August 1924 (copy of the letter and list)—J.J.N. Exter to Jo. VGM, b5511; 27 August 1924. *Wheatfield with Crows* was insured for 20,000 guilders and the *Sunflowers* for 15,000 guilders.

120 'Ik begrijp niet hoe u tot het allerlaatste oogenblik hebt durven wachten met mij te melden dat de tentoonstelling niet door kon gaan.' 'Ik verzoek u dringend mij hierheen te berichten wanneer zij aangekomen zijn en de lijsten terug te zenden.' Jo to J.J.N. Exter. VGM, b5512; 28 August 1924 (copy).

121 'als een schooljongen'. J.J.N. Exter to Jo. VGM, b5513; 30 August 1924.

122 VGM, b6609; 18 April 1924.

123 Otto Fischer to Jo. VGM, b6137; 5 August 1924. Jo to Otto Fischer. VGM, b6139; 11 August 1924.

124 Otto Fischer to Jo. VGM, b6141; 3 September 1924. Jo to Otto Fischer. VGM, b6142; 6 September 1924.

125 Otto Fischer to Jo. VGM, b6144; 15 September—b6146; 15 October 1924. Jo to Otto Fischer. VGM, b6145; 19 September 1924. VGM, b6158–9 (lists of titles and prices).

126 Jo to Hartmann, a colleague of Fischer's. VGM, b6155; 22 November—b6156; 25 November 1924 (quotation). VGM, b6148 (net prices).

127 Otto Fischer to Jo. VGM, b6152; 11 November—b6154; 20 November 1924

128 'Es werden *keine* Ausstellungen mehr in Deutschland gehalten.' Jo to Otto Fischer. VGM, b6153; 14 November 1924.

129 'Het beoordeelen van de echtheid van een schilderij is altijd een moeilijke zaak en zonder het schilderij gezien te hebben kan men er nooit geheel juist over oordeelen. . . . We zouden alleen volkomen zekerheid kunnen hebben indien we het schilderij zelf zagen.' Jo to J.-B. de la Faille. VGM, b7454; 18 August 1924.

130 'niet de alles-beslissende factor'. *NRC*, 2 December 1928 and *Het Vaderland*, 3 December 1928. Shortly afterwards he actually used just such a provenance as an argument (*NRC*, 5 February 1929).

131 VGM, b6925; 26 August 1924 and VGMB, TS 3988.

132 'C'est une interpretation à moi.' Van Gogh, *Letters* 2009, letter 805.

133 'J'ai revécu en vous lisant les meilleurs souvenirs de ma vie. Le cher Catalpa, je le vois devant moi, j'en étais si fière. "Vous êtes en pleine campagne", me disait-on. Dans ce petit coin obscur de Paris, que j'y ai été heureuse et . . . ce que j'y ai souffert. Que ma vie a été tragique et comme elle m'a pris de forces! hélas il ne m'en restent pas beaucoup.' Jo to Paul Gachet. VGM, b1527; 10 September 1924.

134 'Iedere Amsterdammer kent de begaafde vrouw met de ruime artistieke belangstelling, aan wier bewonderenswaardige werkkracht we de boeken met brieven van haar zwager Vincent van Gogh danken,—en kan dus oordeelen over de treffende gelijkenis.' Maria de Klerk-Viola, *NRC*, 24 October 1924.

135 'waarin de warme, intelligente oogen van inwendig leven trillen'. *De Tijd*, 29 October 1924.

136 Jo to Carl Marcus. VGM, b6237; 28 October 1924. Jo to Emil Richter. VGM, b6235; 7 November 1924. Jo to the Kunstverein in Wiesbaden. VGM, b6233; 21 November 1924. Jo to the Neue-Secession in Munich. VGM, b6231; 27 November 1924. Jo to the Kunstverein in Hamburg. VGM, b6229; 2 January 1925.

137 Galerie Marcel Bernheim to Jo. VGM, b5786; 4 April 1924. Jo to Galerie Marcel Bernheim. VGM, b5787; 9 April 1924 (carbon copy).

138 Jo to Bernheim. VGM, b5800; 21 October—b5801; 24 October 1924. Galerie Bernheim to Jo. VGM, b5802; 24 October 1924. A copy of the list is VGM, b5785. As usual, she explained the prices in guilders were *net*. Jo to Bernheim. VGM, b5803; 28 October 1924.

139 Galerie Marcel Bernheim to Jo. VGM, b5808; 17 December 1924.

140 Jo to Marcel Bernheim. VGM, b5809; 19 December 1924. Vincent to Marcel Bernheim. VGM, b5810; 21 December 1924.

141 Marcel Bernheim to Jo. VGM, b5813; 5 January 1925. Jo to Marcel Bernheim. VGM, b5814; undated (copy of the telegram text 'Pas à vendre')—b5815; 6 January 1925.

142 Galerie Marcel Bernheim to Jo. VGM, b5816; 7 January—b5818; 30 January 1925. Jo to Marcel Bernheim. VGM, b5817; 13 January 1925.

143 Jo to Marcel Bernheim. VGM, b5821; 9 February 1925.

144 'Ce n'est pas pour mon plaisir mais pour l'intérêt de l'œuvre de Vincent que j'arrange toutes ces expositions. Une fois que je ne serai plus là, il y aura un fin.' Gachet lent two portraits of Van Gogh to Bernheim and Jo was pleased with the impression of the exhibition he had given her. Jo to Paul Gachet. VGM, b1528; 22 December 1924—b1529; 20 January—b1530; 31 January 1925 (quotation).

145 'tikje schorre, diepe stem'; 'met een beheerste emotionaliteit, een eigen oordeel, een relativerende humor en een zuiver gevoel voor waarden'. Bonger 1986, p. 485.

146 Chair Dirk Wiggers to Jo. VGM, b5516—Jo to Dirk Wiggers. VGM, b5517; both 18 November 1924.

147 'Een bevriend schilder te Parijs maakte mij er attent op dat enkele schilderijen overgespannen moeten worden, dat kan dan misschien meteen gebeuren—natuurlijk voor mijn rekening.' Jo to Reinier Sybrand Bakels. VGM, b5524; 11 February 1925.

148 J.H.C. Vermeer to Jo. VGM, b5527; 27 February 1925. Jo to Dirk Wiggers. VGM, b5528; 14 March 1925. VGM, b5515–16 (frames). This was the last sales list that Jo compiled during her lifetime.

149 Dirk Wiggers to Jo. VGM, b5532; 16 April 1925—b5533 (undated copy of her reply): '*Korenaren*, *f* 3.000,- *Allée te Arles*, *f* 9.000,- *Boeken* *f* 9.500 tezamen *f* 20.000,-. Anderen zijn niet verkoopbaar.'

150 'die alles in een roes van opwinding doet. Dat was hij juist niet, hoe oneindig veel teerheid en fijnheid was er in hem.' 'Ik denk dikwijls: "Wat is het moeilijk de zuivere waarheid omtrent iets vast te stellen."' Jo to Willem Steenhoff. VGM, b7426; 1 April 1925 (photocopy (VGMD) from the documents left by Steenhoff. Private collection).

151 'De belangstelling voor het werk van Van Gogh en voor zijn persoon blijft groeien. De tweede druk van deze interessante brieven is er om het te bewijzen, maar tevens de tentoonstelling van zijn werk in Parijs en hier in Pulchri.' *Het Vaderland*, 25 April 1925.

152 'Schilderijen Koninginneweg: 1 Landschap te Arles—2 Zonsondergang Auvers—3 Cypressen met twee figuren—4 Winterlandschap St. Rémy—5 Toren te Nuenen—6 La Veillée (naar Millet)—7 Dame bij de wieg (Parijs). Naar Berlijn—8 Bloeiende boomgaard (wit)—9 Bloeiende boomgaard (rose)—10 Stilleven vruchten (geel). Schilderijen Waldeck Pyrmontlaan: 1 Slaapkamer. Naar Berlijn—2 Huisje van den schilder te Arles. Naar Berlijn—3 Zelfportret—4 Zee—5 Zaaier—6 Dorscher, naar Millet—7 Schapenscheerster, naar Millet—8 Seine bij Asnières.' VGM, b5535 (Fetter) and b5536 (list).

153 H.E. van Gelder to Vincent and Josina. VGM, b3604; 8 September 1925.

154 Jo to the Pulchri board. VGM, b5539; 26 April 1925—and b5542 (list of the seven works).

155 VGMB, BVG 3468. After the end of the exhibition in October, director Willem Cornelis Schuylenburg asked Vincent to consent to them remaining on show for a brief period. 'Wetende hoezeer Uw moeder erop gesteld was ze weer terug te hebben, zou ik het haar nooit gevraagd hebben, dankbaar als ik reeds was voor haar groote welwillendheid om ze voor onze tentoonstelling beschikbaar te stellen.' ('Knowing how much your mother was counting on getting them back, I would never have asked her, grateful as I was for her great willingness to provide them for our exhibition.') Vincent gave permission for the *Sunflowers* to remain in Utrecht until 1 December 1925 and the *Irises* until 1 April 1926. After the *Sunflowers* returned, it was apparent it was damaged. Vincent must have been upset, but he reacted politely and wrote that there was 'een spijkergat rechts boven in zit, waaromheen de verf voor een deel af is. . . . Wendt U zich tot Uw assuradeur of wilt U soms even aankomen om het schilderij zelf te zien?' ('a nail hole top right, around which some of the paint has flaked off. . . . Would you please contact your insurer, or would you prefer to come and see the painting for yourself?') W.C. Schuylenburg to Vincent. VGM, b5550; 6 October—b3484; 2 November—b5553; 11 December 1925. Vincent to W.C. Schuylenburg. VGM, b5551; 10 December 1925 (quotation).

156 SGVH, no. 49. The announcement of her death is VGM, b1586. Maria de Klerk-Viola wrote in the *Algemeen Handelsblad* of 3 September: 'Wel was mevr. Van Gogh sedert lang af en toe lijdende, maar reeds zoo menigmaal triomfeerde haar energieke, levenskrachtige natuur over de ziekte.' ('Mrs van Gogh had suffered from her illness on and off for years, but so many times her energetic and vigorous character triumphed over her condition.') Reports like this were reprinted in other newspapers, for example in *De Sumatra Post*, 7 October 1925.

157 *NRC*, 4 and 5 September 1925. Exactly fifty years later Vincent wrote that there had been torrential rain. He commented that the Bongers 'waaren zoo opgeschroefd sentimenteel en wilden beredderen' ('were so pretentiously emotional and tried to manage things'). *Vincent's Diary*, 5 September 1975.

158 *NRC*, *Algemeen Handelsblad*, *Het Vaderland* and *De Avondpost* of 5 September 1925. See also Van Gogh 1952–4, p. 249; *Algemeen Handelsblad*, 6 September 1925; *Het Volk*, 16 March 1926 and *Voorwaarts. Sociaal-Democratisch Dagblad*, 23 March 1926.

159 Jo to Theo. VGM, b4272; 2 March 1889: 'Before I forget, I should tell you I was born on 4 October 1863. Could you not work it out, Dries and you, or did neither of you know how old I was? No, but now it's really in earnest.' *Brief Happiness* 1999, p. 193. In February 1957 Vincent paid three hundred guilders to the council for the maintenance of Jo's and Johan's graves. The Vincent van Gogh Foundation took over the responsibility at the end of 1987. VGM, b6929.

160 'onbluschbare geestdrift in haar donkere oogen'. 'Zij heeft op heldhaftige wijze een apostolaat vervuld en daarmee haar eigen leven tot een geestelijke schoonheid vervuld.' 'den waarde-inhoud van Vincent van Gogh, als mensch en als kunstenaar, te leeren inzien' *NRC*, 4 September 1925. Also included in Van Gogh 1952–4, vol. 4, pp. 250–1.

161 'Vergeten wij niet dat het steeds een vrouw is, die al de beslommeringen, démarches enz. enz. voor deze dingen zich op de schouders laadt.' *Haarlems Dagblad*, 15 September 1925. Included in Van Gogh 1952–4, vol. 4, pp. 251–3.

162 Bernard 2012, p. 886.

163 'Vincent's palet, opengebloeid in de gloed van Theo's hart, belichtte en voor de komende geslachten bewaarde'; 'een ongemeen stoere vrouw'. Tralbaut 1953, pp. 2 and 8.

164 'Dan zei ze dat de opvoeding van haar zoon in de goede richting ook een stuk werk voor de maatschappij is. "Dat is dan ook mijn voornaamste werk geweest". Zoo waren precies haar woorden.' *De Proletarische Vrouw*, 10 September 1925.

165 'Ik weet niets heerlijkers dan dat ik jou gelukkig zie. Het is de kroon op mijn leven ook, weet dat wel!' Jo to Vincent. VGM, b2106; 31 October 1914.

166 'Vous savez bien ce qu'elle a fait pendant les derniers trente-cinq années; en même temps c'était pour moi [comme] si elle ne vivait que pour moi.' Vincent to Paul Gachet. VGM, b2807; 1 September—b2808; 4 September 1925 (quotation).

167 *Diary* 3, pp. 137–8; 15 November 1891.

Epilogue: 'An exceptional example for women'

1 *Account Book* 2002, p. 136.

2 'Copy of the estate inventory for inheritance tax concerning the estate of Mrs J.G. Bonger', recorded at the Amsterdam notary R. Nicolaï. VGM, b2219; April 1926. The Leesinrichting was at 486 Singel and from 1922 at 489 Herengracht.

3 'waaronder zeer veel belangrijke werken op allerlei gebied, maar vooral ook op het terrein der kunst en der kunsthistorie van vele landen van Europa.' The library's archive contains no details about this donation. With thanks to librarian Sil Wijnvoord, telephone conversation 19 October 2016.

4 Vincent to art historian Anna Wagner; 2 March 1961. VGMD.

5 'Mijn vader wilde in die tijd beslist zijn Van Gogh-collectie bij elkaar houden, maar er verder niet veel aandacht aan besteden. Hij was bezig met zijn ingenieurscarrière en daarbij wilde hij niet aangesproken worden als de neef van de beroemde schilder. Pas na de oorlog ging hij zich actief met de collectie bemoeien.' Interview with Johan and Anneke van Gogh, 20 June 2003. VGMD, pp. 1 and 4. See also Tromp 2006, pp. 163–4.

6 Speech by Vincent. VGM, b7439; 1 February 1975. See also Van Gogh 1995, p. 4.

7 'een aantal jaren geleden het besluit genomen scheen, uit den voorraad werken van Vincent, nog in Uw bezit, niets meer te verkoopen. Jammer genoeg voor mij . . .'; 'vrij groot aantal'. Johannes de Bois to Vincent. VGM, b5493; 1 July 1926.

8 Van Gogh 1987, pp. 5–6. His position on this point changed. J.H. Gosschalk wrote: 'Inmiddels heb ik gehoord dat U aan verkoopen niet meer denkt' ('I have meanwhile heard that you are no longer thinking of selling'). When F.M. Hübner commented: 'Da Sie mich wissen liessen, dass Sie nicht grundsätzlich gegen Verkäufe seien' ('Because you let me know that you are not fundamentally against sales'), and asked which paintings might be available, Vincent replied that he did not want to sell anything for the time being. J.H. Gosschalk to Vincent. VGM, b5856; 28 January 1926—F.M. Hübner to Vincent. VGM, b6390; 14 August—Vincent to F.M. Hübner. VGM, b6391; 13 September 1926. So that 'for the time being' turned out to be brief.

9 He donated some, and exchanged others for food during the Second World War. There is an overview of the works he sold, donated or exchanged in the Van Gogh Museum's archive.

10 Vincent to Ernest Brown & Phillips. VGM, b5971; 18 December 1926.

11 VGM, b5988; 9 February—b5989; 23 February 1927. Vincent agreed to a discount of 800 guilders for *Trees in the Garden of the Asylum* (F 640 / JH 1800) and *Landscape with Trees and Figures* (F 818 / JH 1848). These two, as well as *Portait of Madame Trabuc*, were immediately sold on to Galerie Thannhauser. See *Thannhauser Gallery* 2017, pp. 164, 176 and 178.

12 Brown 1968, p. 98.

13 This overview, based on De la Faille 1928, is given by Balk 2006, p. 240. Differences in numbers referred to in the introduction to this current biography are caused by including or not including double-sided drawings and sketchbook pages.

14 *Account Book* 2002, p. 9. Her income did, of course, have to cover costs, such as having frames, mounts and shipping crates made. Memorandum by Vincent van Gogh, 27 May 1977 (VGMD).

15 Betsy inherited her brother Henri's estate when he died in 1929. It included four paintings and two drawings by Van Gogh, and after Betsy's death they entered Vincent's collection. Presently in the Van Gogh Museum, they are *Small Bottle with Peonies and Blue Delphiniums* (F 243a / JH 1106); *Trees and Undergrowth* (F 309a / JH 1312); *Field with Farmhouses* (F 576 / JH 1423); *Woman Binding Sheaves (after Jean-François Millet)* (F 700 / JH 1781); *The Vicarage Garden* (F 1132 / JH 463) and *Ditch* (F 1243 / JH 472). See *Account Book* 2002, p. 162, 179. VGM, b2580. With thanks to Johan van Gogh. Cf. the August 1994 memorandum from Han Veenenbos, secretary of the Vincent van Gogh Foundation, and see VGMD. In 1973 Vincent summarized a number of purchases and donations: VGM, b6621; 2 June 1973.

16 Vincent to Paul Gachet. VGM, b2812; 2 March 1926. Paul Gachet to Vincent. VGM, b4577; 17 January 1938: 'Je suis bien content de l'occasion qui me procure le plaisir d'avoir de vos nouvelles: ça me rappelle le temps où votre mère vivait!' ('I am very happy with the opportunity that gives me the pleasure of hearing from you: it reminds of the time when your mother was alive!')

17 'il y a souvent des passages fort intéressants'. Paul Gachet to Vincent. VGM, b3406; 19 March 1926. On the transfer: VGMD, 30 November 1982.

18 A letter from Jo to Annie van Gelder-Pigeaud reveals that Adriaan Barnouw had recommended the publishers Houghton Mifflin Co to Jo as early as 1921. VGM, b3719; 6 October 1921.

19 VGM, b6857 contains the correspondence about the publication. Nico van Suchtelen (WB) to Vincent. VGM, b6857; 16 October 1925 ('attractive proposal')—7 December 1925. Nico van Suchtelen (WB) to Constable and Company. VGM, b6857; 5 March 1926. Vincent to Leo Simons. VGM, b6857; 8 March 1926.

20 Vincent to Constable and Company. VGM, b6857; 11 October 1927.

21 *The Burlington Magazine for Connoisseurs* 51 (November 1927), pp. 253–4; signed by 'J.L.' Cf. Vincent to Paul Gachet. VGM, b2819; 14 December 1927. That same summer Bernheim-Jeune in Paris expressed interest in an edition in French after Vincent had sent him the three volumes of *Brieven aan zijn broeder*. Jean Bernheim Jeune to Vincent. VGM, b5835; 12 July 1927. Vincent specified the following requirement: 'Je suis disposé de faire une révision de la traduction, l'expérience avec la traduction allemande et avec les épreuves anglaises en ayant démontré la nécessité.' ('I am willing to do a revision of the translation, experience with the German translation and with English proofs having demonstrated the need.') Vincent to Jean Bernheim Jeune. VGM, b5835; 27 July 1927 (carbon copy).

22 Contrary to the title, the letters Van Gogh wrote in 1890 were also included. Vincent's foreword was also printed in Van Gogh, *Complete Letters* 1958, pp. IX–XII.

23 On this see Leo Jansen, Hans Luijten and Fieke Pabst, 'Paper Endures: Documentary Research into the Life and Work of Vincent van Gogh', *Van Gogh Museum Journal 2002*. Amsterdam and Zwolle 2002, pp. 26–39.

24 In 1927 in *The Letters* under the title 'Loyalty, Devotion, Love', in 1928 in the second edition of *Briefe an seinen Bruder* as 'Treue, Widmung, Liebe', in 1932 in *Lettres à son frère Vincent* in French, and in *Verzamelde brieven* 1952–4 in Dutch. In the last two of these books the title of the tribute was replaced by Jo's name. Each time, Johan Cohen Gosschalk's drawing of Jo was included.

25 'Mijn vader was niet mededeelzaam over zijn moeder; er werd veel verteld over kunst, maar over haar was hij zwijgzaam.' In conversation with Johan van Gogh, 9 September 2007.

26 William Gravesmill, who worked in the M.H. de Young Memorial Museum in San Francisco during the 1970s, wrote the following on 3 January 2009 in an e-mail to the Van Gogh Museum: 'Dr Van Gogh often talked about the fact that his mother was "the perfect pack rat", because she kept everything and we now have all of those letters' (VGMD).

27 Van Gogh, *Letters* 2009. www.vangoghletters.org. For the book editions based on it, see www.vangoghletters.org/vg/bookedition.html.

28 Meyjes also suggested this. See Meyjes 2007, p. 106. For the later imbalances on the art market, the influence of auction houses and the improbably high sums paid for Van Goghs since the last decades of the twentieth century, see Nathalie Heinich, *The Glory of Van Gogh: An Anthropology of Admiration*. Princeton 1996. She also discusses the effect that commercialism had on Van Gogh's fame.

29 Kōdera 2002, pp. 280–1.

30 *Catalogus Vincent van Gogh. Werken uit de verzameling van ir. V.W. van Gogh in bruikleen afgestaan aan de Gemeente Amsterdam*. Compiled by W. Steenhoff. Amsterdam 1931 (VGMB, BVG 2640 c). Jo was honoured in the foreword (p. 7). This shows that Vincent and Josina had still a considerable number of works in their home in Laren.

31 Conversation with Johan van Gogh, 6 January 2014. See also Van Gogh 1987, pp. 5 and 8.

32 'Het was haar geloof in de waarde van het werk en haar liefde voor de taak, die Vincent zich in zijn werk stelde, welke in feite tot deze onderscheiding heeft geleid.' VGM, b5137 (Medal of Honour) and Silver Carnation (private collection).

33 'De Staat neemt voor zijn rekening de rente en aflossing van een door de stichting te sluiten lening, welke lening tot een bedrag van *f* 18.470.000, ter betaling van de koopprijs, de stichting bereid is aan te gaan.' F.J. Duparc, *Een eeuw strijd voor Nederlands cultureel erfgoed*. The Hague 1975, pp. 338–40, quotation on p. 339. See also Van Gogh

1987, p. 6. During the summer of 2003 the Van Gogh Museum's Sjraar van Heugten, Head of Collections, and Chris Stolwijk, Head of Research, interviewed Johan and Anneke van Gogh (20 June) and Mathilde Cramer-van Gogh (1 August). In his 'Additions' to his interview, Johan stressed: 'Er kan niet genoeg de nadruk op gelegd worden dat het rijk en niet vader het initiatief genomen heeft voor Stichting/Museum.' ('It cannot be sufficiently emphasized that the Dutch State, and not my father, took the initiative for the Foundation/Museum.') Letter to the museum, September 2004 (VGMD). *Vincent's Diary*, 22 October 1971 and 28 May 1972. Van Bronkhorst 1995. Peter de Ruiter, *A.M. Hammacher. Kunst als levensessentie*. Baarn 2000, pp. 263–5. On 13 November 1962 the Special Committee officially approved the contract of 21 July 1962 between the Dutch State and the Vincent van Gogh Foundation (session 6827).

34 Van Gogh, *Letters* 2009, letter 534. VGM, b6621; 2 June 1973.

35 When the foundation was established, it was stipulated that each of the three branches (children) of Vincent van Gogh would provide a board member. The fourth board member is a representative of the Dutch State. The foundation is the collection's owner and must give permission if there are requests for loans. The Van Gogh Museum manages and conserves the collection and conducts research into it.

36 Modderkolk 2014 and Hans Luijten in *Art Market Dictionary* (2022), https://www.degruyter.com/document/doi/10.1515/amd/html.

37 She was also one of the characters in *Langs de kant van de weg*, a four-part television drama about Vincent van Gogh's life, directed by Jan Keja. In the fourth episode, broadcast on 27 April 1990, Jo is 'de schakel—over de dood heen—tussen Vincent en ons' ('the link—transcending death—between Vincent and us'.) The 1991 film *Van Gogh*, written and directed by Maurice Pialat, with Corinne Bourdon as Jo. Claire Cooperstein, *Johanna. A Novel of the Van Gogh Family*. New York etc. 1995. The play *Van Gogh* by Bas Heijne, performed by 'Het Toneel Speelt' in March 2003, with Betty Schuurman as Jo. On 19 October 2005 the one-woman show *Van Gogh and Jo* was performed by its author, Muriel Nussbaum, in the Thomas A. Walsh Art Gallery at the Regina A. Quick Center for the Arts, Fairfield University, Connecticut. The play *Mrs van Gogh* (Musgrove Studio, Maidment Theatre Complex, The University of Auckland, New Zealand) was performed in April 2012 by the Galatea Theatre, with Gina Timberlake playing the part of Jo. The posters stated suggestively: 'All because one woman refused to destroy the hundreds of paintings left to her.' She also figures in the Spanish novel *La viuda de los Van Gogh* by Camilo Sánchez (Buenos Aires 2012). The artist Tang Da Wu staged an exhibition in the Goodman Arts Centre (Singapore) that centred on Jo: 'First Art Council. Third Chapter: Waiting', 5–9 April 2013. Silke Riemann and Ben Verbong wrote *Johanna. De vrouw die Vincent van Gogh beroemd maakte. Een vie romancée*. Translated by Janneke Panders. Amsterdam 2014. Finally, the creative writers William J. Havlicek and David A. Glen have announced the book *Van Gogh's Enduring Legacy: And the Remarkable Woman Who Changed the History of Art* (Amsterdam 2019) and Cinema7films are making a film entitled *Jo, The Van Goghs' Widow*, in which Jo will play a central role: https://cinema7.com/?portfolio_page=jo-the-van-goghs-widow.

38 *Diary* 1, p. 17.

39 *Diary* 1, p. 3.

Illustrations

Plates

Plate 27 Jo van Gogh-Bonger, list of the Van Gogh paintings and the asking prices for Ambroise Vollard in Paris, November 1896. Van Gogh Museum, Amsterdam (Vincent van Gogh Foundation)

Plate 28 Joseph Jessurun de Mesquita (attributed to), *Isaac Israëls*, *c.* 1888. Gelatin printing out paper, 220 × 144 mm. Rijksmuseum, Amsterdam, donated by Mrs O. Vermeulen and Mr F. Diepenbrock

Plate 29 Isaac Israëls, *Jo van Gogh-Bonger*, 1895–6. Drawing from an 1890 photograph (see Plate 16). Red chalk, pencil heightened with white on paper, 300 × 195 mm. Private collection

Plate 30 Isaac Israëls, *Kitten in Different Positions*, 1896. Enclosure with a letter to Jo van Gogh-Bonger. Pencil, red and black watercolour, black chalk on paper, 350 × 256 mm. Private collection

Plate 31 Villa Jacoba, Noordwijk aan Zee, summer 1898. Jo van Gogh-Bonger sits on the chair on the left, Vincent van Gogh sits cross-legged on the ground in front of her. The man with a moustache behind her in the centre may be her brother Henri. On the right, wearing a white apron, is the maid Gerritje. Photograph: Jacob Braakman, Noordwijk aan Zee. Van Gogh Museum, Amsterdam (Vincent van Gogh Foundation)

Plate 32 Calendar page for Wednesday 22 May 1901 with a quotation by Jo van Gogh-Bonger. 'Preserving our children from prejudice and misconceptions is one of the few things we can do to make their life's struggle easier. They are entitled to that.' Van Gogh Museum, Amsterdam (Vincent van Gogh Foundation)

Plate 33 Johan Cohen Gosschalk at his easel on which there is a portrait of a girl, undated. Unknown photographe.r Van Gogh Museum, Amsterdam (Vincent van Gogh Foundation)

Plate 34 Willem Steenhoff in the Rijksmuseum, with Van Gogh's *The Potato Eaters* behind him, *c.* 1918. Unknown photographer. Van Gogh Museum, Amsterdam (Vincent van Gogh Foundation)

Plate 35 Jo Cohen Gosschalk-Bonger, Anna van Gogh-Carbentus and Vincent van Gogh in Bussum, 1903. Unknown photographer. Van Gogh Museum, Amsterdam (Vincent van Gogh Foundation)

Plate 36 Jo Cohen Gosschalk-Bonger, *c.* 1904. Unknown photographer. Van Gogh Museum, Amsterdam (Vincent van Gogh Foundation)

Plate 37 Poster 'Tentoonstelling Vincent van Gogh, Stedelijk Museum Amsterdam, juli-augustus 1905'. Lithograph on paper, 83,4 × 630 mm. Van Gogh Museum, Amsterdam (Vincent van Gogh Foundation)

Plate 38 List of invitees to the opening of the exhibition in the Stedelijk Museum, 1905. Handwriting of Jo Cohen Gosschalk-Bonger and her son Vincent. Van Gogh Museum, Amsterdam (Vincent van Gogh Foundation)

Plate 39 Johan Cohen Gosschalk, *Jo Cohen Gosschalk-Bonger*, *c.* 1905. Charcoal, watercolour, pastels on paper, 350 × 330 mm. Drents Museum, donated by Stichting Schone Kunsten rond 1900

Plate 40 Johan Cohen Gosschalk, *Jo Cohen Gosschalk-Bonger in a Red Dress, Fur Hat and Fur Stole*, 1906. Oil on canvas, 50 × 40 cm. Van Gogh Museum, Amsterdam (Vincent van Gogh Foundation)

Plate 41 Leopold Graf von Kalckreuth, *Portrait of Paul Cassirer*, 1912. Oil on canvas, 61 × 46 cm. Stiftung Stadtmuseum Berlin Photograph: Hans-Joachim Bartsch, Berlin

Plate 42 Pierre Bonnard, *The Bernheim-Jeune Brothers*, 1920. Josse in the foreground and Gaston behind him. Oil on canvas, 166 × 155.5 cm. Musée d'Orsay, Paris Photograph: RMN-Grand Palais (Musée d'Orsay) / Hervé Lewandowski

Plate 43 Anthonius (Toon) Bernardus Kelder, *Portrait of J.H. de Bois, Art Dealer, Haarlem*, 1944. Pencil, ink and watercolour on paper, 239 × 138 mm. Frans Hals Museum, Haarlem Photograph: Arend Velsink

Plate 44 Henri Fantin-Latour, *Flowers*, 1877. Oil on canvas, 54.5 × 61.2 cm. Van Gogh Museum, Amsterdam (Vincent van Gogh Foundation)

Plate 45 Jo van Gogh-Bonger at her desk in the living room at 77 Koninginneweg in Amsterdam, 1909 or later. On the wall behind the desk are Fantin-Latour's *Flowers* and Vincent van Gogh's *Vase of Honesty* (1884), with *Landscape at Twilight* (1890) at the top. Unknown photographer. Van Gogh Museum, Amsterdam (Vincent van Gogh Foundation)

Plate 46 Jo van Gogh-Bonger on the sofa in the living room at 77 Koninginneweg in Amsterdam, 1915. On the wall behind her is Gauguin's *The Mango Trees, Martinique*. Photograph: Bernard Eilers, Amsterdam. Van Gogh Museum, Amsterdam (Vincent van Gogh Foundation)

Plate 47 Paul Gauguin, *The Mango Trees, Martinique*, 1887. Oil on canvas, 86 × 116 cm. Van Gogh Museum, Amsterdam (Vincent van Gogh Foundation)

Plate 48 Johan Cohen Gosschalk, *Self-Portrait*, 1905–10. Oil on panel, 46 × 36 cm. Van Gogh Museum, Amsterdam (Vincent van Gogh Foundation)

Plate 49 Schedule of works by Van Gogh on commission with the Artz & De Bois gallery in The Hague, 12 November 1912. Van Gogh Museum, Amsterdam (Vincent van Gogh Foundation)

Plate 50 Announcement of the Nationale Betoging (national demonstration) in Utrecht—*Bussumsche Courant*, 10 September 1902. www.delpher.nl

Plate 51 Josina Wibaut and Jo van Gogh-Bonger on the road to Aragnouet in the Pyrenees, 1914. Photograph: Vincent van Gogh. Van Gogh Museum, Amsterdam (Vincent van Gogh Foundation)

Figures

Abbreviations

AB Lijst Andries Bonger (VGM, b3055)—List Andries Bonger

ACA Stadsarchief, Amsterdam—Amsterdam City Archives

AHKB Archief voor Hedendaagse Kunst, Brussels—Archives of Contemporary Art

Atria Atria, Kennisinstituut voor Emancipatie en Vrouwengeschiedenis, Amsterdam—Institute on Gender Equality and Women's History

AVP Archief Vollard, Paris. Musées Nationaux, Bibliothèques et Archives. Fonds Vollard, MS 421—Vollard Archives

2,2 'Lettres adressés à Vollard, classées par ordre alphabétique de signataire'

4,1 'Registre des doubles de la correspondance de Vollard, 1899–1922'

4,3 'Registre de caisse, consignant les entrées et sorties 1894–1900'

4,4 'Lettres adressés à Vollard, classées par ordre alphabétique de signataire'

Brinkman *Brinkman's cumulatieve catalogus van boeken* 1833—(accessible digitally in DBNL)—*Brinkman's Cumulative Catalogue of Books*

BSDVC Bond van Sociaal-Democratische Vrouwenclubs—Union of Social Democratic Women's Associations

BWN *Biografisch woordenboek van Nederland* (accessible digitally in Huygens ING)—*Biographical Dictionary of The Netherlands*

BWSA *Biografisch woordenboek van het socialisme en de arbeidersbeweging in Nederland* (accessible digitally in IISG)—*Biographical Dictionary of Socialism and the Labour Movement in the Netherlands*

CZPP Carl Zigrosser Papers, *circa* 1891–1971. University of Pennsylvania. Folder 608

CBG Centraal Bureau voor Genealogie. Centrum voor familiegeschiedenis, The Hague—Institute for Dutch Research on Genealogy

DBNL Digitale Bibliotheek voor de Nederlandse Letteren (www.dbnl.org)—Digital Library for Dutch Literature

F 'Faille': numbers of the Van Gogh works in De la Faille 1970

GAB Gemeentearchief, Baarn—Archives

GAGMN Gemeentearchief Gooise Meren en Huizen, Naarden—Archives

GAH Gemeentearchief, Haarlem—Archives

GAL Gemeentearchief, Leiden—Archives

GAZ Gemeentearchief, Zeist—Archives

HUA Het Utrechts Archief, Utrecht—Archives

Huygens ING Huygens Instituut voor Nederlandse Geschiedenis, Amsterdam—Huygens Research Institute in the Field of History and Culture

IISG Internationaal Instituut voor Sociale Geschiedenis, Amsterdam—International Institute of Social History

JH 'Jan Hulsker': numbers of the Van Gogh works in Hulsker 1996b

KBB Koninklijke Bibliotheek, Brussels—Royal Library

KBH Koninklijke Bibliotheek, The Hague—Royal Library

KBK Koninklijke Bibliotheek, Kopenhagen—Royal Library

LMDH Literatuurmuseum, The Hague—Museum of Literature

NAW National Archives, Washington

NNAB Nieuw Notarieel Archief, Bussum (in SSAN)—Archives

NNBW *Nieuw Nederlandsch Biografisch Woordenboek* (accessible digitally in DBNL)—*New Dutch Biographical Dictionary*

NRC *Nieuwe Rotterdamsche Courant*

RHCM Regionaal Historisch Centrum Limburg, Maastricht—Archives

RHCW Regionaal Historisch Centrum Rijnstreek en Lopikerwaard, Woerden—Archives

RKD Rijksdienst voor Kunsthistorische Documentatie, Nederlands Instituut voor Kunstgeschiedenis, The Hague—Netherlands Institute for Art History

RM 'Related Manuscripts' in Van Gogh, *Letters* 2009—http://vangoghletters.org/vg/overview.html#overview.3

RPK Rijksprentenkabinet, Rijksmuseum, Amsterdam—Print Room

SAKB	Staatsarchiv des Kantons Basel-Stadt, Basel—Archives
SAR	Stadsarchief, Rotterdam—Archives
SDAP	Sociaal-Democratische Arbeiderspartij—Social Democratic Labour Party
SDVC / SDVPC	Sociaal-Democratische Vrouwenpropagandaclub—Social Democratic Women's Party
SGVH	Streekarchief Gooi- en Vechtstreek, Hilversum—Archives
SNVN	Streekarchivariaat Noordwest-Veluwe, Nunspeet—Archives
SSAN	Stads- en Streekarchief, Naarden—Archives
SUBH	Staats- und Universitätsbibliothek, Hamburg—Library
SUD	Spoorwegmuseum, Utrecht—The Railway Museum
TGAL	Tate Gallery Archives, London
UBA	Universiteitsbibliotheek, Amsterdam—University Library
UBL	Universiteitsbibliotheek, Leiden—University Library
VGM	Van Gogh Museum, Amsterdam
VGMB	Van Gogh Museum, Amsterdam. Library
VGMD	Van Gogh Museum, Amsterdam. Documentation
WB	Wereldbibliotheek—publisher in Amsterdam
WNT	*Woordenboek der Nederlandsche Taal* (www.gtb.inl.nl)—*Dictionary of Dutch Language*
WPPW	Walter Pach Papers, 1883–1890. Washington, DC. Archives of American Art, Smithsonian Institution

Bibliography

Adang 2008

Marc Adang, *Voor sociaal-democratie, smaakopvoeding en verheffend genot. De Amsterdamse vereniging Kunst aan het Volk, 1903–1928*. Amsterdam 2008.

Account Book 2002

Chris Stolwijk and Han Veenenbos, *The Account Book of Theo van Gogh and Jo van Gogh-Bonger*. Leiden 2002.

Van Adrichem 2001

Jan van Adrichem, *De ontvangst van de moderne kunst in Nederland, 1910–2000. Picasso als pars pro toto*. Amsterdam 2001.

Agee 1988

William C. Agee, 'Walther Pach and Modernism: A Sampler from New York, Paris, and Mexico City', *Archives of American Art Journal* 28, no. 3 (1988), pp. 2–10.

Art-documents 1952

'Émile Bernard et Vincent van Gogh', *Art-documents*, no. 17 (February 1952), pp. 12–14.

Aurier 1890

G.A. Aurier, 'Les isolés: Vincent van Gogh', *Mercure de France* (January 1890), pp. 24–9.

Bailey 2006

Martin Bailey, 'The British Discover Van Gogh', in exh. cat. Compton Verney 2006, pp. 17–35.

Bailey 2010

Martin Bailey, 'The Van Goghs at the Grafton Galleries', *The Burlington Magazine* 152 (December 2010), pp. 794–8.

Bakker 1995

Nelleke Bakker, *Kind en karakter. Nederlandse pedagogen over opvoeding in het gezin, 1845–1925*. Amsterdam 1995.

Balk 2003

Hildelies Balk, '"De volle grootheid van zijn ziel." Bremmers hartstocht voor het werk van Vincent van Gogh', in Cat. Otterlo 2003, pp. 428–40.

Balk 2006

Hildelies Balk, *De kunstpaus H.P. Bremmer, 1871–1956*. Bussum 2006.

Bank and Van Buuren 2000

Jan Bank and Maarten van Buuren, *1900: The Age of Bourgeois Culture*. With Marianne Braun and Douwe Draaisma. Assen 2004.

Van Beek 2010

N. A. van Beek, *De aanteekeningen van Tante Mietje van Gogh*. The Hague 2010.

Berger 1985

Renate Berger, 'Wilhelmina Jacoba van Gogh (1862–1941). "Du bist sehr tapfer, liebe Schwester"', in *Schwestern berühmter Männer. Zwölf biographische Porträts*. Ed. Louise F. Pusch. Frankfurt am Main 1985, pp. 453–91.

Bernard 1891
Émile Bernard, 'Vincent van Gogh', *Les Hommes d'Aujourd'hui* 8, no. 390. Paris 1891.
Bernard 1994
Émile Bernard, *Propos sur l'art*. 2 vols. Paris 1994.
Bernard 2012
Émile Bernard, les lettres d'un artiste (1884–1941). Ed. Neil McWilliam. Textes recueillis par Lorédana Harscoët-Maire, Neil McWilliam, Bogomila Welsh-Ovcharov. Dijon 2012.
Boekholt and De Booy 1987
Petrus Boekholt and Engelina de Booy, *Geschiedenis van de school in Nederland vanaf de middeleeuwen tot aan de huidige tijd*. Assen and Maastricht 1987.
Blom 2012
Ron Blom, *Frank van der Goes, 1859–1939. Journalist, literator en pionier van het socialisme*. Delft 2012.
Bonger 1974
Henk Bonger, 'Un Amstellodamois à Paris. Extraits des lettres écrites à Paris entre 1880 et 1890 par Andries Bonger à ses parents à Amsterdam', in *Liber amicorum Karel G. Boon*. Ed. Dieuwke de Hoop Scheffer. Amsterdam 1974, pp. 60–70.
Bonger 1986
Henk Bonger, 'Een dierbare herinnering', *Tirade* 30, no. 7/8 (1986), pp. 484–9.
Bonger 1997
Henk Bonger, 'Herinneringen aan mijn oom Dries Bonger.' Unpublished typescript, dated March 1997. VGMD.
Bonger 2019
Jo Bonger, *Dagboeken—Diaries*. Ed. Hans Luijten. Amsterdam 2019. Accessible at www.bongerdiaries.org.
Van der Borch van Verwolde 1937
F. W. M. van der Borch van Verwolde, 'Andries Bonger', in *Jaarboek van de Maatschappij der Nederlandsche Letterkunde 1936–1937*. Leiden 1937, pp. 112–22.
Borrie 1973
G.W.B. Borrie, *Pieter Lodewijk Tak (1848–1907)*. Assen 1973.
Van den Bos 1984
Pieter van den Bos, 'In Bussum begon de victorie voor de Van Goghs', *De Gooi- en Eemlander*, 12 September 1984; also in the *Utrechts Nieuwsblad* of 29 September 1984 under the title 'Van Gogh's victorie begon in Bussum'.
Bosch 2005
Mineke Bosch, *Een onwrikbaar geloof in rechtvaardigheid. Aletta Jacobs, 1854–1929*. Amsterdam 2005.
Bouwman 1992
Dick Bouwman, 'Van Gogh op zolder', *Contactblad Historische Kring Bussum* 8, no. 2 (1992), pp. 59–61.
Van Boven 1992
Erica van Boven, *Een hoofdstuk apart. 'Vrouwenromans' in de literaire kritiek, 1898–1930*. Amsterdam 1992.
Brief Happiness 1999
Brief Happiness: The Correspondence of Theo van Gogh and Jo Bonger. Introduction and commentary by Han van Crimpen. Eds. Leo Jansen and Jan Robert. Amsterdam and Zwolle 1999 (Cahier Vincent 7).
Briefwisseling Van Eeden en Van Deyssel 1981
De briefwisseling tussen Frederik van Eeden en Lodewijk van Deyssel. Eds. H.W. van Tricht and Harry G.M. Prick. Second edition. The Hague 1981.
Van Bronkhorst 1995
Gerald van Bronkhorst, 'Vincent Willem van Gogh and the Van Gogh Museum's pre-history', in *Van Gogh Museum Journal 1995*. Amsterdam 1995, pp. 24–33.
Brown 1968
Exhibition: The Memoirs of Oliver Brown. London 1968.
Brühl 1991
Georg Brühl, *Die Cassirers. Streiter für den Impressionismus*. Leipzig 1991.

Brugmans 1970
I.J. Brugmans, *Stapvoets voorwaarts. Sociale geschiedenis van Nederland in de negentiende eeuw*. Bussum 1970.
Brugmans 1976
I. J. Brugmans, *Paardenkracht en mensenmacht. Sociaal-economische geschiedenis van Nederland, 1795–1940*. The Hague 1976.
Bijl de Vroe 1987
Fusien Bijl de Vroe, *De schilder Jan Veth, 1864–1925. Chroniqueur van een bewogen tijdperk*. Amsterdam and Brussels 1987.

Van Calcar 1886
Elise van Calcar, *Gelukkig—ofschoon getrouwd. Een boek voor gehuwden en ongehuwden*. Haarlem 1886.
Cat. Amsterdam 1987
The Rijksmuseum Vincent van Gogh. Eds. E. van Uitert and M. Hoyle. Amsterdam 1987.
Cat. Amsterdam 1999
Vincent van Gogh: Paintings. Vol. 1: Dutch Period, 1881–1885, Van Gogh Museum. Louis van Tilborgh and Marije Vellekoop. Amsterdam and Blaricum 1999.
Cat. Otterlo 2003
The Paintings of Vincent van Gogh in the Collection of the Kröller-Müller Museum. Jos ten Berge et al. Otterlo 2003.
Cat. Otterlo 2007
Drawings and Prints by Vincent van Gogh in the Collection of the Kröller-Müller Museum. Teio Meedendorp. Otterlo 2007.
Van Crimpen 1988
Han van Crimpen, 'Friends Remember Vincent in 1912', in *Vincent van Gogh: International Symposium Tokyo—October 17–19, 1985*. Eds. Haruo Arikawa et al. Tokyo 1988, pp. 73–90.
Van Crimpen 1993
Han van Crimpen, 'Johanna van Gogh: A Legacy, a Mission', in Kōdera and Rosenberg 1993, pp. 355–73.
Van Crimpen 2002
Han van Crimpen, 'Vincent Willem van Gogh, 1890–1978', in exh. cat. Sapporo 2002, pp. 254–8. English translation of Han van Crimpen, 'Hij kan zulke olijke gezichtjes trekken—zijn eene neusvleugel optrekken of hij zeggen wil "ajakkes"'. Undated and unpublished typescript. VGMD.

Daloze 2015
Marcel Daloze, 'From Eugène Boch to Louis Piérard: The Stages of Van Gogh's Critical Reception in Belgium (1888–1914)', in *Van Gogh in the Borinage. The Birth of an Artist*. Ed. Sjraar van Heugten. Exh. cat. Mons (Musée des Beaux-Arts), 2015. Mons 2015, pp. 184–201.
Doiteau 1940
Victor Doiteau, 'A quel mal succomba Théodore van Gogh?', *Aesculape* 30, no. 1 (1940), pp. 76–87.
Dutch Civil Code
J.A. Fruin, *Nederlandse wetboeken* (1898).

Ebbink 2006
Hans Ebbink, 'De Utrechtse jaren van drukker, uitgever en kunstverzamelaar Willem Scherjon', *Nobelmagazine* 3, no. 2 (2006), pp. 12–14 and pp. 46–50.
Van Eeden 1937
Frederik van Eeden, *Kunstenaarsbrieven*. Ed. Hans van Eeden and H.W. van Tricht. Amsterdam 1937.
Van Eeden 1971
Frederik van Eeden, *Dagboek 1878–1923*. 4 vols. Ed. H.W. van Tricht. Culemborg 1971 (accessible digitally in DBNL).

Eliot 2004

George Eliot, *The Mill on the Floss*, 2004. The Project Gutenberg E-book. Produced by Curtis Weyant and David Maddock. https://www.gutenberg.org/files/6688/6688-h/6688-h.htm.

Etty 2000

Elsbeth Etty, *Henriette Roland Holst, 1869–1952. Liefde is heel het leven niet*. Seventh edition. Amsterdam 2000.

Exh. cat. Amsterdam 1892

Tentoonstelling der nagelaten werken van Vincent van Gogh. Exh. cat. Amsterdam (Kunstzaal Panorama), 1892–3. Amsterdam 1892.

Exh. cat. Amsterdam 1977

Rond de roem van Vincent van Gogh. S.H. Levie et al. Exh. cat. Amsterdam (Rijksmuseum Vincent van Gogh), 1977. Amsterdam 1977.

Exh. cat. Amsterdam 1991

De schilders van Tachtig: Nederlandse schilderkunst, 1880–1895. Eds. C.B. Blotkamp and R. Bionda. Exh. cat. Amsterdam (Rijksmuseum Vincent van Gogh), 1991. Zwolle 1991.

Exh. cat. Amsterdam 1999

Theo van Gogh, 1857–1891. Art Dealer, Collector and Brother of Vincent. Chris Stolwijk and Richard Thomson. With a contribution by Sjraar van Heugten. Exh. cat. Amsterdam (Van Gogh Museum), Paris (Musée d'Orsay), 1999–2000. Amsterdam and Zwolle 1999.

Exh. cat. Amsterdam 2005

Vincent van Gogh: The Drawings. Colta Ives et al. Exh. cat. Amsterdam (Van Gogh Museum), New York (The Metropolitan Museum of Art), 2005. New Haven and London 2005.

Exh. cat. Amsterdam 2012

Isaac Israels in Amsterdam. J.F. Heijbroek and Jessica Voeten. Exh. cat. Amsterdam (City Archives), 2012. Bussum 2012.

Exh. cat. Assen 1991

Johan Cohen Gosschalk, 1873–1912. Han van Crimpen and Jacqueline Boreel. Exh. cat. Assen (Drents Museum) and Amsterdam (Rijksmuseum Vincent van Gogh), 1991. Assen and Amsterdam 1991.

Exh. cat. Breda 2003

Vincent van Gogh. Verloren vondsten. Het mysterie van de Bredase kisten. Ron Dirven and Kees Wouters. Exh. cat. Breda (Breda's Museum), 2003–4. Breda 2003.

Exh. cat. Bremen 2002

Van Gogh: Fields. The Field of Poppies and the Artists' Dispute. Wulf Herzogenrath and Dorothee Hansen. Exh. cat. Bremen (Kunsthalle), 2002–3. Ostfildern 2002.

Exh. cat. Cologne 2012

1912—Mission Moderne. Die Jahrhundertschau des Sonderbundes. Barbara Schaeffer. Exh. cat. Cologne (Wallraf-Richartz-Museum), 2012. Cologne 2012.

Exh. cat. Compton Verney 2006

Van Gogh and Britain: Pioneer Collectors. Martin Bailey. With an essay by Frances Fowle. Exh. cat. Compton Verney (Warwickshire), Edinburgh (The National Gallery—The Dean Gallery), 2006. Edinburgh 2006.

Exh. cat. Copenhagen 1984

Gauguin og van Gogh i København i 1893—Gauguin and Van Gogh in Copenhagen in 1893. Merete Bodelsen. Exh. cat. Copenhagen (Ordrupgaard), 1984–5. Copenhagen 1984.

Exh. cat. Detroit 2022

Van Gogh in America. Detroit (Detroit Institute of Arts), 2022–3.

Exh. cat. Essen 1990

Vincent van Gogh and the Modern Movement: 1890–1914. Vincent van Gogh and Early Modern Art: 1890–1914. Roland Dorn et al. Exh. cat. Essen (Museum Folkwang), Amsterdam (Van Gogh Museum), 1990–1. Freren 1990.

Exh. cat. Essen 2010
"Das schönste Museum der Welt." Museum Folkwang bis 1933. Hartwig Fischer et al. Exh. cat. Essen (Museum Folkwang), 2010. Göttingen 2010.
Exh. cat. Groningen 1999
Jozef Israëls, 1824–1911. Diewertje Dekkers. With contributions by Martha Kloosterboer et al. Exh. cat. Groningen (Groninger Museum), Amsterdam (Joods Historisch Museum), 1999–2000. Zwolle 1999.
Exh. cat. Haarlem 2017
Van Gogh in Haarlem: Kunsthandel J.H. de Bois, 1913–1946. Antoon Erftemeijer, J.F. Heijbroek, E.L. Wouthuysen. Exh. cat. Haarlem (Kunsthandel Kruis-weg68), 2017. Haarlem 2017.
Exh. cat. The Hague 1990
Van Gogh en Den Haag. Michiel van der Mast and Charles Dumas. Exh. cat. The Hague (Haags Historisch Museum), 1990. Zwolle 1990.
Exh. cat. The Hague 2008
Jozef en Isaac Israëls. Vader en zoon. John Sillevis et al. Exh. cat. The Hague (Gemeentemuseum), 2008–9. Zwolle 2008.
Exh. cat. London 2015
Inventing Impressionism. Paul Durand-Ruel and the Modern Art Market. Ed. Sylvie Patry. With contributions by Dorothee Hansen et al. Exh. cat. Paris (Musée du Luxembourg), 2014–15, London (National Gallery), Philadelphia (Philadelphia Museum of Art), 2015. London 2015.
Exh. cat. New York 2006
Cézanne to Picasso: Ambroise Vollard, Patron of the Avant-Garde. Eds. Rebecca A. Rabinow. Douglas W. Druick et al. Exh. cat. New York (The Metropolitan Museum of Art), Chicago (The Art Institute of Chicago), Paris (Musée d'Orsay), 2006–7. New York etc. 2006.
Exh. cat. Paris 1966
Vincent van Gogh, dessinateur. Exh. cat. Paris (Institut néerlandais), 1966. Paris 1966.
Exh. cat. Paris 1988
Van Gogh à Paris. Françoise Cachin and Bogomila Welsh-Ovcharov. Assistées par Monique Nonne. Exh. cat. Paris (Musée d'Orsay), 1988. Paris 1988.
Exh. cat. Paris 1999
Cézanne to Van Gogh: The Collection of Doctor Gachet. Anne Distel and Susan Alyson Stein. Exh. cat. Paris (Galeries Nationales d'Exposition du Grand Palais), New York (The Metropolitan Museum of Art), Amsterdam (Van Gogh Museum), 1999. New York 1999.
Exh. cat. Rotterdam 1999
Isaac Israëls. Hollands impressionist. Saskia de Bodt et al. Exh. cat. Rotterdam (Kunsthal), 1999–2000. Schiedam 1999.
Exh. cat. Sapporo 2002
Vincent & Theo van Gogh. Exh. cat. Sapporo (Hokkaido Museum of Art), Kobe (Hyogo Prefectural Museum of Art), 2002. Sapporo 2002.

De la Faille 1928
J.-B. de la Faille, *L'œuvre de Vincent van Gogh: catalogue raisonné.* Paris 1928.
De la Faille 1970
J.-B. de la Faille, *The Works of Vincent van Gogh: His Paintings and Drawings.* Amsterdam 1970.
Feilchenfeldt 1988
Walter Feilchenfeldt, *Vincent van Gogh & Paul Cassirer, Berlin: The Reception of Van Gogh in Germany from 1901 to 1914.* Catalogue of the drawings compiled by Han Veenenbos. Zwolle 1988 (Cahier Vincent 2).
Feilchenfeldt 1990
Walter Feilchenfeldt, 'Vincent van Gogh—His Collectors and Dealers, in exh. cat. Essen 1990, pp. 39–46.

Feilchenfeldt 2005
Walter Feilchenfeldt, 'Early provenances—Vincent van Gogh and Ambroise Vollard', in *By Appointment Only: Cezanne, Van Gogh and Some Secrets of Art Dealing: Essays and Lectures.* London 2005, pp. 107–21.
Feilchenfeldt 2010
Walter Feilchenfeldt, 'Karl Ernst Osthaus und die Werke Van Goghs', in exh. cat. Essen 2010, pp. 169–77.
Feilchenfeldt 2013
Walter Feilchenfeldt, *Vincent van Gogh: The Years in France. Complete Paintings, 1886–1890. Dealers, Collectors, Exhibitions, Provenance.* London 2013.
Feilchenfeldt and Brandis 2005
Rahel E. Feilchenfeldt and Markus Brandis, *Paul Cassirer Verlag, Berlin 1898–1933. Eine kommentierte Bibliographie.* Second, revised edition. Munich 2005.
Fontijn 1997
Jan Fontijn, *Broeders in bedrog. De biograaf en zijn held.* Amsterdam 1997.
Fontijn 1999
Jan Fontijn, *Tweespalt. Het leven van Frederik van Eeden tot 1901.* Second edition. Amsterdam 1999.
Fontijn 2007
Jan Fontijn, 'Keerpunten in een leven', in *Bespottelijk maar aangenaam. De biografie in Nederland.* Eds. Arjen Fortuin and Joke Linders. Foreword Elsbeth Etty. Amsterdam 2007, pp. 69–83.
France and St Clair 2004
Mapping Lives: The Uses of Biography. Eds. Peter France and William St Clair. Oxford and New York 2004.

Gachet 1956
Paul Gachet, *Deux amis des impressionnistes: le docteur Gachet et Murer.* Paris 1956.
Gachet 1994
Paul Gachet, *Les 70 jours de Van Gogh à Auvers.* Essai d'éphéméride dans le décor de l'époque (20 mai—30 juillet 1890) d'après les lettres, documents, souvenirs et déductions, Auvers-sur-Oise 1959. Commentaires d'Alain Mothe. Paris 1994.
Gauguin, *Lettres* 1983
Paul Gauguin: 45 lettres à Vincent, Theo et Jo van Gogh. Ed. Douglas Cooper. The Hague and Lausanne 1983.
Geel 2011
Rudolf Geel, 'Dirk Bouwman en Van Gogh', *Bussums Historisch Tijdschrift* 27, no. 3 (2011), pp. 25–6.
Van Gelder 1978
J.G. van Gelder, 'Obituary: The "Engineer" Van Gogh', *The Burlington Magazine* 120 (September 1978), p. 602.
De Génestet 1869
De dichtwerken van P.A. de Génestet. 2 vols. Amsterdam 1869.
Geschiedenis 2006
Geschiedenis van Amsterdam. Hoofdstad in aanbouw, 1813–1900. Eds. Remieg Aerts and Piet de Rooy. Amsterdam 2006.
De Glas 1989
Frank de Glas, *Nieuwe lezers voor het goede boek. De Wereldbibliotheek en Ontwikkeling / De Arbeiderspers voor 1940.* Amsterdam 1989.
Goethe 1999
Johann Wolfgang von Goethe, *Faust.* Ed. Albrecht Schöne. 2 vols. Darmstadt 1999.
Goethe 2008
Johan Wolfgang von Goethe, *Faust.* Translated with an Introduction and Notes by David Luke. 2 vols. Oxford 2008.
Van Gogh 1906
Vincent van Gogh, *Briefe.* Ed. M. Mauthner. Berlin 1906.

Van Gogh 1911
Lettres de Vincent van Gogh à Émile Bernard. Ed. Émile Bernard. Paris 1911.
Van Gogh 1913
The Letters of a Post-Impressionist, Being the Familiar Correspondence of Vincent van Gogh. Translated from the German by Anthony M. Ludovici. Boston and New York 1913.
Van Gogh, *Briefe* 1914
Vincent van Gogh, *Briefe an seinen Bruder*. Ed. J. van Gogh-Bonger. 2 vols. Berlin 1914.
Van Gogh, *Brieven* 1914
Vincent van Gogh, *Brieven aan zijn broeder*. Ed. J. van Gogh-Bonger. 3 vols. Amsterdam 1914 (accessible digitally in DBNL).
Van Gogh 1923–4
Vincent van Gogh, *Brieven aan zijn broeder*. Ed. J. van Gogh-Bonger. Second edition. 3 vols. Amsterdam 1923–4.
Van Gogh 1927
V.W. van Gogh, 'In memoriam J. van Gogh-Bonger: Loyalty, Devotion, Love', in Van Gogh 1927–9, vol. 1, pp. LXV-LXXII. As 'Memoir of J. van Gogh-Bonger', in Van Gogh, *Complete Letters* 1958. vol. 1, pp. LIX-LXVII.
Van Gogh 1927–9
The Letters of Vincent van Gogh to His Brother, 1872–1886. 2 vols. London, Boston and New York 1927. *Further Letters of Vincent van Gogh to his Brother, 1886–1889*. London, Boston and New York 1929.
Van Gogh 1928
Vincent van Gogh, *Briefe an seinen Bruder*. Ed. J. van Gogh-Bonger. Second edition. 3 vols. Berlin 1928.
Van Gogh 1932
Théo van Gogh, *Lettres à son frère Vincent*. Amsterdam 1932.
Van Gogh 1952–4
Verzamelde brieven van Vincent van Gogh. Eds. J. van Gogh-Bonger and V.W. van Gogh. 4 vols. Amsterdam and Antwerp 1952–4.
Van Gogh 1958
The Complete Letters of Vincent van Gogh. 3 vols. London 1958.
Van Gogh 1987
Johan van Gogh, 'The History of the Collection', in Cat. Amsterdam 1987, pp. 1–8.
Van Gogh 1995
Johan van Gogh, 'Chronologisch overzicht van het leven van Ir. dr. V.W. van Gogh', September 1995. VGMD.
Van Gogh 2007
Vincent van Gogh, *Painted with Words: The Letters to Émile Bernard*. Eds. Leo Jansen, Hans Luijten and Nienke Bakker. New York 2007.
Van Gogh, *Brieven* 2009
Vincent van Gogh, *De brieven. De volledige, geïllustreerde uitgave*. Eds. Leo Jansen, Hans Luijten and Nienke Bakker. 6 vols. Amsterdam 2009 (the digital edition of the correspondence is accessible at www.vangoghletters.org).
Van Gogh, *Letters* 2009
Vincent van Gogh, *The Letters: The Complete Illustrated and Annotated Edition*. Eds. Leo Jansen, Hans Luijten and Nienke Bakker. 6 vols. London 2009 (the digital edition of the correspondence is accessible at www.vangoghletters.org).
's-Gravesande 1956
G.H. 's-Gravesande, *De geschiedenis van* De Nieuwe Gids. *Brieven en documenten*. Second edition. Arnhem 1956.
Greer 2007
Joan Greer, 'The Artist's Correspondence in Late Nineteenth-Century Publications on Art: The Letters of Vincent van Gogh in the Belgian Periodical *Van Nu & Straks*', in *Current Issues in 19th-Century Art*. Ed. Chris Stolwijk. Zwolle and Amsterdam 2007, pp. 112–35 (Van Gogh Studies 1).
Grever and Waaldijk 1998

Maria Grever and Berteke Waaldijk, *Feministische openbaarheid. De Nationale Tentoonstelling van Vrouwenarbeid in 1898*. Amsterdam 1998.

Grodzinski 2009

Veronica Grodzinski, 'The Art Dealer and Collector as Visionary: Discovering Vincent van Gogh in Wilhelmine Germany, 1900–1914', *Journal of the History of Collections* 21, no. 2 (2009), pp. 221–8.

Hammacher 1978

A.M. Hammacher, 'Vincent Willem van Gogh, 1890–1978', *Museumjournaal* 23, no. 2 (1978), pp. 50–2.

Van Heerikhuizen 1987

Bart van Heerikhuizen, *W.A. Bonger, socioloog en socialist*. Groningen 1987.

Van der Heide 2015a

Marcus van der Heide, 'Een nagekomen Gooise erflater: Jo van Gogh-Bonger (1862–1925). De victorie van Vincent van Gogh in Bussum', *Tussen Vecht en Eem. Tijdschrift voor Regionale Geschiedenis* 33, no. 4 (2015), pp. 284–7.

Van der Heide 2015b

Marcus van der Heide, 'Jo van Gogh-Bonger: in Bussum begint de victorie van Vincent van Gogh (1)', *Bussums Historisch Tijdschrift* 31, no. 2 (2015), pp. 30–3.

Van der Heide 2015c

Marcus van der Heide, 'Jo van Gogh-Bonger: in Bussum begon de victorie van Vincent van Gogh (2)', *Bussums Historisch Tijdschrift* 31, no. 3 (2015), pp. 28–31.

Heijbroek 1991

J.F. Heijbroek, 'Het Rijksmuseum voor Moderne Kunst van Willem Steenhoff: werkelijkheid of utopie?', *Bulletin van het Rijksmuseum* 39, no. 2 (1991), pp. 163–231.

Heijbroek 2012

J.F. Heijbroek, *Frits Lugt, 1884–1970. Living for Art: A Biography*. Bussum and Paris 2012.

Heijbroek and Wouthuysen 1993

J.F. Heijbroek and E.L. Wouthuysen, *Kunst, kennis en commercie: de kunsthandelaar J.H. de Bois (1878–1946)*. Amsterdam 1993.

Heijbroek and Wouthuysen 1999

J.F. Heijbroek and E.L. Wouthuysen, *Portret van een kunsthandel. De firma Van Wisselingh en zijn compagnons, 1938-heden*. Zwolle and Amsterdam 1999.

Heijne 2003

Bas Heijne, 'Kunst en passie: het verhaal van Jo van Gogh-Bonger—Art and Passion: The Story of Jo van Gogh-Bonger', in *Van Gogh Museum: een portret—Van Gogh Museum: A Portrait*. John Leighton et al. Amsterdam and Zwolle 2003, pp. 24–39.

Hemels and Vegt 1993

J. Hemels and R. Vegt, *Het geïllustreerde tijdschrift in Nederland. Bibliografie. Deel 1: 1840–1945*. Amsterdam 1993.

Van Heugten and Pabst 1995

Sjraar van Heugten and Fieke Pabst, *The Graphic Work of Vincent van Gogh*. Zwolle 1995 (Cahier Vincent 6).

Hofsink and Overkamp 2011

Gert Hofsink and Natalie Overkamp, *Grafstenen krijgen een gezicht*. Stichting Begraafplaatsen Ermelo-Veldwijk 2011.

Huishoudboek 1889–91

Huishoudboek van Mevrouw Theodorus van Gogh-Bonger, April 1889—September 1891. VGM, b2211.

Huishoudboek 1893–6

Huishoudboek van Jo van Gogh-Bonger, Oktober 1893—Februari 1896. All expenses are noted in the *Huishoudboek voor Nederlandsche vrouwen*. Second edition. Leiden 1891. VGM, b2213.

Huizinga 1927

Johan Huizinga, *Leven en werk van Jan Veth*. Haarlem 1927.

Huizinga 1989–91
J. Huizinga, *Briefwisseling*. Eds. Léon Hanssen, Wessel Krul and Anton van der Lem. 3 vols. Utrecht and Antwerp 1989–91.

Hulsker 1963
Jan Hulsker, 'Zijn naam is voor het nageslacht', in *150 jaar Koninkrijk der Nederlanden: ontstaan en bestaan*. Eds. P.J. Bouman et al. Amsterdam 1963, pp. 148–55.

Hulsker 1974
Jan Hulsker, 'What Theo Really Thought of Vincent', *Vincent. Bulletin of the Rijksmuseum Vincent van Gogh* 3, no. 2 (1974), pp. 2–28.

Hulsker 1989
Jan Hulsker, 'The Elusive van Gogh, and What his Parents Really Thought of Him', *Simiolus. Netherlands Quarterly for the History of Art* 19, no. 4 (1989), pp. 243–70.

Hulsker 1990
Jan Hulsker, *Vincent and Theo van Gogh: A Dual Biography*. Ann Arbor, Michigan 1990.

Hulsker 1996a
Jan Hulsker, 'De Van Goghs en de Bongers', *Jong Holland* 12, no. 2 (1996), pp. 44–53.

Hulsker 1996b
Jan Hulsker, *The New Complete Van Gogh: Paintings, Drawings, Sketches. Revised and Enlarged Edition of the Catalogue Raisonné of the Works of Vincent van Gogh*. Amsterdam and Philadelphia 1996.

Van Hulst et al. 1969
H. van Hulst, A. Pleysier and A. Scheffer, *Het Roode Vaandel volgen wij. Geschiedenis van de Sociaal Democratische Arbeiderspartij van 1880 tot 1940*. The Hague 1969.

Jobse-Van Putten 1995
Jozien Jobse-van Putten, *Eenvoudig maar voedzaam. Cultuurgeschiedenis van de dagelijkse maaltijd in Nederland*. Nijmegen 1995.

Joosten 1969a
J.M. Joosten, '1. De eerste kennismaking met het werk van Vincent van Gogh in Nederland', *Museumjournaal*, series 14, no. 3 (1969), pp. 154–7.

Joosten 1969b
J.M. Joosten, '2. De Vincent van Gogh-tentoonstellingen bij kunsthandels Buffa in Amsterdam en Oldenzeel in Rotterdam in februari-maart 1892', *Museumjournaal*, series 14, no. 4 (1969), pp. 216–19.

Joosten 1969c
J.M. Joosten, '3. De tentoonstelling van werken van Vincent van Gogh bij de Haagsche Kunstkring van 17 mei tot 6 juni 1892 (1e deel)', *Museumjournaal*, series 14, no. 5 (1969), pp. 269–73.

Joosten 1970a
J.M. Joosten, '4. De tentoonstelling van werken van Vincent van Gogh bij de Haagsche Kunstkring in 1892 (2e deel) en bij Arti et Amicitiae te Amsterdam in 1892 (1e deel)', *Museumjournaal*, series 15, no. 1 (1970), pp. 47–9.

Joosten 1970b
J.M. Joosten, '5. Het vervolg van de besprekingen van de Amsterdamse keuze-tentoonstelling, de tentoonstelling van vroege tekeningen bij de kunsthandel Oldenzeel te Rotterdam en de Van Gogh tentoonstelling in het Panoramagebouw te Amsterdam', *Museumjournaal*, series 15, no. 2 (1970), pp. 100–3.

Joosten 1970c
J.M. Joosten '6. Conclusie', *Museumjournaal*, series 15, no. 3 (1970), pp. 154–8.

Van Kalmthout 1998
A.B.G.M. van Kalmthout, *Muzentempels. Multidisciplinaire kunstkringen in Nederland tussen 1880 en 1914*. Hilversum 1998.

Van Kerckhoven 1980

G. van Kerckhoven, 'Het Van Goghnummer van *Van Nu en Straks*. De rol van Henry van de Velde bij het tot stand komen van het derde nummer van de eerste reeks. Antwerp 1980.' Unpublished typescript. VGMB.

Klarenbeek 2012

Hanna Klarenbeek, *Penseelprinsessen & broodschilderessen. Vrouwen in de beeldende kunst, 1808–1913*. Bussum 2012.

Kocka 1987

Jürgen Kocka, *Bürger und Bürgerlichkeit im 19. Jahrhundert*. Göttingen 1987.

Kōdera 2002

Tsukasa Kōdera, 'Van Gogh and Hyogo Prefecture: Vincent's Stay in Kobe and Terukazu Oishi's Van Gogh Monument', in exh. cat. Sapporo 2002, pp. 278–84.

Kōdera and Rosenberg 1993

The Mythology of Vincent van Gogh. Ed. Tsukasa Kōdera and Yvette Rosenberg. Tokyo etc. 1993.

Kort geluk 1999

Kort geluk. De briefwisseling tussen Theo van Gogh en Jo Bonger. Inleiding en toelichting Han van Crimpen. Eds. Leo Jansen and Jan Robert. Amsterdam and Zwolle 1999 (Cahier Vincent 7).

Kramers et al. 1982

Henk Kramers, Jaak Slangen and Marius Vroegindeweij, *Het Leidse Volkshuis, 1890–1980. Geschiedenis van een stichting sociaal-kultureel werk*. Leiden 1982.

Kunstsalon Cassirer 2011

Kunstsalon Bruno & Paul Cassirer: Die Ausstellungen 1898–1901. 'Das Beste aus aller Welt zeigen.' Kunstsalon Paul Cassirer: Die Ausstellungen 1901–1905. 'Man steht da und staunt.' Eds. Bernard Echte and Walther Feilchenfeldt. Mitarbeit Petra Cordioli. 2 vols. Wädenswil 2011.

Larsson 1993

Håkan Larsson, *Flames from the South: The Introduction of Vincent van Gogh in Sweden before 1900*. Thesis. Lund 1993.

Larsson 1996

Håkan Larsson, *Flames from the South: On the Introduction of Vincent van Gogh to Sweden*. Eslöv 1996.

Leeman 1990

Fred Leeman, 'Van Gogh's Posthumous Rise to Fame in the Low Countries—Holland and Belgium', in exh. cat. Essen 1990, pp. 207–63.

Leeman 2013

Fred Leeman, *Émile Bernard (1868–1941)*. Avec la collaboration de Béatrice Recchi-Altarriba, pétite-fille de l'artiste et Anne Champié. Documentation Lucrezia Argyropoulos-Recchi et Céline Cordier. Paris 2013.

Lenz 1990

Christian Lenz, 'Julius Meier-Graefe and His Relation to Van Gogh', in exh. cat. Essen 1990, pp. 47–59.

De Liagre Böhl 2013

Herman de Liagre Böhl, *Wibaut de Machtige. Een biografie*. Amsterdam 2013.

Liefdesbrieven 1927

Liefdesbrieven gewisseld tusschen Willem Kloos en Jeanne Reyneke van Stuwe van juni 1898 tot 7 september 1899. The Hague 1927.

Lindenburg 1989

A.W. Lindenburg, *Het Instituut Van Kinsbergen te Elburg in de 19e eeuw (met een beknopt overzicht van de 20e eeuw)*. Elburg 1989.

Locher 1973

J.L. Locher, 'De verzamelaar A. Bonger, een voorbeeld van de relatie tussen kunstenaar en publiek omstreeks de laatste eeuwwisseling', in J.L. Locher, *Vormgeving en structuur. Over kunst en kunstbeschouwing in de negentiende en twintigste eeuw*. Amsterdam 1973, pp. 98–125.

Lugt 1938–87
Frits Lugt, *Répertoire des catalogues de ventes publiques intéressant l'art ou la curiosité*. 4 vols. The Hague 1938–87.
Luijten 2019
Hans Luijten, *Alles voor Vincent. Het leven van Jo van Gogh-Bonger*. Amsterdam 2019.

Manheim 1989
Ron Manheim, 'The "Germanic" Van Gogh: A Case Study of Cultural Annexation', *Simiolus. Netherlands Quarterly for the History of Art* 19, no. 4 (1989), pp. 227–88.
McCarthy 2011
Laurette E. McCarthy, *Walter Pach (1883–1958). The Armory Show and the Untold Story of Modern Art*. Pennsylvania 2011.
Meyjes 2007
Irene Meyjes, *Johanna van Gogh-Bonger: kunsthandelaar?* Deventer 2007.
Modderkolk 2014
Linda Modderkolk, 'Johanna Gezina Bonger (1862–1925)', in *Digitaal Lexicon voor Vrouwen in Nederland* (2014). www.resources.huygens.knaw.nl/vrouwenlexicon/lemmata/data/Bonger; included in *1001 vrouwen in de 20ste eeuw*. Ed. Els Kloek. Nijmegen 2018, pp. 123–4.
Moes 1961
Wally Moes, *Heilig ongeduld. Herinneringen uit mijn leven*. Amsterdam 1961.
Molegraaf 2012
Mario Molegraaf, '"Ze zeggen dat ik steeds eender zing." Vincent van Gogh had een dichtende zus', *De Parelduiker* 17, no. 2 (2012), pp. 26–36.
Montijn 2000
Ileen Montijn, *Leven op stand, 1890–1940*. Seventh edition. Amsterdam 2003.
Mooij 1993
Annet Mooij, *Geslachtsziekten en besmettingsangst. Een historisch-sociologische studie, 1850–1990*. Amsterdam 1993.

Naifeh and White Smith 2011
Steven Naifeh and Gregory White Smith, *Vincent van Gogh. The Life*. London 2011.

Op de Coul 1990
Martha Op de Coul, 'De Van Gogh-tentoonstelling in de Haagsche Kunstkring', in exh. cat. The Hague 1990, pp. 166–9.
Op de Coul 2002
Martha Op de Coul, 'In Search of Van Gogh's Nuenen Studio: The Oldenzeel Exhibitions of 1903', in *Van Gogh Museum Journal 2002*. Amsterdam 2002, pp. 104–19.

Pickvance 1992
Ronald Pickvance, *'A Great Artist is Dead': Letters of Condolence on Vincent van Gogh's Death*. Zwolle 1992. (Cahier Vincent 4).
Piérard 1924
Louis Piérard, *La vie tragique de Vincent van Gogh*. Paris 1924.
Pissarro 1980–91
Janine Bailly-Herzberg, *Correspondance de Camille Pissarro*. 5 vols. Paris 1980–91.
Posthumus 1943–64
N.W. Posthumus, *Nederlandse prijsgeschiedenis*. 2 vols. Leiden 1943–64.
Praamstra 2007
Olf Praamstra, *Busken Huet. Een biografie*. Amsterdam 2007.

Pratt 2006

Jonathan Pascoe Pratt, 'Patron or Pirate? Vollard and the Works of Vincent van Gogh', in exh. cat. New York 2006, pp. 48–59.

Predikbeurtenblad 1883–9

Predikbeurtenblad. Godsdienstoefeningen bij de protestantsche gemeente te Amsterdam. ACA, Archives of the Hervormde Gemeente, accession number 376, inv.no. 376.286A (1877), 376.286B (1878), 376.1003 (1882–3), 376.1004 (1883–4), 376.1006 (1885–6).

Prick 1981–6

Harry G.M. Prick, *De briefwisseling tussen Lodewijk van Deyssel en Albert Verwey*. 3 vols. The Hague 1981–6.

Prick 1986

Harry G.M. Prick, 'Lodewijk van Deyssel over Vincent van Gogh', *Maatstaf* 34, no. 3 (1986), pp. 19–25.

Prick 2003

Harry G.M. Prick, *Een vreemdeling op de wegen. Het leven van Lodewijk van Deyssel vanaf 1890*. Amsterdam 2003.

Du Quesne-Van Gogh 1910

E.H. du Quesne-van Gogh, *Vincent van Gogh. Persoonlijke herinneringen aangaande een kunstenaar*. Baarn 1910.

Du Quesne-Van Gogh 1923

E.H. du Quesne-van Gogh, *Vincent van Gogh. Herinneringen aan haar broeder*. Second edition. Baarn 1923.

Redon and Bernard 2009

Odilon Redon and Émile Bernard. Masterpieces from the Andries Bonger Collection. Fred Leeman. With the assistance of Fleur Roos Rosa de Carvalho. Eds. Aukje Vergeest and Chris Stolwijk. Zwolle 2009.

Reisel 1967

Jacob H. Reisel, *Isaac Israëls. Portret van een Hollandse impressionist. Oeuvre en persoonlijkheidsstructuur*. Amsterdam 1967.

Renders 2008

Hans Renders, *De zeven hoofdzonden van de biografie. Over biografen, historici en journalisten*. Amsterdam 2008.

Rewald 1986a

John Rewald, 'Theo van Gogh as Art Dealer', in *Studies in Post-Impressionism*. Eds. Irene Gordon and Frances Weitzenhoffer. London 1986, pp. 7–115.

Rewald 1986b

John Rewald, 'The Posthumous Fate of Vincent van Gogh, 1890–1970', in Rewald 1986a, pp. 244–54. Enlarged edition of John Rewald, 'Vincent van Gogh, 1890–1970: aan dr. ir. V.W. van Gogh voor zijn tachtigste verjaardag—Vincent van Gogh, 1890–1970: To Ing. Dr. V.W. van Gogh on his Eightieth Birthday', *Museumjournaal* 15, no. 4 (1970), pp. 209–19. Also published in exh. cat. Amsterdam 1977, pp. 4–13.

Reyneke van Stuwe 1932

Jeanne Reyneke van Stuwe, 'Theo en Vincent van Gogh', *De Nieuwe Gids* 47 (March 1932), pp. 354–6.

Roodenburg 1992

Klaas Roodenburg, *Kunstenaars op de Noordwest Veluwe, 1880–1930. Een speurtocht...* Ed. C.M.F. de Zwart. Nunspeet 1992.

Rovers 2009a

Eva Rovers, '"He is the key and the antithesis of so much": Helene Kröller-Müller's Fascination with Vincent Van Gogh', *Simiolus. Netherlands Quarterly for the History of Art* 33, no. 4 (2009), pp. 258–72.

Rovers 2009b

Eva Rovers, 'The Art Collector—between Philanthropy and Self-glorification', *Journal of the History of Collections* 21, no. 2 (2009), pp. 157–61.

Rovers 2010

Eva Rovers, *De eeuwigheid verzameld. Helene Kröller-Müller (1869–1939)*. Amsterdam 2010.

Royaards-Sandberg 1981

Jacqueline Royaards-Sandberg, *Ik heb je zoveel te vertellen. Brieven van en aan Lodewijk van Deyssel, Emile en Frans Erens en Isaac Israëls*. Ed. Harry G.M. Prick. Baarn 1981.

Ruberg 2005

Willemijn Ruberg, *Conventionele correspondentie. Briefcultuur van de Nederlandse elite, 1770–1850*. Nijmegen 2005.

Sanchez 2012

Pièrre Sanchez, *Le Salon des XX et de la Libre Esthétique. Répertoire des exposants et liste de leurs œuvres. Bruxelles, 1884–1914*. Dijon 2012.

Schiefler 1974

Gustav Schiefler, *Meine Graphiksammlung*. Ed. Gerhard Schack. Hamburg 1974.

Stein 1986

Van Gogh. A Retrospective. Ed. Susan A. Stein. New York 1986.

Van Stipriaan 2011

René van Stipriaan, *Vincent van Gogh. Ooggetuigen van zijn lange weg naar wereldroem*. Amsterdam 2011.

Stokvis 2005

Pieter Stokvis, *Het intieme burgerleven: huishouden, huwelijk en gezin in de lange negentiende eeuw*. Amsterdam 2005.

Supinen 1988

Marja Supinen, 'Julien Leclercq—Vincent van Goghin varhainen puolustaja', in *Taidehistoriallisia Tutkimuksia. Konsthistoriska Studier* 11. Helsinki 1988, pp. 68–110.

Supinen 1990

Marja Supinen, 'Julien Leclercq: A Champion of the Unknown Vincent van Gogh', *Jong Holland* 6, no. 6 (1990), pp. 5–14.

Tempel 1999

Benno Tempel, '"Such absurdity can never deserve the name of art." Impressionism in the Netherlands', in *Van Gogh Museum Journal 1999*. Amsterdam and Zwolle 1999, pp. 112–29.

Thannhauser Gallery 2017

Stefan Koldehoff and Chris Stolwijk, *The Thannhauser Gallery: Marketing Van Gogh*. With contributions by Megan Fontanella and Günter Herzog. Catalogue of Works compiled by Monique Hageman with Nora Koldehoff. Brussels 2017.

Thys 1956

Walther Thys, De Kroniek *van P.L. Tak. Brandpunt van Nederlandse cultuur in de jaren negentig van de vorige eeuw*. Amsterdam and Antwerp 1956.

Tibbe 2014

Lieske Tibbe, *Verstrengeling van traditie en vernieuwing. Kunstkritiek in Nederland tijdens het fin de siècle, 1885–1905*. Rotterdam 2014.

Van Tilborgh and Vellekoop 1998

Louis van Tilborgh and Marije Vellekoop, 'Van Gogh in Utrecht: The Collection of Gerlach Ribbius Peletier (1856–1930)', in *Van Gogh Museum Journal 1997–1998*. Zwolle 1998, pp. 26–41.

Timmerman 1983

Aegidius W. Timmerman, *Tim's herinneringen*. Ed. Harry G.M. Prick. Amsterdam 1983.

Tralbaut 1953

Mark Edo Tralbaut, *Vincent, Theo, Johanna*. Amsterdam 1953.

Tralbaut 1963

Mark Edo Tralbaut, 'André Bonger, l'ami des frères Van Gogh', *Van Goghiana 1*. Antwerp 1963, pp. 5–54.

Tromp 2006

Henk Tromp, *De strijd om de echte Vincent van Gogh. De kunstexpert als brenger van een onwelkome boodschap, 1900–1970*. Amsterdam 2006.

Van Uildriks, *Dagboek* 2010

De liefde en de vrijheid, natuurlijk! Dagboek van Frederike van Uildriks (1854–1919). Ed. Mineke Bosch. Hilversum 2010.

Van Nu en Straks 1982

Van Nu en Straks, 1893–1901. *Een vrij voorhoede-orgaan gewijd aan de kunst van Nu, nieuwsgierig naar de kunst-nog-in-wording—die van Straks.* Ed. A.M. Musschoot. The Hague 1982.

Van Nu en Straks 1988

Het ontstaan van Van Nu en Straks. *Een brieveneditie, 1890–1894.* Eds. L. van Dijck, J.P. Lissens and T. Saldien. 2 vols. Antwerp 1988.

Van de Velde 1992

Henry van de Velde, *Récit de ma vie. Anvers—Bruxelles—Paris—Berlin, 1863–1900.* Ed. Anne van Loo. With Fabrice van de Kerckhove. Brussels 1992.

Veldhorst 2018

Natascha Veldhorst, *Van Gogh and Music. A Symphony in Blue and Yellow*. New Haven 2015.

Vergeer 1990

Charles Vergeer, *Toen werden schoot en boezem lekkernij. Erotiek van de Tachtigers.* Amsterdam 1990.

Versteegh 2016

Jaap Versteegh, *Fatale kunst. Leven en werk van Sara de Swart (1861–1951).* Nijmegen 2016.

Verwey 1912

Albert Verwey, 'H.P. Bremmer, Vincent van Gogh', *De Beweging. Algemeen Maandschrift voor Letteren, Kunst, Wetenschap en Staatkunde* 8, no. 2 (1912), pp. 94–5.

Voskuil 1992

P.H.A. Voskuil, 'Het medische dossier van Theo van Gogh', *Nederlands Tijdschrift voor Geneeskunde* 136, no. 36 (September 1992), pp. 1777–9. Some responses to it and rejoinders by Voskuil on pp. 2141–4.

Voskuil 2009

Piet H.A. Voskuil, 'De doodsoorzaak van Theo van Gogh (1857–1891)', *Nederlands Tijdschrift voor Geneeskunde* 153, no. 21 (May 2009), pp. 1–3.

De Vries 2011

Boudien de Vries, *Een stad vol lezers. Leescultuur in Haarlem, 1850–1920.* Nijmegen 2011.

Vijselaar 1982

J. Vijselaar, *Krankzinnigen gesticht. Psychiatrische inrichtingen in Nederland, 1880–1910.* Haarlem 1982.

Wagner 1961

Anna Wagner, 'Enkele Van Gogh schilderijen in het werk van Isaac Israëls', *Museumjournaal*, serie 7, no. 5–6 (1961), pp. 131–5.

Wagner 1967

Anna Wagner, *Isaac Israëls*. Rotterdam 1967.

Wagner 1985

Anna Wagner, *Isaac Israëls*. Venlo 1985.

Weissman 1948

'Herinneringen van A.W. Weissman', in *Jaarboek van het Genootschap Amstelodamum* 42 (1948), pp. 87–145.

Welsh-Ovcharov 1974

Van Gogh in Perspective. Ed. Bogomila Welsh-Ovcharov. Englewood Cliffs 1974.

Welsh-Ovcharov 1996

Bogomila Welsh-Ovcharov, '"I shall grow in the tempest": Van Gogh 100 Years Later', in *Van Gogh 100*. Ed. Joseph D. Masheck. Westport, Connecticut and London 1996, pp. 5–18.

Welsh-Ovcharov 2012

Bogomila Welsh-Ovcharov, 'Vincent van Gogh und die Leidenschaft für die Moderne. Die Kunsthändler Heinrich und Justin K. Thannhauser', in *Aufbruch in die Moderne. Sammler, Mäzene und Kunsthändler in Berlin, 1880–1933*. Anna-Dorothea Ludewig et al. Cologne 2012, pp. 66–87.

Westerink 1976

G. Westerink, *Instituut Van Kinsbergen. Instituut van Opvoeding in Elburg*. Zutphen 1976.

Wildenstein 2001

Daniel Wildenstein, *Gauguin. Premier itinéraire d'un sauvage. Catalogue de l'œuvre peint (1873–1888)*. Text and research Sylvie Crussard. Documentation and chronology Martine Heudron. 2 vols. Paris 2001.

Van der Woud 2010

Auke van der Woud, *Koninkrijk vol sloppen. Achterbuurten en vuil in de negentiende eeuw*. Amsterdam 2010.

Zemel 1980

Carol M. Zemel, *The Formation of a Legend: Van Gogh Criticism, 1890–1920*. Ann Arbor 1980.

Zigrosser 1971

Carl Zigrosser, *My Own Shall Come to Me: A Personal Memoir and Picture Chronicle*. Haarlem 1971.

Zwikker 2021

Roelie Zwikker, 'An Offer You *Can* Refuse', *Van Gogh Museum Articles*. Van Gogh Museum Academy, 30 November 2020. https://www.vangoghmuseum.nl/en/about/knowledge-and-research/academy/van-gogh-museum-articles/an-offer-you-can-refuse

Acknowledgements

The Vincent van Gogh Foundation gave me generous access, with no reservations whatsoever, to the surviving documentation. The many conversations I had with family members encouraged me greatly and assisted me significantly in my work. I am profoundly grateful to the members of the Van Gogh family, the board of the Vincent van Gogh Foundation, all my colleagues at the Van Gogh Museum, my fellow art historians, and my family, friends and nearest and dearest for their enduring inspiration and contributions to the creation of this biography. My thanks go to Mathilde ('Til') Cramer-van Gogh, Sylvia Cramer, Machteld van Laer-Cramer, Barbara Vroom-Cramer, Mars Cramer, Anneke van Gogh-Vonhoff, Jantine van Gogh, Josien van Gogh, Janne Heling, Marjolijn de Vries-van Gogh, Willem van Gogh, Han Veenenbos, Els Bonger, Eduard en Marga Josephus Jitta, Axel Rüger, Betty Klaasse, Aggie Langendijk, An Tuijnman, Louis van Tilborgh, Teio Meedendorp, Nienke Bakker, Eva Rovers, Karin Koevoet, Liede Maas, Margje Steenbeek, Mirjam Koelewijn, Ger Luijten, Isolde Cael, Lucinda Timmermans, Anita Hopman, Niek Stafleu, Zibi Dowgwillo, Anita Vriend, Sija Speelman, Monique den Ouden, Ernst-Jan Jonkman, Renske Cohen Tervaert, Renske Suijver, Eelco Zwart, Alex Nikken, Heleen van Driel, Kiona van Rooijen, Serge Taal, Albert Meyer, Martine Blok, Mariëlle Gerritsen, Frédérique Haanen, Maurice Tromp, Marlies Coucke, Esther de Jong, Pieter Plomp, Kriszta Schneider, Chris Stolwijk, Annemarie Kets, Heleen Stockmann-Kouwenaar, Martin Bailey, Freek Heijbroek, Michael Hoyle, H.W. Huidekoper-de Bruijn, Doro Keman, Geraldine McDonald, Andreas Obst, Henk Schouwenaar, Ira Schouwenaar, René van Stipriaan, Jessica Voeten, Piet Voskuil, Mieneke te Hennepe, John Müller, Tine Luyt, Guido van Oorschot, Jolien Hoek, Edwin Venema, Stefan Koldehoff, Marcel Daloze, Yvonne Majoor, Fusien Bijl-de Vroe, Wim Trompert, Jan Snoek, Robert Verhoogt, Paul Steenhoff, Helma Steenhoff-Brokx, Josephine Moonen, Frits Stolk, Henk en Hardy Veldhorst, Robert Veldhorst, Eddy de Jongh, Lammijna Oosterbaan, Willem den Ouden, Gijsbert van der Wal, Wouter van der Veen, Eveline Lambrechtsen, Madeleine Philips, Alinde Bierhuizen, Nadja Louwerse, Richard Bionda, Sjraar van Heugten, Susan A. Stein, Jan Kiviet, Roxanne van den Bosch, Sarah Meijler, Suzan Beijer, Stella Nelissen, Anton van der Lem, Willem Morelis, Karen Harmsen and Barbara Stok.

I am also greatly indebted to Fieke Pabst, Monique Hageman, Kelly Boender and Riet Schenkeveld-van der Dussen for their extremely valuable input, and to Patrick Grant, my main man.

My thanks to Lynne Richards for her friendly collaboration, hard work and meticulous translation.

I want to express special appreciation for the extensive and very valuable comments made by Johan van Gogh, Marije Vellekoop, Leo Jansen, Roelie Zwikker, Suzanne Bogman, Maarten Bonger and Marieke van Oostrom on earlier versions. And above all to Natascha Veldhorst, the light of my life, without whom I would never have been able to write this book.

Index of Names and Titles

Index of people and the titles of their artworks and books referred to in this publication. Page numbers in italics refer to illustrations. The works shown in figures 51 (p. 292), 59 (p. 322), *Plate 55*, and *Plate 56* are not included in this index.